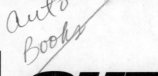

SUZUKI

SAMURAI/SIDEKICK/TRACKER
1986-98 REPAIR MANUAL

Deleted

President	Dean F. Morgantini, S.A.E.
Vice President–Finance	Barry L. Beck
Vice President–Sales	Glenn D. Potere
Executive Editor	Kevin M. G. Maher
Production Manager	Ben Greisler, S.A.E.
Project Managers	Michael Abraham, George B. Heinrich III, S.A.E., Will Kessler, A.S.E., S.A.E., Richard Schwartz
Schematics Editor	Christopher G. Ritchie
Editor	George B. Heinrich III, S.A.E.

CHILTON™ Automotive Books
PUBLISHED BY W. G. NICHOLS, INC.

Manufactured in USA
© 1998 W. G. Nichols
1020 Andrew Drive
West Chester, PA 19380
ISBN 0-8019-9088-2
Library of Congress Catalog Card No. 97-77880
1234567890 7654321098

Contents

Contents

7 DRIVE TRAIN

8 SUSPENSION AND STEERING

9 BRAKES

10 BODY & TRIM

GLOSSARY

MASTER INDEX

SAFETY NOTICE

Proper service and repair procedures are vital to the safe, reliable operation of all motor vehicles, as well as the personal safety of those performing repairs. This manual outlines procedures for servicing and repairing vehicles using safe, effective methods. The procedures contain many NOTES, CAUTIONS and WARNINGS which should be followed, along with standard procedures, to eliminate the possibility of personal injury or improper service which could damage the vehicle or compromise its safety.

It is important to note that repair procedures and techniques, tools and parts for servicing motor vehicles, as well as the skill and experience of the individual performing the work, vary widely. It is not possible to anticipate all of the conceivable ways or conditions under which vehicles may be serviced, or to provide cautions as to all possible hazards that may result. Standard and accepted safety precautions and equipment should be used during cutting, grinding, chiseling, prying, or any other process that can cause material removal or projectiles.

Some procedures require the use of tools specially designed for a specific purpose. Before substituting another tool or procedure, you must be completely satisfied that neither your personal safety, not the performance of the vehicle, will be endangered.

Although information in this manual is based on industry sources and is complete as possible at the time of publication, the possibility exists that some vehicle manufacturers made later changes which could not be included here. While striving for total accuracy, NP/Chilton cannot assume responsibility for any errors, changes or omissions that may occur in the compilation of this data.

PART NUMBERS

Part numbers listed in this reference are not recommendations by Chilton for any product brand name. They are references that can be used with interchange manuals and aftermarket supplier catalogs to locate each brand supplier's discrete part number.

SPECIAL TOOLS

Special tools are recommended by the vehicle manufacturer to perform their specific job. Use has been kept to a minimum, but, where absolutely necessary, they are referred to in the text by the part number of the tool manufacturer. These tools can be purchased, under the appropriate part number, from your local dealer or regional distributor, or an equivalent tool can be purchased locally from a tool supplier or parts outlet. Before substituting any tool for the one recommended, read the SAFETY NOTICE at the top of this page.

ACKNOWLEDGMENTS

NP/Chilton expresses appreciation to Suzuki Motors of America for their generous assistance.

A special thanks to the fine companies who supported the production of this book. Hand tools, supplied by Craftsman, were used during all phases of vehicle teardown and photography. A Rotary lift, the largest automobile lift manufacturer in the world offering the biggest variety of surface and inground lifts available, was also used.

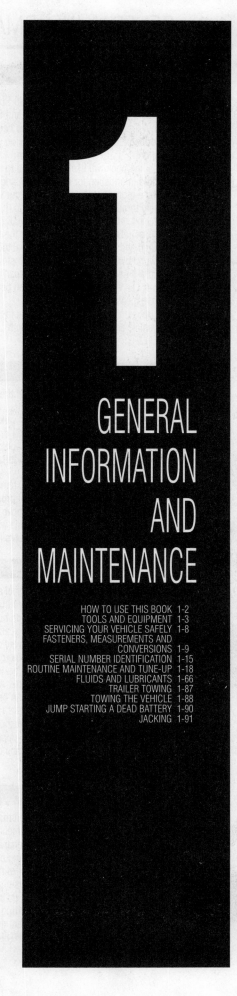

1

GENERAL INFORMATION AND MAINTENANCE

HOW TO USE THIS BOOK

Chilton's Total Car Care manual for the 1986–95 Suzuki Samurai, 1989–98 Suzuki Sidekick, 1996–98 Suzuki X-90 and Sidekick Sport, and 1989–98 Geo/Chevy Tracker models is intended to help you learn more about the inner workings of your vehicle while saving you money on its upkeep and operation.

The beginning of the book will likely be referred to the most, since that is where you will find information for maintenance and tune-up. The other sections deal with the more complex systems of your vehicle. Operating systems from engine through brakes are covered to the extent that the average do-it-yourselfer becomes mechanically involved. This book will not explain such things as rebuilding a differential for the simple reason that the expertise required and the investment in special tools make this task uneconomical. It will, however, give you detailed instructions to help you change your own brake pads and shoes, replace spark plugs, and perform many more jobs that can save you money, give you personal satisfaction and help you avoid expensive problems.

A secondary purpose of this book is a reference for owners who want to understand their vehicle and/or their mechanics better. In this case, no tools at all are required.

Where to Begin

Before removing any bolts, read through the entire procedure. This will give you the overall view of what tools and supplies will be required. There is nothing more frustrating than having to walk to the bus stop on Monday morning because you were short one bolt on Sunday afternoon. So read ahead and plan ahead. Each operation should be approached logically and all procedures thoroughly understood before attempting any work.

All sections contain adjustments, maintenance, removal and installation procedures, and in some cases, repair or overhaul procedures. When repair is not considered practical, we tell you how to remove the part and then how to install the new or rebuilt replacement. In this way, you at least save the labor costs. Backyard repair of some components is just not practical.

Avoiding Trouble

Many procedures in this book require you to "label and disconnect . . ." a group of lines, hoses or wires. Don't be lulled into thinking you can remember where everything goes—you won't. If you hook up vacuum or fuel lines incorrectly, the vehicle will run poorly, if at all. If you hook up electrical wiring incorrectly, you may instantly learn a very expensive lesson.

You don't need to know the official or engineering name for each hose or line. A piece of masking tape on the hose and a piece on its fitting will allow you to assign your own label such as the letter A or a short name. As long as you remember your own code, the lines can be reconnected by matching similar letters or names. Do remember that tape will dissolve in gasoline or other fluids; if a component is to be washed or cleaned, use another method of identification. A permanent felt-tipped marker can be very handy for marking metal parts. Remove any tape or paper labels after assembly.

Maintenance or Repair?

It's necessary to mention the difference between maintenance and repair. Maintenance includes routine inspections, adjustments, and replacement of parts which show signs of normal wear. Maintenance compensates for wear or deterioration. Repair implies that something has broken or is not working. A need for repair is often caused by lack of maintenance. Example: draining and refilling the automatic transmission fluid is maintenance recommended by the manufacturer at specific mileage intervals. Failure to do this can ruin the transmission, requiring very expensive repairs. While no maintenance program can prevent items from breaking or wearing out, a general rule can be stated: MAINTENANCE IS CHEAPER THAN REPAIR.

Two basic mechanic's rules should be mentioned here. First, whenever the left side of the vehicle or engine is referred to, it is meant to specify the driver's side. Conversely, the right side of the vehicle means the passenger's side. Second, most screws and bolts are removed by turning counterclockwise, and tightened by turning clockwise.

Safety is always the most important rule. Constantly be aware of the dangers involved in working on an automobile and take the proper precautions. See the information in this section regarding SERVICING YOUR VEHICLE SAFELY and the SAFETY NOTICE on the acknowledgment page.

Avoiding the Most Common Mistakes

Pay attention to the instructions provided. There are 3 common mistakes in mechanical work:

1. Incorrect order of assembly, disassembly or adjustment. When taking something apart or putting it together, performing steps in the wrong order usually just costs you extra time; however, it CAN break something. Read the entire procedure before beginning disassembly. Perform everything in the order in which the instructions say you should, even if you can't immediately see a reason for it. When you're taking apart something that is very intricate, you might want to draw a picture of how it looks when assembled at one point in order to make sure you get everything back in its proper position. We will supply exploded views whenever possible. When making adjustments, perform them in the proper order; often, one adjustment affects another, and you cannot expect even satisfactory results unless each adjustment is made only when it cannot be changed by any other.

2. Overtorquing (or undertorquing). While it is more common for overtorquing to cause damage, undertorquing may allow a fastener to vibrate loose causing serious damage. Especially when dealing with aluminum parts, pay attention to torque specifications and utilize a torque wrench in assembly. If a torque figure is not available, remember that if you are using the right tool to perform the job, you will probably not have to strain yourself to get a fastener tight enough. The pitch of most threads is so slight that the tension you put on the wrench will be multiplied many times in actual force on what you are tightening. A good example of how critical torque is can be seen in the case of spark plug installation, especially where you are putting the plug into an aluminum cylinder head. Too little torque can fail to crush the gasket, causing leakage of combustion gases and consequent overheating of the plug and engine parts. Too much torque can damage the threads or distort the plug, changing the spark gap.

There are many commercial products available for ensuring that fasteners won't come loose, even if they are not torqued just right (a very common brand is Loctite®). If you're worried about getting something together tight enough to hold, but loose enough to avoid mechanical damage during assembly, one of these products might offer substantial insurance. Before choosing a threadlocking compound, read the label on the package and make sure the product is compatible with the materials, fluids, etc. involved.

3. Crossthreading. This occurs when a part such as a bolt is screwed into a nut or casting at the wrong angle and forced. Crossthreading is more likely to occur if access is difficult. It helps to clean and lubricate fasteners, then to start threading with the part to be installed positioned straight in. Then, start the bolt, spark plug, etc. with your fingers. If you encounter resistance, unscrew the part and start over again at a different angle until it can be inserted and turned several times without much effort. Keep in mind that many parts, especially spark plugs, have tapered threads, so that gentle turning will automatically bring the part you're threading to the proper angle, but only if you don't force it or resist a change in angle. Don't put a wrench on the part until it's been tightened a couple of turns by hand. If you suddenly encounter resistance, and the part has not seated fully, don't force it. Pull it back out to make sure it's clean and threading properly.

Always take your time and be patient; once you have some experience, working on your vehicle may well become an enjoyable hobby.

TOOLS AND EQUIPMENT

◆ **See Figures 1 thru 17**

Naturally, without the proper tools and equipment it is impossible to properly service your vehicle. It would also be virtually impossible to catalog every tool that you would need to perform all of the operations in this book. Of course, It would be unwise for the amateur to rush out and buy an expensive set of tools on the theory that he/she may need one or more of them at some time.

The best approach is to proceed slowly, gathering a good quality set of those tools that are used most frequently. Don't be misled by the low cost of bargain tools. It is far better to spend a little more for better quality. Forged wrenches, 6 or 12-point sockets and fine tooth ratchets are by far preferable to their less expensive counterparts. As any good mechanic can tell you, there are few worse experiences than trying to work on a vehicle with bad tools. Your monetary savings will be far outweighed by frustration and mangled knuckles.

Begin accumulating those tools that are used most frequently: those associated with routine maintenance and tune-up. In addition to the normal assortment of screwdrivers and pliers, you should have the following tools:

• Wrenches/sockets and combination open end/box end wrenches in sizes from ⅛–¾ in. or 3mm–19mm (depending on whether your vehicle uses standard or metric fasteners) and a ¹³⁄₁₆ in. or ⅝ in. spark plug socket (depending on plug type).

➥**If possible, buy various length socket drive extensions. Universal-joint and wobble extensions can be extremely useful, but be careful when using them, as they can change the amount of torque applied to the socket.**

• Jackstands for support.
• Oil filter wrench.
• Spout or funnel for pouring fluids.
• Grease gun for chassis lubrication (unless your vehicle is not equipped with any grease fittings—for details, please refer to information on Fluids and Lubricants found later in this section).
• Hydrometer for checking the battery (unless equipped with a sealed, maintenance-free battery).
• A container for draining oil and other fluids.
• Rags for wiping up the inevitable mess.

In addition to the above items there are several others that are not absolutely necessary, but handy to have around. These include Oil Dry® (or an equivalent oil absorbent gravel—such as cat litter) and the usual

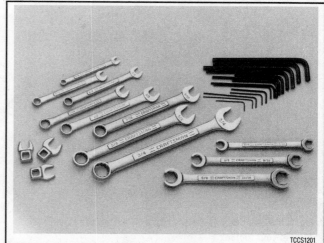

Fig. 2 In addition to ratchets, a good set of wrenches and hex keys will be necessary

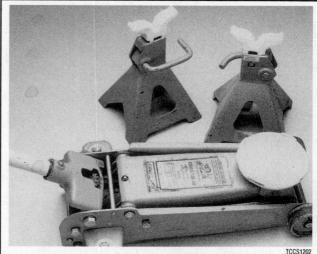

Fig. 3 A hydraulic floor jack and a set of jackstands are essential for lifting and supporting the vehicle

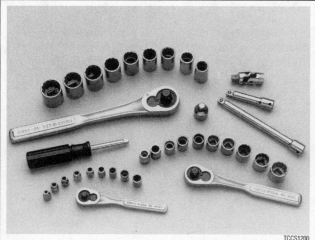

Fig. 1 All but the most basic procedures will require an assortment of ratchets and sockets

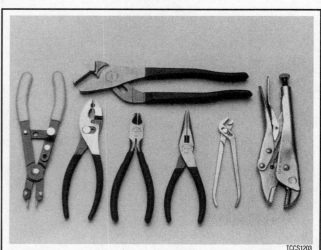

Fig. 4 An assortment of pliers, grippers and cutters will be handy for old rusted parts and stripped bolt heads

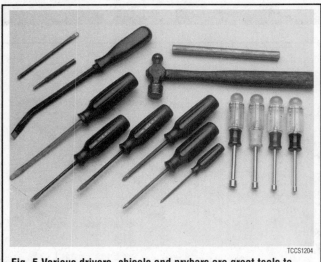

TCCS1204

Fig. 5 Various drivers, chisels and prybars are great tools to have in your toolbox

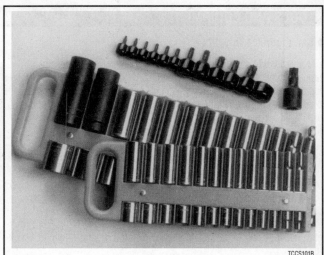

TCCS101B

Fig. 8 . . . these Torx® drivers and magnetic socket holders are just 2 examples of their handy products

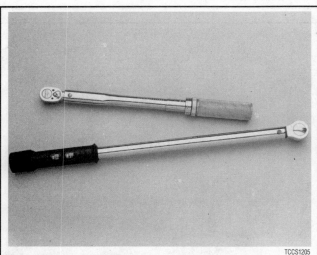

TCCS1205

Fig. 6 Many repairs will require the use of a torque wrench to assure the components are properly fastened

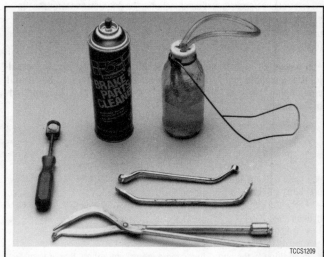

TCCS1209

Fig. 9 Although not always necessary, using specialized brake tools will save time

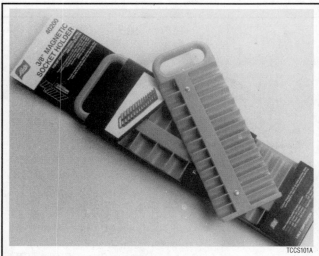

TCCS101A

Fig. 7 Tools from specialty manufacturers such as Lisle® are designed to make your job easier . . .

TCCS1210

Fig. 10 A few inexpensive lubrication tools will make maintenance easier

supply of lubricants, antifreeze and fluids, although these can be purchased as needed. This is a basic list for routine maintenance, but only your personal needs and desire can accurately determine your list of tools.

After performing a few projects on the vehicle, you'll be amazed at the other tools and non-tools on your workbench. Some useful household items are: a large turkey baster or siphon, empty coffee cans and ice trays (to store parts), ball of twine, electrical tape for wiring, small rolls of colored tape for tagging lines or hoses, markers and pens, a note pad, golf tees (for plugging vacuum lines), metal coat hangers or a roll of mechanics's wire (to hold things out of the way), dental pick or similar long, pointed probe, a strong magnet, and a small mirror (to see into recesses and under manifolds).

A more advanced set of tools, suitable for tune-up work, can be drawn up easily. While the tools are slightly more sophisticated, they need not be outrageously expensive. There are several inexpensive tach/dwell meters on the market that are every bit as good for the average mechanic as a professional model. Just be sure that it goes to a least 1200–1500 rpm on the tach scale and that it works on 4, 6 and 8-cylinder engines. (If you have one or more vehicles with a diesel engine, a special tachometer is required

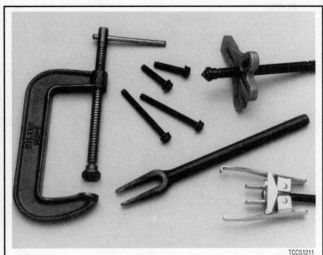

Fig. 11 Various pullers, clamps and separator tools are needed for many larger, more complicated repairs

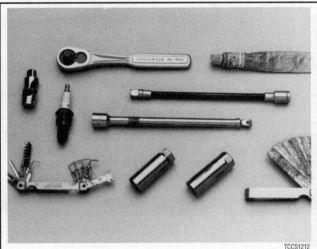

Fig. 12 A variety of tools and gauges should be used for spark plug gapping and installation

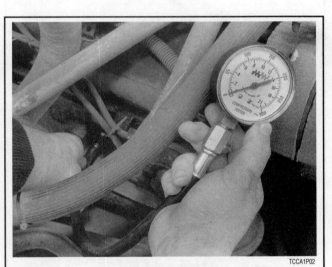

Fig. 14 A screw-in type compression gauge is recommended for compression testing

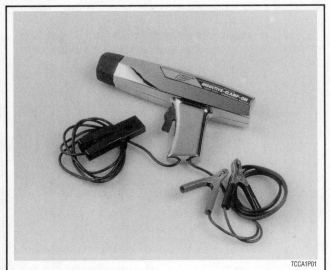

Fig. 13 Inductive type timing light

Fig. 15 A vacuum/pressure tester is necessary for many testing procedures

since diesels don't use spark plug ignition systems). The key to these purchases is to make them with an eye towards adaptability and wide range. A basic list of tune-up tools could include:
- Tach/dwell meter.
- Spark plug wrench and gapping tool.
- Feeler gauges for valve or point adjustment. (Even if your vehicle does not use points or require valve adjustments, a feeler gauge is helpful for many repair/overhaul procedures).

A tachometer/dwell meter will ensure accurate tune-up work on vehicles without electronic ignition. The choice of a timing light should be made carefully. A light which works on the DC current supplied by the vehicle's battery is the best choice; it should have a xenon tube for brightness. On any vehicle with an electronic ignition system, a timing light with an inductive pickup that clamps around the No. 1 spark plug cable is preferred.

In addition to these basic tools, there are several other tools and gauges you may find useful. These include:

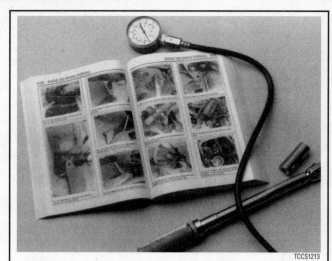

Fig. 17 Proper information is vital, so always have a Chilton Total Car Care manual handy

- Compression gauge. The screw-in type is slower to use, but eliminates the possibility of a faulty reading due to escaping pressure.
- Manifold vacuum gauge.
- 12V test light.
- A combination volt/ohmmeter
- Induction Ammeter. This is used for determining whether or not there is current in a wire. These are handy for use if a wire is broken somewhere in a wiring harness.

As a final note, you will probably find a torque wrench necessary for all but the most basic work. The beam type models are perfectly adequate, although the newer click types (breakaway) are easier to use. The click type torque wrenches tend to be more expensive. Also keep in mind that all types of torque wrenches should be periodically checked and/or recalibrated. You will have to decide for yourself which better fits your purpose.

Special Tools

Normally, the use of special factory tools is avoided for repair procedures, since these are not readily available for the do-it-yourself mechanic. When it is possible to perform the job with more commonly available tools, it will be pointed out, but occasionally, a special tool was designed to perform a specific function and should be used. Before substituting another tool, you should be convinced that neither your safety nor the performance of the vehicle will be compromised.

Special tools can usually be purchased from an automotive parts store or from your dealer. In some cases special tools may be available directly from the tool manufacturer.

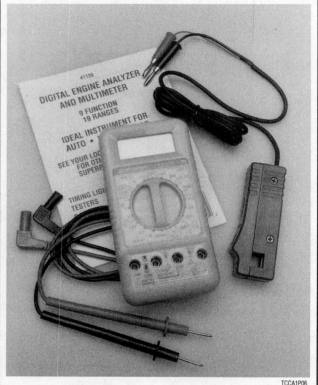

Fig. 16 Most modern automotive multimeters incorporate many helpful features

TCCA1AC1

SERVICING YOUR VEHICLE SAFELY

♦ See Figures 18, 19, 20 and 21

It is virtually impossible to anticipate all of the hazards involved with automotive maintenance and service, but care and common sense will prevent most accidents.

The rules of safety for mechanics range from "don't smoke around gasoline," to "use the proper tool(s) for the job." The trick to avoiding injuries is to develop safe work habits and to take every possible precaution.

Do's

- Do keep a fire extinguisher and first aid kit handy.
- Do wear safety glasses or goggles when cutting, drilling, grinding or prying, even if you have 20–20 vision. If you wear glasses for the sake of vision, wear safety goggles over your regular glasses.
- Do shield your eyes whenever you work around the battery. Batteries contain sulfuric acid. In case of contact with the eyes or skin, flush the area with water or a mixture of water and baking soda, then seek immediate medical attention.

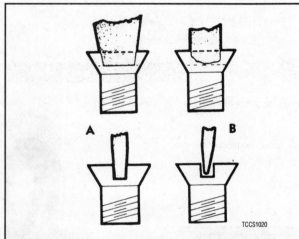

Fig. 18 Screwdrivers should be kept in good condition to prevent injury or damage which could result if the blade slips from the screw

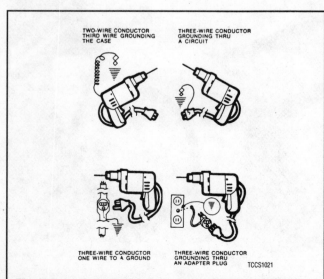

Fig. 19 Power tools should always be properly grounded

Fig. 20 Using the correct size wrench will help prevent the possibility of rounding off a nut

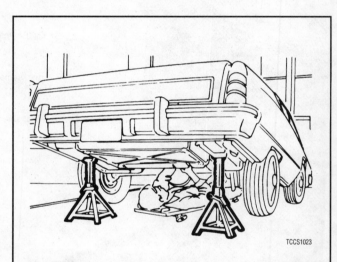

Fig. 21 NEVER work under a vehicle unless it is supported using safety stands (jackstands)

- Do use safety stands (jackstands) for any undervehicle service. Jacks are for raising vehicles; jackstands are for making sure the vehicle stays raised until you want it to come down. Whenever the vehicle is raised, block the wheels remaining on the ground and set the parking brake.
- Do use adequate ventilation when working with any chemicals or hazardous materials. Like carbon monoxide, the asbestos dust resulting from some brake lining wear can be hazardous in sufficient quantities.
- Do disconnect the negative battery cable when working on the electrical system. The secondary ignition system contains EXTREMELY HIGH VOLTAGE. In some cases it can even exceed 50,000 volts.
- Do follow manufacturer's directions whenever working with potentially hazardous materials. Most chemicals and fluids are poisonous if taken internally.
- Do properly maintain your tools. Loose hammerheads, mushroomed punches and chisels, frayed or poorly grounded electrical cords, excessively worn screwdrivers, spread wrenches (open end), cracked sockets, slipping ratchets, or faulty droplight sockets can cause accidents.
- Likewise, keep your tools clean; a greasy wrench can slip off a bolt head, ruining the bolt and often harming your knuckles in the process.

• Do use the proper size and type of tool for the job at hand. Do select a wrench or socket that fits the nut or bolt. The wrench or socket should sit straight, not cocked.

• Do, when possible, pull on a wrench handle rather than push on it, and adjust your stance to prevent a fall.

• Do be sure that adjustable wrenches are tightly closed on the nut or bolt and pulled so that the force is on the side of the fixed jaw.

• Do strike squarely with a hammer; avoid glancing blows.

• Do set the parking brake and block the drive wheels if the work requires a running engine.

Don'ts

• Don't run the engine in a garage or anywhere else without proper ventilation—EVER! Carbon monoxide is poisonous; it takes a long time to leave the human body and you can build up a deadly supply of it in your system by simply breathing in a little every day. You may not realize you are slowly poisoning yourself. Always use power vents, windows, fans and/or open the garage door.

• Don't work around moving parts while wearing loose clothing. Short sleeves are much safer than long, loose sleeves. Hard-toed shoes with neoprene soles protect your toes and give a better grip on slippery surfaces. Jewelry such as watches, fancy belt buckles, beads or body adornment of any kind is not safe working around a vehicle. Long hair should be tied back under a hat or cap.

• Don't use pockets for toolboxes. A fall or bump can drive a screwdriver deep into your body. Even a rag hanging from your back pocket can wrap around a spinning shaft or fan.

• Don't smoke when working around gasoline, cleaning solvent or other flammable material.

• Don't smoke when working around the battery. When the battery is being charged, it gives off explosive hydrogen gas.

• Don't use gasoline to wash your hands; there are excellent soaps available. Gasoline contains dangerous additives which can enter the body through a cut or through your pores. Gasoline also removes all the natural oils from the skin so that bone dry hands will suck up oil and grease.

• Don't service the air conditioning system unless you are equipped with the necessary tools and training. When liquid or compressed gas refrigerant is released to atmospheric pressure it will absorb heat from whatever it contacts. This will chill or freeze anything it touches. Although refrigerant is normally non-toxic, R-12 becomes a deadly poisonous gas in the presence of an open flame. One good whiff of the vapors from burning refrigerant can be fatal.

• Don't use screwdrivers for anything other than driving screws! A screwdriver used as an prying tool can snap when you least expect it, causing injuries. At the very least, you'll ruin a good screwdriver.

• Don't use a bumper or emergency jack (that little ratchet, scissors, or pantograph jack supplied with the vehicle) for anything other than changing a flat! These jacks are only intended for emergency use out on the road; they are NOT designed as a maintenance tool. If you are serious about maintaining your vehicle yourself, invest in a hydraulic floor jack of at least a 1½ ton capacity, and at least two sturdy jackstands.

FASTENERS, MEASUREMENTS AND CONVERSIONS

Bolts, Nuts and Other Threaded Retainers

▶ See Figures 22, 23, 24 and 25

Although there are a great variety of fasteners found in the modern car or truck, the most commonly used retainer is the threaded fastener (nuts, bolts, screws, studs, etc.). Most threaded retainers may be reused, provided that they are not damaged in use or during the repair. Some retainers (such as stretch bolts or torque prevailing nuts) are designed to deform when tightened or in use and should not be reinstalled.

Whenever possible, we will note any special retainers which should be replaced during a procedure. But you should always inspect the condition of a retainer when it is removed and replace any that show signs of damage. Check all threads for rust or corrosion which can increase the torque necessary to achieve the desired clamp load for which that fastener was originally selected. Additionally, be sure that the driver surface of the fastener has not been compromised by rounding or other damage. In some cases a driver surface may become only partially rounded, allowing the driver to catch in only one direction. In many of these occurrences, a fastener may be installed and tightened, but the driver would not be able to grip and loosen the fastener again. (This could lead to frustration down the line should that component ever need to be disassembled again).

If you must replace a fastener, whether due to design or damage, you must ALWAYS be sure to use the proper replacement. In all cases, a retainer of the same design, material and strength should be used. Markings on the heads of most bolts will help determine the proper strength of the fastener. The same material, thread and pitch must be selected to assure proper installation and safe operation of the vehicle afterwards.

POZIDRIVE   PHILLIPS RECESS   TORX®   CLUTCH RECESS

  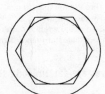

INDENTED HEXAGON   HEXAGON TRIMMED   HEXAGON WASHER HEAD

TCCS1037

Fig. 22 Here are a few of the most common screw/bolt driver styles

Thread gauges are available to help measure a bolt or stud's thread. Most automotive and hardware stores keep gauges available to help you select the proper size. In a pinch, you can use another nut or bolt for a thread gauge. If the bolt you are replacing is not too badly damaged, you can select a match by finding another bolt which will thread in its place. If you find a nut which threads properly onto the damaged bolt, then use that nut to help select the replacement bolt. If however, the bolt you are replacing is so badly damaged (broken or drilled out) that its threads cannot be used as a gauge, you might start by looking for another bolt (from the same assembly or a similar location on your vehicle) which will thread into the damaged bolt's mounting. If so, the other bolt can be used to select a nut; the nut can then be used to select the replacement bolt.

In all cases, be absolutely sure you have selected the proper replacement. Don't be shy, you can always ask the store clerk for help.

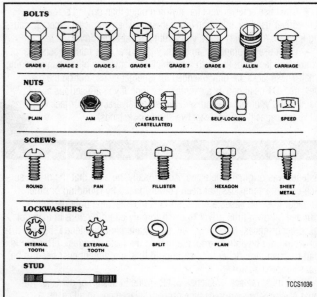

Fig. 23 There are many different types of threaded retainers found on vehicles

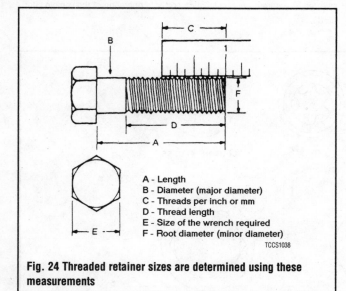

A - Length
B - Diameter (major diameter)
C - Threads per inch or mm
D - Thread length
E - Size of the wrench required
F - Root diameter (minor diameter)

TCCS1038

Fig. 24 Threaded retainer sizes are determined using these measurements

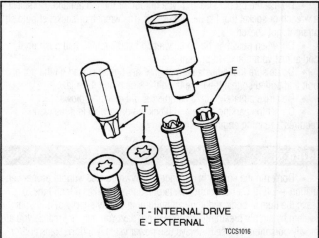

T - INTERNAL DRIVE
E - EXTERNAL

TCCS1016

Fig. 25 Special fasteners such as these Torx® head bolts are used by manufacturers to discourage people from working on vehicles without the proper tools

❉❉ WARNING

Be aware that when you find a bolt with damaged threads, you may also find the nut or drilled hole it was threaded into has also been damaged. If this is the case, you may have to drill and tap the hole, replace the nut or otherwise repair the threads. NEVER try to force a replacement bolt to fit into the damaged threads.

Torque

Torque is defined as the measurement of resistance to turning or rotating. It tends to twist a body about an axis of rotation. A common example of this would be tightening a threaded retainer such as a nut, bolt or screw. Measuring torque is one of the most common ways to help assure that a threaded retainer has been properly fastened.

When tightening a threaded fastener, torque is applied in three distinct areas, the head, the bearing surface and the clamp load. About 50 percent of the measured torque is used in overcoming bearing friction. This is the friction between the bearing surface of the bolt head, screw head or nut face and the base material or washer (the surface on which the fastener is rotating). Approximately 40 percent of the applied torque is used in overcoming thread friction. This leaves only about 10 percent of the applied torque to develop a useful clamp load (the force which holds a joint together). This means that friction can account for as much as 90 percent of the applied torque on a fastener.

TORQUE WRENCHES

▶ **See Figures 26, 27 and 28**

In most applications, a torque wrench can be used to assure proper installation of a fastener. Torque wrenches come in various designs and most automotive supply stores will carry a variety to suit your needs. A torque wrench should be used any time we supply a specific torque value for a fastener. A torque wrench can also be used if you are following the general guidelines in the accompanying charts. Keep in mind that because there is no worldwide standardization of fasteners, the charts are a general guideline and should be used with caution. Again, the general rule of "if you are using the right tool for the job, you should not have to strain to tighten a fastener" applies here.

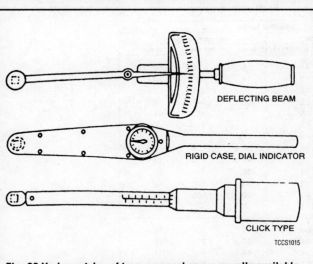

Fig. 26 Various styles of torque wrenches are usually available at your local automotive supply store

Beam Type

▶ **See Figure 29**

The beam type torque wrench is one of the most popular types. It consists of a pointer attached to the head that runs the length of the flexible beam (shaft) to a scale located near the handle. As the wrench is pulled, the beam bends and the pointer indicates the torque using the scale.

Click (Breakaway) Type

▶ **See Figure 30**

Another popular design of torque wrench is the click type. To use the click type wrench you pre-adjust it to a torque setting. Once the torque is reached, the wrench has a reflex signaling feature that causes a momentary breakaway of the torque wrench body, sending an impulse to the operator's hand.

Pivot Head Type

▶ **See Figure 31**

Some torque wrenches (usually of the click type) may be equipped with a pivot head which can allow it to be used in areas of limited access. BUT, it

	Mark		Class		Mark	Class
Hexagon head bolt		4—	4T	Stud bolt		
		5—	5T			
	Bolt head No.	6—	6T		No mark	
		7—	7T			
		8—	8T			4T
		9—	9T			
		10—	10T			
		11—	11T			
	No mark		4T			
Hexagon flange bolt w/ washer hexagon bolt	No mark		4T		Grooved	
Hexagon head bolt	Two protruding lines		5T			6T
Hexagon flange bolt w/ washer hexagon bolt	Two protruding lines		6T	Welded bolt		
Hexagon head bolt	Three protruding lines		7T			4T
Hexagon head bolt	Four protruding lines		8T			

TCCS1240

Fig. 27 Determining bolt strength of metric fasteners—NOTE: this is a typical bolt marking system, but there is not a worldwide standard

Class	Diameter mm	Pitch mm	Specified torque					
			Hexagon head bolt			Hexagon flange bolt		
			N·m	kgf·cm	ft·lbf	N·m	kgf·cm	ft·lbf
4T	6	1	5	55	48 in.·lbf	6	60	52 in.·lbf
	8	1.25	12.5	130	9	14	145	10
	10	1.25	26	260	19	29	290	21
	12	1.25	47	480	35	53	540	39
	14	1.5	74	760	55	84	850	61
	16	1.5	115	1,150	83	—	—	—
5T	6	1	6.5	65	56 in.·lbf	7.5	75	65 in.·lbf
	8	1.25	15.5	160	12	17.5	175	13
	10	1.25	32	330	24	36	360	26
	12	1.25	59	600	43	65	670	48
	14	1.5	91	930	67	100	1,050	76
	16	1.5	140	1,400	101	—	—	—
6T	6	1	8	80	69 in.·lbf	9	90	78 in.·lbf
	8	1.25	19	195	14	21	210	15
	10	1.25	39	400	29	44	440	32
	12	1.25	71	730	53	80	810	59
	14	1.5	110	1,100	80	125	1,250	90
	16	1.5	170	1,750	127	—	—	—
7T	6	1	10.5	110	8	12	120	9
	8	1.25	25	260	19	28	290	21
	10	1.25	52	530	38	58	590	43
	12	1.25	95	970	70	105	1,050	76
	14	1.5	145	1,500	108	165	1,700	123
	16	1.5	230	2,300	166	—	—	—
8T	8	1.25	29	300	22	33	330	24
	10	1.25	61	620	45	68	690	50
	12	1.25	110	1,100	80	120	1,250	90
9T	8	1.25	34	340	25	37	380	27
	10	1.25	70	710	51	78	790	57
	12	1.25	125	1,300	94	140	1,450	105
10T	8	1.25	38	390	28	42	430	31
	10	1.25	78	800	58	88	890	64
	12	1.25	140	1,450	105	155	1,600	116
11T	8	1.25	42	430	31	47	480	35
	10	1.25	87	890	64	97	990	72
	12	1.25	155	1,600	116	175	1,800	130

TCCS1241

Fig. 28 Typical bolt torques for metric fasteners—WARNING: use only as a guide

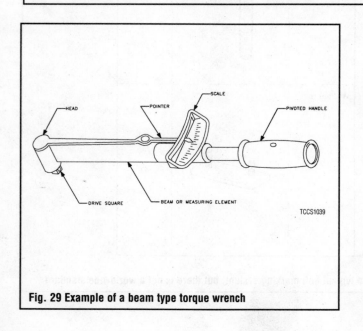

TCCS1039

Fig. 29 Example of a beam type torque wrench

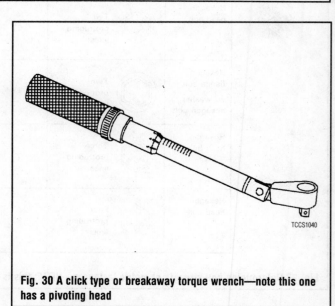

TCCS1040

Fig. 30 A click type or breakaway torque wrench—note this one has a pivoting head

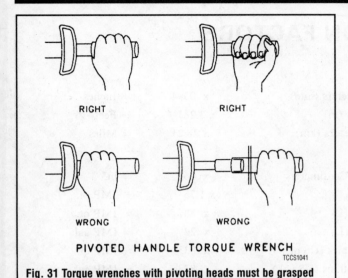

Fig. 31 Torque wrenches with pivoting heads must be grasped and used properly to prevent an incorrect reading

must be used properly. To hold a pivot head wrench, grasp the handle lightly, and as you pull on the handle, it should be floated on the pivot point. If the handle comes in contact with the yoke extension during the process of pulling, there is a very good chance the torque readings will be inaccurate because this could alter the wrench loading point. The design of the handle is usually such as to make it inconvenient to deliberately misuse the wrench.

➡**It should be mentioned that the use of any U-joint, wobble or extension will have an effect on the torque readings, no matter what type of wrench you are using. For the most accurate readings, install the socket directly on the wrench driver. If necessary, straight extensions (which hold a socket directly under the wrench driver) will have the least effect on the torque reading. Avoid any extension that alters the length of the wrench from the handle to the head/driving point (such as a crow's foot). U-joint or Wobble extensions can greatly affect the readings; avoid their use at all times.**

Rigid Case (Direct Reading)

▶ **See Figure 32**

A rigid case or direct reading torque wrench is equipped with a dial indicator to show torque values. One advantage of these wrenches is that they can be held at any position on the wrench without affecting accuracy. These wrenches are often preferred because they tend to be compact, easy to read and have a great degree of accuracy.

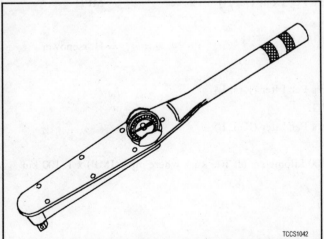

Fig. 32 The rigid case (direct reading) torque wrench uses a dial indicator to show torque

TORQUE ANGLE METERS

▶ **See Figure 33**

Because the frictional characteristics of each fastener or threaded hole will vary, clamp loads which are based strictly on torque will vary as well. In most applications, this variance is not significant enough to cause worry. But, in certain applications, a manufacturer's engineers may determine that more precise clamp loads are necessary (such is the case with many aluminum cylinder heads). In these cases, a torque angle method of installation would be specified. When installing fasteners which are torque angle tightened, a predetermined seating torque and standard torque wrench are usually used first to remove any compliance from the joint. The fastener is then tightened the specified additional portion of a turn measured in degrees. A torque angle gauge (mechanical protractor) is used for these applications.

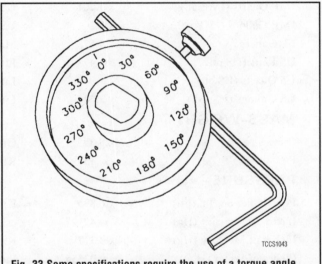

Fig. 33 Some specifications require the use of a torque angle meter (mechanical protractor)

Standard and Metric Measurements

▶ **See Figure 34**

Throughout this manual, specifications are given to help you determine the condition of various components on your vehicle, or to assist you in their installation. Some of the most common measurements include length (in. or cm/mm), torque (ft. lbs., inch lbs. or Nm) and pressure (psi, in. Hg, kPa or mm Hg). In most cases, we strive to provide the proper measurement as determined by the manufacturer's engineers.

Though, in some cases, that value may not be conveniently measured with what is available in your toolbox. Luckily, many of the measuring devices which are available today will have two scales so the Standard or Metric measurements may easily be taken. If any of the various measuring tools which are available to you do not contain the same scale as listed in the specifications, use the accompanying conversion factors to determine the proper value.

The conversion factor chart is used by taking the given specification and multiplying it by the necessary conversion factor. For instance, looking at the first line, if you have a measurement in inches such as "free-play should be 2 in." but your ruler reads only in millimeters, multiply 2 in. by the conversion factor of 25.4 to get the metric equivalent of 50.8mm. Likewise, if the specification was given only in a Metric measurement, for example in Newton Meters (Nm), then look at the center column first. If the measurement is 100 Nm, multiply it by the conversion factor of 0.738 to get 73.8 ft. lbs.

CONVERSION FACTORS

LENGTH–DISTANCE

Inches (in.)	x 25.4	= Millimeters (mm)	x .0394	= Inches
Feet (ft.)	x .305	= Meters (m)	x 3.281	= Feet
Miles	x 1.609	= Kilometers (km)	x .0621	= Miles

VOLUME

Cubic Inches (in3)	x 16.387	= Cubic Centimeters	x .061	= in3
IMP Pints (IMP pt.)	x .568	= Liters (L)	x 1.76	= IMP pt.
IMP Quarts (IMP qt.)	x 1.137	= Liters (L)	x .88	= IMP qt.
IMP Gallons (IMP gal.)	x 4.546	= Liters (L)	x .22	= IMP gal.
IMP Quarts (IMP qt.)	x 1.201	= US Quarts (US qt.)	x .833	= IMP qt.
IMP Gallons (IMP gal.)	x 1.201	= US Gallons (US gal.)	x .833	= IMP gal.
Fl. Ounces	x 29.573	= Milliliters	x .034	= Ounces
US Pints (US pt.)	x .473	= Liters (L)	x 2.113	= Pints
US Quarts (US qt.)	x .946	= Liters (L)	x 1.057	= Quarts
US Gallons (US gal.)	x 3.785	= Liters (L)	x .264	= Gallons

MASS–WEIGHT

Ounces (oz.)	x 28.35	= Grams (g)	x .035	= Ounces
Pounds (lb.)	x .454	= Kilograms (kg)	x 2.205	= Pounds

PRESSURE

Pounds Per Sq. In. (psi)	x 6.895	= Kilopascals (kPa)	x .145	= psi
Inches of Mercury (Hg)	x .4912	= psi	x 2.036	= Hg
Inches of Mercury (Hg)	x 3.377	= Kilopascals (kPa)	x .2961	= Hg
Inches of Water (H_2O)	x .07355	= Inches of Mercury	x 13.783	= H_2O
Inches of Water (H_2O)	x .03613	= psi	x 27.684	= H_2O
Inches of Water (H_2O)	x .248	= Kilopascals (kPa)	x 4.026	= H_2O

TORQUE

Pounds–Force Inches (in–lb)	x .113	= Newton Meters (N·m)	x 8.85	= in–lb
Pounds–Force Feet (ft–lb)	x 1.356	= Newton Meters (N·m)	x .738	= ft–lb

VELOCITY

Miles Per Hour (MPH)	x 1.609	= Kilometers Per Hour (KPH)	x .621	= MPH

POWER

Horsepower (Hp)	x .745	= Kilowatts	x 1.34	= Horsepower

FUEL CONSUMPTION*

Miles Per Gallon IMP (MPG)	x .354	= Kilometers Per Liter (Km/L)
Kilometers Per Liter (Km/L)	x 2.352	= IMP MPG
Miles Per Gallon US (MPG)	x .425	= Kilometers Per Liter (Km/L)
Kilometers Per Liter (Km/L)	x 2.352	= US MPG

*It is common to covert from miles per gallon (mpg) to liters/100 kilometers (1/100 km), where mpg (IMP) x 1/100 km = 282 and mpg (US) x 1/100 km = 235.

TEMPERATURE

Degree Fahrenheit (°F)	= (°C x 1.8) + 32
Degree Celsius (°C)	= (°F – 32) x .56

Fig. 34 Standard and metric conversion factors chart

TCCS1044

SERIAL NUMBER IDENTIFICATION

Vehicle

▶ See Figures 35, 36, 37 and 38

Every vehicle covered by this manual is equipped with a Vehicle Identification Number (VIN), which contains important information regarding your particular vehicle, such as: manufacturer; car line; vehicle series, chassis and restraint system; engine type; design sequence; body type; year of manufacture; assembly plant; and sequential manufacture number.

Throughout this manual you will be required to know with which engine your vehicle was originally equipped. The 6th digit (for Suzuki models) or the 8th digit (for Geo models) in your vehicle's VIN code, when cross-referenced with the accompanying vehicle identification chart, indicates your vehicle's original engine.

→If the engine in your vehicle was replaced with a different one, the VIN code will not reflect this change, since it is illegal to remove or alter the original VIN code tag from the vehicle.

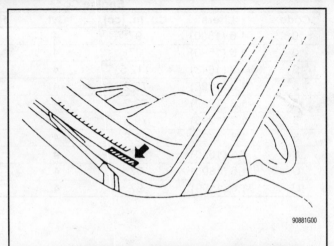

Fig. 37 The VIN code was moved to the top side of the left-hand edge of the instrument panel in 1992 for all Sidekick, Sidekick Sport, Tracker and X-90 models

Fig. 35 The VIN code is located on the left-hand front door pillar on 1986–87 Samurai models

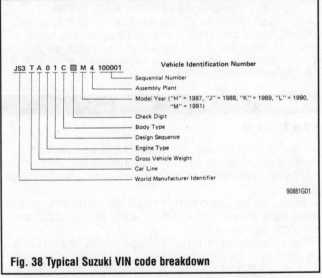

Fig. 38 Typical Suzuki VIN code breakdown

Vehicle Identification Number

JS3 T A 01 C ▨ M 4 100001

- Sequential Number
- Assembly Plant
- Model Year ("H" = 1987, "J" = 1988, "K" = 1989, "L" = 1990, "M" = 1991)
- Check Digit
- Body Type
- Design Sequence
- Engine Type
- Gross Vehicle Weight
- Car Line
- World Manufacturer Identifier

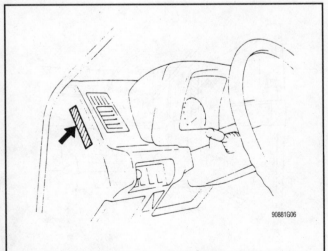

Fig. 36 In 1988, Suzuki moved the VIN code location to the left-hand side of the instrument panel

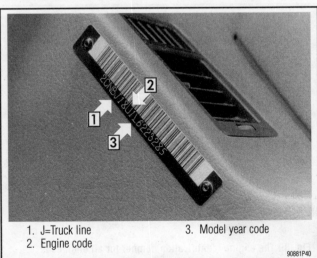

1. J=Truck line
2. Engine code
3. Model year code

The VIN codes used on Geo Tracker models have the digits slightly re-arranged as shown

VEHICLE IDENTIFICATION

Engine Code						Model Year	
Code	Liters	Cu. In. (cc)	Cyl.	Fuel Sys.	Eng. Mfg.	Code	Year
0	1.6 (1590)	97	4	TFI	Suzuki	G	1986
0	1.6 (1590)	97	4	MFI	Suzuki	H	1987
2	1.8 (1843)	112.5	4	MFI	Suzuki	J	1988
3	1.3 (1298)	79.2	4	TFI	Suzuki	K	1989
5	1.3 (1298)	79.2	4	CARB	Suzuki	L	1990
5	1.3 (1298)	79.2	4	TFI	Suzuki	M	1991
5	1.3 (1324)	80.8	4	CARB	Suzuki	N	1992
6	1.6 (1590)	97	4	MFI	Suzuki	P	1993
U	1.6 (1590)	97	4	MFI	Suzuki	R	1994
U	1.6 (1590)	97	4	TFI	Suzuki	S	1995
						T	1996
						V	1997
						W	1998

90881C00

The 10th digit in the VIN code indicates the year of manufacture of your vehicle. Once again, cross-reference the VIN code letter on your vehicle with the vehicle identification chart in this manual.

The VIN code is located on the left, front door pillar on 1986–87 Samurai models, and on the left-hand side of the instrument panel on 1988–95 Samurai and 1989–91 Sidekick and Tracker models. On all 1992–98 Sidekick, X-90, Tracker and Sidekick Sport models, the VIN code is mounted on the top, left-hand side of the instrument panel (visible through the windshield).

Engine

▶ See Figure 39

The engine identification number provides engine information with regards to engine type (1st digit), engine displacement (2nd and 3rd digits), design sequence (4th digit), and manufacturing sequence (5th through 10th digits).

The 2nd and 3rd digits in the engine identification number indicate the engine displacement in liters. Therefore, a code of 18 indicates that the engine displacement is 1.8L.

The engine identification number is stamped onto the left-hand side of the engine block near the flywheel.

Transmission

▶ See Figures 40, 41 and 42

Much like the engine identification number, all transmissions are equipped with an identifying number stamped in their housing. All the transmissions utilize a 7-digit code.

On manual and 3-speed automatic transmissions, the 1st code digit indicates the year of manufacture. The letter code indicates the same year as shown on the vehicle identification chart in this section. The remaining 6 digits are the manufacturing sequence.

The code on the 4-speed transmission can be broken down as follows:

• Digits 1 and 2—assembly year (for example, 95 indicates 1995 as the year of manufacture)
• Digit 3—assembly month (A = January, B = February, etc.—note that the letter I is not used)
• Digits 4 through 7—sequential manufacturing number

The identification number is stamped into the upper, left-hand, front area of the manual transmission, into the lower, left-hand, front area of the 3-speed transmission, and into the lower, left-hand mid-section of the 4-speed transmission.

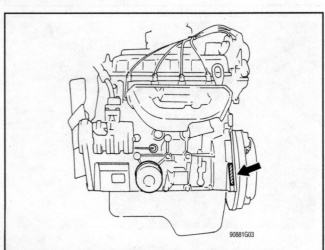

90881G03

Fig. 39 The engine identification number for all engines is located in the same place—lower, left-hand side of the engine block toward the rear edge

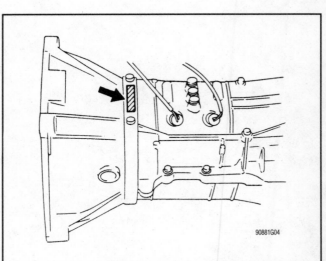

90881G04

Fig. 40 The identification number for manual transmissions is located on the upper, front, left-hand side of the housing

ENGINE IDENTIFICATION

Year	Model	Engine Displacement Liters (cc)	Engine Series (ID/VIN)	Fuel System	No. of Cylinders	Engine Type
1986	Samurai	1.3 (1324)	5	2-BBL.	4	8V-SOHC
1987	Samurai	1.3 (1324)	5	2-BBL.	4	8V-SOHC
1988	Samurai	1.3 (1324)	5	2-BBL.	4	8V-SOHC
1989	Samurai	1.3 (1324)	5	2-BBL.	4	8V-SOHC
	Sidekick	1.3 (1298)	5	2-BBL.	4	8V-SOHC
		1.6 (1590)	0	TFI	4	8V-SOHC
	Tracker	1.6 (1590)	U	TFI	4	8V-SOHC
1990	Samurai	1.3 (1298)	5	TFI	4	8V-SOHC
	Sidekick	1.6 (1590)	0	TFI	4	8V-SOHC
	Tracker	1.6 (1590)	U	TFI	4	8V-SOHC
1991	Samurai	1.3 (1298)	5	TFI	4	8V-SOHC
	Sidekick	1.6 (1590)	0	TFI	4	8V-SOHC
	Tracker	1.6 (1590)	U	TFI	4	8V-SOHC
1992	Samurai	1.3 (1298)	5	TFI	4	8V-SOHC
	Sidekick	1.6 (1590)	0	TFI	4	8V-SOHC
		1.6 (1590)	0	MFI	4	16V-SOHC
	Tracker	1.6 (1590)	U	TFI	4	8V-SOHC
1993	Samurai	1.3 (1298)	3	TFI	4	8V-SOHC
	Sidekick	1.6 (1590)	0	TFI	4	8V-SOHC
		1.6 (1590)	0	MFI	4	16V-SOHC
	Tracker	1.6 (1590)	U	TFI	4	8V-SOHC
1994	Samurai	1.3 (1298)	3	TFI	4	8V-SOHC
	Sidekick	1.6 (1590)	0	TFI	4	8V-SOHC
		1.6 (1590)	0	MFI	4	16V-SOHC
	Tracker	1.6 (1590)	U	TFI	4	8V-SOHC
	①	1.6 (1590)	U	MFI	4	16V-SOHC
1995	Samurai	1.3 (1298)	3	TFI	4	8V-SOHC
	Sidekick	1.6 (1590)	0	TFI	4	8V-SOHC
		1.6 (1590)	0	MFI	4	16V-SOHC
	Tracker	1.6 (1590)	U	TFI	4	8V-SOHC
	①	1.6 (1590)	6	MFI	4	16V-SOHC
1996	X90	1.6 (1590)	0	MFI	4	16V-SOHC
	Sidekick	1.6 (1590)	0	MFI	4	16V-SOHC
	Sport	1.8 (1843)	2	MFI	4	16V-DOHC
	Tracker	1.6 (1590)	6	MFI	4	16V-SOHC
1997	X90	1.6 (1590)	0	MFI	4	16V-SOHC
	Sidekick	1.6 (1590)	0	MFI	4	16V-SOHC
	Sport	1.8 (1843)	2	MFI	4	16V-DOHC
	Tracker	1.6 (1590)	6	MFI	4	16V-SOHC
1998	X90	1.6 (1590)	0	MFI	4	16V-SOHC
	Sidekick	1.6 (1590)	0	MFI	4	16V-SOHC
	Sport	1.8 (1843)	2	MFI	4	16V-DOHC
	Tracker	1.6 (1590)	6	MFI	4	16V-SOHC

2-BBL. – 2 barrel carburetor
TFI – Throttle-body Fuel Injection
MFI – Multi-port Fuel Injection
8V-SOHC – 8 Valve Single Overhead Camshaft
16V-SOHC – 16 Valve Single Overhead Camshaft
16V-DOHC – 16 Valve Double Overhead Camshafts
① California and New York models

90881C01

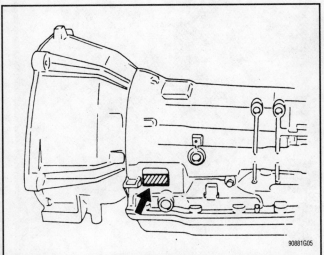

Fig. 41 The 3-speed automatic transmission identifying number is stamped into the lower, front, left-hand side of the case

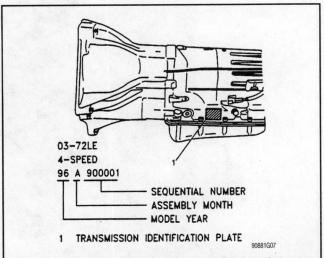

03-72LE
4-SPEED
96 A 900001
— SEQUENTIAL NUMBER
— ASSEMBLY MONTH
— MODEL YEAR

1   TRANSMISSION IDENTIFICATION PLATE

90881G07

Fig. 42 The identification code for the 4-speed automatic transmission is located on the left-hand, mid-section of the case

ROUTINE MAINTENANCE AND TUNE-UP

COMMON UNDERHOOD MAINTENANCE ITEMS

1. Battery
2. Spark plug wires
3. Distributor cap and rotor
4. High-tension coil wire
5. Engine oil fill cap
6. Spark plugs (beneath boot)

7. Brake master cylinder fill cap
8. Air cleaner element housing
9. Coolant reserve tank
10. A/C compressor drive belt
11. Radiator fill cap
12. Water pump drive belt

13. Warning labels (beneath hose)
14. Engine oil level dipstick
15. PCV valve (beneath the air intake case)
16. Upper radiator hose
17. Evaporative (charcoal) canister
18. Windshield washer fluid reservoir

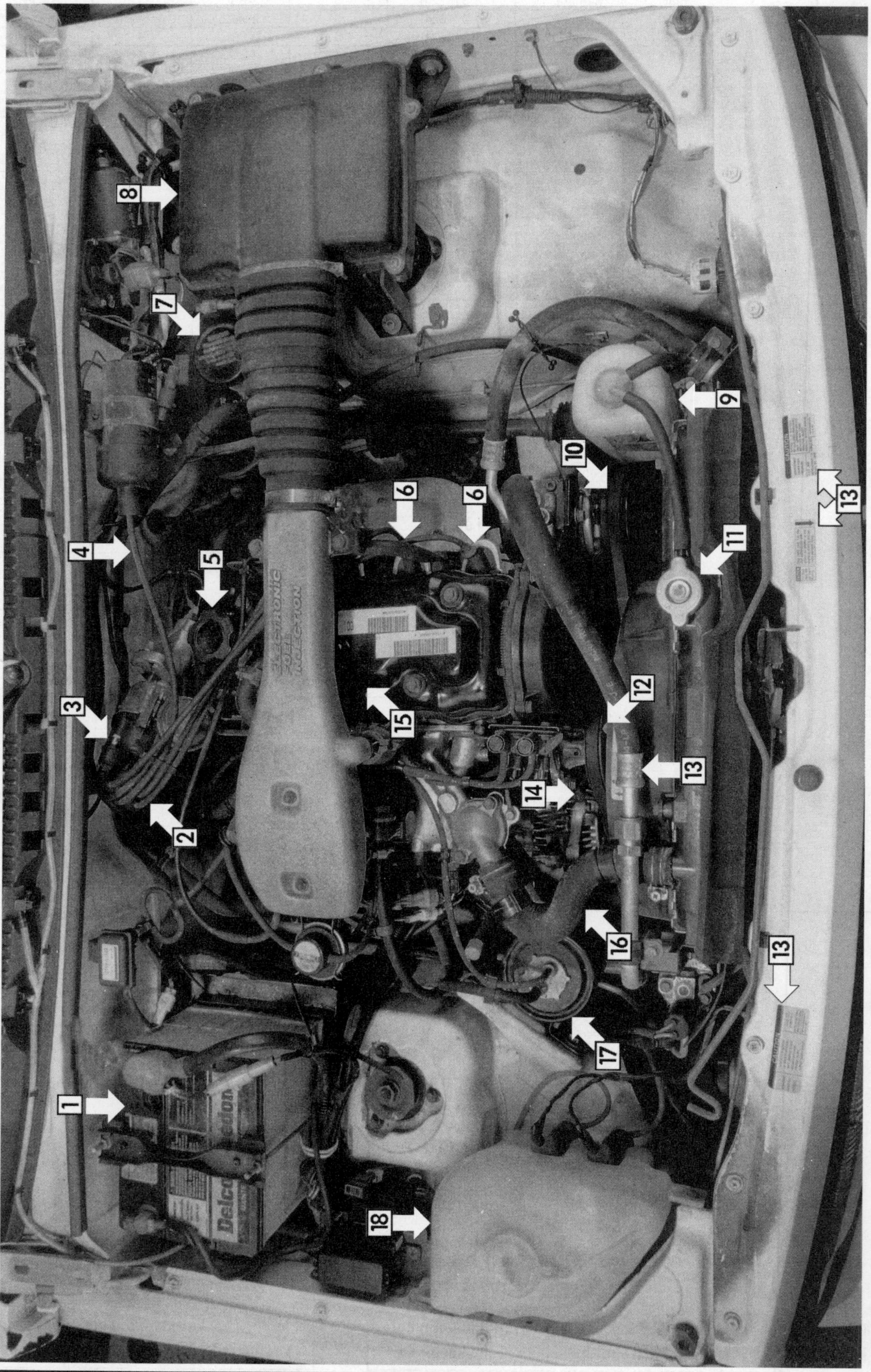

90881P70

COMMON UNDERVEHICLE MAINTENANCE ITEMS

1. Accessory drive belts
2. Front differential fill plug
3. Engine oil filter
4. Front differential drain plug
5. Engine oil drain plug
6. Constant Velocity (CV) boots
7. Universal joint grease points
8. Manual transmission fill plug
9. Manual transmission drain plug
10. Lower radiator hose

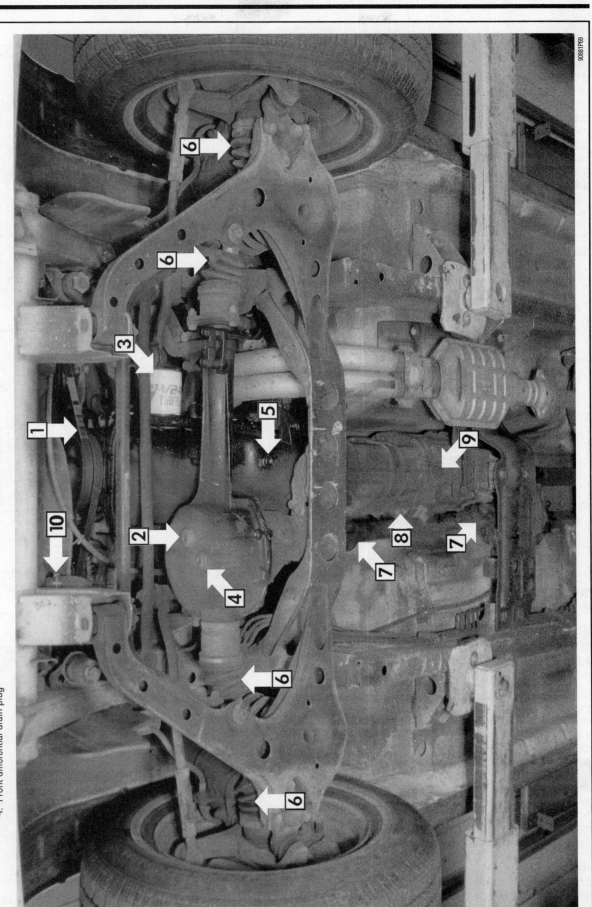

Proper maintenance and tune-up is the key to long and trouble-free vehicle life, and the work can yield its own rewards. Studies have shown that a properly tuned and maintained vehicle can achieve better gas mileage than an out-of-tune vehicle. As a conscientious owner and driver, set aside a Saturday morning, say once a month, to check or replace items which could cause major problems later. Keep your own personal log to jot down which services you performed, how much the parts cost you, the date, and the exact odometer reading at the time. Keep all receipts for such items as engine oil and filters, so that they may be referred to in case of related problems or to determine operating expenses. As a do-it-yourselfer, these receipts are the only proof you have that the required maintenance was performed. In the event of a warranty problem, these receipts will be invaluable.

The literature provided with your vehicle when it was originally delivered includes the factory recommended maintenance schedule. If you no longer have this literature, replacement copies are usually available from the dealer. A maintenance schedule is provided later in this section, in case you do not have the factory literature.

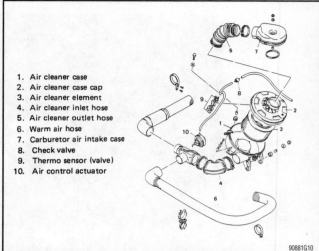

1. Air cleaner case
2. Air cleaner case cap
3. Air cleaner element
4. Air cleaner inlet hose
5. Air cleaner outlet hose
6. Warm air hose
7. Carburetor air intake case
8. Check valve
9. Thermo sensor (valve)
10. Air control actuator

Fig. 44 Exploded view of the air inlet system, including the air cleaner element, used on Samurai models

Fig. 43 To prolong the length and quality of your vehicle's usefulness, it is important to perform periodic preventive maintenance

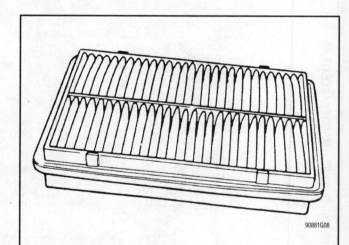

Fig. 45 The Sidekick, Tracker, Sport and X-90 models utilize a rectangular, flat element, rather than the cylindrical one used by Samurai models

Air Cleaner (Element)

REMOVAL & INSTALLATION

▶ See Figures 44 and 45

The air cleaner element helps prevent airborne contaminants from entering the engine through the intake system (carburetor or throttle body, intake manifold, cylinder head). Such airborne contaminants as dirt, soot, smoke, etc. can lead to an increase in engine wear if allowed into the engine. Also, a dirty or dusty air cleaner element can increase fuel consumption and lower engine power output. Therefore, it is important to periodically inspect and replace the air cleaner element.

During normal (non-severe) vehicle usage, the air cleaner element should be replaced with a new one every 30,000 miles (50,000 km) or 30 months, whichever occurs first. If the vehicle is driven under severe conditions, inspect the air cleaner element every 3,000 miles (5,000 km) or 3 months, and replace it at least every 15,000 miles (25,000 km) or 15 months (whichever occurs first).

The Samurai models utilize a cylindrical air cleaner element, whereas the other models use a flat, rectangular element. The air cleaner element is located in a large, black plastic housing (cylindrical for Samurai models and rectangular for all other models) attached to the carburetor/throttle body via large air tubes. To replace the air cleaner element:

To replace the air cleaner element, loosen the cover hold-down screws . . .

. . . then raise the cover and remove the element—note that some models utilize cover hold-down clamps

1. Open the hood.
2. Locate the air cleaner element housing. If unsure of its location, trace the air tube from the carburetor or throttle body (depending on your particular model) back to the black plastic housing.
3. On Samurai models, detach the air cleaner outlet hose (air tube) from the housing cover by loosening the hose clamp with a screwdriver, then by pulling the hose off of the cover flange.
4. Loosen the housing cover hold-down screws or clamps, then lift the cover up and off of the housing.
5. Note the installed position of the element, then pull it out of the housing.
6. Inspect the element by holding a 75W drop light, or similar lamp, inside the element (Samurai models), or on one side of the element (all other models). If light from the lamp can be seen through the element, it is still usable. If no light is visible through the element, or if the element is oily, ripped or otherwise damaged, replace it with a new one. If the element is only a little dusty or dirty and you have access to pressurized air, you can clean the element by blowing air through the element from the engine side of the element. (In other words, you should blow the air through the element in the opposite direction the air going into the engine normally flows during vehicle operation.)
7. Use a clean shop rag to wipe clean the inside of the housing. If there is oil or oily grime present in the housing, inspect the PCV system.

To install:
8. Position the element in the housing, then install the cover onto the housing. Ensure that the groove in the housing cover is properly engaged on the housing lip, then engage the hold-down screws or clamps to securely hold the cover in place.
9. If applicable, reattach the air cleaner outlet hose to the cover flange, and tighten the hose clamp until snug.
10. Close the hood.

Fuel Filter

REMOVAL & INSTALLATION

▶ See Figures 46 thru 53

✳✳ WARNING

This procedure must not be done when the engine is hot. Allow the engine to cool down completely prior to performing this procedure.

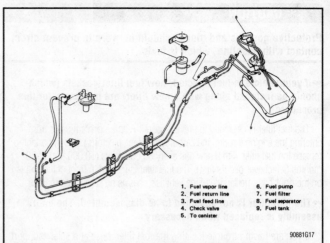

Fig. 46 Fuel supply system on carbureted models, showing the location of the fuel filter in relation to the fuel tank and other fuel system components

1. Fuel vapor line
2. Fuel return line
3. Fuel feed line
4. Check valve
5. To canister
6. Fuel pump
7. Fuel filter
8. Fuel separator
9. Fuel tank

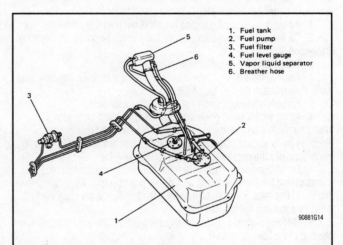

Fig. 47 The fuel filter on fuel-injected Samurai models is located in the same location as on carbureted models, however, the filter is mounted horizontally rather than vertically

1. Fuel tank
2. Fuel pump
3. Fuel filter
4. Fuel level gauge
5. Vapor liquid separator
6. Breather hose

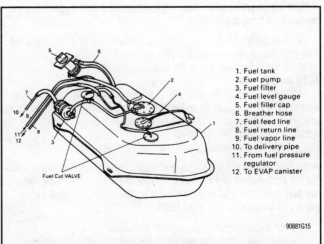

Fig. 48 The fuel filter on fuel-injected Sidekick, Tracker, Sidekick Sport and X-90 models is mounted closer to the fuel tank than the filter used on Samurai models

1. Fuel tank
2. Fuel pump
3. Fuel filter
4. Fuel level gauge
5. Fuel filler cap
6. Breather hose
7. Fuel feed line
8. Fuel return line
9. Fuel vapor line
10. To delivery pipe
11. From fuel pressure regulator
12. To EVAP canister

Fuel Cut VALVE

❊❊ CAUTION

Protective goggles and gloves should be worn to prevent direct contact with gasoline, which is toxic.

➡**If your vehicle is fuel injected, new fuel filter gaskets (which should be included along with a new filter) are necessary for this procedure.**

The fuel filter is designed to prevent gasoline-borne contaminants from entering the engine through the carburetor or fuel injector(s). It is important to replace the fuel filter with a new one every 30,000 miles (50,000 km) or 30 months (whichever occurs first). The fuel filter is located in front of the fuel tank on the right-hand underside of the vehicle's chassis on carbureted models.

➡**The fuel filter is not designed to be disassembled. The entire assembly is replaced when necessary.**

If you are having trouble locating the fuel filter, raise and safely support the rear of the vehicle on jackstands. Crawl under the vehicle and locate the three fuel lines leading from the fuel tank. Trace the fuel lines forward until one of them enters a metal cylindrical object; this is the fuel filter. The fuel filter used on carbureted models is mounted in a vertical orientation (the cylinder points up and down), whereas the fuel filters on fuel-injected models are mounted horizontally.

1. If necessary, allow the engine to cool down until it is completely cold.
2. On fuel-injected vehicles, relieve fuel system pressure, as described in Section 5.
3. Disconnect the negative battery cable.
4. Remove the fuel tank filler cap to release any built-up fuel tank pressure, then reinstall the fuel tank filler cap.
5. Raise and safely support the vehicle on jackstands.
6. Along with a small drain pan and plenty of clean shop rags, crawl under the right-side of the vehicle between the front and rear wheels. Position the drain pan under the fuel filter to catch any fuel in the lines. If necessary, use the rags to soak up any spilled gasoline.
7. On carbureted models, detach the fuel lines from the fuel filter by compressing the fuel line clamp tabs with a pair of pliers. While compressing the clamp tabs, slide the clamp down the fuel line, away from the fuel filter. Perform this to both fuel lines.
8. On fuel-injected models, remove the small pressure relief screw from the end of the filter (to release any residual fuel pressure in the lines). Position an aptly-sized open end wrench on the fuel filter flange and a box end wrench on the fuel line fitting attaching bolt. Use the open end wrench to hold the filter steady while loosening the line bolt with the box end wrench. Disconnect the other fuel line from the filter in the same manner. Once the lines are detached from the filter, pour any residual fuel into the catch pan.

➡**Note the position of the fuel filter inlet and outlet nipples before removing it from the vehicle.**

9. Remove the lower clamp bolt, then loosen the clamp adjusting bolt until the filter can be removed from the mounting clamp.
10. Pull the fuel filter out of the mounting clamp.

To install:

11. Crawl under the vehicle, and slide the new filter into the mounting clamp. Tighten the adjusting bolt until snug, then turn the filter in the clamp until the inlet and outlet nipples are positioned as before removal, then tighten the adjusting bolt securely.
12. Install the lower clamp bolt and tighten it securely.

➡**On carbureted vehicles, the top filter nipple is for the outlet hose (to the carburetor) and the lower nipple is for the inlet hose (from the fuel tank). On fuel-injected models, the filter inlet and outlet ports are marked on the filter itself.**

13. For carbureted vehicles, perform the following:
   a. Insert each fuel line over the applicable filter nipple as far as possible, then compress the fuel line clamp tabs and slide the clamp up the line until it is positioned over the filter nipple.
   b. Position the second clamp in the same manner.

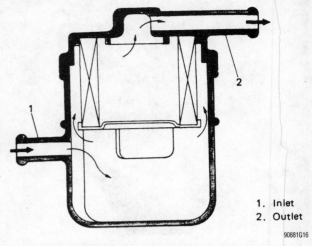

1. Inlet
2. Outlet

90881G16

Fig. 49 Cross-sectional view of the fuel filter used with a carbureted fuel system—arrows indicate the direction of fuel flow

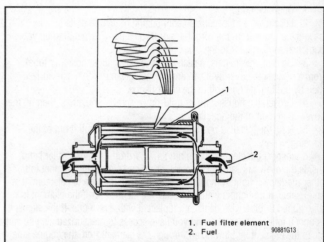

1. Fuel filter element
2. Fuel   90881G13

Fig. 50 The fuel-injection systems' filter is a metal canister surrounding a folded paper element—arrows indicate fuel flow through the filter

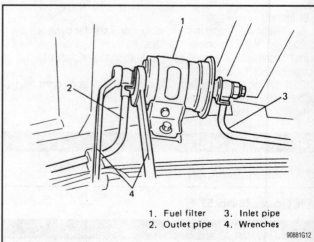

1. Fuel filter   3. Inlet pipe
2. Outlet pipe   4. Wrenches

90881G12

Fig. 51 To prevent damaging the lines or the filter itself, two wrenches should be used to disconnect the fuel lines from the filter—fuel-injected models

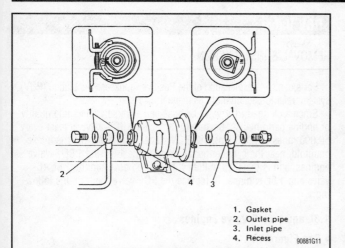

1. Gasket
2. Outlet pipe
3. Inlet pipe
4. Recess

90881G11

Fig. 52 Exploded view of the fuel line-to-fuel filter mounting on fuel-injected models—be sure to utilize new gaskets during assembly

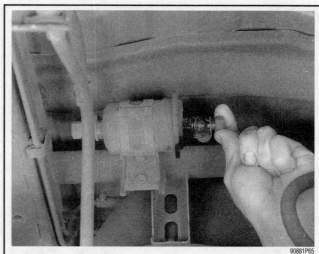

90881P65

Remove the banjo bolts from both ends of the filter and separate the lines from the filter

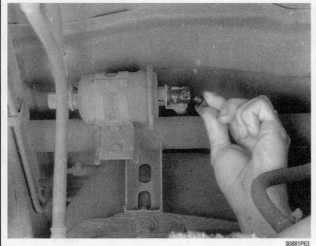

90881P63

For fuel-injected models, remove the small pressure relief screw from one end of the fuel filter . . .

90881P66

Remove the lower clamp bolt . . .

90881P64

. . . then, using two wrenches, loosen the fuel inlet and outlet line banjo bolts

90881P67

. . . then loosen the clamp adjusting bolt . . .

. . . until the filter can be removed from the mounting clamp

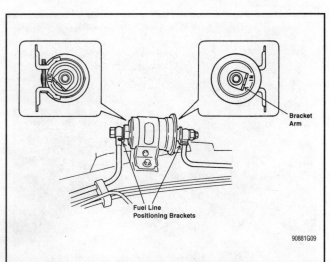

Fig. 53 When attaching the lines to the filter, ensure that they are situated between the two arms of each positioning bracket

➡The clamps should be at least ¼ in. (6mm) from the end of the fuel lines, but should also be positioned over the filter nipples.

14. For fuel-injected models, perform the following:

   a. Install a new gasket on one of the fuel line attaching bolts, then insert the bolt through one of the fuel line fittings.

   b. Install another new gasket on the threaded portion of the bolt protruding from the fuel line fitting.

   c. Position the fuel line fitting against the fuel filter so that the fuel line is positioned between the two arms of the line bracket, and thread the attaching bolt by hand.

   d. Using the open end wrench and a torque wrench and socket, tighten the fuel line attaching bolt to 25 ft. lbs. (34 Nm).

   e. Perform the same for the other fuel line.

   f. Install the small pressure relief screw.

15. Connect the negative battery cable.

16. For carbureted models, start the engine. Allow the engine to idle and check the fuel filter and lines for leaks, then turn the engine **OFF.**

17. For fuel-injected models, turn the ignition switch **ON** for 3 seconds (do not start the engine) to operate the electric fuel pump, then turn the switch **OFF.** Turn the ignition switch **ON** and **OFF** like this three or four times, which will produce fuel pressure in the lines. Inspect the fuel filter and lines for gasoline leaks.

18. Lower the vehicle.

PCV Valve

REMOVAL & INSTALLATION

For a complete explanation of the Positive Crankcase Ventilation (PCV) system, refer to Section 4 of this manual.

Since a clogged PCV valve or hose can adversely affect idle quality or engine performance, be sure to replace the PCV valve at least every 50,000 miles (83,000 km). The PCV valve is threaded into the intake manifold, near the cylinder head cover, on the 1.3L and 1.6L 8-valve engines, and is installed in the cylinder head cover on the 1.6L 16-valve and 1.8L engines. To replace the PCV valve, perform the following:

1.3L and 1.6L 8-Valve Engines

▸ See Figure 54

1. Detach the PCV system hoses from the cylinder head cover, PCV valve, air cleaner assembly and the 3-way junction.

2. Unthread the PCV valve from the intake manifold.

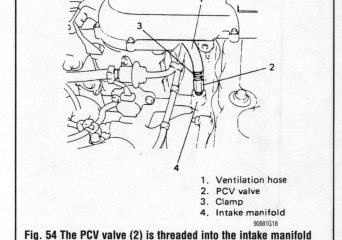

1. Ventilation hose
2. PCV valve
3. Clamp
4. Intake manifold

Fig. 54 The PCV valve (2) is threaded into the intake manifold (4) near the cylinder head cover and carburetor/throttle body

To remove the PCV valve, first detach the rubber hose from it . . .

. . . then loosen the PCV valve with a socket and ratchet . . .

90881P47

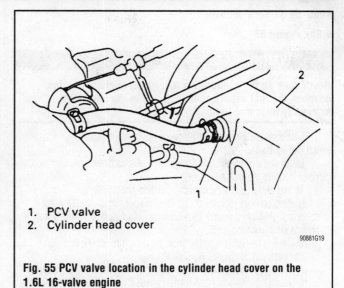

1. PCV valve
2. Cylinder head cover

90881G19

Fig. 55 PCV valve location in the cylinder head cover on the 1.6L 16-valve engine

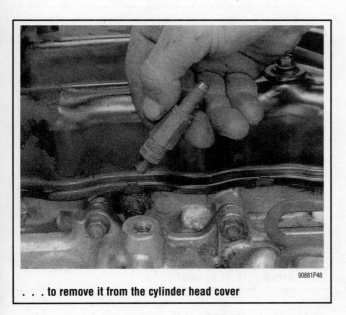

. . . to remove it from the cylinder head cover

90881P48

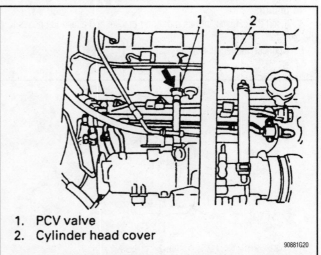

1. PCV valve
2. Cylinder head cover

90881G20

Fig. 56 The PCV valve (1) is mounted in the side of the cylinder head cover (2) on the 1.8L engine

To install:

3. Wrap Teflon® tape around the PCV valve threads, then install the valve in the intake manifold. Tighten the valve to 133–221 inch lbs. (15–25 Nm).

4. Reattach all of the system hoses to the cylinder head cover, valve, air cleaner assembly and 3-way junction.

1.6L 16-Valve and 1.8L Engines

▶ See Figures 55 and 56

1. Disconnect the rubber hose from the PCV valve, mounted in the cylinder head cover, by releasing the hose clamp and pulling the hose off of the valve nipple.

2. Remove the valve from the cylinder head cover.

To install:

3. Install the new valve in the cylinder head cover.

4. Reattach the hose to the PCV valve, and secure it with the hose clamp.

Evaporative Canister

SERVICING

The evaporative (charcoal) canister, known as the vapor storage canister, is a part of the evaporative emission control system. The canister stores fuel vapors when the engine is not running for later use. Inspect the canister periodically, and it should be replaced with a new one every 97,500 miles (162,500 km) or 8 years, whichever occurs first, regardless of its condition.

The evaporative (charcoal) canister is mounted in the engine compartment, near the air cleaner housing.

To inspect and replace the canister, perform the following:

1986–89 Samurai Models

▶ See Figure 57

1. Disconnect the negative battery cable to prevent accidental sparks, which can ignite fuel vapors.

2. Label and detach all of the hoses from the canister, then remove the canister from its mounting bracket.

3. To test and inspect the canister, perform the following:

a. Plug canister nipples **C** and **D** with your fingers (refer to the accompanying illustration), then blow air into nipple **A** strongly. Air should emit from nipple **B**.

b. Unplug the other nipples, then blow air into nipple **B**; no air should pass out of nipples **A, C** or **D**.

c. Blow air into nipple **C**; air should exit from the other 3 nipples.

d. Inspect the canister and related hoses for damage, such as cracks, holes, deterioration, etc.

e. If the canister does not function as stated or exhibits physical damage, it is defective and needs to be replaced with a new one.

To install:

4. Insert the canister into its mounting bracket and attach the hoses to the canister.

5. Connect the negative battery cable.

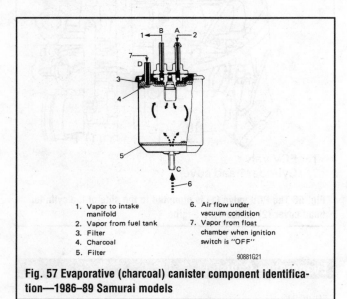

1. Vapor to intake manifold
2. Vapor from fuel tank
3. Filter
4. Charcoal
5. Filter
6. Air flow under vacuum condition
7. Vapor from float chamber when ignition switch is "OFF"

90881G21

Fig. 57 Evaporative (charcoal) canister component identification—1986–89 Samurai models

Except 1986–89 Samurai Models

▶ See Figures 58 and 59

1. Disconnect the negative battery cable to prevent accidental sparks, which can ignite fuel vapors.

2. Label and detach all of the hoses from the canister, then remove the canister from its mounting bracket.

3. To test and inspect the canister, perform the following:

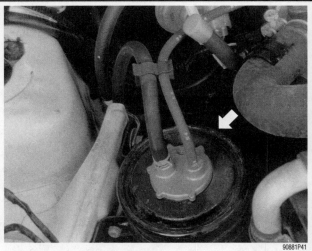

90881P41

The evaporative canister (arrow) is mounted on the inner, right-hand fender

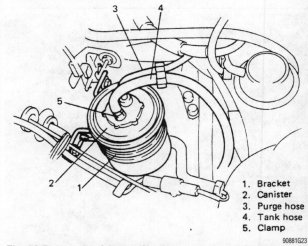

1. Bracket
2. Canister
3. Purge hose
4. Tank hose
5. Clamp

90881G23

Fig. 58 Evaporative (charcoal) canister component identification—except 1986–89 Samurai models

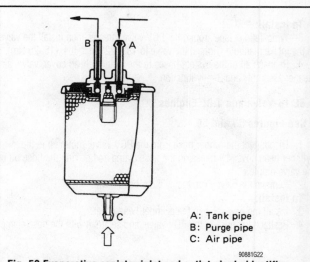

A: Tank pipe
B: Purge pipe
C: Air pipe

90881G22

Fig. 59 Evaporative canister inlet and outlet nipple identification—except 1986–89 Samurai models

a. Plug canister nipples **C** with a finger (refer to the accompanying illustration), then blow air into nipple **A** strongly; air should emit from nipple **B**.

b. Unplug the other nipples, then blow air into nipple **B**; no air should pass out of nipples **A** or **C**.

c. Blow air into nipple **C**; air should exit from the other 2 nipples.

d. Inspect the canister and related hoses for damage, such as cracks, holes, deterioration, etc.

e. If the canister does not function as stated or exhibits physical damage, it is defective and needs to be replaced with a new one.

To install:

4. Insert the canister into its mounting bracket and attach the hoses to the canister.

5. Connect the negative battery cable.

Battery

PRECAUTIONS

Always use caution when working on or near the battery. Never allow a tool to bridge the gap between the negative and positive battery terminals. Also, be careful not to allow a tool to provide a ground between the positive cable/terminal and any metal component on the vehicle. Either of these conditions will cause a short circuit, leading to sparks and possible personal injury.

Do not smoke, have an open flame or create sparks near a battery; the gases contained in the battery are very explosive and, if ignited, could cause severe injury or death.

All batteries, regardless of type, should be carefully secured by a battery hold-down device. If this is not done, the battery terminals or casing may crack from stress applied to the battery during vehicle operation. A battery which is not secured may allow acid to leak out, making it discharge faster; such leaking corrosive acid can also eat away at components under the hood.

Always visually inspect the battery case for cracks, leakage and corrosion. A white corrosive substance on the battery case or on nearby components would indicate a leaking or cracked battery. If the battery is cracked, it should be replaced immediately.

REMOVAL & INSTALLATION

1. Disconnect the negative and then the positive battery cables.
2. Loosen the hold-down clamp or strap retainers.
3. Remove the battery hold-down device.
4. Remove the battery from the vehicle.

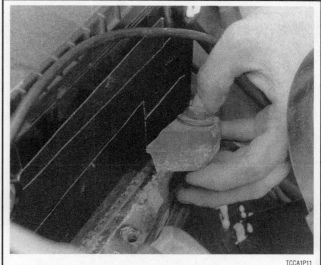

. . . then remove the battery hold-down device

TCCA1P11

Remove the battery from the vehicle

TCCA1P12

Loosen the battery hold-down device retainer . . .

TCCA1P10

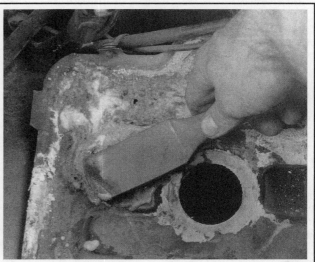

Use a wire brush to clean any rust from the battery tray

TCCA1P13

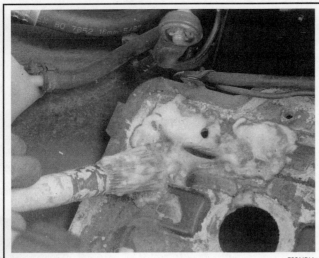

Brush on a solution of baking soda and water to clean the tray

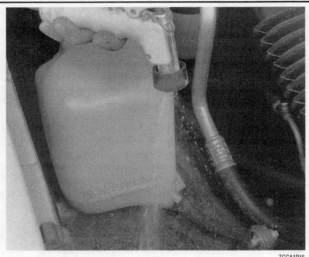

After cleaning the tray thoroughly, wash it off with some water

While the battery is removed, it is a good idea and opportunity to check the condition of the battery tray. Clear it of any debris, and check it for soundness (the battery tray can be cleaned with a baking soda and water solution). Rust should be wire brushed away, and the metal given a couple coats of anti-rust paint.

To install:

5. Install the battery and tighten the hold-down clamp or strap securely. Do not overtighten, as this can crack the battery case.

6. Connect the positive and then the negative battery cables.

GENERAL MAINTENANCE

▶ **See Figure 60**

A battery that is not sealed must be checked periodically for electrolyte level. You cannot add water to a sealed maintenance-free battery (though not all maintenance-free batteries are sealed); however, a sealed battery must also be checked for proper electrolyte level, as indicated by the color of the built-in hydrometer "eye."

Always keep the battery cables and terminals free of corrosion. Check these components about once a year. Refer to the removal, installation and cleaning procedures outlined in this section.

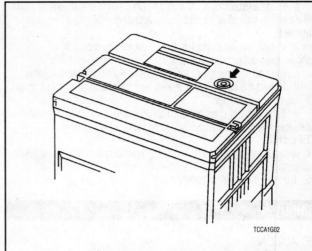

Fig. 60 A typical location for the built-in hydrometer on mainte-nance-free batteries

Keep the top of the battery clean, as a film of dirt can help completely discharge a battery that is not used for long periods. A solution of baking soda and water may be used for cleaning, but be careful to flush this off with clear water. DO NOT let any of the solution into the filler holes. Baking soda neutralizes battery acid and will de-activate a battery cell.

Batteries in vehicles which are not operated on a regular basis can fall victim to parasitic loads (small current drains which are constantly drawing current from the battery). Normal parasitic loads may drain a battery on a vehicle that is in storage and not used for 6–8 weeks. Vehicles that have additional accessories such as a cellular phone, an alarm system or other devices that increase parasitic load may discharge a battery sooner. If the vehicle is to be stored for 6–8 weeks in a secure area and the alarm system, if present, is not necessary, the negative battery cable should be disconnected at the onset of storage to protect the battery charge.

Remember that constantly discharging and recharging will shorten battery life. Take care not to allow a battery to be needlessly discharged.

BATTERY FLUID

Check the battery electrolyte level at least once a month, or more often in hot weather or during periods of extended vehicle operation. On non-sealed batteries, the level can be checked either through the case on translucent batteries or by removing the cell caps on opaque-cased types. The electrolyte level in each cell should be kept filled to the split ring inside each cell, or the line marked on the outside of the case.

If the level is low, add only distilled water through the opening until the level is correct. Each cell is separate from the others, so each must be checked and filled individually. Distilled water should be used, because the chemicals and minerals found in most drinking water are harmful to the battery and could significantly shorten its life.

If water is added in freezing weather, the vehicle should be driven several miles to allow the water to mix with the electrolyte. Otherwise, the battery could freeze.

Although some maintenance-free batteries have removable cell caps for access to the electrolyte, the electrolyte condition and level on all sealed maintenance-free batteries must be checked using the built-in hydrometer "eye." The exact type of eye varies between battery manufacturers, but most apply a sticker to the battery itself explaining the possible readings. When in doubt, refer to the battery manufacturer's instructions to interpret battery condition using the built-in hydrometer.

➡**Although the readings from built-in hydrometers found in sealed batteries may vary, a green eye usually indicates a properly charged battery with sufficient fluid level. A dark eye is normally an indicator of a battery with sufficient fluid, but one which may be** low in charge. And a light or yellow eye is usually an indication that electrolyte supply has dropped below the necessary level for battery (and hydrometer) operation. In this last case, sealed batteries with an insufficient electrolyte level must usually be discarded.

Checking the Specific Gravity

▶ See Figure 61

A hydrometer is required to check the specific gravity on all batteries that are not maintenance-free. On batteries that are maintenance-free, the specific gravity is checked by observing the built-in hydrometer "eye" on the top of the battery case. Check with your battery's manufacturer for proper interpretation of its built-in hydrometer readings.

On non-maintenance-free batteries, the fluid level can be checked through the case on translucent models; the cell caps must be removed on other models

If the fluid level is low, add only distilled water through the opening until the level is correct

✳✳ CAUTION

Battery electrolyte contains sulfuric acid. If you should splash any on your skin or in your eyes, flush the affected area with plenty of clear water. If it lands in your eyes, get medical help immediately.

The fluid (sulfuric acid solution) contained in the battery cells will tell you many things about the condition of the battery. Because the cell plates must be kept submerged below the fluid level in order to operate, maintaining the fluid level is extremely important. And, because the specific gravity of the acid is an indication of electrical charge, testing the fluid can be an aid in determining if the battery must be replaced. A battery in a vehicle with a properly operating charging system should require little maintenance, but careful, periodic inspection should reveal problems before they leave you stranded.

As stated earlier, the specific gravity of a battery's electrolyte level can be used as an indication of battery charge. At least once a year, check the specific gravity of the battery. It should be between 1.20 and 1.26 on the gravity scale. Most auto supply stores carry a variety of inexpensive battery testing hydrometers. These can be used on any non-sealed battery to test the specific gravity in each cell.

The battery testing hydrometer has a squeeze bulb at one end and a nozzle at the other. Battery electrolyte is sucked into the hydrometer until the float is lifted from its seat. The specific gravity is then read by noting the position of the float. If gravity is low in one or more cells, the battery should be slowly charged and checked again to see if the gravity has come up. Generally, if after charging, the specific gravity between any two cells varies more than 50 points (0.50), the battery should be replaced, as it can no longer produce sufficient voltage to guarantee proper operation.

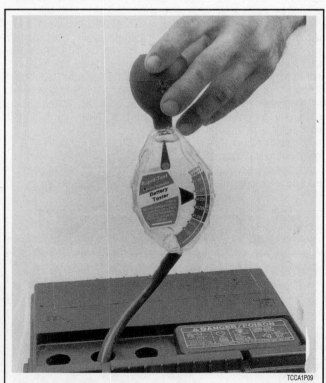

Check the specific gravity of the battery's electrolyte with a hydrometer

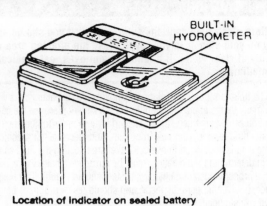

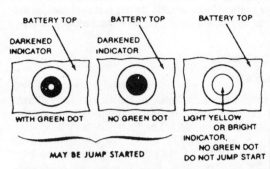

Fig. 61 A typical sealed (maintenance-free) battery with a built-in hydrometer—NOTE that the hydrometer eye may vary between battery manufacturers; always refer to the battery's label

CABLES

▶ **See Figures 62, 63, 64, 65 and 66**

Once a year (or as necessary), the battery terminals and the cable clamps should be cleaned. Loosen the clamps and remove the cables, negative cable first. On batteries with posts on top, the use of a puller specially made for this purpose is recommended. These are inexpensive and available in most auto parts stores. Side terminal battery cables are secured with a small bolt.

Clean the cable clamps and the battery terminal with a wire brush, until all corrosion, grease, etc., is removed and the metal is shiny. It is especially important to clean the inside of the clamp thoroughly (an old knife is useful here), since a small deposit of foreign material or oxidation there will prevent a sound electrical connection and inhibit either starting or charging. Special tools are available for cleaning these parts, one type for conventional top post batteries and another type for side terminal batteries. It is also a good idea to apply some dielectric grease to the terminal, as this will aid in the prevention of corrosion.

After the clamps and terminals are clean, reinstall the cables, negative cable last; DO NOT hammer the clamps onto battery posts. Tighten the clamps securely, but do not distort them. Give the clamps and terminals a thin external coating of grease after installation, to retard corrosion.

Fig. 63 The underside of this special battery tool has a wire brush to clean post terminals

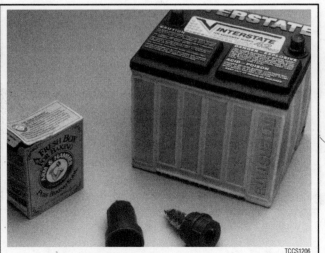

Fig. 62 Maintenance is performed with household items and with special tools like this post cleaner

Fig. 64 Place the tool over the battery posts and twist to clean until the metal is shiny

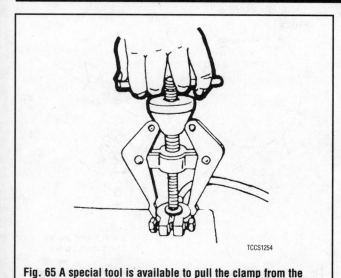

Fig. 65 A special tool is available to pull the clamp from the post

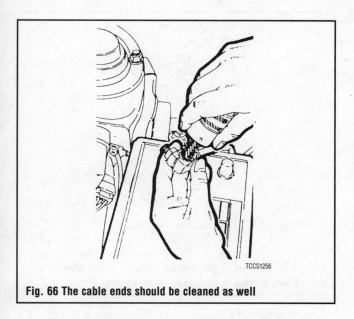

Fig. 66 The cable ends should be cleaned as well

Check the cables at the same time that the terminals are cleaned. If the cable insulation is cracked or broken, or if the ends are frayed, the cable should be replaced with a new cable of the same length and gauge.

CHARGING

❊❊ CAUTION

The chemical reaction which takes place in all batteries generates explosive hydrogen gas. A spark can cause the battery to explode and splash acid. To avoid serious personal injury, be sure there is proper ventilation and take appropriate fire safety precautions when connecting, disconnecting, or charging a battery and when using jumper cables.

A battery should be charged at a slow rate to keep the plates inside from getting too hot. However, if some maintenance-free batteries are allowed to discharge until they are almost "dead," they may have to be charged at a high rate to bring them back to "life." Always follow the charger manufacturer's instructions on charging the battery.

REPLACEMENT

When it becomes necessary to replace the battery, select one with an amperage rating equal to or greater than the battery originally installed. Deterioration and just plain aging of the battery cables, starter motor, and associated wires makes the battery's job harder in successive years. The slow increase in electrical resistance over time makes it prudent to install a new battery with a greater capacity than the old.

Belts

INSPECTION

▶ **See Figures 67 thru 73**

The 1.3L and 1.6L engines utilize only poly-V belts, whereas the 1.8L engine uses one poly-V belt and one serpentine belt. The 1.8L poly-V belt is referred to as the fan drive belt, and the serpentine belt is referred to as the alternator drive belt, although it also drives most of the other accessories as well.

Inspect the belts for signs of glazing or cracking. A glazed belt will be perfectly smooth from slippage, while a good belt will have a slight texture

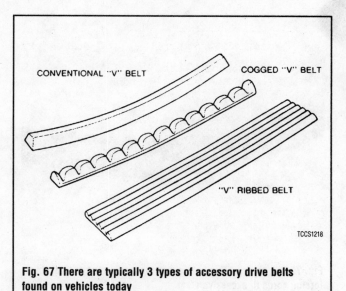

Fig. 67 There are typically 3 types of accessory drive belts found on vehicles today

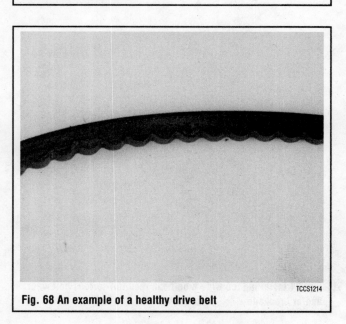

Fig. 68 An example of a healthy drive belt

Fig. 69 Deep cracks in this belt will cause flex, building up heat that will eventually lead to belt failure

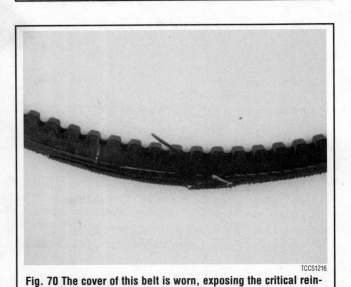

Fig. 70 The cover of this belt is worn, exposing the critical reinforcing cords to excessive wear

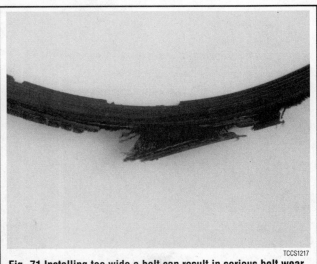

Fig. 71 Installing too wide a belt can result in serious belt wear and/or breakage

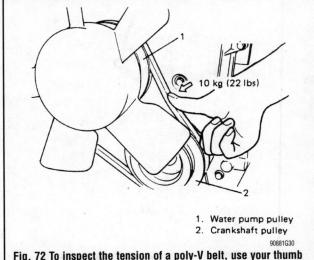

1. Water pump pulley
2. Crankshaft pulley

90881G30

Fig. 72 To inspect the tension of a poly-V belt, use your thumb to depress the belt at the mid-point

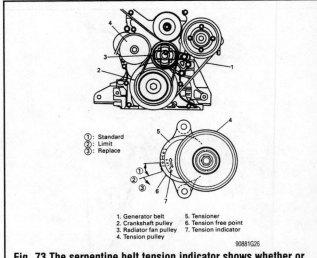

① : Standard
② : Limit
③ : Replace

1. Generator belt
2. Crankshaft pulley
3. Radiator fan pulley
4. Tension pulley
5. Tensioner
6. Tension free point
7. Tension indicator

90881G26

Fig. 73 The serpentine belt tension indicator shows whether or not the belt is properly tensioned—1.8L engine

of fabric visible. Cracks will usually start at the inner edge of the belt and run outward. All worn or damaged drive belts should be replaced immediately. It is best to replace all drive belts at one time, as a preventive maintenance measure, during this service operation.

For poly-V belts, inspect the accessory drive belt tension. The belt should deflect ¼–⅓ in. (6–9mm) under thumb pressure (approximately 22 lbs. or 10 kg) at the mid-point of the belt. If the belt deflection is not as specified, adjust the belt tension.

For the 1.8L engine serpentine belt, tension is indicated by the tension indicator. The serpentine belt tension indicator should point within the proper range (refer to the accompanying illustration). If the indicator does not point in the proper range, the serpentine belt should be replaced.

➡ **It may be necessary to use a mirror to read the serpentine belt indicator position.**

ADJUSTMENT

1.3L and 1.6L Engines

▶ **See Figure 74**

➡ **Although used drive belts should have a belt deflection of ¼–⅓ in. (6–9mm) under thumb pressure (approximately 22 lbs. or 10 kg)**

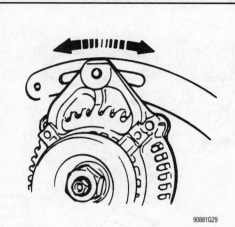

Fig. 74 To adjust the tension of the accessory drive belt, loosen the pivot and adjusting bolts, then move the component until the proper tension is reached

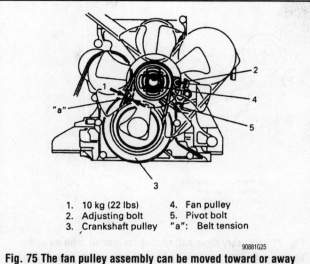

1. 10 kg (22 lbs)
2. Adjusting bolt
3. Crankshaft pulley
4. Fan pulley
5. Pivot bolt
"a": Belt tension

Fig. 75 The fan pulley assembly can be moved toward or away from the crankshaft pulley to adjust the fan drive belt tension

at the mid-point of the belt, when adjusting a new drive belt a deflection of 0.16–0.19 in. (4–5mm).

If the accessory drive belt is too tight or loose, adjust it to specification by moving the alternator, A/C compressor or power steering pump (depending on the particular belt).

1. Disconnect the negative battery cable.
2. Loosen the component's pivot and adjusting bolts until it can be repositioned.

➡ On 4WD Sidekick, X-90 and Tracker models, the rear alternator pivot bolt can be difficult to loosen. The best way to loosen and tighten this bolt is to use a stubby combination wrench on the pivot bolt head and a second wrench on the open end of the stubby wrench for leverage.

3. Using a padded prybar, carefully move the component away from the engine until the belt is properly tensioned, then tighten the adjusting and pivot bolts securely.
4. Connect the negative battery cable.

1.8L Engine

FAN DRIVE BELT

◗ See Figure 75

➡ Although used drive belts should have a belt deflection of ¼–⅓ in. (6–9mm) under thumb pressure (approximately 22 lbs. or 10 kg) at the mid-point of the belt, when adjusting a new drive belt a deflection of 0.16–0.19 in. (4–5mm).

If the accessory drive belt is too tight or loose, adjust it to specification by moving the fan pulley assembly, as follows:

1. Disconnect the negative battery cable.
2. Loosen the fan pulley assembly pivot and adjusting bolts until it can be moved.
3. Using a padded prybar, carefully move the fan pulley assembly away from the crankshaft pulley until the belt is properly tensioned, then tighten the adjusting and pivot bolts to 37 ft. lbs. (50 Nm).
4. Connect the negative battery cable.

ALTERNATOR DRIVE BELT

The serpentine belt utilizes an automatic tensioner assembly, and cannot be manually adjusted. If the belt is out of adjustment, replace it with a new one.

REMOVAL & INSTALLATION

1.3L and 1.6L Engines

◗ See Figures 76 and 77

1. Disconnect the negative battery cable.
2. Loosen the component's pivot and adjusting bolts until it can be repositioned.
3. Push the component toward the engine to release the belt tension, and until the belt can be removed from all applicable pulleys.

To install:

4. Position the accessory drive belt in the pulley grooves, then using a padded prybar, carefully move the component away from the engine until the belt is properly tensioned. Tighten the adjusting and pivot bolts securely.

➡ Although used drive belts should have a belt deflection of ¼–⅓ in. (6–9mm) under thumb pressure (approximately 22 lbs. or 10 kg) at the mid-point of the belt, when adjusting a new drive belt a deflection of 0.16–0.19 in. (4–5mm).

5. Connect the negative battery cable.

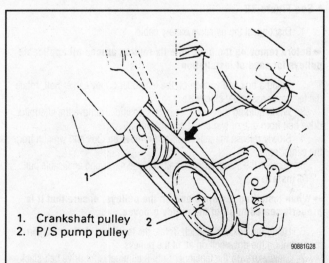

1. Crankshaft pulley
2. P/S pump pulley

Fig. 76 Accessory drive belt routing on models equipped with power steering

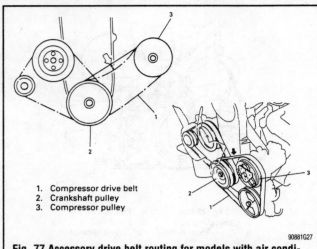

1. Compressor drive belt
2. Crankshaft pulley
3. Compressor pulley

90881G27

Fig. 77 Accessory drive belt routing for models with air conditioning only (left), and with air conditioning with power steering (right)

1.8L Engine

FAN DRIVE BELT

1. Disconnect the negative battery cable.
2. Loosen the fan pulley assembly pivot and adjusting bolts until it can be repositioned.
3. Push the component toward the crankshaft pulley to release the belt tension, and until the belt can be removed from both pulleys.

To install:

4. Position the accessory drive belt in the pulley grooves, then using a padded prybar, carefully move the fan pulley assembly away from the crankshaft pulley until the belt is properly tensioned. Tighten the adjusting and pivot bolts to 37 ft. lbs. (50 Nm).

➡**Although used drive belts should have a belt deflection of ¼–⅓ in. (6–9mm) under thumb pressure (approximately 22 lbs. or 10 kg) at the mid-point of the belt, when adjusting a new drive belt a deflection of 0.16–0.19 in. (4–5mm).**

5. Connect the negative battery cable.

ALTERNATOR DRIVE BELT

♦ **See Figure 78**

1. Disconnect the negative battery cable.

➡**Before removing the belt, note its routing around all applicable pulleys for ease of installation.**

2. Using a box end wrench on the tensioner pulley center bolt, rotate the tensioner assembly clockwise.
3. While holding the tensioner in this position, remove the alternator drive belt from one or two of the applicable pulleys.
4. Slowly release the tensioner, and remove the box end wrench from the center bolt.
5. Remove the alternator drive belt from the remaining applicable pulleys.

To install:

➡**When installing the drive belt on the pulleys, ensure that it is properly seated in all of the pulley grooves.**

6. Using the box end wrench, rotate the tensioner clockwise again, then position the drive belt on all of the pulleys.
7. Slowly release the tensioner until it eliminates all drive belt slack.
8. Inspect the tensioner indicator to be sure that the belt is properly tensioned. If the belt tension is incorrect, the belt should be replaced with a new one, or, if installing a new belt, the belt may not be the correct belt for your vehicle.

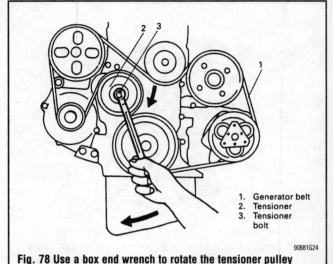

1. Generator belt
2. Tensioner
3. Tensioner bolt

90881G24

Fig. 78 Use a box end wrench to rotate the tensioner pulley assembly clockwise to relieve serpentine belt tension

9. Connect the negative battery cable, then start the engine. Ensure that the drive belt works properly.
10. Stop the engine, then double-check to ensure that the belt is properly seated on all applicable pulleys.

Timing Belts

INSPECTION

♦ **See Figures 79 thru 87**

➡**The 1.6L 16-valve and the 1.8L engines covered by this manual are interference motors. If the timing belt (1.6L) or chain (1.8L) breaks, internal damage to the engine is a very likely result.**

The 1.3 and 1.6L engines covered by this manual utilize a timing belt to drive the camshaft from the crankshaft's turning motion and to maintain proper valve timing. Some manufacturer's schedule periodic timing belt replacement to assure optimum engine performance, to make sure the motorist is never stranded should the belt break (as the engine will stop instantly) and for some (such as the 1.6L 16-valve engine) to prevent the possibility of severe internal engine damage should the belt break.

No!

OIL

TCCS1242

Fig. 79 Do not bend, twist or turn the timing belt inside out. Never allow oil, water or steam to contact the belt

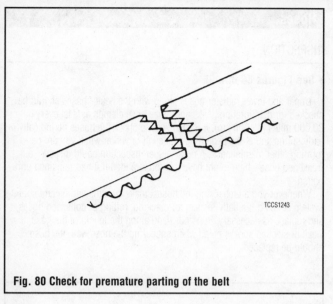

Fig. 80 Check for premature parting of the belt

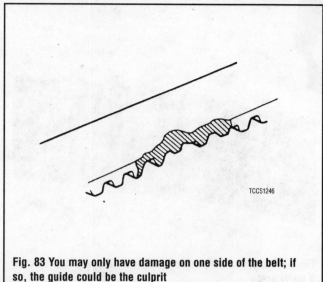

Fig. 83 You may only have damage on one side of the belt; if so, the guide could be the culprit

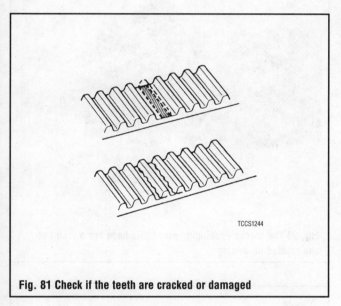

Fig. 81 Check if the teeth are cracked or damaged

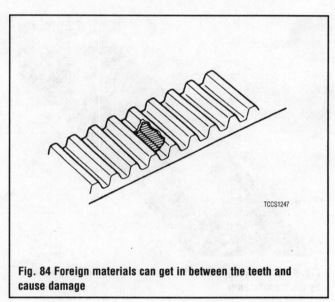

Fig. 84 Foreign materials can get in between the teeth and cause damage

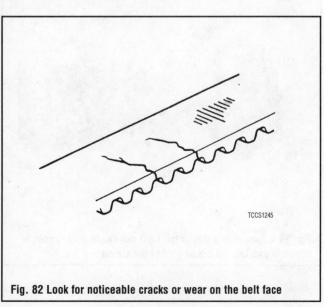

Fig. 82 Look for noticeable cracks or wear on the belt face

Fig. 85 Inspect the timing belt for cracks, fraying, glazing or damage of any kind

Fig. 86 Damage on only one side of the timing belt may indicate a faulty guide

Fig. 87 ALWAYS replace the timing belt at the interval specified by the manufacturer

Although the 1.3L and 1.6L 8-valve engines covered in this manual are not listed as interference motors (they are not listed by Suzuki as motors whose valves might contact the pistons if the camshaft was rotated separately from the crankshaft) the first 2 reasons for periodic replacement still apply.

Whether or not you decide to replace the belt, you would be wise to check it periodically to make sure it has not become damaged or worn. Suzuki recommends replacing the timing belts at least every 60,000 miles (96,000 km), and inspecting them every 30,000 miles (48,000 km) between replacements. Generally speaking, a severely damaged belt will show as engine performance would drop dramatically, but a damaged belt (which could give out suddenly) may not give as much warning. In general, any time the engine timing cover(s) is(are) removed you should inspect the belt for premature parting, severe cracks or missing teeth. Also, an access plug may be provided in the upper portion of the timing cover so that camshaft timing can be checked without cover removal. If timing is found to be off, cover removal and further belt inspection or replacement is necessary.

➥For timing belt cover and belt removal and installation, please refer to Section 3.

INSPECTION

▶ **See Figures 88 thru 95**

Upper and lower radiator hoses along with the heater hoses should be checked for deterioration, leaks and loose hose clamps at least every 30,000 miles (48,000 km). It is also wise to check the hoses periodically in early spring and at the beginning of the fall or winter when you are performing other maintenance. A quick visual inspection could discover a weakened hose which might have left you stranded if it had remained unrepaired.

Whenever you are checking the hoses, make sure the engine and cooling system are cold. Visually inspect for cracking, rotting or collapsed hoses, and replace as necessary. Run your hand along the length of the hose. If a weak or swollen spot is noted when squeezing the hose wall, the hose should be replaced.

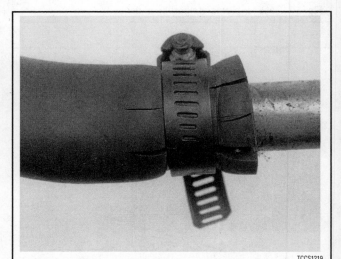

Fig. 88 The cracks developing along this hose are a result of age-related hardening

Fig. 89 A hose clamp that is too tight can cause older hoses to separate and tear on either side of the clamp

Fig. 90 A soft spongy hose (identifiable by the swollen section) will eventually burst and should be replaced

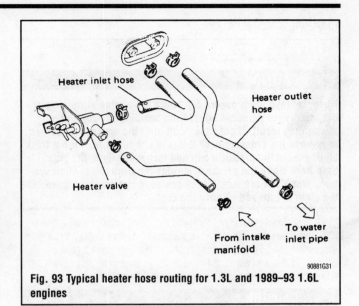

Fig. 93 Typical heater hose routing for 1.3L and 1989–93 1.6L engines

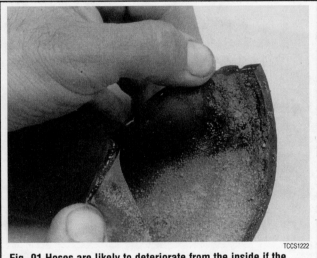

Fig. 91 Hoses are likely to deteriorate from the inside if the cooling system is not periodically flushed

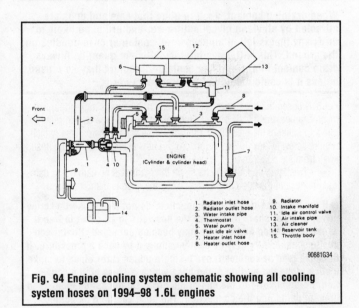

1. Radiator inlet hose
2. Radiator outlet hose
3. Water intake pipe
4. Thermostat
5. Water pump
6. Fast idle air valve
7. Heater inlet hose
8. Heater outlet hose
9. Radiator
10. Intake manifold
11. Idle air control valve
12. Air intake pipe
13. Air cleaner
14. Reservoir tank
15. Throttle body

Fig. 94 Engine cooling system schematic showing all cooling system hoses on 1994–98 1.6L engines

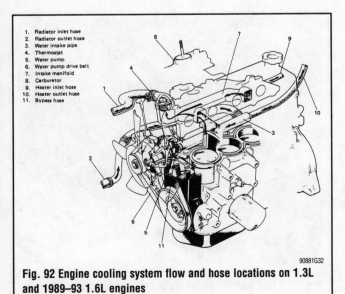

1. Radiator inlet hose
2. Radiator outlet hose
3. Water intake pipe
4. Thermostat
5. Water pump
6. Water pump drive belt
7. Intake manifold
8. Carburetor
9. Heater inlet hose
10. Heater outlet hose
11. Bypass hose

Fig. 92 Engine cooling system flow and hose locations on 1.3L and 1989–93 1.6L engines

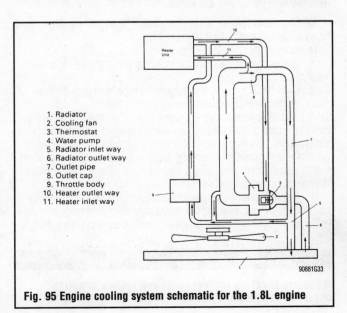

1. Radiator
2. Cooling fan
3. Thermostat
4. Water pump
5. Radiator inlet way
6. Radiator outlet way
7. Outlet pipe
8. Outlet cap
9. Throttle body
10. Heater outlet way
11. Heater inlet way

Fig. 95 Engine cooling system schematic for the 1.8L engine

REMOVAL & INSTALLATION

1. Remove the radiator pressure cap.

> ※※ **CAUTION**
>
> **Never remove the pressure cap while the engine is running or hot, otherwise personal injury from scalding hot coolant or steam may result. If possible, wait until the engine has cooled to remove the pressure cap. If this is not possible, wrap a thick cloth around the pressure cap and turn it slowly to the stop. Step back while the pressure is released from the cooling system. When you are sure all the pressure has been released, use the cloth to turn and remove the cap.**

2. Position a clean container under the radiator and/or engine drain plug, then open the drain and allow the cooling system to drain to an appropriate level. For some upper hoses, only a little coolant must be drained. To remove hoses positioned lower on the engine, such as a lower radiator hose, the entire cooling system must be emptied.

> ※※ **CAUTION**
>
> **When draining coolant, keep in mind that cats and dogs are attracted by ethylene glycol antifreeze, and are quite likely to drink any that is left in an uncovered container or in puddles on the ground. This will prove fatal in sufficient quantity. Always drain coolant into a sealable container. Coolant may be reused unless it is contaminated or several years old.**

3. Loosen the hose clamps at each end of the hose requiring replacement. Clamps are usually either of the spring tension type (which require pliers to squeeze the tabs and loosen) or of the screw tension type (which require screw or hex drivers to loosen). Pull the clamps back on the hose away from the connection.

4. Twist, pull and slide the hose off the fitting, taking care not to damage the neck of the component from which the hose is being removed.

➡ **If the hose is stuck at the connection, do not try to insert a screwdriver or other sharp tool under the hose end in an effort to free it, as the connection and/or hose may become damaged. Heater connections especially may be easily damaged by such a procedure. If the hose is to be replaced, use a single-edged razor blade to make a slice along the portion of the hose which is stuck on the connection, perpendicular to the end of the hose. Do not cut deep so as to prevent damaging the connection. The hose can then be peeled from the connection and discarded.**

5. Clean both hose mounting connections. Inspect the condition of the hose clamps and replace them, if necessary.

To install:

6. Dip the ends of the new hose into clean engine coolant to ease installation.

7. Slide the clamps over the replacement hose, then slide the hose ends over the connections into position.

8. Position and secure the clamps at least ¼ in. (6.35mm) from the ends of the hose. Make sure they are located beyond the raised bead of the connector.

9. Close the radiator or engine drains and properly refill the cooling system with the clean drained engine coolant or a suitable 50/50 mixture of ethylene glycol coolant and water.

10. If available, install a pressure tester and check for leaks. If a pressure tester is not available, run the engine until normal operating temperature is reached (allowing the system to naturally pressurize), then check for leaks.

> ※※ **CAUTION**
>
> **If you are checking for leaks with the system at normal operating temperature, BE EXTREMELY CAREFUL not to**

touch any moving or hot engine parts. Once temperature has been reached, shut the engine OFF, and check for leaks around the hose fittings and connections which were removed earlier.

CV-Boots

INSPECTION

▶ **See Figures 96 and 97**

The Constant Velocity (CV) boots should be checked for damage each time the oil is changed and any other time the vehicle is raised for service. These boots keep water, grime, dirt and other damaging matter from entering the CV-joints. Any of these could cause early CV-joint failure which can be expensive to repair. Heavy grease thrown around the inside of the front wheel(s) and on the brake caliper/drum can be an indication of a torn boot. Thoroughly check the boots for missing clamps and tears. If the boot is damaged, it should be replaced immediately. Please refer to Section 7 for the service procedures.

TCCS1011

Fig. 96 CV-boots must be inspected periodically for damage

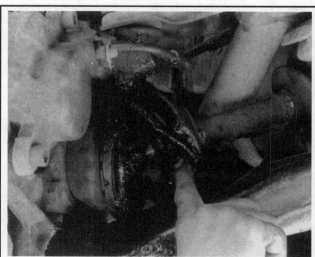

TCCS1010

Fig. 97 A torn boot should be replaced immediately

Spark Plugs

♦ See Figure 98

A typical spark plug consists of a metal shell surrounding a ceramic insulator. A metal electrode extends downward through the center of the insulator and protrudes a small distance. Located at the end of the plug and attached to the side of the outer metal shell is the side electrode. The side electrode bends in at a 90° angle so that its tip is just past and parallel to the tip of the center electrode. The distance between these two electrodes (measured in thousandths of an inch or hundredths of a millimeter) is called the spark plug gap.

The spark plug does not produce a spark, but instead provides a gap across which the current can arc. The coil produces anywhere from 20,000 to 50,000 volts (depending on the type and application) which travels through the wires to the spark plugs. The current passes along the center electrode and jumps the gap to the side electrode, and in doing so, ignites the air/fuel mixture in the combustion chamber.

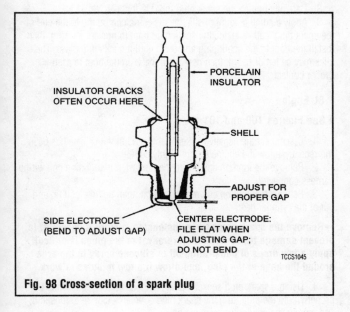

Fig. 98 Cross-section of a spark plug

SPARK PLUG HEAT RANGE

♦ See Figure 99

Spark plug heat range is the ability of the plug to dissipate heat. The longer the insulator (or the farther it extends into the engine), the hotter the plug will operate; the shorter the insulator (the closer the electrode is to the block's cooling passages) the cooler it will operate. A plug that absorbs little heat and remains too cool will quickly accumulate deposits of oil and carbon since it is not hot enough to burn them off. This leads to plug fouling and consequently to misfiring. A plug that absorbs too much heat will have no deposits but, due to the excessive heat, the electrodes will burn away quickly and might possibly lead to pre-ignition or other ignition problems. Pre-ignition takes place when plug tips get so hot that they glow sufficiently to ignite the air/fuel mixture before the actual spark occurs. This early ignition will usually cause a pinging during low speeds and heavy loads.

The general rule of thumb for choosing the correct heat range when picking a spark plug is: if most of your driving is long distance, high speed travel, use a colder plug; if most of your driving is stop and go, use a hotter plug. Original equipment plugs are generally a good compromise between the 2 styles and most people never have the need to change their plugs from the factory-recommended heat range.

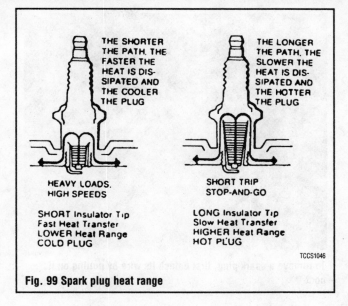

Fig. 99 Spark plug heat range

REMOVAL & INSTALLATION

Suzuki recommends replacing your spark plugs at least every 30,000 miles (48,000 km) or 30 months, whichever occurs first. However, a set of spark plugs may require replacement between 20,000–30,000 miles (32,000–48,000 km), depending on your style of driving. In normal operation plug gap increases about 0.001 in. (0.025mm) for every 2500 miles (4000 km). As the gap increases, the plug's voltage requirement also increases. It requires a greater voltage to jump the wider gap and about two to three times as much voltage to fire the plug at high speeds than at idle. The improved air/fuel ratio control of modern fuel injection combined with the higher voltage output of modern ignition systems will often allow an engine to run significantly longer on a set of standard spark plugs, but keep in mind that efficiency will drop as the gap widens (along with fuel economy and power).

1.3L and 1.6L Engines

When you're removing spark plugs, work on one at a time. Don't start by removing the plug wires all at once, because, unless you number them, they may become mixed up. Take a minute before you begin to number the wires with tape.

1. Disconnect the negative battery cable, and, if the vehicle has been run recently, allow the engine to thoroughly cool.

2. Carefully twist the spark plug wire boot to loosen it, then pull upward and remove the boot from the plug. Be sure to pull on the boot and not on the wire, otherwise the connector located inside the boot may become separated.

3. Using compressed air, blow any water or debris from the spark plug well to assure that no harmful contaminants are allowed to enter the combustion chamber when the spark plug is removed. If compressed air is not available, use a rag or a brush to clean the area.

➡Remove the spark plugs when the engine is cold, if possible, to prevent damage to the threads. If removal of the plugs is difficult, apply a few drops of penetrating oil or silicone spray to the area around the base of the plug, and allow it a few minutes to work.

4. Using a spark plug socket that is equipped with a rubber insert to properly hold the plug, turn the spark plug counterclockwise to loosen it, and remove the spark plug from the bore.

✳✳ WARNING

Be sure not to use a flexible extension on the socket. Use of a flexible extension may allow a shear force to be applied to the plug. A shear force could break the plug off in the cylinder head, leading to costly and frustrating repairs.

To remove a spark plug, first detach its wire by pulling on its boot

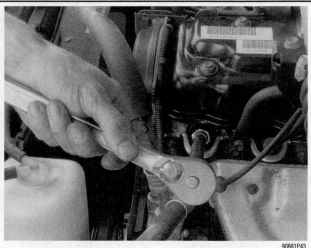

Clean the area around the spark plug, then use a socket and ratchet . . .

. . . to remove the spark plug from the cylinder head

To install:

5. Inspect the spark plug boot for tears or damage. If a damaged boot is found, the spark plug wire must be replaced.

6. Using a wire feeler gauge, check and adjust the spark plug gap. When using a gauge, the proper size should pass between the electrodes with a slight drag. The next larger size should not be able to pass while the next smaller size should pass freely.

7. Carefully thread the plug into the bore by hand. If resistance is felt before the plug is almost completely threaded, back the plug out and begin threading it again. In small, hard to reach areas, an old spark plug wire and boot could be used as a threading tool. The boot will hold the plug while you twist the end of the wire, and the wire is supple enough to twist before it would allow the plug to crossthread.

✲✲ WARNING

Do not use the spark plug socket to thread the plugs. Always carefully thread the plug by hand or using an old plug wire to prevent the possibility of crossthreading and damaging the cylinder head bore.

8. Carefully tighten the spark plug to 20 ft. lbs. (27 Nm).

9. Apply a small amount of silicone dielectric compound to the end of the spark plug lead or inside the spark plug boot to prevent sticking, then install the boot to the spark plug and push until it clicks into place. The click may be felt or heard, then gently pull back on the boot to assure proper contact.

1.8L Engine

▶ See Figures 100 and 101

1. Disconnect the negative battery cable, and, if the vehicle has been run recently, allow the engine to thoroughly cool.

2. Remove the ignition coil cover, then unfasten the ignition coil wiring harness connector.

3. Remove the ignition coil mounting bolt, then pull the coil up and out of the cylinder head cover.

➡**Remove the spark plugs when the engine is cold, if possible, to prevent damage to the threads. If removal of the plugs is difficult, apply a few drops of penetrating oil or silicone spray to the area around the base of the plug, and allow it a few minutes to work.**

4. Using a spark plug socket that is equipped with a rubber insert to properly hold the plug, turn the spark plug counterclockwise to loosen it, and remove the spark plug from the bore.

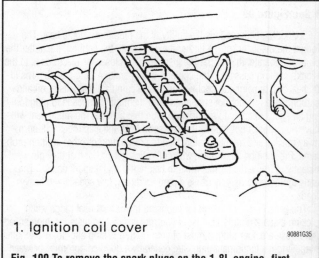

1. Ignition coil cover

Fig. 100 To remove the spark plugs on the 1.8L engine, first remove the ignition coil cover . . .

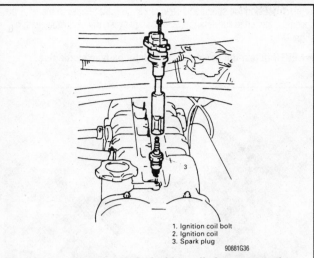

1. Ignition coil bolt
2. Ignition coil
3. Spark plug

90881G36

Fig. 101 . . . then remove the ignition coils for access to the plugs

✳✳ WARNING

Be sure not to use a flexible extension on the socket. Use of a flexible extension may allow a shear force to be applied to the plug. A shear force could break the plug off in the cylinder head, leading to costly and frustrating repairs.

To install:

5. Inspect the ignition coil boot for tears or damage. If a damaged boot is found, the ignition coil must be replaced.

6. Using a wire feeler gauge, check and adjust the spark plug gap. When using a gauge, the proper size should pass between the electrodes with a slight drag. The next larger size should not be able to pass while the next smaller size should pass freely.

7. Carefully thread the plug into the bore by hand. If resistance is felt before the plug is almost completely threaded, back the plug out and begin threading it again. In small, hard to reach areas, a piece of thick vacuum hose which fits snugly onto the spark plug could be used as a threading tool. The hose will hold the plug while you twist the end of it, and the hose is supple enough to twist before it would allow the plug to crossthread.

✳✳ WARNING

If using the spark plug socket to thread the plugs, be especially careful not to force the spark plugs. Always carefully thread the plug by hand or using an old plug wire to prevent the possibility of crossthreading and damaging the cylinder head bore.

8. Carefully tighten the spark plug to 20 ft. lbs. (27 Nm).
9. Apply a small amount of silicone dielectric compound to the inside of the end of the ignition coil.
10. Install the ignition coil and mounting bolt. Tighten the mounting bolt snugly.
11. Install the ignition coil cover.
12. Connect the negative battery cable.

INSPECTION & GAPPING

▶ See Figures 102 thru 111

Check the plugs for deposits and wear. If they are not going to be replaced, clean the plugs thoroughly. Remember that any kind of deposit will decrease the efficiency of the plug. Plugs can be cleaned on a spark plug cleaning machine, which can sometimes be found in service stations, or you can do an acceptable job of cleaning with a stiff brush. If the plugs are cleaned, the electrodes must be filed flat. Use an ignition points file, not

TCCS2135

Fig. 102 A normally worn spark plug should have light tan or gray deposits on the firing tip

TCCS2136

Fig. 103 A carbon fouled plug, identified by soft, sooty, black deposits, may indicate an improperly tuned vehicle. Check the air cleaner, ignition components and engine control system

an emery board or the like, which will leave deposits. The electrodes must be filed perfectly flat with sharp edges; rounded edges reduce the spark plug voltage by as much as 50%.

Check spark plug gap before installation. The ground electrode (the L-shaped one connected to the body of the plug) must be parallel to the cen-ter electrode and the specified size wire gauge (please refer to the tune-up specifications chart for details) must pass between the electrodes with a slight drag.

➡**NEVER adjust the gap on a used platinum type spark plug.**

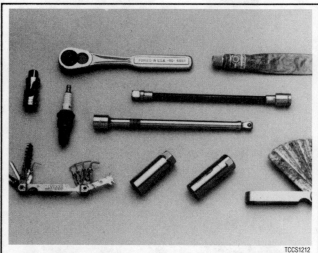

Fig. 104 A variety of tools and gauges are needed for spark plug service

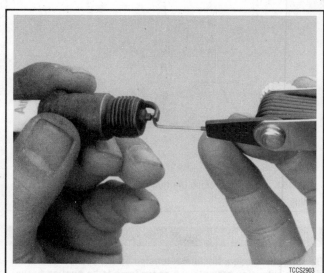

Fig. 106 Checking the spark plug gap with a feeler gauge

Fig. 105 A physically damaged spark plug may be evidence of severe detonation in that cylinder. Watch that cylinder carefully between services, as a continued detonation will not only dam-age the plug, but could also damage the engine

Fig. 107 An oil fouled spark plug indicates an engine with worn piston rings and/or bad valve seals allowing excessive oil to enter the chamber

Always check the gap on new plugs as they are not always set correctly at the factory. Do not use a flat feeler gauge when measuring the gap on a used plug, because the reading may be inaccurate. A round-wire type gapping tool is the best way to check the gap. The correct gauge should pass through the electrode gap with a slight drag. If you're in doubt, try one size smaller and one larger. The smaller gauge should go through easily, while the larger one shouldn't go through at all. Wire gapping tools usually have a bending tool attached. Use that to adjust the side electrode until the proper distance is obtained. Absolutely never attempt to bend the center electrode. Also, be careful not to bend the side electrode too far or too often as it may weaken and break off within the engine, requiring removal of the cylinder head to retrieve it.

Fig. 108 Adjusting the spark plug gap

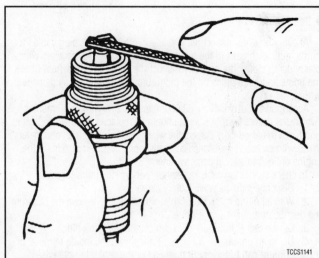

Fig. 110 If the standard plug is in good condition, the electrode may be filed flat—CAUTION: do not file platinum plugs

Fig. 109 This spark plug has been left in the engine too long, as evidenced by the extreme gap—Plugs with such an extreme gap can cause misfiring and stumbling accompanied by a noticeable lack of power

Fig. 111 A bridged or almost bridged spark plug, identified by build-up between the electrodes caused by excessive carbon or oil build-up on the plug

Spark Plug Wires

➡The 1.8L engine does not utilize spark plug wires; each of the engine's four ignition coils is mounted directly over one of the spark plugs.

TESTING

◆ See Figure 114

At every tune-up/inspection, visually check the spark plug cables for burns, cuts, or breaks in the insulation. Start by wiping the wires with a clean, damp cloth. The carefully inspect the surface of the wires. Check the boots and the nipples on the distributor cap. Replace any damaged wiring.

According to Suzuki, every 60,000 miles (96,000 Km) or 60 months (whichever occurs first), the wires should be replaced with new ones. It is good idea to periodically inspect the wires' resistance with an ohmmeter. Wires with excessive resistance can cause misfiring, and may make the engine difficult to start in damp weather.

To check spark plug cable resistance, perform the following:

1. Disconnect the negative battery cable.
2. With all of the spark plug cables still attached, remove the cap from the distributor and position it aside.
3. Detach one of the spark plug cables from its spark plug.
4. Using an ohmmeter, check resistance from the inside terminal of the distributor cap to the spark plug end of the cable. In both cases, resistance of any given spark plug wire should be between 3,000–6700 ohms per foot of wire. Therefore a 2 foot long spark plug wire with 10,000 ohms of resistance would be acceptable (less than the 14,000 ohm max.), while the same wire should be discarded if resistance is 15,000 ohms.

➡If all of the wires must be disconnected from the spark plugs, coil packs or distributor cap at one time, be sure to tag the wires to assure proper installation.

5. If the spark plug cable resistance was below 7,000 ohms per foot of length, reattach it to the spark plug. Otherwise replace it with a new wire.
6. Perform Steps 3 through 5 for each spark plug cable.
7. After each cable is tested, and possibly replaced with a good one, ensure that all of them are properly attached to the distributor cap and spark plugs.
8. Install the distributor cap, and connect the negative battery cable.

REMOVAL & INSTALLATION

.The best possible method for installing a new set of wires is to replace ONE AT A TIME so there can be no mix-up. Do not rely on wiring diagrams or sketches, since the position of the distributor can be changed (unless the distributor is keyed for installation in only one position). Start by replacing the longest wire first.

➡If all of the wires must be disconnected from the spark plugs or distributor cap at one time, be sure to label the wires to assure proper installation.

1. Disconnect the negative battery cable.
2. Remove the longest spark plug cable from the engine by detaching both ends and removing it from any cable retaining clips.
   To install:
3. Install the boot of the new spark plug cable firmly over the applicable spark plug.
4. Route the wire in exactly the same path as the original and connect it to the distributor.
5. Repeat the process for each shorter wire.
6. Connect the negative battery cable.

Distributor Cap and Rotor

It is normally a good idea to inspect the distributor cap and rotor any time you perform a tune-up which includes checking the spark plug wires for wear, damage or excessive resistance.

REMOVAL & INSTALLATION

◆ See Figures 115, 116 and 117

1. Disconnect the negative battery cable for safety.

➡Depending on the reason you have for removing the distributor cap, it may (in some cases) make more sense to leave the spark plug wires attached. This is handy if you are testing spark plug wires or if removal was necessary to access other components (and wire play allows you to reposition the cap out of the way).

2. Tag the spark plug and ignition coil wires and the distributor cap towers for reassembly, then disconnect the wires from the cap. THIS STEP IS CRITICAL. Do not attempt to rewire the cap based only on a diagram, this too often leads to confusion and miswiring.

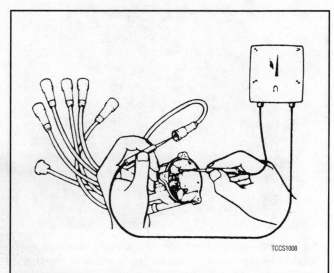

Fig. 114 Checking plug wire resistance through the distributor cap with an ohmmeter

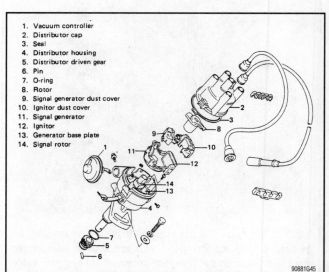

1. Vacuum controller
2. Distributor cap
3. Seal
4. Distributor housing
5. Distributor driven gear
6. Pin
7. O-ring
8. Rotor
9. Signal generator dust cover
10. Ignitor dust cover
11. Signal generator
12. Ignitor
13. Generator base plate
14. Signal rotor

Fig. 115 Exploded view of a distributor which utilizes hold-down clips to secure the cap in place—1986–88 1.3L engines

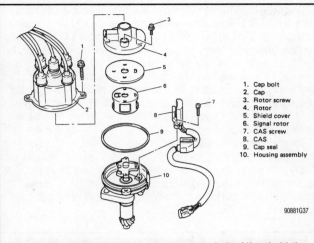

1. Cap bolt
2. Cap
3. Rotor screw
4. Rotor
5. Shield cover
6. Signal rotor
7. CAS screw
8. CAS
9. Cap seal
10. Housing assembly

90881G37

Fig. 116 The 1989–95 1.3L engines use cap bolts (1) to hold the cap (2) on the housing (10)—note that the rotor (4) is retained by a screw (3)

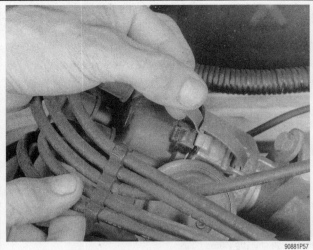

90881P57

. . . otherwise, the wires can stay attached—unfasten the cap hold-down clamps . . .

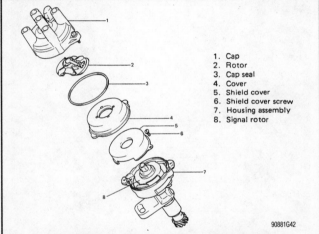

1. Cap
2. Rotor
3. Cap seal
4. Cover
5. Shield cover
6. Shield cover screw
7. Housing assembly
8. Signal rotor

90881G42

Fig. 117 The distributors used on 1.6L engines also utilize screws to hold the cap on the housing, but the rotor does not use a retaining screw

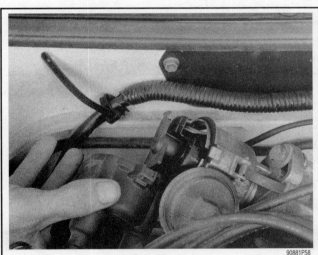

90881P58

. . . and lift the cap up and off of the distributor housing, then set it aside

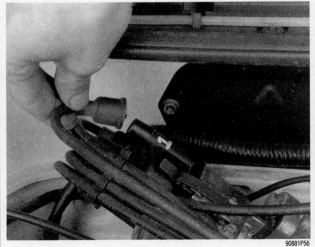

90881P56

If removing the cap for replacement, label and detach all of the spark plug wires . . .

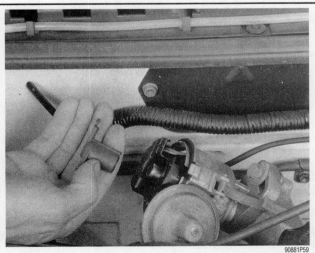

90881P59

Remove the rotor by pulling it up and off of the distributor shaft (check for a retaining screw first)

3. Disengage the two distributor cap hold-down clips or screws, depending on your specific model.

4. Carefully lift the distributor cap STRAIGHT up and off the distributor in order to prevent damage to the rotor blade and spring.

➡**Some models may be equipped with a rotor mounting screw; be sure to remove this screw before attempting to remove the rotor.**

5. If necessary, remove the rotor mounting screw (if equipped), then grasp the rotor by hand and pull upward to remove it from the distributor shaft and armature.

6. Inspect both the distributor cap and rotor for damage (replace, as necessary).

To install:

7. Align the locating boss on the rotor with the flat spot on the distributor shaft, then carefully seat the rotor on the distributor shaft. Make sure the rotor is fully seated, but do not force it, as plastic components often break easily. If equipped, install and tighten the rotor mounting screw snugly.

8. Position the distributor cap on the base and align the cap with the hold-down clips or screws holes.

9. Secure the cap using the hold-down clips/screws.

10. If applicable, connect the ignition coil lead wire to the center tower of the distributor cap; otherwise, attach the wiring harness connector to the distributor.

11. If removed, connect the spark plug wire leads as tagged during removal.

12. Connect the negative battery cable.

INSPECTION

After removing the distributor cap and rotor, clean the components (both inside and outside of the cap) using soap and water. If compressed air is available, carefully dry the components (wearing safety goggles) or allow the parts to air dry. You can dry them with a clean, soft cloth, just don't leave any lint or moisture behind.

Once the cap and rotor have been thoroughly cleaned, check for cracks, carbon tracks, burns or other physical damage. Make sure the distributor cap's carbon button is free of damage. Check the cap terminals for dirt or corrosion. Always check the rotor blade and spring closely for damage. Replace any components where damage is found.

Ignition Timing

GENERAL INFORMATION

Ignition timing is the measurement, in degrees of crankshaft rotation, of the point at which the spark plugs fire in each of the cylinders. It is measured in degrees before or after Top Dead Center (TDC) of the compression stroke.

Because it takes a fraction of a second for the spark plug to ignite the mixture in the cylinder, the spark plug must fire a little before the piston reaches TDC. Otherwise, the mixture will not be completely ignited as the piston passes TDC and the full power of the explosion will not be used by the engine.

The timing measurement is given in degrees of crankshaft rotation before the piston reaches TDC (BTDC). If the setting for the ignition timing is 5° BTDC, the spark plug must fire 5° before each piston reaches TDC. This only holds true, however, when the engine is at idle speed.

As the engine speed increases, the pistons go faster. The spark plugs have to ignite the fuel even sooner if it is to be completely ignited when the piston reaches TDC.

If the ignition is set too far advanced (BTDC), the ignition and expansion of the fuel in the cylinder will occur too soon and tend to force the piston down while it is still traveling up. This causes engine ping. If the ignition spark is set too far retarded, after TDC (ATDC), the piston will have already passed TDC and started on its way down when the fuel is ignited. This will cause the piston to be forced down for only a portion of its travel. This will result in poor engine performance and lack of power.

Timing marks consisting of 0 marks or scales can be found on the rim of the crankshaft pulley and the timing cover. The mark(s) on the pulley correspond(s) to the position of the piston in the number 1 cylinder. A stroboscopic (dynamic) timing light is used, which is hooked into the circuit of the No. 1 cylinder spark plug. Every time the spark plug fires, the timing light flashes. By aiming the timing light at the timing marks while the engine is running, the exact position of the piston within the cylinder can be easily read since the stroboscopic flash makes the pulley appear to be standing still. Proper timing is indicated when the mark and scale are in proper alignment.

Because these vehicles utilize high voltage, electronic ignition systems, only a timing light with an inductive pick-up should be used. This pick-up simply clamps onto the No. 1 spark plug wire, eliminating the adapter. It is not susceptible to cross-firing or false triggering, which may occur with a conventional light, due to the greater voltages produced by electronic ignition.

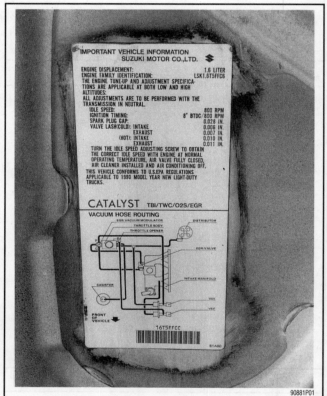

The vehicle information label, located under the hood, provides important tune-up specifications

INSPECTION & ADJUSTMENT

➡**Since manufacturing specifications often change during the model-year, refer to the Vehicle Emission Control Information (VECI) label, located in the engine compartment, for your engine's specific ignition timing specification, prior to adjusting the ignition timing. If the specification indicated on your vehicle's VECI label differs from that given in this procedure, use the VECI label specification.**

1986-88 1.3L Engines

▸ See Figures 118 and 119

1. Remove the rubber plug from the ignition timing inspection hole in the transmission housing (located near the engine/transmission flange).

2. Start the engine and allow it to warm up to normal operating temperature.

3. Be sure that all of the electrical loads, except for the ignition switch, are OFF. If equipped, ensure that the air conditioning is OFF.

4. Apply the parking brake and place the gearshift in Neutral.

5. Check the idle speed to ensure that it is 750–850 rpm. If it is not, adjust the idle speed prior to adjusting ignition timing.

6. Turn the ignition switch **OFF**.

7. Install the inductive timing light according to the manufacturer's instructions. The timing light input lead should always be attached to the No. 1 cylinder spark plug wire.

8. Start the engine and allow it to idle.

✳✳ CAUTION

When using the timing light, be sure to keep yourself and all tools away from moving and hot engine components. Do not wear loose clothing when working around a running engine, otherwise personal injury or death may result.

9. Use the timing light to read the ignition timing by pointing the light at the ignition timing inspection hole and pulling the light's trigger. If the 10 degree BTDC mark is aligned with the timing match mark on the transmission housing, the ignition timing is correct. Otherwise, adjust the ignition timing as follows:

a. Loosen the distributor flange bolt.

b. Rotate the distributor housing until the ignition timing is within specifications. Turn the distributor counterclockwise to advance, and clockwise to retard the ignition timing.

c. Tighten the distributor flange bolt securely.

10. After adjusting the ignition timing and tightening the distributor flange bolts, recheck the ignition timing to ensure that it did not change while tightening the distributor flange bolts.

11. Shut the engine **OFF**, then remove the inductive timing light from the vehicle. Install the ignition timing inspection hole plug.

1989–95 1.3L Engines

▶ See Figures 120 and 121

1. Start the engine and allow it to warm up to normal operating temperature.

2. Turn off the engine, turn the ignition switch **ON** for 5 seconds, then start the engine again and run it at 2000 rpm for 5 minutes. This will ensure that the engine is properly warmed up.

3. Be sure that all of the electrical loads, except for the ignition switch, are OFF. If equipped, ensure that the air conditioning is OFF.

4. Apply the parking brake and place the gearshift in Neutral (manual transmissions) or Park (automatic transmissions).

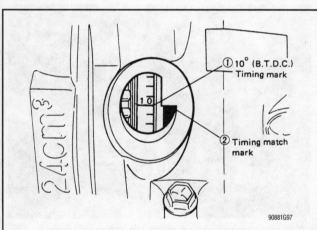

Fig. 118 The ignition timing inspection hole is located on the transmission, near the engine flange—the ignition is correctly set when the 10 degree BTDC mark is aligned with the match-mark at 750–850 rpm

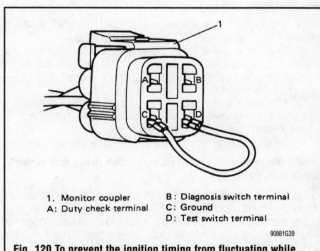

1. Monitor coupler
A: Duty check terminal
B: Diagnosis switch terminal
C: Ground
D: Test switch terminal

Fig. 120 To prevent the ignition timing from fluctuating while checking it, use a jumper wire to ground monitor connector terminal D to terminal C

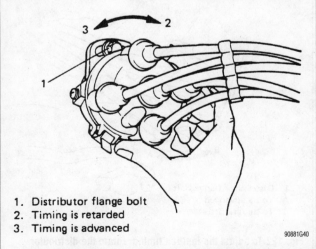

1. Distributor flange bolt
2. Timing is retarded
3. Timing is advanced

Fig. 119 To adjust the ignition timing, loosen the flange bolt(s) and rotate the distributor housing accordingly

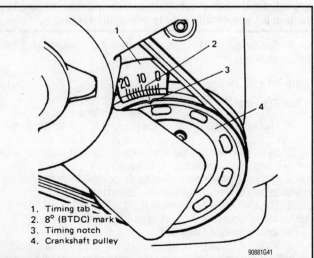

1. Timing tab
2. 8° (BTDC) mark
3. Timing notch
4. Crankshaft pulley

Fig. 121 The ignition timing marks are stamped in a tab protruding from the timing belt cover, above the crankshaft pulley

5. Check the idle speed to ensure that it is 800 rpm. If it is not, adjust the idle speed prior to adjusting ignition timing.

6. Turn the ignition switch **OFF**.

7. Install the inductive timing light according to the manufacturer's instructions. The timing light input lead should always be attached to the No. 1 cylinder spark plug wire.

8. Remove the cover from the monitor connector, located beside the right-hand head light assembly, and, using a jumper wire, connect terminals **C** and **D**. Grounding terminal **C** to terminal **D** will fix the ignition timing (prevent the timing from moving).

9. Start the engine and allow it to idle.

✳✳ CAUTION

When using the timing light, be sure to keep yourself and all tools away from moving and hot engine components. Do not wear loose clothing when working around a running engine, otherwise personal injury or death may result.

10. Use the timing light to read the ignition timing by pointing the light at the timing marks (located on the crankshaft pulley and timing belt cover tab) and pulling the light's trigger.

➡**If the timing fluctuates or changes, terminal D is not properly grounded to terminal C.**

11. If the ignition timing, with terminal **D** properly grounded, is not 7–9 degrees BTDC at 800 rpm engine speed, adjust the timing.

12. To adjust the ignition timing, loosen the distributor flange bolts and rotate it until the proper ignition timing is within specifications. Turn the distributor counterclockwise to advance, and clockwise to retard the ignition timing. Tighten the distributor flange bolts securely.

13. After adjusting the ignition timing and tightening the distributor flange bolts, recheck the ignition timing to ensure that it did not change while tightening the distributor flange bolts.

14. Detach the jumper wire from the monitor connector.

➡**With this jumper wire removed, the ignition timing may fluctuate, which is normal.**

15. Observe the ignition timing marks with the timing light while increasing engine speed. The ignition timing should advance as the engine speed increases. If the engine speed does not advance, inspect the TP sensor, the test switch terminal circuit, the engine start signal circuit and PCM.

✳✳ WARNING

Driving the vehicle with the monitor connector terminals grounded will result in catalytic converter damage; be sure to remove the jumper wire prior to driving the vehicle.

16. Shut the engine **OFF**, then remove the inductive timing light from the vehicle. Install the monitor connector cover.

1989–90 1.6L Engines

▶ **See Figure 122**

1. Start the engine and allow it to warm up to normal operating temperature.

2. Be sure that all of the electrical loads, except for the ignition switch, are OFF. If equipped, ensure that the air conditioning is OFF.

3. Apply the parking brake and place the gearshift in Neutral (manual transmissions) or Park (automatic transmissions).

4. Check the idle speed to ensure that it is 750–850 rpm. If it is not, adjust the idle speed prior to adjusting ignition timing.

5. Turn the ignition switch **OFF**.

6. Install the inductive timing light according to the manufacturer's instructions. The timing light input lead should always be attached to the No. 1 cylinder spark plug wire.

7. Start the engine and allow it to idle.

✳✳ CAUTION

When using the timing light, be sure to keep yourself and all tools away from moving and hot engine components. Do not wear loose clothing when working around a running engine, otherwise personal injury or death may result.

8. Use the timing light to read the ignition timing by pointing the light at the timing marks (located on the crankshaft pulley and timing belt cover tab) and pulling the light's trigger.

9. If the ignition timing, is not 8 degrees BTDC at 750–850 rpm engine speed, adjust the timing.

10. To adjust the ignition timing, loosen the distributor flange bolt(s) and rotate it until the proper ignition timing is within specifications. Turn the distributor counterclockwise to advance, and clockwise to retard the ignition timing. Tighten the distributor flange bolt(s) securely.

11. After adjusting the ignition timing and tightening the distributor flange bolts, recheck the ignition timing to ensure that it did not change while tightening the distributor flange bolts.

12. Shut the engine **OFF**, then remove the inductive timing light from the vehicle.

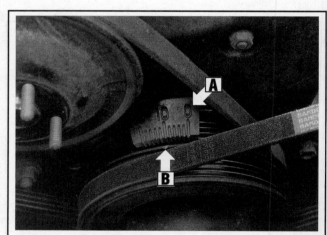

A. Ignition timing mark tab   B. TDC timing mark

90881P55

The ignition timing marks are located on a tab attached to the engine

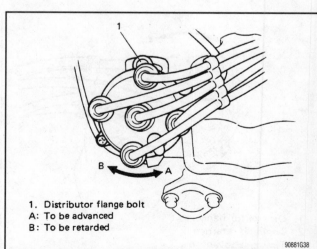

1. Distributor flange bolt
A: To be advanced
B: To be retarded

90881G38

Fig. 122 To adjust the ignition timing, rotate the distributor housing counterclockwise to advance timing and clockwise to retard timing

1991–93 1.6L Engines

1. Start the engine and allow it to warm up to normal operating temperature.

2. Turn off the engine, turn the ignition switch **ON** for 5 seconds, then start the engine again and run it at 2000 rpm for 5 minutes. This will ensure that the engine is properly warmed up.

3. Be sure that all of the electrical loads, except for the ignition switch, are OFF. If equipped, ensure that the air conditioning is OFF.

4. Apply the parking brake and place the gearshift in Neutral (manual transmissions) or Park (automatic transmissions).

5. Check the idle speed to ensure that it is 800 rpm. If it is not, adjust the idle speed prior to adjusting ignition timing.

6. Turn the ignition switch **OFF**.

7. Install the inductive timing light according to the manufacturer's instructions. The timing light input lead should always be attached to the No. 1 cylinder spark plug wire.

8. Remove the cover from the monitor connector, located beside the right-hand head light assembly, and, using a jumper wire, connect terminals **C** and **D**. Grounding terminal **C** to terminal **D** will fix the ignition timing (prevent the timing from moving).

9. Start the engine and allow it to idle.

❊❊ CAUTION

When using the timing light, be sure to keep yourself and all tools away from moving and hot engine components. Do not wear loose clothing when working around a running engine, otherwise personal injury or death may result.

10. Use the timing light to read the ignition timing by pointing the light at the timing marks (located on the crankshaft pulley and timing belt cover tab) and pulling the light's trigger.

➡ **If the timing fluctuates or changes, terminal D is not properly grounded to terminal D.**

11. If the ignition timing, with terminal **D** properly grounded, is not 7–9 degrees BTDC at 800 rpm engine speed, adjust the timing.

12. To adjust the ignition timing, loosen the distributor flange bolts and rotate it until the proper ignition timing is within specifications. Turn the distributor counterclockwise to advance, and clockwise to retard the ignition timing. Tighten the distributor flange bolts securely.

13. After adjusting the ignition timing and tightening the distributor flange bolts, recheck the ignition timing to ensure that it did not change while tightening the distributor flange bolts.

14. Detach the jumper wire from the monitor connector.

➡ **With this jumper wire removed, the ignition timing may fluctuate, which is normal.**

15. Observe the ignition timing marks with the timing light while increasing engine speed. The ignition timing should advance as the engine speed increases. If the engine speed does not advance, inspect the TP sensor, the test switch terminal circuit, the engine start signal circuit and PCM.

❊❊ WARNING

Driving the vehicle with the monitor connector terminals grounded will result in catalytic converter damage; be sure to remove the jumper wire prior to driving the vehicle.

16. Shut the engine **OFF**, then remove the inductive timing light from the vehicle. Install the monitor connector cover.

1994–98 1.6L and 1.8L Engines

▶ **See Figures 123 and 124**

1. Start the engine and allow it to warm up to normal operating temperature.

2. Be sure that all of the electrical loads, except for the ignition switch, are OFF. If equipped, ensure that the air conditioning is OFF.

3. Apply the parking brake and place the gearshift in Neutral (manual transmissions) or Park (automatic transmissions).

4. Check the idle speed to ensure that it is within specifications. If it is not, adjust the idle speed prior to adjusting ignition timing.

5. Turn the ignition switch **OFF**.

6. Install the inductive timing light according to the manufacturer's instructions. The timing light input lead should always be attached to the No. 1 cylinder spark plug wire.

7. Remove the cover from the Duty Check Data Link Connector (DC-DLC), located beside the right-hand headlight assembly (1994–96 models) or next to the battery (1997–98 models), and, using a jumper wire, connect DC-DLC connector cavities **4** and **5**. Grounding cavity **5** to cavity **4** will fix the ignition timing (prevent the timing from moving).

8. Start the engine and allow it to idle.

❊❊ CAUTION

When using the timing light, be sure to keep yourself and all tools away from moving and hot engine components. Do not wear loose clothing when working around a running engine, otherwise personal injury or death may result.

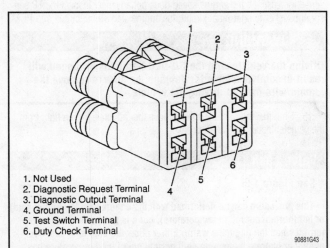

1. Not Used
2. Diagnostic Request Terminal
3. Diagnostic Output Terminal
4. Ground Terminal
5. Test Switch Terminal
6. Duty Check Terminal

90881G43

Fig. 123 Before attempting to inspect the ignition timing, use a small jumper wire to ground the test switch terminal (5) to the ground terminal (4) of the DC-DLC

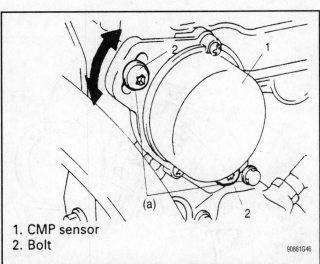

1. CMP sensor
2. Bolt

90881G46

Fig. 124 On 1.8L engines, loosen the CMP sensor bolts and rotate the sensor to adjust ignition timing

9. Use the timing light to read the ignition timing by pointing the light at the timing marks (located on the crankshaft pulley and timing belt cover tab) and pulling the light's trigger.

➡**If the timing fluctuates or changes, cavity 5 is not properly grounded to cavity 4.**

10. If the ignition timing, with terminal **5** properly grounded, is not 4–6 degrees BTDC at 750–850 rpm engine speed, adjust the timing.

11. To adjust the ignition timing, loosen the distributor flange bolts (1.6L engines) or the Camshaft Position (CMP) sensor bolts, and rotate it until the proper ignition timing is within specifications. Turn it counterclockwise to advance, and clockwise to retard the ignition timing. Tighten the distributor flange bolts securely, or tighten the CMP bolts to 133 inch lbs. (15 Nm).

12. After adjusting the ignition timing and tightening the distributor flange bolts, recheck the ignition timing to ensure that it did not change while tightening the distributor flange bolts.

13. Detach the jumper wire from the DC-DLC.

➡**With this jumper wire removed, the ignition timing may fluctuate, which is normal.**

14. Observe the ignition timing marks with the timing light while increasing engine speed. The ignition timing should advance as the engine speed increases. If the engine speed does not advance, inspect the TP sensor, the test switch terminal circuit, the engine start signal circuit and PCM.

❊❊ WARNING

Driving the vehicle with the DC-DLC terminals grounded will result in catalytic converter damage; be sure to remove the jumper wire prior to driving the vehicle.

15. Shut the engine **OFF**, then remove the inductive timing light from the vehicle. Install the DC-DLC cover.

Valve Lash

▶ **See Figure 125**

➡**This procedure can be performed with the engine cold (overnight cold) or hot (normal operating temperature), but it is not a good idea to perform it when the engine is warm. Either allow the engine to cool completely or operate the engine until normal operating temperature has been reached. If you decide to perform the adjustment with the engine hot and it takes too long to complete the procedure, you may need to stop in the middle to warm the engine up again. Therefore, it is better to allow the engine to cool completely before adjusting the valve lash.**

Valve lash refers to the clearance between the rocker arm adjusting screw and the tip of the valve stem. A thickness gauge should be used to measure this gap. Valve lash should be inspected every 15,000 miles (24,000 km) or 15 months, whichever occurs first.

For this procedure you will need a new cylinder head cover gasket.

➡**Throughout this procedure the cylinders are referred to by their number. The number of each cylinder is dependent upon their location; the frontmost cylinder is No. 1 and the numbering proceeds for each cylinder toward the rearmost cylinder, which is No. 4. Therefore, the cylinders are numbered, from front-to-back, 1 through 4.**

INSPECTION & ADJUSTMENT

1986–88 1.3L Engines

▶ **See Figure 126**

1. Remove the cylinder head cover.

2. Remove the rubber ignition timing inspection plug from the clutch housing on the transmission.

3. Using a large wrench, or a socket and large ratchet on the crankshaft pulley center nut, have an assistant turn the crankshaft clockwise (viewing the crankshaft from the front of the engine) until the timing mark line, next to the T mark, on the flywheel is aligned with the match mark on the transmission case.

4. Locate the spark plug wire tower on the distributor cap that corresponds to the No. 1 cylinder spark plug. Matchmark the position of the No. 1 distributor tower with the engine block or other engine component.

5. Remove the distributor cap and ensure that the distributor rotor points toward the matchmark. If the rotor points 180 degrees away from the matchmark (in the opposite direction), have your assistant rotate the crankshaft 360 degrees (one full revolution), then realign the timing line (next to the T mark) with the match mark on the transmission.

  a. The distributor rotor should now point to the No. 1 cylinder distributor cap tower matchmark. The engine is now positioned with the No. 1 cylinder at Top Dead Center (TDC) on the compression stroke.

  b. If it still does not point to the matchmark, you matchmarked the wrong tower. Reinstall the distributor cap and double-check the spark plug tower identification.

6. With the No. 1 cylinder at TDC on the compression stroke, use feeler gauges to check the clearance between the rocker arm adjusting screws and the tips of the valve stems for valves 1, 2, 5 and 7. (Refer to the accompanying illustration for valve numbering.)

1. Adjusting screw lock nut
2. Adjusting screw
3. Valve stem

90881G48

Fig. 125 The valve lash is the clearance (A) between the bottom surface of the adjusting screw (2) and the valve stem tip (3)

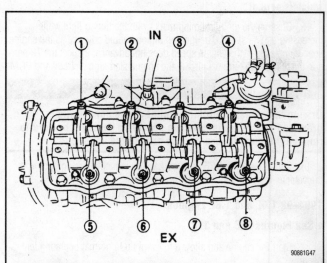

EX

90881G47

Fig. 126 When adjusting the valve lash, valves 1, 2, 5 and 7, and valves 3, 4, 6 and 8 are adjusted at the same time

7. If the valve clearance is not within the specifications shown in the tune-up specifications chart in this section, adjust the clearance as follows:

a. Loosen the adjusting screw locknut of the valve needing adjustment.

b. Pass the appropriately-sized feeler gauge between the adjusting screw and the valve stem tip. Tighten or loosen the adjusting screw until a slight drag can be felt on the feeler gauge.

c. Once this drag is felt, tighten the locknut to 133–168 inch lbs. (15–19 Nm) while holding the adjusting screw to prevent it from turning. This may seem harder than it sounds and may take you several attempts to get the knack for it.

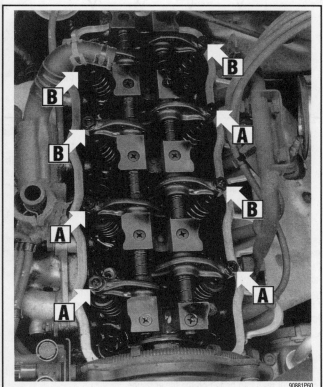

Adjust all A valves with the No. 1 piston at TDC, turn the crankshaft 360 degrees, then adjust all B valves

90881P60

To adjust the valve, loosen the locknut and turn the adjusting screw until the proper gap is attained

90881P61

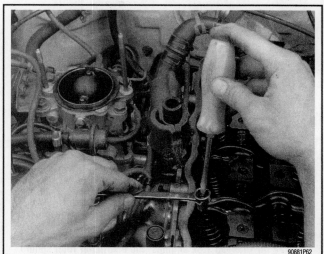

Hold the adjusting screw steady with the screwdriver while tightening the locknut

90881P62

✳✳ WARNING

Although it is important to properly adjust the valve lash, it is better to have too loose of a valve lash clearance than too tight of a clearance. Too tight of a valve lash clearance may cause the valves to burn or prematurely wear, necessitating expensive engine repairs.

d. Once the locknut is tightened, double-check the valve lash of the valve you just adjusted. If the valve lash changed while tightening the locknut, loosen the locknut and readjust the lash. You can double-check the valve lash adjustment by using a feeler gauge that is 0.002 in. [.003] (0.05mm) bigger than the specification. If this larger feeler gauge passes between the adjusting screw and valve stem tip with less than moderate effort, the adjustment is still too loose.

➡ **A set of stepped feeler gauges can also be used to ensure that the clearance is not too great.**

8. Once you have the lash properly adjusted on valves 1, 2, 5 and 7. Have your assistant rotate the crankshaft another full revolution (360 degrees) until the timing marks are once again aligned. At this point, valves 3, 4, 6 and 8 can be adjusted by repeating substeps 7a through 7d for each of them.

9. Once all of the valves have been properly adjusted, install the cylinder head cover and distributor cap.

1989–95 1.3L and 1989–96 1.6L Engines

▶ See Figures 127, 128, 129 and 130

1. If equipped, remove the air intake case.

2. Remove the cylinder head cover.

3. Using a large wrench, or a socket (typically 17mm) and large ratchet on the crankshaft pulley center nut, turn the crankshaft clockwise (viewing the crankshaft from the front of the engine) until the Top Dead Center (TDC) line on the crankshaft pulley is aligned with the 0 mark on the timing mark tab attached to the timing belt cover.

4. Locate the spark plug wire tower on the distributor cap that corresponds to the No. 1 cylinder spark plug. Matchmark the position of the No. 1 distributor tower with the engine block or other engine component.

5. Remove the distributor cap and ensure that the distributor rotor points toward the matchmark. If the rotor points 180 degrees away from the matchmark (in the opposite direction), have your assistant rotate the crankshaft 360 degrees (one full revolution) and realign the timing marks.

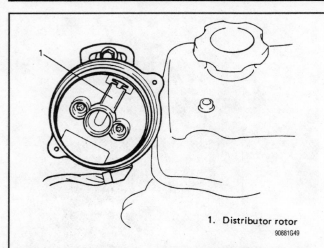

Fig. 127 On 1989–95 1.3L engines, the distributor rotor should point in the direction shown when the No. 1 cylinder is positioned at TDC on the compression stroke

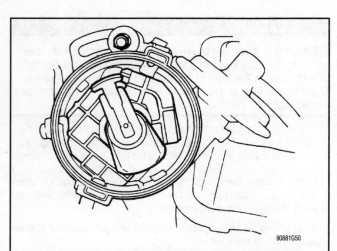

Fig. 128 With No. 1 cylinder at TDC on the compression stroke, the distributor rotor should point as indicated—1.6L engines with 8-valve cylinder heads

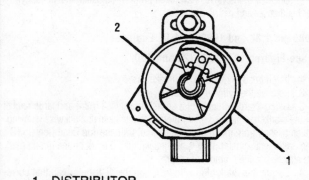

1 DISTRIBUTOR
2 ROTOR

Fig. 129 On 1.6L engines equipped with 16-valve cylinder heads, the distributor rotor should point in the direction shown when the No. 1 cylinder is properly positioned at TDC on the compression stroke

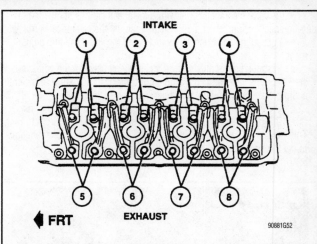

Fig. 130 The valves in 16-valve cylinder heads are paired for identification purposes—adjust both valves in each pair when their number is indicated in the procedure

a. The distributor rotor should now point to the No. 1 cylinder distributor cap tower matchmark. The engine is now positioned with the No. 1 cylinder at Top Dead Center (TDC) on the compression stroke.

b. If the rotor still does not point to the matchmark, you may have matchmarked the wrong tower, or the distributor is installed improperly. Reinstall the distributor cap and double-check the spark plug tower identification by tracing the spark plug wire back to the cylinder.

6. With the No. 1 cylinder at TDC on the compression stroke, use feeler gauges to check the clearance between the rocker arm adjusting screws and the tips of the valve stems for valve-pairs 1, 2, 5 and 7. (Refer to the accompanying illustration for valve numbering.)

7. If the valve clearance is not within the specifications shown in the tune-up specifications chart in this section, adjust the clearance as follows:

a. Loosen the adjusting screw locknut of the valve needing adjustment.

b. Pass the appropriately-sized feeler gauge between the adjusting screw and the valve stem tip. Tighten or loosen the adjusting screw until a slight drag can be felt on the feeler gauge.

➡**Valve lash adjusting tools (such as Suzuki Tool 09917–18210) can be purchased to help make adjusting the valve lash easier, but are by no means necessary for this procedure.**

c. Once this drag is felt, tighten the locknut to 133–168 inch lbs. (15–19 Nm) while holding the adjusting screw to prevent it from turning. This may seem harder than it sounds and may take you several attempts to get the knack for it.

✳✳ WARNING

Although it is important to properly adjust the valve lash, it is better to have too loose of a valve lash clearance than too tight of a clearance. Too tight of a valve lash clearance may cause the valves to burn or prematurely wear, necessitating expensive engine repairs.

d. Once the locknut is tightened, double-check the valve lash of the valve you just adjusted. If the valve lash changed while tightening the locknut, loosen the locknut and readjust the lash. You can double-check the valve lash adjustment by using a feeler gauge that is 0.002 in. (0.05mm) bigger than specification. If this larger feeler gauge passes between the adjusting screw and valve stem tip with less than moderate effort, the adjustment is still too loose.

➡**A set of stepped feeler gauges can also be used to ensure that the clearance is not too great.**

8. Once you have the lash properly adjusted on valve-pairs 1, 2, 5 and 7. Have your assistant rotate the crankshaft another full revolution (360 degrees) until the timing marks are once again aligned. At this point, valve-pairs 3, 4, 6 and 8 can be adjusted by repeating substeps 7a through 7d for each of them.

9. Once all of the valves have been properly adjusted, install the cylinder head cover and distributor cap.

1.8L Engine

The 1.8L engine utilizes automatic hydraulic lash adjusters to maintain proper valve lash at all times. The valve lash for this engine is not manually adjustable. Therefore, periodic valve lash inspection and adjustment is not necessary or possible.

Idle Speed and Mixture

ADJUSTMENTS

Idle Speed

CARBURETD ENGINES

▶ **See Figure 131**

1. Place the transmission gearshift in Neutral and apply the parking brake.

2. Prior to performing the idle speed adjustment procedure, be sure the following are as noted:
- Lead wires and hoses of the engine emission control system are properly connected.
- The accelerator cable has some play (it is not tight).
- All vacuum hoses are securely attached.
- The fuel level in the carburetor should be within the round mark at the center of the level gauge.
- Valve lash should be checked and, if necessary, adjusted.
- The air cleaner element should be inspected and replaced, if necessary.
- All electrical accessories are turned OFF.
- Ignition timing should be inspected and adjusted, if necessary.
- The idle up actuator should not be operating when the engine is idling.

➡**In areas above 4,000 ft. (1,220m) above sea level, the idle up system will normally be in operation. According to the manufacturer, do not attempt to adjust the idle speed.**

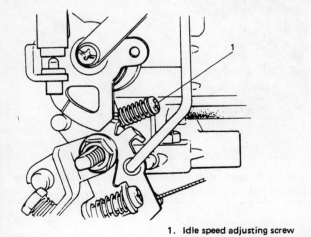

1. Idle speed adjusting screw

90881G53

Fig. 131 Idle speed adjusting screw location on all carbureted engines

3. Install a tachometer to the engine according to the manufacturer's instructions.

4. Start the engine and allow it to idle until it has reached normal operating temperature.

5. Monitor the idle speed and ensure that it is within specifications.

6. If the idle speed is not as specified, adjust the idle speed by turning the idle speed adjusting screw on the carburetor. If the idle speed cannot be adjusted to specifications, it may be due to a faulty throttle valve return or some other defect.

7. After the idle speed is adjusted, check the idle up for proper operation when the lights, heater fan, or rear defogger are turned ON. If the idle up needs adjustment, refer to Section 4.

8. Turn the engine **OFF**, then double-check accelerator cable play is within specifications. For accelerator cable adjustment procedure and specifications, refer to Section 5.

9. Remove the tachometer from the engine.

FUEL-INJECTED ENGINES

▶ **See Figures 132 thru 137**

To adjust the idle speed on MFI- and TFI-equipped engines you will need a tachometer and duty cycle meter, or analog voltmeter (MFI engines only).

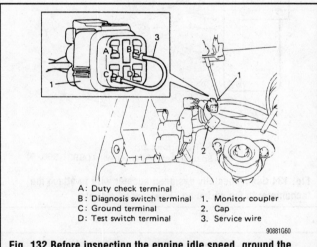

A: Duty check terminal
B: Diagnosis switch terminal
C: Ground terminal
D: Test switch terminal
1. Monitor coupler
2. Cap
3. Service wire

90881G60

Fig. 132 Before inspecting the engine idle speed, ground the diagnosis switch terminal of the DC-DLC (monitor coupler)—TFI-equipped engines

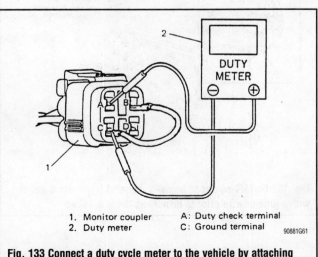

1. Monitor coupler
2. Duty meter
A: Duty check terminal
C: Ground terminal

90881G61

Fig. 133 Connect a duty cycle meter to the vehicle by attaching the positive lead to terminal B and the negative lead to the ground terminal of the DC-DLC (monitor coupler)—TFI-equipped

1. Prior to performing the idle speed adjustment procedure, be sure the following are as noted:

- Lead wires and hoses of the engine emission control system are properly connected.
- The accelerator cable has some play (it is not tight).
- All vacuum hoses are securely attached.
- Valve lash should be checked and, if necessary, adjusted.
- The air cleaner element should be inspected and replaced, if necessary.
- All electrical accessories are turned OFF.

2. Warm the engine up to normal operating temperature, then turn it **OFF**.

3. Using a jumper wire, ground the diagnosis switch terminal in the Duty Check Data Link Connector (DC-DLC), which is located next to the right-hand head light.

4. Attach a duty cycle meter to the duty output (duty check) and ground terminals of the DC-DLC.

5. On MFI-equipped engines, connect a tachometer to the engine according to the manufacturer's instructions.

6. On TFI-equipped engines, detach the noise suppresser connector, then attach Suzuki Adapter wire (or equivalent specific tool) between the suppresser and the detached connector. Attach the tachometer to the adapter wire.

7. For MFI-equipped engines, if using an analog voltmeter for duty cycle inspection, measure and note the battery voltage.

8. Start the engine and check the Idle Air Control (IAC) valve duty cycle and the engine idle speed. The duty cycle should be 50% at 750–850 rpm. If using an analog voltmeter on MFI-equipped models, the voltmeter should register one-half battery voltage (measured earlier) when the duty cycle is at 50%. Therefore, if the battery voltage was measured as 14 volts, the voltmeter will indicate 7 volts when the duty cycle is at 50%.

9. If the duty cycle is out of specifications, adjust it by turning the idle air adjusting screw.

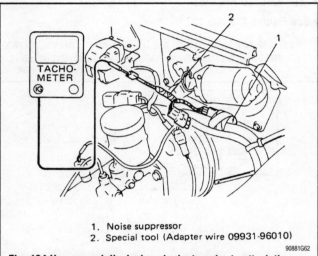

1. Noise suppressor
2. Special tool (Adapter wire 09931-96010)

90881G62

Fig. 134 Use a specially designed adapter wire to attach the tachometer to the wiring on TFI-equipped models

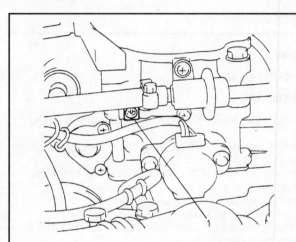

1. Idle speed adjusting screw

90881G59

Fig. 136 The idle speed adjusting screw is located on the side of the throttle-body on the TFI system, as indicated

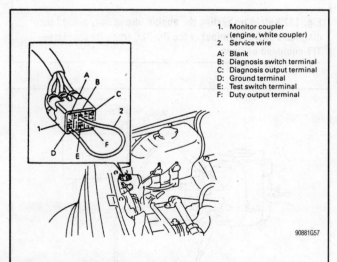

1. Monitor coupler (engine, white coupler)
2. Service wire
A: Blank
B: Diagnosis switch terminal
C: Diagnosis output terminal
D: Ground terminal
E: Test switch terminal
F: Duty output terminal

90881G57

Fig. 135 On MFI-equipped engines, connect terminals B and D with a jumper wire prior to inspecting the idle speed

90881P45

With the throttle body removed, the idle speed adjusting screw location (arrow) is easily seen

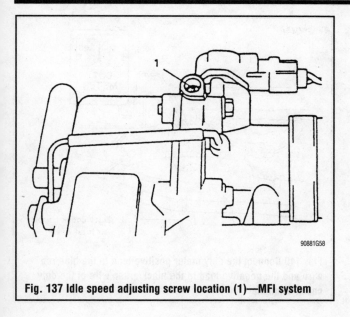

Fig. 137 Idle speed adjusting screw location (1)—MFI system

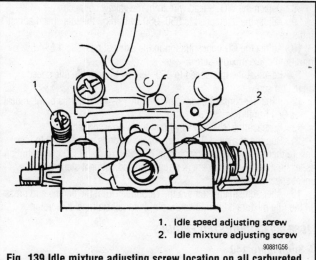

1. Idle speed adjusting screw
2. Idle mixture adjusting screw

Fig. 139 Idle mixture adjusting screw location on all carbureted models

10. Install the adjusting screw cap on the throttle-body.
11. Remove the jumper wire from the DC-DLC.
12. Install the DC-DLC cover.
13. With the engine idling, turn the air conditioning system ON and note the engine idle speed. The idle speed should rise to 1000 rpm, otherwise there may be a malfunction in the A/C ON signal circuit.

Idle Mixture

1986–87 CARBURETED ENGINES

♦ See Figures 138 and 139

The carburetor was calibrated at the factory and should not normally need adjustment, and a Carbon Monoxide (CO) exhaust gas emissions analyzer is necessary for carburetor mixture adjustment. For these two reasons,

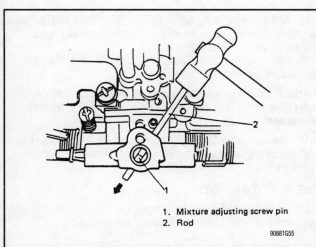

1. Mixture adjusting screw pin
2. Rod

Fig. 138 Remove the carburetor and drive the mixture adjusting screw pin out of the carburetor with a drift and hammer to enable mixture adjustment

if you feel your idle mixture may be out of adjustment, it is a good idea to have your carburetor inspected and serviced by a professional automotive technician.

➡ You will need two new carburetor gaskets, a CO gas tester and a tachometer for this procedure.

To adjust the idle mixture yourself, perform the following:

1. Remove the carburetor from the vehicle so that access to the mixture adjusting screw pin, covering the mixture adjusting screw, can be gained.
2. Using an iron rod approximately 0.18 in. (4.5mm) thick, drive out the mixture adjusting screw pin.
3. Reinstall the carburetor, ensuring that all of the emission control system hoses and lead wires are properly attached. Adjust the accelerator cable, as described in Section 5, and fill the cooling system.
4. Place the transmission gearshift in Neutral, and apply the parking brake.
5. Install a tachometer to the engine, and the CO tester in the exhaust pipe according to the manufacturer's instructions.
6. Prior to performing the idle mixture adjustment procedure, be sure the following are as noted:
   - The fuel level in the carburetor should be within the round mark at the center of the level gauge.
   - Valve lash should be checked and, if necessary, adjusted.
   - The air cleaner element should be inspected and replaced, if necessary.
   - All electrical accessories are turned OFF.
   - Ignition timing should be inspected and adjusted, if necessary.
   - The choke valve opens completely.
   - The idle up actuator does not operate.
7. Start the engine and allow it to warm up to normal operating temperature.

✷✷ CAUTION

Be careful when working around a running engine. Do not wear loose clothing; it may become caught in a moving engine component and cause serious physical injury or death.

8. Detach the WOTS lead wire from the yellow connector.

9. Adjust the idle speed to 850–950 by turning the idle speed adjusting screw.

10. Adjust the CO concentration in the exhaust gases to 1.5–4.5% by turning the idle mixture screw.

11. Readjust the idle speed to 850–950 by turning the idle speed adjusting screw.

12. If the CO concentration is not within 1.5–4.5% at this point, repeat Steps 9–11 until it is.

13. Reattach the WOTS lead wire to the yellow connector.

14. Run the engine at 2,000 rpm for 30 seconds and allow it to idle. Insure that the engine idling speed is 750–850 rpm and CO concentration is less than 0.5%. If they are not, repeat the adjustment steps until they meet specifications.

15. After adjustment, remove the carburetor from the engine and press-fit the idle mixture adjusting screw pin, then reinstall the carburetor.

1988–89 CARBURETED ENGINES

▶ **See Figure 140**

The carburetor was calibrated at the factory and should not normally need adjustment, and a Carbon Monoxide (CO) exhaust gas emissions analyzer is necessary for carburetor mixture adjustment. For these two reasons, if you feel your idle mixture may be out of adjustment, it is a good idea to have your carburetor inspected and serviced by a professional automotive technician.

To inspect the engine idle mixture, perform the following:

1. Attach a tachometer to the engine according to manufacturer's instructions.

2. Warm the engine up to normal operating temperature.

3. Remove the rubber seal of the duty check coupler and attach the positive lead of a duty meter to the blue/red wire and the negative lead to the black/green wire.

4. Run the engine at 1,500–2,000 rpm for 30 seconds, then allow it to idle.

5. Inspect the duty cycle, which should be between 10–50 at 750–850 rpm. If it is out specifications, adjust it as follows:

➡**You will need two new carburetor gaskets, a CO gas tester and a tachometer for this procedure.**

6. Remove the carburetor from the vehicle so that access to the mixture adjusting screw pin, covering the mixture adjusting screw, can be gained.

7. Using a iron rod approximately 0.18 in. (4.5mm) thick, drive the mixture adjusting screw pin out.

8. Reinstall the carburetor, ensuring that all of the emission control system hoses and lead wires are properly attached. Adjust the accelerator cable, as described in Section 5, and fill the cooling system.

9. Place the transmission gearshift in Neutral, and apply the parking brake.

10. Install a tachometer to the engine (if not already done), and the duty meter to the check coupler (if not already done).

11. Prior to performing the idle mixture adjustment procedure, be sure the following are as noted:
  • The fuel level in the carburetor should be within the round mark at the center of the level gauge.
  • Valve lash should be checked and, if necessary, adjusted.

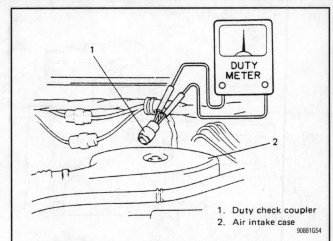

1. Duty check coupler
2. Air intake case

90881G54

Fig. 140 Connect the duty meter positive lead to the blue/red wire and the negative lead to the black/green wire of the duty check connector

  • The air cleaner element should be inspected and replaced, if necessary.
  • All electrical accessories are turned OFF.
  • Ignition timing should be inspected and adjusted, if necessary.
  • The choke valve opens completely.
  • The idle up actuator does not operate.

12. Start the engine and allow it to warm up to normal operating temperature.

❄❄ CAUTION

Be careful when working around a running engine. Do not wear loose clothing; it may become caught in a moving engine component and cause serious physical injury or death.

13. Adjust the idle speed to specifications.

14. Run the engine at 1,500–2,000 rpm for 30 seconds, then allow it to idle.

15. With the engine idling, adjust the idle mixture speed slowly in small increments, allowing time for the duty to stabilize after turning the screw, until a duty cycle of 10–50 is achieved.

16. After achieving a duty cycle of 10–50, readjust the idle speed to specifications, if necessary.

➡**If the adjustment cannot be completed because the duty cycle meter does not deflect, there may be a problem within the feedback system.**

17. After adjustment, install the rubber seal on the duty check coupler. Also, remove the carburetor from the engine and press-fit the idle mixture adjusting screw pin, then reinstall the carburetor.

FUEL-INJECTED ENGINES

The idle mixture on fuel-injected engines is automatically controlled by the Powertrain Control Module (PCM) and is not adjustable.

TUNE-UP SPECIFICATIONS

Year	Model	Engine ID/VIN	Engine Displacement Liters (cc)	Spark Plugs Gap (in.)	Ignition Timing (deg.) MT	Ignition Timing (deg.) AT	Fuel Pump (psi)	Idle Speed (rpm) MT	Idle Speed (rpm) AT	Valve Clearance In.	Valve Clearance Ex.
1986	Samurai	5	1.3 (1324)	0.027-0.031	10B	—	3-4	800	—	0.0051- ① 0.0067	0.0063- ① 0.0079
1987	Samurai	5	1.3 (1324)	0.027-0.031	10B	—	3-4	800	—	0.0051- ① 0.0067	0.0063- ① 0.0079
1988	Samurai	5	1.3 (1324)	0.027-0.031	10B	—	3-4	800	—	0.0051- ① 0.0067	0.0063- ① 0.0079
1989	Samurai	5	1.3 (1324)	0.027-0.031	10B	—	3-4	800	—	0.0051- ① 0.0067	0.0063- ① 0.0079
	Sidekick	5	1.3 (1298)	0.027-0.031	10B	—	34-40	800	—	0.0051- ① 0.0067	0.0063- ① 0.0079
		0	1.6 (1590)	0.027-0.031	8B	8B	34-40	800	800	0.0051- ① 0.0067	0.0063- ① 0.0079
	Tracker	U	1.6 (1590)	0.027-0.031	8B	8B	34-40	800	800	0.0051- ① 0.0067	0.0063- ① 0.0079
1990	Samurai	5	1.3 (1298)	0.027-0.031	10B	—	3-4	800	—	0.0051- ① 0.0067	0.0063- ① 0.0079
	Sidekick	0	1.6 (1590)	0.027-0.031	8B	8B	34-40	800	800	0.0051- ① 0.0067	0.0063- ① 0.0079
	Tracker	U	1.6 (1590)	0.027-0.031	8B	8B	34-40	800	800	0.0051- ① 0.0067	0.0063- ① 0.0079
1991	Samurai	5	1.3 (1298)	0.029	8B	—	34-40	800	—	0.0051- ① 0.0067	0.0063- ① 0.0079
	Sidekick	0	1.6 (1590)	0.029	8B	8B	34-40	800	800	0.0051- ① 0.0067	0.0063- ① 0.0079
	Tracker	U	1.6 (1590)	0.029	8B	8B	34-40	800	800	0.0051- ① 0.0067	0.0063- ① 0.0079
1992	Samurai	5	1.3 (1298)	0.029	8B	—	34-40	800	—	0.0051- ① 0.0067	0.0063- ① 0.0079
	Sidekick	0	1.6 (1590)	0.029	8B	8B	34-40	800	800	0.0051- ① 0.0067	0.0063- ① 0.0079
	Tracker	U	1.6 (1590)	0.029	8B	8B	34-40	800	800	0.0051- ① 0.0067	0.0063- ① 0.0079
1993	Samurai	5	1.3 (1298)	0.029	8B	—	34-40	800	—	0.0051- ① 0.0067	0.0063- ① 0.0079
	Sidekick	0	1.6 (1590)	0.029	8B	8B	34-40	800	800	0.0051- ① 0.0067	0.0063- ① 0.0079
	Tracker	U	1.6 (1590)	0.029	8B	8B	34-40	800	800	0.0051- ① 0.0067	0.0063- ① 0.0079
1994	Samurai	3	1.3 (1298)	0.029	8B	—	34-40	800	—	0.0051- ① 0.0067	0.0063- ① 0.0079
	Sidekick ②	0	1.6 (1590)	0.029	8B	8B	34-40	800	800	0.005- ④ 0.007	0.005- ④ 0.007
	③	0	1.6 (1590)	0.029	5B	5B	34-40	800	800	0.005- ① 0.007	0.006- ⑤ 0.008

90881C02

TUNE-UP SPECIFICATIONS

Year	Model	Engine ID/VIN	Engine Displacement Liters (cc)	Spark Plugs Gap (in.)	Ignition Timing (deg.) MT	AT	Fuel Pump (psi)	Idle Speed (rpm) MT	AT	Valve Clearance In.	Ex.
1994 cont.	Tracker	U	1.6 (1590)	0.029	8B	8B	34-40	800	800	0.0051-⑥ 0.0067	0.0063-⑥ 0.0073
	⑦	U	1.6 (1590)	0.029	8B	8B	36-43	800	800	0.0050-⑧ 0.0070	0.0050-⑧ 0.0070
1995	Samurai	3	1.3 (1298)	0.029	8B	—	34-40	800	—	0.0051-① 0.0067	0.0063-① 0.0079
	Sidekick ②	0	1.6 (1590)	0.029	8B	8B	34-40	800	800	0.005-④ 0.007	0.005-④ 0.007
	③	0	1.6 (1590)	0.029	5B	5B	34-40	800	800	0.005-① 0.007	0.006-⑤ 0.008
	Tracker	U	1.6 (1590)	0.029	8B	8B	34-40	800-850	800-850	0.0051-⑥ 0.0067	0.0063-⑥ 0.0073
	⑦	6	1.6 (1590)	0.029	8B	8B	30-37	800-850	800-850	0.0050-⑧ 0.0070	0.0050-⑧ 0.0070
1996	X90	0	1.6 (1590)	0.029	5B	5B	28-37	800	800	0.0050-⑧ 0.0070	0.0050-⑧ 0.0070
	Sidekick	0	1.6 (1590)	0.029	5B	5B	28-37	800	800	0.0050-⑧ 0.0070	0.0050-⑧ 0.0070
	Sport	2	1.8 (1843)	0.029	5B	5B	31-37	750-800	750-800	HYD.	HYD.
	Tracker	6	1.6 (1590)	0.029	8B	8B	30-37	800-850	800-850	0.0050-⑧ 0.0070	0.0050-⑧ 0.0070
1997	X90	0	1.6 (1590)	0.029	5B	5B	28-37	800	800	0.0050-⑧ 0.0070	0.0050-⑧ 0.0070
	Sidekick	0	1.6 (1590)	0.029	5B	5B	28-37	800	800	0.0050-⑧ 0.0070	0.0050-⑧ 0.0070
	Sport	2	1.8 (1843)	0.029	5B	5B	31-37	750-800	750-800	HYD.	HYD.
	Tracker	6	1.6 (1590)	0.029	8B	8B	30-37	800-850	800-850	0.0050-⑧ 0.0070	0.0050-⑧ 0.0070
1998	X90	0	1.6 (1590)	0.029	5B	5B	28-37	800	800	0.0050-⑧ 0.0070	0.0050-⑧ 0.0070
	Sidekick	0	1.6 (1590)	0.029	5B	5B	28-37	800	800	0.0050-⑧ 0.0070	0.0050-⑧ 0.0070
	Sport	2	1.8 (1843)	0.029	5B	5B	31-37	750-800	750-800	HYD.	HYD.
	Tracker	6	1.6 (1590)	0.029	8B	8B	30-37	800-850	800-850	0.0050-⑧ 0.0070	0.0050-⑧ 0.0070

① – 2-door model / 8 valve engine
② – 4-door model / 16 valve engine
③ – California and New York models.
④ – Cold engine specifications.
⑤ – Cold engine specifications. Hot engine specifications are:
  Intake: 0.0090-0.0110 in.
  Exhaust: 0.0102-0.0118 in.
⑥ – Cold engine specifications. Hot engine specifications are:
  Intake: 0.009-0.011 in.
  Exhaust: 0.0102-0.0118 in.
⑦ – Cold engine specifications. Hot engine specifications are 0.007-0.008 in.
⑧ – Cold engien specifications. Hot engien specifications are 0.010-0.012 in.

90881C03

Air Conditioning System

SYSTEM SERVICE & REPAIR

▶ See Figure 141

➡ **It is recommended that the A/C system be serviced by an EPA Section 609 certified automotive technician utilizing a refrigerant recovery/recycling machine.**

The do-it-yourselfer should not service his/her own vehicle's A/C system for many reasons, including legal concerns, personal injury, environmental damage and cost. The following are some of the reasons why you may decide not to service your own vehicle's A/C system.

According to the U.S. Clean Air Act, it is a federal crime to service or repair (involving the refrigerant) a Motor Vehicle Air Conditioning (MVAC) system for money without being EPA certified. It is also illegal to vent R-12 and R-134a refrigerants into the atmosphere. Selling or distributing A/C system refrigerant (in a container which contains less than 20 pounds of refrigerant) to any person who is not EPA 609 certified is also not allowed by law.

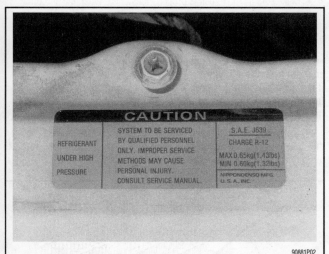

A label in the engine compartment warns that the A/C system should only be serviced by qualified personnel

90881P02

90881G82

Fig. 141 Your A/C system should be serviced only by qualified MVAC technicians, one reason being the extreme toxicity of air conditioning refrigerant

State and/or local laws may be more strict than the federal regulations, so be sure to check with your state and/or local authorities for further information. For further federal information on the legality of servicing your A/C system, call the EPA Stratospheric Ozone Hotline.

➡ **Federal law dictates that a fine of up to $25,000 may be leveled on people convicted of venting refrigerant into the atmosphere. Additionally, the EPA may pay up to $10,000 for information or services leading to a criminal conviction of the violation of these laws.**

When servicing an A/C system you run the risk of handling or coming in contact with refrigerant, which may result in skin or eye irritation or frostbite. Although low in toxicity (due to chemical stability), inhalation of concentrated refrigerant fumes is dangerous and can result in death; cases of fatal cardiac arrhythmia have been reported in people accidentally subjected to high levels of refrigerant. Some early symptoms include loss of concentration and drowsiness (zzzzzzzz).

➡ **Generally, the limit for exposure is lower for R-134a than it is for R-12. Exceptional care must be practiced when handling R-134a.**

Also, refrigerants can decompose at high temperatures (near gas heaters or open flame), which may result in hydrofluoric acid, hydrochloric acid and phosgene (a fatal nerve gas).

R-12 refrigerant can damage the environment because it is a Chlorofluorocarbon (CFC), which has been proven to add to ozone layer depletion, leading to increasing levels of UV radiation. UV radiation has been linked with an increase in skin cancer, suppression of the human immune system, an increase in cataracts, damage to crops, damage to aquatic organisms, an increase in ground-level ozone, and increased global warming.

R-134a refrigerant is a greenhouse gas which, if allowed to vent into the atmosphere, will contribute to global warming (the Greenhouse Effect).

It is usually more economically feasible to have a certified MVAC automotive technician perform A/C system service on your vehicle. Some possible reasons for this are as follows:

• While it is illegal to service an A/C system without the proper equipment, the home mechanic would have to purchase an expensive refrigerant recovery/recycling machine to service his/her own vehicle.

• Since only a certified person may purchase refrigerant—according to the Clean Air Act, there are specific restrictions on selling or distributing A/C system refrigerant—it is legally impossible (unless certified) for the home mechanic to service his/her own vehicle. Procuring refrigerant in an illegal fashion exposes one to the risk of paying a $25,000 fine to the EPA.

R-12 Refrigerant Conversion

If your vehicle still uses R-12 refrigerant, one way to save A/C system costs down the road is to investigate the possibility of having your system converted to R-134a. The older R-12 systems can be easily converted to R-134a refrigerant by a certified automotive technician by installing a few new components and changing the system oil.

The cost of R-12 is steadily rising and will continue to increase, because it is no longer imported or manufactured in the United States. Therefore, it is often possible to have an R-12 system converted to R-134a and recharged for less than it would cost to just charge the system with R-12.

If you are interested in having your system converted, contact local automotive service stations for more details and information.

PREVENTIVE MAINTENANCE

▶ See Figures 142 and 143

Although the A/C system should not be serviced by the do-it-yourselfer, preventive maintenance can be practiced and A/C system inspections can be performed to help maintain the efficiency of the vehicle's A/C system. For preventive maintenance, perform the following:

• The easiest and most important preventive maintenance for your A/C system is to be sure that it is used on a regular basis. Running the system for five minutes each month (no matter what the season) will help ensure that the seals and all internal components remain lubricated.

➡Some newer vehicles automatically operate the A/C system compressor whenever the windshield defroster is activated. When running, the compressor lubricates the A/C system components; therefore, the A/C system would not need to be operated each month.

• In order to prevent heater core freeze-up during A/C operation, it is necessary to maintain proper antifreeze protection. Use a hand-held coolant tester (hydrometer) to periodically check the condition of the antifreeze in your engine's cooling system.

➡Antifreeze should not be used longer than the manufacturer specifies.

• For efficient operation of an air conditioned vehicle's cooling system, the radiator cap should have a holding pressure which meets manufacturer's specifications. A cap which fails to hold these pressures should be replaced.

• Any obstruction of or damage to the condenser configuration will restrict air flow which is essential to its efficient operation. It is, therefore, a good rule to keep this unit clean and in proper physical shape.

➡Bug screens which are mounted in front of the condenser (unless they are original equipment) are regarded as obstructions.

• The condensation drain tube expels any water which accumulates on the bottom of the evaporator housing into the engine compartment. If this tube is obstructed, the air conditioning performance can be restricted and condensation buildup can spill over onto the vehicle's floor.

Fig. 142 A coolant tester can be used to determine the freezing and boiling levels of the coolant in your vehicle

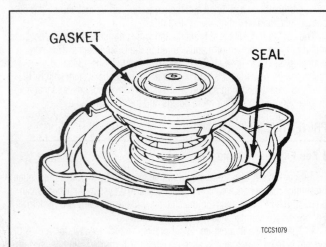

Fig. 143 To ensure efficient cooling system operation, inspect the radiator cap gasket and seal

SYSTEM INSPECTION

▶ See Figure 144

Although the A/C system should not be serviced by the do-it-yourselfer, preventive maintenance can be practiced and A/C system inspections can be performed to help maintain the efficiency of the vehicle's A/C system. For A/C system inspection, perform the following:

The easiest and often most important check for the air conditioning system consists of a visual inspection of the system components. Visually inspect the air conditioning system for refrigerant leaks, damaged compressor clutch, abnormal compressor drive belt tension and/or condition, plugged evaporator drain tube, blocked condenser fins, disconnected or broken wires, blown fuses, corroded connections and poor insulation.

A refrigerant leak will usually appear as an oily residue at the leakage point in the system. The oily residue soon picks up dust or dirt particles from the surrounding air and appears greasy. Through time, this will build up and appear to be a heavy dirt impregnated grease.

For a thorough visual and operational inspection, check the following:
• Check the surface of the radiator and condenser for dirt, leaves or other material which might block air flow.
• Check for kinks in hoses and lines. Check the system for leaks.
• Make sure the drive belt is properly tensioned. When the air conditioning is operating, make sure the drive belt is free of noise or slippage.
• Make sure the blower motor operates at all appropriate positions, then check for distribution of the air from all outlets with the blower on **HIGH** or **MAX**.

➡Keep in mind that under conditions of high humidity, air discharged from the A/C vents may not feel as cold as expected, even if the system is working properly. This is because vaporized moisture in humid air retains heat more effectively than dry air, thereby making humid air more difficult to cool.

• Make sure the air passage selection lever is operating correctly. Start the engine and warm it to normal operating temperature, then make sure the temperature selection lever is operating correctly.

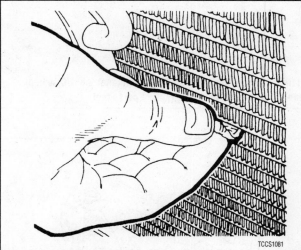

Fig. 144 Periodically remove any debris from the condenser and radiator fins

Windshield Wipers

ELEMENT (REFILL) CARE & REPLACEMENT

▶ See Figures 145 thru 154

For maximum effectiveness and longest element life, the windshield and wiper blades should be kept clean. Dirt, tree sap, road tar and so on will cause streaking, smearing and blade deterioration if left on the glass. It is advisable to wash the windshield carefully with a commercial glass cleaner. at least once a month. Wipe off the rubber blades with the wet rag afterwards. Do not attempt to move wipers across the windshield by hand; damage to the motor and drive mechanism will result.

To inspect and/or replace the wiper blade elements, place the wiper switch in the **LOW** speed position and the ignition switch in the **ACC** position. When the wiper blades are approximately vertical on the windshield, turn the ignition switch to **OFF**.

Examine the wiper blade elements. If they are found to be cracked, broken or torn, they should be replaced immediately. Replacement intervals will vary with usage, although ozone deterioration usually limits element life to about one year. If the wiper pattern is smeared or streaked, or if the blade chatters across the glass, the elements should be replaced. It is easiest and most sensible to replace the elements in pairs.

If your vehicle is equipped with aftermarket blades, there are several different types of refills and your vehicle might have any kind. Aftermarket blades and arms rarely use the exact same type blade or refill as the original equipment. Here are some typical aftermarket blades; not all may be available for your vehicle:

The Anco® type uses a release button that is pushed down to allow the refill to slide out of the yoke jaws. The new refill slides back into the frame and locks in place.

Fig. 147 Pylon® wiper blade and adapter

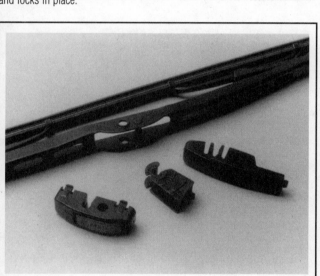

Fig. 145 Bosch® wiper blade and fit kit

Fig. 148 Anco® wiper blade and fit kit

Fig. 146 Lexor® wiper blade and fit kit

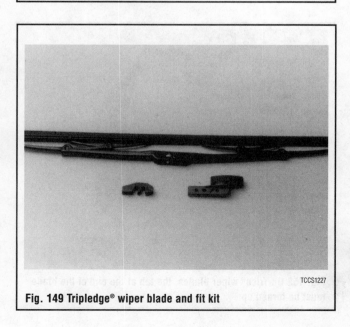

Fig. 149 Tripledge® wiper blade and fit kit

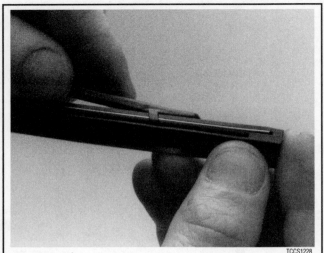

Fig. 150 To remove and install a Lexor® wiper blade refill, slip out the old insert and slide in a new one

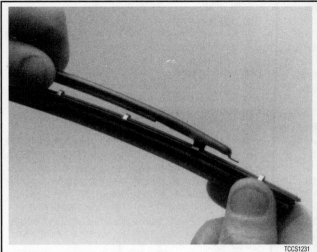

Fig. 153 . . . then the insert can be removed. After installing the replacement insert, bend the tab back

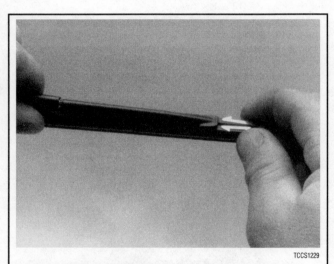

Fig. 151 On Pylon® inserts, the clip at the end has to be removed prior to sliding the insert off

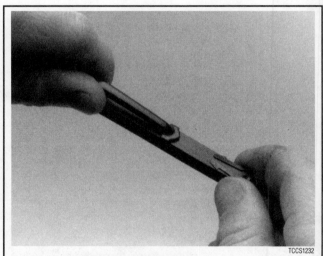

Fig. 154 The Tripledge® wiper blade insert is removed and installed using a securing clip

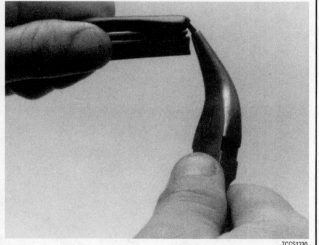

Fig. 152 On Trico® wiper blades, the tab at the end of the blade must be turned up . . .

Some Anco® refills are removed by locating where the metal backing strip or the refill is wider. Insert a small screwdriver blade between the frame and metal backing strip. Press down to release the refill from the retaining tab.

Other types of Anco® refills have two metal tabs which are unlocked by squeezing them together. The rubber filler can then be withdrawn from the frame jaws. A new refill is installed by inserting the refill into the front frame jaws and sliding it rearward to engage the remaining frame jaws. There are usually four jaws; be certain when installing that the refill is engaged in all of them. At the end of its travel, the tabs will lock into place on the front jaws of the wiper blade frame.

Another type of refill is made from polycarbonate. The refill has a simple locking device at one end which flexes downward out of the groove into which the jaws of the holder fit, allowing easy release. By sliding the new refill through all the jaws and pushing through the slight resistance when it reaches the end of its travel, the refill will lock into position.

To replace the Tridon® refill, it is necessary to remove the wiper blade. This refill has a plastic backing strip with a notch about 1 in. (25mm) from the end. Hold the blade (frame) on a hard surface so that the frame is tightly bowed. Grip the tip of the backing strip and pull up while twisting counter-clockwise. The backing strip will snap out of the retaining tab. Do this for the remaining tabs until the refill is free of the blade. The length of these refills is molded into the end and they should be replaced with identical types.

Regardless of the type of refill used, be sure to follow the part manufacturer's instructions closely. Make sure that all of the frame jaws are engaged as the refill is pushed into place and locked. If the metal blade holder and frame are allowed to touch the glass during wiper operation, the glass will be scratched.

Tires and Wheels

Common sense and good driving habits will afford maximum tire life. Fast starts, sudden stops and hard cornering are hard on tires and will shorten their useful life span. Make sure that you don't overload the vehicle or run with incorrect pressure in the tires. Both of these practices will increase tread wear.

➡ **For optimum tire life, keep the tires properly inflated, rotate them often and have the wheel alignment checked periodically.**

Inspect your tires frequently. Be especially careful to watch for bubbles in the tread or sidewall, deep cuts or underinflation. Replace any tires with bubbles in the sidewall. If cuts are so deep that they penetrate to the cords, discard the tire. Any cut in the sidewall of a radial tire renders it unsafe. Also look for uneven tread wear patterns that may indicate the front end is out of alignment or that the tires are out of balance.

TIRE ROTATION

▶ **See Figures 155 and 156**

Tires must be rotated periodically to equalize wear patterns that vary with a tire's position on the vehicle. Tires will also wear in an uneven way as the front steering/suspension system wears to the point where the alignment should be reset.

Rotating the tires will ensure maximum life for the tires as a set, so you will not have to discard a tire early due to wear on only part of the tread. Regular rotation is required to equalize wear.

When rotating "unidirectional tires," make sure that they always roll in the same direction. This means that a tire used on the left side of the vehicle must not be switched to the right side and vice-versa. Such tires should only be rotated front-to-rear or rear-to-front, while always remaining on the same side of the vehicle. These tires are marked on the sidewall as to the direction of rotation; observe the marks when reinstalling the tire(s).

Some styled or "mag" wheels may have different offsets front to rear. In these cases, the rear wheels must not be used up front and vice-versa.

Fig. 156 Unidirectional tires are identifiable by sidewall arrows and/or the word "rotation"

Furthermore, if these wheels are equipped with unidirectional tires, they cannot be rotated unless the tire is remounted for the proper direction of rotation.

➡ **The compact or space-saver spare is strictly for emergency use. It must never be included in the tire rotation or placed on the vehicle for everyday use.**

TIRE DESIGN

▶ **See Figure 157**

For maximum satisfaction, tires should be used in sets of four. Mixing of different types (radial, bias-belted, fiberglass belted) must be avoided. In most cases, the vehicle manufacturer has designated a type of tire on which the vehicle will perform best. Your first choice when replacing tires should be to use the same type of tire that the manufacturer recommends.

When radial tires are used, tire sizes and wheel diameters should be selected to maintain ground clearance and tire load capacity equivalent to the original specified tire. Radial tires should always be used in sets of four.

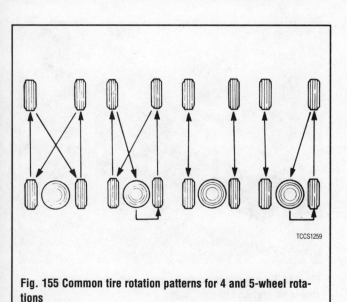

Fig. 155 Common tire rotation patterns for 4 and 5-wheel rotations

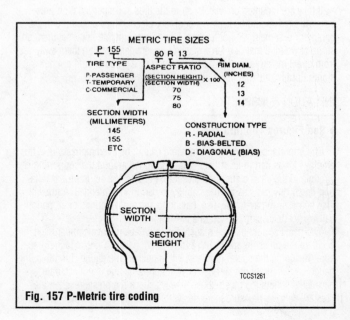

Fig. 157 P-Metric tire coding

✻✻ CAUTION

Radial tires should never be used on only the front axle.

When selecting tires, pay attention to the original size as marked on the tire. Most tires are described using an industry size code sometimes referred to as P-Metric. This allows the exact identification of the tire specifications, regardless of the manufacturer. If selecting a different tire size or brand, remember to check the installed tire for any sign of interference with the body or suspension while the vehicle is stopping, turning sharply or heavily loaded.

Snow Tires

Good radial tires can produce a big advantage in slippery weather, but in snow, a street radial tire does not have sufficient tread to provide traction and control. The small grooves of a street tire quickly pack with snow and the tire behaves like a billiard ball on a marble floor. The more open, chunky tread of a snow tire will self-clean as the tire turns, providing much better grip on snowy surfaces.

To satisfy municipalities requiring snow tires during weather emergencies, most snow tires carry either an M + S designation after the tire size stamped on the sidewall, or the designation "all-season." In general, no change in tire size is necessary when buying snow tires.

Most manufacturers strongly recommend the use of 4 snow tires on their vehicles for reasons of stability. If snow tires are fitted only to the drive wheels, the opposite end of the vehicle may become very unstable when braking or turning on slippery surfaces. This instability can lead to unpleasant endings if the driver can't counteract the slide in time.

Note that snow tires, whether 2 or 4, will affect vehicle handling in all non-snow situations. The stiffer, heavier snow tires will noticeably change the turning and braking characteristics of the vehicle. Once the snow tires are installed, you must re-learn the behavior of the vehicle and drive accordingly.

➡ **Consider buying extra wheels on which to mount the snow tires. Once done, the "snow wheels" can be installed and removed as needed. This eliminates the potential damage to tires or wheels from seasonal removal and installation. Even if your vehicle has styled wheels, see if inexpensive steel wheels are available. Although the look of the vehicle will change, the expensive wheels will be protected from salt, curb hits and pothole damage.**

TIRE STORAGE

If they are mounted on wheels, store the tires at proper inflation pressure. All tires should be kept in a cool, dry place. If they are stored in the garage or basement, do not let them stand on a concrete floor; set them on strips of wood, a mat or a large stack of newspaper. Keeping them away from direct moisture is of paramount importance. Tires should not be stored upright, but in a flat position.

INFLATION & INSPECTION

▶ **See Figures 158 thru 166**

The importance of proper tire inflation cannot be overemphasized. A tire employs air as part of its structure. It is designed around the supporting strength of the air at a specified pressure. For this reason, improper inflation drastically reduces the tire's ability to perform as intended. A tire will lose some air in day-to-day use; having to add a few pounds of air periodically is not necessarily a sign of a leaking tire.

Two items should be a permanent fixture in every glove compartment: an accurate tire pressure gauge and a tread depth gauge. Check the tire pressure (including the spare) regularly with a pocket type gauge. Too often, the gauge on the end of the air hose at your corner garage is not accurate because it suffers too much abuse. Always check tire pressure when the tires are cold, as pressure increases with temperature. If you must move the

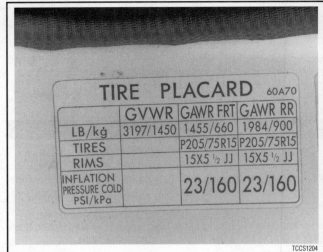

TIRE PLACARD	60A70	
	GVWR	GAWR FRT	GAWR RR
LB/kg	3197/1450	1455/660	1984/900
TIRES		P205/75R15	P205/75R15
RIMS		15X5 ½ JJ	15X5 ½ JJ
INFLATION PRESSURE COLD PSI/kPa		23/160	23/160

TCCS1204

Fig. 158 The recommended tire inflation pressure is provided on a label attached to the driver's side door pillar

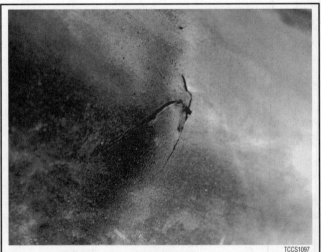

TCCS1097

Fig. 159 Tires should be checked frequently for any sign of puncture or damage

TCCS1095

Fig. 160 Tires with deep cuts, or cuts which show bulging should be replaced immediately

vehicle to check the tire inflation, do not drive more than a mile before checking. A cold tire is generally one that has not been driven for more than three hours.

A plate or sticker is normally provided somewhere in the vehicle (door post, hood, tailgate or trunk lid) which shows the proper pressure for the tires. Never counteract excessive pressure build-up by bleeding off air pressure (letting some air out). This will cause the tire to run hotter and wear quicker.

✳✳ CAUTION

Never exceed the maximum tire pressure embossed on the tire! This is the pressure to be used when the tire is at maximum loading, but it is rarely the correct pressure for everyday driving. Consult the owner's manual or the tire pressure sticker for the correct tire pressure.

Once you've maintained the correct tire pressures for several weeks, you'll be familiar with the vehicle's braking and handling personality. Slight adjustments in tire pressures can fine-tune these characteristics, but never change the cold pressure specification by more than 2 psi. A slightly softer tire pressure will give a softer ride but also yield lower fuel mileage. A

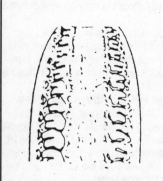
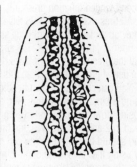

- DRIVE WHEEL HEAVY ACCELERATION
- OVERINFLATION

- HARD CORNERING
- UNDERINFLATION
- LACK OF ROTATION

TCCS1262

Fig. 161 Examples of inflation-related tire wear patterns

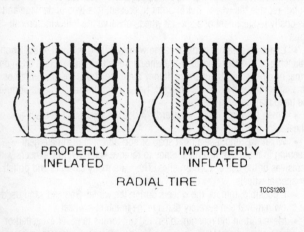

PROPERLY INFLATED

IMPROPERLY INFLATED

RADIAL TIRE

TCCS1263

Fig. 162 Radial tires have a characteristic sidewall bulge; don't try to measure pressure by looking at the tire. Use a quality air pressure gauge

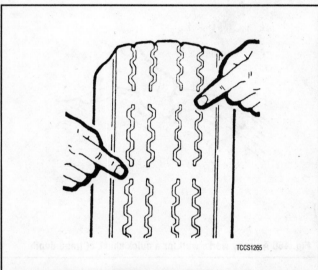

TCCS1265

Fig. 164 Tread wear indicators will appear when the tire is worn

CONDITION	RAPID WEAR AT SHOULDERS	RAPID WEAR AT CENTER	CRACKED TREADS	WEAR ON ONE SIDE	FEATHERED EDGE	BALD SPOTS	SCALLOPED WEAR
EFFECT							
CAUSE	UNDER-INFLATION OR LACK OF ROTATION	OVER-INFLATION OR LACK OF ROTATION	UNDER-INFLATION OR EXCESSIVE SPEED*	EXCESSIVE CAMBER	INCORRECT TOE	UNBALANCED WHEEL OR TIRE DEFECT *	LACK OF ROTATION OF TIRES OR WORN OR OUT-OF-ALIGNMENT SUSPENSION.
CORRECTION		ADJUST PRESSURE TO SPECIFICATIONS WHEN TIRES ARE COOL ROTATE TIRES		ADJUST CAMBER TO SPECIFICATIONS	ADJUST TOE-IN TO SPECIFICATIONS	DYNAMIC OR STATIC BALANCE WHEELS	ROTATE TIRES AND INSPECT SUSPENSION

*HAVE TIRE INSPECTED FOR FURTHER USE.

TCCS1267

Fig. 163 Common tire wear patterns and causes

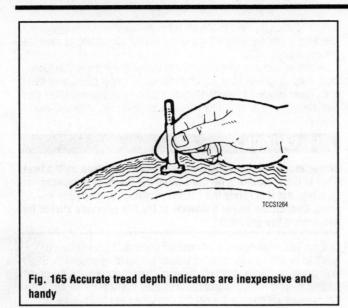

Fig. 165 Accurate tread depth indicators are inexpensive and handy

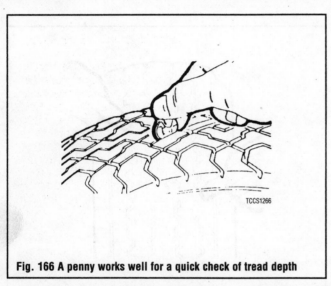

Fig. 166 A penny works well for a quick check of tread depth

slightly harder tire will give crisper dry road handling but can cause skidding on wet surfaces. Unless you're fully attuned to the vehicle, stick to the recommended inflation pressures.

All tires made since 1968 have built-in tread wear indicator bars that show up as ½ in. (13mm) wide smooth bands across the tire when 1/16 in. (1.5mm) of tread remains. The appearance of tread wear indicators means that the tires should be replaced. In fact, many states have laws prohibiting the use of tires with less than this amount of tread.

You can check your own tread depth with an inexpensive gauge or by using a Lincoln head penny. Slip the Lincoln penny (with Lincoln's head upside-down) into several tread grooves. If you can see the top of Lincoln's head in 2 adjacent grooves, the tire has less than 1/16 in. (1.5mm) tread left and should be replaced. You can measure snow tires in the same manner by using the "tails" side of the Lincoln penny. If you can see the top of the Lincoln memorial, it's time to replace the snow tire(s).

CARE OF SPECIAL WHEELS

If you have invested money in magnesium, aluminum alloy or sport wheels, special precautions should be taken to make sure your investment is not wasted and that your special wheels look good for the life of the vehicle.

Special wheels are easily damaged and/or scratched. Occasionally check the rims for cracking, impact damage or air leaks. If any of these are found, replace the wheel. But in order to prevent this type of damage and the costly replacement of a special wheel, observe the following precautions:

• Use extra care not to damage the wheels during removal, installation, balancing, etc. After removal of the wheels from the vehicle, place them on a mat or other protective surface. If they are to be stored for any length of time, support them on strips of wood. Never store tires and wheels upright; the tread may develop flat spots.

• When driving, watch for hazards; it doesn't take much to crack a wheel.

• When washing, use a mild soap or non-abrasive dish detergent (keeping in mind that detergent tends to remove wax). Avoid cleansers with abrasives or the use of hard brushes. There are many cleaners and polishes for special wheels.

• If possible, remove the wheels during the winter. Salt and sand used for snow removal can severely damage the finish of a wheel.

• Make certain the recommended lug nut torque is never exceeded or the wheel may crack. Never use snow chains on special wheels; severe scratching will occur.

FLUIDS AND LUBRICANTS

Fluid Disposal

Used fluids such as engine oil, transmission fluid, antifreeze and brake fluid are hazardous wastes and must be disposed of properly. Before draining any fluids, consult with your local authorities; in many areas, waste oil, antifreeze, etc. are being accepted as a part of recycling programs. A number of service stations and auto parts stores are also accepting waste fluids for recycling.

Be sure of the recycling center's policies before draining any fluids, as many will not accept different fluids that have been mixed together.

Fuel and Engine Oil Recommendations

FUEL

➡**Some fuel additives contain chemicals that can damage the catalytic converter and/or oxygen sensor. Read all of the labels carefully before using any additive in the engine or fuel system.**

All vehicles covered by this manual are designed to run on unleaded fuel. The use of a leaded fuel in a vehicle requiring unleaded fuel will plug the catalytic converter and render it inoperative. It will also increase exhaust

backpressure to the point where engine output will be severely reduced. Obviously, use of leaded fuel should not be a problem, since most companies have stopped selling it for quite some time.

For all models the minimum octane rating of the unleaded fuel being used must be at least 87 (as listed on the pumps), which usually means regular unleaded. Some areas may have 86 or even lower octanes available, which would make 87 mid-grade or even premium. In these cases a minimum fuel octane of 87 should STILL be used.

Fuel should be selected for the brand and octane which performs best with your engine. Judge a gasoline by its ability to prevent pinging, its engine starting capabilities (cold and hot) and general all-weather performance. The use of a fuel too low in octane (a measurement of anti-knock quality) will result in spark knock. Since many factors such as altitude, terrain, air temperature and humidity affect operating efficiency, knocking may result even though the recommended fuel is being used. If persistent knocking occurs, it may be necessary to switch to a different brand or grade of fuel. Continuous or heavy knocking may result in engine damage.

➡**Your engine's fuel requirement can change with time, mainly due to carbon buildup, which will in turn change the compression ratio. If your engine pings or knocks switch to a higher grade of fuel. Sometimes just changing brands will cure the problem.**

The other most important quality you should look for in a fuel is that it contains detergents designed to keep fuel injection systems clean. Many of the major fuel companies will display information right at the pumps telling you that their fuels contain these detergents. The use of a high-quality fuel which contains detergents will help assure trouble-free operation of your car's fuel system.

In Multi-port Fuel Injected (MFI) vehicles, oxygenated fuels, which meet the minimum octane requirement of 87 and the following requirements, may be used in your vehicle.

➡**Oxygenated fuels are fuels which contain oxygen-carrying additives such as MTBE or alcohol.**

Unleaded gasoline containing Methyl Tertiary Butyl Ether (MTBE) may be used in the MFI-equipped models covered by this manual, so long as the MTBE content in the gasoline is less than 15 percent. Gasoline containing MTBE does not contain alcohol.

Blends of unleaded gasoline and ethanol (grain alcohol), also known as gasohol, may be used in your MFI-equipped vehicle so long as the amount of ethanol is not greater than 10 percent. Fuel containing wood alcohol (methanol) may be used in your vehicle so long as the level of methanol is not greater than 5 percent and the fuel contains no co-solvents or corrosion inhibitors.

❄❄ WARNING

Never use fuels containing more than 5 percent methanol, otherwise fuel system damage and/or performance problems will occur.

OIL

▶ **See Figure 167**

When adding oil to the crankcase or changing the oil and filter, it is important that oil of an equal quality to original equipment be used in your car. The use of inferior oils may void the warranty, damage your engine, or both. Suzuki recommends using oil with the API classification of SG, SH, or SH/ILSAC GF-1. If the vehicle is operated in a climate with temperatures above -4°F (-20°C), the manufacturer recommends using SAE 10W-30 oil. Refer to the accompanying chart for all recommended oil viscosities and their associated temperature ranges.

The Society of Automotive Engineers (SAE) grade number of the oil indicates the viscosity of the oil—its ability to lubricate at a given temperature. The lower the SAE number, the lighter the oil; the lower the viscosity, the

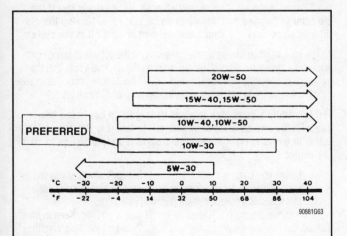

Fig. 167 Select the viscosity of the oil you add to your vehicle based upon the expected temperature range until your next oil change

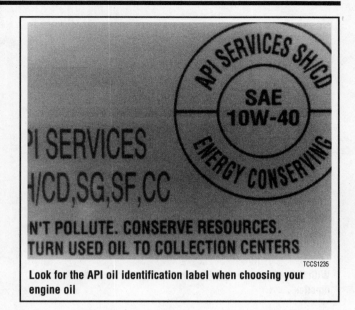

Look for the API oil identification label when choosing your engine oil

easier it is to crank the engine in cold weather, but the less the oil will lubricate and protect the engine in high temperatures. This number is marked on every oil container.

Oil viscosities should be chosen from those oils recommended for the lowest anticipated temperatures during the oil change interval. Due to the need for an oil that embodies both good lubrication at high temperature and easy cranking in cold weather, multigrade oils have been developed. Basically, a multigrade oil is thinner at low temperatures and thicker at high temperatures. For example, a 10W–40 oil (the W stands for winter) exhibits the characteristics of a 10-weight (SAE 10) oil when the car is first started and the oil is cold. Its lighter weight allows it to travel to the lubricating surfaces quicker and offer less resistance to starter motor cranking than a heavier oil. But after the engine reaches operating temperature, the 10W–40 oil begins acting like straight 40-weight (SAE 40) oil. It behaves as a heavier oil, providing greater lubrication and protection against foaming than lighter oils.

The American Petroleum Institute (API) designations, also found on oil containers, indicate the classification of engine oil used for given operating conditions. Only oils designated Service SG (or the latest superseding designation) heavy-duty detergent should be used in your vehicle. Oils of the SG-type perform many functions inside the engine besides their basic lubrication. Through a balanced system of metallic detergents and polymeric dispersants, the oil prevents high and low temperature deposits and also keeps sludge and dirt particles in suspension. Acids, particularly sulfuric, as well as other by-products of engine combustion are neutralized by the oil. If these acids are allowed to concentrate, they can cause corrosion and rapid wear of the internal engine parts.

❄❄ WARNING

Non-detergent motor oils or straight mineral oils should never be used in your engine.

Engine

OIL LEVEL CHECK

Check the engine oil level every time you fill the gas tank. The oil level should be between the upper and lower marks on the dipstick. Make sure that the dipstick is inserted into the crankcase as far as possible and that the vehicle is resting on level ground. Also, allow a few minutes after turning the engine **OFF** for the oil to drain into the pan, otherwise an inaccurate reading may result. One good way to assure enough time for the oil to run back into the pan is to fill the fuel tank first, then check the oil after paying for the gas.

With the vehicle sitting on a level surface, remove the oil level dipstick . . .

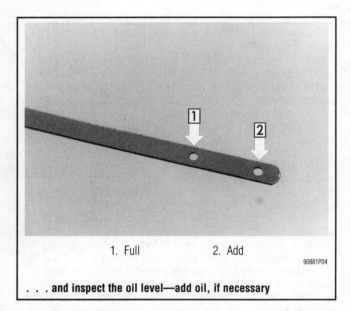

1. Full   2. Add

. . . and inspect the oil level—add oil, if necessary

To add oil to the engine, remove the oil fill cap . . .

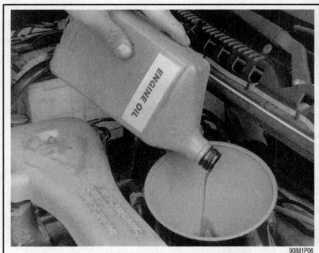

. . . and pour the appropriate amount of clean oil into the engine—using a funnel helps avoid messy spills

1. Open the hood, then locate and remove the engine oil dipstick.
2. Wipe the dipstick with a clean, lint-free rag and reinsert it. Be sure to insert it all the way.
3. Pull out the dipstick and note the oil level. It should be between the upper and the lower marks.

➡ **Use a high quality multigrade oil of the proper viscosity, and add oil to the engine in small amounts so that you do not accidentally overfill it.**

4. If the level is below the lower mark, install the dipstick and add fresh oil to bring the level within the proper range by adding oil through the oil filler cap. Do not overfill the engine.
5. Recheck the oil level and add more engine oil, if necessary.
6. Close the hood.

OIL & FILTER CHANGE

▸ **See Figure 168**

➡ **The engine oil and oil filter should be changed at the recommended intervals on the maintenance interval chart. Though some manufacturers have at times recommended changing the filter only at every other oil change, we recommend that you always change the filter with the oil. The benefit of fresh oil is quickly lost if the old filter is clogged and unable to do its job. Also, leaving the old filter in place leaves a significant amount of dirty oil in the system.**

The oil should be changed more frequently if the vehicle is being operated under severe conditions. Before draining the oil, make sure that the engine is at operating temperature. Hot oil will hold more impurities in suspension and will flow better, allowing the removal of more oil and dirt.

➡ **It is usually a good idea to place your ignition key in the box or bag with the bottles of fresh engine oil. In this way it will be VERY HARD to forget to refill the engine crankcase before you go to start the engine.**

1. Before you crawl under the vehicle, take a look at where you will be working and gather all the necessary tools, such as a few wrenches or a ratchet and assorted sockets, a drain pan, and clean rags.
2. Position the drain pan beneath the oil pan drain plug. Keep in mind that the fast flowing oil, which will spill out as you pull the plug from the pan, will flow with enough force that it could miss the pan. Position the drain pan accordingly and be ready to move the pan more directly beneath the plug as the oil flow lessens to a trickle.
3. Loosen the drain plug with a wrench (or socket and driver), then carefully unscrew the plug with your fingers. Use a rag to shield your fin-

Position the catch pan beneath the drain plug, then loosen it with a wrench or socket and ratchet

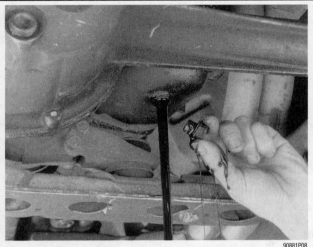

Unthread the plug by hand and quickly withdraw it from the hot oil to prevent painful burns

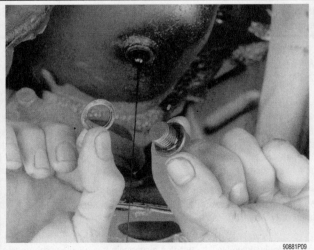

If the drain plug is equipped with a copper or plastic washer, be sure to replace it with a new one

gers from the heat. Push in on the plug as you unscrew it so you can feel when all of the screw threads are out of the hole (and so you will keep the oil from seeping past the threads until you are ready to remove the plug). You can then remove the plug quickly to avoid having hot oil run down your arm. This will also help assure that you have the plug in your hand, not in the bottom of a pan of hot oil.

☀☀ CAUTION

Be careful of the oil; when at operating temperature, it is hot enough to cause a severe burn.

4. Allow the oil to drain until nothing but a few drops come out of the drain hole. Check the drain plug to make sure the threads and sealing surface are not damaged. Carefully thread the plug into position and tighten it with a torque wrench to 22–28 ft. lbs. (30–38 Nm). If a torque wrench is not available, snug the drain plug and give a slight additional turn. You don't want the plug to fall out (as you would quickly become stranded), but the pan threads are EASILY stripped from overtightening (and this can be time consuming and/or costly to fix).

5. The oil filter is located on the front left-hand side of all the engines installed in these vehicles; position the drain pan beneath it.

If you own a 4-wheel drive vehicle, fabricate a small catch container from an empty oil bottle

Loosen, but do not remove, the old oil filter using a strap wrench . . .

. . . then position the catch container on the front axle and steering linkage, against the oil pan

After the catch container is properly situated, remove the oil filter and allow the oil to drain

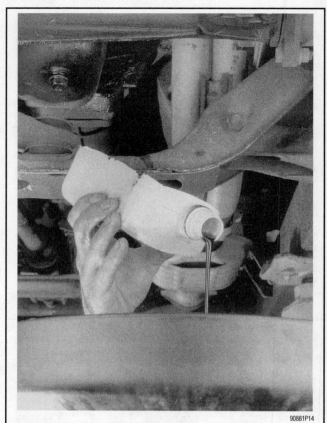

The collected oil can then be poured into a large catch pan

6. When you remove the oil filter from 4-wheel drive models, you will notice that the oil draining from the filter pours directly onto the front axle housing. This causes the oil to run off the housing in multiple directions, making it very difficult to avoid having a messy spill accumulate under your vehicle. This mess can be avoided by fabricating a small catch pan out of an old engine oil bottle as follows:

    a. Remove the cap from the old engine oil bottle.

    b. Using a utility knife, carefully cut the bottle in half vertically (from the neck to the bottom).

    c. You should now have half of an old oil bottle. Position the bottle under the engine oil filter (you can situate the bottle on the axle housing and steering components) so that it will catch the engine oil draining from the filter when you loosen it.

    d. After removing the filter, the drained oil can be neatly poured into the large drain pan (or other container) from the half-bottle.

7. To remove the oil filter, you may need an oil filter wrench, since the filter may have been fitted too tightly and/or the heat from the engine may have made it even tighter. A filter wrench can be obtained at any auto parts store and is well-worth the investment. Loosen the filter with the filter wrench. With a rag wrapped around the filter, unscrew the filter from the boss on the side of the engine. Be careful of hot oil that will drain out of the filter. Make sure that your drain pan (2-wheel drive mod-els) or your half-bottle fabricated container (4-wheel models) is under the filter before you start to remove it from the engine; should some of the hot oil happen to get on you, there will be a place to dump the filter in a hurry and the filter will usually spill a good bit of dirty oil as it is removed.

8. Wipe the base of the mounting boss with a clean, dry cloth. When you install the new filter, smear a small amount of fresh oil on the gasket with your finger, just enough to coat the entire contact surface. When you tighten the filter, rotate it an additional ¾ turn after the gasket contacts the engine block surface.

✵✵ WARNING

Never operate the engine without engine oil, otherwise SEVERE engine damage will result.

9. Refill the engine crankcase with the proper amount of oil. DO NOT WAIT TO DO THIS, because if you forget and someone tries to start the car, severe engine damage will occur.

10. Refill the engine crankcase slowly, checking the level often. You may notice that it usually takes less than the amount of oil listed in the capacity chart to refill the crankcase. But, that is only until the engine is run and the oil filter is filled with oil. To make sure the proper level is obtained, run the engine to normal operating temperature, shut the engine **OFF**, allow the oil to drain back into the oil pan, and recheck the level. Top off the oil at this time to the fill mark.

➡**If the vehicle is not resting on level ground, the oil level reading on the dipstick may be slightly misleading. Be sure to check the level only when the car is sitting level.**

11. Drain your used oil in a suitable container for recycling and clean up your tools, as you will be needing them again in a couple of thousand more miles (kilometers?).

12. Dispose of the used engine oil properly.

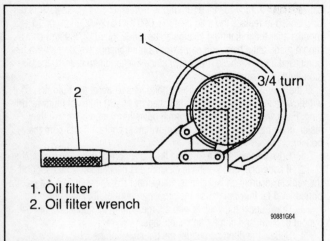

1. Oil filter
2. Oil filter wrench

90881G64

Fig. 168 To properly tighten the oil filter, turn it an additional ¾ turn after the rubber gasket on the filter contacts the engine block surface

Manual Transmission

FLUID RECOMMENDATIONS

♦ See Figure 169

The manufacturer recommends that manual transmissions covered by this manual may use SAE 75W-85, 75W-90 or 80W-90 hypoid gear (depending on the temperature range until the next oil change) oil meeting or exceeding API grade GL-4 for lubrication. DO NOT use any other fluids for lubrication. Use of improper fluids could lead to leaks or transmission damage.

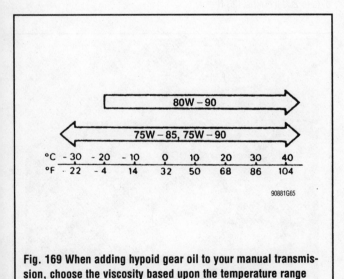

Fig. 169 When adding hypoid gear oil to your manual transmission, choose the viscosity based upon the temperature range expected until the next oil change

LEVEL CHECK

The fluid level should be checked every 7½ months or 7500 miles (12,000 km), and replaced every 22½ months or 22,500 miles (36,000 km), whichever comes first.

Samurai Models

♦ See Figure 170

1. Park the vehicle on a level surface, turn the engine **OFF**, FIRMLY apply the parking brake and block the drive wheels.

➡**Ground clearance may make access to the transmission filler plug impossible without raising and supporting the vehicle, BUT, if this is done, the car MUST be supported at four corners and level. If only the front or rear is supported, an improper fluid level will be indicated. If you are going to place the vehicle on four jackstands, this might be the perfect opportunity to rotate the tires as well.**

2. Remove the oil level plug from the side of the transmission case.
3. When the level plug is removed a slight amount of fluid should dribble out of the hole. If no fluid dribbles out of the hole, insert your finger in the level hole and feel for the fluid level; the fluid level should be even with the bottom of the hole.
4. If additional fluid is necessary, remove the filler hole and add new, clean hypoid gear oil through the filler hole using a siphon pump or squeeze bottle until the fluid level is even with the bottom of the level hole.
5. When you are finished, carefully install the filler and level plugs. Tighten the filler plug to 177–265 inch lbs. (20–30 Nm), and tighten the level plug to 88–142 inch lbs. (10–16 Nm). DO NOT overtighten the plug(s) and damage the housing.

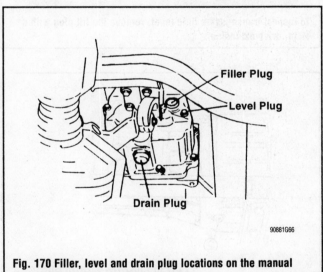

Filler Plug

Level Plug

Drain Plug

90881G66

Fig. 170 Filler, level and drain plug locations on the manual transmission used on Samurai models

Except Samurai Models

♦ See Figure 171

1. Park the vehicle on a level surface, turn the engine **OFF**, FIRMLY apply the parking brake and block the drive wheels.

➡**Ground clearance may make access to the transmission filler plug impossible without raising and supporting the vehicle, BUT, if this is done, the car MUST be supported at four corners and level. If only the front or rear is supported, an improper fluid level will be indicated. If you are going to place the vehicle on four jackstands, this might be the perfect opportunity to rotate the tires as well.**

2. Remove the oil filler plug from the side of the transmission case.
3. When the filler plug is removed a slight amount of fluid should dribble out of the hole. If no fluid dribbles out of the hole, insert your finger in the hole and feel for the fluid level; the fluid level should be even with the bottom of the hole.

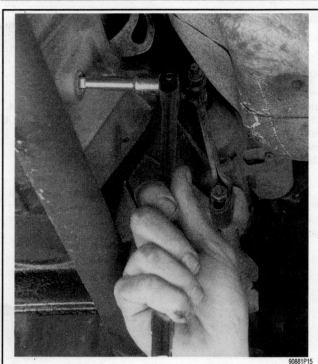

To inspect transmission fluid level, remove the fill plug with a ⅜ in. drive extension

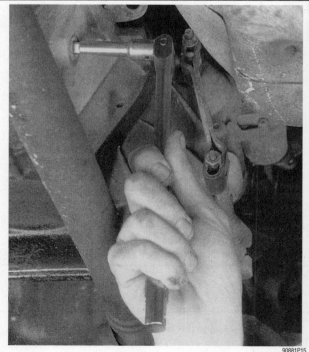

① Oil filler and level plug
② Oil drain plug

Fig. 171 Filler/level and drain plug locations on Sidekick, Tracker, Sport and X-90 manual transmissions

4. If additional fluid is necessary, add it through the filler hole using a siphon pump or squeeze bottle.

5. When you are finished, carefully install and tighten the plug to 162–241 inch lbs. (18–27 Nm). DO NOT overtighten the plug and damage the housing.

DRAIN & REFILL

Under normal conditions, the manufacturer indicates that the manual transmission fluid should be changed at the 7,500 mile (12,000 km) or 7.5 month mark, and every 22,500 miles (36,000 km) or 22.5 months after the initial fluid change. However, if the vehicle is driven under severe conditions (such as towing a trailer; repeated short trips; driving on rough, dusty,

salted and/or muddy roads; or driving in extremely cold weather), it is recommended to replace the fluid every 15,000 miles (24,000 km) or 15 months after the initial fluid change at the 7,500 mile (12,000 km) or 7.5 month mark. Little harm can come from a fluid change when you have just purchased a used vehicle, especially since the condition of the transmission fluid is usually not known.

If the fluid is to be drained, it is a good idea to warm the fluid first so it will flow better. This can be accomplished by 15–20 miles of highway driving. Fluid which is warmed to normal operating temperature will flow faster, drain more completely and remove more contaminants from the housing.

1. Drive the vehicle to assure the fluid is at normal operating temperature.

2. If additional under-vehicle clearance is needed, raise and support the vehicle securely on jackstands. Remember that the vehicle must be supported level (at four points) so the proper amount of fluid can be added.

3. Crawl under the vehicle with a large drain pan, containers of new hypoid gear oil, and some clean shop rags.

4. Situate the drain pan under the transmission housing, below the drain plug. Remember that with drain plugs which are mounted on the side of the transmission case, the fluid will likely flow with some force at first (arcing outward from the transmission), and will not just drip straight downward into the pan. If the transmission in your vehicle is equipped with a side-mounted drain plug, position the drain pan accordingly and move it more directly beneath the drain plug as the flow slows to a trickle.

➡ **To ensure that the fill plug is not frozen or rusted in place, remove it from the transmission BEFORE removing the drain plug. It would be unfortunate to drain all of your transmission fluid and then realize that the fill plug is stripped or frozen in place.**

5. Remove the fill plug, then the drain plug and allow the transmission fluid to drain out.

➡ **The transmission drain plug is usually a square receiver which is designed to accept a ⅜ in. driver such as a ratchet or extension.**

6. Once the transmission fluids stops draining from the case, clean the drain hole and drain plug of all dirt and debris. Install and tighten the drain plug to 200 inch lbs. (23 Nm).

To drain the manual transmission, first remove the fill plug (to ensure that it is not frozen in place) . . .

. . . then loosen the drain plug with a breaker bar—unthread the plug by hand . . .

. . . and withdraw the plug and your hand quickly to avoid the hot transmission oil

Prior to reinstalling the drain plug, be sure to clean the plug and drain hole of all dirt and debris (arrow)

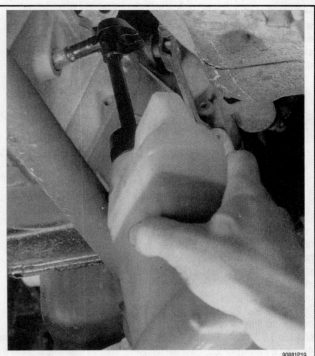

After installing the drain plug, use a pump to fill the transmission with the proper lubricant

7. On Samurai models, remove the small level plug.

8. Fill the transmission until the fluid level is at the bottom edge of the filler hole (Sidekick, Tracker, X-90 and Sidekick Sport models) or level hole (Samurai models) with SAE 75W-90 hypoid gear oil.

9. Reinstall the filler and level (if equipped) plug once you are finished. Tighten the filler plug to 162–241 inch lbs. (18–27 Nm) on Sidekick, Tracker, X-90 and Sidekick Sport models, or to 177–265 inch lbs. (20–30 Nm) for Samurai models. On Samurai models, tighten the level plug to 88–142 inch lbs. (10–16 Nm). DO NOT overtighten the plug(s) and damage the housing.

10. If necessary, remove the jackstands and carefully lower the vehicle.

Automatic Transmission

FLUID RECOMMENDATIONS

The automatic transmissions covered by this manual use Dexron® III Automatic Transmission Fluid for lubrication. DO NOT use improper fluids such as Type-F® or hypoid gear oil. Use of improper fluids could lead to leaks or transmission damage. Always use new, clean ATF whenever adding fluid to the transmission.

LEVEL CHECK

▶ **See Figure 172**

It is very important to maintain the proper fluid level in an automatic transmission. If the level is either too high or too low, poor shifting operation and internal damage are likely to occur. For this reason, inspect the automatic transmission fluid at every engine oil change.

The transmission fluid level must be checked with the engine running at slow idle, the vehicle parked on level ground, and the transmission fluid at least at room temperature (70°F/21°C).

1. Apply the parking brake and start the engine. Allow it to idle for 2 minutes.

2. With your foot on the brake pedal to hold the vehicle from moving, move the transmission gearshift selector through each gear, then move it back to the **P** (Park) position.

➡**Do NOT read the fluid level if you have drive in city traffic in hot weather, if the vehicle was pulling a trailer, or if you have just driven the vehicle for a long time at high speed. Allow the transmission fluid approximately 30 minutes to cool down before checking the fluid level, otherwise the level indicated will be misleading.**

3. Open the hood.

4. Locate the transmission fluid dipstick at the rear of the engine compartment, near the distributor. Pull the dipstick out of its tube and CAREFULLY touch the wet end of the dipstick to ascertain its temperature. The fluid should be at least room temperature (70°F/21°C). If the fluid feels cold, drive the vehicle for a minimum of 5 miles (8 km) before checking the fluid level.

5. If the fluid is room temperature or hotter, wipe the dipstick clean with a shop rag and reinsert it in the dipstick tube. Ensure that the dipstick is fully seated in the dipstick tube.

6. Pull the dipstick out of the tube and, while holding the dipstick horizontal, read the fluid level on the dipstick end. The fluid level should be between the two marks in the cold range on the dipstick if the fluid is not hot (approximately 68°F/20°C for 3-speed models, or 77°F/25°C for 4-speed models). If the fluid is hot (approximately 194°F/90°C for 3-speed models, or 167°F/75°C for 4-speed models), the fluid level should be between the two range marks on the dipstick.

7. If the fluid level is below the specified range, add just enough fluid through the dipstick tube to the transmission until the level is correct. It only takes 0.37 qt. (0.35L) on 3-speed transmissions or 0.32 qt. (0.30L) for 4-speed transmissions, to raise the fluid level from the low cold mark to the full cold mark or from the low hot mark to the full hot mark. Always add a little fluid at a time so that you do not accidentally overfill the transmission, which would require you to drain fluid back out. If the fluid level registers above the specified range, some fluid must be drained out of the transmission to bring the level down within the acceptable range. If some transmission fluid needs to be drained because the level is too high, you might as well remove and clean the transmission fluid pan and replace the filter.

8. Install the dipstick, close the hood and turn the engine **OFF**.

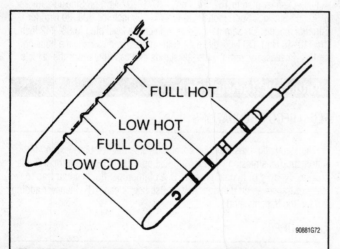

Fig. 172 The Automatic Transmission Fluid (ATF) should fall between the two applicable marks on the dipstick, depending on the temperature of the ATF

DRAIN, PAN/FILTER SERVICE & REFILL

Under normal service, the manufacturer indicates that the Automatic Transmission Fluid (ATF) used in 3-speed models does not require periodic replacement, and the ATF used in 4-speed models only requires replacement every 100,000 miles (160,000 km). However, if a major service is performed to the transmission, if transmission fluid becomes burnt or discolored through severe usage, or if the vehicle is subjected to constant stop-and-go driving in hot weather, frequent trailer towing, long periods of highway use at high speeds, commercial use (such as taxi, police, delivery or rental vehicles) fluid should be changed to prevent transmission damage every 52,500 miles (84,000 km) for 3-speed models, or every 15,000 miles (24,000 km) for 4-speed models.

3-Speed Transmission

▶ **See Figures 173, 174 and 175**

Whenever draining and replacing the ATF, it is good preventive maintenance to always install a new fluid filter.

1. If necessary, raise the vehicle and support it securely on jackstands.

2. Along with a large catch pan, tools (such as sockets, an extension, a ratchet and a gasket scraper), several clean shop rags, and the new fluid filter and pan gasket, crawl under the vehicle.

3. If necessary, matchmark and detach the driveshaft from the front differential, then position it out of the way by suspending it with cord or wire to the side.

4. Place the catch pan under the transmission fluid pan.

➡**Draining transmission fluid can be extremely messy. Work slowly and carefully, be sure to use a very large drain pan, and wear old clothing (ATF stains are very difficult to remove from clothing) when draining the fluid.**

5. Remove the right-hand side, left-hand side and front pan attaching bolts, and loosen the rear pan bolts to within a few turns of complete removal, then carefully break the gasket seal allowing most of the fluid to drain over the front edge of the pan.

✳✳ CAUTION

DO NOT force the pan while breaking the gasket seal. DO NOT allow the pan flange to become bent or otherwise damaged.

6. When fluid has drained to the level of the pan flange, remove the rear pan bolts and carefully lower the pan, doing your best to drain the rest of the fluid into the drain pan.

7. Clean the transmission fluid pan thoroughly using a safe solvent, then allow it to air dry. DO NOT use a cloth to dry the pan which might leave behind bits of lint. Discard the old pan gasket.

8. If necessary, remove the Automatic Transmission Fluid (ATF) filter mounting bolts, then remove the filter by pulling it down and off of the valve body. Make sure any gaskets or seals are removed with the old filter.

9. Install the new oil filter screen making sure all gaskets or seals are in place, then secure using the retaining bolts, if applicable. Tighten the filter mounting bolts to 168 inch lbs. (19 Nm).

10. Clean all of the fluid pan attaching bolts thoroughly, then apply threadlocking compound, such as Suzuki Cement Super 1333B, to the pan bolt threads.

11. Place a new gasket on the fluid pan, then install the pan to the transmission. Tighten the attaching bolts in a crisscross pattern to 115 inch lbs. (13 Nm).

12. Attach the driveshaft to the differential flange so that the matchmarks are aligned, then tighten the driveshaft-to-differential bolts to 36 ft. lbs. (50 Nm).

13. If necessary, remove the jackstands and carefully lower the vehicle.

➡**It is a good idea to add ATF to the transmission slowly and check the level often to avoid overfilling. There are not many frustrating circumstances worse than having to remove the transmission fluid pan a second time to drain out excess ATF, which is necessary to avoid damaging the transmission.**

14. Add the proper amount of Dexron III ATF to the transmission through the filler tube.

15. Start the engine and move the gear selector through all gears in the shift pattern. Allow the engine to reach normal operating temperature.

16. Check the transmission fluid level. Add or remove fluid, as necessary, to obtain the correct level.

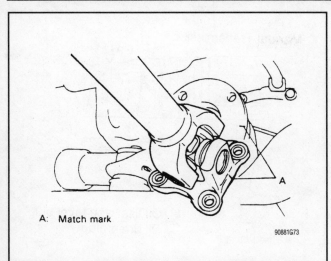

A: Match mark

90881G73

Fig. 173 To drain the ATF from 4-wheel drive models, matchmark and detach the front driveshaft from the differential flange . . .

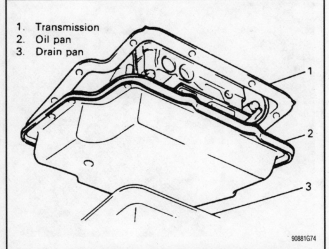

1. Transmission
2. Oil pan
3. Drain pan

90881G74

Fig. 174 . . . then remove most of the pan bolts and allow the fluid to drain into the catch pan

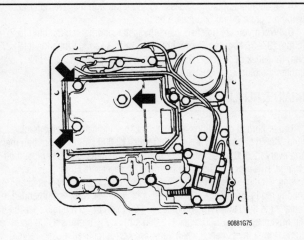

90881G75

Fig. 175 If the fluid filter is to be replaced, remove the attaching bolts (arrows) and pull the filter off of the transmission valve body

4-Speed Transmission

♦ See Figure 176

➡The manufacturer does not indicate that the 4-speed automatic transmissions require any sort of periodic filter replacement. If you would like to change the transmission fluid filter, please refer to Section 7.

1. If necessary, raise the vehicle and support it securely on jackstands.
2. Along with a large catch pan, tools (such as sockets and a ratchet, or a wrench), and several clean shop rags, crawl under the vehicle.
3. Place the catch pan under the transmission fluid pan drain plug.

➡Draining transmission fluid can be extremely messy. Work slowly and carefully, be sure to use a very large drain pan, and wear old clothing (ATF stains are very difficult to remove from clothing) when draining the fluid.

4. Remove the drain plug, allowing the ATF to drain into the catch pan.
5. When fluid has completely drained from the transmission, install the drain plug. Tighten the drain plug to 203 inch lbs. (23 Nm).
6. If necessary, remove the jackstands and carefully lower the vehicle.

➡It is a good idea to add ATF to the transmission slowly, and check the level often to avoid overfilling the engine.

7. Add the proper amount of Dexron III ATF to the transmission through the filler tube.
8. Start the engine and move the gear selector through all gears in the shift pattern. Allow the engine to reach normal operating temperature.
9. Check the transmission fluid level. Add or remove fluid, as necessary, to obtain the correct level.

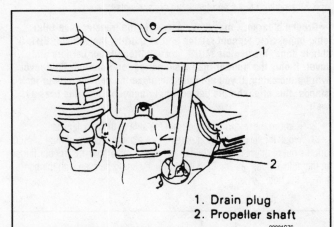

1. Drain plug
2. Propeller shaft

90881G76

Fig. 176 Unlike the 3-speed automatic transmission, the 4-speed transmission is equipped with a fluid drain plug (1)—according to the manufacturer, the ATF filter does not require periodic replacement

Transfer Case

FLUID RECOMMENDATIONS

♦ See Figure 177

➡Only 4-wheel drive models are equipped with transfer cases.

The manufacturer recommends that transfer cases covered by this manual may use SAE 75W-85, 75W-90 or 80W-90 hypoid gear (depending on the temperature range until the next oil change) oil meeting or exceeding API grade GL-4 for lubrication. DO NOT use any other fluids for lubrication. Use of improper fluids could lead to leaks or transfer case damage.

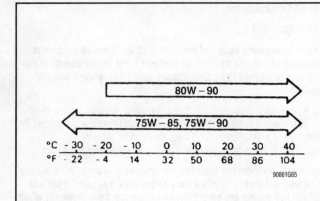

Fig. 177 When adding hypoid gear oil to your transfer case, choose the applicable viscosity based upon the temperature range expected until the next oil change

LEVEL CHECK

▶ **See Figures 178 and 179**

The fluid level should be checked every 7.5 months or 7500 miles (12,000 km), and replaced every 22.5 months or 22,500 miles (36,000 km), whichever comes first.

1. Park the vehicle on a level surface, turn the engine **OFF**, FIRMLY apply the parking brake and block the drive wheels.

➡ **Ground clearance may make access to the transfer case filler plug impossible without raising and supporting the vehicle, BUT, if this is done, the vehicle MUST be supported at four corners and level. If only the front or rear is supported, an improper fluid level will be indicated. If you are going to place the vehicle on four jackstands, this might be the perfect opportunity to rotate the tires as well.**

2. Remove the level/filler plug from the side of the transfer case.
3. When the level/filler plug is removed, a slight amount of fluid should dribble out of the hole. If no fluid dribbles out of the hole, insert your finger in the hole and feel for the fluid level, which should be even with the bottom of the hole.

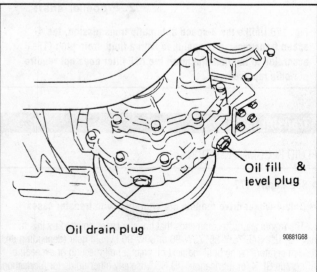

Fig. 178 Fill and drain plug locations on Samurai transfer cases

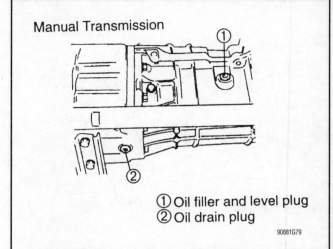

Fig. 179 Sidekick, Sidekick Sport, Tracker and X-90 transfer case fill and drain plug locations

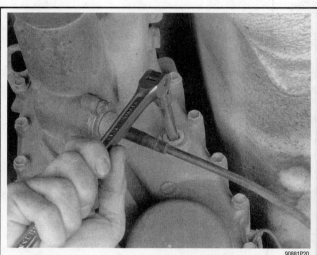

To inspect the transfer case fluid level, remove the fill plug with a breaker bar and ⅜ in. drive extension

4. If additional fluid is necessary, add it through the level/filler hole using a siphon pump or squeeze bottle.
5. When you are finished, carefully install and tighten the plug to 27–39 ft. lbs. (37–53 Nm) for Samurai models, or to 162–241 inch lbs. (18–27 Nm) for Sidekick, Tracker, Sidekick Sport and X-90 models. DO NOT overtighten the plug and damage the housing.

DRAIN & REFILL

Under normal conditions, the manufacturer indicates that the transfer case fluid should be changed at the 7,500 mile (12,000 km) or 7½ month mark, and every 22,500 miles (36,000 km) or 22½ months after the initial fluid change. However, if the vehicle is driven under severe conditions (such as towing a trailer, repeated short trips, driving on rough, dusty, salted and/or muddy roads, or driving in extremely cold weather), it is recommended to replace the fluid every 15,000 miles (24,000 km) or 15 months after the initial fluid change at 7,500 miles (12,000 km) or 7½ months. Little harm can come from a fluid change when you have just purchased a used vehicle, especially since the condition of the transfer case fluid is usually not known.

If the fluid is to be drained, it is a good idea to warm the fluid first so it will flow better. This can be accomplished by 15–20 miles of highway driving. Fluid which is warmed to normal operating temperature will flow faster, drain more completely and remove more contaminants from the housing.

1. Drive the vehicle to assure the fluid is at normal operating temperature.

2. If additional under-vehicle clearance is needed, raise and support the vehicle securely on jackstands. Remember that the vehicle must be supported level (at four points) so the proper amount of fluid can be added.

➡**The Sidekick, Sidekick Sport, Tracker and X-90 transfer case plugs are usually square receiver (pipe) plugs, which are designed to accept a ⅜ in. driver such as a ratchet or extension.**

3. Crawl under the vehicle with a large drain pan, containers of new hypoid gear oil, some clean shop rags and the applicable tools (the Sidekick, Sidekick Sport, Tracker and X-90 transfer cases use ⅜ in. female pipe plugs, and the Samurai transfer case uses large hex-head plugs).

4. Position the drain pan under the transfer case housing, below the drain plug. Remember that with drain plugs which are mounted on the side of the transfer case, the fluid will likely flow with some force at first (arcing outward from the transfer case), and will not just drip straight downward into the pan. If the transfer case in your vehicle is equipped with a side-mounted drain plug, position the drain pan accordingly and move it more directly beneath the drain plug as the flow slows to a trickle.

. . . then unthread the plug by hand to keep inward pressure on it until all threads are free of the hole

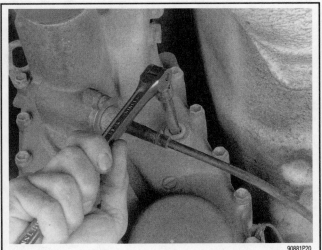

To drain the transfer case fluid, first remove the fill plug to ensure that it is not frozen or stuck in place

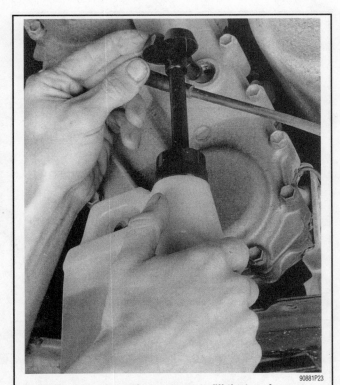

Install the drain plug and use a pump to fill the transfer case with the proper fluid

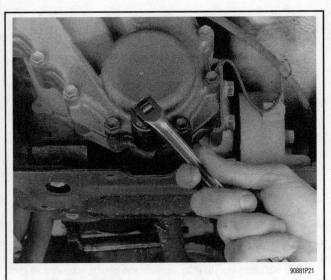

Loosen the drain plug with a breaker bar . . .

➡**To ensure that the fill plug is not frozen or rusted in place, remove it from the transfer case BEFORE removing the drain plug. It would be unfortunate to drain all of your gear oil and then realize that the fill plug is stripped or frozen in place.**

5. Remove the fill plug, then the drain plug and allow the gear oil to drain out.

6. Once the fluid stops draining from the case, install and tighten the drain plug to 27–39 ft. lbs. (37–53 Nm) for Samurai models, or to 162–241 inch lbs. (18–27 Nm) for Sidekick, Tracker, Sidekick Sport and X-90 models.

7. Fill the transmission until the fluid level is at the bottom edge of the level/filler hole with the appropriate hypoid gear oil.

8. Reinstall the level/filler plug once you are finished. Tighten the filler plug to 27–39 ft. lbs. (37–53 Nm) for Samurai models, or to 162–241 inch lbs. (18–27 Nm) for Sidekick, Tracker, Sidekick Sport and X-90 models. DO NOT overtighten the plug(s) and damage the housing.

9. If necessary, remove the jackstands and carefully lower the vehicle.

Drive Axle(s)

➡This procedure applies to both front (4-wheel drive models) and rear drive axle assemblies.

FLUID RECOMMENDATIONS

♦ See Figures 180 and 181

➡Only 4-wheel drive models are equipped with front drive axle assemblies.

The manufacturer recommends that differential case assemblies covered by this manual may use SAE 75W-80, 75W-90 or 80W-90 hypoid gear (depending on the temperature range until the next oil change) oil for 1986–94 models, or 75W-85, 80W-90 or 90 hypoid gear oil for 1995–98 models. All gear oils must meet or exceed API grade GL-5 for lubrication. DO NOT use any other fluids for lubrication. Use of improper fluids could lead to leaks or differential assembly damage.

LEVEL CHECK

♦ See Figures 182, 183 and 184

The fluid level in the front and rear axles should be checked at each oil change. Like the manual transmission, the axles do not have a dipstick to check fluid level. Instead, a filler plug is located in the side of the housing, at a level just barely above the level to which fluid should fill the housing. To check the fluid level:

1. Make sure the transmission is in **P** (A/T) or in gear on a manual, then FIRMLY set the parking brake and block the drive wheels.

2. Check under the vehicle is see if there is sufficient clearance for you to access the filler plug on the side of the differential housing. If not you will have to raise and support the vehicle using jackstands at four points to make sure it is completely level. Failure to support the vehicle level will prevent from properly checking or filling the rear axle fluid.

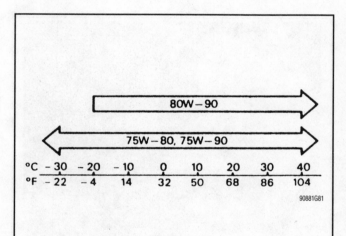

Fig. 180 Front and rear drive axle assembly recommended gear oil viscosities for 1986–94 models

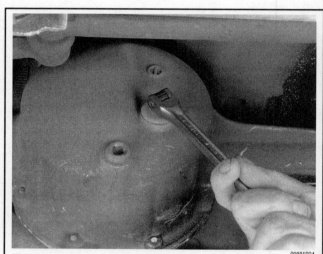

To check the drive axle fluid level, remove the fill plug (front drive axle shown)

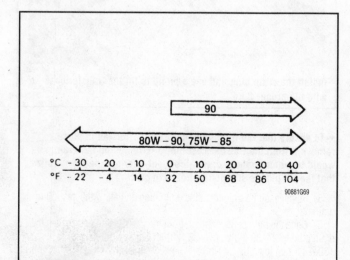

Fig. 181 Front and rear drive axle assembly recommended gear oil viscosities for 1995–98 models

Before installing the fill plug, replace the plastic washer with a new one to prevent leaks

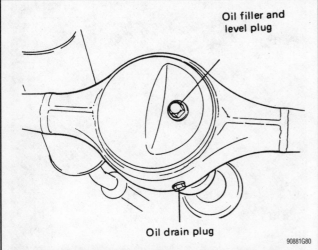

Fig. 182 Fill and drain plug locations for Samurai front and rear drive axle assemblies

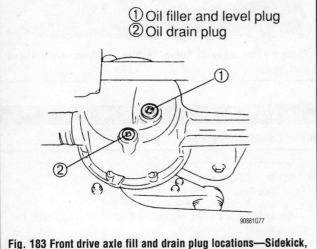

Fig. 183 Front drive axle fill and drain plug locations—Sidekick, Sidekick Sport, Tracker and X-90 models

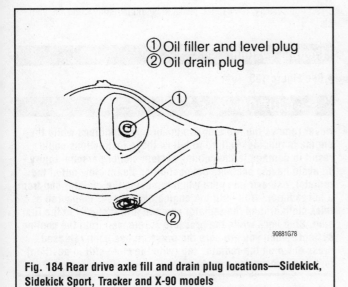

Fig. 184 Rear drive axle fill and drain plug locations—Sidekick, Sidekick Sport, Tracker and X-90 models

3. Thoroughly clean the area surrounding the fill plug. This will prevent any dirt from entering the housing and contaminating the gear oil.

4. Remove the fill plug and make sure that the gear oil is up to the bottom of the fill hole. If a slight amount of lubricant does not drip out of the hole when the plug is removed, additional lubricant should be added. Use the appropriate viscosity hypoid gear lubricant, depending on the temperature range expected until the next fluid change.

5. Once you are finished, install the fill plug, then (if raised) remove the jackstands and lower the vehicle.

DRAIN & REFILL

Under normal conditions, the manufacturer indicates that the drive axle assembly fluid should be changed at the 7,500 mile (12,000 km) or 7.5 month mark, and every 22,500 miles (36,000 km) or 22.5 months after the initial fluid change. However, if the vehicle is driven under severe conditions (such as towing a trailer; repeated short trips; driving on rough, dusty, salted and/or muddy roads; or driving in extremely cold weather), it is recommended to replace the fluid every 15,000 miles (24,000 km) or 15 months after the initial fluid change at the 7,500 mile (12,000 km) or 7.5 month mark. Little harm can come from a fluid change when you have just purchased a used vehicle, especially since the condition of the drive axle assembly fluid is usually not known.

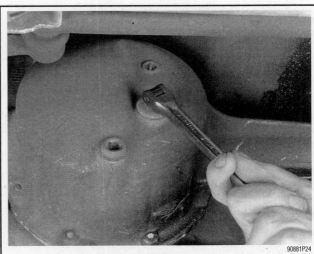

To drain drive axle fluid, first loosen the fill plug to ensure that it is not frozen or rusted in place . . .

. . . then loosen the drain plug

Unscrew the drain plug by hand while maintaining inward pressure against the threads

If the fluid is to be drained, it is a good idea to warm the fluid first so it will flow better. This can be accomplished by 15–20 miles of highway driving. Fluid which is warmed to normal operating temperature will flow faster, drain more completely and remove more contaminants from the housing.

1. Drive the vehicle to assure the fluid is at normal operating temperature.
2. If additional under-vehicle clearance is needed, raise and support the vehicle securely on jackstands. Remember that the vehicle must be supported level (at four points) so the proper amount of fluid can be added.

➡The Sidekick, Sidekick Sport, Tracker and X-90 drive axle assembly plugs are usually square receiver (pipe) plugs, which are designed to accept a ³⁄₈ in. driver such as a ratchet or extension.

3. Crawl under the vehicle with a large drain pan, containers of new hypoid gear oil, some clean shop rags and the applicable tools (the Sidekick, Sidekick Sport, Tracker and X-90 drive axle assemblies use ³⁄₈ in. female pipe plugs, and the Samurai drive axle assembly uses large hex-head plugs).
4. Position the drain pan under the drive axle assembly housing, below the drain plug. Remember that with drain plugs which are mounted on the side of the drive axle, the fluid will likely flow with some force at first (arcing outward from the drive axle), and will not just drip straight downward into the pan. If the drive axle(s) in your vehicle is equipped with a side-mounted drain plug, position the drain pan accordingly and move it more directly beneath the drain plug as the flow slows to a trickle.

➡To ensure that the fill plug is not frozen or rusted in place, remove it from the drive axle BEFORE removing the drain plug. It would be unfortunate to drain all of your gear oil and then realize that the fill plug is stripped or frozen in place.

5. Remove the fill plug, then the drain plug and allow the gear oil to drain out.
6. Once the fluid stops draining from the drive axle, install and tighten the drain plug to the following applicable specification:
Front Drive Axles
• Samurai drain plug—29–51 ft. lbs. (40–70 Nm)
• Sidekick, Sidekick Sport, Tracker and X-90 drain plug—162–241 inch lbs. (18–27 Nm)
Rear Drive Axles
• Samurai drain plug—29–51 ft. lbs. (40–70 Nm)
• Sidekick, Sidekick Sport, Tracker and X-90 drain plug—162–217 inch lbs. (18–25 Nm)
7. Fill the drive axle until the fluid level is at the bottom edge of the fill hole with the appropriate hypoid gear oil.

Using a pump can make filling the drive axle housing easier and less messy

❄❄ WARNING

DO NOT overtighten the plug(s) and damage the housing.

8. Reinstall the fill plug once you are finished. Tighten the fill plug to the following applicable specification:
Front Drive Axles
• Samurai fill plug—26–36 ft. lbs. (35–50 Nm)
• Sidekick, Sidekick Sport, Tracker and X-90 fill plug—26–33 ft. lbs. (35–44 Nm)
Rear Drive Axles
• Samurai fill plug—26–36 ft. lbs. (35–50 Nm)
• Sidekick, Sidekick Sport, Tracker and X-90 fill plug—26–36 ft. lbs. (35–49 Nm)
9. If necessary, remove the jackstands and carefully lower the vehicle.

Cooling System

▸ See Figure 185

❄❄ CAUTION

Never remove the radiator cap under any conditions while the engine is running! Failure to follow these instructions could result in damage to the cooling system and/or personal injury. To avoid having scalding hot coolant or steam blow out of the radiator, use extreme care when removing the radiator cap from a hot radiator. Wait until the engine has cooled, then wrap a thick cloth around the radiator cap and turn it slowly to the first stop. Step back while the pressure is released from the cooling system. When you are sure the pressure has been released, press down on the radiator cap (with the cloth still in position), turn and remove the cap.

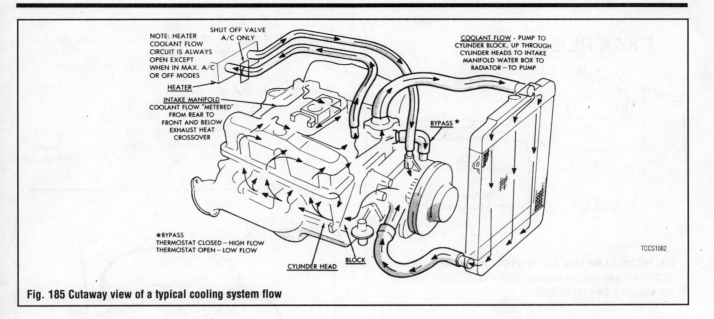

NOTE: HEATER COOLANT FLOW CIRCUIT IS ALWAYS OPEN EXCEPT WHEN IN MAX. A/C OR OFF MODES

SHUT OFF VALVE A/C ONLY

HEATER

INTAKE MANIFOLD COOLANT FLOW "METERED" FROM REAR TO FRONT AND BELOW EXHAUST HEAT CROSSOVER

COOLANT FLOW - PUMP TO CYLINDER BLOCK, UP THROUGH CYLINDER HEADS TO INTAKE MANIFOLD WATER BOX TO RADIATOR — TO PUMP

BYPASS ★

★BYPASS
THERMOSTAT CLOSED — HIGH FLOW
THERMOSTAT OPEN — LOW FLOW

CYLINDER HEAD   BLOCK

TCCS1082

Fig. 185 Cutaway view of a typical cooling system flow

FLUID RECOMMENDATIONS

The recommended coolant for all vehicles covered by this manual is a 50/50 mixture of ethylene glycol antifreeze and distilled water for year-round use. If a 50/50 concentration does not provide adequate protection against freezing (extremely cold climates), follow the instructions on the antifreeze container to obtain the desired freezing point. An antifreeze/coolant testing hydrometer can be used to determine the freezing point of your coolant mixture.

LEVEL CHECK

▶ **See Figures 186 and 187**

Once a week, open your hood and glance at the coolant reserve tank to ensure it is properly filled. When the engine is cold, the coolant level should be at the FULL mark on the reserve tank. If your engine is hot, allow it to cool before checking the coolant level, adding coolant, or any other cooling system service.

If the level is not as specified, top off the cooling system using the recovery tank and its markings as a guideline. Remove the reserve tank cap

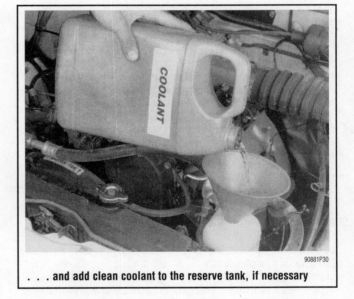

90881P30

. . . and add clean coolant to the reserve tank, if necessary

90881P29

The coolant level can be checked by inspecting the level through the translucent reserve tank . . .

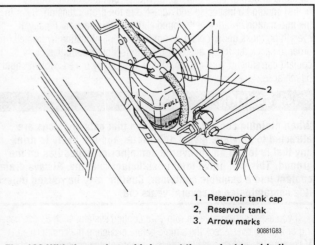

1. Reservoir tank cap
2. Reservoir tank
3. Arrow marks

90881G83

Fig. 186 With the engine cold, inspect the coolant level in the reserve tank and, if necessary, add coolant to bring the level to the FULL mark—Samurai model shown

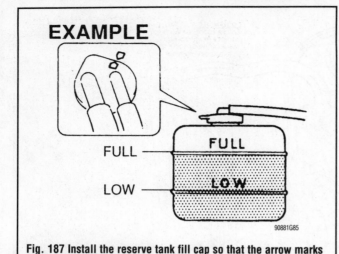

Fig. 187 Install the reserve tank fill cap so that the arrow marks on the tank and cap are aligned—Sidekick, Sidekick Sport, Tracker and X-90 models shown

and pour in new, clean antifreeze/water mixture until the level is at the FULL mark, then install the reserve tank cap so that the arrow mark on the tank and the arrow mark on the cap are aligned.

If you add coolant to the reserve tank, make a note to check it again soon. A coolant level that consistently drops is usually a sign of a small, hard to detect leak, though in the worst scenario it could be a sign of an internal engine leak (blown head gasket/cracked block? . . . check the engine oil for coolant contamination). In most cases, you will be able to trace the leak to a loose fitting or damaged hose (and you might solve a problem before it leaves you stranded). Evaporating ethylene glycol antifreeze will leave small, white (salt-like) deposits, which can be helpful in tracing a leak.

SYSTEM INSPECTION

At least every 30,000 miles (48,000 km) or every 30 months (whichever occurs first), all hoses, fittings and cooling system connections should be inspected for damage, wear or leaks. Hose clamps should be checked for tightness, and soft or cracked hoses should be replaced. Damp spots, or accumulations of rust, dye or white deposits near hoses or fittings indicate possible leakage. These must be corrected before filling the system with fresh coolant. The pressure cap should be examined for signs of deterioration and aging. The fan belt and/or other drive belt(s) should be inspected and adjusted to the proper tension. Refer to the information on drive belts found earlier in this section. Finally, if everything looks good, obtain an antifreeze/coolant testing hydrometer in order to check the freeze and boil-over protection capabilities of the coolant currently in your engine. Old or improperly mixed coolant should be replaced.

✳✳ CAUTION

When draining coolant, keep in mind that cats and dogs are attracted to ethylene glycol antifreeze, and are likely to drink any that is left in an uncovered container or in puddles on the ground. This will prove fatal in sufficient quantity. Always drain coolant into a sealable container. Coolant may be reused unless it is contaminated or several years old.

If you experience problems with your cooling system, such as overheating or boiling-over, check the simple before expecting the complicated. Make sure the system can fully pressurize (are all the connections tight/is the radiator cap on properly, is the cap seal intact?). Ideally, a pressure tester should be connected to the radiator opening and the system should be pressurized and inspected for leaks. If no obvious problems are found,

use a hydrometer antifreeze/coolant tester (available at most automotive supply stores) to check the condition and concentration of the antifreeze in your cooling system. Excessively old coolant or the wrong proportions of water and coolant will hurt the coolant's boiling and freezing points.

Check the Radiator Cap

◗ **See Figure 188**

While you are checking the coolant level, check the radiator cap for a worn or cracked gasket. If the top doesn't seal properly, fluid will be lost and the engine will overheat. Worn caps should be replaced with new ones.

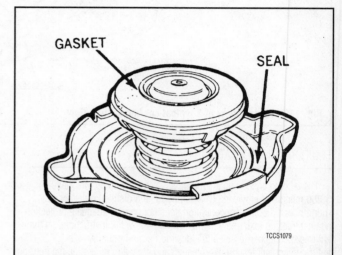

Fig. 188 Be sure the rubber gasket on the radiator cap has a tight seal

Clean Radiator of Debris

◗ **See Figure 189**

Periodically, clean any debris—leaves, paper, insects, etc.—from the radiator fins. Pick the large pieces off by hand. The smaller pieces can be washed away with water pressure from a hose.

Carefully straighten any bent radiator fins with a pair of needle-nosed pliers. Be careful; the fins are very soft. Don't wiggle the fins back and forth too much. Straighten them once and try not to move them again.

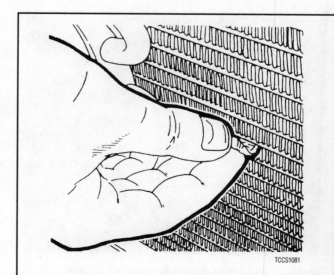

Fig. 189 Periodically remove all debris from the radiator fins

DRAIN & REFILL

▶ **See Figure 190**

➡To properly drain and refill the cooling system, you will need clean shop rags, a large catch pan or similar container, access to clean water (such as a garden hose) and bottles of clean, new ethylene glycol antifreeze.

At least once every 30 months or 30,1890 miles (48,000 km), the engine cooling system should be inspected, flushed and refilled with fresh coolant. If the coolant is left in the system too long, it loses its ability to prevent rust and corrosion. If the coolant has too much water, it won't protect against freezing.

✳✳ CAUTION

When draining coolant, keep in mind that cats and dogs are attracted to ethylene glycol antifreeze, and are likely to drink any that is left in an uncovered container or in puddles on the ground. This will prove fatal in sufficient quantity. Always drain coolant into a sealable container. Coolant may be reused unless it is contaminated or several years old.

  1. If necessary, allow the engine to cool.
  2. Remove the radiator cap by rotating it slowly counterclockwise until a stop is felt. Do not push down on the cap while turning it. Allow any radiator pressure to vent, then depress the cap and continue loosening it.

✳✳ CAUTION

Never remove the radiator cap under any conditions while the engine is running! Failure to follow these instructions could result in damage to the cooling system and/or personal injury. To avoid having scalding hot coolant or steam blow out of the radiator, use extreme care when removing the radiator cap from a hot radiator. Wait until the engine has cooled, then wrap a thick cloth around the radiator cap and turn it slowly to the first stop. Step back while the pressure is released from the cooling system. When you are sure the pressure has been released, press down on the radiator cap (with the cloth still in position), turn and remove the cap.

  3. Remove the reservoir tank by removing the reserve tank cap, then by lifting the tank straight up. Drain the reservoir into the large catch pan.
  4. Position the catch pan under the radiator, beneath the drain plug, then loosen the plug and allow the radiator coolant to empty completely.
  5. Install the reserve tank and fill it to the FULL mark with the proper coolant.

To drain the engine coolant, first remove the caps from the radiator fill neck . . .

. . . and the reserve tank, then lift the reserve tank up and out of the engine compartment to empty it

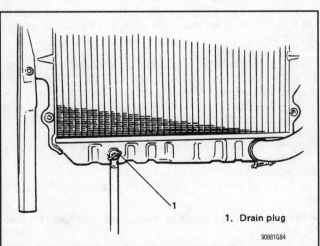

1. Drain plug

Fig. 190 Loosen the radiator drain plug to allow the coolant to empty into the catch pan—the drain plug is located along the bottom edge of the radiator

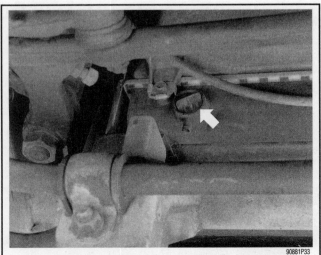

Loosen the radiator drain valve (arrow) and allow all of the coolant to empty into a large catch pan

Install the reserve tank and fill it to the FULL mark . . .

. . . then tighten the drain valve and fill the radiator with clean coolant

➡**The vehicle must be parked on level ground when filling the cooling system.**

6. Install the radiator drain plug, then fill the radiator with the proper coolant and install the radiator cap. When installing the radiator cap, ensure that it is fully tightened.

7. Start the engine and allow it to idle for 2–3 minutes to purge air from the cooling system, then turn the engine **OFF**.

8. Remove the radiator cap and, if necessary, add coolant to the radiator until the coolant level is at the base of the fill neck.

9. Inspect the coolant level in the reserve tank and, if necessary, add coolant to bring the level in the tank to the FULL mark.

FLUSHING & CLEANING THE SYSTEM

➡**To properly flush and clean the cooling system, you will need clean shop rags, a large catch pan or similar container, access to clean water (such as a garden hose) and bottles of clean, new ethylene glycol antifreeze.**

At least once every 30 months or 30,000 miles (48,000 km), the engine cooling system should be inspected, flushed and refilled with fresh coolant.

If the coolant is left in the system too long, it loses its ability to prevent rust and corrosion. If the coolant has too much water, it won't protect against freezing.

✳✳ CAUTION

When draining coolant, keep in mind that cats and dogs are attracted to ethylene glycol antifreeze, and are likely to drink any that is left in an uncovered container or in puddles on the ground. This will prove fatal in sufficient quantity. Always drain coolant into a sealable container. Coolant may be reused unless it is contaminated or several years old.

1. If necessary, allow the engine to cool.
2. Remove the radiator cap by rotating it slowly counterclockwise until a stop is felt. Do not push down on the cap while turning it. Allow any radiator pressure to vent, then depress the cap and continue loosening it.

✳✳ CAUTION

Never remove the radiator cap under any conditions while the engine is running! Failure to follow these instructions could result in damage to the cooling system and/or personal injury. To avoid having scalding hot coolant or steam blow out of the radiator, use extreme care when removing the radiator cap from a hot radiator. Wait until the engine has cooled, then wrap a thick cloth around the radiator cap and turn it slowly to the first stop. Step back while the pressure is released from the cooling system. When you are sure the pressure has been released, press down on the radiator cap (with the cloth still in position), turn and remove the cap.

3. Remove the reservoir tank by removing the reserve tank cap, then by lifting the tank straight up. Drain the reservoir into the large catch pan.

4. Position the catch pan under the radiator, beneath the drain plug, then loosen the plug and allow the radiator coolant to empty completely.

5. Install the reserve tank and fill it to the FULL mark with clean water.

➡**The vehicle must be parked on level ground when filling the cooling system.**

6. Install the radiator drain plug, then fill the radiator with clean water and install the radiator cap. When installing the radiator cap, ensure that it is fully tightened.

7. Start the engine and allow it to idle for 2–3 minutes, to purge air from the cooling system, then turn the engine **OFF**.

8. Remove the radiator cap and, if necessary, add water to the radiator until the level is at the base of the fill neck.

9. Start the engine and allow it to idle until normal operating temperature is reached (the upper radiator hose will get hot), then turn the engine **OFF**.

10. Allow the engine to cool.

11. Remove the radiator cap by rotating it slowly counterclockwise until a stop is felt. Do not push down on the cap while turning it. Allow any radiator pressure to vent, then depress the cap and continue loosening it.

12. Remove the reservoir tank by removing the reserve tank cap, then by lifting the tank straight up. Drain the reservoir into the large catch pan.

13. Position the catch pan under the radiator, beneath the drain plug, then loosen the plug and allow the water in the radiator to empty completely.

14. Repeat Steps 5 through 13 as many times as necessary until the water drained from the radiator is clean and clear.

15. Install the reserve tank and fill it to the FULL mark with the proper coolant.

➡**The vehicle must be parked on level ground when filling the cooling system.**

16. Install the radiator drain plug, then fill the radiator with the proper coolant and install the radiator cap. When installing the radiator cap, ensure that it is fully tightened.

17. Start the engine and allow it to idle for 2–3 minutes to purge air from the cooling system, then turn the engine **OFF**.

18. Remove the radiator cap and, if necessary, add coolant to the radiator until the coolant level is at the base of the fill neck.

19. Inspect the coolant level in the reserve tank and, if necessary, add coolant to bring the level in the tank to the FULL mark.

Brake Master Cylinder

FLUID RECOMMENDATIONS

☀☀ WARNING

BRAKE FLUID EATS PAINT. Take great care not to splash or spill brake fluid on painted surfaces. Should you spill a small amount on the car's finish, don't panic, just flush the area with plenty of water.

When adding fluid to the system ONLY use fresh DOT 3 brake fluid from a sealed container. DOT 3 brake fluid will absorb moisture when it is exposed to the atmosphere, which will lower its boiling point. A container that has been opened once, closed and placed on a shelf will allow enough moisture to enter, over time, to contaminate the fluid within. If your brake fluid is contaminated with water, you could boil the brake fluid under hard braking and loose all/some of the brake system. Don't take the risk, buy fresh brake fluid whenever you must add to the system.

LEVEL CHECK

▶ **See Figure 191**

Brake fluid level and condition is a safety related item and it should be checked ANY TIME the hood is opened. Your vehicle should not use brake fluid rapidly (unless there is a leak in the system), but the level should drop slowly in relation to brake pad wear.

The master cylinder reservoir is located under the hood, on the left side firewall. All vehicles covered by this manual should be equipped with a see-through plastic reservoir. This makes checking the level easy and helps reduce the risk of fluid contamination (since you don't have to expose the fluid by opening the cap to check the level). Fluid should be kept between the MIN and MAX lines. If the brake fluid level is near or below the MIN mark, fill the reservoir to the MAX mark.

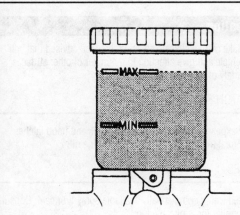

Fig. 191 The brake fluid level in the master cylinder fluid reservoir may fall between the MAX and MIN marks, but should be closer to, or at the MAX mark

If it is necessary to add brake fluid, clean the fill cap, then remove it from the master cylinder . . .

. . . and add the proper amount of fluid—using a funnel will help avoid messy spills

If it becomes necessary to add fluid to the system, take a moment to clean the area around the cap and reservoir. Use a clean rag to wipe away dust and dirt which could enter the reservoir after the cover is removed. If the level of the brake fluid is less than half the volume of the reservoir (and the brake pads are not approaching a replacement point), it is advised that you check the brake system for leaks. Leaks in the hydraulic system often occur at the wheel cylinders.

Clutch Master Cylinder

➡Only the Sidekick Sport is equipped with a hydraulic clutch actuation system and, therefore, is the only vehicle with a clutch master cylinder.

FLUID RECOMMENDATIONS

☀☀ WARNING

The clutch system is filled with glycol-based brake fluid (DOT 3) at the factory; do not use or mix different types of fluids when filling the clutch system master cylinder reservoir.

When adding fluid to the hydraulic clutch system ONLY use fresh DOT 3 brake fluid from a sealed container. DOT 3 brake fluid will absorb moisture when it is exposed to the atmosphere, which will lower its boiling point. A container that has been opened once, closed and placed on a shelf will allow enough moisture to enter, over time, to contaminate the fluid within.

✳✳ WARNING

BRAKE FLUID EATS PAINT. Take great care not to splash or spill brake fluid on painted surfaces. Should you spill a small amount on the car's finish, don't panic, just flush the area with plenty of water.

LEVEL CHECK

▶ **See Figure 192**

Brake fluid level and condition is a safety related item and it should be checked ANY TIME the hood is opened. Your vehicle should not use clutch (brake) fluid rapidly (unless there is a leak in the system).

The clutch master cylinder reservoir is located under the hood, on the left side firewall near the brake master cylinder. The Sidekick Sport is equipped with a see-through plastic reservoir. This makes checking the level easy and helps reduce the risk of fluid contamination (since you don't have to expose the fluid by opening the cap to check the level). Fluid may be kept between the MIN and MAX lines, but the level should ideally be maintained at the MAX mark. If the fluid level is near or below the MIN mark, fill the reservoir to the MAX mark.

If it becomes necessary to add fluid to the system, take a moment to clean the area around the cap and reservoir. Use a clean rag to wipe away dust and dirt which could enter the reservoir after the cover is removed. If the level of the fluid is less than half the volume of the reservoir (and the clutch disc is not approaching a replacement point), it is advised that you check the system for leaks.

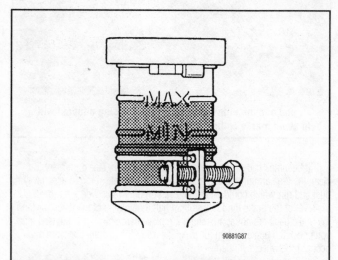

90881G87

Fig. 192 The brake fluid level in the clutch master cylinder fluid reservoir should be kept at the MAX mark

Power Steering Pump Reservoir

FLUID RECOMMENDATIONS

The power steering system covered by this manual uses Dexron® III Automatic Transmission Fluid (ATF) for lubrication. DO NOT use improper fluids such as Type F® ATF, hypoid gear oil, or other types of power steering fluid. Use of improper fluids could lead to leaks or system damage. Always use new, clean Dexron® III ATF whenever adding fluid to the transmission.

LEVEL CHECK

The level of the power steering fluid should be checked in the reservoir periodically, at least once a year. Fluid is checked using the dipstick which is attached to the underside of the reservoir cap. The fluid level, which should be inspected when the power steering fluid is cool, should fall between the MAX and MIN marks on the dipstick. If the level is close to, or below the MIN mark, add enough clean Dexron® III ATF to the power steering pump through the fill cap/dipstick hole.

✳✳ WARNING

Extensive driving with a low power steering fluid level can damage the power steering pump.

1. If the engine is warm or hot, allow it to cool down.
2. Locate the power steering pump reservoir, then remove the cap/dipstick and note the level as indicated by the markings. To be sure of your reading, wipe the dipstick off with a clean shop rag, install the cap back in position, remove it again and double check the level.
3. If the level is close to, or below the MIN mark, add fluid to bring it up to the proper level (a funnel is usually very helpful). As with most automotive fluids, DO NOT overfill.
4. When you are finished, install and tighten the fill cap/dipstick until secure.

Steering Gear

The steering gears used on vehicles equipped with manual steering are sealed units, and do not require periodic fluid service. If there is evidence of fluid leakage from the steering gear, remove it and replace or repair it accordingly.

Chassis Greasing

Chassis greasing should be performed every 12 months or 12,000 miles (19,000 km) for most cars. Greasing can be performed with a commercial pressurized grease gun or at home by using a hand-operated grease gun. Wipe the grease fittings clean before greasing in order to prevent the possibility of forcing any dirt into the component.

There are far less grease points on the modern automotive chassis than there were on cars of yesteryear. The front suspension components and driveshaft U-joints should be checked for grease fittings, and, if equipped, periodically lubricated.

A water resistant long life generic chassis grease should be used for all chassis greasing applications.

Body Lubrication

Whenever you take care of chassis greasing it is also advised that you walk around the vehicle and give attention to a number of other surfaces which require a variety of lubrication/protection.

HOOD/DOOR LATCH & HINGES

Wipe clean any exposed surfaces of the door, trunk and hood latches and hinges. Then, treat the surfaces using clean engine oil.

LOCK CYLINDERS

Should be treated with a commercially available spray lubricant. Consult your local parts supplier for applicable lubricants.

CLUTCH, THROTTLE VALVE (TV) & KICKDOWN LINKAGE

A water resistant long life chassis grease should be used for all linkages.

Wheel Bearings

REPACKING

➡**Sodium based grease is not compatible with lithium based grease. Read the package labels and be careful not to mix the two types. If there is any doubt as to the type of grease used, completely clean the old grease from the bearing and hub before replacing.**

Before handling the bearings, there are a few things that you should remember to do and not to do.

DO the following:

• Remove all outside dirt from the housing before exposing the bearing.
• Treat a used bearing as gently as you would a new one.
• Work with clean tools in clean surroundings.
• Use clean, dry gloves, or at least clean, dry hands.
• Clean solvents and flushing fluids are a must.
• Use clean paper when laying out the bearings to dry.
• Protect disassembled bearings from rust and dirt. Cover them up.
• Use clean, lint-free rags to wipe the bearings.
• Keep the bearings in oil-proof paper when they are to be stored or are not in use.
• Clean the inside of the housing before replacing the bearing.

Do NOT do the following:

• Do not work in dirty surroundings.
• Do not use dirty, chipped or damaged tools.
• Do not work on wooden work benches or use wooden mallets.
• Do not handle bearings with dirty or moist hands.
• Do not use gasoline for cleaning. Use a safe solvent.
• Do not spin dry bearings with compressed air. They will be damaged.
• Do not use cotton waste or dirty cloths to wipe bearings.
• Do not scratch or nick bearing surfaces.

• Do not allow the bearing to come in contact with dirt or rust at any time. The wheel bearings require periodic maintenance. A premium high melting point grease, such as Suzuki Super Grease A or equivalent, must be used. Long fiber type greases must not be used. This service is recommended at least every 15,000 miles (24,000 km) or 15 months (whichever occurs first).

➡**For information on Wheel Bearing removal and installation, refer to Section 8 of this manual.**

1. Remove the wheel bearing.
2. Clean all parts in a non-flammable solvent and let them air dry.

➡**Only use lint-free rags to dry the bearings. Never spin-dry a bearing with compressed air, as this will damage the rollers.**

3. Check for excessive wear and damage. Replace the bearing as necessary.

➡**Packing wheel bearings with grease is best accomplished by using a wheel bearing packer (available at most automotive parts stores).**

4. If a wheel bearing packer is not available, the bearings may be packed by hand.
　　a. Place a "healthy" glob of grease in the palm of one hand.
　　b. Force the edge of the bearing into the grease so that the grease fills the space between the rollers and the bearing cage.
　　c. Keep rotating the bearing while continuing to push grease through it.
　　d. Continue until the grease is forced out the other side of the bearing.

➡**Grease should fill all spaces in the wheel bearing.**

5. Place the packed bearing on a clean surface and cover it until it is time for installation.
6. Install the wheel bearing.

TRAILER TOWING

▶ **See Figure 193**

General Recommendations

Your vehicle was primarily designed to carry passengers and cargo. It is important to remember that towing a trailer will place additional loads on your vehicles engine, drivetrain, steering, braking and other systems. However, if you decide to tow a trailer, using the prior equipment is a must.

✳✳ CAUTION

The vehicles manufactured by Suzuki are only designed to tow light weight trailers of Class 1 designation. Towing any trailer above this classification may lead to vehicle damage and/or decreased vehicle performance, such as handling, acceleration, and especially braking.

Local laws may require specific equipment such as trailer brakes or fender mounted mirrors. Check your local laws.

Trailer Weight

The weight of the trailer is the most important factor. A good weight-to-horsepower ratio is about 35:1, 35 lbs. of Gross Combined Weight (GCW) for every horsepower your engine develops. Multiply the engine's rated horsepower by 35 and subtract the weight of the vehicle passengers and luggage. The number remaining is the approximate ideal maximum weight you should tow, although a numerically higher axle ratio can help compensate for heavier weight.

Hitch (Tongue) Weight

Calculate the hitch weight in order to select a proper hitch. The weight of the hitch is usually 9–11% of the trailer gross weight and should be measured with the trailer loaded. Hitches fall into various categories: those that mount on the frame and rear bumper, the bolt-on type, or the weld-on distribution type used for larger trailers. Axle mounted or clamp-on bumper hitches should never be used.

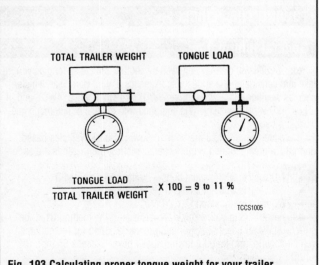

Fig. 193 Calculating proper tongue weight for your trailer

Check the gross weight rating of your trailer. Tongue weight is usually figured as 10% of gross trailer weight. Therefore, a trailer with a maximum gross weight of 2000 lbs. will have a maximum tongue weight of 200 lbs. Class I trailers fall into this category. Class II trailers are those with a gross weight rating of 2000–3000 lbs., while Class III trailers fall into the 3500–6000 lbs. category. Class IV trailers are those over 6000 lbs. and are for use with fifth wheel trucks, only.

✳✳ CAUTION

The vehicles manufactured by Suzuki are only designed to tow light weight trailers of Class 1 designation. Towing any trailer above this classification may lead to vehicle damage and/or decreased vehicle performance, such as handling, acceleration, and especially braking.

When you've determined the hitch that you'll need, follow the manufacturer's installation instructions, exactly, especially when it comes to fastener torques. The hitch will subjected to a lot of stress and good hitches come with hardened bolts. Never substitute an inferior bolt for a hardened bolt.

Cooling

ENGINE

Overflow Tank

One of the most common, if not THE most common, problems associated with trailer towing is engine overheating. If you have a cooling system without an expansion tank, you'll definitely need to get an aftermarket expansion tank kit, preferably one with at least a 2 quart capacity. These kits are easily installed on the radiator's overflow hose, and come with a pressure cap designed for expansion tanks.

Flex Fan

Another helpful accessory for vehicles using a belt-driven radiator fan is a flex fan. These fans are large diameter units designed to provide more airflow at low speeds, by using fan blades that have deeply cupped surfaces. The blades then flex, or flatten out, at high speed, when less cooling air is needed. These fans are far lighter in weight than stock fans, requiring less horsepower to drive them. Also, they are far quieter than stock fans. If you do decide to replace your stock fan with a flex fan, note that if your vehicle has a fan clutch, a spacer will be needed between the flex fan and water pump hub.

TOWING THE VEHICLE

General Information

Your Suzuki vehicle may be towed by another vehicle so long as you take into consideration various characteristics of your particular vehicle, such as whether it is 2-wheel drive (2WD) or 4-wheel drive (4WD), and, if it is a 4WD vehicle, whether it is equipped with manual or automatic free-wheeling hubs.

There are four different methods for towing Suzuki vehicles based upon the aforementioned vehicle characteristics; the methods are as follows:
- 4WD vehicle with manual hubs—method A or method B
- 4WD vehicle with automatic hubs—method B
- 2WD vehicle—method C

Whenever towing your vehicle, regardless of the method used, be sure to ALWAYS use the proper equipment designed for recreational vehicle towing, and that the towing speed never exceeds 55 mph (88 km/h).

Oil Cooler

Aftermarket engine oil coolers are helpful for prolonging engine oil life and reducing overall engine temperatures. Both of these factors increase engine life. While not absolutely necessary in towing Class I and some Class II trailers, they are recommended for heavier Class II and all Class III towing. Engine oil cooler systems usually consist of an adapter, screwed on in place of the oil filter, a remote filter mounting and a multi-tube, finned heat exchanger, which is mounted in front of the radiator or air conditioning condenser.

TRANSMISSION

An automatic transmission is usually recommended for trailer towing. Modern automatics have proven reliable and, of course, easy to operate, in trailer towing. The increased load of a trailer, however, causes an increase in the temperature of the automatic transmission fluid. Heat is the worst enemy of an automatic transmission. As the temperature of the fluid increases, the life of the fluid decreases.

It is essential, therefore, that you install an automatic transmission cooler. The cooler, which consists of a multi-tube, finned heat exchanger, is usually installed in front of the radiator or air conditioning compressor, and hooked in-line with the transmission cooler tank inlet line. Follow the cooler manufacturer's installation instructions.

Select a cooler of at least adequate capacity, based upon the combined gross weights of the vehicle and trailer.

Cooler manufacturers recommend that you use an aftermarket cooler in addition to, and not instead of, the present cooling tank in your radiator. If you do want to use it in place of the radiator cooling tank, get a cooler at least two sizes larger than normally necessary.

➡**A transmission cooler can, sometimes, cause slow or harsh shifting in the transmission during cold weather, until the fluid has a chance to come up to normal operating temperature. Some coolers can be purchased with or retrofitted with a temperature bypass valve which will allow fluid flow through the cooler only when the fluid has reached above a certain operating temperature.**

Handling A Trailer

Towing a trailer with ease and safety requires a certain amount of experience. It's a good idea to learn the feel of a trailer by practicing turning, stopping and backing in an open area such as an empty parking lot.

✳✳ CAUTION

Always utilize safety chains to secure the vehicle being towed in the event of towing component damage or breakage. The safety chains will help avoid causing a dangerous vehicle accident.

Towing Method A

▸ **See Figures 194 and 195**

➡**This method is designed so that all four vehicle wheels are on the ground.**

Prepare the vehicle for towing as follows:
1. Turn the ignition switch to the **ACC** position, which will unlock the steering column.
2. If applied, release the parking brake.

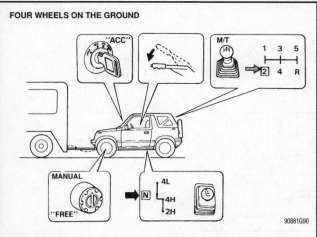

Fig. 194 Towing method A is designed so that all four wheels are on the ground—vehicles equipped with manual transmissions

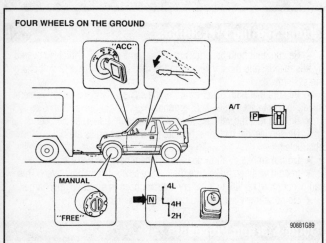

Fig. 195 When towing a vehicle equipped with an automatic transmission using method A, be sure to position the transmission gearshift lever in the P position and the transfer case lever in neutral

3. Position the transmission gearshift lever in 2nd gear (manual transmissions) or in **P** (automatic transmissions).
4. Shift the transfer case lever into neutral.
5. Set the manual free-wheeling hubs to the FREE position.
Every 200 miles (320 km) stop towing the vehicle. Leave the transmission in 2nd gear (manual), or shift it into **D** (automatic), and, with the transfer case still in neutral, start the engine. Rev the engine for approximately one minute to circulate oil in the transfer case.

➥**On manual transmissions, the clutch should be engaged when revving the engine.**

On automatic transmissions, before continuing with towing the vehicle, be sure to shift the transmission back to **P**.

Towing Method B

▸ **See Figure 196**

➥**This method is designed so that the front wheels are on the ground, the rear wheels are on a towing dolly, and the vehicle is towed backward.**

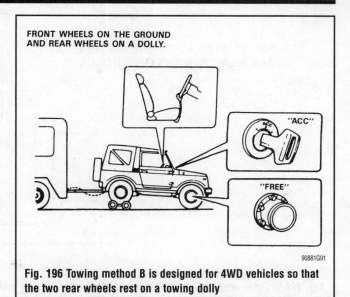

Fig. 196 Towing method B is designed for 4WD vehicles so that the two rear wheels rest on a towing dolly

Prepare the vehicle for towing as follows:
1. For vehicles with automatic free-wheeling hubs, release the hubs as follows:
    a. Stop the vehicle completely.
    b. Disengage the clutch and shift the transfer lever to the 2H position.
    c. Drive the vehicle 4 or 5 ft. (approximately 2 m) in the opposite direction to the direction you were driving before shifting to 2H. The hubs are now unlocked.
2. Secure the rear wheels of the vehicle on the towing dolly according to the manufacturer's instructions.
3. Turn the ignition switch to the **ACC** position, which will unlock the steering column.

❋❋ WARNING

The steering column is not sturdy enough to withstand jolts transmitted from the front wheels during towing, therefore always unlock the steering wheel prior to towing the vehicle.

4. Ensure the front wheels are facing straight rearward and secure the steering wheel with a steering wheel clamping device designed explicitly for this purpose.
5. For vehicle with manual free-wheeling hubs, position the hubs to the FREE position.

Towing Method C

▸ **See Figure 197**

➥**This method is designed so that the front wheels are on the ground, the rear wheels are on a towing dolly, and the vehicle is towed backward.**

Prepare the vehicle for towing as follows:
1. Secure the rear wheels of the vehicle on the towing dolly according to the manufacturer's instructions.
2. Turn the ignition switch to the **ACC** position, which will unlock the steering column.

❋❋ WARNING

The steering column is not sturdy enough to withstand jolts transmitted from the front wheels during towing, therefore always unlock the steering wheel prior to towing the vehicle.

3. Ensure the front wheels are facing straight rearward and secure the steering wheel with a steering wheel clamping device designed explicitly for this purpose.

FRONT WHEELS ON THE GROUND AND REAR WHEELS ON A DOLLY.

"ACC"

90881G88

Fig. 197 Vehicles equipped with 2WD should only be towed using method C

JUMP STARTING A DEAD BATTERY

▶ **See Figure 198**

Whenever a vehicle is jump started, precautions must be followed in order to prevent the possibility of personal injury. Remember that batteries contain a small amount of explosive hydrogen gas which is a by-product of battery charging. Sparks should always be avoided when working around batteries, especially when attaching jumper cables. To minimize the possibility of accidental sparks, follow the procedure carefully.

✳✳ CAUTION

NEVER hook the batteries up in a series circuit or the entire electrical system will go up in smoke, including the starter!

Vehicles equipped with a diesel engine may utilize two 12 volt batteries. If so, the batteries are connected in a parallel circuit (positive terminal to positive terminal, negative terminal to negative terminal). Hooking the batteries up in parallel circuit increases battery cranking power without increasing total battery voltage output. Output remains at 12 volts. On the other hand, hooking two 12 volt batteries up in a series circuit (positive terminal to negative terminal, positive terminal to negative terminal) increases total battery output to 24 volts (12 volts plus 12 volts).

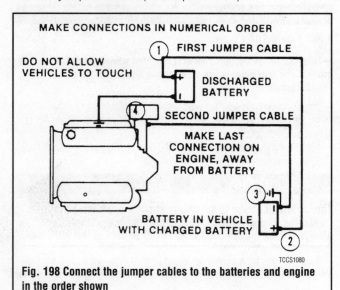

MAKE CONNECTIONS IN NUMERICAL ORDER

DO NOT ALLOW VEHICLES TO TOUCH

① FIRST JUMPER CABLE

DISCHARGED BATTERY

SECOND JUMPER CABLE

MAKE LAST CONNECTION ON ENGINE, AWAY FROM BATTERY

③

② BATTERY IN VEHICLE WITH CHARGED BATTERY

TCCS1080

Fig. 198 Connect the jumper cables to the batteries and engine in the order shown

Jump Starting Precautions

• Be sure that both batteries are of the same voltage. Vehicles covered by this manual and most vehicles on the road today utilize a 12 volt charging system.
• Be sure that both batteries are of the same polarity (have the same terminal, in most cases NEGATIVE grounded).
• Be sure that the vehicles are not touching or a short could occur.
• On serviceable batteries, be sure the vent cap holes are not obstructed.
• Do not smoke or allow sparks anywhere near the batteries.
• In cold weather, make sure the battery electrolyte is not frozen. This can occur more readily in a battery that has been in a state of discharge.
• Do not allow electrolyte to contact your skin or clothing.

Jump Starting Procedure

1. Make sure that the voltages of the 2 batteries are the same. Most batteries and charging systems are of the 12 volt variety.
2. Pull the jumping vehicle (with the good battery) into a position so the jumper cables can reach the dead battery and that vehicle's engine. Make sure that the vehicles do NOT touch.
3. Place the transmissions/transaxles of both vehicles in **Neutral** (MT) or **P** (AT), as applicable, then firmly set their parking brakes.

➡**If necessary for safety reasons, the hazard lights on both vehicles may be operated throughout the entire procedure without significantly increasing the difficulty of jumping the dead battery.**

4. Turn all lights and accessories OFF on both vehicles. Make sure the ignition switches on both vehicles are turned to the **OFF** position.
5. Cover the battery cell caps with a rag, but do not cover the terminals.
6. Make sure the terminals on both batteries are clean and free of corrosion or proper electrical connection will be impeded. If necessary, clean the battery terminals before proceeding.
7. Identify the positive (+) and negative (-) terminals on both batteries.
8. Connect the first jumper cable to the positive (+) terminal of the dead battery, then connect the other end of that cable to the positive (+) terminal of the booster (good) battery.
9. Connect one end of the other jumper cable to the negative (-) terminal on the booster battery and the final cable clamp to an engine bolt head, alternator bracket or other solid, metallic point on the engine with the dead battery. Try to pick a ground on the engine that is positioned away from the

battery in order to minimize the possibility of the 2 clamps touching should one loosen during the procedure. DO NOT connect this clamp to the negative (-) terminal of the bad battery.

> ❊❊ **CAUTION**

Be very careful to keep the jumper cables away from moving parts (cooling fan, belts, etc.) on both engines.

10. Check to make sure that the cables are routed away from any moving parts, then start the donor vehicle's engine. Run the engine at moderate speed for several minutes to allow the dead battery a chance to receive some initial charge.

11. With the donor vehicle's engine still running slightly above idle, try to start the vehicle with the dead battery. Crank the engine for no more than 10 seconds at a time and let the starter cool for at least 20 seconds between tries. If the vehicle does not start in 3 tries, it is likely that something else is also wrong or that the battery needs additional time to charge.

12. Once the vehicle is started, allow it to run at idle for a few seconds to make sure that it is operating properly.

13. Turn ON the headlights, heater blower and, if equipped, the rear defroster of both vehicles in order to reduce the severity of voltage spikes and subsequent risk of damage to the vehicles' electrical systems when the cables are disconnected. This step is especially important to any vehicle equipped with computer control modules.

14. Carefully disconnect the cables in the reverse order of connection. Start with the negative cable that is attached to the engine ground, then the negative cable on the donor battery. Disconnect the positive cable from the donor battery and finally, disconnect the positive cable from the formerly dead battery. Be careful when disconnecting the cables from the positive terminals not to allow the alligator clips to touch any metal on either vehicle or a short and sparks will occur.

JACKING

▶ **See Figures 199, 200, 201, 202 and 203**

Your vehicle was supplied with a jack for emergency road repairs. This jack is fine for changing a flat tire or other short term procedures not requiring you to go beneath the vehicle. If it is used in an emergency situation, carefully follow the instructions provided either with the jack or in your owner's manual. Do not attempt to use the jack on any portions of the vehicle other than specified by the vehicle manufacturer. Always block the diagonally opposite wheel when using a jack.

A more convenient way of jacking is the use of a garage or floor jack. For Sidekick, Sidekick Sport, Tracker and X-90 models, you may use the floor jack beneath either of the axle differential housings (front and rear), or beneath the frame rails behind the front wheels and in front of the rear wheels. Ensure that the jack is supporting the vehicle on a frame rail or axle housing; NOT the floor panels or other body sheet metal. For Samurai models, position the floor jack or tire-changing jack under the leaf spring seats or differential housings only.

Never place the jack under the radiator, engine or transmission components (unless otherwise instructed to do so in a specific repair procedure). Severe and expensive damage will result when the jack is raised. Additionally, never jack under the floorpan or bodywork; the metal will deform.

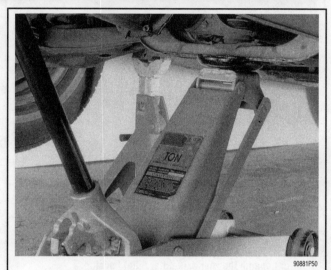

. . . and position the jackstand(s) under the side frame rail(s)

To raise the front of the vehicle with a floor jack, position it beneath the crossmember . . .

To raise the rear end of the vehicle, position the floor jack either under the side frame rail . . .

Whenever you plan to work under the vehicle, you must support it on jackstands or ramps. Never use cinder blocks or stacks of wood to support the vehicle, even if you're only going to be under it for a few minutes. Never crawl under the vehicle when it is supported only by the tire-changing jack or other floor jack.

✳✳ CAUTION

When supported improperly (on cinder blocks, pieces of wood) or on the vehicle tire-changing jack, the vehicle is EXTREMELY unstable and can easily fall. If the vehicle falls from a raised position, severe damage can occur to the vehicle, and, if you are under the vehicle when it falls, severe physical injury or death.

➡**Always position a block of wood or small rubber pad on top of the jack or jackstand to protect the lifting point's finish when lifting or supporting the vehicle.**

. . . or beneath the rear axle differential housing

90881P52

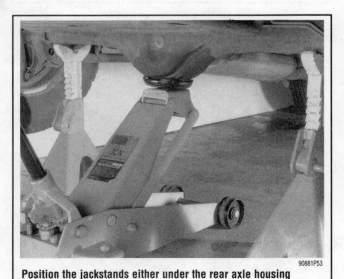

Position the jackstands either under the rear axle housing tubes . . .

90881P53

Small hydraulic, screw, or scissors jacks are satisfactory for raising the vehicle. Drive-on trestles or ramps are also a handy and safe way to both raise and support the vehicle. Be careful though, some ramps may be too steep to drive your vehicle onto without scraping the front bottom panels. Never support the vehicle on any suspension member (unless specifically instructed to do so by a repair manual) or by an underbody panel.

Jacking Precautions

The following safety points cannot be overemphasized:
• Always block the opposite wheel, or wheels, to keep the vehicle from rolling off the jack.
• When raising the front of the vehicle, firmly apply the parking brake.
• When the drive wheels are to remain on the ground, leave the vehicle in gear to help prevent it from rolling.
• Always use jackstands to support the vehicle when you are working underneath. Place the stands beneath the vehicle's jacking brackets. Before climbing underneath, rock the vehicle a bit to make sure it is firmly supported.
• Never raise the vehicle on an inclined or uneven surface.

. . . or beneath the side frame rails (as long as the floor jack is not in the way)

90881P54

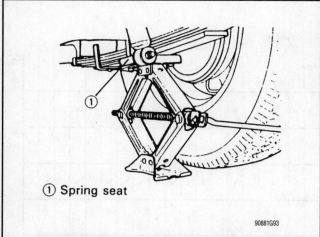

1 Spring seat

90881G93

Fig. 199 When using the tire-changing jack to lift the front of the vehicle, ensure that it is positioned beneath the leaf spring seat (1)—Samurai models

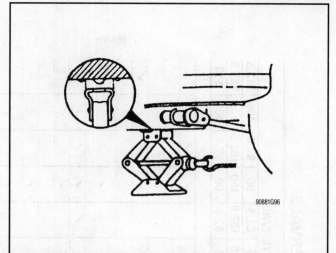

90881G96

Fig. 202 To raise the vehicle when changing a tire, position the jack beneath the side frame rail . . .

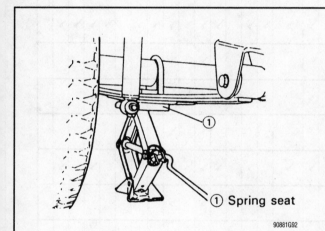

1 Spring seat

90881G92

Fig. 200 The tire-changing jack should also be positioned under the leaf spring seat when raising the rear of the vehicle—Samurai models

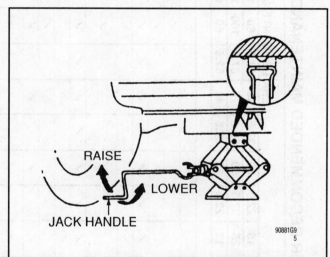

RAISE

LOWER

JACK HANDLE

90881G9
5

Fig. 203 . . . then turn the jack handle clockwise to slowly raise the vehicle—Sidekick, Sidekick Sport, Tracker or X-90 models

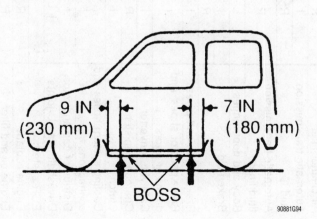

9 IN
(230 mm)

7 IN
(180 mm)

BOSS

90881G94

Fig. 201 When raising a Sidekick, Sidekick Sport, Tracker or X-90 model, position the floor or tire-changing jack at the points indicated

MANUFACTURER RECOMMENDED MAINTENANCE INTERVALS

VEHICLE MAINTENANCE INTERVAL

	Miles (x1000)	7.5	15	22.5	30	37.5	45	52.5	60	67.5	75	82.5	90	97.5	105	112.5
	km (x1000)	12.5	25	37.5	50	62.5	75	87.5	100	112.5	125	137.5	150	162.5	175	187.5
Component	Months / Type of Service	7.5	15	22.5	30	37.5	45	52.5	60	67.5	75	82.5	90	97.5	105	113
Accessory drive belts	I												✓			
Air cleaner filter	R								✓							✓
Automatic transmission fluid ①	I		✓	✓	✓	✓	✓	✓	✓	✓	✓	✓	✓	✓	✓	✓
Automatic transmission fluid lines	R				✓				✓				✓			
Body and door hinges	L	✓	✓	✓	✓	✓	✓	✓	✓	✓	✓	✓	✓	✓	✓	✓
Brake fluid	R		✓				✓				✓				✓	
Brake hoses and pipes	I		✓				✓				✓				✓	
Brake pads or shoes, and drums or rotors	I		✓				✓				✓				✓	
Catalytic converter	I													✓		
Charcoal canister	R								✓					✓		
Clutch	I		✓				✓				✓				✓	
Cooling system hoses and connections	I												✓			
Distributor cap and rotor	I															
Driveshafts and U-joints	I, L		✓		✓	✓			✓	✓			✓		✓	
EGR system ②	R								✓				✓		✓	
Engine coolant	R								✓						✓	
Engine oil and filter	R	✓	✓	✓	✓	✓	✓	✓	✓	✓	✓	✓	✓	✓	✓	✓
Exhaust system	I		✓			✓			✓				✓		✓	
Free wheeling hubs	I	✓	✓	✓	✓	✓	✓	✓	✓	✓	✓	✓	✓	✓	✓	✓
Fuel filter	R								✓							
Fuel lines and connections	I								✓				✓			
Fuel tank cap	R								✓				✓			
Idle speed	I														✓	
Ignition timing	I				✓											
Leaf springs	I												✓			
Oxygen sensor ③	I															

90881C04

MANUFACTURER RECOMMENDED MAINTENANCE INTERVALS

VEHICLE MAINTENANCE INTERVAL

Component	Type of Service	Miles (x1000) 7.5 / km 12.5 / Months 7.5	15 / 25 / 15	22.5 / 37.5 / 22.5	30 / 50 / 30	37.5 / 62.5 / 37.5	45 / 75 / 45	52.5 / 87.5 / 52.5	60 / 100 / 60	67.5 / 112.5 / 67.5	75 / 125 / 75	82.5 / 137.5 / 82.5	90 / 150 / 90	97.5 / 162.5 / 97.5	105 / 175 / 105	112.5 / 187.5 / 113
Parking brake	I		✓		✓		✓		✓		✓		✓		✓	
PCV valve ④																
Shock absorbers	I		✓		✓		✓		✓		✓		✓		✓	
Spark plug wires	R								✓							
Spark plugs	R				✓				✓				✓			
Steering knuckle oil seals	R			✓						✓						✓
Steering system	I	✓	✓	✓	✓	✓	✓	✓	✓	✓	✓	✓	✓	✓	✓	✓
Suspension nuts and bolts	T	✓	✓		✓	✓	✓		✓		✓		✓		✓	
Timing belt	I												✓			
Tires ⑤	I	✓	✓	✓	✓	✓	✓	✓	✓	✓	✓	✓	✓	✓	✓	✓
Transmission ⑥, transfer and differential fluid	R	✓			✓			✓			✓			✓		
Vacuum hoses	I								✓							
Valve lash	I		✓		✓		✓		✓		✓		✓		✓	
Wheel bearings	I, L	✓	✓		✓		✓		✓		✓		✓		✓	

I – Inspect and correct or replace, if necessary.

L – Lubricate.

R – Replace or change.

T – Tighten the fasteners to the specified torque value.

① 3-speed transmission: no replacement required.

4-speed transmission: replace the fluid every 100,000 miles (160,000 km).

② Inspect the EGR system every 50,000 miles (83,000 km).

③ Replace the oxygen sensor every 80,000 miles (133,000 km).

④ Replace the PCV valve every 50,000 miles (83,000 km).

⑤ Whenever inspecting the tires, rotate them to increase longevity.

⑥ Manual transmission.

90881C05

MANUFACTURER RECOMMENDED SEVERE MAINTENANCE INTERVALS①

Component	Type of Service	Vehicle Maintenance Interval ②
Air cleaner filter	I	Every 3,000 miles (5,000 km) or 3 months
3-speed automatic transmission fluid	R	Every 15,000 miles (25,000 km) or 15 months
	I	Every 3,000 miles (5,000 km) or 3 months
	R	Every 52,500 miles (84,000 km) or 52 months
4-speed automatic transmission fluid	I	Every 3,000 miles (5,000 km) or 3 months
	R	Every 15,000 miles (24,000 km) or 15 months
Brake pads or shoes, and drums or rotors	I	Every 6,000 miles (10,000 km) or 6 months
Distributor cap and spark plug wires	I	Every 15,000 miles (25,000 km) or 15 months
Driveshafts and U-joints	I, L	Every 6,000 miles (10,000 km) or 6 months
Engine oil and filter	R	Every 3,000 miles (5,000 km) or 3 months
Exhaust system	I	Every 6,000 miles (10,000 km) or 6 months
Leaf springs	I	Every 15,000 miles (25,000 km) or 15 months
Steering knuckle oil seals	R	Every 15,000 miles (25,000 km) or 15 months
Steering system	I	Every 3,000 miles (5,000 km) or 3 months
Suspension nuts and bolts	T	Every 6,000 miles (10,000 km) or 6 months
Transmission, transfer case and differential fluid	R	Every 15,000 miles (25,000 km) or 15 months after first replacement

I – Inspect and correct or replace, if necessary.

L – Lubricate.

R – Replace or change.

T – Tighten the fasteners to the specified torque value.

① If a vehicle is operated under any of the following conditions it is considered severe service:
- Towing a trailer.
- Repeated short trips.
- Driving on rough, dusty and/or muddy roads.
- Driving in extremely cold weather and/or on salted roads.

All other maintenance service procedures should be performed according to the normal maintenance interval chart.

② Perform the service at either the mileage or the monthly interval (whichever occurs first).

90881C06

CAPACITIES

Year	Model	Engine ID/VIN	Engine Displacement Liters (cc)	Engine Oil with Filter (qts.)	Transmission (pts.) 5-Speed	Auto.	Transfer Case (pts.)	Drive Axle (pts.) Front	Rear	Fuel Tank (gal.)	Cooling System (qts.)
1986	Samurai	5	1.3 (1324)	3.9	2.75	—	1.7	4.2	3.2	10.6	5.3
1987	Samurai	5	1.3 (1324)	3.9	2.75	—	1.7	4.2	3.2	10.6	5.3
1988	Samurai	5	1.3 (1324)	3.9	2.75	—	1.7	4.2	3.2	10.6	5.3
1989	Samurai	5	1.3 (1324)	3.9	2.75	—	1.7	4.2	3.2	10.6	5.3
	Sidekick	5	1.3 (1298)	4.75	①	②	3.6	2.1	4.6	11	5.6
		0	1.6 (1590)	4.75	①	②	3.6	2.1	4.6	11	5.5
	Tracker	U	1.6 (1590)	4.5	3.2	5.8	3.6	2.4	4.6	11	5.5
1990	Samurai	5	1.3 (1298)	3.9	2.75	—	1.7	4.2	3.2	10.6	5.3
	Sidekick	0	1.6 (1590)	4.75	①	②	3.6	2.1	4.6	11	5.5
	Tracker	U	1.6 (1590)	4.5	3.2	5.8	3.6	2.4	4.6	11	5.5
1991	Samurai	5	1.3 (1298)	3.9	2.75	—	1.7	4.2	3.2	10.6	5.3
	Sidekick	0	1.6 (1590)	4.75	①	②	3.6	2.1	4.6	11	5.5
	Tracker	U	1.6 (1590)	4.5	3.2	5.8	3.6	2.4	4.6	11	5.5
1992	Samurai	5	1.3 (1298)	3.9	2.75	—	1.7	4.2	3.2	10.6	5.3
	Sidekick	0	1.6 (1590)	4.75	①	②	3.6	2.1	4.6	11	5.5
	Tracker	U	1.6 (1590)	4.5	3.2	5.8	3.6	2.4	4.6	11	5.5
1993	Samurai	3	1.3 (1298)	3.9	2.75	—	1.7	4.2	3.2	10.6	5.3
	Sidekick	0	1.6 (1590)	4.75	①	②	3.6	2.1	4.6	11	5.5
	Tracker	U	1.6 (1590)	4.5	3.2	5.8	3.6	2.4	4.6	11	5.5
1994	Samurai	3	1.3 (1298)	3.9	2.75	—	1.7	4.2	3.2	10.6	5.3
	Sidekick	0	1.6 (1590)	4.75	①	③	3.6	2.1	4.6	11	5.5
	Tracker	U	1.6 (1590)	4.5	④	②	3.6	2.2	4.6	11	5.5
1995	Samurai	3	1.3 (1298)	3.9	2.75	—	1.7	4.2	3.2	10.6	5.3
	Sidekick	0	1.6 (1590)	4.75	①	③	3.6	2.1	4.6	11	5.5
	Tracker	U, 6	1.6 (1590)	4.5	④	②	3.6	2.2	4.6	11	5.5
1996	X90	0	1.6 (1590)	4.75	①	③	3.6	2.1	4.6	11	5.5
	Sidekick	0	1.6 (1590)	4.75	①	③	3.6	2.1	4.6	⑤	5.5
	Sport	2	1.8 (1843)	5.5	①	③	3.6	2.1	4.6	18.5	5.5
	Tracker	6	1.6 (1590)	4.5	④	②	3.6	2.2	4.6	⑤	5.5
1997	X90	0	1.6 (1590)	4.75	①	③	3.6	2.1	4.6	11	5.5
	Sidekick	0	1.6 (1590)	4.75	①	③	3.6	2.1	4.6	⑤	5.5
	Sport	2	1.8 (1843)	5.5	①	③	3.6	2.1	4.6	18.5	5.5
	Tracker	6	1.6 (1590)	4.5	④	②	3.6	2.2	4.6	⑤	5.5
1998	X90	0	1.6 (1590)	4.75	①	③	3.6	2.1	4.6	11	5.5
	Sidekick	0	1.6 (1590)	4.75	①	③	3.6	2.1	4.6	⑤	5.5
	Sport	2	1.8 (1843)	5.5	①	③	3.6	2.1	4.6	18.5	5.5
	Tracker	6	1.6 (1590)	4.5	④	②	3.6	2.2	4.6	⑤	5.5

Note: All capacities are approximate. Add fluid gradually and check to be sure a proper fluid level is obtained.

① 2-wheel drive model: 4.0 pts.
4-wheel drive model: 3.2 pts.

② Fluid drain, and filter and pan removal only: 5.9 pts.
After complete transmission overhaul: 10.8 pts.

③ 3-speed transmission –
– Fluid drain, and filter and pan removal only: 5.9 pts.
– After complete transmission overhaul: 10.8 pts.
4-speed overdrive transmission –
– Fluid drain, and filter and pan removal only: 5.3 pts.
– After complete transmission overhaul: 14.6 pts.

④ 2-wheel drive model: 3.6 pts.
4-wheel drive model: 3.2 pts.

⑤ 2-door model: 11 gals.
4-door model: 14.5 gals.

90881C07

ENGLISH TO METRIC CONVERSION: MASS (WEIGHT)

Current **mass** measurement is expressed in pounds and ounces (lbs. & ozs.). The metric unit of mass (or weight) is the kilogram (kg). Even although this table does not show conversion of masses (weights) larger than 15 lbs, it is easy to calculate larger units by following the data immediately below.

To convert ounces (oz.) to grams (g): multiply th number of ozs. by 28
To convert grams (g) to ounces (oz.): multiply the number of grams by .035

To convert pounds (lbs.) to kilograms (kg): multiply the number of lbs. by .45
To convert kilograms (kg) to pounds (lbs.): multiply the number of kilograms by 2.2

lbs	kg	lbs	kg	oz	kg	oz	kg
0.1	0.04	0.9	0.41	0.1	0.003	0.9	0.024
0.2	0.09	1	0.4	0.2	0.005	1	0.03
0.3	0.14	2	0.9	0.3	0.008	2	0.06
0.4	0.18	3	1.4	0.4	0.011	3	0.08
0.5	0.23	4	1.8	0.5	0.014	4	0.11
0.6	0.27	5	2.3	0.6	0.017	5	0.14
0.7	0.32	10	4.5	0.7	0.020	10	0.28
0.8	0.36	15	6.8	0.8	0.023	15	0.42

ENGLISH TO METRIC CONVERSION: TEMPERATURE

To convert Fahrenheit (°F) to Celsius (°C): take number of °F and subtract 32; multiply result by 5; divide result by 9

To convert Celsius (°C) to Fahrenheit (°F): take number of °C and multiply by 9; divide result by 5; add 32 to total

Fahrenheit (F)		Celsius (C)		Fahrenheit (F)		Celsius (C)		Fahrenheit (F)		Celsius (C)	
°F	°C	°C	°F	°F	°C	°C	°F	°F	°C	°C	°F
−40	−40	−38	−36.4	80	26.7	18	64.4	215	101.7	80	176
−35	−37.2	−36	−32.8	85	29.4	20	68	220	104.4	85	185
−30	−34.4	−34	−29.2	90	32.2	22	71.6	225	107.2	90	194
−25	−31.7	−32	−25.6	95	35.0	24	75.2	230	110.0	95	202
−20	−28.9	−30	−22	100	37.8	26	78.8	235	112.8	100	212
−15	−26.1	−28	−18.4	105	40.6	28	82.4	240	115.6	105	221
−10	−23.3	−26	−14.8	110	43.3	30	86	245	118.3	110	230
−5	−20.6	−24	−11.2	115	46.1	32	89.6	250	121.1	115	239
0	−17.8	−22	−7.6	120	48.9	34	93.2	255	123.9	120	248
1	−17.2	−20	−4	125	51.7	36	96.8	260	126.6	125	257
2	−16.7	−18	−0.4	130	54.4	38	100.4	265	129.4	130	266
3	−16.1	−16	3.2	135	57.2	40	104	270	132.2	135	275
4	−15.6	−14	6.8	140	60.0	42	107.6	275	135.0	140	284
5	−15.0	−12	10.4	145	62.8	44	112.2	280	137.8	145	293
10	−12.2	−10	14	150	65.6	46	114.8	285	140.6	150	302
15	−9.4	−8	17.6	155	68.3	48	118.4	290	143.3	155	311
20	−6.7	−6	21.2	160	71.1	50	122	295	146.1	160	320
25	−3.9	−4	24.8	165	73.9	52	125.6	300	148.9	165	329
30	−1.1	−2	28.4	170	76.7	54	129.2	305	151.7	170	338
35	1.7	0	32	175	79.4	56	132.8	310	154.4	175	347
40	4.4	2	35.6	180	82.2	58	136.4	315	157.2	180	356
45	7.2	4	39.2	185	85.0	60	140	320	160.0	185	365
50	10.0	6	42.8	190	87.8	62	143.6	325	162.8	190	374
55	12.8	8	46.4	195	90.6	64	147.2	330	165.6	195	383
60	15.6	10	50	200	93.3	66	150.8	335	168.3	200	392
65	18.3	12	53.6	205	96.1	68	154.4	340	171.1	205	401
70	21.1	14	57.2	210	98.9	70	158	345	173.9	210	410
75	23.9	16	60.8	212	100.0	75	167	350	176.7	215	414

TCCS1C01

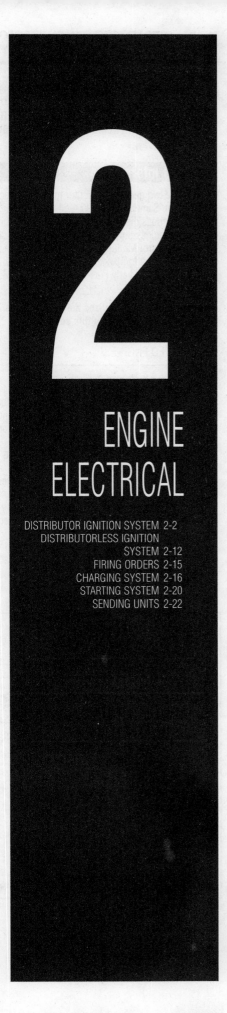

2

ENGINE
ELECTRICAL

DISTRIBUTOR IGNITION SYSTEM

➡For information on understanding electricity and trouble-shooting electrical circuits, please refer to Section 6 of this manual.

General Information

There are two general distributor ignition systems used on the Sidekick, Tracker, Samurai and X-90 models. The earlier system is a conventional breakerless distributor ignition system and is used by 1.3L carbureted engines only. The second system, which is controlled by the Electronic Control Module (ECM) to fine-tune the ignition timing for optimal engine performance, is used on 1.3L and 1.6L engines equipped with either Throttle-body Fuel Injection (TFI) or Multi-point Fuel Injection (MFI).

➡The Sidekick Sport utilizes a distributorless ignition system, which is presented later in this section.

CARBURETED ENGINES

♦ See Figures 1, 2 and 3

The principal components of this simple, yet effective, breakerless ignition system are the spark plugs, the ignition coil and the distributor, which is composed of a rotor, an igniter, a signal generator, a vacuum advance mechanism and a centrifugal advance mechanism.

The signal generator, which manufactures the ignition reference signal, is composed of a signal rotor, a magnet and a pick-up coil. The signal rotor reference signal turns the igniter on and off, which, in turn, switches the ignition coil primary current off, thereby inducing a high voltage current in the secondary windings of the ignition coil. This high voltage current is then routed to the applicable spark plug.

Through the use of mechanical (centrifugal) and vacuum advance mechanisms, the ignition spark timing is automatically advanced or retarded as needed for optimum engine performance.

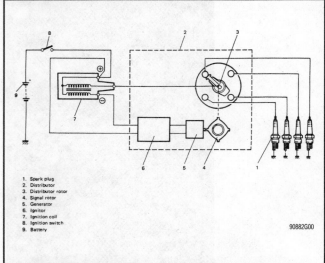

1. Spark plug
2. Distributor
3. Distributor rotor
4. Signal rotor
5. Generator
6. Ignitor
7. Ignition coil
8. Ignition switch
9. Battery

90882G00

Fig. 1 Electrical ignition system schematic—carbureted engines

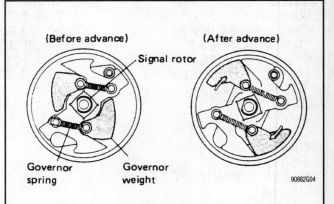

Fig. 2 The distributor used with carbureted engines utilizes a mechanical (centrifugal) advance mechanism, which advances the timing based on engine speed

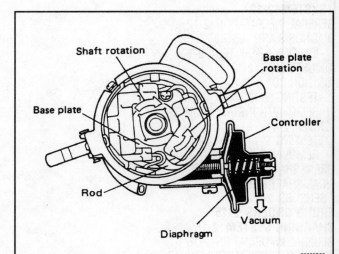

Fig. 3 The distributor also uses a vacuum actuated advance mechanism to control ignition timing based upon engine load

TFI & MFI ENGINES

♦ See Figures 4, 5 and 6

➡Disconnecting the battery cable on some vehicles may interfere with the functions of the on board computer systems and may require the computer to undergo a relearning process, once the negative battery cable is reconnected.

The ignition system used by vehicles equipped with TFI or MFI fuel delivery systems utilizes an Ignition Control (IC) system. The IC system is referred to as the Electronic Spark Advance (ESA) system on 1989–95 models. The IC system is comprised of the following components:

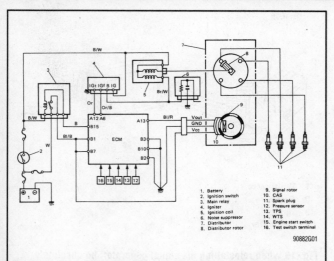

Fig. 4 Electronic ignition system schematic—1990–95 Samurai models

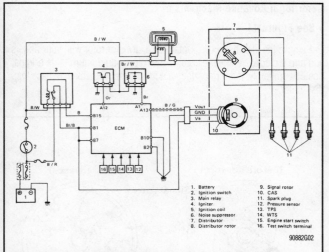

Fig. 5 Electronic ignition system schematic—1989–95 fuel-injected Sidekick and Tracker models

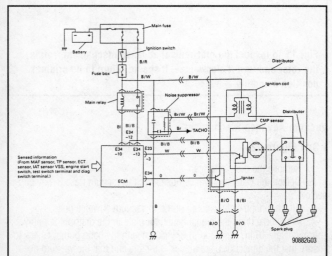

Fig. 6 Electronic ignition system schematic—1996–98 Sidekick, Tracker and X-90 models

- Electronic Control Module (ECM)
- Igniter (power unit)
- Ignition coil
- Distributor
- Spark plugs
- Spark plug wires
- Crank Angle Sensor (CAS)
- Various other sensors, such as the pressure sensor, the Throttle Position Sensor (TPS) and the test switch terminal.

The IC system is controlled by the ECM, which is programmed to provide the most advantageous ignition timing under every engine condition. The ECM receives incoming reference signals from various sensors and switches which convey the current engine condition (such as engine speed, intake air volume, coolant temperature, crankshaft position, etc.). The ECM uses the incoming information to select the most appropriate ignition timing from its memory, and adjusts the ignition timing by exact operation of the igniter.

The ECM reference signal turns the igniter on and off, which, in turn, switches the ignition coil primary current off, thereby inducing a high voltage current in the secondary windings of the ignition coil. This high voltage current is then routed, via the distributor, to the applicable spark plug.

Diagnosis and Testing

CARBURETED ENGINES

Ignition Spark Test

1. Remove the spark plug wire from the No. 1 cylinder spark plug.
2. Install a commercially available spark plug/wire tester in the end of the spark plug wire. If this tester is not available, you may also test for spark by grounding the plug wire by holding its end against a metal part of the engine.

✳✳ CAUTION

When performing this test, wearing rubber gloves and using a pair of insulated pliers to hold the spark plug wire against the engine may help avoid receiving an electrical shock.

3. While watching the spark plug tester or end of the wire, have an assistant inside the vehicle crank the engine with the ignition switch for 3–5 seconds. There should be a visible blue-white spark. If no spark is evident, or if the spark is weak (yellow spark color), inspect the spark plug wire, the ignition coil, the distributor or the spark plug itself for damage.
4. Install the wire to the applicable spark plug.
5. Repeat for each of the spark plugs/wires.

Signal Generator

▶ See Figures 7, 8, 9 and 10

1. Remove the distributor from the vehicle.
2. Remove the igniter and signal generator from the distributor.
3. Remove the dust cover from the igniter.
4. Detach the red and white wires from the igniter.
5. Attach an ohmmeter to the red and white wires, and measure the signal generator resistance. The resistance should be between 130–190 ohms. If the resistance is not within this range, replace the signal generator with a new one.
6. After testing the signal generator, attach the red and white wires to the igniter as shown in the accompanying illustration.

✳✳ WARNING

Never connect the red and white wires to the wrong terminals; damage to the igniter and/or signal generator can occur.

7. Install the signal generator, then the igniter. Inspect the air gap and adjust as necessary.
8. Install the distributor.

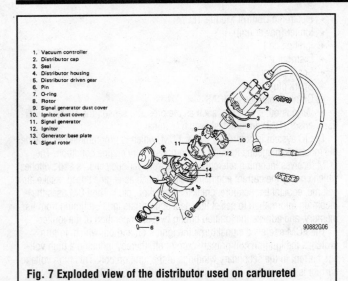

1. Vacuum controller
2. Distributor cap
3. Seal
4. Distributor housing
5. Distributor driven gear
6. Pin
7. O-ring
8. Rotor
9. Signal generator dust cover
10. Ignitor dust cover
11. Signal generator
12. Ignitor
13. Generator base plate
14. Signal rotor

90882G06

Fig. 7 Exploded view of the distributor used on carbureted engines. Note the location of the signal generator

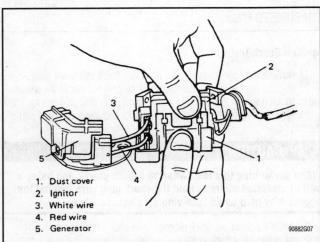

1. Dust cover
2. Ignitor
3. White wire
4. Red wire
5. Generator

90882G07

Fig. 8 To test the signal generator, remove the generator and the igniter from the distributor, then pull the dust covers off of the two components

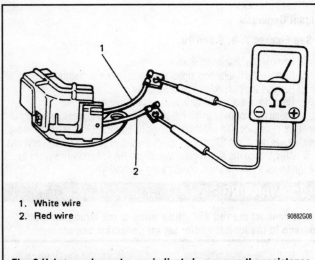

1. White wire
2. Red wire

90882G08

Fig. 9 Using an ohmmeter, as indicated, measure the resistance of the signal generator

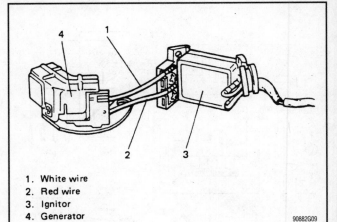

1. White wire
2. Red wire
3. Ignitor
4. Generator

90882G09

Fig. 10 When reinstalling the signal generator, be absolutely sure to connect the red and white wires as indicated, otherwise generator or igniter damage will occur

Centrifugal Advance Mechanism

♦ See Figure 11

Remove the distributor cap. Grasp the distributor rotor with your fingers and turn it clockwise, then release it. The rotor should return to its original position smoothly. If the rotor does not function as described, replace the distributor.

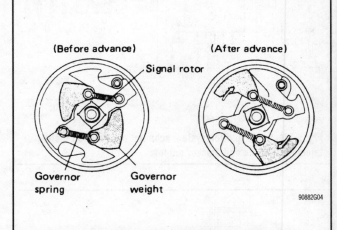

(Before advance)   (After advance)

Signal rotor

Governor   Governor
spring   weight

90882G04

Fig. 11 To inspect the mechanical advance mechanism, rotate the rotor and turn it clockwise—it should return to its original position smoothly

Vacuum Advance Mechanism

♦ See Figure 12

1. Remove the distributor cap.
2. Detach the vacuum advance hose from the vacuum hose 3-way connector.
3. Attach a hand-held vacuum pump to vacuum advance hose.
4. While observing the signal generator plate in the distributor, apply approximately 16 in. Hg (53 kPa) of vacuum with the hand pump. Check to ensure that the generator plate moves smoothly and that the vacuum does not leak down.

If the plate does not move smoothly or if the vacuum leaks down, replace the vacuum advance mechanism.

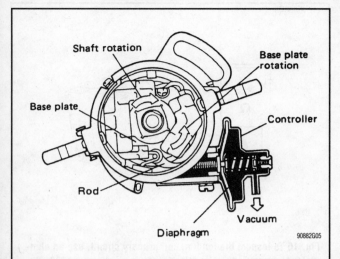

Fig. 12 When applying vacuum to the vacuum advance canister, the generator plate should move smoothly

TFI & MFI ENGINES

Ignition Spark Test

▶ See Figure 13

1. Label and detach the fuel injector(s), the Throttle Position (TP) sensor (if equipped) and the Idle Air Control (IAC) valve (if equipped) wiring harness at the connector(s).

※ CAUTION

Without properly detaching the aforementioned wiring harness, gasoline vapors may build up and leak out of the air intake, which may lead to an explosive and very dangerous condition.

2. Remove the spark plug wire from the No. 1 cylinder spark plug.
3. Install a commercially available spark plug/wire tester in the end of the spark plug wire. If this tester is not available, you may also test for spark by grounding the plug wire by holding its end against a metal part of the engine.

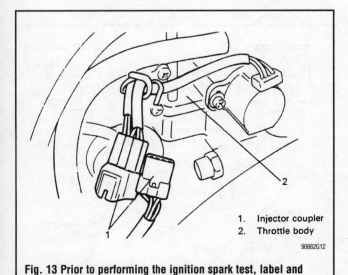

1. Injector coupler
2. Throttle body

Fig. 13 Prior to performing the ignition spark test, label and detach the fuel injector wiring harness connector

※ CAUTION

When performing this test, wearing rubber gloves and using a pair of insulated pliers to hold the spark plug wire against the engine may help avoid receiving an electrical shock.

4. While watching the spark plug tester or end of the wire, have an assistant inside the vehicle crank the engine with the ignition switch for 3–5 seconds. There should be a visible blue-white spark. If no spark is evident, or if the spark is weak (yellow spark color), inspect the spark plug wire, the ignition coil, the distributor or the spark plug itself for damage.
5. Install the wire to the applicable spark plug.
6. Repeat for each of the spark plugs/wires.
7. After the testing is complete, reattach the fuel injector(s), TP sensor (if equipped) and IAC valve (if equipped) wiring harness.

Adjustments

CARBURETED ENGINES

Signal Generator and Rotor Air Gap

▶ See Figures 14 and 15

1. Remove the distributor cap and rotor.
2. Using a feeler gauge, measure the clearance between the signal generator and one of the signal rotor teeth. The clearance should be 0.008–0.016 in. (0.2–0.4mm).
3. If the air gap is not within the specified range, adjust it as follows:

   a. Remove the distributor from the engine, then the igniter from the distributor.

   b. Slightly loosen the two signal generator screws, then, using a flat blade screwdriver, move the signal generator so that the air gap is within specifications.

4. After adjusting the air gap, tighten the two signal generator screws snugly.
5. Recheck the air gap to ensure that it still within specifications.
6. Install the igniter (if an adjustment was made), the rotor and the distributor cap.
7. Install the distributor.

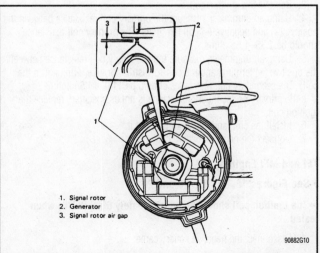

1. Signal rotor
2. Generator
3. Signal rotor air gap

Fig. 14 Use a feeler gauge to inspect the signal generator and rotor air gap

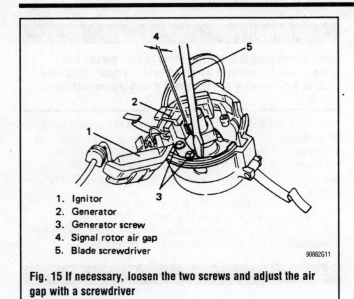

1. Ignitor
2. Generator
3. Generator screw
4. Signal rotor air gap
5. Blade screwdriver

90882G11

Fig. 15 If necessary, loosen the two screws and adjust the air gap with a screwdriver

Ignition Timing

For the ignition timing adjustment, please refer to Section 1 in this manual.

TFI & MFI ENGINES

No adjustments, other than ignition timing, are necessary on these engines. For this procedure, please refer to Section 1 in this manual.

Ignition Coil

TESTING

Carbureted Engines

➡The ignition coil should be approximately 68°F (20°C) when tested.

1. Disconnect the negative battery cable.
2. Detach the lead wires and coil-to-distributor wire from the ignition coil.
3. Remove the ignition coil.
4. Using an ohmmeter, measure the primary coil resistance between the positive (+) and negative (-) coil terminals. The primary coil resistance should be 1.35–1.65 ohms.
5. Using an ohmmeter, measure the secondary coil resistance between the positive (+) terminal and the coil-to-distributor wire terminal (on the coil). The secondary coil resistance should be 11.0–14.5 kilohms.

If the primary or secondary resistance is not as specified, replace the ignition coil.

6. Install the coil, and attach all wires to it.
7. Connect the negative battery cable.

TFI and MFI Engines

▸ **See Figures 16, 17, 18, 19 and 20**

➡The ignition coil should be approximately 68°F (20°C) when tested.

1. Disconnect the negative battery cable.

➡Disconnecting the battery cable on some vehicles may interfere with the functions of the on board computer systems and may require the computer to undergo a relearning process, once the negative battery cable is disconnected.

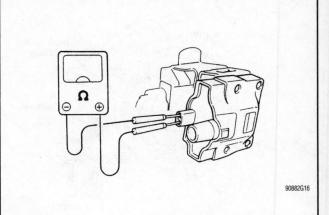

90882G16

Fig. 16 To inspect the ignition coil primary circuit, use an ohmmeter to measure the circuit's resistance as shown—1990–95 Samurai models

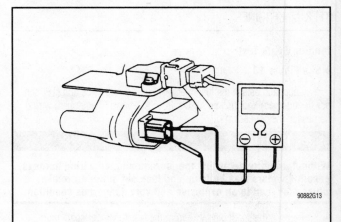

90882G13

Fig. 17 Connect the ohmmeter to the ignition coil as indicated for the primary circuit test—1989–95 fuel-injected Sidekick and Tracker models

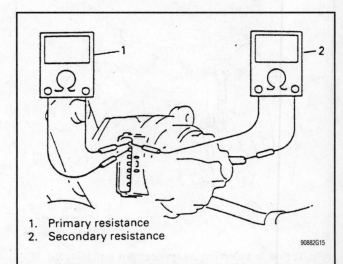

1. Primary resistance
2. Secondary resistance

90882G15

Fig. 18 The ohmmeter should be connected to the terminals shown for ignition coil testing—1996–98 models

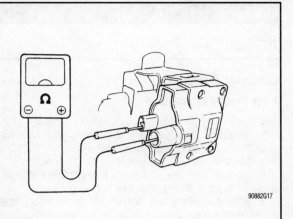

Fig. 19 Measure the secondary circuit resistance by connecting an ohmmeter to the terminals shown—1990–95 Samurai models

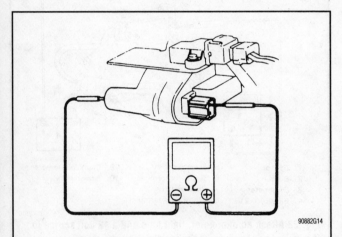

Fig. 20 For 1989–95 fuel-injected Sidekick and Tracker models, attach the ohmmeter to the ignition coil as shown for secondary circuit testing

2. Detach the lead wire connector and coil-to-distributor wire from the ignition coil.

3. Using an ohmmeter, measure the primary coil resistance between the positive (+) and negative (-) coil terminals. The primary coil resistance should be as follows:
- 1.3L engines—0.9–1.1 ohms
- 1989–93 1.6L engines—0.72–0.88 ohms
- 1994–95 1.6L engines—1.08–1.32 ohms
- 1996–98 1.6L engines—0.7–0.9 ohms

4. Using an ohmmeter, measure the secondary coil resistance between the positive (+) terminal and the coil-to-distributor wire terminal (on the coil). The secondary coil resistance should be as follows:
- 1.3L engines—10.2–13.8 kilohms
- 1989–93 1.6L engines—10.2–14.0 kilohms
- 1994–95 1.6L engines—22.1–29.9 kilohms
- 1996–98 1.6L engines—13–18 kilohms

If the primary or secondary resistance is not as specified, replace the ignition coil.

5. Install the coil, and reattach all wires to it.
6. Connect the negative battery cable.

REMOVAL & INSTALLATION

Carbureted Engines

1. Disconect the negative battery cable.
2. Label and detach the positive and negative lead wires from the ignition coil by loosening the wire terminal securing screws.
3. Detach the high-tension coil-to-distributor wire from the ignition coil by grasping the wire BOOT with your fingers and pulling it off of the terminal tower.

> **⁑⁑ WARNING**
>
> **Whenever disconnecting spark plug or coil-to-distributor high-tension wires, always pull on the boot. If you pull on the wire itself, the metal terminal inside the boot may become detached from the wire, requiring you to purchase a new wire.**

4. While supporting the ignition coil, remove its two mounting fasteners, then remove the coil from the engine compartment.

To install:

5. Position the ignition coil in the engine compartment so that the mounting fastener holes are aligned with the coil mounting bracket slots.
6. Install and tighten the two coil mounting fasteners until secure.
7. Reattach the high-tension coil-to-distributor wire; be sure that the wire is fully engaged on the ignition coil terminal tower.
8. Reattach the positive and negative lead wires to the coil and tighten the wire terminal securing screws snugly.
9. Connect the negative battery cable.

TFI and MFI Engines

♦ See Figure 21

➡ Disconnecting the battery cable on some vehicles may interfere with the functions of the on board computer systems and may require the computer to undergo a relearning process, once the negative battery cable is disconnected.

1. Disconect the negative battery cable.
2. Label and detach the lead wire connector from the ignition coil by disengaging the connector retaining tab.
3. Detach the high-tension coil-to-distributor wire from the ignition coil by grasping the wire BOOT with your fingers and pulling it off of the terminal tower.

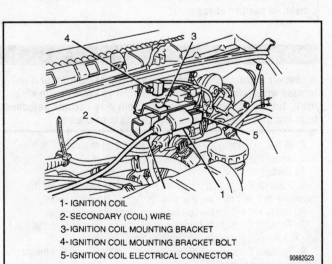

1- IGNITION COIL
2- SECONDARY (COIL) WIRE
3- IGNITION COIL MOUNTING BRACKET
4- IGNITION COIL MOUNTING BRACKET BOLT
5- IGNITION COIL ELECTRICAL CONNECTOR

Fig. 21 The ignition coil is secured to a mounting bracket, which is located on the firewall of the engine compartment

1. Wiring harness connector
2. High tension cable
3. Mounting bolt
4. Ignition coil

90882P00

For removal, detach the wiring harness connector and the high tension cable, then remove the mounting bolts

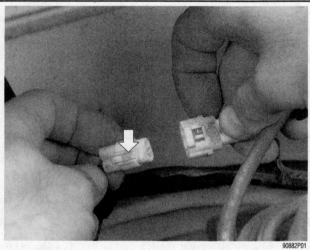

90882P01

The wiring harness connector halves use a retaining tab to maintain positive engagement

❋❋ WARNING

Whenever disconnecting spark plug or coil-to-distributor high-tension wires, always pull on the boot. If you pull on the wire itself, the metal terminal inside the boot may become detached from the wire, requiring you to purchase a new wire.

4. While supporting the ignition coil, remove its mounting fasteners, then remove the coil from the engine compartment.
   To install:
5. Position the ignition coil in the engine compartment so that the mounting fastener holes are aligned with the coil mounting holes.
6. Install and tighten the coil mounting fasteners until secure.
7. Reattach the high-tension coil-to-distributor wire; be sure that the wire is fully engaged on the ignition coil terminal tower.
8. Reattach the lead wire connector to the coil, ensuring that the retaining tab is fully engaged.
9. Connect the negative battery cable.

Igniter

TESTING

Carbureted Engines

▶ **See Figures 22 and 23**

1. Remove the distributor from the vehicle.
2. Remove the igniter and signal generator from the distributor.
3. Remove the dust cover from the igniter.
4. Detach the red and white wires from the igniter.
5. Attach an ohmmeter, a bulb and a 12 volt source to the igniter as shown in the accompanying illustration.
6. Set the ohmmeter to the 1–10 ohm range, then attach the negative lead wire to the red wire terminal of the igniter and the negative ohmmeter lead wire to the white wire terminal. If the light bulb illuminates, the igniter is functioning properly. If the light bulb does not illuminate, replace the igniter with a new one.

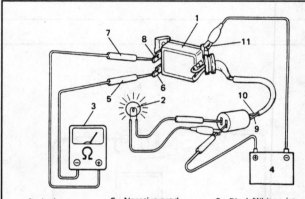

1. Ignitor
2. Bulb
3. Ohmmeter
4. Battery (12V)
5. Negative prod
6. Red wire terminal
7. Positive prod
8. White wire terminal
9. Black/White wire
10. Brown wire
11. Earth

90882G18

Fig. 22 Attach an ohmmeter, light bulb and a 12 volt source to the igniter as shown for proper testing

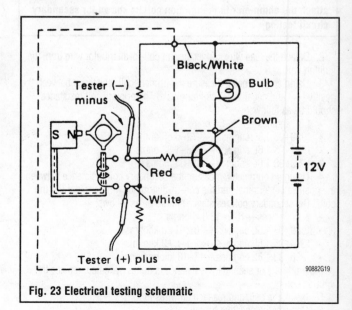

90882G19

Fig. 23 Electrical testing schematic

Never connect the ohmmeter to the wrong wire terminals, and be sure to perform this check quickly (two or three seconds).

7. After testing the igniter, attach the red and white wires to the signal generator as shown in the accompanying illustration, otherwise damage to the igniter and/or signal generator can occur.

Never connect the red and white wires to the wrong terminals; damage to the igniter and/or signal generator can occur.

8. Install the signal generator, then the igniter. Inspect the air gap and adjust as necessary.
9. Install the distributor.

TFI and MFI Engines

▶ See Figures 24 and 25

➡An analog type ohmmeter, a voltmeter and two new 1.5v batteries are needed for this procedure. Prior to performing this check, prepare the two new 1.5v batteries as shown in the accompanying illustration.

1. On 1989–95 models, remove the igniter from the ignition coil bracket.
2. On 1996–98 models, detach the wiring harness connector from the distributor.
3. Arrange the two 1.5v batteries in series (the positive end terminal of one is attached to the negative end terminal of the other) and, using a voltmeter, ensure that the batteries are providing a total of 3 volts.
4. For 1989–95 models, connect the positive terminal of the ohmmeter to terminal **G**, and the negative lead to terminal **OC** of the igniter.
5. For 1996–98 models, connect the positive terminal of the ohmmeter to terminal **4**, and the negative lead to terminal **6** of the distributor connector.
6. Using the ohmmeter, check for continuity between the two terminals. There should be no continuity (infinity).
7. Using the batteries, arranged as previously described, apply 3 volts to terminal **IB** (1989–95 models) or terminal **5** (1996–98 models). To apply this voltage, the wire attached to the positive end of the batteries should be applied to terminal **IB** (1989–95 models) or terminal **5** (1996–98 models),

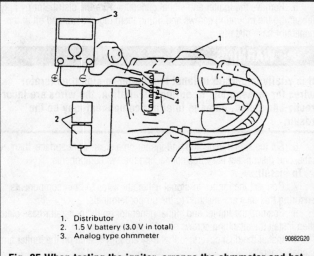

1. Distributor
2. 1.5 V battery (3.0 V in total)
3. Analog type ohmmeter
90882G20

Fig. 25 When testing the igniter, arrange the ohmmeter and batteries as shown—1996–98 models

and the negative lead wire should be applied to terminal **G** (1989–95 models) or terminal **4**. Refer to the accompanying illustrations for additional clarity.
8. Using the ohmmeter once again, recheck for continuity with the 3 volts applied. There should now be continuity.
9. If the igniter does not function as described, it is malfunctioning. Replace the igniter (1989–95 models) or the distributor (1996–98 models) with a new one.

REMOVAL & INSTALLATION

Carbureted Engines

▶ See Figure 26

1. Remove the distributor from the engine.
2. Remove the distributor cap by disengaging the two retaining clamps from the sides of the cap and lifting the cap up and off of the distributor housing.
3. Carefully pull the rotor up and off of the distributor shaft.
4. Remove the igniter and signal generator dust covers from the distributor.

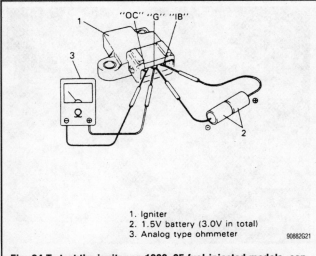

"OC" "G" "IB"

1. Igniter
2. 1.5V battery (3.0V in total)
3. Analog type ohmmeter
90882G21

Fig. 24 To test the igniter on 1989–95 fuel-injected models, connect the ohmmeter and batteries to the igniter as shown

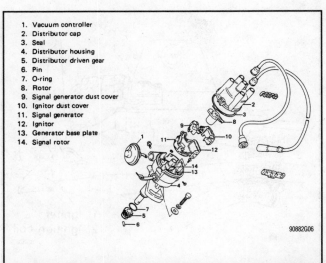

1. Vacuum controller
2. Distributor cap
3. Seal
4. Distributor housing
5. Distributor driven gear
6. Pin
7. O-ring
8. Rotor
9. Signal generator dust cover
10. Ignitor dust cover
11. Signal generator
12. Ignitor
13. Generator base plate
14. Signal rotor

90882G06

Fig. 26 Exploded view of the distributor, showing the location of the igniter—carbureted engines

5. Remove the igniter and signal generator from the distributor by fully loosening the mounting screws and lifting them together up and off of the generator base plate.

✳✳ WARNING

It is vitally important to label the igniter-to-signal generator wires for reassembly. If, during installation, the wires are incorrectly connected, damage to either component may be the result.

6. Set the signal generator and igniter on a clean work surface, then label and disconnect the wires connecting the two components.

To install:

7. Connect the igniter-to-signal generator wires to both components, ensuring that they are attached to the proper terminals.

8. Position the igniter and signal generator on the generator base plate, then install the attaching screws snugly.

9. Install the dust covers so that they are fully seated on the igniter and signal generator.

10. Install the rotor on the distributor shaft by aligning the rotor flat spot (in the rotor mounting hole) and the distributor shaft flat spot, then by carefully, but firmly, pressing the rotor onto the top of the shaft until it is fully seated.

11. Install the distributor cap and engage both hold-down clamps.

12. Install the distributor in the engine.

TFI and MFI Engines

1989–95 MODELS

▶ See Figure 27

➟Disconnecting the battery cable on some vehicles may interfere with the functions of the on board computer systems and may require the computer to undergo a relearning process, once the negative battery cable is disconnected.

1. Disconnect the negative battery cable.

2. Label and detach the wiring harness connector from the igniter (mounted on the ignition coil bracket) by disengaging the connector retaining tab.

3. Remove the igniter attaching screws, and remove the igniter.

To install:

4. Position the igniter on the ignition coil bracket, and install the attaching screws until snug.

5. Insert the wiring harness connector in the igniter terminal, and press it in until the retaining tab is fully engaged.

6. Connect the negative battery cable.

1996–98 MODELS

The igniter in distributors used on 1996–98 models are an integral component of the distributor. If the igniter is found to be defective, the distributor must be replaced as an assembly.

Distributor

REMOVAL & INSTALLATION

➟Disconnecting the battery cable on some vehicles may interfere with the functions of the on board computer systems and may require the computer to undergo a relearning process, once the negative battery cable is reconnected.

1. Disconnect the negative battery terminal at the battery.

2. Label the distributor cap terminal towers to correspond with their applicable cylinders. For example, trace the No. 1 cylinder spark plug wire to the distributor cap and number that cap terminal tower with a "1".

3. Label and disconnect all wires and vacuum hoses from the distributor.

90881P56

Label and detach all of the spark plug wires from the distributor cap, then remove the cap

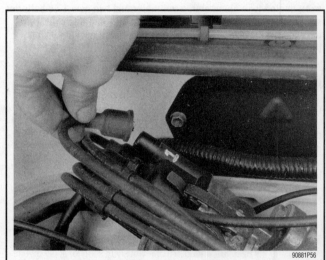

1. Igniter
2. Ignition coil

90882G22

Fig. 27 The igniter (1) is located on the ignition coil (2) mounting bracket

90882P02

Disconnect the rubber hose from the vacuum advance canister . . .

➡️Do not bend or twist the spark plug wires, otherwise internal plug wire damage may result. Grip the wire boot when removing or installing the wires.

4. Matchmark the No. 1 cylinder terminal tower to the distributor housing, then remove the distributor cap.

5. Remove the distributor cap, as described in Section 1.

6. Rotate the crankshaft clockwise until the distributor rotor points to the No. 1 cylinder mark on the distributor housing.

7. Matchmark the distributor housing position on the engine.

8. Remove the distributor flange bolt, and remove the distributor by carefully sliding it up and out of the engine.

➡️Do not crank the engine with the distributor removed.

Remove the distributor hold-down bolt . . .

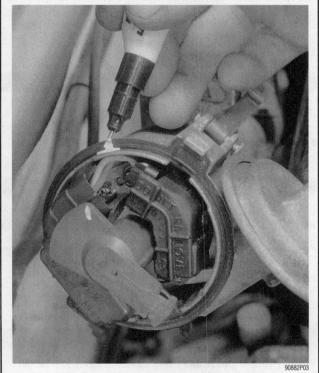

. . . then matchmark the rotor position on the distributor housing . . .

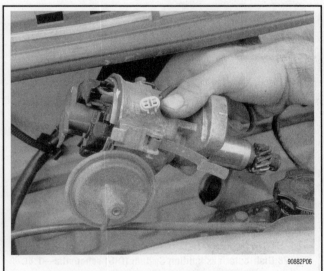

. . . then slide the distributor up and out of the engine

To install:

9. If the crankshaft was not rotated while the distributor was removed from the engine (timing not disturbed), perform the following:

a. Insert the distributor in the engine, ensuring that matchmarks on the distributor housing, engine and rotor are aligned.

b. Tighten the flange bolt until secure, then install the distributor cap.

c. Reattach all of the wiring and vacuum hoses to the distributor.

d. Connect the negative battery cable, then inspect and adjust ignition timing as necessary.

10. If the crankshaft was rotated while the distributor was removed from the engine (timing disturbed), perform the following:

a. Rotate the crankshaft in a clockwise position until the Top Dead Center (TDC) timing mark on the flywheel (1986–88 1.3L engines) or crankshaft pulley (except 1986–88 1.3L engines) is aligned with the TDC timing matchmark on the transmission case (1986–88 1.3L engines) or engine timing mark tab (except 1986–88 1.3L engines).

➡️After aligning the 2 timing marks, remove the cylinder head cover to visually ensure that neither rocker arm is riding on the peak of its camshaft lobe at the No. 1 cylinder. If one (or both) of the arms is (are) found to be riding on the camshaft lobe peaks, turn the crankshaft another 360 degrees until the same 2 marks are realigned.

. . . and the distributor housing position on the mounting flange for ease of installation

b. Turn the distributor rotor so that it points to the No. 1 cylinder terminal tower mark on the distributor housing.

c. Connect all vacuum and electrical wires to the distributor and cap.

d. Connect the negative battery cable and set the timing to specification.

DISTRIBUTORLESS IGNITION SYSTEM

General Information

♦ See Figures 28 and 29

The ignition system used in Sidekick Sport models, which are equipped with the 1.8L engine, are equipped with an electronic Distributorless Ignition System (DIS). The DIS is composed of the following components:

- Electronic Control Module (ECM)
- Igniter
- Ignition coils
- Camshaft Position (CMP) sensor
- Spark plugs
- ECM input sensors: Throttle Position (TP) sensor, Engine Coolant Temperature (ECT) sensor, and Mass Airflow (MAF) sensor

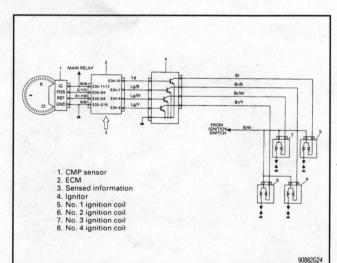

1. CMP sensor
2. ECM
3. Sensed information
4. Ignitor
5. No. 1 ignition coil
6. No. 2 ignition coil
7. No. 3 ignition coil
8. No. 4 ignition coil

Fig. 28 Distributorless Ignition System (DIS) schematic—1.8L engines

90882G24

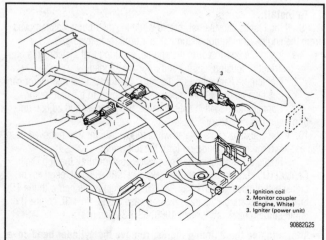

1. Ignition coil
2. Monitor coupler (Engine, White)
3. Igniter (power unit)

90882G25

Fig. 29 The DIS utilizes four separate ignition coils (1), one for each spark plug, instead of a conventional distributor for spark delivery. The coils are controlled by the igniter (3)

Crank Angle and Camshaft Position Sensors

For Crank Angle Sensor (CAS) and camshaft position sensor service/testing procedures, please refer to Section 4 of this manual.

➡ **Since the DIS does not utilize a distributor, each spark plug is equipped with its own ignition coil.**

The ECM monitors incoming reference signals to determine engine speed, engine condition and crankshaft position. The ECM is programmed with the best ignition timing for all engine conditions. The ECM selects the best ignition timing based upon the incoming information and sends a reference signal to the igniter. The igniter turns the primary voltage on and off in each of the ignition coils, which creates the secondary voltage current. The secondary voltage is carried to each of the spark plugs and fires the air/fuel mixture in the applicable cylinder.

Diagnosis and Testing

IGNITION SPARK TEST

♦ See Figures 30 and 31

1. Detach the fuel injector wiring harness connector.

✱✱ CAUTION

If the fuel injector connector is not detached, combustible fuel may be emitted from the spark plug holes during the test, which can result in an explosion or fire.

2. Perform the following steps for each of the four ignition coil/spark plugs, one at a time:

a. Remove the ignition coil and spark plug.

b. Attach the ignition coil connector to the ignition coil, then insert the end of the spark plug into the ignition coil.

✱✱ WARNING

Wearing rubber gloves and using insulated pliers to hold the ignition coil during this test, may help reduce the chance of electrocution.

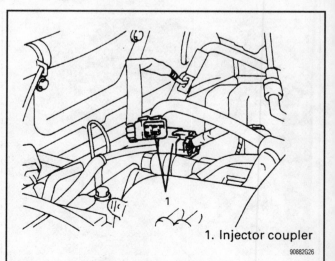

1. Injector coupler

90882G26

Fig. 30 Prior to performing the ignition spark test, always detach the fuel injector wiring harness connector

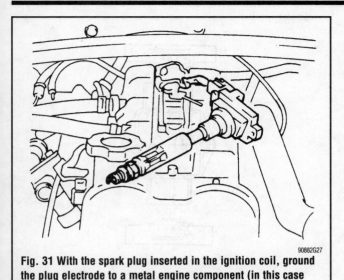

Fig. 31 With the spark plug inserted in the ignition coil, ground the plug electrode to a metal engine component (in this case the cylinder head cover) as shown

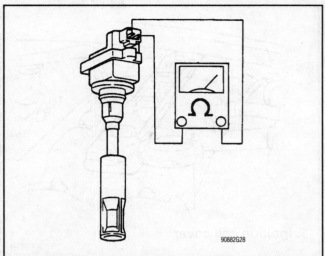

Fig. 32 To test the ignition coil(s), first measure the resistance between the two side connector terminals . . .

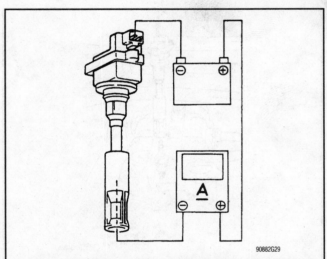

Fig. 33 . . . then measure the current as shown with a 12 volt battery attached to the coil and the DVOM

  c. Ground the spark plug electrode against a metal part of the engine, as shown in the accompanying illustration.

  d. While observing the spark plug electrodes, have an assistant crank the engine for 3–5 seconds with the ignition key. A strong blue-white spark should be observed between the spark plug electrodes. If no spark is observed, ensure that the plug is adequately grounded on a metal engine component. If no spark, or a weak yellowish spark is evident, inspect the spark plug, ignition coil and igniter for malfunctions.

3. Install the spark plug and ignition coil.

4. Repeat substeps 2a through 2d for each of the spark plugs.

Adjustments

No adjustments, other than ignition timing, are necessary on these engines. For this procedure, please refer to Section 1 in this manual.

Ignition Coils

TESTING

▶ See Figures 32 and 33

➡Disconnecting the battery cable on some vehicles may interfere with the functions of the on board computer systems and may require the computer to undergo a relearning process, once the negative battery cable is disconnected.

To properly perform this test, you will need a 12 volt vehicle battery and a Digital Volt-Ohmmeter (DVOM). Perform the following test for each ignition coil suspected of malfunctioning.

1. Remove the ignition coil.

2. Switch the DVOM to the ohm (resistance) setting, then measure the resistance between the two terminals inside the side connector on the coil. The resistance should be between 0.61–0.73 ohms at 68°F (20°C). If the resistance is not within the specified value, replace it with a new one.

3. Switch the DVOM to the amp setting, then connect the 12 volt battery and DVOM to the ignition coil as shown in the accompanying illustration to measure the current. The ammeter should register between 0.3–1.4 milliamps. If the current is not within the specified range, replace the ignition coil with a new one.

4. Detach the battery and DVOM from the ignition coil, then reattach them so that the negative DVOM lead is attached to side connector and the negative battery lead is connected to the spark plug end of the ignition coil. No current should flow through the ignition coil in this configuration; if there is current flow, replace the ignition coil with a new one.

5. If the ignition coil tested satisfactorily, install it in the engine. Otherwise, install a new ignition coil.

REMOVAL & INSTALLATION

▶ See Figures 34 and 35

➡Disconnecting the battery cable on some vehicles may interfere with the functions of the on board computer systems and may require the computer to undergo a relearning process, once the negative battery cable is disconnected.

1. Disconnect the negative battery cable, and, if the vehicle has been run recently, allow the engine to thoroughly cool.

2. Remove the ignition coil cover, then unfasten the ignition coil wiring harness connector.

3. Remove the ignition coil mounting bolt, then pull the coil up and out of the cylinder head cover.

To install:

4. Apply a small amount of silicone dielectric compound to the inside of the end of the ignition coil.

5. Install the ignition coil and mounting bolt. Tighten the mounting bolt snugly.

6. Install the ignition coil cover.

7. Connect the negative battery cable.

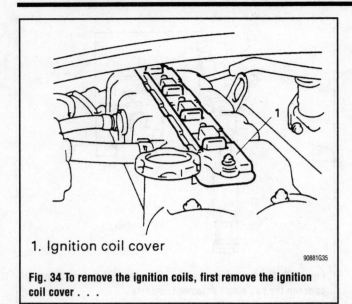

1. Ignition coil cover

90881G35

Fig. 34 To remove the ignition coils, first remove the ignition coil cover . . .

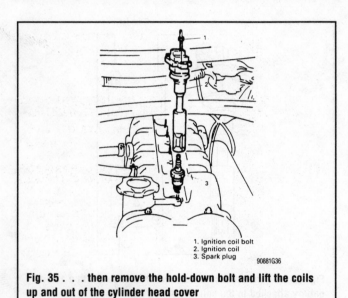

1. Ignition coil bolt
2. Ignition coil
3. Spark plug

90881G36

Fig. 35 . . . then remove the hold-down bolt and lift the coils up and out of the cylinder head cover

Igniter

TESTING

▶ **See Figure 36**

➡**Disconnecting the battery cable on some vehicles may interfere with the functions of the on board computer systems and may require the computer to undergo a relearning process, once the negative battery cable is reconnected.**

Remove the igniter from the firewall. Then, using a Digital Volt-Ohmmeter (DVOM) set to measure resistance (ohms), perform the following steps:

1. With the DVOM positive lead on terminal **E1** and the negative lead on terminal **I1**, measure the resistance. The resistance should register neither 0 nor infinity (∞).

2. With the DVOM positive lead on terminal **E2** and the negative lead on terminal **I2**, measure the resistance. The resistance should register neither 0 nor infinity (∞).

3. With the DVOM positive lead on terminal **E3** and the negative lead on terminal **I3**, measure the resistance. The resistance should register neither 0 nor infinity (∞).

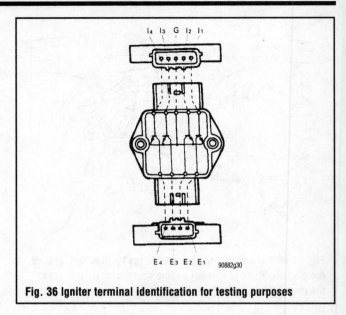

90882g30

Fig. 36 Igniter terminal identification for testing purposes

4. With the DVOM positive lead on terminal **E4** and the negative lead on terminal **I4**, measure the resistance. The resistance should register neither 0 nor infinity (∞).

5. With the DVOM positive lead on terminal **E1** and the negative lead on terminal **G**, measure the resistance. The resistance should register neither 0 nor infinity (∞).

6. With the DVOM positive lead on terminal **E2** and the negative lead on terminal **G**, measure the resistance. The resistance should register neither 0 nor infinity (∞).

7. With the DVOM positive lead on terminal **E3** and the negative lead on terminal **G**, measure the resistance. The resistance should register neither 0 nor infinity (∞).

8. With the DVOM positive lead on terminal **E4** and the negative lead on terminal **G**, measure the resistance. The resistance should register neither 0 nor infinity (∞).

9. With the DVOM positive lead on terminal **I1** and the negative lead on terminal **G**, measure the resistance. The resistance should register neither 0 nor infinity (∞).

10. With the DVOM positive lead on terminal **I2** and the negative lead on terminal **G**, measure the resistance. The resistance should register neither 0 nor infinity (∞).

11. With the DVOM positive lead on terminal **I3** and the negative lead on terminal **G**, measure the resistance. The resistance should register neither 0 nor infinity (∞).

12. With the DVOM positive lead on terminal **I4** and the negative lead on terminal **G**, measure the resistance. The resistance should register neither 0 nor infinity (∞).

13. With the DVOM positive lead on terminal **I1** and the negative lead on terminal **E1**, measure the resistance. The resistance should register infinity (∞).

14. With the DVOM positive lead on terminal **I2** and the negative lead on terminal **E2**, measure the resistance. The resistance should register infinity (∞).

15. With the DVOM positive lead on terminal **I3** and the negative lead on terminal **E3**, measure the resistance. The resistance should register infinity (∞).

16. With the DVOM positive lead on terminal **I4** and the negative lead on terminal **E4**, measure the resistance. The resistance should register infinity (∞).

17. With the DVOM positive lead on terminal **G** and the negative lead on terminal **E1**, measure the resistance. The resistance should register infinity (∞).

18. With the DVOM positive lead on terminal **G** and the negative lead on terminal **E2**, measure the resistance. The resistance should register infinity (∞).

19. With the DVOM positive lead on terminal **G** and the negative lead on terminal **E3**, measure the resistance. The resistance should register infinity (∞).

20. With the DVOM positive lead on terminal **G** and the negative lead on terminal **E4**, measure the resistance. The resistance should register infinity (∞).

21. With the DVOM positive lead on terminal **G** and the negative lead on terminal **I1**, measure the resistance. The resistance should register neither 0 nor infinity (∞).

22. With the DVOM positive lead on terminal **G** and the negative lead on terminal **I2**, measure the resistance. The resistance should register neither 0 nor infinity (∞).

23. With the DVOM positive lead on terminal **G** and the negative lead on terminal **I3**, measure the resistance. The resistance should register neither 0 nor infinity (∞).

24. With the DVOM positive lead on terminal **G** and the negative lead on terminal **I4**, measure the resistance. The resistance should register neither 0 nor infinity (∞).

If, during any step in the testing procedure, the results were not as indicated in that particular step, the igniter is faulty and must be replaced with a new one.

REMOVAL & INSTALLATION

▶ See Figure 37

➡ **Disconnecting the battery cable on some vehicles may interfere with the functions of the on board computer systems and may require the computer to undergo a relearning process, once the negative battery cable is disconnected.**

1. Disconnect the negative battery cable.
2. Label, then detach the wiring harness connectors at the igniter.
3. Remove the igniter mounting fasteners, then remove the igniter.

FIRING ORDERS

▶ See Figures 38 and 39

➡ **To avoid confusion, remove and tag the spark plug wires one at a time, for replacement.**

If a distributor is not keyed for installation with only one orientation, it could have been removed previously and rewired. The resultant wiring

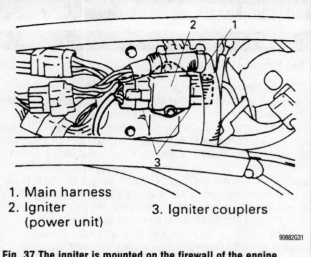

1. Main harness
2. Igniter (power unit)
3. Igniter couplers

90882G31

Fig. 37 The igniter is mounted on the firewall of the engine compartment

To install:

4. Position the igniter against the firewall so that the mounting holes are aligned, then install and tighten the mounting fasteners snugly.
5. Reattach the wiring harness connectors to the igniter.
6. Connect the negative battery cable.

Crankshaft Position and Camshaft Position Sensors

For service and testing procedures of these sensors, please refer to Section 4 of this manual.

would hold the correct firing order, but could change the relative placement of the plug towers in relation to the engine. For this reason it is imperative that you label all wires before disconnecting any of them. Also, before removal, compare the current wiring with the accompanying illustrations. If the current wiring does not match, make notes in your book to reflect how your engine is wired.

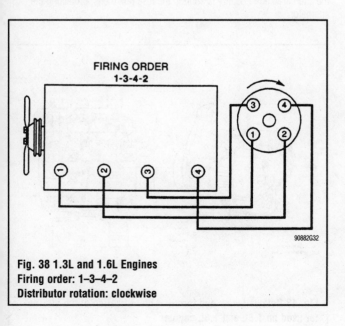

Fig. 38 1.3L and 1.6L Engines
Firing order: 1–3–4–2
Distributor rotation: clockwise

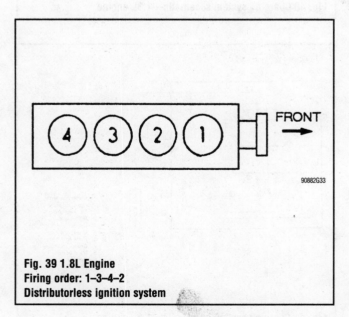

Fig. 39 1.8L Engine
Firing order: 1–3–4–2
Distributorless ignition system

CHARGING SYSTEM

General Information

▶ **See Figures 40, 41, 42, 43 and 44**

The charging system is a negative (-) ground system which consists of an alternator, a regulator (mounted inside the alternator), a charge indicator, a storage battery and wiring connecting the components.

The alternator is belt-driven from the engine. Energy is supplied from the alternator/regulator system to the rotating field through two brushes to two slip-rings. The slip-rings are mounted on the rotor shaft and are connected to the field coil. This energy supplied to the rotating field from the battery is called excitation current and is used to initially energize the field to begin the generation of electricity. Once the alternator starts to generate electricity, the excitation current comes from its own output rather than the battery.

The alternator produces power in the form of alternating current. The alternating current is rectified by diodes into direct current. The direct current is used to charge the battery and power the rest of the electrical system.

When the ignition key is turned **ON**, current flows from the battery, through the charging system indicator light on the instrument panel, to the

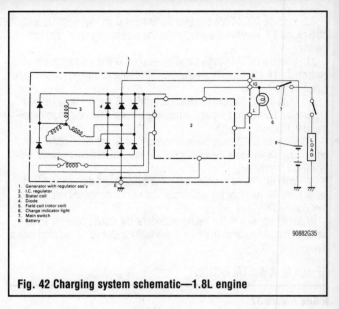

Fig. 42 Charging system schematic—1.8L engine

voltage regulator, and to the alternator. Since the alternator is not producing any current, the alternator warning light comes on. When the engine is started, the alternator begins to produce current and turns the alternator light off. As the alternator turns and produces current, the current is divided in two ways: one part to the battery to charge the battery and power the electrical components of the vehicle, and one part is returned to the alternator to enable it to increase its output. In this situation, the alternator is receiving current from the battery and from itself. A voltage regulator is wired into the current supply to the alternator to prevent it from receiving too much current, which, in turn, would cause it to produce too much current. Conversely, if the voltage regulator does not allow the alternator to receive enough current, the battery will not be fully charged and will eventually drain.

The battery is connected to the alternator at all times, whether the ignition key is turned **ON** or not. If the battery were shorted to ground, the alternator would also be shorted. This would damage the alternator. To prevent this, often a fuse link is installed in the wiring between the battery and the alternator. If the battery is shorted the fuse link melts, protecting the alternator.

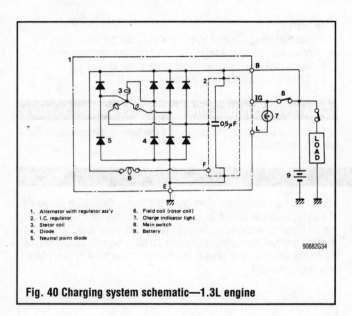

1. Alternator with regulator ass'y
2. I.C. regulator
3. Stator coil
4. Diode
5. Neutral point diode
6. Field coil (rotor coil)
7. Charge indicator light
8. Main switch
9. Battery

Fig. 40 Charging system schematic—1.3L engine

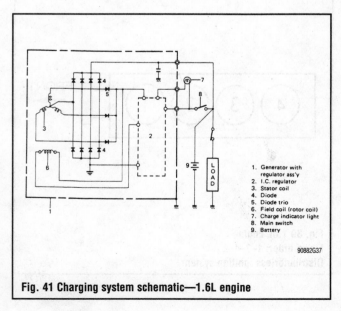

1. Generator with regulator ass'y
2. I.C. regulator
3. Stator coil
4. Diode
5. Diode trio
6. Field coil (rotor coil)
7. Charge indicator light
8. Main switch
9. Battery

Fig. 41 Charging system schematic—1.6L engine

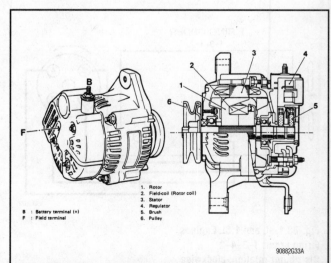

B : Battery terminal (+)
F : Field terminal

1. Rotor
2. Field-coil (Rotor coil)
3. Stator
4. Regulator
5. Brush
6. Pulley

Fig. 43 Cutaway view and terminal identification of the alternator used on 1.3L and 1.6L engines

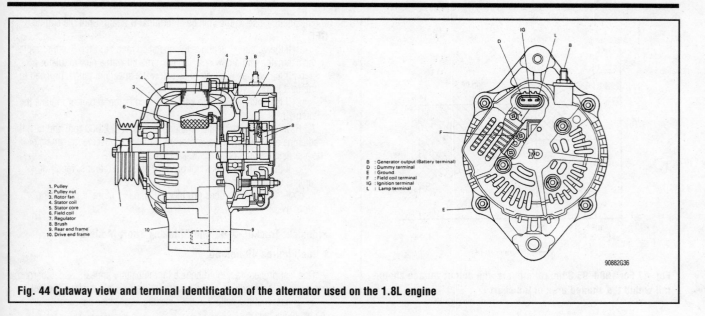

1. Pulley
2. Pulley nut
3. Rotor fan
4. Stator coil
5. Stator core
6. Field coil
7. Regulator
8. Brush
9. Rear end frame
10. Drive end frame

B : Generator output (Battery terminal)
D : Dummy terminal
E : Ground
F : Field coil terminal
IG : Ignition terminal
L : Lamp terminal

90882G36

Fig. 44 Cutaway view and terminal identification of the alternator used on the 1.8L engine

Alternator Precautions

➡**Disconnecting the battery cable on some vehicles may interfere with the functions of the on board computer systems and may require the computer to undergo a relearning process, once the negative battery cable is reconnected.**

Several precautions must be observed with alternator equipped vehicles to avoid damage to the unit.

• If the battery is removed for any reason, be sure to reconnect it with the proper polarity. Reversing the battery connections may result in damage to the one-way rectifiers.

• When utilizing a booster battery as a starting aid, always connect the positive to positive terminals and the negative terminal from the booster battery to a good engine ground on the vehicle being started.

• Never use a fast charge as a booster to start vehicles.

• Disconnect the battery cable when charging the battery with a fast charger.

• Never attempt to polarize the alternator.

• Do not use test lights of more than 12 volts when checking diode continuity.

• Do not short across or ground any of the alternator terminals.

• The polarity of the battery, alternator and regulator must be matched and considered before making any electrical connections within the system.

• Disconnect the battery ground terminal when performing any service on electrical components.

• Disconnect the battery if arc welding is to be done on the vehicle.

Alternator

TESTING

Samurai Models

▸ **See Figures 45, 46, 47 and 48**

This test procedure should be used if the battery appears undercharged, because of slow cranking or the battery indicator is clear with a red dot.

1. Ensure that the battery is not discharged because accessories were inadvertently left on.

2. Inspect the alternator drive belt for the proper tension and condition. This is described in detail in Section 1 of this manual.

3. Inspect the system wiring for defects. Check all connections for tightness and cleanliness, including the slip connectors at the alternator and firewall, the cable connections at the battery, and the starter and ignition ground cable.

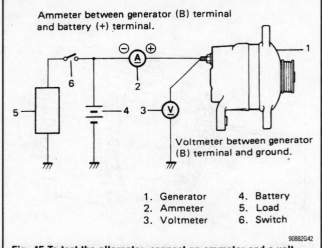

Ammeter between generator (B) terminal and battery (+) terminal.

Voltmeter between generator (B) terminal and ground.

1. Generator	4. Battery
2. Ammeter	5. Load
3. Voltmeter	6. Switch

90882G42

Fig. 45 To test the alternator, connect an ammeter and a voltmeter in the charging circuit, as indicated

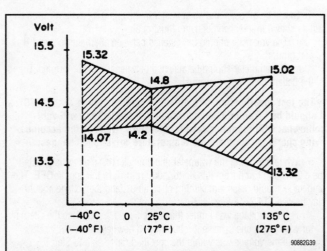

90882G39

Fig. 46 The voltage exhibited by the voltmeter depends upon the temperature of the regulator case. The voltage should fall within the shaded area of the chart—1986–89 Samurai models

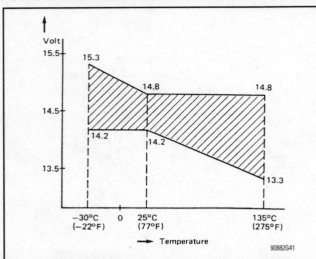

Fig. 47 For 1990–95 Samurai models, the output voltage should fall within the shaded area of the chart

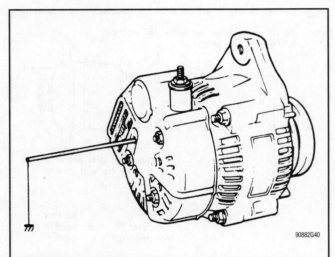

Fig. 48 Use a jumper wire to ground alternator terminal F during the testing procedure

4. Install a voltmeter and an ammeter in the charging system wiring circuit as shown in the accompanying illustration.

a. The voltmeter should be installed between alternator terminal **B** and ground.

b. The ammeter should be attached between alternator terminal **B** and the battery positive (+) terminal.

➡ **The test specifications are given for components at 77°F (25°C). It should be taken into consideration that the voltage will vary somewhat with regulator case temperature. Refer to the accompanying charts for approximate temperature-to-voltage changes.**

5. While observing the voltmeter and ammeter, have an assistant start the engine and run it from idle up to 2,000 rpm. Turn the engine **OFF**. The amperage should reach a maximum of 10 amps, and the voltage should stay between 14.2–14.8 volts

a. If the voltage was higher than specified, either replace the alternator with a new one or have it rebuilt with a new regulator.

b. If the voltage was within the specified range skip to Step 7.

c. If the voltage was lower than the specified minimum, perform the next step.

6. Using a jumper wire, ground alternator terminal **F** and start the

engine again. Observe the voltage at terminal **B** again. Shut the engine **OFF**.

a. If the voltage was above the specified range in Step 5, either replace the alternator with a new one or have it rebuilt with a new regulator.

b. If the voltage was within or below the specified range, proceed to the next step.

c. If the voltage was below the specified range, repair or replace the alternator.

7. Have your assistant, start the engine, run it at 2,000 rpm and turn the headlamps and heater blower motor on, while you observe the ammeter. The alternator should produce at least 20 amps.

a. If the alternator does not produce at least 20 amps, repair or replace the alternator.

b. If the alternator does produce 20 amps or more, it is working properly.

Sidekick, Tracker, X-90 and Sidekick Sport Models

▶ **See Figures 49 and 50**

This test procedure should be used if the battery appears undercharged, because of slow cranking or the battery indicator is clear with a red dot.

1. Ensure that the battery is not discharged because accessories were inadvertently left on.

2. Inspect the alternator drive belt for the proper tension and condition. This is described in detail in Section 1 of this manual.

3. Inspect the system wiring for defects. Check all connections for tightness and cleanliness, including the slip connectors at the alternator and firewall, the cable connections at the battery, and the starter and ignition ground cable.

4. Install a voltmeter and an ammeter in the charging system wiring circuit as shown in the accompanying illustration.

a. The voltmeter should be installed between alternator terminal **B** and ground.

b. The ammeter should be attached between alternator terminal **B** and the battery positive (+) terminal.

5. Turn off all accessories, such as the wipers, the heater blower motor, etc.

➡ **The test specifications are given for components at 68°F (20°C). It should be taken into consideration that the voltage will vary somewhat with regulator case temperature. Refer to the accompanying charts for approximate temperature-to-voltage changes.**

6. While observing the voltmeter and ammeter, have an assistant start the engine and run it from idle up to 2,000 rpm. Turn the engine **OFF**. The amperage should reach a maximum of 10 amps, and the voltage should stay between 14.4–15.0 volts

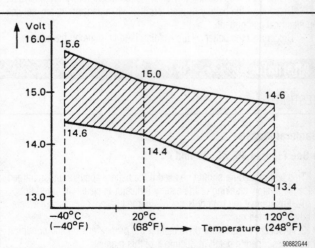

Fig. 49 Depending upon the temperature of the regulator case, the voltage should fall somewhere within the shaded area of the chart—Sidekick, Tracker and X-90 models

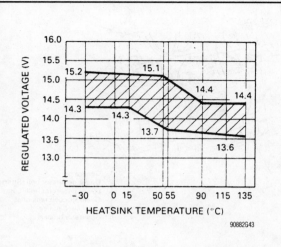

Fig. 50 For Sidekick Sport models, the output voltage should fall within the shaded area of this chart

a. If the voltage was higher than specified, either repair or replace the alternator.

b. If the voltage was within the specified range, perform the next step.

c. If the voltage was lower than the specified minimum, perform the next step.

7. Have your assistant, start the engine, run it at 2,000 rpm and turn the headlamps and heater blower motor on, while you observe the ammeter. The alternator should produce at least 20 amps.

a. If the alternator does not produce at least 20 amps, repair or replace the alternator.

b. If the alternator does produce 20 amps or more, it is working properly.

REMOVAL & INSTALLATION

➡ Disconnecting the battery cable on some vehicles may interfere with the functions of the on board computer systems and may require the computer to undergo a relearning process, once the negative battery cable is reconnected.

Samurai Models

1. Disconnect the negative battery cable.
2. From under the vehicle, label and detach all wiring from the alternator.
3. Disengage the brake pipe from the clamp on the radiator shield, then remove the shield.
4. Loosen the mounting bolts, then remove the alternator drive belt from the pulley.
5. While supporting the alternator, remove the mounting bolts and lower the alternator down and out of the engine compartment.

To install:

6. Hold the alternator in position, then install the mounting bolts finger-tight.
7. Position the alternator drive belt around the pulley, then adjust the drive belt tension as described in Section 1.
8. Tighten the mounting bolts securely.
9. Reattach all wiring to the alternator.
10. Install the lower radiator shield and connect the brake pipe to the mounting clamp.
11. Connect the negative battery cable.

Sidekick, Tracker, X-90 and Sidekick Sport Models

◆ **See Figures 51, 52, 53 and 54**

1. Disconnect the negative battery cable.
2. On Sidekick Sport models, remove the air inlet hose.

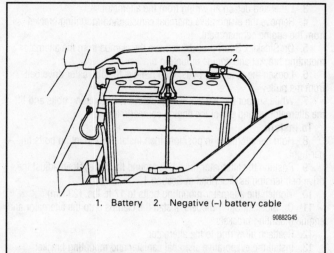

1. Battery   2. Negative (–) battery cable

Fig. 51 To remove the alternator on Sidekick Sport models, disconnect the negative battery cable . . .

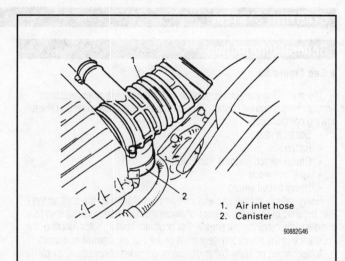

1. Air inlet hose
2. Canister

Fig. 52 . . . then remove the air inlet hose from the throttle body and air cleaner housing

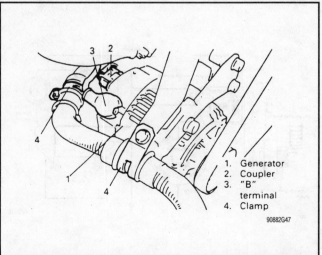

1. Generator
2. Coupler
3. "B" terminal
4. Clamp

Fig. 53 Detach all wiring and any wiring clamps from the alternator

3. Label and detach all wiring from the alternator.

4. Remove the evaporative charcoal canister and mounting bracket from the engine compartment.

5. On Sidekick Sport models, remove the clamps from the alternator mounting bracket and engine mounting bracket.

6. Loosen the mounting bolts, then remove the alternator drive belt from the pulley.

7. While supporting the alternator, remove the mounting bolts and lift the alternator up and out of the engine compartment.

To install:

8. Hold the alternator in position, then install the mounting bolts finger-tight.

9. Position the alternator drive belt around the pulley, then adjust the drive belt tension as described in Section 1.

10. Tighten the alternator mounting bolts to 17 ft. lbs. (23 Nm).

11. On Sidekick Sport models, install the clamps onto the alternator and engine mounting brackets.

12. Reattach all wiring to the alternator.

13. Install the evaporative charcoal canister and mounting bracket.

14. On Sidekick Sport models, install the air inlet hose.

15. Connect the negative battery cable.

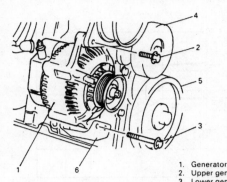

1. Generator
2. Upper generator bolt (Short)
3. Lower generator bolt (Long)
4. Generator belt tensioner
5. Crankshaft pulley
6. Generator bracket

Fig. 54 Remove the alternator mounting bolts and lift the alternator up and out of the engine compartment

STARTING SYSTEM

General Information

▶ **See Figure 55**

The starting system is designed to rotate the engine at a speed fast enough for the engine to start. The starting system is comprised of the following components:

• Starter motor
• Battery
• Clutch switch (manual transmissions)
• Ignition switch
• Heavy circuit wiring

Heavy cables, connectors and switches are utilized by the starting system because of the large amount of amperage this system is required to handle while cranking the engine. For premium starter motor function, the resistance in the starting system must be kept to an absolute minimum.

A discharged or faulty battery, loose or corroded connections, or partially broken cables will result in slower-than-normal cranking speeds. The amount of damage evident may even prevent the starter motor from rotating the engine at all.

Vehicles equipped with manual transmissions are equipped with a clutch switch in the starter circuit, which is designed to prevent the starter motor from operating unless the clutch pedal is depressed. Vehicles equipped with automatic transmissions are equipped with either a Park/Neutral Position (PNP) switch, a Manual Lever Position (MLP) switch or a Transmission Range (TR) sensor in the starter circuit. These switches prevent the starter motor from functioning unless the transmission range selector lever is in Neutral (**N**) or Park (**P**).

The starter motor is a 12 volt assembly, which has the starter solenoid mounted on the drive end-housing. The starter solenoid energizes when the relay contacts are closed. When the solenoid energizes, the starter drive engages with the flywheel ring gear, rotating the crankshaft and starting the engine. An overrunning clutch in the starter drive assembly protects the starter motor from excessive speed when the engine starts.

Starter

TESTING

▶ **See Figures 56, 57, 58 and 59**

✳✳ WARNING

During the following test, the starter motor must not be energized for longer than 5 seconds, otherwise you run the risk of burning out the starter motor coil.

1. Remove the starter motor from the vehicle.

2. Detach the field coil lead from terminal **M** on the starter motor.

3. Using jumper wires, connect a 12 volt battery to the starter motor so that the negative battery terminal is attached to the starter motor housing and to solenoid terminal **M**, and that the positive battery terminal is connected to starter motor solenoid terminal **S**. The starter motor plunger should move outward; if it does not, replace the solenoid with a new one.

4. Detach the negative battery jumper wire from terminal **M** on the starter motor solenoid, and check the plunger for movement. The plunger should remain extended; if the plunger returns to its resting position, replace the solenoid with a new one.

5. While observing the solenoid plunger, detach the negative battery lead from the starter motor housing. The plunger should return to its normal resting position; if it does not, replace the solenoid with a new one.

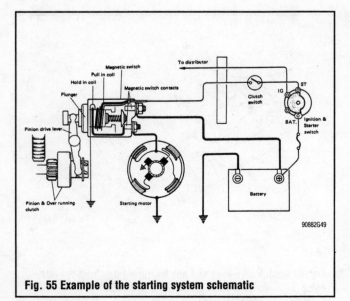

Fig. 55 Example of the starting system schematic

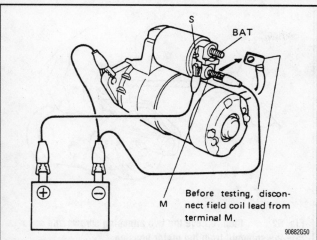

Fig. 56 To test the solenoid plunger, first detach the field coil lead from alternator terminal M, then attach a 12 volt battery to the starter motor as shown . . .

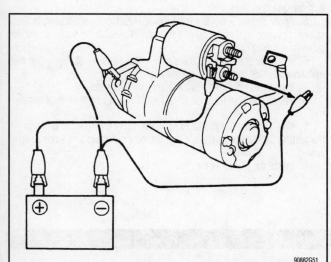

Fig. 57 . . . then detach the negative jumper wire from terminal M. The plunger should remain extended

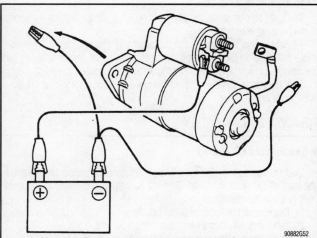

Fig. 58 Detach the other negative lead from the starter motor housing. The solenoid plunger should now retract to its normal resting position

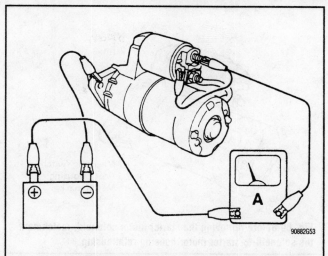

Fig. 59 Use an ammeter to measure the amount of current draw the starter motor uses

6. Reattach the 12 volt battery and install an ammeter to the starter motor as shown in the accompanying illustration. The starter motor should rotate smoothly and steadily with the pinion gear moving out, and the ammeter should display less than 60 amps at 11.5 volts (Samurai models), or 90 amps at 11 volts (Sidekick, Tracker, X-90 and Sidekick Sport models). If the ammeter does not display the specified values, or if the starter motor does not operate smoothly and steadily, replace the starter motor with a new one.

REMOVAL & INSTALLATION

1. Disconnect the negative battery cable.
2. If necessary for added under-vehicle clearance, apply the parking brake, block the rear wheels, then raise and safely support the front of the vehicle on jackstands.
3. From beneath the vehicle, label and detach all wiring from the starter motor solenoid terminals.
4. Remove one of the two starter motor mounting bolts and loosen the other bolt until it can be turned by hand, then support the starter motor with one hand while removing the last starter motor mounting bolt.
5. Lower the starter motor down and away from the engine and transmission.
   To install:
6. Hold the starter motor in position and install the two mounting bolts. Tighten the two bolts securely.
7. Reattach all applicable wiring to the starter motor solenoid. Ensure that the wiring terminals and connectors are clean and free of corrosion.
8. If necessary, lower the vehicle.
9. Connect the negative battery cable.

SOLENOID REPLACEMENT

➧ See Figures 60, 61 and 62

➡Prior to removing the solenoid from the starter motor unit, match-mark the solenoid-to-starter motor housing position, as shown in the accompanying illustration.

1. Remove the starter motor from the vehicle.
2. Detach the solenoid-to-starter motor wire from the solenoid terminal.

➡Do not disassemble the solenoid; if the solenoid is defective, replace the entire unit with a new one.

3. Remove the two attaching screws, then slide the solenoid out of the starter motor housing flange.

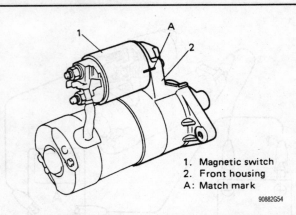

1. Magnetic switch
2. Front housing
A: Match mark

Fig. 60 Before removing the starter motor solenoid, matchmark the solenoid-to-starter motor housing relationship

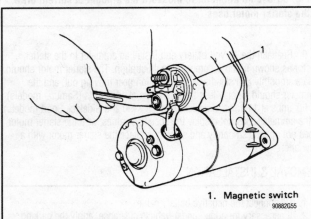

1. Magnetic switch

Fig. 61 Disconnect the field coil lead from the solenoid by loosening the retaining nut . . .

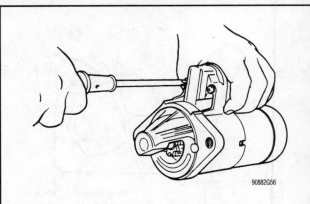

Fig. 62 . . . then remove the two attaching screws and separate the solenoid from the motor housing

To install:

4. Inspect the solenoid plunger joint for wear or other damage. Replace it, if damage is evident.

5. Apply Suzuki Super Grease A (99000–25010) or equivalent, to the solenoid plunger and to the tip of the lever arm (inside the starter motor-to-solenoid housing hole).

6. Insert the solenoid into the starter motor housing, ensuring that the matchmarks made during removal are aligned.

7. Install and tighten the two attaching screws securely.

8. Attach the starter motor-to-solenoid wire to the solenoid terminal.

9. While the starter motor is removed form the vehicle, perform the testing procedure to ensure that the new solenoid functions properly.

10. Install the starter motor.

SENDING UNITS

➡This section describes the operating principles of sending units, warning lights and gauges. Sensors which provide information to the Electronic Control Module (ECM) are covered in Section 4 of this manual.

Instrument panels contain a number of indicating devices (gauges and warning lights). These devices are composed of two separate components. One is the sending unit, mounted on the engine or other remote part of the vehicle, and the other is the actual gauge or light in the instrument panel.

Several types of sending units exist, however most can be characterized as being either a pressure type or a resistance type. Pressure type sending units convert liquid pressure into an electrical signal which is sent to the gauge. Resistance type sending units are most often used to measure temperature and use variable resistance to control the current flow back to the indicating device. Both types of sending units are connected in series by a wire to the battery (through the ignition switch). When the ignition is turned **ON**, current flows from the battery through the indicating device and on to the sending unit.

Coolant Temperature Sender

TESTING

◆ **See Figures 63, 64, 65, 66 and 67**

1. Remove the coolant temperature sender from the engine.

2. Position the sender in a container of water on your stove, as shown in the accompanying illustration.

➡**Refer to the accompanying charts for the approximate resistance at varying temperatures.**

3. Using an ohmmeter, measure and note the sender terminal-to-sender metal housing resistance.

4. Slowly heat the water in the container and observe the sender resistance exhibited on the ohmmeter. The resistance of the sender should smoothly and steadily decrease as the water temperature increases.

5. If the sender resistance does not react as noted, replace the sender with a new one.

REMOVAL & INSTALLATION

◆ **See Figures 68 and 69**

On 1.3L and 1.6L engines, the coolant temperature sender is mounted in the front of the intake manifold. On the 1.8L engine, the sender is mounted next to the water outlet cap.

1. Disconnect the negative battery cable.
2. Label and detach the wire from the sender unit.
3. Drain the cooling system until the coolant level is below the sender.
4. Remove the sender with an open end wrench.

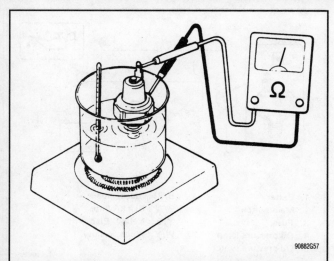

Fig. 63 To test the sender, position it in a container full of water and slowly heat it on your stove

Temperature	Resistance
50°C (122°F)	189.4 – 259.6 Ω
115°C (239°F)	24.2 – 28.1 Ω

90882G60

Fig. 66 If the sender's resistance values are not within the specified ranges at the temperature indicated, replace the sender with a new one—1996–98 1.6L engines

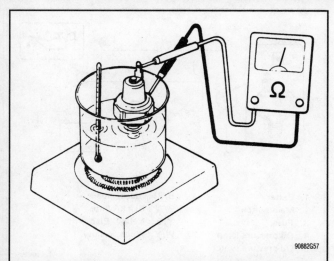

Fig. 64 As the temperature of the water increases, the resistance of the sender should decrease

Temperature	Resistance
50°C (122°F)	190 – 260 Ω
80°C (176°F)	55 – 65 Ω
100°C (212°F)	25 – 35 Ω

90882G61

Fig. 67 The sender used in 1.8L engines should exhibit the indicated values when tested

To install:

5. Clean the sender threads, then wrap Teflon® pipe sealing tape around the sender threads.

6. Install the sender by hand, then tighten the sender to 71 inch lbs. (8 Nm).

7. Reattach the sender wire.

8. Connect the negative battery cable, and refill the cooling system.

Oil Pressure Sender

TESTING

♦ **See Figures 70 and 71**

1. Label and detach the oil pressure switch wire.

2. Using an ohmmeter, measure the resistance between the switch terminal and the engine block. With the engine not running, there should continuity. When the engine is running, there should be no continuity (infinite resistance).

3. If the switch does not function as indicated, replace it with a new one.

Temperature	Resistance
50°C (122°F)	133.9 – 178.9 Ω
80°C (176°F)	47.5 – 56.8 Ω
100°C (212°F)	26.2 – 29.3 Ω

90882G59

Fig. 65 The sender should create the resistances shown in this chart, depending on its temperature—1986–95 1.3L and 1.6L engines

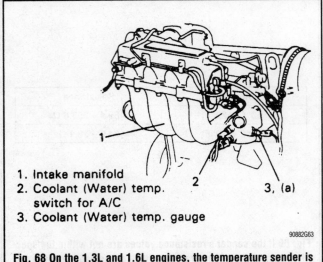

1. Intake manifold
2. Coolant (Water) temp. switch for A/C
3. Coolant (Water) temp. gauge

2   3, (a)

90882G63

Fig. 68 On the 1.3L and 1.6L engines, the temperature sender is mounted in the front of the intake manifold

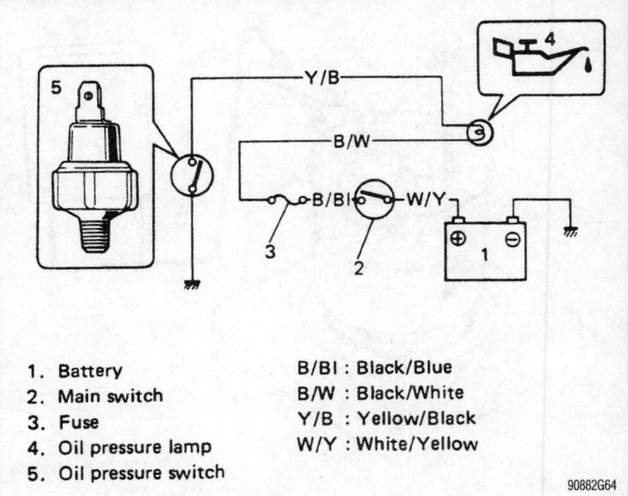

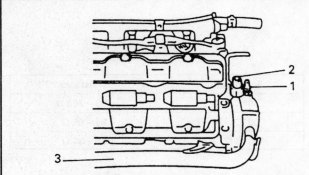

1. Engine coolant temperature sensor (ECT sensor) (for A/C)
2. Engine coolant temperature sensor (ECT sensor)
3. Water outlet pipe

90882G62

Fig. 69 The temperature sender (ECT sensor) used on 1.8L engines is mounted next to the water outlet cap and pipe

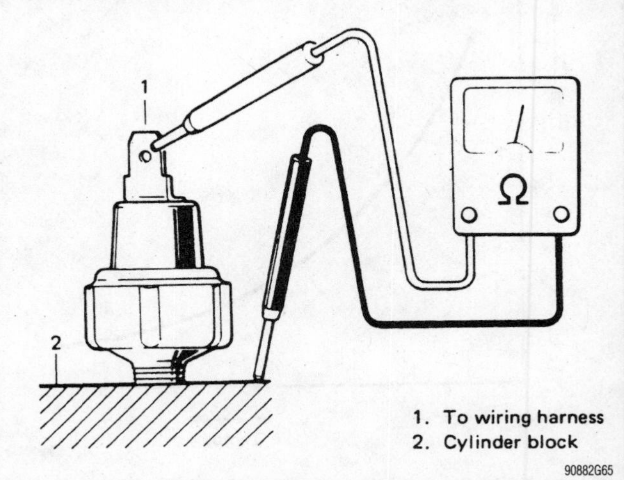

REMOVAL & INSTALLATION

♦ **See Figure 72**

The oil pressure switch is threaded into the cylinder block above the oil filter.
1. Disconnect the negative battery cable.
2. Label and detach the wire from the switch.
3. Remove the sender with an open end wrench.
To install:
4. Clean the sender threads, then install the sender by hand and tighten it until secure.
5. Reattach the sender wire.
6. Connect the negative battery cable.

1. Battery
2. Main switch
3. Fuse
4. Oil pressure lamp
5. Oil pressure switch

B/Bl : Black/Blue
B/W : Black/White
Y/B : Yellow/Black
W/Y : White/Yellow

90882G64

Fig. 70 Oil pressure switch system schematic

1. To wiring harness
2. Cylinder block

90882G65

Fig. 71 Use an ohmmeter to check the resistance between the switch terminal and the engine block

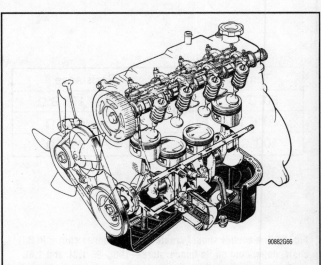

90882G66

Fig. 72 The oil pressure switch is located in the engine block above the oil filter

3

ENGINE AND ENGINE OVERHAUL

1.3L (1,298cc & 1,324cc) ENGINE SPECIFICATIONS

Description	English Specifications	Metric Specifications
Type	Inline Single Overhead Camshaft (SOHC)	
Displacement	80.8 cu. in.	1.3L (1,324cc)
Number of Cylinders	4	
Bore	2.91	74.0mm
Stroke		
1,298cc engine	2.97 in.	75.4mm
1,324cc engine	3.03 in.	77.0mm
Compression ratio		
1986-90 models ①	8.9:1	
1991-95 models	9.5:1	
Compression pressure ②	170-199 psi	1171.3-1371.1 kPa
Allowable variation between cylinders ②	14.2 psi	97.8 kPa
Valve lash (clearance)		
Cold engine		
Intake valve	0.0051-0.0067 in.	0.13-0.17mm
Exhaust valve	0.0063-0.0079 in.	0.16-0.20mm
Hot engine		
Intake valve	0.009-0.011 in.	0.23-0.27mm
Exhaust valve	0.0102-0.0118 in.	0.26-0.30mm
Cylinder head		
Cylinder head-to-engine block surface warpage	0.002 in.	0.05mm
Cylinder head-to-exhaust manifold surface warpage	0.004 in.	0.1mm
Cylinder head-to-intake manifold surface warpage	0.004 in.	0.1mm
Valve guide bore diameter—Intake and exhaust valves	0.4736-0.4743 in.	12.030-12.048mm
Valve seat angle—Intake and exhaust valves	45°	
Valve seat width—Intake and exhaust valves	0.0512-0.0590 in.	1.3-1.5mm
Valves, valve springs and camshaft		
Cam height (base circle + lift)		
Fuel pump lobe	1.5590-1.5748 in.	39.6-40.0mm
Intake and exhaust lobes	1.4724-1.4763 in.	37.4-37.5mm
Camshaft run-out	0.0039 in.	0.10mm
Camshaft thrust clearance	0.0295 in.	0.75mm
Camshaft-to-journal clearance	0.0020-0.0059 in.	0.050-0.150mm
Contact seat width—Intake and exhaust valves	0.0512-0.0590 in.	1.3-1.5mm
Stock allowance of valve stem end face	0.019 in.	0.5mm
Valve guide inside diameter—Intake and exhaust valves	0.2756-0.2761 in.	7.000-7.015mm
Valve guide protrusion—Intake and exhaust valves	0.56 in.	14mm
Valve guide-to-valve stem clearance		
Exhaust valves		
Intake valves	0.0008-0.0027 in.	0.02-0.07mm
Valve head margin		
Exhaust valves	0.0275-0.0390 in.	0.7-1.0mm
Intake valves	0.0236-0.0390 in.	0.6-1.0mm
Valve head radial run-out	0.003 in.	0.08mm
Valve spring free length	1.8937-1.9409 in.	48.1-49.3mm

90883C04

1.3L (1,298cc & 1,324cc) ENGINE SPECIFICATIONS

Description	English Specifications	Metric Specifications
Valves, valve springs and camshaft - Continued		
Valve spring preload—Intake and exhaust valves	50.2-64.3 lbs. @ 1.63 in.	22.8-29.2 kg @ 41.5mm
Valve spring squareness	0.079 in.	2.0mm
Valve stem diameter		
Exhaust valves	0.2737-0.2742 in.	6.950-6.965mm
Intake valves	0.2742-0.2748 in.	6.965-6.980mm
Valve stem end deflection		
Exhaust valves	0.007 in.	0.18mm
Intake valves	0.005 in.	0.14mm
Rocker arm shaft and rocker arms		
Rocker arm inside diameter	0.629-0.630 in.	16.000-16.018mm
Rocker shaft outside diameter	0.628-0.629 in.	15.973-15.988mm
Rocker shaft run-out	0.004 in.	0.12mm
Rocker shaft-to-arm clearance	0.0017-0.0035 in.	0.045-0.09mm
Engine block		
Cylinder bore out-of-round and taper	0.0039 in.	0.10mm
Cylinder bore-to-piston clearance	0.0008-0.0015 in.	0.02-0.04mm
Engine block-to-cylinder head surface warpage	0.0012-0.0024 in.	0.03-0.06mm
Standard cylinder bore	2.9134-2.9193 in.	74.00-74.15mm
Pistons		
Piston pin diameter	0.6691-0.6693 in.	16.995-17.000mm
Piston ring groove width		
Oil ring	0.1106-0.1114 in.	2.81-2.83mm
Second compression ring	0.0594-0.0602 in.	1.51-1.53mm
Top compression ring	0.0480-0.0488 in.	1.22-1.24mm
Standard piston diameter	2.9122-2.9129 in.	73.970-73.990mm
Piston rings		
End-gap		
Oil ring	0.0079-0.0708 in.	0.20-1.8mm
Second compression ring	0.0079-0.0275 in.	0.20-0.70mm
Top compression ring	0.0079-0.0275 in.	0.20-0.70mm
Side clearance		
Second compression ring	0.008-0.0039 in.	0.02-0.10mm
Top compression ring	0.0012-0.0047 in.	0.03-0.12mm
Thickness		
Oil ring	0.0177 in.	0.45mm
Second compression ring	0.0578-0.0586 in.	1.47-1.49mm
Top compression ring	0.0461-0.0468 in.	1.17-1.19mm
Crankshaft and connecting rods		
Bearing-to-journal clearance (oil clearance)	0.0008-0.0023 in.	0.020-0.060mm
Connecting rod bend	0.0020 in.	0.05mm
Connecting rod big end side clearance	0.0039-0.0137 in.	0.10-0.35mm
Connecting rod journal diameter	1.6529-1.6535 in.	41.982-42.000mm
Connecting rod journal out-of-round and taper	0.0004 in.	0.01mm
Connecting rod journal-to-connecting rod clearance	0.0012-0.0031 in.	0.030-0.080mm
Connecting rod small end bore inside diameter	0.6680-0.6684 in.	16.968-16.979mm
Connecting rod twist	0.0039 in.	0.10mm
Crankshaft journal diameter	1.7710-1.7716 in.	44.982-45.000mm
Crankshaft journal out-of-round and taper	0.0004 in.	0.01mm
Crankshaft run-out ③	0.0023 in.	0.06mm
Crankshaft thrust play	0.0044-0.0149 in.	0.11-0.38mm
Flywheel run-out	0.0078 in.	0.2mm
Oil Pump		
Oil pump rotor side clearance	0.0059 in.	0.15mm
Outer rotor-to-oil pump case clearance	0.0122 in.	0.310mm

① Except for 1989 Sidekick models, which was 8.7:1.

② Specification at cranking speed (400 rpm).

③ Measured at the center of the crankshaft.

1.6L (1590cc) 8-VALVE ENGINE SPECIFICATIONS

Description	English Specifications	Metric Specifications
Type	Single Overhead Camshaft (SOHC)	
Displacement	97 cu. in.	1.6L (1590cc)
Number of Cylinders	4	
Bore	2.95 in.	74.9mm
Stroke	3.54 in.	89.9mm
Compression ratio	8.9:1	
Compression pressure	170-199 psi ①	1200-1400 kPa ①
Allowable variation between cylinders	14.2 psi ①	100 kPa ①
Valve lash (clearance)		
Cold engine		
Intake valve	0.0051-0.0067 in.	0.13-0.17mm
Exhaust valve	0.0063-0.0079 in.	0.16-0.20mm
Hot engine		
Intake valve	0.009-0.011 in.	0.23-0.27mm
Exhaust valve	0.0102-0.0118 in.	0.26-0.30mm
Cylinder head		
Camshaft journal bore inside diameter		
Journal No. 1 ②	1.7716-1.7723 in.	45.000-45.016mm
Journal No. 2	1.7638-1.7644 in.	44.800-44.816mm
Journal No. 3	1.7560-1.7565 in.	44.600-44.616mm
Journal No. 4	1.7480-1.7486 in.	44.400-44.416mm
Journal No. 5	1.7402-1.7407 in.	44.200-44.216mm
Cylinder head-to-engine block surface warpage	0.002 in.	0.05mm
Cylinder head-to-intake and exhaust manifold surface warpage	0.004 in.	0.10mm
Valve seat angle—Intake and exhaust valves ③	15° – 45° – 60°	
Valve seat width—Intake and exhaust valves	0.0512-0.0590 in.	1.3-1.5mm
Valves, valve springs and camshaft		
Cam height (base circle + lift)		
Exhaust lobes	1.4724-1.4763 in.	37.400-37.501mm
Intake lobes	1.4724-1.4763 in.	37.400-37.536mm
Camshaft journal outside diameter		
Journal No. 1 ②	1.7687-1.7697 in.	44.925-44.950mm
Journal No. 2	1.7609-1.7618 in.	44.725-44.750mm
Journal No. 3	1.7530-1.7539 in.	44.525-44.550mm
Journal No. 4	1.7451-1.7460 in.	44.325-44.350mm
Journal No. 5	1.7402-1.7407 in.	44.125-44.150mm
Camshaft run-out	0.0039 in.	0.10mm
Camshaft-to-journal clearance	0.0020-0.0059 in.	0.050-0.150mm
Contact seat width—Intake and exhaust valves	0.0512-0.0590 in.	1.3-1.5mm
Stock allowance of valve stem end face	0.019 in.	0.5mm
Valve guide inside diameter—Intake and exhaust valves	0.2756-0.2761 in.	7.000-7.015mm
Valve guide protrusion—Intake and exhaust valves	0.55 in.	14mm
Valve guide-to-valve stem clearance		
Exhaust valves	0.0014-0.0035 in.	0.035-0.090mm
Intake valves	0.0008-0.0027 in.	0.020-0.070mm

90883C07

1.6L (1590cc) 8-VALVE ENGINE SPECIFICATIONS

Description	English Specifications	Metric Specifications
Valves, valve springs and camshaft - Continued		
Valve head margin		
Exhaust valves	0.027-0.039 in.	0.7-1.0mm
Intake valves	0.023-0.039 in.	0.6-1.0mm
Valve head radial run-out	0.003 in.	0.08mm
Valve spring free length	1.9094-1.9866 in.	48.50-50.46mm
Valve spring preload—Intake and exhaust valves	50.2-64.3 lbs. @ 1.63 in.	22.8-29.2 kg @ 41.5mm
Valve spring squareness	0.079 in.	2.0mm
Valve stem diameter		
Exhaust valves	0.2737-0.2742 in.	6.950-6.965mm
Intake valves	0.2742-0.2748 in.	6.965-6.980mm
Exhaust valves	0.007 in.	0.18mm
Intake valves	0.005 in.	0.14mm
Valve stem end deflection		
Rocker arm shaft and rocker arms		
Rocker arm inside diameter	0.629-0.630 in.	16.000-16.018mm
Rocker arm shaft outside diameter	0.628-0.629 in.	15.973-15.988mm
Rocker arm shaft run-out	0.004 in.	0.12mm
Rocker arm shaft-to-arm clearance	0.0005-0.0035 in.	0.012-0.090mm
Oil pump		
Oil pressure at 4000 rpm	46.9-61.1 psi	330-430 kPa
Oil pump outer rotor-to-case clearance	0.0122 in.	0.310mm
Oil pump rotor side clearance	0.0059 in.	0.15mm
Engine block		
Cylinder bore out-of-round and taper	0.0039 in.	0.10mm
Cylinder bore-to-piston clearance	0.0008-0.0015 in.	0.02-0.04mm
Engine block-to-cylinder head surface warpage	0.002 in.	0.05mm
Standard cylinder bore diameter limit	2.9586 in.	75.15mm
Pistons		
Piston pin diameter	0.7478-0.7480 in.	18.995-19.000mm
Standard piston diameter	2.9516-2.9524 in.	74.970-74.990mm
Piston rings		
End-gap		
Oil ring	0.0079-0.0708 in.	0.20-1.80mm
Second compression ring	0.0079-0.0275 in.	0.20-0.70mm
Top compression ring	0.0079-0.0275 in.	0.20-0.70mm
Side clearance		
Second compression ring	0.0008-0.0023 in.	0.02-0.06mm
Top compression ring	0.0012-0.0027 in.	0.03-0.07mm
Crankshaft and connecting rods		
Connecting rod bearing-to-journal clearance (oil clearance)	0.0008-0.0031 in.	0.020-0.080mm
Connecting rod bend	0.0020 in.	0.05mm
Connecting rod big end side clearance	0.0039-0.0137 in.	0.10-0.35mm
Connecting rod journal diameter	1.7316-1.7323 in.	43.982-44.000mm
Connecting rod journal out-of-round and taper	0.0004 in.	0.01mm
Connecting rod journal-to-connecting rod clearance	0.0008-0.0031 in.	0.020-0.080mm
Connecting rod small end bore inside diameter	0.7481-0.7484 in.	19.003-19.011mm
Connecting rod twist	0.0039 in.	0.10mm
Crankshaft bearing-to-journal clearance (oil clearance)	0.0008-0.0023 in.	0.020-0.060mm
Crankshaft journal out-of-round and taper	0.0004 in.	0.01mm
Crankshaft run-out	0.0023 in.	0.06mm
Crankshaft thrust bearing thickness	0.0984 in.	2.5mm
Crankshaft thrust play	0.0044-0.0149 in.	0.11-0.38mm
Flywheel run-out	0.0078 in.	0.2mm

① Specification at cranking speed (400 rpm).
② Starting with the camshaft end closest to the front of the vehicle.
③ The valve seats should be ground with a three-angle valve job.

90883C08

1.6L (1590cc) 16-VALVE ENGINE SPECIFICATIONS

Description	English Specifications	Metric Specifications
Type	Single Overhead Camshaft (SOHC)	
Displacement	97 cu. in.	1.6L (1590cc)
Number of Cylinders	4	
Bore	2.95 in.	74.9mm
Stroke	3.54 in.	89.9mm
Compression ratio	9.5:1	
Compression pressure ①	170-199 psi	1200-1400 kPa
Allowable variation between cylinders ①	14.2 psi	100 kPa
Valve lash (clearance)		
Cold engine	0.0051-0.0067 in.	0.13-0.17mm
Hot engine	0.007-0.008 in.	0.17-0.21mm
Cylinder head		
Camshaft journal bore inside diameter	1.1024-1.1031 in.	28.000-28.021mm
Cylinder head-to-engine block surface warpage	0.002 in.	0.05mm
Cylinder head-to-intake and exhaust manifold surface warpage	0.004 in.	0.10mm
Valve seat angle—Intake and exhaust valves ②	15° – 45°	
Valve seat width—Intake and exhaust valves	0.0433-0.0512 in.	1.1-1.3mm
Valves, valve springs and camshaft		
Cam height (base circle + lift)		
Exhaust lobes	1.4275-1.4376 in.	36.256-36.516mm
Intake lobes	1.4202-1.4303 in.	36.071-36.331mm
Camshaft journal outside diameter	1.1000-1.1008 in.	27.939-27.960mm
Camshaft run-out	0.0039 in.	0.10mm
Camshaft-to-journal clearance	0.0016-0.0047 in.	0.040-0.120mm
Contact seat width—Intake and exhaust valves	0.0433-0.0512 in.	1.1-1.3mm
Valve guide inside diameter—Intake and exhaust valves	0.2166-0.2170 in.	5.500-5.512mm
Valve guide protrusion—Intake and exhaust valves	0.45 in.	11.5mm
Valve guide-to-valve stem clearance		
Exhaust valves	0.0018-0.0035 in.	0.045-0.090mm
Intake valves	0.0008-0.0027 in.	0.020-0.070mm
Valve head margin		
Exhaust valves	0.027-0.047 in.	0.7-1.2mm
Intake valves	0.024-0.047 in.	0.6-1.2mm
Valve spring free length	1.4043-1.4500 in.	35.67-36.83mm
Valve spring preload—Intake and exhaust valves	20.5-27.5 lbs. @ 1.24 in.	9.3-12.5 kg @ 31.5mm
Valve spring squareness	0.079 in.	2.0mm
Valve stem diameter		
Exhaust valves	0.2142-0.2148 in.	5.440-5.455mm
Intake valves	0.2152-0.2157 in.	5.465-5.480mm
Valve stem end deflection		
Exhaust valves	0.007 in.	0.18mm
Intake valves	0.005 in.	0.14mm

90883C10

1.6L (1590cc) 16-VALVE ENGINE SPECIFICATIONS

Description	English Specifications	Metric Specifications
Rocker arm shaft and rocker arms		
Rocker arm inside diameter	0.629-0.630 in.	16.000-16.018mm
Rocker arm shaft outside diameter	0.628-0.629 in.	15.973-15.988mm
Rocker arm shaft run-out	0.008 in.	0.20mm
Rocker arm shaft-to-arm clearance	0.0001-0.0035 in.	0.001-0.090mm
Oil pump		
Oil pressure at 4000 rpm	46.9-61.1 psi	330-430 kPa
Oil pump outer rotor-to-case clearance	0.0122 in.	0.310mm
Oil pump rotor side clearance	0.0059 in.	0.15mm
Engine block		
Cylinder bore out-of-round and taper	0.0039 in.	0.10mm
Cylinder bore-to-piston clearance	0.0008-0.0015 in.	0.02-0.04mm
Engine block-to-cylinder head surface warpage	0.002 in.	0.05mm
Standard cylinder bore diameter limit	2.9586 in.	75.15mm
Pistons		
Piston pin diameter	0.7478-0.7480 in.	18.995-19.000mm
Piston pin-to-connecting rod clearance	0.0001-0.0020 in.	0.003-0.050mm
Standard piston diameter	2.9516-2.9524 in.	74.970-74.990mm
Piston rings		
End-gap		
Top compression ring	0.0079-0.0669 in.	0.20-1.70mm
Second compression ring	0.0079-0.0275 in.	0.20-0.70mm
Oil ring	0.0079-0.0275 in.	0.20-0.70mm
Side clearance		
Second compression ring	0.0008-0.0023 in.	0.02-0.06mm
Top compression ring	0.0012-0.0027 in.	0.03-0.07mm
Crankshaft and connecting rods		
Connecting rod bearing-to-journal clearance (oil clearance)	0.0008-0.0031 in.	0.020-0.080mm
Connecting rod bend	0.0020 in.	0.05mm
Connecting rod big end side clearance	0.0039-0.0137 in.	0.10-0.35mm
Connecting rod journal diameter	1.7316-1.7323 in.	43.982-44.000mm
Connecting rod journal out-of-round and taper	0.0004 in.	0.01mm
Connecting rod small end bore inside diameter	0.7482-0.7486 in.	19.003-19.011mm
Connecting rod twist	0.0039 in.	0.10mm
Crankshaft bearing-to-journal clearance (oil clearance)	0.0008-0.0023 in.	0.020-0.060mm
Crankshaft journal out-of-round and taper	0.0004 in.	0.01mm
Crankshaft run-out	0.0023 in.	0.06mm
Crankshaft thrust bearing thickness	0.0984 in.	2.5mm
Crankshaft thrust play	0.0044-0.0149 in.	0.11-0.38mm
Flywheel run-out	0.0078 in.	0.2mm

① Specification at cranking speed (400 rpm).
② The valve seats should be ground with a two-angle valve job.

90883C11

1.8L (1843cc) ENGINE SPECIFICATIONS

Description	English Specifications	Metric Specifications
Type	Double Overhead Camshaft (DOHC)	
Displacement	112.5 cu. in.	1.8L (1843cc)
Number of Cylinders	4	
Bore	3.31 in.	84.07mm
Stroke	3.27 in.	83.06mm
Compression ratio	9.8:1	
Compression pressure ①	170-199 psi	1200-1400 kPa
Allowable variation between cylinders ①	14.2 psi	100 kPa
Cylinder head		
Camshaft journal bore inside diameter	1.0236-1.0249 in.	26.000-26.033mm
Cylinder head bore-to-lash adjuster clearance	0.0010-0.0059 in.	0.025-0.150mm
Cylinder head-to-engine block surface warpage	0.002 in.	0.05mm
Cylinder head-to-intake and exhaust manifold surface warpage	0.004 in.	0.10mm
Hydraulic lash adjuster cylinder head bore inside diameter	1.2205-1.2214 in.	31.000-31.025mm
Hydraulic lash adjuster outside diameter	1.2189-1.2194 in.	30.959-30.975mm
Valve seat angle		
Exhaust valves ②	15° – 45°	
Intake valves ③	15° – 45° – 60°	
Valve seat width—intake and exhaust valves	0.0433-0.0512 in.	1.1-1.3mm
Valves, valve springs and camshaft		
Cam height (base circle + lift)		
Exhaust lobes	1.5639-1.5780 in.	39.722-40.082mm
Intake lobes	1.5838-1.5917 in.	40.228-40.588mm
Camshaft journal oil clearance	0.0008-0.0047 in.	0.020-0.120mm
Camshaft journal outside diameter	1.0220-1.0228 in.	25.959-25.980mm
Camshaft run-out	0.0039 in.	0.10mm
Contact seat width—intake and exhaust valves	0.0433-0.0512 in.	1.1-1.3mm
Valve guide inside diameter—intake and exhaust valves	0.2362-0.2366 in.	6.000-6.012mm
Valve guide protrusion—intake and exhaust valves	0.53 in.	13.5mm
Valve guide-to-valve stem clearance		
Exhaust valves	0.0018-0.0035 in.	0.045-0.090mm
Intake valves	0.0008-0.0027 in.	0.020-0.070mm
Valve head margin		
Exhaust valves	0.028-0.047 in.	0.7-1.2mm
Intake valves	0.024-0.039 in.	0.6-1.0mm
Valve head radial run-out	0.003 in.	0.08mm
Valve spring free length	1.6339-1.6791 in.	41.50-42.65mm
Valve spring preload—intake and exhaust valves	46.7-56.7 lbs. @ 1.28 in.	21.2-25.7 kg @ 32.6mm
Valve spring squareness	0.079 in.	2.0mm
Valve stem diameter		
Exhaust valves	0.2339-0.2344 in.	5.940-5.955mm
Intake valves	0.2348-0.2354 in.	5.965-5.980mm
Engine block		
Cylinder bore out-of-round and taper	0.0039 in.	0.10mm
Cylinder bore-to-piston clearance ④	0.0008-0.0015 in.	0.02-0.04mm
Engine block-to-cylinder head surface warpage	0.0024 in.	0.06mm
Standard cylinder bore inside diameter		
Identification mark: blue ④	3.3071-3.3074 in.	84.00-84.01mm
Identification mark: red ④	3.3075-3.3078 in.	84.01-84.02mm

90883C12

1.8L (1843cc) ENGINE SPECIFICATIONS

Description	English Specifications	Metric Specifications
Pistons		
Piston pin diameter	0.8267–0.8268 in.	20.997–21.000mm
Standard piston diameter		
Identification No. 1 ④	3.3063–3.3066 in.	83.980–83.990mm
Identification No. 2 ④	3.3059–3.3062 in.	83.97–83.98mm
Piston rings		
End-gap		
Oil ring	0.0079–0.0708 in.	0.20–1.80mm
Second compression ring	0.0138–0.0275 in.	0.35–0.70mm
Top compression ring	0.0079–0.0275 in.	0.20–0.70mm
Side clearance		
Oil ring	0.0023–0.0059 in.	0.06–0.15mm
Second compression ring	0.0008–0.0023 in.	0.02–0.06mm
Top compression ring	0.0012–0.0027 in.	0.03–0.07mm
Crankshaft and connecting rods		
Connecting rod bearing-to-journal clearance (oil clearance)	0.0018–0.0031 in.	0.045–0.080mm
Connecting rod bend	0.0020 in.	0.05mm
Connecting rod big end side clearance	0.0099–0.0157 in.	0.25–0.40mm
Connecting rod journal diameter	1.9678–1.9685 in.	49.982–50.000mm
Connecting rod journal out-of-round and taper	0.0004 in.	0.01mm
Connecting rod small end bore inside diameter	0.8269–0.8272 in.	21.003–21.011mm
Connecting rod small end-to-piston pin clearance	0.0001–0.0005 in.	0.003–0.014mm
Connecting rod twist	0.0039 in.	0.10mm
Crankshaft bearing-to-journal clearance (oil clearance)	0.0010–0.0023 in.	0.026–0.060mm
Crankshaft journal out-of-round and taper	0.0004 in.	0.01mm
Crankshaft run-out	0.0023 in.	0.06mm
Crankshaft thrust bearing thickness	0.0984 in.	2.5mm
Crankshaft thrust play	0.0039–0.0165 in.	0.10–0.42mm
Flywheel run-out	0.0078 in.	0.2mm

① Specification at cranking speed (250–400 rpm).
② The exhaust valve seat should be ground with a two-angle valve job.
③ The intake valve seat should be ground with a three-angle valve job.
④ The red marked cylinder should be paired with a piston marked with a "1" for proper clearance.
   The blue marked cylinder should be paired with a piston marked with a "2" for proper clearance.

90883C13

ENGINE MECHANICAL

Engine

REMOVAL & INSTALLATION

→If your vehicle is equipped with air conditioning, refer to Section 1 for information regarding the implications of servicing your A/C system yourself. Only an MVAC-trained, EPA-certified automotive technician should service the A/C system or its components.

In the process of removing the engine, you will come across a number of steps which call for the removal of a separate component or system, such as "disconnect the exhaust system" or "remove the radiator." In most instances, a detailed removal procedure can be found elsewhere in this manual.

It is virtually impossible to list each individual wire and hose which must be disconnected, simply because so many different model and engine combinations have been manufactured. Careful observation and common sense are the best possible approaches to any repair procedure.

Removal and installation of the engine can be made easier if you follow these basic points:

• If you have to drain any of the fluids, use a suitable container.
• Always tag any wires or hoses and, if possible, the components they came from before disconnecting them.
• Because there are so many bolts and fasteners involved, store and label the retainers from components separately in muffin pans, jars or coffee cans. This will prevent confusion during installation.
• After unbolting the transmission, always make sure it is properly supported.
• If it is necessary to disconnect the air conditioning system, have this service performed by a qualified technician using a recovery/recycling station. If the system does not have to be disconnected, unbolt the compressor and position it aside.
• When unbolting the engine mounts, always make sure the engine is properly supported. When removing the engine, make sure that any lifting devices are properly attached to the engine. It is recommended that if your engine is supplied with lifting hooks, your lifting apparatus be attached to them.
• Lift the engine from its compartment slowly, checking that no hoses, wires or other components are still connected.
• After the engine is clear of the compartment, place it on an engine stand or workbench.
• After the engine has been removed, you can perform a partial or full teardown of the engine using the procedures outlined in this manual.

1.3L Engine

→The engine and transmission are removed together. Once removed from the vehicle, they can be separated for further servicing.

1. Disconnect the negative, then the positive battery cables.
2. Remove the hood.

❊❊ CAUTION

When draining engine coolant, keep in mind that cats and dogs are attracted to ethylene glycol antifreeze and could drink any that is left in an uncovered container or in puddles on the ground. This will prove fatal in sufficient quantities. Always drain coolant into a sealable container. Coolant should be reused unless it is contaminated or is several years old.

❊❊ CAUTION

The EPA warns that prolonged contact with used engine oil may cause a number of skin disorders, including cancer! You should make every effort to minimize your exposure to used engine oil.

Protective gloves should be worn when changing the oil. Wash your hands and any other exposed skin areas as soon as possible after exposure to used engine oil. Soap and water, or waterless hand cleaner should be used.

3. From beneath the vehicle, drain the engine cooling system, the engine oil and the transmission fluid.
4. Label and detach all undervehicle wiring attached to the engine, transmission and related components, then position the wiring harnesses aside.
5. If applicable, label and disconnect any lower vacuum hoses which will interfere with engine and transmission removal.
6. Disconnect any lower cooling system hoses from the engine.
7. Remove the exhaust manifold-to-exhaust pipe fasteners and separate the two components.
8. Disconnect the clutch cable from any mounting brackets and the clutch release lever.
9. Remove the front and rear driveshafts.
10. From inside the vehicle, remove the gearshift lever from the transmission (refer to Section 7).
11. From above the engine compartment, remove the air cleaner (carbureted engines) or the air inlet tube (fuel injected engines).
12. Label and detach all wiring attached to the engine, transmission and related components, then position the wiring harnesses aside.
13. Label and disconnect all vacuum hoses which will interfere with engine and transmission removal.
14. Release fuel system pressure (as described in Section 5), then detach all fuel lines from the engine.
15. Disconnect the accelerator cable from the carburetor or throttle body.
16. Disconnect all cooling system hoses from the engine.
17. Remove the cooling fan, cooling fan clutch, fan shroud and radiator from the vehicle for added clearance.
18. From above the engine compartment, use a large engine hoist and hoist chain attached to the two engine lifting eye hooks (one on the intake manifold side of the engine, the other on the exhaust manifold side of the engine) to support the weight of the engine.
19. From under the vehicle, remove the exhaust center pipe mounting bracket and four transmission mounting bolts.
20. Remove the support bar (connected to the chassis) from beneath the transmission.
21. From above the vehicle, remove the left- and right-hand engine mount attaching fasteners.
22. Slowly and carefully lift the engine and transmission up and out of the engine compartment. When lifting the engine, double check that all wires, hoses and cables have been disconnected and will not hinder engine and transmission removal.
23. Set the engine and transmission on the ground, then remove the clutch lower plate. Remove the transmission-to-engine mounting bolts and separate the transmission from the engine.
24. If necessary, install the engine on an engine work stand.
25. Installation is the reverse of the removal procedure. During installation, be sure to keep the following points in mind:
• When installing the engine and transmission into the engine compartment, do not remove the engine hoist support from the assembly until all of the mount fasteners are fully tightened.
• Tighten the transmission-to-engine bolts to 16–25 ft. lbs. (22–35 Nm), the engine mount-to-frame bolts to 29–43 ft. lbs. (40–60 Nm), the engine mount-to-engine bolts to 37–43 ft. lbs. (50–60 Nm), the engine mounting nuts to 29–37 ft. lbs. (40–50 Nm), and the driveshaft flange bolts and nuts to 17–21 ft. lbs. (23–30 Nm).
• Be sure to adjust the accelerator cable play (Section 5) and the clutch cable play (Section 7).
• If necessary, the emission control label on the underside of the vehicle's hood can be referred to for proper vacuum hose routing.

❋❋ WARNING

Before starting the engine, BE SURE to fill the engine with the proper amount and type of oil and coolant, and the transmission with the proper type of clean lubricant. Otherwise severe, and costly, engine or transmission damage will be the result.

- Be sure to properly tension the water pump drive belt.
- Before starting the engine, double-check the connection and routing of all wires, hoses and cables one last time to prevent avoidable component damage.
- After the engine is started, check for oil, coolant and fuel leaks; repair them, if necessary. Also, listen for any strange engine or transmission sounds, which may indicate unseen internal damage.

1.6L and 1.8L Engines

▶ See Figures 1 thru 6

➡The engine is separated from the transmission in the vehicle and removed by itself.

1. Properly relieve fuel system pressure as described in Section 5.
2. Disconnect the negative, then the positive battery cables.
3. Remove the hood.

❋❋ CAUTION

When draining engine coolant, keep in mind that cats and dogs are attracted to ethylene glycol antifreeze and could drink any that is left in an uncovered container or in puddles on the ground. This will prove fatal in sufficient quantities. Always drain coolant into a sealable container. Coolant should be reused unless it is contaminated or is several years old.

❋❋ CAUTION

The EPA warns that prolonged contact with used engine oil may cause a number of skin disorders, including cancer! You should make every effort to minimize your exposure to used engine oil. Protective gloves should be worn when changing the oil. Wash your hands and any other exposed skin areas as soon as possible after exposure to used engine oil. Soap and water, or waterless hand cleaner should be used.

4. Drain the engine cooling system and the engine oil.
5. Remove the cooling fan, cooling fan clutch, fan shroud and radiator from the vehicle for added clearance.
6. Disconnect the accelerator and, if equipped, transmission kick-down cable from the carburetor or throttle body.
7. If equipped, remove the strut tower reinforcement bar.
8. Remove the air inlet hose and upper case from the throttle body.
9. On models equipped with automatic transmissions, remove the engine oil level gauge and transmission fluid level gauge guide.

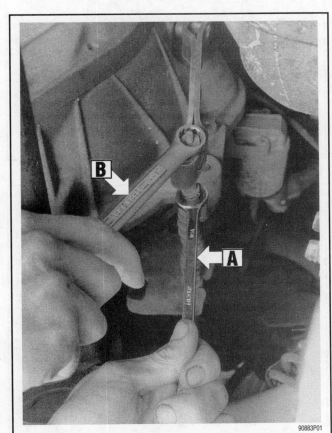

To detach the clutch cable, hold it with one wrench (A) and loosen the end nut with another wrench (B) . . .

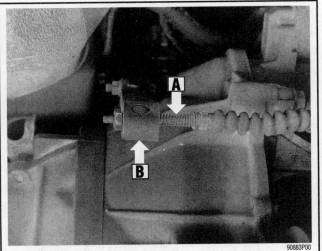

Before removing the engine, the clutch cable (A) must be disconnected from the clutch release lever (B)

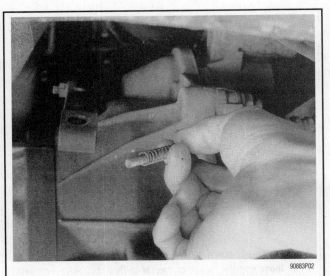

. . . then pull the cable out of the clutch release lever

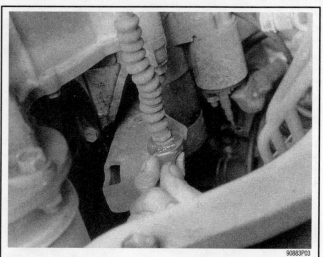

Separate the clutch cable from its mounting bracket by loosening the holding nut . . .

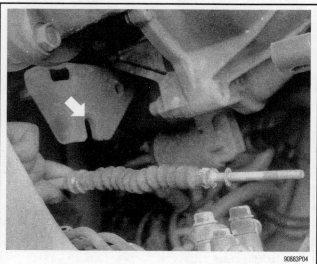

. . . and sliding it out of the mounting groove (arrow)

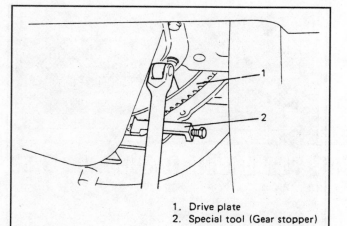

1. Drive plate
2. Special tool (Gear stopper)

Fig. 1 A specific tool can be used to hold the flywheel steady when loosening the torque converter-to-flywheel bolts—models equipped with automatic transmissions

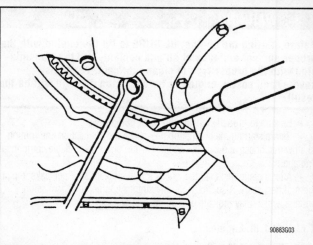

Fig. 2 If a special tool is not readily available, you can use a large prytool to hold the teeth of the flywheel, which will keep the crankshaft from turning

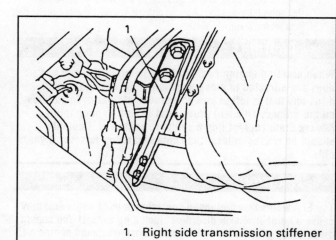

1. Right side transmission stiffener

Fig. 3 Before separating the engine from the transmission, the right side transmission support brace (stiffener) must be removed

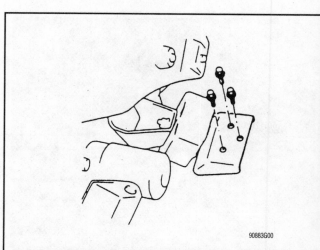

Fig. 4 For 1.6L engines, remove the engine mount-to-chassis bolts from both sides of the engine, before lifting the engine on the hoist

10. Label and detach all wiring attached to the engine and related components (which will inhibit engine removal), then position the wiring harnesses aside. Be sure to disconnect all wiring, even wiring under the vehicle.

11. Label and disconnect all vacuum and cooling system hoses which will interfere with engine removal.

12. Apply the parking brake, block the rear wheels, then raise and safely support the front of the vehicle securely on jackstands.

13. If equipped, remove the front differential housing from the vehicle.

14. Remove the No. 1 exhaust pipe from the exhaust manifold and the No. 2 exhaust pipe.

15. For 1.6L engines, detach the clutch cable from the clutch release lever, then remove the clutch cable mount from the engine block.

16. If applicable, remove the automatic transmission fluid line clamps from the right-hand side transmission support brace, then remove the support brace.

17. Remove the lower transmission inspection cover.

18. For models equipped with automatic transmissions, have an assistant hold the center crankshaft pulley bolt with a large breaker bar while you remove the torque converter-to-flywheel bolts through the lower transmission inspection cover access hole. If an assistant is not available, the crankshaft can be kept from rotating by installing a tool designed for this purpose, or by holding it steady with a large prytool on the flywheel teeth.

19. Lower the vehicle.

20. Remove the starter motor, then support the front edge of the transmission on a jackstand. Use a piece of wood between the jackstand and the transmission to avoid damaging the transmission housing.

✽✽ WARNING

Do not raise or support automatic transmissions from beneath the fluid pan; damage to the fluid pan may result.

21. If equipped, remove the power steering pump and/or A/C compressor and brackets, leaving the hoses attached. Suspend the power steering pump and/or A/C compressor with strong cord or wire from the side frame rail so that it does not leak.

22. Remove the transmission-to-engine block attaching bolts and nuts.

23. Attach the engine lifting hoist to the engine by means of a hoisting chain. The engine comes from the factory equipped with hoisting eye hooks (one on each side of the engine); use these hooks when removing the engine.

24. From above the vehicle, remove the left and right-hand engine-to-mount attaching fasteners.

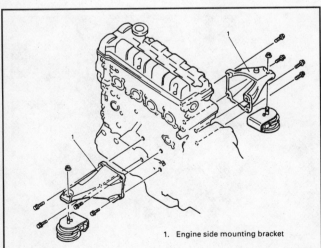

1. Engine side mounting bracket

90883G01

Fig. 5 The engine mounts used with 1.8L engines are attached to the engine brackets with only one nut per side

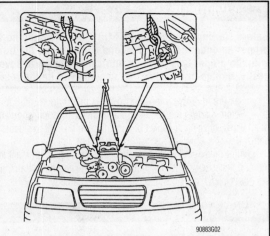

90883G02

Fig. 6 When lifting the engine out of the vehicle, be absolutely sure to attach the hoist chain to the two eye hooks (one on each side of the engine) to avoid damaging any engine components

25. Separate the engine from the transmission by pulling the engine forward. On models with manual transmissions, the engine must be pulled forward enough so that the transmission input shaft clears the clutch disc and pressure plate assembly.

26. Slowly and carefully lift the engine and transmission up and out of the engine compartment. When lifting the engine, double check that all wires, hoses and cables have been disconnected and will not hinder engine and transmission removal.

27. If necessary, install the engine on an engine workstand.

28. Installation is the reverse of the removal procedure. During installation, be sure to keep the following points in mind:

✽✽ WARNING

After lowering the engine into the engine compartment, slide the engine back until it is completely mated with the transmission. Failure to properly seat the engine on the transmission can lead to component damage when the attaching fasteners are tightened.

• When installing the engine into the engine compartment, do not remove the hoist support from the assembly until all of the mount fasteners are fully tightened.

• For 1.6L engines with 8-valve cylinder heads, tighten the transmission-to-engine bolts to 62 ft. lbs. (85 Nm), the engine mount nuts to 29–37 ft. lbs. (40–50 Nm), the engine mount (chassis side) bracket bolts to 37–43 ft. lbs. (50–60 Nm), the engine mount (engine side) bracket bolts to 36–43 ft. lbs. (50–60 Nm), the torque converter bolts to 37–43 ft. lbs. (50–60 Nm), and the No. 1 exhaust pipe nuts to 29–43 ft. lbs. (40–60 Nm).

• For 1.6L engines with 16-valve cylinder heads, tighten the engine-to-transmission nuts and bolts to 51–72 ft. lbs. (70–100 Nm), the torque converter bolts to 47 ft. lbs. (65 Nm), the exhaust pipe nuts and bolts to 37 ft. lbs. (50 Nm), the transmission support brace bolts to 37 ft. lbs. (50 Nm), and the engine mount bolts to 29–43 ft. lbs. (40–60 Nm).

• For 1.8L engines, tighten the transmission-to-engine bolts to 58 ft. lbs. (80 Nm), the engine-to-mount fasteners to 36 ft. lbs. (50 Nm), the torque converter-to-flywheel bolts to 47 ft. lbs. (65 Nm), the transmission support brace bolts to 36 ft. lbs. (50 Nm), and the No. 1 exhaust pipe fasteners to 36 ft. lbs. (50 Nm).

• When installing the power steering pump bracket, install the bolt which points toward the rear of the vehicle first, then the other two bolts.

• Be sure to adjust the accelerator cable play (Section 5) and the clutch cable or kickdown cable play (Section 7).

• If necessary, the emission control label on the underside of the vehicle's hood can be referred to for proper vacuum hose routing.

✷✷ WARNING

Before starting the engine, BE SURE to fill the engine with the proper amount and type of oil and coolant, and the transmission with the proper type of clean lubricant. Otherwise severe, and costly, engine or transmission damage will be the result.

- Be sure to properly tension the water pump drive belt.
- Before starting the engine, double-check the connection and routing of all wires, hoses and cables one last time to prevent avoidable component damage.
- After the engine is started, check for oil, coolant and fuel leaks; repair them, if necessary. Also, listen for any strange engine or transmission sounds, which may indicate unseen internal damage.

Rocker Arm (Valve) Cover

REMOVAL & INSTALLATION

1.3L and 1.6L 8-Valve Engines

▶ See Figure 7

1. Disconnect the negative battery cable.
2. If necessary for added clearance, remove the air inlet hose and air intake case (fuel-injected models) or air cleaner housing (carbureted engines).
3. Detach the PCV valve hose from the PC valve (mounted in the rocker arm cover).
4. Disengage the spark plug wires and the accelerator cable from their clips (mounted on the rocker arm cover).
5. Completely loosen the rocker cover hold-down bolts, then lift the cover up and off of the cylinder head.
6. Discard the old rocker arm cover gasket.

To install:

7. Clean the cylinder head and rocker arm cover mating surfaces of all dirt, grime, oil, etc.
8. Install a new gasket in the groove on the bottom of the rocker arm cover.
9. Position the rocker arm cover on the cylinder head, then install and tighten the hold-down bolts until snug.
10. Engage the spark plug wires and the accelerator cable in the holding clips.
11. Reattach the rubber hose to the PCV valve.
12. If necessary, install the air intake case, or air cleaner housing (as applicable), and the air inlet hose.
13. Connect the negative battery cable.

To remove the rocker arm cover, detach the air inlet hose from the air intake case . . .

. . . then loosen the air intake support bracket bolts . . .

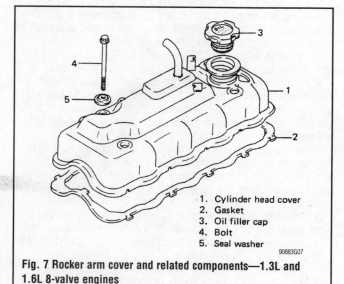

1. Cylinder head cover
2. Gasket
3. Oil filler cap
4. Bolt
5. Seal washer

90883G07

Fig. 7 Rocker arm cover and related components—1.3L and 1.6L 8-valve engines

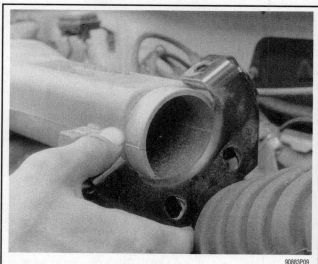

. . . and remove it from the engine

Detach the breather hose from the intake case by compressing the clamp and sliding it down the hose

90883P10

Detach the breather hose from the rocker arm cover . . .

90883P13

Remove the intake case hold-down bolts . . .

90883P11

. . . and disengage the spark plug wires from the routing clips

90883P14

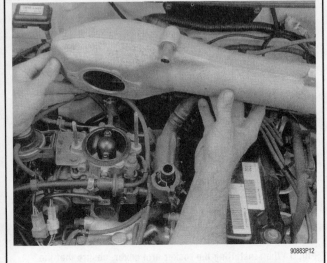

. . . and lift the intake case up and off of the throttle body

90883P12

Loosen the rocker arm cover hold-down bolts . . .

90883P15

. . . then remove the bolts, ensuring that the rubber seals are retained for later use

1.6L 16-Valve Engine

♦ **See Figures 8 and 9**

1. Disconnect the negative battery cable.
2. Remove the throttle body cover.
3. Detach the PCV valve hose from the PCV valve.
4. Disconnect the accelerator cable and the kickdown cable (3-speed automatic models) or the throttle cable (4-speed automatic models) from the throttle body.
5. Remove the air inlet tube and bracket.
6. Label and disengage the spark plug wires from the spark plugs.
7. Completely loosen the rocker cover hold-down bolts, then lift the cover up and off of the cylinder head.
8. Discard the old rocker arm cover gasket and O-rings.

To install:

9. Clean the cylinder head and rocker arm cover mating surfaces of all dirt, grime, oil, etc.
10. Install a new gasket in the groove on the bottom of the rocker arm cover. Also, install new O-rings to the spark plug holes in the rocker arm cover.

Lift the rocker arm cover off of the cylinder head

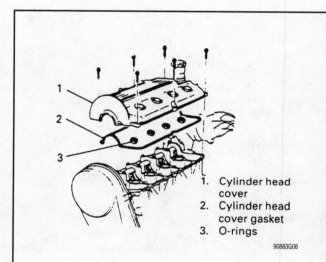

1. Cylinder head cover
2. Cylinder head cover gasket
3. O-rings

Fig. 8 Exploded view of the rocker arm cover mounting

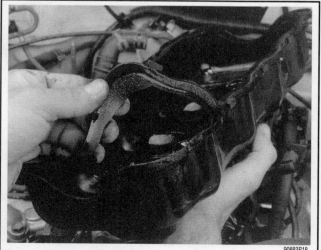

Be sure to discard the old gasket—a new one is necessary for installation

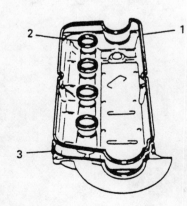

1. Cylinder head cover gasket
2. O-rings
3. Cylinder head cover

Fig. 9 When installing the rocker arm cover, ensure that the gasket and O-rings remain in position

➡When installing the rocker arm cover on the cylinder head, ensure that the gasket or O-rings do not become dislodged from the cover; this could lead to improper sealing and oil leakage.

11. Position the rocker arm cover on the cylinder head, then install and tighten the hold-down bolts until snug.
12. Engage the spark plug wires to their respective spark plugs.
13. Install the air intake tube and bracket.
14. Reattach the accelerator and kickdown, or throttle, cables to the throttle body. Be sure to adjust the play in all of the cables.
15. Reattach the rubber hose to the PCV valve.
16. Install the throttle cover.
17. Connect the negative battery cable.

1.8L Engine

◗ See Figures 10, 11 and 12

1. Disconnect the negative battery cable.
2. Remove the ignition coils.
3. Detach the accelerator cable from its mounting clip.
4. Remove the oil level gauge.
5. Disconnect the breather hose and PCV hose from the rocker arm cover.

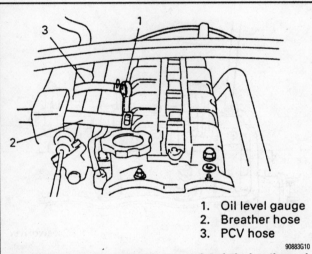

1. Oil level gauge
2. Breather hose
3. PCV hose

90883G10

Fig. 10 To remove the rocker arm cover, detach the breather and PCV hoses, and remove the oil level gauge

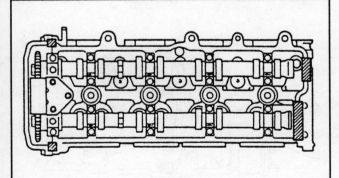

▨ : Area to apply sealant "A"

90883G11

Fig. 11 Before installing the rocker arm cover, apply sealant to the shaded areas for proper sealing

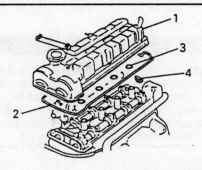

1. Cylinder head cover	4. Cylinder head
2. Cylinder head cover gasket	side seal
3. O-ring	

90883G12

Fig. 12 When positioning the rocker arm cover on the cylinder head, ensure that the gasket, side seal and O-rings do not become dislodged or malpositioned

6. Loosen the rocker arm cover hold-down nuts, then lift the cover up and off of the cylinder head.
7. Discard the old cover gasket and O-rings.

To install:
8. Clean the cylinder head and rocker arm cover mating surfaces of all dirt, grime, oil, etc.
9. Apply sealant (such as Suzuki Sealant 99000–31150) to the cylinder head surface, as shown in the accompanying illustration.
10. Install a new gasket in the groove on the bottom of the rocker arm cover. Also, install new O-rings to the spark plug holes in the rocker arm cover.
11. Install a new side seal in the cylinder head.

➡When installing the rocker arm cover on the cylinder head, ensure that the gasket or O-rings do not become dislodged from the cover; this could lead to improper sealing and oil leakage.

12. Position the rocker arm cover on the cylinder head, then install and tighten the hold-down nuts until snug.
13. Install the ignition coils and cover.
14. Install the oil level gauge.
15. Reattach the breather hose and the PCV hose to the rocker arm cover.
16. Engage the accelerator cable in the mounting clip, then connect the negative battery cable.

Rocker Arms/Shafts

REMOVAL & INSTALLATION

➡During these procedures, identify all components removed from the engine so that they may be reinstalled in their original positions. If discarding the old components so that new components can be installed, identifying the old items is not necessary.

1.3L and 1.6L 8-Valve Engines

◗ See Figures 13 thru 20

➡If your vehicle is equipped with air conditioning, refer to Section 1 for information regarding the implications of servicing your A/C system yourself. Only an MVAC-trained, EPA-certified automotive technician should service the A/C system or its components.

1. Disconnect the negative battery cable and drain the engine cooling system.

❋❋ CAUTION

When draining engine coolant, keep in mind that cats and dogs are attracted to ethylene glycol antifreeze and could drink any that is left in an uncovered container or in puddles on the ground. This will prove fatal in sufficient quantities. Always drain coolant into a sealable container. Coolant should be reused unless it is contaminated or is several years old.

2. Although not indicated by the manufacturer, it may be necessary on Samurai models (as it is on Sidekick models) to remove several components from the front of the vehicle for enough clearance to remove the rocker arm shafts. If this added clearance is necessary for rocker arm shaft removal, perform the following:

❋❋ CAUTION

Some models covered by this manual may be equipped with a Supplemental Restraint System (SRS), which uses an air bag. Whenever working near any of the SRS components, such as the impact sensors, the air bag module, steering column and instrument panel, refer to Section 6 for SRS precautions. Failure to heed all precautions may result in accidental air bag deployment, which could easily result in severe personal injury or death. Also, never attempt any electrical diagnosis or service to the SRS components and wiring; this work should only be performed by a qualified automotive technician.

a. If your vehicle is equipped with air conditioning, the manufacturer states that the compressor must be disconnected from the A/C hoses; refer to Section 1 before servicing any A/C components.
b. Remove the hood.
c. Remove the front grille.
d. Remove the hood lock from the front upper member, then remove the front upper member.
e. Remove the radiator cooling fan, shroud and radiator.
3. Loosen the water pump pulley mounting bolts, then remove the accessory drive belts and water pump pulley.
4. If equipped, remove the air intake case from the throttle body.
5. Remove the rocker arm cover.
6. Loosen all of the valve lash locknuts and adjusting screws so that there is no pressure exerted on the camshaft lobes.

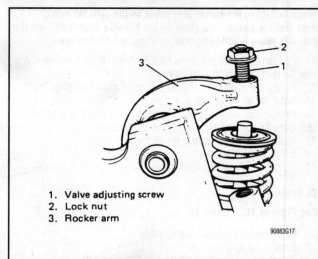

1. Valve adjusting screw
2. Lock nut
3. Rocker arm

90883G17

Fig. 14 . . . then loosen the rocker arm locknuts and adjusting screws to relieve any pressure from the camshaft lobes

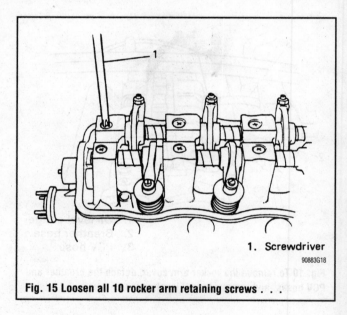

1. Screwdriver

90883G18

Fig. 15 Loosen all 10 rocker arm retaining screws . . .

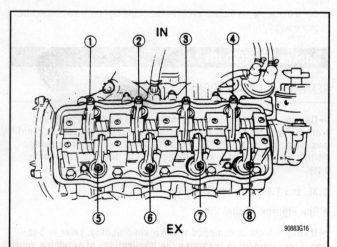

90883G16

Fig. 13 Before removing the rocker arm shafts, be sure to label the rocker arms as shown so that they can be reinstalled in their original positions . . .

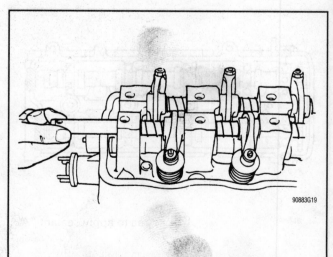

90883G19

Fig. 16 . . . then slowly slide the rocker arm shafts out of the cylinder head and remove each rocker arm one at a time

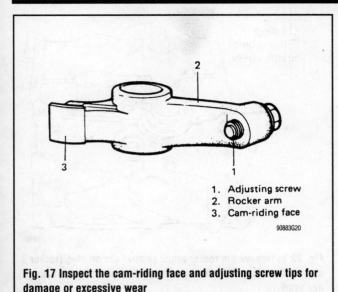

1. Adjusting screw
2. Rocker arm
3. Cam-riding face

90883G20

Fig. 17 Inspect the cam-riding face and adjusting screw tips for damage or excessive wear

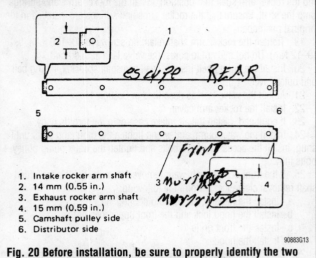

1. Intake rocker arm shaft
2. 14 mm (0.55 in.)
3. Exhaust rocker arm shaft
4. 15 mm (0.59 in.)
5. Camshaft pulley side
6. Distributor side

90883G13

Fig. 20 Before installation, be sure to properly identify the two rocker arm shafts, since they are not identical

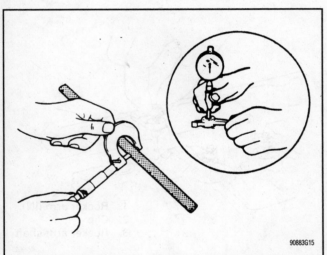

90883G15

Fig. 18 Use a micrometer and a bore gauge to measure and calculate the rocker arm-to-shaft clearance

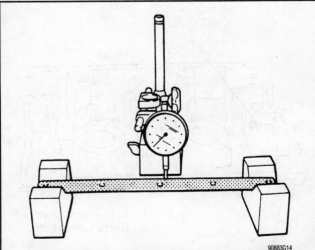

90883G14

Fig. 19 Position the rocker arm shaft on two wooden blocks equipped with V notches to inspect run-out

7. Remove the timing belt cover, timing belt, camshaft sprocket and inside timing belt cover from the engine.

8. Matchmark the rocker arms so that they can be reinstalled in their original positions.

9. Loosen the 10 rocker arm shaft securing screws, then slowly slide one of the rocker arm shafts out of the front of the cylinder head. While withdrawing the rocker arm shaft from the cylinder head, remove the rocker arms and springs. Set the rocker arms and springs aside in order.

10. Remove the other rocker arm shaft in the same manner.

11. Clean the rocker arms, shafts, springs and rocker arm shaft bores in the cylinder head.

To install:

12. Inspect the tip of the adjusting screw for excessive wear; if wear is evident, replace the adjusting screw.

13. Inspect the face of the rocker arm cam-riding surface for wear; if excessive wear is evident, replace the rocker arm.

14. Inspect the rocker arm-to-shaft clearance by using a micrometer to measure the outside diameter of the rocker arm shaft where the rocker arms ride on it. Use a bore gauge to measure the inside diameter of the rocker arm bore. Subtract the rocker arm bore inside diameter from the rocker arm shaft outside diameter to calculate the rocker arm-to-shaft clearance. Compare your findings with the values presented in the engine rebuilding specification charts at the end of this section. If your findings are not within the values in the charts, replace the rocker arm, shaft, or both.

15. Position the rocker arm shaft in two wooden blocks with V cutouts in them (refer to the accompanying illustration). Using a dial indicator, measure the amount of run-out at the center of the rocker arm shaft. If your measurement is not within the values presented in the engine rebuilding specifications chart.

16. Apply clean engine oil to the rocker arms and shafts.

➡ **The two rocker arm shafts are not identical. To distinguish between the two, inspect the stepped ends of the rocker arm shafts. The intake rocker arm shaft stepped end is 0.55 in. (14mm) wide and the exhaust side rocker arm shaft stepped end is 0.59 in. (15mm) wide. Refer to the accompanying illustration.**

17. Insert the intake side rocker arm shaft into the cylinder head bore so that the stepped end is toward the timing belt end of the engine, then slowly slide the rocker arm shaft into position, while installing the rocker arms and springs onto the shaft. Ensure that the rocker arms and springs are installed in their original positions.

18. Install the exhaust side rocker arm shaft in the cylinder head so that the stepped end faces the distributor end of the engine. While slowly slid-

ing the rocker arm shaft into position, install the rocker arms and springs onto the shaft. Ensure that the rocker arms and springs are installed in their original positions.

19. Tighten the rocker arm shaft retaining screws to 80–106 inch lbs. (9–12 Nm). Do not attempt to adjust the valve lash at this point.

20. Install the timing belt inside cover, camshaft sprocket, timing belt and outer cover.

21. Adjust the valve lash as described in Section 1.

22. Install the rocker arm cover.

23. If equipped, install the air intake case onto the throttle body.

24. Install the water pump pulley and tighten the mounting bolts until snug. Install the accessory drive belts and tighten the water pump pulley bolts fully.

25. If the front components were removed from the vehicle for added shaft removal clearance, perform the following:
   a. Install the radiator, shroud and cooling fan.
   b. Install the hood lock and the front upper member.
   c. Install the front grille.
   d. Install the hood.

26. Connect the negative battery cable and fill the engine cooling system.

27. If your vehicle is equipped with air conditioning, have the A/C compressor installed and your system evacuated and recharged by a qualified MVAC technician.

1.6L 16-Valve Engine

▶ **See Figures 21 thru 27**

1. Disconnect the negative battery cable.
2. Remove the camshaft from the cylinder head.
3. Matchmark the positions of the intake rocker arms so that they can be reinstalled in their original positions.
4. Remove the rocker arm shaft plug and timing belt inside cover from the cylinder head.

> ※※ **WARNING**

Be sure not to bend the rocker arm clip during removal.

5. Remove each intake rocker arm with its clip from the rocker arm shaft.
6. Matchmark the positions of the exhaust rocker arms so that they can be reinstalled in their original positions.
7. Remove the rocker arm shaft bolts, then slide the rocker arm shaft toward the rear of the engine until the O-ring is exposed. Remove the O-ring from the rocker arm shaft groove.

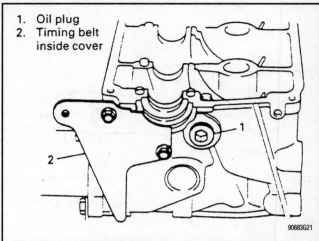

1. Oil plug
2. Timing belt inside cover

Fig. 22 To remove the rocker arms, remove the oil plug (rocker arm shaft plug) and the timing belt inside cover from the cylinder head . . .

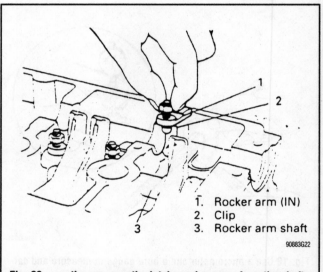

1. Rocker arm (IN)
2. Clip
3. Rocker arm shaft

Fig. 23 . . . then remove the intake rocker arms from the shaft

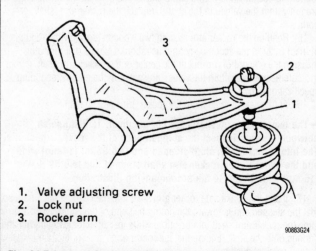

1. Valve adjusting screw
2. Lock nut
3. Rocker arm

Fig. 21 Prior to rocker arm removal, be sure to loosen the exhaust rocker arm locknut and adjusting screw

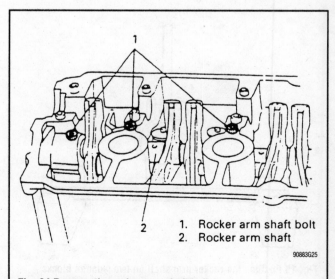

1. Rocker arm shaft bolt
2. Rocker arm shaft

Fig. 24 Remove the rocker arm shaft bolts . . .

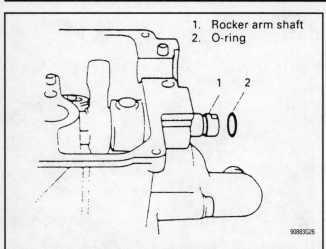

1. Rocker arm shaft
2. O-ring

90883G26

Fig. 25 . . . and slide the rocker arm shaft rearward until the O-ring and groove are exposed, then remove the O-ring and pull the shaft forward

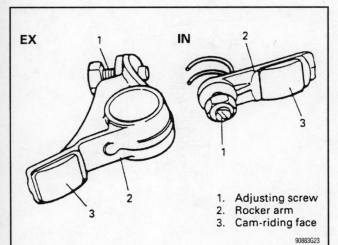

EX IN

1. Adjusting screw
2. Rocker arm
3. Cam-riding face

90883G23

Fig. 26 Inspect the cam-riding faces and adjusting screw tips of the rocker arms for damage or excessive wear

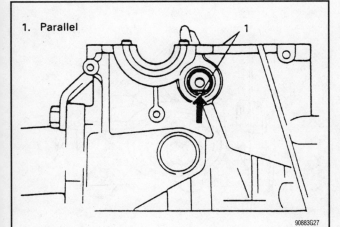

1. Parallel

90883G27

Fig. 27 After installing the rocker arm shaft, rotate it so that the flat on its end is positioned parallel with the cylinder head-to-engine block gasket mating surface

8. Remove the exhaust rocker arms by sliding the rocker arm shaft out of the front of the cylinder head.

9. Position the rocker arms and springs on a clean work surface in order so that they can be reinstalled in their original positions.

10. Clean the rocker arms, springs and rocker arm shaft.

To install:

11. Inspect the tip of the adjusting screw for excessive wear; if wear is evident, replace the adjusting screw.

12. Inspect the face of the rocker arm cam-riding surface for wear; if excessive wear is evident, replace the rocker arm.

13. Inspect the exhaust rocker arm-to-shaft clearance as follows:

    a. Use a micrometer to measure the outside diameter of the rocker arm shaft where the rocker arms ride on it. Use a bore gauge to measure the inside diameter of the rocker arm bore. Subtract the rocker arm bore inside diameter from the rocker arm shaft outside diameter to calculate the rocker arm-to-shaft clearance. Compare your findings with the values presented in the engine rebuilding specification charts at the end of this section. If your findings are not within the values in the charts, replace the rocker arm, shaft, or both.

14. Position the rocker arm shaft in two wooden blocks with V cutouts in them (refer to the accompanying illustration). Using a dial indicator, measure the amount of run-out at the center of the rocker arm shaft. If your measurement is not within the values presented in the engine rebuilding specifications chart.

15. Apply clean engine oil to the rocker arms and shafts.

➡**Ensure that the rocker arm is installed in the cylinder head so that the O-ring groove is toward the distributor end of the engine.**

16. Insert the rocker arm shaft into the cylinder head bore so that the O-ring groove end is toward the distributor end of the engine, while installing the exhaust rocker arms and springs onto the shaft. Ensure that the rocker arms and springs are installed in their original positions.

17. Push the rocker arm out of the back side of the cylinder head until the O-ring groove is exposed. Install a new O-ring into the groove, then slide the rocker arm shaft back into the cylinder head so that both ends are flush with the head. Rotate the shaft so that the flat surface on its front end faces down and is parallel with the cylinder head-to-engine block gasket surface.

18. Install and tighten the rocker arm shaft retaining screws to 97 inch lbs. (11 Nm). Do not attempt to adjust the valve lash at this point.

19. Fill a small amount of clean engine oil into the rocker arm pivot holding part of the rocker arm shaft, then install the intake rocker arms so that their clips are properly engaged on the shaft.

20. Install the camshaft and all other items removed earlier.

21. Adjust the valve lash as described in Section 1, then install the rocker arm cover.

1.8L Engine

The 1.8L DOHC engine does not utilize rocker arms or rocker arm shafts.

Thermostat

REMOVAL & INSTALLATION

◆ **See Figures 28 and 29**

✳✳ CAUTION

When draining engine coolant, keep in mind that cats and dogs are attracted to ethylene glycol antifreeze and could drink any that is left in an uncovered container or in puddles on the ground. This will prove fatal in sufficient quantities. Always drain coolant into a sealable container. Coolant should be reused unless it is contaminated or is several years old.

1. Drain the engine cooling system until the level of coolant is below the level of the thermostat.

2. If working space is constricted, the upper radiator hose may be detached from the thermostat housing.

To remove the thermostat, loosen the thermostat housing mounting bolts . . .

Grasp the thermostat by hand and pull it up and out of the intake manifold

. . . then lift the housing off of the intake manifold, thereby exposing the thermostat (arrow)

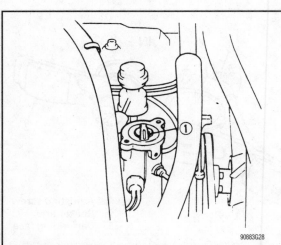

Fig. 28 When installing the thermostat on 1.3L and 1.6L engines, ensure that the air bleed valve (1) is facing toward the front of the engine

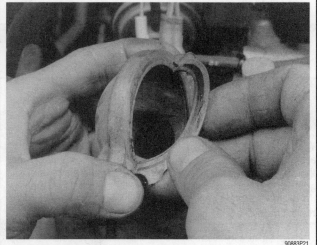

Remove the old gasket from the housing or the intake manifold (depending onto which surface it is stuck)

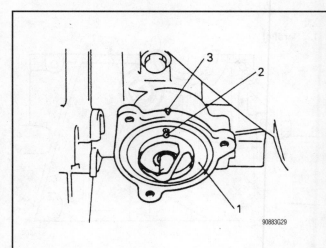

Fig. 29 On 1.8L engines, when installing the thermostat, be sure that the air bleed valve (2) and the matchmark (3) are aligned

3. Remove the thermostat housing mounting bolts, then lift the housing off of the intake manifold.

4. Remove and discard the old gasket.

5. Grasp the thermostat by hand and lift it out of the intake manifold.

6. Clean the thermostat housing-to-intake manifold gasket mating surfaces of all dirt, grime and old gasket material.

To install:

7. On 1.3L and 1.6L engines, position the new thermostat in the intake manifold hole so that the spring side of the thermostat is positioned down, and the air bleed valve is positioned toward the front of the engine.

8. On 1.8L engines, position the new thermostat in the intake manifold hole so that the spring side of the thermostat is positioned down, and the air bleed valve is aligned with the matchmark on the intake manifold.

9. Position a new gasket on the thermostat, then position the thermostat housing over the thermostat and on the intake manifold.

10. Install and tighten the thermostat housing mounting bolts evenly and securely.

11. If necessary, reattach the upper radiator hose to the housing.

12. Fill the cooling system.

13. Start the engine and inspect for coolant leaks.

Intake Manifold

REMOVAL & INSTALLATION

➡**During these procedures, identify all components removed from the engine so that they may be reinstalled in their original positions. If discarding the old components so that new components can be installed, identifying the old items is not necessary.**

1.3L Engine

For the 1.3L engine, the carburetor may be removed prior to separating the intake manifold from the engine, or may be removed along with the intake manifold.

1. Disconnect the negative battery cable.

❊❊ CAUTION

Never open, service or drain the radiator or cooling system when hot; serious burns can occur from the steam and hot coolant. Also, when draining engine coolant, keep in mind that cats and dogs are attracted to ethylene glycol antifreeze and could drink any that is left in an uncovered container or in puddles on the ground. This will prove fatal in sufficient quantities. Always drain coolant into a sealable container. Coolant should be reused unless it is contaminated or is several years old.

2. Drain the cooling system.

3. Remove the air cleaner from the carburetor, and, if desired, the carburetor from the intake manifold.

4. Label and detach all electrical wiring, vacuum hoses and cooling system hoses from the intake manifold.

❊❊ WARNING

Never use a prybar between the intake manifold and cylinder head mating surface to attempt to separate the two components; damage to the intake manifold or cylinder head may occur, necessitating component replacement.

5. Remove the intake manifold mounting fasteners, then remove the intake manifold from the cylinder head. It may be necessary to tap the manifold with a soft-faced mallet to free it from the cylinder head.

6. Insert clean shop rags in the intake holes in the cylinder head to prevent accidentally dropping anything (such as dirt, nuts, bolts, etc.), which would require cylinder head removal, into the cylinders.

7. If not already removed, the carburetor can now be separated from the intake manifold by loosening the mounting fasteners.

8. If a new manifold is to be installed, any components mounted on the intake manifold (such as the PCV valve, EGR valve, gas filter, thermostat, sensors, switches, etc.) may be removed from the intake manifold at this time.

9. Thoroughly clean all gasket mating surfaces of all dirt and old gasket material.

To install:

10. If a new manifold is being installed, transfer any manifold-mounted components to the new manifold.

11. Remove the rags from the cylinder head intake holes.

12. Position a new intake manifold gasket on the cylinder head, then install the intake manifold. Tighten the intake manifold-to-cylinder head bolts to 159–248 inch lbs. (18–28 Nm). Be sure to tighten the center bolts first, then work your way out to both ends of the manifold.

13. Reattach all electrical wiring, vacuum hoses and cooling system hoses to the intake manifold.

14. Install the carburetor onto the intake manifold, and the air cleaner onto the carburetor.

15. Fill the cooling system.

16. Connect the negative battery cable.

17. Start the engine and inspect for engine coolant and fuel leaks.

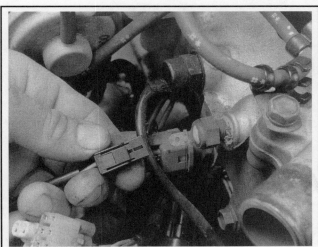

To remove the intake manifold, detach and label all wiring from the intake manifold sensors . . .

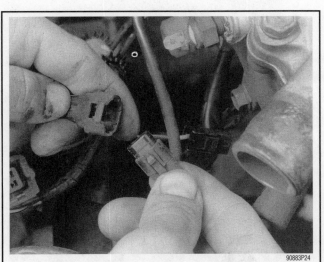

. . . or, when necessary, disengage any wiring connectors for wires leading to the intake manifold

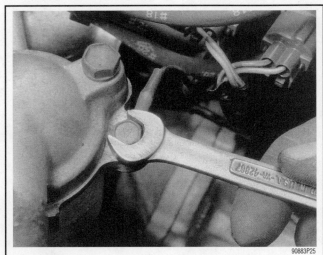

Detach all ground wires from the manifold, including the one attached to the thermostat housing bolt

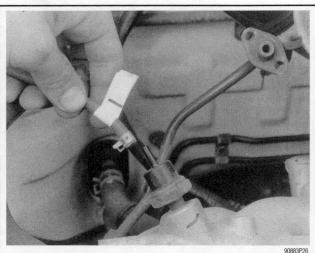

Label and detach all vacuum lines from the intake manifold and related components . . .

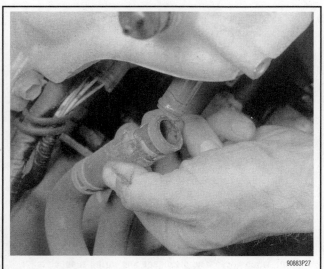

. . . and disconnect all cooling system hoses from the manifold

Before loosening the mounting fasteners, ensure that all wires and hoses are properly disconnected . . .

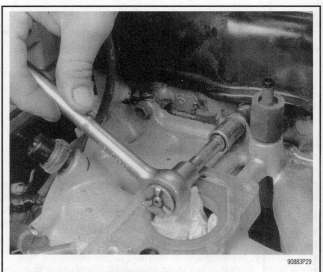

. . . then remove the mounting fasteners

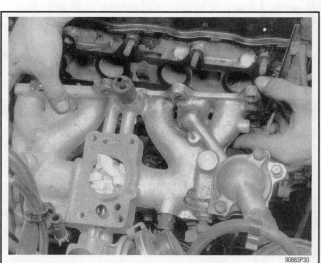

Lift the intake manifold up and off of the cylinder head studs . . .

. . . and insert clean rags or paper towels in the cylinder head intake holes

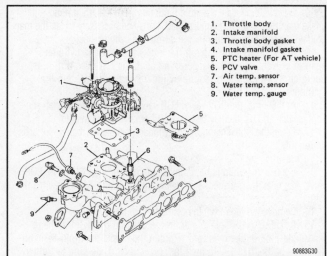

1. Throttle body
2. Intake manifold
3. Throttle body gasket
4. Intake manifold gasket
5. PTC heater (For AT vehicle)
6. PCV valve
7. Air temp. sensor
8. Water temp. sensor
9. Water temp. gauge

Fig. 30 Exploded view of the throttle body and intake manifold mounting

Be sure to remove and discard the old intake manifold-to-cylinder head gasket

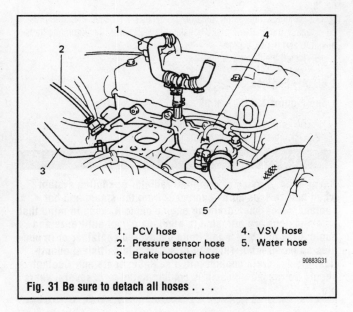

1. PCV hose
2. Pressure sensor hose
3. Brake booster hose
4. VSV hose
5. Water hose

Fig. 31 Be sure to detach all hoses . . .

1.6L TFI Engines

▶ See Figures 30, 31 and 32

1. Remove the throttle body from the intake manifold.
2. Disconnect the PCV hose from the rocker arm cover.
3. Detach the pressure sensor hose from the gas filter.
4. Disconnect the brake booster and automatic transmission (if equipped) vacuum hoses from the intake manifold.
5. Detach the Vacuum Switching Valve (VSV) hose for the throttle opener and EVAP canister from the intake manifold.
6. Detach the upper radiator hose from the thermostat housing, and the heater inlet and water bypass hoses from the intake manifold.
7. Disconnect the EGR valve hoses from the EGR valve.
8. Detach and label all wiring and wiring connectors from components mounted on the intake manifold.

✷✷ WARNING

Never use a prybar between the intake manifold and cylinder head mating surface to attempt to separate the two components; damage to the intake manifold or cylinder head may occur, necessitating component replacement.

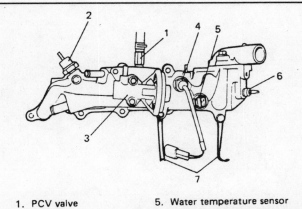

1. PCV valve
2. Gas filter
3. EGR valve
4. Air temperature sensor
5. Water temperature sensor
6. Water temperature gauge
7. Clamp

Fig. 32 . . . as well as vacuum lines and wiring from the intake manifold, prior to removing the attaching fasteners

9. Remove the intake manifold mounting fasteners, then remove the intake manifold from the cylinder head. It may be necessary to tap the manifold with a soft-faced mallet to free it from the cylinder head.

10. Insert clean shop rags in the intake holes in the cylinder head to prevent accidentally dropping anything (such as dirt, nuts, bolts, etc.), which would require cylinder head removal, into the cylinders.

11. At this time, the PCV valve, EGR valve, gas filter, thermostat, sensors, switch and gauge may be removed from the intake manifold.

12. Clean the intake manifold-to-cylinder head gasket mating surfaces thoroughly.

To install:

13. If a new manifold is being installed, transfer the PCV valve, EGR valve, gas filter, thermostat, sensors, switch and gauge to the new manifold.

14. Remove the rags from the cylinder head intake holes.

15. Position a new intake manifold gasket on the cylinder head, then install the intake manifold. Tighten the intake manifold-to-cylinder head bolts to 159–248 inch lbs. (18–28 Nm). Be sure to tighten the center bolts first, then work your way out to both ends of the manifold.

16. Reattach all wiring to the intake manifold and related components.

17. Reconnect the upper radiator, the bypass, the heater inlet, the pressure sensor, the VSV, the brake booster, the EGR valve, the automatic transmission, and the PCV hoses.

18. Install the throttle body.

1.6L MFI Engines

▶ See Figures 33, 34 and 35

1. Relieve the fuel system pressure as described in Section 5.
2. Disconnect the negative battery cable.

✳✳ CAUTION

Never open, service or drain the radiator or cooling system when hot; serious burns can occur from the steam and hot coolant. Also, when draining engine coolant, keep in mind that cats and dogs are attracted to ethylene glycol antifreeze and could drink any that is left in an uncovered container or in puddles on the ground. This will prove fatal in sufficient quantities. Always drain coolant into a sealable container. Coolant should be reused unless it is contaminated or is several years old.

3. Drain the engine cooling system.
4. Remove the air intake pipe.
5. Detach the accelerator cable and automatic transmission kickdown cable (if equipped) from the throttle body.
6. Detach the vacuum hose from the PCV valve.
7. Disengage all wiring from the intake manifold and throttle body which will interfere with removal.
8. Disconnect all vacuum and cooling system hoses from the throttle body and intake manifold which will restrict removal.

✳✳ WARNING

Be sure to plug the fuel lines to prevent dirt or other contaminants, which may cause future fuel system damage, from entering the fuel system.

9. Disconnect and plug the fuel feed line from the junction near the firewall. Be sure to use a second wrench to hold the junction steady while loosening the fuel line flare nut. Also, detach the fuel return line.

10. Remove the alternator adjusting arm brace.
11. Remove the intake manifold brace, the No. 1 brace and the No. 2 brace with the EGR pressure transducer.
12. Detach the cooling system bypass hose from the intake manifold.

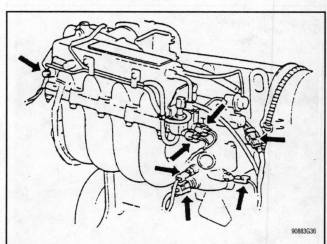

Fig. 34 Prior to removing the intake manifold, be sure to detach all cooling system hoses, vacuum lines and wires (shown by arrows) from the intake manifold, throttle body and surge tank

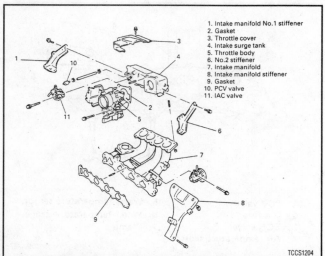

1. Intake manifold No.1 stiffener
2. Gasket
3. Throttle cover
4. Intake surge tank
5. Throttle body
6. No.2 stiffener
7. Intake manifold
8. Intake manifold stiffener
9. Gasket
10. PCV valve
11. IAC valve

Fig. 33 Exploded view of the intake manifold, throttle body and intake surge tank mounting

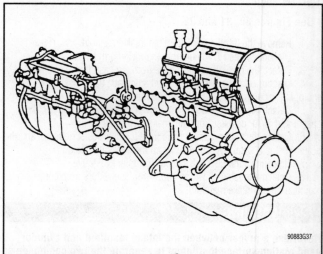

Fig. 35 The throttle body and surge tank are removed along with the intake manifold as an assembly, then they may be separated

✳✳ WARNING

Never use a prybar between the intake manifold and cylinder head mating surface to attempt to separate the two components; damage to the intake manifold or cylinder head may occur, necessitating component replacement.

13. Remove the intake manifold-to-cylinder head mounting fasteners, then separate the intake manifold and throttle body assembly from the engine. It may be necessary to tap the manifold with a soft-faced mallet to free it from the cylinder head. At this point the throttle body and intake surge tank can be separated from the intake manifold by removing the attaching fasteners. Be sure to discard any old gaskets used between these components.

14. Insert clean shop rags in the intake holes in the cylinder head to prevent accidentally dropping anything (such as dirt, nuts, bolts, etc.), which would require cylinder head removal, into the cylinders.

15. Remove and discard the old intake manifold-to-cylinder head gasket.

16. Clean all gasket mating surfaces thoroughly.

To install:

17. If necessary, assemble the intake surge tank and throttle body onto the intake manifold, making sure to use new gaskets and to tighten the attaching fasteners to 203 inch lbs. (23 Nm).

18. Remove the rags from the cylinder head intake holes.

19. Position a new intake manifold gasket on the cylinder head studs, then install the intake manifold and throttle body assembly onto the cylinder head. Be sure to install the wiring clamps on their original studs.

20. Starting in the middle of the intake manifold and working outward toward the ends, tighten the manifold mounting fasteners to 203 inch lbs. (23 Nm).

21. Reattach the cooling system bypass hose to the intake manifold.

22. Install the intake manifold brace, the No. 1 brace and the No. 2 brace with the EGR pressure transducer. Tighten the brace fasteners to 36 ft. lbs. (50 Nm).

23. Install the alternator adjusting arm brace. Tighten the brace bolts to 36 ft. lbs. (50 Nm).

24. Attach the fuel feed line to the junction near the firewall. Be sure to use a second wrench to hold the junction steady while tightening the fuel line flare nut to 32.5 ft. lbs. (45 Nm). Also, reattach the fuel return line.

25. Connect all vacuum and cooling system hoses to the throttle body and intake manifold.

26. Engage all wiring to the intake manifold and throttle body.

27. Connect the PCV vacuum hose to the valve.

28. Reattach the accelerator cable and automatic transmission kickdown cable (if equipped) to the throttle body. Be sure to adjust the accelerator and kickdown (if equipped) cables play. Accelerator cable play adjustment is covered in Section 5, and kickdown cable adjustment is described in Section 7.

29. Install the air intake pipe.

30. Fill the engine cooling system.

31. Connect the negative battery cable.

32. Turn the ignition key **ON**, but do not start the engine; this allows the fuel system to pressurize. Check for fuel system leaks.

33. Afdter checking for fuel system leaks, start the engine and inspect for engine coolant leaks.

1.8L Engine

▶ See Figures 36 and 37

1. Remove the throttle body from the intake manifold.
2. Remove the front and rear intake manifold braces.
3. Detach the water pipe from the intake manifold.

✳✳ WARNING

Never use a prybar between the intake manifold and cylinder head mating surface to attempt to separate the two components; damage to the intake manifold or cylinder head may occur, necessitating component replacement.

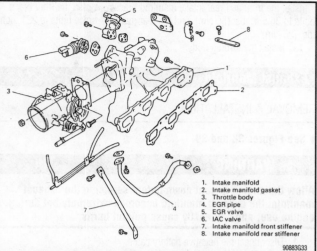

1. Intake manifold
2. Intake manifold gasket
3. Throttle body
4. EGR pipe
5. EGR valve
6. IAC valve
7. Intake manifold front stiffener
8. Intake manifold rear stiffener

90883G33

Fig. 36 Exploded view of the intake manifold and throttle body mounting

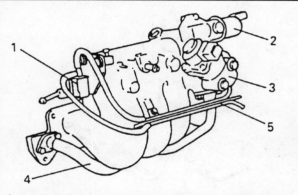

1. EVAP solenoid purge valve	4. EGR pipe
2. IAC valve	5. Vacuum pipe
3. EGR valve	

90883G34

Fig. 37 If a new intake manifold is being installed, transfer all intake manifold components over to the new manifold

4. Remove the intake manifold mounting fasteners, then separate the manifold from the cylinder head. It may be necessary to tap the manifold with a soft-faced mallet to free it from the cylinder head.

5. Insert clean shop rags in the intake holes in the cylinder head to prevent accidentally dropping anything (such as dirt, nuts, bolts, etc.), which would require cylinder head removal, into the cylinders.

6. Remove and discard the old intake manifold gasket. Thoroughly clean all gasket mating surfaces of all dirt and old gasket material.

7. If a new manifold is being installed, remove the EVAP solenoid purge valve, Exhaust Gas Recirculation (EGR) valve, Idle Air Control (IAC) valve, EGR pipe and vacuum pipe from the old intake manifold.

To install:

8. Clean all gasket mating surfaces thoroughly.

9. If necessary, transfer the EVAP solenoid purge valve, Exhaust Gas Recirculation (EGR) valve, Idle Air Control (IAC) valve, EGR pipe and vacuum pipe onto the new intake manifold.

10. Remove the rags from the cylinder head intake holes.

11. Along with a new gasket, install the intake manifold onto the cylinder head. Starting in the middle of the intake manifold and working outward toward the ends, tighten the manifold mounting fasteners to 203 inch lbs. (23 Nm).

12. Connect the water pipe to the intake manifold.

Install the front and rear intake manifold braces. Tighten the front brace bolts to 36.5 ft. lbs. (50 Nm), and the rear manifold brace bolts to 221 inch lbs. (25 Nm).

13. Install the throttle body.

Exhaust Manifold

REMOVAL & INSTALLATION

♦ See Figures 38 and 39

※※ WARNING

Allow the engine to cool down before servicing the exhaust manifold; the exhaust manifold becomes extremely hot during engine use, and can easily cause painful burns.

1. Disconnect the negative battery cable.
2. For 1.8L engines, remove the strut tower bar.
3. On 1.6L and 1.8L engines, if added working room is needed, remove the air cleaner outlet tube and the air inlet pipe.

To remove the exhaust manifold, remove the air intake case brace fasteners . . .

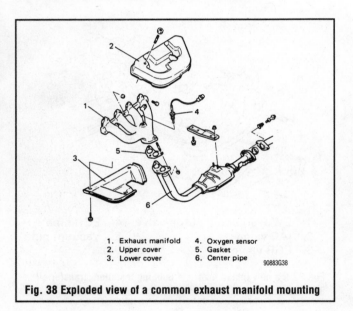

1. Exhaust manifold	4. Oxygen sensor
2. Upper cover	5. Gasket
3. Lower cover	6. Center pipe

90883G38

Fig. 38 Exploded view of a common exhaust manifold mounting

. . . then remove the brace from the engine

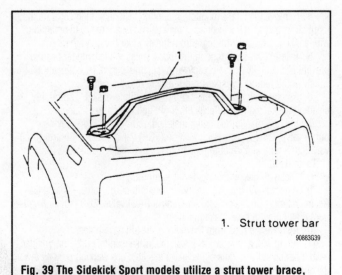

1. Strut tower bar

90883G39

Fig. 39 The Sidekick Sport models utilize a strut tower brace, which must be removed before the exhaust manifold

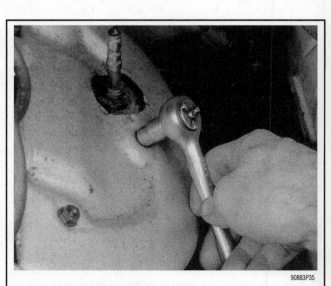

Loosen the manifold shield retaining bolts . . .

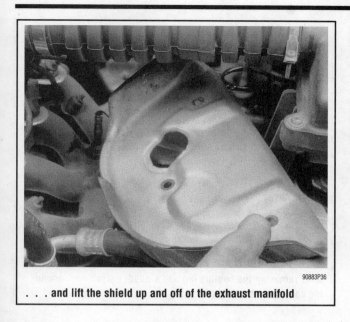

... and lift the shield up and off of the exhaust manifold

Remove the exhaust manifold mounting nuts and bolts . . .

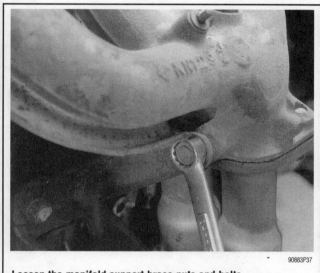

Loosen the manifold support brace nuts and bolts . . .

. . . then separate the manifold from the cylinder head

. . . then remove the brace from the manifold and engine block

Remove and discard the old manifold-to-cylinder head gasket

4. For 1.6L and 1.8L engines, disengage the oxygen sensor wiring harness connector. Remove the air intake case support brace from the engine.

5. Remove the exhaust manifold shield retaining bolts, then separate the shield(s) from the manifold.

6. If equipped, remove the exhaust manifold brace from the engine block and manifold.

7. Detach the exhaust pipe from the manifold by removing the mounting nuts.

8. Remove the exhaust manifold retaining bolts and nuts, then pull the exhaust manifold off of the cylinder head.

9. Remove and discard the old exhaust manifold gasket.

10. Thoroughly clean the manifold-to-cylinder head gasket mating surfaces of all dirt, carbon and old gasket material.

To install:

11. Install a new exhaust manifold-to-cylinder head gasket on the cylinder head studs, then install the exhaust manifold. Tighten the exhaust manifold mounting fasteners to 159–248 inch lbs. (18–28 Nm). Be sure to tighten the center bolts first, then work your way out to both ends of the manifold.

12. On 1.6L and 1.8L engines, install the air intake case support brace, and tighten the mounting bolts to 159–248 inch lbs. (18–28 Nm).

13. Reattach the exhaust pipe to the exhaust manifold, using a new gasket, then tighten the attaching nuts to 29–43 ft. lbs. (40–60 Nm).

14. If equipped, install the exhaust manifold brace, and tighten the brace-to-engine block bolt to 36.5–43 ft. lbs. (50–60 Nm) and the brace-to-exhaust manifold nut to 29–43 ft. lbs. (40–60 Nm).

15. Posiotion the cover on the exhaust manifold and install the retaining bolts. Tighten the retaining bolts securely.

16. On 1.6L and 1.8L engines, reattach the oxygen sensor lead wire to the wiring harness. Be sure to properly retain the wire with the wiring clamp.

17. If removed, install the air cleaner outlet tube and the air inlet pipe.

18. For 1.8L engines, install the strut tower bar. Tighten the mounting nuts and bolts to 66 ft. lbs. (90 Nm).

19. Connect the negative battery cable.

20. Start the engine and inspect for exhaust leaks.

Radiator

REMOVAL & INSTALLATION

◆ See Figure 40

1. Disconnect the negative battery cable.
2. Drain the cooling system.

After removing the cooling fan and shroud, detach any remaining cooling system hoses . . .

. . . and remove all radiator mounting fasteners . . .

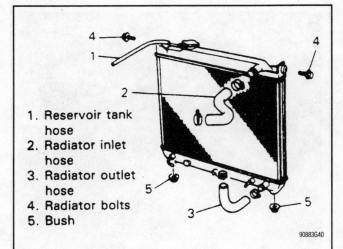

1. Reservoir tank hose
2. Radiator inlet hose
3. Radiator outlet hose
4. Radiator bolts
5. Bush

Fig. 40 Exploded view of the typical cooling system hose connections

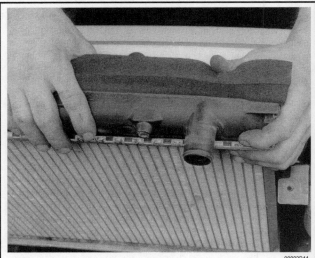

. . . then lift the radiator up and out of the engine compartment

3. If your vehicle is equipped with an automatic transmission, position a small catch pan under the transmission cooler line fittings at the radiator, then disconnect the cooler lines from the radiator. Be sure to plug the cooler lines so that no contaminants, which can lead to transmission failure or accelerated wear, enter the system.

4. Remove the cooling fan and radiator shroud.

5. Detach any cooling system hoses not yet disconnected from the radiator.

6. Remove the radiator retaining bolts, then lift the radiator up and out of the engine compartment.

To install:

7. Set the radiator in position, making sure that the bottom studs are properly positioned in the rubber isolating grommets, then install the mounting bolts. Tighten the bolts until secure.

8. Reattach the cooling system hoses to the radiator.

9. Install the cooling fan and radiator shroud.

10. Fill the cooling system; refer to Section 1.

11. Connect the negative battery cable.

12. Start the engine and inspect for coolant leaks.

Engine Fan

REMOVAL & INSTALLATION

❊❊ CAUTION

Do NOT disconnect the A/C lines during the following procedure. Refer to Section 1 for information regarding the implications of servicing your A/C system yourself. Only an MVAC-trained, EPA-certified, automotive technician should service the A/C system or its components.

1. If equipped with air conditioning, remove the A/C line clamp bolt and move the line toward the engine to provide adequate clearance for fan shroud removal.

2. Drain the cooling system until the coolant level is below the upper radiator hose.

3. Detach the upper radiator hose from the radiator.

4. Remove all of the cooling fan shroud retaining fasteners.

5. Using an open end wrench, break all of the fan/clutch mounting fasteners loose.

6. Remove the water pump drive belt.

. . . and move the line toward the engine to provide adequate clearance for fan shroud removal

Loosen the clamp, then separate the upper hose from the radiator

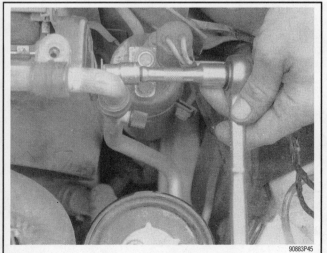

To remove the cooling fan, first remove the A/C line (if equipped) mounting clamp bolt . . .

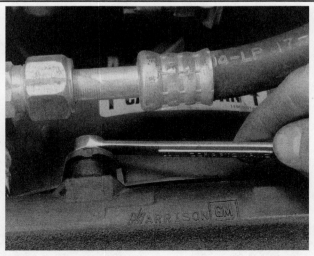

Remove all of the radiator shroud fasteners . . .

※※ WARNING

When lifting the cooling fan and shroud out of the engine compartment, take care not to damage the radiator fins.

7. Remove the cooling fan/clutch mounting fasteners, then lift the fan/clutch assembly and the shroud up and out of the engine bay together.

8. At this point, if necessary, the pulley may be removed from the water pump.

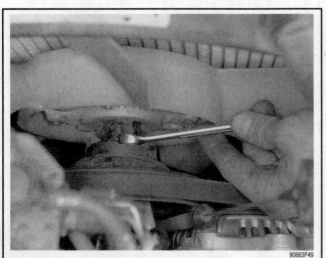

. . . and loosen the cooling fan mounting fasteners, THEN remove the drive belt . . .

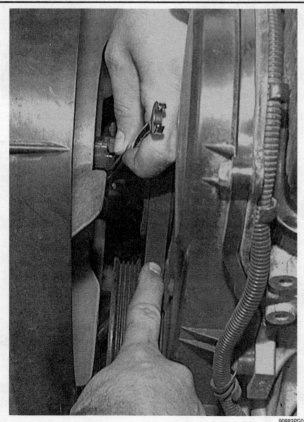

. . . because the drive belt can be used to hold the fan stable while loosening the mounting fasteners

Position the A/C line (if equipped) out of the way . . .

. . . then lift the cooling fan and shroud out of the engine compartment together

To install:

9. If removed, position the pulley on the water pump flange.

10. Lower the cooling fan/clutch assembly and shroud into the engine compartment together.

11. Install the cooling fan/clutch mounting fasteners finger-tight.

12. Position the cooling fan shroud properly, then install the retaining fasteners. Tighten them until snug.

13. Install the water pump drive belt, then tighten the cooling fan/clutch mounting fasteners to 97 inch lbs. (11 Nm).

14. Attach the upper radiator hose to the radiator.

15. If equipped with air conditioning, position the A/C line against the radiator and install the line clamp bolt securely.

16. Fill the cooling system, then start the engine and check for coolant leaks.

Water Pump

REMOVAL & INSTALLATION

➡During these procedures, identify all components removed from the engine so that they may be reinstalled in their original positions. If discarding the old components so that new components can be installed, identifying the old items is not necessary.

1.3L and 1.6L Engines

▶ See Figures 41, 42 and 43

1. Remove the timing belt cover, timing belt, tensioner, plate and spring.

2. Remove the water pump mounting bolts.

3. Remove the one (1.6L MFI engines) or two (1.3L and 1.6L TFI engines) small rubber seals from between the water pump and the oil pump, and the water pump and the cylinder head.

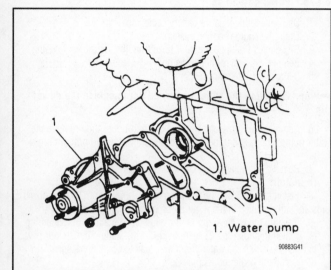

Fig. 41 Exploded view of the water pump mounting

1. Water pump

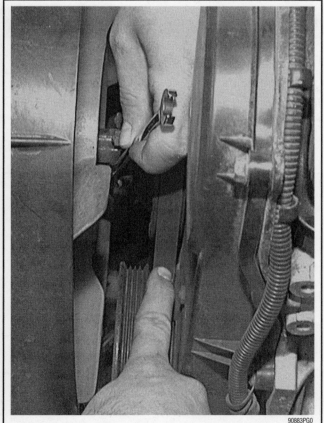

The drive belt can be used to hold the fan stable while loosening the mounting fasteners

4. If necessary for clearance, remove the oil level dipstick tube retaining bolt from the engine block and the alternator adjusting brace.

✳✳ WARNING

Do NOT use a prybar between the water pump housing and the engine block to separate the two components; this can cause scratches and/or gouges, which can prevent proper sealing.

5. Pull the water pump off of the engine block. If the water pump is difficult to remove from the engine block, use a soft-faced mallet to tap the water pump housing until it loosens.

➡ Do not disassemble the water pump; if the water pump is damaged or defective, the entire unit is replaced.

6. Thoroughly clean the water pump gasket mating surfaces of old gasket material and corrosion.

To install:

7. Along with a new gasket, install the water pump on the engine block. Tighten the water pump mounting bolts to 88–115 inch lbs. (10–13 Nm).

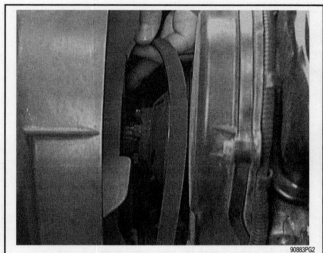

Loosen the fan bolts, then either remove the drive belt before the fan and shroud . . .

. . . or wait to remove the belt, along with the water pump pulley

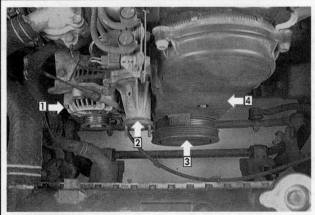

1. Alternator
2. Water pump
3. Crankshaft pulley
4. Timing belt cover

90883PG5

Once the cooling fan and shroud are removed, access can be gained to many of the engine components, including the water pump

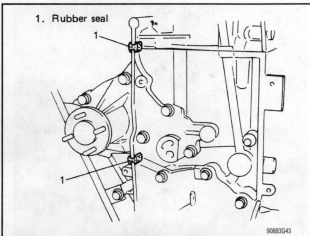

1. Rubber seal

90883G43

Fig. 42 Be sure to install the two rubber seals between the water pump, oil pump and cylinder head before installing the timing belt cover—1.3L and 1.6L TFI engines

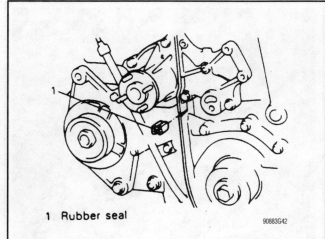

1 Rubber seal

90883G42

Fig. 43 The 1.6L MFI engine uses only one rubber seal between the oil pump and water pump

8. On 1.3L and TFI 1.6L engines, install two new rubber seals: one between the water pump and oil pump, and the other between the water pump and the cylinder head. The MFI 1.6L engines only use one rubber seal, located between the water and oil pumps.

9. If removed, install the alternator adjusting brace and the oil level dipstick retaining bolt.

10. Install the timing belt, tensioner, plate, spring and cover.

1.8L Engine

▶ **See Figures 44 and 45**

1. Disconnect the negative battery cable.
2. Drain the engine cooling system.
3. Disconnect the upper radiator hose from the thermostat housing.
4. Remove the heater outlet pipe bolt.
5. Remove the alternator belt.

➡**When removing the water pump, do not misplace the dowel pin.**

6. Remove the four water pump mounting bolts, then remove the water pump from the engine. Discard the old water pump mounting bolts.

7. Remove the water pump O-ring and discard it.

To install:

8. Install a new O-ring on the water pump, and ensure that the dowel pins are still mounted in the water pump prior to installation.

9. Position the water pump on the engine and install NEW mounting bolts. Tighten the bolts to 221 inch lbs. (25 Nm). Failure to use four new bolts when installing the water pump may lead to coolant leakage.

10. Install the heater outlet pipe bolt.
11. Install the alternator drive belt.
12. Reattach the upper radiator hose to the thermostat housing.
13. Fill the cooling system.
14. Connect the negative battery cable.

Cylinder Head

REMOVAL & INSTALLATION

➡**During these procedures, identify all components removed from the engine so that they may be reinstalled in their original positions. If discarding the old components so that new components can be installed, identifying the old items is not necessary.**

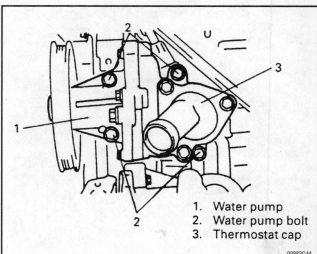

1. Water pump
2. Water pump bolt
3. Thermostat cap

90883G44

Fig. 44 The water pump is mounted next to the thermostat housing

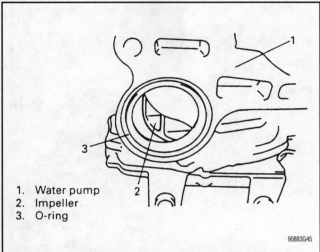

1. Water pump
2. Impeller
3. O-ring

Fig. 45 Be sure to install a new O-ring in the water pump prior to installation, otherwise coolant leakage may occur

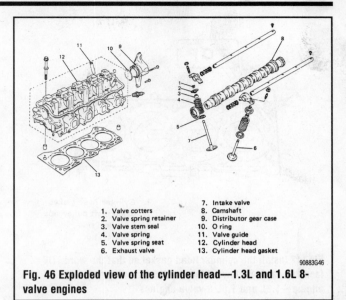

1. Valve cotters	7. Intake valve
2. Valve spring retainer	8. Camshaft
3. Valve stem seal	9. Distributor gear case
4. Valve spring	10. O ring
5. Valve spring seat	11. Valve guide
6. Exhaust valve	12. Cylinder head
	13. Cylinder head gasket

Fig. 46 Exploded view of the cylinder head—1.3L and 1.6L 8-valve engines

1.3L Engine

▶ See Figures 46, 47 and 48

The 1.3L engine uses an 8-valve cylinder head.
1. Disconnect the negative battery cable.

❊❊ CAUTION

Never open, service or drain the radiator or cooling system when hot; serious burns can occur from the steam and hot coolant. Also, when draining engine coolant, keep in mind that cats and dogs are attracted to ethylene glycol antifreeze and could drink any that is left in an uncovered container or in puddles on the ground. This will prove fatal in sufficient quantities. Always drain coolant into a sealable container. Coolant should be reused unless it is contaminated or is several years old.

2. Drain the engine coolant.
3. Remove the timing belt.
4. Remove the intake manifold.
5. Remove the exhaust manifold.
6. Remove the rocker arm cover, then loosen all of the valve lash locknuts and adjusting screws until no pressure is applied to the camshaft.
7. On carbureted models, remove the fuel pump and rod from the cylinder head.

➡**Although the manufacturer does not specify a bolt removal sequence, it is advisable to remove the bolts in reverse of the installation sequence.**

8. Loosen and remove the 10 cylinder head mounting bolts.

❊❊ WARNING

Do not attempt to loosen the cylinder head from the engine block by striking it with a hammer or mallet; the cylinder head is positioned on the engine block by locating pins. If the cylinder head is struck with a hammer or mallet, the cylinder head may be damaged, or the locating pins may shear off in the block.

9. Lift the cylinder head up and off of the engine block. If the cylinder head is difficult to separate from the engine block, lift the cylinder head with a prytool positioned under one of the bolt bosses located on the side of the cylinder head. Do not strike the side of the cylinder head with a mallet or hammer because the head is positioned on the engine block with locating pins.

10. Insert clean shop rags in the cylinder bores to prevent dirt and other contaminants from falling into the cylinder bores.

11. Remove the old gasket from the engine block. Clean all gasket mating surfaces on the engine block and cylinder head, including the intake manifold, exhaust manifold, carburetor/throttle body, and fuel pump.

12. Inspect the locating pins and engine block gasket surface for damage. If the locating pins re damaged, new ones must be installed. Engine block damage will require engine disassembly and must be repaired, preferably by a qualified automotive machine shop.

13. Clean and inspect the cylinder head for damage, as described later in the engine reconditioning portion of this section.

To install:

14. Ensure that the locating pins are properly installed in the engine block.

15. Position the new cylinder head gasket on the engine block so that it is retained by the locating pins. The gasket should be situated so that the word TOP is facing upward (away from the engine block) and toward the front (timing belt end) of the engine.

16. Remove the shop rags from the cylinder bores.

17. Gently set the cylinder head on the engine block ensuring that the intake and exhaust sides of the cylinder head are facing the proper directions.

➡**Although not required by the manufacturer, it is always a good idea to use new cylinder head bolts.**

18. Lightly lubricate the threads of the cylinder head bolts, then install them finger-tight.

19. Using the sequence shown in the accompanying illustration, tighten the cylinder head bolts to 23–25 ft. lbs. (31–34 Nm), then to 35–37 ft. lbs. (48–50 Nm), and finally to 46–50 ft. lbs. (63–70 Nm) for 1986–88 models. For 1989–95 models, use the same sequence, but tighten the bolts to 27 ft. lbs. (37 Nm), then to 40 ft. lbs. (54 Nm), and finally to 52 ft. lbs. (71 Nm).

20. Install the fuel pump and rod, the intake manifold, the exhaust manifold, the timing belt and all other related items.

21. Fill the engine cooling system with the proper amount and type of coolant.

22. Adjust the valve lash for all valves.

23. Install the rocker arm cover.

24. Connect the negative battery cable.

25. Start the engine and check for coolant, fuel, vacuum and exhaust leaks.

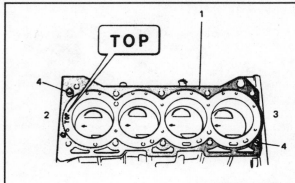

1. Cylinder head gasket
2. Crankshaft pulley side
3. Flywheel side
4. Locating pin

90883G47

Fig. 47 Install the cylinder head gasket so that the word TOP faces upward and toward the crankshaft pulley end of the engine—1.3L and 1.6L 8-valve engines

90883P52

. . . then remove the timing belt and rocker arm cover

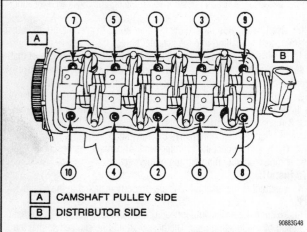

A CAMSHAFT PULLEY SIDE
B DISTRIBUTOR SIDE

90883G48

Fig. 48 When tightening the cylinder head bolts, be sure to follow the sequence shown, otherwise improper cylinder head sealing will result—1.3L and 1.6L 8-valve engines

90883P53

Loosen and remove all of the cylinder head bolts in the proper sequence . . .

90883P51

To remove the cylinder head, detach all hoses, wires and cables from the cylinder head and manifolds . . .

90883P54

. . . and, with the help of an assistant, lift the cylinder head up and off of the engine block

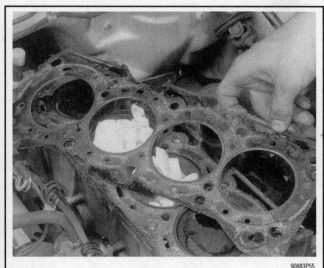

Remove the old gasket from the engine block . . .

. . . and clean the gasket mating surfaces of all traces of old gasket material and dirt

1.6L TFI Engine

The 1.6L TFI engine uses an 8-valve cylinder head.

➡️The manufacturer recommends removing the cylinder head with the distributor, exhaust manifold and intake manifold installed. If desired, these items can be removed from the cylinder head before the head is removed.

1. Relieve fuel system pressure.
2. Disconnect the negative battery cable.

✳️ CAUTION

Never open, service or drain the radiator or cooling system when hot; serious burns can occur from the steam and hot coolant. Also, when draining engine coolant, keep in mind that cats and dogs are attracted to ethylene glycol antifreeze and could drink any that is left in an uncovered container or in puddles on the ground. This will prove fatal in sufficient quantities. Always drain coolant into a sealable container. Coolant should be reused unless it is contaminated or is several years old.

3. Drain the engine cooling system.
4. Remove the air intake case and throttle body.
5. Label and detach all cooling system and vacuum hoses from the intake manifold, throttle body and cylinder head.
6. Label and disengage all electrical wires from the distributor, intake manifold, cylinder head, throttle body and oxygen sensor. Detach the wiring harness from any retaining clamps on the cylinder head.
7. Relieve fuel system pressure as described in Section 5.
8. Detach the fuel lines from the throttle body and pressure regulator.
9. Remove the timing belt.
10. Detach the exhaust pipe from the exhaust manifold by removing the attaching nuts.

➡️**If your vehicle is equipped with air conditioning, refer to Section 1 for information regarding the implications of servicing your A/C system yourself. Only an MVAC-trained, EPA-certified automotive technician should service the A/C system or its components.**

11. If applicable, remove the air conditioning compressor adjusting brace from the cylinder head. Do NOT disconnect any of the A/C refrigerant lines.
12. Remove the rocker arm cover, then loosen all of the valve lash locknuts and adjusting screws until all pressure is relieved from the camshaft.

➡️**Although the manufacturer does not specify a bolt removal sequence, it is advisable to remove the bolts in reverse of the installation sequence.**

13. Loosen and remove the 10 cylinder head mounting bolts.

✳️ WARNING

Do not attempt to loosen the cylinder head from the engine block by striking it with a hammer or mallet; the cylinder head is positioned on the engine block by locating pins. If the cylinder head is struck with a hammer or mallet, the cylinder head may be damaged, or the locating pins may shear off in the block.

14. Lift the cylinder head up and off of the engine block. If the cylinder head is difficult to separate from the engine block, lift the cylinder head with a prytool positioned under one of the bolt bosses located on the side of the cylinder head. Do not strike the side of the cylinder head with a mallet or hammer because the head is positioned on the engine block with locating pins.
15. If desired, the intake manifold, exhaust manifold, distributor and distributor case may now be removed from the cylinder head.
16. Insert clean shop rags in the cylinder bores to prevent dirt and other contaminants from falling into the cylinder bores.
17. Remove the old gasket from the engine block. Clean all gasket mating surfaces on the engine block and cylinder head, including the intake manifold, exhaust manifold, and throttle body.
18. Inspect the locating pins and engine block gasket surface for damage. If the locating pins re damaged, new ones must be installed. Engine block damage will require engine disassembly and must be repaired, preferably by a qualified automotive machine shop.
19. Clean and inspect the cylinder head for damage, as described later in the engine reconditioning portion of this section.

To install:
20. Ensure that the locating pins are properly installed in the engine block.
21. Position the new cylinder head gasket on the engine block so that it is retained by the locating pins. The gasket should be situated so that the word TOP is facing upward (away from the engine block) and toward the front (timing belt end) of the engine.
22. Remove the shop rags from the cylinder bores.
23. If necessary, install the intake manifold, exhaust manifold, distributor case and distributor on the cylinder head. These components can also be installed after the cylinder head is mated to the engine block.

24. Gently set the cylinder head on the engine block ensuring that the intake and exhaust sides of the cylinder head are facing the proper directions.

➡ **Although not required by the manufacturer, it is always a good idea to use new cylinder head bolts.**

25. Lightly lubricate the threads of the cylinder head bolts, then install them finger-tight.

26. Using the sequence shown in the accompanying illustration, tighten the cylinder head bolts to 27 ft. lbs. (37 Nm), then to 40 ft. lbs. (54 Nm), and finally to 52 ft. lbs. (71 Nm).

27. If equipped, install the air conditioning compressor adjusting brace onto the cylinder head.

28. Install the timing belt inside cover, camshaft sprocket, timing belt, outer cover and all other related items, such as the crankshaft pulley, water pump pulley, water pump drive belt, cooling fan and shroud.

29. Reattach all fuel lines, vacuum hoses, cooling system hoses and wiring to their respective components.

30. Reattach the exhaust pipe to the exhaust manifold.

31. Connect the accelerator and, if equipped, the kickdown cables to the throttle body. Adjust cable end-play as described in Section 5 (accelerator cable) and Section 7 (kickdown cable).

32. Fill the engine cooling system with the proper amount and type of coolant.

33. Adjust the valve lash for all valves.

34. Install the rocker arm cover.

35. Install the air intake case.

36. Connect the negative battery cable.

37. Start the engine and check for coolant, fuel, vacuum and exhaust leaks.

1.6L MFI Engine

▶ **See Figures 49, 50, 51, 52 and 53**

The 1.6L MFI engine utilizes a 16-valve cylinder head.
1. Relieve fuel system pressure, as described in Section 5.
2. Disconnect the negative cable.

✳✳ CAUTION

Never open, service or drain the radiator or cooling system when hot; serious burns can occur from the steam and hot coolant. Also, when draining engine coolant, keep in mind that cats and dogs are attracted to ethylene glycol antifreeze and could drink any that is left in an uncovered container or in puddles on the ground. This will prove fatal in sufficient quantities. Always drain coolant into a sealable container. Coolant should be reused unless it is contaminated or is several years old.

3. Drain the cooling system.
4. Remove the intake manifold brace from the engine.
5. Label and detach all wiring and vacuum hoses from the distributor, intake manifold, oxygen sensor, throttle body, and cylinder head.
6. Detach the fuel supply and return lines from the fuel injector supply manifold.
7. Remove the rocker arm cover, then loosen all of the valve lash locknuts and adjusting screws.
8. Disconnect all cooling system hoses from the engine.
9. Remove the timing belt from the engine.
10. Separate the exhaust pipe from the exhaust manifold and remove the exhaust manifold brace.

✳✳ WARNING

Failure to properly loosen the cylinder head bolts may result in cylinder head warpage.

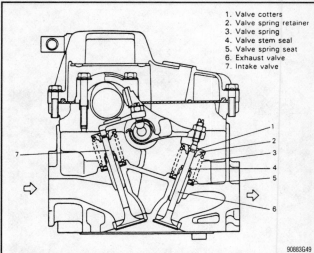

1. Valve cotters
2. Valve spring retainer
3. Valve spring
4. Valve stem seal
5. Valve spring seat
6. Exhaust valve
7. Intake valve

Fig. 49 Cross-sectional view of the cylinder head used on the 1.6L MFI engine

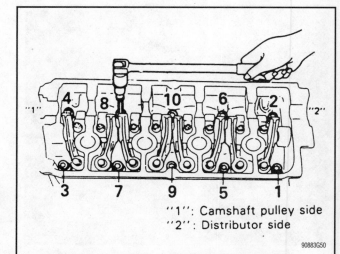

"1": Camshaft pulley side
"2": Distributor side

Fig. 50 Be sure to loosen the 10 cylinder head bolts in the sequence shown, otherwise cylinder head warpage may occur

11. Loosen the cylinder head mounting bolts using Suzuki Tools 09900–00415 (A) and 09900–00411 (B) (or their equivalents) in the order shown in the accompanying illustration, then remove the bolts from the cylinder head.

12. Ensure that all wires, hoses and cables, which would restrict cylinder head removal, have been detached.

✳✳ WARNING

Do not attempt to loosen the cylinder head from the engine block by striking it with a hammer or mallet; the cylinder head is positioned on the engine block by locating pins. If the cylinder head is struck with a hammer or mallet, the cylinder head may be damaged, or the locating pins may shear off in the block.

13. Lift the cylinder head up and off of the engine block. If the cylinder head is difficult to separate from the engine block, lift the cylinder head with a prytool positioned under one of the bolt bosses located on the side of the cylinder head. Do not strike the side of the cylinder head with a mallet or hammer because the head is positioned on the engine block with locating pins.

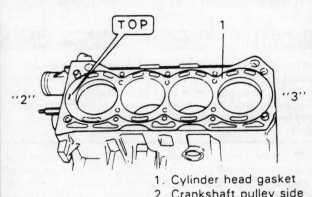

Fig. 51 Install the cylinder head gasket on the engine block so that the word TOP faces upward and is toward the crankshaft pulley side of the engine

1. Cylinder head gasket
2. Crankshaft pulley side
3. Flywheel side

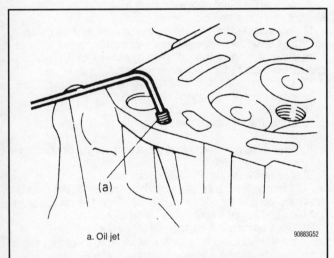

a. Oil jet

Fig. 52 If necessary, tighten the oil jet (venturi plug) to 35–53 inch lbs. (4–6 Nm)

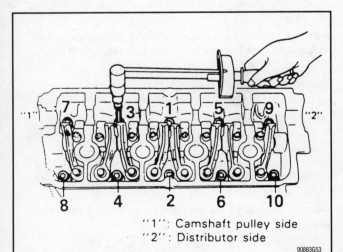

"1": Camshaft pulley side
"2": Distributor side

Fig. 53 Tighten the cylinder head bolts in the sequence shown to ensure proper cylinder head sealing

14. If desired, the intake manifold, exhaust manifold, distributor and distributor case may now be removed from the cylinder head.

15. Insert clean shop rags in the cylinder bores to prevent dirt and other contaminants from falling into the cylinder bores.

16. Remove the old gasket from the engine block. Clean all gasket mating surfaces on the engine block and cylinder head, including the intake manifold, exhaust manifold, and throttle body.

17. Inspect the locating pins and engine block gasket surface for damage. If the locating pins re damaged, new ones must be installed. Engine block damage will require engine disassembly and must be repaired, preferably by a qualified automotive machine shop.

18. Clean and inspect the cylinder head for damage, as described later in the engine reconditioning portion of this section.

To install:

19. Ensure that the locating pins are properly installed in the engine block.

20. Position the new cylinder head gasket on the engine block so that it is retained by the locating pins. The gasket should be situated so that the word TOP is facing upward (away from the engine block) and toward the front (timing belt end) of the engine.

21. Ensure the oil jet (venturi plug) is installed in the cylinder head, and that it is not clogged. If it is not installed, tighten it to 35–53 inch lbs. (4–6 Nm).

22. Remove the shop rags from the cylinder bores.

23. If necessary, install the intake manifold, exhaust manifold, distributor case and distributor on the cylinder head. These components can also be installed after the cylinder head is mated to the engine block.

24. Gently set the cylinder head on the engine block ensuring that the intake and exhaust sides of the cylinder head are facing the proper directions.

➡**Although not required by the manufacturer, it is always a good idea to use new cylinder head bolts.**

25. Lightly lubricate the threads of the cylinder head bolts, then install them finger-tight.

26. Using the sequence shown in the accompanying illustration and using Suzuki Tools 09900–00415 (A) and 09900–00411 (B) (or their equivalents), tighten all of the cylinder head bolts to 25 ft. lbs. (35 Nm), then to 40 ft. lbs. (55 Nm), and finally to 47.5–50.5 ft. lbs. (65–70 Nm).

27. Reattach the exhaust pipe to the exhaust manifold, and install the exhaust manifold brace.

28. Install the timing belt.

29. Connect all cooling system hoses to the engine.

30. Attach the fuel supply and return lines to the fuel injector supply manifold.

31. Reconnect all wiring and vacuum hoses to the distributor, intake manifold, oxygen sensor, throttle body, and cylinder head.

32. Install the intake manifold brace.

33. Fill the cooling system.

34. Connect the negative cable.

35. Adjust the valve lash and the accelerator and kickdown (if equipped) cables.

36. Turn the ignition key **ON**, but do not start the engine; this allows the fuel system to pressurize. Check for fuel system leaks.

37. After checking for fuel system leaks, start the engine and inspect for engine coolant, fuel, vacuum and exhaust leaks.

1.8L Engine

▶ See Figures 54 thru 59

1. Relieve fuel system pressure.
2. Disconnect the negative battery cable.

❉❉ CAUTION

Never open, service or drain the radiator or cooling system when hot; serious burns can occur from the steam and hot coolant. Also, when draining engine coolant, keep in mind that cats and dogs are attracted to ethylene glycol antifreeze and could drink any that is left in an uncovered container or in puddles on the ground. This will prove fatal in sufficient quantities. Always drain coolant into a sealable container. Coolant should be reused unless it is contaminated or is several years old.

3. Drain the engine cooling system.

4. Remove the camshafts and valve lash adjusters.

5. Remove the intake manifold brace from the engine.

6. Label and detach all wiring and vacuum hoses, which will interfere with cylinder head removal, from the intake manifold, oxygen sensor, throttle body, and cylinder head.

7. Detach the fuel supply and return lines from the fuel injector supply manifold.

8. Detach the water pipe from the intake manifold, and disconnect any other cooling system hoses from the engine.

9. Separate the exhaust pipe from the exhaust manifold and remove the exhaust manifold brace.

✳✳ WARNING

Failure to properly loosen the cylinder head bolts may result in cylinder head warpage.

10. Loosen the cylinder head mounting bolts in the order shown in the accompanying illustration, then remove the bolts from the cylinder head.

➡️**Be sure to loosen the small M6 bolt located on the side of the cylinder head, near the crankshaft pulley end.**

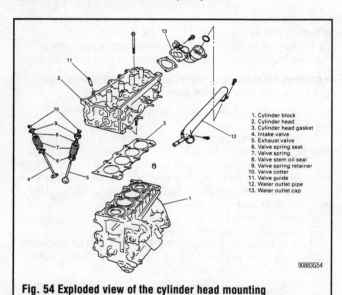

1. Cylinder block
2. Cylinder head
3. Cylinder head gasket
4. Intake valve
5. Exhaust valve
6. Valve spring seat
7. Valve spring
8. Valve stem oil seal
9. Valve spring retainer
10. Valve cotter
11. Valve guide
12. Water outlet pipe
13. Water outlet cap

90883G54

Fig. 54 Exploded view of the cylinder head mounting

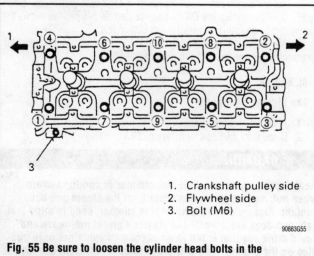

1. Crankshaft pulley side
2. Flywheel side
3. Bolt (M6)

90883G55

Fig. 55 Be sure to loosen the cylinder head bolts in the sequence shown to avoid head warpage—do not forget to loosen the small M6 bolt (3)

11. Ensure that all wires, hoses and cables, which would restrict cylinder head removal, have been detached.

✳✳ WARNING

Do not attempt to loosen the cylinder head from the engine block by striking it with a hammer or mallet; the cylinder head is positioned on the engine block by locating pins. If the cylinder head is struck with a hammer or mallet, the cylinder head may be damaged, or the locating pins may shear off in the block.

12. Lift the cylinder head up and off of the engine block. If the cylinder head is difficult to separate from the engine block, lift the cylinder head with a prytool positioned under one of the bolt bosses located on the side of the cylinder head. Do not strike the side of the cylinder head with a mallet or hammer because the head is held in position on the engine block with locating pins.

13. If desired, the intake manifold, exhaust manifold, and any other items may now be removed from the cylinder head.

14. Insert clean shop rags in the cylinder bores to prevent dirt and other contaminants from falling into the cylinder bores.

15. Remove the old gasket from the engine block. Clean all gasket mating surfaces on the engine block and cylinder head, including the intake manifold and exhaust manifold.

16. Inspect the locating pins and engine block gasket surface for damage. If the locating pins re damaged, new ones must be installed. Engine block damage will require engine disassembly and must be repaired, preferably by a qualified automotive machine shop.

17. Clean and inspect the cylinder head for damage, as described later in the engine reconditioning portion of this section.

To install:

18. Ensure that the locating pins are properly installed in the engine block.

19. Position the new cylinder head gasket on the engine block a shown in the accompanying illustration.

20. Remove the shop rags from the cylinder bores.

21. If necessary, install the intake manifold, exhaust manifold, and any other components on the cylinder head. These components can also be installed after the cylinder head is mated to the engine block.

22. Gently set the cylinder head on the engine block ensuring that the intake and exhaust sides of the cylinder head are facing the proper directions.

➡️**Although not required by the manufacturer, it is always a good idea to use new cylinder head bolts.**

23. Lightly lubricate the threads of the cylinder head bolts, then install them finger-tight.

➡️**Be sure to follow the cylinder head bolt tightening sequence exactly, otherwise improperly cylinder head sealing will occur.**

24. Using the sequence shown in the accompanying illustration, tighten the cylinder head bolts in the following steps:

a. Tighten all cylinder head bolts, in sequence, to 38.5 ft. lbs. (53 Nm).

b. Tighten the head bolts, in sequence, to 61 ft. lbs. (84 Nm).

c. Loosen all of the head bolts in the indicated sequence until they can be rotated by hand.

d. Retighten the head bolts, in sequence, to 27 ft. lbs. (37 Nm).

e. Tighten the cylinder head bolts, in sequence, to 76 ft. lbs. (105 Nm).

➡️**Tighten the small M6 bolt ONLY after the other bolts are fully tightened.**

f. Tighten the small M6 bolt to 97 inch lbs. (11 Nm).

25. Ensure that the crankshaft sprocket key is aligned with the timing mark on the engine block. If it is not aligned, rotate the crankshaft until it is.

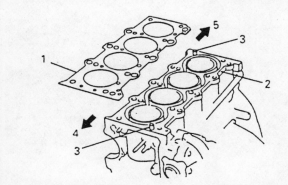

1. Cylinder head gasket
2. Cylinder block
3. Knock pin
4. Camshaft pulley side
5. Flywheel side

90883G56

Fig. 56 Position the new cylinder head gasket on the engine block as shown

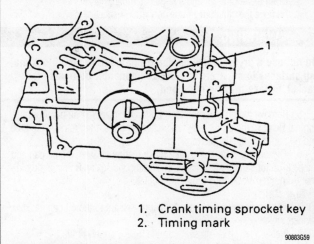

1. Crank timing sprocket key
2. Timing mark

90883G59

Fig. 59 Rotate the crankshaft so that the crankshaft timing sprocket key is aligned with the timing mark on the engine block

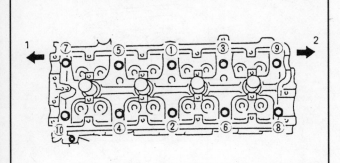

1. Crankshaft pulley side
2. Flywheel side

90883G57

Fig. 57 Tighten the cylinder head bolts in the sequence shown to ensure proper cylinder head sealing

26. Attach the exhaust pipe to the exhaust manifold, and install the exhaust manifold brace.

27. Reattach the water pipe to the intake manifold, and connect any other cooling system hoses to the engine.

28. Reattach the fuel supply and return lines to the fuel injector supply manifold.

29. Attach all applicable wiring and vacuum hoses to the intake manifold, oxygen sensor, throttle body, and cylinder head.

30. Install the intake manifold brace from the engine.

31. Install the camshafts, valve lash adjusters and all other related components.

32. Fill the cooling system.

33. Connect the negative cable.

34. Adjust the accelerator and kickdown (if equipped) cables, as described in Section 5 (accelerator cable) or Section 7 (kickdown cable).

35. Turn the ignition key **ON**, but do not start the engine; this allows the fuel system to pressurize. Check for fuel system leaks.

36. After checking for fuel system leaks, start the engine and inspect for engine coolant, fuel, vacuum and exhaust leaks.

Oil Pan

REMOVAL & INSTALLATION

1.3L Engine

▶ See Figures 60, 61 and 62

1. If added undervehicle clearance is needed, apply the parking brake and block the rear wheels, then raise and safely support the front of the vehicle on jackstands.

2. If equipped, remove the undervehicle skid plate.

✵✵ CAUTION

The EPA warns that prolonged contact with used engine oil may cause a number of skin disorders, including cancer! You should make every effort to minimize your exposure to used engine oil. Protective gloves should be worn when changing the oil. Wash your hands and any other exposed skin areas as soon as possible after exposure to used engine oil. Soap and water, or waterless hand cleaner should be used.

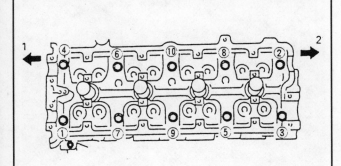

1. Crankshaft pulley side
2. Flywheel side

90883G58

Fig. 58 When loosening the cylinder head bolts during installation, be sure to do so in the sequence indicated

3. Drain the engine oil into a large catch pan.
4. Remove the clutch or torque converter inspection cover.

✳✳ WARNING

Do not use a prytool between the oil pan and engine block mating surfaces to separate the two components, otherwise the gasket surface may be damaged.

5. Remove the oil pan mounting bolts and lower the oil pan from the engine. Remove the oil pick-up tube retaining bolts, then remove the tube and oil pan from the engine together.
6. Thoroughly clean the engine block mating surface, the oil pan and the pick-up tube of all oil, grime and old silicone sealer. Remove the old seal from the pick-up tube mounting hole.

To install:

7. Apply a continuous bead of silicone sealant to the oil pan gasket surface.
8. Install a new pick-up seal into the tube mounting hole.
9. Raise the oil pan and oil pump pick-up into position. Install the pick-up tube, and tighten the retaining bolts to 80–106 inch lbs. (9–12 Nm).

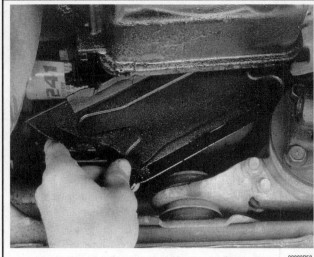

. . . then remove the inspection plate from the transmission

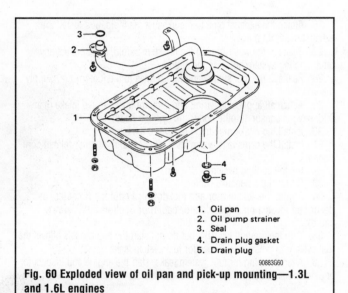

1. Oil pan
2. Oil pump strainer
3. Seal
4. Drain plug gasket
5. Drain plug

Fig. 60 Exploded view of oil pan and pick-up mounting—1.3L and 1.6L engines

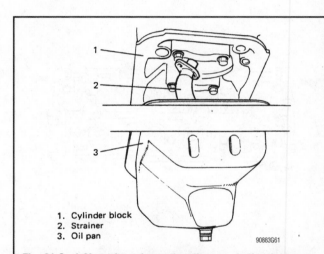

1. Cylinder block
2. Strainer
3. Oil pan

Fig. 61 On 1.3L engines, lower the oil pan and allow it to rest on the crossmember, then detach the pick-up tube from the oil pump—remove both components together from the vehicle

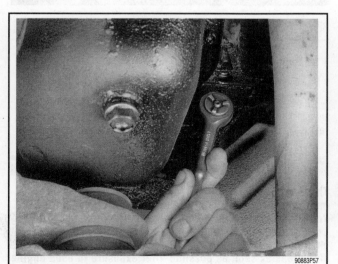

To remove the oil pan, loosen the lower inspection plate retaining bolts . . .

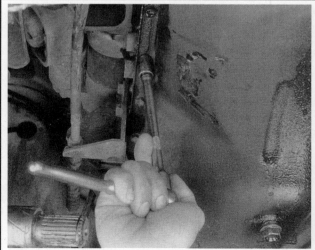

On 1.6L engines, loosen all of the oil pan retaining bolts . . .

10. Position the oil pan against the engine block and install all of the mounting bolts finger-tight.

11. Tighten the oil pan mounting bolts to 80–106 inch lbs. (9–12 Nm) by starting at the center of the oil pan and working your way toward both ends.

12. Install the oil pan drain plug, along with a new washer. Tighten the drain plug to 22–28 ft. lbs. (30–40 Nm).

13. Install the lower clutch or torque converter inspection cover.

14. If applicable, install the undervehicle skid plate, and lower the vehicle.

Remove the two bolts . . .

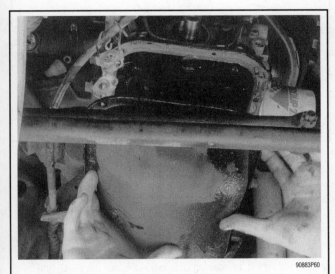

. . . then remove the oil pan from the engine

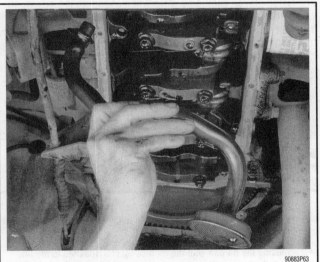

. . . and detach the pick-up and screen from the oil pump

Once the oil pan is lowered, the two pick-up mounting bolts (arrows) can be accessed

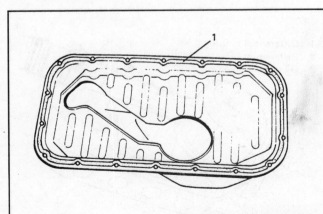

1. Sealant (99000-31150)

Fig. 62 On 1.3L and 1.6L engines, apply a continuous bead of silicone sealant to the oil pan mating flange to properly seal the engine block-to-oil pan joint

Wait at least 30 minutes after tightening the oil pan mounting bolts before adding oil to the engine. This time period will allow the silicone sealant to set properly.

15. Fill the engine with the proper amount and type of engine oil. Refer to section 1 for details.
16. Start the engine and check for oil leaks from the oil pan perimeter.

1.6L Engine

▶ See Figures 63 and 64

1. Apply the parking brake and block the rear wheels, then raise and safely support the front of the vehicle on jackstands.
2. On 4-wheel drive models, remove the front differential from the vehicle.
3. On MFI engines, remove the Crankshaft Position (CKP) sensor.

The EPA warns that prolonged contact with used engine oil may cause a number of skin disorders, including cancer! You should make every effort to minimize your exposure to used engine oil. Protective gloves should be worn when changing the oil. Wash your hands and any other exposed skin areas as soon as possible after exposure to used engine oil. Soap and water, or waterless hand cleaner should be used.

4. Drain the engine oil into a large catch pan.
5. On MFI engines equipped with automatic transmissions, remove the left-hand side transmission brace.
6. Remove the clutch or torque converter inspection cover.

Do not use a prytool between the oil pan and engine block mating surfaces to separate the two components, otherwise the gasket surface may be damaged.

7. Remove the oil pan mounting bolts and lower the oil pan from the engine. Remove the oil pick-up tube retaining bolt(s), then remove the tube from the engine.

➡**If removing the oil pan with the oil pick-up still attached to the oil pump is difficult, lower the oil pan as far as possible, detach the pick-up attaching bolts, then remove the pan with the pick-up from the vehicle.**

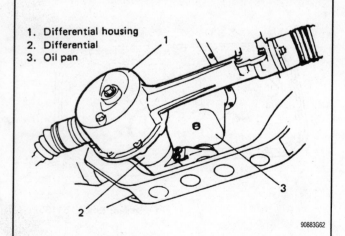

1. Differential housing
2. Differential
3. Oil pan

90883G62

Fig. 63 On 4-wheel drive models, remove the front differential from the vehicle for oil pan removal

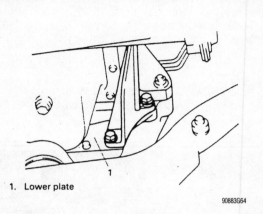

1. Lower plate

90883G64

Fig. 64 On 1.6L MFI engines mated to automatic transmissions, the left-hand side transmission brace must be removed before the torque converter inspection plate

8. Thoroughly clean the engine block gasket surface, the oil pan and the pick-up tube of all oil, grime and old silicone sealant. Remove the old seal from the pick-up tube mounting hole.

To install:

9. Apply a continuous bead of silicone sealant (such as Suzuki Sealant 99000–31150) to the oil pan gasket surface.
10. Install a new pick-up seal into the tube mounting hole.
11. Raise the oil pan and oil pump pick-up into position. Install the pick-up tube, and tighten the retaining bolts to 80–106 inch lbs. (9–12 Nm).
12. Position the oil pan against the engine block and install all of the mounting bolts finger-tight.
13. Tighten the oil pan mounting bolts to 80–106 inch lbs. (9–12 Nm) by starting at the center of the oil pan and working your way toward both ends.
14. Install the oil pan drain plug, along with a new washer. Tighten the drain plug to 22–28 ft. lbs. (30–40 Nm).
15. Install the lower clutch or torque converter inspection cover.
16. If applicable, install the left-hand side transmission brace, and tighten the mounting bolts to 36 ft. lbs. (50 Nm).
17. If applicable, install the front differential assembly.
18. Refill the front differential with the proper type and amount of lubricant. Refer to section 1 for details.
19. If equipped, install the CKP sensor.
20. Lower the vehicle.

Wait at least 30 minutes after tightening the oil pan mounting bolts before adding oil to the engine. This time period will allow the silicone sealant to set properly.

21. Fill the engine with the proper amount and type of engine oil. Refer to section 1 for details.
22. Start the engine and check for oil leaks from the oil pan perimeter.

1.8L Engine

▶ See Figures 65, 66 and 67

1. Break loose the lug nuts on both front wheels.
2. Apply the parking brake and block the rear wheels, then raise and safely support the front of the vehicle on jackstands.
3. Remove the engine oil dipstick and tube from the engine.
4. Remove the front wheels, then remove the differential from the vehicle.
5. Remove the tie rods, center link and idler arm from the vehicle, as described in Section 8.

6. Drain the engine oil into a large catch pan.
7. Remove the clutch or torque converter inspection cover.

☀☀ WARNING

Do not use a prytool between the oil pan and engine block mating surfaces to separate the two components, otherwise the gasket surface may be damaged.

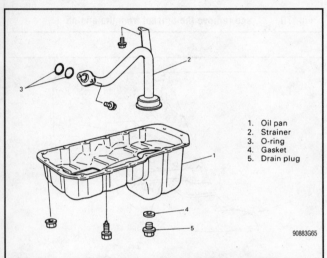

1. Oil pan
2. Strainer
3. O-ring
4. Gasket
5. Drain plug

90883G65

Fig. 65 Exploded view of the oil pan and oil pump pick-up and screen mounting

8. Remove the oil pan mounting bolts and lower the oil pan from the engine; temporarily support it on the vehicle crossmember. Using an open end wrench inserted between the lowered oil pan and the engine block, remove the oil pick-up tube retaining bolt(s). Separate the pick-up tube from the oil pump, then remove the tube and oil pan from the vehicle together.

9. Thoroughly clean the engine block gasket surface, the oil pan and the pick-up tube of all oil, grime and old silicone sealant. Remove the old seal from the pick-up tube mounting hole.

To install:

10. Apply a continuous bead of silicone sealant (such as Suzuki Sealant 99000–31150) to the oil pan mating surface.

11. Install a new pick-up seal into the tube mounting hole.

12. Raise the oil pan and oil pump pick-up into position. Install the pick-up tube, and tighten the retaining bolts to 80–106 inch lbs. (9–12 Nm).

13. Position the oil pan against the engine block and install all of the mounting bolts finger-tight.

14. Tighten the oil pan mounting bolts to 80–106 inch lbs. (9–12 Nm) by starting at the center of the oil pan and working your way toward both ends.

15. Install the oil pan drain plug, along with a new washer. Tighten the drain plug to 22–28 ft. lbs. (30–40 Nm).

16. Install the lower clutch or torque converter inspection cover.

17. Install the tie rods, center link and idler arm.

18. Install the front differential assembly.

19. Refill the front differential with the proper type and amount of lubricant. Refer to section 1 for details.

20. Install the engine oil level dipstick and tube.

21. Lower the vehicle.

☀☀ WARNING

Wait at least 30 minutes after tightening the oil pan mounting bolts before adding oil to the engine. This time period will allow the silicone sealant to set properly.

22. Fill the engine with the proper amount and type of engine oil. Refer to section 1 for details.

23. Start the engine and check for oil leaks from the oil pan perimeter.

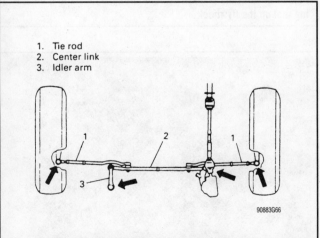

1. Tie rod
2. Center link
3. Idler arm

90883G66

Fig. 66 The tie rods, center link and idler arm must be removed for oil pan removal—detach the steering components at the points indicated (black arrows)

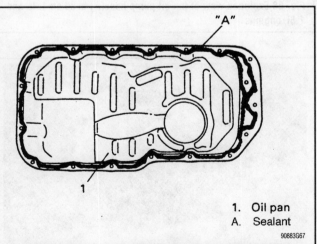

1. Oil pan
A. Sealant

90883G67

Fig. 67 Be sure to apply a continuous bead of silicone sealant to the oil pan mating flange prior to installation, otherwise oil leakage may occur

Oil Pump

REMOVAL & INSTALLATION

1.3L and 1.6L Engines

▶ **See Figures 68 thru 94**

1. Disconnect the negative battery cable.
2. Remove the timing belt and tensioner.
3. Remove the alternator and mounting bracket.

➡**If your vehicle is equipped with air conditioning, refer to Section 1 for information regarding the implications of servicing your A/C system yourself. Only an MVAC-trained, EPA-certified automotive technician should service the A/C system or its components.**

4. If equipped, remove the air conditioning compressor bracket bolts and support the compressor out of the way. Do NOT disconnect any of the A/C refrigerant lines.
5. Apply the parking brake and block the rear wheels, then raise and safely support the front of the vehicle on jackstands.

Fig. 70 . . . and remove the bracket from the engine

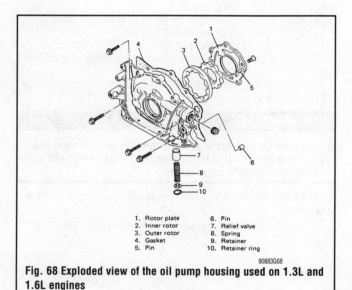

1. Rotor plate
2. Inner rotor
3. Outer rotor
4. Gasket
5. Pin
6. Pin
7. Relief valve
8. Spring
9. Retainer
10. Retainer ring

Fig. 68 Exploded view of the oil pump housing used on 1.3L and 1.6L engines

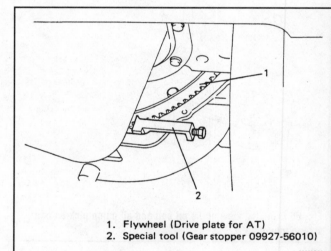

1. Flywheel (Drive plate for AT)
2. Special tool (Gear stopper 09927-56010)

Fig. 71 Prevent the crankshaft from turning by installing a holding tool on the flywheel . . .

Fig. 69 To remove the oil pump, remove the timing belt, then loosen the P/S pump bracket bolts . . .

Fig. 72 . . . or you can use a large prybar to hold the flywheel steady

6. Drain the engine and front differential oil.

7. Remove the lower transmission (clutch or torque converter) inspection cover.

8. Remove the crankshaft timing belt sprocket by loosening the center bolt, while preventing the crankshaft from rotating. To hold the crankshaft from turning, you can use Suzuki Tool 09927–56010 (or equivalent), or a large prybar inserted in the transmission housing slot and the flywheel teeth (also shown in the accompanying photographs).

9. Remove the oil pan and oil pump pick-up.

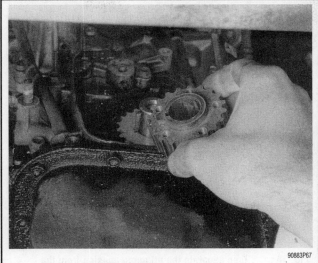

Fig. 75 . . . then slide the sprocket . . .

Fig. 73 To use the prybar, insert it in the transmission case groove (arrow) and between two flywheel teeth

Fig. 76 . . . and the timing belt guide off of the crankshaft

Fig. 74 With the crankshaft secured, loosen the timing belt sprocket retaining bolt . . .

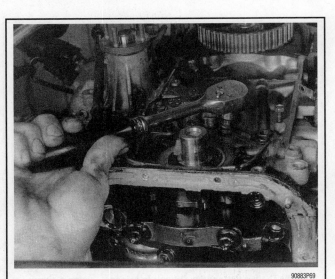

Fig. 77 Loosen all 7 oil pump housing mounting bolts . . .

Fig. 78 . . . then separate the oil pump housing from the engine block

10. Loosen the seven mounting bolts, and remove the oil pump housing. If the housing is difficult to separate from the engine block, use a small prytool against one of the mounting bolt bosses—do NOT slide the prybar between the oil pump housing and engine block mating surfaces.

11. If the oil pump is to be inspected, disassemble and inspect it as follows:

    a. Remove the oil level dipstick tube bracket bolt, then pull the dipstick and tube out of the oil pump housing.

    b. Remove the oil pump rotor plate by loosening the five retaining screws. The rotor plate retaining screws can be difficult to remove, be sure not to strip the Philips grooves in the heads of the screws, otherwise the screw will need to be drilled out of the housing.

    c. Remove the outer and inner rotors from the housing.

    d. Without scratching the oil seal bore surface, use a small punch to drive the oil seal, or a seal removal tool to pry the oil seal, from the housing.

    e. Remove the oil pressure relief retaining snap-ring from the housing bore, then remove the retainer cap, spring and piston from the housing. Ensure that the piston bore is thoroughly cleaned when cleaning the housing.

    f. Clean the oil pump housing, rotors and pressure regulating components until free of all dirt and oil.

Fig. 79 If the oil pump is to be inspected, remove the 5 cover screws and remove the cover from the housing

Fig. 81 Remove the oil pressure relief retaining snapring . . .

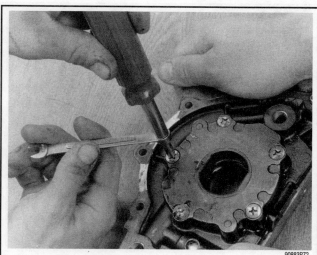

Fig. 80 The screws can be difficult to remove—using a screwdriver with wrenchable flats will increase leverage

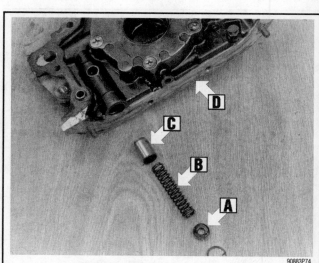

Fig. 82 . . . then extract the retainer cap (A), spring (B) and piston (C) from the housing (D)

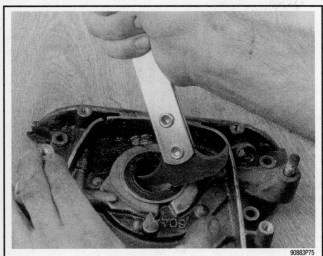

Fig. 83 Use a seal prytool to remove the old oil seal from its bore

g. Install the inner and outer rotors in the oil housing bore. The outer rotor should be installed so that the small dot, marked on one of its faces, points away from the housing. The inner rotor will only fit in the housing in one orientation: the raised ring must face away from the housing.

h. Using feeler gauges, measure the clearance between the outer rotor and bore wall. Then, using a straightedge spanning the oil pump housing and rotors, measure the clearance between the edge of the straightedge and oil pump rotors. Compare your findings with the engine rebuilding specification charts at the end of this section.

i. If the measurements were not within the specified ranges, or one or more oil pump components shows evidence of excessive wear or damage, the oil pump components should be replaced.

To install:

12. If the oil pump was disassembled for inspection, assemble it as follows:

a. Using an oil seal installer, or an aptly-sized socket, drive the new oil seal into the seal bore. Ensure that the seal is driven in straight and is fully seated in the housing.

b. Apply a thin coat of clean engine oil to the oil pump rotors, the oil seal lip, the inside surfaces of the oil pump housing (including the regulator bore), and to the oil pressure piston (relief valve).

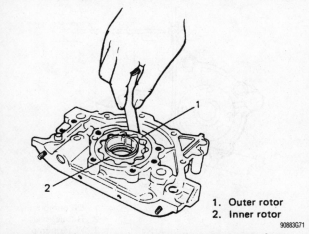

1. Outer rotor
2. Inner rotor

Fig. 84 Use feeler gauges to measure the outer rotor-to-bore wall clearance—if the clearance is out of specifications, the oil pump components must be replaced

Fig. 86 Use an oil seal installer, or a large socket, and a hammer to drive the new seal into the housing

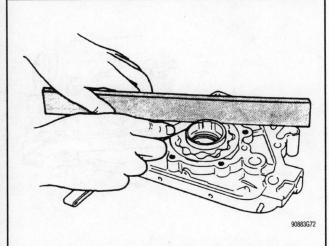

Fig. 85 Using a straightedge and feeler gauges, also measure the amount of rotor side clearance

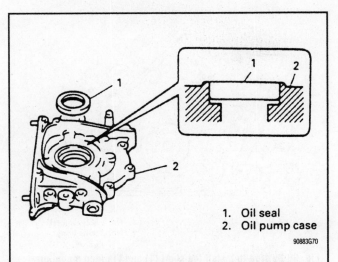

1. Oil seal
2. Oil pump case

Fig. 87 Drive the oil seal into the housing until its outer edge is flush with the oil pump housing surface

Fig. 88 When installing the rotors, ensure that the dot (arrow) on the outer rotor faces away from the housing

c. Install the relief valve, the spring, the retainer cap and a new snap-ring in the housing bore.

d. Install the inner and outer pump rotors in the housing.

e. Position the rotor plate on the housing, then install and tighten the five retaining screws securely. After tightening the screws, ensure that the oil pump rotors spin smoothly by hand.

f. Install a new oil level dipstick tube seal in the housing, then insert the end of the tube in the housing. Install the tube bracket bolt and tighten it securely.

13. Ensure the two oil pump locating pins are installed in the engine block, then install a new oil pump housing-to-engine block gasket.

14. Install Suzuki Tool 09926–18210, or its equivalent, onto the crankshaft. Apply a thin coating of clean engine oil onto the outer surfaces of the tool. This tool will prevent the new oil seal lip from being damaged when the oil pump housing is installed on the engine block.

15. Ensure the flats on the inside of the oil pump bore are aligned with the flats on the crankshaft, then carefully slide the oil pump housing onto the crankshaft and against the engine block until flush. Install the oil pump housing mounting bolts and tighten them to 97 inch lbs. (11 Nm). When installing the oil pump mounting bolts, be sure to install the shorter oil pump bolts as indicated in the accompanying illustration. The three other bolts are slightly longer and should be installed in the lower holes.

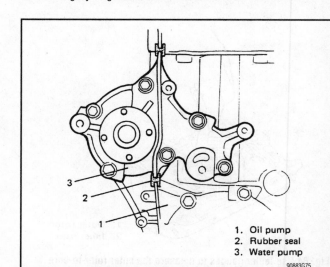

1. Crankshaft
2. Special tool
   (Oil seal guide (Vinyl resin) 09926-18210)

Fig. 89 Install the special tool over the crankshaft so that the new oil seal lip will not be damaged when the oil pump housing is installed

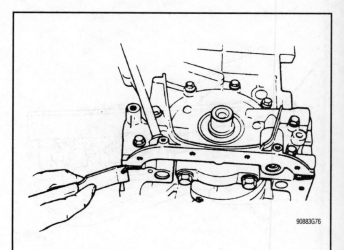

1. Oil pump
2. Rubber seal
3. Water pump

Fig. 91 Install a new rubber seal between the oil pump and the water pump before installing the timing belt outer cover

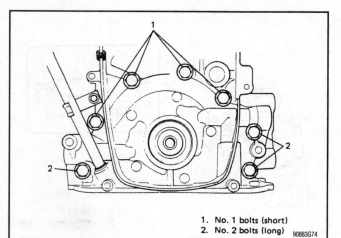

1. No. 1 bolts (short)
2. No. 2 bolts (long)

Fig. 90 Be sure to install the short (1) and the long mounting bolts (2) in the correct positions during oil pump housing installation

Fig. 92 After installing the oil pump housing, cut any protruding gasket material off flush with the oil pan mating surface

16. Install a new rubber seal between the oil pump and the water pump.

17. Inspect the lower oil pump edge to ensure that the gasket is not protruding past the surface. If the gasket protrudes from the oil pump, cut it flush with a sharp knife.

18. Install the timing belt guide, key and crankshaft timing belt sprocket.

19. Install the timing belt, tensioner, oil pump pick-up, oil pan and all other related components.

20. On 4-wheel drive models, install the front differential unit.

✷✷ WARNING

Operating the engine without the proper amount and type of engine oil can result in severe engine damage.

21. Adjust the valve lash on all valves, then refill the engine with the proper type and amount of engine oil.

22. If equipped, refill the front differential with the proper type and amount of lubricant.

23. Connect the negative battery cable.

24. After filling the engine with engine oil, start the vehicle and inspect the oil pressure as follows:

   a. Remove the oil pressure switch from the engine block.

   b. Install an oil pressure gauge in the oil pressure switch threaded hole. Ensure that your oil pressure gauge hose is equipped with the same thread pitch and size as the oil pressure switch, otherwise damage to the oil pressure switch hole will result.

   c. Start the engine and allow it to warm up to normal operating temperature.

   d. Place the transmission in Neutral (manual models) or Park (automatic models), apply the parking brake and block the drive wheels.

   e. Raise the engine speed to 3000 rpm and read the value indicated by the oil pressure gauge. The oil pressure should match the values presented in the engine rebuilding specifications charts at the end of this section. If the oil pressure is not as indicated, there is a defect in the engine lubrication system.

   f. After inspecting the oil pressure, stop the engine and remove the oil pressure gauge.

   g. Install the oil pressure switch, making sure to wrap its threads with Teflon® sealing tape. Tighten the switch to 124 inch lbs. (14 Nm). Cut off any exposed Teflon® tape.

25. Start the engine and inspect the oil pan and pressure switch for leaks.

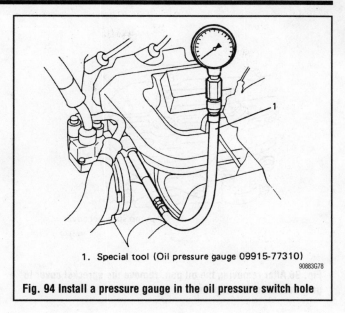

1. Special tool (Oil pressure gauge 09915-77310)

90883G78

Fig. 94 Install a pressure gauge in the oil pressure switch hole

1.8L Engine

♦ See Figures 95 thru 103

1. Disconnect the negative battery cable.

2. Remove the oil pan and oil pump pick-up.

3. Remove the oil pump sprocket cover mounting bolts, then separate the cover from the engine.

➡**When separating the pump from the engine, do not loose the small locating dowels; they will be needed upon installation.**

4. Remove the oil pump mounting bolts, and remove the oil pump from the lower crankcase. If the oil pump is difficult to separate from the engine, tap it lightly with a soft-faced mallet until it works loose.

✷✷ WARNING

Do NOT remove the sprocket from the oil pump, otherwise damage to the oil pump center shaft and abnormal pump operation may be the result.

5. Clean the oil pump-to-engine mating surface thoroughly.

6. If the oil pump is to be inspected, disassemble and inspect it as follows:

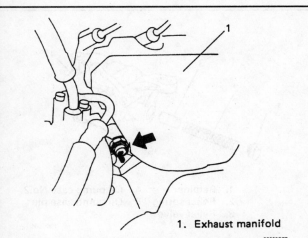

1. Exhaust manifold

90883G77

Fig. 93 To test the engine oil pressure, remove the oil pressure switch (arrow), which is threaded into the engine block, next to the exhaust manifold

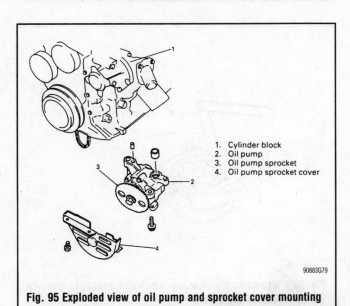

1. Cylinder block
2. Oil pump
3. Oil pump sprocket
4. Oil pump sprocket cover

90883G79

Fig. 95 Exploded view of oil pump and sprocket cover mounting

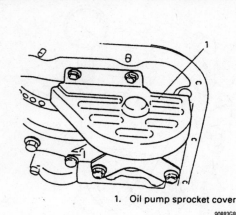

1. Oil pump sprocket cover

90883G80

Fig. 96 After removing the oil pan, remove the sprocket cover to gain access to the oil pump

a. Separate the two oil pump case halves by loosening the five attaching screws.

b. Remove the outer and inner rotors from the housing.

c. Remove the oil pressure relief retainer from the housing, then remove the spring and piston (relief valve) from the housing. Ensure that the piston bore is thoroughly cleaned when cleaning the housing.

d. Clean the oil pump housing, rotors and pressure relief components until free of all dirt and oil.

e. Install the inner and outer rotors in the oil housing bore.

f. Using feeler gauges, measure the clearance between the outer rotor and bore wall. Then, using a straightedge spanning the oil pump housing and rotors, measure the clearance between the edge of the straightedge and oil pump rotors. Compare your findings with the engine rebuilding specification charts at the end of this section.

g. If the measurements were not within the specified ranges, or one or more oil pump components shows evidence of excessive wear or damage, the oil pump should be replaced.

To install:

7. If the oil pump was disassembled for inspection, assemble it as follows:

a. Apply a thin coat of clean engine oil to the oil pump rotors, the inside surfaces of the oil pump housing (including the relief bore), and to the oil pressure piston (relief valve).

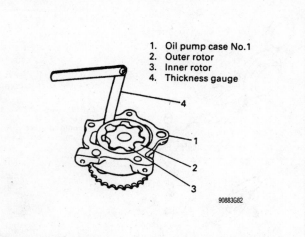

1. Oil pump case No.1	4. Relief valve
2. Oil pump case No.2	5. Relief spring
3. Outer rotor	6. Retainer

90883G81

Fig. 97 Exploded view of the oil pump assembly

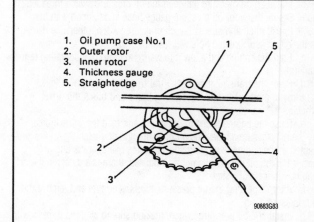

1. Oil pump case No.1
2. Outer rotor
3. Inner rotor
4. Thickness gauge
5. Straightedge

90883G83

Fig. 99 . . . and the rotor side clearance—if the clearances measured are not within the specified ranges, replace the oil pump

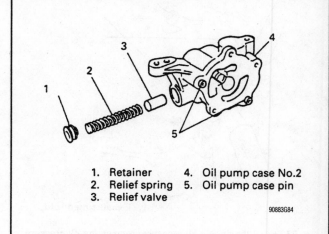

1. Oil pump case No.1
2. Outer rotor
3. Inner rotor
4. Thickness gauge

90883G82

Fig. 98 If inspecting the oil pump, use feeler gauges to measure the outer rotor-to-pump bore . . .

1. Retainer	4. Oil pump case No.2
2. Relief spring	5. Oil pump case pin
3. Relief valve	

90883G84

Fig. 100 Before assembling the two oil pump case halves, ensure that the locating (case) pins are installed

b. Install the relief valve, the spring, and the retainer in the housing bore.

c. Install the inner and outer pump rotors in the housing.

d. Assemble the two oil pump halves, then install and tighten the five retaining screws to 106 inch lbs. (12 Nm). After tightening the screws, ensure that the oil pump gear spins smoothly by hand.

→ **When installing the oil pump, do not allow the locating dowels to fall out of position.**

8. Ensure the locating dowels are installed in the pump, then position the oil pump sprocket in the drive chain and the pump housing against the lower crankcase. Install and tighten the mounting bolts to 177 inch lbs. (20 Nm).

9. Install the oil pump sprocket cover and tighten the mounting bolts to 97 inch lbs. (11 Nm).

10. Install the oil pump pick-up and oil pan.

11. Refill the engine with the proper type and amount of engine oil.

※※ WARNING

Operating the engine without the proper amount and type of engine oil can result in severe engine damage.

12. Connect the negative battery cable.

13. After filling the engine with engine oil, start the vehicle and inspect the oil pressure as follows:

a. Remove the oil pressure switch from the engine block.

b. Install an oil pressure gauge in the oil pressure switch threaded hole. Ensure that your oil pressure gauge hose is equipped with the same threads as the oil pressure switch, otherwise damage to the oil pressure switch hole will result.

c. Start the engine and allow it to warm up to normal operating temperature.

d. Place the transmission in Neutral (manual models) or Park (automatic models), apply the parking brake and block the drive wheels.

e. Raise the engine speed to 4000 rpm and read the value indicated by the oil pressure gauge. The oil pressure should be 55–66 psi (390–470 kPa). If the oil pressure is not as indicated, there is a defect in the engine lubrication system.

f. After inspecting the oil pressure, stop the engine and remove the oil pressure gauge.

g. Install the oil pressure switch, making sure to wrap its threads with Teflon® sealing tape. Tighten the switch to 124 inch lbs. (14 Nm). Cut off any exposed Teflon® tape.

h. Start the engine and inspect the oil pan and pressure switch for leaks.

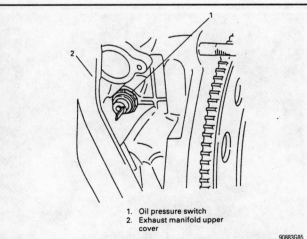

1. Oil pressure switch
2. Exhaust manifold upper cover

90883G85

Fig. 101 To inspect the oil pump output pressure, remove the oil pressure sender, located near the flywheel on the left-hand side of the engine . . .

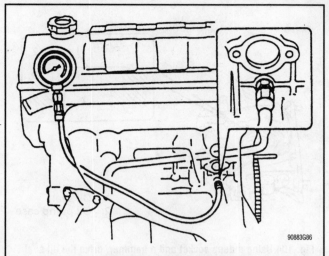

90883G86

Fig. 102 . . . then install an oil pressure gauge—run the engine at 4000 rpm and observe the gauge for oil pump output pressure

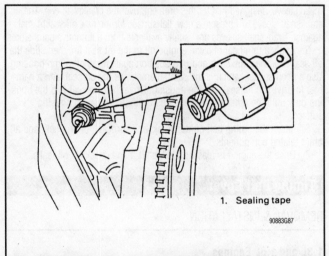

1. Sealing tape

90883G87

Fig. 103 Wrap the oil pressure sender threads with sealing tape prior to installation

OIL SEAL REPLACEMENT

◆ **See Figure 104**

→ **This procedure only applies to the 1.3L and 1.6L engines; the 1.8L engine oil pump does not use an oil seal. This procedure is also written for oil seal replacement only. If you must remove the oil pump for other service, the procedures presented under oil pump removal and installation include oil seal replacement.**

1. Remove the timing belt, crankshaft sprocket and belt guide.

2. Using a small prytool, carefully pry the old oil seal out of the oil pump housing bore. Take care not to scratch the oil pump housing bore, otherwise oil leakage may occur. Wrapping a piece of tape around the end of the prytool may help reduce the change of scoring the bore by covering any sharp corners on the tool.

3. Clean the oil pump housing bore and the crankshaft.

4. If the oil seal is being removed because of oil leakage, inspect the crankshaft surface where the oil seal contacts it. If there is a wear groove on the crankshaft, a new oil seal will probably not cure the oil leak. Before removing the crankshaft and replacing it, attempt to repair it by installing a

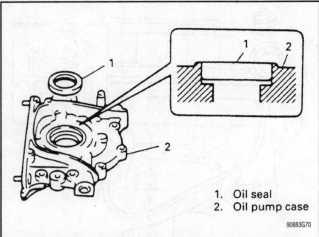

1. Oil seal
2. Oil pump case

90883G70

Fig. 104 Using a deep socket and a hammer, drive the oil seal into the housing until its outer edge is flush with the oil pump housing surface

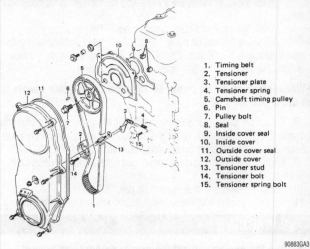

1. Timing belt
2. Tensioner
3. Tensioner plate
4. Tensioner spring
5. Camshaft timing pulley
6. Pin
7. Pulley bolt
8. Seal
9. Inside cover seal
10. Inside cover
11. Outside cover seal
12. Outside cover
13. Tensioner stud
14. Tensioner bolt
15. Tensioner spring bolt

90883GA3

Fig. 105 Exploded view of timing belt, cover and camshaft sprocket mounting

metal sleeve, designed just for this problem, over the crankshaft end. The crankshaft sleeve will present a new, flat surface for the new oil seal to seal against. Crankshaft sleeves are usually available from automotive parts stores.

5. Apply a thin coat of clean engine oil to the oil seal lip, then slide the oil seal over the crankshaft and into position against the oil pump housing. Use a deep socket, which is the same diameter as the oil seal, and a hammer to drive the oil seal into the housing. Drive the new seal into the housing only until the outer seal edge is flush with the oil pump housing surface.

6. Install the timing belt guide, crankshaft sprocket, timing belt, and all other related components.

7. Once the engine is reassembled, start it and check for oil leaks.

Timing Belt Cover

REMOVAL & INSTALLATION

1.3L and 1.6L Engines

▶ See Figure 105

➡**If your vehicle is equipped with air conditioning, refer to Section 1 for information regarding the implications of servicing your A/C system yourself. Only an MVAC-trained, EPA-certified automotive technician should service the A/C system or its components.**

1. If your vehicle is equipped with air conditioning, have your A/C system evacuated by a qualified MVAC technician.
2. Disconnect the negative battery cable.
3. Remove the engine cooling fan and fan shroud.
4. If equipped, detach the A/C compressor suction flexible hose from the pipe. Also, remove the A/C compressor drive belt.
5. Remove the water pump drive belt and the water pump pulley.
6. Remove the crankshaft pulley by loosening the outer retaining bolts and pulling it off of the end of the crankshaft.

➡**The crankshaft pulley center bolt does not hold the pulley on the crankshaft (it secures the timing belt sprocket on the crankshaft) and should not be loosened at this time.**

7. Remove the timing belt outer cover retaining fasteners, then pull the cover off of the engine block and cylinder head.
8. Clean the timing belt cover, engine block gasket mating surface, and seal of all dirt and grime. Inspect the seal for damage, such as tears, rips, crumbling, excessive hardening, etc. Replace the seal if any damage is evident.

90883PG6

To remove the crankshaft pulley, loosen the mounting bolts . . .

90883PG7

. . . then remove the pulley and bolts from the crankshaft

Loosen the timing belt cover retaining bolts . . .

90883PG8

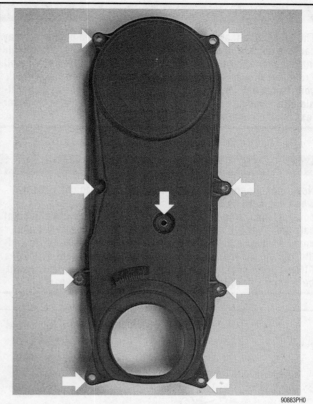

The timing cover is held onto the engine with bolts at nine points (arrows)

90883PH0

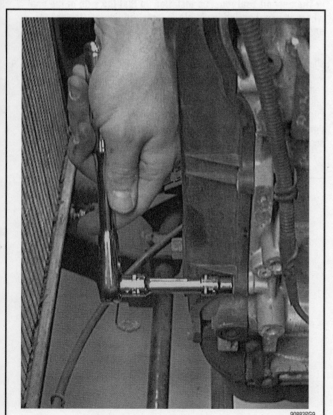

. . . and be sure to locate all of the retaining bolts, including the ones at the bottom of the cover

90883PG9

To install:

9. Install the timing belt cover gasket in the groove on the inside of the cover. Position the cover on the engine block and cylinder head, then install the retaining fasteners. Tighten the fasteners until snug.

10. Slide the crankshaft pulley on the end of the crankshaft so that the keyway in the pulley is aligned with the key on the crankshaft. Install the pulley retaining bolts, and tighten them to 80–106 inch lbs. (9–12 Nm).

11. Install the water pump pulley and the accessory drive belts.

12. Install the engine cooling fan and shroud.

13. If equipped, reconnect the air conditioner compressor suction flexible hose and pipe.

14. Adjust the accessory drive belt tension, as described in Section 1.

15. Connect the negative battery cable.

16. If equipped, have the A/C system evacuated and recharged by a qualified MVAC technician.

Timing Chain Cover and Seal

REMOVAL & INSTALLATION

1.8L Engine

▶ See Figures 106, 107, 108, 109 and 110

➡It is a good idea to keep your ignition keys with the new oil containers so that you do not accidentally start the engine before filling it with oil.

1. Disconnect the negative battery cable.

The EPA warns that prolonged contact with used engine oil may cause a number of skin disorders, including cancer! You should make every effort to minimize your exposure to used engine oil. Protective gloves should be worn when changing the oil. Wash your hands and any other exposed skin areas as soon as possible after exposure to used engine oil. Soap and water, or waterless hand cleaner should be used.

2. Drain the engine oil.

Never open, service or drain the radiator or cooling system when hot; serious burns can occur from the steam and hot coolant. Also, when draining engine coolant, keep in mind that cats and dogs are attracted to ethylene glycol antifreeze and could drink any that is left in an uncovered container or in puddles on the ground. This will prove fatal in sufficient quantities. Always drain coolant into a sealable container. Coolant should be reused unless it is contaminated or is several years old.

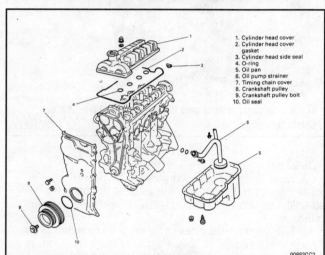

1. Cylinder head cover
2. Cylinder head cover gasket
3. Cylinder head side seal
4. O-ring
5. Oil pan
6. Oil pump strainer
7. Timing chain cover
8. Crankshaft pulley
9. Crankshaft pulley bolt
10. Oil seal

90883GC2

Fig. 106 Exploded view of timing chain cover and crankshaft pulley mounting

3. Drain the engine coolant.
4. Remove the oil pan and oil pump pick-up.
5. Remove the rocker arm cover.
6. Remove the water bypass pipe and bypass hose No. 2.
7. Remove the cooling fan, pulley and accessory drive belt.
8. Remove the alternator drive belt.
9. Remove the water pump pulley.
10. Remove the alternator drive belt tensioner and idler pulley.
11. Detach the upper radiator hose from the thermostat housing.
12. If equipped, without disconnecting the A/C hoses, separate the A/C compressor from the compressor mounting bracket. Position the compressor aside and secure it with strong cord or wire.
13. If equipped, remove the A/C compressor mounting bracket from the engine.
14. Using a long breaker bar and socket, remove the crankshaft pulley bolt. To secure the crankshaft from rotating, install a pulley holding tool (such as Suzuki Tool 09917–68221). Use M8, P1.25 bolts with a strength rating of at least 7T to attach the holding tool to the pulley.
15. Once the bolt is removed, install a steering wheel puller on the crankshaft drive belt pulley, then draw the pulley off of the end of the crankshaft.
16. Remove the timing chain cover retaining fasteners, then pull the cover off of the engine and cylinder head.
17. Clean the gasket mating surfaces on the timing chain cover, engine block, and cylinder head of all oil, dirt and old sealant material.

Take care not to damage the oil seal bore during removal, otherwise oil leakage may occur.

18. Remove the crankshaft oil seal from the cover by using a seal pry-tool, or by driving it out of the cover with a drift and hammer.

To install:

➡ The new oil seal must be installed so that the side of the seal where the seal spring is visible is installed inward (toward the engine block).

19. Use a seal installation tool should be used to install a new crankshaft oil seal in the timing chain cover. If the driving tool is not available, a large socket and hammer can be used. The socket diameter should be the same as the metal part of the oil seal. Drive the seal into the cover bore until the outer surface of the seal is flush with the timing chain cover.
20. Apply silicone sealant, such as Suzuki sealant 99000–31150, to the timing chain cover on the cover-to-engine mating surface. Refer to the accompanying illustration for sealant application.

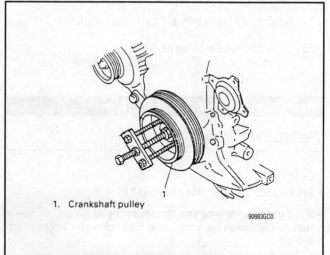

1. Crankshaft pulley

90883GC0

Fig. 107 A steering wheel puller will be necessary to draw the accessory drive belt pulley off of the end of the crankshaft

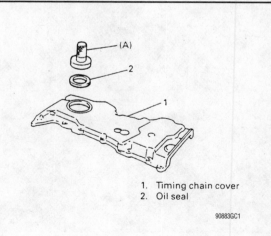

(A)
2
1

1. Timing chain cover
2. Oil seal

90883GC1

Fig. 108 Use a seal installer (A) and hammer to drive the new oil seal into the cover bore until the outer edge of the seal is flush with the cover surface

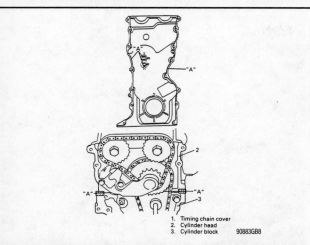

Fig. 109 Prior to installing the timing chain cover on the engine block and cylinder head, apply silicone sealant to the cover as indicated (areas marked A)

1. Timing chain cover
2. Cylinder head
3. Cylinder block   90883GB8

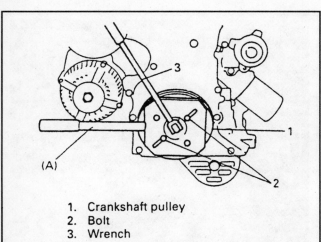

1. Crankshaft pulley
2. Bolt
3. Wrench

90883GB9

Fig. 110 Use a spanner tool (A) to hold the crankshaft pulley steady while tightening the center bolt to 109 ft. lbs. (150 Nm)

21. Ensure that the timing chain cover locating dowel is installed in the engine block. Apply a thin coat of clean engine oil to the crankshaft oil seal lip, then install the cover. Tighten the cover retaining bolts to 97 inch lbs. (11 Nm).

22. Slide the crankshaft pulley onto the end of the crankshaft and install the center bolt. Install the crankshaft holding tool, then tighten the center bolt to 109 ft. lbs. (150 Nm). The center bolt will draw the pulley onto the crankshaft when tightened to the specified torque value.

23. If equipped, install the A/C compressor mounting bracket. Tighten the bolts to 40 ft. lbs. (55 Nm).

24. Install the alternator drive belt idler pulley. Tighten the retaining nut to 33 ft. lbs. (45 Nm).

25. Reattach the upper radiator hose to the thermostat housing.

26. Install the alternator drive belt tensioner. Tighten the tensioner mounting bolts to 19 ft. lbs. (25 Nm).

27. Install the cooling fan belt, pulley and fan.

28. Install the water pump pulley.

29. Install the alternator drive belt.

30. Install the water bypass pipe and bypass hose No. 2. Tighten the bolts to 203 inch lbs. (23 Nm).

31. Install the rocker arm cover.

32. Install the oil pump pick-up and the oil pan.

33. Adjust the cooling fan drive belt tension, as described in Section 1.

34. Refill the cooling system with the proper amount and type of coolant.

35. Refill the front differential (if applicable) with the proper amount and type of lubricant.

※※ WARNING

Operating the engine without the proper amount and type of engine oil can result in severe engine damage.

36. Refill the engine with the proper amount and type of clean engine oil.

37. Start the engine and check for coolant, oil and exhaust leaks.

38. Have your front wheel alignment inspected.

OIL SEAL REPLACEMENT

Oil seal replacement is covered in the cover removal and installation procedure. However, if the oil seal needs to be replaced but the cover does not need to removed, use the following procedure.

1. Disconnect the negative battery cable.

2. If extra clearance is necessary for crankshaft drive belt pulley removal is necessary, remove the cooling fan, pulley and accessory drive belt.

3. Remove the alternator drive belt.

4. Using a long breaker bar and socket, remove the crankshaft pulley bolt. To secure the crankshaft from rotating, install a pulley holding tool (such as Suzuki Tool 09917–68221). Use M8, P1.25 bolts with a strength rating of at least 7T to attach the holding tool to the pulley.

5. Once the bolt is removed, install a steering wheel puller on the crankshaft drive belt pulley, then draw the pulley off of the end of the crankshaft.

※※ WARNING

Take care not to damage the oil seal bore during removal, otherwise oil leakage may occur.

6. Using a small prytool, carefully pry the old oil seal out of the cover bore. Take care not to scratch the oil pump housing bore, otherwise oil leakage may occur. Wrapping a piece of tape around the end of the prytool may help reduce the change of scoring the bore by covering any sharp corners on the tool.

7. Clean the oil seal bore and the crankshaft.

8. If the oil seal is being removed because of oil leakage, inspect the crankshaft surface where the oil seal contacts it. If there is a wear groove on the crankshaft, a new oil seal will probably not cure the oil leak. Before removing the crankshaft and replacing it, explore the possibility of repairing it by installing a metal sleeve, designed just for this problem, over the crankshaft end. The crankshaft sleeve will present a new, flat surface, with which the new oil seal can make contact. Crankshaft sleeves are usually available from automotive parts stores.

To install:

9. Apply a thin coat of clean engine oil to the oil seal lip, then slide the oil seal over the crankshaft and into position against the timing chain cover. Use a deep socket, which is the same diameter as the oil seal, and a hammer to drive the oil seal into the housing. Drive the new seal into the housing only until the outer seal edge is flush with the cover surface.

➡The new oil seal must be installed so that the side of the seal where the seal spring is visible is installed inward (toward the engine block).

10. Slide the crankshaft pulley onto the end of the crankshaft and install the center bolt. Install the crankshaft holding tool, then tighten the center bolt to 109 ft. lbs. (150 Nm). The center bolt will draw the pulley onto the crankshaft when tightened to the specified torque value.

11. Install the cooling fan belt, pulley and fan.

12. Install the alternator drive belt.

13. Adjust the cooling fan drive belt tension, as described in Section 1.

14. Start the engine and check oil leakage from the new oil seal.

Timing Belt and Sprockets (Pulleys)

REMOVAL & INSTALLATION

➡During these procedures, identify all components removed from the engine so that they may be reinstalled in their original positions. If discarding the old components so that new components can be installed, identifying the old items is not necessary.

1.3L and 1.6L 8-Valve Engines

◆ See Figures 111 thru 117

➡Do not rotate the crankshaft counterclockwise or attempt to rotate the crankshaft by turning the camshaft sprocket.

1. Remove the timing belt cover.
2. If the timing belt is not already marked with a directional arrow, use white paint, a grease pencil or correction fluid to do so.
3. Disconnect one end of the tensioner spring. Loosen the timing belt tensioner bolt and stud, then, using your finger, press the tensioner plate up and remove the timing belt from the crankshaft and camshaft sprockets.

. . . however, if not already marked, use paint or correction fluid to indicate the direction of travel

Remove the outer timing belt cover from the engine . . .

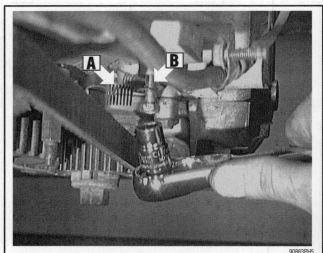

If necessary, when removing the tensioner spring (A), loosen the spring anchor bolt (B)

The timing belt may already be marked (arrow) with the proper direction of travel . . .

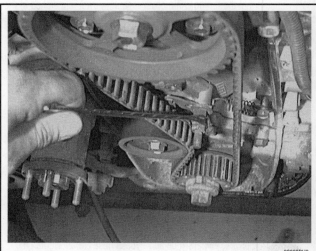

Loosen the tension plate, spring bolt and stud nut to remove the plate from the engine . . .

4. Remove the timing belt tensioner, tensioner plate and spring from the engine.

5. Insert a metal rod through the hole in the camshaft to lock the camshaft from rotating. Loosen the camshaft sprocket retaining bolt, then pull the camshaft sprocket off of the end of the camshaft.

6. Remove the crankshaft timing belt sprocket by loosening the center bolt, while preventing the crankshaft from rotating. To hold the crankshaft from turning, you can use Suzuki Tool 09927–56010 (or equivalent), or a large prybar inserted in the transmission housing slot and the flywheel teeth. Pull the sprocket off of the end of the crankshaft. Be sure to retain the crankshaft sprocket key and belt guide for assembly.

7. If necessary, remove the timing belt inside cover from the cylinder head.

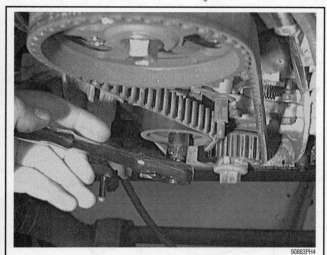

. . . then loosen the tension adjuster pulley center bolt for adjuster removal

Remove the timing belt from crankshaft and camshaft sprockets

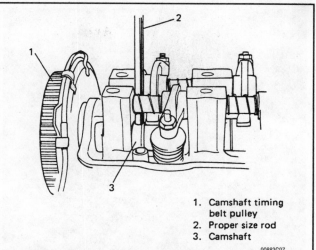

1. Camshaft timing belt pulley
2. Proper size rod
3. Camshaft

90883G97

Fig. 111 Use a metal rod (2) inserted through the camshaft hole to secure it from rotating . . .

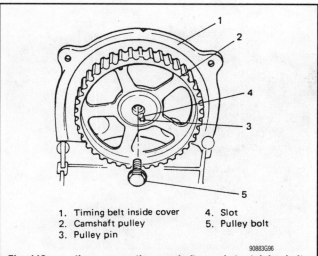

1. Timing belt inside cover
2. Camshaft pulley
3. Pulley pin
4. Slot
5. Pulley bolt

90883G96

Fig. 112 . . . then remove the camshaft sprocket retaining bolt and the sprocket from the end of the camshaft

To remove the crankshaft sprocket, have an assistant hold the flywheel from turning . . .

. . . while you loosen the crankshaft sprocket retaining bolt

Slide the sprocket off of the end of the crankshaft . . .

. . . and be sure to retain the timing belt guide for reassembly

To install:

8. If necessary, install the timing belt inside cover.

9. Slide the timing belt guide on the crankshaft so that the concave side faces the oil pump, then install the sprocket key in the groove in the crankshaft.

10. Slide the pulley onto the crankshaft, and install the center retaining bolt. Tighten the center bolt to 48–54 ft. lbs. (65–75 Nm) for 1986–88 1.3L engines, to 76–83 ft. lbs. (105–115 Nm) for 1989–95 1.3L engines, or to 58–65 ft. lbs. (80–90 Nm) for 1.6L engines. To hold the crankshaft from turning, you can use Suzuki Tool 09927–56010 (or equivalent), or a large prybar inserted in the transmission housing slot and the flywheel teeth.

11. Install the timing belt camshaft sprocket, ensuring that the slot in the sprocket engages the camshaft (pulley) pin; this ensures that the sprocket is properly positioned on the end of the camshaft. Secure the camshaft with the metal rod used during removal, then tighten the sprocket bolt to 41–46 ft. lbs. (56–64 Nm).

12. Assemble the timing belt tensioner plate and the tensioner, making sure that the lug of the tensioner plate engages the tensioner.

13. Install the timing belt tensioner, tensioner plate and spring on the engine. Tighten the mounting bolt and stud only finger-tight at this time. Ensure that when the tensioner is moved in a counterclockwise direction, the tensioner moves in the same direction. If the tensioner does not move, remove it and the tensioner plate to reassemble them properly.

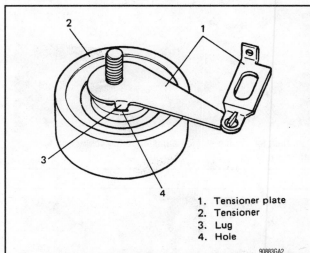

1. Tensioner plate
2. Tensioner
3. Lug
4. Hole

Fig. 113 Assemble the tensioner (2) and the plate (1) so that the lug (3) engages the hole (4) in the tensioner

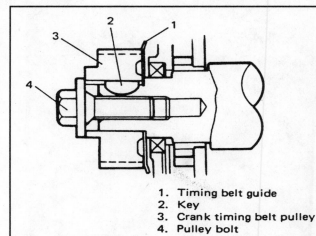

1. Timing belt guide
2. Key
3. Crank timing belt pulley
4. Pulley bolt

Fig. 114 When installing the crankshaft sprocket (pulley), ensure that the concave side of the timing belt guide is facing the engine

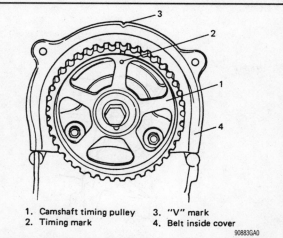

1. Camshaft timing pulley   3. "V" mark
2. Timing mark   4. Belt inside cover

90883GA0

Fig. 115 Before installing the timing belt, position the camshaft sprocket (1) so that the timing mark on the sprocket (2) is aligned with the notch (3) on the inside timing belt cover (4) . . .

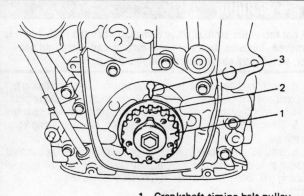

1. Crankshaft timing belt pulley
2. Punch mark
3. Arrow mark on oil pump case

90883GA1

Fig. 116 . . . and ensure that the crankshaft sprocket (1) timing mark (2) is aligned with the mark on the oil pump (3)

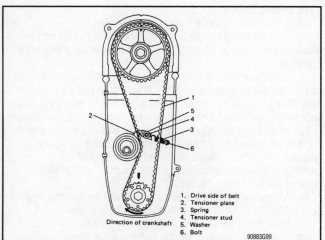

Direction of crankshaft

1. Drive side of belt
2. Tensioner plate
3. Spring
4. Tensioner stud
5. Washer
6. Bolt

90883G99

Fig. 117 Install the timing belt on the sprockets so that there is no slack in the drive side of the belt (1), then install the tensioning assembly

90883PH2

To properly tension the timing belt, rotate the crankshaft through two full revolutions

14. Loosen all rocker arm valve lash locknuts and adjusting screws. This will permit movement of the camshaft without any rocker arm associated drag, which is essential for proper timing belt tensioning. If the camshaft does not rotate freely (free of rocker arm drag), the belt will not be properly tensioned.

15. Rotate the camshaft sprocket clockwise until the timing mark on the sprocket and the V mark on the timing belt inside cover are aligned.

16. Using a 17mm wrench, or socket and breaker bar, on the crankshaft sprocket center bolt, turn the crankshaft clockwise until the punch mark on the sprocket is aligned with the arrow mark on the oil pump.

17. With the camshaft and crankshaft marks properly aligned, push the tensioner up with your finger and install the timing belt on the two sprockets, ensuring that the drive side of the belt is free of all slack. Release your finger from the tensioner. Be sure to install the timing belt so that the directional arrow is pointing in the appropriate direction.

➡ **In this position, the No. 4 cylinder is at Top Dead Center (TDC) on the compression stroke.**

18. Rotate the crankshaft clockwise two full revolutions, then tighten the tensioner stud to 18–21 ft. lbs. (24–30 Nm) for 1986–88 models, or to 80–106 inch lbs. (9–12 Nm) for 1989–95 models. Then, tighten the tensioner bolt to 18–21 ft. lbs. (24–30 Nm).

19. Ensure that all four timing marks are still aligned as before; if they are not, remove the timing belt, and install and tension it again.

20. Install the timing belt cover and all related components.

1.6L 16-Valve Engine

▶ **See Figures 118 thru 124**

The 1.6L 16-valve engine is known as an interference motor, because it is fabricated with such close tolerances between the pistons and valves that, if the timing belt is incorrectly positioned, jumps teeth on one of the sprockets or breaks, the valve and pistons will come into contact. This can cause severe internal engine damage. Therefore, it is vitally important to inspect and replace the timing belt as indicated in the maintenance intervals charts in Section 1.

➡ **Do not rotate the crankshaft counterclockwise or attempt to rotate the crankshaft by turning the camshaft sprocket.**

1. Remove the timing belt cover.

2. If the timing belt is not already marked with a directional arrow, use white paint, a grease pencil or correction fluid to do so.

3. Rotate the crankshaft clockwise until the timing mark on the camshaft sprocket and the V mark on the timing belt inside cover are aligned, and the punch mark on the crankshaft sprocket is aligned with the mark on the engine.

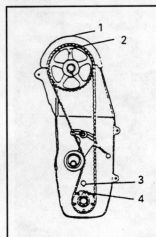

1. "V" mark on cylinder head cover
2. Timing mark by "E" on camshaft timing belt pulley
3. Arrow mark on oil pump case
4. Punch mark on crankshaft timing belt pulley

90883G95

Fig. 118 Prior to timing belt removal, rotate the crankshaft clockwise until the camshaft and crankshaft sprocket marks are aligned with the marks on the engine . . .

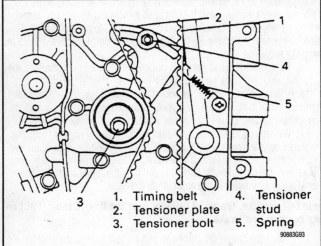

1.	Timing belt	4.	Tensioner
2.	Tensioner plate		stud
3.	Tensioner bolt	5.	Spring

90883G93

Fig. 119 . . . then remove the timing belt and tensioner assembly from the engine

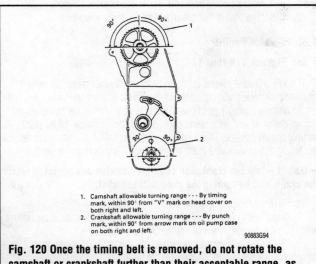

1. Camshaft allowable turning range - - - By timing mark, within 90° from "V" mark on head cover on both right and left.
2. Crankshaft allowable turning range - - - By punch mark, within 90° from arrow mark on oil pump case on both right and left.

90883G94

Fig. 120 Once the timing belt is removed, do not rotate the camshaft or crankshaft further than their acceptable range, as indicated

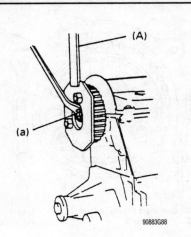

90883G88

Fig. 121 Use a spanner tool (A) to hold the camshaft sprocket steady while loosening the retaining bolt (a)

✳ WARNING

Do not rotate the crankshaft or camshaft once the timing belt is removed, because the valves and pistons can come into contact, which may cause internal engine damage.

4. Disconnect one end of the tensioner spring. Loosen the timing belt tensioner bolt and stud, then, using your finger, press the tensioner plate up and remove the timing belt from the crankshaft and camshaft sprockets.

5. Remove the timing belt tensioner, tensioner plate and spring from the engine.

6. Install Suzuki Tool 09917–68220, or equivalent, onto the camshaft sprocket to hold the camshaft from rotating. Loosen the camshaft sprocket retaining bolt, then pull the camshaft sprocket off of the end of the camshaft.

7. Remove the crankshaft timing belt sprocket by loosening the center bolt, while preventing the crankshaft from rotating. To hold the crankshaft from turning, you can use Suzuki Tool 09927–56010 (or equivalent), or a large prybar inserted in the transmission housing slot and the flywheel teeth. Pull the sprocket off of the end of the crankshaft. Be sure to retain the crankshaft sprocket key and belt guide for assembly.

8. If necessary, remove the timing belt inside cover from the cylinder head.

To install:

9. If necessary, install the timing belt inside cover.

10. Slide the timing belt guide on the crankshaft so that the concave side faces the oil pump, then install the sprocket key in the groove in the crankshaft.

11. Slide the pulley onto the crankshaft, and install the center retaining bolt. Tighten the center bolt to 80 ft. lbs. (110 Nm). To hold the crankshaft from turning, you can use Suzuki Tool 09927–56010 (or equivalent), or a large prybar inserted in the transmission housing slot and the flywheel teeth.

12. Install the timing belt camshaft sprocket, ensuring that the slot in the sprocket engages the camshaft (pulley) pin; this ensures that the sprocket is properly positioned on the end of the camshaft. Secure the camshaft with the holding tool used during removal, then tighten the sprocket bolt to 44 ft. lbs. (60 Nm).

13. Assemble the timing belt tensioner plate and the tensioner, making sure that the lug of the tensioner plate engages the tensioner.

14. Install the timing belt tensioner, tensioner plate and spring on the engine. Tighten the mounting bolt and stud only finger-tight at this time. Ensure that when the tensioner is moved in a counterclockwise direction, the tensioner moves in the same direction. If the tensioner does not move, remove it and the tensioner plate to reassemble them properly.

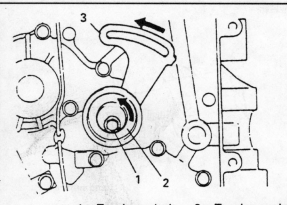

1. Tensioner bolt   3. Tensioner plate
2. Tensioner

90883G90

Fig. 122 After installing the tensioner and plate, ensure that the plate moves when the tensioner is rotated in a counterclockwise direction

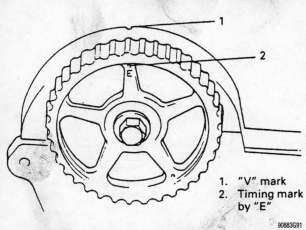

1. "V" mark
2. Timing mark by "E"

90883G91

Fig. 123 Before installing the timing belt, ensure that the camshaft sprocket mark is aligned with the notch in the inside timing belt cover . . .

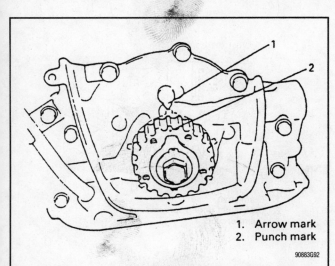

1. Arrow mark
2. Punch mark

90883G92

Fig. 124 . . . and be sure that the crankshaft sprocket marks are also aligned

15. Loosen all rocker arm valve lash locknuts and adjusting screws. This will permit movement of the camshaft without any rocker arm associated drag, which is essential for proper timing belt tensioning. If the camshaft does not rotate freely (free of rocker arm drag), the belt will not be properly tensioned.

16. Rotate the camshaft sprocket clockwise until the timing mark on the sprocket and the V mark on the timing belt inside cover are aligned.

17. Using a wrench, or socket and breaker bar, on the crankshaft sprocket center bolt, turn the crankshaft clockwise until the punch mark on the sprocket is aligned with the arrow mark on the oil pump.

18. With the camshaft and crankshaft marks properly aligned, push the tensioner up with your finger and install the timing belt on the two sprockets, ensuring that the drive side of the belt is free of all slack. Release your finger from the tensioner. Be sure to install the timing belt so that the directional arrow is pointing in the appropriate direction.

➡️**In this position, the No. 4 cylinder is at Top Dead Center (TDC) on the compression stroke.**

19. Rotate the crankshaft clockwise two full revolutions, then tighten the tensioner stud to 97 inch lbs. (11 Nm). Then, tighten the tensioner bolt to 18 ft. lbs. (24 Nm).

20. Ensure that all four timing marks are still aligned as before; if they are not, remove the timing belt, and install and tension it again.

21. Install the timing belt cover and all related components.

Timing Chain(s) and Sprockets (Gears)

REMOVAL & INSTALLATION

1.8L Engine

▶ **See Figures 125 thru 138**

➡️**During this procedure, identify all components removed from the engine so that they may be reinstalled in their original positions. If discarding the old components so that new components can be installed, identifying the old items is not necessary.**

1. Remove the timing chain cover from the engine.

2. Rotate the crankshaft clockwise until the crankshaft sprocket, idler sprocket, camshaft sprocket and engine timing marks are positioned as shown in the accompanying illustration.

➡️**Ensuring the crankshaft, idler sprocket and camshafts are correctly positioned is vital for timing chain installation.**

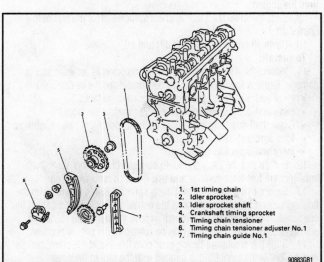

1. 1st timing chain
2. Idler sprocket
3. Idler sprocket shaft
4. Crankshaft timing sprocket
5. Timing chain tensioner
6. Timing chain tensioner adjuster No.1
7. Timing chain guide No.1

90883GB1

Fig. 125 Exploded view of the outer timing chain, sprockets and tensioner assembly mounting

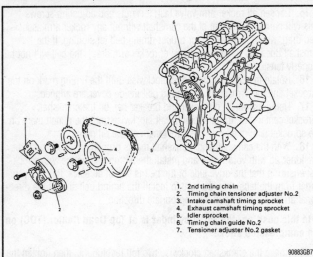

Fig. 126 Exploded view of the inner timing chain, sprockets and tensioner assembly mounting

1. 2nd timing chain
2. Timing chain tensioner adjuster No.2
3. Intake camshaft timing sprocket
4. Exhaust camshaft timing sprocket
5. Idler sprocket
6. Timing chain guide No.2
7. Tensioner adjuster No.2 gasket

90883GB7

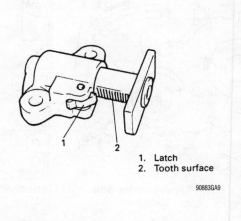

1. Latch
2. Tooth surface

90883GA9

Fig. 127 Inspect the latch and tooth surfaces of the inner chain tension adjuster mechanism for damage or excessive wear

3. Remove the outer timing chain tension adjuster mounting bolts, then remove the adjuster from the cylinder head by rotating the intake camshaft counterclockwise a little while depressing the adjuster contact pad.

4. Hold the intake camshaft steady by using an open end wrench on the hexagonal section of the camshaft, then loosen the camshaft sprocket retaining bolt. Loosen the exhaust camshaft sprocket retaining bolt in the same manner.

5. Remove the camshaft sprockets from the ends of the camshafts, then lift the sprockets and chain up and off of the engine.

❄❄ WARNING

Do not rotate the crankshaft or camshafts once the outer timing chain is removed from the engine, otherwise damage to the pistons and/or valves may occur.

6. Remove the inner timing chain guide by loosening the mounting fasteners and separating it from the engine block.

7. Remove the inner timing chain tension adjuster and contact arm (tensioner) from the engine block.

8. Remove the timing chain idler pulley from the cylinder head, drop the idler sprocket and inner timing chain down to disengage it from the crankshaft sprocket, then remove the inner timing chain and idler pulley from the engine.

9. Slide the crankshaft timing chain sprocket off of the end of the crankshaft.

10. Clean all components of all dirt and oil.

To install:

11. Inspect the following timing chain components for wear and/or damage. Replace any items found to be worn, defective or damaged:
- Inner and outer timing chain guide contact surfaces
- Inner and outer timing chain tensioner contact surfaces
- Crankshaft and camshaft timing chain sprocket teeth and bushings
- Idler sprocket teeth and bushing
- Inner and outer timing chains

12. Ensure that the latch and tooth surfaces of the inner timing chain tensioner are free from damage and that the latch functions properly.

13. Ensure that the crankshaft timing sprocket key is aligned with the timing mark on the engine block. If the engine was assembled so that the crankshaft is not properly positioned, remove the hydraulic valve lash adjusters so that the crankshaft may be rotated to the proper position.

14. Slide the crankshaft timing gear onto the end of the crankshaft so that the key in the crankshaft is aligned with the slot in the gear.

15. Apply clean engine oil to the idler gear bushing, then drape the inner timing chain on the idler sprocket so that the dark blue chain piece is

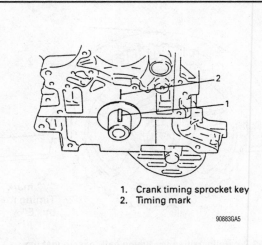

1. Crank timing sprocket key
2. Timing mark

90883GA5

Fig. 128 Ensure that the crankshaft key is aligned with the timing mark on the engine block . . .

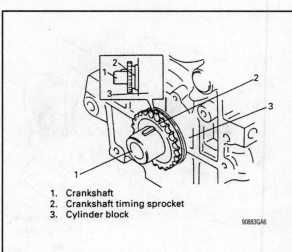

1. Crankshaft
2. Crankshaft timing sprocket
3. Cylinder block

90883GA6

Fig. 129 . . . then slide the sprocket on the end of the crankshaft, as shown

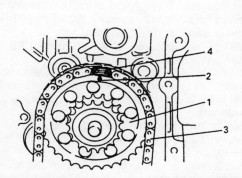

1. Idler sprocket
2. Match mark on idler sprocket
3. 1st timing chain
4. Dark blue plate

90883GA7

Fig. 130 Install the inner timing chain so that the dark blue chain link is aligned with the matchmark on the idler sprocket . . .

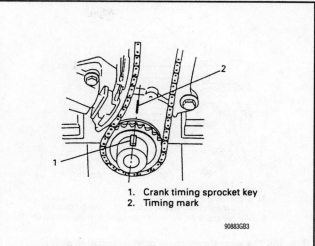

1. Crank timing sprocket key
2. Timing mark

90883GB3

Fig. 133 To install the outer chain, ensure that the crankshaft sprocket is still aligned with the mark on the engine block . . .

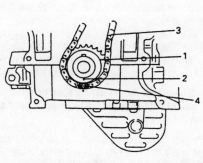

1. Crankshaft timing sprocket
2. Match mark
3. 1st timing chain
4. Yellow plate

90883GA8

Fig. 131 . . . and the yellow link is aligned with the matchmark on the crankshaft sprocket

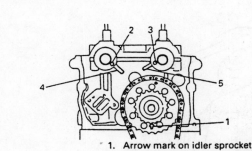

1. Arrow mark on idler sprocket
2. Knock pin of intake camshaft
3. Knock pin of exhaust camsaft
4. Timing mark of intake side
5. Timing mark of exhaust side

90883GB4

Fig. 134 . . . then align the camshafts so that they are positioned as shown

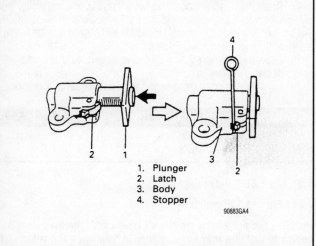

1. Plunger
2. Latch
3. Body
4. Stopper

90883GA4

Fig. 132 Prior to installing the tension adjuster, depress the plunger and insert a pin to hold it in this position

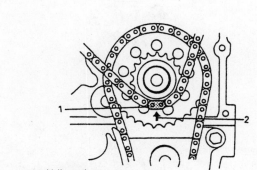

1. Yellow plate
2. Match mark of 2nd timing chain (Arrow mark)

90883GB5

Fig. 135 Install the outer chain on the idler sprocket so that the yellow link is aligned with the arrow mark on the sprocket

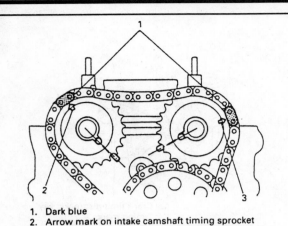

1. Dark blue
2. Arrow mark on intake camshaft timing sprocket
3. Arrow mark on exhaust camshaft timing sprocket

90883GB6

Fig. 136 The outer timing chain must be installed on the camshaft sprockets so that the dark blue links are aligned with the arrow marks on the sprockets

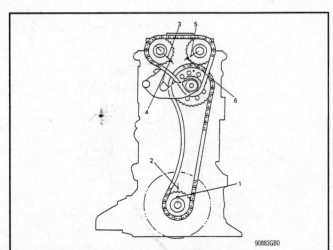

1. Plunger
2. Body
3. Stopper

90883GB2

Fig. 137 Depress the plunger and install a push-pin in the adjuster to hold the plunger in during installation

90883GB0

Fig. 138 After installation, rotate the crankshaft through two full revolutions and ensure that all of the timing marks realign properly

aligned with the matchmark on the idler sprocket. Position the timing chain around and under the crankshaft sprocket so that the yellow chain piece is aligned with the matchmark on the crankshaft sprocket. Install the idler sprocket and sprocket shaft in the cylinder head.

16. Install the inner timing chain contact arm (tensioner), then tighten the pivot bolt to 19 ft. lbs. (25 Nm).

17. With the latch of the inner timing chain tension adjuster returned and the plunger fully depressed into the adjuster, insert a pin into the latch and adjuster body. With the pin installed, the plunger should not come out of the adjuster body.

18. Install the inner timing chain tension adjuster onto the engine block, then tighten the mounting bolts to 97 inch lbs. (11 Nm). Pull the pin out of the adjuster.

19. Install the inner timing chain guide, making sure that the spacer is installed on the upper mounting bolt. Tighten the mounting fasteners to 97 inch lbs. (11 Nm).

20. Double check that the dark blue and yellow chain pieces are still aligned with the idler and crankshaft sprocket matchmarks (respectively), and that the crankshaft timing sprocket mark is still aligned with the mark on the engine block..

21. Ensure that the locating dowels of the intake and exhaust camshafts are aligned with the timing marks on the cylinder head, as shown in the accompanying illustration.

22. Hold both of the camshaft sprockets and have an assistant drape the outer timing chain over them so that the blue chain pieces are aligned with the matchmarks on the sprockets. It may be necessary to turn the chain around if the blue marks are too far apart. Position the sprockets and chain so that the chain is engaged on the underside of the idler sprocket, and the yellow chain link is aligned with the mark (arrow) on the idler sprocket. Once the chain is properly positioned with respect to all three sprockets, install the intake and exhaust camshaft sprockets on their respective camshafts.

➡ **The camshaft sprockets do not have a specific direction of orientation; either side of both sprockets may be positioned so that they face away from the camshaft.**

23. Install the camshaft sprocket retaining bolts finger-tight, then secure the camshafts (one at a time) with an open end wrench. Tighten both sprocket retaining bolts to 44 ft. lbs. (60 Nm).

24. With the plunger of the outer timing chain tension adjuster fully depressed into the adjuster, insert a push-pin into the latch and adjuster body. With the push-pin installed, the plunger should not come out of the adjuster body.

25. Install the outer timing chain tension adjuster, along with a new gasket, onto the cylinder head. Tighten the mounting bolts to 97 inch lbs. (11 Nm) and the idler sprocket nut to 33 ft. lbs. (45 Nm).

26. Pull the push-pin out of the adjuster body to tension the outer timing chain.

27. Rotate the crankshaft clockwise two full revolutions, and realign the crankshaft sprocket timing mark with the mark on the engine block. Ensure that the camshaft and idler sprocket marks are still aligned with the timing marks on the engine block and cylinder head.

28. Lubricate the timing chains, guides, tensioners, adjusters, and sprockets with clean engine oil.

29. Install the timing chain cover and all related engine components.

Camshaft, Bearings and Lifters

REMOVAL & INSTALLATION

1.3L and 1.6L 8-Valve Engines

▶ **See Figures 139 and 140**

➡ **During this procedure, identify all components removed from the engine so that they may be reinstalled in their original positions. If discarding the old components so that new components can be installed, identifying the old items is not necessary.**

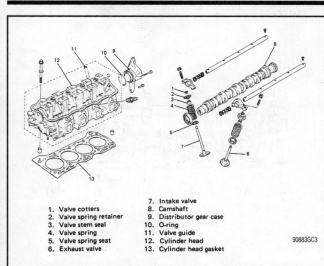

1. Valve cotters
2. Valve spring retainer
3. Valve stem seal
4. Valve spring
5. Valve spring seat
6. Exhaust valve
7. Intake valve
8. Camshaft
9. Distributor gear case
10. O-ring
11. Valve guide
12. Cylinder head
13. Cylinder head gasket

90883GC3

Fig. 139 Exploded view of the cylinder head, showing camshaft mounting

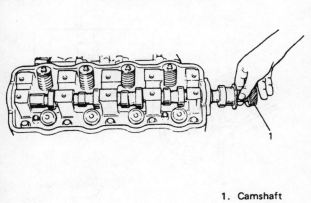

1. Camshaft

90883GC4

Fig. 140 Carefully slide the camshaft out of the rear end of the cylinder head

1. Remove the cylinder head.
2. Remove the intake and exhaust manifolds, the rocker arms and shafts, and the camshaft sprocket from the cylinder head.
3. Remove the distributor from the distributor case.
4. Remove the distributor case mounting fasteners, then separate the case from the cylinder head.
5. Carefully slide the camshaft out of the rear (distributor) end of the cylinder head.
6. Using a seal removal tool or small prytool, carefully pry the old camshaft oil seal out of the front of the cylinder head bore. Take care not to scratch the camshaft oil seal bore, otherwise oil leakage may occur. If using a small prytool, wrapping a piece of tape around the end of the tool may help reduce the change of scoring the bore by covering any sharp corners on the tool.
7. Clean the cylinder head, camshaft, rocker arms and shafts and all gasket mating surfaces of all dirt, corrosion and oil.

To install:

8. Apply a thin coat of clean engine oil to the oil seal lip, then drive the new seal into the housing only until the outer seal edge is flush with the cover surface.

➡The new oil seal must be installed so that the side of the seal where the seal spring is visible is installed inward (toward the engine block).

9. Apply clean engine oil to the camshaft, then carefully slide it into the rear end of the cylinder head.
10. Install the distributor case and tighten the mounting fasteners until secure.
11. Install the rocker arm shafts and rocker arms, the inside timing belt cover, the timing belt sprocket, the intake and exhaust manifolds, and the distributor.
12. Install the cylinder head on the engine block. Install all related items.

1.6L 16-Valve Engine

▶ See Figures 141 thru 146

➡During this procedure, identify all components removed from the engine so that they may be reinstalled in their original positions. If discarding the old components so that new components can be installed, identifying the old items is not necessary.

1. Disconnect the negative battery cable.

❋❋ CAUTION

Some models covered by this manual may be equipped with a Supplemental Restraint System (SRS), which uses an air bag. Whenever working near any of the SRS components, such as the impact sensors, the air bag module, steering column and instrument panel, refer to Section 6 for SRS precautions. Failure to heed all precautions may result in accidental air bag deployment, which could easily result in severe personal injury or death. Also, never attempt any electrical diagnosis or service to the SRS components and wiring; this work should only be performed by a qualified automotive technician.

2. Remove the hood.
3. Remove the front grille.
4. Remove the hood lock from the front upper member, then remove the front upper member.
5. Remove the radiator.
6. Remove the timing belt cover, timing belt, camshaft sprocket and inside timing belt cover from the engine.
7. Remove the rocker arm cover.
8. Remove the distributor and distributor case from the cylinder head. When removing the distributor case, position a small catch pan or rag beneath it to catch any oil which may leak during removal.
9. Loosen all of the valve lash locknuts and adjusting screws so that there is no pressure exerted on the camshaft lobes.

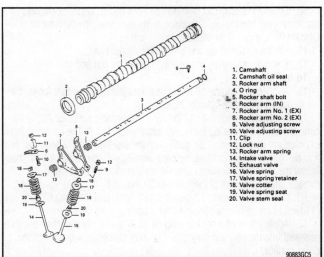

1. Camshaft
2. Camshaft oil seal
3. Rocker arm shaft
4. O ring
5. Rocker shaft bolt
6. Rocker arm (IN)
7. Rocker arm No. 1 (EX)
8. Rocker arm No. 2 (EX)
9. Valve adjusting screw
10. Valve adjusting screw
11. Clip
12. Lock nut
13. Rocker arm spring
14. Intake valve
15. Exhaust valve
16. Valve spring
17. Valve spring retainer
18. Valve cotter
19. Valve spring seat
20. Valve stem seal

90883GC5

Fig. 141 Exploded view of the camshaft and valve train components

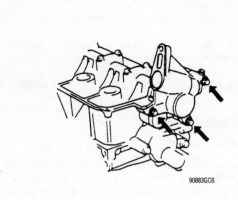

Fig. 142 To remove the distributor case, loosen the three mounting bolts (arrows), then separate it from the cylinder head

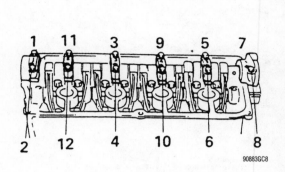

Fig. 144 Tighten the camshaft housing mounting bolts in the sequence shown and in four steps to 97 inch lbs. (11 Nm)

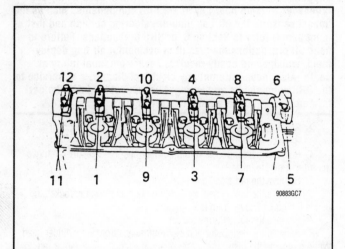

Fig. 143 Be sure to loosen the camshaft housing (bearing cap) bolts only in the sequence shown to avoid camshaft warpage

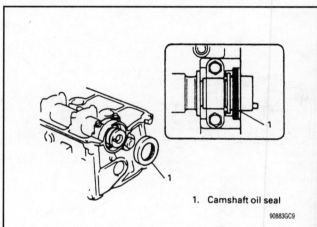

1. Camshaft oil seal

Fig. 145 After installing the camshaft, install a new oil seal—when installing the oil seal, drive it in the bore until it is flush with the cylinder head surface

10. Loosen the camshaft bearing cap bolts in the sequence shown in the accompanying illustration, then remove the caps from the cylinder head. Discard the old camshaft oil seal.

11. Lift the camshaft up and off of the cylinder head.

12. Clean the camshaft and bearing caps of all dirt and oil.

To install:

13. Apply clean engine oil to the camshaft journals and cam lobes, then set the camshaft on the cylinder head.

14. Apply clean engine oil to the camshaft bearing surfaces. Apply silicone sealant to the mating surface of bearing cap No. 6. The camshaft bearing caps are marked with their position numbers (No. 1 is the foremost cap, and No. 6 is the rearmost bearing cap). Install bearing cap No. 1 first, then install the remaining bearing caps. Oil the camshaft bearing cap bolt threads, then tighten all of them first to 24 inch lbs. (2.7 Nm), then to 48 inch lbs. (5.4 Nm), then to 72 inch lbs. (8.2 Nm), and finally to 97 inch lbs. (11 Nm) in the sequence shown in the accompanying illustration.

15. Apply a thin coat of clean engine oil to the oil seal lip, then drive the new seal into the housing only until the outer seal edge is flush with the cover surface.

➡The new oil seal must be installed so that the open side of the seal is installed inward (toward the cylinder head).

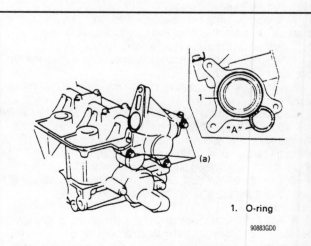

1. O-ring

Fig. 146 Apply silicone sealant to the distributor case at the area marked A—tighten the mounting bolts (a) to 97 inch lbs. (11 Nm)

16. Apply silicone sealant on the distributor case, as shown in the accompanying illustration, then install the distributor case on the cylinder head. Tighten the mounting fasteners to 97 inch lbs. (11 Nm). Install the distributor to the distributor case.

17. Install the timing belt cover, timing belt, camshaft sprocket and inside timing belt cover on the engine.

18. Install the radiator.

19. Install the remove the front upper member, then install the hood lock onto the front upper member.

20. Install the front grille.

21. Install the hood.

22. Adjust rocker arm valve lash.

23. Install the rocker arm cover.

24. Connect the negative battery cable.

25. Fill the cooling system with the proper type and amount of engine coolant.

26. Start the engine and check for coolant and fuel leaks.

1.8L Engine

▶ See Figures 147 thru 156

➡During this procedure, identify all components removed from the engine so that they may be reinstalled in their original positions. If discarding the old components so that new components can be installed, identifying the old items is not necessary.

1. Disconnect the negative battery cable.

❋❋ CAUTION

The EPA warns that prolonged contact with used engine oil may cause a number of skin disorders, including cancer! You should make every effort to minimize your exposure to used engine oil. Protective gloves should be worn when changing the oil. Wash your hands and any other exposed skin areas as soon as possible after exposure to used engine oil. Soap and water, or water-less hand cleaner should be used.

2. Drain the engine oil.

3. Remove the oil pan and oil pump pick-up.

4. Remove the rocker arm cover.

5. Remove the timing chain cover.

6. Remove the outer timing chain.

7. Remove the Camshaft Position (CMP) sensor.

8. After removing the outer timing chain, rotate the crankshaft 90 degrees clockwise (as shown in the accompanying illustration) so that interference between the valves and pistons is avoided.

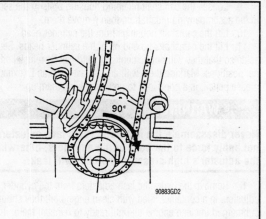

Fig. 148 After removing the outer timing chain, rotate the crankshaft 90 degrees (¼ turn) clockwise so that the valves and pistons will not come into contact

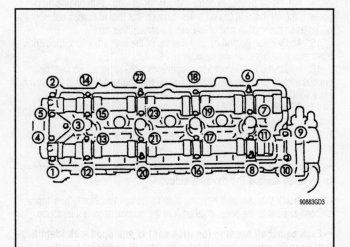

Fig. 149 Loosen the camshaft housing mounting bolts only in the sequence shown, otherwise camshaft warpage may occur

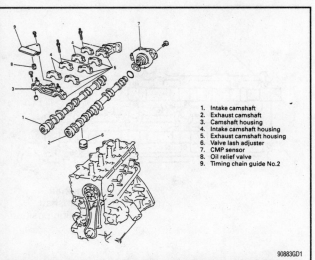

1. Intake camshaft
2. Exhaust camshaft
3. Camshaft housing
4. Intake camshaft housing
5. Exhaust camshaft housing
6. Valve lash adjuster
7. CMP sensor
8. Oil relief valve
9. Timing chain guide No.2

Fig. 147 Exploded view of camshaft mounting on the cylinder head

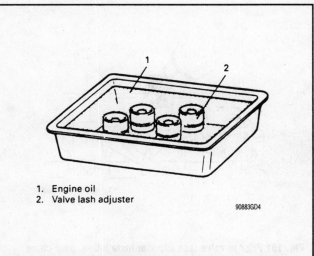

1. Engine oil
2. Valve lash adjuster

Fig. 150 Keep the hydraulic valve lash adjusters submerged in clean engine oil until ready for installation

9. Loosen the camshaft retaining housing bolts in the sequence shown in the accompanying illustration, then remove them.

10. Lift the camshaft housings from the cylinder head.

11. Lift the camshafts up and off of the cylinder heads. Set the camshaft aside so that they will not be confused, and can be reinstalled in their original positions. Marking them with an I (intake) and an E (exhaust) with a grease pencil, is a good idea to prevent mixing them up.

✖✖ WARNING

Never disassemble the hydraulic valve lash adjusters. Also, do not apply force to the body of the adjusters, otherwise the oil in the adjuster's high pressure chamber will leak.

12. Remove the hydraulic lash adjusters from the cylinder head. Set the adjusters in a container filled with clean engine oil; they should be kept submerged in clean engine oil until ready to reinstall them. If a container of clean engine oil is not available, only set the lash adjusters with their bucket bodies facing down. NEVER set the lash adjusters on their sides or with their bucket bodies facing up.

13. Clean the camshaft journals on the cylinder head, the camshaft housings (caps) and the camshafts of all dirt, grime and oil.

To install:

14. Fill the oil passages of the cylinder head with clean engine oil by pouring the oil through the oil holes. Ensure that the oil comes out from the oil holes in the sliding part of the valve lash adjuster bore.

15. Apply clean engine oil to the sides of the lash adjusters, then slide them into their bores in the cylinder head.

16. Rotate the crankshaft 1¾ revolutions (630 degrees) so that the crankshaft key is aligned with the mark on the engine block and the timing mark (dot) on the idler gear is positioned up.

17. Oil the camshaft journals and lobes, and lubricate the camshaft seats in the cylinder head, then set the camshafts on the cylinder head. Rotate the camshafts so that the locating pins on their front ends are positioned as shown in the accompanying illustration.

➡**Install the camshafts so that the end with the CMP sensor groove is oriented toward the exhaust side.**

18. Install the camshaft housing pins in the cylinder head, then apply silicone sealant to the areas marked A in the accompanying illustration.

➡**Each camshaft housing (bearing cap) is equipped with identification as to whether it is an intake or exhaust camshaft housing, what position it should take from the timing chain end of the engine, and an arrow (should point to the timing chain end of the engine).**

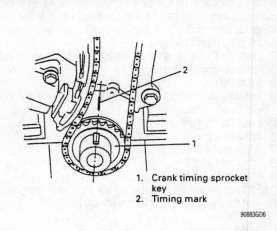

1. Crank timing sprocket key
2. Timing mark

90883GD6

Fig. 152 Before installing the camshafts, rotate the crankshaft so that the matchmarks are aligned

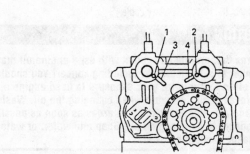

1. Knock pin of intake camshaft
2. Knock pin of exhaust camshaft
3. Match mark of intake camshaft
4. Match mark of exhaust camshaft

90883GD7

Fig. 153 After installing the camshafts, rotate them so that the locating dowels are positioned as shown

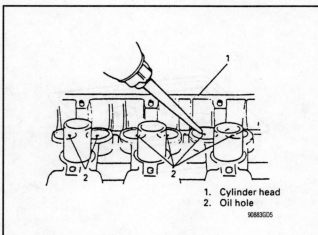

1. Cylinder head
2. Oil hole

90883GD5

Fig. 151 Prior to valve lash adjuster installation, pour clean engine oil through the oil holes in the cylinder head until it exits the holes in the adjuster bores

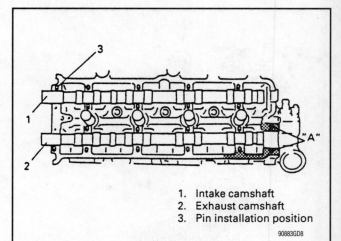

1. Intake camshaft
2. Exhaust camshaft
3. Pin installation position

90883GD8

Fig. 154 Apply sealant to the cylinder head in the areas marked A . . .

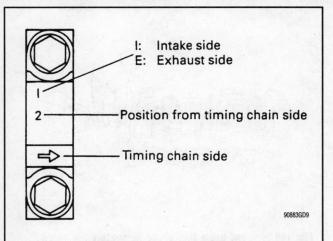

Fig. 155 . . . then install the camshaft housings—the housings are stamped with identification marks, which help with housing positioning during installation

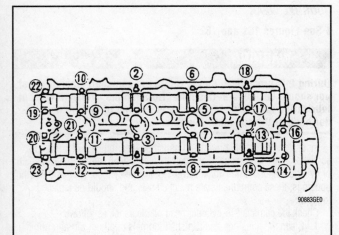

Fig. 156 Tighten the camshaft housing mounting bolts ONLY in the sequence shown

19. Lubricate the camshaft housing-to-camshaft surfaces with clean engine oil, then position the housings on the cylinder head.

20. Lubricate the housing mounting bolts with clean engine oil, then install them finger-tight.

21. Using an inch-pound torque wrench and the sequence shown in the accompanying illustration, tighten all of the housing mounting bolts first to 24 inch lbs. (2.7 Nm), then to 48 inch lbs. (5.4 Nm), then to 72 inch lbs. (8.2 Nm), and finally to 97 inch lbs. (11 Nm).

22. Install the CMP sensor.

23. Install the outer timing chain.

24. Install the timing chain cover.

25. Install the rocker arm cover.

26. Install the oil pan and pump pick-up.

27. Install the cooling system and all other components.

28. Refill the cooling system with coolant, the front differential with gear oil and the engine with clean engine oil.

✲✲✲ WARNING

Do not turn the camshafts or start the engine for approximately ½ hour after installing the valve lash adjusters and camshafts;

it takes time for the valves to settle in place. Operating the engine before this time period may result n interference between the valves and pistons, which can easily cause expensive and time-consuming internal engine damage.

29. After a half hour period, start the engine. Check the ignition timing and adjust it as necessary.

30. If the valve lash adjusters make a tapping sound when the engine started, air may be trapped in the adjuster(s). In such a case, run the engine at 2000 rpm for approximately ½ hour, after which the air should be bled from the adjuster(s). If the tapping sound continues, the adjuster is most likely defective. To check the adjuster, perform the following:

    a. Remove the rocker arm cover.

    b. With you thumb, press down on each of the adjusters with a force of less than 44 lbs. (20 kg) when the valve adjuster is resting against the camshaft lobe base circle. If clearance exists between the adjuster and the camshaft, that adjuster is defective.

    c. Perform this inspection for all 16 adjusters. Replace any that are found to be defective.

    d. Install the rocker arm cover.

INSPECTION

1.3L and 1.6L 8-Valve Engines

LOBE WEAR

▶ See Figure 157

Using a micrometer, measure the height of each of the camshaft lobes at its highest point. If the measured height is below the allowable range, replace the camshaft(s).

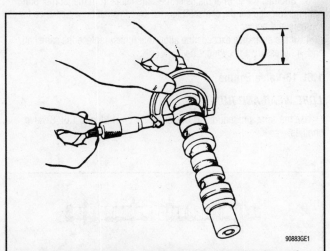

Fig. 157 Use a micrometer to measure the highest point on the camshaft lobe—if the height is not within the specified range, replace the camshaft

RUN-OUT

▶ See Figure 158

Position the camshaft so that both ends of the camshaft sit in V notches cut into wooden blocks. The center of the camshaft should not be supported. Situate a dial indicator so that it is reading off of the center camshaft journal. Spin the camshaft and observe the dial indicator; the total range measured is the total amount of run-out. If the run-out measured is not within the specified range, replace the camshaft.

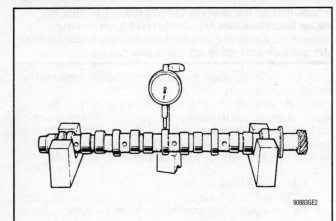

Fig. 158 Place both ends of the camshaft in V-notches cut into wooden blocks, position a dial indicator on the middle journal, then spin the camshaft and observe the dial indicator to measure run-out

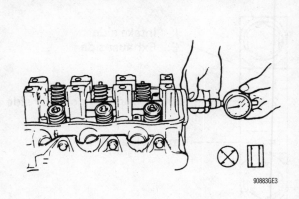

Fig. 160 . . . and use a bore gauge to measure the inside diameter of the camshaft journal bores in the cylinder head—subtract the journal measurements from the bore diameters to calculate oil clearance

JOURNAL WEAR

▶ See Figures 159 and 160

1. Using a micrometer, measure each of the camshaft journals at four places (every 90 degrees) around its circumference, and record the findings. Do this for all camshaft journals.

2. Using a bore gauge, measure each of the camshaft bores in the cylinder head, also at four positions for each bore, then record the measurements. Measure all of the camshaft bores.

3. Subtract the journal diameter measurements from the journal bore findings to calculate the camshaft journal-to-camshaft bore clearance for all journals and bores.

4. If the clearance exceeds the allowable limits, replace the camshaft, and, if necessary, the cylinder head.

1.6L 16-Valve Engine

LOBE WEAR AND RUN-OUT

Use the same procedures as presented for the 1.3L and 1.6L 8-valve engines.

JOURNAL WEAR

▶ See Figures 161 and 162

> **✳✳ WARNING**
>
> **During this procedure, do not rotate the camshaft since it is not, nor should be, oiled at this time. Rotating the camshaft without lubrication may cause scratching or scoring of either the cylinder head or the camshaft journals.**

Inspect the camshaft journal and housings (bearing caps) for pitting, scratches, wear or damage. If any defects are evident, replace the camshaft or cylinder head and housings. Never replace the cylinder head and not the housings; these components are matched sets and should be replaced together.

Check the camshaft-to-cylinder head oil clearance as follows:

1. Clean the housings and camshaft journals of all oil, dirt and grime.

2. Set the camshaft on the cylinder head.

3. Position a piece of Plastigage® along the full width of each of the camshaft journals. (The Plastigage® should be set on the camshaft journal so that it runs parallel to the camshaft rotational axis.)

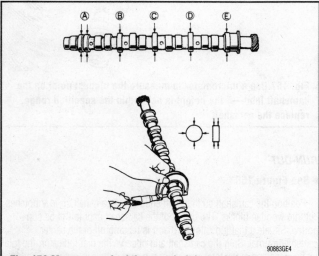

Fig. 159 Measure each of the camshaft journals in four positions around their circumferences . . .

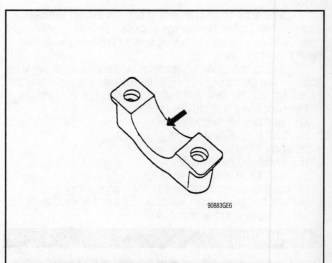

Fig. 161 Inspect the camshaft housing surfaces for scratches, pitting, wear or damage

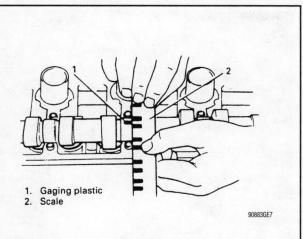

Fig. 162 Use the scale included with the Plastigage® kit to measure the piece of flattened Plastigage® for clearance

1. Gaging plastic
2. Scale

4. Install the camshaft housings (bearing caps) and tighten the mounting bolts as described in the removal and installation procedure.

5. Remove the camshaft housings and measure the Plastigage® width with the scale enclosed with the Plastigage® kit.

6. If the specifications are not within the allowable range, use a micrometer to measure the camshaft journals and a bore gauge to measure the camshaft bores (with the housings installed). Replace the component which is out of specifications.

1.8L Engine

LOBE WEAR AND RUN-OUT

Use the same procedures as presented for the 1.3L and 1.6L 8-valve engines.

JOURNAL WEAR

Use the same procedures as presented for the 1.6L 16-valve engine.

HYDRAULIC VALVE LASH ADJUSTER WEAR

▶ See Figure 163

Inspect the adjuster for pitting, scratches, or other damage. If any defects are found, replace the lash adjuster.

Measure the inside diameter of the lash adjuster bores and the outside diameter of the lash adjusters. Subtract the adjuster diameter from the bore measurement to calculate the adjuster-to-bore clearance. If the clearance exceeds the allowable value, replace the cylinder head or lash adjuster.

Idler Shaft

REMOVAL & INSTALLATION

1.8L Engine

Idler shaft and sprocket removal/installation is covered under the timing chain(s) and sprockets removal/installation procedure, located earlier in this section.

Rear Main Seal

REMOVAL & INSTALLATION

1.3L and 1.6L Engines

RECOMMENDED METHOD

▶ See Figure 164

It is recommended to replace the oil seal by dropping the oil pan and removing the entire rear main seal housing. It is possible to remove the oil seal without doing this, but it is often difficult because the oil seal is extremely stiff and can easily cock in the bore. If you wish to try to replace the seal without removing the oil pan, refer to the alternative method.

1. Remove the transmission, the flywheel and the oil pan from the vehicle.

2. Loosen the five rear main seal housing mounting bolts, then separate the housing from the back of the engine block. Discard the old gasket.

3. Position the housing on wooden blocks so that the outer side is facing down and the seal is not being supported. Use a blunt drift and hammer to drive the old seal out of the housing.

4. Clean the rear main seal housing and engine block mating surfaces of all dirt, grime, oil and old gasket material.

To install:

5. Position the rear main seal housing with the outer surface facing up, and on a flat, clean piece of wood.

6. Position the new oil seal in the seal housing bore and using a seal driver, or a large flat block of wood, and a hammer seat the seal in the housing until the outer edge of the seal is flush with the outer surface of the housing.

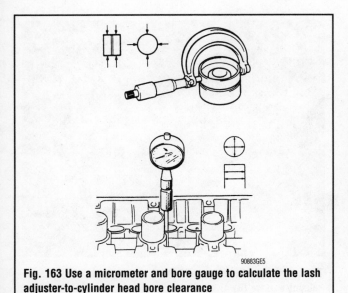

Fig. 163 Use a micrometer and bore gauge to calculate the lash adjuster-to-cylinder head bore clearance

To remove the oil seal (A) and housing (B), remove the transmission, then the oil pan (C) from the vehicle

The oil seal housing is secured to the engine block with five bolts (A), and to the oil pan with two (B)

Position the seal driver against the new oil seal . . .

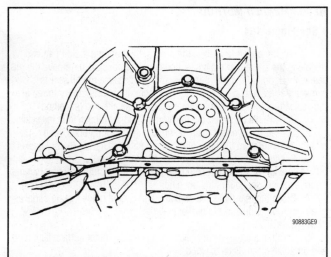

Fig. 164 After tightening the oil seal housing mounting bolts, trim any protruding gasket from the oil pan mating surface

. . . and carefully tap the seal into position with a mallet

7. Apply a thin coat of clean engine oil to the oil seal lip.

8. Along with a new gasket, position the oil seal housing against the engine block, and install the mounting bolts finger-tight.

9. Tighten the housing mounting bolts to 80–106 inch lbs. (9–12 Nm).

10. After the oil seal housing mounting bolts are tightened, the gasket may protrude out from the bottom of the housing. Use a sharp knife or razor blade to trim the gasket flush with the oil pan mating surface.

11. Install the oil pan, flywheel and transmission.

☀ WARNING

Operating the engine without the proper amount and type of engine oil can result in severe engine damage.

12. Be sure to fill the engine with clean engine oil before starting it.

ALTERNATIVE METHOD

1. Remove the transmission and flywheel from the engine.

2. Using a small prytool, carefully remove the old rear main oil seal from the oil seal housing. Be careful not to scratch or gouge the oil seal bore.

To install:

3. Apply a thin coat of clean engine oil to the new oil seal lip.

4. Position the new oil seal in the seal housing bore and using a seal

The outer edge of the new seal (A) should sit flush with the housing surface (B)

driver and a hammer seat the seal in the housing until the outer edge of the seal is flush with the outer surface of the housing.

5. Install the flywheel and transmission.

1.8L Engine

◆ **See Figure 165**

1. Remove the transmission and flywheel from the engine.
2. Using a small prytool, carefully remove the old rear main oil seal from the oil seal housing. Be careful not to scratch or gouge the oil seal bore.

To install:

3. Apply a thin coat of clean engine oil to the new oil seal lip.
4. Using Suzuki Tools 09911–97710 and 09911–97810, or their equivalents, install the new oil seal in the seal housing bore. Seat the seal in the housing until the outer edge of the seal is flush with the outer surface of the housing.
5. Install the flywheel and transmission.

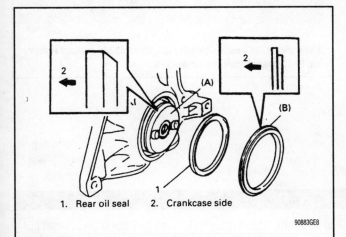

1. Rear oil seal 2. Crankcase side

90883GE8

Fig. 165 Use the two Suzuki tools 0991–97710 (A) and 09911–97810 (B), or their equivalents, to drive the new seal into the seal bore

Flywheel/Flexplate

REMOVAL & INSTALLATION

1. Remove the transmission from the vehicle.
2. On models equipped with manual transmission, remove the pressure plate and clutch disc from the flywheel.
3. Matchmark the relationship between the flywheel and the crankshaft.
4. Using a flywheel holding tool to keep the crankshaft from rotating, loosen the flywheel-to-crankshaft mounting bolts.
5. Remove the flywheel from the crankshaft.
6. If equipped with a manual transmission, drive the old clutch pilot bearing out of the center flywheel hole.
7. Clean the flywheel and flywheel bolts of all dirt and oil.

To install:

8. If applicable, drive a new clutch pilot bearing in the flywheel until it is flush with the flywheel surface.
9. Position the flywheel on the crankshaft so that the matchmarks are aligned.
10. Apply Loctite® 414, or equivalent to the threads of the flywheel bolts.

❉❉ WARNING

Do not apply too much Loctite® on the bolt threads, otherwise the sealant may overflow the bolt seat. This could result in the bolt breaking loose during vehicle usage.

Use the Suzuki flywheel holding tool or, if not available, this generic type of flywheel holding tool . . .

. . . while loosening the flywheel retaining bolts . . .

. . . then pull the flywheel off of the crankshaft

11. Install and tighten the flywheel mounting bolts finger-tight first, then tighten them to 42–47 ft. lbs. (57–65 Nm) for the 1.3L engine, to 58 ft. lbs. (78 Nm) for the 1.6L engine, and to 51 ft. lbs. (70 Nm) for the 1.8L engine in a crisscross pattern. Secure the flywheel with the holding tool.

12. On manual transmissions, install the pressure plate and clutch disc, as described in Section 7.

13. Install the transmission.

Tighten the flywheel bolts in a crisscross pattern, as in the sequence shown, to the specified value

90883P88

90883P89

The clutch pilot bearing (arrow) can be replaced without removing the flywheel from the crankshaft

EXHAUST SYSTEM

Inspection

➡Safety glasses should be worn at all times when working on or near the exhaust system. Older exhaust systems will almost always be covered with loose rust particles which will shower you when disturbed. These particles are more than a nuisance and could injure your eye.

❈❈ CAUTION

Do NOT perform exhaust repairs or inspection with the engine or exhaust hot. Allow the system to cool completely before attempting any work. Exhaust systems are noted for sharp edges, flaking metal and rusted bolts. Gloves and eye protection are required. A healthy supply of penetrating oil and rags is highly recommended.

Your vehicle must be raised and supported safely to inspect the exhaust system properly. By placing 4 safety stands under the vehicle for support should provide enough room for you to slide under the vehicle and inspect the system completely. Start the inspection at the exhaust manifold or turbocharger pipe where the header pipe is attached and work your way to the back of the vehicle. On dual exhaust systems, remember to inspect both sides of the vehicle. Check the complete exhaust system for open seams, holes loose connections, or other deterioration which could permit exhaust fumes to seep into the passenger compartment. Inspect all mounting brackets and hangers for deterioration, some models may have rubber O-rings that can be overstretched and non-supportive. These components will need

to be replaced if found. It has always been a practice to use a pointed tool to poke up into the exhaust system where the deterioration spots are to see whether or not they crumble. Some models may have heat shield covering certain parts of the exhaust system, it will be necessary to remove these shields to have the exhaust visible for inspection also.

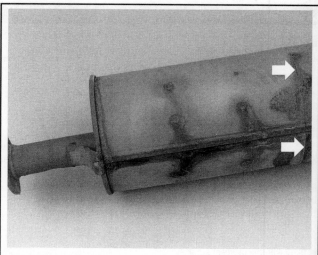

TCCA3P73

Cracks in the muffler are a guaranteed leak

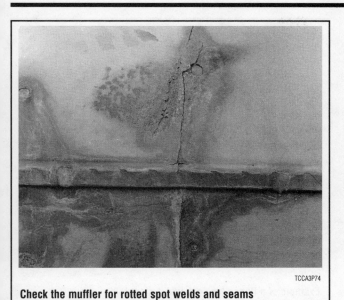

Check the muffler for rotted spot welds and seams

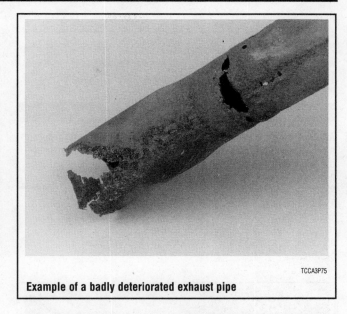

Example of a badly deteriorated exhaust pipe

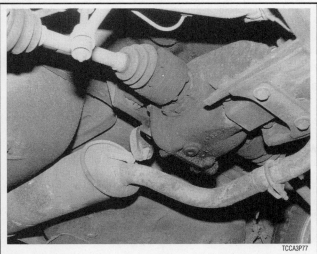

Make sure the exhaust components are not contacting the body or suspension

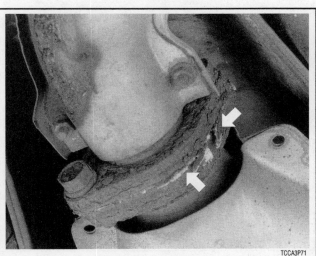

Inspect flanges for gaskets that have deteriorated and need replacement

Check for overstretched or torn exhaust hangers

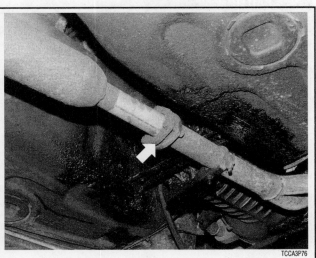

Some systems, like this one, use large O-rings (donuts) in between the flanges

REPLACEMENT

There are basically two types of exhaust systems. One is the flange type where the component ends are attached with bolts and a gasket in-between. The other exhaust system is the slip joint type. These components slip into one another using clamps to retain them together.

✳ CAUTION

Allow the exhaust system to cool sufficiently before spraying a solvent exhaust fasteners. Some solvents are highly flammable and could ignite when sprayed on hot exhaust components.

Before removing any component of the exhaust system, ALWAYS squirt a liquid rust dissolving agent onto the fasteners for ease of removal. A lot of knuckle skin will be saved by following this rule. It may even be wise to spray the fasteners and allow them to sit overnight.

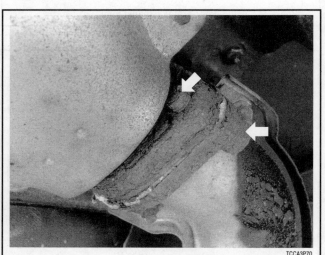

TCCA3P70

Nuts and bolts will be extremely difficult to remove when deteriorated with rust

Flange Type

✳ CAUTION

Do NOT perform exhaust repairs or inspection with the engine or exhaust hot. Allow the system to cool completely before attempting any work. Exhaust systems are noted for sharp edges, flaking metal and rusted bolts. Gloves and eye protection are required. A healthy supply of penetrating oil and rags is highly recommended. Never spray liquid rust dissolving agent onto a hot exhaust component.

Before removing any component on a flange type system, ALWAYS squirt a liquid rust dissolving agent onto the fasteners for ease of removal. Start by unbolting the exhaust piece at both ends (if required). When unbolting the headpipe from the manifold, make sure that the bolts are free before trying to remove them. if you snap a stud in the exhaust manifold, the stud will have to be removed with a bolt extractor, which often means removal of the manifold itself. Next, disconnect the component from the mounting; slight twisting and turning may be required to remove the component completely from the

TCCA3P72

Example of a flange type exhaust system joint

vehicle. You may need to tap on the component with a rubber mallet to loosen the component. If all else fails, use a hacksaw to separate the parts. An oxy-acetylene cutting torch may be faster but the sparks are DANGEROUS near the fuel tank, and at the very least, accidents could happen, resulting in damage to the under-car parts, not to mention yourself.

Slip Joint Type

Before removing any component on the slip joint type exhaust system, ALWAYS squirt a liquid rust dissolving agent onto the fasteners for ease of removal. Start by unbolting the exhaust piece at both ends (if required). When unbolting the headpipe from the manifold, make sure that the bolts are free before trying to remove them. if you snap a stud in the exhaust manifold, the stud will have to be removed with a bolt extractor, which often means removal of the manifold itself. Next, remove the mounting U-bolts from around the exhaust pipe you are extracting from the vehicle. Don't be surprised if the U-bolts break while removing the nuts. Loosen the exhaust pipe from any mounting brackets retaining it to the floor pan and separate the components.

TCCA3P79

Example of a common slip joint type system

ENGINE RECONDITIONING

Determining Engine Condition

Anything that generates heat and/or friction will eventually burn or wear out (i.e. a light bulb generates heat, therefore its life span is limited). With this in mind, a running engine generates tremendous amounts of both; friction is encountered by the moving and rotating parts inside the engine and heat is created by friction and combustion of the fuel. However, the engine has systems designed to help reduce the effects of heat and friction and provide added longevity. The oiling system reduces the amount of friction encountered by the moving parts inside the engine, while the cooling system reduces heat created by friction and combustion. If either system is not maintained, a break-down will be inevitable. Therefore, you can see how regular maintenance can affect the service life of your vehicle. If you do not drain, flush and refill your cooling system at the proper intervals, deposits will begin to accumulate in the radiator, thereby reducing the amount of heat it can extract from the coolant. The same applies to your oil and filter; if it is not changed often enough it becomes laden with contaminates and is unable to properly lubricate the engine. This increases friction and wear.

There are a number of methods for evaluating the condition of your engine. A compression test can reveal the condition of your pistons, piston rings, cylinder bores, head gasket(s), valves and valve seats. An oil pressure test can warn you of possible engine bearing, or oil pump failures. Excessive oil consumption, evidence of oil in the engine air intake area and/or bluish smoke from the tail pipe may indicate worn piston rings, worn valve guides and/or valve seals. As a general rule, an engine that uses no more than one quart of oil every 1000 miles is in good condition. Engines that use one quart of oil or more in less than 1000 miles should first be checked for oil leaks. If any oil leaks are present, have them fixed before determining how much oil is consumed by the engine, especially if blue smoke is not visible at the tail pipe.

COMPRESSION TEST

A noticeable lack of engine power, excessive oil consumption and/or poor fuel mileage measured over an extended period are all indicators of internal engine wear. Worn piston rings, scored or worn cylinder bores, blown head gaskets, sticking or burnt valves, and worn valve seats are all possible culprits. A check of each cylinder's compression will help locate the problem.

➡A screw-in type compression gauge is more accurate than the type you simply hold against the spark plug hole. Although it takes slightly longer to use, it's worth the effort to obtain a more accurate reading.

TCCS3801

A screw-in type compression gauge is more accurate and easier to use without an assistant

1. Make sure that the proper amount and viscosity of engine oil is in the crankcase, then ensure the battery is fully charged.
2. Warm-up the engine to normal operating temperature, then shut the engine **OFF**.
3. Disable the ignition system.
4. Label and disconnect all of the spark plug wires from the plugs.
5. Thoroughly clean the cylinder head area around the spark plug ports, then remove the spark plugs.
6. Set the throttle plate to the fully open (wide-open throttle) position. You can block the accelerator linkage open for this, or you can have an assistant fully depress the accelerator pedal.
7. Install a screw-in type compression gauge into the No. 1 spark plug hole until the fitting is snug.

❄❄ WARNING

Be careful not to crossthread the spark plug hole.

8. According to the tool manufacturer's instructions, connect a remote starting switch to the starting circuit.
9. With the ignition switch in the **OFF** position, use the remote starting switch to crank the engine through at least five compression strokes (approximately 5 seconds of cranking) and record the highest reading on the gauge.
10. Repeat the test on each cylinder, cranking the engine approximately the same number of compression strokes and/or time as the first.
11. Compare the highest readings from each cylinder to that of the others. The indicated compression pressures are considered within specifications if the lowest reading cylinder is within 75 percent of the pressure recorded for the highest reading cylinder. For example, if your highest reading cylinder pressure was 150 psi (1034 kPa), then 75 percent of that would be 113 psi (779 kPa). So the lowest reading cylinder should be no less than 113 psi (779 kPa).
12. If a cylinder exhibits an unusually low compression reading, pour a tablespoon of clean engine oil into the cylinder through the spark plug hole and repeat the compression test. If the compression rises after adding oil, it means that the cylinder's piston rings and/or cylinder bore are damaged or worn. If the pressure remains low, the valves may not be seating properly (a valve job is needed), or the head gasket may be blown near that cylinder. If compression in any two adjacent cylinders is low, and if the addition of oil doesn't help raise compression, there is leakage past the head gasket. Oil and coolant in the combustion chamber, combined with blue or constant white smoke from the tail pipe, are symptoms of this problem. However, don't be alarmed by the normal white smoke emitted from the tail pipe during engine warm-up or from cold weather driving. There may be evidence of water droplets on the engine dipstick and/or oil droplets in the cooling system if a head gasket is blown.

OIL PRESSURE TEST

Check for proper oil pressure at the sending unit passage with an externally mounted mechanical oil pressure gauge (as opposed to relying on a factory installed dash-mounted gauge). A tachometer may also be needed, as some specifications may require running the engine at a specific rpm.

1. With the engine cold, locate and remove the oil pressure sending unit.
2. Following the manufacturer's instructions, connect a mechanical oil pressure gauge and, if necessary, a tachometer to the engine.
3. Start the engine and allow it to idle.
4. Check the oil pressure reading when cold and record the number. You may need to run the engine at a specified rpm, so check the specifications chart located earlier in this section.
5. Run the engine until normal operating temperature is reached (upper radiator hose will feel warm).
6. Check the oil pressure reading again with the engine hot and record the number. Turn the engine **OFF**.

7. Compare your hot oil pressure reading to that given in the chart. If the reading is low, check the cold pressure reading against the chart. If the cold pressure is well above the specification, and the hot reading was lower than the specification, you may have the wrong viscosity oil in the engine. Change the oil, making sure to use the proper grade and quantity, then repeat the test.

Low oil pressure readings could be attributed to internal component wear, pump related problems, a low oil level, or oil viscosity that is too low. High oil pressure readings could be caused by an overfilled crankcase, too high of an oil viscosity or a faulty pressure relief valve.

Buy or Rebuild?

Now that you have determined that your engine is worn out, you must make some decisions. The question of whether or not an engine is worth rebuilding is largely a subjective matter and one of personal worth. Is the engine a popular one, or is it an obsolete model? Are parts available? Will it get acceptable gas mileage once it is rebuilt? Is the car it's being put into worth keeping? Would it be less expensive to buy a new engine, have your engine rebuilt by a pro, rebuild it yourself or buy a used engine from a salvage yard? Or would it be simpler and less expensive to buy another car? If you have considered all these matters and more, and have still decided to rebuild the engine, then it is time to decide how you will rebuild it.

➡**The editors at Chilton feel that most engine machining should be performed by a professional machine shop. Don't think of it as wasting money, rather, as an assurance that the job has been done right the first time. There are many expensive and specialized tools required to perform such tasks as boring and honing an engine block or having a valve job done on a cylinder head. Even inspecting the parts requires expensive micrometers and gauges to properly measure wear and clearances. Also, a machine shop can deliver to you clean, and ready to assemble parts, saving you time and aggravation. Your maximum savings will come from performing the removal, disassembly, assembly and installation of the engine and purchasing or renting only the tools required to perform the above tasks. Depending on the particular circumstances, you may save 40 to 60 percent of the cost doing these yourself.**

A complete rebuild or overhaul of an engine involves replacing all of the moving parts (pistons, rods, crankshaft, camshaft, etc.) with new ones and machining the non-moving wearing surfaces of the block and heads. Unfortunately, this may not be cost effective. For instance, your crankshaft may have been damaged or worn, but it can be machined undersize for a minimal fee.

So, as you can see, you can replace everything inside the engine, but, it is wiser to replace only those parts which are really needed, and, if possible, repair the more expensive ones. Later in this section, we will break the engine down into its two main components: the cylinder head and the engine block. We will discuss each component, and the recommended parts to replace during a rebuild on each.

Engine Overhaul Tips

Most engine overhaul procedures are fairly standard. In addition to specific parts replacement procedures and specifications for your individual engine, this section is also a guide to acceptable rebuilding procedures. Examples of standard rebuilding practice are given and should be used along with specific details concerning your particular engine.

Competent and accurate machine shop services will ensure maximum performance, reliability and engine life. In most instances it is more profitable for the do-it-yourself mechanic to remove, clean and inspect the component, buy the necessary parts and deliver these to a shop for actual machine work.

Much of the assembly work (crankshaft, bearings, piston rods, and other components) is well within the scope of the do-it-yourself mechanic's tools and abilities. You will have to decide for yourself the depth of involvement you desire in an engine repair or rebuild.

TOOLS

The tools required for an engine overhaul or parts replacement will depend on the depth of your involvement. With a few exceptions, they will be the tools found in a mechanic's tool kit (see Section 1 of this manual). More in-depth work will require some or all of the following:

- A dial indicator (reading in thousandths) mounted on a universal base
- Micrometers and telescope gauges
- Jaw and screw-type pullers
- Scraper
- Valve spring compressor
- Ring groove cleaner
- Piston ring expander and compressor
- Ridge reamer
- Cylinder hone or glaze breaker
- Plastigage®
- Engine stand

The use of most of these tools is illustrated in this section. Many can be rented for a one-time use from a local parts jobber or tool supply house specializing in automotive work.

Occasionally, the use of special tools is called for. See the information on Special Tools and the Safety Notice in the front of this book before substituting another tool.

OVERHAUL TIPS

Aluminum has become extremely popular for use in engines, due to its low weight. Observe the following precautions when handling aluminum parts:

- Never hot tank aluminum parts (the caustic hot tank solution will eat the aluminum.
- Remove all aluminum parts (identification tag, etc.) from engine parts prior to the tanking.
- Always coat threads lightly with engine oil or anti-seize compounds before installation, to prevent seizure.
- Never overtighten bolts or spark plugs especially in aluminum threads.

When assembling the engine, any parts that will be exposed to frictional contact must be prelubed to provide lubrication at initial start-up. Any product specifically formulated for this purpose can be used, but engine oil is not recommended as a prelube in most cases.

When semi-permanent (locked, but removable) installation of bolts or nuts is desired, threads should be cleaned and coated with Loctite® or another similar, commercial non-hardening sealant.

CLEANING

Before the engine and its components are inspected, they must be thoroughly cleaned. You will need to remove any engine varnish, oil sludge and/or carbon deposits from all of the components to insure an accurate inspection. A crack in the engine block or cylinder head can easily become overlooked if hidden by a layer of sludge or carbon.

Most of the cleaning process can be carried out with common hand tools and readily available solvents or solutions. Carbon deposits can be chipped away using a hammer and a hard wooden chisel. Old gasket material and varnish or sludge can usually be removed using a scraper and/or cleaning solvent. Extremely stubborn deposits may require the use of a power drill with a wire brush. If using a wire brush, use extreme care around any critical machined surfaces (such as the gasket surfaces, bearing saddles, cylinder bores, etc.). USE OF A WIRE BRUSH IS NOT RECOMMENDED ON ANY ALUMINUM COMPONENTS. Always follow any safety recommendations given by the manufacturer of the tool and/or solvent. You should always wear eye protection during any cleaning process involving scraping, chipping or spraying of solvents.

An alternative to the mess and hassle of cleaning the parts yourself is to drop them off at a local garage or machine shop. They will, more than likely, have the necessary equipment to properly clean all of the parts for a nominal fee.

Use a gasket scraper to remove the old gasket material from the mating surfaces

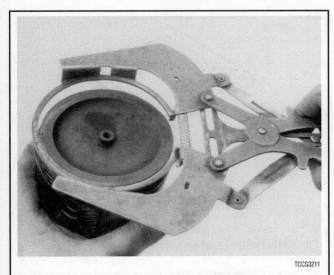

Use a ring expander tool to remove the piston rings

Clean the piston ring grooves using a ring groove cleaner tool, or . . .

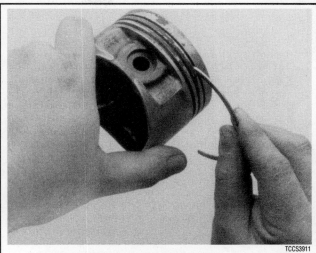

. . . use a piece of an old ring to clean the grooves. Be careful, the ring can be quite sharp

✼✼ CAUTION

Always wear eye protection during any cleaning process involving scraping, chipping or spraying of solvents.

Remove any oil galley plugs, freeze plugs and/or pressed-in bearings and carefully wash and degrease all of the engine components including the fasteners and bolts. Small parts such as the valves, springs, etc., should be placed in a metal basket and allowed to soak. Use pipe cleaner type brushes, and clean all passageways in the components. Use a ring expander and remove the rings from the pistons. Clean the piston ring grooves with a special tool or a piece of broken ring. Scrape the carbon off of the top of the piston. You should never use a wire brush on the pistons. After preparing all of the piston assemblies in this manner, wash and degrease them again.

✼✼ WARNING

Use extreme care when cleaning around the cylinder head valve seats. A mistake or slip may cost you a new seat.

When cleaning the cylinder head, remove carbon from the combustion chamber with the valves installed. This will avoid damaging the valve seats.

REPAIRING DAMAGED THREADS

▶ **See Figures 166, 167, 168, 169 and 170**

Several methods of repairing damaged threads are available. Heli-Coil (shown here), Keenserts, and Microdot, are among the most widely used. All involve basically the same principle—drilling out stripped threads, tapping the hole and installing a prewound insert—making welding, plugging and oversize fasteners unnecessary.

Two types of thread repair inserts are usually supplied: a standard type for most inch coarse, inch fine, metric course and metric fine thread sizes and a spark lug type to fit most spark plug port sizes. Consult the individual tool manufacturer's catalog to determine exact applications. Typical thread repair kits will contain a selection of prewound threaded inserts, a tap (corresponding to the outside diameter threads of the insert) and an installation tool. Spark plug inserts usually differ because they require a tap equipped with pilot threads and a combined reamer/tap section. Most manufacturers also supply blister-packed thread repair inserts separately in addition to a master kit containing a variety of taps and inserts plus installation tools.

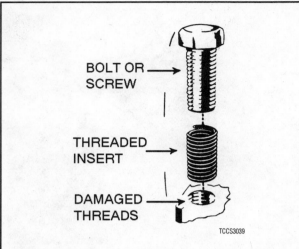

Fig. 166 Damaged bolt hole threads can be replaced with thread repair inserts

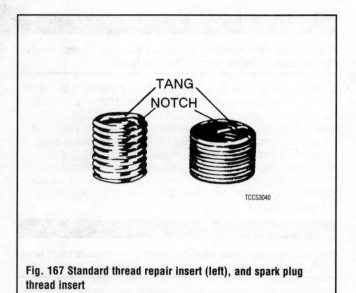

Fig. 167 Standard thread repair insert (left), and spark plug thread insert

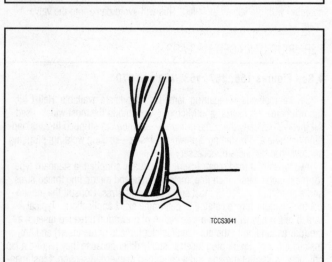

Fig. 168 Drill out the damaged threads with the specified size bit. Be sure to drill completely through the hole or to the bottom of a blind hole

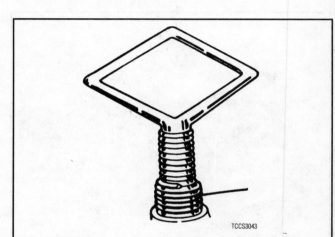

Fig. 169 Using the kit, tap the hole in order to receive the thread insert. Keep the tap well oiled and back it out frequently to avoid clogging the threads

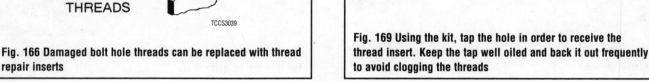

Fig. 170 Screw the insert onto the installer tool until the tang engages the slot. Thread the insert into the hole until it is 1/4–1/2 turn below the top surface, then remove the tool and break off the tang using a punch

Before attempting to repair a threaded hole, remove any snapped, broken or damaged bolts or studs. Penetrating oil can be used to free frozen threads. The offending item can usually be removed with locking pliers or using a screw/stud extractor. After the hole is clear, the thread can be repaired, as shown in the series of accompanying illustrations and in the kit manufacturer's instructions.

Engine Preparation

To properly rebuild an engine, you must first remove it from the vehicle, then disassemble and diagnose it. Ideally you should place your engine on an engine stand. This affords you the best access to the engine components. Follow the manufacturer's directions for using the stand with your particular engine. Remove the flywheel or flexplate before installing the engine to the stand.

Now that you have the engine on a stand, and assuming that you have drained the oil and coolant from the engine, it's time to strip it of all but the necessary components. Before you start disassembling the engine, you may want to take a moment to draw some pictures, or fabricate some labels or containers to mark the locations of various components and the bolts and/or studs which fasten them. Modern day engines use a lot of little brackets and clips which hold wiring harnesses and such, and these holders are often mounted on studs and/or bolts that can be easily mixed up. The manufacturer spent a lot of time and money designing your vehicle, and they wouldn't have wasted any of it by haphazardly placing brackets, clips or fasteners on the vehicle. If it's present when you disassemble it, put it back when you assemble, you will regret not remembering that little bracket which holds a wire harness out of the path of a rotating part.

You should begin by unbolting any accessories still attached to the engine, such as the water pump, power steering pump, alternator, etc. Then, unfasten any manifolds (intake or exhaust) which were not removed during the engine removal procedure. Finally, remove any covers remaining on the engine such as the rocker arm, front or timing cover and oil pan. Some front covers may require the vibration damper and/or crank pulley to be removed beforehand. The idea is to reduce the engine to the bare necessities (cylinder head(s), valve train, engine block, crankshaft, pistons and connecting rods), plus any other `in block' components such as oil pumps, balance shafts and auxiliary shafts.

Finally, remove the cylinder head(s) from the engine block and carefully place on a bench. Disassembly instructions for each component follow later in this section.

Cylinder Head

There are two basic types of cylinder heads used on today's automobiles: the Overhead Valve (OHV) and the Overhead Camshaft (OHC). The latter can also be broken down into two subgroups: the Single Overhead Camshaft (SOHC) and the Dual Overhead Camshaft (DOHC). Generally, if there is only a single camshaft on a head, it is just referred to as an OHC head. Also, an engine with a OHV cylinder head is also known as a pushrod engine.

Most cylinder heads these days are made of an aluminum alloy due to its light weight, durability and heat transfer qualities. However, cast iron was the material of choice in the past, and is still used on many vehicles today. Whether made from aluminum or iron, all cylinder heads have valves and seats. Some use two valves per cylinder, while the more hi-tech engines will utilize a multi-valve configuration using 3, 4 and even 5 valves per cylinder. When the valve contacts the seat, it does so on precision machined surfaces, which seals the combustion chamber. All cylinder heads have a valve guide for each valve. The guide centers the valve to the seat and allows it to move up and down within it. The clearance between the valve and guide can be critical. Too much clearance and the engine may consume oil, lose vacuum and/or damage the seat. Too little, and the valve can stick in the guide causing the engine to run poorly if at all, and possibly causing severe damage. The last component all cylinder heads have are valve springs. The spring holds the valve against its seat. It also returns the valve to this position when the valve has been opened by the valve train or camshaft. The spring is fastened to the valve by a retainer and valve locks (sometimes called keepers). Aluminum heads will also have a valve spring shim to keep the spring from wearing away the aluminum.

An ideal method of rebuilding the cylinder head would involve replacing all of the valves, guides, seats, springs, etc. with new ones. However, depending on how the engine was maintained, often this is not necessary. A major cause of valve, guide and seat wear is an improperly tuned engine. An engine that is running too rich, will often wash the lubricating oil out of the guide with gasoline, causing it to wear rapidly. Conversely, an engine which is running too lean will place higher combustion temperatures on the valves and seats allowing them to wear or even burn. Springs fall victim to the driving habits of the individual. A driver who often runs the engine rpm to the redline will wear out or break the springs faster then one that stays well below it. Unfortunately, mileage takes it toll on all of the parts. Generally, the valves, guides, springs and seats in a cylinder head can be machined and re-used, saving you money. However, if a valve is burnt, it

may be wise to replace all of the valves, since they were all operating in the same environment. The same goes for any other component on the cylinder head. Think of it as an insurance policy against future problems related to that component.

Unfortunately, the only way to find out which components need replacing, is to disassemble and carefully check each piece. After the cylinder head(s) are disassembled, thoroughly clean all of the components.

DISASSEMBLY

Whether it is a single or dual overhead camshaft cylinder head, the disassembly procedure is relatively unchanged. One aspect to pay attention to is careful labeling of the parts on the dual camshaft cylinder head. There will be an intake camshaft and followers as well as an exhaust camshaft and followers and they must be labeled as such. In some cases, the components are identical and could easily be installed incorrectly. DO NOT MIX THEM UP! Determining which is which is very simple; the intake camshaft and components are on the same side of the head as was the intake manifold. Conversely, the exhaust camshaft and components are on the same side of the head as was the exhaust manifold.

TCCA3P54

Exploded view of a valve, seal, spring, retainer and locks from an OHC cylinder head

Example of a multi-valve cylinder head. Note how it has 2 intake and 2 exhaust valve ports

Cup Type Camshaft Followers

➡Only the 1.8L engine is equipped with cup type camshaft followers; the 1.3L and 1.6L engines utilize rocker arms.

C-clamp type spring compressor and an OHC spring removal tool (center) for cup type followers

Most cup type follower cylinder heads retain the camshaft using bolt-on bearing caps

Position the OHC spring tool in the follower bore, then compress the spring with a C-clamp type tool

Most cylinder heads with cup type camshaft followers will have the valve spring, retainer and locks recessed within the follower's bore. You will need a C-clamp style valve spring compressor tool, an OHC spring removal tool (or equivalent) and a small magnet to disassemble the head.

1. If not already removed, remove the camshaft(s) and/or followers. Mark their positions for assembly.

2. Position the cylinder head to allow use of a C-clamp style valve spring compressor tool.

➡️ **It is preferred to position the cylinder head gasket surface facing you with the valve springs facing the opposite direction and the head laying horizontal.**

3. With the OHC spring removal adapter tool positioned inside of the follower bore, compress the valve spring using the C-clamp style valve spring compressor.

4. Remove the valve locks. A small magnetic tool or screwdriver will aid in removal.

5. Release the compressor tool and remove the spring assembly.

6. Withdraw the valve from the cylinder head.

7. If equipped, remove the valve seal.

➡️ **Special valve seal removal tools are available. Regular or needle nose type pliers, if used with care, will work just as well. If using ordinary pliers, be sure not to damage the follower bore. The follower and its bore are machined to close tolerances and any damage to the bore will effect this relationship.**

8. If equipped, remove the valve spring shim. A small magnetic tool or screwdriver will aid in removal.

9. Repeat Steps 3 through 8 until all of the valves have been removed.

Rocker Arm Type Camshaft Followers

➡️ **Only the 1.3L and 1.6L engines utilize rocker arms; the 1.8L engine is equipped with cup type camshaft followers.**

Most cylinder heads with rocker arm-type camshaft followers are easily disassembled using a standard valve spring compressor. However, certain models may not have enough open space around the spring for the standard tool and may require you to use a C-clamp style compressor tool instead.

1. If not already removed, remove the rocker arms and/or shafts and the camshaft. If applicable, also remove the hydraulic lash adjusters. Mark their positions for assembly.

2. Position the cylinder head to allow access to the valve spring.

3. Use a valve spring compressor tool to relieve the spring tension from the retainer.

➡️ **Due to engine varnish, the retainer may stick to the valve locks. A gentle tap with a hammer may help to break it loose.**

4. Remove the valve locks from the valve tip and/or retainer. A small magnet may help in removing the small locks.

5. Lift the valve spring, tool and all, off of the valve stem.

Another example of the rocker arm type OHC head. This model uses a follower under the camshaft

Before the camshaft can be removed, all of the followers must first be removed . . .

Example of the shaft mounted rocker arms on some OHC heads

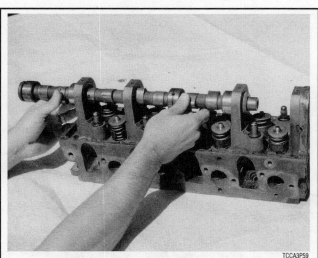
. . . then the camshaft can be removed by sliding it out (shown), or unbolting a bearing cap (not shown)

Compress the valve spring . . .

TCCA3P57

Remove the valve seal from the guide. Some gentle prying or pliers may help to remove stubborn ones

TCCA3P55

. . . then remove the valve locks from the valve stem and spring retainer

TCCA3P58

All aluminum and some cast iron heads will have these valve spring shims. Remove all of them as well

TCCA3P52

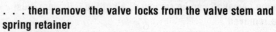
Remove the valve spring and retainer from the cylinder head

TCCA3P56

6. If equipped, remove the valve seal. If the seal is difficult to remove with the valve in place, try removing the valve first, then the seal. Follow the steps below for valve removal.

7. Position the head to allow access for withdrawing the valve.

➡**Cylinder heads that have seen a lot of miles and/or abuse may have mushroomed the valve lock grove and/or tip, causing difficulty in removal of the valve. If this has happened, use a metal file to carefully remove the high spots around the lock grooves and/or tip. Only file it enough to allow removal.**

8. Remove the valve from the cylinder head.

9. If equipped, remove the valve spring shim. A small magnetic tool or screwdriver will aid in removal.

10. Repeat Steps 3 though 9 until all of the valves have been removed.

INSPECTION

Now that all of the cylinder head components are clean, it's time to inspect them for wear and/or damage. To accurately inspect them, you will need some specialized tools:

- A 0–1 inch micrometer for the valves
- A dial indicator or inside diameter gauge for the valve guides
- A spring pressure test gauge

If you do not have access to the proper tools, you may want to bring the components to a shop that does.

Valves

The first thing to inspect are the valve heads. Look closely at the head, margin and face for any cracks, excessive wear or burning. The margin is the best place to look for burning. It should have a squared edge with an even width all around the diameter. When a valve burns, the margin will look melted and the edges rounded. Also inspect the valve head for any signs of tulipping. This will show as a lifting of the edges or dishing in the center of the head and will usually not occur to all of the valves. All of the heads should look the same, any that seem dished more than others are probably bad. Next, inspect the valve lock grooves and valve tips. Check for any burrs around the lock grooves, especially if you had to file them to remove the valve. Valve tips should appear flat, although slight rounding with high mileage engines is normal. Slightly worn valve tips will need to be machined flat. Last, measure the valve stem diameter with the micrometer. Measure the area that rides within the guide, especially towards the tip where most of the wear occurs. Take several measurements along its length and compare them to each other. Wear should be even along the length with little to no taper. If no minimum diameter is given in the speci-

fications, then the stem should not read more than 0.001 in. (0.025mm) below the specification. Any valves that fail these inspections should be replaced.

Springs, Retainers and Valve Locks

The first thing to check is the most obvious, broken springs. Next check the free length and squareness of each spring. If applicable, insure to distinguish between intake and exhaust springs. Use a ruler and/or carpenters square to measure the length. A carpenters square should be used to check the springs for squareness. If a spring pressure test gauge is available, check each springs rating and compare to the specifications chart. Check the readings against the specifications given. Any springs that fail these inspections should be replaced.

The spring retainers rarely need replacing, however they should still be checked as a precaution. Inspect the spring mating surface and the valve lock retention area for any signs of excessive wear. Also check for any signs of cracking. Replace any retainers that are questionable.

Valve locks should be inspected for excessive wear on the outside contact area as well as on the inner notched surface. Any locks which appear worn or broken and its respective valve should be replaced.

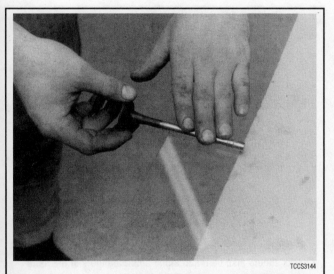

Valve stems may be rolled on a flat surface to check for bends

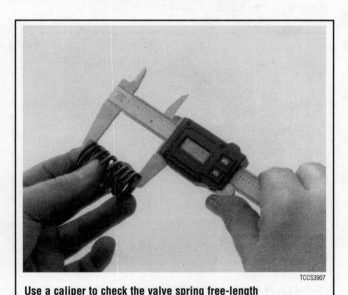

Use a caliper to check the valve spring free-length

Use a micrometer to check the valve stem diameter

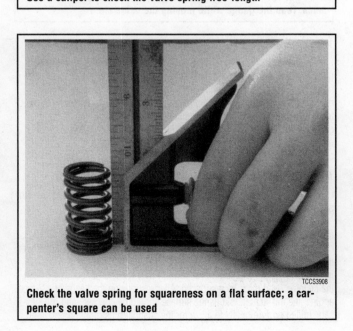

Check the valve spring for squareness on a flat surface; a carpenter's square can be used

Cylinder Head

There are several things to check on the cylinder head: valve guides, seats, cylinder head surface flatness, cracks and physical damage.

VALVE GUIDES

Now that you know the valves are good, you can use them to check the guides, although a new valve, if available, is preferred. Before you measure anything, look at the guides carefully and inspect them for any cracks, chips or breakage. Also if the guide is a removable style (as in most aluminum heads), check them for any looseness or evidence of movement. All of the guides should appear to be at the same height from the spring seat. If any seem lower (or higher) from another, the guide has moved. Mount a dial indicator onto the spring side of the cylinder head. Lightly oil the valve stem and insert it into the cylinder head. Position the dial indicator against the valve stem near the tip and zero the gauge. Grasp the valve stem and wiggle towards and away from the dial indicator and observe the readings. Mount the dial indicator 90 degrees from the initial point and zero the gauge and again take a reading. Compare the two readings for a out of round condition. Check the readings against the specifications given. An Inside Diameter (I.D.) gauge designed for valve guides will give you an accurate valve guide bore measurement. If the I.D. gauge is used, compare the readings with the specifications given. Any guides that fail these inspections should be replaced or machined.

A dial gauge may be used to check valve stem-to-guide clearance; read the gauge while moving the valve stem

VALVE SEATS

A visual inspection of the valve seats should show a slightly worn and pitted surface where the valve face contacts the seat. Inspect the seat carefully for severe pitting or cracks. Also, a seat that is badly worn will be recessed into the cylinder head. A severely worn or recessed seat may need to be replaced. All cracked seats must be replaced. A seat concentricity gauge, if available, should be used to check the seat run-out. If run-out exceeds specifications the seat must be machined (if no specification is given use 0.002 in. or 0.051mm).

CYLINDER HEAD SURFACE FLATNESS

After you have cleaned the gasket surface of the cylinder head of any old gasket material, check the head for flatness.

Place a straightedge across the gasket surface. Using feeler gauges, determine the clearance at the center of the straightedge and across the cylinder head at several points. Check along the centerline and diagonally on the head surface. If the warpage exceeds 0.003 in. (0.076mm) within a 6.0 in. (15.2cm) span, or 0.006 in. (0.152mm) over the total length of the head, the cylinder head must be resurfaced. After resurfacing the heads of a V-type engine, the intake manifold flange surface should be checked, and if necessary, milled proportionally to allow for the change in its mounting position.

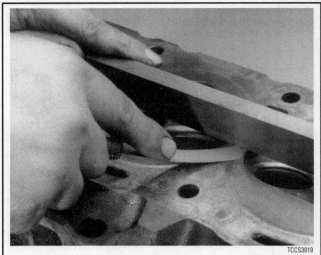

Check the head for flatness across the center of the head surface using a straightedge and feeler gauge

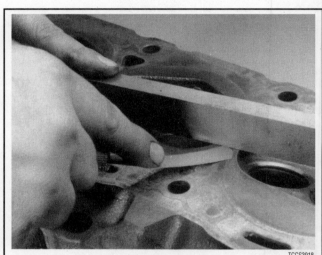

Checks should also be made along both diagonals of the head surface

CRACKS AND PHYSICAL DAMAGE

Generally, cracks are limited to the combustion chamber, however, it is not uncommon for the head to crack in a spark plug hole, port, outside of the head or in the valve spring/rocker arm area. The first area to inspect is always the hottest: the exhaust seat/port area.

A visual inspection should be performed, but just because you don't see a crack does not mean it is not there. Some more reliable methods for inspecting for cracks include Magnaflux®, a magnetic process or Zyglo®, a dye penetrant. Magnaflux® is used only on ferrous metal (cast iron) heads. Zyglo® uses a spray on fluorescent mixture along with a black light to reveal the cracks. It is strongly recommended to have your cylinder head checked professionally for cracks, especially if the engine was known to have overheated and/or leaked or consumed coolant. Contact a local shop for availability and pricing of these services.

Physical damage is usually very evident. For example, a broken mounting ear from dropping the head or a bent or broken stud and/or bolt. All of these defects should be fixed or, if irreparable, the head should be replaced.

Camshaft and Followers

Inspect the camshaft(s) and followers as described earlier in this section.

REFINISHING & REPAIRING

Many of the procedures given for refinishing and repairing the cylinder head components must be performed by a machine shop. Certain steps, if the inspected part is not worn, can be performed yourself inexpensively. However, you spent a lot of time and effort so far, why risk trying to save a couple bucks if you might have to do it all over again?

Valves

Any valves that were not replaced should be refaced and the tips ground flat. Unless you have access to a valve grinding machine, this should be done by a machine shop. If the valves are in extremely good condition, as well as the valve seats and guides, they may be lapped in without performing machine work.

It is a recommended practice to lap the valves even after machine work has been performed and/or new valves have been purchased. This insures a positive seal between the valve and seat.

LAPPING THE VALVES

➡**Before lapping the valves to the seats, read the rest of the cylinder head section to insure that any related parts are in acceptable enough condition to continue.**

➡**Before any valve seat machining and/or lapping can be performed, the guides must be within factory recommended specifications.**

1. Invert the cylinder head.
2. Lightly lubricate the valve stems and insert them into the cylinder head in their numbered order.
3. Raise the valve from the seat and apply a small amount of fine lapping compound to the seat.
4. Moisten the suction head of a hand-lapping tool and attach it to the head of the valve.
5. Rotate the tool between the palms of both hands, changing the position of the valve on the valve seat and lifting the tool often to prevent grooving.
6. Lap the valve until a smooth, polished circle is evident on the valve and seat.
7. Remove the tool and the valve. Wipe away all traces of the grinding compound and store the valve to maintain its lapped location.

❄ WARNING

Do not get the valves out of order after they have been lapped. They must be put back with the same valve seat they were lapped with.

Springs, Retainers and Valve Locks

There is no repair or refinishing possible with the springs, retainers and valve locks. If they are found to be worn or defective, they must be replaced with new (or known good) parts.

Cylinder Head

Most refinishing procedures dealing with the cylinder head must be performed by a machine shop. Read the sections below and review your inspection data to determine whether or not machining is necessary.

VALVE GUIDE

➡**If any machining or replacements are made to the valve guides, the seats must be machined.**

Unless the valve guides need machining or replacing, the only service to perform is to thoroughly clean them of any dirt or oil residue.

There are only two types of valve guides used on automobile engines: the replaceable-type (all aluminum heads) and the cast-in integral-type (most cast iron heads). There are four recommended methods for repairing worn guides.

- Knurling
- Inserts
- Reaming oversize
- Replacing

Knurling is a process in which metal is displaced and raised, thereby reducing clearance, giving a true center, and providing oil control. It is the least expensive way of repairing the valve guides. However, it is not necessarily the best, and in some cases, a knurled valve guide will not stand up for more than a short time. It requires special knurling and precision reaming tools to obtain proper clearances. It would not be cost effective to purchase these tools, unless you plan on rebuilding several of the same cylinder head.

Installing a guide insert involves machining the guide to accept a bronze insert. One style is the coil-type which is installed into a threaded guide. Another is the thin-walled insert where the guide is reamed oversize to accept a split-sleeve insert. After the insert is installed, a special tool is then run through the guide to expand the insert, locking it to the guide. The insert is then reamed to the standard size for proper valve clearance.

Reaming for oversize valves restores normal clearances and provides a true valve seat. Most cast-in type guides can be reamed to accept an valve with an oversize stem. The cost factor for this can become quite high as you will need to purchase the reamer and new, oversize stem valves for all guides which were reamed. Oversizes are generally 0.003 to 0.030 in. (0.076 to 0.762mm), with 0.015 in. (0.381mm) being the most common.

To replace cast-in type valve guides, they must be drilled out, then reamed to accept replacement guides. This must be done on a fixture which will allow centering and leveling off of the original valve seat or guide, otherwise a serious guide-to-seat misalignment may occur making it impossible to properly machine the seat.

Replaceable-type guides are pressed into the cylinder head. A hammer and a stepped drift or punch may be used to install and remove the guides. Before removing the guides, measure the protrusion on the spring side of the head and record it for installation. Use the stepped drift to hammer out the old guide from the combustion chamber side of the head. When installing, determine whether or not the guide also seals a water jacket in the head, and if it does, use the recommended sealing agent. If there is no water jacket, grease the valve guide and its bore. Use the stepped drift, and hammer the new guide into the cylinder head from the spring side of the cylinder head. A stack of washers the same thickness as the measured protrusion may help the installation process.

VALVE SEATS

➡**Before any valve seat machining can be performed, the guides must be within factory recommended specifications.**

➡**If any machining or replacements were made to the valve guides, the seats must be machined.**

If the seats are in good condition, the valves can be lapped to the seats, and the cylinder head assembled. See the valves section for instructions on lapping.

If the valve seats are worn, cracked or damaged, they must be serviced by a machine shop. The valve seat must be perfectly centered to the valve guide, which requires very accurate machining.

CYLINDER HEAD SURFACE

If the cylinder head is warped, it must be machined flat. If the warpage is extremely severe, the head may need to be replaced. In some instances, it may be possible to straighten a warped head enough to allow machining. In either case, contact a professional machine shop for service.

➡**Any OHC cylinder head that shows excessive warpage should have the camshaft bearing journals align bored after the cylinder head has been resurfaced.**

❄ WARNING

Failure to align bore the camshaft bearing journals could result in severe engine damage including but not limited to: valve and piston damage, connecting rod damage, camshaft and/or crankshaft breakage.

CRACKS AND PHYSICAL DAMAGE

Certain cracks can be repaired in both cast iron and aluminum heads. For cast iron, a tapered threaded insert is installed along the length of the crack. Aluminum can also use the tapered inserts, however welding is the preferred method. Some physical damage can be repaired through brazing or welding. Contact a machine shop to get expert advice for your particular dilemma.

ASSEMBLY

The first step for any assembly job is to have a clean area in which to work. Next, thoroughly clean all of the parts and components that are to be assembled. Finally, place all of the components onto a suitable work space and, if necessary, arrange the parts to their respective positions.

Cup Type Camshaft Followers

➡Only the 1.8L engine is equipped with cup type camshaft followers; the 1.3L and 1.6L engines utilize rocker arms.

To install the springs, retainers and valve locks on heads which have these components recessed into the camshaft follower's bore, you will need a small screwdriver-type tool, some clean white grease and a lot of patience. You will also need the C-clamp style spring compressor and the OHC tool used to disassemble the head.

1. Lightly lubricate the valve stems and insert all of the valves into the cylinder head. If possible, maintain their original locations.
2. If equipped, install any valve spring shims which were removed.
3. If equipped, install the new valve seals, keeping the following in mind:
• If the valve seal presses over the guide, lightly lubricate the outer guide surfaces.
• If the seal is an O-ring type, it is installed just after compressing the spring but before the valve locks.
4. Place the valve spring and retainer over the stem.
5. Position the spring compressor and the OHC tool, then compress the spring.
6. Using a small screwdriver as a spatula, fill the valve stem side of the lock with white grease. Use the excess grease on the screwdriver to fasten the lock to the driver.
7. Carefully install the valve lock, which is stuck to the end of the screwdriver, to the valve stem then press on it with the screwdriver until the grease squeezes out. The valve lock should now be stuck to the stem.
8. Repeat Steps 6 and 7 for the remaining valve lock.
9. Relieve the spring pressure slowly and insure that neither valve lock becomes dislodged by the retainer.

Once assembled, check the valve clearance and correct as needed

TCCA3P64

10. Remove the spring compressor tool.
11. Repeat Steps 2 through 10 until all of the springs have been installed.
12. Install the followers, camshaft(s) and any other components that were removed for disassembly.

Rocker Arm Type Camshaft Followers

➡Only the 1.3L and 1.6L engines utilize rocker arms; the 1.8L engine is equipped with cup type camshaft followers.

1. Lightly lubricate the valve stems and insert all of the valves into the cylinder head. If possible, maintain their original locations.
2. If equipped, install any valve spring shims which were removed.
3. If equipped, install the new valve seals, keeping the following in mind:
• If the valve seal presses over the guide, lightly lubricate the outer guide surfaces.
• If the seal is an O-ring type, it is installed just after compressing the spring but before the valve locks.
4. Place the valve spring and retainer over the stem.
5. Position the spring compressor tool and compress the spring.
6. Assemble the valve locks to the stem.
7. Relieve the spring pressure slowly and insure that neither valve lock becomes dislodged by the retainer.
8. Remove the spring compressor tool.
9. Repeat Steps 2 through 8 until all of the springs have been installed.
10. Install the camshaft(s), rockers, shafts and any other components that were removed for disassembly.

Engine Block

GENERAL INFORMATION

A thorough overhaul or rebuild of an engine block would include replacing the pistons, rings, bearings, timing belt/chain assembly and oil pump. For OHV engines also include a new camshaft and lifters. The block would then have the cylinders bored and honed oversize (or if using removable cylinder sleeves, new sleeves installed) and the crankshaft would be cut undersize to provide new wearing surfaces and perfect clearances. However, your particular engine may not have everything worn out. What if only the piston rings have worn out and the clearances on everything else are still within factory specifications? Well, you could just replace the rings and put it back together, but this would be a very rare example. Chances are, if one component in your engine is worn, other components are sure to follow, and soon. At the very least, you should always replace the rings, bearings and oil pump. This is what is commonly called a "freshen up".

Cylinder Ridge Removal

Because the top piston ring does not travel to the very top of the cylinder, a ridge is built up between the end of the travel and the top of the cylinder bore.

Pushing the piston and connecting rod assembly past the ridge can be difficult, and damage to the piston ring lands could occur. If the ridge is not removed before installing a new piston or not removed at all, piston ring breakage and piston damage may occur.

➡It is always recommended that you remove any cylinder ridges before removing the piston and connecting rod assemblies. If you know that new pistons are going to be installed and the engine block will be bored oversize, you may be able to forego this step. However, some ridges may actually prevent the assemblies from being removed, necessitating its removal.

There are several different types of ridge reamers on the market, none of which are inexpensive. Unless a great deal of engine rebuilding is anticipated, borrow or rent a reamer.

1. Turn the crankshaft until the piston is at the bottom of its travel.
2. Cover the head of the piston with a rag.

3. Follow the tool manufacturers instructions and cut away the ridge, exercising extreme care to avoid cutting too deeply.

4. Remove the ridge reamer, the rag and as many of the cuttings as possible. Continue until all of the cylinder ridges have been removed.

DISASSEMBLY

▶ See Figure 171

The engine disassembly instructions following assume that you have the engine mounted on an engine stand. If not, it is easiest to disassemble the engine on a bench or the floor with it resting on the bell housing or transmission mounting surface. You must be able to access the connecting rod fasteners and turn the crankshaft during disassembly. Also, all engine covers (timing, front, side, oil pan, whatever) should have already been removed. Engines which are seized or locked up may not be able to be completely disassembled, and a core (salvage yard) engine should be purchased.

If not done during the cylinder head removal, remove the timing chain/belt and/or gear/sprocket assembly. Remove the oil pick-up and pump assembly and, if necessary, the pump drive. If equipped, remove any balance or auxiliary shafts. If necessary, remove the cylinder ridge from the top of the bore. See the cylinder ridge removal procedure earlier in this section.

Rotate the engine over so that the crankshaft is exposed. Use a number punch or scribe and mark each connecting rod with its respective cylinder number. The cylinder closest to the front of the engine is always number 1. However, depending on the engine placement, the front of the engine could either be the flywheel or damper/pulley end. Generally the front of the engine faces the front of the vehicle. Use a number punch or scribe and also mark the main bearing caps from front to rear with the front most cap being number 1 (if there are five caps, mark them 1 through 5, front to rear).

✸✸ WARNING

Take special care when pushing the connecting rod up from the crankshaft because the sharp threads of the rod bolts/studs will score the crankshaft journal. Insure that special plastic caps are installed over them, or cut two pieces of rubber hose to do the same.

Again, rotate the engine, this time to position the number one cylinder bore (head surface) up. Turn the crankshaft until the number one piston is at the bottom of its travel, this should allow the maximum access to its connecting rod. Remove the number one connecting rods fasteners and cap and place two lengths of rubber hose over the rod bolts/studs to protect the crankshaft from damage. Using a sturdy wooden dowel and a hammer, push the connecting rod up about 1 in. (25mm) from the crankshaft

Place rubber hose over the connecting rod studs to protect the crankshaft and cylinder bores from damage

TCCS3804

Carefully tap the piston out of the bore using a wooden dowel

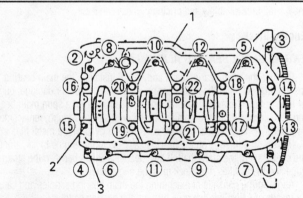

1. Lower crankcase
2. Bolt (10 mm thread diameter)
3. Bolt (8 mm thread diameter)

90883GF2

Fig. 171 Be sure to loosen the crankcase mounting bolts in the sequence shown to avoid warpage

and remove the upper bearing insert. Continue pushing or tapping the connecting rod up until the piston rings are out of the cylinder bore. Remove the piston and rod by hand, put the upper half of the bearing insert back into the rod, install the cap with its bearing insert installed, and hand-tighten the cap fasteners. If the parts are kept in order in this manner, they will not get lost and you will be able to tell which bearings came form what cylinder if any problems are discovered and diagnosis is necessary. Remove all the other piston assemblies in the same manner. On V-style engines, remove all of the pistons from one bank, then reposition the engine with the other cylinder bank head surface up, and remove that banks piston assemblies.

✳✳ WARNING

On the 1.8L engine, be sure to loosen the crankcase mounting bolts in the sequence, shown in the accompanying illustration, to avoid crankcase warpage.

The only remaining component in the engine block should now be the crankshaft. Loosen the main bearing caps evenly until the fasteners can be turned by hand, then remove them and the caps. Remove the crankshaft from the engine block. Thoroughly clean all of the components.

INSPECTION

Now that the engine block and all of its components are clean, it's time to inspect them for wear and/or damage. To accurately inspect them, you will need some specialized tools:

- Two or three separate micrometers to measure the pistons and crankshaft journals
- A dial indicator
- Telescoping gauges for the cylinder bores
- A rod alignment fixture to check for bent connecting rods

If you do not have access to the proper tools, you may want to bring the components to a shop that does.

Generally, you shouldn't expect cracks in the engine block or its components unless it was known to leak, consume or mix engine fluids, it was severely overheated, or there was evidence of bad bearings and/or crankshaft damage. A visual inspection should be performed on all of the components, but just because you don't see a crack does not mean it is not there. Some more reliable methods for inspecting for cracks include Magnaflux®, a magnetic process or Zyglo®, a dye penetrant. Magnaflux® is used only on ferrous metal (cast iron). Zyglo® uses a spray on fluorescent mixture along with a black light to reveal the cracks. It is strongly recommended to have your engine block checked professionally for cracks, especially if the engine was known to have overheated and/or leaked or consumed coolant. Contact a local shop for availability and pricing of these services.

Engine Block

ENGINE BLOCK BEARING ALIGNMENT

Remove the main bearing caps and, if still installed, the main bearing inserts. Inspect all of the main bearing saddles and caps for damage, burrs or high spots. If damage is found, and it is caused from a spun main bearing, the block will need to be align-bored or, if severe enough, replacement. Any burrs or high spots should be carefully removed with a metal file.

Place a straightedge on the bearing saddles, in the engine block, along the centerline of the crankshaft. If any clearance exists between the straightedge and the saddles, the block must be align-bored.

Align-boring consists of machining the main bearing saddles and caps by means of a flycutter that runs through the bearing saddles.

DECK FLATNESS

The top of the engine block where the cylinder head mounts is called the deck. Insure that the deck surface is clean of dirt, carbon deposits and old gasket material. Place a straightedge across the surface of the deck along its centerline and, using feeler gauges, check the clearance along several points. Repeat the checking procedure with the straightedge placed along both diagonals of the deck surface. If the reading exceeds 0.003 in. (0.076mm) within a 6.0 in. (15.2cm) span, or 0.006 in. (0.152mm) over the total length of the deck, it must be machined.

CYLINDER BORES

The cylinder bores house the pistons and are slightly larger than the pistons themselves. A common piston-to-bore clearance is 0.0015–0.0025 in.

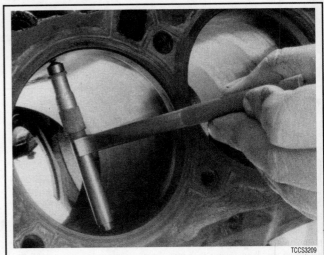

TCCS3209

Use a telescoping gauge to measure the cylinder bore diameter—take several readings within the same bore

(0.0381mm–0.0635mm). Inspect and measure the cylinder bores. The bore should be checked for out-of-roundness, taper and size. The results of this inspection will determine whether the cylinder can be used in its existing size and condition, or boring to the next oversize is required (or in the case of removable sleeves, have replacements installed).

The amount of cylinder wall wear is always greater at the top of the cylinder than at the bottom. This wear is known as taper. Any cylinder that has a taper of 0.0012 in. (0.305mm) or more, must be machined (bored). Measurements are taken at a number of positions in each cylinder: at the top, middle and bottom and at two points at each position; that is, at a point 90 degrees from the crankshaft centerline, as well as a point parallel to the crankshaft centerline. The measurements are made with either a special dial indicator or a telescopic gauge and micrometer. If the necessary precision tools to check the bore are not available, take the block to a machine shop and have them mike it. Also if you don't have the tools to check the cylinder bores, chances are you will not have the necessary devices to check the pistons, connecting rods and crankshaft. Take these components with you and save yourself an extra trip.

For our procedures, we will use a telescopic gauge and a micrometer. You will need one of each, with a measuring range which covers your cylinder bore size.

1. Position the telescopic gauge in the cylinder bore, loosen the gauges lock and allow it to expand.

➡**Your first two readings will be at the top of the cylinder bore, then proceed to the middle and finally the bottom, making a total of six measurements.**

2. Hold the gauge square in the bore, 90 degrees from the crankshaft centerline, and gently tighten the lock. Tilt the gauge back to remove it from the bore.

3. Measure the gauge with the micrometer and record the reading.

4. Again, hold the gauge square in the bore, this time parallel to the crankshaft centerline, and gently tighten the lock. Again, you will tilt the gauge back to remove it from the bore.

5. Measure the gauge with the micrometer and record this reading. The difference between these two readings is the out-of-round measurement of the cylinder.

6. Repeat steps 1 through 5, each time going to the next lower position, until you reach the bottom of the cylinder. Then go to the next cylinder, and continue until all of the cylinders have been measured.

The difference between these measurements will tell you all about the wear in your cylinders. The measurements which were taken 90 degrees from the crankshaft centerline will always reflect the most wear. That is because at this position is where the engine power presses the piston against the cylinder bore the hardest. This is known as thrust wear. Take your top, 90 degree measurement and compare it to your bottom, 90 degree measurement. The difference between them is the taper. When you measure your pistons, you will compare these readings to your piston sizes and determine piston-to-wall clearance.

Crankshaft

Inspect the crankshaft for visible signs of wear or damage. All of the journals should be perfectly round and smooth. Slight scores are normal for a used crankshaft, but you should hardly feel them with your fingernail. When measuring the crankshaft with a micrometer, you will take readings at the front and rear of each journal, then turn the micrometer 90 degrees and take two more readings, front and rear. The difference between the front-to-rear readings is the journal taper and the first-to-90 degree reading is the out-of-round measurement. Generally, there should be no taper or out-of-roundness found, however, up to 0.0005 in. (0.0127mm) for either can be overlooked. Also, the readings should fall within the factory specifications for journal diameters.

If the crankshaft journals fall within specifications, it is recommended that it be polished before being returned to service. Polishing the crankshaft insures that any minor burrs or high spots are smoothed, thereby reducing the chance of scoring the new bearings.

Pistons and Connecting Rods

PISTON

The piston should be visually inspected for any signs of cracking or burning (caused by hot spots or detonation), and scuffing or excessive wear on the skirts. The wristpin attaches the piston to the connecting rod. The piston should move freely on the wrist pin, both sliding and pivoting. Grasp the connecting rod securely, or mount it in a vise, and try to rock the piston back and forth along the centerline of the wristpin. There should not be any excessive play evident between the piston and the pin. If there are C-clips retaining the pin in the piston then you have wrist pin bushings in the rods. There should not be any excessive play between the wrist pin and the rod bushing. Normal clearance for the wrist pin is approx. 0.001–0.002 in. (0.025mm–0.051mm).

Use a micrometer and measure the diameter of the piston, perpendicular to the wrist pin, on the skirt. Compare the reading to its original cylinder measurement obtained earlier. The difference between the two readings is the piston-to-wall clearance. If the clearance is within specifications, the piston may be used as is. If the piston is out of specification, but the bore is not, you will need a new piston. If both are out of specification, you will need the cylinder machined (bored) and oversize pistons installed. Generally, if two or more pistons/bores are out of specification, it is best to bore the entire block and purchase a complete set of oversize pistons.

CONNECTING ROD

You should have the connecting rod checked for straightness at a machine shop. If the connecting rod is bent, it will unevenly wear the bearing and piston, as well as place greater stress on these components. Any bent or twisted connecting rods must be replaced. If the rods are straight and the wrist pin clearance is within specifications, then only the bearing end of the rod need be checked. Place the connecting rod into a vice, with the bearing inserts in place, install the cap to the rod and torque the fasteners to specifications. Use a telescoping gauge and carefully measure the inside diameter of the bearings. Compare this reading to the rods original crankshaft journal diameter measurement. The difference is the oil clearance. If the oil clearance is not within specifications, install new bearings in the rod and take another measurement. If the clearance is still out of specifications, and the crankshaft is not, the rod will need to be reconditioned by a machine shop.

➡You can also use Plastigage® to check the bearing clearances. The assembling section has complete instructions on its use.

Camshaft

Inspect the camshaft and lifters/followers as described earlier in this section.

Bearings

All of the engine bearings should be visually inspected for wear and/or damage. The bearing should look evenly worn all around with no deep scores or pits. If the bearing is severely worn, scored, pitted or heat blued, then the bearing, and the components that use it, should be brought to a machine shop for inspection. Full-circle bearings (used on most camshafts, auxiliary shafts, balance shafts, etc.) require specialized tools for removal and installation, and should be brought to a machine shop for service.

Oil Pump

➡The oil pump is responsible for providing constant lubrication to the whole engine and so it is recommended that a new oil pump be installed when rebuilding the engine.

Completely disassemble the oil pump and thoroughly clean all of the components. Inspect the oil pump gears and housing for wear and/or damage. Insure that the pressure relief valve operates properly and there is no binding or sticking due to varnish or debris. If all of the parts are in proper working condition, lubricate the gears and relief valve, and assemble the pump.

REFINISHING

Almost all engine block refinishing must be performed by a machine shop. If the cylinders are not to be machined, then the cylinder glaze can be

Measure the piston's outer diameter, perpendicular to the wrist pin, with a micrometer

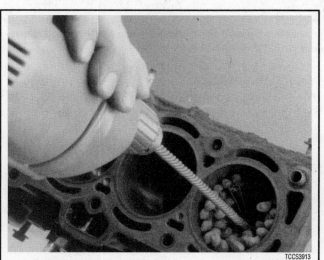

Use a ball type cylinder hone to remove any glaze and provide a new surface for seating the piston rings

removed with a ball hone. When removing cylinder glaze with a ball hone, use a light or penetrating type oil to lubricate the hone. Do not allow the hone to run dry as this may cause excessive scoring of the cylinder bores and wear on the hone. If new pistons are required, they will need to be installed to the connecting rods. This should be performed by a machine shop as the pistons must be installed in the correct relationship to the rod or engine damage can occur.

Pistons and Connecting Rods

Only pistons with the wrist pin retained by C-clips are serviceable by the home-mechanic. Press fit pistons require special presses and/or heaters to remove/install the connecting rod and should only be performed by a machine shop.

All pistons will have a mark indicating the direction to the front of the engine and the must be installed into the engine in that manner. Usually it is a notch or arrow on the top of the piston, or it may be the letter F cast or stamped into the piston.

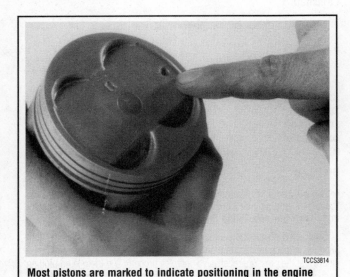

Most pistons are marked to indicate positioning in the engine (usually a mark means the side facing the front)

TCCS3814

C-CLIP TYPE PISTONS

1. Note the location of the forward mark on the piston and mark the connecting rod in relation.
2. Remove the C-clips from the piston and withdraw the wrist pin.

➡**Varnish build-up or C-clip groove burrs may increase the difficulty of removing the wrist pin. If necessary, use a punch or drift to carefully tap the wrist pin out.**

3. Insure that the wrist pin bushing in the connecting rod is usable, and lubricate it with assembly lube.
4. Remove the wrist pin from the new piston and lubricate the pin bores on the piston.
5. Align the forward marks on the piston and the connecting rod and install the wrist pin.
6. The new C-clips will have a flat and a rounded side to them. Install both C-clips with the flat side facing out.
7. Repeat all of the steps for each piston being replaced.

ASSEMBLY

▶ **See Figure 172**

Before you begin assembling the engine, first give yourself a clean, dirt free work area. Next, clean every engine component again. The key to a good assembly is cleanliness.

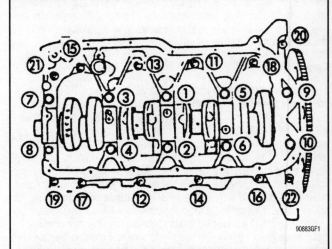

90883GF1

Fig. 172 When tightening the crankcase mounting bolts, be sure to adhere to the sequence shown—1.8L Engine

Mount the engine block into the engine stand and wash it one last time using water and detergent (dish washing detergent works well). While washing it, scrub the cylinder bores with a soft bristle brush and thoroughly clean all of the oil passages. Completely dry the engine and spray the entire assembly down with an anti-rust solution such as WD-40® or similar product. Take a clean lint-free rag and wipe up any excess anti-rust solution from the bores, bearing saddles, etc. Repeat the final cleaning process on the crankshaft. Replace any freeze or oil galley plugs which were removed during disassembly.

Crankshaft

➡**The 1.8L engine does not use individual main bearing caps, it utilizes a one-piece crankcase to secure the crankshaft in the engine. When tightening the crankcase mounting bolts, be sure to follow the sequence shown in the accompanying illustration.**

1. Remove the main bearing inserts from the block and bearing caps.
2. If the crankshaft main bearing journals have been refinished to a definite undersize, install the correct undersize bearing. Be sure that the bearing inserts and bearing bores are clean. Foreign material under inserts will distort bearing and cause failure.
3. Place the upper main bearing inserts in bores with tang in slot.

➡**The oil holes in the bearing inserts must be aligned with the oil holes in the cylinder block.**

4. Install the lower main bearing inserts in bearing caps.
5. Clean the mating surfaces of block and rear main bearing cap.
6. Carefully lower the crankshaft into place. Be careful not to damage bearing surfaces.
7. Check the clearance of each main bearing by using the following procedure:
   a. Place a piece of Plastigage® or its equivalent, on bearing surface across full width of bearing cap and about ¼ in. off center.
   b. Install the caps (1.3L and 1.6L engines), or crankcase (1.8L engine) and tighten bolts to specifications. Do not turn crankshaft while Plastigage® is in place.
   c. Remove the caps or crankcase. Using the supplied Plastigage® scale, check width of Plastigage® at widest point to get maximum clearance. Difference between readings is taper of journal.
   d. If clearance exceeds specified limits, try a 0.001 in. or 0.002 in. undersize bearing in combination with the standard bearing. Bearing clearance must be within specified limits. If standard and 0.002 in. undersize bearing does not bring clearance within desired limits, refinish crankshaft journal, then install undersize bearings.
8. After the bearings have been fitted, apply a light coat of engine oil to the journals and bearings.

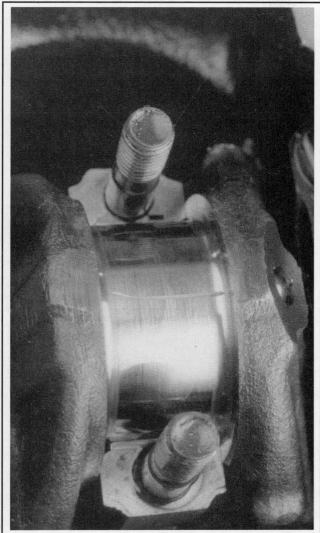

Apply a strip of gauging material to the bearing journal, then install and torque the cap

A dial gauge may be used to check crankshaft end-play

Carefully pry the crankshaft back and forth while reading the dial gauge for end-play

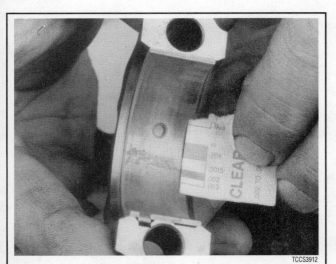

After the cap is removed again, use the scale supplied with the gauging material to check the clearance

9. For the 1.3L and 1.6L engines, perform the following:

a. Install the rear main bearing cap. Install all bearing caps except the thrust bearing cap. Be sure that main bearing caps are installed in original locations. Tighten the bearing cap bolts to specifications.

b. Install the thrust bearing cap with bolts finger-tight.

c. Pry the crankshaft forward against the thrust surface of upper half of bearing.

d. Hold the crankshaft forward and pry the thrust bearing cap to the rear. This aligns the thrust surfaces of both halves of the bearing.

e. Retain the forward pressure on the crankshaft. Tighten the cap bolts to specifications.

10. For the 1.8L engine, perform the following:

a. Apply a coat of clean engine to the crankcase mounting bolt threads.

b. Apply Suzuki sealant 99000–31150, or its equivalent, to the crankcase-to-engine mating surface as shown in the accompanying illustration.

c. Position the crankcase on the engine and install the mounting bolts finger-tight.

❉❉ WARNING

It is vitally important to tighten the crankcase mounting bolts in the proper sequence and to the specified value.

d. Using a torque wrench, tighten the crankcase-to-engine block bolts, in the sequence shown, to 115 inch lbs. (13 Nm) for all 8mm bolts, and to 21 ft. lbs. (29 Nm) for the 10mm bolts. Then, tighten the bolts, in the proper sequence, to 177 inch lbs. (20 Nm) for all 8mm bolts, and to 32 ft. lbs. (44 Nm) for all 10mm bolts. Finally, tighten the bolts, in the correct order, to 20 ft. lbs. (27 Nm) for the 8mm bolts, and to 42 ft. lbs. (58 Nm) for the 10mm bolts.

11. Rotate the crankshaft by hand to ensure that it rotates smoothly.

12. Measure the crankshaft end-play as follows:

    a. Mount a dial gauge to the engine block and position the tip of the gauge to read from the crankshaft end.

    b. Carefully pry the crankshaft toward the rear of the engine and hold it there while you zero the gauge.

    c. Carefully pry the crankshaft toward the front of the engine and read the gauge.

    d. Confirm that the reading is within specifications. If not, install a new thrust bearing and repeat the procedure. If the reading is still out of specifications with a new bearing, have a machine shop inspect the thrust surfaces of the crankshaft, and if possible, repair it.

13. Rotate the crankshaft so as to position the first rod journal to the bottom of its stroke.

14. Install the rear main seal.

Pistons and Connecting Rods

1. Before installing the piston/connecting rod assembly, oil the pistons, piston rings and the cylinder walls with light engine oil. Install connecting rod bolt protectors or rubber hose onto the connecting rod bolts/studs. Also perform the following:

    a. Select the proper ring set for the size cylinder bore.

    b. Position the ring in the bore in which it is going to be used.

    c. Push the ring down into the bore area where normal ring wear is not encountered.

    d. Use the head of the piston to position the ring in the bore so that the ring is square with the cylinder wall. Use caution to avoid damage to the ring or cylinder bore.

    e. Measure the gap between the ends of the ring with a feeler gauge. Ring gap in a worn cylinder is normally greater than specification. If the ring gap is greater than the specified limits, try an oversize ring set.

    f. Check the ring side clearance of the compression rings with a feeler gauge inserted between the ring and its lower land according to specification. The gauge should slide freely around the entire ring circumference without binding. Any wear that occurs will form a step at the inner portion of the lower land. If the lower lands have high steps, the piston should be replaced.

2. Unless new pistons are installed, be sure to install the pistons in the

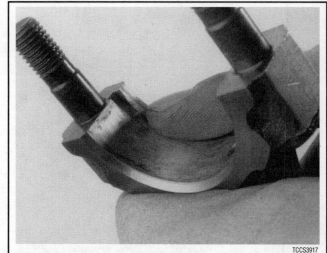

The notch on the side of the bearing cap matches the tang on the bearing insert

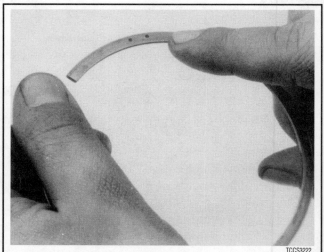

Most rings are marked to show which side of the ring should face up when installed to the piston

Checking the piston ring-to-ring groove side clearance using the ring and a feeler gauge

Install the piston and rod assembly into the block using a ring compressor and the handle of a hammer

cylinders from which they were removed. The numbers on the connecting rod and bearing cap must be on the same side when installed in the cylinder bore. If a connecting rod is ever transposed from one engine or cylinder to another, new bearings should be fitted and the connecting rod should be numbered to correspond with the new cylinder number. The notch on the piston head goes toward the front of the engine.

3. Install all of the rod bearing inserts into the rods and caps.

4. Install the rings to the pistons. Install the oil control ring first, then the second compression ring and finally the top compression ring. Use a piston ring expander tool to aid in installation and to help reduce the chance of breakage.

5. Make sure the ring gaps are properly spaced around the circumference of the piston. Fit a piston ring compressor around the piston and slide the piston and connecting rod assembly down into the cylinder bore, pushing it in with the wooden hammer handle. Push the piston down until it is only slightly below the top of the cylinder bore. Guide the connecting rod onto the crankshaft bearing journal carefully, to avoid damaging the crankshaft.

6. Check the bearing clearance of all the rod bearings, fitting them to the crankshaft bearing journals. Follow the procedure in the crankshaft installation above.

7. After the bearings have been fitted, apply a light coating of assembly oil to the journals and bearings.

8. Turn the crankshaft until the appropriate bearing journal is at the bottom of its stroke, then push the piston assembly all the way down until the connecting rod bearing seats on the crankshaft journal. Be careful not to allow the bearing cap screws to strike the crankshaft bearing journals and damage them.

9. After the piston and connecting rod assemblies have been installed, check the connecting rod side clearance on each crankshaft journal.

10. Prime and install the oil pump and the oil pump intake tube.

11. Install the cylinder head(s) using new gaskets.

12. Install the timing sprockets/gears and the belt/chain assemblies.

Engine Covers and Components

Install the timing cover(s) and oil pan. Refer to your notes and drawings made prior to disassembly and install all of the components that were removed. Install the engine into the vehicle.

Engine Start-up and Break-in

STARTING THE ENGINE

Now that the engine is installed and every wire and hose is properly connected, go back and double check that all coolant and vac-

uum hoses are connected. Check that you oil drain plug is installed and properly tightened. If not already done, install a new oil filter onto the engine. Fill the crankcase with the proper amount and grade of engine oil. Fill the cooling system with a 50/50 mixture of coolant/water.

1. Connect the vehicle battery.

2. Start the engine. Keep your eye on your oil pressure indicator; if it does not indicate oil pressure within 10 seconds of starting, turn the vehicle off.

❄❄ WARNING

Damage to the engine can result if it is allowed to run with no oil pressure. Check the engine oil level to make sure that it is full. Check for any leaks and if found, repair the leaks before continuing. If there is still no indication of oil pressure, you may need to prime the system.

3. Confirm that there are no fluid leaks (oil or other).

4. Allow the engine to reach normal operating temperature (the upper radiator hose will be hot to the touch).

5. If necessary, set the ignition timing.

6. Install any remaining components such as the air cleaner (if removed for ignition timing) or body panels which were removed.

BREAKING IT IN

Make the first miles on the new engine, easy ones. Vary the speed but do not accelerate hard. Most importantly, do not lug the engine, and avoid sustained high speeds until at least 100 miles. Check the engine oil and coolant levels frequently. Expect the engine to use a little oil until the rings seat. Change the oil and filter at 500 miles, 1500 miles, then every 3000 miles past that.

KEEP IT MAINTAINED

Now that you have just gone through all of that hard work, keep yourself from doing it all over again by thoroughly maintaining it. Not that you may not have maintained it before, heck you could have had 100,000–200,000 miles on it before doing this. However, you may have bought the vehicle used, and the previous owner did not keep up on maintenance. Which is why you just went through all of that hard work. See?

TORQUE SPECIFICATIONS

Engine	Component	Ft. Lbs.	Nm
1.3L Engine			
	Camshaft timing belt sprocket	41-46	56-64
	Connecting rod bearing cap nut	24-26	33-37
	Cooling fan/clutch mounting fasteners	97 inch lbs.	11
	Crankshaft main bearing cap bolt	37-41	50-57
	Crankshaft pulley retaining bolts	80-106 inch lbs.	9-12
	Crankshaft timing belt sprocket center retaining bolt		
	1986-88 models	48-54	65-75
	1989-95 models	76-83	105-115
	Cylinder head bolts ①		
	1986-88 models		
	Step 1	23-25	31-34
	Step 2	35-37	48-50
	Step 3	46-50	63-70
	1989-95 models		
	Step 1	27	37
	Step 2	40	54
	Step 3	52	71
	Driveshaft flange bolts and nuts	17-21	23-30
	Engine mount-to-engine bolts	37-43	50-60
	Engine mount-to-frame bolts	29-43	40-60
	Engine mounting nuts	29-37	40-50
	Exhaust manifold-to-cylinder head mounting fasteners	159-248 inch lbs.	18-28
	Exhaust pipe-to-exhaust manifold attaching nuts	29-43	40-60
	Flywheel-to-crankshaft mounting bolts	58	78
	Intake manifold-to-cylinder head bolts	159-248 inch lbs.	18-28
	Oil filter stand bolts	177-221 inch lbs.	20-25
	Oil pan drain plug	22-28	30-40
	Oil pan mounting bolts	80-106 inch lbs.	9-12
	Oil pressure switch	124 inch lbs.	14
	Oil pump housing mounting bolts and tighten them	97 inch lbs.	11
	Oil pump pick-up tube bolts	80-106 inch lbs.	9-12
	Oil pump rotor plate screws	80-106 inch lbs.	9-12
	Rear main oil seal housing mounting bolts	80-106 inch lbs.	9-12
	Rocker arm shaft retaining screws	80-106 inch lbs.	9-12
	Spark plug	177-265 inch lbs.	20-30
	Timing belt tensioner bolt	18-21	24-30
	Timing belt tensioner stud		
	1986-88 models	18-21	24-30
	1989-95 models	80-106 inch lbs.	9-12
	Transmission-to-engine bolts	16-25	22-35
	Water pump mounting bolts	88-115 inch lbs.	10-13
	Water pump mounting bolts	88-115 inch lbs.	10-13
1.6L 8-Valve Engine			
	Air intake case support brace bolts	159-248 inch lbs.	18-28
	Camshaft timing belt sprocket	41-46	56-64
	Connecting rod bearing cap nut	24-26	33-37
	Cooling fan/clutch mounting fasteners	97 inch lbs.	11
	Crankshaft pulley retaining bolts	80-106 inch lbs.	9-12
	Crankshaft timing belt sprocket center retaining bolt	58-65	80-90

TORQUE SPECIFICATIONS

Engine	Component	Ft. Lbs.	Nm
1.6L 8-Valve Engine - Continued			
	Cylinder head bolts ①		
	Step 1	27	37
	Step 2	40	54
	Step 3	52	71
	Engine mount chassis side bracket bolts	37-43	50-60
	Engine mount engine side bracket bolts	36-43	50-60
	Engine mount nuts	29-37	40-50
	Exhaust manifold brace-to-engine block bolt	36.5-43	50-60
	Exhaust manifold brace-to-exhaust manifold nut	29-43	40-60
	Exhaust manifold-to-cylinder head mounting fasteners	159-248 inch lbs.	18-28
	Exhaust pipe-to-exhaust manifold attaching nuts	29-43	40-60
	Flywheel-to-crankshaft mounting bolts ②	58	78
	Intake manifold-to-cylinder head bolts	159-248 inch lbs.	18-28
	Left-hand side transmission brace bolts	37	50
	No.1 exhaust pipe nuts	29-43	40-60
	Oil filter stand bolts	177-221 inch lbs.	20-25
	Oil pan bolts	80-106 inch lbs.	9-12
	Oil pan drain plug	22-28	30-40
	Oil pressure switch	124 inch lbs.	14
	Oil pump housing mounting bolts and tighten them	97 inch lbs.	11
	Oil pump pick-up bolts	80-106 inch lbs.	9-12
	Oil pump rotor plate screws	80-106 inch lbs.	9-12
	Rear main oil seal housing mounting bolts	80-106 inch lbs.	9-12
	Rocker arm shaft retaining screws	80-106 inch lbs.	9-12
	Spark plug	177-265 inch lbs.	20-30
	Timing belt tensioner bolt	18-21	24-30
	Timing belt tensioner stud	80-106 inch lbs.	9-12
	Torque converter bolts	37-43	50-60
	Transmission-to-engine bolts	62	85
	Water pump mounting bolts	88-115 inch lbs.	10-13
1.6L 16-Valve Engine			
	Air intake case support brace bolts	159-248 inch lbs.	18-28
	Alternator adjusting arm brace bolts	37	50
	Camshaft bearing cap bolts ①		
	Step 1	24 inch lbs.	2.7
	Step 2	48 inch lbs.	5.4
	Step 3	72 inch lbs.	8.2
	Step 4	97 inch lbs.	11
	Camshaft timing belt sprocket bolt	44	60
	Connecting rod bearing cap nuts	26	35
	Cooling fan/clutch mounting fasteners	97 inch lbs.	11
	Crankshaft main bearing cap bolts	39	54
	Crankshaft pulley retaining bolts	80-106 inch lbs.	9-12
	Crankshaft timing belt sprocket center retaining bolt	80	110
	Cylinder head bolts ①		

90883C01

TORQUE SPECIFICATIONS

Engine	Component	Ft. Lbs.	Nm
1.6L 16-Valve Engine - Continued			
	Engine mount bolts	29-43	40-60
	Engine-to-transmission nuts and bolts	51-72	70-100
	Exhaust manifold brace-to-engine block bolt	37-43	50-60
	Exhaust manifold brace-to-exhaust manifold nut	29-43	40-60
	Exhaust manifold-to-cylinder head mounting fasteners	159-248 inch lbs.	18-28
	Exhaust pipe nuts and bolts	37	50
	Exhaust pipe-to-exhaust manifold attaching nuts	29-43	40-60
	Flywheel-to-crankshaft mounting bolts ②	58	78
	Fuel feed line firewall junction flare nut	32.5	45
	Intake manifold brace the No. 1 and 2 brace fasteners	37	50
	Intake manifold-to-cylinder head mounting fasteners	203 inch lbs.	23
	Intake surge tank-to-intake manifold mounting bolts	203 inch lbs.	23
	Left-hand side transmission brace bolts	37	50
	Oil jet venturi plug	35-53 inch lbs.	4-6
	Oil pan bolts	80-106 inch lbs.	9-12
	Oil pan drain plug	22-28	30-40
	Oil pressure switch	124 inch lbs.	14
	Oil pump housing mounting bolts and tighten them	97 inch lbs.	11
	Oil pump pick-up bolts	80-106 inch lbs.	9-12
	Rear main oil seal housing mounting bolts	80-106 inch lbs.	9-12
	Rocker arm shaft retaining screws	97 inch lbs.	11
	Throttle body-to-intake manifold attaching fasteners	203 inch lbs.	23
	Timing belt tensioner bolt	18	24
	Timing belt tensioner stud	97 inch lbs.	11
	Torque converter bolts	47	65
	Transmission support brace bolts	37	50
	Water pump mounting bolts	88-115 inch lbs.	10-13
1.8L Engine			
	A/C compressor mounting bracket bolts	40	55
	Air intake case support brace bolts	159-248 inch lbs.	18-28
	Alternator drive belt idler	33	45
	Alternator drive belt tensioner mounting bolts	19	25
	Camshaft housing-to-cylinder head bolts ①		
	Step 1	24 inch lbs.	2.7
	Step 2	48 inch lbs.	5.4
	Step 3	72 inch lbs.	8.2
	Step 4	97 inch lbs.	11 .
	Camshaft timing chain gear retaining bolts	44	60
	Connecting rod bearing cap nuts	33	45
	Cooling fan/clutch mounting fasteners	97 inch lbs.	11
	Crankcase-to-engine block bolts ①		
	Step 1		
	10mm bolts	21	29
	8mm bolts	115 inch lbs.	13
	Step 2		
	10mm bolts	32	44
	8mm bolts	177 inch lbs.	20
	Step 3		
	10mm bolts	42	58
	8mm bolts	20	27

90883C02

TORQUE SPECIFICATIONS

Engine	Component	Ft. Lbs.	Nm
1.8L Engine - Continued			
	Crankshaft pulley center bolt	109	150
	Cylinder head bolts ①		
	Step 1	39	53
	Step 2	61	84
	Step 3	loosen all bolts completely	
	Step 4	27	37
	Step 5	76	105
	Step 6 (tighten the small M6 bolt)	97 inch lbs.	11
	Engine-to-mount fasteners	37	50
	Exhaust manifold brace-to-engine block bolt	36.5-43	50-60
	Exhaust manifold brace-to-exhaust manifold nut	29-43	40-60
	Exhaust manifold-to-cylinder head mounting fasteners	159-248 inch lbs.	18-28
	Exhaust pipe-to-exhaust manifold attaching nuts	29-43	40-60
	Flywheel-to-crankshaft mounting bolts	51	70
	Front and rear intake manifold braces bolts	37	50
	Inner timing chain contact arm tensioner pivot bolt	19	25
	Inner timing chain guide mounting fasteners	97 inch lbs.	11
	Inner timing chain tension adjuster mounting bolts	97 inch lbs.	11
	Intake manifold-to-cylinder head mounting fasteners	203 inch lbs.	23
	No. 1 exhaust pipe fasteners	37	50
	Oil pan bolts	80-106 inch lbs.	9-12
	Oil pan drain plug	22-28	30-40
	Oil pressure switch	124 inch lbs.	14
	Oil pump housing retaining screws	106 inch lbs.	12
	Oil pump housing-to-engine bolts	177 inch lbs.	20
	Oil pump pick-up bolts	80-106 inch lbs.	9-12
	Oil pump relief valve plug	21	29
	Oil pump sprocket cover bolts	97 inch lbs.	11
	Outer timing chain tension adjuster mounting bolts	97 inch lbs.	11
	Rear manifold brace bolts	221 inch lbs.	25
	Strut tower bar mounting nuts and bolts	66	90
	Timing chain cover retaining bolts	97 inch lbs.	11
	Timing chain idler gear nut	33	45
	Torque converter-to-flywheel bolts	47	65
	Transmission support brace bolts	37	50
	Transmission-to-engine bolts	58	79
	Water bypass pipe and bypass hose No. 2 bolts	203 inch lbs.	23
	Water pump mounting bolts ③	221 inch lbs.	25

① Refer to the text for the proper tightening sequence.
② Manual and automatic transmissions.
③ New bolts are necessary for installation.

90883C03

USING A VACUUM GAUGE

White needle = steady needle   *Dark needle = drifting needle*

The vacuum gauge is one of the most useful and easy-to-use diagnostic tools. It is inexpensive, easy to hook up, and provides valuable information about the condition of your engine.

Indication: Normal engine in good condition

Gauge reading: Steady, from 17–22 in./Hg.

Indication: Sticking valve or ignition miss

Gauge reading: Needle fluctuates from 15–20 in./Hg. at idle

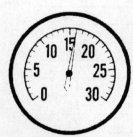

Indication: Late ignition or valve timing, low compression, stuck throttle valve, leaking carburetor or manifold gasket.

Gauge reading: Low (15–20 in./Hg.) but steady

Indication: Improper carburetor adjustment, or minor intake leak at carburetor or manifold

NOTE: Bad fuel injector O-rings may also cause this reading.

Gauge reading: Drifting needle

Indication: Weak valve springs, worn valve stem guides, or leaky cylinder head gasket (vibrating excessively at all speeds).

NOTE: A plugged catalytic converter may also cause this reading.

Gauge reading: Needle fluctuates as engine speed increases

Indication: Burnt valve or improper valve clearance. The needle will drop when the defective valve operates.

Gauge reading: Steady needle, but drops regularly

Indication: Choked muffler or obstruction in system. Speed up the engine. Choked muffler will exhibit a slow drop of vacuum to zero.

Gauge reading: Gradual drop in reading at idle

Indication: Worn valve guides

Gauge reading: Needle vibrates excessively at idle, but steadies as engine speed increases

TCCS3C01

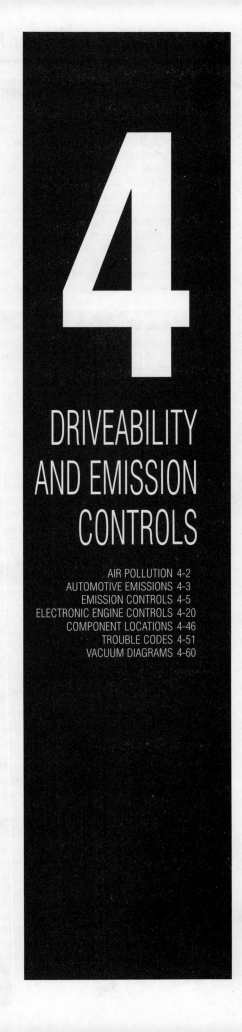

4

DRIVEABILITY AND EMISSION CONTROLS

AIR POLLUTION

The earth's atmosphere, at or near sea level, consists approximately of 78 percent nitrogen, 21 percent oxygen and 1 percent other gases. If it were possible to remain in this state, 100 percent clean air would result. However, many varied sources allow other gases and particulates to mix with the clean air, causing our atmosphere to become unclean or polluted.

Some of these pollutants are visible while others are invisible, with each having the capability of causing distress to the eyes, ears, throat, skin and respiratory system. Should these pollutants become concentrated in a specific area and under certain conditions, death could result due to the displacement or chemical change of the oxygen content in the air. These pollutants can also cause great damage to the environment and to the many man made objects that are exposed to the elements.

To better understand the causes of air pollution, the pollutants can be categorized into 3 separate types, natural, industrial and automotive.

Natural Pollutants

Natural pollution has been present on earth since before man appeared and continues to be a factor when discussing air pollution, although it causes only a small percentage of the overall pollution problem. It is the direct result of decaying organic matter, wind born smoke and particulates from such natural events as plain and forest fires (ignited by heat or lightning), volcanic ash, sand and dust which can spread over a large area of the countryside.

Such a phenomenon of natural pollution has been seen in the form of volcanic eruptions, with the resulting plume of smoke, steam and volcanic ash blotting out the sun's rays as it spreads and rises higher into the atmosphere. As it travels into the atmosphere the upper air currents catch and carry the smoke and ash, while condensing the steam back into water vapor. As the water vapor, smoke and ash travel on their journey, the smoke dissipates into the atmosphere while the ash and moisture settle back to earth in a trail hundreds of miles long. In some cases, lives are lost and millions of dollars of property damage result.

Industrial Pollutants

Industrial pollution is caused primarily by industrial processes, the burning of coal, oil and natural gas, which in turn produce smoke and fumes. Because the burning fuels contain large amounts of sulfur, the principal ingredients of smoke and fumes are sulfur dioxide and particulate matter. This type of pollutant occurs most severely during still, damp and cool weather, such as at night. Even in its less severe form, this pollutant is not confined to just cities. Because of air movements, the pollutants move for miles over the surrounding countryside, leaving in its path a barren and unhealthy environment for all living things.

Working with Federal, State and Local mandated regulations and by carefully monitoring emissions, big business has greatly reduced the amount of pollutant introduced from its industrial sources, striving to obtain an acceptable level. Because of the mandated industrial emission clean up, many land areas and streams in and around the cities that were formerly barren of vegetation and life, have now begun to move back in the direction of nature's intended balance.

Automotive Pollutants

The third major source of air pollution is automotive emissions. The emissions from the internal combustion engines were not an appreciable problem years ago because of the small number of registered vehicles and the nation's small highway system. However, during the early 1950's, the trend of the American people was to move from the cities to the surrounding suburbs. This caused an immediate problem in transportation because the majority of suburbs were not afforded mass transit conveniences. This lack of transportation created an attractive market for the automobile manufacturers, which resulted in a dramatic increase in the number of vehicles produced and sold, along with a marked increase in highway construction

between cities and the suburbs. Multi-vehicle families emerged with a growing emphasis placed on an individual vehicle per family member. As the increase in vehicle ownership and usage occurred, so did pollutant levels in and around the cities, as suburbanites drove daily to their businesses and employment, returning at the end of the day to their homes in the suburbs.

It was noted that a smoke and fog type haze was being formed and at times, remained in suspension over the cities, taking time to dissipate. At first this "smog," derived from the words "smoke" and "fog," was thought to result from industrial pollution but it was determined that automobile emissions shared the blame. It was discovered that when normal automobile emissions were exposed to sunlight for a period of time, complex chemical reactions would take place.

It is now known that smog is a photo chemical layer which develops when certain oxides of nitrogen (NOx) and unburned hydrocarbons (HC) from automobile emissions are exposed to sunlight. Pollution was more severe when smog would become stagnant over an area in which a warm layer of air settled over the top of the cooler air mass, trapping and holding the cooler mass at ground level. The trapped cooler air would keep the emissions from being dispersed and diluted through normal air flows. This type of air stagnation was given the name "Temperature Inversion."

TEMPERATURE INVERSION

In normal weather situations, surface air is warmed by heat radiating from the earth's surface and the sun's rays. This causes it to rise upward, into the atmosphere. Upon rising it will cool through a convection type heat exchange with the cooler upper air. As warm air rises, the surface pollutants are carried upward and dissipated into the atmosphere.

When a temperature inversion occurs, we find the higher air is no longer cooler, but is warmer than the surface air, causing the cooler surface air to become trapped. This warm air blanket can extend from above ground level to a few hundred or even a few thousand feet into the air. As the surface air is trapped, so are the pollutants, causing a severe smog condition. Should this stagnant air mass extend to a few thousand feet high, enough air movement with the inversion takes place to allow the smog layer to rise above ground level but the pollutants still cannot dissipate. This inversion can remain for days over an area, with the smog level only rising or lowering from ground level to a few hundred feet high. Meanwhile, the pollutant levels increase, causing eye irritation, respiratory problems, reduced visibility, plant damage and in some cases, even disease.

This inversion phenomenon was first noted in the Los Angeles, California area. The city lies in terrain resembling a basin and with certain weather conditions, a cold air mass is held in the basin while a warmer air mass covers it like a lid.

Because this type of condition was first documented as prevalent in the Los Angeles area, this type of trapped pollution was named Los Angeles Smog, although it occurs in other areas where a large concentration of automobiles are used and the air remains stagnant for any length of time.

HEAT TRANSFER

Consider the internal combustion engine as a machine in which raw materials must be placed so a finished product comes out. As in any machine operation, a certain amount of wasted material is formed. When we relate this to the internal combustion engine, we find that through the input of air and fuel, we obtain power during the combustion process to drive the vehicle. The by-product or waste of this power is, in part, heat and exhaust gases with which we must dispose.

The heat from the combustion process can rise to over 4000°F (2204°C). The dissipation of this heat is controlled by a ram air effect, the use of cooling fans to cause air flow and a liquid coolant solution surrounding the combustion area to transfer the heat of combustion through the cylinder walls and into the coolant. The coolant is then directed to a thin-finned, multi-tubed radiator, from which the excess heat is transferred to the atmosphere by 1 of the 3 heat transfer methods, conduction, convection or radiation.

The cooling of the combustion area is an important part in the control of exhaust emissions. To understand the behavior of the combustion and transfer of its heat, consider the air/fuel charge. It is ignited and the flame front burns progressively across the combustion chamber until the burning charge reaches the cylinder walls. Some of the fuel in contact with the walls is not hot enough to burn, thereby snuffing out or quenching the combustion process. This leaves unburned fuel in the combustion chamber. This unburned fuel is then forced out of the cylinder and into the exhaust system, along with the exhaust gases.

Many attempts have been made to minimize the amount of unburned fuel in the combustion chambers due to quenching, by increasing the coolant temperature and lessening the contact area of the coolant around the combustion area. However, design limitations within the combustion chambers prevent the complete burning of the air/fuel charge, so a certain amount of the unburned fuel is still expelled into the exhaust system, regardless of modifications to the engine.

AUTOMOTIVE EMISSIONS

Before emission controls were mandated on internal combustion engines, other sources of engine pollutants were discovered along with the exhaust emissions. It was determined that engine combustion exhaust produced approximately 60 percent of the total emission pollutants, fuel evaporation from the fuel tank and carburetor vents produced 20 percent, with the final 20 percent being produced through the crankcase as a by-product of the combustion process.

Exhaust Gases

The exhaust gases emitted into the atmosphere are a combination of burned and unburned fuel. To understand the exhaust emission and its composition, we must review some basic chemistry.

When the air/fuel mixture is introduced into the engine, we are mixing air, composed of nitrogen (78 percent), oxygen (21 percent) and other gases (1 percent) with the fuel, which is 100 percent hydrocarbons (HC), in a semi-controlled ratio. As the combustion process is accomplished, power is produced to move the vehicle while the heat of combustion is transferred to the cooling system. The exhaust gases are then composed of nitrogen, a diatomic gas (N_2), the same as was introduced in the engine, carbon dioxide (CO_2), the same gas that is used in beverage carbonation, and water vapor (H_2O). The nitrogen (N_2), for the most part, passes through the engine unchanged, while the oxygen (O_2) reacts (burns) with the hydrocarbons (HC) and produces the carbon dioxide (CO_2) and the water vapors (H_2O). If this chemical process would be the only process to take place, the exhaust emissions would be harmless. However, during the combustion process, other compounds are formed which are considered dangerous. These pollutants are hydrocarbons (HC), carbon monoxide (CO), oxides of nitrogen (NOx), oxides of sulfur (SOx) and engine particulates.

HYDROCARBONS

Hydrocarbons (HC) are essentially fuel which was not burned during the combustion process or which has escaped into the atmosphere through fuel evaporation. The main sources of incomplete combustion are rich air/fuel mixtures, low engine temperatures and improper spark timing. The main sources of hydrocarbon emission through fuel evaporation on most vehicles used to be the vehicle's fuel tank and carburetor float bowl.

To reduce combustion hydrocarbon emission, engine modifications were made to minimize dead space and surface area in the combustion chamber. In addition, the air/fuel mixture was made more lean through the improved control which feedback carburetion and fuel injection offers and by the addition of external controls to aid in further combustion of the hydrocarbons outside the engine. Two such methods were the addition of air injection systems, to inject fresh air into the exhaust manifolds and the installation of catalytic converters, units that are able to burn traces of hydrocarbons without affecting the internal combustion process or fuel economy.

To control hydrocarbon emissions through fuel evaporation, modifications were made to the fuel tank to allow storage of the fuel vapors during periods of engine shut-down. Modifications were also made to the air intake system so that at specific times during engine operation, these vapors may be purged and burned by blending them with the air/fuel mixture.

CARBON MONOXIDE

Carbon monoxide is formed when not enough oxygen is present during the combustion process to convert carbon (C) to carbon dioxide (CO_2). An increase in the carbon monoxide (CO) emission is normally accompanied by an increase in the hydrocarbon (HC) emission because of the lack of oxygen to completely burn all of the fuel mixture.

Carbon monoxide (CO) also increases the rate at which the photo chemical smog is formed by speeding up the conversion of nitric oxide (NO) to nitrogen dioxide (NO_2). To accomplish this, carbon monoxide (CO) combines with oxygen (O_2) and nitric oxide (NO) to produce carbon dioxide (CO_2) and nitrogen dioxide (NO_2). ($CO + O_2 + NO = CO_2 + NO_2$).

The dangers of carbon monoxide, which is an odorless and colorless toxic gas are many. When carbon monoxide is inhaled into the lungs and passed into the blood stream, oxygen is replaced by the carbon monoxide in the red blood cells, causing a reduction in the amount of oxygen supplied to the many parts of the body. This lack of oxygen causes headaches, lack of coordination, reduced mental alertness and, should the carbon monoxide concentration be high enough, death could result.

NITROGEN

Normally, nitrogen is an inert gas. When heated to approximately 2500°F (1371°C) through the combustion process, this gas becomes active and causes an increase in the nitric oxide (NO) emission.

Oxides of nitrogen (NOx) are composed of approximately 97–98 percent nitric oxide (NO). Nitric oxide is a colorless gas but when it is passed into the atmosphere, it combines with oxygen and forms nitrogen dioxide (NO_2). The nitrogen dioxide then combines with chemically active hydrocarbons (HC) and when in the presence of sunlight, causes the formation of photochemical smog.

Ozone

To further complicate matters, some of the nitrogen dioxide (NO_2) is broken apart by the sunlight to form nitric oxide and oxygen. (NO_2 + sunlight = NO + O). This single atom of oxygen then combines with diatomic (meaning 2 atoms) oxygen (O_2) to form ozone (O_3). Ozone is one of the smells associated with smog. It has a pungent and offensive odor, irritates the eyes and lung tissues, affects the growth of plant life and causes rapid deterioration of rubber products. Ozone can be formed by sunlight as well as electrical discharge into the air.

The most common discharge area on the automobile engine is the secondary ignition electrical system, especially when inferior quality spark plug cables are used. As the surge of high voltage is routed through the secondary cable, the circuit builds up an electrical field around the wire, which acts upon the oxygen in the surrounding air to form the ozone. The faint glow along the cable with the engine running that may be visible on a dark night, is called the "corona discharge." It is the result of the electrical field passing from a high along the cable, to a low in the surrounding air, which forms the ozone gas. The combination of corona and ozone has been a major cause of cable deterioration. Recently, different and better quality insulating materials have lengthened the life of the electrical cables.

Although ozone at ground level can be harmful, ozone is beneficial to the earth's inhabitants. By having a concentrated ozone layer called the "ozonosphere," between 10 and 20 miles (16–32 km) up in the atmosphere, much of the ultra violet radiation from the sun's rays are absorbed and screened. If this ozone layer were not present, much of the earth's surface would be burned, dried and unfit for human life.

OXIDES OF SULFUR

Oxides of sulfur (SOx) were initially ignored in the exhaust system emissions, since the sulfur content of gasoline as a fuel is less than $\frac{1}{10}$ of 1 percent. Because of this small amount, it was felt that it contributed very little to the overall pollution problem. However, because of the difficulty in solving the sulfur emissions in industrial pollutions and the introduction of catalytic converter to the automobile exhaust systems, a change was mandated. The automobile exhaust system, when equipped with a catalytic converter, changes the sulfur dioxide (SO_2) into sulfur trioxide (SO_3).

When this combines with water vapors (H_2O), a sulfuric acid mist (H_2SO_4) is formed and is a very difficult pollutant to handle since it is extremely corrosive. This sulfuric acid mist that is formed, is the same mist that rises from the vents of an automobile battery when an active chemical reaction takes place within the battery cells.

When a large concentration of vehicles equipped with catalytic converters are operating in an area, this acid mist may rise and be distributed over a large ground area causing land, plant, crop, paint and building damage.

PARTICULATE MATTER

A certain amount of particulate matter is present in the burning of any fuel, with carbon constituting the largest percentage of the particulates. In gasoline, the remaining particulates are the burned remains of the various other compounds used in its manufacture. When a gasoline engine is in good internal condition, the particulate emissions are low but as the engine wears internally, the particulate emissions increase. By visually inspecting the tail pipe emissions, a determination can be made as to where an engine defect may exist. An engine with light gray or blue smoke emitting from the tail pipe normally indicates an increase in the oil consumption through burning due to internal engine wear. Black smoke would indicate a defective fuel delivery system, causing the engine to operate in a rich mode. Regardless of the color of the smoke, the internal part of the engine or the fuel delivery system should be repaired to prevent excess particulate emissions.

Diesel and turbine engines emit a darkened plume of smoke from the exhaust system because of the type of fuel used. Emission control regulations are mandated for this type of emission and more stringent measures are being used to prevent excess emission of the particulate matter. Electronic components are being introduced to control the injection of the fuel at precisely the proper time of piston travel, to achieve the optimum in fuel ignition and fuel usage. Other particulate after-burning components are being tested to achieve a cleaner emission.

Good grades of engine lubricating oils should be used, which meet the manufacturers specification. Cut-rate oils can contribute to the particulate emission problem because of their low flash or ignition temperature point. Such oils burn prematurely during the combustion process causing emission of particulate matter.

The cooling system is an important factor in the reduction of particulate matter. The optimum combustion will occur, with the cooling system operating at a temperature specified by the manufacturer. The cooling system must be maintained in the same manner as the engine oiling system, as each system is required to perform properly in order for the engine to operate efficiently for a long time.

Crankcase Emissions

Crankcase emissions are made up of water, acids, unburned fuel, oil fumes and particulates. These emissions are classified as hydrocarbons (HC) and are formed by the small amount of unburned, compressed air/fuel mixture entering the crankcase from the combustion area (between the cylinder walls and piston rings) during the compression and power strokes. The head of the compression and combustion help to form the remaining crankcase emissions.

Since the first engines, crankcase emissions were allowed into the atmosphere through a road draft tube, mounted on the lower side of the engine block. Fresh air came in through an open oil filler cap or breather. The air passed through the crankcase mixing with blow-by gases. The motion of the vehicle and the air blowing past the open end of the road draft tube caused a low pressure area (vacuum) at the end of the tube. Crankcase emissions were simply drawn out of the road draft tube into the air.

To control the crankcase emission, the road draft tube was deleted. A hose and/or tubing was routed from the crankcase to the intake manifold so the blow-by emission could be burned with the air/fuel mixture. However, it was found that intake manifold vacuum, used to draw the crankcase emissions into the manifold, would vary in strength at the wrong time and not allow the proper emission flow. A regulating valve was needed to control the flow of air through the crankcase.

Testing, showed the removal of the blow-by gases from the crankcase as quickly as possible, was most important to the longevity of the engine. Should large accumulations of blow-by gases remain and condense, dilution of the engine oil would occur to form water, soots, resins, acids and lead salts, resulting in the formation of sludge and varnishes. This condensation of the blow-by gases occurs more frequently on vehicles used in numerous starting and stopping conditions, excessive idling and when the engine is not allowed to attain normal operating temperature through short runs.

Evaporative Emissions

Gasoline fuel is a major source of pollution, before and after it is burned in the automobile engine. From the time the fuel is refined, stored, pumped and transported, again stored until it is pumped into the fuel tank of the vehicle, the gasoline gives off unburned hydrocarbons (HC) into the atmosphere. Through the redesign of storage areas and venting systems, the pollution factor was diminished, but not eliminated, from the refinery standpoint. However, the automobile still remained the primary source of vaporized, unburned hydrocarbon (HC) emissions.

Fuel pumped from an underground storage tank is cool but when exposed to a warmer ambient temperature, will expand. Before controls were mandated, an owner might fill the fuel tank with fuel from an underground storage tank and park the vehicle for some time in warm area, such as a parking lot. As the fuel would warm, it would expand and should no provisions or area be provided for the expansion, the fuel would spill out of the filler neck and onto the ground, causing hydrocarbon (HC) pollution and creating a severe fire hazard. To correct this condition, the vehicle manufacturers added overflow plumbing and/or gasoline tanks with built in expansion areas or domes.

However, this did not control the fuel vapor emission from the fuel tank. It was determined that most of the fuel evaporation occurred when the vehicle was stationary and the engine not operating. Most vehicles carry 5–25 gallons (19–95 liters) of gasoline. Should a large concentration of vehicles be parked in one area, such as a large parking lot, excessive fuel vapor emissions would take place, increasing as the temperature increases.

To prevent the vapor emission from escaping into the atmosphere, the fuel systems were designed to trap the vapors while the vehicle is stationary, by sealing the system from the atmosphere. A storage system is used to collect and hold the fuel vapors from the carburetor (if equipped) and the fuel tank when the engine is not operating. When the engine is started, the storage system is then purged of the fuel vapors, which are drawn into the engine and burned with the air/fuel mixture.

EMISSION CONTROLS

Crankcase Ventilation System

OPERATION

▶ See Figure 1

The Positive Crankcase Ventilation (PCV) system is designed to prevent engine blow-by gases, containing unburned hydrocarbons (HC) and carbon monoxide (CO), from being released into the atmosphere, and also helps to keep the engine oil clean, by ridding the crankcase of moisture and corrosive fumes. The PCV valve system vents crankcase gases into the incoming air charge entering the engine, where they are burned with the fuel and air mixture.

1986–90 Models

Crankcase blow-by gases flow through a passage in the engine block into the cylinder head. The gases exit the cylinder head through an opening in the rocker arm cover, and through a hose to a 3-way connector. At the 3-way connector, fresh incoming air from the air cleaner assembly is mixed with the blow-by gases. The fresh air/blow-by gas mixture is routed through a hose to the intake manifold. The mixture is introduced to the incoming air charge in the intake manifold, and is burned along with the air charge.

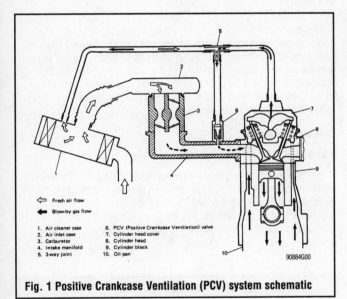

Fresh air flow
Blow-by gas flow

1. Air cleaner case
2. Air inlet case
3. Carburetor
4. Intake manifold
5. 3-way joint
6. PCV (Positive Crankcase Ventilation) valve
7. Cylinder head cover
8. Cylinder head
9. Cylinder block
10. Oil pan

90884G00

Fig. 1 Positive Crankcase Ventilation (PCV) system schematic

1991–98 Models

TFI ENGINES

Crankcase blow-by gases flow through a passage in the engine block into the cylinder head. Under the rocker arm cover, fresh incoming air from the air cleaner assembly is mixed with the blow-by gases. The fresh air/blow-by gas mixture exits the cylinder head through an opening in the rocker arm cover, and through a hose to the intake manifold. The mixture is introduced to the incoming air charge in the intake manifold, and is burned along with the air charge.

MFI ENGINES

Crankcase blow-by gases flow through a passage in the engine block into the cylinder head. The blow-by gases exit the cylinder head through the PCV valve and into a hose leading to the intake manifold. The gases are introduced to the incoming air charge in the intake manifold, and is burned along with the air charge.

COMPONENT TESTING

Never adjust the idle speed without checking the PCV valve and hoses first, because a stuck PCV valve, plugged hose, or vacuum leakage from a PCV line can cause a rough idle.

PCV Hoses

Inspect all PCV system hoses for loose connections, leaks, clogs, and deterioration. Replace any faulty hoses with new ones.

PCV Valve

CARBURETED AND TFI ENGINES

▶ See Figure 2

1. Detach the PCV hoses from the 3-way connection (1986–90 models), or from the rocker arm cover (1991–95 models).
2. Start the engine and allow it to idle.
3. Position your thumb over the end of the disconnected PCV valve hose, and check for vacuum.
4. If no vacuum is evident, check the hose for a clog or other obstruction. Replace the hose, if necessary.
5. Turn the engine off.

✳✳ CAUTION

NEVER suck air through the PCV valve. Residual toxic gasoline and blow-by fumes may be inhaled, which can cause severe internal injuries.

6. Disconnect the PCV valve hose from the valve. Attach a new hose to the valve, then blow air through the new hose and into the PCV valve. The air should pass with difficulty through the PCV valve (from the rocker arm side to the intake manifold side of the PCV valve).
7. If the air passes easily through the valve, it is stuck in the open position. Replace the valve with a new one.
8. If a new valve is to be installed, wrap Teflon® sealing tape around the PCV valve threads, then install it in the intake manifold.
9. Reattach all of the system hoses to the 3-way connection (1986–90 models only), the PCV valve, and to the rocker arm cover.

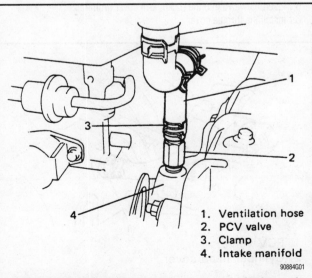

1. Ventilation hose
2. PCV valve
3. Clamp
4. Intake manifold

90884G01

Fig. 2 The PCV valve is threaded into a boss in the intake manifold

MFI ENGINES

▶ **See Figures 3 and 4**

1. Remove the throttle cover from the engine.
2. Remove the PCV valve, with the hose attached, by pulling it out of the rocker arm cover.
3. Start the engine and allow it to idle.
4. Place the tip of one of your fingers over the exposed end of the PCV valve to feel for vacuum. If no vacuum is present, check the valve and hose for an obstruction or clogging; replace either component, if necessary.
5. Stop the engine.
6. Detach the valve from the hose, and shake it. Listen to valve, while shaking it, to check the needle inside; if the valve does not emit a rattling noise, replace it with a new one.
7. Reattach the hose to the valve, and insert the valve into the rocker arm cover grommet.
8. Install the throttle cover.

REMOVAL & INSTALLATION

PCV Valve

CARBURETED AND TFI ENGINES

1. Detach the ventilation system hose from the PCV valve.

➡**The PCV valve is threaded into the intake manifold.**

2. Using an open end wrench, or a socket and ratchet, remove the PCV valve from the intake manifold.

To install:
3. If installing the old PCV valve, clean the threads.
4. Wrap Teflon® sealing tape around the valve threads.
5. Thread the valve into the intake manifold by hand, to avoid crossthreading it.
6. Tighten the valve to 133–221 inch lbs. (15–25 Nm).
7. Reattach the ventilation hose to the valve.

MFI ENGINES

1. Remove the throttle cover from the engine.
2. Remove the PCV valve, with the hose attached, by pulling it out of the rocker arm cover.
3. Detach the valve from the hose.

To install:
4. Attach the hose to the valve, and secure them with a hose clamp.
5. Insert the valve into the rocker arm cover grommet.
6. Install the throttle cover.

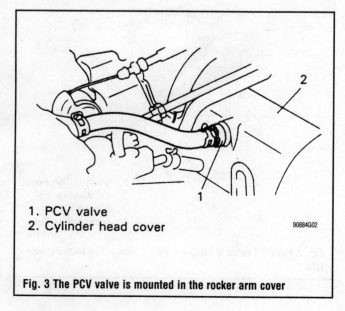

1. PCV valve
2. Cylinder head cover

90884G02

Fig. 3 The PCV valve is mounted in the rocker arm cover

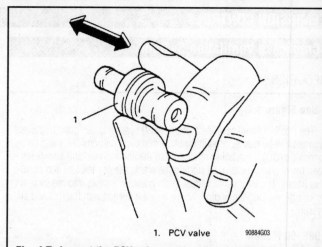

1. PCV valve   90884G03

Fig. 4 To inspect the PCV valve, remove it from the rocker arm cover and vacuum hose, then shake it and listen for a rattling sound

Evaporative Emission Controls

OPERATION

The evaporative emission control system is designed to prevent to release of gasoline fumes, containing environmentally damaging unburned hydrocarbons, into the air. The system does this by storing the fuel vapors until the engine is started, at which time the vapors are vented into the incoming air charge to be burned by the engine. The system uses a container, known as the vapor storage container, filled with activated charcoal to trap the fuel vapors until needed.

Carbureted Engine

▶ **See Figure 5**

On carbureted engines, the major evaporative emission control system components are the vapor storage container, the vent solenoid (mounted on the side of the carburetor), and the liquid vapor separator (mounted near the fuel tank). On these models, the (switch) vent solenoid controls when the fuel vapors are drawn out of the storage canister and into the air stream.

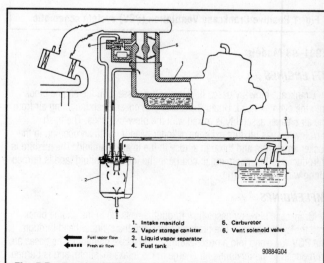

1. Intake manifold   5. Carburetor
2. Vapor storage canister   6. Vent solenoid valve
3. Liquid vapor separator
4. Fuel tank

⬅ Fuel vapor flow
⬅ Fresh air flow

90884G04

Fig. 5 Evaporative (EVAP) emission control system schematic— carbureted engines

1.3L TFI Engine

◆ See Figure 6

On 1.3L TFI engines, the major evaporative emission control system components are the vapor storage canister, the Bi-metal Vacuum Switching Valve (BVSV), and the vapor liquid separator. The BVSV blocks the fuel vapor lines when the engine coolant is too cold, thereby preventing fuel vapors from being introduced to the air stream when the engine is not at normal operating temperature.

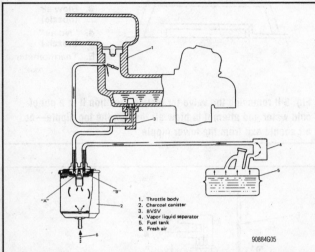

1. Throttle body
2. Charcoal canister
3. BVSV
4. Vapor liquid separator
5. Fuel tank
6. Fresh air

90884G05

Fig. 6 Evaporative (EVAP) emission control system schematic— 1.3L TFI engines

1.6L TFI Engine

◆ See Figure 7

On 1.6L TFI engines, the major evaporative emission control system components are the vapor storage canister, the Canister Purge Vacuum Switching Valve (CP VSV), the 2-way check valve and the vapor liquid separator.

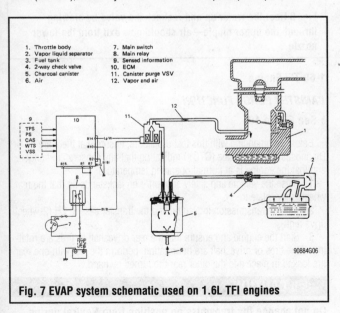

1. Throttle body
2. Vapor liquid separator
3. Fuel tank
4. 2-way check valve
5. Charcoal canister
6. Air
7. Main switch
8. Main relay
9. Sensed information
10. ECM
11. Canister purge VSV
12. Vapor and air

90884G06

Fig. 7 EVAP system schematic used on 1.6L TFI engines

➡On newer models, the CP VSV is referred to as the EVAP Solenoid Purge Valve (EVAP SP Valve), and the 2-way check valve is known as the Tank Pressure Control (TPC) valve. The CP VSV and EVAP SP Valve function identically, only the name was changed. The 2-way check valve and TPC valve also function identically and perform the same job on the vehicle.

The CP VSV controls when the fuel vapors, stored in the vapor storage canister, are routed to the incoming air stream. The CP VSV is electronically controlled by the Engine Control Module (ECM), which controls the CP VSV based on engine conditions (such as engine temperature and speed).

The 2-way check valve is installed in the hose leading from the vapor liquid separator to the vapor storage canister. The valve is designed to maintain a constant pressure in the fuel tank. When the pressure in the fuel tank builds to a specified value, the check valve opens and allows the fuel vapors to flow to the storage canister. On the other hand, when the pressure in the fuel tank drops too low, the check valves opens to allow air to flow into the fuel tank to raise the dropping pressure.

1.6L and 1.8L MFI Engines

➡1.6L MFI engines are available with two different evaporative emission systems: EVAP I and EVAP II. EVAP I models include all 1992–95 models, 1996 4-door Sidekick and Tracker models, 1996 X-90 (except California with automatic transmission) models, and 1996 Sidekick Sport (1.8L engine) models. EVAP II models include 1996 2-door Sidekick and Tracker models, 1996 California X-90 models with automatic transmissions, and all 1997–98 models.

EVAP I MODELS

The major EVAP I emission control system components are the vapor storage canister, the EVAP Solenoid Purge (EVAP SP) valve, the Tank Pressure Control (TPC) valve and the vapor liquid separator.

The EVAP SP valve controls when the fuel vapors, stored in the vapor storage canister, are routed to the incoming air stream. The EVAP SP valve is electronically controlled by the Engine Control Module (ECM), which controls the EVAP SP valve based on engine conditions (such as engine temperature and speed).

The TPC valve is installed in the hose leading from the vapor liquid separator to the vapor storage canister. The valve is designed to maintain a constant pressure in the fuel tank. When the pressure in the fuel tank builds to a specified value, the check valve opens and allows the fuel vapors to flow to the storage canister. On the other hand, when the pressure in the fuel tank drops too low, the check valves opens to allow air to flow into the fuel tank to raise the dropping pressure.

EVAP II MODELS

The major EVAP II system, also referred to as the enhanced evaporative emission control system, components are the EVAP Canister Surge (EVAP CS) tank, the Fuel Tank Pressure Control (FTPC) valve, the Fuel Tank Pressure (FTP) sensor, the EVAP Canister Vent Solenoid (EVAP CVS), the EVAP Tank Pressure Control Solenoid Vacuum (EVAP TPCSV) valve, and the EVAP Canister Purge (EVAP CP) valve.

The EVAP II system functions in much the same manner as the EVAP I system, with the exception of a few added components to fine-tune EVAP system functioning. The additional components are the EVAP CVS, EVAP TPCSV valve, and FTP sensor.

The EVAP CVS and the FTP sensor are utilized so that the ECM can diagnose fuel vapor leakage from the EVAP II system. The EVAP CVS is usually open, but is closed by the ECM whenever it checks for leaks.

The FTP sensor is similar to the Manifold Absolute Pressure (MAP) sensor, in that it measures the difference between the air pressure (or vacuum) in the fuel tank and the atmospheric pressure. The ECM provides a 5 volt reference signal and a ground to the sensor. The sensor sends a voltage signal between 0.1 and 4.9 volts back to the ECM. When the fuel cap is removed from the fuel tank, the pressure in the fuel tank equalizes to atmospheric pressure, at which time the FTP sensor output signal voltage will range from 2.0 to 2.5 volts.

COMPONENT TESTING

Carbureted Engine

HOSES

Inspect all evaporative emission control system hoses for loose connections, leaks, clogs, and deterioration. Replace any faulty hoses with new ones.

VAPOR STORAGE CANISTER

The vapor storage canister testing procedure is presented in Section 1 of this manual.

VENT SOLENOID

✳✳ CAUTION

NEVER suck air through the vent solenoid. Residual toxic gasoline fumes can be inhaled, which can cause severe internal injuries.

1. Detach and label the vapor storage canister hose from the vent solenoid (mounted on the side of the carburetor).
2. Connect a new hose to the nipple on the solenoid.
3. With the ignition switch **OFF**, attempt to blow air through the hose connected to the vent solenoid. Air should pass freely through the solenoid.
4. Turn the ignition switch **ON**, but do not start the engine. Once again, attempt to blow air through the vent solenoid hose. Air should pass freely through the solenoid.
5. Start the engine, then blow air through the vent solenoid hose again. The air should not pass through the solenoid while the engine is running.
6. If the vent solenoid did not function as indicated, replace it with a new one.
7. Remove the new hose, connected to the solenoid, and reattach the old hose.

1.3L TFI Engine

HOSES

Inspect all evaporative emission control system hoses for loose connections, leaks, clogs, and deterioration. Replace any faulty hoses with new ones.

VAPOR STORAGE CANISTER

The vapor storage canister testing procedure is presented in Section 1 of this manual.

BI-METAL VACUUM SWITCHING VALVE (BVSV)

▶ **See Figures 8 and 9**

➡ **This procedure can also be performed by removing the BVSV and warming it up in a pot of water on a stove.**

1. Allow the vehicle to sit, unused, overnight so that the engine is completely cold (below 131°F/55°C).
2. Disconnect and label the vacuum hoses from the BVSV.
3. Attach two new hoses to the BVSV nipples.
4. Blow through the hose attached to the upper BVSV nipple (3) and ensure that no air comes out of the end of the other hose (4).
5. Start the engine and allow it to warm up (above 149°F/65°C).
6. Once again, blow through the hose attached to the upper BVSV nipple (3) and ensure that air does come out of the end of the other hose (4).
7. If the BVSV does not function as indicated, replace it with a new one.
8. Reattach the original vacuum hoses to the BVSV.

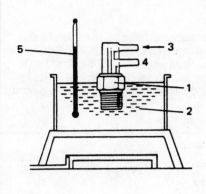

1.	BVSV
2.	Cool water
3.	Blow air (nozzle)
4.	"No air" (nozzle)
5.	Thermometer

90884G15

Fig. 8 If removing the valve for testing, position it in a pot of cold water and attempt to blow air through the top nipple—no air should exit from the lower nipple

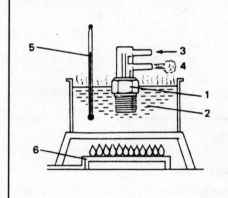

1.	BVSV
2.	Hot water
3.	Blow air (nozzle)
4.	Air (nozzle)
5.	Thermometer
6.	Heater

90884G16

Fig. 9 Heat the water up and recheck the valve by blowing through the upper nipple—air should now exit from the lower nozzle

1.6L TFI Engine

CANISTER PURGE FUNCTION

▶ **See Figure 10**

Before commencing with this test procedure, ensure that there are no Diagnostic Trouble Codes (DTC's) indicating that any sensors are faulty, and that the engine is at normal operating temperature.

1. Raise the vehicle and safely support it on jackstands so that the rear wheels may rotate freely.
2. Set the transmission in Neutral and the transfer case in 2H (2-wheel drive high).
3. Start the engine and ensure that the rear driveshaft or tires are rotating. If the tires or driveshaft are not rotating, perform the test with one rear tire locked in place and the other rear tire turned by hand.

✳✳ CAUTION

Do not change the transmission position from Neutral during this test, otherwise the rear wheels may spin at a high speed, which causes a dangerous condition.

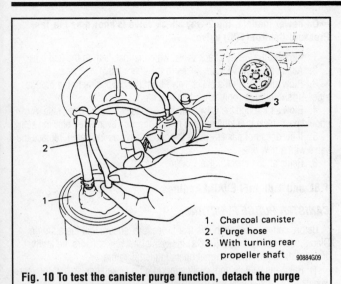

Fig. 10 To test the canister purge function, detach the purge hose from the canister and check for vacuum

1. Charcoal canister
2. Purge hose
3. With turning rear propeller shaft

90884G09

4. Start the engine and allow it to idle until normal operating temperature is reached. You know the engine has reached normal operating temperature when the upper radiator hose becomes warm to the touch.

5. Detach the purge hose from the canister. Position the tip of your finger against the disconnected end of the purge hose. With the engine idling, ensure that no vacuum is felt from the purge vacuum hose.

6. With your finger still over the disconnected end of the purge vacuum hose, increase engine speed to 1500 rpm or more; vacuum should be felt with the engine speed above 1500 rpm.

7. If vacuum from the purge hose did not function as indicated, check the vacuum passage, the vacuum hoses, the CP VSV, the wiring harness and the ECM for damage or blockages.

VACUUM PASSAGE

▶ See Figure 11

1. Start the engine and allow it to run at idle.
2. Place the tip of one of your fingers over the open end of the vacuum nipple.
3. Ensure that vacuum is felt at the vacuum nipple.
4. If no vacuum is felt, clean the passage by blowing compressed air into the passage.

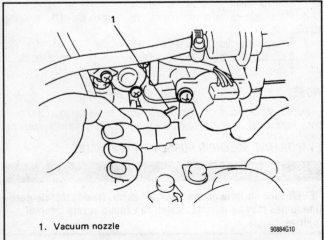

1. Vacuum nozzle

90884G10

Fig. 11 Use your finger to check for vacuum at the vacuum passage in the intake manifold—if no vacuum is present, the passage is blocked

HOSES

Inspect all evaporative emission control system hoses for loose connections, leaks, clogs, and deterioration. Replace any faulty hoses with new ones.

CANISTER PURGE VACUUM SWITCHING VALVE (CP VSV)

▶ See Figures 12, 13 and 14

❊❊ CAUTION

NEVER suck air through the CP VSV. Residual toxic gasoline fumes may be inhaled, which can cause severe internal injuries.

➡ On newer models, the CP VSV is referred to as the EVAP Solenoid Purge Valve (EVAP SP Valve).

1. With the ignition switch **OFF**, detach the wiring harness connector from the CP VSV.

2. Using an ohmmeter, measure the resistance between the two CP VSV terminals. Resistance should be 30–38 ohms. If the resistance of the CP VSV is not as specified, replace it with a new one.

3. Detach the CP VSV vacuum hoses from the intake manifold and the vapor storage canister.

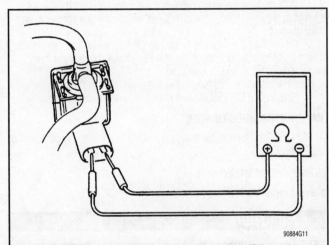

90884G11

Fig. 12 Measure the resistance between the two VSV terminals—if the resistance is not within the specified range, replace it with a new one

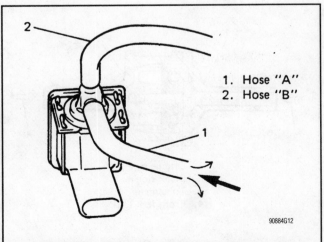

1. Hose "A"
2. Hose "B"

90884G12

Fig. 13 With the wiring harness disengaged from the CP VSV, attempt to blow air through hose A—no air should exit from hose B

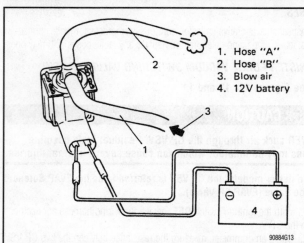

1. Hose "A"
2. Hose "B"
3. Blow air
4. 12V battery

90884G13

Fig. 14 Apply 12 volts DC current to the CP VSV terminals and once again attempt to blow air through hose A—air should now exit from hose B

4. With the wiring harness connector still detached from the CP VSV, attempt to blow air through the CP VSV as indicated in the accompanying illustration. Air should not pass through the valve.

5. Connect a 12 volt battery to the two CP VSV wiring harness terminal, then attempt to blow air through the valve again. Air should pass freely through the valve while it is energized.

6. If the valve does not function as indicated, replace it with a new one.

7. Reattach the CP VSV vacuum lines and wiring harness connector.

VAPOR STORAGE CANISTER

The vapor storage canister testing procedure is presented in Section 1 of this manual.

2-WAY CHECK VALVE

♦ See Figure 15

✳✳ CAUTION

NEVER suck air through the 2-way check valve. Residual toxic gasoline fumes may be inhaled, which can cause severe internal injuries.

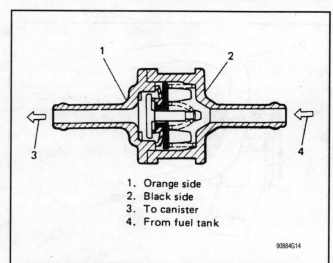

1. Orange side
2. Black side
3. To canister
4. From fuel tank

90884G14

Fig. 15 Air should pass through the 2-way check valve from the fuel tank side only when blowing hard

➡On newer models, the 2-way check valve is known as the Tank Pressure Control (TPC) valve.

1. Remove the 2-way check valve, which is installed on the fuel tank.
2. Attach two new vacuum hoses to the check valve.
3. Blow air through the check valve from the black side to the orange side. Air should pass only when blowing hard.
4. Blow air through the valve from the orange side to the black side. Air should pass freely through the valve in this direction even when blowing softly.
5. If air does not pass through the check valve as indicated, replace the valve with a new one.
6. Reinstall the check valve.

1.6L and 1.8L MFI EVAP I Engines

CANISTER PURGE FUNCTION

Before commencing with this test procedure, ensure that there are no Diagnostic Trouble Codes (DTC's) indicating that any sensors are faulty, and that the engine is at normal operating temperature.

1. Raise the vehicle and safely support it on jackstands so that the rear wheels may rotate freely.
2. Set the transmission in Neutral and the transfer case in 2H (2-wheel drive high).
3. Start the engine and ensure that the rear driveshaft or tires are rotating. If the tires or driveshaft are not rotating, perform the test with one rear tire locked in place and the other rear tire turned by hand.

✳✳ CAUTION

Do not change the transmission position from Neutral during this test, otherwise the rear wheels may spin at a high speed, which causes a dangerous condition.

4. Start the engine and allow it to idle until normal operating temperature is reached. You know the engine has reached normal operating temperature when the upper radiator hose becomes warm to the touch.
5. Detach the purge hose from the canister. Position the tip of your finger against the disconnected end of the purge hose. With the engine idling, ensure that no vacuum is felt from the purge vacuum hose.
6. With your finger still over the disconnected end of the purge vacuum hose, increase engine speed to 1500 rpm or more; vacuum should be felt with the engine speed above 1500 rpm.
7. If vacuum from the purge hose did not function as indicated, check the vacuum passage, the vacuum hoses, the EVAP SP valve, the wiring harness and the ECM for damage or blockages.

VACUUM PASSAGE

1. Start the engine and allow it to run at idle.
2. Place the tip of one of your fingers over the open end of the vacuum nipple.
3. Ensure that vacuum is felt at the vacuum nipple.
4. If no vacuum is felt, clean the passage by blowing compressed air into the passage.

HOSES

Inspect all evaporative emission control system hoses for loose connections, leaks, clogs, and deterioration. Replace any faulty hoses with new ones.

EVAPORATIVE SOLENOID PURGE (EVAP SP) VALVE

✳✳ CAUTION

NEVER suck air through the EVAP SP valve. Residual toxic gasoline fumes may be inhaled, which can cause severe internal injuries.

1. With the ignitions witch **OFF**, detach the wiring harness connector from the EVAP SP valve.

2. Using an ohmmeter, measure the resistance between the two EVAP SP valve terminals. Resistance should be 28–36 ohms. If the resistance of the EVAP SP valve is not as specified, replace it with a new one.

3. Detach the EVAP SP valve vacuum hoses from the intake manifold and the vapor storage canister.

4. With the wiring harness connector still detached from the EVAP SP valve, attempt to blow air through the EVAP SP valve as indicated in the accompanying illustration. Air should not pass through the valve.

5. Connect a 12 volt battery to the two EVAP SP valve wiring harness terminal, then attempt to blow air through the valve again. Air should pass freely through the valve while it is energized.

6. If the valve does not function as indicated, replace it with a new one.

7. Reattach the EVAP SP valve vacuum lines and wiring harness connector.

VAPOR STORAGE CANISTER

The vapor storage canister testing procedure is presented in Section 1 of this manual.

TANK PRESSURE CONTROL (TPC) VALVE

❊❊ CAUTION

NEVER suck air through the TPC valve. Residual toxic gasoline fumes may be inhaled, which can cause severe internal injuries.

1. Remove the TPC valve, which is installed on the fuel tank.
2. Attach two new vacuum hoses to the check valve.
3. Blow air through the check valve from the black side to the orange side. Air should pass only when blowing hard.
4. Blow air through the valve from the orange side to the black side. Air should pass freely through the valve in this direction even when blowing softly.
5. If air does not pass through the check valve as indicated, replace the valve with a new one.
6. Reinstall the check valve.

1.6L and 1.8L MFI EVAP II Engines

EVAP II CANISTER PURGE SYSTEM INSPECTION

1. Allow the engine to cool down to room temperature.
2. Start the engine.
3. Disconnect the purge hose from the vapor storage canister.
4. Position a finger tip against the disconnected end of the purge hose, and check for vacuum. Vacuum should not be felt when the engine is below normal operating temperature.
5. Connect the purge hose to the canister and allow the engine to warm up to normal operating temperature.
6. Once again, disconnect the purge hose from the vapor storage canister.
7. Check the purge hose for vacuum again. Vacuum should now be felt.

➡ The EVAP II system does not purge the canister unless the engine is sufficiently warmed up and the heated oxygen sensor is fully activated. When the purge hose is disconnected in Step 6, some air may be pulled into the purge line. As a result, the ECM may detect a change in the purge gas concentration and stop purging the system. This is normal, and may be the cause of a failure to detect vacuum in Step 7. If no vacuum is evident in Step 7, continue testing the EVAP II system components to avoid replacing a good component.

8. If vacuum from the purge hose did not function as indicated, inspection of the EVAP II system is necessary.

HOSES

Inspect all evaporative emission control system hoses for loose connections, leaks, clogs, and deterioration. Replace any faulty hoses with new ones.

VAPOR STORAGE CANISTER

The vapor storage canister testing procedure is presented in Section 1 of this manual.

EVAP CANISTER PURGE (EVAP CP) VALVE

▶ See Figure 16

❊❊ CAUTION

NEVER suck air through the EVAP CP valve. Residual toxic gasoline fumes may be inhaled, which can cause severe internal injuries.

1. With the ignition switch **OFF**, detach the wiring harness connector from the EVAP CP valve.

2. Using an ohmmeter, measure the resistance between the two EVAP CP valve terminals. Resistance should be 28–36 ohms at 68°F (20°C). If the resistance of the EVAP CP valve is not as specified, replace it with a new one.

3. Detach the EVAP CP valve vacuum hoses from the intake manifold and the vapor storage canister.

4. With the wiring harness connector still detached from the EVAP CP valve, attempt to blow air through the EVAP CP valve as indicated in the accompanying illustration. Air should not pass through the valve.

5. Connect a 12 volt DC battery to the two EVAP CP valve wiring harness terminal, then attempt to blow air through the valve again. Air should pass freely through the valve while it is energized.

6. If the valve does not function as indicated, replace it with a new one.

7. Reattach the EVAP CP valve vacuum lines and wiring harness connector.

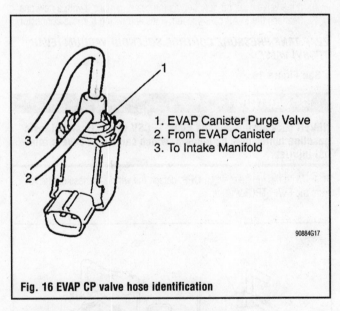

1. EVAP Canister Purge Valve
2. From EVAP Canister
3. To Intake Manifold

90884G17

Fig. 16 EVAP CP valve hose identification

EVAP CANISTER VENT SOLENOID (EVAP CVS)

▶ See Figure 17

❊❊ CAUTION

NEVER suck air through the EVAP CVS. Residual toxic gasoline fumes may be inhaled, which can cause severe internal injuries.

1. With the ignition switch **OFF**, detach the wiring harness connector from the EVAP CVS.

2. Using an ohmmeter, measure the resistance between the two EVAP CVS terminals. Resistance should be 25–30 ohms at 68°F (20°C). If the resistance of the EVAP CVS is not as specified, replace it with a new one.

3. Detach the EVAP CVS vacuum hoses from the intake manifold and the vapor storage canister.

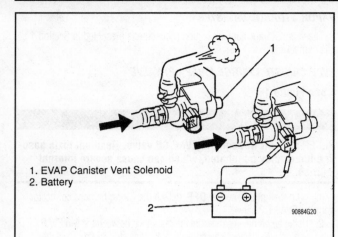

1. EVAP Canister Vent Solenoid
2. Battery

90884G20

Fig. 17 When the EVAP CVS is not energized, the air blown into the valve should exit through the side hose—when the valve is energized, the air should not exit through the other hose

4. With the wiring harness connector still detached from the EVAP CVS, attempt to blow air through the EVAP CVS as indicated in the accompanying illustration. Air should pass freely through the valve.

5. Connect a 12 volt DC battery to the two EVAP CVS wiring harness terminal, then attempt to blow air through the solenoid again. Air should not pass freely through the solenoid while it is energized.

6. If the valve does not function as indicated, replace it with a new one.

7. Reattach the EVAP CVS vacuum lines and wiring harness connector.

EVAP TANK PRESSURE CONTROL SOLENOID VACUUM (EVAP TPCSV) VALVE

▶ See Figure 18

❋❋ CAUTION

NEVER suck air through the EVAP TPCSV valve. Residual toxic gasoline fumes may be inhaled, which can cause severe internal injuries.

1. With the ignitions witch **OFF**, detach the wiring harness connector from the EVAP TPCSV valve.

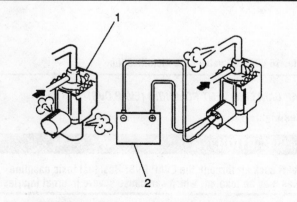

1. EVAP Tank Pressure Control Solenoid Vacuum Valve
2. Battery

90884G19

Fig. 18 When the EVAP TPCSV is not energized, the air blown into the valve should exit through the filter—when the valve is energized, the air should exit through the other hose

2. Using an ohmmeter, measure the resistance between the two EVAP TPCSV valve terminals. Resistance should be 28–36 ohms at 68°F (20°C). If the resistance of the EVAP TPCSV valve is not as specified, replace it with a new one.

3. Detach the EVAP TPCSV valve vacuum hoses from the intake manifold and the vapor storage canister.

4. With the wiring harness connector still detached from the EVAP TPCSV valve, attempt to blow air through the EVAP TPCSV valve as indicated in the accompanying illustration. Air should not pass through the valve.

5. Connect a 12 volt DC battery to the two EVAP TPCSV valve wiring harness terminal, then attempt to blow air through the valve again. Air should pass freely through the valve while it is energized.

6. If the valve does not function as indicated, replace it with a new one.

7. Reattach the EVAP TPCSV valve vacuum lines and wiring harness connector.

TANK PRESSURE CONTROL (TPC) VALVE

▶ See Figure 19

1. Attach a long piece of new vacuum hose to the TPC valve nipple marked TANK.

2. Blow hard into the vacuum hose. Air should pass SLOWLY through the valve and out the port marked CAN.

3. Remove the vacuum hose from the TANK nipple, and connect it to the CAN port of the TPC valve.

4. Blow lightly through the vacuum hose. Air should pass freely through the valve and out the TANK nipple.

5. If the TPC valve did not function as indicated, replace it with a new one.

6. Reattach the vacuum hose to the TANK port on the TPC valve.

7. Using a hand-held vacuum pump, apply vacuum to the vacuum port of the TPC valve.

8. With vacuum applied to the TPC valve, blow through the vacuum hose. Air should pass easily through the valve and out the CAN port of the TPC valve.

9. If the TPC valve did not function as indicated, replace it with a new one.

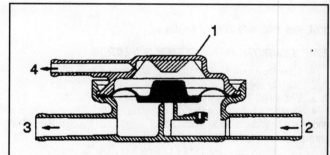

1. Fuel Tank Pressure Control Valve
2. From Fuel Tank
3. To EVAP Canister
4. Vacuum Port

90884G18

Fig. 19 Cross-sectional view of the TPC valve—nozzle 2 is marked TANK, and nozzle 3 is marked CAN

REMOVAL & INSTALLATION

1.3L Carbureted Engine

VAPOR STORAGE CANISTER

The vapor storage canister removal and installation procedure is presented in Section 1 of this manual.

VENT SOLENOID

1. Disconnect the negative battery cable.
2. If necessary, remove the carburetor from the vehicle.
3. Detach and label the vent solenoid wiring connector.
4. Remove the solenoid-to-carburetor mounting bolts and washers.
5. Carefully pull the vent solenoid off of the carburetor.
6. Remove and discard the old gasket.

To install:

7. Along with a new gasket, position the vent solenoid against the carburetor.
8. Install the vent solenoid mounting bolts and washers. Tighten them until snug.
9. Reattach the solenoid wiring harness connector.
10. If applicable, install the carburetor.
11. Connect the negative battery cable.

1.3L TFI Engine

VAPOR STORAGE CANISTER

The vapor storage canister removal and installation procedure is presented in Section 1 of this manual.

BI-METAL VACUUM SWITCHING VALVE (BVSV)

1. Drain the engine cooling system until the coolant level is below the BVSV, mounted in the intake manifold.
2. Detach and label the vacuum lines from the BVSV.
3. Using an open end wrench, loosen the BVSV, then remove it from the intake manifold.

To install:

4. If the old BVSV is to be installed, clean the threads thoroughly.
5. Wrap Teflon® sealing tape around the BVSV threads, then install it by hand.
6. Tighten the BVSV until secure, then reattach the vacuum lines.
7. Fill the cooling system.

1.6L TFI Engine

VAPOR STORAGE CANISTER

The vapor storage canister removal and installation procedure is presented in Section 1 of this manual.

CANISTER PURGE VACUUM SWITCHING VALVE (CP VSV)

1. Disconnect the negative battery cable.
2. Detach and label the wiring harness connector from the CP VSV.
3. Disconnect and label the vacuum lines from the CP VSV.
4. Loosen the CP VSV mounting bracket fasteners, then remove the valve from the intake manifold.

To install:

5. Position the CP VSV on the intake manifold, and install the mounting fasteners until secure.
6. Reattach the vacuum hoses to the CP VSV.
7. Insert the wiring harness connector in the CP VSV until the retaining latch is fully engaged.
8. Connect the negative battery cable.

2-WAY CHECK VALVE

1. Disconnect the negative battery cable.
2. If necessary for added accessibility, lower the fuel tank from the vehicle.
3. Remove the hose clamps and detach the vapor hoses from the 2-way check valve.
4. Remove the check valve from the vehicle.

To install:

5. Install the check valve in position and reattach the vapor hoses to it.
6. Install the vapor hose clamps and tighten them until snug.
7. If necessary, install the fuel tank.
8. Install the negative battery cable.

1.6L and 1.8L MFI EVAP I Engines

VAPOR STORAGE CANISTER

The vapor storage canister removal and installation procedure is presented in Section 1 of this manual.

EVAPORATIVE SOLENOID PURGE (EVAP SP) VALVE

1. Disconnect the negative battery cable.
2. Detach and label the wiring harness connector from the EVAP SP valve.
3. Disconnect and label the vacuum lines from the EVAP SP valve.
4. Loosen the EVAP SP valve mounting bracket fasteners, then remove the valve from the intake manifold.

To install:

5. Position the EVAP SP valve on the intake manifold, and install the mounting fasteners until secure.
6. Reattach the vacuum hoses to the EVAP SP valve.
7. Insert the wiring harness connector in the EVAP SP valve until the retaining latch is fully engaged.
8. Connect the negative battery cable.

TANK PRESSURE CONTROL (TPC) VALVE

1. Disconnect the negative battery cable.
2. If necessary for added accessibility, lower the fuel tank from the vehicle.
3. Remove the hose clamps and detach the vapor hoses from the TPC valve.
4. Remove the check valve from the vehicle.

To install:

5. Install the check valve in position and reattach the vapor hoses to it.
6. Install the vapor hose clamps and tighten them until snug.
7. If necessary, install the fuel tank.
8. Install the negative battery cable.

1.6L and 1.8L MFI EVAP II Engines

VAPOR STORAGE CANISTER

The vapor storage canister removal and installation procedure is presented in Section 1 of this manual.

EVAP CVS, EVAP TPCSV, AND EVAP CP VALVES

1. Disconnect the negative battery cable.
2. Detach and label the wiring harness connector from the valve/solenoid.
3. Disconnect and label the vacuum lines from the valve/solenoid.
4. Loosen the mounting bracket fasteners, then remove the component from the intake manifold (EVAP CVS) or from the right-hand inner fenderwell (EVAP TPCSV and EVAP CP).

To install:

5. Position the component on the intake manifold, or right-hand inner fenderwell, and install the mounting fasteners until secure.
6. Reattach the vacuum hoses to the component.
7. Insert the wiring harness connector in the valve/solenoid until the retaining latch is fully engaged.
8. Connect the negative battery cable.

TANK PRESSURE CONTROL (TPC) VALVE

1. Remove the hose clamps and detach the vapor hoses from the TPC valve, mounted next to the vapor storage canister.
2. Remove the valve from the engine compartment.

To install:

3. Install the valve in position and reattach the vapor hoses to it.
4. Install the vapor hose clamps and tighten them until snug.

FUEL TANK PRESSURE (FTP) SENSOR

1. Disconnect the negative battery cable.
2. Remove the fuel tank from the vehicle.

3. Detach and label the FTP sensor wiring harness connector.

4. Loosen the two mounting bolts, then lift the sensor off of the fuel tank.

To install:

5. Install the FTP sensor on the fuel tank so that the wiring harness connector terminals face the fuel level sensor.

6. Install the two mounting bolts, and tighten then to 11–18 inch lbs. (1.2–2.0 Nm).

7. Reattach the wiring harness connector to the sensor. Ensure that the connector is fully engaged to the sensor.

8. Install the fuel tank in the vehicle.

9. Connect the negative battery cable.

Exhaust Gas Recirculation (EGR) System

OPERATION

The Exhaust Gas Recirculation (EGR) system reduces the emission Oxides of Nitrogen (NOx) into the atmosphere by rerouting exhaust gas back into the intake manifold. The incoming charge of exhaust gas dilutes the air/fuel mixture entering the cylinders, and, thereby, reduces peak combustion temperature. Lower peak combustion temperatures result in lower levels of NOx.

The EGR system is controlled by vacuum and the Engine Control Module (ECM), based on engine speed, temperature and load.

Carbureted Models

▶ See Figure 20

The EGR system used on 1986–89 Samurai vehicles is composed of the EGR modulator, the EGR valve, a Bi-Metal Vacuum Switching Valve (BVSV), and the Three-Way Solenoid Valve (TWSV).

The EGR system is controlled largely by vacuum as follows: the BVSV is mounted in the vacuum line leading from the intake manifold to the EGR modulator, and threaded into the coolant passage of the intake manifold. The BVSV's main function is to sense engine coolant temperature, and to open or close based on the coolant temperature. When the engine coolant temperature is too cold, the BVSV closes, thereby stopping engine vacuum from reaching the EGR modulator.

The EGR modulator senses the amount of backpressure in the exhaust valve, and, in turn, controls the amount of vacuum applied to the EGR valve.

Mounted in the vacuum line from the EGR modulator to the EGR valve, is the TWSV. The main function of this component is to block vacuum from

reaching the EGR valve when the ECM deems it necessary (depending on transmission gear and operation of the heating-air conditioning system). Therefore, the vacuum must travel through the BVSV, through the EGR modulator and through the TWSV before it reaches the EGR valve.

If vacuum is allowed to reach the EGR valve, it pulls the EGR valve pintle up and off of its seat, thereby allowing exhaust gas to flow into the intake manifold.

Fuel Injected Models

1.3L AND 1.6L ENGINES

▶ See Figure 21

The EGR system used on Sidekick, Tracker, X-90 and 1990–95 Samurai vehicles is composed of the EGR modulator, the EGR valve, the EGR Temperature (EGRT) sensor, and the EGR Solenoid Vacuum (EGR SV) valve.

➡ **On newer vehicles, the EGR modulator is referred to as the EGR pressure transducer. Both components are identical and perform the same job, regardless of which name you decide to call them.**

The EGR system is controlled largely by vacuum as follows: the EGR SV valve is mounted in the vacuum line leading from the intake manifold to the EGR modulator. The EGR SV valve's main function is to open or close based on signals from the Engine Control Module (ECM), thereby allowing or preventing (respectively) engine vacuum from reaching the EGR modulator. The ECM sends signals to the EGR SV valve depending on engine temperature, barometric pressure, engine speed, and engine load.

The EGR modulator senses the amount of backpressure in the exhaust valve, and, in turn, controls the amount of vacuum applied to the EGR valve. Therefore, the vacuum must travel through the EGR SV valve and through the EGR modulator before it reaches the EGR valve.

If vacuum is allowed to reach the EGR valve, it pulls the EGR valve pintle up and off of its seat, thereby allowing exhaust gas to flow into the intake manifold.

The 1990–95 California models are equipped with the EGRT sensor, which is used by the ECM to monitor EGR valve operation. The operation of the EGR valve is monitored by the change in temperature in the exhaust gases.

The 1996–98 models are equipped with two additional components, both of which are used for EGR system diagnosis by the ECM. The Manifold Differential Pressure (MDP) sensor and the EGR Bypass (EGRB) valve (mounted in the vacuum line between the EGR modulator and the EGR valve. The ECM uses these components to compare the pressure in the EGR system with the pressure in the intake manifold to check for a blockage.

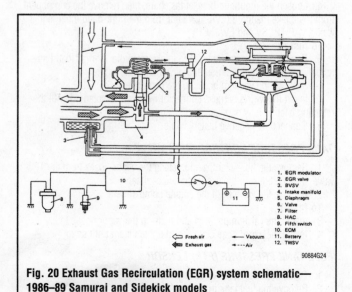

1. EGR modulator
2. EGR valve
3. BVSV
4. Intake manifold
5. Diaphragm
6. Valve
7. Filter
8. HAC
9. Fifth switch
10. ECM
11. Battery
12. TWSV

⇦ Fresh air   ⟵ Vacuum
⇦ Exhaust gas   ⟵--- Air

90884G24

Fig. 20 Exhaust Gas Recirculation (EGR) system schematic—1986–89 Samurai and Sidekick models

1. Ignition switch
2. Main relay
3. ECM
4. Sensed information
5. SV valve
6. EGR modulator
7. EGR valve
8. EGRT sensor (California spec. vehicle only)
9. Intake manifold
10. Throttle body
11. Exhaust gas
12. Vacuum
13. Air

ECT sensor
MAP sensor
CMP sensor
TP sensor
VSS
EGRT sensor

⟵ 11
⟵ 12
⟵-- 13

90884G27

Fig. 21 Exhaust Gas Recirculation (EGR) system schematic—1990–98 Sidekick, Tracker, X-90 and Samurai models

1.8L ENGINE

▶ **See Figure 22**

The EGR system used on Sidekick Sport models is composed of only the EGR valve and exhaust gas piping. The EGR valve is controlled solely by the ECM, unlike the other EGR systems covered in this manual. The ECM decides when to initiate EGR system function based on input information from the Camshaft Position (CMP) sensor, Engine Coolant Temperature (ECT) sensor, Mass Air Flow (MAF) sensor and the Vehicle Speed Sensor (VSS).

The EGR system is turned off when the engine is too cold, the throttle valve is opening less than specification calls for, when the engine is operated under heavy load, and when the vehicle is stopped.

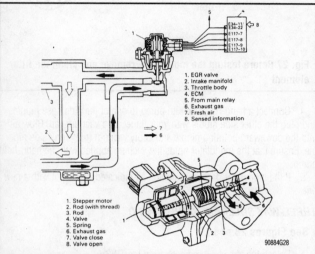

1. EGR valve
2. Intake manifold
3. Throttle body
4. ECM
5. From main relay
6. Exhaust gas
7. Fresh air
8. Sensed information

1. Stepper motor
2. Rod (with thread)
3. Rod
4. Valve
5. Spring
6. Exhaust gas
7. Valve close
8. Valve open

Fig. 22 Exhaust Gas Recirculation (EGR) system schematic— Sidekick Sport models

COMPONENT TESTING

Carbureted Models

EGR SYSTEM INSPECTION

▶ **See Figures 23 and 24**

➡ Before commencing with this procedure, ensure that you are not at an altitude of more than 4000 ft. (1220m) and that the gear shift lever is in Neutral. If you are at an altitude of more than 4000 ft. (1220m), be sure to detach the HAC wiring harness connector.

✷✷ CAUTION

During the following procedure, it may be necessary to wear gloves to avoid burning your finger when the EGR valve becomes hot.

1. If the engine is hot, allow the engine to cool down to room temperature.
2. Start the engine and allow it to idle. Check that the EGR valve diaphragm is not operating by touching it with your finger.
3. Warm the engine up to normal operating temperature, then race the engine. While racing the engine, ensure that the diaphragm moves toward the wide end of the EGR valve (1) during acceleration and toward the narrow end of the valve (2) during deceleration.
4. If the EGR valve does not function as indicated, test the EGR system components to find the defective item.

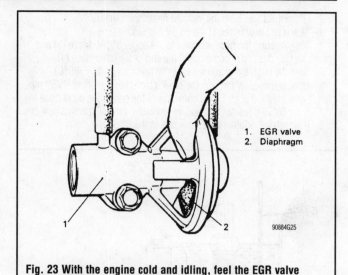

1. EGR valve
2. Diaphragm

Fig. 23 With the engine cold and idling, feel the EGR valve diaphragm to ensure that the valve is not operating

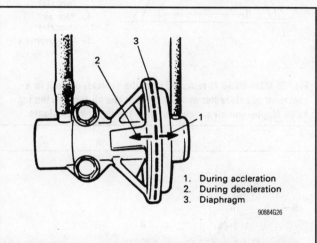

1. During accleration
2. During deceleration
3. Diaphragm

Fig. 24 When the engine is warm, rev the engine and ensure that the diaphragm moves toward (1) during acceleration and toward (2) during deceleration

HOSES

Inspect all EGR system hoses for loose connections, leaks, clogs, and deterioration. Replace any faulty hoses with new ones.

EGR VALVE

1. Detach the vacuum hose from the TWSV.
2. Attach a hand-held vacuum pump to the disconnected end of the vacuum hose.
3. Slowly apply vacuum to the EGR valve diaphragm. The EGR valve diaphragm should move smoothly as vacuum is applied, and it should hold its position (open) when more than 7.9 in. Hg (20 cmHg) vacuum is applied.
4. If the diaphragm did not move smoothly, or did not hold its position, replace the EGR valve.
5. Reattach the vacuum hose to the TWSV.

BI-METAL VACUUM SWITCHING VALVE (BVSV)

▶ **See Figures 25 and 26**

➡ This procedure can also be performed by removing the BVSV and warming it up in a pot of water on a stove.

1. Allow the vehicle to sit, unused, overnight so that the engine is completely cold (below 127°F/53°C).

2. Disconnect and label the vacuum hoses from the BVSV.

3. Attach two new hoses to the BVSV nipples.

4. Blow through the hose attached to the upper BVSV nipple (3) and ensure that air does NOT come out of the end of the other hose (4).

5. Start the engine and allow it to warm up (above 149°F/65°C).

6. Once again, blow through the hose attached to the upper BVSV nipple (3) and ensure that air DOES come out of the end of the other hose (4).

7. If the BVSV does not function as indicated, replace it with a new one.

8. Reattach the original vacuum hoses to the BVSV.

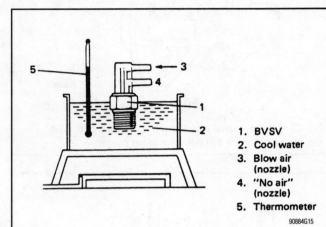

1. BVSV
2. Cool water
3. Blow air (nozzle)
4. "No air" (nozzle)
5. Thermometer

90884G15

Fig. 25 If the BVSV is removed from the vehicle, place it in a container of cold water and attempt to blow air through the top valve nipple—no air should exit from the lower valve nipple

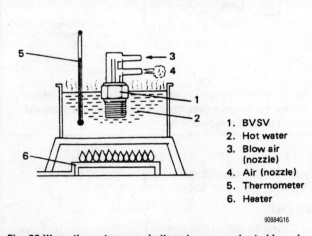

1. BVSV
2. Hot water
3. Blow air (nozzle)
4. Air (nozzle)
5. Thermometer
6. Heater

90884G16

Fig. 26 Warm the water up and attempt, once again, to blow air through the upper valve nipple—the air should now exit from the lower nozzle

EGR MODULATOR

▶ See Figure 27

1. Remove the modulator from the vehicle.

2. Remove the cap and inspect the filter for contamination and/or damage. Use compressed air to blow the dirt out of the filter.

3. Reassemble the filter and cap, then plug one of the side hose nipples and blow compressed air into the other side nipple. Ensure that the air passes through the air filter and out the modulator cap.

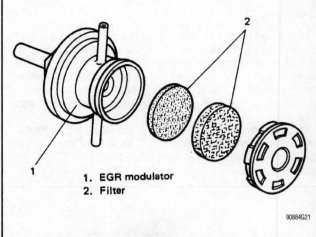

1. EGR modulator
2. Filter

90884G21

Fig. 27 Before testing the modulator, remove and clean the filter element

4. Connect a hand-held vacuum pump to one of the side hose nipples and plug the other side nipple with your finger, or a vacuum cap. Blow air into the downward pointing nipple and apply vacuum to the one side nipple. Ensure that the modulator holds the vacuum applied with the hand-held pump.

5. If the modulator does not function as indicated, replace it with a new one.

THREE-WAY SOLENOID VALVE (TWSV)

▶ See Figures 28 and 29

1. Detach the two vacuum hoses from the TWSV.

2. Attach two new vacuum hoses to the TWSV, then attempt to blow air through hose 1 (refer to the accompanying illustration). The air should exit from the other hose (2) and NOT out of the filter (3).

3. Detach the wiring harness connector from the TWSV, then connect a 12 volt DC battery to the two terminals to energize the TWSV.

4. Once again, attempt to blow air through hose 1. The air should now exit through the filter and NOT from hose 2.

5. If the TWSV did not function as indicated, replace it with a new one.

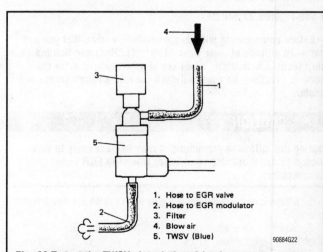

1. Hose to EGR valve
2. Hose to EGR modulator
3. Filter
4. Blow air
5. TWSV (Blue)

90884G22

Fig. 28 To test the TWSV, detach the wiring harness connector from the valve, then blow air into the upper valve hose—the air should exit from the lower hose

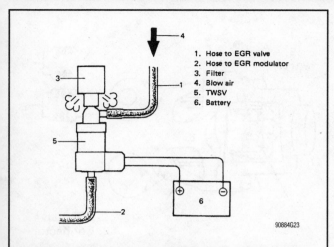

Fig. 29 Apply 12 volts DC current to the valve and once again blow air into the upper vacuum hose—the air should now exit from the filter and NOT from the lower hose

Fuel Injected Models—1.3L and 1.6L Engines

EGR SYSTEM INSPECTION

➡Before commencing with this procedure, ensure that you are not at an altitude of more than 8,200 ft. (2500m), that the atmospheric pressure is 23 in. Hg (585 mmHg) or higher, that the transmission is in Neutral, that the parking brake lever is engaged, and that the VSS, ECT sensor, TP sensor and MAP sensor are in good operating condition.

✳✳ CAUTION

During the following procedure, it may be necessary to wear gloves to avoid burning your finger when the EGR valve becomes hot.

1. For 1994–96 models, perform the following:
  a. Raise and safely support the rear of the vehicle on jackstands so that rear wheels can spin freely.
  b. Position the transfer case in 2H.
  c. Start the engine and release the parking brake lever; the rear wheels should turn. If the wheels are not turning, have an assistant rotate one of the wheels during the test. This is necessary only on 1994–96 models since the ECM knows if the rear drive wheels are spinning or not; the EGR system will not function if the ECM thinks the vehicle is standing still.
2. If the engine is hot, allow the engine to cool down to room temperature.
3. Start the engine, then while racing the engine to 3500 rpm or higher, check that the EGR valve diaphragm is not operating by touching it with your finger.
4. Warm the engine up to normal operating temperature, then race the engine to at least 3500 rpm. While racing the engine, ensure that the diaphragm moves toward the wide end of the EGR valve (1) during acceleration and toward the narrow end of the valve (2) during deceleration. (Refer to the accompanying illustration.) If the EGR valve does not function as indicated, test the EGR system components to find the defective item.
5. Keep the engine idling, then open the EGR valve by hand: the engine should either stop or reduce its speed. If neither occurs, the EGR passage is most likely clogged. Clean the passage and retest.

HOSES

Inspect all EGR system hoses for loose connections, leaks, clogs, and deterioration. Replace any faulty hoses with new ones.

EGR VALVE

1. Detach the vacuum hose from the EGR modulator.
2. Attach a hand-held vacuum pump to the disconnected end of the vacuum hose.
3. Slowly apply vacuum to the EGR valve diaphragm. The EGR valve diaphragm should move smoothly as vacuum is applied, and it should hold its position (open) when more than 7.9 in. Hg (20 cmHg) vacuum is applied.
4. If the diaphragm did not move smoothly, or did not hold its position, replace the EGR valve.
5. Reattach the vacuum hose to the EGR modulator.

EGR MODULATOR

1. Remove the modulator from the vehicle.
2. Remove the cap and inspect the filter for contamination and/or damage. Use compressed air to blow the dirt out of the filter.
3. Reassemble the filter and cap, then plug one of the side hose nipples and blow compressed air into the other side nipple. Ensure that the air passes through the air filter and out the modulator cap.
4. Connect a hand-held vacuum pump to one of the side hose nipples and plug the other side nipple with your finger, or a vacuum cap. Blow air into the downward pointing nipple and apply vacuum to the one side nipple. Ensure that the modulator holds the vacuum applied with the hand-held pump.
5. If the modulator does not function as indicated, replace it with a new one.

EGR SOLENOID VACUUM (EGR SV) VALVE

✳✳ CAUTION

NEVER suck air through the EGR SV valve. Residual toxic gasoline fumes may be inhaled, which can cause severe internal injuries.

1. With the ignitionswitch **OFF**, detach the wiring harness connector from the EGR SV valve.
2. Using an ohmmeter, measure the resistance between the two EGR SV valve terminals. Resistance should be 33–39 ohms at 68°F (20°C) for 1990–93 models, 30–38 ohms at 68°F (20°C) for 1994–96 models, or 28–36 ohms at 68°F (20°C) for 1997–98 models. If the resistance of the EGR SV valve is not as specified, replace it with a new one.
3. Detach the EGR SV valve vacuum hoses from the EGR modulator and throttle body.

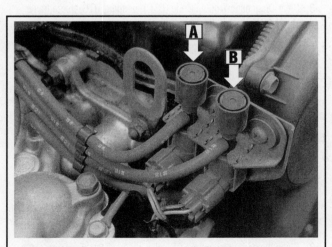

A. EGR TWSV   B. Throttle opener valve

The EGR SV valve is mounted on the front of the engine, next to the throttle opener vacuum switching valve

4. With the wiring harness connector still detached from the EGR SV valve, attempt to blow air through the EGR SV valve hose A (as indicated in the accompanying illustration). Air should emit from hose B.

5. Connect a 12 volt DC battery to the two EGR SV valve wiring harness terminals, then attempt to blow air through the valve again. Air should exit from the filter, NOT from hose B while it is energized.

6. If the valve does not function as indicated, replace it with a new one.

7. Reattach the EGR SV valve vacuum lines and wiring harness connector.

EGR BYPASS (EGRB) VALVE

❋❋ CAUTION

NEVER suck air through the EGRB valve. Residual toxic gasoline fumes may be inhaled, which can cause severe internal injuries.

1. With the ignitions witch **OFF**, detach the wiring harness connector from the EGRB valve.

2. Using an ohmmeter, measure the resistance between the two EGRB valve terminals. Resistance should be 37–44 ohms at 68°F (20°C). Measure the resistance between the EGRB valve body and the wiring connector terminals; the resistance should be 1 megaohm or greater.

3. Detach the EGRB valve vacuum hoses from the EGR modulator and throttle body.

4. With the wiring harness connector still detached from the EGRB valve, attempt to blow air through the EGR SV valve hose A (as indicated in the accompanying illustration). Air should emit from hose B.

5. Connect a 12 volt DC battery to the two EGRB valve wiring harness terminals, then attempt to blow air through the valve again. Air should exit from the filter, NOT from hose B while it is energized.

6. If the valve does not function as indicated, replace it with a new one.

7. Reattach the EGRB valve vacuum lines and wiring harness connector.

Fuel Injected Models—1.8L Engine

EGR SYSTEM INSPECTION

➡**A scan tool, such as Suzuki scan tool with OBD-II cartridge, is necessary for this system inspection.**

1. Connect the scan tool to the DLC with the ignition switch **OFF**.

2. Start the engine and warm it up to normal operating temperature (176–212°F/80–100°C).

3. Clear Diagnostic Trouble Code (DTC), pending DTC, freeze frame data in ECM memory with the scan tool.

4. With the engine, and without depressing the accelerator pedal, open the EGR valve by using the MISC TEST mode.

5. In this state, the more the EGR valve opens, the lower the engine idle speed should drop. If the idle speed does not drop, the possible causes could be a clogged EGR gas passage, a stuck or faulty EGR valve, poor performance of the ECT sensor or TP sensor, or DTC's and/or pending DTC's are stored in ECM memory.

EGR VALVE

▶ **See Figure 30**

1. Remove the EGR valve from the engine.

2. Measure the resistance between EGR valve terminals A and B, C and B, F and E, and D and E. All resistances should be between 20–24 ohms. If the one or more of the values measured is not within this range, replace the EGR valve with a new one.

3. Clean the carbon from the EGR valve gas passage.

❋❋ WARNING

Do not use a sharp-edged implement to remove the carbon. Be careful not to damage the EGR valve, valve seat or rod.

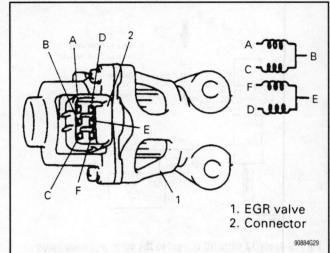

1. EGR valve
2. Connector

90884G29

Fig. 30 EGR valve terminal identification for testing—Sidekick Sport models

4. Inspect the EGR valve, valve seat and rod for defects, such as cracks, bends or other damage. If any such damage is evident, replace the valve with a new one.

MANIFOLD DIFFERENTIAL PRESSURE (MDP) SENSOR

Testing procedures for the Manifold Differential Pressure (MDP) sensor a covered later in this section, under electronic engine controls.

REMOVAL & INSTALLATION

Except 1.8L Engine

EGR VALVE

1. Detach and label the vacuum hoses from the EGR valve.

2. Loosen the two EGR valve mounting bolts, then separate the valve from the intake manifold.

3. Remove and discard the old gasket.

4. Clean the EGR valve-to-intake manifold gasket mating surface of all carbon, dirt and old gasket material.

To install:

5. Position a new gasket on the intake manifold, then install the EGR valve. Tighten the EGR valve bolts evenly to 15 ft. lbs. (20 Nm).

6. Reattach the vacuum hoses to the valve.

EGR MODULATOR

➡**This component is also referred to as the EGR Pressure Transducer.**

1. Detach and label the vacuum hoses from the EGR modulator.

2. Disengage the modulator from the mounting clips.

To install:

3. Engage the modulator securely in the mounting clips.

4. Reattach the vacuum hoses to the modulator.

BVSV, TWSV, EGR SV, AND EGRB VALVES

1. Disconnect the negative battery cable.

2. Detach and label the vacuum hoses from the valve.

3. Disengage the wiring harness connector from the valve.

4. Loosen the two retaining screws, then separate the valve from the mounting bracket.

To install:

5. Position the valve on the mounting bracket, then install the retaining screws until snug.

6. Reattach the wiring harness connector in the valve, ensuring that the locking tab is fully engaged.

7. Connect the vacuum hoses to the valve.

8. Connect the negative battery cable.

1.8L Engine

EGR VALVE

1. Disconnect the negative battery cable.

2. Detach the EGR valve connection from the valve.

3. Loosen the EGR valve mounting bolts, then separate the valve from the intake manifold.

4. Remove and discard the old gasket.

5. Clean the EGR valve-to-intake manifold gasket mating surface of all carbon, dirt and old gasket material.

To install:

6. Position a new gasket on the intake manifold, then install the EGR valve. Tighten the EGR valve bolts evenly to 15 ft. lbs. (20 Nm).

7. Reattach the EGR valve connection to the valve.

8. Connect the negative battery cable.

MANIFOLD DIFFERENTIAL PRESSURE (MDP) SENSOR

The removal and installation of this sensor is described later in this section.

Feedback Carburetor System

OPERATION

The feedback carburetor system is only used on 1986–89 1.3L engines. The primary purpose of this system is to maintain a controlled air/fuel mixture, which reduces the emission of Oxides of Nitrogen (NOx), hydrocarbons, carbon monoxide, and to improve fuel economy at the same time. The system is composed of an oxygen sensor and the Engine Control Module (ECM). The ECM uses information gathered by the oxygen sensor to manipulate the mixture control solenoid in the carburetor, thereby altering the air/fuel mixture of the carburetor.

The ECM controls many systems, such as the fuel cut system, idle-up system, bowl vent system, EGR system and the secondary throttle valve system, as well as the feedback carburetor system. The ECM is located under the glove compartment of the instrument panel.

The ECM receives incoming information from several components, namely: oxygen (O2) sensor, Engine Coolant Thermal (ECT) switch, Throttle Position (TP) micro-switches, ignition coil, 5th switch, Barometric Pressure (BP) switch, and underhood temperature sensor. The ECM also monitors the heater fan circuit, the rear defogger circuit (if equipped), and the tail light, side marker light and license plate light circuits for excessive electrical loads.

➡**The oxygen sensor and engine coolant temperature sensors are described later in this section, under Electronic Engine Controls.**

The two throttle position switches (wide open switch and idle switch) are mounted on the carburetor, and indicate the position of the carburetor throttle. The ECM uses this information in conjunction with the other sensors to determine the proper amount of fuel that should be introduced into the air stream for the correct air/fuel mixture.

The ignition coil is used by the ECM to determine engine speed (rpm).

The 5th switch is designed to send a signal to the ECM whenever the transmission gearshift lever is moved to the 5th gear position.

The barometric pressure sensor is used by the ECM to determine the altitude of the vehicle. Since air density changes with respect to changes in altitude, the amount of fuel needed for the proper air/fuel mixture is different at various altitudes.

The underhood temperature sensor is designed to monitor the temperature of the air in the engine compartment, and to relay that information to the ECM, which uses the information to correctly alter the air/fuel mixture. When the air temperature is low (cold), the ECM enriches the mixture slightly to allow for better combustion. Likewise, when the air temperature is high (hot), it leans the mixture out slightly.

TESTING

System Operation

◗ **See Figures 31 and 32**

The operation of the feedback carburetor system can be conveyed by the CHECK ENGINE light in the instrument cluster. The CHECK ENGINE light automatically flashes at the 50,000 mile (80,000km), the 80,000 mile (128,000km), and the 100,000 mile (162,000km) marks when the engine is warmed up. The automatic flashing indicates that the feedback carburetor system is functioning properly.

Should any of the following conditions occurs, the feedback system can be tested manually.

• Fuel consumption increases excessively, even during normal operation.

• Engine tends to stall.

• Engine is hard to start.

Inspect the feedback carburetor system, as follows:

1. Turn the cancel switch or check switch, located under the driver's side instrument panel, on.

2. Turn the ignition switch **ON**, without starting the engine. At this time,

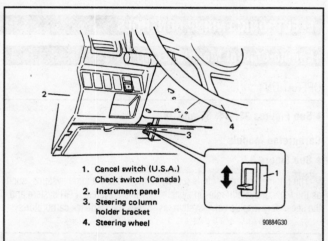

1. Cancel switch (U.S.A.)
   Check switch (Canada)
2. Instrument panel
3. Steering column holder bracket
4. Steering wheel

90884G30

Fig. 31 The CHECK ENGINE light can be cleared by actuating the cancel switch, mounted under the left-hand side of the instrument panel

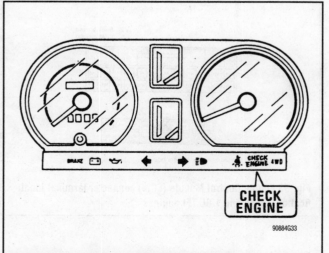

90884G33

Fig. 32 The operation of the feedback carburetor is conveyed through the CHECK ENGINE light, located in the instrument cluster

the CHECK ENGINE light should illuminate, but NOT flash. If the light does not illuminate, ensure that the light bulb is not blown and inspect the wiring harness for an open or short circuit.

3. After confirming proper CHECK LIGHT function, start the engine and allow it to reach normal operating temperature.

4. Once the engine reaches normal operating temperature, run the engine at 1500–2000 rpm. While operating the engine at this speed, ensure that the CHECK LIGHT flashes, which indicates the system is functioning properly. If the light does not flash, the problem could be caused by one or more of the following:

- Defective oxygen sensor.
- Defective mixture control solenoid valve.
- Defective carburetor or maladjusted idle mixture.
- Defective Engine Coolant Thermal (ECT) switch.
- Detached or loose emission control system wiring harness connectors.
- Defective Engine Control Module (ECM).
- Defective micro-switches (idle and WOT).

5. Check the preceding switches and sensors, then replace any that require it. Retest the system.

6. After ensuring the CHECK ENGINE light flashes when it should, turn the cancel switch off.

7. Turn the engine **OFF**.

ELECTRONIC ENGINE CONTROLS

Engine Control Module (ECM)

OPERATION

▶ **See Figures 33, 34, 35 and 36**

Carbureted Models

▶ **See Figure 37**

The Engine Control Module (ECM) controls many engine systems, such as the fuel cut system, idle-up system, bowl vent system, EGR system and the secondary throttle valve system, as well as the feedback carburetor sys-

Components

The testing of the individual feedback carburetor system sensors and switches are covered later in this section, under Electronic Engine Controls.

REMOVAL & INSTALLATION

The removal and installation of the individual feedback carburetor system sensors and switches are covered later in this section, under Electronic Engine Controls. For ignition coil removal, refer to Section 2 of this manual.

Emission Warning Lamps

The CHECK ENGINE light automatically comes on at the 50,000 mile (80,000km), 80,000 mile (128,000km) and 100,000 mile (160,000km) marks.

RESETTING

The lamp reset switch is located on the left side of the dashboard, mounted on the steering column support or to the left speaker. The lamp can be reset by moving the switch upwards and then downwards. If the switch remains on after being reset, check the system.

tem. The ECM utilizes reference signals from various sensors and switches to determine the current condition of the engine, then decides on the proper response. The ECM is located under the glove compartment of the instrument panel.

TFI and MFI Models

▶ **See Figures 38 and 39**

The ECM is a precision unit consisting of one microcomputer chip, an Analog/Digital (A/D) converter, and an Input/Output (I/O) unit. The ECM is an essential component of the electronic control system, and controls all major systems, such as the fuel injectors, idle air control valve, throttle opener solenoid vacuum valve, etc. The ECM also performs on-board self-diagnostic, back-up, and fail safe functions.

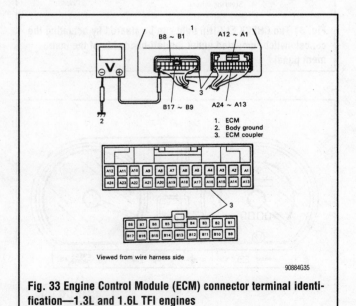

Fig. 33 Engine Control Module (ECM) connector terminal identification—1.3L and 1.6L TFI engines

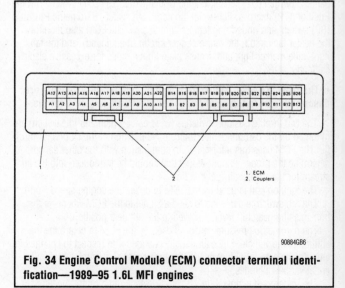

Fig. 34 Engine Control Module (ECM) connector terminal identification—1989-95 1.6L MFI engines

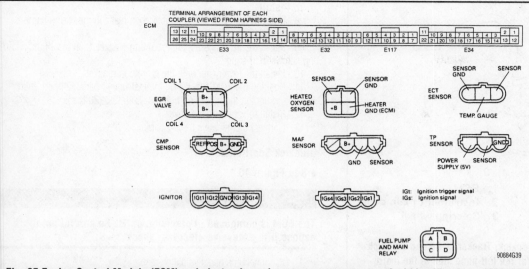

Fig. 35 Engine Control Module (ECM) and electronic engine sensor connector terminal identification—1996–98 1.6L MFI engines, and 1.8L engines equipped with the EVAP I system and/or manual transmission

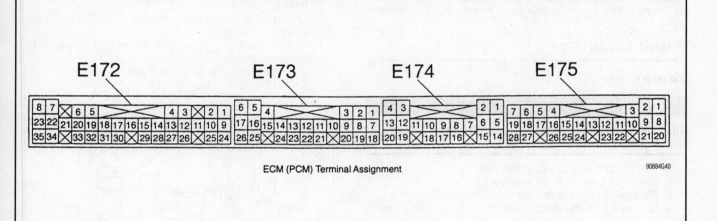

Fig. 36 Engine Control Module (ECM) connector terminal identification—1.8L engines equipped with the EVAP II system and/or the automatic transmission

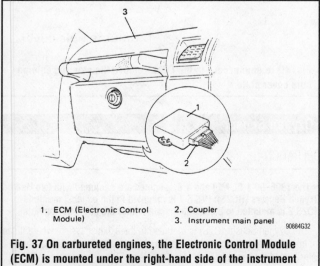

Fig. 37 On carbureted engines, the Electronic Control Module (ECM) is mounted under the right-hand side of the instrument panel, behind the glove compartment

1. ECM (Electronic Control Module)
2. Coupler
3. Instrument main panel

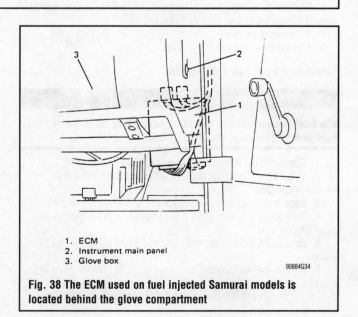

Fig. 38 The ECM used on fuel injected Samurai models is located behind the glove compartment

1. ECM
2. Instrument main panel
3. Glove box

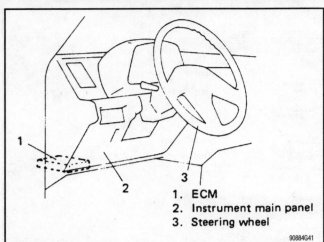

1. ECM
2. Instrument main panel
3. Steering wheel

90884G41

Fig. 39 The ECM used on Sidekick, Tracker, X-90 and Sidekick Sport models is located under the left-hand side of the instrument panel

The ECM used on Sidekick, Tracker, X-90 and Sidekick Sport models is mounted under the left-hand side of the instrument panel. The ECM used on Samurai models is mounted under the right-hand side of the instrument panel.

REMOVAL & INSTALLATION

Samurai Models

> **⁕⁕ WARNING**
>
> **The ECM is composed of precision parts. Be careful not to expose it to excessive electrical shock.**

1. Disconnect the negative battery cable.
2. Remove the glove box to gain access to the ECM.
3. Disengage the wiring harness connectors from the ECM.
4. Loosen the ECM retaining bolts, then remove the unit from the firewall.

To install:

5. Position the ECM on the inner firewall, then install and tighten the retaining bolts until secure.
6. Reattach the wiring harness connectors to the ECM. Ensure that the connector retaining latches are fully engaged.
7. Install the glove box.
8. Connect the negative battery cable.

Sidekick, Tracker and X-90 Models

> **⁕⁕ WARNING**
>
> **The ECM is composed of precision parts. Be careful not to expose it to excessive electrical shock.**

1. Disconnect the negative battery cable.
2. Remove the two screws from the left-hand front speaker cover on the instrument panel.
3. Remove the speaker mounting screws, and remove the speaker.
4. Remove the two bolts and the ECM bracket from the instrument panel support brace.
5. Remove the two screws, and separate the fuse panel from the ECM bracket.
6. Remove the two screws, and remove the ECM from the mounting bracket.
7. Disengage and label the wiring harness connectors from the ECM.

To install:

8. Position the ECM in the vehicle, then reattach the wiring harness connectors to it.
9. Install the ECM against the mounting bracket, then install the retaining screws until snug.
10. Install the fuse panel onto the mounting bracket.
11. Position the ECM bracket on the instrument panel support, then install and tighten the mounting bolts to 15 ft. lbs. (20 Nm).
12. Install the speaker and cover.
13. Connect the negative battery cable.

Sidekick Sport Models

▶ See Figure 40

> **⁕⁕ WARNING**
>
> **The ECM is composed of precision parts. Be careful not to expose it to excessive electrical shock.**

1. Disconnect the negative battery cable.
2. Remove the steering column hole cover plate.
3. Disengage the wiring harness connectors from the ECM.
4. Loosen the ECM retaining bolts, then remove the unit from the mounting bracket.

To install:

5. Position the ECM on the mounting bracket, then install and tighten the retaining bolts until secure.
6. Reattach the wiring harness connectors to the ECM. Ensure that the connector retaining latches are fully engaged.
7. Install the steering column hole cover plate.
8. Connect the negative battery cable.

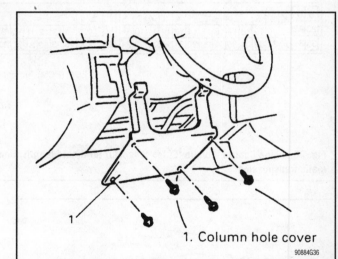

1. Column hole cover

90884G36

Fig. 40 To gain access to the ECM, remove the steering column hole cover plate

Oxygen Sensor

OPERATION

➡ **The 1996–98 1.6L MFI and 1.8L engines are equipped with two Heated Oxygen Sensors (HO2S): HO2S 1 is mounted in the exhaust manifold, HO2S 2 is mounted in the exhaust system after the catalytic converter.**

The Oxygen Sensor (O2S) is mounted in the exhaust system where it can monitor the oxygen content of the exhaust gases. Starting in 1991, electrically-heated oxygen sensors were used. Heated Oxygen Sensors (HO2S) reach operating temperature sooner, which allows earlier activation of the closed loop fuel control.

The O2S has the ability to produce a low voltage signal that feeds the information on the engine's exhaust content to the Engine Control Module (ECM). The O2S is constructed from a material (zirconium/platinum) that conducts electricity under certain conditions. At operating temperature (600°F/315°C), the element becomes a semiconductor. A platinum coating on the outer surface of the element stimulates further combustion of the exhaust gases right at the surface, which keeps sensor heated to the proper temperature. The O2S is constructed with an inner cavity, which is filled with atmospheric (reference) air. The atmosphere is composed of approximately 21% oxygen. In this electrical circuit, the inner cavity is the positive terminal. The outer surface of the sensor is exposed to the exhaust gas stream, and is the negative (ground) terminal. The oxygen concentration difference between the reference air and the exhaust gases produces a small voltage signal.

All oxygen sensors operate in the same manner. The voltage ranges differ from approximately 0.1 volt (high O2/lean mixture) to 0.9 volt (low O2/rich mixture). The voltages are monitored and used by the ECM to fine tune the air/fuel ratio mixture to achieve the ideal mixture desired. The ECM sends a reference signal of 450 millivolts. This reference serves to run the engine when it is in open loop mode of operation. When the air/fuel ratio is correct, the ECM will display 450 millivolts. When the engine is operating with a rich air/fuel mixture, there is a reduction of free oxygen in the exhaust stream and the oxygen voltage rises above the reference signal. When the engine is running lean, the voltage drops below the reference voltage due to excess oxygen in the exhaust gases. The O2S provides the feedback information for the closed loop operating mode of the fuel delivery system.

The oxygen sensor is located on the left-hand side of the engine, mounted in the upper side of the exhaust manifold.

TESTING

1.3L Carbureted Engine

1. Perform a visual inspection of the connector to ensure that it is properly connected and all terminals are straight, tight and free from corrosion or damage.
2. Start the engine and allow it to reach normal operating temperature.
3. Detach the oxygen sensor connector from the wiring harness.
4. Set a Digital Volt-Ohmmeter (DVOM) to the voltmeter setting, then attach the positive lead to the oxygen sensor terminal and the ground lead to a good engine ground. Be sure to use a digital voltmeter, otherwise an inaccurate reading may occur.

✳✳ WARNING

Never apply voltage to the oxygen sensor, otherwise it may be damaged. Also, never connect an ohmmeter (or a DVOM set on the ohm function) to the oxygen sensor; it will damage the sensor.

5. Run the engine at 1500–2000 rpm and turn the wide open microswitch OFF by moving the lever with your finger. Measure the voltage of the oxygen sensor with the DVOM; the value should be approximately 0.8 volt.
6. Run the engine between 1000–1500 rpm and disconnect the Mixture Control Valve (MCV) solenoid vacuum hose from the intake manifold. Check the voltage of the oxygen sensor again, and ensure that it is below 0.2 volt.
7. If the oxygen sensor did not function as noted, replace it with a new one.
8. When done inspecting the oxygen sensor, reconnect the MCV solenoid vacuum hose to the intake manifold.

1.3L and 1.6L TFI Engines

Before performing the oxygen sensor test procedures, ensure that the following items are in good working order:
• The air cleaner is not clogged.
• There are no vacuum leaks.

• The spark plugs are in good condition.
• The spark plug wires are in good condition.
• The distributor cap and rotor are in good condition.
• The ignition timing is correct.
• Engine compression is satisfactory.

If a Diagnostic Trouble Code (DTC) No. 13 and another code are indicated together, the latter code takes priority over Code No. 13. Therefore, check and correct any other DTC components indicated by the ECM first, then perform the following tests.

PERFORMANCE TEST

✳✳ CAUTION

When performing this procedure, be sure to keep out of the way of moving or hot engine components. Refrain from wearing loose clothing.

1. Perform a visual inspection of the connector to ensure that it is properly connected and all terminals are straight, tight and free from corrosion or damage.
2. Start the engine and allow the engine to reach normal operating temperature.
3. Run the engine at 2000 rpm.
4. Detach the wiring harness connector from the O2 sensor.
5. Measure the voltage between the terminal on the sensor and a good ground (a metal part of the engine). The sensor voltage should fluctuate between 0–900 millivolts.
   a. If the voltage does not fluctuate, or reads 0 millivolts, replace the O2 sensor.
   b. If the voltage does not fluctuate between 0–450 millivolts, skip to the next step.
6. Observe the voltmeter and remove the MAP sensor vacuum line. The O2 sensor voltage should jump to 900 millivolts.
   a. If the voltage does not fluctuate between 0–450 millivolts, or jump to 900 millivolts, replace the O2 sensor.
   b. If the voltage increases to 900 millivolts, the O2 sensor is functioning properly.

HEATING ELEMENT TEST

➡**This test only applies to 1991 and later models; earlier models do not utilize an electrically-heated oxygen sensor.**

1. If the engine is warm, allow it to cool down.
2. Turn the ignition switch OFF.
3. Detach the wiring harness connector from the oxygen sensor.
4. Connect a Digital Volt-Ohmmeter (DVOM), set on the ohmmeter function, to the two heating element terminals of the oxygen sensor.
5. Measure the resistance of the heating circuit in the sensor. The resistance should be between 3.0–5.5 ohms at 68°F (20°C).
   a. If the ohm values are within specifications, the heating element if functioning properly.
   b. If the ohm readings are not within the specified range, replace the HO2 sensor with a new one.

1.6L MFI Engine

1. Perform a visual inspection of the connector to ensure that it is properly connected and all terminals are straight, tight and free from corrosion or damage.
2. Detach the wiring harness connector from the oxygen sensor, and check the resistance between terminals 1 and 4 of the sensor. Resistance should be between 10–15 ohms at 70°F (21°C). If the resistance is not within the specified range, replace the oxygen sensor with a new one.
3. If the resistance was within specification, check for battery (B+) between the wiring harness connector terminals 1 and 4 with the ignition switch ON. If battery positive voltage is not present at the connector, check oxygen sensor circuit continuity back to the ECM. If the circuits are good, the ECM may be defective.
4. Check the sensor voltage between terminal 2 and the sensor body

with the ignition switch **OFF**. Voltage should be between 350–500 milli-volts. If the voltage is not within specification, replace the sensor with a new one.

5. If the voltage was as specified, recheck the voltage after heating the engine to normal operating temperature. With the engine running at 1200 rpm, the sensor voltage should vary between 100–900 millivolts. If the voltage does not fluctuate, or is not within the specified range, replace the sensor with a new one.

6. If the voltage was within the specified range, check the oxygen sensor circuits back to the ECM. If the sensor and circuits are functional, the ECM is most likely defective.

1.8L Engine

▶ See Figure 41

1. Start the engine and allow it to warm up to normal operating temperature.
2. Run the engine at 2000 rpm for at least 2 minutes.
3. Turn the ignition switch **OFF**, then disengage the wiring harness connector from the oxygen sensor.
4. Connect a Digital Volt-Ohmmeter (DVOM), set on the voltmeter function, to terminals 1 and 2 of the oxygen sensor.
5. Start the engine and have an assistant repeatedly rev the engine while you observe the voltmeter. The oxygen sensor voltage should fluctuate from below 0.5 volt to above 0.5 volt.
6. If the oxygen sensor voltage never rises above 0.5 volt or falls below 0.5 volt, it is defective and should be replaced.
7. If the voltage does fluctuate between <0.5 volt and >0.5 volt, there is a defect in the wiring circuit. Inspect all connectors for a tight fit, the ECM for a malfunction, and the circuit for an open or poor connection.

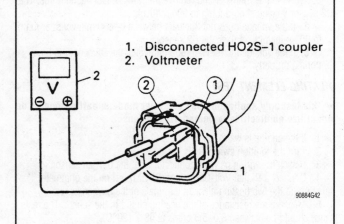

1. Disconnected HO2S–1 coupler
2. Voltmeter

Fig. 41 Use a DVOM set on the voltmeter function to measure the oxygen sensor output voltage

REMOVAL & INSTALLATION

▶ See Figures 42 and 43

➡The 1996–98 1.6L MFI and 1.8L engines are equipped with two heated oxygen sensors: HO2S 1, mounted in the exhaust manifold, and HO2S 2, mounted in the exhaust system after the catalytic converter.

The oxygen sensor uses a permanently attached pigtail and connector. The pigtail should not be removed from the sensor. Damage or removal of the pigtail or connector could affect proper operation of the oxygen sensor.

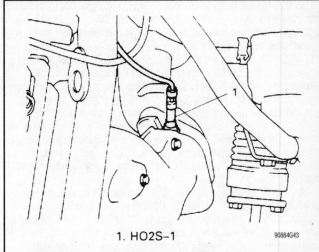

1. HO2S–1

Fig. 42 All models are equipped with an oxygen sensor mounted in the exhaust manifold . . .

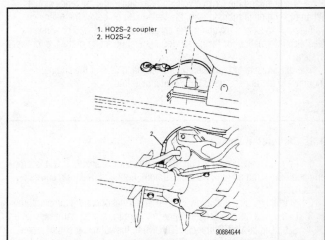

1. HO2S–2 coupler
2. HO2S–2

Fig. 43 . . . but the 1996–98 engines are equipped with a second oxygen sensor, mounted in the exhaust pipe after the catalytic converter

✳✳ WARNING

Take care when handling the oxygen sensor. The inline electrical connector and louvered end of the sensor must be kept free of grease, dirt or other contaminants. Also, avoid using cleaning solvents of any type on the sensor.

1. Run the engine until it has warmed up to normal operating temperature.
2. If removing HO2S 2, raise and securely support the front of the vehicle on jackstands. Apply the parking brake and block the rear wheels.

✳✳ CAUTION

Be cautious when working on and around the hot exhaust system. Painful burns will result if naked skin is exposed to the exhaust system pipes or manifold.

3. Disconnect the negative battery cable.
4. Detach the wiring harness connector from the sensor connector.

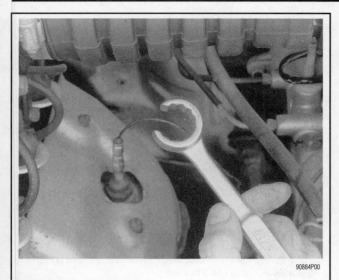

Using a flare nut wrench . . .

90884P00

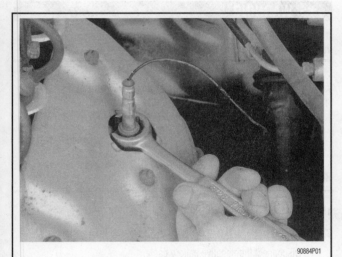

. . . loosen the oxygen sensor from the manifold or exhaust pipe

90884P01

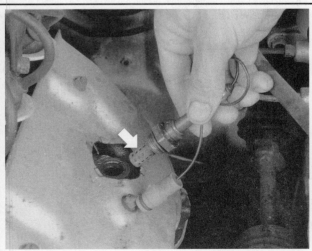

Remove the sensor, being careful not to damage the sensor tip

90884P02

✳✳ WARNING

The oxygen sensor may be difficult to remove when the engine temperature is below 120°F (48°C). Excessive force may damage the threads in the exhaust manifold or pipe.

5. Carefully remove the oxygen sensor from the exhaust manifold or pipe. If may be necessary to use a socket that is designed specifically for this purpose.

To install:

➡A special anti-seize compound is used on the oxygen sensor threads. The compound consists of a liquid graphite and glass beads. The graphite will burn away, but the glass beads will remain, making it easier to remove the sensor. New sensors will already have the compound applied to the threads. If a sensor is removed from an engine and is to be reinstalled, the threads must have an anti-seize compound applies prior to installation.

6. Thread the sensor into the exhaust manifold or pipe, and tighten it to 29–36 ft. lbs. (40–50 Nm).
7. Reattach the wiring harness to the sensor connector.
8. If necessary, lower the vehicle and remove the rear wheel blocks.
9. Connect the negative battery cable.
10. Start the engine and verify proper sensor operation.

Idle Air Control (IAC) Valve

➡Only the 1992–98 1.6L and 1.8L engines are equipped with an Idle Air Control (IAC) valve.

OPERATION

The purpose of the Idle Air Control (IAC) valve is to control engine idle speeds while preventing stalling due to changes in engine load. The IAC valve performs four important functions, namely:
- To maintain specified engine idle speed at all times.
- To improve engine starting.
- To compensate the air/fuel mixture ratio during deceleration (dash-pot effect).
- To improve driveability when the engine is at normal operating temperature.

The IAC assembly, mounted on the right side of the throttle body, controls bypass air around the throttle plate. By extending or retracting a conical valve, a controlled amount of air can move around the throttle plate. If engine speed (rpm) is too low, more air is diverted around the throttle plate to increase engine speed.

During idle, the proper position of the IAC valve is calculated by the ECM based on battery voltage, coolant temperature, engine load and engine speed. If the engine speed drops below a specified rate with the throttle plate closed, the ECM will then calculate a new valve position.

On 1.6L engines, four different possible designs of the IAC conical valve may be used on these engines. The first design utilizes a single taper shape, while the second design uses a dual taper shape. The third design uses a blunt-tipped valve, whereas the fourth design uses a rotating shutter. Care should be taken to ensure use of the proper design when service replacement is necessary.

TESTING

1992–98 1.6L Engines

TFI MODELS

1. Perform a visual inspection of the valve connector to ensure it is properly engaged. Inspect the connector to ensure there are no bent, corroded, loose or damaged terminals.
2. Detach the wiring harness from the IAC valve connector.
3. Connect the positive lead of a Digital Volt-Ohmmeter (DVOM), set on

the voltmeter function, to the wiring harness connector terminal 2, and the negative lead to a good engine ground.

4. Turn the ignition switch **ON**, and measure the amount of voltage from terminal 2. The proper amount of voltage should be 8.5–9.5 volts. If the voltage measured at terminal 2 is not within the specified range, there is a malfunction in the IAC valve circuit or in the ECM.

5. Turn the ignition switch **OFF**.

6. Switch the DVOM to the ohmmeter setting, then connect the DVOM leads to terminals 1 and 2 of the IAC valve.

7. Measure the IAC valve resistance, which should be 11–14 ohms at 68°F (20°C). If the resistance is not within the specified range, replace the valve with a new one. If the resistance is within the specified range, the IAC valve is functioning properly.

MFI MODELS

1. Perform a visual inspection of the valve connector to ensure it is properly engaged. Inspect the connector to ensure there are no bent, corroded, loose or damaged terminals.

2. Detach the wiring harness from the IAC valve connector.

3. Connect the leads of a Digital Volt-Ohmmeter DVOM, switched to the ohmmeter setting, to terminals 1 and 2 of the IAC valve.

4. Measure the IAC valve resistance, which should be 11–14 ohms at 68°F (20°C). If the resistance is not within the specified range, replace the valve with a new one. If the resistance is within the specified range, the IAC valve is functioning properly.

5. If the resistance value was within the specified range, connect a fused jumper wire between IAC valve terminal 2 to the positive battery terminal, and another jumper wire between terminal 1 and a good engine ground. With both jumper wires connected, air should be able to pass through the intake hose at the top of the valve. If air does not pass freely, the valve is defective.

6. If the valve is functional, check the IAC valve circuits back to the ECM for continuity.

7. If the IAC valve circuit checks out to be fine, the ECM may be defective.

1.8L Engine

▶ See Figure 44

1. Attach a tachometer to the engine, according to the manufacturer's instructions.

2. Start the engine and allow it to reach normal operating temperature.

3. Turn the ignition switch **OFF**.

4. Remove any component necessary to gain access to the ECM.

5. Detach ECM E33–24 terminal from the ECM connector.

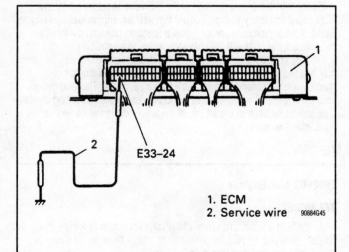

1. ECM
2. Service wire

Fig. 44 With the ignition switch turned OFF, use a jumper wire to ground ECM terminal E33–24

6. Start the engine and check the engine idle speed.

7. With the ignition switch **ON**, reattach E33–24 terminal to the ECM connector.

8. With the ignition switch **OFF**, use a jumper wire to ground E33–24 terminal of the ECM connector to a good chassis ground.

9. Start the engine and recheck the engine idle speed. The idle speed should now be higher than the idle speed registered in Step 6.

   a. If the idle speed results are as described, the IAC valve and its circuit are in good condition.

   b. If the idle speed results were not as described, jump to the next step.

10. With the ignition switch **OFF**, detach the wiring harness connector from the IAC valve.

11. Use a Digital Volt-Ohmmeter (DVOM), switched to the ohmmeter setting, to measure the resistance between the two IAC valve terminals. The IAC valve resistance should be 11–14 at 68°F (20°C).

   a. If the resistance is within the specified range, proceed to the next step.

   b. If the IAC valve resistance was not within the specified range, replace the IAC valve with a new one.

12. With the IAC valve disconnected from the wiring harness, start the engine and observe the idle speed registered on the tachometer.

❊❊❊ WARNING

If the battery is connected to the wrong IAC valve terminals, the valve will be damaged beyond repair.

13. While the engine idles, attach a 12 volt DC battery to the two IAC valve terminals as shown in the accompanying illustration. Recheck the idle speed, which should now be higher than measured in Step 12.

   a. If the idle speed in Step 13 is higher than that of Step 12, inspect the IAC valve circuit for problems.

   b. If the idle speed in Step 12 is higher than that registered in Step 13, replace the IAC valve with a new one.

REMOVAL & INSTALLATION

1992–98 1.6L Engines

TFI MODELS

1. Disconnect the negative battery cable.

2. Disengage the wiring harness connector from the IAC valve.

3. Remove the EGR modulator from its mounting bracket.

4. Detach the fast idle valve hose from the IAC valve.

5. Drain the engine coolant into a large catch pan.

6. Remove the two clamps, then detach the two engine coolant hoses from the IAC valve.

7. Remove the IAC valve mounting bolts, then separate the valve from the throttle body.

To install:

8. Clean the IAC valve gasket mating surface, then install a new gasket.

9. Place the IAC valve assembly into position, then install and tighten the mounting screws to 44 inch lbs. (5 Nm).

10. Install the two engine coolant hoses and clamps to the IAC valve.

11. Reattach the fast idle valve hose to the IAC valve.

12. Attach the wiring harness connector to the valve.

13. Connect the negative battery cable.

14. Refill the cooling system with the proper amount and type of engine coolant.

15. Start the engine and verify proper IAC valve operation. Check for engine coolant leakage.

MFI MODELS

1. Disconnect the negative battery cable.

2. Drain the engine coolant into a large catch pan.

3. Remove the throttle cover mounting bolts, then remove the cover from the throttle body.

4. Remove the IAC valve air intake hose, then detach the wiring harness connector from the valve.

5. Disconnect the engine coolant hoses from the IAC valve.

6. Remove the mounting fasteners, then separate the IAC valve from the throttle body.

To install:

7. Clean the IAC valve gasket surfaces thoroughly, then install a new gasket on the IAC valve.

8. Position the valve on the throttle body, then install the mounting bolts. Tighten the bolts to 13.5–20.0 ft. lbs. (18–28 Nm).

9. Reattach the engine coolant hoses, the wiring harness connector and the air intake hose to the IAC valve.

10. Install the throttle cover, and secure it on the engine with the three retaining bolts.

11. Connect the negative battery cable.

12. Fill the engine cooling system.

13. Start the engine and inspect for coolant leaks. Ensure that the IAC valve functions properly.

1.8L Engine

1. Disconnect the negative battery cable.

2. Disengage the wiring harness connector from the valve.

3. Remove the mounting fasteners, then separate the IAC valve from the intake manifold.

To install:

4. Clean the IAC valve gasket surfaces thoroughly, then install a new gasket on the IAC valve.

5. Position the valve on the intake manifold, then install the mounting bolts.

6. Reattach the wiring harness connector to the IAC valve.

7. Connect the negative battery cable.

8. Start the engine and ensure that the IAC valve functions properly.

Idle Speed Control Solenoid (ISCS) Valve

➡ **Only the 1.3L TFI and 1989–91 1.6L engines are equipped with an Idle Speed Control Solenoid (ISCS) valve.**

OPERATION

The purpose of the Idle Speed Control Solenoid (ISCS) valve is to control engine idle speeds while preventing stalling due to changes in engine load. The ISCS valve performs four important functions, namely:

- To maintain specified engine idle speed at all times.
- To improve engine starting.
- To compensate the air/fuel mixture ratio during deceleration (dash-pot effect).
- To improve driveability when the engine is at normal operating temperature.

The ISCS valve assembly controls bypass air around the throttle plate. By closing or opening the bypass air passage, a controlled amount of air can move around the throttle plate. If engine speed (rpm) is too low, more air is diverted around the throttle plate to increase engine speed.

During idle, the proper cycle of the ISCS valve is calculated by the ECM based on engine condition. Engine condition is calculated by the ECM based upon incoming information (such as battery voltage, coolant temperature, engine load, engine speed, etc.) from numerous sensors. If the engine speed drops below a specified rate with the throttle plate closed, the ECM will then alter the frequency of the valve cycle.

TESTING

1.3L TFI and 1991 1.6L TFI Engines

♦ **See Figures 45 and 46**

1. Ensure the ignition switch is **OFF**, then detach the wiring harness connector from the valve.

2. Using a Digital Volt-Ohmmeter (DVOM), switched to the ohmmeter

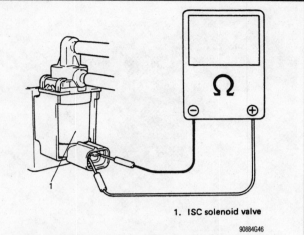

1. ISC solenoid valve

90884G46

Fig. 45 Use a DVOM to measure the resistance of the ISCS valve, and replace the valve if the resistance is not within the specified ranges

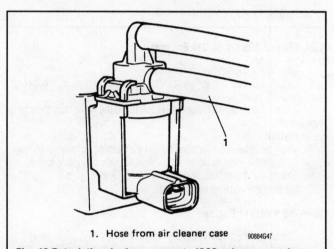

1. Hose from air cleaner case

90884G47

Fig. 46 Detach the air cleaner case-to-ISCS valve vacuum hose from the air cleaner, and ensure that no air is being drawn into the hose

setting, measure the resistance between the two valve terminals. The resistance should be between 30–33 ohms for 1.3L TFI engines, and 11–14 ohms for 1991 1.6L TFI engines at 68°F (20°C). If the value observed is not within this specified range, replace the valve with a new one.

3. Start the engine and allow it to reach normal operating temperature.

4. With the engine idling and the wiring harness still detached from the valve, disconnect the air cleaner housing-to-ISCS valve vacuum hose from the air cleaner housing. Ensure that no air is being drawn in the hose.

5. Connect a 12 volt DC battery to the ISCS valve terminals, then check that air is being drawn into the disconnected end of the air cleaner housing-to-ISCS valve vacuum hose.

6. If the valve did not perform as described, replace it with a new one.

1989–90 1.6L TFI Engines

1. Ensure the ignition switch is **OFF**, then detach the wiring harness connector from the valve.

2. Using a Digital Volt-Ohmmeter (DVOM), switched to the ohmmeter setting, measure the resistance between the two valve terminals. The resistance should be between 5.4–6.6 ohms at 68°F (20°C). If the value observed is not within this specified range, replace the valve with a new one.

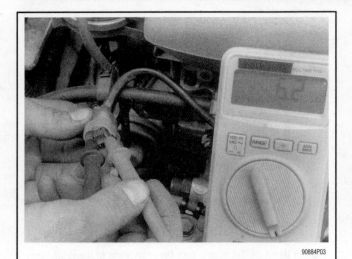

Use a DVOM to measure the resistance of the ISCS valve—
1989–90 1.6L engine shown

REMOVAL & INSTALLATION

1.3L TFI and 1991 1.6L TFI Engines

1. Disconnect the negative battery cable.
2. Detach and label the wiring harness connector and vacuum hoses from the ISCS valve.
3. Loosen the retaining fasteners, then remove the valve from the engine compartment.

To install:

4. Install the valve in position and tighten the retaining fasteners until snug.
5. Reattach the vacuum hoses and wiring harness connector to the valve. Ensure that the connector retaining latch is fully engaged.
6. Connect the negative battery cable.

1989–90 1.6L TFI Engines

1. Disconnect the negative battery cable.
2. Detach and label the wiring harness connector from the ISCS valve wiring.
3. Using a thin, metal prytool, such as a scratch awl, disengage the wiring terminals from the TP sensor/ISCS valve plastic connector.

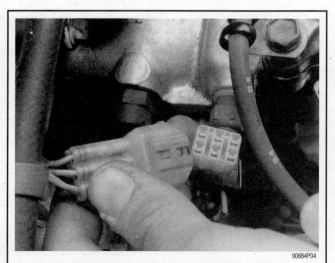

To remove the ISCS valve, disengage the wiring harness connector from the valve wiring . . .

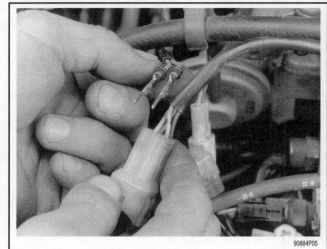

. . . then separate the two wire terminals from the ISCS valve/TP sensor connector

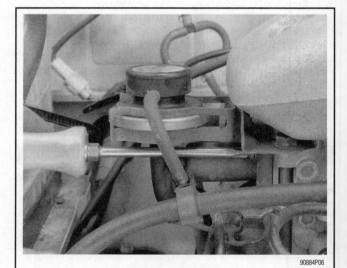

Loosen the ISCS valve mounting screws . . .

. . . then separate the valve from the throttle body assembly

4. Loosen the retaining fasteners, then remove the valve from the throttle body.

To install:

5. Along with a new gasket, install the valve on the throttle body, then tighten the retaining screws until secure.

6. Insert the wiring terminals in the TP sensor/ISCS valve connector until they are fully engaged. Give both wires a slight tug to ensure that they will not back out of the connector.

7. Reattach the wiring harness connector to the valve wiring. Ensure that the connector retaining latch is fully engaged.

8. Connect the negative battery cable.

Engine Coolant Temperature (ECT) Sensor/Switch

OPERATION

Carbureted Engine

The Engine Coolant Thermal (ECT) switch, often referred to as simply the thermal switch, provides temperature information to the ECM for driveability. The ECT switch opens and closes depending on the engine coolant temperature. The switch is closed when the engine is cold, and opens when the engine warms to above 116°F (46.5°C). The ECM monitors the ECT switch circuit, and knows the engine is warmed up when the circuit registers infinite resistance (the switch is open).

Fuel Injected Engines

The Engine Coolant Temperature (ECT) sensor is a thermistor (a resistor which changes its value based on the temperature it encounters) mounted in a coolant passage. Low coolant temperature produces a high resistance, while high temperature causes a low resistance.

The ECM supplies a 5 volt reference signal to the ECT through a resistor in the ECM, and measures the voltage. By measuring the voltage the ECM calculates the engine coolant temperature. Engine coolant temperature affects most systems that are controlled by the ECM.

A failure in the ECT sensor should set a Diagnostic Trouble Code (DTC). Remember that these DTC's indicate a failure somewhere in the ECT circuit, so proper use of the component testing will either lead to repairing a wiring problem, replacing the sensor and/or replacing the ECM to properly repair the fault.

The ECT used on the 1.6L TFI engine is located on the right-hand side of the engine, mounted in the intake manifold.

The ECT sensor used on 1.6L MFI engines is mounted in the intake manifold, next to the thermostat housing.

TESTING

Carbureted Engine

▶ See Figures 47 and 48

1. Drain the engine coolant into a large catch pan.
2. Remove the ECT switch from the intake manifold.
3. Position the switch and a thermometer in a container of cold water (86°F/30°C or below) on a stove.
4. Using an ohmmeter, measure the resistance between the two switch terminals. There should be continuity, because the switch should be closed.
5. Slowly heat the water in the container to above 116°F (46.5°C) and check the resistance once again. There should now be no continuity (infinite resistance).
6. If the switch functioned as described, it is good. Otherwise, replace it with a new one.
7. Install the switch and fill the engine cooling system.

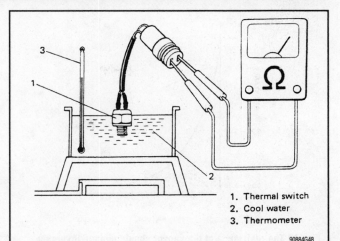

1. Thermal switch
2. Cool water
3. Thermometer

90884G48

Fig. 47 To test the ECT sensor/switch, position the sensor/switch in a container of cold water and note the resistance (for sensors) or continuity (for switches)

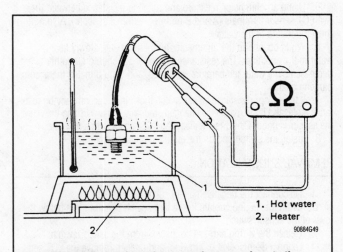

1. Hot water
2. Heater

90884G49

Fig. 48 Heat the container of water and once again note the resistance (sensor) or continuity (switch)—replace the sensor/switch if it does not perform as specified

Fuel Injected Engines

▶ See Figure 49

➡The ECT sensor may be tested by measuring the temperature-to-resistance values with an ohmmeter. A cold ECT sensor should have a high resistance value, whereas a warm sensor should exhibit a low resistance value.

Some models may be equipped with ECT sensors with three wire terminals. On these vehicles, terminals A and B are the signal terminals, and terminal C supplies voltage to the coolant temperature gauge in the instrument cluster.

1. Drain the engine coolant into a large catch pan.
2. Perform a visual inspection of the ECT sensor connector to ensure that it is properly engaged, and that there are no bent, corroded, loose or damaged terminals.
3. Remove the ECT sensor from the intake manifold.
4. Position the sensor and a thermometer in a container of cold water (86°F/30°C or below) on a stove.

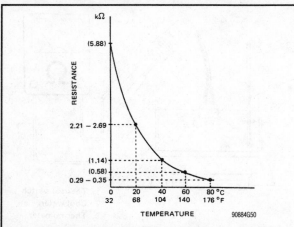

Fig. 49 The resistance of the sensor should change inversely from the temperature of the water—if the resistance of the ECT sensor does not approximately match the values shown in the chart, replace the sensor

5. Using an ohmmeter, measure and note the resistance between the two ECT sensor terminals (A and B on three-terminal sensors). Also note the temperature of the water.

6. While observing the ohmmeter and thermometer, slowly heat the water in the container. The resistance of the sensor should smoothly decrease as the water temperature increases, and should match the accompanying chart.

7. If the sensor resistance values match those in the accompanying resistance table, and if the resistance changed smoothly while warming the water, the sensor is good. Otherwise, replace the ECT sensor with a new one.

8. Install the switch and fill the engine cooling system.

REMOVAL & INSTALLATION

1. Disconnect the negative battery cable.

2. Drain the engine coolant into a large catch pan until it is below the level of the sensor/switch.

3. Detach the wiring harness connector from the sensor/switch.

4. Using a deep socket or crowfoot and ratchet, remove the ECT sensor/switch from the intake manifold.

To install:

5. If the old ECT sensor/switch is going to be reinstalled, clean the threads thoroughly.

6. Apply silicone sealant on, or wrap Teflon® sealing tape around, the sensor/switch threads.

7. Thread the sensor/switch into the intake manifold by hand until finger-tight, then tighten it to 9–12 ft. lbs. (12–17 Nm).

8. Reattach the wiring harness connector to the sensor/switch. Push the connector onto the terminal until an audible click is heard, then pull back gently to ensure that it is fully engaged.

9. Fill the engine cooling system.

10. Connect the negative battery cable.

11. Start the engine and inspect for coolant leaks. Ensure proper ECT sensor/switch operation.

Intake Air Temperature (IAT) and Air Temperature Sensors (ATS)

OPERATION

♦ See Figure 50

➡The Intake Air Temperature (IAT) sensor is not used on carbureted engines. Also, it is referred to as the Air Temperature Sensor (ATS) on 1.3L TFI engines.

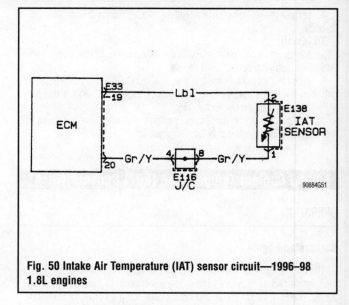

Fig. 50 Intake Air Temperature (IAT) sensor circuit—1996–98 1.8L engines

The Intake Air Temperature (IAT) sensor is a thermistor (a resistor which changes its value based on the temperature it encounters) mounted in the incoming air stream. Low incoming air temperature produces a high resistance, while high temperature causes a low resistance.

The ECM supplies a 5 volt reference signal to the IAT sensor through a resistor in the ECM, and measures the voltage. By measuring the voltage the ECM calculates the temperature of the incoming air. The ECM uses the IAT information to calculate air density, which affects air/fuel mixture. The IAT sensor is used to control air/fuel mixture, spark timing, and delays in the EGR system when the intake air is cold.

A failure in the IAT sensor should set a Diagnostic Trouble Code (DTC). Remember that these DTC's indicate a failure somewhere in the component's circuit, so a DTC does not necessarily mean that the sensor itself is bad. Once a DTC is set, the ECM will use an artificial default value for the IAT sensor and some engine performance will return.

The ATS used on 1.3L TFI engines is mounted in the intake manifold. The IAT sensor used on the 1.6L TFI engine is located on the right-hand side of the engine, mounted in the intake manifold below the throttle body. The IAT sensor used on 1.6L and 1.8L MFI engines is mounted in the backside of the air cleaner housing.

TESTING

♦ See Figures 51 and 52

➡The IAT sensor/ATS may be tested by measuring the temperature-to-resistance values with an ohmmeter. A cold sensor should have a high resistance value, whereas a warm sensor should exhibit a low resistance value.

1. Perform a visual inspection of the sensor connector to ensure that it is properly engaged, and that there are no bent, corroded, loose or damaged terminals.

2. Remove the sensor from the intake manifold (TFI engines) or from the air cleaner housing (MFI engines).

3. As shown in the accompanying illustration, position the sensor and a thermometer in a container of cold water on a stove.

4. Using an ohmmeter, measure and note the resistance between the two sensor terminals. Also note the temperature of the water.

5. While observing the ohmmeter and thermometer, slowly heat the water in the container. The resistance of the sensor should smoothly decrease as the water temperature increases, and should match the accompanying chart.

6. If the sensor resistance values match those in the accompanying resistance table, and if the resistance changed smoothly while warming the water, the sensor is good. Otherwise, replace the sensor with a new one.

7. Install the sensor.

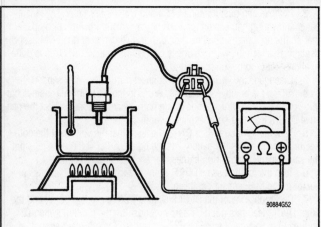

Fig. 51 Situate the IAT/ATS sensor so that the temperature probe is positioned in a container of cold water, then measure the resistance of the sensor

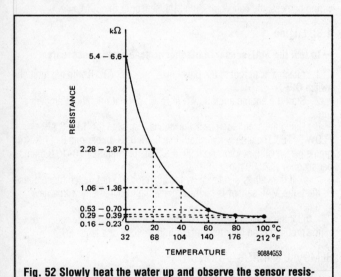

Fig. 52 Slowly heat the water up and observe the sensor resistance—the sensor resistance should match the values provided

REMOVAL & INSTALLATION

1.3L and 1.6L TFI Engines

1. Disconnect the negative battery cable.
2. Detach the wiring harness connector from the sensor.
3. Remove the sensor from the intake manifold.

To install:
4. If the old sensor is going to be reinstalled, clean the sensor threads thoroughly.
5. Apply silicone sealant on, or wrap Teflon® sealing tape around, the sensor threads.
6. Thread the sensor into the intake manifold by hand until finger-tight, then tighten the sensor to 9–12 ft. lbs. (12–17 Nm).
7. Reattach the wiring harness connector to the sensor.
8. Connect the negative battery cable.
9. Start the engine and ensure proper sensor operation.

1.6L MFI and 1.8L Engines

1. Disconnect the negative battery cable.
2. Detach the wiring harness connector from the sensor.
3. Remove the IAT sensor from the air cleaner housing.

To install:
4. Insert the sensor into the air cleaner housing.
5. Reattach the wiring harness connector to the sensor.
6. Connect the negative battery cable.
7. Start the engine and ensure proper IAT sensor operation.

Mass Airflow (MAF) Sensor

OPERATION

▶ **See Figures 53, 54 and 55**

➡ **Only the 1.6L MFI and 1.8L engines use Mass Airflow (MAF) sensors.**

The Mass Airflow (MAF) sensor consists of a heat resistor, a metering duct, a straightening net and a control circuit.

The MAF sensor detects the amount of airflow through the throttle body, and sends a reference signal to the ECM. The ECM utilizes this information to help manage the engine.

The MAF sensor is a thermal control type and includes a heat resistor and a control circuit. The heat resistor is cooled by the incoming air stream entering the throttle body opening. The control circuit manages the electri-

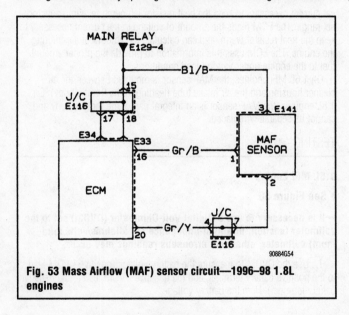

Fig. 53 Mass Airflow (MAF) sensor circuit—1996–98 1.8L engines

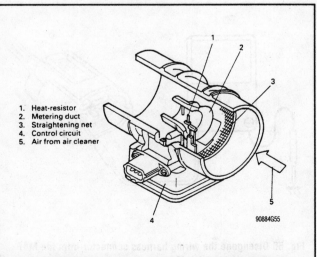

1. Heat-resistor
2. Metering duct
3. Straightening net
4. Control circuit
5. Air from air cleaner

Fig. 54 The MAF sensor used on 1.6L engines is mounted between the air intake tube and the air cleaner housing

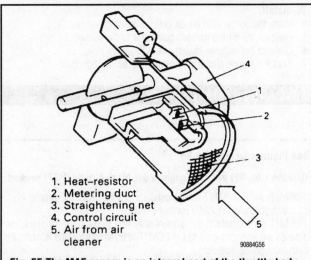

1. Heat–resistor
2. Metering duct
3. Straightening net
4. Control circuit
5. Air from air cleaner

90884G56

Fig. 55 The MAF sensor is an integral part of the throttle body on 1.8L engines

cal current necessary to keep the heat resistor temperature within a factory-set range. The ECM reads the amount of voltage in the current necessary to keep the heat resistor warm, and can calculate the amount of air entering the engine. The ECM uses this information to provide the proper amount fuel to the engine under varying load conditions.

On 1.6L MFI engines, the MAF sensor is mounted between the air cleaner housing and the air intake tube (leading to the throttle body). On 1.8L engines, the MAF sensor is an integral part of the throttle body and cannot be separately replaced.

TESTING

1.6L MFI Engine

▶ See Figure 56

➡ It is necessary to use a Digital Volt-Ohmmeter (DVOM) set to the voltmeter function, or a high-impedance (10 kilohms/volts minimum) voltmeter, otherwise erroneous readings may occur.

1. Use the DVOM to measure the battery voltage (positive DVOM lead to the positive battery terminal, and the negative DVOM lead to the negative battery terminal). Note the battery voltage.

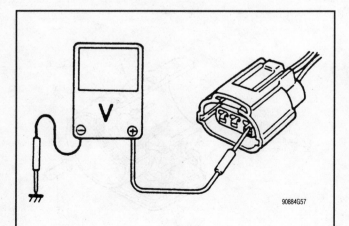

90884G57

Fig. 56 Disengage the wiring harness connector from the MAF sensor, then attach a DVOM (set to the voltmeter function) to the B+ terminal of the sensor connector and a good ground

2. Remove and position the ECM along with its bracket, relays, fuse panel and wiring harness on the floor of the vehicle. Position clean paper or mat on the floor first so that no hair, dirt or dust can enter the ECM accidentally. Reattach the wiring harness connectors to the ECM. This is done to allow access to the unit during testing.

3. Disengage the wiring harness connector from the MAF sensor.

4. Attach the positive lead of the DVOM to the B+ terminal (positive battery voltage) of the MAF sensor wiring harness connector. Connect the negative DVOM lead to a good engine ground.

5. Turn the ignition switch **ON** and ensure that the voltage at the connector is the same as the battery voltage noted earlier. If the voltage is not the same, inspect the wiring harness for an open or short circuit.

6. Turn the ignition switch **OFF**, then reattach the wiring harness connector to the MAF sensor connector.

7. Backprobe one of the DVOM leads to ECM terminal E32–9, and the other DVOM lead to a good chassis ground. Turn the ignition switch **ON** and read the voltage of terminal E32–9. The voltage observed should be 1.0–1.6 volts.

8. Start the engine and once again check the voltage at terminal E32–9. The voltage should be lower than 5 volts (exact specification is 1.7–2.0 volts) at idle and gradually rise as you increase engine speed (rpm).

9. If the voltage did not react as described, there is a problem in the wiring harness, the connectors, the MAF sensor or the ECM.

1.8L Engine

➡ To test the MAF sensor, a diagnostic scan tool is necessary.

1. Attach a scan tool to the Data Link Connector (DLC) with the ignition switch **OFF**.

2. Start the engine and allow it to reach normal operating temperature.

3. Using the scan tool, check the values displayed for "MASS AIR FLOW RATE." The airflow rate should be 0.20–0.53 lb. per minute (1.5–4.0 grams per second) at idle, and 0.66–1.32 lbs. per minute (5.0–10.0 grams per second) at 2,500 rpm.

   a. If the values displayed by the scan tool do not match those specified, the MAF sensor is faulty; replace the throttle body with a new one.

   b. If the values displayed by your scan tool match those specified, the problem is an intermittent fault in the circuit or a faulty ECM.

REMOVAL & INSTALLATION

1.6L MFI Engine

1. Disconnect the negative battery cable.
2. Disengage the wiring harness connector from the MAF sensor.
3. Remove the air cleaner upper housing retainers, then lift the housing and MAF sensor up and out of the engine compartment.
4. Separate the MAF sensor from the upper air cleaner housing.

❊❊ WARNING

To avoid accidental MAF sensor damage, do not attempt to disassemble the MAF sensor. Also, do not expose the MAF sensor to electrical shocks, and do not insert fingers or any other object into the MAF sensor hole. Do not touch the air-straightening net.

To install:

5. Inspect the MAF sensor seal for deterioration or damage.
6. Install the MAF sensor in the air cleaner upper housing, ensuring that the seal is properly engaged.
7. Install the upper housing and MAF sensor onto the lower air cleaner housing, then tighten the retainers securely.
8. Reattach the wiring harness connector to the MAF sensor.
9. Conenct the negative battery cable.
10. Start the engine and ensure MAF sensor operation.

1.8L Engine

The MAF sensor is an integral part of the throttle body and cannot be separated from it. For throttle body removal and installation procedures, refer to Section 5.

Manifold Absolute Pressure (MAP) and Manifold Differential Pressure (MDP) Sensors

OPERATION

◗ See Figures 57 and 58

➡Only TFI-equipped engines use a MAP sensor for fuel delivery control. The MFI-equipped engines use a MDP sensor for EGR system diagnostics.

The Manifold Absolute Pressure (MAP) sensor measures and responds to the changes in the intake manifold pressure. As manifold pressure changes, the electrical resistance of the sensor also changes. By monitoring the sensor's output voltage, the ECM can calculate the engine load condition, and determine the engine's fuel requirements. When there is high

pressure (low vacuum) in the intake manifold, the engine requires more fuel. When there is low pressure (high vacuum) in the intake manifold, the engine requires less fuel. High intake manifold pressure produces a high voltage MAP sensor signal, whereas low intake manifold pressure produces a low voltage MAP sensor signal.

The MAP sensor is also used to measure barometric pressure under certain conditions, which allows the ECM to automatically adjust for different altitudes.

➡The 1996–98 1.6L MFI and 1.8L engines use a Manifold Differential Pressure (MDP) sensor, which functions exactly like the MAP sensor. However, the ECM uses the MDP sensor information only for EGR system self-diagnostics.

The MAP/MDP sensor is mounted on the right-hand side of the firewall.

TESTING

1.3L TFI, 1.6L MFI and 1.8L Engines

◗ See Figures 59, 60 and 61

➡The 1.3L TFI engine uses a MAP sensor, whereas the 1.6L and 1.8L MFI engines utilize a MDP sensor.

1. Detach the vacuum hose from the sensor, then disengage the wiring harness connector from the MAP/MDP sensor.

2. Remove the MAP/MDP sensor retaining bolts, then lift the sensor out of the engine compartment.

3. Arrange 3 new 1.5 volt batteries in series (positive-to-negative, positive-to-negative, etc.). Using jumper wires connect the battery assembly negative end to the ground terminal of the sensor, and the positive end of the battery assembly to the Vin terminal.

4. Using a Digital Volt-Ohmmeter (DVOM), switched to the voltmeter function, measure the voltage between the ground terminal and the VOUT terminal of the sensor. For this measurement, ensure that the negative DVOM lead is attached to the ground terminal, and the positive lead is connected to the VOUT terminal. Compare the voltage reading with the accompanying chart.

➡If unfamiliar with metric pressure measurements, divide the barometric pressure column numbers of the chart by 2.54 to calculate the applicable barometric pressure in inches of Mercury (in. Hg).

5. Connect a hand-held vacuum pump to the MAP/MDP sensor vacuum nipple. While observing the voltage of the sensor (as described in Step 4), slowly

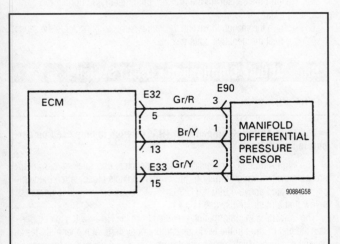

Fig. 57 Manifold Differential Pressure (MDP) sensor circuit— 1996–98 MFI engines

1. Output voltage
2. Reference voltage
3. Ground
4. Semi-conductor type pressure converting element
5. Filter
6. Intake manifold pressure (Vacuum)

Fig. 58 Cutaway view of the internal Manifold Absolute Pressure (MAP) sensor components

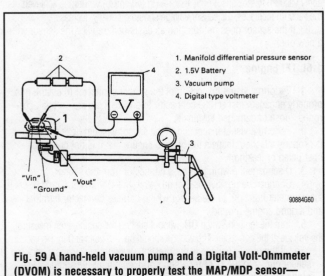

1. Manifold differential pressure sensor
2. 1.5V Battery
3. Vacuum pump
4. Digital type voltmeter

Fig. 59 A hand-held vacuum pump and a Digital Volt-Ohmmeter (DVOM) is necessary to properly test the MAP/MDP sensor— MFI engine shown

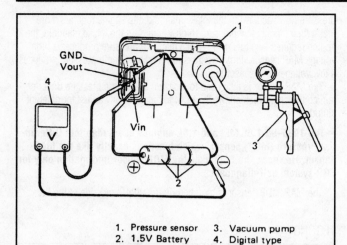

1. Pressure sensor
2. 1.5V Battery (4.5V in total)
3. Vacuum pump
4. Digital type voltmeter

90884G61

Fig. 60 Although different in appearance, the MAP sensor used on 1.3L TFI engines is tested the same as on MFI engines

Applied vacuum valve (mmHg)	Manifold differential pressure sensor output voltage (V)
200	2.40 – 4.40
250	2.13 – 4.13
300	1.86 – 3.86
350	1.59 – 3.59
400	1.32 – 3.32

90884CM1

Fig. 61 Compare the voltage reading of the MAP sensor to this chart

apply vacuum to the sensor until 15.7 in. Hg (40 cmHg) vacuum is achieved. As the vacuum increases, the sensor voltage should gradually decrease.

6. If the sensor does not function as described, replace the sensor with a new one.

1.6L TFI Engine

1. Perform a visual inspection of the sensor connector to ensure it is properly engaged. Inspect the connector to ensure there are no bent, corroded, loose or damaged terminals.

2. Perform a visual inspection of the sensor vacuum hose to ensure it is properly attached. Inspect the hose to ensure that it is not cracked, obstructed or leaking.

3. Disengage the wiring harness connector from the sensor.

4. Connect the positive lead of a Digital Volt-Ohmmeter (DVOM), set to the voltmeter function, to the sensor wiring harness connector terminal 1 and a good engine ground.

5. Turn the ignition switch **ON**, without starting the engine, then measure the voltage at the connector. The voltage should be 4–5 volts at 0 in. Hg vacuum.

   a. If the proper voltage is not present, working backwards, check the sensor circuit to the ECM for a short or open circuit. Be sure to back-probe the circuit connectors; NEVER pierce the wiring.

   b. If the voltage is present, proceed to the next step.

6. Turn the ignition switch **OFF**.

7. Reattach the wiring harness connector to the MAP sensor.

8. Connect the positive lead of the Digital Volt-Ohmmeter (DVOM), set to the voltmeter function, to the sensor wiring harness connector terminal 2 and a good engine ground.

9. Connect a hand-held vacuum pump to the vacuum port of the MAP sensor.

10. Turn the ignition switch **ON**.

11. Using the vacuum pump, apply 10 in. Hg of vacuum slowly to the sensor and observe the DVOM. The sensor's resistance should decrease smoothly to 1.32–1.50 volts.

   a. If the reading is within the specified range, the MAP sensor is good.

   b. If the values observed are not within the specified range, or do not change smoothly, the MAP sensor is faulty. Replace the sensor with a new one.

REMOVAL & INSTALLATION

1. Disconnect the negative battery cable.
2. Detach the vacuum hose from the sensor.
3. Disengage the wiring harness connector from the sensor.
4. Loosen the mounting bolt(s), and remove the sensor from the firewall.

To install:

5. Position the sensor on the firewall, then install and tighten the mounting bolt(s) securely.

6. Reattach the vacuum hose and the wiring harness connector to the sensor.

7. Connect the negative battery cable.

High Altitude Compensator (HAC) Switch

OPERATION

➡**The High Altitude Compensator (HAC) switch is only used on carbureted models.**

The High Altitude Compensator (HAC) switch is essentially a barometric pressure switch, which turns on (the switch contacts close) when the vehicle is operated above 4,000 ft. (1220m). Whenever the vehicle is operated below that altitude, the switch is open.

The ECM uses the information provided from the HAC switch to compensate the fuel mixture in the feedback carburetor system. At higher altitudes air density declines, which means that the amount of fuel needed by the vehicle drops because there is less air to mix with the fuel. If the feedback carburetor system does not compensate for a difference in altitude, eventually the air/fuel mixture will become too rich for the engine to operate efficiently.

The HAC switch is mounted on the right-hand side of the firewall, in the engine compartment. It is small (about 2.5 inches from top to bottom), cylindrical in shape and secured to the firewall by two mounting bolts.

TESTING

1. Detach the wiring harness connector from the HAC switch, then attach an ohmmeter to the terminals of the switch.

2. Check the resistance of the switch.

   a. If your altitude is 4,000 ft. (1220m) or higher, the switch should show 0 ohms (the switch contacts are closed).

   b. If the altitude is below 4,000 ft. (1220m), the switch should show infinite resistance (no continuity).

3. If the switch resistance values were not as specified, or if the switch exhibited any ohm value other than 0 or infinity, the switch is defective and should be replaced with a new one.

REMOVAL & INSTALLATION

1. Disconnect the negative battery cable.
2. Disengage the wiring harness connector from the sensor.
3. Loosen the mounting bolts, and remove the sensor from the firewall.

To install:

4. Position the sensor on the firewall, then install and tighten the mounting bolt(s) securely.

5. Reattach the wiring harness connector to the sensor.

6. Connect the negative battery cable.

Thermal Engine Room Switch

OPERATION

➡The thermal engine room switch, essentially an underhood temperature switch, is only used on carbureted models as part of the feedback carburetor system.

The thermal engine room switch provides temperature information to the ECM for driveability. The switch opens and closes depending on the engine compartment temperature. The switch is closed when the air in the engine compartment is cold, and opens when the engine compartment air warms to above 67°F (19.5°C). The ECM monitors the switch circuit, and knows the underhood air is warmed up when the circuit registers infinite resistance (the switch is open).

The switch is mounted on the right-hand side of the firewall, just above the HAC switch.

TESTING

1. Detach the wiring harness connector from the switch, then attach an ohmmeter to the terminals of the switch.

2. Check the resistance of the switch.

   a. If the ambient air temperature is below 44°F (7°C), the switch should show 0 ohms (the switch contacts are closed).

   b. If the air temperature is above 67°F (19.5°C), the switch should show infinite resistance (no continuity).

➡To simulate colder temperatures during warm weather, place the sensor in the freezer for a few minutes, then measure the sensor resistance.

3. If the switch resistance values were not as specified, or if the switch exhibited any ohm value other than 0 or infinity, the switch is defective and should be replaced with a new one.

REMOVAL & INSTALLATION

1. Disconnect the negative battery cable.

2. Disengage the wiring harness connector from the switch.

3. Loosen the mounting bolts, and remove the switch from the firewall.

To install:

4. Position the switch on the firewall, then install and tighten the mounting bolt(s) securely.

5. Reattach the wiring harness connector to the switch.

6. Connect the negative battery cable.

Throttle Position Sensor (TPS)

OPERATION

▸ See Figure 62

➡The Throttle Position (TP) sensor is used only on fuel injected engines; carbureted engines utilize throttle position micro-switches, which is described later in this section.

The Throttle Position Sensor (TPS) consists of a contact switch (for idle position) and a potentiometer mounted on the throttle body, and is connected to the throttle valve shaft. The TPS's only function is to convey the positioning of the throttle valve to the ECM. Throttle position when the engine is idling is detected by the contact switch, which turns ON only during idle. An opening of the throttle valve beyond idle is detected by the

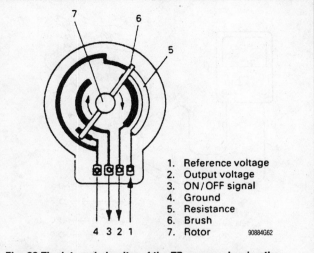

1. Reference voltage
2. Output voltage
3. ON/OFF signal
4. Ground
5. Resistance
6. Brush
7. Rotor

90884G62

Fig. 62 The internal circuitry of the TP sensor, showing the rotating contact arms

potentiometer. The ECM supplies a 5 volt reference signal to the TPS, and as the sensor brush moves across the print resistance according to the position of the throttle valve position, the return voltage to the ECM varies accordingly. By monitoring the return voltage, the ECM can detect the exact position of the throttle valve at any point in time.

TPS information is used by the ECM to calculate fuel delivery for starting, acceleration and deceleration, as well as an input for idle speed control. TPS data is also used by the ECM for torque converter clutch control.

A broken or loose TPS may cause intermittent bursts of fuel from an injector, which may cause an unstable idle because the ECM detects the throttle is moving.

The TPS is mounted on the side of the throttle body.

TESTING

▸ See Figures 63, 64, 65 and 66

1. Disconnect the negative battery cable.

2. Detach the wiring harness connector from the TPS.

Resistance between C and D terminals (Idle switch)	When throttle lever-to-stop screw clearance is 0.3 mm (0.012 in.)	0 – 500 Ω
	When throttle lever-to-stop screw clearance is 0.5 mm (0.020 in.)	∞ (Infinity)
Resistance between A and D terminals	———	3.5 – 6.5 kΩ
Resistance between B and D terminals	When throttle valve is at idle position	0.3 – 2 kΩ
	When throttle valve is fully open	2 – 6.5 kΩ

NOTE:
• When checking resistance at idle position, apply –50 cmHg vacuum to throttle opener to move throttle valve to idle position.
• There should be more than 2 kΩ resistance difference between when throttle valve is at idle position and when it is fully open.

90884G63

Fig. 63 Throttle Position (TP) sensor test chart for TFI engines

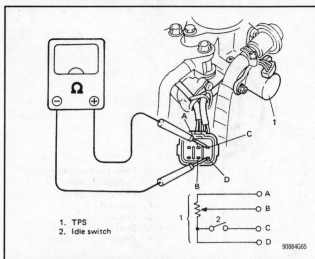

1. TPS
2. Idle switch

90884G65

Fig. 64 TP sensor connector terminal identification for TFI-equipped models

TERMINALS	CONDITION	RESISTANCE
Between A and B terminals (Idle switch)	When throttle lever-to-stop screw clearance is 0.5 mm (0.020 in.)	0 – 500 Ω
	When throttle lever-to-stop screw clearance is 0.8 mm (0.031 in.)	∞ (Infinity)
Between A and D terminals	—	3.5 – 6.5 kΩ
Between A and C terminals	Throttle valve is at idle position	0.3 – 2.0 kΩ
	Throttle valve is fully opened	2.0 – 6.5 kΩ

NOTE:
There should be more than 2 kΩ resistance difference between when throttle valve is at idle position and when it is fully open.

90884G66

Fig. 65 Throttle Position (TP) sensor inspection chart for MFI engines

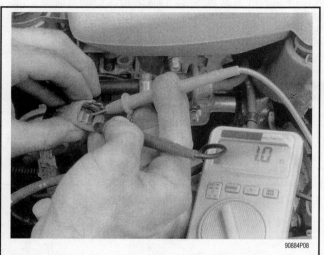

On TFI engines, first check the resistance when the lever-to-stop screw clearance is 0.012 in. (0.3mm) . . .

90884P08

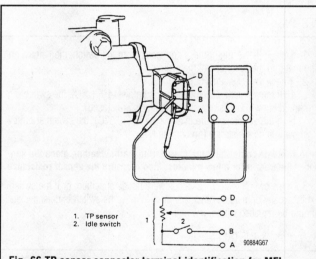

1. TP sensor
2. Idle switch

90884G67

Fig. 66 TP sensor connector terminal identification for MFI-equipped models

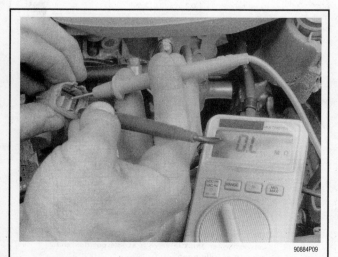

. . . then measure the TP sensor resistance when the clearance is 0.020 in. (0.5mm)

90884P09

3. Using an ohmmeter, measure the resistance between the terminals of the TPS according to the accompanying test chart.

4. If the resistance values observed during the inspection do not match those presented in the test chart, adjust the installed angle of the TPS. Recheck the sensor after adjusting its position.

5. If the resistance values are still not satisfactory, replace the TPS with a new one.

ADJUSTMENT

1.3L TFI Engine

▶ See Figures 67 and 68

1. Disconnect the negative battery cable.
2. Detach the wiring harness connector from the TPS.
3. Disconnect and label the throttle opener vacuum hose from the Vacuum Solenoid Valve (VSV), then attach a hand-held vacuum pump to the throttle opener. Apply 19.7 in. Hg (50 cmHg) vacuum to the throttle opener unit, which should move the throttle valve to the idle position.
4. Insert a 0.012 in. (0.3mm) thick feeler gauge between the throttle valve lever and the throttle stop screw.

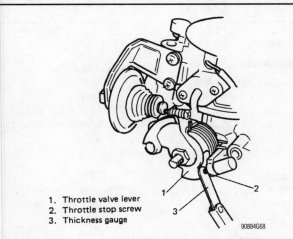

1. Throttle valve lever
2. Throttle stop screw
3. Thickness gauge

90884G68

Fig. 67 Insert a 0.012 in. (0.3mm) thick feeler gauge between the throttle stop screw and the throttle valve lever to properly adjust the TP sensor

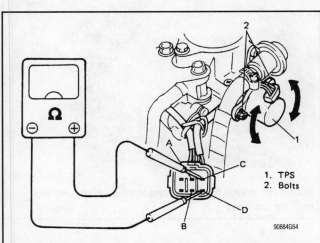

1. TPS
2. Bolts

90884G64

Fig. 68 Slowly rotate the TP sensor until the ohmmeter changes from infinite resistance to 0 ohms (continuity), then tighten the TP sensor screws

5. Loosen the TPS mounting bolts, then attach an ohmmeter to TPS terminals C and D.

6. Rotate the TPS fully clockwise, then turn it slowly counterclockwise until the ohmmeter changes from infinite resistance to 0 ohms (continuity).

7. Tighten the TPS mounting bolts to 31 inch lbs. (3.5 Nm).

8. Insert a 0.016 in. (0.4mm) thick feeler gauge between the throttle valve lever and the throttle stop screw, and recheck the sensor resistance between terminals C and D. Resistance should be infinite.

9. Insert a 0.8 in. (0.2mm) thick feeler gauge between the throttle valve lever and the throttle stop screw, and recheck the sensor resistance between terminals C and D. Resistance should be 0–500 ohms.

10. If the TPS resistance values are not as specified in Steps 8 and 9, the sensor is incorrectly adjusted; perform the adjustment procedure again.

✳✳ WARNING

The throttle stop screw is precisely adjusted at the factory—never remove or adjust it.

11. Reconnect all wiring harness connectors and vacuum hoses after the test is complete.

1.6L TFI Engine

1. Disconnect the negative battery cable.

2. Detach the wiring harness connector from the TPS.

3. Disconnect and label the throttle opener vacuum hose from the Vacuum Solenoid Valve (VSV), then attach a hand-held vacuum pump to the throttle opener. Apply 19.7 in. Hg (50 cmHg) vacuum to the throttle opener unit, which should move the throttle valve to the idle position.

4. Insert a 0.016 in. (0.4mm) thick feeler gauge between the throttle valve lever and the throttle stop screw.

5. Loosen the TPS mounting bolts, then attach an ohmmeter to TPS terminals C and D.

6. Rotate the TPS fully clockwise, then turn it slowly counterclockwise until the ohmmeter changes from infinite resistance to 0 ohms (continuity).

7. Tighten the TPS mounting bolts to 31 inch lbs. (3.5 Nm).

8. Insert a 0.020 in. (0.5mm) thick feeler gauge between the throttle valve lever and the throttle stop screw, and recheck the sensor resistance between terminals C and D. Resistance should be infinite.

9. Insert a 0.012 in. (0.3mm) thick feeler gauge between the throttle valve lever and the throttle stop screw, and recheck the sensor resistance between terminals C and D. Resistance should be 0–500 ohms.

10. If the TPS resistance values are not as specified in Steps 8 and 9, the sensor is incorrectly adjusted; perform the adjustment procedure again.

✳✳ WARNING

The throttle stop screw is precisely adjusted at the factory—never remove or adjust it.

11. Reconnect all wiring harness connectors and vacuum hoses after the test is complete.

1.6L MFI Engine

▶ See Figure 69

1. Disconnect the negative battery cable.

2. Detach the wiring harness connector from the TPS.

3. Insert a 0.026 in. (0.65mm) thick feeler gauge between the throttle valve lever and the throttle stop screw.

4. Loosen the TPS mounting bolts, then attach an ohmmeter to TPS terminals A and B.

5. Rotate the TPS fully counterclockwise, then turn it slowly clockwise until the ohmmeter changes from continuity to no continuity (infinite resistance).

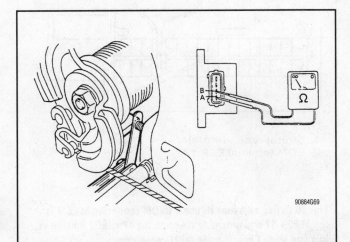

90884G69

Fig. 69 When adjusting the TP sensor, ensure that there is no continuity between terminals A and B when a 0.037 in. (0.8mm) feeler gauge is inserted between the throttle stop screw and lever

6. Tighten the TPS mounting bolts to 31 inch lbs. (3.5 Nm).

7. Insert a 0.037 in. (0.8mm) thick feeler gauge between the throttle valve lever and the throttle stop screw, and recheck the sensor resistance between terminals A and B. Resistance should be infinite.

8. Insert a 0.020 in. (0.5mm) thick feeler gauge between the throttle valve lever and the throttle stop screw, and recheck the sensor resistance between terminals A and B. The sensor should exhibit continuity.

9. If the TPS resistance values are not as specified in Steps 7 and 8, the sensor is incorrectly adjusted; perform the adjustment procedure again.

❋❋ WARNING

The throttle stop screw is precisely adjusted at the factory—never remove or adjust it.

10. Reconnect all wiring harness connectors and vacuum hoses after the test is complete.

1.8L Engine

▶ **See Figure 70**

1. Start the engine and allow it to reach normal operating temperature.

2. Ensure that the fast idle cam and cam follower lever are not in contact with each other.

3. Loosen the TPS mounting bolts.

4. Remove the ECM with the wiring harness attached to it. Position it on the floor of the vehicle.

5. Connect the positive lead of a Digital Volt-Ohmmeter (DVOM), switched to the voltmeter function, to ECM terminal E33-17, and the negative lead to a good chassis ground.

6. While you observe the DVOM, have an assistant slowly rotate the TPS clockwise and counterclockwise until a voltage of 0.35–0.65 volt (0.5 volt is preferred) is achieved.

7. Tighten the TPS mounting bolts to 22 inch lbs. (2.5 Nm).

8. Have your assistant open the throttle valve to the Wide Open Throttle (WOT) position. Observe the DVOM; the voltage should be 3.5–4.5 volts (4.0 volt is preferred).

9. Reinstall the ECM.

REMOVAL & INSTALLATION

TFI Engines

▶ **See Figures 71, 72 and 73**

1. Disconnect the negative battery cable.

2. Detach the wiring harness connector from the TPS.

3. Remove the TP sensor wire terminals from the harness plastic connector by using a thin, pointed tool to disengage the terminals' retaining latches. Pull the terminals out of the connector body.

4. Remove the mounting bolts, then pull the TPS off of the throttle body.

To install:

5. If necessary, clean the TPS-to-throttle body mating surface of all dirt, grime or oil.

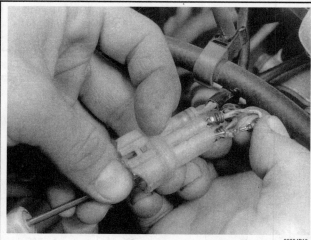

Use an awl or similar tool to disengage the wiring terminals from the connector

90884P10

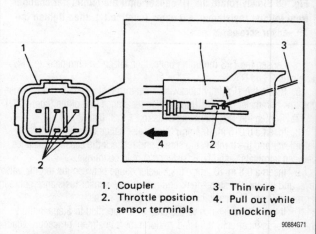

1. Digital type voltmeter
2. ECM terminal E33-17

90884G70

Fig. 70 During adjustment, use a DVOM connected to ECM terminal E33–17 and ground to measure the TP sensor voltage at idle and Wide Open Throttle (WOT) positions

1. Coupler
2. Throttle position sensor terminals
3. Thin wire
4. Pull out while unlocking

90884G71

Fig. 71 The thin metal tool is used to depress the plastic retaining tab so that the terminal can be withdrawn from connector body

Loosen the two TP sensor mounting bolts . . .

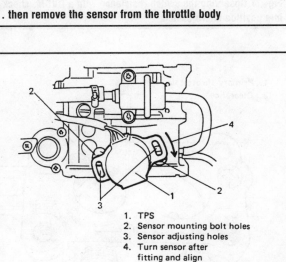

. . . then remove the sensor from the throttle body

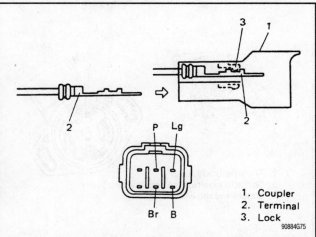

Fig. 73 Re-engage the wiring terminals in the plastic connector housing—give each wire a slight tug to ensure that they will not back out of the connector

6. Position the TPS on the throttle body so that the mounting bolt slots are slightly askew from the bolt holes in the throttle body (as shown in the illustration). After the TPS is flush against the throttle body, rotate the sensor clockwise until the sensor slots are aligned with the throttle body holes. Install and hand tighten the sensor mounting bolts.

7. Insert the four TPS wire terminals into the plastic connector until they are properly engaged. Give each wire a slight tug to ensure that they will not come out of the connector.

8. Adjust the TPS angle, as described under TPS testing.

9. Tighten the sensor mounting bolts to 31 inch lbs. (3.5 Nm).

10. Reconnect the wiring harness connector to the TPS.

11. Conenct the negative battery cable.

MFI Engines

▶ See Figures 74 and 75

1. Disconnect the negative battery cable.

2. Detach the wiring harness connector from the TPS.

3. Remove the mounting bolts, then pull the TPS off of the throttle body.

To install:

4. If necessary, clean the TPS-to-throttle body mating surface of all dirt, grime or oil.

1. TPS
2. Sensor mounting bolt holes
3. Sensor adjusting holes
4. Turn sensor after fitting and align holes

Fig. 72 When installing the TP sensor, slide onto the throttle body so that the mounting slots are slightly askew from the bolts holes, then rotate the sensor until the holes align

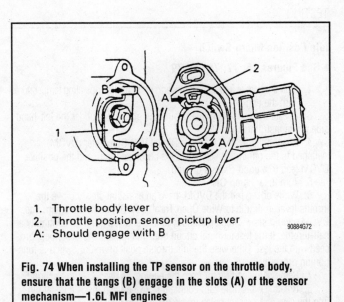

1. Throttle body lever
2. Throttle position sensor pickup lever
A: Should engage with B

Fig. 74 When installing the TP sensor on the throttle body, ensure that the tangs (B) engage in the slots (A) of the sensor mechanism—1.6L MFI engines

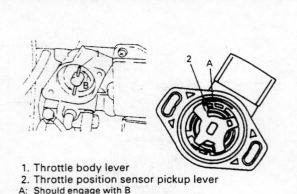

1. Throttle body lever
2. Throttle position sensor pickup lever
A: Should engage with B

90884G73

Fig. 75 On 1.8L engines, the slots (A) of the sensor mechanism should retain the two small pins (B) of the throttle valve shaft

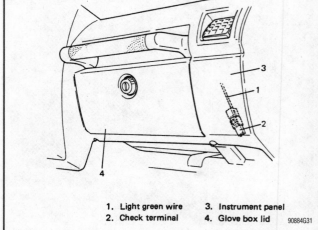

1. Light green wire
2. Check terminal
3. Instrument panel
4. Glove box lid

90884G31

Fig. 76 The micro-switch test terminal is located behind the glove compartment door, under the instrument panel

5. Position the TPS on the throttle body so that the sensor pick-up lever can properly engage with the throttle body lever tangs (B).
6. Install and hand-tighten the sensor mounting bolts.
7. Insert the four TPS wire terminals into the plastic connector until they are properly engaged. Give each wire a slight tug to ensure that they will not come out of the connector.
8. Adjust the TPS angle, as described under TPS testing.
9. Reconnect the wiring harness connector to the TPS.
10. Conenct the negative battery cable.

Throttle Position Micro-Switches

OPERATION

The throttle position is indicated to the ECM by two position micro-switches: the idle position micro-switch and the wide open position micro-switch.

The idle position micro-switch closes its circuit when the throttle valve in the idle position. The wide open throttle micro-position switch closes its circuit when the throttle valve is in the Wide Open Throttle (WOT) position. By monitoring these two circuits, the ECM can detect extreme throttle valve positions, and alter the air/fuel mixture accordingly.

TESTING

Idle Position Micro-Switch

▶ See Figures 76, 77, 78 and 79

1. Start the engine and allow it to warm up to normal operating temperature.
2. Turn the engine **OFF**.
3. Locate the check terminal behind the glove box, under the left-hand side of the instrument panel.
4. Attach the negative lead of a Digital Volt-Ohmmeter (DVOM), switched to the ohmmeter setting, to the check terminal, and the positive DVOM lead to a good chassis ground.
5. Turn the ignition **ON**.
6. While observing the DVOM, have an assistant slowly move the throttle lever from idle to Wide Open Throttle (WOT) and back again. The DVOM should show circuit continuity at idle and WOT, but no continuity at half-throttle. If the test terminal circuit does not function as described, proceed with the test. Otherwise the idle throttle position micro-switch is functioning properly.
7. Remove the carburetor from the engine, as described in Section 5.
8. Rotate the fast idle cam counterclockwise, then insert a metal pin into the cam and bracket holes to secure them in position.

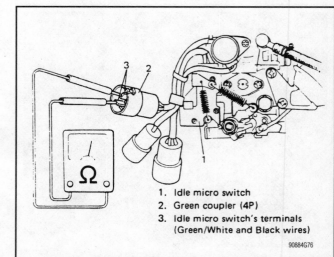

1. Idle micro switch
2. Green coupler (4P)
3. Idle micro switch's terminals (Green/White and Black wires)

90884G76

Fig. 77 Observing the switch resistance with a DVOM, check the idle position micro-switch

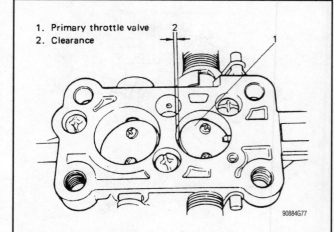

1. Primary throttle valve
2. Clearance

90884G77

Fig. 78 The resistance shown on the DVOM should switch from 0 ohms to infinite resistance when the throttle valve-to-bore clearance is 0.014–0.024 in. (0.36–0.62mm)

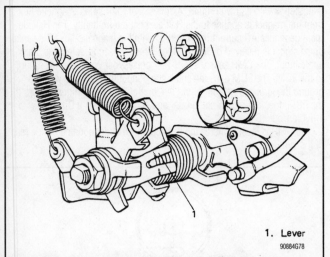

Fig. 79 Adjust the throttle valve-to-bore clearance by bending the lever indicated

1. Lever

90884G78

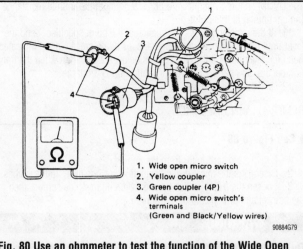

1. Wide open micro switch
2. Yellow coupler
3. Green coupler (4P)
4. Wide open micro switch's terminals
(Green and Black/Yellow wires)

90884G79

Fig. 80 Use an ohmmeter to test the function of the Wide Open Throttle (WOT) micro-switch—attach the ohmmeter to the switch connectors as shown

9. Attach the DVOM, set on the ohmmeter function, to the idle position micro-switch terminals. Check for switch continuity (0 ohms) when the throttle valve is in the idle position. If the switch resistance observed was not as described, replace the switch with a new one.

10. Open the throttle valve ¼ to ½, then observe the switch resistance again. The switch should register infinite resistance (no continuity). If the switch resistance observed was not as described, replace the switch with a new one.

11. Observe the DVOM, and slowly open the throttle valve until the throttle valve-to-carburetor bore clearance is 0.014–0.024 in. (0.36–0.62mm). The DVOM should switch from 0 ohms (continuity) to infinite resistance (no continuity) at this point.

12. If the resistance does not change at the point specified, bend the lever until the resistance transition happens at the precise point indicated. Bend the lever down if the clearance is below specification when the transition occurs, and bend it up if the specification is too large.

13. Install the carburetor.

Wide Open Throttle (WOT) Position Micro-Switch

▶ See Figures 80, 81 and 82

1. Start the engine and allow it to warm up to normal operating temperature.
2. Turn the engine **OFF**.
3. Locate the check terminal behind the glove box, under the left-hand side of the instrument panel.
4. Attach the negative lead of a Digital Volt-Ohmmeter (DVOM), switched to the ohmmeter setting, to the check terminal, and the positive DVOM lead to a good chassis ground.
5. Turn the ignition **ON**.
6. While observing the DVOM, have an assistant slowly move the throttle lever from idle to Wide Open Throttle (WOT) and back again. The DVOM should show circuit continuity at idle and WOT, but no continuity at half-throttle. If the test terminal circuit does not function as described, proceed with the test. Otherwise the idle throttle position micro-switch is functioning properly.
7. Remove the carburetor from the engine, as described in Section 5.
8. Attach the DVOM, set on the ohmmeter function, to the WOT position micro-switch terminals. Check for switch continuity (0 ohms) when the throttle valve is in the idle position. If the switch resistance observed was not as described, replace the switch with a new one.
9. Open the throttle valve to the WOT position, then observe the switch resistance again. The switch should register infinite resistance (no continuity). If the switch resistance observed was not as described, replace the switch with a new one.
10. Observe the DVOM, and slowly open the throttle valve until the throttle valve-to-carburetor bore clearance is 0.24–0.28 in. (6.0–7.2mm).

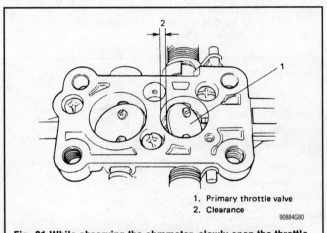

1. Primary throttle valve
2. Clearance

90884G80

Fig. 81 While observing the ohmmeter, slowly open the throttle valve until the valve-to-bore clearance is 0.24–0.28 in. (6.0–7.2mm)—the resistance should change from 0 ohms to infinite resistance

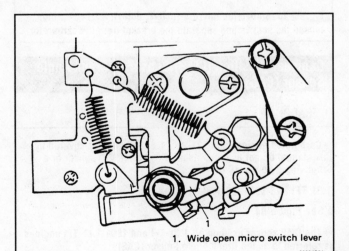

1. Wide open micro switch lever

90884G81

Fig. 82 To adjust the valve-to-bore clearance, bend the lever (1) until the proper clearance is reached

The DVOM should switch from 0 ohms (continuity) to infinite resistance (no continuity) at this point.

11. If the resistance does not change at the point specified, bend the lever until the resistance transition happens at the precise point indicated. Bend the lever down if the clearance is below specification when the transition occurs, and bend it up if the specification is too large.

12. Install the carburetor.

REMOVAL & INSTALLATION

▶ **See Figure 83**

1. Remove the carburetor from the engine.
2. Disengage the micro-switch actuating springs from both switches.
3. Loosen the micro-switch bracket retaining machine screws, then pull the bracket and switches of the carburetor.

※※ WARNING

Do not disassemble the micro-switches from the mounting bracket; replace the bracket and switches together as a unit.

To install:

4. Install the bracket and switches onto the side of the carburetor, then tighten the retaining machine screws until secure.
5. Reattach the actuating springs to the micro-switches.
6. Install the carburetor on the engine.

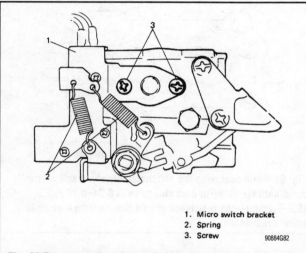

1. Micro switch bracket
2. Spring
3. Screw
90884G82

Fig. 83 To remove the micro-switches, detach the two springs, loosen the screws and separate the bracket from the carburetor

Camshaft Position (CMP) Sensor or Crank Angle Sensor (CAS)

OPERATION

➡**Carbureted engines and 1989–90 1.6L TFI engines covered by this manual do not use a Camshaft Position (CMP) sensor or a Crank Angle Sensor (CAS).**

1.3L TFI and 1991–98 1.6L Engines

▶ **See Figure 84**

➡**The CMP sensor used on all 1.3L TFI and 1991 1.6L TFI engines is referred to as the Crank Angle Sensor (CAS).**

The Camshaft Position (CMP) sensor is located inside the distributor assembly. The CMP sensor consists of a signal rotor, a stationary magnet, and a stationary Hall-effect switch, which is supplied ignition voltage, and

is equipped with its own ground. As the signal rotor spins, magnetic flux from the magnet is applies to the Hall element intermittently. The Hall element generates AC current in proportion with the magnetic flux. The sensor pulse signal is received by the ECM, by which it used to determine crank angle input. The CMP sensor sends four pulses, per complete revolution, to the ECM. The ECM uses the crank angle input to determine when to ground the igniter, thus controlling the ignition coil and ignition timing. If the ECM does not receive the proper signal, it should set a Diagnostic Trouble Code (DTC).

The CMP is located inside the distributor, which is mounted on the rear of the cylinder head.

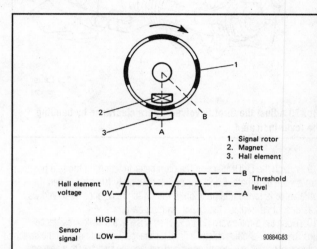

1. Signal rotor
2. Magnet
3. Hall element

Fig. 84 The Camshaft Position (CMP) sensor, or the Crank Angle Sensor (CAS), produces four voltage pulses for each camshaft revolution

1.8L Engine

The Camshaft Position (CMP) sensor is mounted on the rear of the cylinder head and is comprised of the signal generator (photo transistors) and the signal rotor (slot plate).

The signal generator produces reference signal pulses through two types of slots in the signal rotor, both of which are turned by the camshaft.

The CMP sensor generates 4 pulse signals, each of which has a different wave form, for each camshaft rotation. The ECM uses these signals for piston position at 10° Before Top Dead Center (BTDC). The sensor also generates a second set of 360 pulse signals for each camshaft generation, which is used by the ECM for engine speed and precise piston positioning.

TESTING

1.3L TFI Engine

➡**For all Engine Control Module (ECM) terminal identification, refer to the illustrations earlier in this section.**

1. Remove all necessary components for access to the ECM. Remove the ECM with the wiring harness connected, then set it on the floor of the vehicle for access during the test procedure. Ensure that the wiring harness connectors are fully engaged with the ECM.
2. Disengage the yellow connector from the ECM.
3. Using a Digital Volt-Ohmmeter (DVOM) set on the voltmeter function, connect the positive lead to terminal B1 on the green ECM connector, and the negative lead to terminal A13 on the detached yellow ECM connector. Refer to the ECM terminal identification illustrations earlier in this section.
4. Turn the ignition **ON**.
5. While observing the DVOM, have an assistant rotate the crankshaft with a large socket and ratchet on the center crankshaft pulley bolt. Turn the crankshaft so that it travels through 3 or 4 full revolutions.

6. The voltage observed on the DVOM should fluctuate from 0–1 volt to battery voltage four times for each crankshaft revolution.

a. If the voltage did not fluctuate four times for each revolution, or does not oscillate from 0–1 volt to battery voltage, inspect the wiring harness for an open or short circuit, or, if available, substitute a known good distributor and recheck the system. If the circuit checks out okay, replace the distributor assembly.

b. If the voltage functioned as described, inspect the ECM, the wiring harness and related components.

1.6L Engine

➡ **For all Engine Control Module (ECM) terminal identification, refer to the illustrations earlier in this section.**

1991 MODELS

1. Turn the ignition switch **OFF**.
2. Remove all necessary components for access to the ECM. Remove the ECM with the wiring harness connected, then set it on the floor of the vehicle for access during the test procedure. Ensure that the wiring harness connectors are fully engaged with the ECM.
3. Disengage the yellow connector from the ECM.
4. Using a Digital Volt-Ohmmeter (DVOM) set on the voltmeter function, connect the positive lead to terminal B1 on the green ECM connector (which should still be attached to the ECM), and the negative lead to terminal A13 on the detached yellow ECM connector.
5. Turn the ignition **ON**.
6. While observing the DVOM, have an assistant rotate the crankshaft with a large socket and ratchet on the center crankshaft pulley bolt. Turn the crankshaft so that it travels through 3 or 4 full revolutions.
7. The voltage observed on the DVOM should fluctuate from 0–1 volt to battery voltage four times for each crankshaft revolution.

a. If the voltage did not fluctuate four times for each revolution, or does not oscillate from 0–1 volt to battery voltage, inspect the wiring harness for an open or short circuit, or, if available, substitute a known good distributor and recheck the system. If the circuit checks out okay, replace the distributor assembly.

b. If the voltage functioned as described, inspect the ECM, the wiring harness and related components.

1992–98 MODELS

1. Turn the ignition switch **OFF**.
2. Remove all necessary components for access to the ECM. Remove the ECM with the wiring harness connected, then set it on the floor of the vehicle for access during the test procedure. Ensure that the wiring harness connectors are fully engaged with the ECM.
3. Using a Digital Volt-Ohmmeter (DVOM) set on the voltmeter function, attach the positive lead to ECM connector terminal B3 (1992–95 models) or terminal E33–3 (1996–98 models), and the negative lead to a good chassis ground.
4. Turn the ignition **ON**.
5. While observing the DVOM, have an assistant rotate the crankshaft clockwise (viewing the crankshaft from the front of the engine) with a large socket and ratchet on the center crankshaft pulley bolt. Turn the crankshaft so that it travels through 3 or 4 full revolutions.
6. The voltage observed on the DVOM should fluctuate from 0–1 volt to 3–5 volts (1992–95 models) or 3–5.25 volts (1996–98 models) four times for each crankshaft revolution. The voltage presented on the DVOM should read 0–1 volt whenever the signal rotor is not between the Hall-effect switch and the magnet, whereas the voltage should be 3–5 (1992–95 models) or 3–5.25 volts (1996–98 models) when the rotor is positioned between the two components.

a. If the voltage did not fluctuate four times for each revolution, or does not oscillate from 0–1 volt to battery voltage, inspect the wiring

harness for an open or short circuit, or, if available, substitute a known good distributor and recheck the system. If the circuit checks out okay, replace the distributor assembly.

b. If the voltage functioned as described, inspect the ECM, the wiring harness and related components.

1.8L Engine

▶ **See Figure 85**

➡ **For all Engine Control Module (ECM) terminal identification, refer to the illustrations earlier in this section.**

1. Turn the ignition switch **OFF**.
2. Detach the wiring harness connector from the CMP sensor.
3. Using a Digital Volt-Ohmmeter (DVOM) set on the voltmeter function, attach the positive lead to CMP sensor wiring harness connector terminal 2, and the negative lead to terminal 3.
4. Turn the ignition switch **ON**, and measure the voltage on the DVOM. Voltage should be the same as battery voltage; if the voltage is not battery voltage, inspect the wiring harness for open or short circuits.
5. Turn the ignition switch **OFF**.
6. Reattach the wiring harness connector to the CMP sensor.
7. Remove all necessary components for access to the ECM. Remove the ECM with the wiring harness connected, then set it on the floor of the vehicle for access during the test procedure. Ensure that the wiring harness connectors are fully engaged with the ECM.
8. For 1996–97 vehicles, perform the following:

a. Using a Digital Volt-Ohmmeter (DVOM) set on the voltmeter function, attach the positive lead to ECM connector terminal E33–5 or E33–6, and the negative lead to a good chassis ground.

b. Turn the ignition **ON**.

c. While observing the DVOM, have an assistant rotate the crankshaft clockwise (viewing the crankshaft from the front of the engine) with a large socket and ratchet on the center crankshaft pulley bolt. Turn the crankshaft so that it travels through 3 or 4 full revolutions.

d. The voltage observed on the DVOM should fluctuate from 0–1 volt to 4–6 volts four times for each crankshaft revolution.

e. Turn the ignition **OFF**.

f. Now attach the positive lead to ECM connector terminal E33–3 or E33–4, and the negative lead to a good chassis ground.

g. Turn the ignition **ON**.

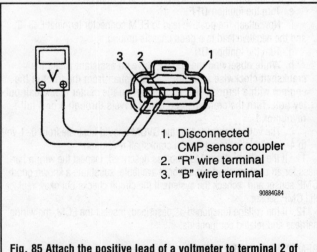

1. Disconnected CMP sensor coupler
2. "R" wire terminal
3. "B" wire terminal

90884G84

Fig. 85 Attach the positive lead of a voltmeter to terminal 2 of the CMP sensor wiring harness connector, and the negative lead to terminal 3 of the connector

h. While observing the DVOM, have an assistant rotate the crankshaft clockwise (viewing the crankshaft from the front of the engine) with a large socket and ratchet on the center crankshaft pulley bolt. Turn the crankshaft so that it travels through 3 or 4 full revolutions.

i. The voltage observed on the DVOM should fluctuate from 0–1 volt to 4–6 volts four times for each crankshaft revolution.

9. For 1998 vehicles equipped with automatic transmissions or the EVAP II system, perform the following:

a. Using a Digital Volt-Ohmmeter (DVOM) set on the voltmeter function, attach the positive lead to ECM connector terminal E175–10, and the negative lead to a good chassis ground.

b. Turn the ignition **ON**.

c. While observing the DVOM, have an assistant rotate the crankshaft clockwise (viewing the crankshaft from the front of the engine) with a large socket and ratchet on the center crankshaft pulley bolt. Turn the crankshaft so that it travels through 3 or 4 full revolutions.

d. The voltage observed on the DVOM should fluctuate from 0–1 volt to 4–6 volts four times for each crankshaft revolution.

e. Turn the ignition **OFF**.

f. Now attach the positive lead to ECM connector terminal E175–22, and the negative lead to a good chassis ground.

g. Turn the ignition **ON**.

h. While observing the DVOM, have an assistant rotate the crankshaft clockwise (viewing the crankshaft from the front of the engine) with a large socket and ratchet on the center crankshaft pulley bolt. Turn the crankshaft so that it travels through 3 or 4 full revolutions.

i. The voltage observed on the DVOM should fluctuate from 0–1 volt to 4–6 volts four times for each crankshaft revolution.

10. For 1998 vehicles, other than those equipped with automatic transmissions or the EVAP II system, perform the following:

a. Using a Digital Volt-Ohmmeter (DVOM) set on the voltmeter function, attach the positive lead to ECM connector terminal E33–5, and the negative lead to a good chassis ground.

b. Turn the ignition **ON**.

c. While observing the DVOM, have an assistant rotate the crankshaft clockwise (viewing the crankshaft from the front of the engine) with a large socket and ratchet on the center crankshaft pulley bolt. Turn the crankshaft so that it travels through 3 or 4 full revolutions.

d. The voltage observed on the DVOM should fluctuate from 0–1 volt to 4–6 volts four times for each crankshaft revolution.

e. Turn the ignition **OFF**.

f. Now attach the positive lead to ECM connector terminal E33–3, and the negative lead to a good chassis ground.

g. Turn the ignition **ON**.

h. While observing the DVOM, have an assistant rotate the crankshaft clockwise (viewing the crankshaft from the front of the engine) with a large socket and ratchet on the center crankshaft pulley bolt. Turn the crankshaft so that it travels through 3 or 4 full revolutions.

i. The voltage observed on the DVOM should fluctuate from 0–1 volt to 4–6 volts four times for each crankshaft revolution.

11. If the voltage did not function as described, inspect the wiring harness for an open or short circuit, or, if available, substitute a known good CMP sensor and recheck the system. If the circuit checks out okay, replace the CMP sensor.

12. If the voltage functioned as described, inspect the ECM, the wiring harness and related components.

REMOVAL & INSTALLATION

1.3L and 1.6L Engines

The CMP sensor/CAS cannot be individually replaced; the entire distributor assembly must be replaced if the sensor is found to be defective. Distributor removal and installation is described in Section 2 of this manual.

1.8L Engine

‣ See Figures 86 and 87

✳✳ WARNING

Do not attempt to disassemble the CMP sensor; the sensor must be replaced as a unit if found defective.

1. Disconnect the negative battery cable.
2. Detach the wiring harness connector from the CMP sensor.
3. Loosen the two CMP sensor retaining bolts, then pull the sensor off of the rear side of the cylinder head.
4. Remove and discard the old O-ring from the CMP sensor.

To install:

5. Install a new O-ring, lubricated with clean engine oil, onto the CMP sensor.

6. Install the sensor by fitting the tangs of the sensor coupling in the camshaft end slots. The tangs of the sensor coupling are slightly offset. Therefore, if the tangs are difficult to mate with the camshaft slots, rotate the sensor shaft 180 degrees and reinsert it.

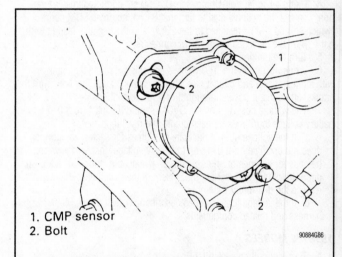

1. CMP sensor
2. Bolt

90884G86

Fig. 86 Loosen the CMP sensor mounting screws, then remove the sensor from the camshaft

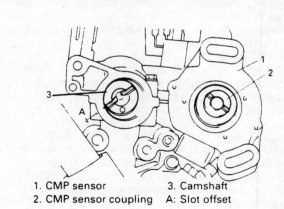

1. CMP sensor
2. CMP sensor coupling
3. Camshaft
A: Slot offset

90884G85

Fig. 87 When installing the CMP sensor on the camshaft, ensure that the coupling slots of the camshaft are properly engaged by the tangs on the sensor

7. Install and tighten the sensor mounting bolts to 133 inch lbs. (15 Nm).
8. Reattach the wiring harness connector to the CMP sensor.
9. Connect the negative battery cable.
10. Adjust the ignition timing.

Crankshaft Position (CKP) Sensor

OPERATION

▶ **See Figure 88**

➡ **Only the 1996–98 1.6L engines utilize a Crankshaft Position (CKP) sensor.**

The CKP sensor is located on the front flange of the oil pan and consists of a signal generator (pick-up coil and magnet) and signal rotor (on the crankshaft timing belt sprocket).

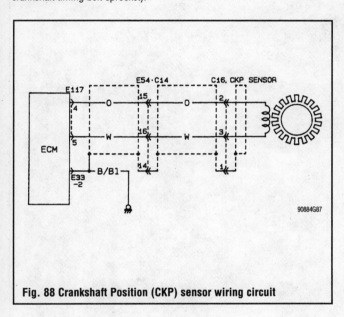

Fig. 88 Crankshaft Position (CKP) sensor wiring circuit

As the crankshaft rotates, AC voltage is generated in the pick-up coil. This current is sent to the ECM, where it is used to calculate the variation of crankshaft speed, which detects if a cylinder misfired).

TESTING

1. Disconnect the negative battery.
2. Detach the wiring harness connector from the CKP sensor.
3. Use a Digital Volt-Ohmmeter (DVOM), switched to the ohmmeter function, to measure the resistance between the two CKP sensor terminals. The resistance should be 360–460 ohms. If the resistance is not as specified, replace it with a new one and retest. Otherwise, inspect the CKP sensor wiring harness for an open or short circuit.
4. Reattach the wiring harness connector to the CKP sensor.
5. Connect the negative battery cable.

REMOVAL & INSTALLATION

The CKP sensor is mounted in the oil pan front gasket flange.
1. If additional undervehicle clearance is needed, raise and safely support the front of the vehicle securely on jackstands. Apply the parking brake and block the rear wheels.
2. Disconnect the negative battery.
3. Detach the wiring harness connector from the CKP sensor.
4. Loosen the CKP sensor retaining bolt, then pull the sensor down and out of the front of the engine.
To install:
5. Insert the sensor into the engine block and install the retaining bolt securely.
6. Reattach the wiring harness connector to the CKP sensor.
7. If necessary, lower the vehicle and remove the rear wheel blocks.
8. Connect the negative battery cable.

COMPONENT LOCATIONS

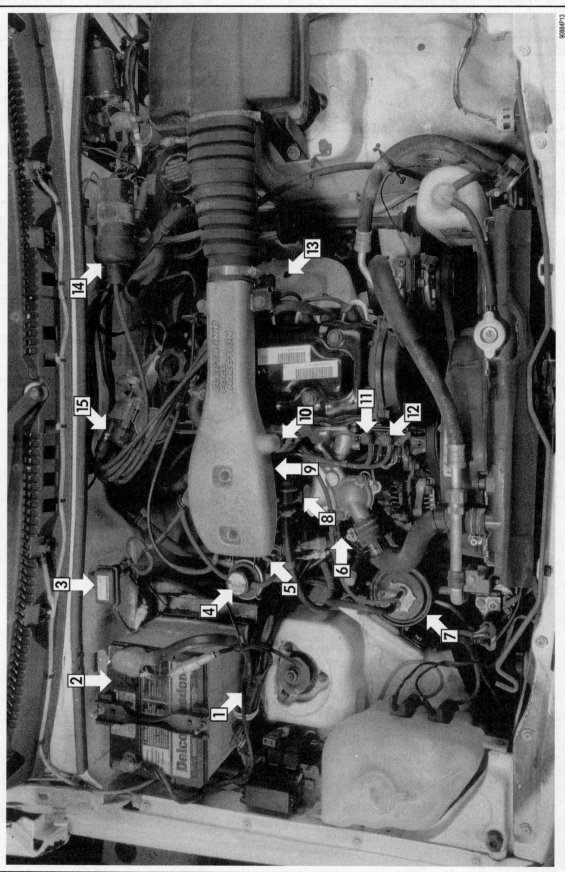

ELECTRONIC ENGINE CONTROL COMPONENTS—1989–90 1.6L TFI ENGINES

1. Diagnostic monitor connector
2. Battery
3. Manifold Absolute Pressure (MAP) sensor
4. EGR modulator
5. Idle Speed Control Solenoid (ISCS) valve
6. Intake Air Temperature (IAT) sensor
7. EGR vapor (charcoal) canister
8. Throttle Position (TP) sensor
9. Throttle opener assembly
10. Positive Crankcase Ventilation (PCV) valve
11. EGR Vacuum Solenoid Valve (VSV)
12. Throttle opener VSV
13. Oxygen (O₂) sensor
14. Ignition coil
15. Crank Angle Sensor (CAS)—(inside the distributor)

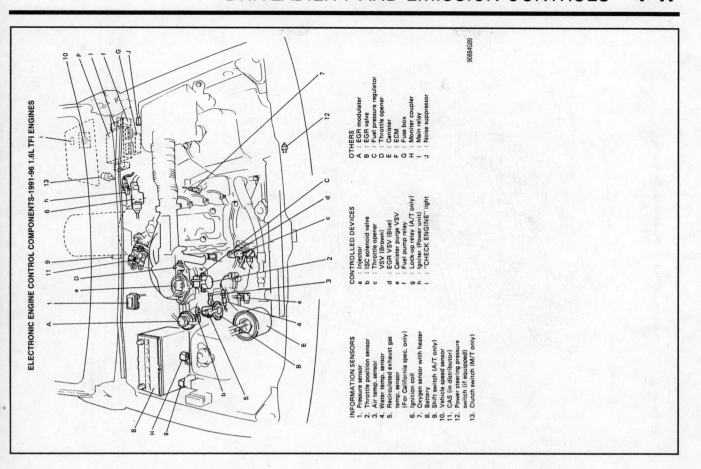

ELECTRONIC ENGINE CONTROL COMPONENTS-1991-96 1.6L TFI ENGINES

INFORMATION SENSORS
1. Pressure sensor
2. Throttle position sensor
3. Air temp. sensor
4. Water temp. sensor
5. Recirculated exhaust gas temp. sensor
   (For California spec. only)
6. Ignition coil
7. Oxygen sensor with heater
8. Battery
9. Shift switch (A/T only)
10. Vehicle speed sensor
11. CAS (in distributor)
12. Power steering pressure switch (if equipped)
13. Clutch switch (M/T only)

CONTROLLED DEVICES
a. Injector
b. ISC solenoid valve
c. Throttle opener
d. VSV (Brown)
e. EGR VSV (Blue)
f. Canister purge VSV (For California spec. only)
g. Fuel pump relay
h. Lock-up relay (A/T only)
i. Igniter (Power unit)
j. "CHECK ENGINE" light

OTHERS
A. EGR modulater
B. EGR valve
C. Fuel pressure regulator
D. Throttle opener
E. Canister
F. ECM
G. Fuse box
H. Moniter coupler
I. Main relay
J. Noise suppressor

90844G89

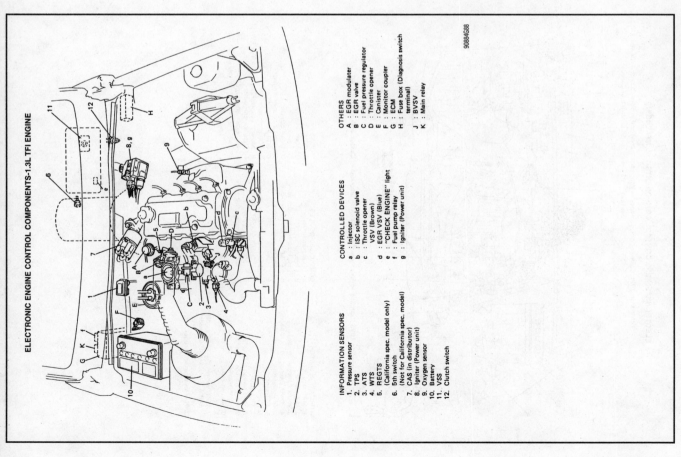

ELECTRONIC ENGINE CONTROL COMPONENTS-1.3L TFI ENGINE

INFORMATION SENSORS
1. Pressure sensor
2. TPS
3. ATS
4. WTS
5. REGTS (California spec. model only)
6. 5th switch (Not for California spec. model)
7. CAS (in distributor)
8. Igniter (Power unit)
9. Oxygen sensor
10. Battery
11. VSS
12. Clutch switch

CONTROLLED DEVICES
a. Injector
b. ISC solenoid valve
c. Throttle opener
d. VSV (Brown)
e. EGR VSV (Blue)
f. "CHECK ENGINE" light
g. Fuel pump relay
h. Igniter (Power unit)

OTHERS
A. EGR modulater
B. EGR valve
C. Fuel pressure regulator
D. Throttle opener
F. Canister
G. Monitor coupler
H. Fuse box (Diagnosis switch terminal)
J. BVSV
K. Main relay

90844G88

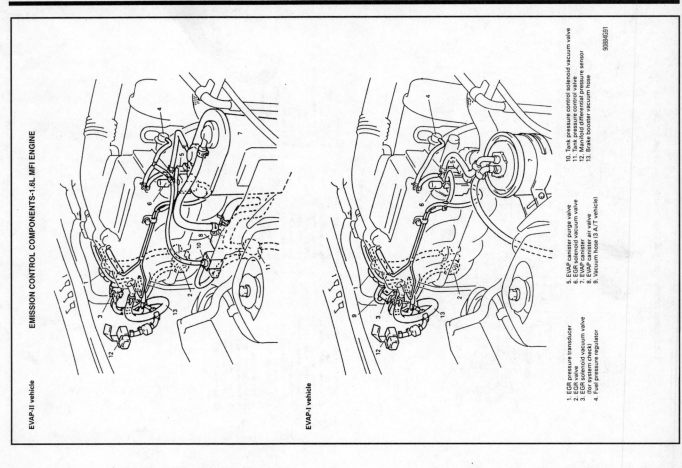

EMISSION CONTROL COMPONENTS-1.6L MFI ENGINE

EVAP-II vehicle

EVAP-I vehicle

1. EGR pressure transducer
2. EGR valve
3. EGR solenoid vacuum valve (for system check)
4. Fuel pressure regulator
5. EVAP canister purge valve
6. EGR solenoid vacuum valve
7. EVAP canister air valve
8. EVAP canister
9. Vacuum hose (3 A/T vehicle)
10. Tank pressure control solenoid vacuum valve
11. Tank pressure control valve
12. Manifold differential pressure sensor
13. Brake booster vacuum hose

90884G91

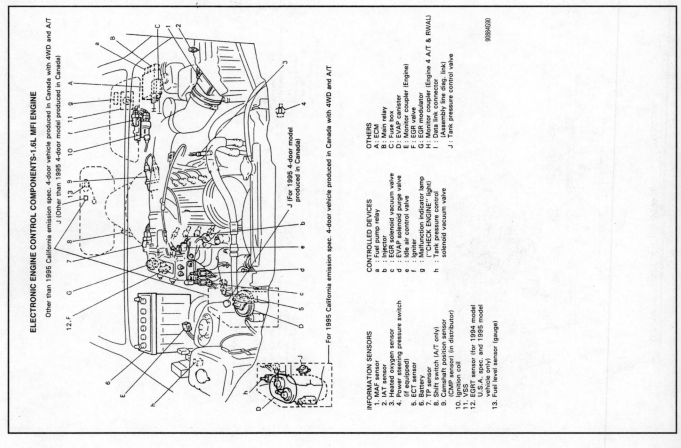

ELECTRONIC ENGINE CONTROL COMPONENTS-1.6L MFI ENGINE

Other than 1995 California emission spec. 4-door vehicle produced in Canada with 4WD and A/T

J (Other than 1995 4-door model produced in Canada)

J (For 1995 4-door model produced in Canada)

— For 1995 California emission spec. 4-door vehicle produced in Canada with 4WD and A/T

INFORMATION SENSORS
1. MAF sensor
2. IAT sensor
3. Heated oxygen sensor
4. Power steering pressure switch (if equipped)
5. ECT sensor
6. Battery
7. TP sensor
8. Shift switch (A/T only)
9. Camshaft position sensor (CMP sensor) (in distributor)
10. Ignition coil
11. VSS
12. EGRT sensor (for 1994 model U.S.A. spec. and 1995 model vehicle only)
13. Fuel level sensor (gauge)

CONTROLLED DEVICES
a : Fuel pump relay
b : Injector
c : EGR solenoid vacuum valve
d : EVAP solenoid purge valve
e : Idle air control valve
f : Igniter
g : Malfunction indicator lamp ("CHECK ENGINE" light)
h : Tank pressure control solenoid vacuum valve

OTHERS
A : ECM
B : Main relay
C : Fuse box
D : EVAP canister
E : Monitor coupler (Engine)
F : EGR modulator
G : EGR valve
H : Monitor coupler (Engine 4 A/T & RWAL)
I : Data link connector (Assembly line diag. link)
J : Tank pressure control valve

90884G90

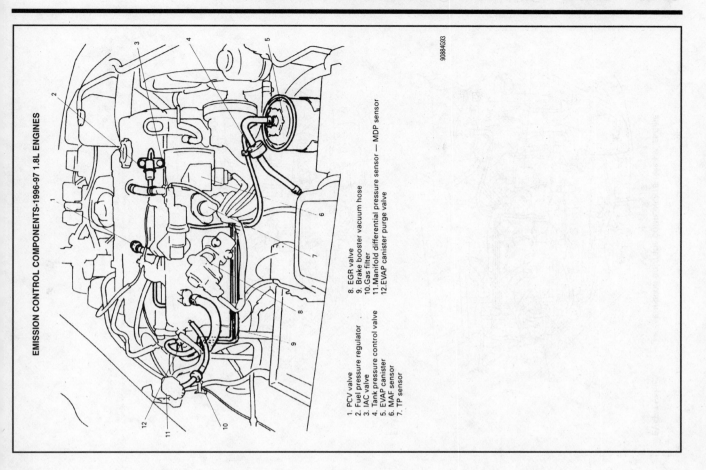

EMISSION CONTROL COMPONENTS-1996-97 1.8L ENGINES

90884G93

1. PCV valve
2. Fuel pressure regulator
3. IAC valve
4. Tank pressure control valve
5. EVAP canister
6. MAF sensor
7. TP sensor
8. EGR valve
9. Brake booster vacuum hose
10. Gas filter
11. Manifold differential pressure sensor — MDP sensor
12. EVAP canister purge valve

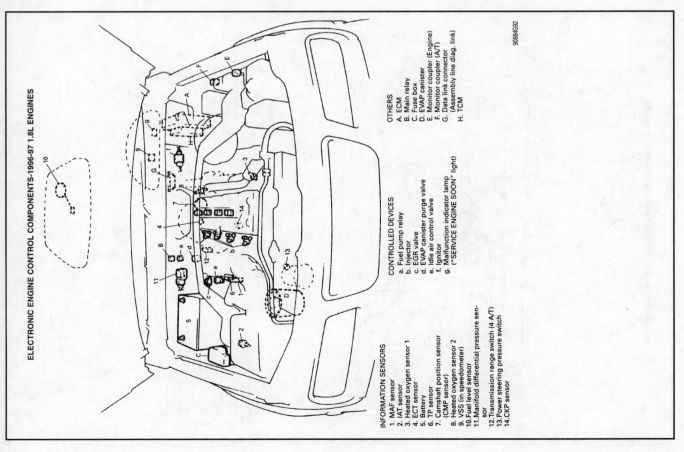

ELECTRONIC ENGINE CONTROL COMPONENTS-1996-97 1.8L ENGINES

90884G92

INFORMATION SENSORS
1. MAF sensor
2. IAT sensor
3. Heated oxygen sensor 1
4. ECT sensor
5. Battery
6. TP sensor
7. Camshaft position sensor (CMP sensor)
8. Heated oxygen sensor 2
9. VSS (in speedometer)
10. Fuel level sensor
11. Manifold differential pressure sensor
12. Transmission range switch (4 A/T)
13. Power steering pressure switch
14. CKP sensor

CONTROLLED DEVICES
a. Fuel pump relay
b. Injector
c. EGR valve
d. EVAP canister purge valve
e. Idle air control valve
f. Ignitor
9. Malfunction indicator lamp ("SERVICE ENGINE SOON" light)

OTHERS
A. ECM
B. Main relay
C. Fuse box
D. EVAP canister
E. Monitor coupler (Engine)
F. Monitor coupler (A/T)
G. Data link connector (Assembly line diag. link)
H. TCM

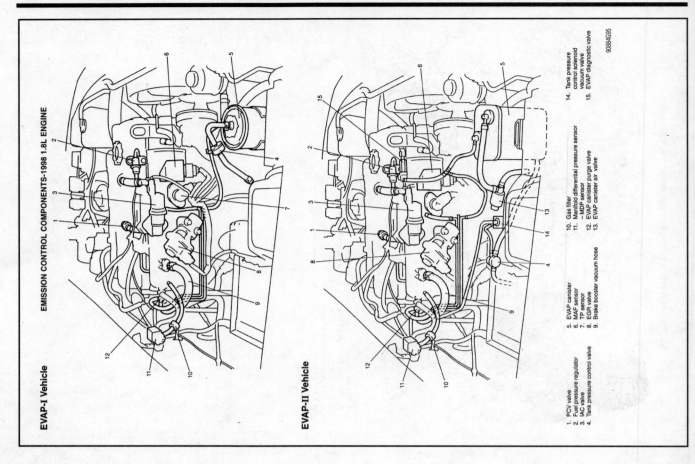

EMISSION CONTROL COMPONENTS-1998 1.8L ENGINE

EVAP-I Vehicle

EVAP-II Vehicle

1. PCV valve
2. Fuel pressure regulator
3. IAC valve
4. Tank pressure control valve
5. EVAP canister
6. MAF sensor
7. TP sensor
8. EGR valve
9. Brake booster vacuum hose
10. Gas filter
11. Manifold differential pressure sensor – MDP sensor
12. EVAP canister purge valve
13. EVAP canister air valve
14. Tank pressure control solenoid vacuum valve
15. EVAP diagnostic valve

90884G95

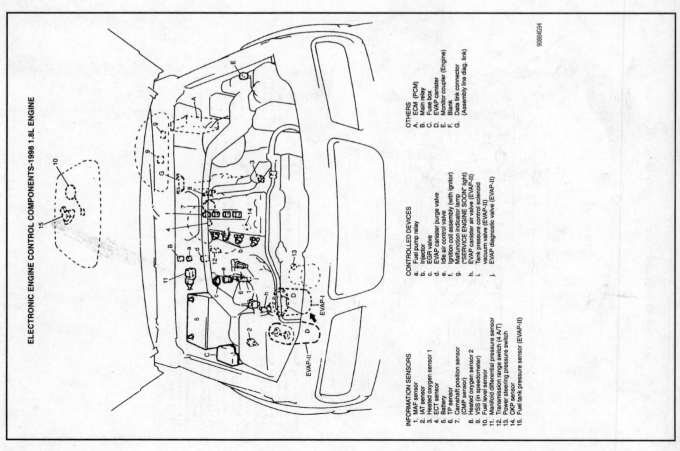

ELECTRONIC ENGINE CONTROL COMPONENTS-1998 1.8L ENGINE

INFORMATION SENSORS
1. MAF sensor
2. IAT sensor
3. Heated oxygen sensor 1
4. ECT sensor
5. Battery
6. TP sensor
7. Camshaft position sensor (CMP sensor)
8. Heated oxygen sensor 2
9. VSS (in speedometer)
10. Fuel level sensor
11. Manifold differential pressure sensor
12. Transmission range switch (4 A/T)
13. Power steering pressure switch
14. CKP sensor
15. Fuel tank pressure sensor (EVAP-II)

CONTROLLED DEVICES
a. Fuel pump relay
b. Injector
c. EGR valve
d. EVAP canister purge valve
e. Idle air control valve
f. Ignition coil assembly (with ignitor)
g. Malfunction indicator lamp ("SERVICE ENGINE SOON" light)
h. EVAP canister air valve (EVAP-II)
i. Tank pressure control solenoid vacuum valve (EVAP-II)
j. EVAP diagnostic valve (EVAP-II)

OTHERS
A. ECM (PCM)
B. Main relay
C. Fuse box
D. EVAP canister
E. Monitor coupler (Engine)
F. Blank
G. Data link connector (Assembly line diag. link)

90884G94

TROUBLE CODES

General Information

TFI & 1992–95 MFI ENGINES

➡**The ECM used with carbureted engines, which utilize the feedback system, do not store Diagnostic Trouble Codes. For feedback carburetor system diagnosis, refer to the procedure earlier in this section.**

The Engine Control Module (ECM), used to control the fuel and ignition systems on fuel injected vehicles, is equipped with a self-diagnostic mode. The ECM constantly monitors the incoming and outgoing signals to and from the various electronic engine control components. The ECM compares these signals with factory-programmed parameters for each sensor, switch or valve. When the signal from a sensor is not within the normal parameters, or when information from one of more sensors conflict with other information from different sensors, the ECM takes note of it.

These discrepancies, or malfunctions, are stored in the memory of the ECM, and are known as Diagnostic Trouble Codes (DTC's). The ECM will store, or save, a DTC even if the problem was only temporary. DTC's are not erased from the ECM memory until power is disconnected from the ECM for more than 20 seconds. Whenever the ECM stores one or more DTC's, the CHECK ENGINE light in the instrument cluster illuminates.

Whenever a problem in the fuel injection system arises, these DTC's can be retrieved in order to help with component and circuit diagnosis. The DTC will, however, only refer you to which component AND circuit was defective. Therefore, either the circuit, the component itself, or both may be the problem; it is just as important to inspect the circuit wiring harness for open and short circuits, as it is to inspect the sensor, switch or valve.

1996–98 MFI ENGINES

The engine and emission control systems on engines equipped with Multi-port Fuel Injection (MFI) are controlled by the Engine Control Module (ECM). The ECM is equipped with a On-Board Diagnostic (OBD) system, which can detect malfunctions within the system, and any abnormalities of those components which influence engine exhaust emissions.

The MFI-equipped engines are quipped with the following functions, which are compliant with federal OBD-II regulations.
• When the ignition switch is turned **ON**, without starting the engine, the Malfunction Indicator Lamp (MIL) should illuminate. The lamp illuminates under this condition so that the MIL circuit and bulb can be checked for proper operation.
• Whenever the ECM detects a malfunction in the vehicle emission system during engine operation, it illuminates the MIL and saves a Diagnostic Trouble Code (DTC) in its memory. The only exception to this is when the ECM detects a cylinder misfire (which can damage the catalytic converter), in which case the MIL flashes rather than staying illuminated. The MIL is located in the instrument cluster.

➡**The MIL will turn off if, after 3 complete driving cycles, the malfunction is no longer detected by the ECM. The stored DTC will, however, remain until the ECM memory is cleared.**

• Whenever a DTC is stored to ECM memory, the engine data at that moment is saved as freeze frame data, which can later be retrieved to help with diagnosis.
• You can communicate with the ECM with either the Suzuki Scan

Tool (Tech-1) or a generic OBD-II scan tool which complies with SAEJ1978.

Driving Cycle

A driving cycle is defined as the cycle from starting the engine to turning the engine **OFF**.

Two Driving Cycle Detection Logic

Whenever a malfunction is detected for the first time (during a driving cycle), it is stored in ECM memory in the form of a pending DTC and freeze frame data. However, the MIL will not illuminate at this time. The MIL will light up only if the same malfunction is detected during the next driving cycle as well.

Pending DTC

The term "pending DTC" indicates that a DTC has been detected by the ECM's Two Driving Cycle Detection Logic, and stored temporarily after the first driving cycle.

Freeze Frame Data

The ECM stores the engine and driving conditions at the time of the first detection of the malfunction in its memory. This data is referred to as "freeze frame data."

Therefore, the ECM can present engine condition information, as well as the specific circuit of the malfunction detected. This information can be very helpful when diagnosing an engine control problem. Unfortunately however, the ECM can store the freeze frame data for only one malfunction at any given time, therefore specific malfunctions take precedent over other malfunctions when the ECM is deciding on which freeze frame data to keep. Malfunctions dealing with misfiring (DTC's P0300 to P0304), fuel system too lean (DTC P0171), and Fuel system too lean (DTC P0172) are stored before any other DTC's.

Diagnostic Connector

GENERAL INFORMATION & LOCATION

1989–95 Fuel Injected Engines

The 1.3L TFI engine, used in the Samurai model, does not use a diagnostic connector for DTC retrieval.

The 1989–95 1.6L TFI and MFI engines use a diagnostic monitor coupler, which is located in the engine compartment near the battery.

1996–98 Fuel Injected Engines

▶ **See Figure 89**

The engine and emission control systems utilize a Data Link Connector (DLC) so that a scan tool can communicate with the ECM, thereby reading stored DTC's and freeze frame data for component testing. The DLC used with these engines complies with SAE regulation J1962 in location, shape and terminal identification.

An OBD-II serial data line is used for either the Suzuki scan tool (Tech-1) or a generic scan tool to communicate with the ECM. Only the Suzuki scan tool can be used to communicate with other control modules, such as the airbag module and the ABS control module, etc., in these vehicles.

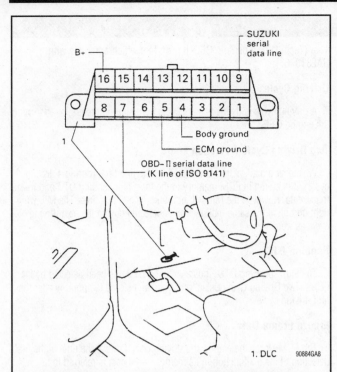

Fig. 89 The Data Link Connector (DLC) uses the standard federally-mandated On-Board Diagnostics (OBD-II) terminal positions—a scan tool is necessary to retrieve the DTC's used by these engines

Reading Codes

1.3L TFI ENGINE

▶ See Figure 90

The CHECK ENGINE light, located in the instrument cluster, can be used to retrieve DTC's stored in the ECM. The DTC's are double-digit numbers, which are conveyed by the CHECK ENGINE light as flashes. Each digit of the code is presented as a series of flashes, so that code No. 32 would be presented as three flashes close together, then 2 flashes after a one second pause. Three seconds after the first code, the next

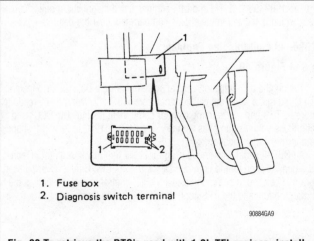

1. Fuse box
2. Diagnosis switch terminal

Fig. 90 To retrieve the DTC's used with 1.3L TFI engines, install a spare fuse in the position marked 2—this will ground the test circuit and actuate the CHECK ENGINE light

When using a scan tool, be sure to follow the manufacturer's instructions carefully to ensure proper diagnosis

code will be flashed in the CHECK ENGINE light. The DTC's can be retrieved as follows:

1. Without starting the engine, turn the ignition switch **ON**. The CHECK ENGINE light should illuminate (not flash); if it doesn't there is a problem in the CHECK ENGINE light circuit.
2. Install a spare fuse into the diagnosis switch terminal, located on the end off the fuse box, under the left-hand side of the instrument panel. Installing the spare fuse will ground the diagnosis circuit.
3. Observe the CHECK ENGINE light and write down any codes flashed. If the only code flashed out by the CHECK ENGINE light is No. 12, no malfunctions were recorded. If the CHECK ENGINE light stay illuminated and does not flash any codes, not even No. 12, there is a problem in the CHECK ENGINE light circuit.
4. After all codes have been flashed and noted, repair or service the defective circuits and components.
5. Remove the spare fuse from the diagnosis terminal.
6. Clear the DTC's.
7. Start the engine and allow it to reach normal operating temperature.
8. Turn the engine **OFF**.
9. Once again install the spare fuse and ensure that code No. 12 is the only DTC flashed by the CHECK ENGINE light.
10. Turn the ignition switch **OFF**, and remove the spare fuse from fuse panel.

1989–95 1.6L ENGINES

▶ See Figures 91 and 92

The CHECK ENGINE light, located in the instrument cluster, can be used to retrieve DTC's stored in the ECM. The DTC's are double-digit numbers, which are conveyed by the CHECK ENGINE light as flashes. Each digit of the code is presented as a series of flashes, so that code No. 32 would be presented as three flashes close together, then 2 flashes after a one second pause. Three seconds after the first code, the next code will be flashed in the CHECK ENGINE light. The DTC's can be retrieved as follows:

1. Sit in the driver's seat so that you can see the CHECK ENGINE light in the instrument cluster.
2. Without starting the engine, turn the ignition switch **ON**. The CHECK ENGINE light should illuminate (not flash); if it doesn't there is a problem in the CHECK ENGINE light circuit.
3. Have a helper connect a jumper wire between terminals B and C (1989–93 models) or terminals B and D (for 1994–95 models) of the monitor coupler, which will ground the diagnosis circuit.
4. Observe the CHECK ENGINE light and note all codes flashed. If the only code flashed out by the CHECK ENGINE light is No. 12, no malfunctions were recorded by the ECM. If the CHECK ENGINE light stays illumi-

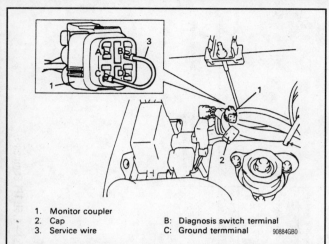

1. Monitor coupler
2. Cap
3. Service wire

B: Diagnosis switch terminal
C: Ground termminal

90884GB0

Fig. 91 To read the DTC's, use a jumper wire to ground terminal B to terminal C, which will activate the CHECK ENGINE light— 1989–93 1.6L engines

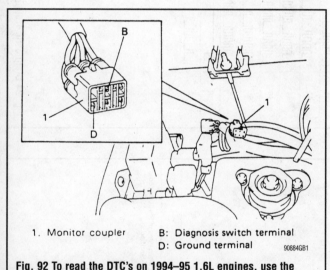

1. Monitor coupler

B: Diagnosis switch terminal
D: Ground terminal

90884GB1

Fig. 92 To read the DTC's on 1994–95 1.6L engines, use the jumper wire to connect terminals B and D

nated and does not flash any codes, not even No. 12, there is a problem with the CHECK ENGINE light circuit.

5. After all codes have been flashed and noted, repair or service the defective circuits and components.

6. Remove the jumper wire from the diagnosis monitor coupler.

7. Clear the DTC's.

8. Start the engine and allow it to reach normal operating temperature.

9. Turn the engine **OFF**.

10. Once again have your assistant install the jumper wire on the monitor coupler, and ensure that code No. 12 is the only DTC flashed by the CHECK ENGINE light.

11. Turn the ignition switch **OFF**, and remove the jumper wire from the monitor coupler.

1996–98 1.6L & 1.8L ENGINES

➡️**If you want to retrieve DTC's or freeze frame data, do NOT disconnect the negative battery cable; this will erase all stored information from the ECM.**

Since the DTC's used by the OBD-II compliant ECM, which is used with all MFI engines, are alpha-numeric (comprising both numbers and letters), the DTC's cannot be retrieved from the MIL as can those of the TFI systems. A scan tool is absolutely necessary to retrieve the DTC's.

To read the DTC's and freeze frame data, refer to the individual scan tool manufacturer's instructions.

Clearing Codes

1989–95 ENGINES

To clear all of the stored DTC's, disconnect the negative battery cable from the battery for at least 20 seconds, then reconnect it. The codes should now be erased from the ECM memory.

1996–98 ENGINES

The DTC's and freeze frame data can either be cleared from ECM memory by utilizing the same scan tool that was used to read the information, or by simply disconnecting the negative battery cable from the battery for at least 30 seconds. The information stored in the ECM will also be cleared if the malfunction is not detected again within 40 driving cycles of the last malfunction occurrence.

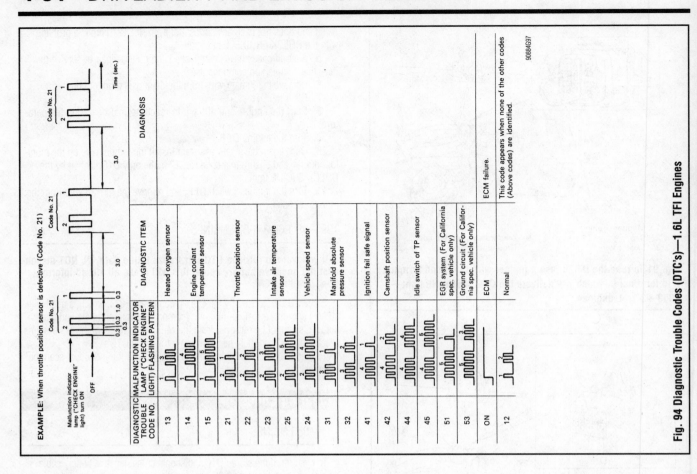

EXAMPLE: When throttle position sensor is defective (Code No. 21)

DIAGNOSTIC TROUBLE CODE NO.	MALFUNCTION INDICATOR LAMP ("CHECK ENGINE" LIGHT) FLASHING PATTERN	DIAGNOSTIC ITEM	DIAGNOSIS
13		Heated oxygen sensor	
14		Engine coolant temperature sensor	
15			
21		Throttle position sensor	
22			
23		Intake air temperature sensor	
25			
24		Vehicle speed sensor	
31		Manifold absolute pressure sensor	
32			
41		Ignition fail safe signal	
42		Camshaft position sensor	
44		Idle switch of TP sensor	
45			
51		EGR system (For California spec. vehicle only)	
53		Ground circuit (For California spec. vehicle only)	
ON		ECM	ECM failure.
12		Normal	This code appears when none of the other codes (Above codes) are identified.

Fig. 94 Diagnostic Trouble Codes (DTC's)—1.6L TFI Engines

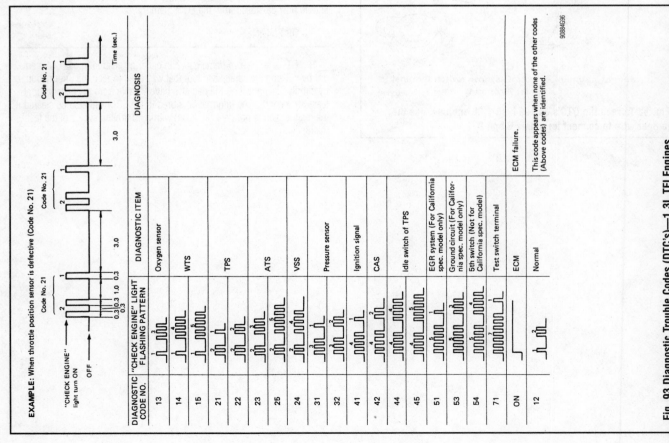

EXAMPLE: When throttle position sensor is defective (Code No. 21)

DIAGNOSTIC TROUBLE CODE NO.	"CHECK ENGINE" LIGHT FLASHING PATTERN	DIAGNOSTIC ITEM	DIAGNOSIS
13		Oxygen sensor	
14		WTS	
15			
21		TPS	
22			
23		ATS	
25			
24		VSS	
31		Pressure sensor	
32			
41		Ignition signal	
42		CAS	
44		Idle switch of TPS	
45			
51		EGR system (For California spec. model only)	
53		Ground circuit (For California spec. model only)	
54		5th switch (Not for California spec. model)	
71		Test switch terminal	
ON		ECM	ECM failure.
12		Normal	This code appears when none of the other codes (Above codes) are identified.

Fig. 93 Diagnostic Trouble Codes (DTC's)—1.3L TFI Engines

DTC NO.	DETECTED ITEM	DETECTING CONDITION (DTC will set when detecting:)	MIL
P0101	Mass air flow circuit performance problem	Poor performance of MAF sensor	2 driving cycles
P0102	Mass air flow circuit low input	Sensor output too low	1 driving cycle
P0103	Mass air flow circuit high input	Sensor output too high	1 driving cycle
P0112	Intake air temp. circuit low input	High temperature–low voltage (or IAT sensor circuit shorted to ground)	1 driving cycle
P0113	Intake air temp. circuit high input	Low temperature–high voltage (or IAT sensor circuit open)	1 driving cycle
P0117	Engine coolant temp. circuit low input	High temperature–low voltage (or ECT sensor circuit shorted to ground)	1 driving cycle
P0118	Engine coolant temp. circuit high input	Low-temperature–high voltage (or ECT sensor circuit open)	1 driving cycle
P0121	Throttle position circuit performance problem	Poor performance of TP sensor	2 driving cycles
P0122	Throttle position circuit low input	Low voltage (or TP sensor circuit shorted to ground)	1 driving cycle
P0123	Throttle position circuit high input	High voltage (or TP sensor circuit open)	1 driving cycle
P0125	Insufficient coolant temp. for closed loop fuel control	Coolant temp. not reaching closed loop temp. within specified time after engine start (or poor performance of ECT sensor)	2 driving cycles
P0131	HO2S-1 circuit low voltage	Max. output voltage of HO2S-1 is lower than specification (or HO2S-1 circuit open)	2 driving cycles (*)
P0132	HO2S-1 circuit high voltage	Min. output voltage of HO2S-1 is higher than specification	2 driving cycles (*)
P0133	HO2S-1 circuit slow response	Response time of HO2S-1 output voltage is longer than specification	2 driving cycles (*)
P0134	HO2S-1 no activity detected	Output voltage of HO2S-1 fails to go above specification (or HO2S-1 circuit shorted to ground)	2 driving cycles
P0135	HO2S-1 heater circuit malfunction	Terminal voltage is out of specification or electric current of heater is out of specification at heater ON	2 driving cycles
P0136	HO2S-2 circuit malfunction	HO2S-2 output voltage is out of specification on avarage (or HO2S-2 circuit open or short)	2 driving cycles
P0141	HO2S-2 heater circuit malfunction	Terminal voltage is out of specification or electric current of heater is out of specification at heater ON	2 driving cycles (*)

Fig. 96 Diagnostic Trouble Codes (DTC's)—1996–98 1.6L Engines

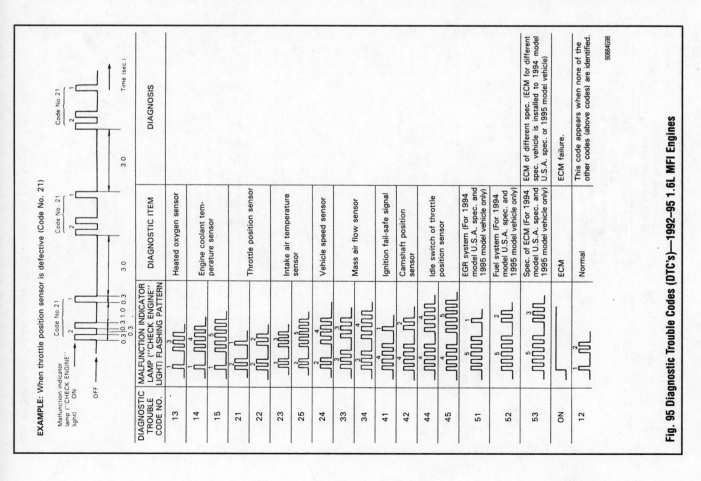

Fig. 95 Diagnostic Trouble Codes (DTC's)—1992–95 1.6L MFI Engines

DTC NO.	DETECTED ITEM	DETECTING CONDITION (DTC will set when detecting:)	MIL
P0500	Vehicle speed sensor malfunction	No signal during fuel cut	1 driving cycle
P0505	Idle air control system malfunction	Difference between desired idle speed and actual idle speed continues to exceed specified value for longer than specified time.	2 driving cycles
			(*)
P0510	Closed throttle position switch malfunction	ON/OFF state of CTP switch is not appropriate as compared with driving condition.	1 driving cycle
P0601	Internal control module memory check sum error	Data write error when written in to ECM	1 driving cycle
P0603	Internal control module keep alive memory error	Data read error when read from ROM in ECM	1 driving cycle
P1408	Manifold differential pressure sensor circuit malfunction	Manifold differential pressure sensor output voltage is higher or lower than specified value (or sensor circuit shorted to ground or open)	2 driving cycles
P1410 (EVAP-II vehicle)	Fuel tank pressure control system malfunction	Terminal voltage is lower than specification at valve OFF or it is higher than specification at valve ON.	2 driving cycles
P1450	Barometric pressure sensor circuit malfunction	Barometric pressure is lower or higher than specification.	1 driving cycle
P1451	Barometric pressure sensor performance problem	Difference between intake manifold pressure and barometric pressure is larger than specification during fuel shut off.	2 driving cycles
P1500	Engine starter signal circuit malfunction	Engine starts with no starter signal or signal input during long period after start.	2 driving cycles
P1510	ECM back-up power supply malfunction	No back-up power after starting engine.	1 driving cycle
P1530	Ignition timing adjustment switch circuit malfunction	Test switch terminal shorted to ground while driving vehicle.	1 driving cycle
P1600 (4A/T vehicle)	Serial communication problem between ECM and TCM	Serial communication line open or short.	1 driving cycle
P1715 (A/T vehicle)	Park/Neutral position switch circuit malfunction	Engine start is detected in other than P/N range or high load, high speed condition are detected in P/N range.	2 driving cycles

NOTE:
- For star (*) marked items in MIL column, MIL in Canada spec. vehicle does not light even when DTC is detected. Bear this in mind when diagnosing troubles.
- For definition of EVAP-I and EVAP-II, refer to GENERAL DESCRIPTION of Section 6E1.

Fig. 98 Diagnostic Trouble Codes (DTC's)—1996–98 1.6L Engines (continued)

DTC NO.	DETECTED ITEM	DETECTING CONDITION (DTC will set when detecting:)	MIL
P0171	Fuel system too lean	Short or long term fuel trim and total trim (short and long terms multiplied) are larger than specification for specified time or longer. (Fuel trim toward rich side is large.)	2 driving cycles
			(*)
P0172	Fuel system too rich	Short or long term fuel trim and total trim (short and long terms multiplied) are smaller than specification for specified time or longer. (Fuel trim toward lean side is large.)	2 driving cycles
			(*)
P0300	Random misfire detected	Misfire of such level as to cause damage to three way catalyst.	MIL blinks during actual misfire and remain continuously illuminated otherwise.
P0301	Cylinder 1 misfire detected		
P0302	Cylinder 2 misfire detected		
P0303	Cylinder 3 misfire detected		
P0304	Cylinder 4 misfire detected	Misfire of such level as to deteriorate emission but not to cause damage to three way catalyst.	2 driving cycles (*)
P0335	Crankshaft position sensor circuit malfunction	No signal during engine running	1 driving cycle
P0340	Camshaft position sensor circuit malfunction	No signal for 3 sec. during engine cranking	1 driving cycle
P0400	Exhanst gas recirculation flow malfunction	Excessive or insufficient EGR flow	2 driving cycles (*)
P0420	Catalyst system efficiency below threshold	Output wave forms of HO2S-1 and HO2S-2 are similar.	2 driving cycles (*)
P0440 (EVAP-II vehicle)	Evaporative emission control system malfunction	Leakage from EVAP system exceeds specification.	2 driving cycles (*)
P0443 (EVAP-I vehicle)	Evaporative emission control system incorrect purge flow	Malfunction of purge control valve. (When control duty of purge control valve changes while warmed engine is running at specified idle speed, variation in IAC duty and engine charging efficiency is less than specification.)	2 driving cycles (*)
P0450 (EVAP-II vehicle)	Evaporative emission control system pressure sensor malfunction	High or low voltage (or pressure sensor circuit shorted to ground or open.)	2 driving cycles
P0461	Fuel level sensor circuit performance	In spite of specified amount of fuel being consumed, fuel level signal voltage change is smaller than specification.	2 driving cycles
P0463	Fuel level sensor circuit high input	Fuel level sensor circuit open (high voltage)	2 driving cycles

Fig. 97 Diagnostic Trouble Codes (DTC's)—1996–98 1.6L Engines (continued)

DTC NO. ("OD/OFF")	DETECTED ITEM	DETECTING CONDITION (DTC will set when detecting:)	MIL
P1710	Back-up signal for speed sensor circuit malfunction	Back-up speed sensor signal is not inputted while output speed sensor signal being inputted.	2 driving cycles
P1875	4WD low switch circuit malfunction	Output speed/back-up speed ratio of 4WD low range is detected when 4WD low switch is turned OFF or output speed/back-up speed ratio of range other than that is detected when it is turned ON.	2 driving cycles

90884GA3

Fig. 100 Diagnostic Trouble Codes (DTC's)—1996–98 1.6L Engines (continued)

3A/T

DTC NO.	DETECTED ITEM	DETECTING CONDITION (DTC will set when detecting:)	MIL
P0740 or P0770	TCC solenoid malfunction	Vehicle speed/engine speed ratio for TCC OFF is detected when TCC ON signal is output and that for TCC ON when TCC OFF signal is output.	2 driving cycles

4A/T

DTC NO. ("OD/OFF")	DETECTED ITEM	DETECTING CONDITION (DTC will set when detecting:)	MIL
P0705 (34)	Transmission range switch circuit malfunction	D and other range signals inputted simultaneously or N, D, 2 or L range signal not inputted while running at 60km/h.	1 driving cycle
P0720 (31)	Output speed sensor circuit malfunction	Output speed sensor signal not inputted while VSS signal being inputted.	2 driving cycles
P0725 (52)	Engine speed input circuit malfunction	Engine speed signal not inputted while engine running (while engine coolant temp. signal being inputted in normal way).	2 driving cycles
P0751 (27)	Shift solenoid A(#1) performance or stuck off	Gear change control from TCM to A/T does not agree with actual gear position of A/T.	2 driving cycles
P0753 (21 or 22)	Shift solenoid A(#1) electrical	Monitor signal OFF is detected when shift solenoid A(#1) is ON or monitor signal ON is detected when it is OFF.	1 driving cycle
P0756 (28)	Shift solenoid B(#2) performance or stuck off	Gear change control from TCM to A/T does not agree with actual gear position of A/T.	2 driving cycles
P0758 (23 or 24)	Shift solenoid B(#2) electrical	Monitor signal OFF is detected when shift solenoid B(#2) is ON or monitor signal ON is detected when it is OFF.	1 driving cycle
P0741 or P0771 (29)	TCC (lock-up) solenoid performance or stuck off	Actual TCC operation does not agree with ON/OFF control from TCM to TCC.	2 driving cycles
P0743 or P0773 (25 or 26)	TCC (lock-up) solenoid electrical	Monitor signal OFF is detected when TCC control solenoid is ON or monitor signal ON is detected when it is OFF.	1 driving cycle
P1700 (32 or 33)	Throttle position signal input malfunction	Pulse signal ON (0V) time from ECM to TCM is out of specification.	1 driving cycle
P1705 (34)	Engine coolant temp. signal input malfunction	Pulse signal from ECM to TCM being OFF (10–14V) is detected or 100% ON is detected for 15 min.	1 driving cycle

90884GA2

Fig. 99 Diagnostic Trouble Codes (DTC's)—1996–98 1.6L Engines (continued)

DTC NO.	DETECTED ITEM	DETECTING CONDITION (DTC will set when detecting:)	MIL
P0171	Fuel system too lean	Total trim (short and long terms added) is larger than specification for specified time or longer. (Fuel trim toward rich side is large.)	2 driving cycles
P0172	Fuel system too rich	Total trim (short and long terms added) is smaller than specification for specified time or longer. (Fuel trim toward lean side is large.)	2 driving cycles
P0300	Random misfire detected	Misfire of such level as to cause damage to three way catalyst.	MIL blinks during actual misfire and remain continuously illuminated otherwise.
P0301	Cylinder 1 misfire detected		
P0302	Cylinder 2 misfire detected		
P0303	Cylinder 3 misfire detected		
P0304	Cylinder 4 misfire detected	Misfire of such level as to deteriorate emission but not to cause damage to three way catalyst.	2 driving cycles
P0335	Crankshaft position sensor circuit malfunction	No signal during engine running	1 driving cycle
P0340	Camshaft position sensor circuit malfunction	No signal for 5 sec. during engine cranking	1 driving cycle
P0400	Exhaust gas recirculation flow malfunction	Excessive or insufficient EGR flow	2 driving cycles
P0420	Catalyst system efficiency below threshold	Output wave forms of HO2S-1 and HO2S-2 are similar.	2 driving cycles
P0440 (EVAP-II)	Evaporative emission control system malfunction	Leakage from EVAP system exceeds specification	2 driving cycles
P0443 (EVAP-I)	Evaporative emission control system incorrect purge flow	Malfunction of purge control valve. (When control duty of purge control valve changes while warmed engine is running at specified idle speed, idle speed change is less than specification.)	2 driving cycles
P0450 (EVAP-II)	Evaporative emission control system pressure sensor malfunction	High or low voltage (or pressure sensor circuit shorted to ground or open)	2 driving cycles
P0451 (EVAP-II)	Evaporative emission control system pressure sensor range/performance	Tank pressure is out of specified value while vehicle running.	2 driving cycles
P0455 (EVAP-II)	Evaporative emission control system leak detected (Gross leak)	Excessive leakage from EVAP system (due to fuel filler cap being loosened, etc.) or purge line clogged.	1 driving cycle
P0461	Fuel level sensor circuit performance	In spite of specified amount of fuel being consumed, fuel level signal voltage change is smaller than specification.	2 driving cycles
P0463	Fuel level sensor circuit high input	Fuel level sensor circuit open (high voltage)	2 driving cycles

Fig. 102 Diagnostic Trouble Codes (DTC's)—1.8L Engines (continued)

DTC NO.	DETECTED ITEM	DETECTING CONDITION (DTC will set when detecting:)	MIL
P0101	Mass air flow circuit performance problem	Poor performance of MAF sensor	2 driving cycles
P0102	Mass air flow circuit low input	Sensor output too low	1 driving cycle
P0103	Mass air flow circuit high input	Sensor output too high	1 driving cycle
P0111	Intake air temp. circuit range/performance problem	Intake air temp. is high or low and temp. change is smaller than specification.	2 driving cycles
P0112	Intake air temp. circuit low input	High temperature-low voltage (or IAT sensor circuit shorted to ground)	1 driving cycle
P0113	Intake air temp. circuit high input	Low temperature-high voltage (or IAT sensor circuit open)	1 driving cycle
P0117	Engine coolant temp. circuit low input	High temperature-low voltage (or ECT sensor circuit shorted to ground)	1 driving cycle
P0118	Engine coolant temp. circuit high input	Low-temperature-high voltage (or ECT sensor circuit open)	1 driving cycle
P0121	Throttle position circuit performance problem	Poor performance of TP sensor	2 driving cycles
P0122	Throttle position circuit low input	Low voltage (or TP sensor circuit shorted to ground)	1 driving cycle
P0123	Throttle position circuit high input	High voltage (or TP sensor circuit open)	1 driving cycle
P0125	Insufficient coolant temp. for closed loop fuel control	Coolant temp. not reaching closed loop temp. within specified time after engine start (or poor performance of ECT sensor)	2 driving cycles
P0131	HO2S-1 circuit low voltage	Max. output voltage of HO2S-1 is lower than specification (or HO2S-1 circuit shorted to ground)	2 driving cycles
P0132	HO2S-1 circuit high voltage	Min. output voltage of HO2S-1 is higher than specification	2 driving cycles
P0133	HO2S-1 circuit slow response	Response time of HO2S-1 output voltage is longer than specification	2 driving cycles
P0134	HO2S-1 no activity detected	Output voltage of HO2S-1 fails to go above specification (or HO2S-1 circuit open)	2 driving cycles
P0135	HO2S-1 heater circuit malfunction	Terminal voltage is out of specification or electric current of heater is out of specification at heater ON	2 driving cycles
P0136	HO2S-2 circuit malfunction	HO2S-2 output voltage is out of specification on average (or HO2S-2 circuit open or short)	2 driving cycles
P0141	HO2S-2 heater circuit malfunction	Terminal voltage is out of specification or electric current of heater is out of specification at heater ON	2 driving cycles

Fig. 101 Diagnostic Trouble Codes (DTC's)—1.8L Engines

DTC NO.	DETECTED ITEM	DETECTING CONDITION (DTC will set when detecting:)	MIL
P0753	Shift solenoid A(#1) electrical	Monitor signal OFF is detected when shift solenoid A(#1) is ON or monitor signal ON is detected when it is OFF.	1 driving cycle
P0756	Shift solenoid B(#2) performance or stuck off	Gear change control from PCM to A/T does not agree with actual gear position of A/T.	2 driving cycles
P0758	Shift solenoid B(#2) electrical	Monitor signal OFF is detected when shift solenoid B(#2) is ON or monitor signal ON is detected when it is OFF.	1 driving cycle
P1875	4WD low switch circuit malfunction	Output speed/back-up speed ratio of 4WD low range is detected when 4WD low switch is turned OFF or output speed/back-up speed ratio of range other than that is detected when it is turned ON.	2 driving cycles

Fig. 104 Diagnostic Trouble Codes (DTC's)—1.8L Engines (continued)

DTC NO.	DETECTED ITEM	DETECTING CONDITION (DTC will set when detecting:)	MIL
P0500	Vehicle speed sensor malfunction	No signal during fuel cut	1 driving cycle
P0505	Idle air control system malfunction	Difference between desired idle speed and actual idle speed continues to exceed specified value for longer than specified time.	2 driving cycles
P0601	Internal control module memory check sum error	Data write error when written in to ECM	1 driving cycle
P0603	Internal control module keep alive memory error	Data read error when read from ROM in ECM	1 driving cycle
P1408	Manifold differential pressure sensor circuit malfunction	Manifold differential pressure sensor output voltage is higher or lower than specified value (or sensor circuit shorted to ground or open)	2 driving cycles
P1410	Fuel tank pressure control system malfunction	Monitor signal of tank pressure control solenoid vacuum valve is different from command signal. (Circuit open or short)	2 driving cycles
P1450	Barometric pressure sensor circuit malfunction	Barometric pressure is lower or higher than specification.	1 driving cycle
P1451	Barometric pressure sensor performance problem	Difference between intake manifold pressure and barometric pressure is larger than specification.	2 driving cycles
P1500	Engine starter signal circuit malfunction	Engine starts with no starter signal or signal input during long period after start.	2 driving cycles
P1510	ECM back-up power supply malfunction	No back-up power after starting engine.	1 driving cycle
P1530	Ignition timing adjustment switch circuit malfunction	Test switch terminal shorted to ground while driving vehicle.	1 driving cycle

A/T

DTC NO.	DETECTED ITEM	DETECTING CONDITION (DTC will set when detecting:)	MIL
P0705	Transmission range switch circuit malfunction	Multiple signals inputted simultaneously or R, N, D, 2 or L range signal not inputted while running at 60km/h or more.	2 driving cycles
P0720	Output speed sensor circuit malfunction	Output speed sensor signal not inputted while VSS signal being inputted.	2 driving cycles
P0741	TCC (lock-up) solenoid performance or stuck off	Actual TCC operation does not agree with ON/OFF control from PCM to TCC.	2 driving cycles
P0743	TCC (lock-up) solenoid electrical	Monitor signal OFF is detected when TCC control solenoid is ON or monitor signal ON is detected when it is OFF.	1 driving cycle
P0751	Shift solenoid A(#1) performance or stuck off	Gear change control from PCM to A/T does not agree with actual gear position of A/T.	2 driving cycles

Fig. 103 Diagnostic Trouble Codes (DTC's)—1.8L Engines (continued)

VACUUM DIAGRAMS

Following are vacuum diagrams for most of the engine and emissions package combinations covered by this manual. Because vacuum circuits will vary based on various engine and vehicle options, always refer first to the vehicle emission control information label, if present. Should the label be missing, or should vehicle be equipped with a different engine from the vehicle's original equipment, refer to the diagrams below for the same or similar configuration.

If you wish to obtain a replacement emissions label, most manufacturers make the labels available for purchase. The labels can usually be ordered from a local dealer.

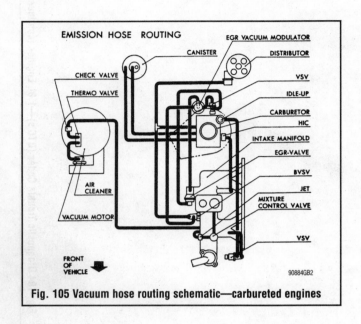

Fig. 105 Vacuum hose routing schematic—carbureted engines

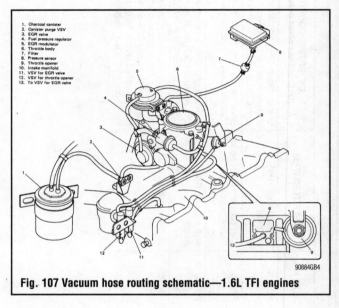

Fig. 107 Vacuum hose routing schematic—1.6L TFI engines

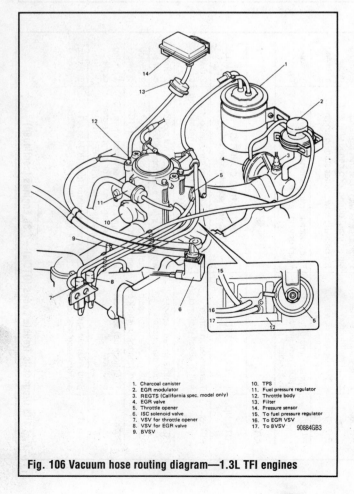

Fig. 106 Vacuum hose routing diagram—1.3L TFI engines

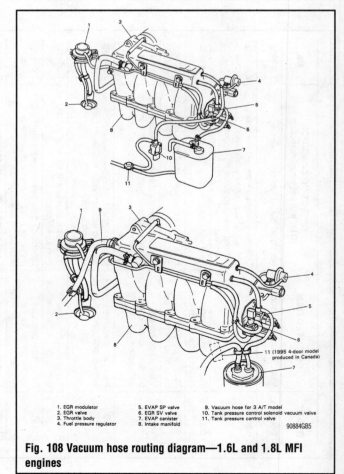

Fig. 108 Vacuum hose routing diagram—1.6L and 1.8L MFI engines

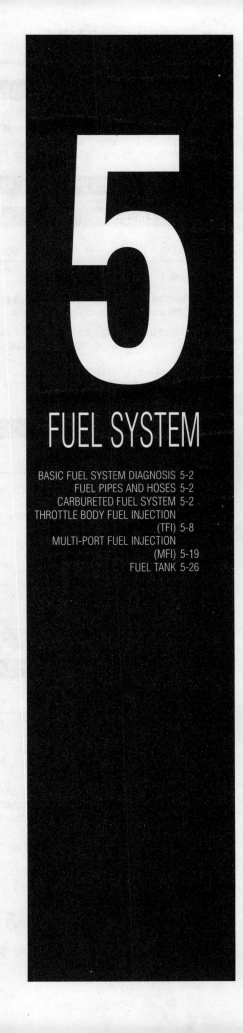

5

FUEL SYSTEM

BASIC FUEL SYSTEM DIAGNOSIS

When there is a problem starting or driving a vehicle, two of the most important checks involve the ignition and the fuel systems. The questions most mechanics attempt to answer first, "is there spark?" and "is there fuel?" will often lead to solving most basic problems. For ignition system diagnosis and testing, please refer to the information on engine electrical components and ignition systems found earlier in this manual. If the ignition system checks out (there is spark), then you must determine if the fuel system is operating properly (is there fuel?).

FUEL PIPES AND HOSES

Carbureted Engines

PRECAUTIONS & INSPECTION

▶ **See Figure 1**

➡**The carbureted fuel system is not under high pressure, and, therefore, does not utilize special screw fittings.**

The fuel hoses use conventional screw-type hose clamps. Position the hose clamps on the hoses as indicated in the accompanying illustration for proper hose sealing.

Inspect the fuel lines for evidence of fuel leakage, hose cracking and deterioration, or other damage. Ensure all hose clamps are secure. If any damage is evident, replace all necessary fuel lines.

Fuel Injected Engines

PRECAUTIONS & INSPECTION

Due to the fact that the fuel supply lines are under high pressure, the fuel supply lines use screw couplings. Any time these fittings are loosened or tightened, ensure that a back-up wrench is used, and that they are tightened to 29–36 ft. lbs. (40–50 Nm).

The fuel return hoses use conventional screw-type hose clamps. Position the hose clamps on the hoses as indicated in the accompanying illustration for proper hose sealing.

Inspect the fuel lines for evidence of fuel leakage, hose cracking and deterioration, or other damage. Ensure all hose clamps are secure. If any damage is evident, replace all necessary fuel lines.

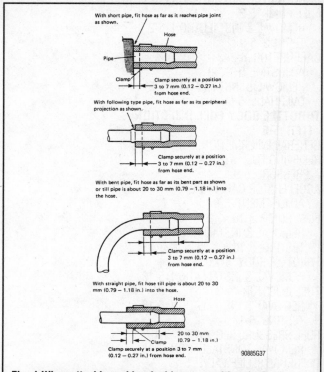

Fig. 1 When attaching rubber fuel hoses, position the hose clamps as indicated

CARBURETED FUEL SYSTEM

Fuel Pump

REMOVAL & INSTALLATION

▶ **See Figures 2, 3 and 4**

1. Disconnect the negative battery cable.
2. Remove the fuel tank cap to release any fuel tank vapor pressure. Reinstall the fuel tank cap.
3. Using a screwdriver, loosen the fuel pump hose clamps, then slide the clamps down the hoses away from the pump assembly.
4. Detach the fuel hoses from the pump, and drain the residual fuel from the hoses into a small metal catch can.
5. Loosen the fuel pump mounting bolts, then separate the pump from the cylinder head.
6. Remove the fuel pump actuating rod from the cylinder head, then remove and discard the old gasket.

To install:

7. Clean the fuel pump-to-cylinder head gasket surfaces thoroughly.
8. Apply a coat of clean engine oil to the actuating rod, then insert it into the cylinder head.
9. Install the fuel pump, along with a new gasket, onto the cylinder head. Install and tighten the mounting bolts securely.

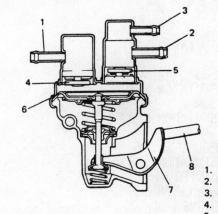

1. Inlet
2. Outlet
3. Return tube
4. Inlet valve
5. Outlet valve
6. Diaphragm
7. Rocker arm
8. Fuel pump rod

Fig. 2 Cross-sectional view of the mechanical fuel pump used on all carbureted engines covered by this manual

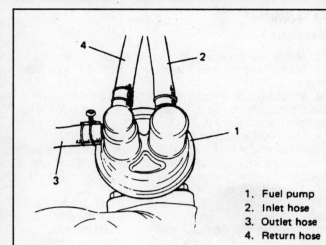

1. Fuel pump
2. Inlet hose
3. Outlet hose
4. Return hose

90885G00

Fig. 3 To remove the fuel pump, first disconnect and label all of the fuel lines from it

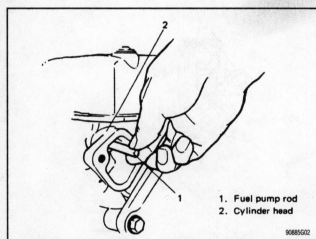

1. Fuel pump rod
2. Cylinder head

90885G02

Fig. 4 After removing the fuel pump from the cylinder head, the fuel pump actuating rod can also be removed and inspected for damage

10. Reattach the fuel hoses to the fuel pump, then slide the retaining clamps up the hoses. The clamps should be positioned as shown in the accompanying illustration. Tighten the clamp screw until secure.

11. Clean any spilled fuel from the engine.

❊❊ CAUTION

If any fuel was spilled near the battery, or on the engine, allow the fuel fumes to dissipate before reconnecting the negative battery cable. Sparks and fuel vapor can cause fatal explosions.

12. Connect the negative battery cable.

TESTING

1. Remove the fuel tank cap to release any fuel tank vapor pressure. Reinstall the fuel tank cap.

2. Using a screwdriver, loosen the fuel pump hose clamps, then slide the clamps down the hoses away from the pump assembly.

3. Detacch the fuel pump-to-carburetor hose from the pump, and drain the residual fuel from the hose into a small metal catch can.

4. Install a new piece of fuel line to the fuel pump. The new piece of fuel line should be long enough to reach 3 or 4 ft. (1m) away from the vehicle.

5. Position the disconnected end of the new fuel hose into a metal catch container; a metal coffee can works well.

6. Have an assistant sit inside the vehicle and, using the ignition switch, crank the engine for 8–12 seconds. Have your helper perform this 4 or 5 times, while you observe the disconnected end of the fuel hose. Fuel should emit from the fuel hose into the metal catch pan. If no fuel is emitted from the hose, inspect the fuel lines for obstructions and also check the fuel pump actuating rod. If there are no problems with the fuel lines or fuel actuating rod, install a known good fuel pump and retest. If the retest is works okay, the old fuel pump was faulty.

7. Remove the new fuel pump hose.

8. Reattach the original fuel hoses to the fuel pump, then slide the retaining clamps up the hoses. The clamps should be positioned as shown in the accompanying illustration. Tighten the clamp screw until secure.

9. Clean any spilled fuel from the engine.

❊❊ CAUTION

If any fuel was spilled near the battery, or on the engine, allow the fuel fumes to dissipate before reconnecting the negative battery cable. Sparks and fuel vapor can cause fatal explosions.

Carburetor

ADJUSTMENTS

Idle Speed and Mixture

For the idle speed and mixture adjustments, refer to Section 1 of this manual.

Accelerator Cable Play

◆ See Figure 5

1. With the engine cold, measure and note the amount of deflection of the accelerator cable at the carburetor, as shown in the accompanying illustration.

2. Start the engine and allow it to reach normal operating temperature.

3. Measure and note the cable play again once the engine is completely warmed up.

4. If the cable play was not within either of the specified ranges, adjust the cable play as follows:
   a. Loosen the adjusting locknut.
   b. Turn the adjusting nut until the cable play is within the specified range.
   c. Tighten the adjusting locknut securely.

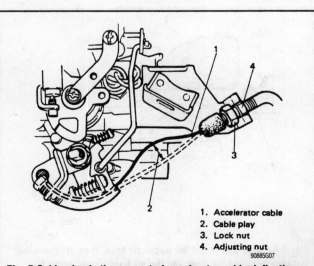

1. Accelerator cable
2. Cable play
3. Lock nut
4. Adjusting nut

90885G07

Fig. 5 Cable play is the amount of accelerator cable deflection when the accelerator pedal is fully disengaged

5. Allow the engine to cool down, then perform the test procedure again to double check the adjustment.

Float Level

▶ **See Figures 6 and 7**

1. Inspect the float level by looking through the level inspection window in the side of the carburetor. The float level should fall within the round mark at the center of the level window.

2. If the float level is not within the round mark in the window, proceed with the adjustment. Otherwise, the float level is correct.

3. Remove the upper air horn from the carburetor and turn it upside-down. Be sure to remove the air horn gasket prior to measuring the float level.

➡**Measure the float level with the all of the float weight applied to the needle valve.**

4. Using a drill bit or bolt of the proper diameter, measure the distance between the float and the gasket surface of the air horn. The distance should be 0.31 in. (8mm). If the float level is not as specified, adjust it by bending the tongue up or down.

5. Install the air horn on the carburetor.

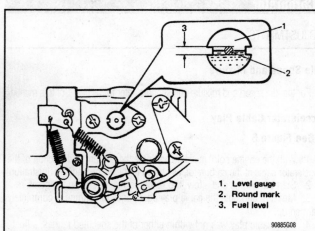

1. Level gauge
2. Round mark
3. Fuel level

90885G08

Fig. 6 Before removing the upper carburetor air horn, observe the fuel level gauge on the side of the carburetor—if the round mark does not fall in the middle of the level gauge, remove the air horn for adjustment

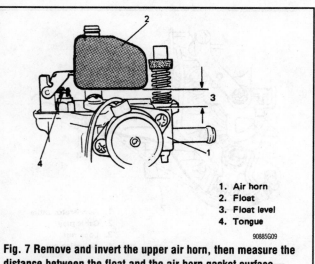

1. Air horn
2. Float
3. Float level
4. Tongue

90885G09

Fig. 7 Remove and invert the upper air horn, then measure the distance between the float and the air horn gasket surface—bend the tongue (4) to adjust as necessary

Idle-Up Operation

▶ **See Figure 8**

1. Start the engine, and allow it to reach normal operating temperature.

2. Ensure that the idle speed is correct; refer to Section 1 for the proper procedure.

3. While turning the tail lights, license plate lights and side marker lights ON, ensure that the idle-up actuator rod moves down (indicating that the idle-up is working).

4. Ensure that the heater fan, rear defogger, and air conditioner (if equipped) are all turned OFF. Turn the headlights ON, then check the engine idle-up speed (rpm). The idle-up speed should be 900–1000 rpm. If the idle-up speed is not as specified, adjust it by turning the adjusting screw.

5. Turn the headlights and other lights OFF.

6. Turn the rear defogger ON, and ensure that the idle-up actuator rod moves down, as in Step 3. Perform this step also with the air conditioner and the heater fan. In all three cases, the idle-up actuator rod should move down and increase the vehicle's idle speed to 900–1000 rpm.

7. If the actuator rod does not move as indicated, there is a problem with the Three-Way Switching Valve (TWSV), the TWSV circuit, or the actuator itself.

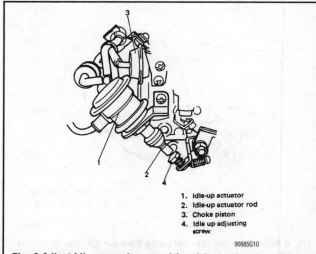

1. Idle-up actuator
2. Idle-up actuator rod
3. Choke piston
4. Idle up adjusting screw

90885G10

Fig. 8 Adjust idle-up engine speed (rpm) by turning the adjusting screw until the proper rpm is achieved

Choke Operation

Perform the following adjustment with the air intake case removed from the engine, and the engine should be cold.

1. Using your finger, check the choke valve for smooth movement.

2. When the ambient temperature is below 77°F (25°C) and the engine is cold, ensure that the choke valve is almost completely closed.

3. Ensure that the choke valve-to-carburetor bore clearance is within 0.004–0.023 in. (0.1–0.6mm) when the ambient air temperature is 77°F (25°C), and within 0.05–0.11 in. (1.3–2.8mm) when the air temperature is 104°F (40°C).

4. If the choke valve-to-carburetor bore clearance is not within the specified ranges, inspect the choke spring, choke piston and each actuating link in the choke system for smooth operation. Lubricate the choke valve shaft and each actuating link with spray lubricant, if necessary.

5. If the choke valve-to-carburetor bore clearance is still not within the specified ranges, remove the carburetor from the intake manifold, then remove the idle-up actuator from the carburetor.

6. Turn the fast idle cam counterclockwise and insert a metal pin into the cam and bracket holes to secure it in place.

7. Bend the choke lever up or down with a pair of pliers. Bending the lever up closes the choke valve, and bending the lever don opens the choke valve.

8. Install the idle-up actuator, the carburetor and the air intake case.

9. Start the engine and allow it to reach normal operating temperature.

10. Stop the engine once it is warmed up, remove the air intake case, and ensure that the choke valve is fully open.

11. If the choke valve does not open fully, the wax element or the link system is defective.

Fast Idle Speed

♦ See Figures 9 and 10

➥Fast idle inspection and adjustment should be performed when the ambient air temperature is between 71–82°F (22–28°C), and only if the idle-up system is functioning normally.

1. Park the vehicle in a garage where the ambient air temperature is 71–82°F (22–28°C) for at least four hours.

2. Remove the carburetor and allow it rest for one hour in the same place as the vehicle (the temperature must be 71–82°F (22–28°C) for the carburetor).

3. After one hour, inspect the cam and cam follower to ensure that the cam mark is positioned as shown.

4. Detach the vacuum hose from the Three-Way Switching Valve (TWSV), and connect a hand-held vacuum pump to the idle-up actuator.

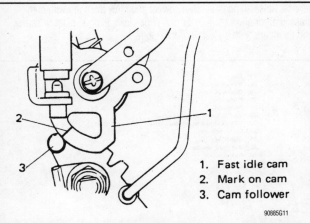

1. Fast idle cam
2. Mark on cam
3. Cam follower

90885G11

Fig. 9 After the carburetor is allowed to sit in an area where the temperature is 71–82°F (22–28°C) for at least one hour, observe the fast idle cam and cam follower—ensure that they are properly aligned, as shown

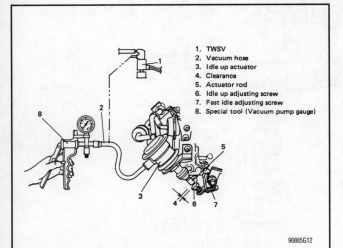

1. TWSV
2. Vacuum hose
3. Idle up actuator
4. Clearance
5. Actuator rod
6. Idle up adjusting screw
7. Fast idle adjusting screw
8. Special tool (Vacuum pump gauge)

90885G12

Fig. 10 Using a hand-held vacuum pump, apply 15.7 in. Hg (40cm Hg) of vacuum to the idle-up actuator

5. Apply 15.7 in. Hg (40cm Hg) of vacuum to the idle-up actuator, then measure the clearance between the actuator rod and the idle-up adjusting screw. The clearance should be 0.10–0.12 in. (2.5–3.0mm).

6. If the clearance was not within the specified range, adjust it by turning the fast idle adjusting screw.

Unloader Operation

♦ See Figure 11

This procedure should be performed when the engine is cold.

1. Remove the air intake case.

2. Ensure that the choke valve is completely closed.

3. Open the choke valve fully, and check that the choke valve-to-carburetor bore clearance is 0.10–0.12 in. (2.5–3.0mm).

4. If the clearance was not within the specified range, adjust it by bending the unloader arm until the proper clearance is achieved.

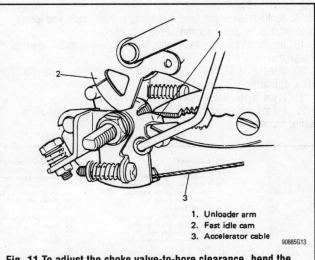

1. Unloader arm
2. Fast idle cam
3. Accelerator cable

90885G13

Fig. 11 To adjust the choke valve-to-bore clearance, bend the unloader arm with a pair of pliers

REMOVAL & INSTALLATION

1. Disconnect the negative battery cable.

✳✳ CAUTION

Never open, service or drain the radiator or cooling system when hot; serious burns can occur from the steam and hot coolant. Also, when draining engine coolant, keep in mind that cats and dogs are attracted to ethylene glycol antifreeze and could drink any that is left in an uncovered container or in puddles on the ground. This will prove fatal in sufficient quantities. Always drain coolant into a sealable container. Coolant should be reused unless it is contaminated or is several years old..

2. Drain the engine coolant.

3. Remove the air intake case from the carburetor.

4. Detach and label all of the wiring connectors from the micro-switches, switch vent solenoid valve, fuel cut-off solenoid valve and mixture control solenoid valve.

5. Detach the wiring connector from the Vacuum Switching Valve (VSV).

6. Remove the EGR modulator and Three-Way Switching Valve (TWSV) from the carburetor.

7. Detach the engine coolant hoses from the carburetor.

8. Disconnect the accelerator cable from the carburetor.

9. Disconnect and label the vacuum hoses from the idle-up actuator and the carburetor.

10. Remove the fuel tank filler cap, then reinstall it. This will release fuel tank pressure.

11. Detach the fuel inlet hose from the carburetor, and drain any residual fuel from the hose into a small metal catch pan.

12. Check around the carburetor for any other wires, hoses or cables which will inhibit carburetor removal.

13. Loosen the carburetor-to-intake manifold mounting bolts, then lift the carburetor up and off of the intake manifold.

14. Install clean shop rags in the intake manifold hole to prevent accidentally dropping nuts or bolts into the engine.

To install:

15. Clean the carburetor-to-intake manifold gasket surface thoroughly.

16. Along with a new carburetor gasket, install the carburetor on the intake manifold. Be sure to remove the shop rags from the intake manifold inlet hole prior to installing the carburetor.

17. Install and tighten the carburetor mounting nuts evenly to 159–248 inch lbs. (18–28 Nm).

18. Reattach all vacuum lines, fuel hoses, coolant hoses, and wiring connectors to the carburetor and related components.

19. Reconnect the accelerator cable, then adjust it as described earlier in this section.

20. Install the EGR modulator and Three-Way Switching Valve (TWSV) to the carburetor.

21. Install the air intake case.

22. Fill the engine cooling system with the proper amount and type of engine coolant.

OVERHAUL

◆ See Figures 12 and 13

Efficient carburetion depends greatly on careful cleaning and inspection during overhaul, since dirt, gum, water, or varnish in or on the carburetor parts are often responsible for poor performance.

Overhaul your carburetor in a clean, dust-free area. Carefully disassemble the carburetor, referring often to the exploded views and directions packaged with the rebuilding kit. Keep all similar and look-alike parts segregated during disassembly and cleaning to avoid accidental interchange during assembly. Make a note of all jet sizes.

When the carburetor is disassembled, wash all parts in clean carburetor solvent, with the following exceptions:

- Micro-switches
- Switch vent solenoid
- Fuel cut solenoid valve
- Mixture control solenoid valve
- Secondary diaphragm, choke piston and idle-up actuator
- Gaskets and parts made of rubber or resin
- Thermo-wax (thermo element)

Do not leave parts in the solvent any longer than it is necessary to sufficiently loosen the deposits. Excessive cleaning may remove the special finish from the float bowl and choke valve bodies, leaving these parts unfit for service. Rinse all parts in clean solvent and blow them dry with compressed air or allow them to air dry. Wipe clean all cork, plastic, leather, and fiber parts with a clean, lint-free cloth.

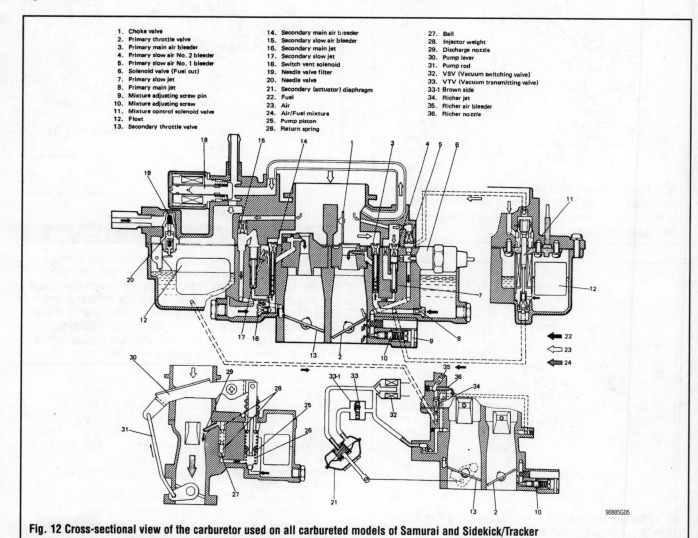

1. Choke valve
2. Primary throttle valve
3. Primary main air bleeder
4. Primary slow air No. 2 bleeder
5. Primary slow air No. 1 bleeder
6. Solenoid valve (Fuel cut)
7. Primary slow jet
8. Primary main jet
9. Mixture adjusting screw pin
10. Mixture adjusting screw
11. Mixture control solenoid valve
12. Float
13. Secondary throttle valve

14. Secondary main air bleeder
15. Secondary slow air bleeder
16. Secondary main jet
17. Secondary slow jet
18. Switch vent solenoid
19. Needle valve filter
20. Needle valve
21. Secondary (actuator) diaphragm
22. Fuel
23. Air
24. Air/Fuel mixture
25. Pump piston
26. Return spring

27. Ball
28. Injector weight
29. Discharge nozzle
30. Pump lever
31. Pump rod
32. VSV (Vacuum switching valve)
33. VTV (Vacuum transmitting valve)
33-1. Brown side
34. Richer jet
35. Richer air bleeder
36. Richer nozzle

Fig. 12 Cross-sectional view of the carburetor used on all carbureted models of Samurai and Sidekick/Tracker

90885G05

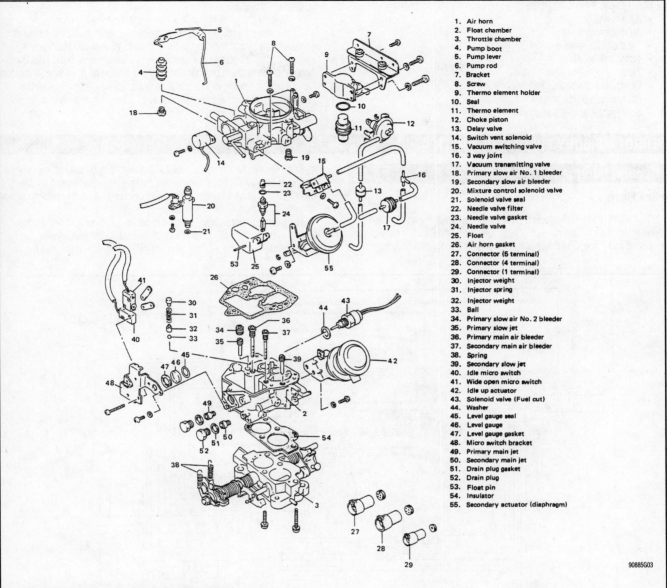

1. Air horn
2. Float chamber
3. Throttle chamber
4. Pump boot
5. Pump lever
6. Pump rod
7. Bracket
8. Screw
9. Thermo element holder
10. Seal
11. Thermo element
12. Choke piston
13. Delay valve
14. Switch vent solenoid
15. Vacuum switching valve
16. 3 way joint
17. Vacuum transmitting valve
18. Primary slow air No. 1 bleeder
19. Secondary slow air bleeder
20. Mixture control solenoid valve
21. Solenoid valve seal
22. Needle valve filter
23. Needle valve gasket
24. Needle valve
25. Float
26. Air horn gasket
27. Connector (5 terminal)
28. Connector (4 terminal)
29. Connector (1 terminal)
30. Injector weight
31. Injector spring
32. Injector weight
33. Ball
34. Primary slow air No. 2 bleeder
35. Primary slow jet
36. Primary main air bleeder
37. Secondary main air bleeder
38. Spring
39. Secondary slow jet
40. Idle micro switch
41. Wide open micro switch
42. Idle up actuator
43. Solenoid valve (Fuel cut)
44. Washer
45. Level gauge seal
46. Level gauge
47. Level gauge gasket
48. Micro switch bracket
49. Primary main jet
50. Secondary main jet
51. Drain plug gasket
52. Drain plug
53. Float pin
54. Insulator
55. Secondary actuator (diaphragm)

90885G03

Fig. 13 Exploded view of the Suzuki carburetor

Blow out all passages and jets with compressed air and be sure that there are no restrictions or blockages. Never use wire or similar tools to clean jets, fuel passages, or air bleeds. Clean all jets and valve separately to avoid accidental interchange.

Check all parts for wear or damage. If wear or damage is found, replace the defective parts. Especially check the following:

1. Check the float needle and seat for wear. If wear is found, replace the complete assembly.

2. Check the float hinge pin for wear and the float for dents or distortion. Replace the float if fuel has leaked into it.

3. Check the throttle and choke shaft bores for wear or out-of-round condition. Damage or wear to the throttle arm, shaft, or shaft bore will often require replacement of the throttle body. These parts require a close tolerance of fit; wear may allow air leakage, which could affect starting and idling.

➡Throttle shafts and bushings are not included in overhaul kits. They can be purchased separately.

4. Inspect the idle mixture adjusting needles for burrs or grooves. Any such condition requires replacement of the needle, since you will not be able to obtain a satisfactory idle.

5. Test the accelerator pump check valves. They should pass air one way, but not the other way. Test for proper seating by blowing and sucking on the valve. Replace the valve check ball and spring as necessary. If the valve is satisfactory, wash the valve parts again to remove breath moisture.

6. Check the bowl cover for warped surfaces with a straightedge.

7. Closely inspect the accelerator pump plunger for wear and damage, replacing as necessary.

8. After the carburetor is assembled, check the choke valve for freedom of operation.

Carburetor overhaul kits are recommended for each overhaul. These kits contain all gaskets and new parts to replace those that deteriorate most rapidly. Failure to replace all parts supplied with the kits (especially gaskets) can result in poor performance later.

Some carburetor manufacturers supply overhaul kits of three basic types: minor repair, major repair, and gasket kits. Basically, they contain the following:

Minor Repair Kits:
• All gaskets
• Float needle valve
• All diagrams
• Spring for the pump diaphragm

Major Repair Kits:
- All jets and gaskets
- All diaphragms
- Float needle valve
- Pump ball valve
- Float
- Complete intermediate rod
- Intermediate pump lever
- Some cover hold-down screws and washers

Gasket Kits:
- All gaskets

After cleaning and checking all components, reassemble the carburetor, using new parts and referring to the exploded view. When reassembling, make sure that all screws and jets are tight in their seats, but do not over-tighten as the tips will be distorted. Tighten all screws gradually, in rotation. Do not tighten needle valves into their seats; uneven jetting will be the result. Always use new gaskets. Be sure to adjust the float level during reassembly.

THROTTLE BODY FUEL INJECTION (TFI)

General Information

▶ See Figure 14

The Throttle body Fuel Injection (TFI) system supplies the combustion chambers with an air/fuel mixture of optimized ratio under widely diverse driving conditions. The TFI system utilizes a single-point throttle body fuel injection system, which injects fuel into the throttle body through one injector.

The TFI system is composed of two major sub-systems: air/fuel delivery and electronic engine controls. The electronic engine control sub-system is covered in Section 4 of this manual.

The main components of the air/fuel delivery sub-system are the fuel tank, fuel pump, fuel filter, throttle body (including the fuel injector, the fuel pressure regulator, the air valve and the ISC valve), fuel lines, and the air

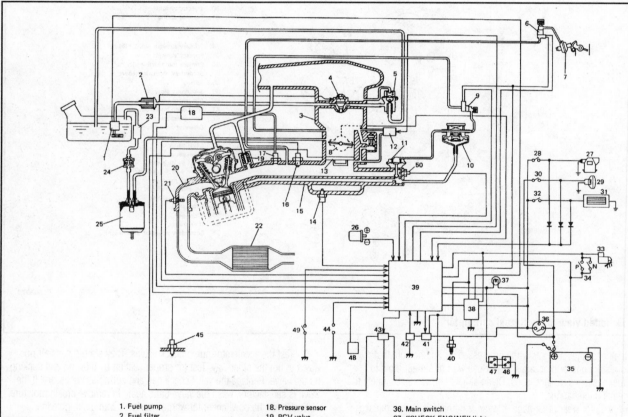

1. Fuel pump
2. Fuel filter
3. Throttle body
4. Injector
5. Fuel pressure regulator
6. Throttle opener VSV (Vacuum Switching Valve)
7. Throttle opener
8. Throttle position sensor
9. EGR VSV
10. EGR modulator
11. EGR valve
12. ISC (Idle Speed Control) solenoid valve
13. PTC (Positive Temperature Coefficient) heater (For AT vehicle)
14. Water temperature sensor
15. Intake manifold
16. Air temperature sensor
17. Gas filter
18. Pressure sensor
19. PCV valve
20. Exhaust manifold
21. Oxygen sensor
22. Three-way catalyst
23. Fuel vapor separator
24. 2-way check valve
25. Charcoal canister
26. Ignition coil
27. Heater fan motor
28. Heater fan switch
29. Small, tail, side marker & license lights
30. Small, tail, side marker & license lights switch
31. Rear defogger
32. Rear defogger switch
33. Starter motor
34. Shift switch (For AT vehicle)
35. Battery
36. Main switch
37. "CHECK ENGINE" light
38. Control relay
39. ECM (Electronic Control Module)
40. Brake pedal switch (Stop light switch)
41. Lock-up relay (For AT vehicle)
42. Lock-up solenoid (For AT vehicle)
43. PTC relay
44. Diagnosis terminal
45. 5th switch (For MT vehicle)
46. Mileage sensor (For Federal Specification only)
47. Cancel switch (For Federal Specification only)
48. Air-conditioner amplifier (For vehicle with air-conditioner)
49. Power steering pump pressure switch (For vehicle with power steering system)
50. Recirculated exhaust gas temperature sensor (California spec. only)

90885G38

Fig. 14 Throttle body Fuel Injection (TFI) system schematic showing all related components

cleaner. The fuel filter and air cleaner are both covered in Section 1, and the air valve and ISC valve are covered in Section 4 of this manual.

Relieving Fuel System Pressure

♦ See Figure 15

✳✳ CAUTION

This procedure can NOT be performed when the engine is hot. If done so, it may cause an adverse effect to the catalytic converter, or create a dangerous, explosive condition.

1. Place the transmission gearshift lever in Neutral (manual transmissions) or Park (automatic transmissions), apply the parking brake, and block the drive wheels.
2. Detach the wiring harness connector from the fuel pump relay, located under the left-hand side (Sidekick and Tracker models) or right-hand side (Samurai models) of the instrument panel near the ECM.
3. Remove the fuel tank filler cap to release fuel vapor pressure in the fuel tank. Reinstall the filler cap.
4. Start the engine and run it until it stops from lack of fuel. Crank the engine 2 or 3 times for a three second period. The fuel lines should now be depressurized.
5. After servicing the component(s), reattach the wiring harness connector to the fuel pump relay.

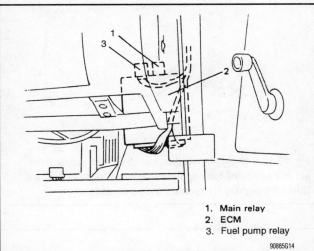

1. Main relay
2. ECM
3. Fuel pump relay

90885G14

Fig. 15 The fuel pump relay is located under the right-hand side of the instrument panel on Samurai models

Accelerator Cable

ADJUSTMENT

Samurai and 1989–93 Sidekick/Tracker Models

♦ See Figures 16 and 17

➡The engine should not be running during this inspection.

1. Ensure that the accelerator pedal is fully released.

➡When measuring the deflection, do not press on the cable so much that the throttle lever moves.

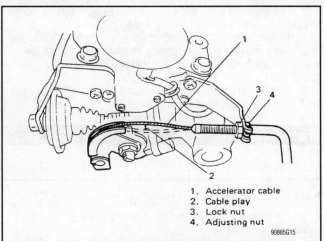

1. Accelerator cable
2. Cable play
3. Lock nut
4. Adjusting nut

90885G15

Fig. 16 Accelerator cable (1) play is the amount of deflection (2) of the cable at the throttle body—to adjust the play, loosen the locknut . . .

90885P03

Fig. 17 . . . then turn the adjusting nut with a wrench to change the accelerator cable play

2. Using a finger, press the cable as shown in the accompanying illustration and measure the deflection. The deflection should be 0.4–0.6 in. (10–15mm).
3. If the deflection is not within the specified range, loosen the locknut and turn the adjusting nut until the desired deflection is obtained. Tighten the locknut securely, and recheck the deflection.
4. Depress the throttle opener rod so that it is not touching the throttle lever, and remeasure the cable deflection, which should now be 0.12–0.20 in. (3–5mm). If the deflection is not as specified, perform Step 3 again.

1994–95 Sidekick and Tracker Models

1. With throttle valve completely closed, inspect the accelerator pedal play (the amount of pedal movement before the accelerator cable causes the throttle lever to move), which should be 0.08–0.27 in. (2–7mm).

➡The adjusting nut and locknut are located on the accelerator cable bracket, mounted on the throttle body.

2. If the pedal play is not within the specified range, loosen the locknut and turn the adjusting nut until the proper play is obtained.

3. Have an assistant sit in the vehicle and fully depress the accelerator pedal, then inspect the clearance between the throttle lever and the lever stopper (throttle body). The clearance should be 0.02–0.07 in. (0.5–2.0mm).

4. If the clearance is not within the indicated range, turn the pedal stopper bolt until the proper clearance is obtained.

Fuel Pump

REMOVAL & INSTALLATION

▶ **See Figures 18 and 19**

The fuel pump is mounted in the fuel tank, which must be removed to service the fuel pump.

1. Remove the fuel tank from the vehicle, as described later in this section.

2. Loosen the fuel pump retaining bolts, then lift the fuel pump up and out of the fuel tank.

3. Remove and discard the old fuel pump gasket.

To install:

4. Position the fuel pump, along with a new gasket, in the fuel tank, ensuring that the fuel pump retaining bolt holes are aligned.

5. Install and tighten the fuel pump retaining bolts securely and evenly.

6. Install the fuel tank into the vehicle.

TESTING

On-Vehicle Inspection

▶ **See Figures 20 and 21**

1. Remove the fuel tank filler cap.

2. Have an assistant turn the ignition **ON**, while you listen at the fuel filler tube opening. The operation of the fuel pump should be heard from the fuel filler tube opening for approximately 3 seconds, then it should stop.

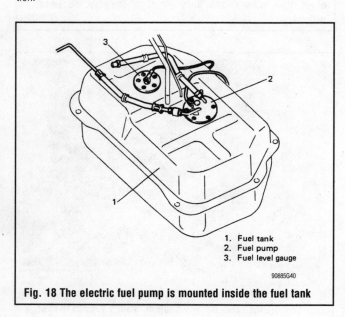

1. Fuel tank
2. Fuel pump
3. Fuel level gauge

90885G40

Fig. 18 The electric fuel pump is mounted inside the fuel tank

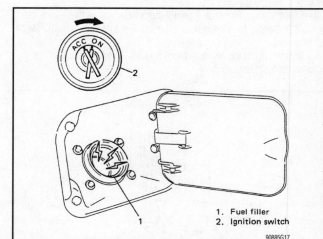

1. Fuel filler
2. Ignition switch

90885G17

Fig. 20 After turning the ignition switch ON, the sound of the electric fuel pump running should be heard from the fuel tank filler tube opening for approximately 3 seconds

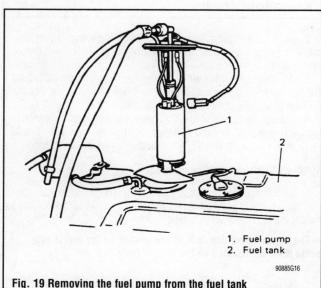

1. Fuel pump
2. Fuel tank

90885G16

Fig. 19 Removing the fuel pump from the fuel tank

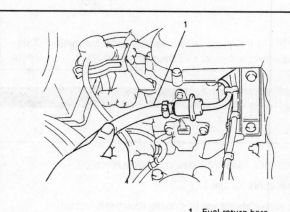

1. Fuel return hose

90885G18

Fig. 21 Fuel pressure should be felt at the fuel return line for 3 seconds after the ignition switch is turned ON as well—if either of these is missing, there is a problem with the fuel pump or its circuit

3. Turn the ignition switch **OFF**.

4. Open the hood to gain access to the fuel return line, connected to the fuel pressure regulator mounted on the throttle body.

5. Once again, have your assistant turn the ignition **ON**, while you feel for fuel pressure at the fuel return line near the throttle body. Fuel pressure should be felt at the return line for approximately 3 seconds after the ignition switch is turned **ON**.

6. If the fuel pump is not heard operating, or if no fuel pressure is felt at the return line, there is a problem with the fuel pump or its circuit.

7. Reinstall the fuel tank filler cap.

Fuel Pump Circuit and Fuel Pressure Inspection

▶ **See Figures 22 thru 27**

For the inspection of the fuel pump circuit or fuel pressure, refer to the accompanying diagnostic charts.

For the fuel pressure inspection, it will be necessary to install a fuel pressure gauge as follows:

1. Relieve the fuel system pressure.

2. Raise and safely support the vehicle on jackstands.

3. Remove the small plug bolt from the fuel filter union bolt.

4. Attach a fuel pressure gauge set (such as Suzuki Tool 09912–58412) to the fuel filter union bolt.

Fuel Pump Relay Inspection

▶ **See Figures 28, 29 and 30**

When testing the fuel pump circuit, it may be necessary to inspect the fuel pump relay for defects. Test the relay as follows:

1. Disconnect the negative battery cable.

2. Remove the fuel pump relay from its mounting bracket after disengaging the wiring harness connector from it.

3. Using a Digital Volt-Ohmmeter (DVOM) set on the ohmmeter func-

Fig. 22 Typical fuel pump circuit schematic for TFI engines

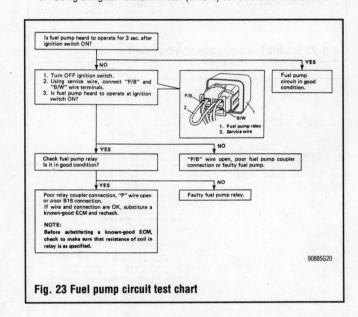

Fig. 23 Fuel pump circuit test chart

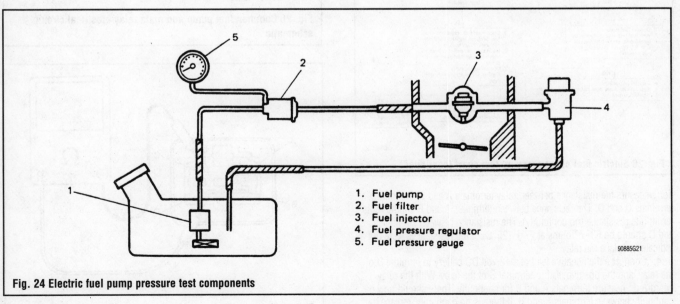

1. Fuel pump
2. Fuel filter
3. Fuel injector
4. Fuel pressure regulator
5. Fuel pressure gauge

Fig. 24 Electric fuel pump pressure test components

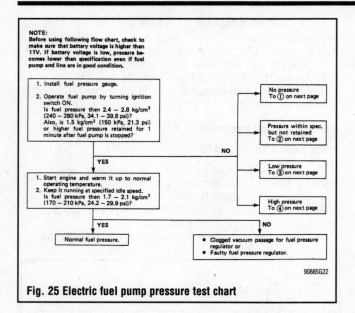

Fig. 25 Electric fuel pump pressure test chart

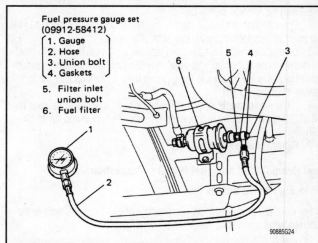

Fig. 27 When testing the fuel pump pressure, a fuel pressure gauge must be connected to the fuel supply system at the fuel filter, as shown

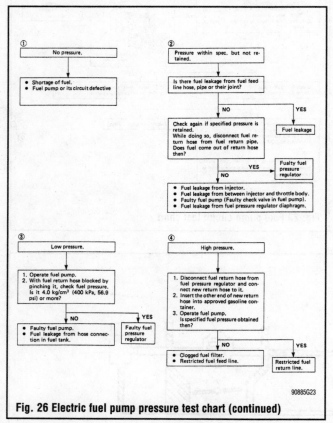

Fig. 26 Electric fuel pump pressure test chart (continued)

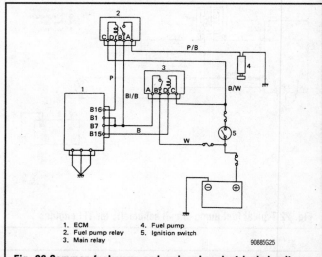

1. ECM
2. Fuel pump relay
3. Main relay
4. Fuel pump
5. Ignition switch

Fig. 28 Common fuel pump and main relay electrical circuit schematic

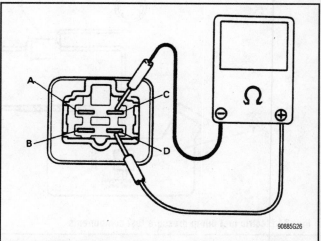

Fig. 29 Measure the fuel pump relay resistance with a Digital Volt-Ohmmeter (DVOM)—if the resistance is not within the specified range, replace the relay with a new one

tion, measure the resistance between relay terminals A and B, and between terminals C and D. The resistance between terminals A and B should register infinite resistance (no continuity). The resistance between terminals C and D should be 63–77 ohms at 77°F (25°C). If the resistances were not as indicated, replace the relay.

4. Connect a the negative lead of a 12 volt DC battery to terminal D of the relay, and the positive lead to terminal C of the relay. With the relay energized, measure terminals A and B for continuity. There should now be continuity between terminals A and B. If there is no continuity, replace the relay with a new one.

5. Install the relay, and reattach the wiring harness connector to it.

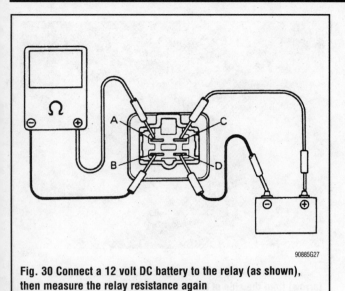

Fig. 30 Connect a 12 volt DC battery to the relay (as shown), then measure the relay resistance again

Throttle Body

REMOVAL & INSTALLATION

▶ See Figure 31

✳✳ CAUTION

Do not perform this procedure when the engine is hot. If fuel comes into contact with hot engine parts, a dangerous explosive condition is created.

1. If necessary, allow the engine to cool down completely.
2. Relieve fuel system pressure.
3. Disconnect the negative battery cable.
4. Drain the engine cooling system into a large, clean catch pan.
5. Remove the air intake case from the throttle body and air cleaner hose.
6. Detach the fuel supply line from the throttle body.
7. Detach the fuel return line from the fuel pressure regulator.
8. Disconnect the accelerator cable and automatic transmission kick-down cable (if equipped) from the throttle lever. Loosen the accelerator cable mounting bracket bolts, then separate the bracket from the side of the throttle body.
9. Detach and label all vacuum hoses from the throttle body.
10. Disconnect the engine cooling system hoses from the throttle body.
11. Detach and label the wiring harness connectors from the fuel injector, the TPS and the ISCS or IAC valve.
12. Remove the throttle body retaining bolts, then lift the throttle body and old gasket up and off of the intake manifold.
13. While the throttle body is removed from the intake manifold, install clean shop rags into the intake manifold opening to prevent accidentally dropping anything into the engine.

To install:

14. Clean the throttle body-to-intake manifold gasket surfaces thoroughly.
15. Install a new gasket onto the intake manifold, then set the throttle body onto the intake manifold.

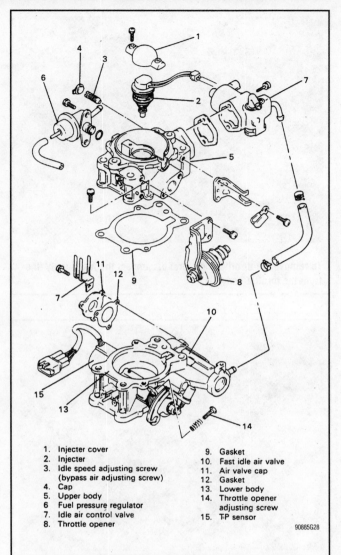

1. Injecter cover
2. Injecter
3. Idle speed adjusting screw (bypass air adjusting screw)
4. Cap
5. Upper body
6. Fuel pressure regulator
7. Idle air control valve
8. Throttle opener
9. Gasket
10. Fast idle air valve
11. Air valve cap
12. Gasket
13. Lower body
14. Throttle opener adjusting screw
15. T-P sensor

Fig. 31 Exploded view of the throttle body, showing all of the engine control components mounted on it

16. Install and tighten the retaining bolts to 160–248 inch lbs. (18–28 Nm).
17. Reattach all wiring connectors, vacuum hoses, cooling system hoses, cables and the fuel return hose to the throttle body.
18. Adjust the accelerator cable play.
19. Install a new O-ring onto the end of the fuel supply line, then lubricate the O-ring with gasoline. Attach the fuel supply line to the throttle body, and tighten the attaching bolts to 71–106 inch lbs. (8–12 Nm).
20. Fill the engine cooling system with the proper type and amount of coolant. The original coolant may be reused so long as it is not more than 1 year old and it is clean (free of debris and corrosion).
21. Connect the negative battery cable.
22. Turn the ignition switch **ON** without starting the engine, and inspect the fuel lines around the throttle body for leaks.
23. Install the air intake case.
24. Start the engine and check for coolant leaks.

To remove the throttle body, first disconnect the fuel supply line from the throttle body . . .

. . . then detach the fuel return hose from the pressure regulator (arrow)

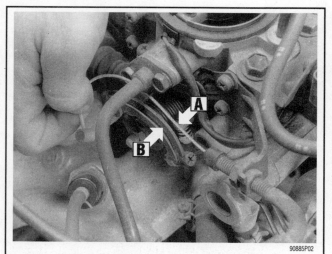

Disengage the accelerator cable (A) from the throttle lever (B) . . .

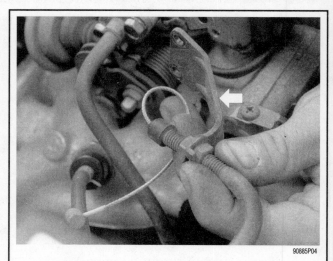

. . . then unfasten the accelerator cable mounting bracket (arrow) from the side of the throttle body

Detach and label all of the vacuum lines . . .

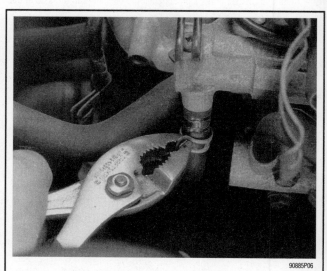

. . . and engine cooling system hoses from the throttle body

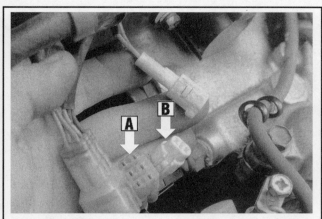

A. ISCS valve and TP sensor connector
B. Fuel injector connector

90885P07

Disengage all of the wiring harness connectors from the throttle body components

90885P08

Loosen all of the throttle body-to-intake manifold bolts . . .

90885P09

. . . then lift the throttle body up and off of the intake manifold

90885P10

Clean the throttle body-to-intake manifold gasket surfaces thoroughly of all old gasket material and dirt

Fuel Injector

REMOVAL & INSTALLATION

1. Release fuel system pressure.
2. Disconnect the negative battery cable.
3. Remove the air intake case from the throttle body.
4. Remove the fuel feed pipe clamp from the intake manifold and disconnect the fuel feed pipe from the throttle body.
5. Remove the injector cover.
6. Disconnect the injector coupler, release its wire harness from the clamp and remove its grommet from the throttle body.
7. Place a cloth over the injector, and a hand on top of the rag. Using an air gun, gently blow low pressure compressed air into the fuel inlet port of the throttle body to unseat the injector. Pull the injector up and out of the throttle body assembly.

✳✳ WARNING

Be careful when using the compressed air. Using excessively high pressure may force the injector to jump out and may cause damage, not only to the injector itself, but also to other parts. Also, never immerse the fuel injector in any type of liquid solvent or cleaner, as damage will occur.

90885P16

To remove the fuel injector, first loosen the fuel supply line attaching bolts . . .

. . . then disconnect the line from the throttle body

Lift the cover off of the fuel injector (arrow) . . .

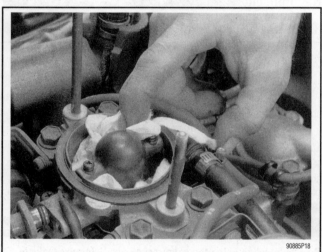

Insert clean rags in the throttle body bore to prevent dropping anything into the engine . . .

. . . then remove the old air intake case-to-throttle body gasket

. . . then loosen the fuel injector cover screws

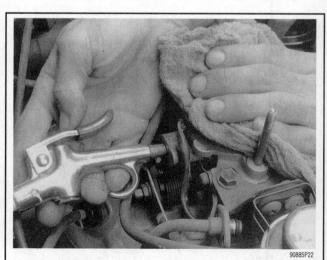

Cover the fuel injector with a rag and your hand, then use compressed air to unseat the injector

Remove the fuel injector from the throttle body

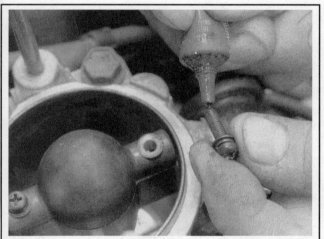

Apply a thin coat of threadlocking compound to the fuel injector cover screws before assembly

8. Using a thin metal prytool, disengage the fuel injector wires from the six-terminal connector.

To install:

9. Insert the wire terminals into the six terminal connector until properly engaged. Give each wire a slight tug to ensure that they will not back out of the connector.

10. Apply a thin coat of gasoline to the new O-rings, then install the fuel injector in the throttle body. Ensure that the injector wiring harness fits in the groove in the throttle body securely.

✳✳ WARNING

Do not apply force to the wiring harness-to-injector connection; it is easily damaged.

11. Reattach the wiring harness connector to the fuel injector, then install the injector cover. Apply a thin coat of locking compound to the screws, then tighten the injector cover screws snugly. The locking compound will keep the screws from backing out and falling into the engine during operation.

12. Apply a thin coat of gasoline to the fuel supply line O-ring, then reconnect the fuel supply line to the throttle body.

13. Connect the negative battery cable and turn the ignition repeatedly **ON** and **OFF** (leaving the ignition switch **ON** for 3 seconds each cycle), until fuel pressure is felt at the return hose.

14. Install the air intake case assembly.

15. Secure all wires and check for any leaks in the system.

TESTING

1. Disconnect the negative battery cable.

2. Detach the wiring harness connector from the fuel injector connector.

3. Attach the leads of a Digital Volt-Ohmmeter (DVOM), set on the ohmmeter function, to the two fuel injector terminals. Measure the resistance of the fuel injector, which should be 0.8–1.8 ohms at 68°F (20°C). If the resistance is not within the specified range, replace the fuel injector with a new one.

4. Reattach the wiring harness connector to the fuel injector.

5. Remove the air intake case from the throttle body.

6. Connect the negative battery cable.

7. While you feel the fuel return hose, have an assistant turn the ignition switch **ON**. Fuel pressure should be felt at the return hose for 3 seconds after the ignition switch is turned **ON**.

To test the fuel injector, detach the wiring harness connector from the fuel injector wiring . . .

. . . then measure the resistance between the two injector terminals—replace the injector if not within specifications

When working around a running engine, remember to keep clear of all moving engine components (such as the engine cooling fan) and hot exhaust parts. Do not wear any loose clothing, which may accidentally be caught in a moving component and cause strangulation.

8. Start or crank the engine, and observe the spray pattern of the fuel injector. The fuel spray pattern should be conical in shape. If no fuel is injected, inspect the wiring harness for continuity, and the wiring harness connectors for proper engagement. If fuel is being injected into the engine, but the spray pattern is not conical in shape, replace the fuel injector with a new one.

9. Stop cranking the engine, or turn the engine **OFF**, and inspect the fuel injector for gasoline leakage. If a leakage of more than one drop of fuel per minute is detected, replace the fuel injector with a new one.

10. Install the air intake case.

Fuel Pressure Regulator

REMOVAL & INSTALLATION

1. Relieve fuel system pressure, as described earlier in this section.
2. Disconnect the negative battery cable.
3. Position a clean shop rag beneath the fuel pressure regulator to soak up any residual fuel.
4. Detach the fuel return and vacuum hoses from the fuel pressure regulator.
5. Loosen the fuel pressure regulator retaining bolts, then pull the regulator off of the throttle body housing.
6. If the original pressure regulator is to be reinstalled, remove and discard the old pressure regulator O-ring.

To install:

7. Install a new O-ring onto the fuel pressure regulator, then apply a thin coat of gasoline on the O-ring.
8. Install the pressure regulator on the throttle body. Tighten the retaining bolts to 31 inch lbs. (3.5 Nm).
9. Reconnect the fuel return and vacuum hoses to the fuel pressure regulator. Tighten the return hose clamp securely.
10. Remove the shop rag, then connect the negative battery cable.
11. Turn the ignition switch **ON**, and inspect the fuel return hose and pressure regulator for fuel leaks.

. . . then detach the fuel return and vacuum hoses from the regulator

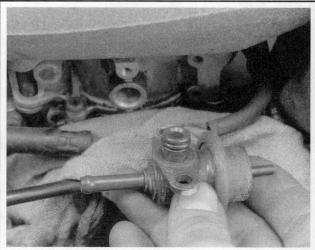

Loosen the fuel pressure regulator mounting screws . . .

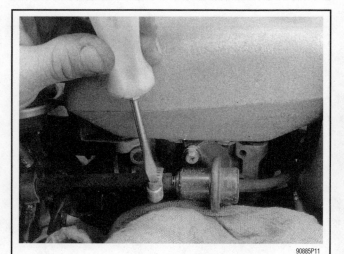

To remove the pressure regulator, loosen the fuel return hose clamp . . .

. . . and remove the regulator from the side of the throttle body

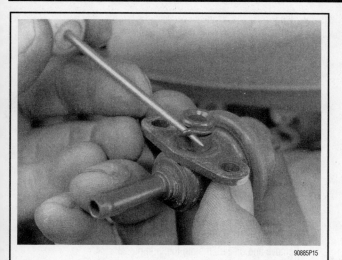

Be sure to remove and discard the regulator O-ring—install a new one prior to installation

Pressure Relief Valve

REMOVAL & INSTALLATION

The Fuel Tank Purge (FTP) and Two-Way Check valves are covered in Section 4 of this manual, under Evaporative Emission Control System.

MULTI-PORT FUEL INJECTION (MFI)

General Information

▶ **See Figure 32**

The Multi-port Fuel Injection (MFI) system supplies the combustion chambers with an air/fuel mixture of optimized ratio under widely diverse driving conditions. The MFI system injects fuel into each intake port of the cylinder head sequentially.

The MFI system is composed of two major sub-systems: air/fuel delivery and electronic engine controls. The electronic engine control sub-system is covered in Section 4 of this manual.

The main components of the air/fuel delivery sub-system are the fuel tank, fuel pump, fuel filter, throttle body, fuel pressure regulator, fuel pulsation damper, fuel injectors and fuel lines. The fuel filter is covered in Section 1.

Relieving Fuel System Pressure

✳✳ CAUTION

This procedure can NOT be performed when the engine is hot. If done so, it may cause an adverse effect to the catalytic converter, or create a dangerous, explosive condition.

1. Place the transmission gearshift lever in Neutral (manual transmissions) or Park (automatic transmissions), apply the parking brake, and block the drive wheels.
2. Detach the wiring harness connector from the fuel pump relay, located under the left-hand side of the instrument panel near the ECM.
3. Remove the fuel tank filler cap to release fuel vapor pressure in the fuel tank. Reinstall the filler cap.

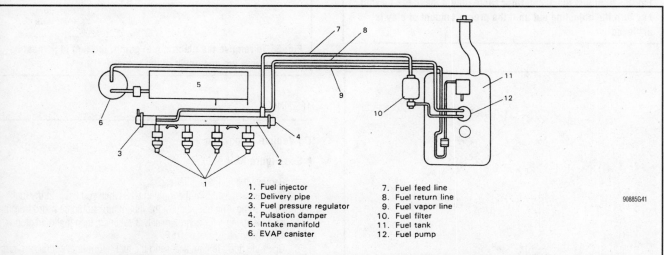

1. Fuel injector
2. Delivery pipe
3. Fuel pressure regulator
4. Pulsation damper
5. Intake manifold
6. EVAP canister
7. Fuel feed line
8. Fuel return line
9. Fuel vapor line
10. Fuel filter
11. Fuel tank
12. Fuel pump

90885G41

Fig. 32 Multi-port Fuel Injection (MFI) fuel delivery system schematic—the fuel injectors fire sequentially to deliver the optimum amount of fuel to each cylinder

4. Start the engine and run it until it stops from lack of fuel. Crank the engine 2 or 3 times for three second periods. The fuel lines should now be depressurized.

5. After servicing the component(s), reattach the wiring harness connector to the fuel pump relay.

Accelerator Cable

ADJUSTMENT

▶ **See Figures 33 and 34**

1. With throttle valve completely closed, inspect the accelerator pedal play (the amount of pedal movement before the accelerator cable causes the throttle lever to move), which should be 0.08–0.27 in. (2–7mm).

➡**The adjusting nut and locknut are located on the accelerator cable bracket, mounted on the throttle body.**

2. If the pedal play is not within the specified range, loosen the locknut and turn the adjusting nut until the proper play is obtained.

3. Have an assistant sit in the vehicle and fully depress the accelerator

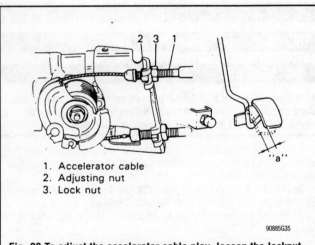

1. Accelerator cable
2. Adjusting nut
3. Lock nut

90885G35

Fig. 33 To adjust the accelerator cable play, loosen the locknut and turn the adjusting nut until the proper amount of play is achieved

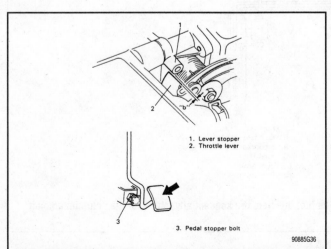

1. Lever stopper
2. Throttle lever

3. Pedal stopper bolt

90885G36

Fig. 34 With the accelerator pedal fully depressed, there should be 0.02–0.07 in. (0.5–2.0mm) clearance (b) between the lever stopper and the throttle lever

pedal, then inspect the clearance between the throttle lever and the lever stopper (throttle body). The clearance should be 0.02–0.07 in. (0.5–2.0mm).

4. If the clearance is not within the indicated range, turn the pedal stopper bolt until the proper clearance is obtained.

Fuel Pump

REMOVAL & INSTALLATION

▶ **See Figure 35**

The fuel pump is mounted in the fuel tank, which must be removed to service the fuel pump.

1. Remove the fuel tank from the vehicle.
2. Loosen the fuel pump retaining bolts, then lift the fuel pump up and out of the fuel tank.
3. Remove and discard the old fuel pump gasket.

To install:

4. Position the fuel pump, along with a new gasket, in the fuel tank, ensuring that the fuel pump retaining bolt holes are aligned.
5. Install and tighten the fuel pump retaining bolts securely and evenly.
6. Install the fuel tank into the vehicle.

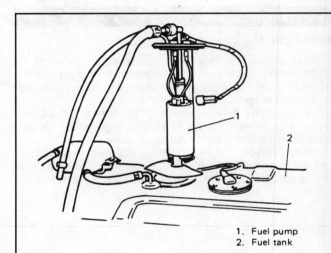

1. Fuel pump
2. Fuel tank

90885G16

Fig. 35 To remove the electric fuel pump, the fuel tank must be lowered from the underside of the vehicle

TESTING

On Vehicle Inspection

▶ **See Figure 36**

1. Remove the fuel tank filler cap.
2. Have an assistant turn the ignition **ON**, while you listen at the fuel filler tube opening. The operation of the fuel pump should be heard from the fuel filler tube opening for approximately 3 seconds, then it should stop.
3. Turn the ignition switch **OFF**.
4. Open the hood to gain access to the fuel return line, connected to the fuel pressure regulator mounted on the throttle body.
5. Once again have your assistant turn the ignition **ON**, while you feel for fuel pressure at the fuel return line near the throttle body. Fuel pressure should be felt at the return line for approximately 3 seconds after the ignition switch is turned **ON**.
6. If the fuel pump is not heard operating or if no fuel pressure is felt at the return line, there is a problem with the fuel pump or its circuit.
7. Reinstall the fuel tank filler cap.

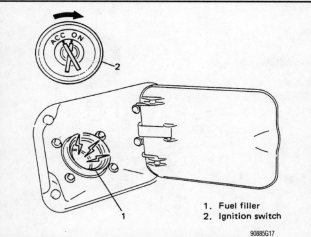

Fig. 36 Sounds from the electric fuel pump should be heard from the fuel tank filler tube opening for approximately 3 seconds after the ignition switch is turned ON

1. Fuel filler
2. Ignition switch

90885G17

Fuel Pump Circuit Inspection

▶ See Figure 37

For the inspection of the fuel pump circuit, refer to the accompanying diagnostic chart.

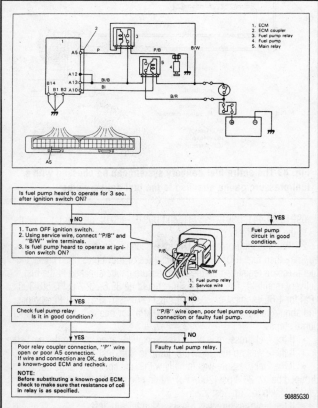

Fig. 37 Perform this fuel pump circuit test to determine whether the fuel pump circuit is functioning properly or not

FUEL PUMP RELAY CHECK

▶ See Figures 38, 39, 40 and 41

When testing the fuel pump circuit, it may be necessary to inspect the fuel pump relay for defects. Test the relay as follows:

1. Disconnect the negative battery cable.

2. Remove the fuel pump relay from its mounting bracket after disengaging the wiring harness connector from it.

3. Using a Digital Volt-Ohmmeter (DVOM) set on the ohmmeter function, measure the resistance between relay terminals A and B, and between terminals C and D. The resistance between terminals A and B should register infinite resistance (no continuity). The resistance between terminals C and D should be 63–77 ohms at 77°F (25°C). If the resistances were not as indicated, replace the relay.

4. Connect a the negative lead of a 12 volt DC battery to terminal D of the relay, and the positive lead to terminal C of the relay. With the relay

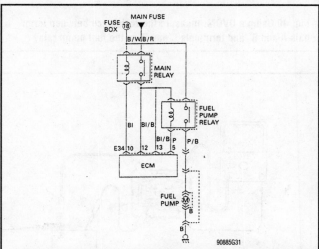

Fig. 38 Common fuel pump and main relay electrical circuit schematic

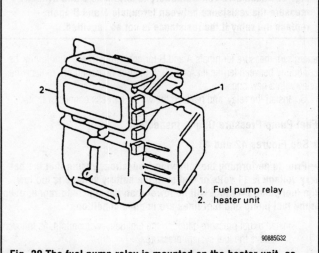

1. Fuel pump relay
2. heater unit

90885G32

Fig. 39 The fuel pump relay is mounted on the heater unit, as shown

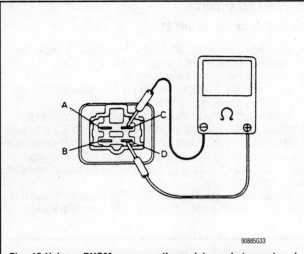

Fig. 40 Using a DVOM, measure the resistance between terminals A and B, and terminals C and D on the fuel pump relay

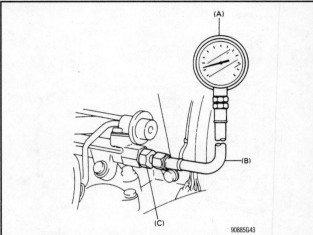

Fig. 42 Install a fuel pressure gauge (A) onto the end of the fuel delivery pipe (supply manifold) using a fitting (C) and flexible hose (B) designed specifically for this purpose

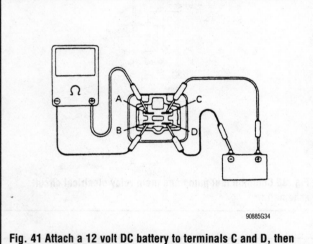

Fig. 41 Attach a 12 volt DC battery to terminals C and D, then measure the resistance between terminals A and B again—replace the relay if the resistance is not as specified

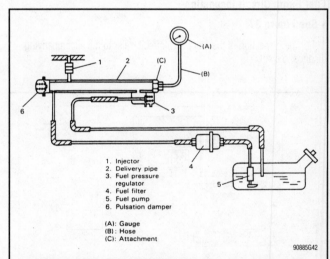

1. Injector
2. Delivery pipe
3. Fuel pressure regulator
4. Fuel filter
5. Fuel pump
6. Pulsation damper

(A): Gauge
(B): Hose
(C): Attachment

Fig. 43 The entire fuel delivery system can be checked with a fuel pressure gauge attached to the fuel delivery pipe

energized, measure terminals A and B for continuity. There should now be continuity between terminals A and B. If there is no continuity, replace the relay with a new one.

5. Install the relay, and reattach the wiring harness connector to it.

Fuel Pump Pressure Output Inspection

▶ See Figures 42 and 43

➡Prior to performing the following inspection, ensure that the battery voltage is 11 volts or higher. If the battery voltage is too low, the fuel pump pressure will be lower than the specified range, even if the fuel pump and fuel lines are in good condition.

1. Install a fuel pressure gauge to the fuel delivery manifold, as follows:
   a. Relieve the fuel system pressure.
   b. Open the hood.
   c. Using a back-up wrench, loosen the small plug bolt from the end of the fuel delivery pipe (fuel supply manifold).
   d. Attach a fuel pressure gauge set (including Suzuki Tools

09912–58441, 09912–58431, and 09919–46010, or their equivalents) to the fuel delivery pipe.

2. Turn the ignition switch **ON** for 3 seconds (without starting the engine), then turn it **OFF**. Repeat this three or four times, then check the fuel pressure registered on the fuel pressure gauge attached to the fuel delivery manifold. The fuel pressure should be 35.6–42.7 psi (250–300 kPa) for 1.6L engines, or 38.4–44.0 psi (270–310 kPa) for 1.8L engines, and should remain above 28.4 psi (200 kPa) for one minute after the fuel pump stops.
   • If the fuel pressure is within the specified range, skip to the next step.
   • If there was no fuel pressure, jump to Sub-Test 1.
   • If the fuel pressure was initially within the specified range but dropped below 28.4 psi (200 kPa) within one minute after the fuel pump stopped, skip to Sub-Test 2.
   • If the fuel pressure was too low, skip to Sub-Test 3.
   • If the fuel pressure was too high, skip to Sub-Test 4.
3. Start the engine and allow it to reach normal operating temperature.
4. Allow the engine to idle and observe the fuel pressure on the gauge.

The fuel pressure should be within 29.8–37.0 psi (210–260 kPa) for 1.6L engines, or within 31.3–37.0 psi (220–260 kPa) for 1.8L engines. If the fuel pressure is not as specified, the problem is most likely a clogged vacuum passage for the fuel pressure regulator, or a faulty fuel pressure regulator. If the fuel pressure was within the specified range, the fuel pump and fuel delivery system is functioning normally.

SUB-TEST 1

1. Install a hose pinch clamp on the fuel return hose (attached to the fuel pressure regulator), and pinch the hose closed.

2. Turn the ignition switch **ON** for 3 seconds (without starting the engine), then turn it **OFF**. Repeat this three or four times, then check the fuel pressure registered on the fuel pressure gauge attached to the fuel delivery manifold. If there is now the specified amount of fuel pressure, the fuel pressure regulator is faulty. If there is still no fuel pressure, the problem is a shortage of fuel in the fuel tank, or the fuel pump or its circuit is defective.

SUB-TEST 2

1. Inspect the fuel feed line hose, pipe and connections for fuel leaks; fix any leaks found.

2. If no leaks were found, detach the fuel return hose from the fuel pressure regulator. Install a new hose to the pressure regulator, and position the open end of the new hose into a container designed to hold gasoline.

3. Turn the ignition switch **ON** for 3 seconds (without starting the engine), then turn it **OFF**. Repeat this three or four times, then check the fuel pressure registered on the fuel pressure gauge attached to the fuel delivery manifold. If, after activating the fuel pump, fuel leaks from the open end of the new regulator hose, the pressure regulator is defective. Otherwise, the problem may lie in one or more of the following:
- Leaking fuel injector
- Faulty fuel pump check valve
- Leaking fuel pressure regulator diaphragm

SUB-TEST 3

1. Install a hose pinch clamp on the fuel return hose (attached to the fuel pressure regulator), and pinch the hose closed.

2. Turn the ignition switch **ON** for 3 seconds (without starting the engine), then turn it **OFF**. Repeat this three or four times, then check the fuel pressure registered on the fuel pressure gauge attached to the fuel delivery manifold. If there is now the specified amount of fuel pressure, the fuel pressure regulator is faulty. If the fuel pressure is still too low, the problem may be one or more of the following:
- Clogged fuel filter
- Restricted fuel feed hose or pipe
- Faulty fuel pump
- Fuel leakage from the hose connection in the fuel tank

SUB-TEST 4

1. Detach the fuel return hose from the fuel pressure regulator.

2. Install a new hose to the pressure regulator, and position the open end of the new hose into a container designed to hold gasoline.

3. Turn the ignition switch **ON** for 3 seconds (without starting the engine), then turn it **OFF**. Repeat this three or four times, then check the fuel pressure registered on the fuel pressure gauge attached to the fuel delivery manifold. If the fuel pressure is now within the specified range, the problem is a restricted fuel return hose or pipe. Otherwise, the pressure regulator is defective.

Throttle Body

REMOVAL & INSTALLATION

▶ **See Figures 44, 45 and 46**

1. Disonnect the negative battery cable.

2. Drain the engine cooling system in a large, clean catch pan. The coolant can be reused, if it is clean and less than 2 years old.

3. Remove the throttle cover, then detach the accelerator cable and, if equipped, the automatic transmission throttle cable from the throttle body.

4. Remove the air intake pipe and hose.

5. Detach all wiring harness connectors from the throttle body.

6. Disconnect all vacuum and engine cooling system hoses from the throttle body.

7. Loosen the throttle body retaining nuts and bolts, then slide the throttle body off of the intake manifold.

8. Clean the throttle body-to-intake manifold gasket surfaces thoroughly.

✳✳ WARNING

If you are going to clean the throttle body, keep the following points in mind to prevent damaging the throttle body:

- The TP sensor, fast idle air valve or other components fabricated with rubber should not be placed in solvent or parts cleaner. The rubber may swell, harden or distort.
- Do not use drills or wires to clean the passages in the throttle body. It can damage the passages.

To install:

9. Install a new throttle body gasket on the intake manifold.

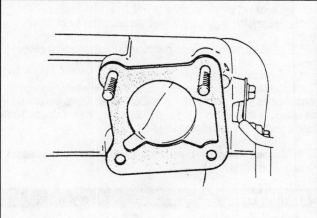

Fig. 44 Be sure to use a new gasket when installing the throttle body onto the intake manifold—using an old gasket may result in vacuum leaks at this juncture

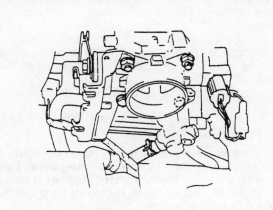

Fig. 45 Install and tighten the throttle body-to-intake manifold retaining fasteners (2 bolts and 2 nuts) in a crisscross pattern to 203 inch lbs. (23 Nm)

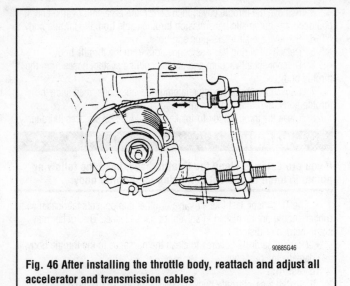

Fig. 46 After installing the throttle body, reattach and adjust all accelerator and transmission cables

10. Install the throttle body on the intake manifold. Tighten the retaining nuts and bolts to 159–248 inch lbs. (18–28 Nm).

11. Reattach the engine cooling and vacuum hoses to the throttle body.

12. Attach the wiring harness connectors to the throttle body components.

13. Install the air intake pipe and hose.

14. Connect the accelerator and automatic transmission (if equipped) throttle cables to the throttle body. Adjust cable play. Accelerator cable adjustment is covered earlier in this section; automatic transmission throttle cable adjustment is described in Section 7.

15. Refill the engine cooling system.

16. Connect the negative battery cable, then start the engine and check for coolant leaks.

Fuel Injectors

REMOVAL & INSTALLATION

♦ **See Figures 47, 48 and 49**

1. Release fuel system pressure as previously described.
2. Disconnect the negative battery cable.
3. For 1.6L engines, remove the throttle cover, then remove the air intake pipe and hose. Detach the intake manifold No. 2 brace from the intake manifold.
4. Detach and label each fuel injector wiring harness connector.
5. Remove the fuel pressure regulator from the fuel delivery manifold, then drain the residual fuel from the delivery manifold into a small metal catch container.
6. Loosen the clamp bolts for the clamps holding the supply and return lines.
7. Loosen the fuel delivery manifold mounting bolts, then lift the manifold and injectors up and off of the engine.

➡**Insert clean shop rags, or paper towels, into the fuel injector holes in the intake manifold to prevent accidentally dropping nuts, bolts or other small parts into the engine. If something is dropped into the engine, the intake manifold, and perhaps the cylinder head, will need to be removed to retrieve the object.**

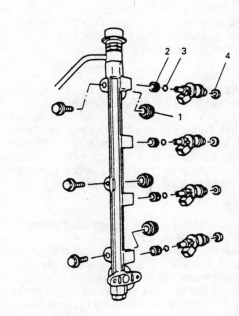

1. Insulator
2. Grommet
3. O ring
4. Cushion

Fig. 47 Exploded view of the fuel injector-to-delivery pipe installation—be sure to use new grommets, O-rings and cushions during installation

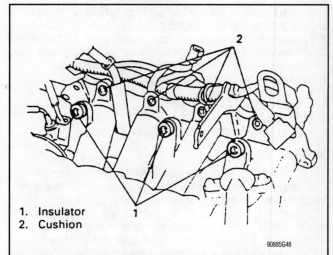

1. Insulator
2. Cushion

Fig. 48 Install the insulators and cushions on the intake manifold, then install the fuel delivery pipe with the fuel injectors

8. Carefully separate the fuel injectors from the delivery manifold.
9. Remove and discard the O-ring from each fuel injector.
10. Remove the fuel injector bosses on the intake manifold of all dirt, grime and gum.

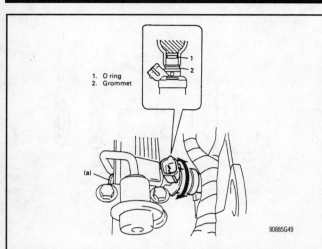

Fig. 49 Once the fuel delivery pipe and injectors are installed, the fuel injectors should spin freely in their seats—if they do not, one of the O-rings was improperly installed

To install:

11. Install new O-rings onto the fuel injectors, then install the grommets.

12. Inspect the delivery manifold insulators and fuel injector cushions for damage, such as scoring; if any damage is evident, replace the insulators with new ones.

13. Install the insulators and cushions on the intake manifold.

14. Apply a thin coat of clean engine oil onto the fuel injector O-rings, then install the fuel injectors onto the delivery manifold. Install the delivery manifold and fuel injectors onto the intake manifold, ensuring that the fuel injectors are properly seated in their bores. Do not attempt to tighten the delivery manifold mounting bolts to force the fuel injectors into place; they may not be properly aligned with the bores in the intake manifold.

15. Ensure that the fuel injectors spin freely in their bores. If they do not, the cause is the improper installation of their O-rings. Remove the fuel injectors and install NEW O-rings again.

16. Tighten the delivery manifold mounting bolts to 159–248 inch lbs. (18–28 Nm).

17. Install the fuel pressure regulator onto the delivery manifold.

18. Reattach the fuel supply and return lines.

19. Attach the wiring harness connectors to the fuel injectors.

20. For 1.6L engines, install the air intake pipe and hose.

21. Connect the negative battery cable.

22. Turn the ignition switch **ON** without starting the engine, and inspect the fuel supply and return lines, as well as the delivery manifold, for fuel leaks.

TESTING

➡**A stethoscope and Digital Volt-Ohmmeter (DVOM) are necessary for this test procedure.**

1. Start the engine and allow it to idle.

2. Use the stethoscope to listen to each of the fuel injectors while the engine is idling. The fuel injectors should produce an operating sound. If no sound or an unusual sound is heard, inspect the fuel injector and circuit for a defect.

3. Disengage the wiring harness connector from each of the fuel injectors.

4. Use the DVOM, set on the ohmmeter function, to measure the resistance between the two terminals of each fuel injector. The resistance should be 12–17 ohms for 1.6L engines, or 10.8–13.2 ohms for 1.8L engines. If any of the fuel injectors do not register a resistance value within the specified range, replace it with a new one.

5. Reattach the wiring harness connectors to the fuel injectors.

Fuel Pressure Regulator

REMOVAL & INSTALLATION

♦ **See Figures 50 and 51**

1. Release the fuel system pressure, as described earlier in this section.

2. Disconnect the negative battery cable.

➡**On 1.8L engines, it may be necessary (because of inaccessibility) to separate the pressure regulator from the delivery manifold before detaching the vacuum and fuel hoses from it.**

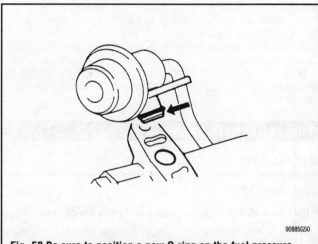

Fig. 50 Be sure to position a new O-ring on the fuel pressure regulator prior to installation—otherwise, fuel leakage may occur, resulting in low fuel pressure and driveability problems

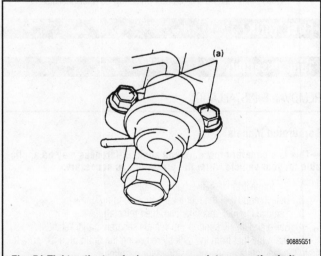

Fig. 51 Tighten the two fuel pressure regulator mounting bolts (a) to 71–106 inch lbs. (8–12 Nm)

3. Detach the vacuum hose from the fuel pressure regulator.

4. Loosen the clamp, then separate the fuel return hose from the fuel pressure regulator. Drain any residual fuel from the return hose into a small metal catch can.

5. Position a clean shop rag under the fuel pressure regulator to absorb any residual fuel leakage during removal. Loosen the mounting bolts, then remove the fuel pressure regulator and fuel pipe from the fuel delivery manifold.

6. Remove and discard the old fuel pressure regulator O-ring.

To install:

7. Apply a thin coat of gasoline to a new O-ring, then install the new O-ring onto the fuel pressure regulator.

➡**For 1.8L engines, it may be necessary to reconnect the fuel and vacuum hoses to the pressure regulator prior to installing the regulator on the delivery manifold.**

8. Install the fuel pressure regulator and pipe onto the delivery manifold. Tighten the fuel pressure regulator mounting bolts to 71–106 inch lbs. (8–12 Nm).

9. Reattach the fuel return hose to the fuel pressure regulator, and tighten the clamp securely.

10. Reconnect the vacuum hose to the pressure regulator, then connect the negative battery cable.

11. Turn the ignition switch **ON**, without starting the engine. Inspect the fuel delivery manifold, the pressure regulator and the return fuel hose for gasoline leaks.

Fuel Pulsation Damper

REMOVAL & INSTALLATION

▶ **See Figure 52**

➡**Only the 1.6L MFI engine utilizes a fuel pulsation damper.**

1. Release the fuel system pressure, as described earlier in this section.
2. Disconnect the negative battery cable.
3. Loosen the fuel supply hose mounting clamp bolt.
4. Position a clean shop rag under the fuel pulsation damper to absorb any residual fuel leakage during removal. Using a back-up wrench, loosen the fuel pulsation damper, then remove it from the fuel delivery manifold.
5. Remove and discard the old fuel pulsation damper gaskets.

FUEL TANK

Tank Assembly

REMOVAL & INSTALLATION

Carbureted Models

➡**This is a general procedure and slight differences may be applicable for your vehicle. Alter the procedure as necessary.**

1. Disconnect the negative battery cable.
2. Detach and label the fuel level gauge sending unit wire.
3. Remove the fuel tank filler cap, then reinstall it.
4. Raise and safely support the vehicle securely on jackstands.
5. Drain the fuel from the tank by removing the drain plug. Be sure to drain the fuel into a container designed for gasoline.

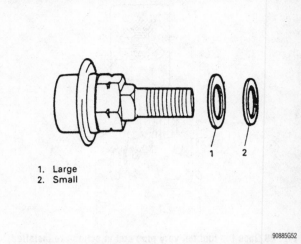

1. Large
2. Small

Fig. 52 Be sure to not only install new gaskets prior to assembly, but to also position the gaskets as shown for proper sealing

To install:

6. Apply a thin coat of engine oil to the new gaskets, then install the new gaskets onto the fuel pulsation damper.

7. Install the fuel pulsation damper in the delivery manifold. Using a back-up wrench, tighten the fuel pulsation damper to 19–25 ft. lbs. (25–35 Nm).

8. Reattach the fuel supply hose to the fuel pressure regulator, and tighten the clamp securely.

9. Reconnect the negative battery cable.

10. Turn the ignition switch **ON**, without starting the engine. Inspect the fuel delivery manifold, the pulsation damper and the supply hose for gasoline leaks.

Pressure Relief Valve

REMOVAL & INSTALLATION

The Fuel Tank Purge (FTP) and Two-Way Check valves are covered in Section 4 of this manual, under Evaporative Emission Control System.

6. Remove the filler hose protector, then detach the filler hose from the tank.

7. Detach the fuel lines and pipes from the fuel tank.

8. Position a floor jack beneath the fuel tank, then remove the fuel tank mounting fasteners. Slowly lower the fuel tank down from the vehicle.

To install:

9. Position the fuel tank on the floor jack, then slowly raise it up into position beneath the vehicle. Install the mounting fasteners and tighten them until secure.

10. Reattach the fuel lines, pipes and fuel level gauge sending unit wire.

11. Reconnect the fuel filler hose, then install the filler hose protector.

12. Install and tighten the fuel tank drain plug to 22–32 ft. lbs. (30–45 Nm).

13. Connect the negative battery cable.

14. Turn the ignition switch **ON** without starting the engine, then inspect the fuel tank and associated lines for fuel leaks.

Fuel Injected Models

▶ **See Figures 53, 54, 55 and 56**

➡**This is a general procedure and slight differences may be applicable for your vehicle. Change the procedure as necessary.**

1. Release the fuel system pressure.
2. Disconnect the negative battery cable.
3. Remove the fuel tank filler cap, then reinstall it.
4. Raise and safely support the vehicle securely on jackstands.
5. Detach and label the fuel level gauge sending unit and fuel pump wires.
6. Due to the lack of a drain plug, drain the fuel from the tank through the filler tube with a pump designed for this purpose.
7. Remove the upper filler hose protector, then detach the breather hose from the filler neck and the vapor hose from the separator.
8. Remove the lower filler hose protector, then disconnect the filler hose from the fuel tank.

9. Detacch the fuel filter inlet pipe from the filter.
10. Detach the fuel line and pipe clamps from the chassis, then remove the fuel filter inlet pipe from the clamp.
11. Position a floor jack beneath the fuel tank, then remove the fuel tank mounting fasteners. Slowly lower the fuel tank slightly until the fuel supply and return lines can be disconnected from the fuel tank, then lower the tank completely from the vehicle.

To install:

12. Position the fuel tank on the floor jack, then slowly raise it up into position beneath the vehicle. Reattach the fuel supply and return lines to the fuel tank, then raise the fuel tank fully. Install the mounting fasteners and tighten them to 36.5 ft. lbs. (50 Nm).
13. Install the fuel filter inlet pipe to the clamp, then reattach the fuel line and pipe clamps to the chassis.
14. Reattach the fuel filter inlet pipe to the filter, ensuring that you use new gaskets. Tighten the fuel filter union bolt to 22–28 ft. lbs. (30–40 Nm).

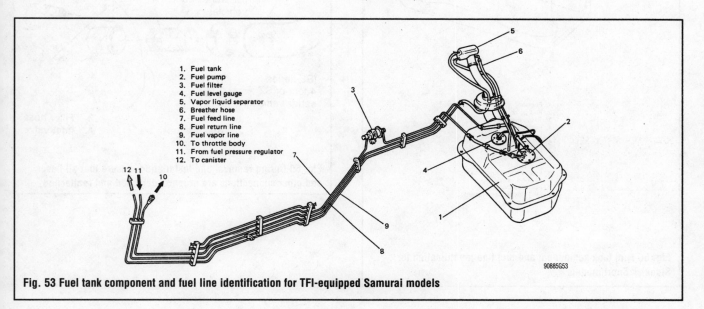

1. Fuel tank
2. Fuel pump
3. Fuel filter
4. Fuel level gauge
5. Vapor liquid separator
6. Breather hose
7. Fuel feed line
8. Fuel return line
9. Fuel vapor line
10. To throttle body
11. From fuel pressure regulator
12. To canister

90885G53

Fig. 53 Fuel tank component and fuel line identification for TFI-equipped Samurai models

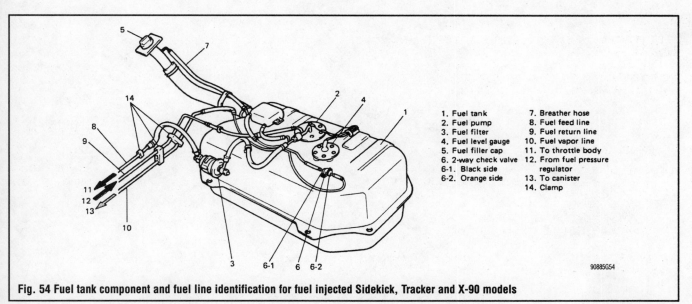

1. Fuel tank
2. Fuel pump
3. Fuel filter
4. Fuel level gauge
5. Fuel filler cap
6. 2-way check valve
6-1. Black side
6-2. Orange side
7. Breather hose
8. Fuel feed line
9. Fuel return line
10. Fuel vapor line
11. To throttle body
12. From fuel pressure regulator
13. To canister
14. Clamp

90885G54

Fig. 54 Fuel tank component and fuel line identification for fuel injected Sidekick, Tracker and X-90 models

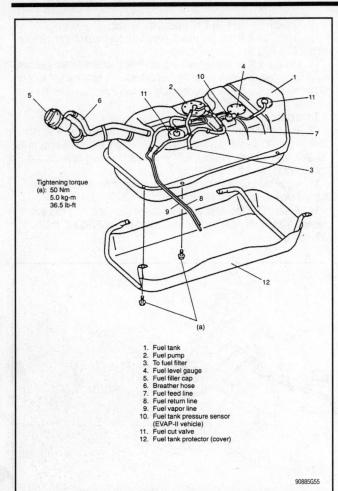

Tightening torque
(a): 50 Nm
5.0 kg-m
36.5 lb-ft

(a)

1. Fuel tank
2. Fuel pump
3. To fuel filter
4. Fuel level gauge
5. Fuel filler cap
6. Breather hose
7. Fuel feed line
8. Fuel return line
9. Fuel vapor line
10. Fuel tank pressure sensor
    (EVAP-II vehicle)
11. Fuel cut valve
12. Fuel tank protector (cover)

90885G55

Fig. 55 Fuel tank component and fuel line identification for Sidekick Sport models

15. Reattach the filler hose to the fuel tank, then install the lower filler hose protector.

16. Reconnect the breather hose to the filler neck, and the vapor hose to the separator. Install the upper filler hose protector.

17. Reattach the fuel level gauge sending unit and fuel pump wires.

18. Lower the vehicle.

19. Connect the negative battery cable.

20. Turn the ignition switch **ON** without starting the engine, then inspect the fuel tank and associated lines for fuel leaks.

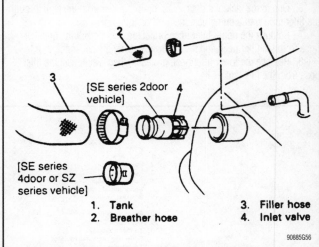

[SE series 2door vehicle]

[SE series 4door or SZ series vehicle]

1. **Tank**
2. **Breather hose**
3. **Filler hose**
4. **Inlet valve**

90885G56

Fig. 56 During removal and installation, ensure that all hoses and other connections are properly detached and reattached

6

CHASSIS ELECTRICAL

UNDERSTANDING AND TROUBLESHOOTING ELECTRICAL SYSTEMS

Basic Electrical Theory

▶ **See Figure 1**

For any 12 volt, negative ground, electrical system to operate, the electricity must travel in a complete circuit. This simply means that current (power) from the positive terminal (+) of the battery must eventually return to the negative terminal (-) of the battery. Along the way, this current will travel through wires, fuses, switches and components. If, for any reason, the flow of current through the circuit is interrupted, the component fed by that circuit will cease to function properly.

Perhaps the easiest way to visualize a circuit is to think of connecting a light bulb (with two wires attached to it) to the battery—one wire attached to the negative (-) terminal of the battery and the other wire to the positive (+) terminal. With the two wires touching the battery terminals, the circuit would be complete and the light bulb would illuminate. Electricity would follow a path from the battery to the bulb and back to the battery. It's easy to see that with longer wires on our light bulb, it could be mounted anywhere. Further, one wire could be fitted with a switch so that the light could be turned on and off.

The normal automotive circuit differs from this simple example in two ways. First, instead of having a return wire from the bulb to the battery, the current travels through the chassis of the vehicle. Since the negative (-) battery cable is attached to the chassis and the chassis is made of electrically conductive metal, the chassis of the vehicle can serve as a ground wire to complete the circuit. Secondly, most automotive circuits contain multiple components which receive power from a single circuit. This lessens the amount of wire needed to power components on the vehicle.

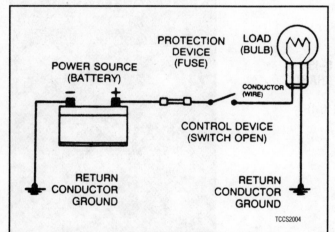

Fig. 1 This example illustrates a simple circuit. When the switch is closed, power from the positive (+) battery terminal flows through the fuse and the switch, and then to the light bulb. The light illuminates and the circuit is completed through the ground wire back to the negative (-) battery terminal. In reality, the two ground points shown in the illustration are attached to the metal chassis of the vehicle, which completes the circuit back to the battery

THE WATER ANALOGY

Electricity is the flow of electrons—hypothetical particles thought to constitute the basic "stuff" of electricity. Many people have been taught electrical theory using an analogy with water. In a comparison with water flowing through a pipe, the electrons would be the water.

The flow of electricity can be measured much like the flow of water through a pipe. The unit of measurement used is amperes, frequently abbreviated as amps (a). When connected to a circuit, an ammeter will measure the actual amount of current flowing through the circuit. When relatively few electrons flow through a circuit, the amperage is low. When many electrons flow, the amperage is high.

Just as water pressure is measured in units such as pounds per square inch (psi), electrical pressure is measured in units called volts (v). When a voltmeter is connected to a circuit, it is measuring the electrical pressure. The higher the voltage, the more current will flow through the circuit. The lower the voltage, the less current will flow.

While increasing the voltage in a circuit will increase the flow of current, the actual flow depends not only on voltage, but also on the resistance of the circuit. Resistance is the amount of force necessary to push the current through the circuit. The standard unit for measuring resistance is an ohm (W or omega). Resistance in a circuit varies depending on the amount and type of components used in the circuit. The main factors which determine resistance are:

• Material—some materials have more resistance than others. Those with high resistance are said to be insulators. Rubber is one of the best insulators available, as it allows little current to pass. Low resistance materials are said to be conductors. Copper wire is among the best conductors. Most vehicle wiring is made of copper.

• Size—the larger the wire size being used, the less resistance the wire will have. This is why components which use large amounts of electricity usually have large wires supplying current to them.

• Length—for a given thickness of wire, the longer the wire, the greater the resistance. The shorter the wire, the less the resistance. When determining the proper wire for a circuit, both size and length must be considered to design a circuit that can handle the current needs of the component.

• Temperature—with many materials, the higher the temperature, the greater the resistance. This principle is used in many of the sensors on the engine.

OHM'S LAW

The preceding definitions may lead the reader into believing that there is no relationship between current, voltage and resistance. Nothing can be further from the truth. The relationship between current, voltage and resistance can be summed up by a statement known as Ohm's law.

Voltage (E) is equal to amperage (I) times resistance (R): $E = I \times R$
Other forms of the formula are $R = E/I$ and $I = E/R$

In each of these formulas, E is the voltage in volts, I is the current in amps and R is the resistance in ohms. The basic point to remember is that as the resistance of a circuit goes up, the amount of current that flows in the circuit will go down, if voltage remains the same.

Electrical Components

POWER SOURCE

The power source for 12 volt automotive electrical systems is the battery. In most modern vehicles, the battery is a lead/acid electrochemical device consisting of six 2 volt subsections (cells) connected in series, so that the unit is capable of producing approximately 12 volts of electrical pressure. Each subsection consists of a series of positive and negative plates held a short distance apart in a solution of sulfuric acid and water.

The two types of plates are of dissimilar metals. This sets up a chemical reaction, and it is this reaction which produces current flow from the battery when its positive and negative terminals are connected to an electrical load. The power removed from the battery is replaced by the alternator, which forces electrons back through the battery, reversing the normal flow, and restoring the battery to its original chemical state.

GROUND

Two types of grounds are used in automotive electric circuits. Direct ground components are grounded through their mounting points. All other components use some sort of ground wire which is attached to the body or chassis of the vehicle. The electrical current runs through the chassis of the vehicle and returns to the battery through the ground (-) cable; if you look, you'll see that the battery ground cable connects between the battery and the body or chassis of the vehicle.

➡ **It should be noted that a good percentage of electrical problems can be traced to bad grounds.**

PROTECTIVE DEVICES

▶ See Figure 2

It is possible for large surges of current to pass through the electrical system of your vehicle. If this surge of current were to reach the load in the circuit, it could burn it out or severely damage it. To prevent this, fuses, circuit breakers and/or fusible links are connected into the supply wires of the electrical system. These items are nothing more than a built-in weak spot in the system. When an abnormal amount of current flows through the system, these protective devices work as follows to protect the circuit:

• Fuse—when an excessive electrical current passes through a fuse, the fuse "blows" (the conductor melts) and opens the circuit, preventing the passage of current.

• Circuit Breaker—a circuit breaker is basically a self-repairing fuse. It will open the circuit in the same fashion as a fuse, but when the surge subsides, the circuit breaker can be reset and does not need replacement.

• Fusible Link—a fusible link (fuse link or main link) is a short length of special, Hypalon high temperature insulated wire that acts as a fuse. When an excessive electrical current passes through a fusible link, the thin gauge wire inside the link melts, creating an intentional open to protect the circuit. To repair the circuit, the link must be replaced. Some newer type fusible links are housed in plug-in modules, which are simply replaced like a fuse, while older type fusible links must be cut and spliced if they melt. Since this link is very early in the electrical path, it's the first place to look if nothing on the vehicle works, but the battery seems to be charged and is properly connected.

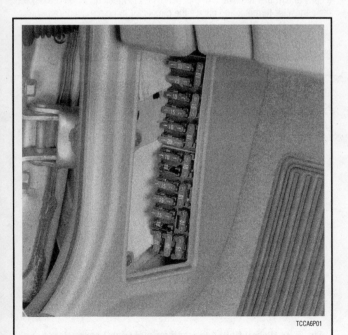

TCCA6P01

Fig. 2 Most vehicles use one or more fuse panels. This one is located in the driver's side kick panel

SWITCHES & RELAYS

▶ See Figures 3 and 4

Switches are used in electrical circuits to control the passage of current. The most common use is to open and close circuits between the battery and the various electric devices in the system. Switches are rated according to the amount of amperage they can handle. If a sufficient amperage rated switch is not used in a circuit, the switch could overload and cause damage.

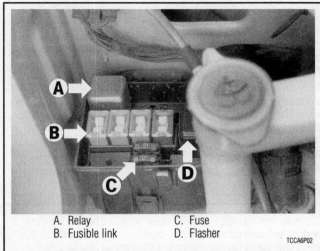

| A. Relay | C. Fuse |
| B. Fusible link | D. Flasher |

TCCA6P02

Fig. 3 The underhood fuse and relay panel usually contains fuses, relays, flashers and fusible links

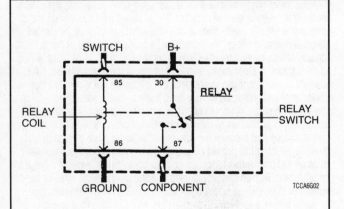

TCCA6G02

Fig. 4 Relays are composed of a coil and a switch. These two components are linked together so that when one operates, the other operates at the same time. The large wires in the circuit are connected from the battery to one side of the relay switch (B+) and from the opposite side of the relay switch to the load (component). Smaller wires are connected from the relay coil to the control switch for the circuit and from the opposite side of the relay coil to ground

Some electrical components which require a large amount of current to operate use a special switch called a relay. Since these circuits carry a large amount of current, the thickness of the wire in the circuit is also greater. If this large wire were connected from the load to the control switch on the dashboard, the switch would have to carry the high amperage load and the dash would be twice as large to accommodate the increased size of the wiring harness. To prevent these problems, a relay is used.

Relays are composed of a coil and a switch. These two components are linked together so that when one operates, the other operates at the same time. The large wires in the circuit are connected from the battery to one side of the relay switch and from the opposite side of the relay switch to the load. Most relays are normally open, preventing current from passing through the circuit. Additional, smaller wires are connected from the relay coil to the control switch for the circuit and from the opposite side of the relay coil to ground. When the control switch is turned on, it grounds the smaller wire to the relay coil, causing the coil to operate. The coil pulls the relay switch closed, sending power to the component without routing it through the inside of the vehicle. Some common circuits which may use relays are the horn, headlights, starter, electric fuel pump and rear window defogger systems.

LOAD

Every complete circuit must include a "load" (something to use the electricity coming from the source). Without this load, the battery would attempt to deliver its entire power supply from one pole to another. The electricity would take a short cut to ground and cause a great amount of damage to other components in the circuit by developing a tremendous amount of heat. This condition could develop sufficient heat to melt the insulation on all the surrounding wires and reduce a multiple wire cable to a lump of plastic and copper.

WIRING & HARNESSES

The average automobile contains about 1/2 mile of wiring, with hundreds of individual connections. To protect the many wires from damage and to keep them from becoming a confusing tangle, they are organized into bundles, enclosed in plastic or taped together and called wiring harnesses. Different harnesses serve different parts of the vehicle. Individual wires are color coded to help trace them through a harness where sections are hidden from view.

Automotive wiring or circuit conductors can be either single strand wire, multi-strand wire or printed circuitry. Single strand wire has a solid metal core and is usually used inside such components as alternators, motors, relays and other devices. Multi-strand wire has a core made of many small strands of wire twisted together into a single conductor. Most of the wiring in an automotive electrical system is made up of multi-strand wire, either as a single conductor or grouped together in a harness. All wiring is color coded on the insulator, either as a solid color or as a colored wire with an identification stripe. A printed circuit is a thin film of copper or other conductor that is printed on an insulator backing. Occasionally, a printed circuit is sandwiched between two sheets of plastic for more protection and flexibility. A complete printed circuit, consisting of conductors, insulating material and connectors for lamps or other components is called a printed circuit board. Printed circuitry is used in place of individual wires or harnesses in places where space is limited, such as behind instrument panels.

Since automotive electrical systems are very sensitive to changes in resistance, the selection of properly sized wires is critical when systems are repaired. A loose or corroded connection or a replacement wire that is too small for the circuit will add extra resistance and an additional voltage drop to the circuit.

The wire gauge number is an expression of the cross-section area of the conductor. The most common system for expressing wire size is the American Wire Gauge (AWG) system. As gauge number increases, area decreases and the wire becomes smaller. An 18 gauge wire is smaller than a 4 gauge wire. A wire with a higher gauge number will carry less current than a wire with a lower gauge number. Gauge wire size refers to the size of the strands of the conductor, not the size of the complete wire. It is possible, therefore, to have two wires of the same gauge with different diameters because one may have thicker insulation than the other.

12 volt automotive electrical systems generally use 10, 12, 14, 16 and 18 gauge wire. Main power distribution circuits and larger accessories usually use 10 and 12 gauge wire. Battery cables are usually 4 or 6 gauge, although 1 and 2 gauge wires are occasionally used.

It is essential to understand how a circuit works before trying to figure out why it doesn't. An electrical schematic shows the electrical current paths when a circuit is operating properly. Schematics break the entire electrical system down into individual circuits. In a schematic, no attempt is made to represent wiring and components as they physically appear on the vehicle; switches and other components are shown as simply as possible. Face views of harness connectors show the cavity or terminal locations in all multi-pin connectors to help locate test points.

CONNECTORS

▶ **See Figures 5 and 6**

Three types of connectors are commonly used in automotive applications—weatherproof, molded and hard shell.

• Weatherproof—these connectors are most commonly used in the engine compartment or where the connector is exposed to the elements. Terminals are protected against moisture and dirt by sealing rings which provide a weathertight seal. All repairs require the use of a special terminal and the tool required to service it. Unlike standard blade type terminals, these weatherproof terminals cannot be straightened once they are bent. Make certain that the connectors are properly seated and all of the sealing rings are in place when connecting leads.

• Molded—these connectors require complete replacement of the connector if found to be defective. This means splicing a new connector assembly into the harness. All splices should be soldered to insure proper contact. Use care when probing the connections or replacing terminals in them, as it is possible to create a short circuit between opposite terminals. If this happens to the wrong terminal pair, it is possible to damage certain components. Always use jumper wires between connectors for circuit checking and NEVER probe through weatherproof seals.

• Hard Shell—unlike molded connectors, the terminal contacts in hard-shell connectors can be replaced. Replacement usually involves the use of a special terminal removal tool that depresses the locking tangs (barbs) on the connector terminal and allows the connector to be removed from the rear of the shell. The connector shell should be replaced if it shows any evidence of burning, melting, cracks, or breaks. Replace individual terminals that are burnt, corroded, distorted or loose.

TCCA6P03

Fig. 5 Hard shell (left) and weatherproof (right) connectors have replaceable terminals

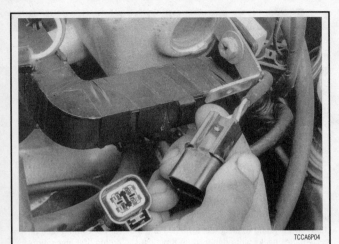

Fig. 6 Weatherproof connectors are most commonly used in the engine compartment or where the connector is exposed to the elements

Test Equipment

Pinpointing the exact cause of trouble in an electrical circuit is most times accomplished by the use of special test equipment. The following describes different types of commonly used test equipment and briefly explains how to use them in diagnosis. In addition to the information covered below, the tool manufacturer's instructions booklet (provided with the tester) should be read and clearly understood before attempting any test procedures.

JUMPER WIRES

✳✳ CAUTION

Never use jumper wires made from a thinner gauge wire than the circuit being tested. If the jumper wire is of too small a gauge, it may overheat and possibly melt. Never use jumpers to bypass high resistance loads in a circuit. Bypassing resistances, in effect, creates a short circuit. This may, in turn, cause damage and fire. Jumper wires should only be used to bypass lengths of wire.

Jumper wires are simple, yet extremely valuable, pieces of test equipment. They are basically test wires which are used to bypass sections of a circuit. Although jumper wires can be purchased, they are usually fabricated from lengths of standard automotive wire and whatever type of connector (alligator clip, spade connector or pin connector) that is required for the particular application being tested. In cramped, hard-to-reach areas, it is advisable to have insulated boots over the jumper wire terminals in order to prevent accidental grounding. It is also advisable to include a standard automotive fuse in any jumper wire. This is commonly referred to as a "fused jumper". By inserting an in-line fuse holder between a set of test leads, a fused jumper wire can be used for bypassing open circuits. Use a 5 amp fuse to provide protection against voltage spikes.

Jumper wires are used primarily to locate open electrical circuits, on either the ground (-) side of the circuit or on the power (+) side. If an electrical component fails to operate, connect the jumper wire between the component and a good ground. If the component operates only with the jumper installed, the ground circuit is open. If the ground circuit is good, but the component does not operate, the circuit between the power feed and component may be open. By moving the jumper wire successively back from the component toward the power source, you can isolate the area of the circuit where the open is located. When the component stops functioning, or the power is cut off, the open is in the segment of wire between the jumper and the point previously tested.

You can sometimes connect the jumper wire directly from the battery to the "hot" terminal of the component, but first make sure the component uses 12 volts in operation. Some electrical components, such as fuel injectors, are designed to operate on about 4 volts, and running 12 volts directly to these components will cause damage.

TEST LIGHTS

♦ **See Figure 7**

The test light is used to check circuits and components while electrical current is flowing through them. It is used for voltage and ground tests. To use a 12 volt test light, connect the ground clip to a good ground and probe wherever necessary with the pick. The test light will illuminate when voltage is detected. This does not necessarily mean that 12 volts (or any particular amount of voltage) is present; it only means that some voltage is present. It is advisable before using the test light to touch its ground clip and probe across the battery posts or terminals to make sure the light is operating properly.

✳✳ WARNING

Do not use a test light to probe electronic ignition spark plug or coil wires. Never use a pick-type test light to probe wiring on computer controlled systems unless specifically instructed to do so. Any wire insulation that is pierced by the test light probe should be taped and sealed with silicone after testing.

Like the jumper wire, the 12 volt test light is used to isolate opens in circuits. But, whereas the jumper wire is used to bypass the open to operate the load, the 12 volt test light is used to locate the presence of voltage in a circuit. If the test light illuminates, there is power up to that point in the circuit; if the test light does not illuminate, there is an open circuit (no power). Move the test light in successive steps back toward the power source until the light in the handle illuminates. The open is between the probe and a point which was previously probed.

The self-powered test light is similar in design to the 12 volt test light, but contains a 1.5 volt penlight battery in the handle. It is most often used in place of a multimeter to check for open or short circuits when power is isolated from the circuit (continuity test).

The battery in a self-powered test light does not provide much current. A weak battery may not provide enough power to illuminate the test light even when a complete circuit is made (especially if there is high resistance in the circuit). Always make sure that the test battery is strong. To check the battery, briefly touch the ground clip to the probe; if the light glows brightly, the battery is strong enough for testing.

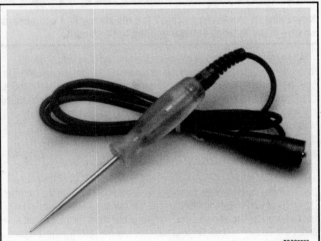

Fig. 7 A 12 volt test light is used to detect the presence of voltage in a circuit

➡**A self-powered test light should not be used on any computer controlled system or component. The small amount of electricity transmitted by the test light is enough to damage many electronic automotive components.**

MULTIMETERS

Multimeters are an extremely useful tool for troubleshooting electrical problems. They can be purchased in either analog or digital form and have a price range to suit any budget. A multimeter is a voltmeter, ammeter and ohmmeter (along with other features) combined into one instrument. It is often used when testing solid state circuits because of its high input impedance (usually 10 megaohms or more). A brief description of the multimeter main test functions follows:

• Voltmeter—the voltmeter is used to measure voltage at any point in a circuit, or to measure the voltage drop across any part of a circuit. Voltmeters usually have various scales and a selector switch to allow the reading of different voltage ranges. The voltmeter has a positive and a negative lead. To avoid damage to the meter, always connect the negative lead to the negative (-) side of the circuit (to ground or nearest the ground side of the circuit) and connect the positive lead to the positive (+) side of the circuit (to the power source or the nearest power source). Note that the negative voltmeter lead will always be black and that the positive voltmeter will always be some color other than black (usually red).

• Ohmmeter—the ohmmeter is designed to read resistance (measured in ohms) in a circuit or component. All ohmmeters will have a selector switch which permits the measurement of different ranges of resistance (usually the selector switch allows the multiplication of the meter reading by 10, 100, 1,000 and 10,000). Since the meters are powered by an internal battery, the ohmmeter can be used as a self-powered test light. When the ohmmeter is connected, current from the ohmmeter flows through the circuit or component being tested. Since the ohmmeter's internal resistance and voltage are known values, the amount of current flow through the meter depends on the resistance of the circuit or component being tested. The ohmmeter can also be used to perform a continuity test for suspected open circuits. In using the meter for making continuity checks, do not be concerned with the actual resistance readings. Zero resistance, or any ohm reading, indicates continuity in the circuit. Infinite resistance indicates an opening in the circuit. A high resistance reading where there should be none indicates a problem in the circuit. Checks for short circuits are made in the same manner as checks for open circuits, except that the circuit must be isolated from both power and normal ground. Infinite resistance indicates no continuity to ground, while zero resistance indicates a dead short to ground.

⁂ WARNING

Never use an ohmmeter to check the resistance of a component or wire while there is voltage applied to the circuit.

• Ammeter—an ammeter measures the amount of current flowing through a circuit in units called amperes or amps. At normal operating voltage, most circuits have a characteristic amount of amperes, called "current draw" which can be measured using an ammeter. By referring to a specified current draw rating, then measuring the amperes and comparing the two values, one can determine what is happening within the circuit to aid in diagnosis. An open circuit, for example, will not allow any current to flow, so the ammeter reading will be zero. A damaged component or circuit will have an increased current draw, so the reading will be high. The ammeter is always connected in series with the circuit being tested. All of the current that normally flows through the circuit must also flow through the ammeter; if there is any other path for the current to follow, the ammeter reading will not be accurate. The ammeter itself has very little resistance to current flow and, therefore, will not affect the circuit, but it will measure current draw only when the circuit is closed and electricity is flowing. Excessive current draw can blow fuses and drain the battery, while a reduced current draw can cause motors to run slowly, lights to dim and other components to not operate properly.

Troubleshooting

When diagnosing a specific problem, organized troubleshooting is a must. The complexity of a modern automotive vehicle demands that you approach any problem in a logical, organized manner. There are certain troubleshooting techniques which are standard:

• Establish when the problem occurs. Does the problem appear only under certain conditions? Were there any noises, odors or other unusual symptoms?

• Isolate the problem area. To do this, make some simple tests and observations, then eliminate the systems that are working properly. Check for obvious problems, such as broken wires and loose or dirty connections. Always check the obvious before assuming something complicated is the cause.

• Test for problems systematically to determine the cause once the problem area is isolated. Are all the components functioning properly? Is there power going to electrical switches and motors. Performing careful, systematic checks will often turn up most causes on the first inspection, without wasting time checking components that have little or no relationship to the problem.

• Test all repairs after the work is done to make sure that the problem is fixed. Some causes can be traced to more than one component, so a careful verification of repair work is important in order to pick up additional malfunctions that may cause a problem to reappear or a different problem to arise. A blown fuse, for example, is a simple problem that may require more than another fuse to repair. If you don't look for a problem that caused a fuse to blow, a shorted wire (for example) may go undetected.

Experience has shown that most problems tend to be the result of a fairly simple and obvious cause, such as loose or corroded connectors, bad grounds or damaged wire insulation which causes a short. This makes careful visual inspection of components during testing essential to quick and accurate troubleshooting.

Testing

OPEN CIRCUITS

▶ **See Figure 8**

1. Isolate the circuit from power and ground.
2. Connect the self-powered test light or ohmmeter ground clip to a good ground and probe sections of the circuit sequentially.

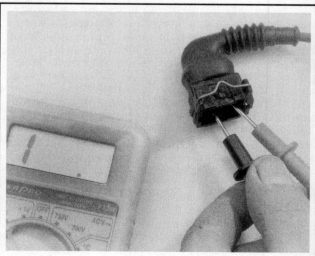

TCCA6P10

Fig. 8 The infinite reading on this multimeter (1 .) indicates that the circuit is open

3. If the light is out or there is infinite resistance, the open is between the probe and the circuit ground.

4. If the light is on or the meter shows continuity, the open is between the probe and end of the circuit toward the power source.

SHORT CIRCUITS

→**Never use a self-powered test light to perform checks for opens or shorts when power is applied to the electrical system under test. The 12 volt vehicle power will quickly burn out the light bulb in the test light.**

1. Isolate the circuit from power and ground.

2. Connect the self-powered test light or ohmmeter ground clip to a good ground and probe any easy-to-reach test point in the circuit.

3. If the light comes on or there is continuity, there is a short somewhere in the circuit.

4. To isolate the short, probe a test point at either end of the isolated circuit (the light should be on or the meter should indicate continuity).

5. Leave the test light probe engaged and sequentially open connectors or switches, remove parts, etc. until the light goes out or continuity is broken.

6. When the light goes out, the short is between the last two circuit components which were opened.

VOLTAGE

▶ **See Figures 9 and 10**

This test determines voltage available from the battery and should be the first step in any electrical troubleshooting procedure. Many electrical problems, especially on computer controlled systems, can be caused by a low state of charge in the battery. Excessive corrosion at the battery cable terminals can cause poor contact that will prevent proper charging and full battery current flow.

1. Set the voltmeter selector switch to the 20V position.

2. Connect the multimeter negative lead to the battery's negative (-) post or terminal and the positive lead to the battery's positive (+) post or terminal.

3. Turn the ignition switch **ON** to provide a load.

4. A well charged battery should register over 12 volts. If the meter reads below 11.5 volts, the battery power may be insufficient to operate the electrical system properly.

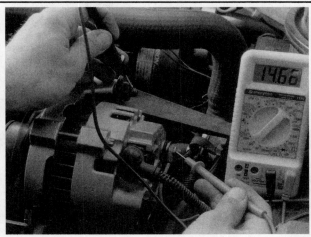

Fig. 10 Testing voltage output between the alternator's BAT terminal and ground. This voltage reading is normal

VOLTAGE DROP

▶ **See Figure 11**

When current flows through a load, the voltage beyond the load drops. This voltage drop is due to the resistance created by the load and also by small resistances created by corrosion at the connectors and damaged insulation on the wires. The maximum allowable voltage drop under load is critical, especially if there is more than one load in the circuit, since all voltage drops are cumulative.

1. Set the voltmeter selector switch to the 20 volt position.

2. Connect the multimeter negative lead to a good ground.

3. Operate the circuit and check the voltage prior to the first component (load).

4. There should be little or no voltage drop in the circuit prior to the first component. If a voltage drop exists, the wire or connectors in the circuit are suspect.

5. While operating the first component in the circuit, probe the ground side of the component with the positive meter lead and observe the voltage

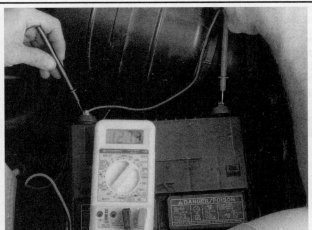

Fig. 9 Using a multimeter to check battery voltage. This battery is fully charged

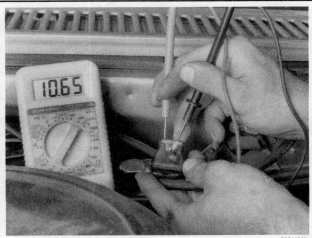

Fig. 11 This voltage drop test revealed high resistance (low voltage) in the circuit

readings. A small voltage drop should be noticed. This voltage drop is caused by the resistance of the component.

6. Repeat the test for each component (load) down the circuit.

7. If a large voltage drop is noticed, the preceding component, wire or connector is suspect.

RESISTANCE

▶ See Figures 12 and 13

❊❊ WARNING

Never use an ohmmeter with power applied to the circuit. The ohmmeter is designed to operate on its own power supply. The normal 12 volt automotive electrical system current could damage the meter!

1. Isolate the circuit from the vehicle's power source.

2. Ensure that the ignition key is **OFF** when disconnecting any components or the battery.

3. Where necessary, also isolate at least one side of the circuit to be checked, in order to avoid reading parallel resistances. Parallel circuit resistances will always give a lower reading than the actual resistance of either of the branches.

4. Connect the meter leads to both sides of the circuit (wire or component) and read the actual measured ohms on the meter scale. Make sure the selector switch is set to the proper ohm scale for the circuit being tested, to avoid misreading the ohmmeter test value.

TCCA6P08

Fig. 12 Checking the resistance of a coolant temperature sensor with an ohmmeter. Reading is 1.04 kilohms

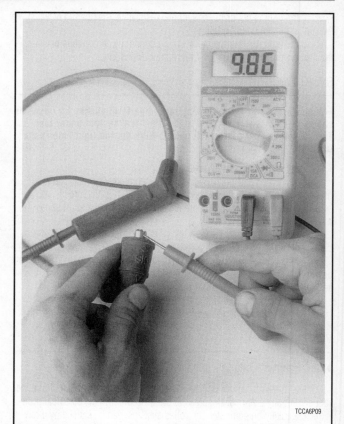

TCCA6P09

Fig. 13 Spark plug wires can be checked for excessive resistance using an ohmmeter

Wire and Connector Repair

Almost anyone can replace damaged wires, as long as the proper tools and parts are available. Automotive wire and terminals are available to fit almost any need. Even the specialized weatherproof, molded and hard shell connectors are now available from aftermarket suppliers.

Be sure the ends of all the wires are fitted with the proper terminal hardware and connectors. Wrapping a wire around a stud is never a permanent solution and will only cause trouble later. Replace wires one at a time to avoid confusion. Always route wires exactly the same as the factory.

➡**If connector repair is necessary, only attempt it if you have the proper tools. Weatherproof and hard shell connectors require special tools to release the pins inside the connector. Attempting to repair these connectors with conventional hand tools will damage them.**

BATTERY CABLES

Disconnecting the Cables

When working on any electrical component on the vehicle, it is always a good idea to disconnect the negative (-) battery cable. This will prevent potential damage to many sensitive electrical components such as the Engine Control Module (ECM), radio, alternator, etc.

➡**Any time you disengage the battery cables, it is recommended that you disconnect the negative (-) battery cable first. This will prevent your accidentally grounding the positive (+) terminal to the body of the vehicle when disconnecting it, thereby preventing damage to the above mentioned components.**

Before you disconnect the cable(s), first turn the ignition to the **OFF** position. This will prevent a draw on the battery which could cause arcing (electricity trying to ground itself to the body of a vehicle, just like a spark plug jumping the gap) and, of course, damaging some components such as the alternator diodes.

When the battery cable(s) are reconnected (negative cable last), be sure to check that your lights, windshield wipers and other electrically operated safety components are all working correctly. If your vehicle contains an Electronically Tuned Radio (ETR), don't forget to also reset your radio stations. Ditto for the clock.

AIR BAG (SUPPLEMENTAL RESTRAINT) SYSTEM

General Information

✳✳ CAUTION

Some vehicles are equipped with an air bag system, also known as the Supplemental Inflatable Restraint (SIR) or Supplemental Restraint System (SRS). The system must be disabled before performing service on or around system components, steering column, instrument panel components, wiring and sensors. Failure to follow safety and disabling procedures could result in accidental air bag deployment, possible personal injury and unnecessary system repairs.

SERVICE PRECAUTIONS

Several precautions must be observed when handling the inflator module to avoid accidental deployment and possible personal injury.
- Never carry the inflator module by the wires or connector on the underside of the module.
- When carrying a live inflator module, hold securely with both hands, and ensure that the bag and trim cover are pointed away.
- Place the inflator module on a bench or other surface with the bag and trim cover facing up.
- With the inflator module on the bench, never place anything on or close to the module which may be thrown in the event of an accidental deployment.
- Never use air bag component parts from another vehicle.
- If the vehicle will be exposed to temperatures above 200°F (93°C), remove the air bag module from the steering wheel.
- If there is a chance of electrical shock to any of the air bag components, remove the air bag module before servicing the vehicle.

DISARMING THE SYSTEM

▶ See Figure 14

✳✳ CAUTION

The Supplemental Inflatable Restraint (SIR) system must be disarmed before performing service around SIR components or SIR wiring. Failure to do so may cause accidental deployment of the air bag, resulting in unnecessary SIR system repairs and/or personal injury.

1. Turn the steering wheel so the front wheels are in the straight ahead position.
2. Turn the ignition switch to the **LOCK** position and remove the key.
3. Remove the AIR BAG fuse from the air bag fuse box.
4. Remove the steering wheel side cap and disengage the yellow connector inside the inflator module housing.
5. Remove the glove box, by disengaging both glove box stoppers from each side, then unplug the yellow passenger air bag inflator module connector.

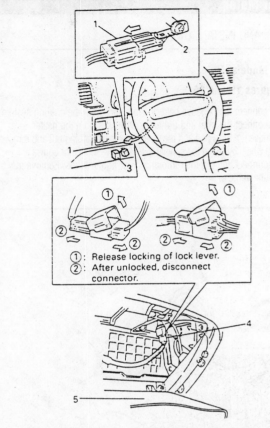

①: Release locking of lock lever.
②: After unlocked, disconnect connector.

1. Yellow connector of driver air bag (inflator) module
2. Connector stay
3. Air bag fuse box
4. Yellow connector of passenger air bag (inflator) module
5. Glove box

90886G00

Fig. 14 To disable the air bag system, the air bag fuse needs to be removed and the yellow air bag module connector needs to be disengaged

ARMING THE SYSTEM

1. Turn the steering wheel so the front wheels are in the straight ahead position.
2. Turn the ignition switch to the **LOCK** position.
3. Engage the passenger air bag inflator module yellow connector. Install glove box.
4. Engage the yellow connector inside the inflator module housing on the driver's air bag. Install the inflator module onto the connector stay.
5. Install the plastic access cover.
6. Turn the ignition switch to the **ON** position. Verify that the air bag indicator lamp flashes 7 times and then turns OFF. If the lamp does not function as specified, there is a malfunction in the SIR system.

HEATING AND AIR CONDITIONING

Blower Motor

REMOVAL AND INSTALLATION

Samurai Models

▶ **See Figures 15 and 16**

1. Disconnect the negative battery cable and drain the cooling system.
2. Disconnect the inlet and outlet heater hoses from the heater core.
3. Remove the horn pad and the steering wheel retaining nut and remove the steering wheel by using the special tool (09944–36010) or equivalent.
4. Disconnect and tag the radio and cigar lighter wires. Remove the radio from the vehicle.

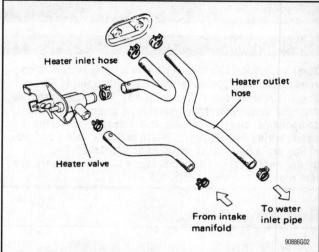

Fig. 16 After installing the heater case assembly, be sure to reconnect the heater core hoses to the proper pipes

5. Remove the ash tray and mounting plate.
6. Disconnect the hood release cable from the release lever.
7. Disconnect and tag the heater control cables and wires at the controls.
8. Remove the heater control lever knobs and facing plate. Loosen the lever case screws.
9. Remove the defroster and side ventilator hoses.
10. Disconnect the lead wires and speedometer cable from the speedometer and remove the lead wires from the heater controls.
11. Disconnect the wiring harness clamps from the instrument panel.

➡ **When separating the instrument panel from the firewall, be sure that all wires, cables and hoses are disconnected.**

12. Loosen the instrument panel mounting screws and remove the instrument panel.

➡ **When removing the heater lever case which is fitted in the steering column holder, be very careful not to damage it.**

13. Loosen the front door opening stop screws and remove the steering column bracket.
14. Detach and tag the blower motor and resistor connections at the coupler.
15. Loosen the heater case securing nut on the engine side.
16. Remove the heater assembly from the vehicle.
17. Remove the blower motor from the case.
To install:
18. Install the blower motor in the heater case and install the assembly in the vehicle.
19. Tighten the heater case securing nut on the engine side.
20. Install the blower motor and resistor connections at the coupler.
21. Tighten the front door opening stop screws and install the steering column holder.
22. Tighten the instrument panel mounting screws and replace the instrument panel.
23. Reconnect the wiring harness clamps to the instrument panel.
24. Reconnect the lead wires and speedometer cable to the speedometer.
25. Install the defroster and side ventilator hoses.
26. Install the heater control knobs and plate, and tighten the lever case screws.

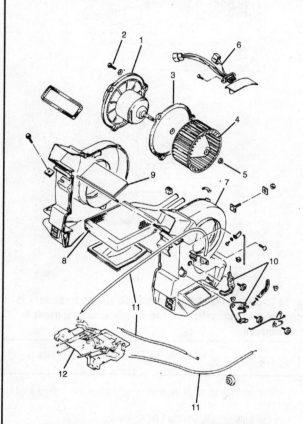

1. Blower motor	7. Heater case assembly
2. Blower motor mounting screw	8. Heater core
3. Blower motor mounting gasket	9. Air control flap
4. Blower motor fan	10. Air control cable levers
5. Blower motor fan mounting nut	11. Air control cables
6. Wiring harness and connectors	12. Heater control panel unit

90886G01

Fig. 15 Exploded view of the heater case assembly, showing the locations of the blower motor and heater core

27. Reconnect the heater control cables at the controls.
28. Reconnect the hood release cable to the release lever.
29. Install the ash tray and mounting plate.
30. Reconnect the radio and cigar lighter wires. Install the radio in the vehicle.
31. Install the horn pad and steering wheel retaining nut and install the steering wheel.
32. Reconnect the inlet and outlet heater hoses to heater core.
33. Refill the cooling system with the proper coolant. Reconnect the negative battery cable.

Sidekick, Tracker, Sidekick Sport and X-90 Models

◗ See Figures 17 and 18

1. Disconnect the negative battery cable.
2. On models with air bags, disable the system.
3. Remove the glove box assembly by opening it, and loosening the pivot and retaining screws from inside the glove box with a screwdriver.
4. On 1996–98 models, remove the instrument panel assist holder (lower brace).
5. Remove the relays and relay bracket from the blower motor case.
6. Disengage the blower motor and resistor wire connectors.

. . . then remove the glove box from the instrument panel

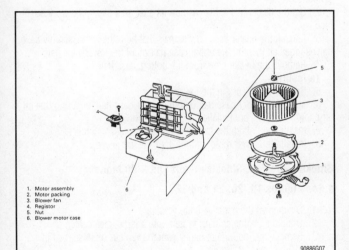

1. Motor assembly
2. Motor packing
3. Blower fan
4. Registor
5. Nut
6. Blower motor case

Fig. 17 Exploded view of the blower motor mounting in the heater case

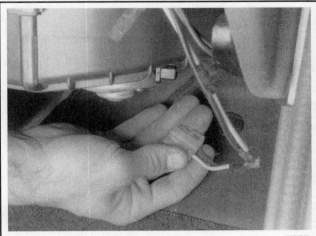

From beneath the instrument panel, detach the wiring harness connectors . . .

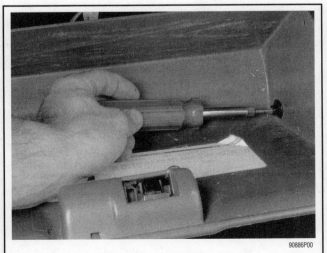

To remove the blower motor, open the glove box and loosen the box pivot and retaining screws . . .

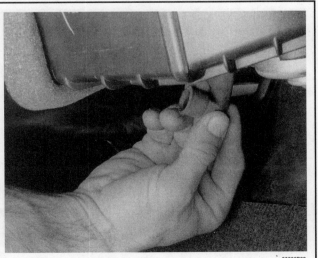

. . . and hoses from the blower motor

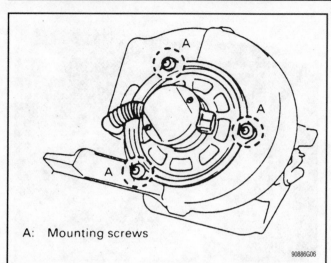

A: Mounting screws

90886G06

Fig. 18 Blower motor mounting bolt locations on the bottom of the heater case

90886P04

Loosen all of the blower motor-to-heater case assembly mounting bolts . . .

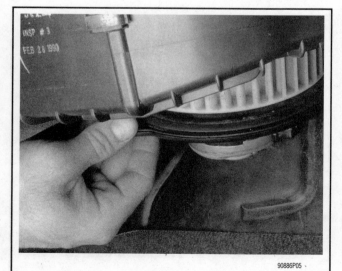

90886P05

. . . then lower the blower motor out of the heater case assembly

7. Disconnect the fresh air control cable from the blower motor case.
8. Remove the 3 blower motor mounting screws.
9. Remove the blower motor.

To install:
10. Install the blower motor and secure with the 3 screws.
11. Connect the fresh air control cable to the blower motor case.
12. Connect the electrical connectors and install the glove box assembly.
13. Install the relay bracket and relays on the blower motor case.
14. On 1996–98 models, install the instrument panel assist holder.
15. Connect the negative battery cable.
16. If applicable, enable the air bag system.
17. Check for proper blower motor operation.

Heater Core

REMOVAL & INSTALLATION

Samurai Models

1. Remove the heater system blower motor, as described earlier in this section.
2. Set the heater assembly case on its side on a clean, flat work surface.
3. Loosen the heater assembly screws that hold the two assembly case halves together, then lift the upper case half off of the lower case half.
4. Remove the heater core from the bottom case half.

To install:
5. Set the heater core in the lower case half.
6. Install the upper case half onto the lower case half, ensuring that all air control flap pins are installed in the proper holes.
7. Install and tighten the case half attaching bolts securely.
8. Install the blower motor and heater case in the vehicle.

Sidekick, Tracker, Sidekick Sport and X-90 Models
▶ See Figures 19, 20, 21 and 22

1. Disconnect the negative battery cable.
2. Drain the engine cooling system into a large, clean catch pan.
3. Remove the instrument panel from the vehicle, as described in Section 10.

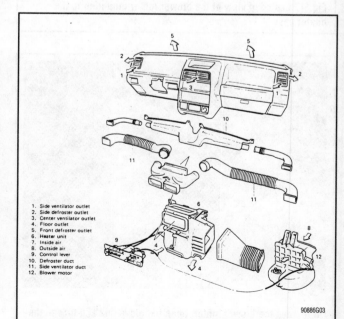

1. Side ventilator outlet
2. Side defroster outlet
3. Center ventilator outlet
4. Floor outlet
5. Front defroster outlet
6. Heater unit
7. Inside air
8. Outside air
9. Control lever
10. Defroster duct
11. Side ventilator duct
12. Blower motor

90886G03

Fig. 19 Exploded view of the air distribution (ducting) system

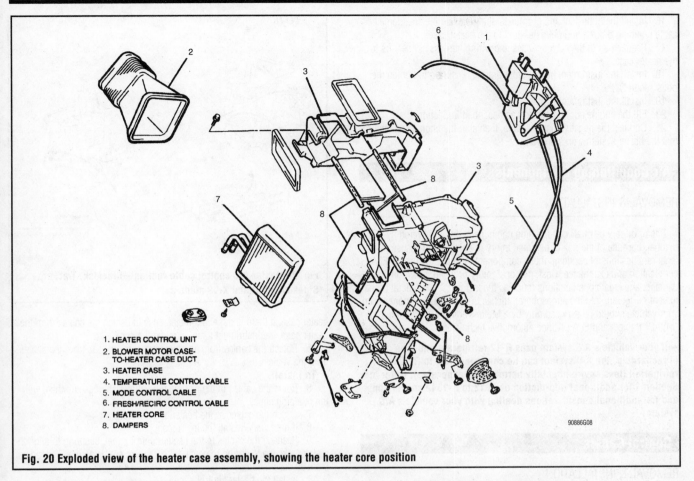

1. HEATER CONTROL UNIT
2. BLOWER MOTOR CASE-
   TO-HEATER CASE DUCT
3. HEATER CASE
4. TEMPERATURE CONTROL CABLE
5. MODE CONTROL CABLE
6. FRESH/RECIRC CONTROL CABLE
7. HEATER CORE
8. DAMPERS

90886G08

Fig. 20 Exploded view of the heater case assembly, showing the heater core position

4. Remove the instrument panel center support from the firewall.
5. Detach and label all wiring harness connectors from the heater case.
6. Disconnect all of the cables from the heater case.
7. Detach the two heater hoses from the heater case.
8. Remove the defroster duct and speedometer cable retaining bracket from the heater case.
9. Remove the grommets and floor duct from the case.
10. Open the hood, then remove the heater case-to-firewall mounting nuts from the engine side of the firewall.
11. Remove the two mounting bolts from inside the passengers' com-
partment, then remove the case from the vehicle.
12. Loosen the heater core retaining bolts, then slide the heater core out of the heater case.

To install:
13. Install the heater core in the heater case, then tighten the retaining bolts securely.
14. Position the heater case in the vehicle, against the firewall, and install the mounting bolts. Tighten them securely.
15. From the engine compartment, install and tighten the heater case mounting nuts securely.

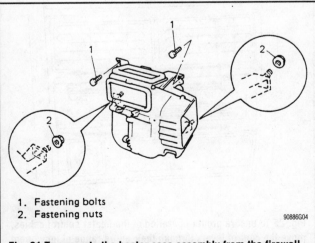

1. Fastening bolts
2. Fastening nuts

90886G04

Fig. 21 To separate the heater case assembly from the firewall, remove the two nuts from the engine compartment, and the two bolts from inside the passengers' compartment

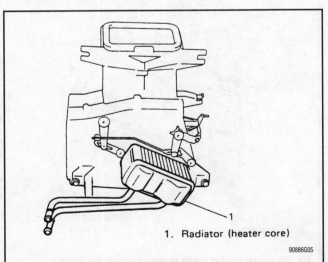

1. Radiator (heater core)

90886G05

Fig. 22 Remove the heater core retaining fasteners, then slide the core out of the heater case assembly

16. Install the floor duct and grommets, then reattach the speedometer cable retaining bracket and defroster duct to the heater case.

17. Reattach all of the cables, hoses and wiring harness connectors to the heater case.

18. Install the instrument panel center bracket, ensuring to tighten the bolts securely.

19. Install the instrument panel.

20. Fill the engine cooling system, as described in Section 1.

21. Connect the negative battery cable, then start the engine and ensure that the heater system works properly.

Air Conditioning Components

REMOVAL & INSTALLATION

Repair or service of air conditioning components is not covered by this manual, because of the risk of personal injury or death, and because of the legal ramifications of servicing these components without the proper EPA certification and experience. Cost, personal injury or death, environmental damage, and legal considerations (such as the fact that it is a federal crime to vent refrigerant into the atmosphere), dictate that the A/C components on your vehicle should be serviced only by a Motor Vehicle Air Conditioning (MVAC) trained, and EPA certified automotive technician.

➡**If your vehicle's A/C system uses R-12 refrigerant and is in need of recharging, the A/C system can be converted over to R-134a refrigerant (less environmentally harmful and expensive). Refer to Section 1 for additional information on R-12 to R-134a conversions, and for additional considerations dealing with your vehicle's A/C system.**

Control Cables

REMOVAL & INSTALLATION

▶ **See Figures 23 and 24**

1. Remove the heater control panel.
2. Matchmark the positions of the control cable housings on the retaining clips.
3. Detach the cables from the control panel levers.
4. Working under the instrument panel, disconnect the cables from the

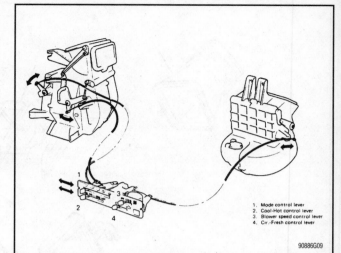

Fig. 24 Heater-A/C control cable routing—Sidekick, Tracker, Sidekick Sport and X-90 models

1. Mode control lever
2. Cool-Hot control lever
3. Blower speed control lever
4. Cir.-Fresh control lever

90886G09

heater case. If there is not enough clearance to detach the cables from the heater case, the instrument panel must be removed.

5. Detach the cables from any retaining clips, then remove the cables from the vehicle.

To install:

6. Route the cables in their original positions, then secure them with the retaining clips.

7. Attach the cables to the heater case levers.

8. If necessary, install the instrument panel.

9. Reattach the cables to the heater control panel, ensuring to align the matchmarks made during removal. If new cables are being installed, adjust them as described later in this section.

10. Install the heater control panel.

ADJUSTMENT

▶ **See Figures 25 thru 32**

The heater control cables are adjusted by positioning the cable sleeves in the retaining clips of the control panel so that when the cables are attached to the control levers, the heating system air is properly routed

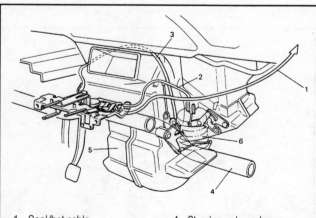

1. Cool/hot cable
2. Circulating/fresh air cable
3. Room/defroster cable
4. Steering column brace
5. Heater case
6. Defroster hose

90886G10

Fig. 23 Heater control cable routing for Samurai models

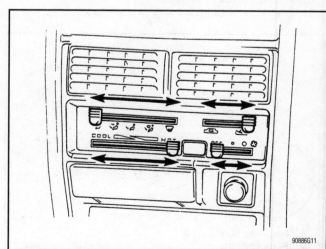

90886G11

Fig. 25 To ensure proper operation of the heater control cables, move the control levers through their entire range of movement and check for binding or improper air flow

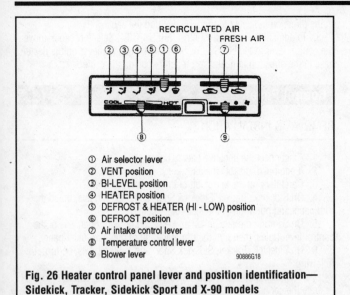

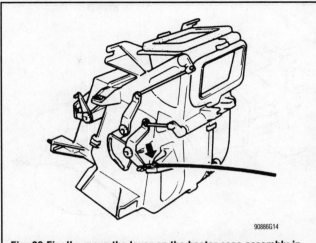

Fig. 26 Heater control panel lever and position identification—Sidekick, Tracker, Sidekick Sport and X-90 models

Fig. 29 Finally, move the lever on the heater case assembly in the direction of the arrow to fix the cable and rod in the proper position

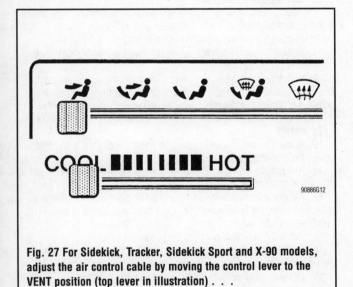

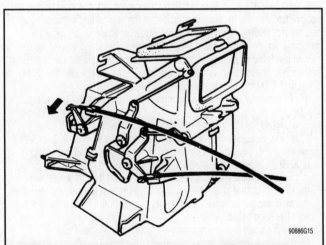

Fig. 27 For Sidekick, Tracker, Sidekick Sport and X-90 models, adjust the air control cable by moving the control lever to the VENT position (top lever in illustration) . . .

Fig. 30 To adjust the heater control cable, position the lever at COOL, then move the heater case assembly lever in the direction of the arrow

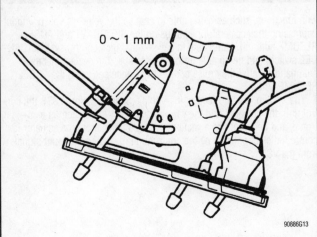

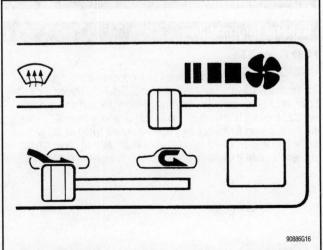

Fig. 28 . . . then attach the cable sleeve to the retaining clip as specified in the procedure—Canadian-built model shown

Fig. 31 To adjust the fresh air control cable, move the control lever to the FRESH position (bottom lever in illustration) . . .

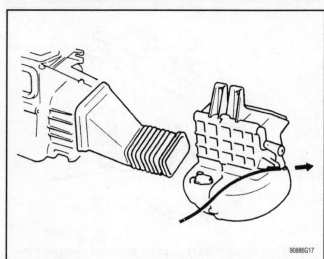

Fig. 32 . . . then move the cable and lever in the direction of the black arrow

throughout the ducting. After installing the cables, but before installing the control panel in the instrument panel, start the engine and operate the various control levers of the control panel, ensuring that they all function smoothly and the air is routed properly. If the levers are not quite right, loosen the cable sleeve retaining clips and reposition the sleeve in relation to the clips. Retest the operation of the lever. For Sidekick, Tracker, Sidekick Sport and X-90 models, perform the following:

1. To correctly adjust the air control cable, perform the following steps:

a. Move the control lever to the VENT position.

b. For vehicles manufactured in Canada (refer to section 1 for VIN information), position the end of the cable sleeve so that it projects 0.00–0.04 in. (0–1mm) from the retaining clip.

c. For vehicles manufactured in Japan, insert the cable sleeve into the retainer until it stops, then clamp it securely. If the cable sleeve does not stop and projects past the retainer clamp, pull it back until it is flush with the edge of the clamp.

d. As shown in the accompanying illustration, push the door (damper) linkage fully in the direction of the arrow to affix the cable and rod into the proper position.

2. To adjust the Heater Control (HOT-COOL Selector) cable, move the control lever to the COOL position. Then, push the lever on the heater case

in the direction indicated to properly position the cable.

3. To adjust the Fresh Air Control (FRESH-CIRC Selector) cable, move the control lever to the FRESH position. Then, push the lever on the heater case in the direction indicated to properly position the cable.

Control Panel

REMOVAL & INSTALLATION

1. Disconnect the negative battery cable.
2. If equipped, disable the air bag system.
3. Carefully pull the knobs off of the control levers.
4. On Sidekick, Tracker, Sidekick Sport and X-90 models, grasp the trim panel and pull it off of the instrument panel.
5. On Samurai models, insert an L-shaped hook through one of the control lever holes, then pull the trim panel off of the instrument panel.
6. On Sidekick, Tracker, Sidekick Sport and X-90 models, perform the following:

a. Remove the ashtray and center garnish mounting screw, then separate the garnish from the instrument panel.

b. Remove the glove box, lower steering column cover and knee bolster from the instrument panel.

c. Remove the instrument panel glove box compartment, then detach the control cables from the blower motor unit and heater case.

7. Remove the control panel mounting fasteners.
8. Detach the wiring harness connector from the blower motor switch, mounted in the control panel.
9. Withdraw the heater-A/C control panel from the instrument panel. The control panel for Sidekick, Tracker, Sidekick Sport and X-90 models pulls out of the instrument panel, whereas the control panel for Samurai models must be pushed into the instrument panel and removed from below.

To install:

10. Install the control panel in the instrument panel, then install and tighten the mounting fasteners.
11. Reattach the wiring and control cables to the control panel. Adjust the cables as described earlier in this section.
12. If applicable, install the instrument panel glove box compartment, the knee bolster, the lower steering column cover and the glove box. Also, install the garnish and ashtray in the instrument panel.
13. Install the control panel mounting fasteners securely.
14. Position the control panel over the control levers, then press it in until it is fully engaged in the instrument panel.
15. Install the control level knobs on the levers.

CRUISE CONTROL

General Information

▶ **See Figure 33**

The cruise control system (known as the speed control system on Tracker models) was an available option for Sidekick, Tracker, Sidekick Sport and X-90 models. The system is designed to maintain a preset vehicle speed while driving at high speeds (highway driving). It allows the driver to operate his/her vehicle at a constant speed as desired within the range of 25–75 mph (40–120 km/h) without depressing the accelerator pedal (constant cruising speed). The system is also equipped

with functions, such as being able to change the vehicle's speed without depressing the accelerator pedal (using the SET COAST and ACCEL RESUME buttons), being able to cancel the cruise control system (CANCEL switch) and being able to resume the speed in system memory automatically after the cruise control was canceled (using the ACCEL RESUME button).

The system is comprised of the Vehicle Speed Sensor (VSS), the control unit, the actuator, and the various switches. The system is electronic, and does not use a vacuum-controlled actuator. The actuator is controlled electronically by the control unit, based on the input signals from the VSS.

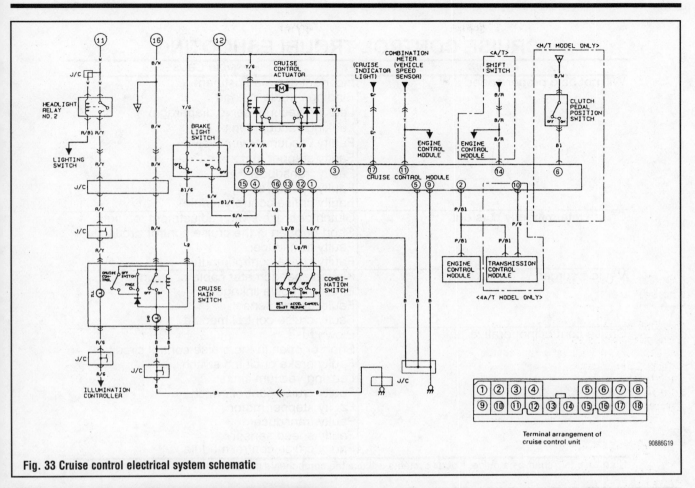

Fig. 33 Cruise control electrical system schematic

Actuator Cable

ADJUSTMENT

▶ See Figure 34

It may be necessary to disconnect the actuator cable from the throttle body lever during various engine procedures. After reattaching the actuator cable to the throttle lever, adjust its end-play as follows:

1. Remove the actuator cover.
2. Loosen the locknuts.
3. Move the actuator cable sleeve in the mounting bracket so that 0.04–0.08 in. (1–2mm) of cable end-play is achieved when the actuator lever is at the fully closed position. (Actually, the lever can deviate from the fully closed position by no more than 0.08–0.12 in. (2–3mm), which is "a" in the accompanying illustration. However, try to get the lever as closed as possible for this adjustment.)
4. Tighten the locknuts to 53 inch lbs. (6 Nm).
5. Install the actuator cover.

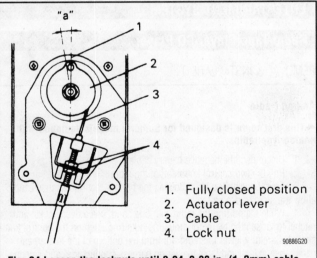

1. Fully closed position
2. Actuator lever
3. Cable
4. Lock nut

Fig. 34 Loosen the locknuts until 0.04–0.08 in. (1–2mm) cable end-play is achieved

CRUISE CONTROL TROUBLESHOOTING

Problem	Possible Cause
Will not hold proper speed	Incorrect cable adjustment
	Binding throttle linkage
	Leaking vacuum servo diaphragm
	Leaking vacuum tank
	Faulty vacuum or vent valve
	Faulty stepper motor
	Faulty transducer
	Faulty speed sensor
	Faulty cruise control module
Cruise intermittently cuts out	Clutch or brake switch adjustment too tight
	Short or open in the cruise control circuit
	Faulty transducer
	Faulty cruise control module
Vehicle surges	Kinked speedometer cable or casing
	Binding throttle linkage
	Faulty speed sensor
	Faulty cruise control module
Cruise control inoperative	Blown fuse
	Short or open in the cruise control circuit
	Faulty brake or clutch switch
	Leaking vacuum circuit
	Faulty cruise control switch
	Faulty stepper motor
	Faulty transducer
	Faulty speed sensor
	Faulty cruise control module

Note: Use this chart as a guide. Not all systems will use the components listed.

TCCA6C01

ENTERTAINMENT SYSTEMS

Radio/Tape Player/CD Player

REMOVAL & INSTALLATION

Analog Radio

➡This procedure is designed for Samurai models equipped with analog-type radios.

1. Disconnect the negative battery cable.
2. Pull the two control knobs off of the radio.
3. From beneath the radio, loosen the bottom mounting screws and allow the radio to drop slightly.
4. While supporting the radio with one hand, use a deep socket and ratchet to loosen the two front mounting nuts (mounted on the control knob shafts). Carefully lower the radio out from the bottom of the instrument panel, then detach and label the wiring harness connector(s) and antenna cable from the back of the radio.

To install:

5. Reattach the wiring and antenna cable to the back of the radio.
6. Position the radio beneath the instrument panel so that the control shafts protrude through their mounting holes.
7. If equipped, position the radio trim plate over the two control shafts and flush against the instrument panel, then install and tighten the front radio mounting nuts snugly.
8. Install and tighten the bottom mounting screws securely.
9. Press the control knobs on the shafts, ensuring that the alignment flat on the shaft is aligned with the flat in the shaft bore of the knob.
10. Connect the negative battery cable.
11. Crank up the tunes on the radio to ensure that it is working properly.

Electronic Radio

⧫ See Figures 35, 36 and 37

➡This procedure includes Samurai models equipped with electronic tuning radios.

1. Disconnect the negative battery cable.

➡Be sure to keep track of all the little screws, nuts and bolts during removal, so that they can be reinstalled in their original positions. Use small plastic bags to keep all related parts together, and all unrelated parts apart.

2. If equipped, disable the air bag system.
3. Pull the heater control lever knobs off of the levers.
4. On 1996–98 models, separate the heater control trim panel from the control unit by pulling it straight away from the instrument panel. Allow the trim panel to hang loose.
5. Open the ashtray, then depress the ashtray retainer and remove the ashtray from the sliding track. While it is removed from the vehicle, now would be a good time to wash it out.
6. Loosen the two retaining screws, then remove the ashtray track from the instrument panel center trim bezel.
7. On 1989–95 Sidekick and Tracker models, remove the trim panel by prying it carefully away from the instrument panel.
8. On 1996–98 models, remove the center trim bezel from the instrument panel by loosening the four retaining screws and maneuvering the heater control trim through the appropriate hole. Set the bezel out of the way.
9. Use a screwdriver to loosen the one rear mounting bracket-to-radio screw; access can be gained to this screw through the ashtray hole.
10. Remove the four radio front retaining screws, then pull the radio out

Depress the retaining tab, then pull the ashtray out of the panel. Take this opportunity to wash it out

On older models, remove the radio trim piece by carefully prying it away from the instrument panel

Loosen the retaining screws . . .

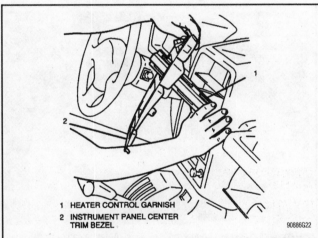

1 HEATER CONTROL GARNISH
2 INSTRUMENT PANEL CENTER TRIM BEZEL

Fig. 35 On newer models, remove the heater control trim panel, then maneuver the center trim bezel through the hole in the heater control garnish and remove the garnish from the vehicle

. . . then remove the ashtray guide track from the instrument panel

Pull the radio out of the instrument panel until . . .

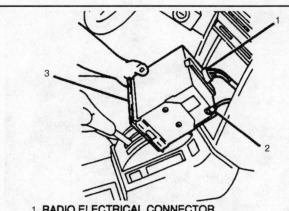

1 RADIO ELECTRICAL CONNECTOR
2 ANTENNA CONNECTOR
3 RADIO

90886G23

Fig. 36 . . . the wires attached to the back side of the radio can be accessed . . .

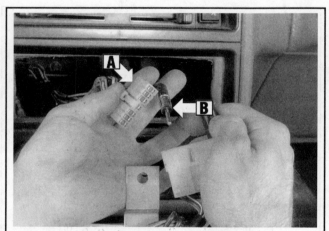

A. Wiring harness connector   B. Antenna cable

90886P11

. . . then detach all of the wires, including the antenna cable, from the radio

1 SIDE MOUNTING BRACKET
2 REAR MOUNTING BRACKET

90886G24

Fig. 37 Once the radio is removed from the vehicle, the side and rear mounting brackets can be separated from it

of the instrument panel just far enough so that the electrical connections on the rear of the radio can be accessed.

11. Detach and label the wiring from the radio. Also, detach the antenna cable from the rear face of the radio.

12. Remove the radio from the vehicle.

13. If necessary, the side mounting and rear mounting brackets can be separated from the radio by loosening the mounting bracket screws.

To install:

14. If removed, install the mounting brackets on the radio unit.

15. Position the radio close enough to the instrument panel hole so that the wiring connectors and antenna cable can be reattached to it. Reattach the wiring and antenna cable to the radio.

16. Slide the radio into the instrument panel opening, then install and tighten the four front mounting screws securely. However, do not tighten the screws so tight that if you ever need to remove the radio again, you will end up stripping the screw heads.

17. Insert the heater control trim through the hole in the center trim bezel, then position the center trim bezel on the instrument panel. Install and tighten the mounting screws snugly.

18. Install the ashtray track, ensuring to tighten the mounting screws securely. Insert the ashtray in the opening, then close it.

19. Position the heater control trim panel over the control levers and against the control unit. Push the trim against the panel until it is properly engaged.

20. Install all of the control lever knobs, then connect the negative battery cable.

21. If applicable, enable the air bag system.

22. Crank up the tunes on the radio to ensure that it is working properly.

Speakers

REMOVAL & INSTALLATION

Front Speakers

▶ See Figure 38

1. Disconnect the negative battery cable.

2. Loosen the two front speaker grille mounting screws, then pull the grille off of the speaker.

3. Loosen the two front speaker mounting screws, then remove the speaker from the instrument panel.

4. Detach and label the speaker wires from the speaker terminals.

To install:

5. Reattach the speaker wires to the speaker terminals.

6. Position the speaker in the mounting hole on the instrument panel, then tighten the two front speaker mounting screws securely.

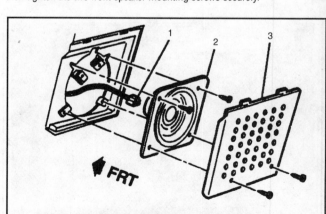

1 FRONT SPEAKER ELECTRICAL CONNECTOR
2 FRONT SPEAKER
3 FRONT SPEAKER GRILLE

90886G26

Fig. 38 Exploded view of the front speaker mounting—Sidekick, Tracker, Sidekick Sport and X-90 shown

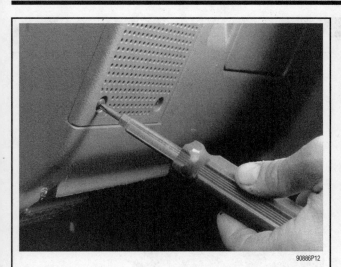

To remove the front speaker, first loosen the speaker grille retaining screws . . .

. . . then remove the grille from the instrument panel

Loosen the speaker mounting screws . . .

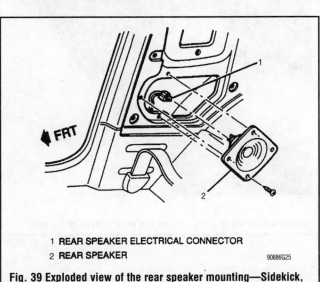

. . . then remove the speaker and detach the wiring harness connectors from it

7. Place the grille over the speaker, then install and tighten the two front speaker grille mounting screws.
8. Connect the negative battery cable.

Rear Speakers

▶ **See Figure 39**

1. Disconnect the negative battery cable.
2. Loosen the front seat belt trim bezel retaining screw, then pull the rear quarter interior trim panel off of the body, disengaging the plastic clips.
3. Loosen the speaker mounting screws, then remove the speaker from the rear inner quarter panel.
4. Detach and label the speaker wires from the speaker terminals.

To install:

5. Reattach the speaker wires to the speaker terminals.
6. Position the speaker in the mounting hole on the rear inner quarter panel, then tighten the speaker mounting screws securely.
7. Place the rear quarter trim panel in position on the body, then press it into place so that the plastic retaining clips engage.
8. Install and tighten the front seat belt trim bezel retaining screw.
9. Connect the negative battery cable.

1 REAR SPEAKER ELECTRICAL CONNECTOR
2 REAR SPEAKER

Fig. 39 Exploded view of the rear speaker mounting—Sidekick, Tracker, Sidekick Sport and X-90 shown

WINDSHIELD WIPERS AND WASHERS

Windshield Wiper Blade and Arm

REMOVAL & INSTALLATION

Front

▶ See Figure 40

1. Turn the ignition switch **ON** without starting the engine. Operate the wipers so that they go through one full cycle, then turn the wipers OFF.

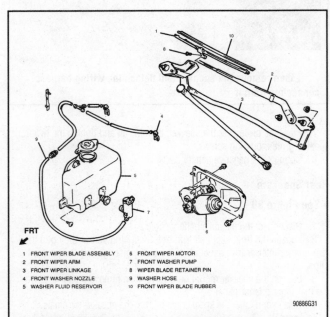

1 FRONT WIPER BLADE ASSEMBLY
2 FRONT WIPER ARM
3 FRONT WIPER LINKAGE
4 FRONT WASHER NOZZLE
5 WASHER FLUID RESERVOIR
6 FRONT WIPER MOTOR
7 FRONT WASHER PUMP
8 WIPER BLADE RETAINER PIN
9 WASHER HOSE
10 FRONT WIPER BLADE RUBBER

90886G31

Fig. 40 Exploded view of the front windshield wiper and washer system—except Samurai models

90886P13

To remove the wiper arms, remove the wiper arm retaining nut . . .

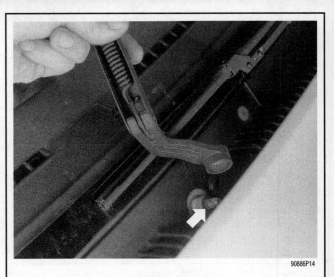

90886P14

. . . then lift the wiper arm up and off of the linkage stud

Ensure that they stop in the park position (bottom-most position). Turn the ignition switch **OFF**.

2. Measure and note the distance from the wiper arm to the top edge of the windshield bottom trim piece.

3. If equipped, remove the plastic wiper arm retaining nut cover from the wiper arm base.

4. Remove the wiper arm retaining nut.

5. Pull the wiper arm off of the wiper linkage stud.

To install:

6. Install the wiper arm on the linkage stud so that the blade is positioned the same distance from the top edge of the windshield bottom trim piece as when removed.

7. Tighten the wiper arm retaining nut to 177 inch lbs. (20 Nm).

8. If equipped, install the retaining nut cover.

Rear

▶ See Figure 41

➡Rear wipers were an option on hard-top Sidekick, Tracker and Sidekick Sport models only.

1. Turn the ignition switch **ON** without starting the engine. Operate the wiper arm so that it goes through one full cycle, then turn the wiper OFF. Ensure that it stops in the park position (vertical position). Turn the ignition switch **OFF**.

2. Make a small matchmark on the rear window with a grease pencil to indicate where the wiper blade tip was positioned.

3. Remove the spare tire from the tire mounting bracket.

4. If equipped, remove the plastic wiper arm retaining nut cover from the wiper arm base.

5. Remove the wiper arm retaining nut.

6. Pull the wiper arm off of the wiper linkage stud.

To install:

7. Slide the wiper arm onto the linkage stud so that the arm is aligned with the matchmark made earlier.

8. Tighten the wiper arm retaining nut to 177 inch lbs. (20 Nm).

9. If equipped, install the retaining nut cover.

10. Install the spare tire onto the mounting bracket.

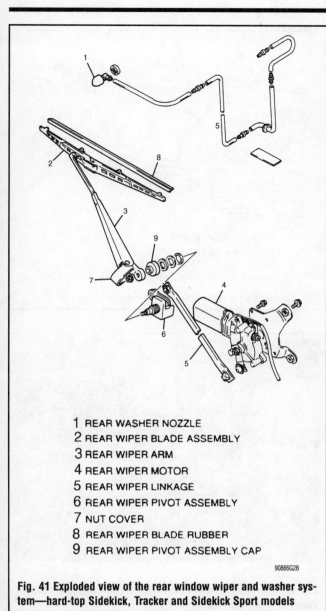

1 REAR WASHER NOZZLE
2 REAR WIPER BLADE ASSEMBLY
3 REAR WIPER ARM
4 REAR WIPER MOTOR
5 REAR WIPER LINKAGE
6 REAR WIPER PIVOT ASSEMBLY
7 NUT COVER
8 REAR WIPER BLADE RUBBER
9 REAR WIPER PIVOT ASSEMBLY CAP

90886G28

Fig. 41 Exploded view of the rear window wiper and washer system—hard-top Sidekick, Tracker and Sidekick Sport models

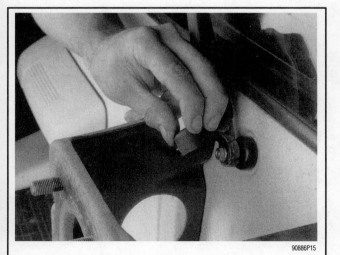

90886P15

To remove the rear wiper arm, first remove the spare tire, then pull the plastic cover off of the wiper arm base

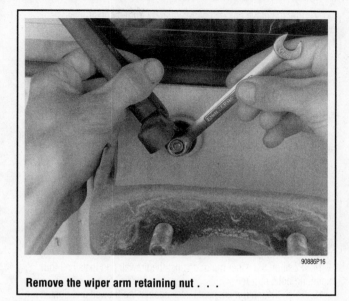

90886P16

Remove the wiper arm retaining nut . . .

90886P17

. . . then separate the wiper arm from the linkage stud

Windshield Wiper Motor

REMOVAL & INSTALLATION

Front

SAMURAI MODELS

The windshield wiper motor is mounted on the upper right-hand corner of the firewall, under the instrument panel, in the passengers' compartment.

1. Disconnect the negative battery cable.
2. Using a plastic or wooden prytool, remove the upper instrument panel mounting bolt plastic covers from the top of the instrument panel.
3. Loosen the upper instrument mounting bolts and pull the instrument panel away from the firewall slightly.
4. Open the glove box, then remove the glove box compartment mounting bolts.
5. Open the hood.
6. Matchmark the positions of the hood latch mechanism and mounting fasteners with white paint, correction fluid, a grease pencil, or a scribing tool, then remove the hood latch. Detach the actuating cable from the hood latch.

7. Pull the glove box compartment away from the instrument panel, withdrawing the hood latch actuating cable as well. Position the glove box compartment aside. For an easier installation, do not pull the glove box so far back that the entire actuating cable is removed form the firewall.

8. Gaining access through the glove box compartment opening, remove the two wiper motor lower mounting bolts.

9. Loosen the remaining two fasteners from the top of the instrument panel, through the right-hand instrument panel mounting bolt hole.

10. Pull the motor away from the firewall until the wiper motor-to-crank arm retaining nut can be accessed from the top of the instrument panel. Use an open end wrench to remove the retaining nut.

11. Detach the wiring harness connector from the motor, then withdraw it through glove box compartment opening.

To install:

12. Position the wiper motor close enough to the firewall so that the wiring harness connector can be reattached to the motor.

13. Position the motor up near the linkage opening, then install the linkage onto the wiper motor shaft. Install the retaining nut and tighten it to 177 inch lbs. (20 Nm).

14. Position the wiper motor against the firewall and install all four mounting bolts securely.

15. Push the instrument panel back against the firewall and tighten the upper mounting bolts securely.

16. Position the glove box compartment in the instrument panel, then, from the engine compartment, pull the hood latch actuating cable out of the passengers' compartment.

17. Install the glove box compartment mounting screws securely.

18. Reattach the hood latch actuating cable to the hood latch mechanism, then install the hood latch mechanism so that the matchmarks (made during removal) are aligned. Tighten the hood latch mechanism mounting fasteners thoroughly.

19. Close the hood carefully, and ensure that the hood latch engages properly.

20. Close the glove box.

21. Install the upper instrument panel plastic trim covers.

22. Connect the negative battery cable.

SIDEKICK, TRACKER, SIDEKICK SPORT AND X-90 MODELS

▶ **See Figures 42, 43, 44, 45 and 46**

1. Turn the ignition switch **ON** without starting the engine. Operate the wipers so that they go through one full cycle, then turn the wipers OFF. Ensure that they stop in the park position (bottom-most position). Turn the ignition switch **OFF**.

2. Open the hood.

3. Disconnect the negative battery cable.

4. Detach the wiring harness connector from the wiper motor, mounted on the driver's side of the engine compartment firewall.

5. Loosen the four mounting bolts, then gently pull the motor away from the firewall.

❊❊ WARNING

Do NOT loosen the wiper motor-to-crank nut in the following step. Be sure to separate the linkage rod from the wiper motor crank arm.

6. Using a small prytool, separate the wiper linkage from the wiper motor crank arm.

❊❊ WARNING

The wiper motor crank arm is not to be removed from the wiper motor. A new wiper motor should come with the crank arm already installed. The position of the crank arm is very important; it is oriented so that the wiper arms will be properly positioned when the motor settles in the park position.

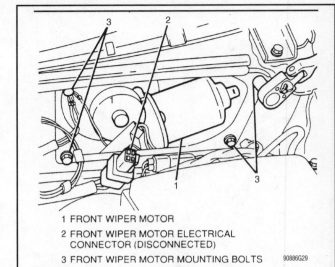

1 FRONT WIPER MOTOR
2 FRONT WIPER MOTOR ELECTRICAL CONNECTOR (DISCONNECTED)
3 FRONT WIPER MOTOR MOUNTING BOLTS   90886G29

Fig. 42 Windshield wiper motor component identification

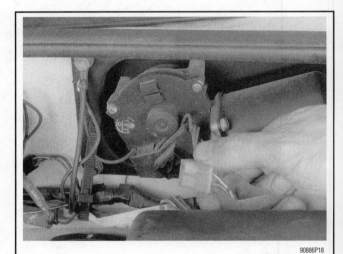

Fig. 43 To remove the wiper motor, first detach the wiring harness connector from the motor . . .

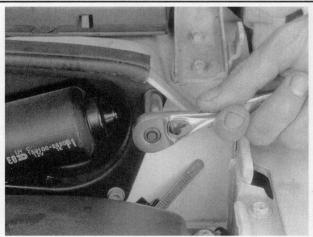

Fig. 44 . . . then loosen all of the wiper motor-to-firewall mounting bolts

Fig. 45 Gently pull the wiper motor away from the firewall . . .

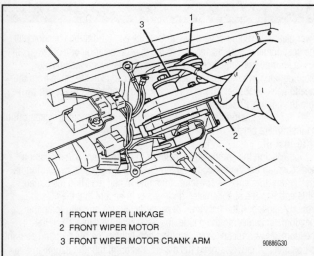

1 FRONT WIPER LINKAGE
2 FRONT WIPER MOTOR
3 FRONT WIPER MOTOR CRANK ARM

90886G30

Fig. 46 . . . until the linkage can be separated from the motor crank arm with a small prytool

To install:

7. Position the wiper motor close to the linkage hole in the firewall, then reattach the linkage to the motor crank arm. Be sure that the linkage is positively engaged by the linkage. It may be necessary to use a large pair of pliers to re-engage the linkage and crank arm.

8. Set the motor against the firewall, then install the mounting bolts. Tighten the mounting bolts to 177 inch lbs. (20 Nm).

9. Reattach the wiring harness connector to the wiper motor.

10. Connect the negative battery cable.

Rear

▶ **See Figure 47**

➡ Rear wipers were an option on hard-top Sidekick, Tracker and Sidekick Sport models only.

1. Disconnect the negative battery cable.

Before proceeding with this procedure, purchase new inner back door panel retainers from a dealership or an aftermarket automotive parts store. The retainers are plastic, and the old ones will most likely break during panel removal.

2. If applicable, remove the spare tire from the mounting bracket.

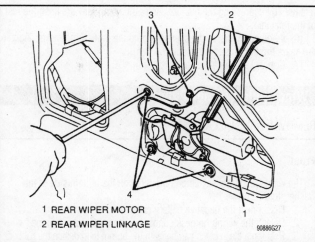

1 REAR WIPER MOTOR
2 REAR WIPER LINKAGE

90886G27

Fig. 47 To remove the rear wiper motor, loosen the three mounting screws with a screwdriver, then withdraw the motor out of the door through the large, lower hole

3. Open the back door.

4. Remove the inner back door panel plastic retainers by pressing the center pin of the retainer in until the retainer is fully disengaged, then pull the entire retainer out of the inner back door panel. Separate the panel from the back door.

5. Carefully remove the watershield from the inside of the back door. If the watershield is not damaged during removal, it can be reused. Otherwise a new one must be purchased, or you can fabricate one out of a plastic lawn bag.

6. Disengage the wiring harness connector from the rear wiper motor.

7. Remove the wiper motor ground strap retaining screw.

8. Loosen the three mounting bolts, then gently pull the motor away from the back door.

✳✳ WARNING

Do NOT loosen the wiper motor-to-crank nut in the following step. Be sure to separate the linkage rod from the wiper motor crank arm.

9. Using a small prytool, separate the wiper linkage from the wiper motor crank arm.

✳✳ WARNING

The wiper motor crank arm is not to be removed from the wiper motor. A new wiper motor should come with the crank arm already installed. The position of the crank arm is very important; it is oriented so that the wiper arms will be properly positioned when the motor settles in the park position.

To install:

10. Position the wiper motor close to the linkage in the back door, then reattach the linkage to the motor crank arm. Be sure that the linkage is positively engaged by the linkage. It may be necessary to use a large pair of pliers to re-engage the linkage and crank arm.

11. Set the motor against the back door, then install the mounting bolts. Tighten the mounting bolts to 177 inch lbs. (20 Nm).

12. Position the ground strap against the back door metal, then install the retaining screw securely.

13. Apply a continuos bead of sealant on the inside of the back door, then install the watershield.

14. Position the inner back door panel against the inside of the back door.

15. Insert new plastic retainers in the panel mounting holes. Engage the

retainers by depressing the retainer center pins until they are flush the rest of the retainer.

16. If equipped, install the spare tire onto the mounting bracket. Tighten the spare tire lug nuts to 40 ft. lbs. (54 Nm).

17. Connect the negative battery cable.

Windshield Washer Pump

REMOVAL & INSTALLATION

Front

The windshield washer pump is mounted on the bottom side of the washer fluid reservoir.

1. Disconnect the negative battery cable.
2. Detach the wiring harness connectors from the washer pump.
3. Position a clean catch pan beneath the pump, then detach the rubber hose from the pump nozzle and drain the washer fluid in the hose into the catch pan. If the catch pan is clean, the windshield washer fluid may be reused.
4. Pull the washer pump out of the washer fluid reservoir and allow the remainder of the fluid to drain into the catch pan.

INSTRUMENTS AND SWITCHES

Instrument Cluster

REMOVAL & INSTALLATION

Samurai Models

▶ See Figure 48

The instrument cluster is referred to as the combination meter on Samurai models.

1. Disconnect the negative battery cable.
2. Loosen the retaining screws, then remove the lower steering column cover from the instrument panel.
3. Remove the upper steering column retaining fasteners, then gently lower the steering column away from the instrument panel.
4. Remove the four attaching screws, then pull the combination meter cover off of the meter.
5. Gaining access to the back of the combination meter up through the

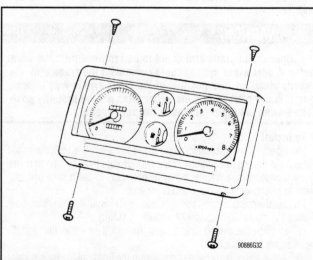

Fig. 48 Loosen the four mounting screws in order to remove the cover from the instrument cluster (combination meter)

To install:

5. Inspect the pump-to-washer fluid reservoir grommet for damage, such as rips, tears, cracking, brittleness, crumbling, etc. Replace the grommet with a new one if any such damage is found.

6. Install the pump into the washer fluid reservoir by pressing it in until fully engaged.

7. Pour a small amount of washer fluid into the reservoir container to double-check that the pump grommet is sealing properly. If fluid leaks out past the grommet, remove the pump and grommet and inspect the grommet for damage; reinstall the pump and grommet.

8. Reattach the rubber fluid hose to the washer pump nipple.

9. Engage the wiring harness connector to the washer pump, ensuring that the pump terminal retainer is properly engaged.

10. Connect the negative battery cable.

Rear

➡Rear wipers were an option on hard-top Sidekick, Tracker and Sidekick Sport models only.

The rear washer pump is also installed in the bottom side of the windshield wiper fluid reservoir, located in the engine compartment. Refer to the front pump procedure for the removal and installation of the rear pump.

lower steering column cover hole, detach the cable from the speedometer. The speedometer cable is secured to the speedometer by one of two methods: a knurled nut, which can be loosened in a conventional manner; or a retaining latch, which must be depressed to disengage the cable from the speedometer. Also, detach the wiring harness connectors (there are two) from the combination meter.

6. Loosen the mounting screws, then pull the combination meter out of the instrument cluster.

To install:

7. Position the combination meter in the instrument panel opening, then reach up behind the combination meter to reattach the two wiring harness connectors and the speedometer cable. When inserting the square cable end into the speedometer, do it gently to ensure that the flats are properly aligned. If the flats are not properly aligned and you force the speedometer cable into the gauge, the gauge can be damaged. If the speedometer was retained by a knurled nut, tighten the nut by hand as tight as possible. Otherwise, insert the cable far enough into the gauge so that retaining latch is properly engaged.

8. Install and tighten the mounting screws securely.

9. Position the combination meter cover over the meter, then install and tighten the four retaining screws snugly.

10. Raise the steering column and install the upper retaining fasteners to 97–150 inch lbs. (11–17 Nm).

11. Install the lower steering column cover.

12. Connect the negative battery cable.

Sidekick, Tracker, Sidekick Sport and X-90 Models

▶ See Figures 49 and 50

1. Disconnect the negative battery cable.
2. Loosen the four retaining screws, then remove the instrument cluster trim bezel.
3. Loosen the four retaining screws, then pull the instrument cluster away from the instrument panel until the back face of the cluster can be accessed.
4. Detach the cable from the back of the speedometer. The speedometer cable is secured to the speedometer by one of two methods: a knurled nut, which can be loosened in a conventional manner; or a retaining latch, which must be depressed to disengage the cable from the speedometer. Also, detach the wiring harness connectors (there are three) from the cluster.
5. Remove the cluster from the vehicle.

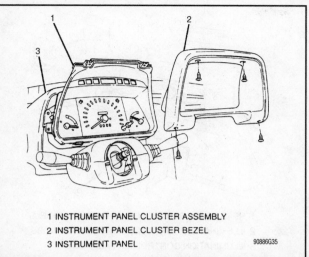

1 INSTRUMENT PANEL CLUSTER ASSEMBLY
2 INSTRUMENT PANEL CLUSTER BEZEL
3 INSTRUMENT PANEL

90886G35

Fig. 49 Exploded view of the instrument cluster trim and bezel mounting on early models

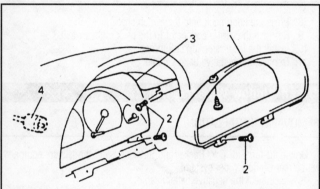

1. Meter cluster hood   3. Speedometer assy
2. Screw   4. Speedometer cable

90886G33

Fig. 50 Exploded view of the instrument cluster trim bezel mounting. To remove the cluster, remove the mounting screws and detach the cable from the speedometer

To install:

6. Position the cluster close enough to the instrument panel opening to reattach the three wiring harness connectors and the speedometer cable. When inserting the square cable end into the speedometer gauge, do it gently to ensure that the flats are properly aligned. If the flats are not properly aligned and you force the speedometer cable into the gauge, the gauge can be damaged. To align the flats of the speedometer and the cable, turn the speedometer gauge shaft slightly until the cable end inserts easily into the gauge. If the speedometer was retained by a knurled nut, tighten the nut by hand as tight as possible. Otherwise, insert the cable far enough into the gauge so that retaining latch is properly engaged.

7. Position the cluster in the instrument panel, then install and tighten the mounting screws securely.

8. Position the trim bezel over the cluster, then install and tighten the retaining screws snugly.

9. Connect the negative battery cable.

Gauges

REMOVAL & INSTALLATION

Samurai Models

▶ **See Figure 51**

✳✳ WARNING

When disassembling the instrument panel, it is a good idea to use a grounding strap to prevent from accidentally introducing electrical shocks to the fragile electronic components. Although static electrical shocks do not seem that damaging, the voltage of static electricity can often reach as high as 50,000 volts; plenty strong enough to damage electronic components.

The individual gauges can be replaced individually by disassembling the instrument cluster. (Refer to the accompanying illustration.) To disassemble the instrument cluster, remove the front and rear cluster half attaching screws, then separate the two halves. The individual gauges can be removed from the back half of the cluster housing.

When installing the gauges, ensure that they are properly positioned and secured in the housing. Reassemble the two halves and tighten the cluster half attaching screws securely.

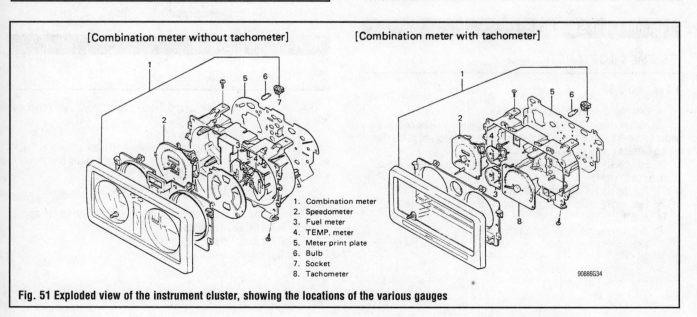

[Combination meter without tachometer]   [Combination meter with tachometer]

1. Combination meter
2. Speedometer
3. Fuel meter
4. TEMP. meter
5. Meter print plate
6. Bulb
7. Socket
8. Tachometer

90886G34

Fig. 51 Exploded view of the instrument cluster, showing the locations of the various gauges

Sidekick, Tracker, Sidekick Sport and X-90 Models

♦ **See Figure 52**

❄❄ WARNING

When disassembling the instrument panel, it is a good idea to use a grounding strap to prevent from accidentally introducing electrical shocks to the fragile electronic components. Although static electrical shocks do not seem that damaging, the voltage of static electricity can often reach as high as 50,000 volts; plenty strong enough to damage electronic components.

The the fuel gauge, the temperature gauge and the speedometer/tachometer (if equipped) gauges can be removed from the instrument cluster by disassembling the instrument cluster. (Refer to the accompanying illustration.) To disassemble the instrument cluster, remove the front and rear cluster half attaching screws, then separate the two halves. The individual gauges can be removed from the back half of the cluster housing.

When installing the gauges, ensure that they are properly positioned and secured in the housing. Reassemble the two halves and tighten the cluster half attaching screws securely.

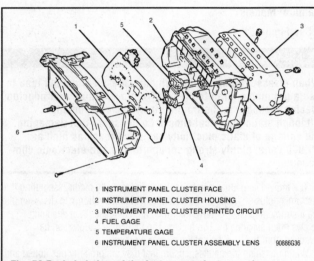

1 INSTRUMENT PANEL CLUSTER FACE
2 INSTRUMENT PANEL CLUSTER HOUSING
3 INSTRUMENT PANEL CLUSTER PRINTED CIRCUIT
4 FUEL GAGE
5 TEMPERATURE GAGE
6 INSTRUMENT PANEL CLUSTER ASSEMBLY LENS   90886G36

Fig. 52 Exploded view of the instrument cluster used on Sidekick, Tracker, Sidekick Sport and X-90 models

Dimmer Light Switch

REMOVAL & INSTALLATION

♦ **See Figure 53**

1. Disconnect the negative battery cable.
2. Remove the lower steering column cover, then reach up behind the wiper switch (through the steering column cover opening) and detach the wiring harness connector from the back of the switch.
3. Pull the knob off of the switch shaft, then loosen the securing nut from the switch shaft.
4. Pull the washer and face plate off of the switch shaft.
5. Remove the switch out from the rear of the instrument panel.
To install:
6. Install the switch in the instrument panel.
7. Install the face plate, washer and securing nut. Tighten the securing nut snugly.

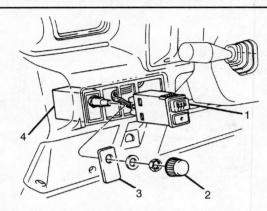

1 REAR DEFOGGER SWITCH — HARDTOP MODELS
2 ILLUMINATION CONTROLLER ADJUSTING KNOBS
3 ILLUMINATION CONTROLLER FACEPLATE
4 ILLUMINATION CONTROLLER   90886G37

Fig. 53 Exploded view of the light dimmer switch and rear defogger switch mounting

8. Press the knob back onto the switch shaft.
9. Reattach the wiring connector to the back of the switch.
10. Install the lower steering column cover.
11. Connect the negative battery cable.

Rear Window Wiper Switch

REMOVAL & INSTALLATION

Only hard-top Sidekick, Tracker and Sidekick Sport models are equipped with a rear window wiper system.
1. Disconnect the negative battery cable.
2. Remove the lower steering column cover, then reach up behind the wiper switch (through the steering column cover opening) and detach the wiring harness connector from the back of the switch.
3. Remove the switch from the instrument panel.
To install:
4. Install the switch in the instrument panel, then reattach the wiring connector to the back of the switch.
5. Install the lower steering column cover.
6. Connect the negative battery cable.

Rear Defogger Switch

REMOVAL & INSTALLATION

Only hard-top Sidekick, Tracker and Sidekick Sport models are equipped with a rear window wiper system.
1. Disconnect the negative battery cable.
2. Remove the lower steering column cover, then reach up behind the wiper switch (through the steering column cover opening) and detach the wiring harness connector from the back of the switch.
3. Remove the switch from the instrument panel.
To install:
4. Install the switch in the instrument panel, then reattach the wiring connector to the back of the switch.
5. Install the lower steering column cover.
6. Connect the negative battery cable.

LIGHTING

Headlights

REMOVAL & INSTALLATION

Samurai Models

▶ **See Figures 54 and 55**

1. Remove the grille from the front of the vehicle by loosening the five retaining screws.

2. Loosen the three mounting screws from the headlight retaining ring, then rotate the ring counterclockwise and pull the ring off of the headlight.

3. Carefully pull the headlight bulb out of the mounting bracket, then pull the wiring harness connector off of the bulb terminals.

To install:

4. Hold the new bulb close enough to the bulb mounting bracket so that the wiring harness connector can be reattached. Push the connector onto the light bulb until it is properly engaged.

5. Position the light bulb in the mounting bracket, then install the retaining ring. Tighten the three retaining ring screws securely.

6. Install the front grille on the vehicle.

Sidekick, Tracker, Sidekick Sport and X-90 Models

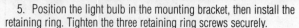

Do not touch the new glass bulb with your fingers. Oil from your fingers can severely shorten the life of the bulb. If necessary, wipe off any dirt or oil from the bulb with rubbing alcohol before completing installation.

1. Open the vehicle's hood and secure it in an upright position.

2. Depress the wiring harness connector retaining latch, then pull the connector off of the light bulb.

3. Unfasten the locking ring which secures the bulb and socket assembly, then withdraw the assembly rearward.

Fig. 54 To remove the headlight, loosen the three ring retaining screws, rotate the ring counterclockwise, then remove the ring

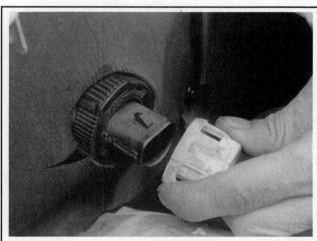

To remove the headlight bulb, first detach the wiring harness connector from it . . .

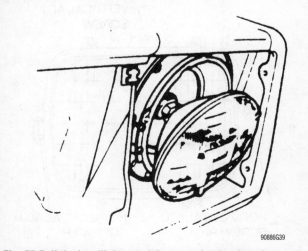

Fig. 55 Pull the headlight out of the mounting bracket, then detach the wiring harness connector from it

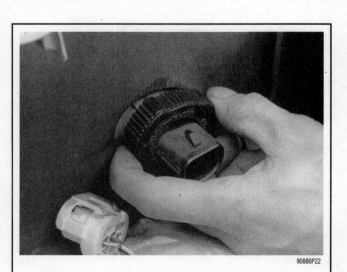

. . . then disengage the retaining ring by turning it counterclockwise

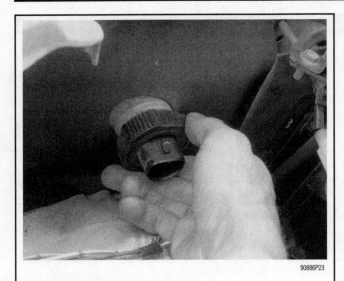

Slide the retaining ring off of the bulb . . .

90886P23

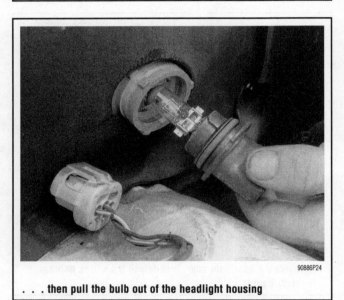

. . . then pull the bulb out of the headlight housing

90886P24

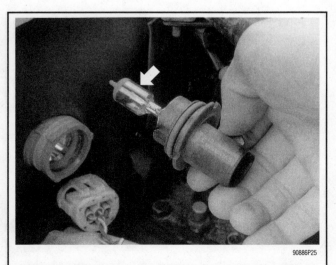

NEVER touch the glass portion (arrow) of the bulb with your bare hands

90886P25

To install:

4. Before installing a light bulb into the socket, ensure that all electrical contact surfaces are free of corrosion or dirt.

5. Position the headlight bulb and secure it with the locking ring.

6. Insert the wiring harness connector onto the light bulb, and push the connector onto the bulb until the retaining latch is properly engaged.

7. To ensure that the replacement bulb functions properly, activate the applicable switch to illuminate the bulb which was just replaced. (If this is a combination low and high beam bulb, be sure to check both intensities.) If the replacement light bulb does not illuminate, either it too is faulty or there is a problem in the bulb circuit or switch. Correct if necessary.

8. Close the vehicle's hood.

AIMING

▶ **See Figures 56, 57, 58, 59 and 60**

The headlights must be properly aimed to provide the best, safest road illumination. The lights should be checked for proper aim and adjusted as necessary. Certain state and local authorities have requirements for headlight aiming; these should be checked before adjustment is made.

✳✳ CAUTION

About once a year, when the headlights are replaced or any time front end work is performed on your vehicle, the headlight should be accurately aimed by a reputable repair shop using the proper equipment. Headlights not properly aimed can make it virtually impossible to see and may blind other drivers on the road, possibly causing an accident. Note that the following procedure is a temporary fix, until you can take your vehicle to a repair shop for a proper adjustment.

Headlight adjustment may be temporarily made using a wall, as described below, or on the rear of another vehicle. When adjusted, the lights should not glare in oncoming car or truck windshields, nor should they illuminate the passenger compartment of vehicles driving in front of you. These adjustments are rough and should always be fine-tuned by a repair shop which is equipped with headlight aiming tools. Improper adjustments may be both dangerous and illegal.

For Samurai vehicles, horizontal and vertical aiming of each sealed beam unit is provided by two adjusting screws which move the retaining ring and adjusting plate against the tension of a coil spring. There is no adjustment for focus; this is done during headlight manufacturing.

Because the composite headlight assembly used on Sidekick, Tracker, and Sidekick Sport models is bolted into position, no adjustment should be

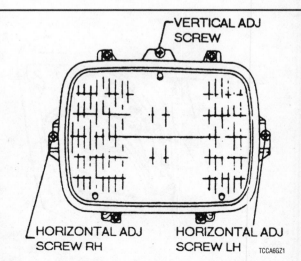

Fig. 56 Location of the aiming screws on most vehicles with sealed beam headlights

TCCA6GZ1

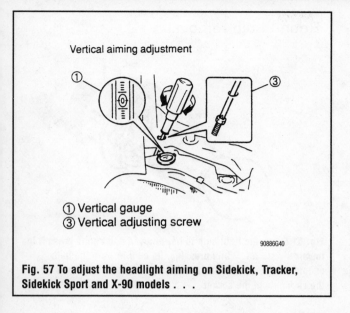

Vertical aiming adjustment

① Vertical gauge
③ Vertical adjusting screw

90886G40

Fig. 57 To adjust the headlight aiming on Sidekick, Tracker, Sidekick Sport and X-90 models . . .

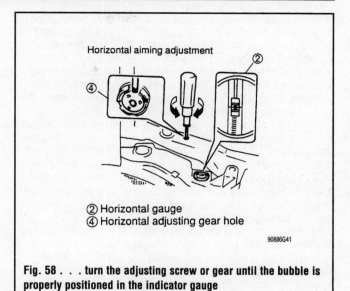

Horizontal aiming adjustment

② Horizontal gauge
④ Horizontal adjusting gear hole

90886G41

Fig. 58 . . . turn the adjusting screw or gear until the bubble is properly positioned in the indicator gauge

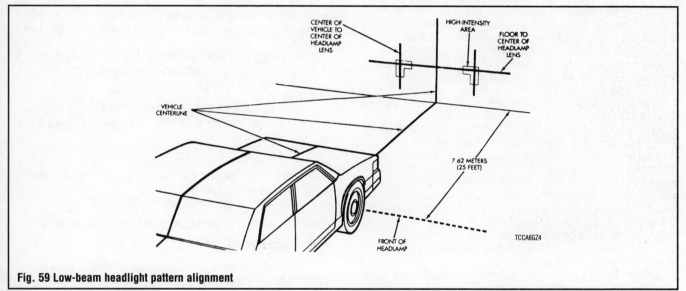

Fig. 59 Low-beam headlight pattern alignment

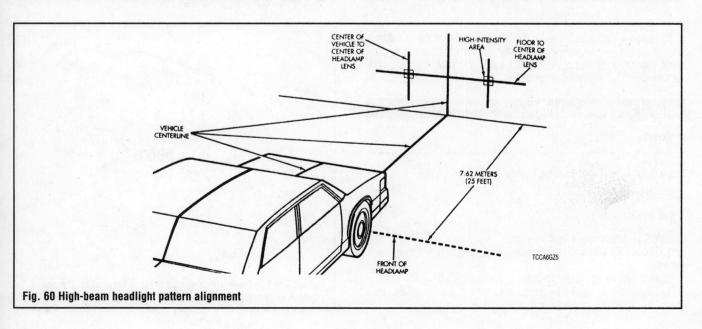

Fig. 60 High-beam headlight pattern alignment

necessary or possible. The headlight assemblies on some models, however, are bolted to an adjuster plate or may be retained by adjusting screws. If so, follow this procedure when adjusting the lights, BUT always have the adjustment checked by a reputable shop.

Before removing the headlight bulb or disturbing the headlamp in any way, note the current settings in order to ease headlight adjustment upon reassembly. If the high or low beam setting of the old lamp still works, this can be done using the wall of a garage or a building:

1. Park the vehicle on a level surface, with the fuel tank about ½ full and with the vehicle empty of all extra cargo (unless normally carried). The vehicle should be facing a wall which is no less than 6 feet (1.8m) high and 12 feet (3.7m) wide. The front of the vehicle should be about 25 feet from the wall.

2. If aiming is to be performed outdoors, it is advisable to wait until dusk in order to properly see the headlight beams on the wall. If done in a garage, darken the area around the wall as much as possible by closing shades or hanging cloth over the windows.

3. Turn the headlights **ON** and mark the wall at the center of each light's low beam, then switch on the brights and mark the center of each light's high beam. A short length of masking tape which is visible from the front of the vehicle may be used. Although marking all four positions is advisable, marking one position from each light should be sufficient.

4. If neither beam on one side is working, and if another like-sized vehicle is available, park the second one in the exact spot where the vehicle was and mark the beams using the same-side light. Then switch the vehicles so the one to be aimed is back in the original spot. It must be parked no closer to or farther away from the wall than the second vehicle.

5. Perform any necessary repairs, but make sure the vehicle is not moved, or is returned to the exact spot from which the lights were marked. Turn the headlights **ON** and adjust the beams to match the marks on the wall.

6. Have the headlight adjustment checked as soon as possible by a reputable repair shop.

The headlight assemblies used on X-90 models are equipped with aiming gauges, which consist of a graduated glass tube filled with liquid. There is a small air bubble in the liquid, the position of which indicates the aiming position. When the headlight assembly is correctly aimed, the air bubble should be at the center of the gauge (the vehicle must be parked on a level surface with a person sitting in the driver's seat for this to be true). If the air bubble is not located at the center of the gauge, adjust the aiming as follows:

7. Place the vehicle on a level surface.

8. Be sure that any items, other than the original vehicle equipment, are not in the vehicle, and the fuel tank is full.

9. Double-check the air pressure in all of the tires. If the air pressure is not correct, add or remove air from the tries, as necessary.

10. Have someone weighing the same as the driver sit in the driver's seat.

11. Open the hood.

12. Observe the horizontal and vertical aiming gauges. If the air bubbles (in both gauges) are not at the center of the gauges, turn the adjusting screw (for vertical aiming) or the adjusting gear (for horizontal aiming) until the air bubble is at the center of the gauge.

Signal and Marker Lights

REMOVAL & INSTALLATION

Front Turn Signal and Parking Lights

SAMURAI MODELS

▶ See Figure 61

1. Disconnect the negative battery cable.

2. Using a Phillips screwdriver, remove the light assembly lens retaining screws.

3. Pull the lens and gasket off of the light assembly.

4. Inspect the lens gasket for tearing or crumbling. If any such damage is evident, replace the old gasket with a new one upon installation.

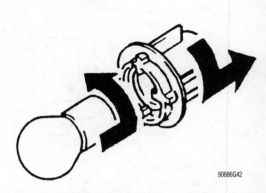

Round bulb removal

90886G42

Fig. 61 Grasp the light bulb to be removed and gently press it in toward its socket. While pressing the bulb in, turn the bulb counterclockwise until the two little pins on the bulb base clear the channels in the socket

5. Once the lens is removed from the light assembly, the individual light bulb(s) can be removed. To remove the light bulb(s):

a. Grasp the light bulb to be removed and gently press it in toward its socket.

b. While pressing the bulb in, turn the bulb counterclockwise until the two little pins on the bulb base clear the channels in the socket.

c. Pull the bulb up and out of its socket.

To install:

6. If the old bulb is being reinstalled, inspect the light bulb contacts; they should be clean and free of corrosion. Otherwise, clean the contacts or purchase a new bulb.

7. Install the light bulb in the socket by pressing it in and turning it clockwise until the bulb pins are fully engaged.

8. Install the lens and gasket on the housing. Tighten the lens retaining screws until they are snug.

9. Connect the negative battery cable.

SIDEKICK, TRACKER, SIDEKICK SPORT AND X-90 MODELS

▶ See Figures 62, 63 and 64

1. Open the hood; the bulb socket is accessible from the in the engine compartment and is located on the outboard side of the headlight.

2. Disconnect the negative battery cable.

90886G44

Fig. 62 The front turn signal bulb socket is located on the outboard side of the headlight bulb socket

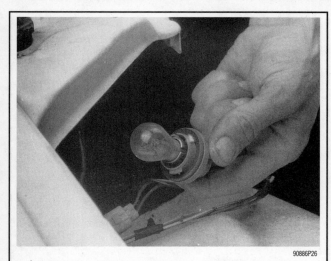

Fig. 63 Separate the light bulb socket from the light assembly housing . . .

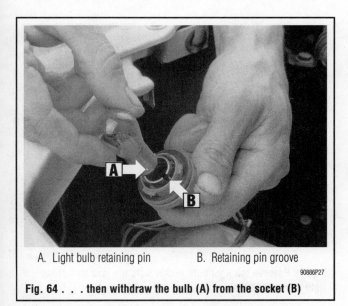

A. Light bulb retaining pin   B. Retaining pin groove

Fig. 64 . . . then withdraw the bulb (A) from the socket (B)

3. Remove the bulb socket from the light assembly housing by turning it counterclockwise and pulling it out of the housing.

4. Once the lens is removed from the light assembly, the individual light bulb(s) can be removed. To remove the light bulb(s):

   a. Grasp the light bulb to be removed and gently press it in toward its socket.

   b. While pressing the bulb in, turn the bulb counterclockwise until the two little pins on the bulb base clear the channels in the socket.

   c. Pull the bulb out of the socket.

To install:

5. If the old bulb is being reinstalled, inspect the light bulb contacts; they should be clean and free of corrosion. Otherwise, clean the contacts or purchase a new bulb. Also inspect the metal terminals of the bulb socket.

6. Install the light bulb in the socket by pressing it in and turning it clockwise until the bulb pins are fully engaged.

7. Insert the bulb and socket into the light assembly housing, then turn it clockwise until it stops. Give the socket a slight tug to ensure that it is properly retained in the housing.

8. Connect the negative battery cable.

9. Close the hood.

Side Marker Light

SAMURAI MODELS

♦ See Figure 65

1. Disconnect the negative battery cable.

2. Using a Phillips screwdriver, remove the light assembly lens retaining screws.

3. Pull the lens and gasket off of the light assembly.

4. Inspect the lens gasket for tearing or crumbling. If any such damage is evident, replace the old gasket with a new one upon installation.

5. Remove the bulb from the socket by pulling it straight out of the socket.

To install:

6. If the old bulb is being reinstalled, inspect the light bulb contacts; they should be clean and free of corrosion. Otherwise, clean the contacts or purchase a new bulb.

7. Press the bulb straight into the socket until it is fully seated.

8. INstall the lens and gasket on the housing. Tighten the lens retaining screws until they are snug.

9. Connect the negative battery cable.

Small oval bulb removal

Fig. 65 To remove the bulb from the socket, simply pull it straight out of the socket

SIDEKICK, TRACKER, SIDEKICK SPORT AND X-90 MODELS— 2-DOOR HARD TOP REAR LIGHTS

♦ See Figures 66 thru 71

1. Disconnect the negative battery cable.

2. Using a Phillips screwdriver, remove the light assembly retaining screw.

3. Pull the light assembly and gasket off of the rear fender.

4. loosen the light assembly attaching screw, then remove the lens and gasket from the housing.

5. Inspect the gasket for tearing or crumbling. If any such damage is evident, replace the old gasket with a new one upon installation.

6. Remove the bulb from the socket by pulling it straight out of the socket.

To install:

7. If the old bulb is being reinstalled, inspect the light bulb contacts; they should be clean and free of corrosion. Otherwise, clean the contacts or purchase a new bulb.

8. Press the bulb straight into the socket until it is fully seated.

9. Reassemble the light housing and secure it with the attaching screw.

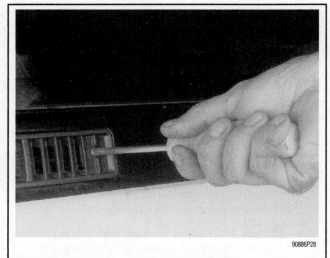

Fig. 66 To remove the rear side marker light bulb on 2-door hard top models, first loosen the light housing mounting screw . . .

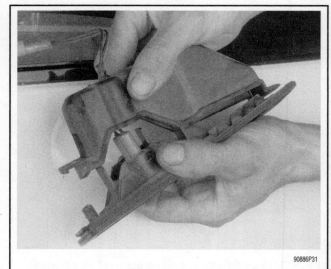

Fig. 69 . . . then disassemble the light assembly housing

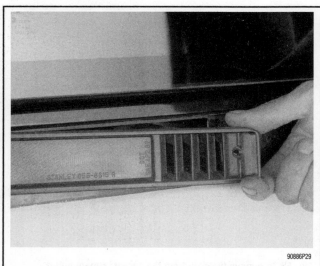

Fig. 67 . . . then pull the housing out of the fender

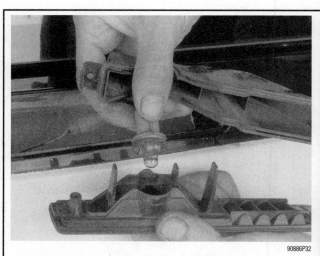

Fig. 70 Remove the light bulb socket from the lens half of the light assembly housing . . .

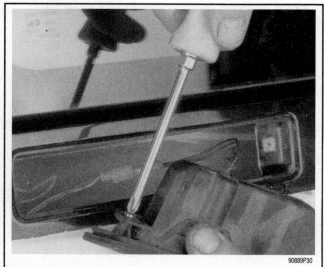

Fig. 68 Loosen the housing-to-lens attaching screw . . .

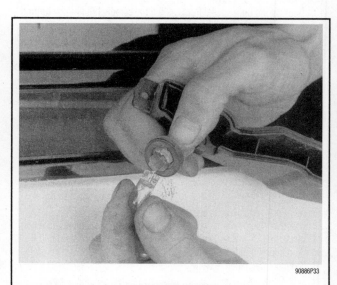

Fig. 71 . . . then pull the old bulb out of the socket

10. Install the light housing on the fender. Tighten the retaining screw until it is snug.

11. Connect the negative battery cable.

SIDEKICK, TRACKER, SIDEKICK SPORT AND X-90 MODELS— EXCEPT 2-DOOR HARD TOP REAR LIGHTS

▶ See Figures 72, 73, 74, 75 and 76

1. Disconnect the negative battery cable.

2. Remove the light housing by pulling outward on the outboard end of the housing (toward the rear of the vehicle for the rear light housing, toward the front of the vehicle for the front light housing) and sliding the housing toward the passenger door.

3. Remove the bulb socket from the light assembly housing by turning it counterclockwise and pulling it out of the housing.

4. Remove the bulb from the socket by pulling it straight out of the socket.

To install:

5. If the old bulb is being reinstalled, inspect the light bulb contacts; they should be clean and free of corrosion. Otherwise, clean the contacts or purchase a new bulb.

6. Press the bulb straight into the socket until it is fully seated.

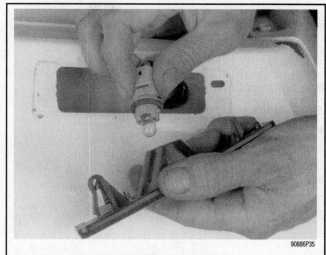

Fig. 74 Twist ¼ turn and pull the light bulb socket out of the light assembly housing . . .

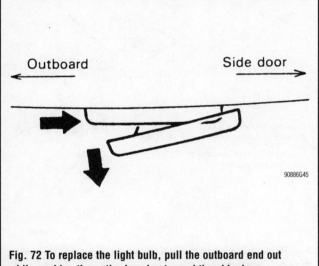

Fig. 72 To replace the light bulb, pull the outboard end out while pushing the entire housing toward the side door . . .

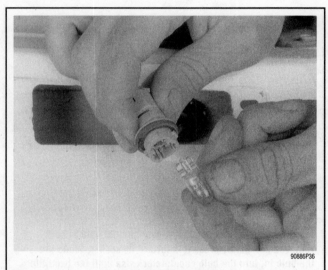

Fig. 75 . . . then pull the light bulb straight out of the socket

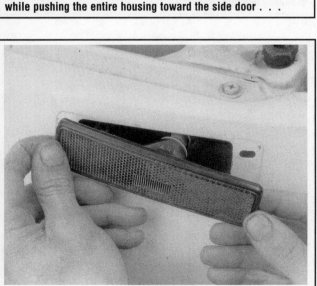

Fig. 73 . . . then separate the light housing from the fender

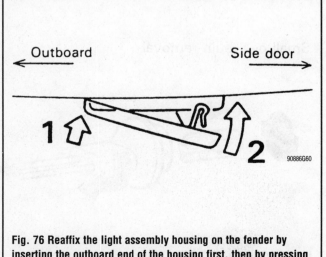

Fig. 76 Reaffix the light assembly housing on the fender by inserting the outboard end of the housing first, then by pressing the door end in against the fender until it is properly engaged

7. Install the light bulb in the socket by pressing it in and turning it clockwise until the bulb pins are fully engaged.

8. INstall the light housing on the fender by first pushing the outboard end of the light housing in, then by pushing the other end in.

9. Connect the negative battery cable.

Rear Turn Signal, Brake and Parking Lights

SAMURAI MODELS

▶ See Figures 77 and 78

1. Disconnect the negative battery cable.

2. Using a Phillips screwdriver, remove the light assembly lens retaining screws.

3. Pull the lens and gasket off of the light assembly.

4. Inspect the lens gasket for tearing or crumbling. If any such damage is evident, replace the old gasket with a new one upon installation.

5. Once the lens is removed from the light assembly, the individual light bulb(s) can be removed. To remove the light bulb(s):

   a. Grasp the light bulb to be removed and gently press it in toward its socket.

   b. While pressing the bulb in, turn the bulb counterclockwise until the two little pins on the bulb base clear the channels in the socket.

   c. Pull the bulb up and out of its socket.

To install:

6. If the old bulb is being reinstalled, inspect the light bulb contacts; they should be clean and free of corrosion. Otherwise, clean the contacts or purchase a new bulb.

7. Install the light bulb in the socket by pressing it in and turning it clockwise until the bulb pins are fully engaged.

8. INstall the lens and gasket on the housing. Tighten the lens retaining screws until they are snug.

9. Connect the negative battery cable.

SIDEKICK, TRACKER, SIDEKICK SPORT AND X-90 MODELS

▶ See Figures 79, 80, 81, 82 and 83

1. Disconnect the negative battery cable.

2. Using a Phillips screwdriver, remove the light assembly retaining screws.

3. Pull the light assembly and gasket off of the rear fender.

4. Inspect the gasket for tearing or crumbling. If any such damage is evident, replace the old gasket with a new one upon installation.

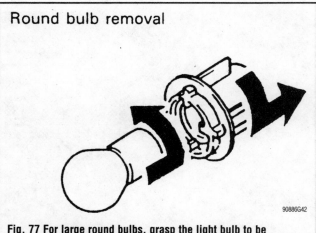

Fig. 77 For large round bulbs, grasp the light bulb to be removed and gently press it in toward its socket. While pressing the bulb in, turn the bulb counterclockwise until the two little pins on the bulb base clear the channels in the socket

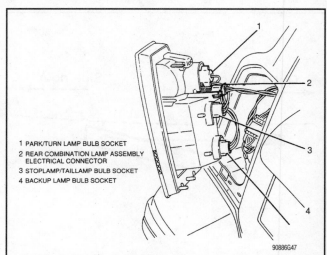

1 PARK/TURN LAMP BULB SOCKET
2 REAR COMBINATION LAMP ASSEMBLY ELECTRICAL CONNECTOR
3 STOPLAMP/TAILLAMP BULB SOCKET
4 BACKUP LAMP BULB SOCKET

Fig. 79 Identification of the lights mounted in the rear taillight assembly housing

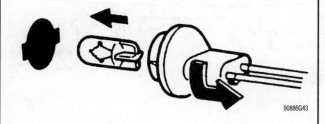

Fig. 78 To remove a small oval bulb from its socket, simply pull it straight out of the socket

Fig. 80 To remove the rear light bulbs, first loosen the light assembly housing mounting screws . . .

5. Remove the bulb socket from the light assembly housing by turning it counterclockwise and pulling it out of the housing.

➡**There are a possible of two types of bulbs used in this housing: larger bulbs with a round metal base and smaller bulbs without any metal base.**

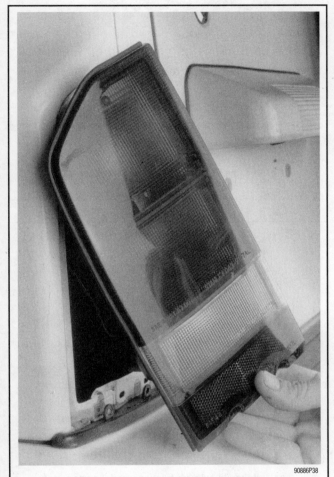

Fig. 81 . . . then separate the housing from the rear fender

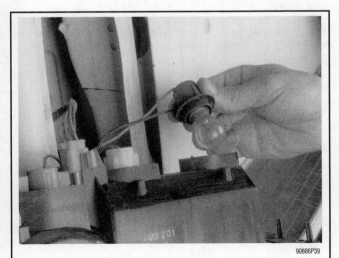

Fig. 82 Remove the bulb socket from the inboard face of the housing . . .

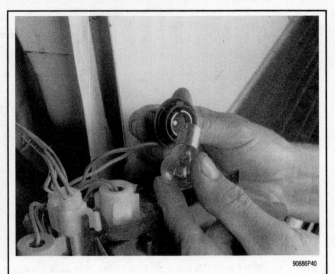

Fig. 83 . . . then remove the light bulb from the socket

6. To remove the larger bulbs equipped with metal bases:
   a. Grasp the light bulb to be removed and gently press it in toward its socket.
   b. While pressing the bulb in, turn the bulb counterclockwise until the two little pins on the bulb base clear the channels in the socket.
   c. Pull the bulb up and out of its socket.
7. To remove the smaller bulbs with a metal base, pull the bulb straight out of the socket.
   To install:
8. If the old bulb is being reinstalled, inspect the light bulb contacts; they should be clean and free of corrosion. Otherwise, clean the contacts or purchase a new bulb.
9. For the metal-based bulbs, install the light bulb in the socket by pressing it in and turning it clockwise until the bulb pins are fully engaged.
10. For the all glass bulbs, simply press the bulb straight into the socket until it is fully seated.
11. Install the light bulb socket in the housing by inserting it and turning it fully clockwise.
12. INstall the light housing and gasket on the fender. Tighten the retaining screws until they are snug.
13. Connect the negative battery cable.

High-Mounted Brake Light

CONVERTIBLE MODELS

➤ **See Figure 84**

1. Disconnect the negative battery cable.
2. Open the rear window.
3. Using a Phillips screwdriver, remove the light assembly retaining screws.
4. Pull the light assembly and gasket off of the body.
5. Inspect the gasket for tearing or crumbling. If any such damage is evident, replace the old gasket with a new one upon installation.
6. Remove the bulb socket from the light assembly housing by turning it counterclockwise and pulling it out of the housing.
7. To remove the bulbs, perform the following:
   a. Grasp the light bulb to be removed and gently press it in toward its socket.
   b. While pressing the bulb in, turn the bulb counterclockwise until the two little pins on the bulb base clear the channels in the socket.
   c. Pull the bulb up and out of its socket.
   To install:
8. If the old bulb is being reinstalled, inspect the light bulb contacts; they should be clean and free of corrosion. Otherwise, clean the contacts or purchase a new bulb.

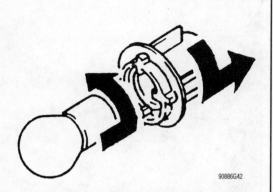

Fig. 84 Grasp the light bulb to be removed and gently press it in toward its socket. While pressing the bulb in, turn the bulb counterclockwise until the two little pins on the bulb base clear the channels in the socket

9. Install the light bulb in the socket by pressing it in and turning it clockwise until the bulb pins are fully engaged.

10. Install the light bulb socket in the housing by inserting it and turning it fully clockwise.

11. Install the light housing on the body. Tighten the retaining screws until they are snug.

12. Connect the negative battery cable.

HARD TOP MODELS

1. Disconnect the negative battery cable.
2. Open the rear door.
3. Remove the light assembly by disengaging the two retaining clips.
4. Pull the light assembly and gasket off of the body.
5. Inspect the gasket for tearing or crumbling. If any such damage is evident, replace the old gasket with a new one upon installation.
6. Remove the bulb socket from the light assembly housing by turning it counterclockwise and pulling it out of the housing.
7. To remove the bulbs, perform the following:
   a. Grasp the light bulb to be removed and gently press it in toward its socket.
   b. While pressing the bulb in, turn the bulb counterclockwise until the two little pins on the bulb base clear the channels in the socket.
   c. Pull the bulb up and out of its socket.

To install:

8. If the old bulb is being reinstalled, inspect the light bulb contacts; they should be clean and free of corrosion. Otherwise, clean the contacts or purchase a new bulb.

9. Install the light bulb in the socket by pressing it in and turning it clockwise until the bulb pins are fully engaged.

10. Install the light bulb socket in the housing by inserting it and turning it fully clockwise.

11. Install the light housing on the body by pressing it into position until the retaining clips are fully engaged.

12. Connect the negative battery cable.

Dome Light

SAMURAI MODELS

1. Disconnect the negative battery cable.
2. Remove the light assembly lens by pressing on the lens cover at the end points, then by pulling the lens down and off of the light housing.
3. Once the lens is removed from the light assembly, the individual light bulb can be removed. To remove the light bulb, pull it straight down from between the metal contacts.

To remove the dome light bulb, first remove the dome light lens . . .

. . . then pull the old bulb out from between the two metal contacts

To install:

4. Inspect the light housing metal contact terminals and, if the old bulb is being reinstalled, the contacts on the light bulb; they should be clean and free of corrosion. Otherwise, clean the contacts on the light housing or purchase a new bulb.

5. Install the light bulb in the socket by pressing it up between the metal terminals until it is fully seated.

6. Position the lens over the light housing, then press up until the retaining latches engage.

7. Connect the negative battery cable.

SIDEKICK, TRACKER, SIDEKICK SPORT AND X-90 MODELS

1. Disconnect the negative battery cable.
2. Remove the light assembly lens by carefully prying the lens cover off of the light housing.
3. Once the lens is removed from the light assembly, the individual light bulb can be removed. To remove the light bulb, pull it straight down from between the metal contacts.

To install:

4. Inspect the light housing metal contact terminals and, if the old bulb is being reinstalled, the contacts on the light bulb; they should be clean and

free of corrosion. Otherwise, clean the contacts on the light housing or purchase a new bulb.

5. Install the light bulb in the socket by pressing it up between the metal terminals until it is fully seated.

6. Position the lens over the light housing, then press up until the retaining latches engage.

7. Connect the negative battery cable.

Interior Reading Lights

SIDEKICK, TRACKER, SIDEKICK SPORT AND X-90 MODELS

1. Disconnect the negative battery cable.

2. Remove the light assembly cover by loosening the retaining screws, then by pulling the lens down and off of the light housing.

3. Once the lens is removed from the light assembly, the individual light bulb can be removed. To remove the light bulb, pull it straight down from between the metal contacts.

To install:

4. Inspect the light housing metal contact terminals and, if the old bulb is being reinstalled, the contacts on the light bulb; they should be clean and free of corrosion. Otherwise, clean the contacts on the light housing or purchase a new bulb.

5. Install the light bulb in the socket by pressing it up between the metal terminals until it is fully seated.

6. Position the lens over the light housing, then install the retaining screws until snug.

7. Connect the negative battery cable.

License Plate Lights

SAMURAI MODELS

1. Disconnect the negative battery cable.

2. Using a Phillips screwdriver, remove the light assembly lens retaining screws.

3. Pull the lens and gasket off of the light assembly.

4. Inspect the lens gasket for tearing or crumbling. If any such damage is evident, replace the old gasket with a new one upon installation.

5. Once the lens is removed from the light assembly, the individual light bulb can be removed. To remove the light bulb, pull it straight out of the socket.

To install:

6. If the old bulb is being reinstalled, inspect the light bulb contacts; they should be clean and free of corrosion. Otherwise, clean the contacts or purchase a new bulb.

7. Install the light bulb in the socket by pressing it in until fully seated in the socket.

8. INstall the lens and gasket on the housing. Tighten the lens retaining screws until they are snug.

9. Connect the negative battery cable.

SIDEKICK, TRACKER, SIDEKICK SPORT AND X-90 MODELS

▶ **See Figures 85 and 86**

1. Disconnect the negative battery cable.

2. Using a Phillips screwdriver, remove the light assembly retaining screws.

3. Pull the light assembly and gasket off of the body.

4. Inspect the gasket for tearing or crumbling. If any such damage is evident, replace the old gasket with a new one upon installation.

5. Remove the bulb socket from the light assembly housing by turning it counterclockwise and pulling it out of the housing.

➡**There are a possible of two types of bulbs which may be used in this housing: larger bulbs with a round metal base and smaller bulbs without any metal base.**

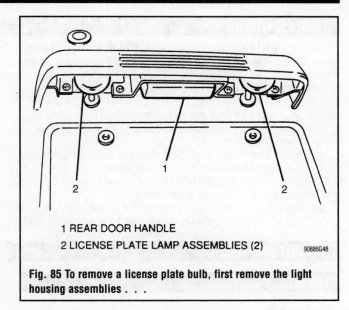

1 REAR DOOR HANDLE
2 LICENSE PLATE LAMP ASSEMBLIES (2)   90886G48

Fig. 85 To remove a license plate bulb, first remove the light housing assemblies . . .

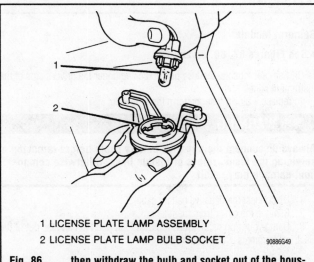

1 LICENSE PLATE LAMP ASSEMBLY
2 LICENSE PLATE LAMP BULB SOCKET   90886G49

Fig. 86 . . . then withdraw the bulb and socket out of the housing

6. To remove the larger bulbs equipped with metal bases:

a. Grasp the light bulb to be removed and gently press it in toward its socket.

b. While pressing the bulb in, turn the bulb counterclockwise until the two little pins on the bulb base clear the channels in the socket.

c. Pull the bulb up and out of its socket.

7. To remove the smaller bulbs with a metal base, pull the bulb straight out of the socket.

To install:

8. If the old bulb is being reinstalled, inspect the light bulb contacts; they should be clean and free of corrosion. Otherwise, clean the contacts or purchase a new bulb.

9. For the metal-based bulbs, install the light bulb in the socket by pressing it in and turning it clockwise until the bulb pins are fully engaged.

10. For the all glass bulbs, simply press the bulb straight into the socket until it is fully seated.

11. Install the light bulb in the socket by pressing it in and turning it clockwise until the bulb pins are fully engaged.

12. Install the light housing and gasket on the fender. Tighten the retaining screws until they are snug.

13. Connect the negative battery cable.

TRAILER WIRING

Wiring the vehicle for towing is fairly easy. There are a number of good wiring kits available and these should be used, rather than trying to design your own.

All trailers will need brake lights and turn signals as well as tail lights and side marker lights. Most areas require extra marker lights for overwide trailers. Also, most areas have recently required back-up lights for trailers, and most trailer manufacturers have been building trailers with back-up lights for several years.

Additionally, some Class I, most Class II and just about all Class III trailers will have electric brakes. Add to this number an accessories wire, to operate trailer internal equipment or to charge the trailer's battery, and you can have as many as seven wires in the harness.

Determine the equipment on your trailer and buy the wiring kit necessary. The kit will contain all the wires needed, plus a plug adapter set which includes the female plug, mounted on the bumper or hitch, and the male plug, wired into, or plugged into the trailer harness.

When installing the kit, follow the manufacturer's instructions. The color coding of the wires is usually standard throughout the industry. One point to note: some domestic vehicles, and most imported vehicles, have separate turn signals. On most domestic vehicles, the brake lights and rear turn signals operate with the same bulb. For those vehicles without separate turn signals, you can purchase an isolation unit so that the brake lights won't blink whenever the turn signals are operated.

One, final point, the best kits are those with a spring loaded cover on the vehicle mounted socket. This cover prevents dirt and moisture from corroding the terminals. Never let the vehicle socket hang loosely; always mount it securely to the bumper or hitch.

CIRCUIT PROTECTION

Fuses

REPLACEMENT

Samurai Models

▶ **See Figures 87, 88, 89 and 90**

On Samurai models, the fuse box is located under the driver's side of the instrument panel.

To replace a blown fuse, perform the following:

❊❊ WARNING

Always disconnect the negative battery cable before removing or servicing the fuses, relays or fusible links. Otherwise component damage may result.

1. Disconnect the negative battery cable.
2. Remove the cover from the fuse box.
3. Using your fingers or a fuse removal tool, pull the bad fuse out of the electrical terminals in the fuse block.

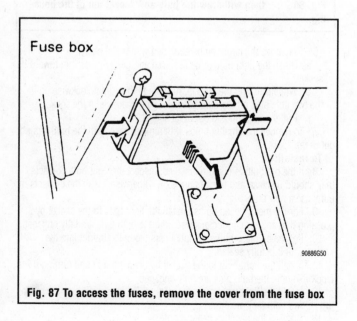

Fuse box

90886G50

Fig. 87 To access the fuses, remove the cover from the fuse box

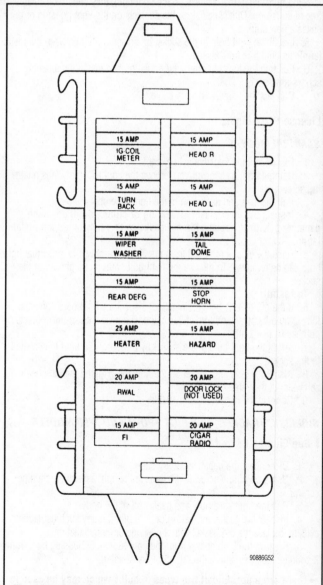

15 AMP IG COIL METER	15 AMP HEAD R
15 AMP TURN BACK	15 AMP HEAD L
15 AMP WIPER WASHER	15 AMP TAIL DOME
15 AMP REAR DEFG	15 AMP STOP HORN
25 AMP HEATER	15 AMP HAZARD
20 AMP RWAL	20 AMP DOOR LOCK (NOT USED)
15 AMP FI	20 AMP CIGAR RADIO

90886G52

Fig. 88 Layout of the fuse box used with Samurai models

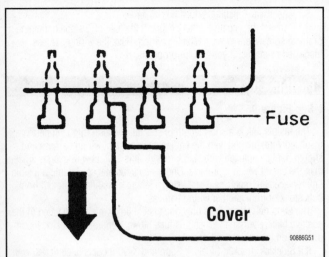

Fig. 89 The hook on the end of the fuse box cover can be used as a fuse removal tool

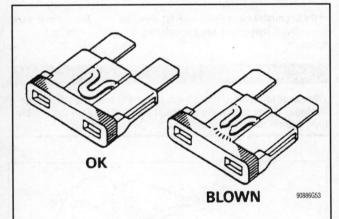

Fig. 90 If the small connective wire in the fuse is broken, the fuse is bad and must be replaced with a fuse of the SAME amp rating

To install:

✳✳ WARNING

Always be sure of the fuse rating of the fuse you are replacing. Component damage or perhaps a vehcle fire may be the result of installing an improper fuse. Refer to your owner's manual for the proper fuse ratings, or look at the fuse you are removing.

4. Insert a new fuse into the fuse block. Ensure that it is fully seated between the electrical terminals.
5. Install the fuse box cover.
6. Connect the negative battery cable. If the fuse blows again, there is a problem somewhere in your vehicle's wiring. Have the wiring harness inspected or inspect it yourself for problems.

Sidekick, Tracker, Sidekick Sport and X-90 Models

▶ **See Figures 91, 92, 93 and 94**

The Sidekick, Tracker, Sidekick Sport and X-90 models, use three types of fuses:

• Main fuse—The main fuse takes current directly from the battery. If your vehicle is equipped with A/C, the main fuse is actually a fusible link located at the battery positive terminal.

• Primary fuse—The primary fuses are situated in the circuit between the main fuse and the individual fuses, mounted in the fuse panel. The primary fuses are used to protect electrical load groups in the vehicle wiring system.

• Individual fuses—The individual fuses are designed to protect individual electrical circuits.

The main fuse and primary fuses are located in the engine compartment. If the main fuse blows, no electrical component will function. If a primary fuse blows, no electrical component in the corresponding load group will function. When replacing the main fuse or a primary fuse, the manufacturer states that a genuine Suzuki fuse must be used.

To replace a blown fuse, perform the following:

✳✳ WARNING

Always disconnect the negative battery cable before removing or servicing the fuses, relays or fusible links. Otherwise component damage may result.

1. Disconnect the negative battery cable.
2. If applicable, remove the cover from the fuse box.
3. Using your fingers or a fuse removal tool, pull the bad fuse out of the electrical terminals in the fuse block.

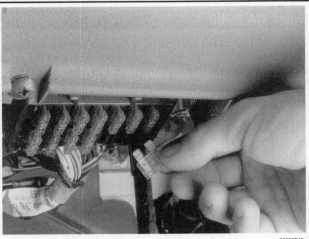

Fig. 91 To remove a fuse, first disconnect the negative battery cable, then separate the cover from the fuse box

Fig. 92 Pull the defective fuse out from between the metal terminals

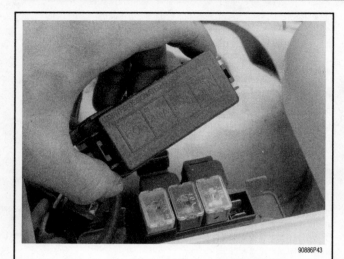

Fig. 93 To access the main or primary fuses, remove the cover lid from the housing

Fig. 94 Remove a fuse by pulling it straight up and out of the housing

To install:

❊❊❊ WARNING

Always be sure of the fuse rating of the fuse you are replacing. Component damage or perhaps a vehicle fire may be the result of installing an improper fuse. Refer to your owner's manual for the proper fuse ratings, or look at the fuse you are removing.

4. Insert a new fuse into the fuse block. Ensure that it is fully seated between the electrical terminals.

5. If necessary, install the fuse box cover.
6. Connect the negative battery cable. If the fuse blows again, there is a problem somewhere in your vehicle's wiring. Have the wiring harness inspected or inspect it yourself for problems.

Fusible Links

▶ **See Figure 95**

The fusible link is a short length of special, Hypalon (high temperature) insulated wire, integral with the engine compartment wiring harness and should not be confused with standard wire. It is several wire gauges smaller than the circuit which it protects. Under no circumstances should a fusible link replacement repair be made using a length of standard wire cut from bulk stock or from another wiring harness.

The Samurai vehicles use only one fusible link, which is attached to the positive battery terminal. When this fuse blows, none of the electrical components on the vehicle will operate.

If a Sidekick, Tracker, Sidekick Sport and X-90 models is equipped with A/C, the main fuse is actually a fusible link located at the battery positive terminal.

When replacing the fusible link, the manufacturer recommends using only a Suzuki fusible link.

➡**Do not mistake a resistor wire for a fusible link. The resistor wire is generally longer and has print stating, "Resistor: don't cut or splice."**

❊❊❊ WARNING

Whenever the fusible link blows, inspect the wiring system for damage. Never substitute a normal piece of wire for the fusible link, even if only for a short time.

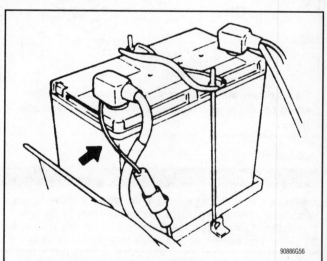

Fig. 95 The fusible link used on all models covered by this manual is attached directly to the positive battery terminal

Flashers

REPLACEMENT

▶ **See Figures 96, 97 and 98**

To replace the flasher unit, perform the following:
1. Disconnect the negative battery cable.

2. If necessary, remove the flasher cover.
3. Pull the indicator flasher straight out of its holder.
To install:
4. Align the indicator flasher with the holder and press it into place until it is fully seated.
5. If applicable, install the flasher cover.
6. Connect the negative battery cable.

FUSE NO.	NAME	COLOR/SIZE (AMPS)	CIRCUIT PROTECTED
	FUSES AND FUSIBLE LINKS		
	MAIN (Fusible link)	GREEN/0.5 mm²	All Electric Load.
1	HEAD-R	RED (10)	Right Side Headlight.
2	HEAD-L	RED (10)	Left Side Headlight.
3	TAIL/DOME	BLUE (15)	Dome Light; Highbeam Indicator; Door Warning; License Plate Light; Instrument Panel Illumination. Rear Park/Rear/Marker; Front Park/Front/Marker.
4	STOP/HORN	BLUE (15)	Stop Light. Horn.
5	HAZARD	BLUE (15)	Hazard, Radio, Clock
6	RADIO/CIGAR	YELLOW (20)	Radio, Cigar Lighter, Clock
7	FI	BLUE (15)	Engine Computer;
8	IG COIL/METER	BLUE (15)	Ignition Coil; Distributor; Fuel Gauge; Temperature Gauge; Indicators: Oil/Temp/Brake/Charging/Fasten Belts/Sensor.
9	TURN/BACK	RED (10)	Turn Signal Flasher; Back-Up Light.
10	WIPER/WASHER	BLUE (15)	Wiper and Washer.
11	REAR DEF	BLUE (15)	Rear Defogger.
12	HEATER	YELLOW (20)	Heater Control.

90886G58

Fig. 96 Fuse and fusible link application chart—Samurai models

NAME	COLOR/SIZE (AMPS)	PROTECTED CIRCUIT
	FUSES AND FUSIBLE LINKS	
MAIN FUSE	YELLOW (60)	All Electric Load.
	RED (50)	CIGAR/RADIO, I.G. COIL/METER, WIPER/WASHER, REAR DEF, TURN/BACK, HEATER.
	GREEN (40)	HEAD-R, HEAD-L, TAIL/DOME, STOP/HORN, HAZARD.
	PINK (30)	Rear Wheel Anti-lock Brake System
HEAD-R	BLUE (15)	Right Side Headlamp.
HEAD-L	BLUE (15)	Left Side Headlamp, High Beam Indicator
TAIL/DOME	BLUE (15)	Dome Lamp, Rear Park/Rear/Marker, License Plate Lamp, Front Park/Front/Marker, Instrument Panel Illumination.
STOP/HORN	BLUE (15)	Stop Lamp Horn.
HAZARD	BLUE (15)	Hazard.
DOOR LOCK	YELLOW (20)	Door Lock Control.
CIGAR RADIO	YELLOW (20)	Cigar lighter, Radio.
I.G. COIL/METER	BLUE (15)	Ignition Coil, Distributor, Fuel Gage, Temperature Gage, Fuel injection controller, Indicators; Oil/Temp./Fuel/Brake/Charging/ Fasten Belts/Check Engine/Four Wheel Drive.
TURN/BACK	BLUE (15)	Turn Signal Flasher, Back Up Lamp.
WIPER/WASHER	BLUE (15)	Front Wiper and Washer/Rear Wiper and Washer.
REAR DEFG	BLUE (15)	Rear Defogger.
HEATER	CLEAR (25)	Heater Control.
RWAL	YELLOW (20)	Rear Wheel Anti-Lock Brake System
FI	BLUE (15)	Electronic Fuel Injection System
AIR COND. MAIN FUSE	TAN 0.3 mm² fusible link	Air conditioning.
*AIR COND.	YELLOW (20)	Air conditioning.

NOTE: *AC Fuse in engine compartment.

90886G57

Fig. 97 Common fuse and fusible link application chart—early Sidekick, Tracker, Sidekick Sport and X-90 models

FUSES AND FUSIBLE LINKS				
NAME		**COLOR/SIZE (AMPS)**	**PROTECTED CIRCUIT**	
MAIN FUSE BOX	BATT	BLACK (80)	All Electric Load.	In engine compartment
	ABS	RED (50)	Anti-lock Brake System	
	IG	YELLOW (60)	CIGAR/RADIO, I.G. COIL/METER, WIPER/WASHER, REAR DEF, TURN/BACK, HEATER.	
	LAMP	PINK (30)	TAIL/DOME, STOP/HORN, HAZARD.	
	HEAD-R	BLUE (15)	Right Side Headlamp.	
	HEAD-L	BLUE (15)	Left Side Headlamp, High Beam Indicator	
FI		BLUE (15)	Electronic Fuel Injection System	
A/C		CLEAR (25)	Air conditioning.	
TAIL/DOME		BLUE (15)	Dome Lamp, Rear Park/Rear/Marker, License Plate Lamp, Front Park/Front/Marker, Instrument Panel Illumination.	
STOP/HORN		BLUE (15)	Stop Lamp Horn.	
HAZARD		BLUE (15)	Hazard.	
DOOR LOCK		YELLOW (20)	Door Lock Control.	
CIGAR RADIO		YELLOW (20)	Cigar lighter, Radio.	
I.G. COIL/METER		BLUE (15)	Ignition Coil, Distributor, Fuel Gage, Engine Coolant Temperature Gage, Fuel injection controller, Indicators; Oil/Temp./Fuel/Brake/Charging/Fasten Belts/Malfunction/Four Wheel Drive.	
TURN/BACK		BLUE (15)	Turn Signal Flasher, Back Up Lamp.	
WIPER/WASHER		BLUE (15)	Front Wiper and Washer/Rear Wiper and Washer.	
REAR DEFG		BLUE (15)	Rear Defogger.	
HEATER		CLEAR (25)	Heater Control.	

90886G59

Fig. 98 Common fuse and fusible link application chart—late Sidekick, Tracker, Sidekick Sport and X-90 models

WIRING DIAGRAMS

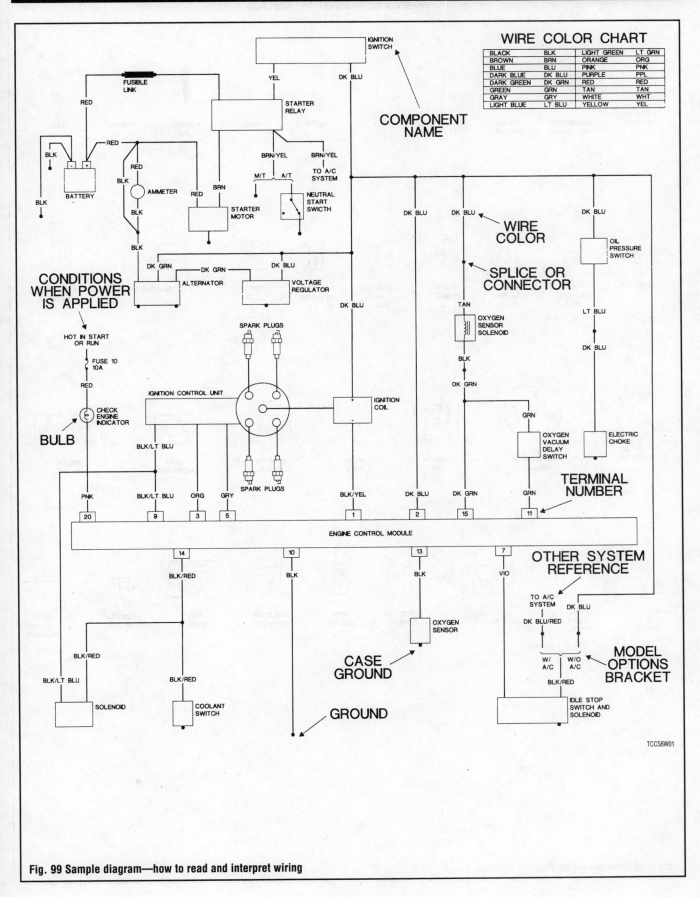

Fig. 99 Sample diagram—how to read and interpret wiring

WIRING DIAGRAM SYMBOLS

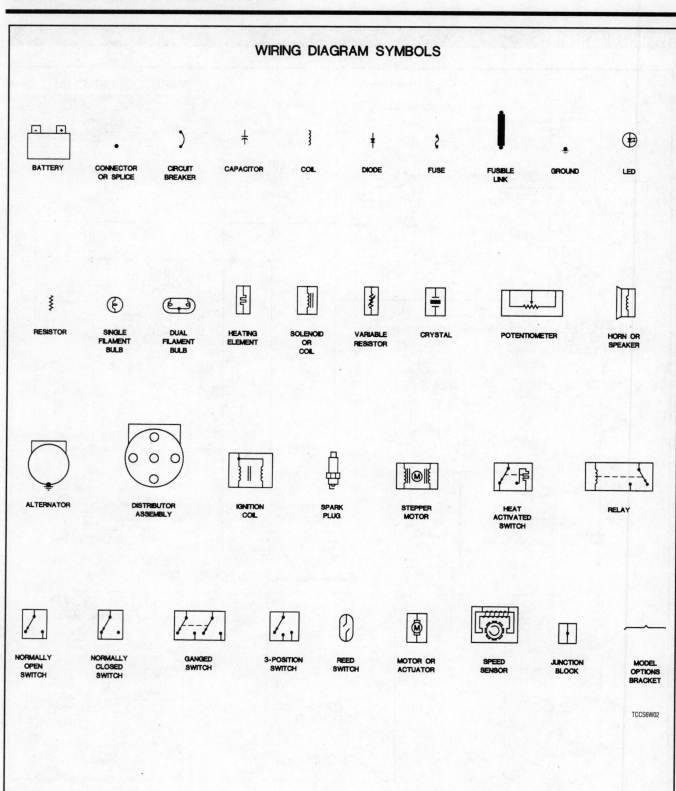

Fig. 100 Common wiring diagram symbols

TCCS6W02

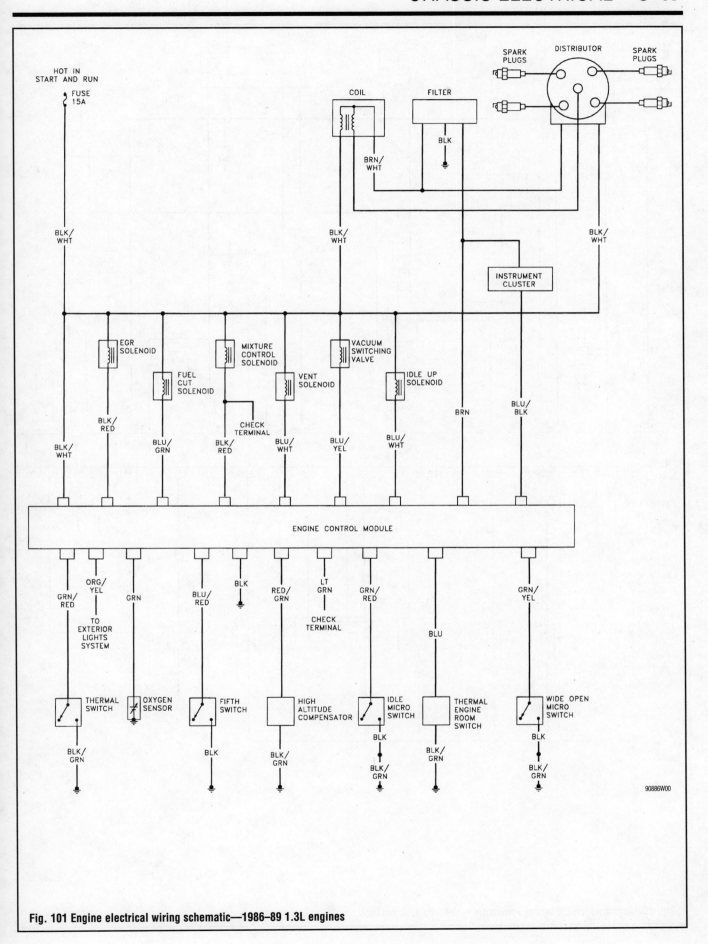

Fig. 101 Engine electrical wiring schematic—1986–89 1.3L engines

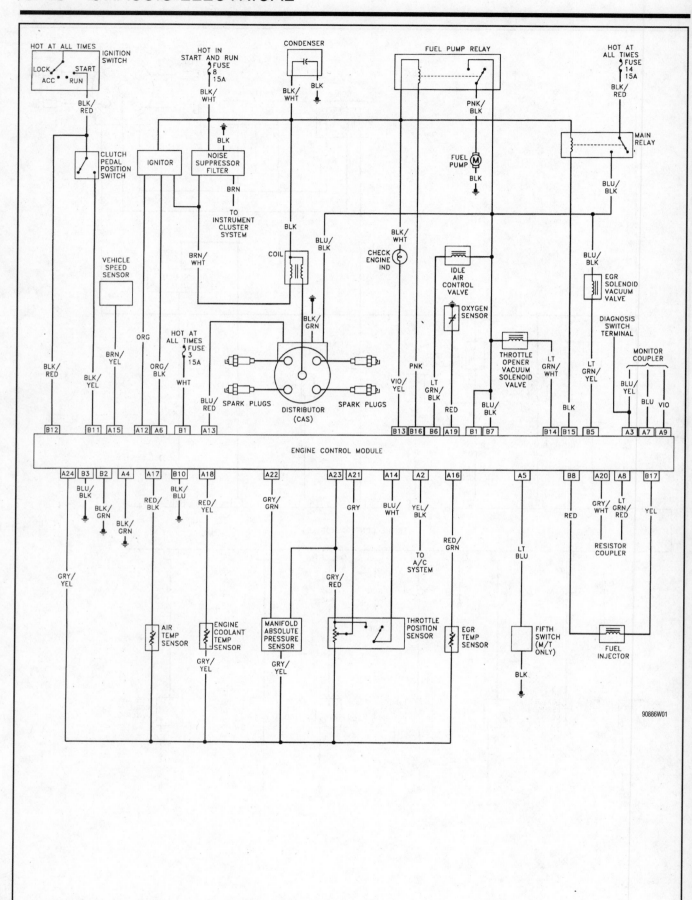

Fig. 102 Engine electrical wiring schematic—1990–95 1.3L engines

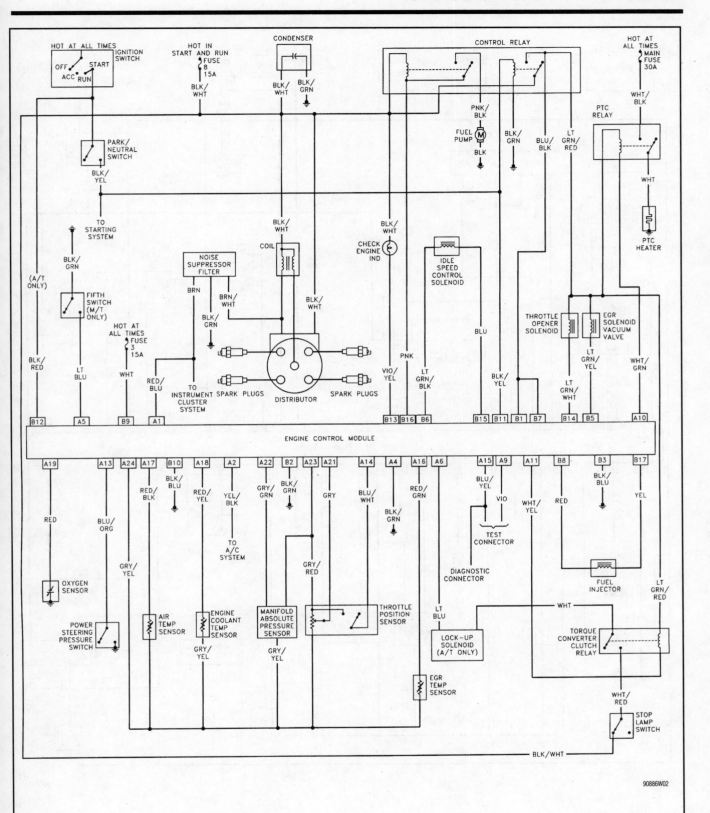

Fig. 103 Engine electrical wiring schematic—1989–90 1.6L TFI engines

90886W02

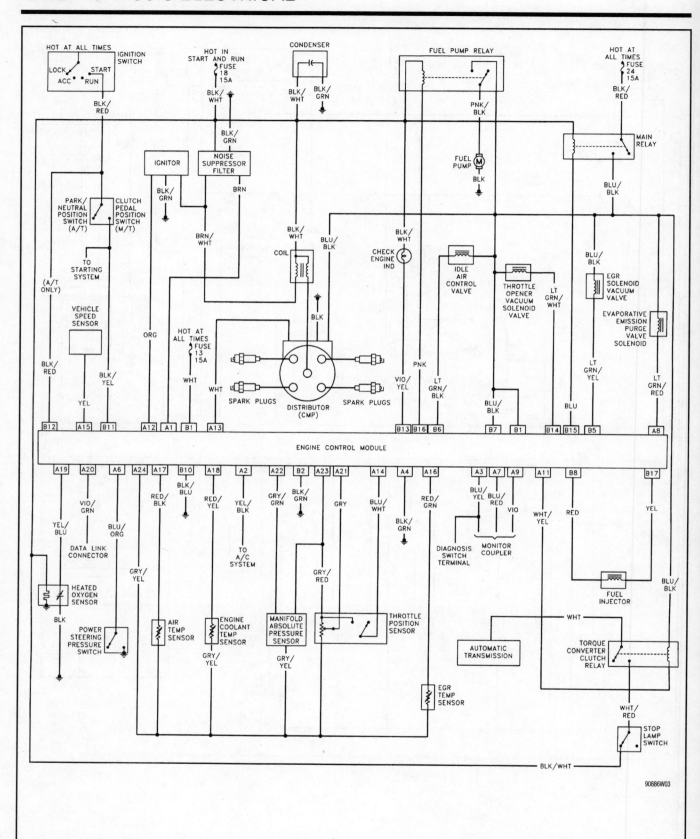

Fig. 104 Engine electrical wiring schematic—1991–95 1.6L TFI engines

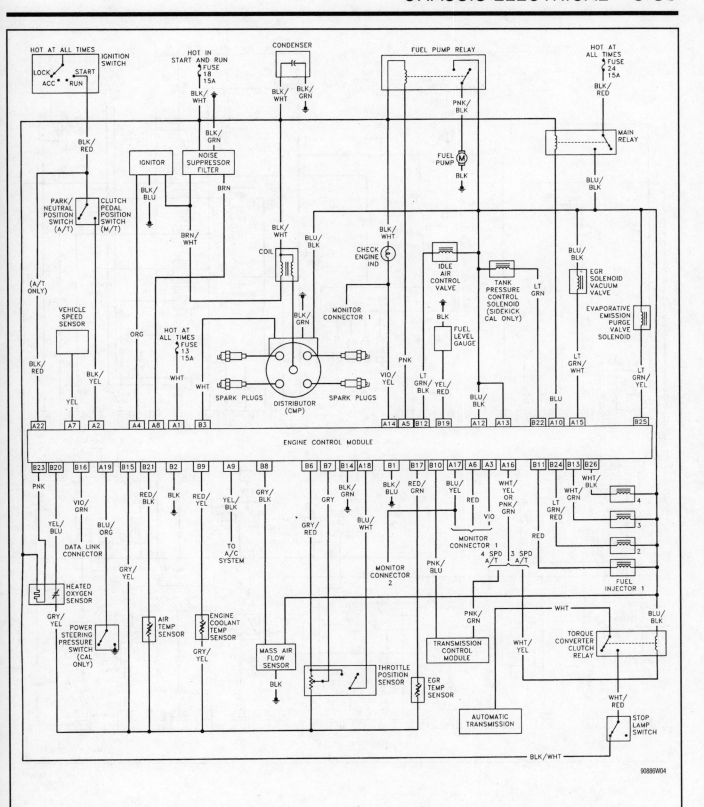

Fig. 105 Engine electrical wiring schematic—1992–95 1.6L MFI engines

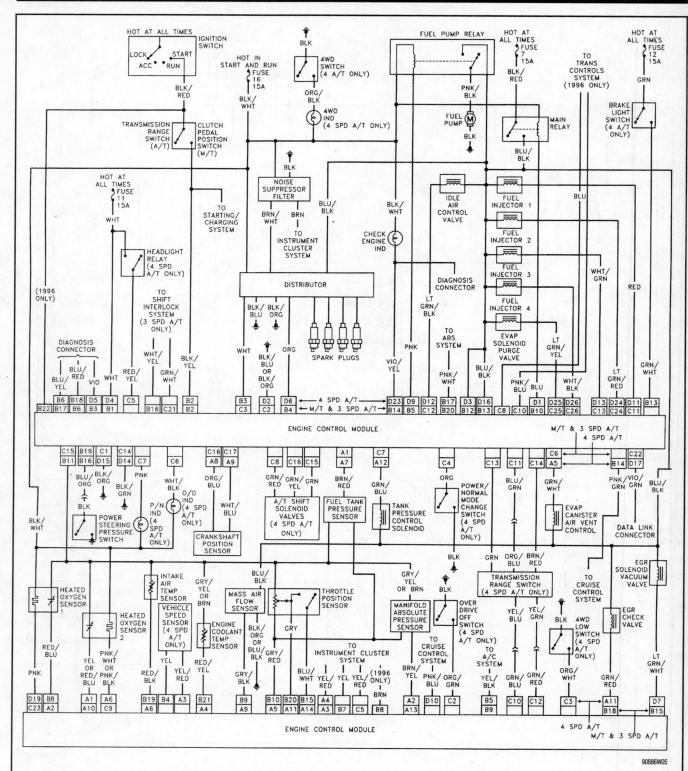

Fig. 106 Engine electrical wiring schematic—1996–98 1.6L MFI engines

90886W05

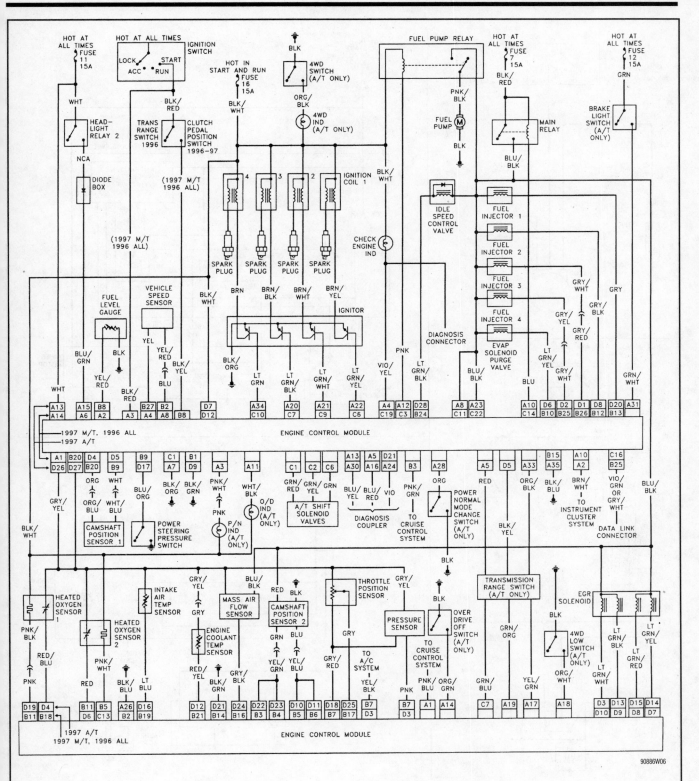

Fig. 107 Engine electrical wiring schematic—1.8L engines

90886W06

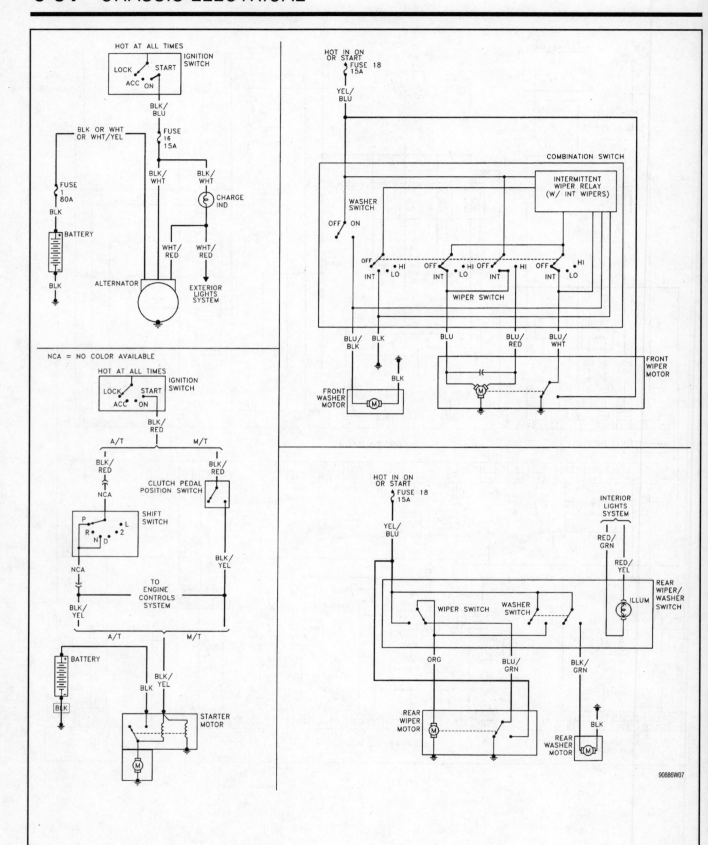

Fig. 108 Chassis wiring schematic—all models

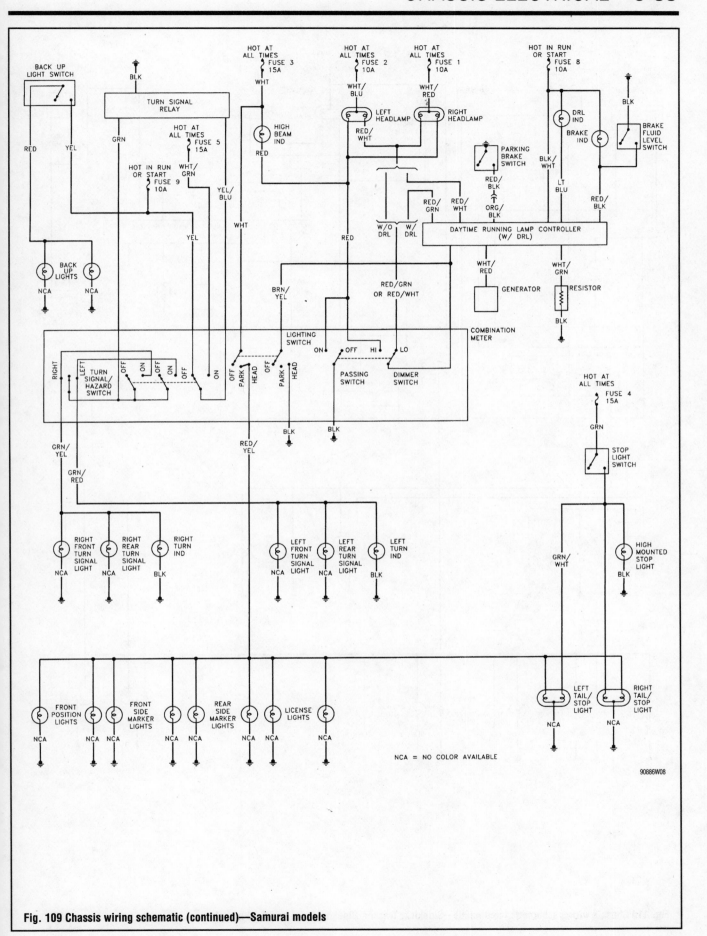

Fig. 109 Chassis wiring schematic (continued)—Samurai models

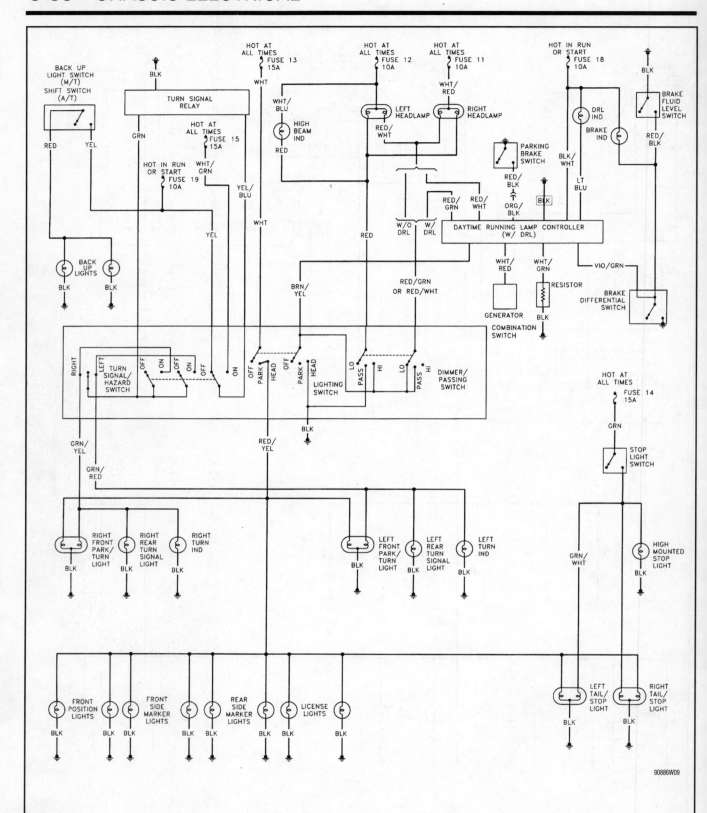

Fig. 110 Chassis wiring schematic (continued)—Sidekick, Tracker, Sidekick Sport and X-90 models

7
DRIVE TRAIN

MANUAL TRANSMISSION

Understanding the Manual Transmission

Because of the way an internal combustion engine breathes, it can produce torque (or twisting force) only within a narrow speed range. Most overhead valve pushrod engines must turn at about 2500 rpm to produce their peak torque. Often by 4500 rpm, they are producing so little torque that continued increases in engine speed produce no power increases.

The torque peak on overhead camshaft engines is, generally, much higher, but much narrower.

The manual transmission and clutch are employed to vary the relationship between engine RPM and the speed of the wheels so that adequate power can be produced under all circumstances. The clutch allows engine torque to be applied to the transmission input shaft gradually, due to mechanical slippage. The vehicle can, consequently, be started smoothly from a full stop.

The transmission changes the ratio between the rotating speeds of the engine and the wheels by the use of gears. 4-speed or 5-speed transmissions are most common. The lower gears allow full engine power to be applied to the rear wheels during acceleration at low speeds.

The clutch driveplate is a thin disc, the center of which is splined to the transmission input shaft. Both sides of the disc are covered with a layer of material which is similar to brake lining and which is capable of allowing slippage without roughness or excessive noise.

The clutch cover is bolted to the engine flywheel and incorporates a diaphragm spring which provides the pressure to engage the clutch. The cover also houses the pressure plate. When the clutch pedal is released, the driven disc is sandwiched between the pressure plate and the smooth surface of the flywheel, thus forcing the disc to turn at the same speed as the engine crankshaft.

The transmission contains a mainshaft which passes all the way through the transmission, from the clutch to the driveshaft. This shaft is separated at one point, so that front and rear portions can turn at different speeds.

Power is transmitted by a countershaft in the lower gears and reverse. The gears of the countershaft mesh with gears on the mainshaft, allowing power to be carried from one to the other. Countershaft gears are often integral with that shaft, while several of the mainshaft gears can either rotate independently of the shaft or be locked to it. Shifting from one gear to the next causes one of the gears to be freed from rotating with the shaft and locks another to it. Gears are locked and unlocked by internal dog clutches which slide between the center of the gear and the shaft. The forward gears usually employ synchronizers; friction members which smoothly bring gear and shaft to the same speed before the toothed dog clutches are engaged.

Shifter Handle

REMOVAL & INSTALLATION

Samurai Models

▶ **See Figures 1 and 2**

1. Disconnect the negative battery cable for safety.
2. Locate the shifter handle inside the passenger compartment. If equipped, remove the console cover.
3. Remove the 4 gear shift boot mounting bolts and slide the upper boot (shift boot No. 2) upwards on the gear shifter away from the center floor tunnel.

❊❊ WARNING

When working with the shift boots, be careful not to force and tear them. The older the boot is, the more easily it can be damaged.

4. Check the lower boot (shift boot No. 1) for a retaining clamp, and if equipped, release the boot clamp. Slide the lower boot, upward toward the shift knob in order to expose the shifter case cover retaining bolts.

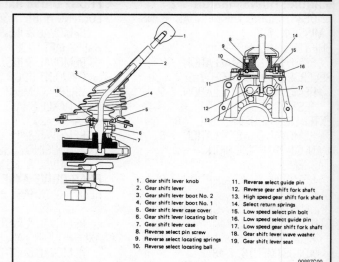

1. Gear shift lever knob	11. Reverse select guide pin
2. Gear shift lever	12. Reverse gear shift fork shaft
3. Gear shift lever boot No. 2	13. High speed gear shift fork shaft
4. Gear shift lever boot No. 1	14. Select return springs
5. Gear shift lever case cover	15. Low speed select pin bolt
6. Gear shift lever locating bolt	16. Low speed select guide pin
7. Gear shift lever case	17. Low speed gear shift fork shaft
8. Reverse select pin screw	18. Gear shift lever wave washer
9. Reverse select locating springs	19. Gear shift lever seat
10. Reverse select locating ball	

90887G00

Fig. 1 Cut-away view of the manual transmission shifter assembly—Samurai models

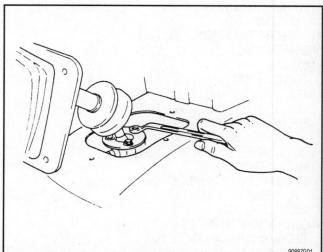

90887G01

Fig. 2 To free the lever from the housing, remove the retaining bolts from the top of the shift lever case cover—Samurai models

5. Loosen the gear shift lever case cover bolts (there are usually 3) and pull the gear shift lever out of the transmission case.
6. Cover the opening in the top of the transmission to prevent dirt, debris or loose bolts from falling in. This can be done with a piece of duct tape or using a plastic bag with a rubber band stretched around the case opening. Or a clean rag may be placed in the opening.

To install:

7. Remove the protective cover (tape, plastic bag or rag) from the top of the transmission case.
8. Clean and inspect the wear surfaces at the bottom of the shift lever. Apply a thin coat of lithium grease to the shifter ball friction surfaces at the bottom of the handle (between the shift lever and lever seat, as well as between the lever and lever case). Also, apply a small dab of grease to the tip of the shifter locating bolt, found inside the shift lever housing.
9. Install the shifter handle into the top of the case, then position the case cover and install the retaining bolts. Tighten the bolts to 35–62 inch lbs. (4–7 Nm).
10. Apply a thin coat of lithium grease to the lower boot (shift boot No. 1) on the surface which seals with the shift lever case cover. Then slide the

boot down the shift handle into position. If equipped, secure the boot retaining clamp. If the clamp was missing or damaged you should replace it with a similar type of band clamp (but in a pinch, a wire tie should be sufficient).

11. Slide the upper boot down the shift lever and into position. Secure the boot to the floor center tunnel using the retaining bolts.

12. If equipped, install the console cover.

13. Connect the negative battery cable.

Sidekick, Tracker, Sidekick Sport and X-90 Models

▶ See Figures 3 thru 13

There are 3 separate boots on the shift lever assembly for these vehicles. An upper boot you can touch from the driver's seat and that is mostly for looks (called the upper boot by Geo or boot No. 3 by Suzuki), a middle boot that seals the passenger compartment from the hole in the vehicle's floor pan (called the lower boot by Geo or boot No. 2 by Suzuki) and a lower boot that seals the shift lever to the shift lever housing on the top of the transmission (called the lever case boot by Geo or boot No. 1 by Suzuki). For simplicity, the following procedure will refer to them as upper, middle and lower in reference to how they are physically mounted on the shift lever.

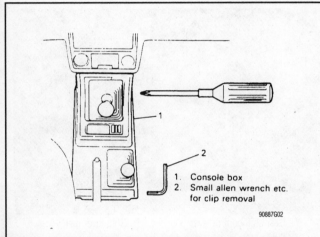

Fig. 3 Each center console is retained by 2 screws at the front and 2 snap retainers at the rear—Sidekick, Tracker, Sidekick Sport and X-90 models

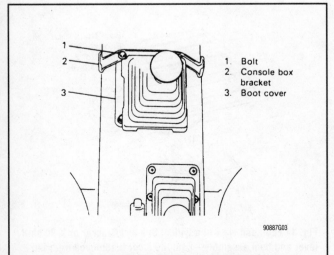

Fig. 4 The center console must be removed for access to the angled console bracket and the middle boot cover

1. Disconnect the negative battery cable for safety.

2. From inside the passenger compartment remove the console cover or, on certain late-model vehicles, both the front and rear console covers. If equipped with 2 console covers, start at the rear one. To free a console cover, remove the 2 screws and the two plastic retainers, then carefully lift the cover from the floor of the vehicle.

➡ The plastic retainers are removed by first pushing the center inward using a small hex key or punch. The center will gently snap inward telling you that fastener is now free. At this point you should be able to pull it back and out by gently grabbing the edges. DO NOT force a retainer out using a prytool unless the center snap has pushed inwards releasing the fastener or it will break and require replacement.

3. The gearshift knob and upper boot should be removed for easier access to the components below. Carefully unscrew the gearshift knob (counterclockwise) from the top of the shift lever. Then gently pull the boot upward and off the shaft. It is very important to be careful not to damage the boot.

✳✳ WARNING

When working with the shift boots, be careful not to force and tear them. The older the boot is, the more easily it can be damaged.

4. Remove the 4 console boot cover and bracket mounting bolts. The carpet may have to be gently held aside for access to 1 or more of the bolts.

5. Carefully remove the console bracket from the front of the middle boot cover. On some models this angled bracket is partially tucked under the carpet. Be careful when removing it not to rip the carpet or to tear the middle shift boot.

6. Remove the boot cover and carefully pull the middle boot upward to expose the lower boot. Although this boot can be removed from the shift lever, it can be very difficult to do without tearing the boot. And, since this boot is what seals the passenger compartment from the undercarriage, we recommend that you simply turn the boot gently inside-out on the lever for access and otherwise leave it in place.

7. Release the lower boot clamp by opening the retaining tabs and gently prying the end of the clamp free. If the clamp is difficult to release, you can carefully cut it using a pair of dikes, but be sure to replace it during installation.

8. Push downward on the gear shift control lever case (the round guide which the lever passes through on the way into the top of the case) and turn the case guide counterclockwise to release it. With the case guide released, pull upward to remove it and the shift control lever from the transmission.

Fig. 5 Loosen and remove the middle boot cover and angled bracket retaining bolts . . .

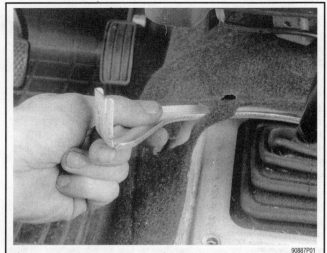

Fig. 6 . . . then carefully withdraw the angled console bracket from under the carpet

90887P01

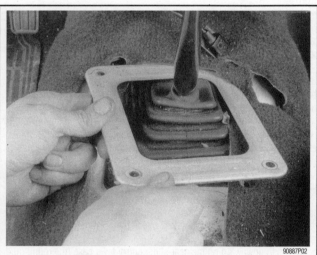

Fig. 7 Lift the boot cover from the assembly, being careful not to damage the middle boot

90887P02

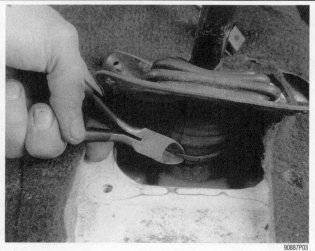

Fig. 8 If the lower clamp cannot be released, it can be CARE-FULLY cut

90887P03

Fig. 9 Lift the lower boot to expose the case cover guide

90887P04

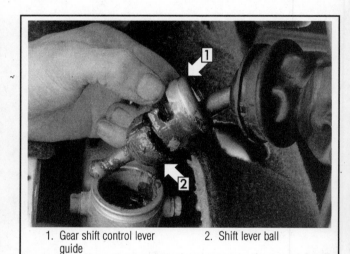

1. Gear shift control lever guide
2. Shift lever ball

Fig. 10 Once the guide is released, carefully withdraw the lever and pivot assembly from the case

90887P05

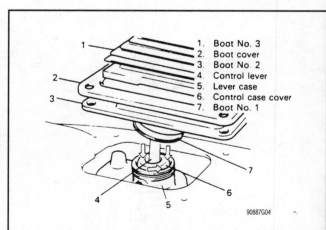

1. Boot No. 3
2. Boot cover
3. Boot No. 2
4. Control lever
5. Lever case
6. Control case cover
7. Boot No. 1

Fig. 11 Exploded view of a typical Sidekick/Tracker or X-90 shift lever and boot assembly—note the lever is removed from the top of the housing by pushing downward on the case cover guide while turning it counterclockwise

90887G04

9. Cover the opening in the top of the transmission shift case to prevent dirt, debris or loose bolts from falling in. This can be done with a piece of duct tape or using a plastic bag with a rubber band stretched around the case opening. Or a clean rag may be placed in the opening.

To install:

10. Remove the protective cover (tape, plastic bag or rag) from the top of the transmission case.

11. Clean and inspect the wear surfaces at the bottom of the shift lever. Apply a thin coat of lithium grease to the shifter ball friction surfaces at the bottom of the handle (on the lever, ball and the guide).

12. Insert the shift lever into position, then push downward on the guide while turning it clockwise to lock the assembly into the top of the transmission shift case. Check the shifter for proper feel and gear engagement.

13. Reposition the lower boot and secure using a suitable clamp. If the original clamp was damaged and no replacement is available, a wire tie may suffice.

14. Reposition the middle boot and the boot cover, making sure to achieve a proper seal that will keep dirt, moisture and fumes out of the passenger compartment. Position the angled console bracket, then install the bracket and boot cover retaining screws to secure the assembly.

15. Install the upper boot over the shift lever, then screw the gearshift knob back into place on top of the shift lever.

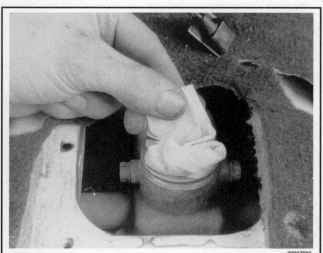

Fig. 12 Cover the case opening or place a clean rag in it to keep dirt, debris or stray bolts out

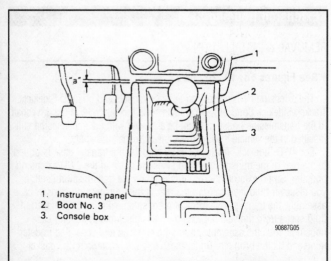

1. Instrument panel
2. Boot No. 3
3. Console box

Fig. 13 After installation, check the console-to-dash clearance, dimension "a"

16. Install the console cover (or covers) using the retaining screws and snap fasteners. To secure the snap fasteners, remove the center portion and insert the large piece into the hole, then gently insert the center portion of the fastener until it is flush with the top of the outer portion. Pull back gently to assure it is secure.

17. Check for the proper clearance between the front of the console cover and the bottom of the dash. There should be about 0.08 in (2mm) of clearance. If not, the angled boot bracket may not be properly installed.

18. Make sure that the flare end of the upper boot is properly engaged with the console cover.

19. Connect the negative battery cable, but double-check shifter action before attempting to start the vehicle.

Reverse Light Switch

REMOVAL & INSTALLATION

▶ **See Figure 14**

For Suzuki vehicles, the manual transmission reverse light switch is usually threaded into the side or top of the transmission housing. The switch will almost always be found on the upper left side of the transmission case, just behind the bell housing. Do not confuse the switch with the 4WD switch which is usually mounted further back, on top of the transfer case (which is integral with the transmission on all but Samurai models).

Before attempting replacement, check the position of the switch, relative to the position of the transmission filler plug. If it is located higher on the transmission case then the plug, you should be able to replace the switch without losing any transmission gear oil. But if the switch is equal to or lower of the case than the plug, you should have a drain pan handy to catch any escaping fluid. In this second case, you should still be able to replace the switch without having to completely drain the fluid. The trick is to have the replacement in one hand while you unthread the old switch. Once the old switch is loose, quickly withdraw it while positioning and threading the replacement in its place. If done correctly, a minimum amount of gear oil will escape.

1. Disconnect the negative battery cable for safety.

2. Raise the hood and check to see if access is possible from underhood or if you will need to raise and support the vehicle for access. On most late-model Sidekick, Tracker or X-90 models, access from underhood is possible, but it is a bit of a reach.

3. If necessary for better access, block the rear wheels, then raise and support the front of the vehicle safely using jackstands.

4. Disenage the switch wiring connector.

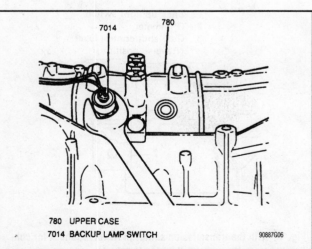

780 UPPER CASE
7014 BACKUP LAMP SWITCH

Fig. 14 The reverse light switch is threaded into the top or side of the transmission housing—this Sidekick/Tracker has the switch on the upper left side, just behind the bell housing

➡Most Suzuki models utilize a switch whose pigtail is permanently attached to the base of the switch. On these models, follow the switch wiring back through the rubberized-plastic coated metal wiring clips to locate the harness connector. Carefully release the lock-tab and disconnect the wiring.

5. Clean the area around the switch to help prevent dirt from falling into the transmission as the switch is removed.

6. If you have decided that the switch is mounted low enough to warrant a drain pan, position it beneath the transmission.

7. Using a wrench or a suitable sensor socket (either flare-end or a deep socket with cut-outs to accommodate the switch wiring), carefully loosen and remove the switch from the transmission housing.

To install:

8. If you are reinstalling the original switch, check for an O-ring or for sealant on the threads. Replace a worn O-ring or re-coat the threads with sealant, as applicable. If you are installing a new switch, check that it is of the same design as the original. For instance, if the original used an O-ring and the replacement does not have one, either you have the wrong switch or the replacement was designed to use a bit of sealant on the threads.

☼☼ WARNING

DO NOT overtighten the switch, you could damage the switch or the aluminum transmission housing.

TESTING

♦ See Figures 15, 16 and 17

If the reverse lights stop working, and a voltage check shows NO POWER to the reverse light sockets when the transmission shift lever is in reverse, check the switch for proper continuity using an ohmmeter. The test can either be conducted directly across the 2 terminals on the switch wiring connector, or for Sidekick, Tracker and X-90 models, it can also be checked underhood using the harness connector at the back of the intake manifold. If the second option is taken, release the wiring from the clamp at the back of the manifold, separate the wiring and check for at terminals 3 and 4 (at one end of the 6 terminal connector).

The switch should test continuous ONLY when the transmission shift lever is in Reverse.

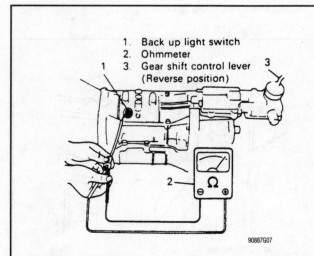

1. Back up light switch
2. Ohmmeter
3. Gear shift control lever (Reverse position)

Fig. 15 With the transmission shifter in Reverse, check for continuity across the switch's 2 wiring terminals

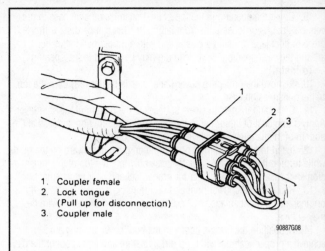

1. Coupler female
2. Lock tongue (Pull up for disconnection)
3. Coupler male

Fig. 16 On late-model vehicles, a harness connector is located behind the intake that you can use for testing . . .

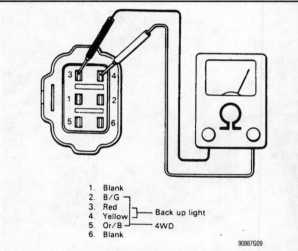

1. Blank
2. B/G
3. Red
4. Yellow ⎫ Back up light
5. Or/B ⎭ 4WD
6. Blank

Fig. 17 . . . at this connector the reverse light circuit is checked between terminals 3 and 4

Extension Housing Seal

REMOVAL & INSTALLATION

♦ See Figures 18, 19, 20 and 21

The extension housing seal on Samurai models and on 2WD Sidekick, Tracker, Sidekick Sport or X-90 models seals the slip-yoke of the driveshaft to the transmission housing. It can be accessed with the transmission still installed in the vehicle if you remove the driveshaft assembly.

For 4WD Sidekick, Tracker or X-90 models, the transfer case is bolted to the rear of the transmission and takes the place of the 2WD extension housing. So no external fluid seal is used on the transmission itself. If you discover fluid leaking from the rear of the transmission/transfer case assembly, the transfer case extension housing seal must be replaced. If fluid seeps from the seal between the transmission and transfer case housings, then the assembly should be removed and separated to determine and fix the problem. Under these rare circumstances, the gasket mating surfaces along with the rest of the transmission and transfer case housing assemblies should be carefully inspected for cracks or deformities.

But no matter which type of vehicle you are talking about, the extension housing seal (whether it is in the transmission or the transfer case) is replaced in the same manner.

1. Block the front wheels of the vehicle, then raise and support the rear of the vehicle safely using jackstands. The rear of the vehicle is supported in this case to place the seal above the fluid-level line in the extension housing.

2. Matchmark and remove the rear driveshaft from the vehicle.

✳✳ WARNING

Take care NOT to damage either the sealing surface of the extension housing or the output shaft during seal removal, or the new seal won't solve your problem.

3. Using a small, suitable prytool or a specially designed seal remover (such as the one produced by Lisle®), carefully pry the old seal from the end of the extension housing.

➡If seal removal is especially difficult you can use a slide hammer with a special oil seal remover attachment, but this should not be necessary for most cases.

To install:

4. Inspect the sealing surface of the output shaft and the extension housing for scores which might prevent sealing or small burrs which could tear a new seal as it was driven into position.

5. Place a thin coating of high temperature lithium grease on the lips of the new seal.

6. Position the seal at the opening of the extension housing and carefully drive it into position using a suitably sized seal driver and a plastic hammer. Drive the seal in until it is flush with the housing surface or just beneath the surface by no more than 0.04 in (1mm).

7. Align and install the driveshaft. Be careful not to tear the new seal with the slip-yoke.

8. If fluid was lost during the procedure or prior to it, make sure the vehicle is completely level. Then check the transmission fluid and top-off, as necessary.

9. If not done already, remove the jackstands and carefully lower the vehicle.

Fig. 18 Remove the driveshaft for access to the extension housing seal (arrow)—this one's in the transfer case

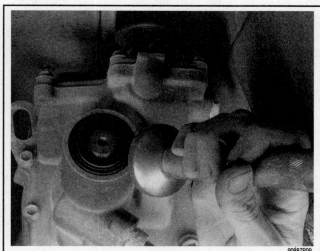

Fig. 20 . . . then carefully drive the new seal into position using a suitably sized driver

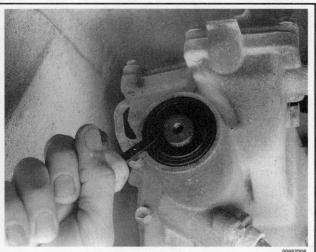

Fig. 19 Use a small prybar or seal tool to carefully pry the old seal from extension housing . . .

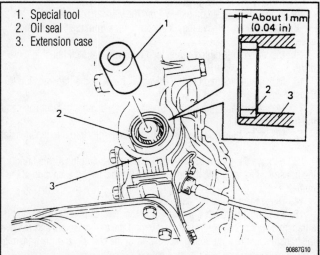

1. Special tool
2. Oil seal
3. Extension case

About 1mm (0.04 in)

Fig. 21 Use a suitably-sized driver and a plastic hammer to carefully install the new extension housing seal

Manual Transmission Assembly

REMOVAL & INSTALLATION

Samurai Models

▶ **See Figures 22 and 23**

1. Disconnect the negative battery cable for safety.
2. From inside the passenger compartment, remove the transmission shift handle.
3. Raise and support the vehicle safely at a height which will be convenient to work from both above and below the vehicle.

➡ **Later in this procedure, the exhaust center pipe must be removed for clearance. If you do not have air tools (which make exhaust fastener removal MUCH easier) take a moment now to spray the exhaust center pipe fasteners with penetrating oil to help loosen them.**

4. Either drain the oil from the transmission case or have a transmission case plug handy for the extension housing (some aftermarket tool companies like Lisle® make plastic transmission plugs for just this purpose. If a plug is not available, a large plastic bag can be stretched across the extension housing and secured with a rubber band. This second method will catch some fluid, but if the transmission is left with the rear downward for any length of time you will wind up with smelly gear oil on the garage floor or in the driveway.
5. Locate the switch wiring which is run through tab rubber-coated metal wiring guides on the top of the transmission housing. Detach the back-up light and fifth switch lead wires at the electrical connector.

This is usually most convenient at the wiring to chassis harness connector.

➡ **Make sure any wires which are left connected to the transmission are positioned in the wiring guides and will not catch on something during transmission removal.**

6. Tag and disconnect the lead wires from the starter motor which is mounted to the engine, through the transmission bell housing. This step can be avoided on some models, if the starter motor can be positioned out of the way, with the wiring still connected. You'll have to use your judgment here, but if you try this, be sure that the starter is properly supported (so as not to stress or damage any of the wiring) and be careful that the starter does not get in the way during transmission removal.
7. Remove the starter mounting bolts and either support the starter motor aside or remove it completely from the vehicle.
8. If applicable, remove the fuel hose clamps from the transmission case.
9. Disconnect the clutch cable, then remove the clutch housing lower plate.
10. Matchmark and remove the driveshaft between the transmission to transfer case.
11. Matchmark and remove the driveshaft between the transfer case and the front differential.
12. Disconnect the bolts fastening the cylinder block to the transmission case.
13. Remove the transmission cross-over protection pipe located under the transmission case. The mounting bolts are located on each side of the frame.
14. Disconnect the center exhaust pipe.
15. Position a transmission jack (or a floor jack with a block of wood if a transmission jack is not available), support the transmission, and remove the transmission rear mounting member from the chassis and the transmission housing.

➡ **Make one final check to be sure that all connections have been removed from the transmission. Make sure any wiring and the starter (if still in the vehicle) will not be caught by the transmission during removal.**

16. If you do not have a transmission jack, this is a good time to get some help from a friend or neighbor. Carefully pull the transmission straight back until the input shaft is free of the clutch assembly. Then carefully lower the transmission from the vehicle.

To install:

17. Clean and inspect the transmission components located in the bell housing. Check the throwout bearing, fork and pivots, along with the input shaft for wear. Now is a very good time to check or replace the clutch and throwout bearing.
18. Apply a light coating of high temperature lithium grease to the input shaft pilot and splines. Be careful not to apply too much grease which could contaminate the clutch and pressure plate assembly.
19. Apply a light coating of high temperature lithium grease to the thrust surfaces of the throwout bearing.
20. Carefully raise the transmission into position using the transmission jack and/or a friend. With the transmission raised to the proper height, carefully slide the transmission forward inserting the input shaft through the clutch and pressure plate until the splines mesh.

✳✳ WARNING

DO NOT force the input shaft into the clutch since damage may occur to the input shaft or the clutch and pressure plate. If the

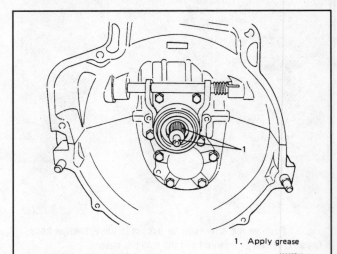

1. Apply grease

90887G11

Fig. 22 Before installation, be sure to clean, inspect and lightly grease the input shaft—Samurai models

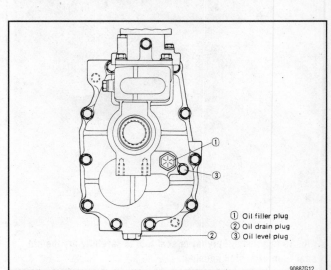

① Oil filler plug
② Oil drain plug
③ Oil level plug

90887G12

Fig. 23 After installation, don't forget to check and top-off the transmission assembly with gear lube

splines do not easily mesh, pull the transmission back enough to carefully insert your CLEAN hand and turn the shaft slightly. Another method (when the friend comes in handy again) is to temporarily insert the driveshaft into the back of the transmission and rotate it to turn the input shaft as the transmission is carefully pushed toward the engine. Of course this second trick only works when the transmission is in gear.

21. Once the transmission is in place, install the transmission-to-engine bolts finger-tight.

22. Install the engine rear mounting member, then tighten member retaining bolts and the transmission-to-engine bolts to 159–248 inch lbs. (18–28 Nm).

23. The balance of the installation procedure is the reverse of removal. If the transmission was drained, or even if it wasn't but some fluid leaked during the procedure, be sure to check and fill the transmission when you are finished.

24. If the clutch was replaced, or if the adjuster was disturbed when removing the cable, check and adjust the clutch before attempting to drive the vehicle.

25. When you are finished, double check all wiring connections, wiring clamps, breather hoses, etc. to make sure everything is back the way you found it.

26. Connect the negative battery cable. Start the engine; check for any leaks and proper clutch operation.

Sidekick, Tracker, Sidekick Sport and X-90 Models

▶ **See Figures 24 thru 44**

On 4WD models, the transmission and transfer case are removed as an assembly, since the transfer case is bolted directly to the rear of the transmission and takes the place of an extension housing.

1. Disconnect the negative battery cable for safety.

2. From inside the passenger compartment, remove the transmission shift handle.

3. On 4WD vehicles, remove the transfer case shift handle from inside the passenger compartment.

➡Although removal of the transfer case shift handle is recommended, it is not always necessary. If you would like to leave the handle in place, just remove the shift knob (which uses a setscrew), boot and boot cover. But, be very careful not to damage the shift lever when lowering the transmission/transfer case assembly from the vehicle. If the lever is left in place, it may be necessary to shift the transfer case lever to different positions while lowering or raising the assembly.

4. Free the transmission breather hose from the clamp at the rear of the cylinder head.

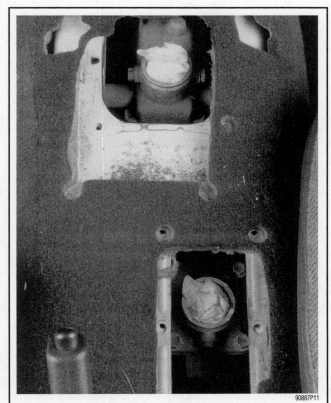

Fig. 25 Cover the openings left by the transmission and transfer case shift levers (as applicable)

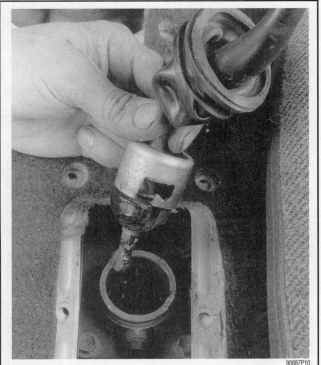

Fig. 24 Before removing the transmission, you should start by removing the shift lever(s)

Fig. 26 Matchmark and remove the driveshaft(s)—the front driveshaft of a 4WD is pictured here

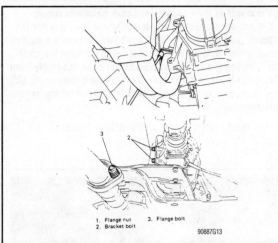

1. Flange nut   3. Flange bolt
2. Bracket bolt

90887G13

Fig. 27 Three sets of fasteners must be removed to free the center exhaust pipe—2WD shown (4WD similar, but bracket bolts are under transmission)

90887P15

Fig. 30 Remove the center pipe converter-to-transmission bracket bolts . . .

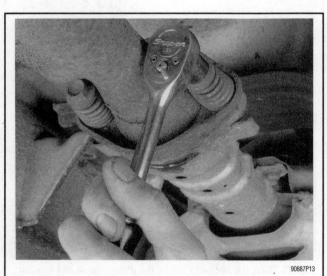

90887P13

Fig. 28 Loosen and remove the center pipe fasteners . . .

90887P16

Fig. 31 . . . then carefully lower the center pipe and converter assembly from the vehicle

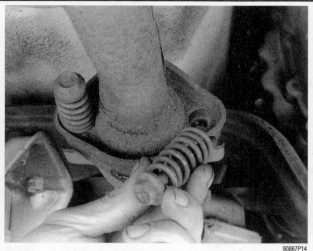

90887P14

Fig. 29 . . . these spring loaded through-bolts are found on the flange at the rear of the converter

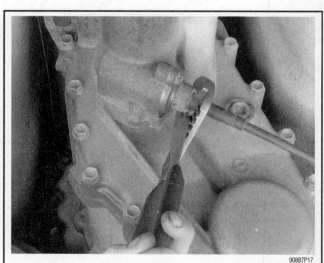

90887P17

Fig. 32 Turn the knurled knob counterclockwise to loosen the speedometer cable . . .

Fig. 33 . . . then withdraw the cable end from the speedometer gear—on 4WDs this is located on the transfer case

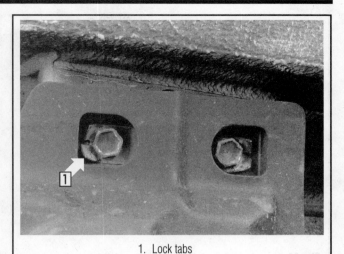

1. Lock tabs

Fig. 36 Remember that mount bolts on the passenger side have lock tabs . . .

Fig. 34 With the transmission supported, loosen and remove the rear mount-to-chassis bolts . . .

Fig. 37 . . . which must be bent away from the bolt heads before they can be loosened

Fig. 35 . . . and the rear mount-to-transmission bolts

Fig. 38 With all of the fasteners removed, the rear transmission mount is easily lowered from the vehicle

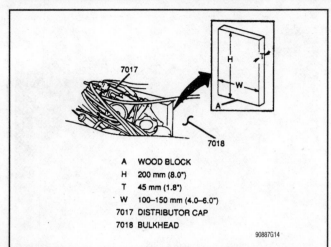

A WOOD BLOCK
H 200 mm (8.0")
T 45 mm (1.8")
W 100–150 mm (4.0–6.0")
7017 DISTRIBUTOR CAP
7018 BULKHEAD

90887G14

Fig. 39 A wooden block should be positioned between the engine and firewall to prevent the possibility of damage if the engine should pivot back while the transmission is being removed

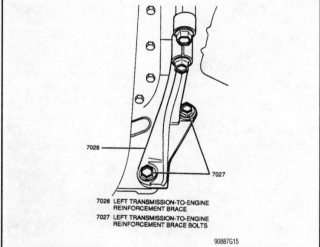

7026 LEFT TRANSMISSION-TO-ENGINE REINFORCEMENT BRACE
7027 LEFT TRANSMISSION-TO-ENGINE REINFORCEMENT BRACE BOLTS

90887G15

Fig. 40 Some models are equipped with a left transmission-to-engine reinforcement brace . . .

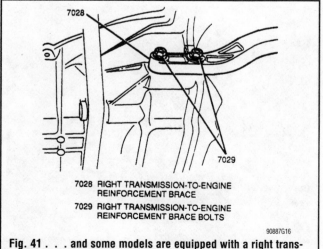

7028 RIGHT TRANSMISSION-TO-ENGINE REINFORCEMENT BRACE
7029 RIGHT TRANSMISSION-TO-ENGINE REINFORCEMENT BRACE BOLTS

90887G16

Fig. 41 . . . and some models are equipped with a right transmission-to-engine reinforcement brace (yours might have one, both or none).

90887P24

Fig. 42 Pull the transmission assembly STRAIGHT back until the input shaft is clear of the pressure plate . . .

90887P25

Fig. 43 . . . and the bell housing is free of the lower engine studs/bolts, then lower the transmission assembly from the vehicle

Fig. 44 Before installation, be sure to clean, inspect and lightly grease the thrust surfaces in the bell housing

5. Bend back the rubber-coated metal clamp at the rear of the intake manifold to free up the wiring harness. Then, disconnect the harness coupler.

6. Tag and disconnect the lead wires from the starter motor which is mounted to the transmission bell housing through an engine mounted flange. This step can be avoided, if the starter motor is supported to hold its position relative to the engine and the engine mounted flange which sits between the engine and transmission bell housing. You'll have to use your judgment here, but if you try this, be sure that the starter is properly supported (so as not to stress or damage any of the wiring). This can be done with a combination of a large block of wood below the starter motor, leaving the upper starter mounting bolt in place (after removing the nut) and using a few creative wire ties or bungee cords.

➡ **If you decide to remove the starter, you will need an ignition wrench or a creative combination of ¼ in. drive tools to reach the wiring retainers.**

7. Remove the starter mounting bolts and remove it completely from the vehicle, or remove the lower mounting bolt and remove the nut from the transmission side of the upper mounting bolt, then secure the starter in position so the wiring will not be damaged.

8. Remove the 2 upper transmission-to-engine mounting bolts. Unfortunately, this is another tight spot. You will either need a large breaker bar with a very short socket or a large combination wrench with a slight offset to really get at the bolt on the driver's side of the vehicle.

9. Unbolt the fan shroud (usually 4 bolts) and hang it from the front of the engine. This will allow the engine to pivot slightly on the motor mounts once the transmission is removed, without jeopardizing the cooling fan.

10. Raise and support the vehicle safely at a height which will be convenient to work from both above and below the vehicle.

➡ **Later in this procedure, the exhaust center pipe must be removed for clearance. If you do not have air tools (which make exhaust fastener removal MUCH easier) take a moment now to spray the exhaust center pipe fasteners with penetrating oil to help loosen them. Spray both the 3 nuts and studs at the exhaust manifold and the 2 through-bolts at the rear of the converter.**

11. If equipped, remove the front skid plate for better access.

12. On 2WD vehicles, either drain the oil from the transmission case or have a transmission case plug handy for the extension housing (some aftermarket tool companies like Lisle® make plastic transmission plugs for just this purpose. If a plug is not available, a large plastic bag can be stretched across the extension housing and secured with a rubber band. This second method will catch some fluid, but if the transmission is left with the rear downward for any length of time you will wind up with smelly gear oil on the garage floor or in the driveway.

13. On 4WD vehicles, you do not have to drain the transmission, but it is probably smartest to drain the transfer case. If you are really adamant about not draining either, you've got 2 options. Either buy 2 transmission plugs that will fit where the front and rear driveshaft slip-yokes go or buy 1 plug and leave the front driveshaft in position, just unbolted at the front differential. Both have the potential to be a pain and to be really messy, but it's your call.

14. Matchmark and remove the rear driveshaft from the vehicle.

15. On 4WD vehicles, matchmark and remove the front driveshaft between the transfer case and the front differential.

16. Disconnect the clutch cable from the throwout arm, then remove the clutch housing lower plate.

17. Unbolt and remove the center exhaust pipe:

   a. First, use a long extension (or a few shorter ones) and a deep socket to loosen and remove the 3 center pipe-to-exhaust manifold stud nuts.

   b. Second, loosen the 2 spring loaded center pipe through-bolts at the rear of the converter.

   c. Finally, hold the center pipe and remove the 2 converter bracket-to-transmission bolts (located on the side of the transmission for 2WD vehicles or underneath the transmission on 4WD vehicles.

➡ **Center pipe removal is another item you may be able to get away without, but ONLY on 2WD vehicles. Although the exhaust pipe itself does not really interfere with transmission removal (it does make it a little more awkward), the problem occurs with the 4WD converter-to-transmission bracket. If you do not remove the bracket, you CANNOT remove the transmission. And, the seemingly easier solution of removing the bracket from the converter is usually impossible because the fasteners which attach the bracket to the top of the converter are so badly cooked and rusted from the extreme heat that they break off on the first attempt (TRUST US ON THIS ONE).**

18. Remove the 2 nuts from the studs attaching the bottom of the transmission bell housing to the back of the engine.

19. Disconnect the speedometer cable from the transmission (2WD) or the transfer case (4WD), as applicable. On some models there is a ground wire bolted to the case by the speedometer cable retainer, be sure to remove the ground wire before lowering the transmission.

20. Position a transmission jack to take the weight off of the rear transmission mount (crossmember).

21. Unbolt the rear transmission mount from the chassis at either side and from the transmission at the center, then remove the mount from the vehicle.

➡ **The 2 bolts on the passenger side of the transmission mount are locked in place using small metal tabs. This is done to help assure they cannot loosen, since the mount simply hangs from the bolts on that side and there is no ledge for it to sit on should they come out. Be sure to carefully bend these tabs out of the way before trying to loosen those 2 bolts.**

22. Place a wooden block 8 in. (200mm) tall X 4–6 in. (100–150mm) wide X 1.8 in. (45mm) thick on its side below the distributor cap, between the cylinder head distributor housing and the firewall. Lower the transmission jack slightly, to preload the wood. This wood will keep the engine from pivoting any further and possibly causing damage to the distributor or to the motor mounts.

23. If equipped, remove the 2 bolts from the right and or left transmission-to-engine reinforcement braces.

24. Carefully pull the transmission (and transfer case assembly on 4WD vehicles) toward the rear of the vehicle until the input shaft pulls clear of the clutch and pressure plate assembly, and until the bell housing pulls off of the lower engine-to-transmission studs/bolts. Although one person can do this, if you don't have a transmission jack we REALLY recommend that you get a friend to help you with this step. Lower the transmission from the vehicle.

To install:

25. Clean and inspect the transmission components located in the bell housing. Check the throwout bearing, fork and pivots, along with the input shaft for wear. Now is a very good time to check or replace the clutch and throwout bearing.

26. Apply a light coating of high temperature lithium grease to the input shaft pilot and splines. Be careful not to apply too much grease which could contaminate the clutch and pressure plate assembly.

27. Apply a light coating of high temperature lithium grease to the thrust surfaces of the throwout bearing.

➡There should be 1 or 2 metal bushings which press into the transmission housing at the lower bell housing bolt holes or they may be left on the lower engine-to-transmission bolts/studs. If used on your application, make sure they are in position before you crawl under with the transmission assembly.

28. Carefully raise the transmission assembly into position using the transmission jack and/or a friend. With the transmission raised to the proper height, carefully slide the assembly forward inserting the input shaft through the clutch and pressure plate until the splines mesh.

✳✳ WARNING

DO NOT force the input shaft into the clutch since damage may occur to the input shaft or the clutch and pressure plate. If the splines do not easily mesh, pull the transmission back enough to carefully insert your CLEAN hand and turn the shaft slightly. Another method (when the friend comes in handy again) is to temporarily insert the driveshaft into the back of the transmission and rotate it to turn the input shaft as the transmission is carefully pushed toward the engine. Of course this second trick only works when the transmission is in gear.

29. Once the transmission is in place, install the transmission-to-engine bolts and nuts finger-tight.

30. Lift the transmission jack slightly to pivot the engine forward and remove the wooden block.

31. Install the engine rear mounting member, then tighten member retaining bolts 29–43 ft. lbs. (40–60 Nm).

32. Remove the transmission jack and install the left and/or right transmission-to-engine reinforcement bracket bolts, as applicable. Tighten the reinforcement bracket bolts to 44–51 ft. lbs. (60–70 Nm).

➡Some of the Geo factory manuals list a specification for the reinforcement bracket bolts of 51–72 ft. lbs. (70–100 Nm), but on 2 of our teardown vehicles the bolts began to strip before that specification was reached. Some of the Suzuki technical manuals don't mention these brackets, while others use a lower bolt torque. We recommend that the lower torque be used in order to prevent possible damage to the transmission case or the engine block. If you are at all unsure, use a thread locking compound such as Loctite® to be certain that these bolts won't loosen in service.

33. Position the center exhaust pipe using a new pipe-to-manifold gasket. Torque the mounting bolts, spring-loaded bolts and stud nuts all to 29–43 ft. lbs. (40–60 Nm).

34. Tighten the engine-to-transmission bolts and nuts to 51–72 ft. lbs. (70–100 Nm).

35. The balance of the installation procedure is the reverse of removal. If the transmission and/or transfer case was drained, or even if it wasn't but some fluid leaked during the procedure, be sure to check and fill the transmission when you are finished.

36. If the clutch was replaced, or if the adjuster was disturbed when removing the cable, check and adjust the clutch before attempting to drive the vehicle.

37. When you are finished, double check all wiring connections, wiring clamps, breather hoses, etc. to make sure everything is back the way you found it.

38. Connect the negative battery cable. Start the engine; check for any leaks and proper clutch operation.

CLUTCH

✳✳ CAUTION

The clutch driven disc may contain asbestos, which has been determined to be a cancer causing agent. Never clean clutch surfaces with compressed air! Avoid inhaling any dust from any clutch surface! When cleaning clutch surfaces, use a commercially available brake cleaning fluid.

Understanding the Clutch

▶ See Figure 45

The purpose of the clutch is to disconnect and connect engine power at the transmission. A vehicle at rest requires a lot of engine torque to get all that weight moving. An internal combustion engine does not develop a high starting torque (unlike steam engines) so it must be allowed to operate without any load until it builds up enough torque to move the vehicle. To a point, torque increases with engine rpm. The clutch allows the engine to build up torque by physically disconnecting the engine from the transmission, relieving the engine of any load or resistance.

The transfer of engine power to the transmission (the load) must be smooth and gradual; if it weren't, drive line components would wear out or break quickly. This gradual power transfer is made possible by gradually releasing the clutch pedal. The clutch disc and pressure plate are the connecting link between the engine and transmission. When the clutch pedal is released, the disc and plate contact each other (the clutch is engaged) physically joining the engine and transmission. When the pedal is pushed in, the disc and plate separate (the clutch is disengaged) disconnecting the engine from the transmission.

Most clutch assemblies consists of the flywheel, the clutch disc, the clutch pressure plate, the throwout bearing and fork, the actuating linkage and the pedal. The flywheel and clutch pressure plate (driving members)

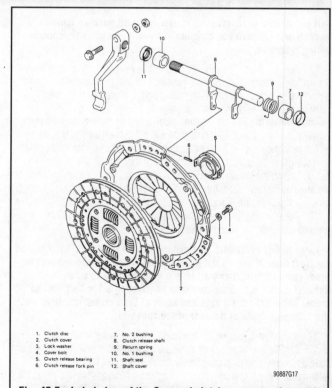

1. Clutch disc
2. Clutch cover
3. Lock washer
4. Cover bolt
5. Clutch release bearing
6. Clutch release fork pin
7. No. 2 bushing
8. Clutch release shaft
9. Return spring
10. No. 1 bushing
11. Shaft seal
12. Shaft cover

90887G17

Fig. 45 Exploded view of the Samurai clutch, pressure plate and throwout bearing assembly—Sidekick, Tracker, Sidekick Sport and X-90 are all almost identical

are connected to the engine crankshaft and rotate with it. The clutch disc is located between the flywheel and pressure plate, and is splined to the transmission shaft. A driving member is one that is attached to the engine and transfers engine power to a driven member (clutch disc) on the transmission shaft. A driving member (pressure plate) rotates (drives) a driven member (clutch disc) on contact and, in so doing, turns the transmission shaft.

There is a circular diaphragm spring within the pressure plate cover (transmission side). In a relaxed state (when the clutch pedal is fully released) this spring is convex; that is, it is dished outward toward the transmission. Pushing in the clutch pedal actuates the attached linkage. Connected to the other end of this is the throwout fork, which hold the throwout bearing. When the clutch pedal is depressed, the clutch linkage pushes the fork and bearing forward to contact the diaphragm spring of the pressure plate. The outer edges of the spring are secured to the pressure plate and are pivoted on rings so that when the center of the spring is compressed by the throwout bearing, the outer edges bow outward and, by so doing, pull the pressure plate in the same direction—away from the clutch disc. This action separates the disc from the plate, disengaging the clutch and allowing the transmission to be shifted into another gear. A coil type clutch return spring attached to the clutch pedal arm permits full release of the pedal. Releasing the pedal pulls the throwout bearing away from the diaphragm spring resulting in a reversal of spring position. As bearing pressure is gradually released from the spring center, the outer edges of the spring bow outward, pushing the pressure plate into closer contact with the clutch disc. As the disc and plate move closer together, friction between the two increases and slippage is reduced until, when full spring pressure is applied (by fully releasing the pedal) the speed of the disc and plate are the same. This stops all slipping, creating a direct connection between the plate and disc which results in the transfer of power from the engine to the transmission. The clutch disc is now rotating with the pressure plate at engine speed and, because it is splined to the transmission shaft, the shaft now turns at the same engine speed.

The clutch is operating properly if:

1. It will stall the engine when released with the vehicle held stationary.

2. The shift lever can be moved freely between 1st and reverse gears when the vehicle is stationary and the clutch disengaged.

Clutch Assembly

✳✳ CAUTION

The clutch driven disc may contain asbestos, which has been determined to be a cancer causing agent. Never clean clutch surfaces with compressed air! Avoid inhaling any dust from any clutch surface! When cleaning clutch surfaces, use a commercially available brake cleaning fluid.

REMOVAL & INSTALLATION

▶ See Figures 46 thru 58

1. Disconnect the negative battery cable for safety.
2. Remove the transmission from the vehicle.
3. Hold the flywheel from turning using a large prytool or a special flywheel holding tool which locks the flywheel teeth. With the flywheel held stationary, loosen and remove the pressure plate mounting bolts.

✳✳ WARNING

In case you plan on using the pressure plate again, be careful to loosen the bolts gradually, one turn at a time, in a star pattern. This gradual release of the pressure plate spring tension helps to prevent possible warping and damage to the plate and spring assembly.

Fig. 46 Remove the transmission assembly for access to the clutch disc and pressure plate

Fig. 47 Loosen the pressure plate bolts gradually, using several passes of a crisscross sequence . . .

Fig. 48 . . . then remove the pressure plate along with the clutch disc beneath it

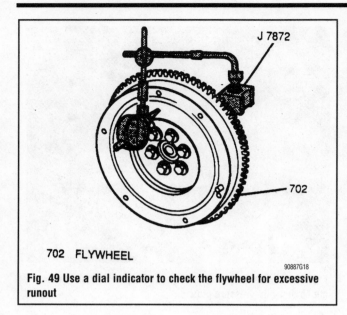

702 FLYWHEEL

90887G18

Fig. 49 Use a dial indicator to check the flywheel for excessive runout

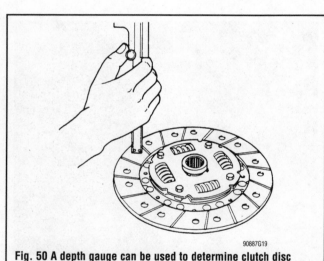

90887G19

Fig. 50 A depth gauge can be used to determine clutch disc wear—measure the depth of the rivet head below the friction surface

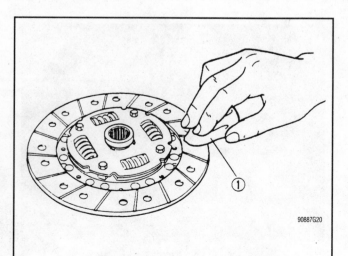

90887G20

Fig. 51 A light glaze can be broken using 120-200 grit sandpaper (1)

90887P30

Fig. 52 Remove the throwout bearing for cleaning and inspection—but DO NOT submerge a sealed bearing in solvent

4. Remove the pressure plate and the clutch disc from the flywheel.

5. Inspect the flywheel for wear and/or scoring and machine or replace, as necessary. Check the flywheel for excessive runout using a dial indicator; if runout exceeds 0.0078 in. (0.2mm) the flywheel should be machined or replaced.

6. Inspect the clutch disc and pressure plate for wear or damage. Check the depth of the rivet heads on the clutch disc. Standard depth is 0.05 in (1.2mm) for the Samurai or 0.06 in. (1.6mm) for other models. The wear limit is 0.02 in. (0.5mm) for all models. Any clutch disc showing wear equal to or greater than the wear limit should be replaced.

7. Check the clutch disc, pressure plate and flywheel for light burnt or glazed surfaces. A glazed component will have a glass-like surface. If found, break the glass-like finish of light glazing using 120-200 grit sandpaper.

8. Clean and inspect the clutch release bearing and the input shaft. Many of the late-model trucks covered by this manual utilize a sealed release bearing. DO NOT submerge a sealed bearing in or soak it with solvent.

➡**The clutch release bearing is a relatively inexpensive part, that performs a very important function. ALWAYS replace the bearing when a new disc and pressure plate is installed. For that matter, it is not a bad idea to replace it even when other components are being reused.**

9. Make sure that the pressure plate retaining bolts and the bolt holes in the flywheel are clean and free of grease or oil to assure proper fastening during installation.

To install:

10. Apply a high temperature lithium grease to the thrust surfaces on the throwout bearing and input shaft. Be careful not to apply too much grease which could come off and contaminate the surfaces of the clutch disc.

11. Make sure the clutch disc, pressure plate and flywheel surfaces are clean and free of all grease, oil or other possible contaminants.

12. Using a clutch alignment arbor (preferably the exact one with the proper sized pilot and proper splines), position and hold the clutch disc against the flywheel.

➡**There are several inexpensive clutch alignment tools on the market. One company even makes small plastic replicas of the input shaft. These plastic alignment tools are well designed and work perfectly for most applications.**

13. Install the pressure plate over the disc, flywheel and alignment arbor assembly, then carefully finger-tighten the bolts.

14. Check to make sure that the clutch disc is properly aligned to the pressure plate and flywheel. To do this, first look down the length of the alignment arbor and make sure it seems perfectly straight. Next, grasp the end of the arbor and withdraw it gently (note the pressure plate bolts must

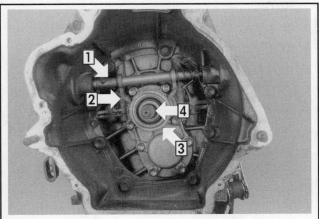

1. Throwout pivot
2. Throwout arm
3. Throwout bearing
4. Input shaft

90887P31

Fig. 53 Clean the components in the bell housing to determine if any require replacement and to prepare them for fresh grease

1. Bearing retaining pin
2. Bearing case slot

90887P32

Fig. 56 When installing the throwout bearing, be sure to locate the retaining pin on the throwout arm within the slot on the bearing case

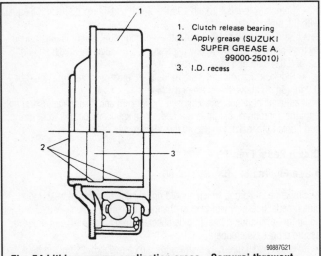

1. Clutch release bearing
2. Apply grease (SUZUKI SUPER GREASE A, 99000-25010)
3. I.D. recess

90887G21

Fig. 54 Lithium grease application areas—Samurai throwout bearing

90887P33

Fig. 57 Position the clutch disc to the flywheel using a clutch alignment tool . . .

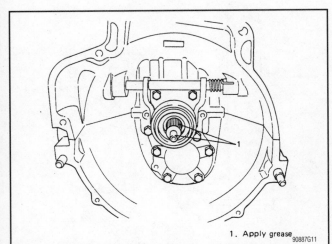

1. Apply grease

90887G11

Fig. 55 Be sure to coat all thrust surfaces of the throwout bearing and input shaft with a light application of high temperature lithium grease

90887P34

Fig. 58 . . . then place the pressure plate assembly over top and secure using the retaining bolts once both components are centered

have been tightened sufficiently to hold the clutch plate at this stage or it will fall out of alignment the second that the arbor is removed). If the clutch disc is properly aligned, the arbor will slide smoothly out from the flywheel pilot and the clutch splines. The arbor should also insert back into both without any hesitation.

15. Once you are satisfied that the disc is properly aligned, tighten the pressure plate bolts and evenly using multiple passes of a star pattern until all are tightened to 159–248 inch lbs. (18–28 Nm).

16. Remove the clutch disc alignment tool.

17. Install the transmission.

18. Check and adjust the clutch, as necessary.

19. Connect the negative battery cable.

ADJUSTMENTS

Clutch Pedal Height

▶ See Figures 59, 60 and 61

The clutch pedal height should not be a periodic adjustment, but may be checked from time-to-time. More importantly, it should be checked after components of the mechanical clutch system have been replaced.

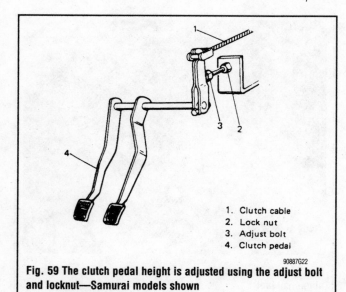

1. Clutch cable
2. Lock nut
3. Adjust bolt
4. Clutch pedal

90887G22

Fig. 59 The clutch pedal height is adjusted using the adjust bolt and locknut—Samurai models shown

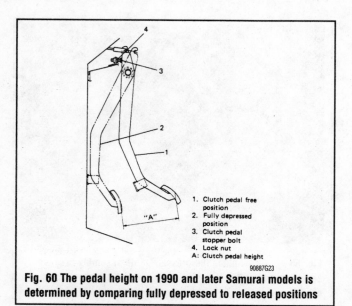

1. Clutch pedal free position
2. Fully depressed position
3. Clutch pedal stopper bolt
4. Lock nut
A: Clutch pedal height

90887G23

Fig. 60 The pedal height on 1990 and later Samurai models is determined by comparing fully depressed to released positions

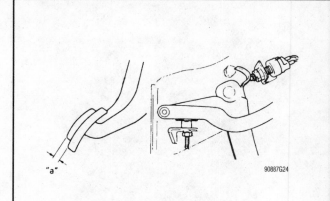

90887G24

Fig. 61 On Sidekick, Tracker and X-90 models the clutch pedal height should be 0.2 in. (5mm) above the brake pedal height (measured as dimension "a")

The proper height varies slightly from model-to-model:

• Samurai Models through 1989—clutch pedal height should be equal with the brake pedal

• Samurai Models 1990 and later—clutch pedal height is determined by total pedal travel. From fully depressed-to-released the pedal should travel 5.83–6.06 in. (148–154 mm).

• Sidekick, Tracker and X-90 models—clutch pedal height should be 0.2 in. (5mm) above the brake pedal height.

If adjustment is necessary, loosen the locknut and turn the adjusting bolt until the appropriate height is reached. Once set, keep the bolt from turning and tighten the locknut to secure the adjustment.

Clutch Pedal Free-Play

▶ See Figures 62, 63, 64 and 65

Unlike pedal height, which should not change because of wear, the clutch pedal free-play will tend to change as the clutch disc wears. The pedal free-play should therefore be checked from time-to-time in order to assure proper clutch operation.

To check pedal free-play depress the clutch pedal, but stop and hold the moment that clutch resistance is felt. Measure the distance that the pedal traveled from the point it was released to the point where resistance was first felt. The resulting measurement is free-play.

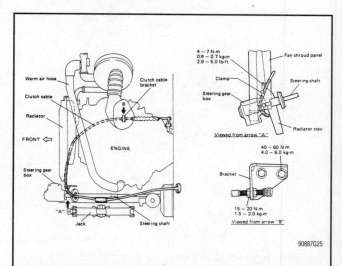

90887G25

Fig. 62 Clutch cable routing—Samurai shown, other models are similar

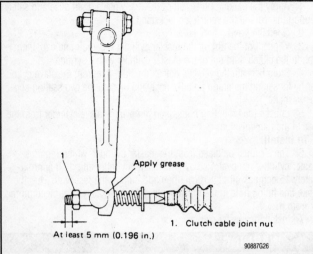

Fig. 63 On the Samurai, clutch pedal free-play is adjusted at the cable joint nut

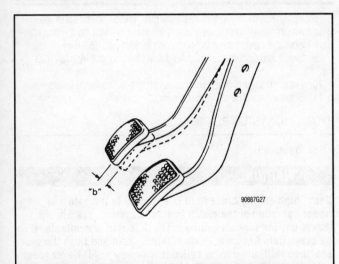

Fig. 64 Clutch pedal free-play is the distance the pedal moves before resistance is felt (dimension "b")

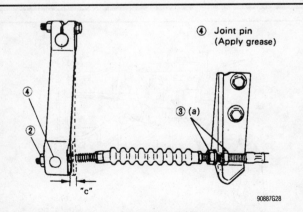

Fig. 65 For the Sidekick, Tracker and X-90, pedal free-play is adjusted at the joint nut (2), while keeping the outer cable nuts (3) tightened around the center cable thread portion—when finished the release arm free travel ("c") should be 0.02–0.06 in. (0.5–1.5mm).

Proper clutch free-play should be:
- Samurai Models—0.8–1.2 in. (20–30mm).
- Sidekick, Tracker and X-90 Models—0.6–1.1 in. (15–25mm).

1. If the free-play must be adjusted on Samurai models, turn the clutch cable outer nut until the proper measurement is obtained at the pedal. Once adjustment is completed, measure the amount of clutch cable that protrudes past the joint nut, it must be at least 0.196 in. (5mm).

2. If the free-play must be adjusted on Sidekick, Tracker or X-90 models, turn the joint nut (2) located at the transmission end of the clutch cable in or out, as necessary to achieve the proper play. But, make sure that the outer cable nuts (3) are tightened around the center of the outer cable thread portion. Once the correct pedal free-play is obtained, check the free-play on the release arm itself (c), it should be 0.02–0.06 in. (0.5–1.5mm).

3. On all models, once you are finished, check pedal adjustment and clutch function with the engine running.

Clutch Master Cylinder

▶ **See Figure 66**

➡ **Only the Sidekick Sport utilizes a hydraulic clutch actuation system.**

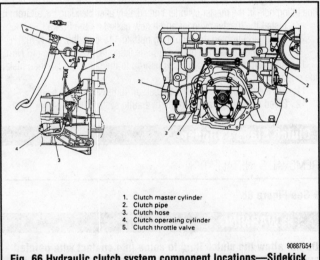

1. Clutch master cylinder
2. Clutch pipe
3. Clutch hose
4. Clutch operating cylinder
5. Clutch throttle valve

Fig. 66 Hydraulic clutch system component locations—Sidekick Sport models only

REMOVAL & INSTALLATION

▶ **See Figure 67**

1. Open the hood.
2. Wipe all of the dirt off the master cylinder reservoir and cap, then siphon the clutch fluid out of the master cylinder with a syringe.
3. From inside the vehicle, remove the pushrod clevis pin, connecting the master cylinder pushrod to the clutch pedal.
4. Loosen the clutch fluid line fitting, then detach the line from the master cylinder.

✳✳ WARNING

Do not allow the clutch fluid to come into contact with painted surfaces; if it does, wash the fluid off immediately.

5. Loosen the mounting nuts, then remove the master cylinder and gasket from the firewall.

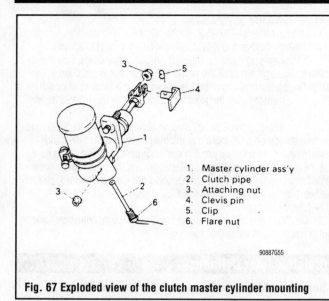

Fig. 67 Exploded view of the clutch master cylinder mounting

1. Master cylinder ass'y
2. Clutch pipe
3. Attaching nut
4. Clevis pin
5. Clip
6. Flare nut

90887G55

To install:

6. To bleed air from the master cylinder, tilt the master cylinder approximately 15 degrees off of vertical, then add fluid to the reservoir. Plug the brake line fitting hole in the master cylinder immediately after bleeding the air from it.

7. Install the master cylinder and a new gasket on the firewall.

8. Install and tighten the mounting nuts to 115 inch lbs. (13 Nm).

9. Install and tighten the brake fluid line fitting to 142 inch lbs. (16 Nm).

10. Reattach the master cylinder pushrod to the clutch pedal, then install the pushrod clevis pin.

11. Fill the master cylinder fluid reservoir to the maximum level.

12. Bleed all residual air from the hydraulic system.

Clutch Slave Cylinder

REMOVAL & INSTALLATION

♦ See Figure 68

❋❋ WARNING

Do not allow the clutch fluid to come into contact with painted surfaces; if it does, wash the fluid off immediately.

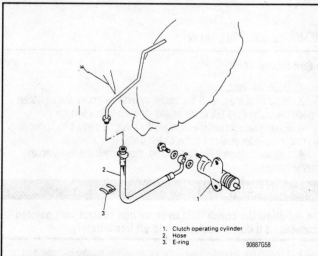

1. Clutch operating cylinder
2. Hose
3. E-ring

90887G58

Fig. 68 Exploded view of the slave cylinder mounting—only the Sidekick Sport uses a hydraulic clutch actuation system

1. Apply the parking brake, block the rear wheels, then raise and safely support the front of the vehicle on jackstands.

2. Open the hood.

3. Wipe all of the dirt off the master cylinder reservoir and cap, then siphon the clutch fluid out of the master cylinder with a syringe.

4. From beneath the vehicle, detach the fluid line from the slave cylinder by loosening the union bolt. Remove and discard the two sealing copper washers.

5. Loosen the mounting bolts, then remove the slave cylinder from the side of the transmission.

To install:

6. The air must be bleed from the master cylinder, which requires master cylinder removal. Remove the master cylinder and tilt it approximately 15 degrees off of vertical, then add fluid to the reservoir. Plug the brake line fitting hole in the master cylinder immediately after bleeding the air from it.

7. Install the master cylinder.

❋❋ WARNING

Do not allow any grease to get on the slave cylinder rubber boot.

8. Apply a small amount of multi-purpose grease on the tip of the slave cylinder actuating rod, then install the slave cylinder on the transmission. Install and tighten the mounting bolts to 36 ft. lbs. (50 Nm).

9. Install and tighten the brake fluid line fitting to 203 inch lbs. (23 Nm).

10. Fill the master cylinder fluid reservoir to the maximum level.

11. Bleed all residual air from the hydraulic system.

HYDRAULIC SYSTEM BLEEDING

♦ See Figure 69

❋❋ WARNING

Clean, high quality brake fluid is essential to the safe and proper operation of the clutch hydraulic system. You should always buy the highest quality brake fluid that is available. If the brake fluid becomes contaminated, drain and flush the system, then refill the master cylinder with new fluid. Never reuse any brake fluid. Any brake fluid that is removed from the system should be discarded. Also, do not allow any brake fluid to come in contact with a painted surface; it will damage the paint.

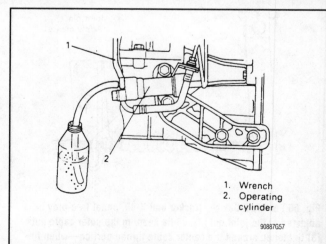

1. Wrench
2. Operating cylinder

90887G57

Fig. 69 The hydraulic clutch system bleeder valve is located on the slave cylinder—use a clear plastic hose and container when bleeding the system

✳✳ CAUTION

Brake fluid contains polyglycol ethers and polyglycols. Avoid contact with the eyes and wash your hands thoroughly after handling brake fluid. If you do get brake fluid in your eyes, flush your eyes with clean, running water for 15 minutes. If eye irritation persists, or if you have taken brake fluid internally, IMMEDIATELY seek medical assistance.

The clutch system bleeder valve is located on the slave cylinder.

1. Apply the parking brake, block the rear wheels, then raise and safely support the front of the vehicle on jackstands.

2. Fill the master cylinder reservoir to the MAX line with clean brake fluid and keep it at least half full throughout the bleeding procedure.

3. From beneath the vehicle, remove the bleeder plug cap, then attach a clear vinyl tube to the slave cylinder bleeder plug. Insert the open end of the hose into a container.

4. Have an assistant depress the clutch pedal, and while your helper holds the pedal in the depressed position, loosen the bleeder plug one-third to one-half of a turn (or until brake fluid starts to exit the bleeder valve).

5. When the fluid pressure is almost gone, retighten the bleeder plug, THEN have your assistant release the clutch pedal. It is very important that the pedal stay depressed while the bleeder valve is open, because air will be sucked into the clutch system if the pedal is released while the valve is still open.

6. If the fluid is level in the master cylinder is low, fill it with clean DOT 3 fluid.

7. Repeat Steps 3 through 5 until all air bubbles are gone from the hydraulic fluid, which is emitted from the bleeder valve.

8. If equipped, install the bleeder plug cap.

9. After completing the bleeding procedure, have your assistant apply fluid pressure to the pipe line (by depressing the clutch pedal) while you check for fluid leaks.

10. Fill the clutch master cylinder fluid reservoir to the specified full level.

11. Check clutch pedal for a spongy feeling; if any sponginess exists, repeat the entire procedure.

AUTOMATIC TRANSMISSION

Understanding Automatic Transmissions

The automatic transmission allows engine torque and power to be transmitted to the rear wheels within a narrow range of engine operating speeds. It will allow the engine to turn fast enough to produce plenty of power and torque at very low speeds, while keeping it at a sensible rpm at high vehicle speeds (and it does this job without driver assistance). The transmission uses a light fluid as the medium for the transmission of power. This fluid also works in the operation of various hydraulic control circuits and as a lubricant. Because the transmission fluid performs all of these functions, trouble within the unit can easily travel from one part to another. For this reason, and because of the complexity and unusual operating principles of the transmission, a very sound understanding of the basic principles of operation will simplify troubleshooting.

TORQUE CONVERTER

▶ **See Figure 70**

The torque converter replaces the conventional clutch. It has three functions:

1. It allows the engine to idle with the vehicle at a standstill, even with the transmission in gear.

2. It allows the transmission to shift from range-to-range smoothly, without requiring that the driver close the throttle during the shift.

3. It multiplies engine torque to an increasing extent as vehicle speed drops and throttle opening is increased. This has the effect of making the transmission more responsive and reduces the amount of shifting required.

The torque converter is a metal case which is shaped like a sphere that has been flattened on opposite sides. It is bolted to the rear end of the engine's crankshaft. Generally, the entire metal case rotates at engine speed and serves as the engine's flywheel.

The case contains three sets of blades. One set is attached directly to the case. This set forms the torus or pump. Another set is directly connected to the output shaft, and forms the turbine. The third set is mounted on a hub which, in turn, is mounted on a stationary shaft through a one-way clutch. This third set is known as the stator.

A pump, which is driven by the converter hub at engine speed, keeps the torque converter full of transmission fluid at all times. Fluid flows continuously through the unit to provide cooling.

Under low speed acceleration, the torque converter functions as follows:

The torus is turning faster than the turbine. It picks up fluid at the center of the converter and, through centrifugal force, slings it outward. Since the outer edge of the converter moves faster than the portions at the center, the fluid picks up speed.

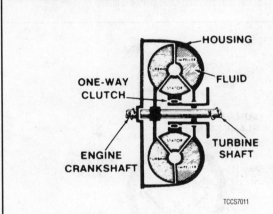

Fig. 70 The torque converter housing is rotated by the engine's crankshaft, and turns the impeller—The impeller then spins the turbine, which gives motion to the turbine shaft, driving the gears

The fluid then enters the outer edge of the turbine blades. It then travels back toward the center of the converter case along the turbine blades. In impinging upon the turbine blades, the fluid loses the energy picked up in the torus.

If the fluid was now returned directly into the torus, both halves of the converter would have to turn at approximately the same speed at all times, and torque input and output would both be the same.

In flowing through the torus and turbine, the fluid picks up two types of flow, or flow in two separate directions. It flows through the turbine blades, and it spins with the engine. The stator, whose blades are stationary when the vehicle is being accelerated at low speeds, converts one type of flow into another. Instead of allowing the fluid to flow straight back into the torus, the stator's curved blades turn the fluid almost 90° toward the direction of rotation of the engine. Thus the fluid does not flow as fast toward the torus, but is already spinning when the torus picks it up. This has the effect of allowing the torus to turn much faster than the turbine. This difference in speed may be compared to the difference in speed between the smaller and larger gears in any gear train. The result is that engine power output is higher, and engine torque is multiplied.

As the speed of the turbine increases, the fluid spins faster and faster in the direction of engine rotation. As a result, the ability of the stator to redirect the fluid flow is reduced. Under cruising conditions, the stator is eventually forced to rotate on its one-way clutch in the direction of engine rotation. Under these conditions, the torque converter begins to behave almost like a solid shaft, with the torus and turbine speeds being almost equal.

PLANETARY GEARBOX

♦ **See Figures 71, 72 and 73**

The ability of the torque converter to multiply engine torque is limited. Also, the unit tends to be more efficient when the turbine is rotating at relatively high speeds. Therefore, a planetary gearbox is used to carry the power output of the turbine to the driveshaft.

Planetary gears function very similarly to conventional transmission gears. However, their construction is different in that three elements make up one gear system, and, in that all three elements are different from one another. The three elements are: an outer gear that is shaped like a hoop, with teeth cut into the inner surface; a sun gear, mounted on a shaft and located at the very center of the outer gear; and a set of three planet gears, held by pins in a ring-like planet carrier, meshing with both the sun gear and the outer gear. Either the outer gear or the sun gear may be held stationary, providing more than one possible torque multiplication factor for each set of gears. Also, if all three gears are forced to rotate at the same speed, the gearset forms, in effect, a solid shaft.

Most automatics use the planetary gears to provide various reductions ratios. Bands and clutches are used to hold various portions of the gearsets to the transmission case or to the shaft on which they are mounted. Shifting is accomplished, then, by changing the portion of each planetary gearset which is held to the transmission case or to the shaft.

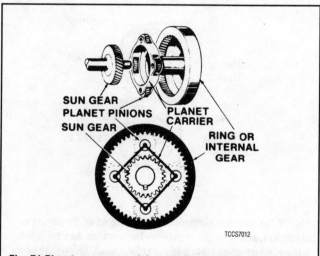

Fig. 71 Planetary gears work in a similar fashion to manual transmission gears, but are composed of three parts

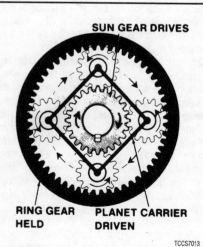

Fig. 72 Planetary gears in the maximum reduction (low) range. The ring gear is held and a lower gear ratio is obtained

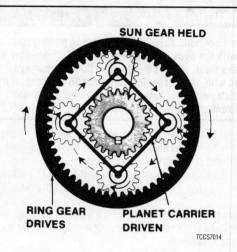

Fig. 73 Planetary gears in the minimum reduction (drive) range. The ring gear is allowed to revolve, providing a higher gear ratio

SERVOS & ACCUMULATORS

♦ **See Figure 74**

The servos are hydraulic pistons and cylinders. They resemble the hydraulic actuators used on many other machines, such as bulldozers. Hydraulic fluid enters the cylinder, under pressure, and forces the piston to move to engage the band or clutches.

The accumulators are used to cushion the engagement of the servos. The transmission fluid must pass through the accumulator on the way to the servo. The accumulator housing contains a thin piston which is sprung away from the discharge passage of the accumulator. When fluid passes through the accumulator on the way to the servo, it must move the piston against spring pressure, and this action smoothes out the action of the servo.

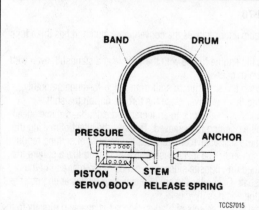

Fig. 74 Servos, operated by pressure, are used to apply or release the bands, to either hold the ring gear or allow it to rotate

HYDRAULIC CONTROL SYSTEM

The hydraulic pressure used to operate the servos comes from the main transmission oil pump. This fluid is channeled to the various servos through the shift valves. There is generally a manual shift valve which is operated by the transmission selector lever and an automatic shift valve for each automatic upshift the transmission provides.

➡Many new transmissions are electronically controlled. On these models, electrical solenoids are used to better control the hydraulic fluid. Usually, the solenoids are regulated by an electronic control module.

There are two pressures which affect the operation of these valves. One is the governor pressure which is effected by vehicle speed. The other is the modulator pressure which is effected by intake manifold vacuum or throttle position. Governor pressure rises with an increase in vehicle speed, and modulator pressure rises as the throttle is opened wider. By responding to these two pressures, the shift valves cause the upshift points to be delayed with increased throttle opening to make the best use of the engine's power output.

Most transmissions also make use of an auxiliary circuit for downshifting. This circuit may be actuated by the throttle linkage the vacuum line which actuates the modulator, by a cable or by a solenoid. It applies pressure to a special downshift surface on the shift valve or valves.

The transmission modulator also governs the line pressure, used to actuate the servos. In this way, the clutches and bands will be actuated with a force matching the torque output of the engine.

Neutral Safety (Selector/Reverse Light) Switch

REMOVAL, INSTALLATION & ADJUSTMENT

◆ **See Figures 75, 76 and 77**

The neutral safety and reverse light switch is mounted on and actuated by the transmission select shaft which protrudes from the side of the transmission housing. It is located directly underneath the select lever and select cable assembly which is used to control the select shaft from the linkage in the passenger compartment.

The shifter select cable is attached at one end to the shift linkage by an e-ring and a cable end clip (though the center console must be removed and the manual shift linkage assembly must be unbolted and repositioned for access). But, the other end of the cable is attached to the transmission manual select lever with a threaded end that may require adjustment if any of the mechanical components in the linkage are replaced or if the lock and adjusting nuts are ever disturbed. Be careful not to touch the nuts on the select cable or it will require adjustment after the switch is replaced. If the cable is ever replaced, or the nuts are turned, then simply adjust the cable so that there is little or no play when both the manual select lever (on the transmission) and the gear select lever (on the floor the passenger compartment) are both in neutral.

1. On 4WD vehicles, make sure the transfer case is in the 2WD position.
2. Place the transmission in Neutral **(N)** using the gear select lever in the passenger compartment.
3. Raise support the rear of the vehicle safely using jackstands. Block the wheels to prevent the vehicle from moving.

➡Although you will be able to access the switch fine whether the front of the rear of the vehicle is raised, we recommend raising the rear in case you need to spin the rear driveshaft to check if the transmission is in gear or not.

4. Disconnect the wiring from the neutral safety switch (4-speed models) or from the harness connector(s) located under the intake manifold (3-speed models), as applicable.
5. Remove the nut, washer and manual shift lever from the manual shift shaft on the side of the transmission housing.
6. For the 4-speed transmission, unstake the lock plate behind the manual shaft nut, then loosen the nut and remove the lock plate from the switch.
7. Remove the 1 retaining bolt and slide the neutral switch from the shift shaft.

To install:

8. If the transmission shaft was rotated, set it back into neutral. To do this, turn the select lever as far clockwise (downward) as possible. Then rotate the selector counterclockwise 3 notches and verify that the rear driveshaft will spin freely.

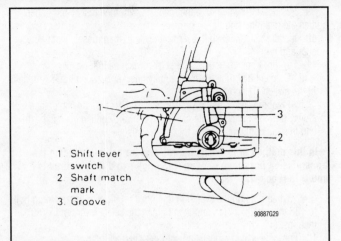

1. Shift lever switch
2. Shaft match mark
3. Groove

90887G29

Fig. 75 The neutral safety position (shift lever) switch is mounted to the side of the transmission assembly—4-speed models shown

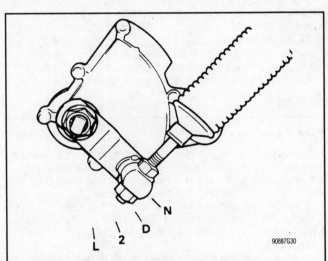

90887G30

Fig. 76 Before tightening the fasteners, make sure the switch and selector lever are both in Neutral

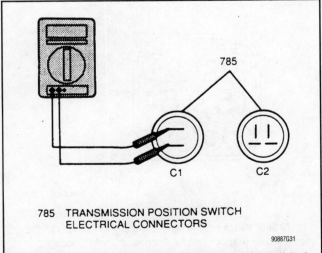

785 TRANSMISSION POSITION SWITCH ELECTRICAL CONNECTORS

90887G31

Fig. 77 On 3-speed models, switch adjustment is accomplished by checking continuity across the 2 terminals of connector C1

9. Position the switch onto the manual shaft, then install and finger-tighten the retaining bolt.

10. Install the manual shift lever on the shaft, then loosely install the washer and nut.

11. For the 3-speed models, adjust the switch as follows:

a. Connect a ohmmeter or continuity checker between the 2 terminals of the switch C1 connector.

b. Pivot the switch as far clockwise (downward) as possible, then slowly turn the switch counterclockwise (upward) until a click is heard and there is continuity across the 2 terminals.

→In this method of locating neutral you are actually placing the transmission in L, then moving it through two different detents 2 and D to reach N.

c. While holding the switch in this position, tighten the retaining bolt to 186 inch lbs. (21 Nm) and then tighten the select lever nut to 169 inch lbs. (19 Nm).

12. For the 4-speed models, adjust the switch as follows:

a. Verify that the transmission is in neutral by turning the drive-shaft.

b. Tighten the shift selector lever nut to 44 inch lbs. (5 Nm), then bend the claws of the lock washer over the nut.

c. Make sure the neutral reference line and the cut-out in the neutral safety switch are both aligned, then while holding the switch in this position, tighten the retaining bolt to 115 inch lbs. (13 Nm)

13. Engage the wiring harness connector to the switch (4-speed) or to the harness located under the intake manifold (3-speed), as applicable.

14. Remove the jackstands and carefully lower the vehicle.

15. Make sure that the transmission operates properly in all positions.

INSPECTION

♦ See Figures 78, 79, 80 and 81

The neutral safety switch is designed to keep the engine from starting in any gear, only allowing the starter to operate in Park **(P)** or Neutral **(N)**. The switch also functions as the reverse light switch, but should ONLY turn these lights on in Reverse **(R)**. To verify proper switch operation:

1. Firmly apply the parking brake and block the drive wheels.

2. Place the gear selector lever in **P**, then turn the ignition switch to **START** and verify that the starter motor operates. Quickly turn the ignition switch to **OFF**.

3. Return the ignition switch to **ON** (with the engine NOT RUNNING) and place the gear selector lever in **R**, then check to make sure the reverse lights are on.

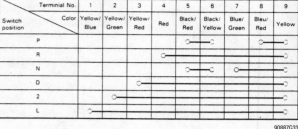

Terminal No.	1	2	3	4	5	6	7	8	9
Switch position \ Color	Yellow/Blue	Yellow/Green	Yellow/Red	Red	Black/Red	Black/Yellow	Blue/Green	Bleu/Red	Yellow
P					O——O				O
R				O					O
N					O——O	O——O			O
D			O						O
2		O							O
L	O								O

90887G33

Fig. 79 Use this chart to check continuity across the shift switch coupler terminals in various gear positions—early-model 4-door Sidekick (except Sport) and Tracker

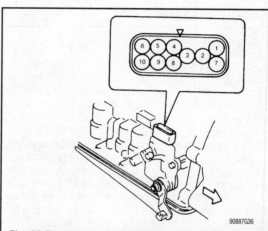

90887G36

Fig. 80 For the late-model Sidekicks, Trackers and the Sidekick Sport, the switch connector is mounted directly to the top of the selector switch and the terminals are arranged differently than on the early-model 4-door Sidekick or Tracker

1. Shift switch coupler

90887G32

Fig. 78 Shift switch coupler terminal identification for early-model 4-door Sidekick (except Sport) and Tracker models equipped with 4-speed transmissions—the switch condition can be checked using the shift switch coupler

Terminal No. \ Switch position	5	4	9	8	2	3	10	7	6
P					O——O	O——O	O		
R					O————————				O
N					O——O	O————	O		O
D				O————————					O
2		O————————							O
L	O————————								O

90887G37

Fig. 81 Use this chart to check continuity across the shift switch coupler terminals in various gear positions—late-model Sidekick, Tracker and Sidekick Sport models

4. Place the gear selector lever in **N**, then turn the ignition switch to **START** and verify that the starter motor operates. Quickly turn the ignition switch to **OFF**.

5. FIRMLY apply pressure to the brake pedal and hold, then check each of the remaining gear selector positions and verify that the starter does NOT try to operate in any other position than **P** or **N**.

6. If any of the previous conditions are not met the switch should be adjusted.

7. On 4-speed models, if faulty operation cannot be corrected by adjustment, a test may be conducted to determine switch condition. To do so, disengage the wiring connector from the shift switch coupler and check continuity across the various terminals as shown in the accompanying chart. For instance, continuity should exist between terminals 5 and 6, as-well-as between 8 and 9 when the selector lever is in **P**.

➡️**The 4-speed shift switch coupler is usually found above the transmission housing in the transmission tunnel. Although access to it may be possible from the passenger compartment on most early 4-door models (if you remove the selector lever), it is probably easier in most cases to get at it from under the truck. To do this, trace the wires back from the switch at the side of the transmission until you can disengage the connector from the vehicle harness. For late-model Sidekicks and Trackers, along with the Sidekick Sport, the wiring connector is mounted directly on top of the switch.**

8. If the switch does not pass these tests and cannot be adjusted, it must be replaced for safety reasons.

Vacuum Modulator

The vacuum modulator is used to sense any changes in torque input to the transmission. It then transmits this signal to the pressure regulator which controls line pressure so that all transmission torque requirements are properly met. This helps to keep shifts smooth at all throttle openings.

REMOVAL & INSTALLATION

▶ **See Figure 82**

1. Raise and support the vehicle safely using jackstands.
2. Disconnect the vacuum pipe from the transmission.
3. Check to see if the driveshaft will interfere with access to the modulator assembly. If so, matchmark and unbolt the shaft from the flange, then reposition and support it aside.

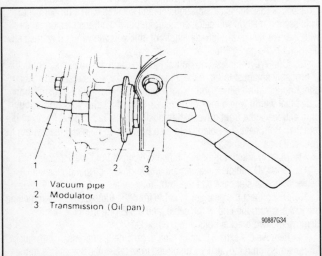

1 Vacuum pipe
2 Modulator
3 Transmission (Oil pan)

90887G34

Fig. 82 The vacuum modulator must be removed using a special flat wrench

4. Use a large-mouthed, but flat-bladed wrench to loosen and remove the vacuum modulator. A special tool No. J-23100 is made for this purpose.

5. Test the modulator for wear or damage and replace, if necessary.

To install:

6. If the old modulator is being reused, be sure to obtain a NEW O-ring and modulator plunger.

7. Install the modulator, being careful not to overtighten it.

8. Connect the vacuum pipe.

9. Remove the jackstands and carefully lower the vehicle.

10. Check the transmission fluid and add, as necessary.

TESTING

▶ **See Figure 83**

A faulty modulator could cause one or more of the following symptoms:
- Harsh shifting (up and/or down)
- Delayed upshifting
- Soft shifting (up and/or down)
- Slips in **L, D** or **R**
- Transmission overheating
- Engine burning of transmission fluid (through the vacuum line)

1. Remove the modulator from the transmission.

2. Turn the modulator so that the vacuum line stem faces straight downward. If transmission fluid comes out of the modulator stem then the vacuum diaphragm is bad and the unit must be replaced.

➡️**Keep in mind that gasoline and/or water vapor may settle in the vacuum side of the modulator and this is OK, unless the vehicle may be exposed to temperatures below 10°F (−12°C), then the modulator must be replaced to prevent operational problems.**

3. Use a hand-held vacuum pump to check movement of the vacuum plunger. Connect the pump to the vacuum stem and apply 20 in. Hg (500mm Hg) while watching the plunger.

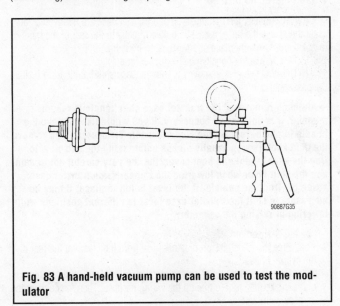

90887G35

Fig. 83 A hand-held vacuum pump can be used to test the modulator

Extension Housing Seal

REMOVAL & INSTALLATION

▶ **See Figure 84**

The extension housing oil seal for automatic transmission vehicles is replaced in the same manner as that on manual transmissions. For details, please refer to that procedure found earlier in this section.

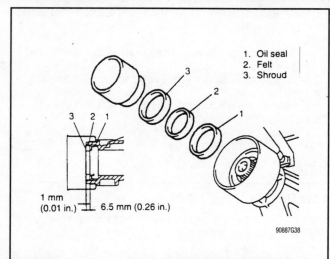

1. Oil seal
2. Felt
3. Shroud

1 mm (0.01 in.)   6.5 mm (0.26 in.)

90887G38

Fig. 84 Exploded view of the oil seal, felt and shroud used on some late-model 4-speeds such as the Sidekick Sport

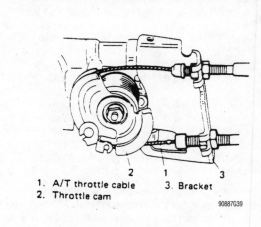

1. A/T throttle cable
2. Throttle cam
3. Bracket

90887G39

Fig. 85 Before removing the transmission, disconnect the throttle cable from the throttle cam and bracket

➡️**A few of the automatic transmissions covered by this manual (such as the one found on the late-model Sidekick Sport) may utilize a felt and shroud assembly along with the oil seal. On these models, make sure that all 3 components are removed and replaced.**

Automatic Transmission Assembly

REMOVAL & INSTALLATION

♦ **See Figures 85 thru 90**

On 4WD models, the transmission and transfer case are removed as an assembly, since the transfer case is bolted directly to the rear of the transmission and takes the place of an extension housing.
1. Disconnect the negative battery cable for safety.
2. On 4WD vehicles, remove the transfer case shift handle from inside the passenger compartment.

➡️**Although removal of the transfer case shift handle is recommended, it is not always necessary. If you would like to leave the handle in place, remove the center console for access, then remove the shift knob (which usually means unthreading the setscrew to free the knob), boot and boot cover. But, be very careful not to damage the shift lever when lowering the transmission/transfer case assembly from the vehicle. If the lever is left in place, it may be necessary to shift the transfer case lever to different positions while lowering or raising the assembly.**

3. For 3-speed models:
   a. Free the transmission breather hose from the clamp at the rear of the cylinder head.
   b. Bend back the rubber-coated metal clamp usually found at the rear of the intake manifold to free up the wiring harness. Then, disconnect the harness couplers.
   c. Disconnect the kick-down cable at the throttle body.
   d. Remove the vacuum modulator hose at the intake manifold.
4. For 4-speed models:
   a. Remove the battery, dipstick and oil filler tube.
   b. Disconnect the throttle cable from the throttle cam and bracket.
   c. Tag and disconnect the wiring harness couplers.
5. Remove the starter mounting bolts, leaving the starter wiring connected, then secure the starter in position or slightly out of the way so the wiring will not be damaged.
6. Remove the 2 upper transmission-to-engine mounting bolts. This is

a tight spot. You will either need a large breaker bar with a very short socket or a large combination wrench with a slight offset to really get at the bolt on the driver's side of the vehicle.

➡️**On some of the models covered by this manual (including all 4-speed transmissions) the right side upper transmission-to-engine bolt is longer. This may make the bolt somewhat more difficult to remove, and be sure not to mix it up with the shorter bolt on the opposite side come installation time.**

7. Raise and support the vehicle safely at a height which will be convenient to work from both above and below the vehicle.

➡️**Later in this procedure, the exhaust center pipe must be removed for clearance. If you do not have air tools (which make exhaust fastener removal MUCH easier) take a moment now to spray the exhaust center pipe fasteners with penetrating oil to help loosen them. Spray both the 3 nuts and studs at the exhaust manifold and the 2 through-bolts at the rear of the converter.**

8. If equipped, remove the front skid plate for better access.
9. On 2WD vehicles, either drain the oil from the transmission case or have a transmission case plug handy for the extension housing (some aftermarket tool companies like Lisle® make plastic transmission plugs for just this purpose. If a plug is not available, a large plastic bag can be stretched across the extension housing and secured with a rubber band. This second method will catch some fluid, but if the transmission is left with the rear downward for any length of time you will wind up with smelly gear oil on the garage floor or in the driveway.
10. On 4WD vehicles, you do not have to drain the transmission, but it is probably smartest to drain the transfer case. If you are really adamant about not draining either, you've got 2 options. Either buy 2 transmission plugs that will fit where the front and rear driveshaft slip-yokes go or buy 1 plug and leave the front driveshaft in position, just unbolted at the front differential. Both have the potential to be a pain and to be really messy, but it's your call.
11. Matchmark and remove the rear driveshaft from the vehicle.
12. On 4WD vehicles, matchmark and remove the front driveshaft between the transfer case and the front differential.
13. Disconnect the gear select cable from the transmission by removing the locknut from the end of the cable, and the E-ring from the bracket. Remove the two bracket bolts and the bracket.
14. Remove the exhaust center pipe to provide the necessary clearance for transmission removal. This pipe runs from the exhaust manifold to the flange at the front of the muffler pipe. On most late-model vehicles it is a 2 piece unit, one from the manifold to a flange at the front of the converter, and

the second which contains the converter and bolts to the front of the muffler pipe. This 2 piece unit can usually be removed as an assembly, which saves you the trouble of breaking one gasket surface and one set of bolts free.

➡️**On vehicles which utilize a 2 piece center pipe assembly, it may be possible to only remove the converter portion. If this is attempted, take great care not to damage the downpipe which remains attached to the bottom of the exhaust manifold. But, remember, nothing is gained if you later decide to remove the downpipe, since you now have one more exhaust joint to seal during installation than you would have if you had removed the 2 piece center pipe as an assembly.**

15. Loosen the clamps, then disconnect and plug the transmission oil cooler hoses from the cooler pipes.

16. Remove the torque converter housing lower plate and disconnect and plug the oil cooler lines.

17. Hold the flywheel in place with Special tool 09927–56010, or an equivalent flywheel holding tool and remove the three torque converter mounting bolts at the flywheel.

➡️**There are many different types of flywheel tools available. The most convenient (but more rare and expensive) are the types that bolt in place leaving your other hands free. But others are available which are essentially prytools that can be used to hold the teeth of the flywheel to keep if from turning. You can usually get away with using a large prybar, but if this is attempted be VERY CAREFUL not to damage the flywheel teeth.**

18. Remove the speedometer end nut, and disconnect the cable.

19. If equipped, remove the left-side transmission case stiffener bracket.

20. If equipped, unbolt the right-side transmission case stiffener bracket from the transmission. On certain models this right-side bracket is attached to the engine using 3 bolts, if this is so on your vehicle remove the rear 2, but only loosen the front-most bracket-to-engine retaining bolt.

21. Remove the transmission-to-engine retaining nuts.

22. Position a transmission jack to take the weight off of the rear transmission mount (crossmember).

23. Unbolt the rear transmission mount from the chassis at either side and from the transmission at the center, then remove the mount from the vehicle.

➡️**The 2 bolts on the passenger side of the transmission mount are locked in place using small metal tabs. This is done to help assure they cannot loosen, since the mount simply hangs from the bolts on that side and there is no ledge for it to sit on should they come out. Be sure to carefully bend these tabs out of the way before trying to loosen those 2 bolts.**

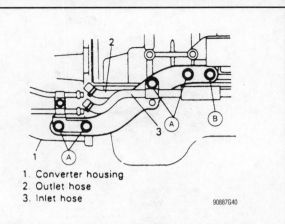

1. Converter housing
2. Outlet hose
3. Inlet hose

90887G40

Fig. 87 Some vehicles utilize a right transmission case-to-engine stiffener bracket that looks like this—On these models remove the rear-most 4 bolts (A), but only loosen the front most bracket-to-engine bolt (B)

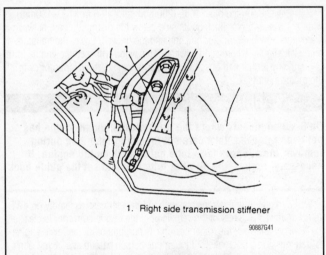

1. Right side transmission stiffener

90887G41

Fig. 88 The Sidekick Sport utilizes a different right transmission case-to-engine stiffener bracket than the other models

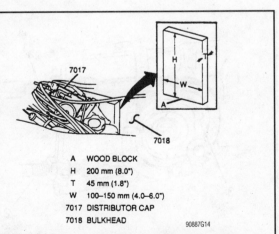

A WOOD BLOCK
H 200 mm (8.0")
T 45 mm (1.8")
W 100–150 mm (4.0–6.0")
7017 DISTRIBUTOR CAP
7018 BULKHEAD

90887G14

Fig. 86 A wooden block should be positioned between the engine and firewall to prevent the possibility of damage if the engine should pivot back while the transmission is being removed

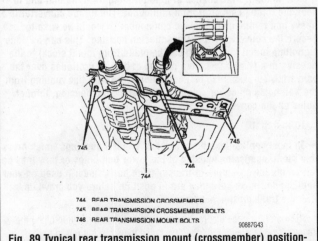

744 REAR TRANSMISSION CROSSMEMBER
745 REAR TRANSMISSION CROSSMEMBER BOLTS
746 REAR TRANSMISSION MOUNT BOLTS

90887G43

Fig. 89 Typical rear transmission mount (crossmember) positioning on these vehicles—2WD shown, but 4WD mounts the same way (only difference on the 4WD is the elimination of 1 right-angled portion of the bracket to leave room for the transfer case)

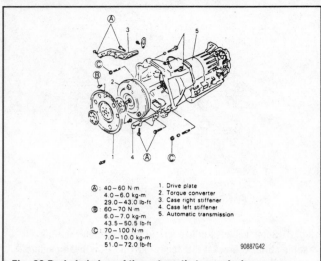

A : 40–60 N·m
4.0–6.0 kg·m
29.0–43.0 lb·ft
B : 60–70 N·m
6.0–7.0 kg·m
43.5–50.5 lb·ft
C : 70–100 N·m
7.0–10.0 kg·m
51.0–72.0 lb·ft

1. Drive plate
2. Torque converter
3. Case right stiffener
4. Case left stiffener
5. Automatic transmission

90887G42

Fig. 90 Exploded view of the automatic transmission case, torque converter and flywheel mounting

24. Place a wooden block 8 in. (200mm) tall X 4–6 in. (100–150mm) wide X 1.8 in. (45mm) thick on its side below the distributor cap, between the cylinder head distributor housing and the firewall. Lower the transmission jack slightly, to preload the wood. This wood will keep the engine from pivoting any further and possibly causing damage to the distributor or to the motor mounts.

✳✳ WARNING

On 3-speed models where the transmission dipstick tube has not been removed, take care not to damage the tube during removal. Also, check for a tube guide hook on the engine. If necessary, remove the oil filler tube bolt and set the guide hook free.

25. Carefully pull the transmission (and transfer case assembly on 4WD vehicles) toward the rear of the vehicle until the torque converter is clear of the flywheel and until the transmission casing pulls off of the lower engine-to-transmission studs/bolts. Although one person can do this, if you don't have a transmission jack we REALLY recommend that you get a friend to help you with this step. Lower the transmission from the vehicle.

➡️Do your best to keep the transmission level while it is being lowered to minimize the chance of fluid draining from the unit and to keep the torque converter from falling out. The torque converter is a heavy and relatively expensive component, it would be wise to secure the converter to the transmission housing. This can be done by bolting metal tabs (which can be made from metal stock) to the housing in a position where a portion of the tab protrudes over the converter. This can also be done using large wire ties running from the bolt holes on either side of the transmission housing, through holes on the converter.

To install:

➡️On most applications there are 1 or 2 metal bushings which press into the transmission housing at the lower bolt holes or they may be left on the lower engine-to-transmission bolts/studs. If used on your application, make sure they are in position before you crawl under with the transmission assembly.

26. Carefully raise the transmission assembly into position using the transmission jack and/or a friend. With the transmission raised to the proper height, carefully slide the assembly forward to mate the torque converter to the flywheel.

27. Once the transmission is in place, install the transmission-to-engine bolts and nuts finger-tight.

28. Lift the transmission jack slightly to pivot the engine forward and remove the wooden block.

29. Install the engine rear mounting member, then tighten member retaining bolts 29–43 ft. lbs. (40–60 Nm).

30. Remove the transmission jack and install the left and/or right transmission-to-engine reinforcement bracket bolts, as applicable. Tighten the reinforcement bracket bolts to 44–51 ft. lbs. (60–70 Nm).

31. Align the bolt holes in the flywheel and the torque converter, then install the flywheel-to-converter bolts and tighten gradually (using multiple passes) to 44–51 ft. lbs. (60–70 Nm).

32. Position the center exhaust pipe using a new pipe-to-manifold gasket and new flange gasket rings (where required). Torque the mounting bolts, spring-loaded bolts and stud nuts (as used) to 29–43 ft. lbs. (40–60 Nm).

33. Tighten the engine-to-transmission bolts and nuts to 51–72 ft. lbs. (70–100 Nm).

34. The balance of the installation procedure is the reverse of removal. If the transmission and/or transfer case was drained, or even if it wasn't but some fluid leaked during the procedure, be sure to check and fill the transmission when you are finished.

35. When you are finished, double check all wiring connections, wiring clamps, breather hoses, etc. to make sure everything is back the way you found it.

36. Check and adjust the select cable (which should not have changed unless the adjusting nut was disturbed, or unless other mechanical components vary, such as a different transmission was installed).

37. Check and adjust the throttle cable, as necessary.

38. Connect the negative battery cable. Start the engine; check for any leaks and proper operation.

ADJUSTMENTS

Throttle (Kickdown) Cable

▶ **See Figures 91, 92, 93 and 94**

The throttle or kickdown cable can also be known as the Throttle Valve (TV) cable. The purpose of the cable is to signal the transmission that a downshift should occur when the accelerator is pushed all the way to the floor. To check and adjust the cable:

1. Check the accelerator cable end-play and make sure it is within specification. There should be 0.4–0.6 in. (10-15mm) of end-play. If not, loosen the cable locknut located at the bracket on the throttle body and turn the adjusting nut until the proper play is achieved. Hold the adjusting nut and tighten the locknut when you are finished.

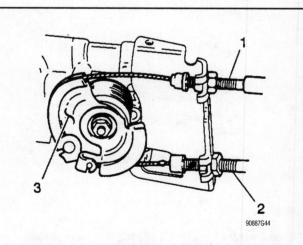

90887G44

Fig. 91 Before checking the throttle cable (2) adjustment at the throttle cam (3), make sure the accelerator pedal cable (1) end-play is within specification

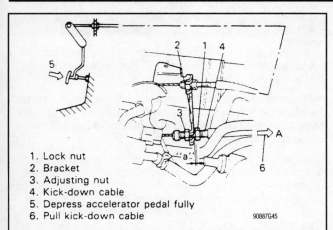

1. Lock nut
2. Bracket
3. Adjusting nut
4. Kick-down cable
5. Depress accelerator pedal fully
6. Pull kick-down cable

90887G45

Fig. 92 When adjusting the throttle cable on 3-speed models, make sure that clearance "a" is 0.0–0.039 in. (0–1mm) with the pedal fully depressed and the cable housing pulled tight away from the throttle body (direction A)

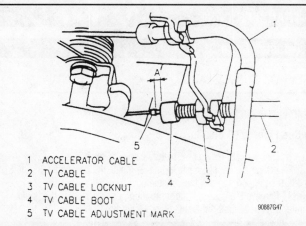

1 ACCELERATOR CABLE
2 TV CABLE
3 TV CABLE LOCKNUT
4 TV CABLE BOOT
5 TV CABLE ADJUSTMENT MARK

90887G47

Fig. 94 Throttle cable adjustment on the 4-speed is a relatively simple matter of obtaining a 0.031–0.059 in. (0.8–1.5mm) measurement between the cable tip end adjustment mark and the end of the boot.

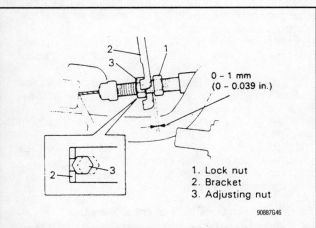

0 – 1 mm
(0 – 0.039 in.)

1. Lock nut
2. Bracket
3. Adjusting nut

90887G46

Fig. 93 While adjusting the cable on 3-speed models, make sure the adjusting nut is fit into the adjusting bracket (as shown with the dotted lines) while holding the specified clearance, then tighten the locknut nut against the bracket.

➡The accelerator cable is the upper cable, while the transmission throttle (kickdown) cable is the lower of the 2 cables on the throttle cam and bracket. If you are in doubt, follow the cables back, one will go through the fire-wall, while the other will continue down to the automatic transmission.

2. Make sure the ignition switch is in the **LOCK** position and have an assistant fully depress and hold the accelerator pedal. If an assistant is not available, a large brick should suffice, but make it is heavy enough that the pedal does not move during adjustment

3. For 3-speed models:

a. Loosen the locknut and adjusting nut so that both are loose and not in contact with the TV cable bracket on the throttle body.

b. Pull the throttle cable casing AWAY from the throttle body until tight and no cable deflection exists, then with the cable held in this position, tighten the cable locknut to within 0.0–0.039 in. (0–1mm) of the cable bracket.

➡**Make sure that the cable adjusting nut is not in contact with the bracket at this point.**

c. Release the accelerator pedal while keeping the cable locknut-to-cable bracket clearance at 0.039 in. (1mm).

d. Tighten the cable adjusting nut until it engages and fits into the cable bracket.

e. Now, with the adjusting nut positioned flush with the cable bracket, fully tighten the cable locknut.

4. For 4-speed models:

a. Measure the distance between the tip end of the cable adjustment mark and the end of the boot. The distance should be 0.031–0.059 in. (0.8–1.5mm). If not, loosen the locknut and turn the adjusting nut until this measurement is achieved.

b. Snug the throttle cable locknut with the throttle cable pulled tight.

c. Double-check the measurement between the tip end of the cable and the adjustment mark to make sure it did not change while tightening the locknut.

5. Operate the vehicle and verify that the transmission kickdown shift is occurring properly.

Shifter Select Cable

The shifter select cable attaches the manual gear selector in the passenger compartment to the shift shaft in the side of the transmission housing. It should not require periodic attention, but may need adjustment if other mechanical components at either end of the cable are replaced. Adjustment is simply a case of removing excessive play from the transmission end of the cable using the adjusting nut and locknut on the threaded portion of the cable which passes through the shift shaft. For more details, please refer to procedures for the Neutral Safety Switch information.

TRANSFER CASE

Transfer Case Shift Lever

REMOVAL & INSTALLATION

Samurai Models

▶ See Figures 95 and 96

1. Disconnect the negative battery cable for safety.
2. Locate the transfer case shift lever inside the passenger compartment. If equipped, remove the console cover.
3. Remove the gear shift boot mounting bolts and slide the upper shifter boot upwards on the shift lever away from the center floor tunnel.

✳✳ WARNING

When working with the shift boots, be careful not to force and tear them. The older the boot is, the more easily it can be damaged.

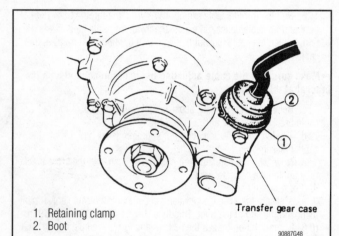

1. Retaining clamp
2. Boot

90887G48

Fig. 95 The shift lever on the 4WD Samurai transfer case is sealed to the top of the case with a boot (2) and a retaining clamp (1)

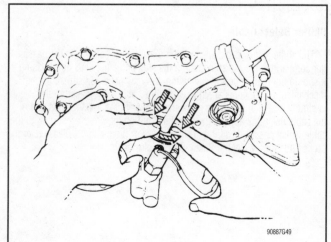

90887G49

Fig. 96 To release the lever from the top of the case, push the lever guide downward while rotating it counterclockwise

4. Check the lower shifter boot for a retaining clamp, and if equipped, release the boot clamp. Slide the lower boot, upward toward the shift knob in order to expose the shift lever guide.

➡**Depending on the amount of clearance that is available through the hole in the floor, it may be easier to access the lower boot and clamp from underneath the vehicle. If so, raise and support the vehicle safely using jackstands.**

5. Push downward on the shift lever guide (the round housing which the lever passes through on the way into the top of the transfer case) and turn the guide counterclockwise to release it. With the guide released, pull upward to remove it and the shift control lever from the transfer case.
6. Cover the opening in the top of the transfer case to prevent dirt, debris or loose bolts from falling in. This can be done with a piece of duct tape or using a plastic bag with a rubber band stretched around the case opening. Or a clean rag may be placed in the opening.

To install:

7. Remove the protective cover (tape, plastic bag or rag) from the top of the transfer case.
8. Clean and inspect the wear surfaces at the bottom of the shift lever. Apply a thin coat of lithium grease to the shifter ball friction surfaces at the bottom of the handle (between the shift lever and lever seat, as well as between the shift lever and lever case).
9. Insert the shift lever into position, then push downward on the guide while turning it clockwise to lock the assembly into the top of the transfer case.
10. Apply a thin coat of lithium grease to the lower boot on the surface which seals with the transfer case. Then slide the boot down the shift handle into position. If equipped, secure the boot retaining clamp. If the clamp was missing or damaged you should replace it with a similar type of band clamp (but in a pinch, a wire tie should be sufficient).
11. Slide the upper boot down the shift lever and into position. Secure the boot to the floor center tunnel using the retaining bolts.
12. If equipped, install the console cover.
13. Connect the negative battery cable.

Sidekick, Tracker, Sidekick Sport and X-90 Models

▶ See Figures 97 thru 102

1. Disconnect the negative battery cable for safety.
2. From inside the passenger compartment remove the console cover or, on certain late-model vehicles, both the front and rear console covers, as necessary. When removing both console covers start with the rear one. To free a console cover, remove the 2 screws and the two plastic retainers, then carefully lift the cover from the floor of the vehicle.

➡**The plastic retainers are removed by first pushing the center inward using a small hex key or punch. The center will gently snap inward telling you that fastener is now free. At this point you should be able to pull it back and out by gently grabbing the edges. DO NOT force a retainer out using a prytool unless the center snap has pushed inwards releasing the fastener or it will break and require replacement.**

3. The shift lever knob and upper boot must be removed for access to the components below. Loosen the knob setscrew and remove the knob from the top of the shift lever.
4. Remove the retaining screws from around the edge of the shift lever boot cover, then remove the cover and boot from the lever.

✳✳ WARNING

When working with the shift boots, be careful not to force and tear them. The older the boot is, the more easily it can be damaged. This boot is especially important, as it seals the passenger compartment from the truck's undercarriage.

5. Release the lower boot clamp by opening the retaining tabs and gently prying the end of the clamp free. If the clamp is difficult to release, you can carefully cut it using a pair of dikes, but be sure to replace it during installation.

6. Push downward on the shift control lever pivot (the round guide which the lever passes through on the way into the top of the case) and turn the pivot counterclockwise to release it. With the pivot released, pull upward to remove it and the shift control lever from the transfer case.

7. Cover the opening in the top of the transfer case to prevent dirt, debris or loose bolts from falling in. This can be done with a piece of duct tape or using a plastic bag with a rubber band stretched around the case opening. Or a clean rag may be placed in the opening.

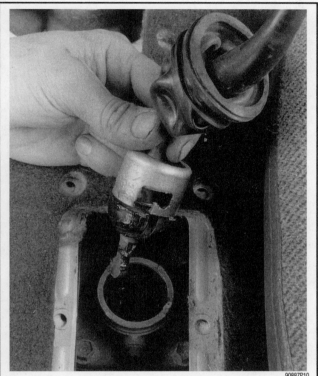

Fig. 97 Remove the shift lever before removing the transfer case/transmission assembly

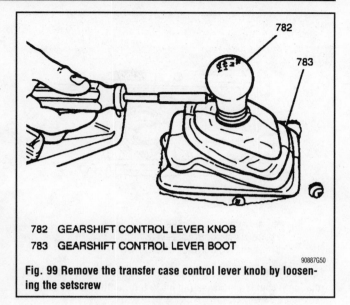

782   GEARSHIFT CONTROL LEVER KNOB
783   GEARSHIFT CONTROL LEVER BOOT

Fig. 99 Remove the transfer case control lever knob by loosening the setscrew

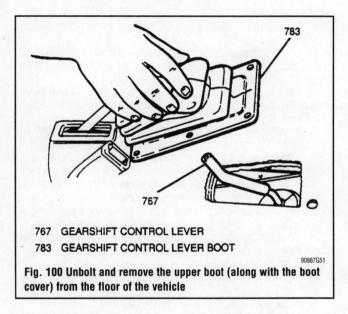

767   GEARSHIFT CONTROL LEVER
783   GEARSHIFT CONTROL LEVER BOOT

Fig. 100 Unbolt and remove the upper boot (along with the boot cover) from the floor of the vehicle

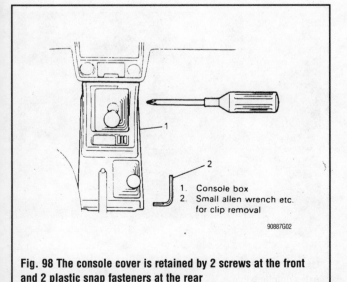

1. Console box
2. Small allen wrench etc. for clip removal

Fig. 98 The console cover is retained by 2 screws at the front and 2 plastic snap fasteners at the rear

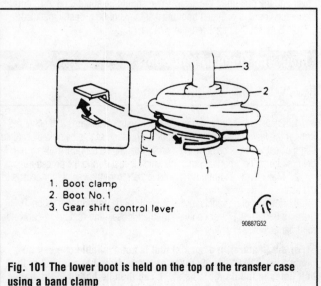

1. Boot clamp
2. Boot No.1
3. Gear shift control lever

Fig. 101 The lower boot is held on the top of the transfer case using a band clamp

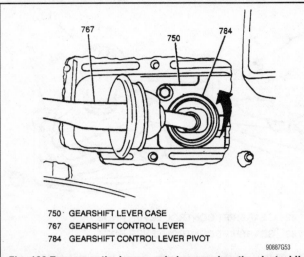

750 · GEARSHIFT LEVER CASE
767 GEARSHIFT CONTROL LEVER
784 GEARSHIFT CONTROL LEVER PIVOT

90887G53

Fig. 102 To remove the lever, push downward on the pivot while rotating it counterclockwise (about ¼ turn, until it is released)

To install:

8. Remove the protective cover (tape, plastic bag or rag) from the top of the transmission case.

9. Clean and inspect the wear surfaces at the bottom of the shift lever. Apply a thin coat of lithium grease to the shifter ball friction surfaces at the bottom of the handle (on the lever, ball and the pivot).

10. Insert the shift lever into position, then push downward on the pivot while turning it clockwise to lock the assembly into the top of the transfer case. Check the shifter for proper feel.

11. Reposition the lower boot and secure using a suitable clamp. If the original clamp was damaged and no replacement is available, a wire tie may suffice.

12. Install the upper boot over the shift lever, making sure to achieve a proper seal that will keep dirt, moisture and fumes out of the passenger compartment. Install the boot cover and retaining screws to secure the assembly.

13. Install the shift knob into place on top of the shift lever and secure using the setscrew. The setscrew must be installed fairly tight or it will buzz during vehicle operation, just be careful not to overtighten and strip the screw head.

14. Install the console cover (or covers) using the retaining screws and snap fasteners. To secure the snap fasteners, remove the center portion and insert the large piece into the hole, then gently insert the center portion of the fastener until it is flush with the top of the outer portion. Pull back gently to assure it is secure.

15. Check for the proper clearance between the front of the console cover and the bottom of the dash. There should be about 0.08 in (2mm) of clearance. If not, the angled boot bracket may not be properly installed.

16. Connect the negative battery cable.

Input and Output Shaft Seals

REMOVAL & INSTALLATION

1. Raise and support the vehicle safely using jackstands. Lift either the front or the rear of the vehicle, depending on which seal is being replaced, so that the seal which is being worked on will be angled upward. This should help minimize the amount of gear oil which is lost during the procedure.

2. Matchmark and remove the driveshaft from the vehicle for access to the seal.

3. For Samurai models, use a special flange holding tool (such as Suzuki's 09930-40113 or equivalent), then loosen and remove the universal joint flange nut.

➡️**For the Samurai, if a special tool is not available one can be made from a VERY sturdy piece of stock, drilled to match 2 of the bolt holes in the flange. The stock can then be bolted to the flange and used as a lever to keep it from turning.**

Take care NOT to damage either the sealing surface of the transfer case housing or the shaft during seal removal, or the new seal won't solve your problem.

4. Using a small, suitable prytool or a specially designed seal remover (such as the one produced by Lisle®), carefully pry the old seal from the end of the extension housing.

➡️**If seal removal is especially difficult you can use a slide hammer with a special oil seal remover attachment, but this should not be necessary for most cases.**

To install:

5. Inspect the sealing surface of the shaft and the transfer case for scores which might prevent sealing or small burrs which could tear a new seal as it was driven into position.

6. Place a thin coating of high temperature lithium grease on the lips of the new seal.

7. Position the seal at the opening of the transfer case housing and carefully drive it into position using a suitably sized seal driver and a plastic hammer. Drive the seal in until it is flush with or just below the housing surface.

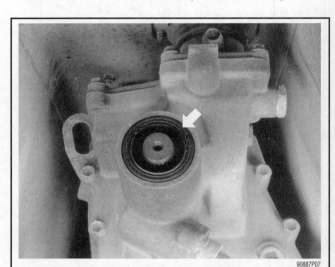

Remove the driveshaft for access to the extension housing seal (this one's in the transfer case)

90887P07

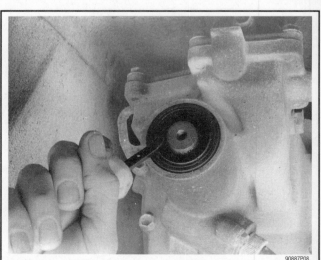

Use a small prybar or seal tool to carefully pry the old seal from extension housing . . .

90887P08

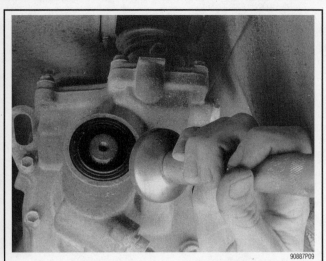

. . . then carefully drive the new seal into position using a suitably sized driver

8. For the Samurai, install the universal joint flange and secure using the retaining nut. Tighten the nut to 80–108 ft. lbs. (110–150 Nm).

9. Align and install the driveshaft. On all models except for the Samurai, be careful not to tear the new seal with the slip-yoke.

10. If fluid was lost during the procedure or prior to it, make sure the vehicle is completely level. Then check the transfer case fluid and top-off, as necessary.

11. Remove the jackstands and carefully lower the vehicle.

Transfer Case Assembly

REMOVAL & INSTALLATION

Samurai Models

➡Even the 2WD Samurai uses a transfer case. Rather than use a straight line driveshaft from the transmission to the differential, the Samurai leaves the transfer case in place and replaces its internal working with a simple offset gear mechanism, thus keeping 2 of the 3 driveshafts used in the 4WD vehicle.

1. On 4WD vehicles, remove the transfer case shift lever.
2. Raise and support the vehicle safely.
3. Drain the oil from the transfer case.
4. Matchmark and remove the driveshafts from the transfer case assembly. Not all of the driveshafts need to be completely removed from the vehicle, just unbolted from the case flanges. In most cases, the shaft or shafts on one side of the transfer case can be repositioned and supported out of the way.
5. Support the transfer case using a suitable transmission jack.
6. Disconnect the speedometer cable from the transfer case.
7. On 4WD vehicles, disconnect the 4WD switch lead wire at the coupler.
8. Remove the three mounting bolts and/or nuts securing the transfer case to the chassis, as applicable.
9. Carefully lower the transfer case from the vehicle.

To install:

10. Position and install the transfer case. Tighten the mounting bolts to 159–248 inch lbs. (18–28 Nm) and/or the mounting nuts to 19–25 ft. lbs. (25–34 Nm).
11. On 4WD vehicles, connect the 4WD switch lead wire at the coupler.
12. Connect the speedometer cable to the transfer case.
13. Properly refill the transfer case with an approved type of gear oil.
14. Align and install the driveshafts to the transfer case.
15. On 4WD vehicles, install the transfer case shift lever.
16. Remove the jackstands and carefully lower the vehicle.

Sidekick, Tracker, Sidekick Sport and X-90 Models

On these models the transfer case is bolted to the transmission and takes the place of the 2WD transmission's extension housing. Therefore, transfer case is removed or installed as part of the transmission assembly.

DRIVELINE

Driveshafts

REMOVAL & INSTALLATION

Samurai Models

▸ See Figures 103 and 104

The 4WD Samurai uses three separate driveshafts, the shafts are designated as No. 1, No. 2, and No. 3: the No. 1 shaft connects the transmission to the transfer case, the No. 2 shaft connects the transfer case to the front differential, the No. 3 shaft connects the transfer case to the rear differential.

The 2WD vehicle uses two separate driveshafts the No. 1 and No. 3 driveshafts. The driveshafts are used in the 2WD vehicles the same way as they are used in the 4WD vehicles.

1. Raise and safely support the vehicle on jackstands.
2. Matchmark the driveshafts to the yokes on the transfer case, or transmission, and the differential.

3. Support the driveshaft and remove the attaching bolts.
4. Remove the driveshaft from the vehicle.

➡The transmission side end of the No. 1 shaft does not have a flange piece; the end is splined and slides onto the output shaft inside the extension case. To remove the shaft, after detaching the transfer case end, just pull the shaft out of the extension case. When removing the No. 1 shaft, the transmission fluid will not leak if the front and the rear of the vehicle are raised evenly and the transmission fluid is filled to specification. If the vehicle is raised unevenly or the fluid is above specification, drain the transmission fluid prior to removing the No. 1 shaft.

To install:

5. The No. 2 and No. 3 shafts are equipped with slip joints on the shafts so that the driveshaft can expand (lengthen) or contract (shorten) itself. Pull the driveshaft apart and liberally fill the driveshaft splines with chassis grease. When reassembling the driveshaft, align the matchmarks on the splines and the shaft to prevent noise or vibration. Verify that the rubber boot is pulled over and is protecting the driveshaft splines.

6. Install the driveshaft, by aligning the matchmarks made during disassembly.

7. Install and tighten the mounting bolts to 37–43 ft. lbs. (50–60 Nm).

8. Lubricate the driveshaft U-joints at the grease fittings and lower the vehicle.

9. If fluid was drained (or leaked), refill the transmission to the proper level with the proper lubricant.

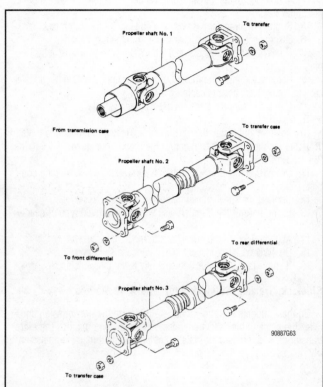

Fig. 103 The Samurai uses three driveshafts—driveshaft No. 1 connects the transmission to the transfer case, No. 2 connects the transfer to the front differential, No. 3 connects the transfer to the rear differential

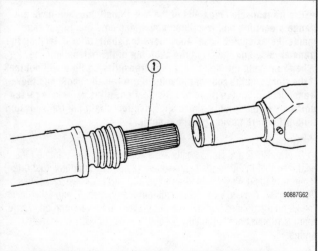

Fig. 104 Apply multi-purpose grease to the slip joint splines (1), then assemble the driveshaft halves

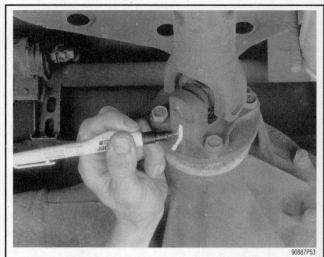

To remove the typical driveshaft, matchmark the driveshaft to the differential flange . . .

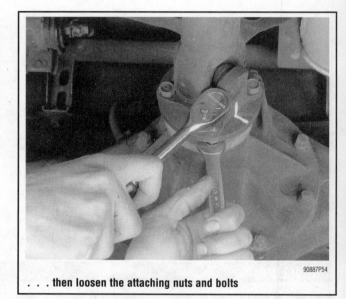

. . . then loosen the attaching nuts and bolts

It may be necessary to use a plastic mallet to break the driveshaft free of the differential flange

Lower the end of the driveshaft . . .

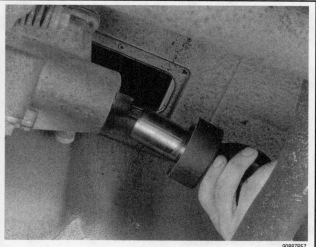

. . . then slide the other end out of the transmission/transfer case—some models use another flange on this end as well

Sidekick, Tracker, Sidekick Sport and X-90 Models

▶ See Figure 105

1. Raise and safely support the vehicle on jackstands.
2. Matchmark the driveshaft(s) yokes to the flanges on the transfer case, or transmission, and the differential.
3. On 4WD models, drain the transfer case oil.
4. Support the driveshaft and remove the attaching nuts and bolts.
5. Remove the driveshaft from the vehicle.
To install:
6. Install the driveshaft, by aligning the matchmarks on the yoke with those on the flanges.
7. Tighten the driveshaft yoke-to-flange bolts and nuts to 40 ft. lbs. (55 Nm).
8. On 4WD models, refill the transfer case. Apply Loctite® pipe sealant to the threads of the oil lever filler plug, then install the plug in the transfer case.
9. Safely lower the vehicle.

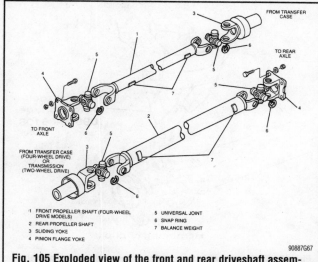

Fig. 105 Exploded view of the front and rear driveshaft assemblies used on Sidekick, Tracker, Sidekick Sport and X-90 models

U-Joints

DISASSEMBLY & ASSEMBLY

▶ See Figures 106, 107 and 108

1. Remove the driveshaft from the vehicle.
2. Remove the two snaprings from the pinion flange.
3. Use a 18mm socket as a driver and a 24mm socket as a cup. Place the driveshaft in a soft jaw vice with the 18mm socket against one of the bearing caps and the 24mm positioned so the bearing cap will slide into the socket. Compress the vice until the bearing cap has moved out 3–4mm.
4. Remove the driveshaft and sockets from the vice. Reposition the driveshaft so the vice jaws can be clamped down on the exposed portion of the bearing cap. With the cap clamped snugly, tap upward on the driveshaft until the cap comes free.
5. Using the 18mm socket and a hammer remove the other bearing cap by driving it out of the pinion flange.

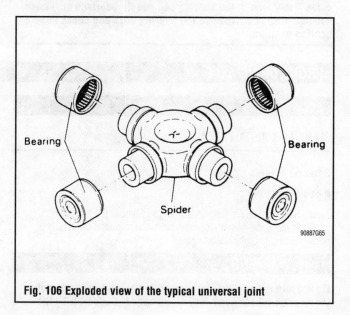

Fig. 106 Exploded view of the typical universal joint

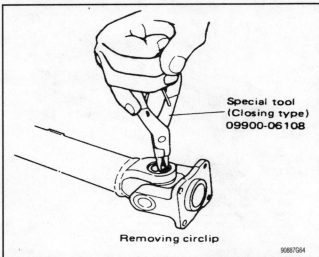

Fig. 107 To disassemble the U-joint, remove the two snaprings from the universal joint pinion flange

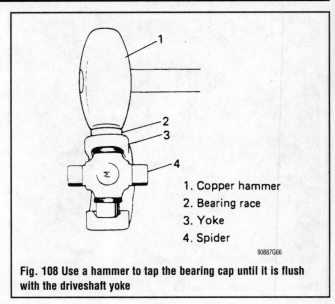

1. Copper hammer
2. Bearing race
3. Yoke
4. Spider

Fig. 108 Use a hammer to tap the bearing cap until it is flush with the driveshaft yoke

6. Remove the pinion flange.
7. Remove the two snaprings from the driveshaft yoke.
8. Use a 18mm socket as a driver and a 24mm socket as a cup. Place the driveshaft in a soft jaw vice with the 18mm socket against one of the bearing caps and the 24mm positioned so the bearing cap will slide into the socket. Compress the vice until the bearing cap has moved out 3–4mm.
9. Remove the driveshaft and sockets from the vice. Reposition the driveshaft so the vice jaws can be clamped down on the exposed portion of the bearing cap. With the cap clamped snugly, tap upward on the driveshaft until the cap comes free.
10. Using the 18mm socket and a hammer remove the other bearing cap by driving it out of the driveshaft.
11. Remove the U-joint.
To assemble:
12. Install the U-joint into the driveshaft yoke.

✳✳ WARNING

DO NOT force the bearing caps into place. If the U-joint will not move freely, one of the bearing cap needle bearings may have become unseated. Remove the bearing caps and check needle bearing position.

FRONT DRIVE AXLE

Locking Hubs

REMOVAL & INSTALLATION

Samurai Models

▶ **See Figure 109**

1. Raise and safely support the vehicle. Remove the front wheels.
2. Remove the caliper mounting bolts and move the caliper out of position with the brake line attached.

✳✳ WARNING

Do not allow the caliper to hang on the brake hose, otherwise the flexible rubber hose may be damaged. Support it by the mounting bracket.

13. Install one bearing cap into the driveshaft yoke. Fit the end of the U-joint into the bearing cap and using a hammer lightly tap the cap until it is flush with the yoke. Using an 18mm socket, tap the bearing cap down until the snapring groove is visible.
14. Install the second bearing cap and position the U-joint so the it is part way into each bearing cap. Lightly tap the second bearing cap into place. Using an 18mm socket tap the U-joint down until the snapring groove is visible.
15. Install the two snaprings.
16. Verify the U-joint moves freely.
17. Install the pinion flange over the U-joint.
18. Install one bearing cap into the pinion flange yoke. Fit the end of the U-joint into the bearing cap and using a hammer lightly tap the cap until it is flush with the yoke. Using an 18mm socket, tap the bearing cap down until the snapring groove is visible.
19. Install the second bearing cap and position the U-joint so the it is part way into each bearing cap. Lightly tap the second bearing cap into place. Using an 18mm socket tap the U-joint down until the snapring groove is visible.
20. Install the two snaprings.
21. Verify the U-joint moves freely.
22. Lubricate the U-joint at the grease fitting and install the driveshaft in the vehicle.

3. Install 2 (8mm) bolts into the threaded holes and tighten evenly. This will remove the rotor from the hub assembly.
4. Thread a bolt into the axle shaft and pull the axle shaft out towards you. Remove the snapring.
5. Remove the locking hub body assembly.
To install:
6. Install a new gasket onto the locking hub assembly.
7. Install the locking hub body assembly to the wheel hub flange and tighten the hub body bolts to 212 inch lbs. (24 Nm).
8. Thread a bolt into the axle shaft and pull the axle shaft out towards you. Install the snapring and remove the bolt from the axle shaft.
9. Install a new gasket in the manual locking hub cover.
10. Before installing the locking hub cover, make sure of the following:
   • The selector knob is in the FREE position.
   • The clutch should be lifted (retracted) towards the cover. The clutch must be positioned properly to ensure proper hub operations.
   • The gasket is centered and installed correctly.

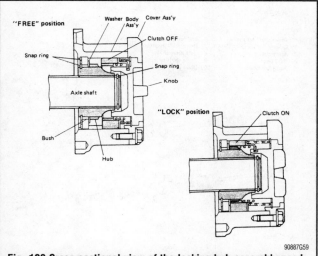

Fig. 109 Cross-sectional view of the locking hub assembly used by Samurai models

11. Install the locking hub cover and tighten the bolts to 115 inch lbs. (13 Nm).

➡ **The mark on the hub knob must be facing the FREE position.**

12. Check that the hub assembly is working correctly. If there are problems with the operation, Remove the hub cover and repeat steps 9–12.

13. Install the brake rotor.

14. Place the brake caliper into position and install the caliper mounting bolts.

15. If removed, reconnect the locking hub assembly and install the front wheels.

16. Lower the vehicle.

17. Pump the brake pedal several times to seat the front brake pads. Road test the vehicle and verify proper operation.

Sidekick, Tracker, Sidekick Sport and X-90 Models

AUTOMATIC LOCKING HUBS

1. Apply the parking brake, block the rear wheels, then raise and safely support the front of the vehicle on jackstands.

2. Unscrew the automatic hub cover and remove the cover and O-ring.

To remove the automatic locking hub, loosen the cover—an oil filter wrench does a good job

Remove the cover from the automatic locking hub assembly . . .

. . . then loosen the six mounting screws . . .

. . . and pull the hub assembly off of the end of the halfshaft

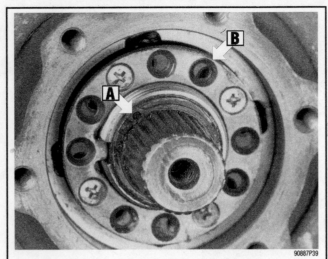

Once the hub is removed, the axle shaft retaining snapring (A) and bearing lockwasher (B) can be accessed

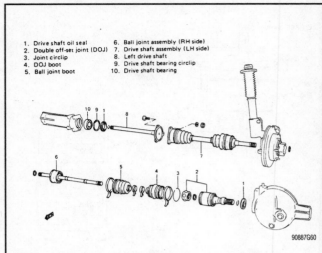

1. Drive shaft oil seal
2. Double off-set joint (DOJ)
3. Joint circlip
4. DOJ boot
5. Ball joint boot
6. Ball joint assembly (RH side)
7. Drive shaft assembly (LH side)
8. Left drive shaft
9. Drive shaft bearing circlip
10. Drive shaft bearing

Fig. 110 Exploded view of the left- and right-hand halfshaft (referred to as a drive shaft by Suzuki) assemblies

3. Remove the hub assembly mounting bolts and remove the hub assembly.

To install:

4. Install a new O-ring on the hub assembly.
5. Install the hub assembly onto the wheel flange. Make sure the tab on the hub fits into the notch on the spindle.
6. Install the six mounting bolts and tighten to 221 inch lbs. (25 Nm).
7. Install a new O-ring on the hub cover.
8. Install the hub cover.
9. Lower the vehicle and remove the wheel blocks.

MANUAL LOCKING HUBS

1. Apply the parking brake, block the rear wheels, then raise and safely support the front of the vehicle.
2. Remove the six manual hub cover mounting bolts and remove the manual hub cover and gasket.
3. Remove the six manual hub mounting bolts.
4. Remove the manual hub and O-ring.

To install:

5. Install a new O-ring on the manual hub body.
6. Install the manual hub onto the wheel flange and install the six mounting bolts. Tighten the mounting bolts to 159 inch lbs. (25 Nm).
7. Install a new gasket on the manual hub cover.
8. Install the hub cover on the hub. The lever must be in the **FREE** position with the clutch pulled out toward the cover.
9. Install the six mounting bolts. Tighten the bolts to 106 inch lbs. (12 Nm).
10. Lower the vehicle and remove the wheel blocks.

Halfshaft

REMOVAL & INSTALLATION

Sidekick, Tracker, Sidekick Sport and X-90 Models

♦ See Figure 110

1. Loosen all of the front wheel lug nuts ½ turn.
2. Apply the parking brake, block the rear wheels, then raise and safely support the front of the vehicle on jackstands.
3. If equipped, remove the front skid plate.
4. Remove the front wheel(s).
5. If equipped, remove the locking hub.
6. Remove the snapring from the end of the halfshaft and remove the spindle washer.

To remove a halfshaft, remove the locking hub, then use a pair of snapring pliers . . .

1. Snapring
2. Washer
3. Halfshaft

. . . to remove the snapring and washer from the halfshaft

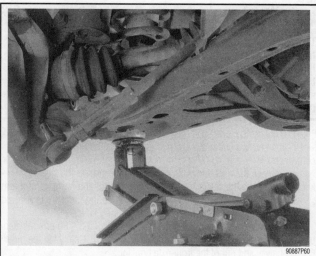

Since the coil spring is under tremendous pressure, support the lower control arm with a floor jack . . .

. . . until the halfshaft is free of the bearing hub

. . . then remove the strut-to-steering knuckle nuts and bolts, and separate the lower ball joint from the knuckle

Use a small prytool to separate the right-hand halfshaft from the differential housing . . .

Pull the steering knuckle away from the vehicle . . .

. . . or matchmark the left-hand halfshaft to the differential housing . . .

7. Remove the sway bar nut from the lower control arm.

8. Remove the cotter pin and nut from the tie rod end ball stud. Separate the tie rod end from the steering knuckle.

9. Remove the brake caliper from the knuckle and suspend with wire, without disconnecting the brake line. Do not let the caliper hang from the brake hose.

90887P46

. . . and loosen the attaching nuts and bolts

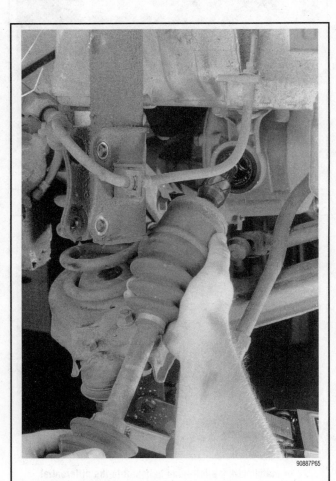

90887P65

Remove the halfshaft from the vehicle

✳✳ CAUTION

The coil spring is under extreme pressure. Make sure the control arm is firmly supported with a hydraulic jack before removing the lower ball joint nut. After the lower ball joint nut has been removed, lower the hydraulic jack slowly to relieve coil spring pressure. If this precaution is not observed, serious bodily injury may result.

10. Support the lower control arm with a hydraulic jack.

11. Remove the cotter pin and nut attaching the ball joint to the lower control arm.

12. Remove the nuts and bolts connecting the strut to the steering knuckle. Separate the steering knuckle from the strut and lower control arm.

13. Slowly lower the hydraulic jack until coil spring pressure is relieved.

14. Remove the outer CV-joint from the steering knuckle.

15. If removing the right side halfshaft, place tool J 37780 or equivalent, between the front axle housing and the inner CV-joint. Gently tap the inner CV-joint away and out of the front axle housing.

16. If removing the left side halfshaft, scribe a reference mark on the left inner axle shaft flange and the inner CV-joint flange to ensure correct installation. Remove the three bolts and three nuts and separate the inner CV-joint from the left inner axle shaft.

17. Remove the halfshaft from the vehicle.

To install:

18. If installing the right halfshaft, install the inner CV-joint into the axle housing, making sure the snapring seats in the differential side gear.

19. If installing the left halfshaft, install the left inner axle shaft flange to the inner CV-joint flange, aligning the reference marks made during removal. Install the three bolts and three nuts and tighten to 36 ft. lbs. (50 Nm).

20. Install the outer CV-joint into the steering knuckle.

21. Support the lower control arm with the hydraulic jack.

22. Attach the steering knuckle and lower ball joint to the lower control arm. Tighten the strut bolts and nuts to 65 ft. lbs. (90 Nm). Tighten the ball joint nut to 42 ft. lbs. (58 Nm) and install a new cotter pin.

23. Remove the hydraulic jack from the lower control arm.

24. Install the brake caliper to the knuckle.

25. Install the tie rod end to the steering knuckle and tighten the nut to 30 ft. lbs. (40 Nm). Install a new cotter pin.

26. Install the spindle washer and snapring to the end of the halfshaft.

27. If equipped, install the locking hub.

28. Install the front wheel.

29. Install the skid plate, if equipped.

30. Lower the vehicle.

CV-JOINT BOOT REPLACEMENT

▶ See Figures 111, 112 and 113

➡ During differential-side and wheel-side joint service, index marks (reference marks) should be placed on the differential-side joint and wheel-side housing. A corresponding matching mark should be placed on the drive axle shaft as well. This will establish the joint to axle position and ensure that all components are installed in the same position from which they were removed. If this precaution is not observed and the components are installed in a different position, uneven or premature component wear may result.

1. Raise and safely support the vehicle.

2. Remove the halfshaft from the vehicle.

3. Secure the shaft in a vise, placing wood or soft metal between the jaws to protect the shaft.

4. Remove the large differential-side boot clamp from the differential-side boot by drawing the clamp hooks together.

5. Remove the small differential-side boot clamp from the differential-side boot. Temporarily slide the differential-side boot toward the center of the drive axle shaft. Place an index mark (reference mark) on the differential-side joint housing and drive axle shaft to ensure correct assembly.

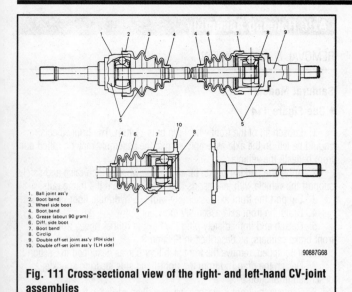

1. Ball joint ass'y
2. Boot band
3. Wheel side boot
4. Boot band
5. Grease (about 90 gram)
6. Diff. side boot
7. Boot band
8. Circlip
9. Double off-set joint ass'y (RH side)
10. Double off-set joint ass'y (LH side)

90887G68

Fig. 111 Cross-sectional view of the right- and left-hand CV-joint assemblies

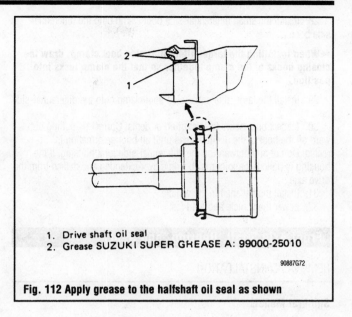

1. Drive shaft oil seal
2. Grease SUZUKI SUPER GREASE A: 99000-25010

90887G72

Fig. 112 Apply grease to the halfshaft oil seal as shown

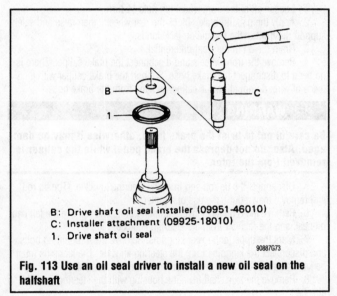

B: Drive shaft oil seal installer (09951-46010)
C: Installer attachment (09925-18010)
1. Drive shaft oil seal

90887G73

Fig. 113 Use an oil seal driver to install a new oil seal on the halfshaft

6. Remove the snapring securing the differential-side joint housing.

7. Remove the differential-side joint housing from the joint. Place an index mark (reference mark) on the joint and drive axle shaft to ensure correct reassembly.

8. Remove the snapring and joint from the drive axle shaft.

9. Remove the differential-side boot from the drive axle shaft.

10. Remove the large wheel-side boot clamp from the wheel-side boot.

11. Remove the small wheel-side boot clamp from the wheel-side boot.

12. Remove the wheel-side boot from the drive axle shaft. Place an index mark(reference mark) on the wheel-side joint and the drive axle shaft to ensure correct assembly.

13. Remove the wheel-side joint from the drive axle shaft by expanding the wheel-side joint snapring.

❊❊ WARNING

Do not disassemble the joints. If any abnormality is found in the joint, replace it as an assembly. Do not wash drive axle boots in solvent. Washing drive axle boots in degreaser or other solvents causes deterioration of boots. DO NOT wash the differential side joint in degreaser. Washing the joint in degreaser will remove all lubrication in the joint needle bearings. Clean the joint assembly and drive axle boots with a clean, dry, solvent-free rag.

To install:
14. Clean the differential-side and the wheel-side boots with a clean, dry, solvent-free cloth.

15. Clean the differential side joint and the wheel-side joint with a clean, dry, solvent-free cloth.

16. Inspect the differential-side and the wheel-side boots for tears, damage or fatigue. Replace as necessary.

17. Inspect the differential side joint for excessive wear or damage. If any excessive wear, damage or abnormality is found, replace the joint as an assembly.

18. Inspect the wheel-side joint for excessive wear or damage. If any excessive wear, damage or abnormality is found, replace the wheel-side joint as an assembly.

19. Align the reference marks on the wheel-side joint and drive axle shaft made during wheel-side joint removal.

20. Install the wheel-side joint onto the drive axle shaft by expanding the wheel-side snapring and slide wheel-side joint onto the drive axle shaft. After installing the wheel-side joint onto the drive axle shaft, make sure the wheel-side joint snapring is securely seated into the groove in the drive axle shaft.

21. Install the wheel-side boot onto the drive axle shaft. Temporarily install the large and small wheel-side boot clamps onto the drive axle shaft. Do not crimp. Pack the wheel-side joint with approximately 4.6–5.3 oz. (130–150 g) of black grease provided in the wheel-side boot kit.

22. Install the small wheel-side boot clamp onto the wheel-side boot.

23. Install the large wheel-side boot clamp onto the wheel-side boot. Temporarily install the large and small differential-side boot clamps onto the drive axle shaft. Do not crimp.

24. Install the differential-side boot onto the drive axle shaft.

➡**When installing the differential side joint onto the drive axle shaft, place the joint onto the drive axle shaft with the short sided splines facing toward the differential-side boot (away from transmission).**

25. Install the differential side joint onto the drive axle shaft aligning reference marks made during disassembly; secure with the snapring. Pack the differential-side joint housing with approximately 8.1–8.8 oz. (230–250 g) of the lubricant provided in the differential-side boot kit.

26. Install the differential-side joint housing onto joint aligning reference marks made during disassembly.

27. Secure the differential-side housing with the snap ring.

28. Install the small differential-side boot clamp onto the differential-side boot.

➡**When installing the large differential-side boot clamp, draw the closing hooks of the clamp together so that the clamp locks into position.**

29. Install the large differential-side boot clamp onto the differential-side boot.

30. Inspect both boots for distortion or dents. Correct by pulling outward on the boot in the desired areas until all boot deformation is corrected. Do not pull outward on the differential-side joint housing. If the housing is pulled, the joint may become over-extended and detach from the drive axle.

31. Install the halfshaft in the vehicle.

32. Lower the vehicle and road test.

Front Axle Shaft, Bearing, and Seal

REMOVAL & INSTALLATION

Samurai Models

1. Loosen all of the front wheel lug nuts ½ turn.

2. Apply the parking brake, block the rear wheels, then raise and safely support the front of the vehicle on jackstands.

3. Drain the oil in the front differential.

4. Remove the front wheels and disconnect the brake caliper. There is no need to disconnect the brake hose. Support the brake caliper with a piece of wire; do not allow the caliper to hang from the brake hose.

✳✳ WARNING

Be careful not to twist the brake hose, otherwise it may be damaged. Also, do not depress the brake pedal while the caliper is removed from the rotor.

5. Disconnect the tie rod end from the steering knuckle. (The tie rod end removal may require the use of a puller.)

6. Remove the 8 oil seal cover mounting bolts and remove the felt pad, oil seal, and the retainer from the steering knuckle.

7. Mark the upper and lower kingpins. Remove the 4 mounting bolts and disconnect the kingpins from the steering knuckle. The kingpins must be kept separated so as to prevent an error during reassembly.

8. Remove the axle shaft from the housing with the steering knuckle attached.

➡**At this time, the lower kingpin bearing sometimes falls out. So remove the bearing while pulling off the knuckle gradually.**

9. If necessary, remove the oil seal from the axle shaft taking note of the original positioning of the seal on the shaft.

To install:

10. If the front axle shaft seal was removed, apply grease to the lip portion of the seal, and slide the seal into place on the axle shaft.

11. If a new axle shaft is being installed, transfer the steering knuckle to the new axle shaft. Install the axle shaft into the differential housing.

12. Install the lower kingpin bearing and the upper and lower kingpins in their correct location. Tighten the mounting bolts to 177–265 inch lbs. (20–30 Nm).

13. Install the steering knuckle oil seal, felt pad, retainer, and the 8 mounting bolts. Tighten the mounting bolts to 71–106 inch lbs. (8–12 Nm).

14. Connect the tie rod end to the steering knuckle and tighten the nut to 22–39 ft. lbs. (30–55 Nm). Install a new cotter pin.

15. Install the front brake caliper assembly. If the brake line was disconnected, bleed the brake system.

16. Install the front wheels and refill the differential with the proper fluid.

17. Lower the vehicle.

Axle Housing Assembly

REMOVAL & INSTALLATION

Samurai Models

▶ **See Figure 114**

1. Loosen all of the front wheel lug nuts ½ turn. The front wheels should be left on the axle assembly so that the assembly may be rolled out from beneath the vehicle.

2. Apply the parking brake, block the rear wheels, then raise and safely support the vehicle with jackstands positioned beneath the frame rails.

3. Support the front axle assembly with two hydraulic floor jacks.

4. Drain the front axle assembly lubricant.

5. Detach and immediately plug the flexible rubber hoses from the front brake calipers, as described in Section 9.

6. If equipped, remove the front stabilizer bar, as described in Section 8.

7. Detach the drag rod from the right-hand side steering knuckle, as described in Section 9.

8. Remove the front driveshaft, as described earlier in this section.

9. Remove the front shock absorbers, as described in Section 8.

10. Remove the front leaf springs, as described in Section 8.

11. Carefully lower the front axle assembly with the floor jacks, ensuring that no cables, wires or other components will inhibit axle assembly removal.

12. Roll the front axle assembly out from beneath the vehicle.

13. The front axle assembly may now be disassembled.

To install:

14. Assemble the front axle assembly as necessary.

15. Roll the front axle assembly into position beneath the vehicle, then slowly raise the axle on two floor jacks.

16. Install the front leaf springs, shock absorbers, and driveshaft. Be sure that the driveshaft and differential flange matchmarks are properly aligned before bolting the two together.

17. Reattach the drag rod to the steering knuckle.

18. If applicable, install the front stabilizer bar.

19. Connect the flexible brake hoses to the front brake calipers.

20. Bleed the brake system, as described in Section 9.

21. Refill the front differential with lubricant, as described in Section 1.

22. Lower the vehicle, then tighten the front wheel lug nuts to the specified value, as described in Section 8.

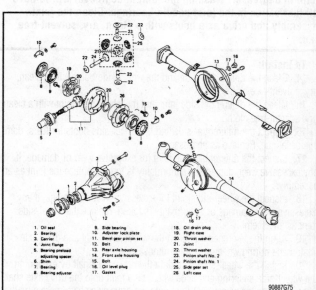

1. Oil seal	9. Side bearing	18. Oil drain plug
2. Bearing	10. Adjuster lock plate	19. Right case
3. Carrier	11. Bevel gear pinion set	20. Thrust washer
4. Joint flange	12. Bolt	21. Nut
5. Bearing preload	13. Rear axle housing	22. Thrust washer
adjusting spacer	14. Front axle housing	23. Pinion shaft No. 2
6. Shim	15. Bolt	24. Pinion shaft No. 1
7. Bearing	16. Oil level plug	25. Side gear set
8. Bearing adjuster	17. Gasket	26. Left case

90887G75

Fig. 114 Exploded view of the front and rear axle housing assemblies

Sidekick, Tracker, Sidekick Sport and X-90 Models

▶ **See Figures 115 thru 129**

1. Apply the parking brake, block the rear wheels, then raise and safely support the vehicle with jackstands positioned beneath the frame rails.

2. Support the front axle assembly with two hydraulic floor jacks, or one transmission jack. If using the transmission jack, it is a good idea to secure the assembly to the jack with a strap or piece of rope.

3. Drain the front axle assembly lubricant.

4. Detach the breather hose from the differential housing.

5. Detach the front driveshaft from the differential flange by removing the 4 mounting bolts, then suspend the end of the driveshaft with strong cord or wire.

6. Loosen the four left mounting bracket bolts.

7. Mathmark the left-hand halfshaft and differential case for reassembly, then remove the three left-hand halfshaft flange bolts to detach the left-hand halfshaft from the differential assembly.

8. Remove the two differential rear crossmember mount bolts, then remove the three mounting bolts on the right-hand of the housing.

9. Using two small prytools as levers, separate the right-hand halfshaft joint from the differential, then lower the differential assembly from the vehicle.

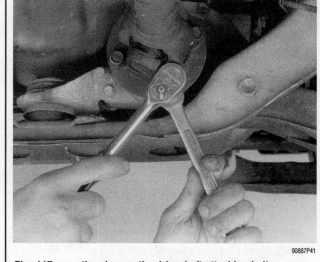

Fig. 117 . . . then loosen the driveshaft attaching bolts

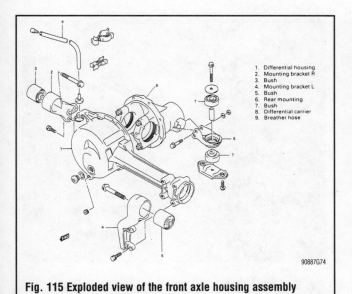

1. Differential housing
2. Mounting bracket R
3. Bush
4. Mounting bracket L
5. Bush
6. Rear mounting
7. Bush
8. Differential carrier
9. Breather hose

Fig. 115 Exploded view of the front axle housing assembly

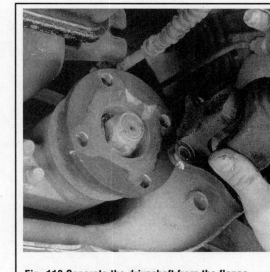

Fig. 118 Separate the driveshaft from the flange . . .

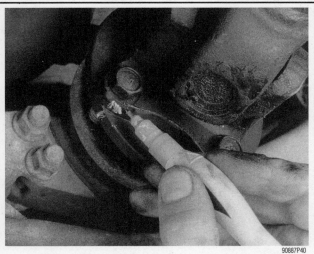

Fig. 116 To remove the front axle/differential assembly, first matchmark the driveshaft and differential flange . . .

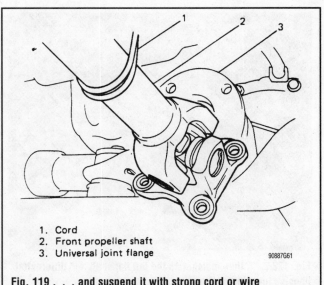

1. Cord
2. Front propeller shaft
3. Universal joint flange

Fig. 119 . . . and suspend it with strong cord or wire

Fig. 120 Support the axle assembly with a transmission jack—secure it to the jack with a strap or rope

Fig. 121 Remove the four left-hand mounting bolts . . .

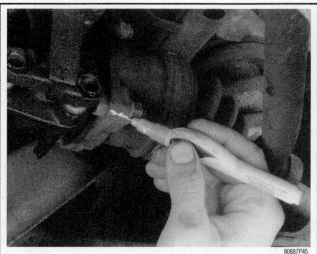

Fig. 122 . . . then matchmark the left halfshaft and differential housing for reinstallation

Fig. 123 Loosen the left halfshaft attaching nuts and bolts, then separate the halfshaft from the differential housing

Fig. 124 Loosen the two rear crossmember mounting bolts . . .

Fig. 125 . . . then remove the right-hand mounting bolts

To install:

10. Raise the differential assembly into position and reinstall the right-hand halfshaft in the assembly. Press the halfshaft into the differential until fully engaged.

11. Install the three right-hand differential assembly mounting bolts, then the two rear mounting bolts. Tighten the bolts until snug.

12. Reattach the left-hand halfshaft to the differential assembly and install the three attaching bolts. Tighten the halfshaft-to-differential flange bolts to 36–43 ft. lbs. (50–60 Nm).

13. Install the four left-hand differential mounting bolts. Tighten all of the differential assembly mounting bolts to 36–43 ft. lbs. (50–60 Nm).

14. Reattach the front driveshaft to the differential assembly, then tighten the mounting bolts to 36–43 ft. lbs. (50–60 Nm).

15. Reattach the breather hose to the differential housing.

16. Fill the front axle assembly with lubricant, as described in Section 1.

17. Lower the vehicle and remove the wheel blocks.

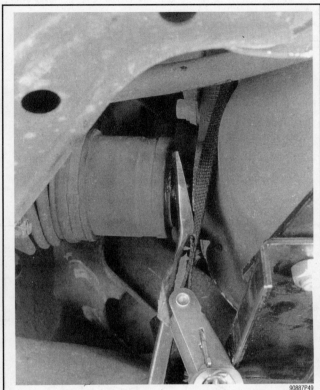

Fig. 126 Use a prytool to disengage the right halfshaft from the differential housing . . .

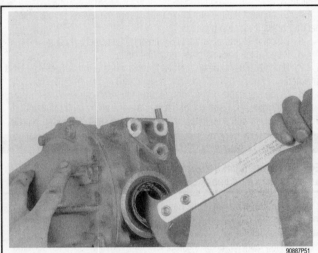

Fig. 128 If necessary, the halfshaft oil seals can be removed from the housing while it is out of the vehicle . . .

Fig. 127 . . . then lower the housing out of the vehicle

Fig. 129 . . . just ensure to use a mallet and the proper size driver to seat the new oil seals in place

REAR DRIVE AXLE

Rear Axle Shaft, Bearing, and Seal

REMOVAL & INSTALLATION

Samurai Models

♦ See Figure 130

1. Raise and safely support the vehicle. Drain the rear differential assembly.
2. Make sure the rear parking brake is released.
3. Remove the rear wheels and remove the rear brake drums from the vehicle.
4. Disconnect the parking brake cables from the levers. Remove the parking brake lever stop plates.
5. Disconnect and plug the brake lines to the wheel cylinders.
6. Remove the backing plate mounting bolts.
7. Using a slide hammer, remove the rear axles with the backing plates attached.
8. Using a suitable prying tool, remove the axle seal from the housing.
9. If the axle, axle bearing, or backing plate is being replaced, support the axle in a vise with additional support under the shaft next to the bearing.

✳✳ CAUTION

Eye protection must be worn during the following 3 steps. Failure to do so could cause injury.

10. With the axle shaft supported properly, grind the top and bottom of the axle bearing retainer. This will enable it to be removed without damaging the axle shaft.
11. Using a chisel, break the retainer and remove the retainer from the axle shaft.
12. Using a press or suitable bearing puller, remove the axle shaft bearing from the axle shaft.
13. Remove the backing plate from the axle shaft.
To install:
14. Using a seal driver, install the new seal with the lip facing the housing to the same depth as the old seal.
15. Install the backing plate on the axle shaft and using a press, install the bearing and the retainer on the axle shaft.

16. Install the axle shaft in the housing.
17. Install the backing plate mounting bolts and torque them to 159–248 inch lbs. (18–28 Nm). Connect the brake lines to the wheel cylinders.
18. Install the parking brake lever stop plates and connect the brake cables to the parking brake lever.
19. Install the rear brake drums and install the rear wheels.
20. Adjust the brakes and bleed the brake hydraulic system.
21. Refill the rear differential and safely lower the vehicle.

Sidekick, Tracker, Sidekick Sport and X-90 Models

♦ See Figures 131 thru 143

1. Raise and safely support the vehicle.
2. Remove the rear wheels and remove the rear brake drums from the vehicle.
3. Drain the gear oil from the rear axle housing.
4. Remove the rear brake return springs.

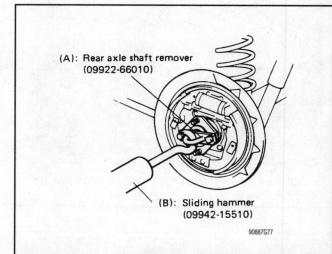

(A): Rear axle shaft remover (09922-66010)

(B): Sliding hammer (09942-15510)

90887G77

Fig. 131 To pull the axle shaft out of the rear housing, it may be necessary to use a slide hammer and adapter, as shown

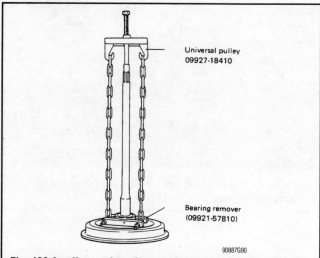

Universal pulley 09927-18410

Bearing remover (09921-57810)

90887G90

Fig. 130 A puller, such as the one shown, must be used to pull the bearing off of the axle shaft

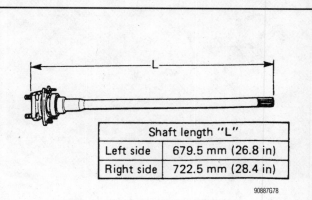

Shaft length "L"	
Left side	679.5 mm (26.8 in)
Right side	722.5 mm (28.4 in)

90887G78

Fig. 132 If removing both of the rear axle shafts from the housing, be sure to mark the shafts so that they can be reinstalled in their original positions—if you mix the shafts up, measure their length

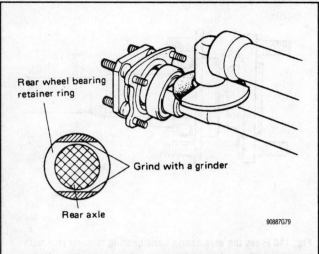

Fig. 133 Use an angle grinder to shave the rear axle shaft bearing retainer ring as shown (shaded areas) . . .

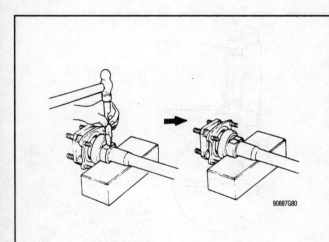

Fig. 134 . . . then use a chisel and hammer to break the retainer ring in half

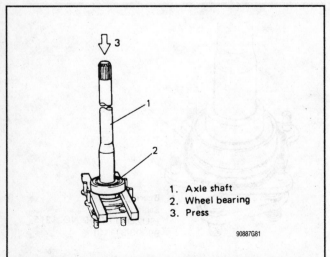

Fig. 135 Remove the axle shaft bearing by pressing it off, as shown

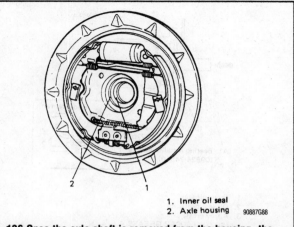

1. Inner oil seal
2. Axle housing

Fig. 136 Once the axle shaft is removed from the housing, the inner oil seal should be pried out of the housing—whenever the axle shaft is removed, the oil seal should be replaced with a new one

→If both axles are being removed mark the axles left and right. The axles are different lengths and must be installed in the correct position.

5. Remove the rear wheel bearing retainer nuts from the rear axle housing.
6. Using an axle puller remove the axle shaft from the housing.

⁑ WARNING

Do not remove the backing plate with the axle; this may cause damage to the inner seal.

7. If the axle, axle bearing or seal is being replaced, support the axle in a vise with additional support under the shaft next to the bearing.

⁑ CAUTION

Eye protection must be worn during rear axle bearing and seal removal. Failure to do so could cause injury.

8. With the axle shaft supported properly, grind the top and bottom of the axle bearing retainer until they are flat. DO NOT grind the axle, component failure could result.
9. Using a chisel and hammer, finish removing the retainer from the axle shaft.
10. Using a press or suitable bearing puller, remove the axle shaft bearing from the axle shaft.
11. Using a prying tool, remove the seal from the axle housing.
To install:
12. Using a seal driver, install the new seal with the lip facing the housing to the same depth as the old seal.
13. Apply grease to the axle shaft inner oil seal lip.
14. Install the new bearing and the retainer on the axle shaft using a suitable press.
15. Apply a bead of sealant on the outer face of the bearing retainer.
16. Install the axle shaft into the rear axle housing and replace the rear wheel bearing retaining nuts, tighten to 159–248 inch lbs. (18–28 Nm). When sliding the axle shaft into the housing, be careful not to damage the inner oil seal.
17. Install the rear brake return springs.
18. Replace the rear brake drums and replace the rear tires on the vehicle.
19. Refill the rear axle housing with the proper gear oil and safely lower the vehicle.

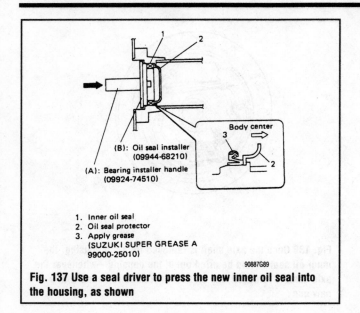

1. Inner oil seal
2. Oil seal protector
3. Apply grease
   (SUZUKI SUPER GREASE A
   99000-25010)

(B): Oil seal installer
(09944-68210)

(A): Bearing installer handle
(09924-74510)

Body center

90887G89

Fig. 137 Use a seal driver to press the new inner oil seal into the housing, as shown

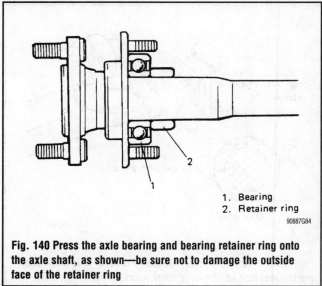

1. Bearing
2. Retainer ring

90887G84

Fig. 140 Press the axle bearing and bearing retainer ring onto the axle shaft, as shown—be sure not to damage the outside face of the retainer ring

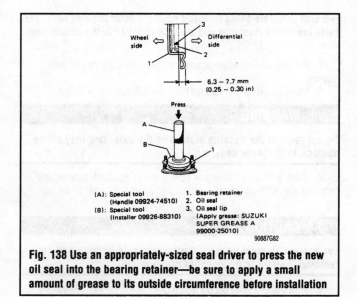

Wheel side

Differential side

6.3 – 7.7 mm
(0.25 – 0.30 in)

Press

(A): Special tool
(Handle 09924-74510)
(B): Special tool
(Installer 09926-88310)

1. Bearing retainer
2. Oil seal
3. Oil seal lip
   (Apply grease: SUZUKI
   SUPER GREASE A
   99000-25010)

90887G82

Fig. 138 Use an appropriately-sized seal driver to press the new oil seal into the bearing retainer—be sure to apply a small amount of grease to its outside circumference before installation

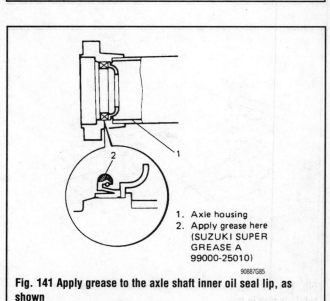

1. Axle housing
2. Apply grease here
   (SUZUKI SUPER
   GREASE A
   99000-25010)

90887G85

Fig. 141 Apply grease to the axle shaft inner oil seal lip, as shown

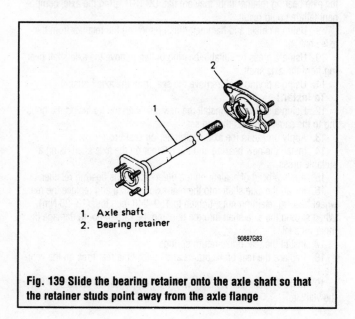

1. Axle shaft
2. Bearing retainer

90887G83

Fig. 139 Slide the bearing retainer onto the axle shaft so that the retainer studs point away from the axle flange

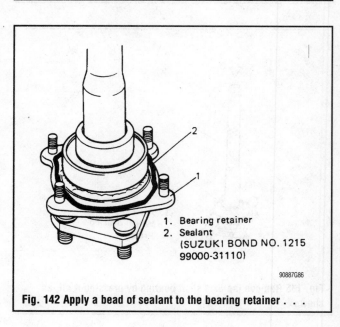

1. Bearing retainer
2. Sealant
   (SUZUKI BOND NO. 1215
   99000-31110)

90887G86

Fig. 142 Apply a bead of sealant to the bearing retainer . . .

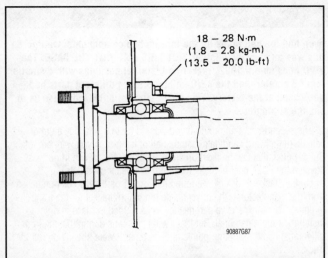

Fig. 143 . . . then slide the axle shaft into the housing—tighten the bearing retainer stud nuts to 159–248 inch lbs. (18–28 Nm)

Axle Housing Assembly

REMOVAL & INSTALLATION

Samurai Models

▶ **See Figure 144**

1. Loosen all of the rear wheel lug nuts ½ turn. The rear wheels should be left on the axle assembly so that the assembly may be rolled out from beneath the vehicle.
2. Block the front wheels, then raise and safely support the rear of the vehicle with jackstands positioned beneath the frame rails.
3. Support the axle housing assembly with two hydraulic floor jacks.
4. Drain the axle housing assembly lubricant.
5. Detach and immediately plug the flexible rubber hose attaching the body brake line to the axle brake line from the axle brake line.
6. If equipped, remove the rear stabilizer bar.
7. Remove the rear driveshaft, as described earlier in this section.
8. Remove the rear shock absorbers, as described in Section 8.

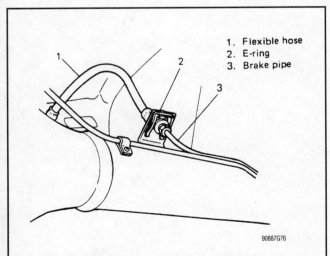

1. Flexible hose
2. E-ring
3. Brake pipe

Fig. 144 Before removing the axle housing, the flexible brake hose must be disconnected

9. Remove the rear leaf springs, as described in Section 8.
10. Carefully lower the axle assembly with the floor jacks, ensuring that no cables, wires or other components will inhibit axle assembly removal.
11. Roll the axle assembly out from beneath the vehicle.
12. The axle assembly may now be disassembled. The brake components and axle shaft procedures are covered elsewhere in this manual. The disassembly of the differential unit should be left to a professional automotive technician, unless you have extensive prior knowledge of this sort.

To install:

13. Assemble the axle assembly as necessary.
14. Roll the axle assembly into position beneath the vehicle, then slowly raise the axle on the two floor jacks.
15. Install the leaf springs, shock absorbers, and driveshaft. Be sure that the driveshaft and differential flange matchmarks are properly aligned before bolting the two together.
16. If applicable, install the stabilizer bar.
17. Connect the flexible brake hose to the rear brake line.
18. Bleed the brake system, as described in Section 9.
19. Refill the differential with lubricant, as described in Section 1.
20. Lower the vehicle, then tighten the rear wheel lug nuts to the specified value, as described in Section 8.

Sidekick, Tracker, Sidekick Sport and X-90 Models

1. Loosen all of the rear wheel lug nuts ½ turn. The rear wheels should be left on the axle assembly so that the assembly may be rolled out from beneath the vehicle.
2. Block the front wheels, then raise and safely support the rear of the vehicle with jackstands positioned beneath the frame rails.
3. Support the axle housing assembly with two hydraulic floor jacks.
4. Drain the axle housing assembly lubricant.
5. Detach and label all wiring harness connectors from the rear axle assembly.
6. Detach and immediately plug the flexible rubber hose attaching the body brake line to the axle brake line from the axle brake line.
7. If equipped, remove the rear stabilizer bar.
8. Remove the rear driveshaft, as described earlier in this section.
9. Remove the rear shock absorbers, as described in Section 8.
10. Remove the rear coil springs, as described in Section 8.
11. Remove the trailing and upper arms, as described in Section 8.
12. Carefully lower the axle assembly with the floor jacks, ensuring that no cables, wires or other components will inhibit axle assembly removal.
13. Roll the axle assembly out from beneath the vehicle.
14. The axle assembly may now be disassembled. The brake components and axle shaft procedures are covered elsewhere in this manual. The disassembly of the differential unit should be left to a professional automotive technician, unless you have extensive prior knowledge of this sort.

To install:

15. Assemble the axle assembly as necessary.
16. Roll the axle assembly into position beneath the vehicle, then slowly raise the axle on the two floor jacks.
17. Install the trailing and upper arms, the coil springs, the shock absorbers, and the driveshaft. Be sure that the driveshaft and differential flange matchmarks are properly aligned before bolting the two together.
18. If applicable, install the stabilizer bar.
19. Reattach all applicable wiring harness connectors to the rear axle assembly.
20. Connect the flexible brake hose to the rear brake line.
21. Bleed the brake system, as described in Section 9.
22. Refill the differential with lubricant, as described in Section 1.
23. Lower the vehicle, then tighten the rear wheel lug nuts to the specified value, as described in Section 8.

FOUR-BY-FOUR CONVERSION

Because of the often-times tremendous difference in prices between 2 and 4-wheel drive trucks some people purchase the 2WD out of necessity, only later to find that they wish they had been able to buy the 4WD. Or, some might even purchase the 2WD on purpose in order to save money up front and then take on the task of conversion to 4WD at a later time.

On the whole, the vehicles covered by this manual make EXCELLENT candidates for this. One of the reasons this is true would be because of Suzuki (and Geo's) approach to building vehicles. For such relatively low production numbers (compared to many of the world's vehicle platforms) it does not make economic sense to build too many unique parts for sub-sets of these vehicles (2WD vs. 4WD or even 2-door vs. 4-door in some cases).

The Samurai, for instance, uses a transfer case whether the vehicle was a 2WD or 4WD model from the factory. That meant every vehicle coming off their assembly line got the same 2 driveshafts to transfer power to the rear wheels (and 4WD models got a third in the form of the transfer case-to-front differential shaft). But more importantly, this means that the owner of a 2WD has one of the major headaches of a typical 4WD conversion already solved. One could easily remove the 2WD transfer case and just bolt the 4WD unit in its place.

One of the vehicles that we tore down in research for this manual was put through such a conversion. One of our editors actually had a 2WD Tracker which was in relatively nice shape, but was not worth selling to replace with a 4WD model. He located a 4WD that had some minor body damage and a bad case of neglect, which, because of these 2 reasons, was selling rather inexpensively.

In case you would like to undertake a similar project, here are a few things we learned during this process. The first and most important thing to do is to get your hands on the manufacturer's parts information. In the case of Suzuki and Geo it is normally in the form of microfiche. Studying the fiche for these 2 vehicles told us that the VAST MAJORITY of parts on this vehicle (even down to most of the suspension and drivetrain) were the same from the factory.

➡**One warning here, we also learned that although certain REPLACEMENT parts were the same, this may not have been the case during assembly. An example is the front hub and bearing assembly, which showed identical part numbers for both the 2WD and 4WD assemblies, meaning that the halfshafts from the 4WD unit should fit right through the 2WD hubs. And, since the 2WD hub**

even had the bolt holes for the locking hub components, we figured this was an easy installation. **BUT THIS WAS NOT THE CASE. The 2WD hubs on our 1992 Tracker had internal bushings with a smaller inner diameter than the 4WD units, meaning different parts had been used at the factory. This didn't stop us, but it did cause us to change strategies.**

The second best thing to do if you want to try this is to buy a donor vehicle (a junkyard candidate is fine, if all of the pieces you want are intact). But a runner, that can be fixed up and sold as a 2WD (which in our case covered the FULL cost of the conversion) is a better candidate.

On the Tracker/Sidekick, we found that only 1 part had to be purchased from the manufacturer; the driver's side mounting bracket for the front differential. This inexpensive part needed to be welded in place in order to install the front differential. But that wasn't bad considering that the front differential had 3 mounting points and the other 2 were already on our 2WD truck.

All other parts in the conversion were taken from the donor vehicle, and they included:
- Front differential
- Front left and right halfshafts
- Front hub and bearing assemblies
- Transmission and transfer case assembly
- Transmission rear crossmember
- Front and rear driveshafts
- Front coil springs (they had one more coil on the 4WD units)
- Rear coil springs
- Instrument cluster (the only way to bring the 4WD lights, unless we wanted to create our own)

A confession on the hub and bearing assemblies. Because hub removal requires the use of a special spindle nut socket (essentially a spanner wrench in socket form) that is capable of 155 ft. lbs. (210 Nm) of torque, we decided to cheat and found any easy answer (no special tools needed). Considering that we already had to swap coil springs, we just took that procedure a little further and finished unbolting the steering knuckles. We swapped the steering knuckles, taking the hub and bearing assemblies with them.

We were also looking into the installation of aftermarket locking differentials, but could not have that information available by press time.

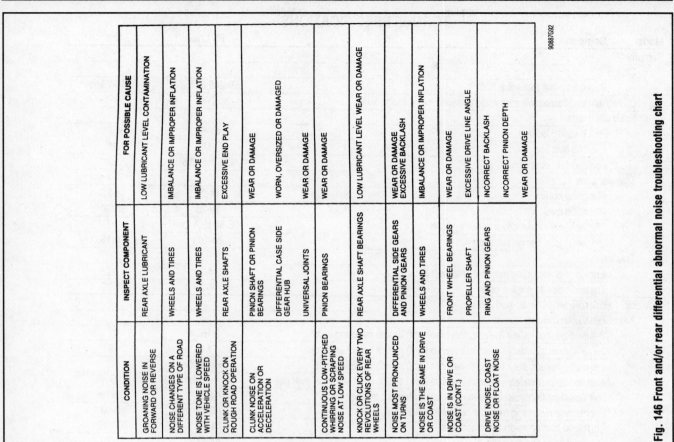

CONDITION	INSPECT COMPONENT	FOR POSSIBLE CAUSE
GROANING NOISE IN FORWARD OR REVERSE	REAR AXLE LUBRICANT	LOW LUBRICANT LEVEL CONTAMINATION
NOISE CHANGES ON A DIFFERENT TYPE OF ROAD	WHEELS AND TIRES	IMBALANCE OR IMPROPER INFLATION
NOISE TONE IS LOWERED WITH VEHICLE SPEED	WHEELS AND TIRES	IMBALANCE OR IMPROPER INFLATION
CLUNK OR KNOCK ON ROUGH ROAD OPERATION	REAR AXLE SHAFTS	EXCESSIVE END PLAY
CLUNK NOISE ON ACCELERATION OR DECELERATION	PINION SHAFT OR PINION BEARINGS	WEAR OR DAMAGE
	DIFFERENTIAL CASE SIDE GEAR HUB	WORN, OVERSIZED OR DAMAGED
	UNIVERSAL JOINTS	WEAR OR DAMAGE
CONTINUOUS LOW-PITCHED WHIRRING OR SCRAPING NOISE AT LOW SPEED	PINION BEARINGS	WEAR OR DAMAGE
KNOCK OR CLICK EVERY TWO REVOLUTIONS OF REAR WHEELS	REAR AXLE SHAFT BEARINGS	LOW LUBRICANT LEVEL WEAR OR DAMAGE
NOISE MOST PRONOUNCED ON TURNS	DIFFERENTIAL SIDE GEARS AND PINION GEARS	WEAR OR DAMAGE EXCESSIVE BACKLASH
NOISE IS THE SAME IN DRIVE OR COAST	WHEELS AND TIRES	IMBALANCE OR IMPROPER INFLATION
NOISE IS IN DRIVE OR COAST (CONT.)	FRONT WHEEL BEARINGS	WEAR OR DAMAGE
	PROPELLER SHAFT	EXCESSIVE DRIVE LINE ANGLE
DRIVE NOISE, COAST NOISE OR FLOAT NOISE	RING AND PINION GEARS	INCORRECT BACKLASH
		INCORRECT PINION DEPTH
		WEAR OR DAMAGE

90887G92

Fig. 146 Front and/or rear differential abnormal noise troubleshooting chart

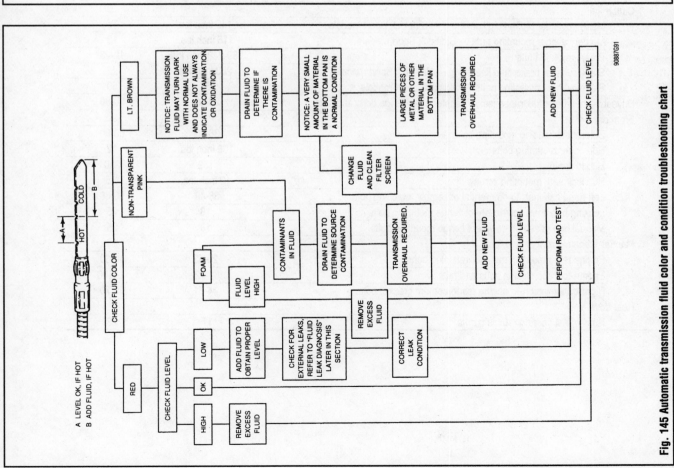

90887G91

Fig. 145 Automatic transmission fluid color and condition troubleshooting chart

TORQUE SPECIFICATIONS

Model	Component	Ft. Lbs.	Nm
Samurai			
Clutch			
	Pressure plate mounting bolts	159-248 inch lbs.	18-28
Driveshaft-to-differential/transmission/transfer case flange bolts		37-43	50-60
Front drive axle			
	Hub bearing locknut	44-65	60-90
	Locking hub body bolts	18	24
	Locking hub cover bolts	115 inch lbs.	13
Transfer case			
	Mounting bolts	14-20	18-28
	Mounting nuts	19-25	25-34
	Shifter handle case cover retaining bolts	35-62 inch lbs.	4-7
	Universal joint flange retaining nut	80-108	110-150
Transmission			
	Engine rear mounting member retaining bolts	14-20	18-28
	Transmission-to-engine bolts	14-20	18-28
Sidekick, Tracker, Sidekick Sport and X-90			
Automatic transmission			
	3-speed neutral safety (selector/reverse light) switch retaining bolt	15	21
	3-speed neutral safety (selector/reverse light) switch select lever nut	14	19
	4-speed neutral safety (selector/reverse light) switch retaining bolt	115 inch lbs.	13
	4-speed neutral safety (selector/reverse light) switch shift selector lever nut	44 inch lbs.	5
	Left and right transmission-to-engine reinforcement bracket bolts	44-51	60-70
	Engine rear mounting member retaining bolts	29-43	40-60
	Engine-to-transmission bolts and nuts	51-72	70-100
	Flywheel-to-converter bolts	44-51	60-70
Clutch			
	Master cylinder brake fluid line fitting — Sidekick Sport models	142 inch lbs.	16
	Master cylinder mounting nuts — Sidekick Sport models	115 inch lbs.	13
	Pressure plate bolts	159-248 inch lbs.	18-28
	Slave cylinder brake fluid line fitting — Sidekick Sport models	203 inch lbs.	23
	Slave cylinder mounting bolts — Sidekick Sport models	36	50
Driveshaft-to-differential/transmission/transfer case flange bolts and nuts		36-43	50-60
Front drive axle			
	Differential housing mounting bolts	36-43	50-60
	Hub cover mounting bolts	106 inch lbs.	12
	Hub lock nut	152	210
	Hub lockplate mounting screws	12 inch lbs.	1.5
	Left-hand halfshaft-to-differential assembly attaching bolts	36-43	50-60
	Locking hub assembly-to-wheel flange mounting bolts	18	25
	Manual hub assembly-to-wheel flange mounting bolts	18	25
Manual Transmission			
	Engine rear mounting member retaining bolts	29-43	40-60
	Engine-to-transmission bolts and nuts	51-72	70-100
	Right transmission-to-engine reinforcement bracket bolts	44-51	60-70
Rear drive axle			
	Rear wheel bearing retaining nuts	17	23

90887C00

8

SUSPENSION AND STEERING

WHEELS

Wheels

REMOVAL & INSTALLATION

▶ **See Figure 1**

1. Park the vehicle on a level surface.
2. Remove the jack, tire iron and, if necessary, the spare tire from their storage compartments.
3. Check the owner's manual or refer to Section 1 of this manual for the jacking points on your vehicle. Then, place the jack in the proper position.
4. If equipped with lug nut trim caps, remove them by either unscrewing or pulling them off the lug nuts, as appropriate. Consult the owner's manual, if necessary.
5. If equipped with a wheel cover or hub cap, insert the tapered end of the tire iron in the groove and pry off the cover.
6. Apply the parking brake and block the diagonally opposite wheel with a wheel chock or two.

➡**Wheel chocks may be purchased at your local auto parts store, or a block of wood cut into wedges may be used. If possible, keep one or two of the chocks in your tire storage compartment, in case any of the tires has to be removed on the side of the road.**

7. If equipped with an automatic transmission, place the selector lever in **P** or Park; with a manual transmission, place the shifter in Reverse.
8. With the tires still on the ground, use the tire iron/wrench to break the lug nuts loose.

➡**If a nut is stuck, never use heat to loosen it or damage to the wheel and bearings may occur. If the nuts are seized, one or two heavy hammer blows directly on the end of the bolt usually loosens the rust. Be careful, as continued pounding will likely damage the brake drum or rotor.**

9. Using the jack, raise the vehicle until the tire is clear of the ground. Support the vehicle safely using jackstands.
10. Remove the lug nuts, then remove the tire and wheel assembly.

To install:

11. Make sure the wheel and hub mating surfaces, as well as the wheel lug studs, are clean and free of all foreign material. Always remove rust from the wheel mounting surface and the brake rotor or drum. Failure to do so may cause the lug nuts to loosen in service.
12. Install the tire and wheel assembly and hand-tighten the lug nuts.
13. Using the tire wrench, tighten all the lug nuts, in a crisscross pattern, until they are snug.
14. Raise the vehicle and withdraw the jackstand, then lower the vehicle.
15. Using a torque wrench, tighten the lug nuts in a crisscross pattern to 37–57 ft. lbs. (50–80 Nm) for Samurai models and 1986–90 Sidekick, Tracker, Sidekick Sport and X-90 models, or to 58–80 ft. lbs. (80–110 Nm) for 1991–98 Sidekick, Tracker, Sidekick Sport and X-90 models. Check your owner's manual or refer to Section 1 of this manual for the proper tightening sequence.

✳✳ WARNING

Do not overtighten the lug nuts, as this may cause the wheel studs to stretch or the brake disc (rotor) to warp.

16. If so equipped, install the wheel cover or hub cap. Make sure the valve stem protrudes through the proper opening before tapping the wheel cover into position.
17. If equipped, install the lug nut trim caps by pushing them or screwing them on, as applicable.
18. Remove the jack from under the vehicle, and place the jack and tire iron/wrench in their storage compartments. Remove the wheel chock(s).
19. If you have removed a flat or damaged tire, place it in the storage compartment of the vehicle and take it to your local repair station to have it fixed or replaced as soon as possible.

INSPECTION

Inspect the tires for lacerations, puncture marks, nails and other sharp objects. Repair or replace as necessary. Also check the tires for treadwear and air pressure as outlined in Check the wheel assemblies for dents, cracks, rust and metal fatigue. Repair or replace as necessary.

Wheel Lug Studs

REMOVAL & INSTALLATION

Disc Brakes

▶ **See Figures 2, 3 and 4**

1. Raise and support the appropriate end of the vehicle safely using jackstands, then remove the wheel.
2. Remove the brake pads and caliper. Support the caliper aside using wire or a coat hanger. For details, please refer to Section 9 of this manual.
3. Remove the brake rotor, as described in Section 9.
4. Properly support the rotor using press bars, then drive the stud out using an arbor press.

➡**If a press is not available, CAREFULLY drive the old stud out using a blunt drift. MAKE SURE the rotor is properly and evenly supported otherwise it may be damaged.**

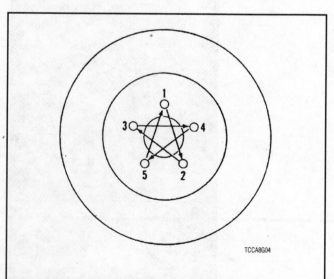

TCCA8G04

Fig. 1 Typical wheel lug tightening sequence

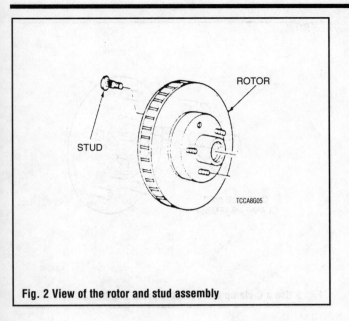

Fig. 2 View of the rotor and stud assembly

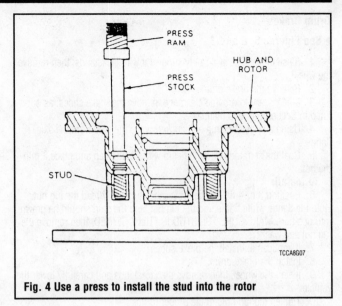

Fig. 4 Use a press to install the stud into the rotor

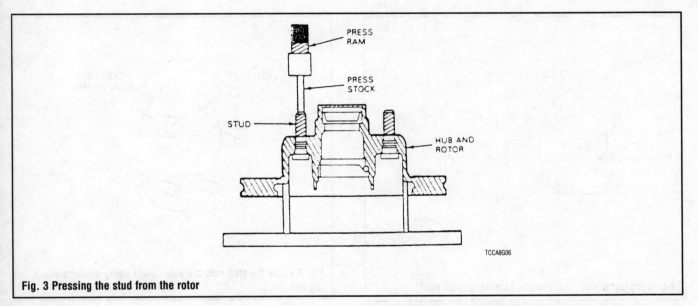

Fig. 3 Pressing the stud from the rotor

To install:

5. Clean the stud hole with a wire brush and start the new stud with a hammer and drift pin. Do not use any lubricant or thread sealer.

6. Finish installing the stud with the press.

➡If a press is not available, start the lug stud through the bore in the hub, then position 3 or 4 flat washers over the protruding end of the stud and thread the lug nut. Hold the hub/rotor while tightening the lug nut, and the stud should be drawn into position. **MAKE SURE THE STUD IS FULLY SEATED, then remove the lug nut and washers.**

7. Install the rotor and adjust the wheel bearings, if applicable.

8. Install the brake caliper and pads.

9. Install the wheel, then remove the jackstands and carefully lower the vehicle.

10. Tighten the lug nuts to the proper torque.

Drum Brakes

▶ **See Figures 5, 6 and 7**

1. Raise the vehicle and safely support it with jackstands, then remove the wheel.

2. Remove the brake drum.

3. If necessary to provide clearance, remove the brake shoes, as outlined in Section 9 of this manual.

4. Using a large C-clamp and socket, press the stud from the axle flange.

5. Coat the serrated part of the stud with liquid soap and place it into the hole.

To install:

6. Position 3 or 4 flat washers over the stud and thread the lug nut. Hold the flange while tightening the lug nut, and the stud should be drawn into position. MAKE SURE THE STUD IS FULLY SEATED, then remove the lug nut and washers.

7. If applicable, install the brake shoes.

8. Install the brake drum.

9. Install the wheel, then remove the jackstands and carefully lower the vehicle.

10. Tighten the lug nuts to the proper torque.

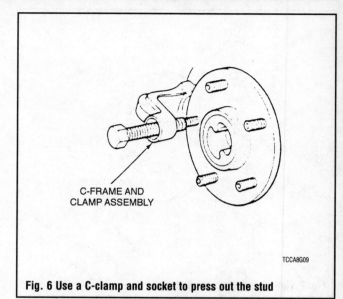

Fig. 6 Use a C-clamp and socket to press out the stud

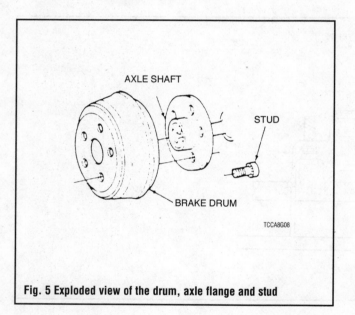

Fig. 5 Exploded view of the drum, axle flange and stud

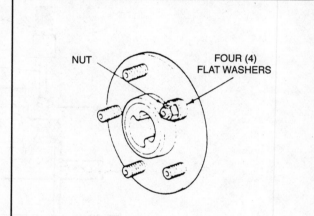

Fig. 7 Force the stud onto the axle flange using washers and a lug nut

FRONT SUSPENSION

COIL SPRING FRONT SUSPENSION COMPONENT LOCATIONS

1. Lower control arms
2. Lower ball joints
3. Steering knuckles
4. Coil springs
5. Stabilizer bar end links
6. Strut assemblies
7. Stabilizer bar

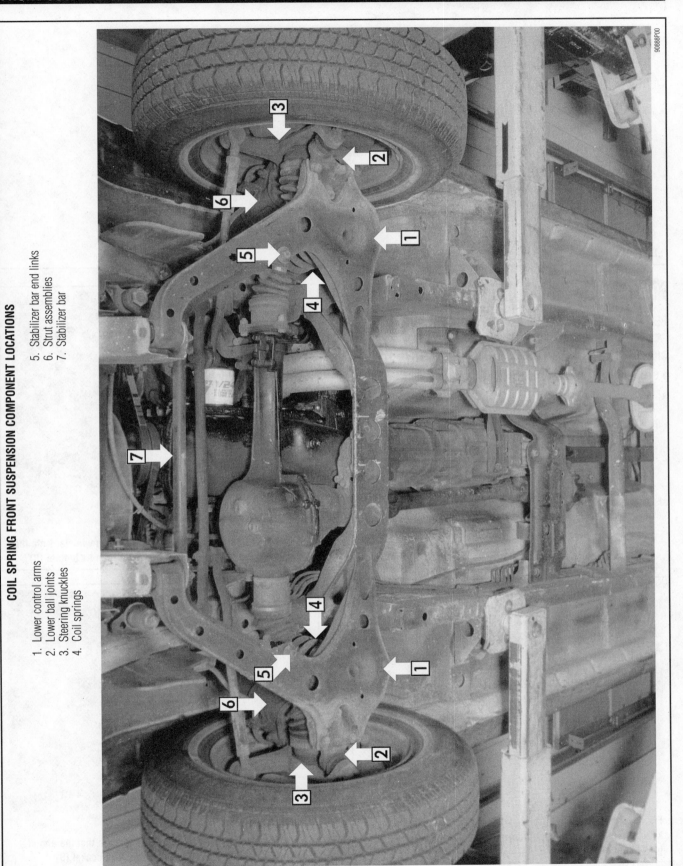

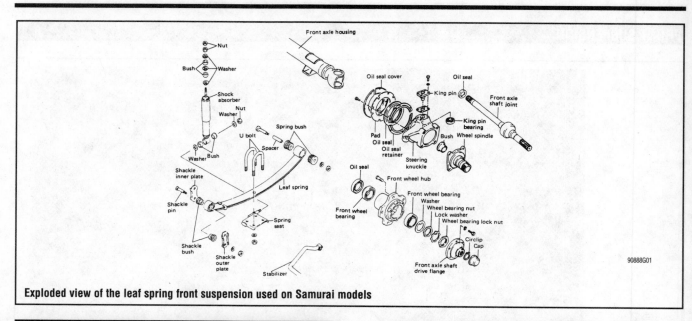

Exploded view of the leaf spring front suspension used on Samurai models

Coil Springs

REMOVAL & INSTALLATION

Sidekick, Tracker, Sidekick Sport and X-90 Models

▶ **See Figures 8, 9 and 10**

1. Loosen all of the front wheel lug nuts ½ turn.
2. Apply the parking brake, block the rear wheels, then raise and safely support the front of the vehicle securely on jackstands.
3. Remove the front wheel. Unbolt the brake caliper and suspend it out of the way.
4. Remove the engine skid plate, if equipped.
5. Support the lower control arm with a floor jack.
6. Remove the 3 nuts and bolts from the control arm, or remove the castellated nut from the ball joint, and separate the control arm from the steering knuckle.
7. Disconnect the stabilizer bar from the control arm.

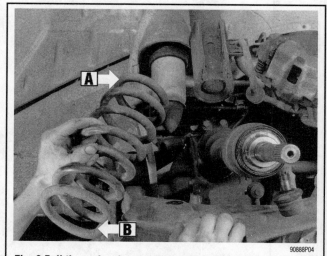

Fig. 9 Pull the spring down and away from the vehicle. Note that the spring's top (A) is a smaller diameter than its bottom (B)

Fig. 8 To remove the coil spring, first remove the steering knuckle. Next, lower and pull down on the control arm and grasp hold of the spring

Fig. 10 When installing the spring, make sure that the end of the coil (A) is fully seated in the control arm pocket (B)

The coil spring is under pressure. Make sure control arm is firmly supported with a hydraulic jack before continuing with procedure. If this precaution is not observed, serious bodily injury may result.

8. Remove the lower strut mounting bracket bolts and disconnect the strut bracket from the steering knuckle.

9. Lower the control arm enough to remove the steering knuckle assembly.

10. Lower the jack until all tension is removed from the coil spring. Remove the coil spring from the vehicle.

To install:

11. Install the coil spring onto the control arm and slowly raise the jack.

➡**The bottom of the spring has a larger diameter than the top. Make sure that the spring is installed correctly.**

12. Install the strut-to-knuckle mounting nuts and bolts and tighten to specifications.

13. Connect the stabilizer link to the control arm. Tighten the nut to the value specified in the torque chart located at the end of this section.

14. If removed, install the 3 nuts and bolts connecting the control arm and ball joint. Tighten the nuts to 51–75 ft. lbs. (70–100 Nm).

15. If removed, install and tighten the ball joint castle nut to 33–50 ft. lbs. (45–70 Nm). Insert a new cotter pin through the castle nut and ball joint stud holes, then bend the cotter pin ends over. If none of the castle nut grooves are aligned with the hole in the ball joint stud hole, continue tightening the castle nut until one of the grooves is aligned with the stud hole, then install the cotter pin.

16. Install the engine skid plate. Tighten the bolts to 40 ft. lbs. (54 Nm).

17. Install the brake caliper and the front wheels, then lower the vehicle.

Leaf Springs

REMOVAL & INSTALLATION

Samurai Models

▶ **See Figure 11**

1. Loosen all of the front wheel lug nuts ½ turn.

2. Apply the parking brake, block the rear wheels, then raise and safely support the front of the vehicle on jackstands, allowing the front suspension to hang free.

3. Remove the front wheel.

4. Remove the stabilizer bar pivot bolt.

5. Support the front axle assembly with an adjustable stand or hydraulic floor jack.

6. Remove the leaf spring to spring plate mounting U-bolts.

7. Remove the lower shock mounting bolt and remove the spring plate.

8. Remove the shackle pin and the nut from the front of the leaf spring.

9. Disconnect the leaf spring bolt at the rear of the spring and remove the leaf spring.

➡**Removal of the leaf spring causes the axle housing to hang from the other leaf spring and the driveshaft. Be sure to support it with a jackstand or floor jack to prevent it from damaging the U-joint of the driveshaft.**

To install:

10. Install the leaf spring and leaf spring rear bolt. Tighten the rear mounting bolt after the vehicle is lowered.

11. Install the shackle pin and nut to the front of the leaf spring. Tighten the nut after the vehicle is lowered.

12. Install the spring plate and U-bolts. Tighten the U-bolt nuts to 44–57 ft. lbs. (60–80 Nm).

13. Connect the shock to its lower mount and install the mounting nut.

14. Install the stabilizer bar pivot bolt. Tighten the stabilizer pivot bolts to 51–65 ft. lbs. (70–90 Nm).

15. Remove the axle housing support, and lower the vehicle.

16. After the vehicle is on the ground, tighten the rear mounting bolt and front shackle nut to the value shown in the torque chart at the end of this section.

Shock Absorbers

REMOVAL & INSTALLATION

Samurai Models

▶ **See Figure 12**

1. Raise and safely support the vehicle.

2. Support the axle assembly and remove the upper shock absorber mounting nut.

3. Remove the lower shock absorber mounting nut and remove the shock absorber.

To install:

4. Install the shock absorber and install the lower mounting nut to the bolt.

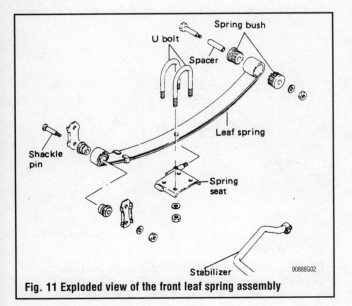

Fig. 11 Exploded view of the front leaf spring assembly

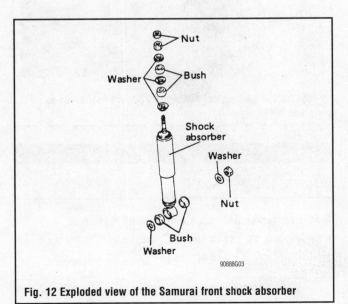

Fig. 12 Exploded view of the Samurai front shock absorber

5. Tighten the upper mounting nut to 16–25 ft. lbs. (22–35 Nm), and the lower nut to 23–39 ft. lbs. (35–55 Nm).

6. Remove the axle support and lower the vehicle.

TESTING

The purpose of the shock absorber is simply to limit the motion of the spring during compression and rebound cycles. If the vehicle is not equipped with these motion dampers, the up and down motion would multiply until the vehicle was alternately trying to leap off the ground and to pound itself into the pavement.

Countrary to popular rumor, the shocks do not affect the ride height of the vehicle. This is controlled by other suspension components such as springs and tires. Worn shock absorbers can affect handling; if the front of the vehicle is rising or falling excessively, the "footprint" of the tires changes on the pavement and steering is affected.

The simplest test of the shock absorber is simply push down on one corner of the unladen vehicle and release it. Observe the motion of the body as it is released. In most cases, it will come up beyond it original rest position, dip back below it and settle quickly to rest. This shows that the damper is controlling the spring action. Any tendency to excessive pitch (up-and-down) motion or failure to return to rest within 2–3 cycles is a sign of poor function within the shock absorber. Oil-filled shocks may have a light film of oil around the seal, resulting from normal breathing and air exchange. This should NOT be taken as a sign of failure, but any sign of thick or running oil definitely indicates failure. Gas filled shocks may also show some film at the shaft; if the gas has leaked out, the shock will have almost no resistance to motion.

While each shock absorber can be replaced individually, it is recommended that they be changed as a pair (both front or both rear) to maintain equal response on both sides of the vehicle. Chances are quite good that if one has failed, its mate is weak also.

When fluid is seeping out of the shock absorber, it's time to replace it

TCCA8P73

Struts

REMOVAL & INSTALLATION

Sidekick, Tracker, Sidekick Sport and X-90 Models

▶ **See Figures 13, 14, 15 and 16**

1. Raise and safely support the vehicle. Allow the front suspension to hang free.

2. Remove the front wheel.

Fig. 13 To remove the front strut, first remove the brake hose-to-strut retaining clip and pull the hose free from the bracket

90888P06

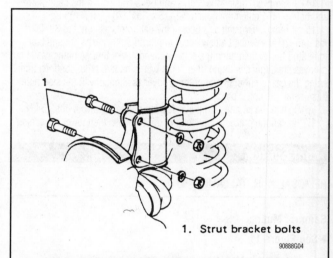

1. Strut bracket bolts

90888G04

Fig. 14 Next, support the lower control arm and remove the lower strut bracket bolts . . .

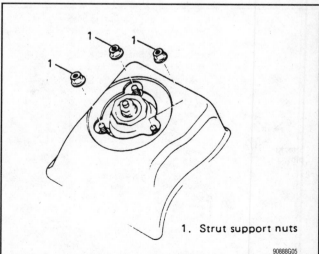

1. Strut support nuts

90888G05

Fig. 15 . . . followed by the upper strut mount attaching nuts—be sure to support the strut before removing the last nut!

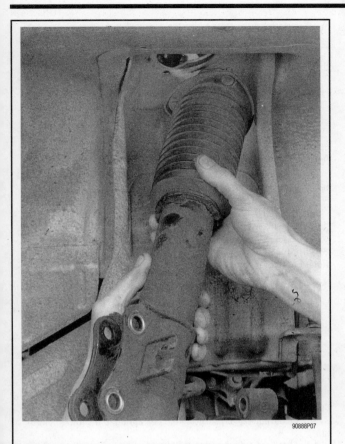

Fig. 16 Finally, pull the strut from the vehicle

3. Disconnect the E-clip mounting the brake hose and remove the brake hose from the strut bracket.

4. Support the control arm with a stand or floor jack.

⁂ CAUTION

The coil spring is under extreme pressure. Make sure control arm is firmly supported with a hydraulic jack before continuing with procedure. If this precaution is not observed, serious bodily injury may result.

5. Matchmark the strut lower bracket to the steering knuckle. Remove the strut-to-knuckle bolts.

6. Remove the upper strut mounting nuts. Hold the strut to prevent it from falling. Remove the strut assembly from the vehicle.

To install:

7. Install the strut assembly and tighten the upper strut mounting nuts to 15–22 ft. lbs. (20–30 Nm).

8. Install the strut-to-knuckle bolts, ensuring that the matchmarks are aligned, then tighten the nuts and bolts to 58–75 ft. lbs. (80–100 Nm).

9. Remove the stand or jack.

10. Connect the brake hose to the strut bracket using the E-clip.

11. Install the front wheels and lower the vehicle.

12. Check the vehicle's alignment.

Lower Ball Joints

INSPECTION

Inspect the ball joint stud dust seal (boot) for grease leaks, detachment, tearing or other damage.

Raise and support the vehicle on jackstands so that the suspension control arms hang and the wheels are off of the ground. Use a floor jack to support the lower control arm, then attempt to wobble the wheel in a vertical motion by holding the top of the tire with one hand and the bottom of the tire with the other. If any movement is felt, have an assistant wobble the wheel while you look for movement between the lower control arm and the spindle; the spindle and arm should not move independently of each other. If there is movement, replace the lower ball joint.

If the ball joint appears fine, check the front wheel bearings, then repeat this test to ensure the ball joint is in good condition.

REMOVAL & INSTALLATION

Sidekick, Tracker, Sidekick Sport and X-90 Models

♦ See Figures 17, 18, 19, 20 and 21

1. Loosen all of the front wheel lug nuts ½ turn.

2. Apply the parking brake, block the rear wheels, then raise and safely support the front of the vehicle on jackstands.

3. Remove the front wheel.

4. Position a hydraulic floor jack beneath the lower control arm, then raise the floor jack until it supports the lower control arm.

5. On 4-wheel drive models, remove the wheel hub, as described later in this section.

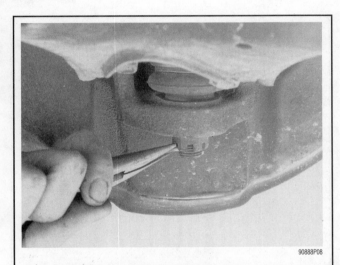

Fig. 17 To remove the lower ball joint, first remove the cotter pin from the ball joint stud and castellated nut . . .

Fig. 18 . . . then loosen and remove the nut. Make sure to support the lower control arm!

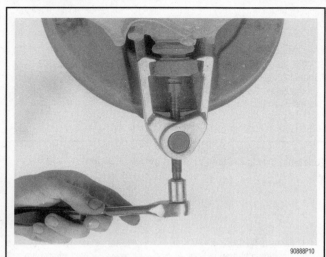

Fig. 19 Using a ball joint separator tool, detach the joint from the steering knuckle

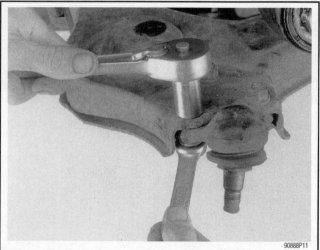

Fig. 20 With the steering knuckle out of the way, remove the three ball joint-to-lower control arm attaching bolts and nuts . . .

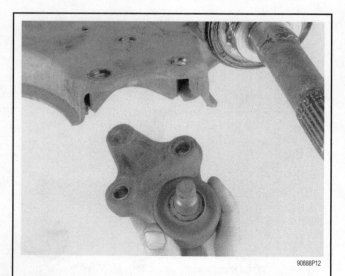

Fig. 21 . . . and remove the ball joint from the control arm

6. Detach the tie rod end from the steering knuckle arm.

7. Secure the bottom of the coil spring to the lower control arm with a chain. This will prevent the spring from accidentally dislodging form the control arm and possibly causing personal injury.

8. Withdraw the lower ball joint castle nut cotter pin, then remove the castle nut.

9. Detach the lower ball joint from the steering knuckle by tapping its end with a mallet, or by using a ball joint separator tool.

10. While slowly raising the floor jack, pull outward on the spindle/knuckle assembly to detach it from the ball joint stud. Support the spindle/knuckle assembly aside.

11. Lower the control arm to relieve the spring pressure and unbolt the ball joint from the control arm.

To install:

12. Position the new ball joint on the control arm. Install the bolts and tighten the nuts to 51–75 ft. lbs. (70–100 Nm).

➡**During installation ensure that the coil spring is properly positioned on its lower and upper seats.**

13. Raise the floor jack enough to allow the spindle/knuckle assembly to clear the ball joint stud.

14. While slowly lowering the floor jack, position the spindle/knuckle assembly onto the lower ball joint stud.

15. Install and tighten the ball joint castle nut to 33–50 ft. lbs. (45–70 Nm). Insert a new cotter pin through the castle nut and ball joint stud holes, then bend the cotter pin ends over. If none of the castle nut grooves are aligned with the hole in the ball joint stud hole, continue tightening the castle nut until one of the grooves is aligned with the stud hole, then install the cotter pin.

16. Remove the chain securing the coil spring to the lower control arm.

17. Attach the tie rod end to the steering knuckle arm, then tighten the tie rod end castle nut to 22–39 ft. lbs. (30–55 Nm). Insert a new cotter pin through the castle nut and tie rod end stud holes, then bend the cotter pin ends over. If none of the castle nut grooves are aligned with the hole in the tie rod end stud hole, continue tightening the castle nut until one of the grooves is aligned with the stud hole, then install the cotter pin.

18. On 4-wheel drive models, install the hub.

19. Lower the floor jack and remove it from beneath the lower control arm.

20. Install the front wheel.

21. Lower the vehicle and remove the rear whee blocks.

22. Tighten all of the front wheel lug nuts.

Stabilizer (Sway) Bar

REMOVAL & INSTALLATION

Samurai Models

▶ **See Figure 22**

1. Apply the parking brake, block the rear wheels, then raise and safely support the front of the vehicle on jackstands.

2. Disconnect the stabilizer bar pivot bolts.

3. Remove the stabilizer bar mount bushing bracket bolts and nuts.

4. Remove the stabilizer bar.

To install:

5. Install the new stabilizer bar, using new bushings.

6. Tighten the stabilizer bar pivot bolts to 51–65 ft. lbs. (70–90 Nm), and the mounting bracket nuts to 160–248 inch lbs. (18–28 Nm).

7. Lower the vehicle.

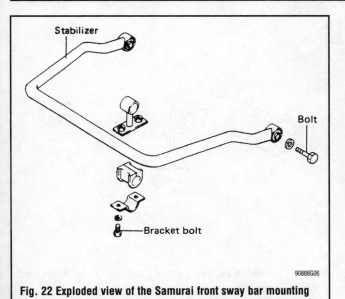

Fig. 22 Exploded view of the Samurai front sway bar mounting

Sidekick, Tracker, Sidekick Sport and X-90 Models

▶ See Figures 23, 24, 25 and 26

1. Apply the parking brake, block the rear wheels, then raise and safely support the front of the vehicle on jackstands.
2. Remove the engine skid plate, if equipped.
3. Disconnect the left and the right sway links from the lower control arm.
4. Remove the sway bar mount bushing bracket bolts and nuts.
5. Remove the sway bar.
6. Remove the sway bar link nuts from the sway bar and remove the sway bar links.

To install:

7. Install the sway bar links to the sway bar and install the nuts. Tighten the nuts to 29–43 ft. lbs. (40–60 Nm).
8. Install the sway bar, using new bushings. Install the sway bar bracket bushing bolts and nuts and connect the sway bar link kits. DO NOT tighten any mounting hardware until all nuts and bolts are in place and the sway bar is centered in the vehicle.
9. Tighten the sway bar link nuts to the lower control arm to 16–25 ft. lbs. (22–35 Nm).

Fig. 24 To remove the front sway bar, first disconnect the bar from the control arm at the end links by removing the attaching nut

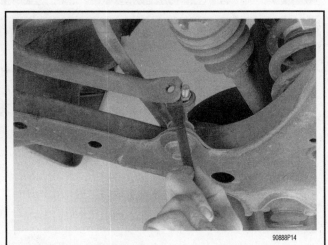

Fig. 25 Some gentle prying may be necessary to remove the link from the sway bar end. Remove the bushing bracket bolts, bracket and bar

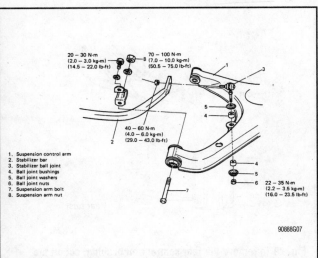

Fig. 23 Exploded view of the coil spring suspension's sway bar assembly

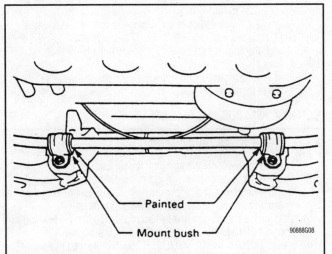

Fig. 26 When installing the sway bar, make sure that the paint marks are aligned with the bushings

10. Tighten the sway bar bracket bolts to 18 ft. lbs. (25 Nm), and the sway bar bracket nuts to 62 ft. lbs. (85 Nm).

11. Install the engine skid plate, if removed.

12. Lower the vehicle.

Lower Control Arms

REMOVAL & INSTALLATION

Sidekick, Tracker, Sidekick Sport and X-90 Models

1. Loosen all of the front wheel lug nuts ½ turn.

2. Apply the parking brake, block the rear wheels, then raise and safely support the front of the vehicle on jackstands.

3. Remove the front wheel.

4. Remove the engine skid plate, if equipped.

5. Support the lower control arm with a floor jack.

6. Remove the 3 nuts and bolts from the control arm, separating the control arm from the ball joint.

7. Disconnect the stabilizer bar from the control arm.

✴✴ CAUTION

The coil spring is under pressure. Make sure control arm is firmly supported with a hydraulic jack before continuing with procedure. If this precaution is not observed, serious bodily injury may result.

8. Remove the lower strut mounting bracket bolts and disconnect the strut bracket from the steering knuckle.

9. Lower the jack until all tension is removed from the coil spring. Remove the coil spring from the vehicle.

10. Remove the front and rear through-bolts from the control arm and remove the control arm from the vehicle.

To install:

11. Install the new control arm, then tighten the front bolt and nut to 51–75 ft. lbs. (70–100 Nm), and the rear bolt and nut to 65–101 ft. lbs. (90–140 Nm).

12. Install the coil spring onto the control arm and slowly raise the jack.

➡The bottom of the spring has a larger diameter than the top. Make sure that the spring is installed correctly.

13. Install the strut-to-knuckle mounting nuts and bolts and tighten to 58–75 ft. lbs. (80–100 Nm).

14. Connect the stabilizer link to the control arm, then tighten the nut to 16–25 ft. lbs. (22–35 Nm).

15. Install the 3 nuts and bolts connecting the control arm and ball joint, and tighten the nuts to 51–75 ft. lbs. (70–100 Nm).

16. Install the engine skid plate. Tighten the bolts to 40 ft. lbs. (54 Nm).

17. Install the front wheels, then lower the vehicle.

18. Tighten the wheel lug nuts.

CONTROL ARM BUSHING REPLACEMENT

▶ **See Figures 27, 28, 29, 30 and 31**

1. Remove the lower control arm from the vehicle.

2. Position the lower control arm in a padded vise.

3. Using a hacksaw, cut off approximately 0.20 in. (5mm) from the front bushing flange, as shown in the accompanying illustration.

4. Position the control arm in a hydraulic press so that the bushing can be pressed out of the control arm using Suzuki press adapters 09951–16060, 09924–74510, and 09951–46020 or their equivalents.

5. Use a knife to cut off the bushing flange surface of the rear bushing.

6. Use the hydraulic press to drive the rear bushing out of the lower control arm with Suzuki tools 09951–16040 or their equivalent.

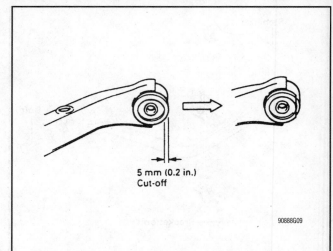

90888G09

Fig. 27 To remove the front control arm bushing, cut off the front flange as shown . . .

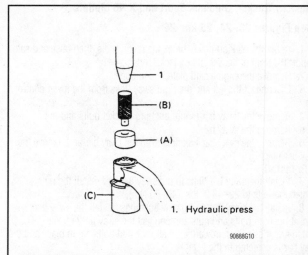

90888G10

Fig. 28 . . . then press the bushing from the control arm using the special tools (A, B and C) as shown

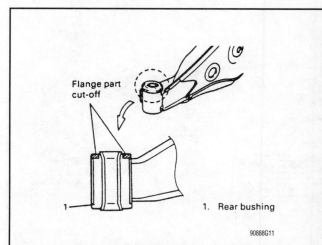

90888G11

Fig. 29 To remove the rear control arm bushing, cut off the flange with a knife, then press the bushing out in a similar manner as the front

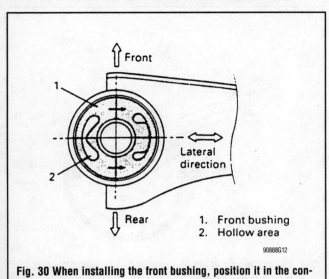

Fig. 30 When installing the front bushing, position it in the control arm as shown

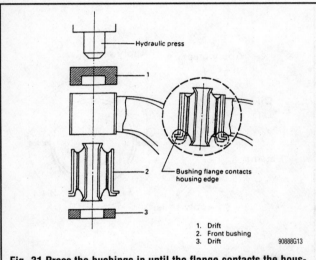

Fig. 31 Press the bushings in until the flange contacts the housing edge

To install:

➡**When installing the front bushing, position it so that the hollow areas are placed as shown in the accompanying illustration. Also, applying a thin coat of grease to the inside of the control arm will make installation much easier.**

7. To install the front bushing, use the hydraulic press to drive the new bushing into the lower control arm until the bushing flange contacts the edge of the lower arm housing. Use the appropriate hydraulic press adapters and spacers, as shown in the accompanying illustration.

➡**Applying a thin coat of soapy water on the outside surface of the bushing will help facilitate installation.**

8. To install the rear bushing, use the hydraulic press to drive the new bushing into the lower control arm until the bushing flange contacts the edge of the lower arm housing. Use the appropriate hydraulic press adapters (D) and spacers (Suzuki tool 09951–16040 or equivalent), as shown in the accompanying illustration.

9. Install the lower control arm on the vehicle.

Knuckle and Spindle

REMOVAL & INSTALLATION

Samurai Models

▶ **See Figure 32**

1. Remove the front wheel hub, as described later in this section.
2. Loosen the king pin upper and lower retaining bolts, but do NOT remove the king pins at this time.

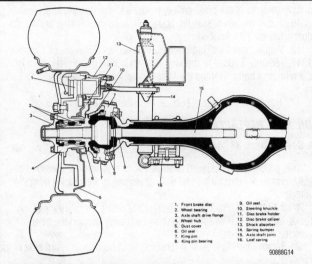

Fig. 32 Cross-sectional view of the Samurai steering knuckle and related components

3. Remove the brake rotor dust cover, brake caliper holder and the wheel spindle from the knuckle.
4. Loosen the tie rod end castle nut, then disengage the tie rod end from the knuckle arm with a tie rod end separator tool.
5. Remove all of the joint seal bolts, then pull the oil seal cover, pad, oil seal and retainer from the knuckle.
6. Identify the upper and lower king pins with white paint or correction fluid, then remove both king pins from the knuckle. When removing the king pins, count the number of shims under each king pin; the same amount of shims must be installed as were removed.
7. Carefully pull the steering knuckle off of the front drive axle. When pulling the knuckle off of the axle, catch the lower king pin bearing when it falls off.. Be sure to identify the upper and lower king pins during disassembly so that they can be reinstalled in their original positions.

To install:

8. Inspect the steering knuckle oil seal for wear or damage. If any defects are found, replace the seal with a new one. The oil seal used at the spherical sliding joint between the knuckle and the inner case accomplishes the additional purpose of keeping out road dust and as acting as a damper from the steering wheel. As this seal wears, its damping effect decreases, which causes the front wheels to develop a tendency to "shimmy."

9. Apply Suzuki Super Grease A (99000–25010) or equivalent, to the king pin bearing rollers.
10. Install the king pin bearings and slide the steering knuckle fully onto the front drive axle.
11. Install the proper amount of shims on each of the king pins, apply Suzuki Sealing Compound 366E (99000–31090) or its equivalent to the king pins as shown in the accompanying illustration. Install the king pins into the steering knuckle.

➥**Before installing a new steering knuckle oil seal, ensure to apply Suzuki Super Grease A (99000–25010) or its equivalent to the oil seal lip.**

12. Install the oil seal retainer, oil seal, pad, and oil seal cover onto the steering knuckle. Start the oil seal cover bolts by hand, then tighten them to 71–106 inch lbs. (8–12 Nm).

13. Attach the tie rod end to the knuckle arm, then tighten the tie rod end castle nut to 22–39 ft. lbs. (30–55 Nm). Insert a new cotter pin through the castle nut and tie rod end stud holes, then bend the cotter pin ends over. If none of the castle nut grooves are aligned with the hole in the tie rod end stud hole, continue tightening the castle nut until one of the grooves is aligned with the stud hole, then install the cotter pin.

14. Apply Sealing Compound 366E (99000–31090) or equivalent to the mating surfaces of the brake caliper holder and the steering knuckle.

15. Install the wheel spindle, brake caliper holder, and the brake rotor dust cover onto the knuckle.

16. Apply thread locking compound (such as Suzuki Lock Cement 1342—99000–32050) to the king pin retaining bolt threads, then install the retaining bolts. Tighten the king pin upper and lower retaining bolts to .

17. Install the front wheel hub, as described later in this section.

OIL SEAL REPLACEMENT

▶ **See Figures 33, 34 and 35**

This procedure is designed to allow you to replace your damaged or leaking steering knuckle oil seal without removing the knuckle from the vehicle.

1. If additional undervehicle clearance is needed, apply the parking brake, block the rear wheels, then raise and safely support the front of the vehicle on jackstands.

2. Remove the eight oil seal retaining bolts from the inboard side of the joint.

3. Slide the oil seal cover and felt packing inward on the drive axle housing.

4. Cut the old oil seal in half and remove it from the joint. Discard the old seal.

5. Using a pair of scissors, cut the new oil seal in one spot, as shown in the accompanying illustration.

6. Install the new seal in the retainer, ensuring that the cut portion of the seal is positioned upward and approximately 30 degrees from the matching face of the oil seal retainer.

7. Apply grease (such as Suzuki Super Grease H—99000–25120) to the inside of the oil seal, then apply sealing compound (such as Suzuki Sealing Compound "Cemedine" 366E—99000–31090) to the mating sur-

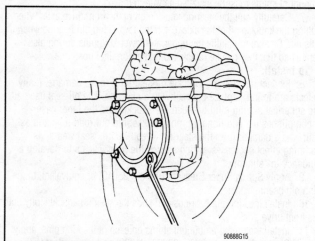

Fig. 33 Remove the eight oil seal retaining ring attaching bolts and slide the ring, packing and seal back. Cut the old seal to remove it

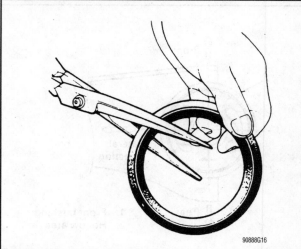

Fig. 34 Cut one part of the new seal and fit it around the axle with the cut facing upwards

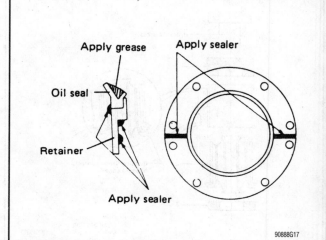

Fig. 35 Apply sealer and grease to the seal and retaining plate as shown

face around the entire circumference of the oil seal; this will help prevent the entry of water into the joint.

8. Install the felt packing and oil seal cover against the oil seal, then install the eight retaining bolts. Tighten the bolts in a crisscross pattern to 71–106 inch lbs. (8–12 Nm).

9. If necessary, lower the vehicle and remove the wheel blocks.

Sidekick, Tracker, Sidekick Sport and X-90 Models

▶ **See Figures 36 thru 41**

1. Loosen all of the front wheel lug nuts ½ turn.

2. Apply the parking brake, block the rear wheels, then raise and safely support the front of the vehicle on jackstands.

3. Remove the front wheel.

4. Position a hydraulic floor jack beneath the lower control arm, then raise the floor jack until it supports the lower control arm.

5. Remove the wheel hub, as described later in this section.

6. Detach the tie rod end from the steering knuckle arm.

7. Secure the bottom of the coil spring to the lower control arm with a chain. This will prevent the spring from accidentally dislodging form the control arm and possibly causing personal injury.

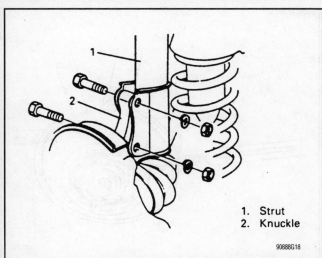

1. Strut
2. Knuckle

90888G18

Fig. 36 To remove the steering knuckle, remove the two lower strut-to-knuckle bolts and the lower ball joint castellated nut

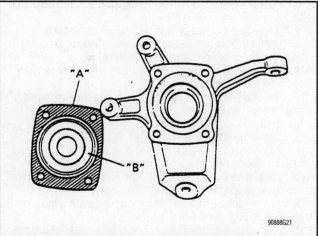

90888G21

Fig. 39 When installing the spindle to the knuckle, apply sealer to surface (A) and grease in recess (B). Make sure to use the proper types

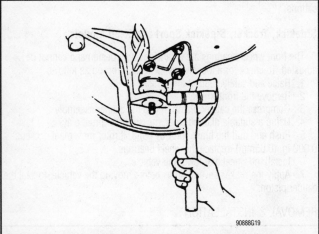

90888G19

Fig. 37 Detach the lower ball joint stud from the steering knuckle by tapping the knuckle with a mallet, or use a ball joint separator tool

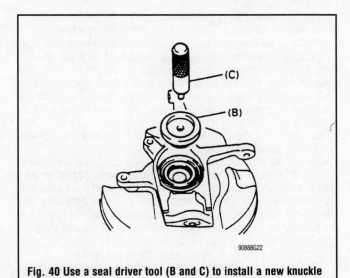

90888G22

Fig. 40 Use a seal driver tool (B and C) to install a new knuckle oil seal

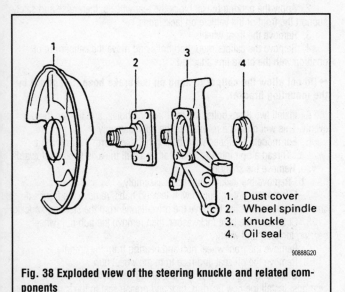

1. Dust cover
2. Wheel spindle
3. Knuckle
4. Oil seal

90888G20

Fig. 38 Exploded view of the steering knuckle and related components

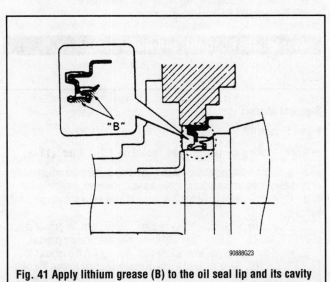

90888G23

Fig. 41 Apply lithium grease (B) to the oil seal lip and its cavity as shown

8. Withdraw the lower ball joint castle nut cotter pin, then remove the castle nut.

9. Remove the lower strut-to-steering knuckle bolts and nuts.

10. Detach the lower ball joint from the steering knuckle by tapping its end with a mallet, or by using a ball joint separator tool.

11. While slowly lowering the floor jack, remove the spindle/knuckle assembly from the vehicle.

12. If necessary, remove the knuckle oil seal, dust cover and wheel spindle from the steering knuckle.

To install:

13. Clean all spindle/knuckle components thoroughly.

14. Apply Suzuki Sealant 99000–31110 or its equivalent to the wheel spindle and steering knuckle mating surfaces.

15. Fill the wheel spindle recess with approximately 0.35 oz. (10g) of lithium grease (such as Suzuki Grease 99000–25010).

16. Install the spindle onto the knuckle, then tighten the spindle-to-knuckle bolts to 36 ft. lbs. (50 Nm).

17. Using a seal driver tool (such as Suzuki Tools 09944–66010 and 09924–74510), install a new knuckle oil seal into the inboard side of the knuckle. Drive the new seal into the knuckle until its inner edge contacts the stepped surface of the knuckle.

18. Apply lithium grease to the oil seal lip and into the oil seal hollow until it is approximately 60% full.

19. While slowly raising the floor jack, position the spindle/knuckle assembly onto the lower ball joint stud and between the strut brackets.

20. Install the lower strut-to-steering knuckle bolts and nuts hand-tight.

21. Install and tighten the ball joint castle nut to 33–50 ft. lbs. (45–70 Nm). Insert a new cotter pin through the castle nut and ball joint stud holes, then bend the cotter pin ends over. If none of the castle nut grooves are aligned with the hole in the ball joint stud hole, continue tightening the castle nut until one of the grooves is aligned with the stud hole, then install the cotter pin.

22. Tighten the lower strut-to-steering knuckle mounting bolts and nuts to 58–75 ft. lbs. (80–100 Nm).

23. Remove the chain securing the coil spring to the lower control arm.

24. Attach the tie rod end to the steering knuckle arm, then tighten the tie rod end castle nut to 22–39 ft. lbs. (30–55 Nm). Insert a new cotter pin through the castle nut and tie rod end stud holes, then bend the cotter pin ends over. If none of the castle nut grooves are aligned with the hole in the tie rod end stud hole, continue tightening the castle nut until one of the grooves is aligned with the stud hole, then install the cotter pin.

25. Install the wheel hub, as described later in this section.

26. Lower the floor jack and remove it from beneath the lower control arm.

27. Install the front wheel.

28. Lower the vehicle and remove the rear wheel blocks.

29. Tighten all of the front wheel lug nuts.

Front Wheel Bearings and Hubs

ADJUSTMENT

Samurai Models

▶ **See Figure 42**

➡**Wheel bearing starting preload should be 2.2–6.6 lbs. (13 kg).**

1. Raise the front end of the vehicle, and remove the front wheels.

2. Remove the wheel bearing locknut and lockwasher.

3. Tighten the bearing nut to 57 ft. lbs. (80 Nm) while spinning the hub by hand.

4. Loosen the nut to completely, and then tighten it to the proper torque of 7–10 ft. lbs. (10–15 Nm). This will give the proper bearing preload.

5. Insert the lockwasher after adjustment, and tighten the locknut to 44–65 ft. lbs. (60–90 Nm). Bend a part of the lockwasher toward the bearing nut (on body side), and another toward the locknut (outside); this will lock the two nuts.

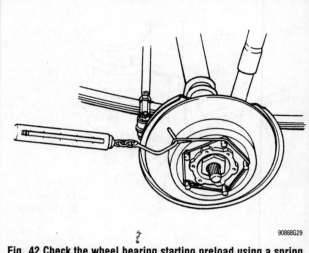

Fig. 42 Check the wheel bearing starting preload using a spring scale as shown

6. Recheck the bearing starting preload, making sure it is within specifications.

Sidekick, Tracker, Sidekick Sport and X-90 Models

The front wheel bearings are a cartridge type design and cannot be adjusted. To check for a loose wheel bearing, proceed as follows:

1. Raise and safely support the vehicle.

2. Remove the front wheel.

3. Compress the caliper piston to free the caliper assembly.

4. Using a suitable dial indicator, measure the thrust play.

5. Push and pull the brake rotor by hand. If rotor movement exceeds 0.002 in. (0.05mm), replace the wheel bearings.

6. Install the wheel and lower the vehicle.

7. Apply the brakes several times before moving the vehicle, to seat the caliper piston.

REMOVAL & INSTALLATION

Samurai Models

▶ **See Figures 43, 44, 45, 46 and 47**

1. Loosen all of the front/rear wheel lug nuts ½ turn.

2. Apply the parking brake, block the rear wheels, then raise and safely support the front of the vehicle on jackstands.

3. Remove the front wheels.

4. Remove the caliper mounting bolts and move the caliper out of position with the brake line attached.

➡**Do not allow the caliper to hang on the brake hose. Support it by the mounting bracket.**

5. Install two 8mm bolts into the threaded holes, and tighten them evenly. This will draw the rotor off of the hub assembly.

6. For models equipped with locking hubs, perform the following:

   a. Thread a bolt into the axle shaft and pull the axle shaft out towards you. Remove the snapring.

   b. Remove the locking hub body assembly.

7. For models not equipped with locking hubs, remove the front axle shaft cap and the circlip. Remove the drive flange from the steering knuckle.

8. Straighten the bent lockwasher, then remove the hub nut (wheel bearing locknut) and washer.

9. Remove the front wheel hub and bearing from the spindle.

10. Remove the oil seal and race from the wheel hub.

11. Clean and inspect the hub and bearing seats. Repack the wheel bearings. Install the new bearing, race and grease seal in the same position.

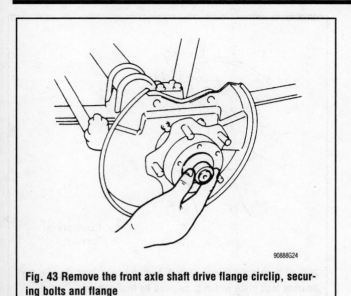

Fig. 43 Remove the front axle shaft drive flange circlip, securing bolts and flange

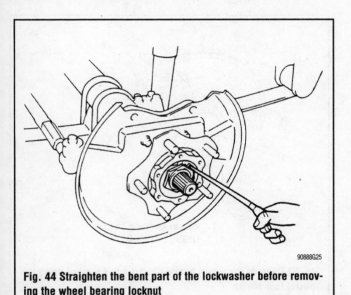

Fig. 44 Straighten the bent part of the lockwasher before removing the wheel bearing locknut

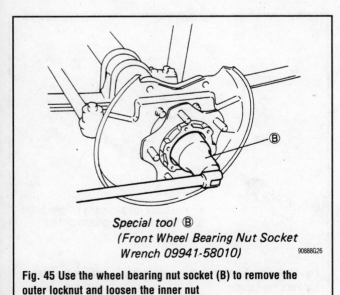

Special tool ⓑ
(Front Wheel Bearing Nut Socket Wrench 09941-58010)

Fig. 45 Use the wheel bearing nut socket (B) to remove the outer locknut and loosen the inner nut

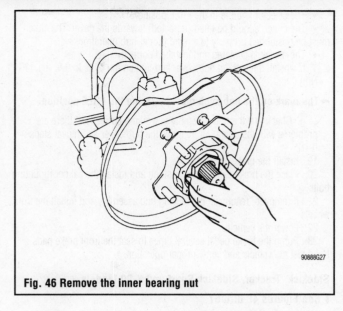

Fig. 46 Remove the inner bearing nut

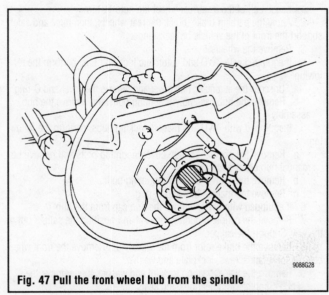

Fig. 47 Pull the front wheel hub from the spindle

To install:

12. Install the front wheel hub and bearing to the knuckle.

13. Tighten the bearing nut to 57 ft. lbs. (80 Nm) while spinning the hub by hand.

14. Loosen the nut to 0 ft. lbs., and then tighten it to the proper torque of 7–10 ft. lbs. (10–15 Nm). This will give the proper bearing preload.

15. Insert the lockwasher after adjustment, and tighten the locknut to 44–65 ft. lbs. (60–90 Nm). Bend a part of the lockwasher toward the bearing nut (on body side), and another toward the locknut (outside). this will lock the two nuts.

16. Install the drive flange to the steering knuckle.

17. For models equipped with free wheeling hubs, install the front axle cap and circlip. Connect the rotor to the hub assembly.

18. For models equipped with locking hubs, perform the following:

   a. Install a new gasket onto the locking hub assembly.

   b. Install the locking hub body assembly to the wheel hub flange and tighten the hub body bolts to 18 ft. lbs. (24 Nm).

   c. Thread a bolt into the axle shaft and pull the axle shaft out towards you. Install the snapring and remove the bolt from the axle shaft.

   d. Install a new gasket in the manual locking hub cover.

   e. Before installing the locking hub cover, make sure of the following:

• The selector knob is in the FREE position.
• The clutch should be lifted (retracted) towards the cover. The clutch must be positioned properly to ensure proper hub operations.
• The gasket is centered and installed correctly.

f. Install the locking hub cover and tighten the bolts to 9 ft. lbs. (13 Nm).

➡ **The mark on the hub knob must be facing the FREE position.**

g. Check that the hub assembly is working correctly. If there are problems with the operation, Remove the hub cover and repeat steps 9–12.

19. Install the brake rotor.
20. Place the brake caliper into position and install the caliper mounting bolts.
21. If removed, reconnect the locking hub assembly and install the front wheels.
22. Lower the vehicle.
23. Pump the brake pedal several times to seat the front brake pads. Road test the vehicle and verify proper operation.

Sidekick, Tracker, Sidekick Sport and X-90 Models

▶ **See Figures 48 thru 57**

1. Loosen all of the front/rear wheel lug nuts ½ turn.
2. Apply the parking brake, block the rear wheels, then raise and safely support the front of the vehicle on jackstands.
3. Remove the wheels.
4. If equipped with 4WD and automatic locking hubs, perform the following:

a. Unscrew the automatic hub cover and remove the cover and O-ring.
b. Remove the hub assembly mounting bolts and remove the hub assembly.

5. If equipped with 4WD and manual locking hubs, perform the following:

a. Remove the six manual hub cover mounting bolts and remove he manual hub cover and gasket.
b. Remove the six manual hub mounting bolts.
c. Remove the manual hub and O-ring.

6. If equipped with 2WD, remove the hub cap from the hub.
7. Remove the caliper mounting bracket and position the caliper out of the way. Support the caliper.
8. Remove the brake rotor from the wheel hub. Remove the front wheel bearing lockplate screws, lockplate and washer.
9. Remove the wheel bearing locknut and washer, then remove the wheel hub complete with bearings and seals.

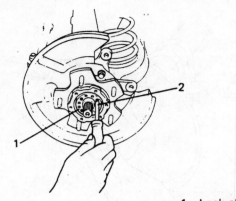

1. Lock plate
2. Screws

90888G30

Fig. 49 To remove the wheel hub and bearings, first remove the bearing lock plate which is secured by four screws

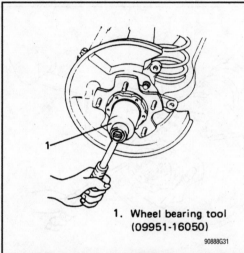

1. Wheel bearing tool (09951-16050)

90888G31

Fig. 50 Remove the wheel bearing locknut and washer using the special tool shown

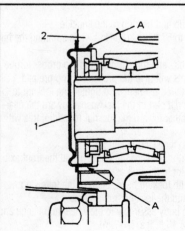

1. Hub cap
2. Wheel hub
A: Apply water tight sealant (99000-31090)

90888G39

Fig. 48 Cross-sectional view of the 2WD front hub and bearing components

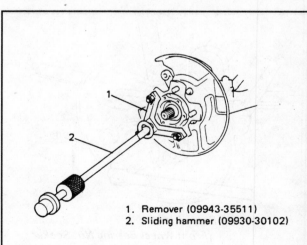

1. Remover (09943-35511)
2. Sliding hammer (09930-30102)

90888G32

Fig. 51 A slide hammer may be necessary to remove the assembly from the spindle

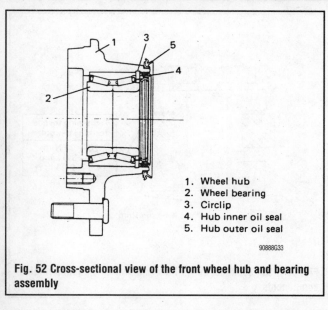

1. Wheel hub
2. Wheel bearing
3. Circlip
4. Hub inner oil seal
5. Hub outer oil seal

90888G33

Fig. 52 Cross-sectional view of the front wheel hub and bearing assembly

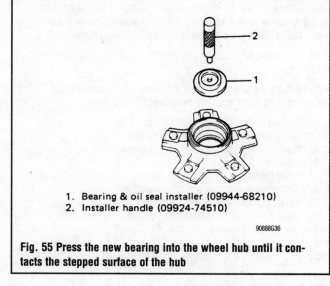

1. Bearing & oil seal installer (09944-68210)
2. Installer handle (09924-74510)

90888G36

Fig. 55 Press the new bearing into the wheel hub until it contacts the stepped surface of the hub

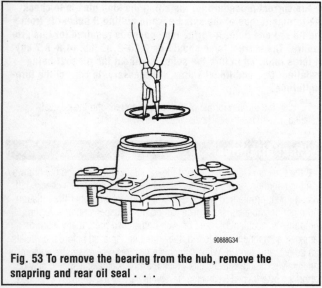

90888G34

Fig. 53 To remove the bearing from the hub, remove the snapring and rear oil seal . . .

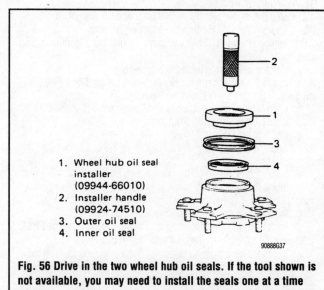

1. Wheel hub oil seal installer (09944-66010)
2. Installer handle (09924-74510)
3. Outer oil seal
4. Inner oil seal

90888G37

Fig. 56 Drive in the two wheel hub oil seals. If the tool shown is not available, you may need to install the seals one at a time

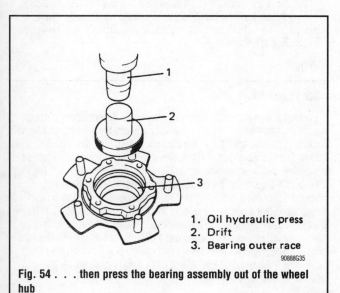

1. Oil hydraulic press
2. Drift
3. Bearing outer race

90888G35

Fig. 54 . . . then press the bearing assembly out of the wheel hub

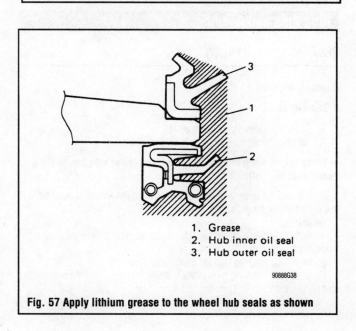

1. Grease
2. Hub inner oil seal
3. Hub outer oil seal

90888G38

Fig. 57 Apply lithium grease to the wheel hub seals as shown

➡**If wheel hub cannot be removed by hand, use special tool J37781 with a J2619–01 for the Tracker or 09943–35511 with 09930–30102 for the Sidekick, Sidekick Sport and X-90 models, or their equivalents. These tools are a hub remover and sliding hammer.**

10. If equipped with ABS brakes, remove the sensor rotor from the wheel hub.

➡**Pull out the sensor rotor from the wheel hub gradually and evenly. Pulling it out partially may cause it to deform.**

11. Remove the inner bearing grease seal.
12. Remove the snapring and remove the inner bearing.
13. Clean and inspect the hub and bearing seats.

To install:

14. Install the inner race, wheel bearing snapring and seal in the hub. Apply lithium grease to the lip portion of the oil seal.
15. If equipped with ABS brakes, install the sensor rotor.
16. Install the hub on the spindle and install the outer bearing, locknut, washer, and lockplate. Tighten the locknut to 123–180 ft. lbs. (170–250 Nm).

17. Install the four lockplate mounting screws. Tighten the screws to 8.8–17.7 inch lbs. (1–2 Nm).
18. Install the brake rotor.
19. Install the caliper and tighten the bolts to 61 ft. lbs. (85 Nm).
20. If equipped with 2WD, install the locking hub cap.
21. If equipped with 4WD and automatic locking hubs, perform the following:
    a. Install a new O-ring on the hub assembly.
    b. Install the hub assembly onto the wheel flange. Make sure the tab on the hub fits into the notch on the spindle.
    c. Install the six mounting bolts and tighten to 18 ft. lbs. (25 Nm).
    d. Install a new O-ring on the hub cover.
    e. Install the hub cover.
22. If equipped with 4WD and manual locking hubs, complete the following sub-steps:
    a. Install a new O-ring on the manual hub body.
    b. Install the manual hub onto the wheel flange and install the six mounting bolts. Tighten the mounting bolts to 18 ft. lbs. (25 Nm).
    c. Install a new gasket on the manual hub cover.
    d. Install the hub cover on the hub. The lever must be in the **FREE** position with the clutch pulled out toward the cover.
    e. Install the six mounting bolts. Tighten the bolts to 71–106 inch lbs. (8–12 Nm).
23. Install the wheels and lower the vehicle.

King Pins and Bushings

REMOVAL & INSTALLATION

Samurai Models

◆ **See Figure 58**

1. Raise and safely support the vehicle.
2. Remove the steering knuckle from the vehicle.

➡**When the steering knuckle is pulled, the lower king pin bearing sometimes falls off.**

3. Remove the upper and the lower king pins, mark them. Check the number of shims on each side.

To install:

4. Install the new king pin bearings in the steering knuckle holding them in with grease.
5. Install the steering knuckle on the axle assembly.
6. Install the new king pins in the steering knuckle, shim them correctly and tighten the bolts to 17 ft. lbs. (23 Nm).

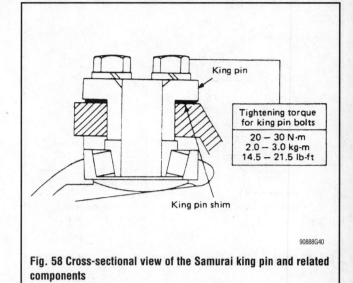

Fig. 58 Cross-sectional view of the Samurai king pin and related components

➡**The correct procedure for installing the king pins is to check the turning torque of the spindle while pulling it outwards from the tie rod end hole. A spring type gauge is required for this procedure. The correct force should be 2.20–3.96 lbs. (4.8–8.7 kg) of force required to turn the spindle without the oil seal being installed. Use additional shims, if necessary, to correct the turning torque.**

7. With the turning torque of the spindle correct and the oil seal installed, install the front wheels and lower the vehicle.

Wheel Alignment

If the tires are worn unevenly, if the vehicle is not stable on the highway or if the handling seems poor, the wheel alignment should be checked. If an alignment problem is suspected, first check for improper tire inflation and other possible causes. These can be worn suspension or steering components, accident damage or even unmatched tires. If any worn or damaged components are found, they must be replaced before the wheels can be properly aligned. Wheel alignment requires very expensive equipment and involves minute adjustments which must be accurate; it should only be performed by a trained technician. Take your vehicle to a properly equipped shop.

Following is a description of the alignment angles which are adjustable on most vehicles and how they affect vehicle handling. Although these angles can apply to both the front and rear wheels, usually only the front suspension is adjustable.

CASTER

◆ **See Figure 59**

Looking at a vehicle from the side, caster angle describes the steering axis rather than a wheel angle. On Samurai models, the steering knuckle is attached to the axle yoke through ball joints or king pins. On Sidekick, Tracker, Sidekick Sport and X-90 models, the steering knuckle is attached to a control arm or strut at the top and a control arm at the bottom. The wheel pivots around the line between these points to steer the vehicle. When the upper point is tilted back, this is described as positive caster. Having a positive caster tends to make the wheels self-centering, increasing directional stability. Excessive positive caster makes the wheels hard to steer, while an uneven caster will cause a pull to one side. Overloading the vehicle or sagging rear springs will affect caster, as will raising the rear of the vehicle. If the rear of the vehicle is lower than normal, the caster becomes more positive.

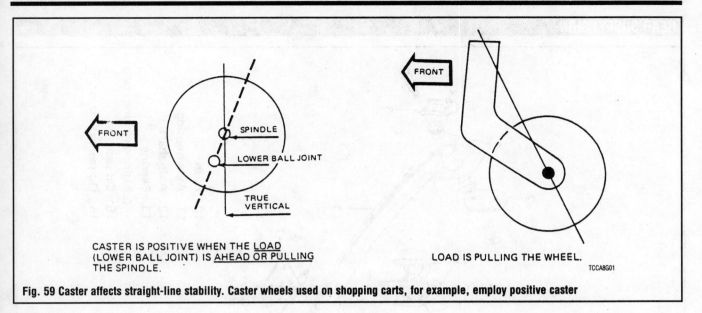

Fig. 59 Caster affects straight-line stability. Caster wheels used on shopping carts, for example, employ positive caster

CAMBER

♦ **See Figure 60**

Looking from the front of the vehicle, camber is the inward or outward tilt of the top of wheels. When the tops of the wheels are tilted in, this is negative camber; if they are tilted out, it is positive. In a turn, a slight amount of negative camber helps maximize contact of the tire with the road. However, too much negative camber compromises straight-line stability, increases bump steer and torque steer.

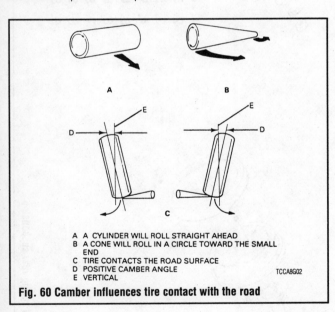

A A CYLINDER WILL ROLL STRAIGHT AHEAD
B A CONE WILL ROLL IN A CIRCLE TOWARD THE SMALL END
C TIRE CONTACTS THE ROAD SURFACE
D POSITIVE CAMBER ANGLE
E VERTICAL

Fig. 60 Camber influences tire contact with the road

TOE

♦ **See Figure 61**

Looking down at the wheels from above the vehicle, toe angle is the distance between the front of the wheels relative to the distance between the back of the wheels. If the wheels are closer at the front, they are said to be toed-in or to have negative toe. A small amount of negative toe enhances directional stability and provides a smoother ride on the highway.

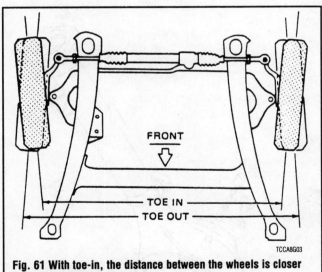

Fig. 61 With toe-in, the distance between the wheels is closer at the front than at the rear

REAR SUSPENSION

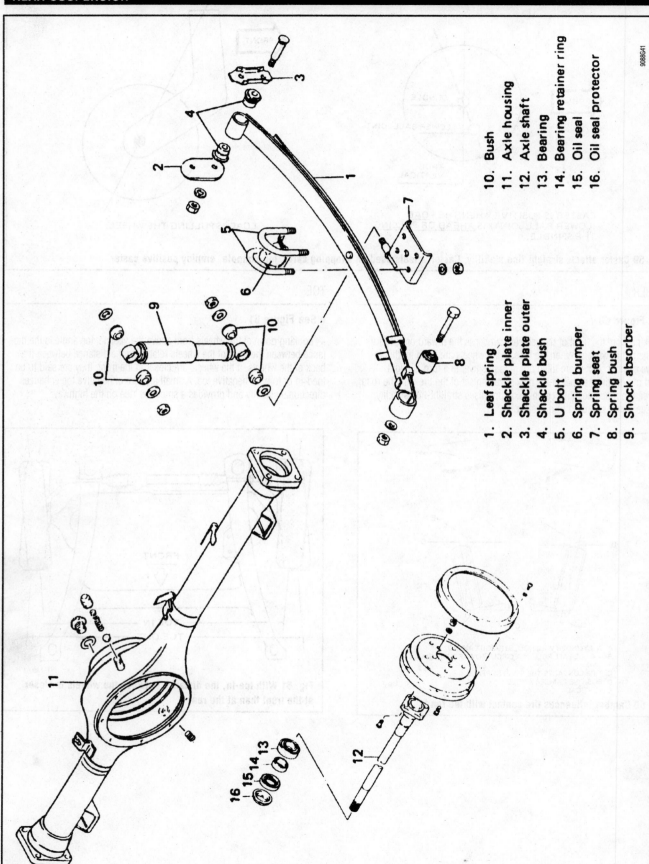

1. Leaf spring
2. Shackle plate inner
3. Shackle plate outer
4. Shackle bush
5. U bolt
6. Spring bumper
7. Spring seat
8. Spring bush
9. Shock absorber
10. Bush
11. Axle housing
12. Axle shaft
13. Bearing
14. Bearing retainer ring
15. Oil seal
16. Oil seal protector

Fig. 62 Exploded view of the leaf spring rear suspension

COIL SPRING REAR SUSPENSION COMPONENT LOCATIONS

1. Shock absorbers
2. Coil springs
3. Trailing arms
4. Upper control arms

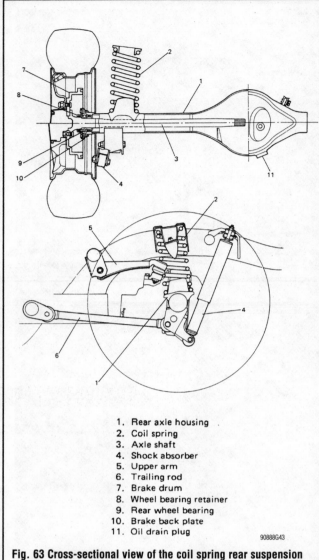

1. Rear axle housing
2. Coil spring
3. Axle shaft
4. Shock absorber
5. Upper arm
6. Trailing rod
7. Brake drum
8. Wheel bearing retainer
9. Rear wheel bearing
10. Brake back plate
11. Oil drain plug

90888G43

Fig. 63 Cross-sectional view of the coil spring rear suspension

Shock Absorbers

REMOVAL & INSTALLATION

Samurai Models

1. Block the rear wheels, then raise and safely support the rear of the vehicle on jackstands. Support the rear axle housing with a hydraulic floor jack.
2. Remove the upper and lower shock absorber mounting bolts.
3. Remove the rear shock absorber.
To install:
4. Install the rear shock absorber.
5. Tighten the mounting bolts to 23–39 ft. lbs. (35–55 Nm).
6. Remove the rear axle support and lower the vehicle. Remove the wheel blocks.

Sidekick, Tracker, Sidekick Sport and X-90 Models

▶ **See Figures 64, 65, 66 and 67**

1. Block the rear wheels, then raise and safely support the rear of the vehicle on jackstands.
2. Support the rear axle housing with a hydraulic floor jack to prevent it from lowering.

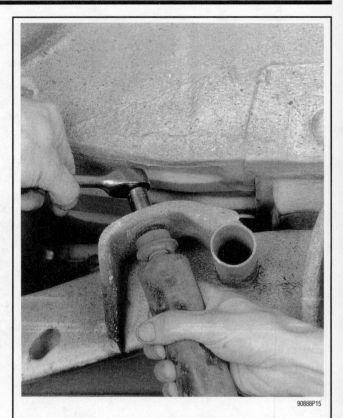

90888P15

Fig. 64 To remove the rear shock absorber, first remove the upper shock mount locknut . . .

90888P16

Fig. 65 . . . then remove the lower mounting bolt. Hold the shock when you remove the bolt, to keep it from falling

Fig. 66 Remove the shock absorber from the vehicle

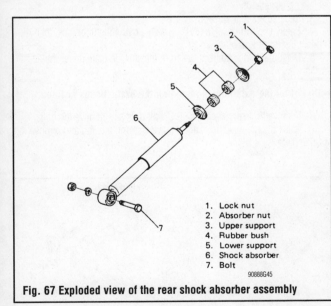

1. Lock nut
2. Absorber nut
3. Upper support
4. Rubber bush
5. Lower support
6. Shock absorber
7. Bolt

Fig. 67 Exploded view of the rear shock absorber assembly

3. Remove the shock absorber upper locknut and retaining nut.
4. Remove the lower shock absorber from the axle housing by removing the mounting nut and bolt.
5. Remove the rear shock absorber.

To install:

6. Install the rear shock absorber.
7. Install the lower mounting nut and bolt. The lower bolt's head should point in toward the center of the vehicle.
8. Install the upper retaining nut and locknut.

9. Tighten the upper mounting nuts to 16–25 ft. lbs. (22–35 Nm), and the lower mounting nuts and bolts to 51–72 ft. lbs. (70–100 Nm).
10. Remove the floor jack from the rear axle assembly.
11. Lower the vehicle and remove the wheel blocks.

TESTING

Refer to the testing procedure given for front suspension shock absorbers, located earlier in this section.

Coil Springs

REMOVAL & INSTALLATION

Sidekick, Tracker, Sidekick Sport and X-90 Models

▶ See Figures 68, 69, 70 and 71

1. Loosen all of the rear wheel lug nuts ½ turn.
2. Block the rear wheels, then raise and safely support the rear of the vehicle on jackstands.
3. Remove the rear wheels.
4. Support the rear axle housing with a hydraulic floor jack.
5. Remove the shock absorber lower mounting nut and bolt. Remove the bolts and nuts from both shock absorbers.
6. Disconnect the parking brake cables from the hangers on the trailing arms.
7. Lower the rear axle housing so the coil spring can be removed.

☀☀ WARNING

Take care to avoid stretching the brake hose!

8. Remove the coil spring from the vehicle.

To install:

9. Install the coil spring to the spring seat and raise the axle housing. Make sure the spring is seated correctly.
10. Install the lower shock absorber mounting bolts and nuts but do not tighten.
11. Connect the parking brake cable hangers and install the rear wheels.
12. Lower the vehicle and tighten the lower shock absorber nuts to the value shown in the torque chart at the end of this section.
13. Remove the wheel blocks.

Fig. 68 To remove the rear springs, first disconnect both lower shock absorber mounts and parking brake cable mounts (shown)

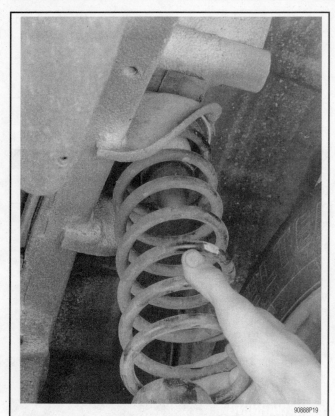

Fig. 69 Slowly lower the rear axle housing until the spring can clear the lower spring perch

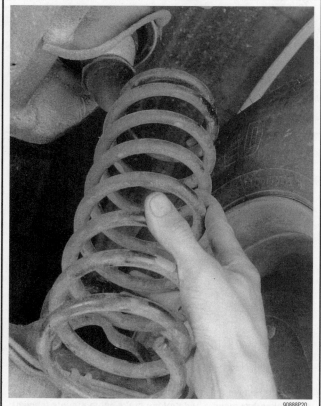

Fig. 70 Remove the spring by pulling it downward from the upper spring seat

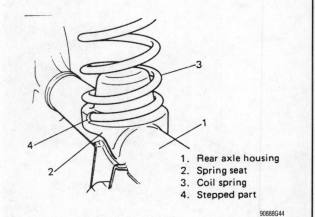

1. Rear axle housing
2. Spring seat
3. Coil spring
4. Stepped part

Fig. 71 When installing the rear coil spring, make sure to position the coil end into the stepped part (4) of the spring seat

Leaf Springs

REMOVAL & INSTALLATION

Samurai Models

♦ See Figure 72

1. Loosen all of the rear wheel lug nuts ½ turn.
2. Block the rear wheels, then raise and safely support the rear of the vehicle on jackstands.
3. Remove the rear wheels.
4. Safely support the axle housing with a hydraulic floor jack, then disconnect the lower end of the shock absorber.
5. Disconnect the stabilizer bar from the shackle plate under the leaf spring.

➡ **Do not let the axle housing hang on the brake hoses or lines.**

6. Remove the rear axle housing U-bolt nuts and remove the bolts.
7. Raise the rear axle housing to release spring tension and remove the shackle plate.

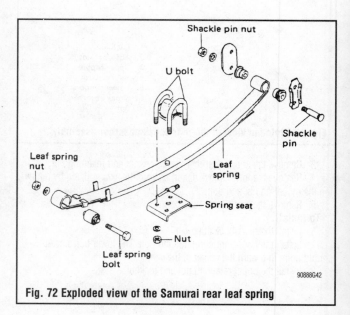

Fig. 72 Exploded view of the Samurai rear leaf spring

8. Support the leaf spring and disconnect the rear leaf spring mounting bolts.

9. Remove the leaf spring assembly.

To install:

10. Install the leaf spring and shackle assembly and tighten the mounting bolts after the vehicle is lowered.

11. Install the U-bolt nuts and tighten to 44–57 ft. lbs. (60–80 Nm).

12. Connect the stabilizer bar under the shackle plate. Install the shock absorber, and tighten the mounting nuts to 23–39 ft. lbs. (35–55 Nm).

13. Install the rear wheels, remove the axle housing support, and lower the vehicle.

14. With the vehicle on the ground, tighten the rear leaf spring mounting bolts to 44–61 ft. lbs. (60–85 Nm). Tighten the rear leaf spring shackle pin nuts to 22–40 ft. lbs. (30–55 Nm).

15. Remove the wheel blocks.

Upper Control Arms

REMOVAL & INSTALLATION

Sidekick, Tracker, Sidekick Sport and X-90 Models

▶ See Figures 73, 74, 75 and 76

1. Loosen all of the rear wheel lug nuts ½ turn.

2. Block the rear wheels, then raise and safely support the rear of the vehicle on jackstands.

3. Remove the tire and wheel assembly.

4. If necessary, remove bracket from upper control arm.

5. Position a jack under the axle.

6. Remove the four bolts securing the ball joint to the differential carrier.

7. Remove the upper control arm-to-body mounting nut and through-bolt.

8. Remove the control arm.

9. If the control arm is being replaced, remove the ball joint assembly from the control arm as follows:

    a. Remove the cotter pin from ball joint.

    b. Remove ball joint castle nut.

    c. Using a bearing puller, remove bracket from ball joint stud bolt.

    d. Remove ball joint boot set ring and ball joint boot.

To install:

10. If the ball joint was removed from the upper control arm, install it as follows:

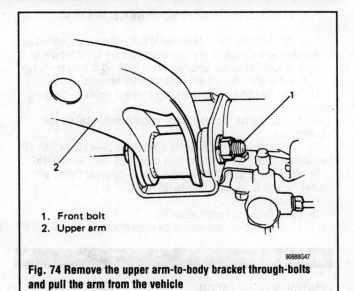

1. Front bolt
2. Upper arm

90888G47

Fig. 74 Remove the upper arm-to-body bracket through-bolts and pull the arm from the vehicle

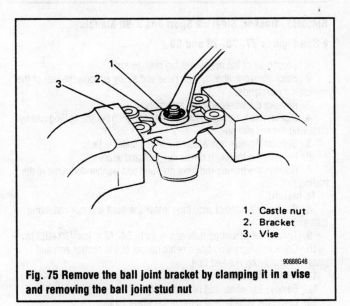

1. Castle nut
2. Bracket
3. Vise

90888G48

Fig. 75 Remove the ball joint bracket by clamping it in a vise and removing the ball joint stud nut

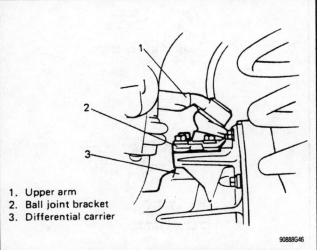

1. Upper arm
2. Ball joint bracket
3. Differential carrier

90888G46

Fig. 73 To remove the rear upper control arm, remove the four ball joint bracket-to-axle housing attaching bolts

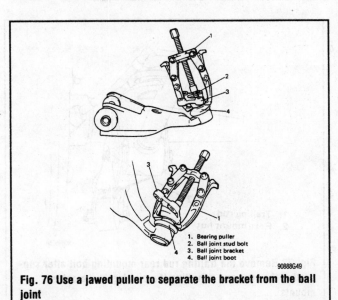

1. Bearing puller
2. Ball joint stud bolt
3. Ball joint bracket
4. Ball joint boot

90888G49

Fig. 76 Use a jawed puller to separate the bracket from the ball joint

a. When installing ball joint boot, be sure to fit boot set wire into ring groove in boot.

b. After installing ball joint bracket to ball joint stud bolt, tighten castle nut till split pin hole in stud bolt aligns with slot in nut but within range of specified torque. Specified torque is 33–50 ft. lbs. (45–70 Nm).

c. Install new cotter pin and bend cotter pin securely.

11. Install the upper control arm to the body and install the mounting nut and through-bolts.

12. Connect the ball joint to the axle assembly and install the four mounting bolts.

13. Tighten the ball joint bracket-to-axle bolts to 29–43 ft. lbs. (40–60 Nm) and the control arm mounting bolts to 58–72 ft. lbs. (80–100 Nm).

14. If necessary, connect the upper bracket to the upper control arm. Tighten the bolts to 13–20 ft. lbs. (18–28 Nm).

15. Remove the jack.

16. Install the tire and wheel assembly.

17. Lower the vehicle, and remove the wheel blocks.

Trailing Arms

REMOVAL & INSTALLATION

Sidekick, Tracker, Sidekick Sport and X-90 Models

♦ See Figures 77, 78, 79 and 80

1. Loosen all of the rear wheel lug nuts ½ turn.

2. Block the front wheels, then raise and safely support the rear of the vehicle on jackstands.

3. Remove the wheel and tire assembly.

4. Disconnect the parking brake cable hanger from the trailing rod by removing the nut and bolt.

5. Support the rear axle assembly with a suitable jack.

6. Remove the trailing rod rear nut, bolt and washer.

7. Remove the trailing rod front nut, bolt and washer and remove the trailing rod.

To install:

8. Position the control arm, then install the front and rear mounting nuts and bolts.

9. Tighten the mounting nuts and bolts to 58–72 ft. lbs. (80–100 Nm).

10. Connect the parking brake cable hanger to the control arm and install the mounting nut and bolt.

11. Remove the jack.

12. Remove the wheel and tire assembly.

13. Lower the vehicle, and remove the wheel blocks.

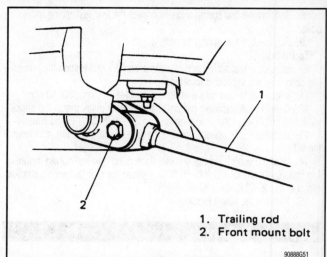

1. Trailing rod
2. Front mount bolt

90888G51

Fig. 78 . . . then remove the trailing rod front mounting bolt and remove the rod from the vehicle

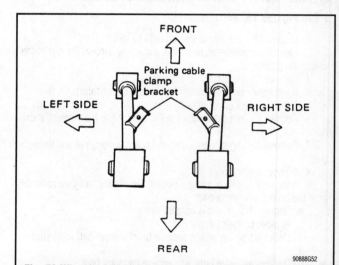

FRONT

Parking cable clamp bracket

LEFT SIDE   RIGHT SIDE

REAR

90888G52

Fig. 79 When installing the rod, make sure to install the correct rod for the correct side of the vehicle

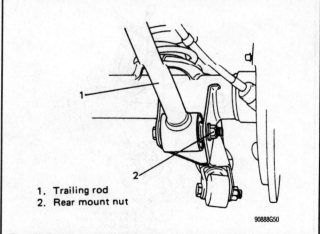

1. Trailing rod
2. Rear mount nut

90888G50

Fig. 77 Remove the trailing rod rear mounting bolt after supporting the rear and unbolting the parking brake cable mounts . . .

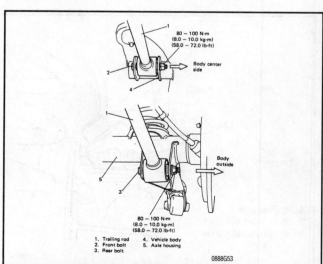

80 – 100 N·m
(8.0 – 10.0 kg-m)
(58.0 – 72.0 lb-ft)

Body center side

Body outside

80 – 100 N·m
(8.0 – 10.0 kg-m)
(58.0 – 72.0 lb-ft)

1. Trailing rod   4. Vehicle body
2. Front bolt   5. Axle housing
3. Rear bolt

0888G53

Fig. 80 Bolt positioning and tightening specifications for the trailing rods

STEERING

STEERING COMPONENT LOCATIONS—COIL SPRING SUSPENSION

1. Steering knuckles
2. Outer tie rod ends
3. Tie rod adjuster and locknuts
4. Inner tie rod ends
5. Center link
6. Idler arm
7. Pitman arm and steering gear

Steering Wheel

REMOVAL & INSTALLATION

1986–95 Models

▶ **See Figures 81, 82, 83, 84 and 85**

1. Disconnect the negative battery cable.
2. Disconnect the horn button and remove the steering wheel shaft nut.
3. Make matchmarks on the steering wheel and the shaft to use as a guide during reinstallation.
4. Remove the steering wheel, using a steering wheel puller.

To install:

5. Install the steering wheel onto the shaft, aligning the matchmarks.
6. Install and tighten the shaft nut to 19–28 ft. lbs. (25–40 Nm).
7. Install the horn button and connect the negative battery cable.

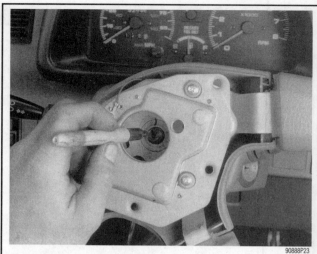

Fig. 83 Matchmark the steering shaft to the wheel for alignment when installing

Fig. 81 To remove the steering wheel, first remove the horn pad . . .

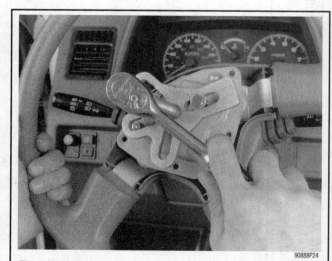

Fig. 84 Assemble a puller to the steering wheel and tighten the center bolt to press the wheel from the shaft

Fig. 82 . . . then loosen and remove the steering wheel shaft nut

Fig. 85 Pull the steering wheel from the shaft

1996–98 Models

◆ **See Figures 86, 87 and 88**

✳✳ CAUTION

The Supplemental Inflatable Restraint (SIR) system must be disarmed before removing the steering wheel. Failure to do so may cause accidental deployment of the air bag, resulting in unnecessary SIR system repairs and/or personal injury.

1. Disable the air bag system.
2. Disconnect the negative battery cable.
3. Remove the steering wheel side cap from the right side and disconnect the horn connectors.
4. Remove the air bag module attaching bolts and the air bag assembly from the vehicle.

✳✳ CAUTION

When carrying a live air bag, make sure the bag and trim cover are pointed away from the body. In the unlikely event of an accidental deployment, the bag will then deploy with minimal chance of injury. When placing a live inflator module on a bench or other surface, always place the bag and trim cover up, away from the surface. This will reduce the motion of the module if it is accidentally deployed.

✳✳ WARNING

The air bag system coil assembly is easily damaged if the correct steering wheel puller tools are not used.

5. Remove the steering wheel nut.
6. Scribe alignment marks across the steering wheel and shaft to ease installation.
7. Using a suitable puller (such as Suzuki tool 09944–36010), remove the steering wheel.

   To install:
8. Make sure the wheels are facing forward and the contact coil is centered.
9. Center the contact coil as follows:
   a. Check that the vehicle's wheels are facing straight ahead.
   b. Check that the ignition switch is at the LOCK position.
   c. Turn the contact coil counterclockwise slowly with a light force. Turn the coil until the contact coil will not turn any further.
   d. From the position where contact coil became unable to turn any further, turn it back clockwise about two and a half rotations and align the center mark with the alignment mark.
10. Install the steering wheel onto the steering column shaft. Be sure to match up the alignment marks that were made during removal.

➡When installing the steering wheel, make sure to install the steering wheel to the steering shaft with the two lugs contact coil fitted in the two grooves in the back of the steering wheel.

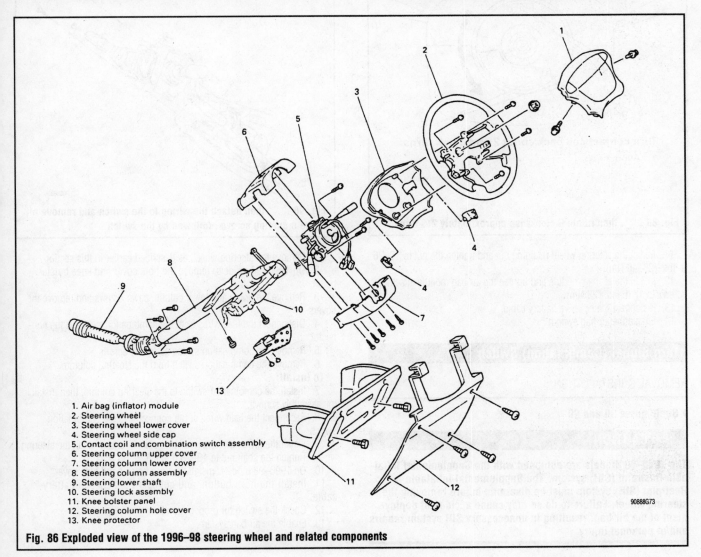

1. Air bag (inflator) module
2. Steering wheel
3. Steering wheel lower cover
4. Steering wheel side cap
5. Contact coil and combination switch assembly
6. Steering column upper cover
7. Steering column lower cover
8. Steering column assembly
9. Steering lower shaft
10. Steering lock assembly
11. Knee bolster panel
12. Steering column hole cover
13. Knee protector

90888G73

Fig. 86 Exploded view of the 1996–98 steering wheel and related components

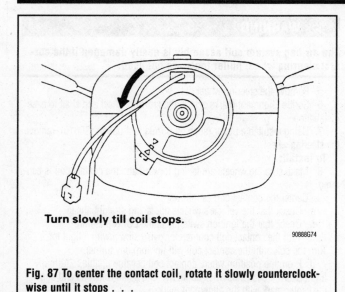

Turn slowly till coil stops.

90888G74

Fig. 87 To center the contact coil, rotate it slowly counterclockwise until it stops . . .

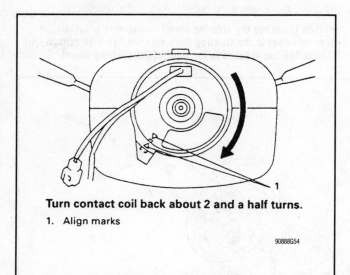

Turn contact coil back about 2 and a half turns.
1. Align marks

90888G54

Fig. 88 . . . then rotate it clockwise approximately 2½ turns

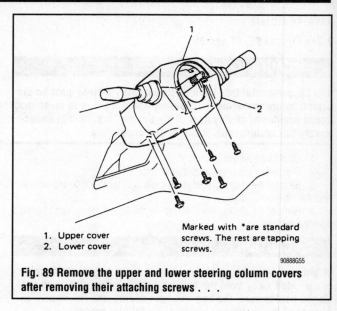

1. Upper cover
2. Lower cover

Marked with *are standard screws. The rest are tapping screws.

90888G55

Fig. 89 Remove the upper and lower steering column covers after removing their attaching screws . . .

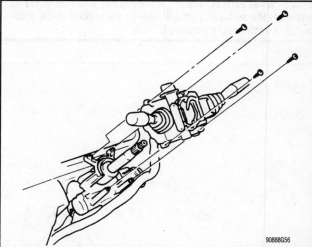

90888G56

Fig. 90 . . . then detach the wiring to the switch and remove all of the mounting screws, followed by the switch

11. Install the steering wheel retaining nut and tighten the nut to 19–28 ft. lbs. (25–40 Nm).
12. Install the air bag module and tighten the air bag module attaching screws to 17 ft. lbs. (23 Nm).
13. Reconnect the negative battery cable.
14. Enable the air bag system.

Turn Signal (Combination) Switch

REMOVAL & INSTALLATION

♦ See Figures 89 and 90

❊❊ CAUTION

The 1996–98 models are equipped with the Supplemental Inflatable Restraint (SIR) system. The Supplemental Inflatable Restraint (SIR) system must be disarmed before removing the steering wheel. Failure to do so may cause accidental deployment of the air bag, resulting in unnecessary SIR system repairs and/or personal injury.

1. Remove the steering wheel, as described earlier in this section.
2. On 1996–98 models, remove the hole cover and knee bolster panel.
3. Remove the upper and lower column cover screws and remove the covers.
4. Disconnect the lead wires from the combination switch at the connector.
5. Remove the combination switch assembly screws.
6. Remove the combination switch from the steering column.
To install:
7. Install the combination switch to the steering column, then install the assembly screws.
8. Reconnect the lead wires at the connector to the combination switch.
9. Install the lower and upper column covers, and reinstall the steering wheel. Tighten the shaft nut to 19–28 ft. lbs. (26–38 Nm).
10. On 1996–98 models, install the knee bolster and hole cover.
11. Install the horn button, and connect the negative battery cable.
12. Check the switch for proper operation.
13. Enable the air bag system.

Ignition Switch and Lock

REMOVAL & INSTALLATION

Samurai Models

1. Disconnect the negative battery cable.
2. Remove the steering wheel from the vehicle with special tool 09944–36010 or equivalent.
3. Disconnect the wire connector at the ignition switch.
4. With the ignition switch in the **OFF** position, remove the mounting bolts and remove the switch.

To install:

5. With the ignition switch in the **OFF** position, install the switch and the mounting bolts.
6. Connect the wire connector at the ignition switch.
7. Install the steering wheel and horn pad.
8. Connect the negative battery cable.

Sidekick, Tracker, Sidekick Sport and X-90 Models

▶ See Figures 91, 92 and 93

1. Disconnect the negative battery cable.
2. If equipped with an air bag, disable the air bag system.
3. Remove the steering wheel from the vehicle.
4. Remove the steering column from the vehicle and place in a vise with jaw protectors.
5. Using a hammer and chisel, create slots on the top of the ignition switch mounting bolts. Insert a flat bladed tool into the slots and remove the bolts (refer to the graphic). It is possible to remove the bolts with a hammer and center punch.
6. Remove the switch by turning the ignition key to **ACC** or **ON** position and removing the ignition switch assembly from steering column.

To install:

7. Position the oblong hole in the steering shaft in the center of the hole in the steering column.
8. Turn the ignition switch key to **ACC** or **ON** position and install the

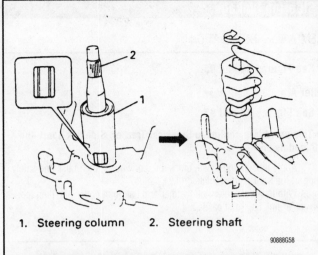

1. Steering column   2. Steering shaft

90888G58

Fig. 92 Align the oblong hole in the steering shaft, then install the lock. Rotate the shaft to ensure that the ignition lock has engaged the oblong hole and locked the shaft

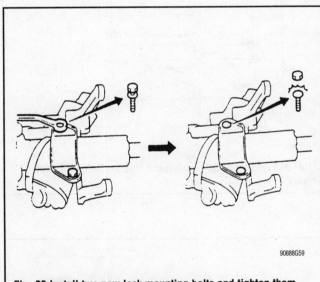

90888G59

Fig. 93 Install two new lock mounting bolts and tighten them until the head breaks off on each one

steering lock assembly onto the column. Do not completely tighten the two bolts holding the ignition switch to the column.

9. Turn the ignition switch to the **LOCK** position and pull out key.
10. Align the hub on the lock with the oblong hole in the steering column shaft and rotate the shaft to assure that the steering shaft is locked.
11. Tighten two new bolts attaching the ignition switch to steering column until the head of each bolt is broken off.
12. Turn ignition key to **ACC** or **ON** position and check to be sure that steering shaft rotates smoothly. Also check for lock operation.
13. Install the steering column in the vehicle.
14. Connect the electrical connector to the ignition switch.
15. If equipped with an air bag, enable the air bag.
16. Connect the negative battery cable.

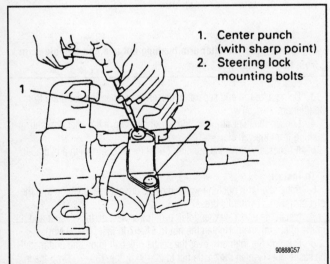

1. Center punch (with sharp point)
2. Steering lock mounting bolts

90888G57

Fig. 91 To remove the ignition lock, first remove the steering column and place in a vise. Next, use a sharp chisel and a hammer to remove the steering lock mounting bolts

Steering Linkage

REMOVAL & INSTALLATION

▶ **See Figures 94 and 95**

Idler Arm

▶ **See Figures 96 and 97**

➡ **This procedure applies to Sidekick, Tracker, Sidekick Sport and X-90 models only.**

1. Apply the parking brake, block the rear wheels, then raise and safely support the front of the vehicle on jackstands.

2. Withdraw the center link-to-idler arm ball joint cotter pin, then loosen the center link ball joint castle nut.

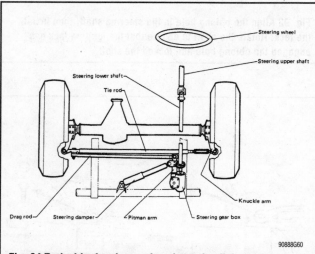

Fig. 94 Typical leaf spring equipped steering linkage components

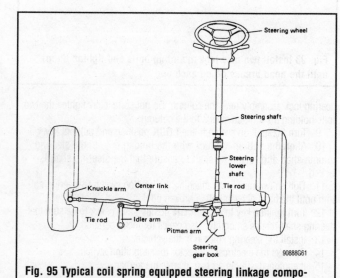

Fig. 95 Typical coil spring equipped steering linkage components

1. Idler arm
2. Center link
3. Castle nut
4. Split pin

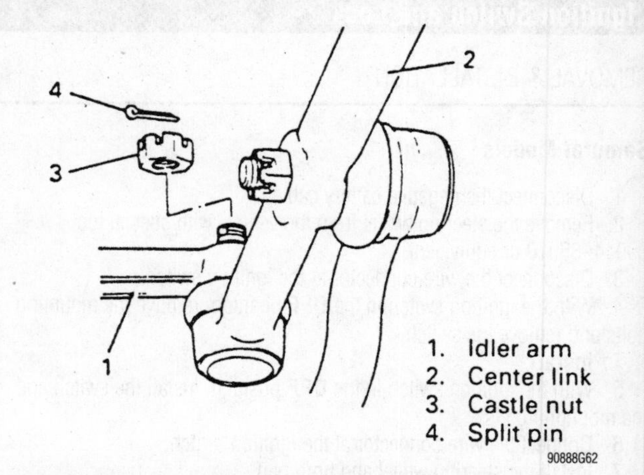

Fig. 96 Remove the idler arm-to-center link cotter pin and castellated nut, then disconnect them with a tie rod separator tool

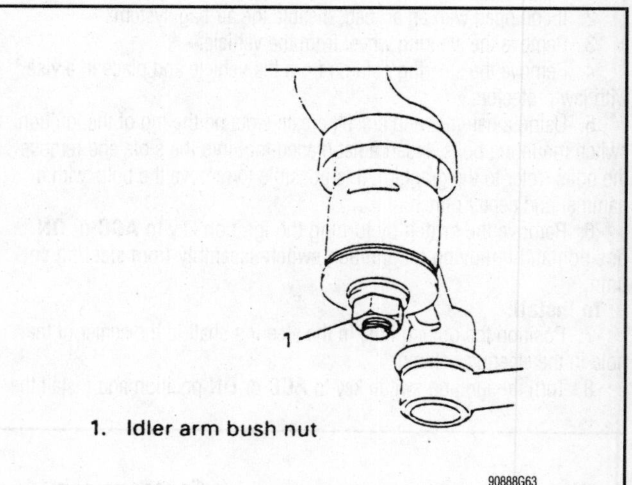

1. Idler arm bush nut

Fig. 97 Remove the idler arm bushing nut and pull the idler arm from the vehicle

3. Using a tie rod end separator, detach the center link ball joint from the idler arm.

4. Loosen the idler arm bushing nut, then remove the idler arm and bushing from the vehicle.

5. If necessary, drive the bushing out of the idler arm with a hydraulic press.

To install:

6. If the idler arm bushing was removed, drive a new bushing into the idler arm with a hydraulic press.

7. Install the upper washer, idler arm, lower washer, lockwasher and nut on the idler arm shaft. Tighten the nut to 51–57 ft. lbs. (70–80 Nm).

8. Position the idler arm over the center link ball joint stud and install the castle nut. Tighten the castle nut to 22–50 ft. lbs. (30–70 Nm). Insert a new cotter pin through the castle nut and center link stud holes, then bend the cotter pin ends over. If none of the castle nut grooves are aligned with the hole in the center link stud hole, continue tightening the castle nut until one of the grooves is aligned with the stud hole, then install the cotter pin.

9. Lower the vehicle and remove the rear wheel blocks.

Tie Rod Ends

▶ See Figures 98, 99, 100 and 101

SIDEKICK, TRACKER, SIDEKICK SPORT, AND X-90 MODELS

1. Loosen all of the front wheel lug nuts ½ turn.

2. Apply the parking brake, block the rear wheels, then raise and safely support the rear of the vehicle on jackstands.

3. Remove the wheels.

4. Remove the cotter pin and castle nut from the outer tie rod end.

5. Separate the outer tie rod end from the steering knuckle, using a tie rod end remover tool.

6. Mark the outer tie rod end jam nut position on the inner tie rod threads.

7. Loosen the jam nut, then remove the outer tie rod end from the inner tie rod.

To install:

8. Install the tie rod end onto the inner tie rod. Align the jam nut with the mark on the tie rod thread, and tighten the jam nut to 37–58 ft. lbs. (50–80 Nm).

9. Connect the tie rod end to the steering knuckle. Tighten the castle nut until the holes of the split pin are aligned but only within the specified torque of 22–39 ft. lbs. (30–55 Nm). Install a new cotter pin.

10. Install the tires.

Fig. 100 Use a tie rod separator tool to disconnect the tie rod end from the steering knuckle

Fig. 98 To remove a tie rod end, first remove the cotter pin from the castellated nut . . .

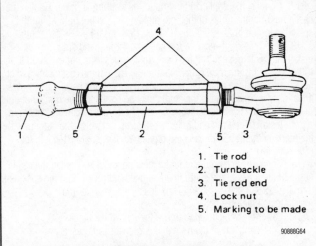

1. Tie rod
2. Turnbackle
3. Tie rod end
4. Lock nut
5. Marking to be made

Fig. 101 Loosen the adjusting (turnbuckle) locknut, then remove the tie rod end

11. Lower the vehicle, and remove the rear wheel blocks.

12. Check and adjust the front end alignment as necessary.

SAMURAI MODELS—LEFT-HAND TIE ROD END

1. Loosen all of the front wheel lug nuts ½ turn.

2. Apply the parking brake, block the rear wheels, then raise and safely support the rear of the vehicle on jackstands.

3. Remove the wheels.

4. Remove the cotter pin and castle nut from the outer tie rod end.

5. Separate the outer tie rod end from the steering knuckle, using a tie rod end remover tool.

6. Mark the outer tie rod end jam nut position on the inner tie rod threads.

7. Loosen the jam nut, then remove the outer tie rod end from the inner tie rod.

To install:

8. Install the tie rod end onto the inner tie rod. Align the jam nut with the mark on the tie rod thread, and tighten the jam nut to 51–72 ft. lbs. (70–100 Nm).

9. Connect the tie rod end to the steering knuckle. Tighten the castle nut until the holes of the split pin are aligned but only within the specified torque of 22–39 ft. lbs. (30–55 Nm). Install a new cotter pin.

Fig. 99 . . . then loosen and remove the nut

10. Install the tires.
11. Lower the vehicle, and remove the rear wheel blocks.
12. Check and adjust the front end alignment as necessary.

SAMURAI MODELS—RIGHT-HAND TIE ROD END

1. Loosen all of the front wheel lug nuts ½ turn.
2. Apply the parking brake, block the rear wheels, then raise and safely support the rear of the vehicle on jackstands.
3. Remove the wheels.
4. Remove the cotter pin and castle nut from the left-hand outer tie rod end.
5. Separate the left-hand outer tie rod end from the steering knuckle, using a tie rod end remover tool.
6. Mark the outer tie rod end jam nut position on the inner tie rod threads.
7. Loosen the jam nut, then remove the outer tie rod end from the inner tie rod.
8. Withdraw the drag rod-to-right tie rod end ball joint cotter pin, then loosen the castle nut.
9. Using a tie rod end separator, detach the drag rod from the right-hand tie rod.
10. Remove the cotter pin and castle nut from the right-hand tie rod end.
11. Separate the right-hand tie rod end from the steering knuckle, using a tie rod end remover tool.
    To install:
12. Connect the right-hand tie rod to the steering knuckle. Tighten the castle nut until the holes of the split pin are aligned but only within the specified torque of 22–39 ft. lbs. (30–55 Nm). Install a new cotter pin.
13. Insert the right-hand tie rod ball stud through the drag rod hole. Install the castle nut hand-tight. Then, tighten the castle nut to 22–39 ft. lbs. (30–55 Nm). Insert a new cotter pin through each of the castle nuts and stud holes, then bend the cotter pin ends over. If none of the castle nut grooves are aligned with the hole in the stud, continue tightening the castle nut until one of the grooves is aligned with the stud hole, then install the cotter pin.
14. Install the tie rod end onto the inner tie rod. Align the jam nut with the mark on the tie rod thread, and tighten the jam nut to 51–72 ft. lbs. (70–100 Nm).
15. Connect the tie rod end to the steering knuckle. Tighten the castle nut until the holes of the split pin are aligned but only within the specified torque of 22–39 ft. lbs. (30–55 Nm). Install a new cotter pin.
16. Install the tires.
17. Lower the vehicle, and remove the rear wheel blocks.
18. Check and adjust the front end alignment as necessary.

Center Link

➡**This procedure applies to Sidekick, Tracker, Sidekick Sport and X-90 models only.**

1. Apply the parking brake, block the rear wheels, then raise and safely support the front of the vehicle on jackstands.
2. Withdraw the center link-to-idler arm and center link-to-Pitman arm ball joint cotter pins, then loosen the center link ball joint castle nuts.
3. Using a tie rod end separator, detach the center link ball joints from the idler and Pitman arms.
4. Withdraw the center link-to-outer tie rod end ball joint cotter pins, then loosen the outer tie rod end ball joint castle nuts.
5. Using a tie rod end separator, detach the center link from the outer tie rod ends.
   To install:
6. Insert the outer tie rod end ball studs through the center link holes. Install the castle nuts hand-tight.
7. Engage the idler arm and Pitman arm with the center link ball joint studs, then install the castle nuts hand-tight.
8. Tighten all of the castle nuts to 22–50 ft. lbs. (30–70 Nm). Insert a new cotter pin through each of the castle nuts and stud holes, then bend the cotter pin ends over. If none of the castle nut grooves are aligned with the hole in the stud, continue tightening the castle nut until one of the grooves is aligned with the stud hole, then install the cotter pin.
9. Lower the vehicle and remove the rear wheel blocks.

Drag Rod

➡**This procedure applies to Samurai models only.**

1. If necessary, apply the parking brake, block the rear wheels, then raise and safely support the front of the vehicle on jackstands.
2. Withdraw the drag rod-to-Pitman arm ball joint cotter pin, then loosen the castle nut.
3. Using a tie rod end separator, detach the drag rod from the Pitman arm.
4. Withdraw the drag rod-to-right tie rod end ball joint cotter pin, then loosen the castle nut.
5. Using a tie rod end separator, detach the drag rod from the right-hand tie rod.
   To install:
6. Insert the right-hand tie rod ball stud through the drag rod hole. Install the castle nut hand-tight.
7. Engage the Pitman arm with the drag rod, then install the castle nut hand-tight.
8. Tighten all of the castle nuts to 22–39 ft. lbs. (30–55 Nm). Insert a new cotter pin through each of the castle nuts and stud holes, then bend the cotter pin ends over. If none of the castle nut grooves are aligned with the hole in the stud, continue tightening the castle nut until one of the grooves is aligned with the stud hole, then install the cotter pin.
9. If necessary, lower the vehicle and remove the rear wheel blocks.

Manual Steering Gear

REMOVAL & INSTALLATION

Samurai Models

1. Remove the steering shaft coupler bolt, then disconnect the coupler from the gear.
2. Apply the parking brake, block the rear wheels, then raise and support the vehicle safely.
3. Remove the radiator under cover and disconnect the Pitman arm from the drag link.
4. Disconnect the steering damper from the Pitman arm.
5. Support the steering gear and remove the mounting bolts.
6. Remove the steering gear from the vehicle.
   To install:
7. Install the steering gear in the vehicle and tighten the mounting nuts to 51–65 ft. lbs. (70–90 Nm).
8. Install the steering damper to the Pitman arm, then tighten the nut to 30 ft. lbs. (40 Nm).
9. Connect the drag link to the Pitman arm, and tighten the nut to 50 ft. lbs. (70 Nm).
10. Install the radiator under cover.
11. Connect the steering coupler to the steering box, and tighten the bolt to 15–21 ft. lbs. (20–30 Nm).
12. Lower the vehicle.

Sidekick and Tracker Models

▶ **See Figures 102, 103, 104 and 105**

1. Raise and support the vehicle safely.
2. Remove the lower skid plate.
3. Disconnect the steering lower shaft mounting bolts.
4. Using special tool J29107 or equivalent, disconnect the center link end from the Pitman arm.
5. Remove the 3 steering gear box mounting bolts.
6. Disconnect the steering lower shaft joint and remove the steering gear.
7. If replacing the steering gear, remove the nut connecting the Pitman arm to the steering gear. Use a Pitman arm puller to remove the Pitman arm from the steering gear.

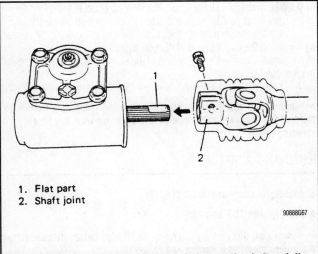

1. Flat part
2. Shaft joint

90888G67

Fig. 102 Remove the lower steering shaft mounting bolt and disconnect the shaft from the gear box

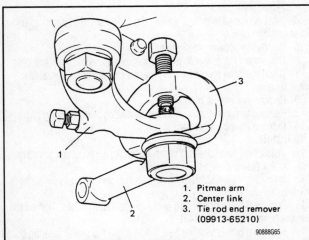

1. Pitman arm
2. Center link
3. Tie rod end remover
   (09913-65210)

90888G65

Fig. 103 Remove the center link-to-Pitman arm attaching nut and, using a tie rod end remover, press out the link from the arm

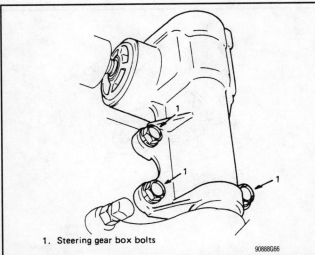

1. Steering gear box bolts

90888G66

Fig. 104 Remove the three steering gear box attaching bolts and remove the box from the vehicle

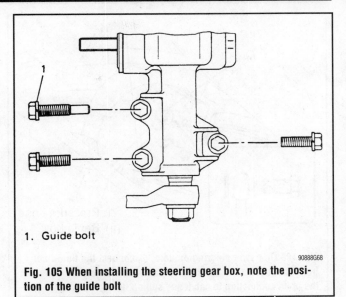

1. Guide bolt

90888G68

Fig. 105 When installing the steering gear box, note the position of the guide bolt

To install:

8. Connect the Pitman arm to the steering gear, then install the nut. Tighten the nut to 101–129 ft. lbs. (140–180 Nm).
9. Install the steering gear box by connecting to the lower shaft joint.

➡**Align the flat part of the steering gear worm shaft with the bolt hole of the lower shaft joint.**

10. Install the steering gear box mounting bolts, then tighten them to 51–72 ft. lbs. (70–100 Nm).
11. Attach the center link to the Pitman arm, then tighten the nut to 22–50 ft. lbs. (30–70 Nm).
12. Connect the lower steering shaft mounting bolts, then tighten them to 15–22 ft. lbs. (20–30 Nm).
13. Install the lower skid plate.
14. Lower the vehicle.

Power Steering Gear

REMOVAL & INSTALLATION

Sidekick, Tracker, Sidekick Sport and X-90 Models

▶ **See Figures 106 and 107**

1. Remove the coolant reservoir tank from the radiator.
2. Disconnect the steering column lower shaft from the gear box by removing the bolt.
3. Raise and safely support the vehicle.
4. Remove the center link nut and lockwasher holding the Pitman arm to the center link. Using a Pitman arm puller, disconnect the center link from the Pitman arm.
5. Lower the vehicle and place a fluid catch pan under the power steering gear box. Remove the pressure hose from the power steering gear assembly and plug the line.
6. Disconnect the return hose and plug the line.
7. Remove the three power steering gear mounting bolts.
8. Remove the power steering gear.
9. Remove the nut holding the Pitman arm to the power steering box. Place alignment marks on the Pitman arm and steering box. Using a Pitman arm puller, remove the Pitman arm from the steering box.
   To install:
10. Align the matchmarks on the Pitman arm and the power steering gear sector shaft. Install the Pitman arm to the gear assembly and tighten the nut to 101–129 ft. lbs. (140–180 Nm).

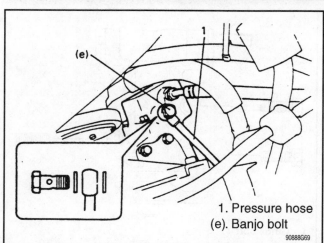

1. Pressure hose
(e). Banjo bolt

Fig. 106 On power steering models, disconnect the fluid lines from the gear box. A small catch can should be placed beneath the open connection to catch any spilled fluid

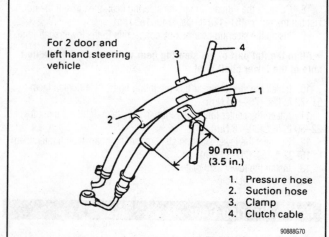

For 2 door and left hand steering vehicle

90 mm (3.5 in.)

1. Pressure hose
2. Suction hose
3. Clamp
4. Clutch cable

Fig. 107 When installing the power steering lines, make sure to route and position them as shown

11. Install the power steering gear assembly on the vehicle, then tighten the mounting bolts to 59–73 ft. lbs. (80–100 Nm).

12. Connect the power steering pressure and return hoses. Using new gaskets, tighten the union bolt for the pressure line to 26 ft. lbs. (35 Nm).

13. Raise and safely support the vehicle.

14. Install the center link to the Pitman arm and tighten the nut to 22–50 ft. lbs. (30–70 Nm). Lower the vehicle.

15. Connect the steering column lower shaft to the gear assembly, then tighten the bolts to 15–22 ft. lbs. (20–30 Nm).

16. Install the coolant reservoir tank to the radiator.

17. Refill and bleed the power steering pump.

Power Steering Pump

BLEEDING

1. Apply the parking brake, block the rear wheels, then raise and support the vehicle safely.

2. Fill the power steering reservoir to the specified level.

3. Run the engine for 3–5 minutes, stop the engine and add fluid if necessary to reach specified level.

4. With the engine stopped, turn the steering wheel to the left and to the right as far as it turns. Repeat a few times and refill the reservoir.

5. With the engine running at idle speed, bleed the air from the system by loosening the bleeder valve at the gear assembly.

6. Repeat the side-to-side turning of the steering wheel until all the foam is gone.

7. Tighten the bleed valve securely. Recheck the fluid level in the reservoir.

➡**When air bleeding is not complete, it is indicated by a foaming fluid on the level indicator or a humming noise from the power steering pump.**

REMOVAL & INSTALLATION

Sidekick, Tracker and X-90 Models

▶ **See Figures 108 and 109**

➡**Remove all dirt and grease from the fittings before disconnecting the power steering pressure and return lines.**

1. Remove the power steering belt.

2. Remove the coolant reservoir tank from the radiator.

3. If equipped with A/C, loosen the air conditioning compressor adjusting and pivot bolts.

4. If not equipped with A/C, loosen the power steering pump adjusting and mounting bolts.

5. Remove the power steering belt.

6. Disconnect the power steering pressure and return hose and plug.

7. Disconnect the power steering pressure switch lead wire at the switch terminal.

8. Remove the engine oil filter.

9. Remove the power steering pump mounting and adjusting bolts.

10. Remove the power steering pump.

To install:

11. Install the power steering pump and replace the pump mounting bolts. Do not tighten.

12. Install the power steering pump pressure switch lead wire to the switch terminal.

13. Replace the power steering pressure and return hoses. Tighten the pressure hose union bolt to 44 ft. lbs. (60 Nm).

14. Install the power steering belt, then tighten the power steering pump mounting bolts to 21 ft. lbs. (28 Nm).

15. If equipped with A/C, tighten the air conditioning compressor mounting bolts to 21 ft. lbs. (28 Nm).

16. Replace the coolant reservoir tank to the radiator. Refill the power steering pump.

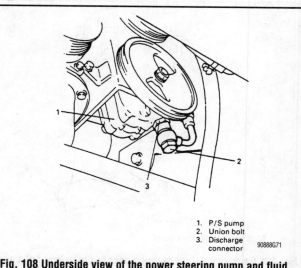

1. P/S pump
2. Union bolt
3. Discharge connector

Fig. 108 Underside view of the power steering pump and fluid line connection

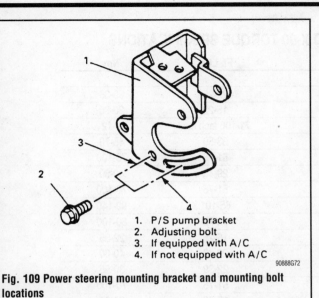

1. P/S pump bracket
2. Adjusting bolt
3. If equipped with A/C
4. If not equipped with A/C

90888G72

Fig. 109 Power steering mounting bracket and mounting bolt locations

17. Replace the oil filter and fill the crankcase to the proper level.
18. Run the engine and operate the power steering. Check for any leaks.

Sidekick Sport Model

➡**Remove all dirt and grease from the fittings before disconnecting the power steering pressure and return lines.**

1. Remove the coolant reservoir tank from the radiator.
2. Remove the air cleaner outlet hose.
3. Remove the alternator drive belt.
4. Using a syringe, remove the fluid from the power steering pump.
5. Disconnect the power steering pressure switch lead wire at the switch terminal.
6. Disconnect the power steering pump discharge hose from the power steering pump. Plug the line to prevent fluid from spilling from the line.
7. Remove the union bolt and disconnect the suction line from the power steering pump. Hold the discharge connector with a wrench to prevent it from getting loose and draining power steering fluid.
8. Remove the three mounting bolts from the power steering pump.
9. Remove the power steering pump from the engine.

To install:

10. Install the power steering pump with the three mounting bolts. Tighten the bolts to 37 ft. lbs. (50 Nm).
11. Connect the pressure hose and suction hose to the power steering pump. Tighten the union bolt to 44 ft. lbs. (60 Nm). Use new gaskets for the union bolt.
12. Connect the power steering pressure switch lead wire to the switch terminal.
13. Install the alternator belt.
14. Install the air cleaner outlet hose.
15. Fill the power steering pump with Dexron®III or superseding A/T fluid.
16. Bleed the air in the power steering pump.
17. Start the engine and check for leaks.

SAMURAI TORQUE SPECIFICATIONS

System	Component	Ft. Lbs.	Nm
Front Suspension			
	Axle shaft drive flange bolt	15-21	20-30
	Differential oil drain lug	160-221 inch lbs.	18-25
	Differential oil filler and level plug	26-36	35-50
	Joint seal bolt	71-106 inch lbs.	8-12
	Kingpin upper and lower bolts	15-21	20-30
	Leaf spring bumper bolt	160-248 inch lbs.	18-28
	Leaf spring nut	44-61	60-85
	Leaf spring U-bolt nut	44-57	60-80
	Shackle pin nut	22-40	30-55
	Shock absorber lower nut	23-39	35-55
	Shock absorber upper locknut	16-25	22-35
	Sway bar bolt	51-65	70-90
	Sway bar mounting bracket bolt	160-248 inch lbs.	18-28
	Sway bar nut	16-25	22-35
	Wheel bearing locknut	44-65	60-90
	Wheel bearing nut	88-133 inch lbs.	10-15
	Wheel lug nut	37-57	50-80
Rear Suspension			
	Differential oil drain lug	160-221 inch lbs.	18-25
	Differential oil filler and level plug	26-36	35-50
	Hub nut	37-57	50-80
	Leaf spring nut	44-61	60-85
	Leaf spring U-bolt nut	44-57	60-80
	Shackle pin nut	22-40	30-55
	Shock absorber nuts	23-39	35-55
	Wheel lug nut	37-57	50-80
Steering			
	Drag rod castle nut	22-39	30-55
	Steering column bolt and nut	97-150 inch lbs.	11-17
	Steering damper nut	26-39	35-55
	Steering damper pin nut	16-25	22-35
	Steering damper stay nut	160-248 inch lbs.	18-28
	Steering gear box nuts	51-65	70-90
	Steering shaft joint flange bolt	15-21	20-30
	Steering shaft rubber joint bolt	133-221 inch lbs.	15-25
	Steering wheel-to-shaft nut	19-28	25-40
	Tie rod end castle nut	22-39	30-55
	Tie rod end jam nut	51-72	70-100

90888C01

SIDEKICK, TRACKER, SIDEKICK SPORT AND X-90 TORQUE SPECIFICATIONS

System	Component	Ft. Lbs.	Nm
Front Suspension			
	4WD Locking hub bolt — automatic type	22-25	30-35
	4WD Locking hub bolt — manual type	15-22	20-30
	4WD locking hub cover bolt	71-106 inch lbs.	8-12
	Ball joint castle nut	33-50	45-70
	Ball joint-to-lower control arm bolts	51-75	70-100
	Bump stopper	29-43	40-60
	Control arm front nut	51-75	70-100
	Control arm rear nut	65-101	90-140
	Strut-to-knuckle mounting nuts	58-75	80-100
	Sway bar end link-to-control arm nut	16-25	22-35
	Sway bar-to-end link nut	29-43	40-60
	Tie rod end castle nut	22-39	30-55
	Upper center strut mounting nut	51-75	70-100
	Upper peripheral strut mounting nuts	15-22	20-30
	Wheel bearing locknut	123-180	170-250
	Wheel bearing lockplate screw	8.8-17.7 inch lbs.	1-2
	Wheel lug nuts — 1986-90 models	37-58	50-80
	Wheel lug nuts — 1991-98 models	58-79	80-110
Rear Suspension			
	Ball joint bracket bolt	29-43	40-60
	Ball joint castle nut	33-50	45-70
	Bearing retainer nut	160-248 inch lbs.	18-28
	Brake drum nut	37-57	50-80
	Differential carrier nut	37-43	50-60
	Differential gear oil drain plug	160-221 inch lbs.	18-25
	Differential gear oil filler plug	26-36	35-50
	Driveshaft nuts	37-43	50-60
	Shock absorber locknut	16-25	22-35
	Shock absorber lower nut	51-72	70-100
	Shock absorber upper nut	16-25	22-35
	Trailing rod nuts	58-72	80-100
	Upper control arm front nut	58-72	80-100
	Wheel lug nuts — 1986-90 models	37-58	50-80
	Wheel lug nuts — 1991-98 models	58-79	80-110
Steering			
	Centerlink castle nut	22-50	30-70
	Driver air bag (inflator) module bolts	17	23
	Idler arm nut	51-57	70-80
	Pitman arm nut	101-129	140-180
	Steering column bolts — 1996-98 models	17	23
	Steering column lower bolts — 1989-95 models	97-150 inch lbs.	11-17
	Steering column upper bolts — 1989-95 models	124 inch lbs.	14
	Steering gear box bolt	51-72	70-100
	Steering shaft joint bolt	15-22	20-30
	Steering wheel-to-steering shaft nut	19-28	25-40
	Tie rod end castle nut	22-39	30-55
	Tie rod end jam nut	37-58	50-80

90888C02

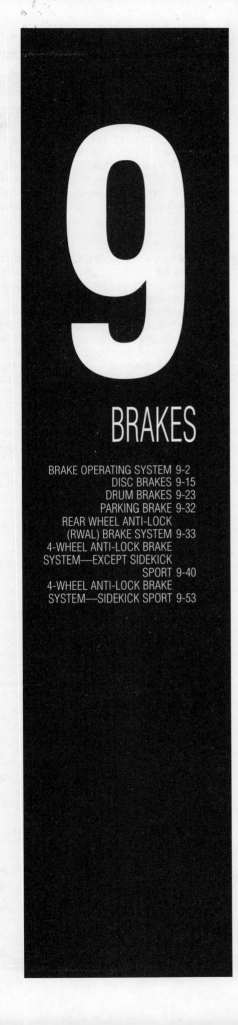

9

BRAKES

BRAKE OPERATING SYSTEM

Basic Operating Principles

Hydraulic systems are used to actuate the brakes of all modern automobiles. The system transports the power required to force the frictional surfaces of the braking system together from the pedal to the individual brake units at each wheel. A hydraulic system is used for two reasons.

First, fluid under pressure can be carried to all parts of an automobile by small pipes and flexible hoses without taking up a significant amount of room or posing routing problems.

Second, a great mechanical advantage can be given to the brake pedal end of the system, and the foot pressure required to actuate the brakes can be reduced by making the surface area of the master cylinder pistons smaller than that of any of the pistons in the wheel cylinders or calipers.

The master cylinder consists of a fluid reservoir along with a double cylinder and piston assembly. Double type master cylinders are designed to separate the front and rear braking systems hydraulically in case of a leak. The master cylinder coverts mechanical motion from the pedal into hydraulic pressure within the lines. This pressure is translated back into mechanical motion at the wheels by either the wheel cylinder (drum brakes) or the caliper (disc brakes).

Steel lines carry the brake fluid to a point on the vehicle's frame near each of the vehicle's wheels. The fluid is then carried to the calipers and wheel cylinders by flexible tubes in order to allow for suspension and steering movements.

In drum brake systems, each wheel cylinder contains two pistons, one at either end, which push outward in opposite directions and force the brake shoe into contact with the drum.

In disc brake systems, the cylinders are part of the calipers. At least one cylinder in each caliper is used to force the brake pads against the disc.

All pistons employ some type of seal, usually made of rubber, to minimize fluid leakage. A rubber dust boot seals the outer end of the cylinder against dust and dirt. The boot fits around the outer end of the piston on disc brake calipers, and around the brake actuating rod on wheel cylinders.

The hydraulic system operates as follows: When at rest, the entire system, from the piston(s) in the master cylinder to those in the wheel cylinders or calipers, is full of brake fluid. Upon application of the brake pedal, fluid trapped in front of the master cylinder piston(s) is forced through the lines to the wheel cylinders. Here, it forces the pistons outward, in the case of drum brakes, and inward toward the disc, in the case of disc brakes. The motion of the pistons is opposed by return springs mounted outside the cylinders in drum brakes, and by spring seals, in disc brakes.

Upon release of the brake pedal, a spring located inside the master cylinder immediately returns the master cylinder pistons to the normal position. The pistons contain check valves and the master cylinder has compensating ports drilled in it. These are uncovered as the pistons reach their normal position. The piston check valves allow fluid to flow toward the wheel cylinders or calipers as the pistons withdraw. Then, as the return springs force the brake pads or shoes into the released position, the excess fluid reservoir through the compensating ports. It is during the time the pedal is in the released position that any fluid that has leaked out of the system will be replaced through the compensating ports.

Dual circuit master cylinders employ two pistons, located one behind the other, in the same cylinder. The primary piston is actuated directly by mechanical linkage from the brake pedal through the power booster. The secondary piston is actuated by fluid trapped between the two pistons. If a leak develops in front of the secondary piston, it moves forward until it bottoms against the front of the master cylinder, and the fluid trapped between the pistons will operate the rear brakes. If the rear brakes develop a leak, the primary piston will move forward until direct contact with the secondary piston takes place, and it will force the secondary piston to actuate the front brakes. In either case, the brake pedal moves farther when the brakes are applied, and less braking power is available.

All dual circuit systems use a switch to warn the driver when only half of the brake system is operational. This switch is usually located in a valve body which is mounted on the firewall or the frame below the master cylin-

der. A hydraulic piston receives pressure from both circuits, each circuit's pressure being applied to one end of the piston. When the pressures are in balance, the piston remains stationary. When one circuit has a leak, however, the greater pressure in that circuit during application of the brakes will push the piston to one side, closing the switch and activating the brake warning light.

In disc brake systems, this valve body also contains a metering valve and, in some cases, a proportioning valve. The metering valve keeps pressure from traveling to the disc brakes on the front wheels until the brake shoes on the rear wheels have contacted the drums, ensuring that the front brakes will never be used alone. The proportioning valve controls the pressure to the rear brakes to lessen the chance of rear wheel lock-up during very hard braking.

Warning lights may be tested by depressing the brake pedal and holding it while opening one of the wheel cylinder bleeder screws. If this does not cause the light to go on, substitute a new lamp, make continuity checks, and, finally, replace the switch as necessary.

The hydraulic system may be checked for leaks by applying pressure to the pedal gradually and steadily. If the pedal sinks very slowly to the floor, the system has a leak. This is not to be confused with a springy or spongy feel due to the compression of air within the lines. If the system leaks, there will be a gradual change in the position of the pedal with a constant pressure.

Check for leaks along all lines and at wheel cylinders. If no external leaks are apparent, the problem is inside the master cylinder.

DISC BRAKES

Instead of the traditional expanding brakes that press outward against a circular drum, disc brake systems utilize a disc (rotor) with brake pads positioned on either side of it. An easily-seen analogy is the hand brake arrangement on a bicycle. The pads squeeze onto the rim of the bike wheel, slowing its motion. Automobile disc brakes use the identical principle but apply the braking effort to a separate disc instead of the wheel.

The disc (rotor) is a casting, usually equipped with cooling fins between the two braking surfaces. This enables air to circulate between the braking surfaces making them less sensitive to heat buildup and more resistant to fade. Dirt and water do not drastically affect braking action since contaminants are thrown off by the centrifugal action of the rotor or scraped off the by the pads. Also, the equal clamping action of the two brake pads tends to ensure uniform, straight line stops. Disc brakes are inherently self-adjusting. There are three general types of disc brake:

1. A fixed caliper.
2. A floating caliper.
3. A sliding caliper.

The fixed caliper design uses two pistons mounted on either side of the rotor (in each side of the caliper). The caliper is mounted rigidly and does not move.

The sliding and floating designs are quite similar. In fact, these two types are often lumped together. In both designs, the pad on the inside of the rotor is moved into contact with the rotor by hydraulic force. The caliper, which is not held in a fixed position, moves slightly, bringing the outside pad into contact with the rotor. There are various methods of attaching floating calipers. Some pivot at the bottom or top, and some slide on mounting bolts. In any event, the end result is the same.

DRUM BRAKES

Drum brakes employ two brake shoes mounted on a stationary backing plate. These shoes are positioned inside a circular drum which rotates with the wheel assembly. The shoes are held in place by springs. This allows them to slide toward the drums (when they are applied) while keeping the linings and drums in alignment. The shoes are actuated by a wheel cylinder which is mounted at the top of the backing plate. When the brakes are applied, hydraulic pressure forces the wheel cylinder's actuating links outward. Since these links bear directly against the top of the brake shoes, the tops of the shoes are then forced against the inner side of the drum. This action forces the bottoms of the two shoes to contact the brake drum by rotating the entire assembly slightly (known as servo action). When pressure within the wheel cylinder is relaxed, return springs pull the shoes back away from the drum.

Most modern drum brakes are designed to self-adjust themselves during application when the vehicle is moving in reverse. This motion causes both shoes to rotate very slightly with the drum, rocking an adjusting lever, thereby causing rotation of the adjusting screw. Some drum brake systems are designed to self-adjust during application whenever the brakes are applied. This on-board adjustment system reduces the need for maintenance adjustments and keeps both the brake function and pedal feel satisfactory.

POWER BOOSTERS

Virtually all modern vehicles use a vacuum assisted power brake system to multiply the braking force and reduce pedal effort. Since vacuum is always available when the engine is operating, the system is simple and efficient. A vacuum diaphragm is located on the front of the master cylinder and assists the driver in applying the brakes, reducing both the effort and travel he must put into moving the brake pedal.

The vacuum diaphragm housing is normally connected to the intake manifold by a vacuum hose. A check valve is placed at the point where the hose enters the diaphragm housing, so that during periods of low manifold vacuum brakes assist will not be lost.

Depressing the brake pedal closes off the vacuum source and allows atmospheric pressure to enter on one side of the diaphragm. This causes the master cylinder pistons to move and apply the brakes. When the brake pedal is released, vacuum is applied to both sides of the diaphragm and springs return the diaphragm and master cylinder pistons to the released position.

If the vacuum supply fails, the brake pedal rod will contact the end of the master cylinder actuator rod and the system will apply the brakes without any power assistance. The driver will notice that much higher pedal effort is needed to stop the car and that the pedal feels harder than usual.

Vacuum Leak Test

1. Operate the engine at idle without touching the brake pedal for at least one minute.
2. Turn off the engine and wait one minute.
3. Test for the presence of assist vacuum by depressing the brake pedal and releasing it several times. If vacuum is present in the system, light application will produce less and less pedal travel. If there is no vacuum, air is leaking into the system.

System Operation Test

1. With the engine **OFF**, pump the brake pedal until the supply vacuum is entirely gone.
2. Put light, steady pressure on the brake pedal.
3. Start the engine and let it idle. If the system is operating correctly, the brake pedal should fall toward the floor if the constant pressure is maintained.

Power brake systems may be tested for hydraulic leaks just as ordinary systems are tested.

✳✳ WARNING

Clean, high quality brake fluid is essential to the safe and proper operation of the brake system. You should always buy the highest quality brake fluid that is available. If the brake fluid becomes contaminated, drain and flush the system, then refill the master cylinder with new fluid. Never reuse any brake fluid. Any brake fluid that is removed from the system should be discarded.

Brake Light Switch

REMOVAL & INSTALLATION

▶ See Figure 1

➡ **The brake light switch is mounted on the brake pedal brace, beneath the instrument panel.**

1. Disconnect the negative battery cable.
2. From beneath the instrument panel, detach the wiring harness connector from the brake (stop) light switch.
3. Using an open end wrench, loosen the locknut, then remove the switch from the mounting bracket.
   To install:
4. Position the switch in the mounting bracket.
5. Pull the brake pedal toward you and, while holding it in this position, adjust the switch position so that the clearance between the end of the switch threads and the brake pedal return cushion is as follows:
   - Samurai models—0.02–0.04 in. (0.5–1.0mm)
   - 1989–95 Sidekick and Tracker models—0.02–0.04 in. (0.5–1.0mm)

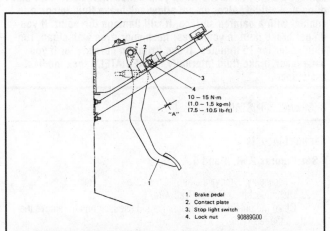

1. Brake pedal
2. Contact plate
3. Stop light switch
4. Lock nut   90889G00

Fig. 1 The brake (stop) light switch is mounted on the brake pedal bracket. The switch should be adjusted until the proper clearance between the switch and the brake pedal contact plate is achieved

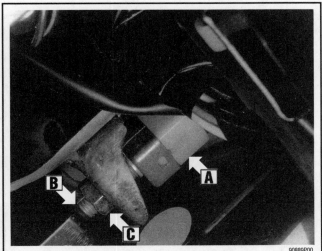

90889P00

To adjust the brake switch, rotate the switch (A) until the clearance (B) is correct, then tighten the locknut (C)

- 1996–98 Sidekick, Tracker, Sidekick Sport and X-90 models—
0.06–0.08 in. (1.5–2.0mm)
6. Tighten the switch locknut to 88–133 inch lbs. (10–15 Nm).
7. Reattach the wiring harness connector to the switch.
8. Connect the negative battery cable.

Master Cylinder

✳✳ WARNING

Clean, high quality brake fluid is essential to the safe and proper operation of the brake system. You should always buy the highest quality brake fluid that is available. If the brake fluid becomes contaminated, drain and flush the system, then refill the master cylinder with new fluid. Never reuse any brake fluid. Any brake fluid that is removed from the system should be discarded.

✳✳ CAUTION

Brake fluid contains polyglycol ethers and polyglycols. Avoid contact with the eyes and wash your hands thoroughly after handling brake fluid. Also, do not allow any brake fluid to come in contact with a painted surface; it will damage the paint. If you do get brake fluid in your eyes, flush your eyes with clean, running water for 15 minutes. If eye irritation persists, or if you have taken brake fluid internally, IMMEDIATELY seek medical assistance.

REMOVAL & INSTALLATION

Samurai Models

▶ See Figures 2, 3, 4 and 5

1. If necessary, remove the air cleaner case.
2. Disconnect the reservoir lead wire.
3. Clean the outside of the reservoir, and use a siphon to remove the fluid from the reservoir.
4. Disconnect and plug the two brake fluid lines at the master cylinder.

✳✳ WARNING

Do not allow brake fluid to sit on painted surfaces; the brake fluid will eat away the paint finish.

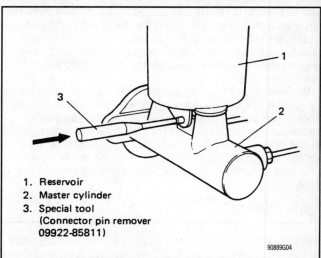

1. Reservoir
2. Master cylinder
3. Special tool
   (Connector pin remover
   09922-85811)

90889G04

Fig. 3 For 1990–95 models, separate the reservoir from the master cylinder by driving the retaining pin out

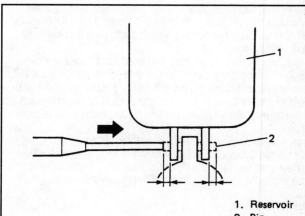

1. Reservoir
2. Pin

90889G02

Fig. 4 When driving a new retaining pin into the reservoir and master cylinder, ensure that it is positioned so that both protruding ends of the pin are even

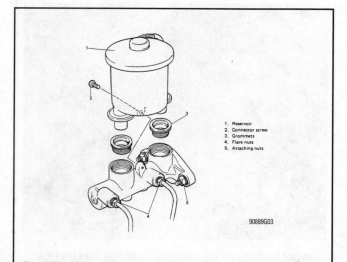

1. Reservoir
2. Connector screw
3. Grommets
4. Flare nuts
5. Attaching nuts

90889G03

Fig. 2 The fluid reservoir is attached to the master cylinder with a retaining screw—1986–89 models

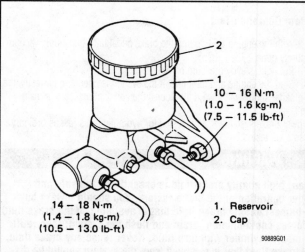

10 – 16 N·m
(1.0 – 1.6 kg-m)
(7.5 – 11.5 lb-ft)

14 – 18 N·m
(1.4 – 1.8 kg-m)
(10.5 – 13.0 lb-ft)

1. Reservoir
2. Cap

90889G01

Fig. 5 When installing the master cylinder, tighten the mounting nuts and brake line fittings to the specified values

5. Remove the two master cylinder to booster mounting bolts and remove the master cylinder.

6. At this point, the reservoir can be separated from the master cylinder by either removing the reservoir retaining screw (1986–89 models), or by driving the retaining pin out with a thin punch. Remove the reservoir from the master cylinder.

To install:

7. If the reservoir was separated from the master cylinder, position the reservoir on the master cylinder and either install the retaining screw (1986–89 models), or drive the retaining pin (1990–95 models) through the reservoir and master cylinder holes.

8. Bleed the master cylinder.

9. Install the new master cylinder and tighten the mounting bolts to 88–141 inch lbs. (10–16 Nm).

10. Install the hydraulic brake lines to the master cylinder and tighten and tighten the flare nuts to 124–159 inch lbs. (14–18 Nm).

✸✸ WARNING

Clean, high quality brake fluid is essential to the safe and proper operation of the brake system. You should always buy the highest quality brake fluid that is available. If the brake fluid becomes contaminated, drain and flush the system, then refill the master cylinder with new fluid. Never reuse any brake fluid. Any brake fluid that is removed from the system should be discarded.

11. Fill the reservoir with the specified brake fluid.

12. Connect the reservoir lead wire. Install the air cleaner case, if removed.

13. Bleed the air from the brake hydraulic system and check the brake pedal play.

Sidekick, Tracker and X-90 Models

1989–93 MODELS

▶ See Figures 6 and 7

✸✸ WARNING

Do not allow brake fluid to come in contact with painted surfaces; the brake fluid can damage paint.

1. If necessary for added clearance, remove the air cleaner case assembly.

2. If equipped, detach the wiring harness connectors from the fluid reservoir, from the Proportioning and Differential (P+D) valve and the pressure limit valve.

3. Clean the outside of the reservoir, then siphon the brake fluid from the reservoir.

4. Disconnect and plug brake fluid lines A, B, and C from the master cylinder, 2-way joint and the P+D valve.

5. Remove the heat shield from the master cylinder bracket.

6. Remove the master cylinder mounting nuts, then remove the master cylinder, 2-way joint and P+D valve together from the booster.

To remove the master cylinder, first siphon all of the brake fluid out of the reservoir . . .

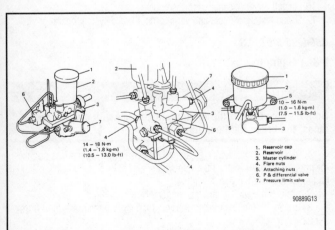

Fig. 6 The 1989–93 models equipped with the RWAL ABS system are designed with the P+D and pressure limit valves mounted on the master cylinder, while models without ABS have the proportioning valve mounted on a frame rail

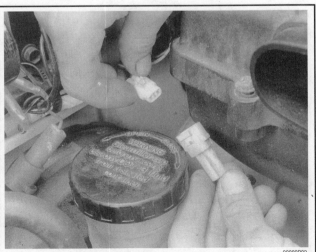

. . . then detach the wiring harness connector(s) from the master cylinder

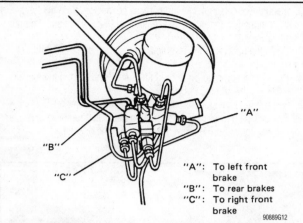

"A": To left front brake
"B": To rear brakes
"C": To right front brake

90889G12

Fig. 7 For models equipped with P+D and pressure limit valves mounted on the master cylinder, detach and plug brake fluid lines A, B and C only—On models not equipped with these two valves . . .

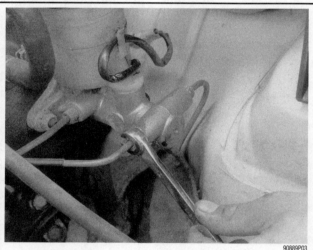

90889P03

. . . detach the brake fluid lines from the master cylinder, then plug them to prevent fluid loss or contamination

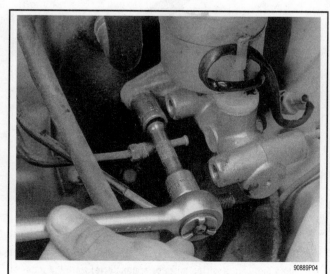

90889P04

Loosen the master cylinder-to-brake booster retaining nuts . . .

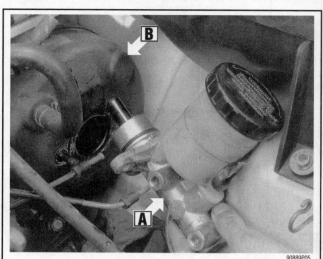

90889P05

. . . then separate the master cylinder (A) from the brake booster (B). Be sure to wipe up all spilled brake fluid

To install:

7. Adjust the booster piston rod-to-master cylinder clearance.
8. Bleed the master cylinder.
9. Install the master cylinder, along with the 2-way joint and P+D valve.
10. Install and tighten the mounting nuts to 88–141 inch lbs. (10–16 Nm).
11. Reattach all of the hydraulic brake lines to the master cylinder, 2-way joint and P+D valve, then tighten the fittings to 124–159 inch lbs. (14–18 Nm).
12. Install the heat shield on the master cylinder bracket.
13. Reattach all of the wiring harness connectors.

✳✳ WARNING

Clean, high quality brake fluid is essential to the safe and proper operation of the brake system. You should always buy the highest quality brake fluid that is available. If the brake fluid becomes contaminated, drain and flush the system, then refill the master cylinder with new fluid. Never reuse any brake fluid. Any brake fluid that is removed from the system should be discarded.

14. Fill the reservoir with the specified brake fluid.
15. Bleed the air from the brake hydraulic system, check the brake pedal play, and inspect the master cylinder fittings for fluid leaks.
16. Install the air cleaner case assembly.
17. Road test the vehicle and verify proper brake system operation.

1994–95 MODELS

▶ See Figure 8

✳✳ WARNING

Do not allow brake fluid to come in contact with painted surfaces; the brake fluid can damage paint.

1. If necessary for added clearance, detach the wiring harness connector from the air flow meter, then remove the air intake hose, air flow meter and air cleaner case assembly lid.
2. Detach the wiring harness connector from the fluid reservoir.
3. Clean the outside of the reservoir, then siphon the brake fluid from the reservoir.
4. Depress the brake pedal a few times, which will make removal easier.
5. Disconnect and plug the three brake fluid lines from the master cylinder.
6. Remove the master cylinder mounting nuts, then remove the master cylinder from the booster.

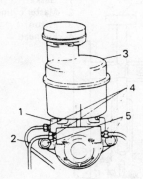

1. Master cylinder
2. Brake pipe
3. Reservoir tank
4. Flare nut
5. Master cylinder

90889G05

Fig. 8 Identification of common master cylinder and related components

✳✳ WARNING

The brake master cylinder should not be disassembled. If the master cylinder is faulty, replace the entire unit with a new one.

To install:

7. Adjust the booster piston rod-to-master cylinder clearance.
8. Bleed the master cylinder.
9. Position the master cylinder against the booster, then install and tighten the mounting nuts to 88–141 inch lbs. (10–16 Nm).
10. Reattach all of the hydraulic brake lines to the master cylinder, then tighten the fittings to 124–159 inch lbs. (14–18 Nm).
11. Reattach all of the wiring harness connectors.

✳✳ WARNING

Clean, high quality brake fluid is essential to the safe and proper operation of the brake system. You should always buy the highest quality brake fluid that is available. If the brake fluid becomes contaminated, drain and flush the system, then refill the master cylinder with new fluid. Never reuse any brake fluid. Any brake fluid that is removed from the system should be discarded.

12. Fill the reservoir with the specified brake fluid.
13. Bleed the air from the brake hydraulic system, check the brake pedal play, and inspect the master cylinder fittings for fluid leaks.
14. Install the air cleaner case assembly lid, the air flow meter, and the air intake hose, then reattach the wiring harness connector to the air flow meter.
15. Road test the vehicle and verify proper brake system operation.

1996–98 MODELS

➡1996–98 Sidekick, Tracker and X-90 models equipped with the Anti-Lock Brake System (ABS) require a scan tool to properly bleed the brake system. If you are servicing such a vehicle, please refer to the applicable ABS section located at the end of this section BEFORE you perform any brake procedures.

1. If necessary for added clearance, remove the air cleaner case assembly.
2. If equipped, detach the wiring harness connectors from the fluid reservoir, from the Proportioning and Differential (P+D) valve, and the pressure limit valve.

✳✳ WARNING

Clean, high quality brake fluid is essential to the safe and proper operation of the brake system. You should always buy the highest quality brake fluid that is available. If the brake fluid becomes contaminated, drain and flush the system, then refill the master cylinder with new fluid. Never reuse any brake fluid. Any brake fluid that is removed from the system should be discarded. Also, do not allow any brake fluid to come in contact with a painted surface; it will damage the paint.

✳✳ CAUTION

Brake fluid contains polyglycol ethers and polyglycols. Avoid contact with the eyes and wash your hands thoroughly after handling brake fluid. If you do get brake fluid in your eyes, flush your eyes with clean, running water for 15 minutes. If eye irritation persists, or if you have taken brake fluid internally, IMMEDIATELY seek medical assistance

3. Clean the outside of the reservoir, then siphon the brake fluid from the reservoir.
4. For vehicles without ABS, disconnect and plug the brake fluid lines from the master cylinder.
5. For vehicles with ABS, disconnect pipes 1 and 2 from the master cylinder and ABS actuator, and pipe 3 from the ABS actuator.
6. Remove the master cylinder mounting nuts, then remove the master cylinder from the booster.

To install:

7. Bleed the master cylinder.
8. Install the new master cylinder. Tighten the mounting nuts to 9.5 ft. lbs. (13 Nm).
9. Install the hydraulic brake lines to the master cylinder and tighten and tighten the flare nuts to 11 ft. lbs. (15 Nm).
10. Reconnect the reservoir lead wire.

✳✳ WARNING

Clean, high quality brake fluid is essential to the safe and proper operation of the brake system. You should always buy the highest quality brake fluid that is available. If the brake fluid becomes contaminated, drain and flush the system, then refill the master cylinder with new fluid. Never reuse any brake fluid. Any brake fluid that is removed from the system should be discarded.

11. Fill the reservoir with the specified brake fluid.
12. Bleed the air from the brake hydraulic system and check the brake pedal play.
13. Road test the vehicle and verify proper brake system operation.

Sidekick Sport Models

✳✳ WARNING

Do not allow brake fluid to come in contact with painted surfaces; the brake fluid can damage paint.

1. Clean the outside of the master cylinder and reservoir, then siphon all of the brake fluid out of the reservoir.
2. Remove the brake fluid pressure proportioning valve switch electrical connection.
3. Disconnect the brake lines from the proportioning valve.
4. Remove the one bolt securing both the 2-way joint and the proportioning valve to the retaining bracket.
5. Remove the master cylinder level switch electrical connector.
6. Disconnect the brake lines from the master cylinder.
7. Remove the attaching nuts and washers from the master cylinder.

8. Loosen the brake booster attaching nuts to allow enough room to remove the master cylinder.

9. Turn the master cylinder and brake booster slightly and remove the master cylinder from the vehicle.

To install:

10. Adjust the clearance between the booster piston and the primary piston.

11. Bleed the master cylinder.

12. Turn the brake booster slightly and install the master cylinder to the brake booster.

13. Tighten the brake booster nuts to 115 inch lbs. (13 Nm).

14. Install and tighten the master cylinder attaching bolts to 115 inch lbs. (13 Nm).

15. Install the brake lines to the master cylinder, then tighten the fittings to 141 inch lbs. (16 Nm).

16. Connect the master cylinder electrical connector.

17. Install the proportioning valve to the master cylinder, then install and tighten the bolt to 88 inch lbs. (10 Nm).

18. Connect and tighten the four brake lines to the proportioning valve to 141 inch lbs. (16 Nm).

19. Reattach all wiring harness connectors.

✳✳ WARNING

Clean, high quality brake fluid is essential to the safe and proper operation of the brake system. You should always buy the highest quality brake fluid that is available. If the brake fluid becomes contaminated, drain and flush the system, then refill the master cylinder with new fluid. Never reuse any brake fluid. Any brake fluid that is removed from the system should be discarded.

20. Refill the brake fluid reservoir with DOT approved brake fluid.

21. Bleed the brake system.

ADJUSTMENT

Piston Rod Clearance

▶ **See Figures 9, 10 and 11**

➡ **This procedure applies to all models.**

The length of the booster piston rod is adjusted to provide the specified clearance between the piston rod end and the master cylinder pis-

Booster piston rod gauge

90889G06

Fig. 9 To properly measure and adjust the master cylinder-to-brake booster piston rod clearance, this tool is necessary

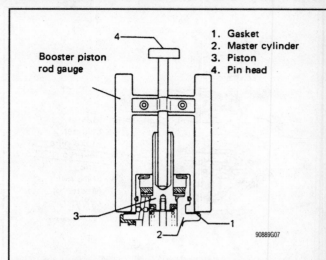

1. Gasket
2. Master cylinder
3. Piston
4. Pin head

90889G07

Fig. 10 Position the measuring tool on the master cylinder as shown . . .

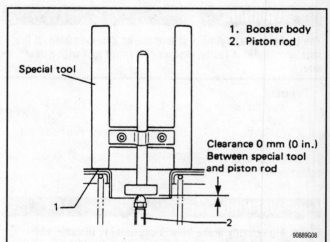

1. Booster body
2. Piston rod

Clearance 0 mm (0 in.) Between special tool and piston rod

90889G08

Fig. 11 . . . then turn the tool around and position it against the booster—there should be zero clearance between the tool pin head and the booster rod

ton. The specified clearance is designed to allow optimum operation of the master cylinder, but to prevent master cylinder damage from excessive booster rod pressure.

1. Remove the master cylinder from the booster.

2. Push the piston rod several times to ensure that the reaction disc inside the booster is in the proper position.

3. Install a new gasket on the master cylinder.

➡ **The inside of the booster should be kept at atmospheric pressure for an accurate measurement.**

4. Position the Booster Piston Rod Gauge 09950–96010, or equivalent, on the master cylinder. Depress the tool pin until it contacts the master cylinder piston.

5. Turn the tool around and position it against the brake power booster. The pin head of the tool should just contact the booster piston rod. If the pin head does not touch, or is moved by the piston rod, adjust the piston rod position by turning it with the Suzuki Booster Piston Rod Adjuster 09952–16010, or equivalent. There should be no clearance (0 in./0mm) between the pin head and the piston rod.

6. Install the master cylinder on the booster.

BLEEDING THE MASTER CYLINDER

※※ CAUTION

Brake fluid contains polyglycol ethers and polyglycols. Avoid contact with the eyes and wash your hands thoroughly after handling brake fluid. If you do get brake fluid in your eyes, flush your eyes with clean, running water for 15 minutes. If eye irritation persists, or if you have taken brake fluid internally, IMMEDIATELY seek medical assistance

If the master cylinder has been removed or disconnected, it must be bled before any brake unit is bled. To bleed the master cylinder:

1. Disconnect the front brake line from the master cylinder and allow fluid to flow from the front connector port.
2. Reconnect the line to the master cylinder and tighten it until it is fluid tight.
3. Have a helper press the brake pedal down one time and hold it down.
4. Loosen the front brake line connection at the master cylinder. This will allow trapped air to escape, along with some fluid.
5. Again tighten the line, release the pedal slowly and repeat the sequence (Sub-steps 3, 4 and 5) until only fluid runs from the port. No air bubbles should be present in the fluid.
6. Final tighten the line fitting at the master cylinder to 11 ft. lbs.
7. After all the air has been bled from the front connection, bleed the master cylinder at the rear connection by repeating Steps 1 through 6.

Power Brake Booster

REMOVAL & INSTALLATION

▶ **See Figures 12 and 13**

※※ WARNING

Clean, high quality brake fluid is essential to the safe and proper operation of the brake system. You should always buy the highest quality brake fluid that is available. If the brake fluid becomes contaminated, drain and flush the system, then refill the master cylinder with new fluid. Never reuse any brake fluid. Any brake fluid that is removed from the system should be discarded. Also, do not allow any brake fluid to come in contact with a painted surface; it will damage the paint.

➡**1996–98 Sidekick, Tracker and X-90 models equipped with the Anti-Lock Brake System (ABS) require a scan tool to properly bleed the brake system. If you are servicing such a vehicle, please refer to the applicable ABS section located at the end of this section BEFORE you perform any brake procedures.**

1. For 1996–98 Sidekick, Tracker and X-90 models equipped with 4-wheel ABS, remove the ABS actuator from the engine compartment.

※※ CAUTION

Brake fluid contains polyglycol ethers and polyglycols. Avoid contact with the eyes and wash your hands thoroughly after handling brake fluid. If you do get brake fluid in your eyes, flush your eyes with clean, running water for 15 minutes. If eye irritation persists, or if you have taken brake fluid internally, IMMEDIATELY seek medical assistance.

2. Remove the master cylinder.
3. Disconnect the vacuum hose from the booster.
4. From inside the vehicle, remove the pushrod clevis pin and cotter pin from the brake pedal arm.
5. Loosen the brake booster mounting nuts, then remove the brake booster from the vehicle.
6. If another booster is going to be installed, disconnect the pedal attachment (the clevis and nut) from the booster.

※※ WARNING

Never disassemble the brake power booster, which would damage the brake booster beyond repair. If it is found to be defective, replace it with a new one.

To install:
7. If necessary, connect the pedal attachment to the booster.

➡**Before installing the brake power booster, measure and, if necessary, adjust the pushrod clevis length.**

8. Position the booster on the firewall so that the booster studs protrude through the firewall into the passenger's compartment of the vehicle.
9. Install the retaining nuts, then tighten the mounting nuts to 88–141 inch lbs. (10–16 Nm).
10. Install the pushrod clevis pin and cotter pin to the brake pedal arm.
11. Connect the vacuum hose to the booster.

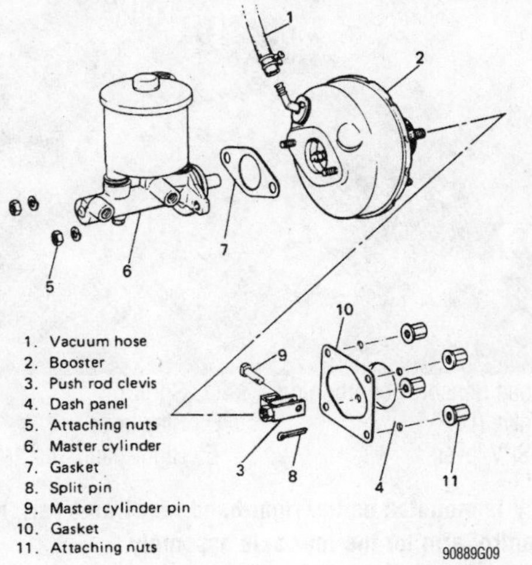

1. Vacuum hose
2. Booster
3. Push rod clevis
4. Dash panel
5. Attaching nuts
6. Master cylinder
7. Gasket
8. Split pin
9. Master cylinder pin
10. Gasket
11. Attaching nuts

90889G09

Fig. 12 Exploded view of the power brake booster mounting

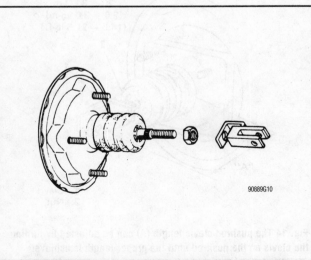

90889G10

Fig. 13 If another booster is going to be installed, transfer the clevis and nut from the old booster to the new one

→ Before installing the master cylinder on the brake power booster, adjust the master cylinder-to-booster piston rod clearance, as described in the master cylinder procedure.

12. For 1996–98 models, apply silicone grease to the master cylinder piston.

13. Mount the master cylinder on the booster, then install all related components (including the ABS actuator for 1996–98 Sidekick, Tracker and X-90 models equipped with ABS).

✳✳ WARNING

Clean, high quality brake fluid is essential to the safe and proper operation of the brake system. You should always buy the highest quality brake fluid that is available. If the brake fluid becomes contaminated, drain and flush the system, then refill the master cylinder with new fluid. Never reuse any brake fluid. Any brake fluid that is removed from the system should be discarded.

14. Fill the brake fluid reservoir, then bleed the brake hydraulic system.

15. After bleeding the system, check brake pedal height and play.

CLEVIS LENGTH CHECK

▶ **See Figure 14**

1. Before installing the brake power booster, ensure that the pushrod clevis length is correct. If the length is incorrect, the brake pedal will not properly engage the booster and master cylinder, and may possibly cause premature master cylinder or booster malfunctioning.

2. Remove the brake booster.

3. Measure the distance from the hole in the clevis to the booster-to-firewall mating surface (on the booster). This measurement is A in the accompanying illustration. The distance should be 4.94–4.98 in. (12.55–12.65cm) for Samurai models, or 4.96–5.00 in. (12.61–12.71cm) for Sidekick, Tracker, Sidekick Sport and X-90 models.

4. If the measurement is not within the specified range, adjust the clevis length by turning the clevis until the proper length is achieved.

5. Tighten the clevis locknut to 15–21 ft. lbs. (20–30 Nm).

6. Install the brake power booster.

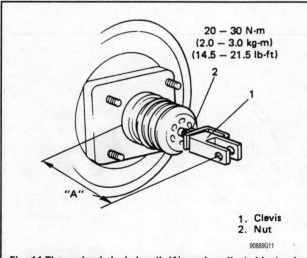

Fig. 14 The pushrod clevis length (A) can be adjusted by turning the clevis on the pushrod until the proper length is achieved

1. Clevis
2. Nut

90889G11

Load Sensing Proportioning Valve (LSPV)

REMOVAL & INSTALLATION

▶ **See Figures 15 and 16**

✳✳ WARNING

Clean, high quality brake fluid is essential to the safe and proper operation of the brake system. You should always buy the highest quality brake fluid that is available. If the brake fluid becomes contaminated, drain and flush the system, then refill the master cylinder with new fluid. Never reuse any brake fluid. Any brake fluid that is removed from the system should be discarded. Also, do not allow any brake fluid to come in contact with a painted surface; it will damage the paint.

→ 1996–98 Sidekick, Tracker and X-90 models equipped with the Anti-Lock Brake System (ABS) require a scan tool to properly bleed the brake system. If you are servicing such a vehicle, please refer to the applicable ABS section located at the end of this section BEFORE you perform any brake procedures.

1. Raise and safely support the vehicle.

2. Disconnect and plug the hydraulic brake lines from the proportioning valve assembly.

✳✳ CAUTION

Brake fluid contains polyglycol ethers and polyglycols. Avoid contact with the eyes and wash your hands thoroughly after handling brake fluid. If you do get brake fluid in your eyes, flush your eyes with clean, running water for 15 minutes. If eye irritation persists, or if you have taken brake fluid internally, IMMEDIATELY seek medical assistance.

3. Remove the proportioning valve from the vehicle body.

→ The proportioning valve should be removed with the spring attached. Do not separate the LSPV spring and lever.

To install:

4. Apply multi-purpose grease to the upper and lower joints of the coil spring.

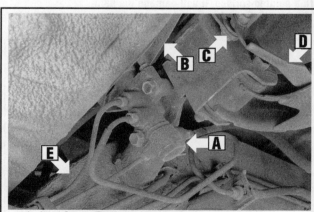

A. Load Sensor Proportioning Valve (LSPV)
B. LSPV lever
C. Spring
D. Stay lever
E. Right-hand, rear frame rail

90889P06

The LSPV is mounted on the right-hand rear frame rail, near the upper control arm for the rear axle assembly

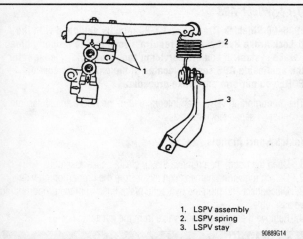

1. LSPV assembly
2. LSPV spring
3. LSPV stay

90889G14

Fig. 15 The LSPV must be removed with the spring and stay lever attached, then the spring and stay lever can be separated from the LSPV assembly

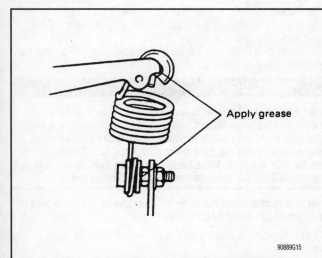

Apply grease

90889G15

Fig. 16 During installation, be sure to apply multi-purpose grease to both ends of the spring, for smooth operation

5. Install the proportioning valve to the vehicle body, then tighten the mounting bolts to 203 inch lbs. (23 Nm).
6. Connect the hydraulic brake lines to the proportioning valve and tighten the flare nuts to 141 inch lbs. (16 Nm).
7. Fill the brake reservoir to the proper level and bleed the brake hydraulic system. Lower the vehicle.

➡Bleed the air from the proportioning valve bleeder valve.

Proportioning and Differential Valve

REMOVAL & INSTALLATION

❊❊ CAUTION

Brake fluid contains polyglycol ethers and polyglycols. Avoid contact with the eyes and wash your hands thoroughly after handling brake fluid. If you do get brake fluid in your eyes, flush your eyes with clean, running water for 15 minutes. If eye irritation persists, or if you have taken brake fluid internally, IMMEDIATELY seek medical assistance.

➡The Samurai model does not use this type of proportioning valve; it only uses a LSPV.

Sidekick, Tracker, and X-90 Models

WITHOUT ABS

❊❊ WARNING

Do not allow brake fluid to come into contact with painted surfaces; the brake fluid can easily damage painted finishes.

➡The proportioning valve is mounted on the inboard side of the front, right-hand frame rail, near the firewall.

1. Apply the parking brake, block the rear wheels, then raise and safely support the front of the vehicle on jackstands.
2. If equipped, detach the wiring harness connector from the proportioning valve.
3. Disconnect and plug the hydraulic brake lines from the proportioning valve assembly.
4. Remove the proportioning valve from the frame rail.

❊❊ WARNING

Never disassemble the proportioning valve, which would damage the component beyond repair. If it is found to be defective, replace it with a new one.

To install:
5. Install the proportioning valve onto the frame rail, then tighten the mounting bolts to 20 ft. lbs. (27 Nm).
6. Attach all of the hydraulic brake lines to the proportioning valve, then tighten the fittings to 124–159 inch lbs. (14–18 Nm).

❊❊ WARNING

Clean, high quality brake fluid is essential to the safe and proper operation of the brake system. You should always purchase the highest quality brake fluid that is available. If the brake fluid becomes contaminated, drain and flush the system, then refill the master cylinder with new fluid. NEVER reuse any brake fluid. Brake fluid that is removed from the hydraulic system should be discarded.

➡Be sure to also bleed the air from the proportioning valve bleeder screw (if equipped) during the bleeding procedure.

90889P07

The proportioning valve (arrow) is mounted on the right-hand, front frame rail

7. Fill the brake reservoir to the proper level and bleed the brake hydraulic system.

8. Lower the vehicle and remove the wheel blocks.

WITH REAR WHEEL ANTI-LOCK (RWAL) SYSTEM

♦ See Figure 17

✸✸ WARNING

Do not allow brake fluid to come into contact with painted surfaces; the brake fluid can easily damage painted finishes.

1. Open the hood, then remove the air cleaner case assembly.
2. Detach the wiring harness connector from the proportioning valve.
3. Disconnect and plug the hydraulic brake lines from the proportioning valve assembly.
4. Remove the proportioning valve from the master cylinder.

✸✸ WARNING

Never disassemble the proportioning valve, which would damage the component beyond repair. If it is found to be defective, replace it with a new one.

To install:

5. Install the proportioning valve to the master cylinder, then tighten the mounting bolts to 20 ft. lbs. (27 Nm).
6. Attach all of the hydraulic brake lines to the proportioning valve, then tighten the fittings to 124–159 inch lbs. (14–18 Nm).

✸✸ WARNING

Clean, high quality brake fluid is essential to the safe and proper operation of the brake system. You should always purchase the highest quality brake fluid that is available. If the brake fluid becomes contaminated, drain and flush the system, then refill the master cylinder with new fluid. NEVER reuse any brake fluid. Brake fluid that is removed from the hydraulic system should be discarded.

➡Be sure to also bleed the air from the proportioning valve bleeder valve during the bleeding procedure.

7. Fill the brake reservoir to the proper level and bleed the brake hydraulic system.

WITH 4-WHEEL ABS

➡**1996–98 Sidekick, Tracker and X-90 models equipped with the Anti-Lock Brake System (ABS) require a scan tool to properly bleed the brake system. If you are servicing such a vehicle, please refer to the applicable ABS section located at the end of this section BEFORE you perform any brake procedures.**

The proportioning valve is an integral part of the ABS actuator assembly, and cannot be separately removed.

Sidekick Sport Models

1. Open the hood, then remove the air cleaner case assembly.
2. Detach the wiring harness connector from the proportioning valve.
3. Disconnect and plug the hydraulic brake lines from the proportioning valve assembly.
4. Remove the proportioning valve from the master cylinder.

✸✸ WARNING

Never disassemble the proportioning valve, which would damage the component beyond repair. If it is found to be defective, replace it with a new one.

To install:

5. Install the proportioning valve to the master cylinder, then tighten the mounting bolts to 20 ft. lbs. (27 Nm).
6. Attach all of the hydraulic brake lines to the proportioning valve, then tighten the fittings to 124–159 inch lbs. (14–18 Nm).

✸✸ WARNING

Clean, high quality brake fluid is essential to the safe and proper operation of the brake system. You should always purchase the highest quality brake fluid that is available. If the brake fluid becomes contaminated, drain and flush the system, then refill the master cylinder with new fluid. NEVER reuse any brake fluid. Brake fluid that is removed from the hydraulic system should be discarded.

➡Be sure to also bleed the air from the proportioning valve bleeder valve during the bleeding procedure.

7. Fill the brake reservoir to the proper level and bleed the brake hydraulic system.

Brake Hoses and Pipes

✸✸ WARNING

Clean, high quality brake fluid is essential to the safe and proper operation of the brake system. You should always buy the highest quality brake fluid that is available. If the brake fluid becomes contaminated, drain and flush the system, then refill the master cylinder with new fluid. Never reuse any brake fluid. Any brake fluid that is removed from the system should be discarded. Also, do not allow any brake fluid to come in contact with a painted surface; it will damage the paint.

Metal lines and rubber brake hoses should be checked frequently for leaks and external damage. Metal lines are particularly prone to crushing and kinking under the vehicle. Any such deformation can restrict the proper flow of fluid and therefore impair braking at the wheels. Rubber hoses should be checked for cracking or scraping; such damage can create a weak spot in the hose and it could fail under pressure.

Any time the lines are removed or disconnected, extreme cleanliness must be observed. Clean all joints and connections before disassembly (use a stiff bristle brush and clean brake fluid); be sure to plug the lines and ports as soon as they are opened. New lines and hoses should be flushed clean with brake fluid before installation to remove any contamination.

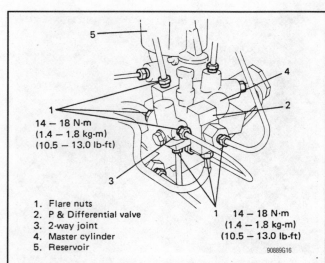

14 – 18 N·m
(1.4 – 1.8 kg-m)
(10.5 – 13.0 lb-ft)

1 14 – 18 N·m
(1.4 – 1.8 kg-m)
(10.5 – 13.0 lb-ft)

1. Flare nuts
2. P & Differential valve
3. 2-way joint
4. Master cylinder
5. Reservoir

90889G16

Fig. 17 During installation, be sure to properly tighten the mounting bolts and brake line fittings to the specified values

Brake fluid contains polyglycol ethers and polyglycols. Avoid contact with the eyes and wash your hands thoroughly after handling brake fluid. If you do get brake fluid in your eyes, flush your eyes with clean, running water for 15 minutes. If eye irritation persists, or if you have taken brake fluid internally, IMMEDIATELY seek medical assistance.

REMOVAL & INSTALLATION

➡1996–98 Sidekick, Tracker and X-90 models equipped with the Anti-Lock Brake System (ABS) require a scan tool to properly bleed the brake system. If you are servicing such a vehicle, please refer to the applicable ABS section located at the end of this section BEFORE you perform any brake procedures.

  1. Disconnect the negative battery cable.
  2. Raise and safely support the vehicle on jackstands.
  3. Remove any wheel and tire assemblies necessary for access to the particular line you are removing.

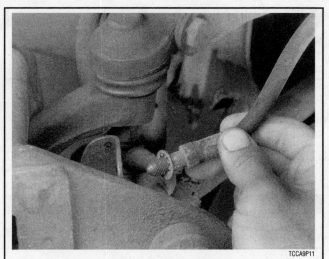

Any gaskets/crush washers should be replaced with new ones during installation

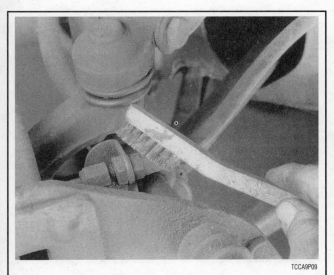

Use a brush to clean the fittings of any debris

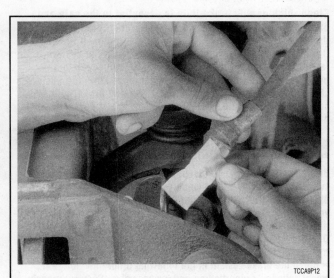

Tape or plug the line to prevent contamination

  4. Thoroughly clean the surrounding area at the joints to be disconnected.
  5. Place a suitable catch pan under the joint to be disconnected.
  6. Using two wrenches (one to hold the joint and one to turn the fitting), disconnect the hose or line to be replaced.
  7. Disconnect the other end of the line or hose, moving the drain pan if necessary. Always use a back-up wrench to avoid damaging the fitting.
  8. Disconnect any retaining clips or brackets holding the line and remove the line from the vehicle.

➡If the brake system is to remain open for more time than it takes to swap lines, tape or plug each remaining clip and port to keep contaminants out and fluid in.

  To install:
  9. Install the new line or hose, starting with the end farthest from the master cylinder. Connect the other end, then confirm that both fittings are correctly threaded and turn smoothly using finger pressure. Make sure the new line will not rub against any other part. Brake lines must be at least 1/2 in. (13mm) from the steering column and other moving parts. Any protective shielding or insulators must be reinstalled in the original location.

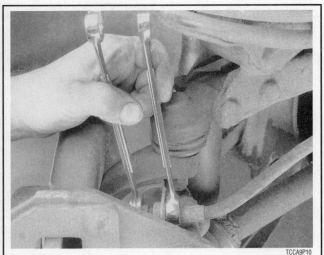

Use two wrenches to loosen the fitting. If available, use flare nut type wrenches

✳✳ WARNING

Make sure the hose is NOT kinked or touching any part of the frame or suspension after installation. These conditions may cause the hose to fail prematurely.

10. Using two wrenches as before, tighten each fitting.
11. Install any retaining clips or brackets on the lines.
12. If removed, install the wheel and tire assemblies, then carefully lower the vehicle to the ground.
13. Refill the brake master cylinder reservoir with clean, fresh brake fluid, meeting DOT 3 specifications. Properly bleed the brake system.
14. Connect the negative battery cable.

Brake System Bleeding

MODELS WITHOUT ABS

▶ See Figures 18, 19 and 20

✳✳ WARNING

Clean, high quality brake fluid is essential to the safe and proper operation of the brake system. You should always buy the highest quality brake fluid that is available. If the brake fluid becomes contaminated, drain and flush the system, then refill the master cylinder with new fluid. Never reuse any brake fluid. Any brake fluid that is removed from the system should be discarded. Also, do not allow any brake fluid to come in contact with a painted surface; it will damage the paint.

✳✳ CAUTION

Brake fluid contains polyglycol ethers and polyglycols. Avoid contact with the eyes and wash your hands thoroughly after handling brake fluid. If you do get brake fluid in your eyes, flush your eyes with clean, running water for 15 minutes. If eye irritation persists, or if you have taken brake fluid internally, IMMEDIATELY seek medical assistance.

➡ Bleed the brake system in the following order only: left rear wheel cylinder, proportioning and bypass valve (Samurai models only), right front wheel caliper, left front wheel caliper.

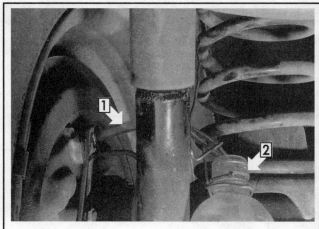

1. Clear plastic hose   2. Catch container

90889P08

Attaching a clear plastic hose to the bleeder valve helps avoid messy brake fluid spills—rear wheel cylinder shown

90889P09

A clear hose (arrow) also allows you to view the emitted brake fluid and check for air bubbles—front caliper shown

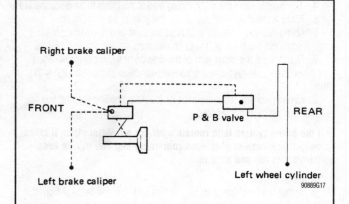

90889G17

Fig. 18 On Samurai models, bleed the hydraulic brake system at the four points shown, starting at the furthest point and working your way closer to the master cylinder

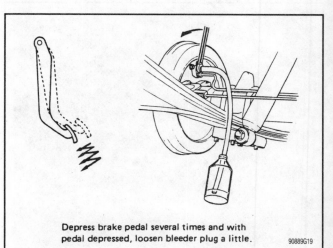

Depress brake pedal several times and with pedal depressed, loosen bleeder plug a little.

90889G19

Fig. 19 Have an assistant depress the brake pedal repeatedly then hold the pedal depressed. Loosen the bleeder valve until brake fluid exits

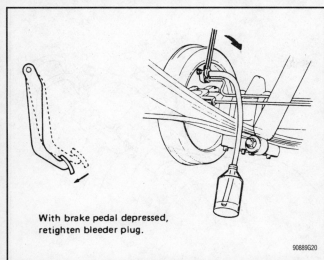

With brake pedal depressed, retighten bleeder plug.

90889G20

Fig. 20 Only once you tighten the bleeder valve can your assistant release the brake pedal

1. Fill the master cylinder reservoir to the MAX line with brake fluid and keep it at least half full throughout the bleeding procedure.

2. Remove the bleeder plug cap, then attach a clear vinyl tube to the wheel cylinder bleeder plug. Insert the open end of the hose into a container.

3. Have an assistant depress the brake pedal several times. While your helper holds the pedal in the depressed position, loosen the bleeder plug one-third to one-half of a turn (or until brake fluid starts to exit the bleeder valve).

4. When the fluid pressure is almost gone, retighten the bleeder plug, THEN have your assistant release the brake pedal. It is very important that the brake pedal stay depressed while the bleeder valve is open, because air will be sucked into the brake system if the pedal is released while the valve is still open.

5. If the fluid is level is low, fill the brake master cylinder fluid reservoir with clean DOT 3 fluid.

6. Repeat Steps 3 through 5 until all air bubbles are gone from the hydraulic fluid.

7. If equipped, install the bleeder plug cap.

8. Proceed to the next item to bleed; remember to bleed the vehicle in the proper order. For Samurai models, start with the left rear wheel cylinder, then the P+D valve, then right front caliper, and finally the left front caliper. For all other models, start with the left rear wheel cylinder, then right front caliper, and finally the left front caliper.

9. Doublecheck that all bleeder plugs are tightened to 22 inch lbs. (2.5 Nm) after completion.

10. After completing the bleeding procedure, apply fluid pressure to the pipe line while checking for leaks.

11. Fill the brake fluid reservoir to the specified full level.

12. Check brake pedal for a spongy feeling; if any evidence exists, repeat the entire procedure.

MODELS WITH ABS

▶ **See Figure 21**

➡ **1996–98 Sidekick, Tracker and X-90 models equipped with the Anti-Lock Brake System (ABS) require a scan tool to properly bleed the brake system. If you are servicing such a vehicle, please refer to the applicable ABS section located at the end of this section BEFORE you perform any brake procedures.**

The ABS systems used on 1990–95 models and Sidekick Sport models should be bled exactly like the non-ABS systems; refer to the previous bleeding procedure.

The 1996–98 Sidekick, Tracker and X-90 models equipped with the ABS system are bled using a special method and tool, refer to the specific ABS section for this procedure.

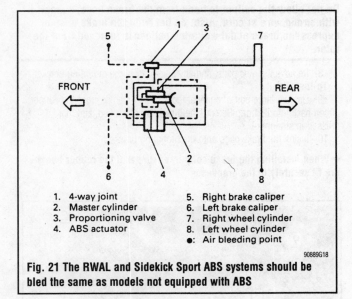

FRONT

REAR

1. 4-way joint
2. Master cylinder
3. Proportioning valve
4. ABS actuator
5. Right brake caliper
6. Left brake caliper
7. Right wheel cylinder
8. Left wheel cylinder
●: Air bleeding point

90889G18

Fig. 21 The RWAL and Sidekick Sport ABS systems should be bled the same as models not equipped with ABS

DISC BRAKES

▶ See Figure 22

Brake Pads

REMOVAL & INSTALLATION

▶ See Figure 23

➡**Always replace all of the brake pads on the same axle at the same time; never replace the pads from one wheel only.**

✳ CAUTION

Brake pads or shoes may contain asbestos, which has been determined to be a cancer causing agent. Never clean the brake surfaces with compressed air! Avoid inhaling any dust from any brake surface! When cleaning brake surfaces, use a commercially available brake cleaning fluid.

1. Siphon approximately ⅔ of the fluid out of the master cylinder.

2. Loosen all of the front wheel lug nuts ½ turn.

3. Apply the parking brake, block the rear wheels, then raise and safely support the front of the vehicle on jackstands.

4. Remove the wheels.

5. On Samurai models, use a small prytool to remove the caliper anti-rattle clip from the outboard side of the caliper.

6. Remove the two guide pin caps (if equipped), then loosen the two guide pins with a wrench.

7. Lift the brake caliper off of the rotor, pads and pad mounting bracket, but do NOT disconnect the brake hose from the caliper.

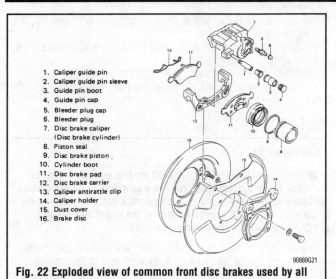

1. Caliper guide pin
2. Caliper guide pin sleeve
3. Guide pin boot
4. Guide pin cap
5. Bleeder plug cap
6. Bleeder plug
7. Disc brake caliper
   (Disc brake cylinder)
8. Piston seal
9. Disc brake piston
10. Cylinder boot
11. Disc brake pad
12. Disc brake carrier
13. Caliper antirattle clip
14. Caliper holder
15. Dust cover
16. Brake disc

Fig. 22 Exploded view of common front disc brakes used by all Suzuki models covered in this manual

※ WARNING

Do not allow the caliper to hang from the brake hose; support it with strong wire or cord. Also, do not twist the brake hose or depress the brake pedal while the caliper is removed from the rotor.

8. Remove the disc pads, and any shims, from the mounting bracket.

To install:

9. Using a large pair of channel locks or a C-clamp, press the caliper piston back into its bore. Be sure the piston is not cocked, and that it is pressed in straight.

10. Install the brake pads onto the mounting bracket.

➡ When installing the brake caliper, ensure that the rubber boots are fit securely in the grooves.

1. Brake rotor
2. Backing plate
3. Caliper and pad mounting bracket
4. Brake pad shim
5. Brake caliper
6. Outboard brake pad
7. Inboard brake pad
8. Upper caliper guide pin
9. Flexible brake hose
10. Union bolt
11. Lower caliper guide pin

Identification of front disc brake components mounted on the vehicle

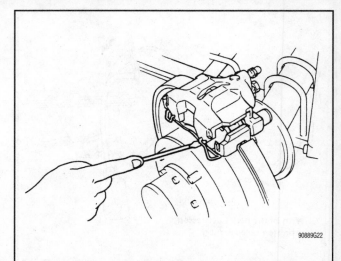

Fig. 23 On Samurai models, use a small prytool to remove the anti-rattle clips from the outboard side of the caliper

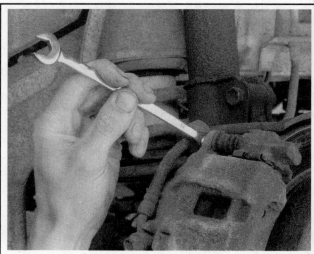

Loosen the upper and lower guide pins . . .

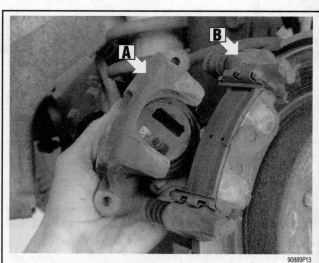

. . . then lift the caliper up and off of the brake pads (A) and mounting bracket (B)

11. Install the brake caliper over the brake rotor, pads and mounting bracket.

12. Install and tighten the guide pins to 19–21 ft. lbs. (25–30 Nm) for Samurai models, to 16–23 ft. lbs. (22–32 Nm) for Sidekick, Tracker and X-90 models, or the upper mounting bolt to 36 ft. lbs. (50 Nm) and the lower bolt to 42 ft. lbs. (58 Nm) for Sidekick Sport models.

13. If equipped, install the guide pin caps.

14. On Samurai models, install the anti-rattle clip on the outboard side of the caliper.

15. Install the front wheels.

16. Lower the vehicle, and fully tighten the wheel lug nuts.

If the caliper is difficult to remove, use a large C-clamp to seat the caliper piston

Be sure to support the caliper aside with strong cord or wire; do not allow it to hang by the brake hose

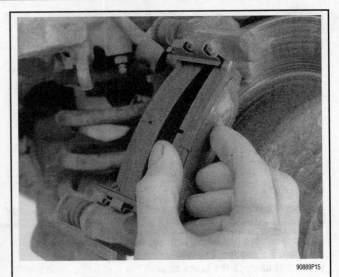

Remove the outer brake pad . . .

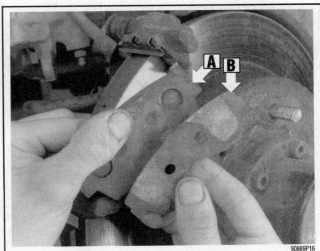

. . . and separate the brake pad (A) from the shims (B), if any were used

Do the same for the inboard brake pads as well

✳✳ CAUTION

Do not attempt to drive the vehicle until after the following step is performed.

17. Depress the brake pedal repeatedly until a firm pedal is obtained. Do not attempt to drive the vehicle unless a firm pedal is obtained.
18. Check the fluid level in the master cylinder. Add fresh brake fluid, as necessary.
19. Road test the vehicle.

INSPECTION

▶ See Figure 24

✳✳ WARNING

Never polish the pad lining with sandpaper, because hard particles from the sandpaper will become imbedded in the lining, which will damage the brake rotor. If the pad lining is damaged or worn excessively or unevenly, replace the pads with new ones.

To inspect the brake pad lining, remove the brake caliper without disconnecting the flexible brake hose from it. Then, inspect the brake pad lining for damage, such as crumbling, missing chunks, uneven wear, etc. Also, measure the combined thickness of the pad lining and the pad backing. The minimum allowable brake pad lining thickness should be as follows:
- Samurai models—0.236 in. (6mm)
- 1989–95 Sidekick and Tracker models—0.315 in. (8mm)
- 1996–98 2-door Sidekick, Tracker and X-90 models—0.236 in. (6mm)
- 1996–98 4-door Sidekick and Tracker models—0.295 in. (7.5mm)
- 1996–98 Sidekick Sport models—0.275 in. (7mm)

If there are signs of damage, or if the lining and backing thickness is less than specified, replace the pads with new ones.

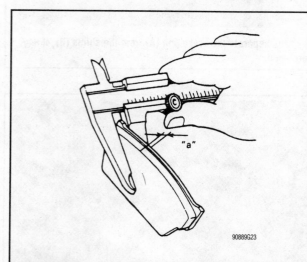

Fig. 24 Use a vernier caliper to measure the brake pad lining and backing thickness. Install new pads if they are worn too thin

Brake Caliper

REMOVAL & INSTALLATION

✳✳ CAUTION

Older brake pads or shoes may contain asbestos, which has been determined to be a cancer causing agent. Never clean the brake surfaces with compressed air! Avoid inhaling any dust from any brake surface! When cleaning brake surfaces, use a commercially available brake cleaning fluid.

➡1996–98 Sidekick, Tracker and X-90 models equipped with the Anti-Lock Brake System (ABS) require a scan tool to properly bleed the brake system. If you are servicing such a vehicle, please refer to the applicable ABS section located at the end of this section BEFORE you perform any brake procedures.

✳✳ CAUTION

Brake fluid contains polyglycol ethers and polyglycols. Avoid contact with the eyes and wash your hands thoroughly after handling brake fluid. If you do get brake fluid in your eyes, flush your eyes with clean, running water for 15 minutes. If eye irritation persists, or if you have taken brake fluid internally, IMMEDIATELY seek medical assistance

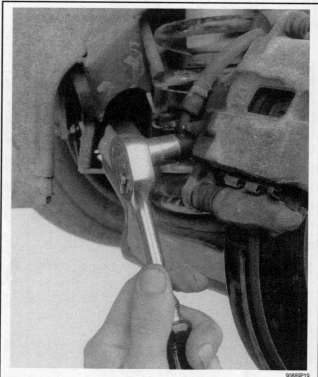

To remove the caliper, loosen the brake hose-to-caliper union bolt . . .

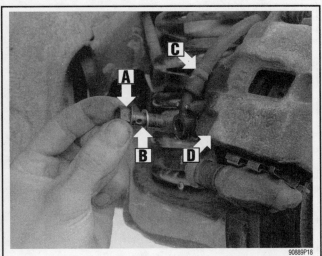

. . . then remove the union bolt (A) and washer (B), thereby detaching the brake hose (C) from the caliper (D)

Be sure to remove BOTH copper washers from the brake hose and caliper. New ones will be needed during assembly

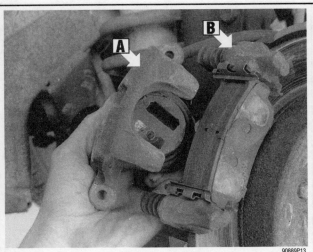

Loosen the caliper guide pins, then lift the caliper up and off of the rotor and brake pads

1. Loosen all of the front wheel lug nuts ½ turn.
2. Apply the parking brake, block the rear wheels, then raise and safely support the front of the vehicle on jackstands.
3. Remove the front wheels.
4. Clean the brake caliper with commercially available brake cleaning spray.
5. Disconnect and plug the flexible brake line.
6. Remove the caliper mounting bolts (guide pins), then remove the caliper from the brake pad mounting bracket.

To install:

7. Install the caliper over the brake pads and mounting bracket.
8. Install and tighten the mounting bolts (guide pins) to 19–21 ft. lbs. (25–30 Nm) for Samurai, Sidekick, Tracker and X-90 models, or the bottom bolt to 37 ft. lbs. (50 Nm) and the top bolt to 42 ft. lbs. (58 Nm) for Sidekick Sport models.
9. Connect the hydraulic brake line, using two new washers, to the caliper. Tighten the flexible hose union bolt to 177–221 inch lbs. (20–25 Nm).
10. Install the front wheels.
11. Lower the vehicle, then fully tighten the front wheel lug nuts.

✳✳ WARNING

Clean, high quality brake fluid is essential to the safe and proper operation of the brake system. You should always purchase the highest quality brake fluid that is available. If the brake fluid becomes contaminated, drain and flush the system, then refill the master cylinder with new fluid. NEVER reuse any brake fluid. Brake fluid that is removed from the hydraulic system should be discarded.

12. Fill the brake reservoir and bleed the hydraulic brake system.

OVERHAUL

▶ **See Figures 25 thru 32**

➡Some vehicles may be equipped dual piston calipers. The procedure to overhaul the caliper is essentially the same with the exception of multiple pistons, O-rings and dust boots.

1. Remove the caliper from the vehicle and place on a clean workbench.

✳✳ CAUTION

NEVER place your fingers in front of the pistons in an attempt to catch or protect the pistons when applying compressed air. This could result in personal injury!

➡Depending upon the vehicle, there are two different ways to remove the piston from the caliper. Refer to the brake pad replacement procedure to make sure you have the correct procedure for your vehicle.

2. The first method is as follows:
    a. Stuff a shop towel or a block of wood into the caliper to catch the piston.
    b. Remove the caliper piston using compressed air applied into the caliper inlet hole. Inspect the piston for scoring, nicks, corrosion and/or worn or damaged chrome plating. The piston must be replaced if any of these conditions are found.
3. For the second method, you must rotate the piston to retract it from the caliper.
4. If equipped, remove the anti-rattle clip.
5. Use a prytool to remove the caliper boot, being careful not to scratch the housing bore.
6. Remove the piston seals from the groove in the caliper bore.
7. Carefully loosen the brake bleeder valve cap and valve from the caliper housing.

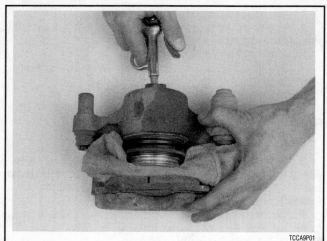

Fig. 25 For some types of calipers, use compressed air to drive the piston out of the caliper, but make sure to keep your fingers clear

Fig. 28 Use a prytool to carefully pry around the edge of the boot . . .

Fig. 26 Withdraw the piston from the caliper bore

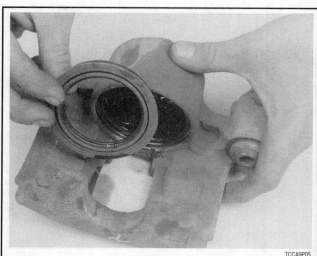

Fig. 29 . . . then remove the boot from the caliper housing, taking care not to score or damage the bore

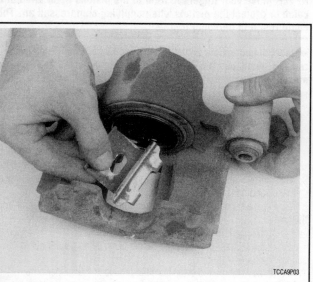

Fig. 27 On some vehicles, you must remove the anti-rattle clip

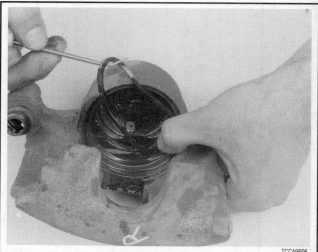

Fig. 30 Use extreme caution when removing the piston seal; DO NOT scratch the caliper bore

8. Inspect the caliper bores, pistons and mounting threads for scoring or excessive wear.

9. Use crocus cloth to polish out light corrosion from the piston and bore.

10. Clean all parts with denatured alcohol and dry with compressed air.

To assemble:

11. Lubricate and install the bleeder valve and cap.

12. Install the new seals into the caliper bore grooves, making sure they are not twisted.

13. Lubricate the piston bore.

14. Install the pistons and boots into the bores of the calipers and push to the bottom of the bores.

15. Use a suitable driving tool to seat the boots in the housing.

16. Install the caliper in the vehicle.

17. Install the wheel and tire assembly, then carefully lower the vehicle.

18. Properly bleed the brake system.

Brake Disc (Rotor)

REMOVAL & INSTALLATION

✳✳ CAUTION

Brake pads or shoes may contain asbestos, which has been determined to be a cancer causing agent. Never clean the brake surfaces with compressed air! Avoid inhaling any dust from any brake surface! When cleaning brake surfaces, use a commercially available brake cleaning fluid.

➡1996–98 Sidekick, Tracker and X-90 models equipped with the Anti-Lock Brake System (ABS) require a scan tool to properly bleed the brake system. If you are servicing such a vehicle, please refer to the applicable ABS section located at the end of this section BEFORE you perform any brake procedures.

TCCA9P07

Fig. 31 Use the proper size driving tool and a mallet to properly seal the boots in the caliper housing

90889P21

To remove the brake rotor, first loosen the caliper mounting bracket bolts (not the caliper guide pins) . . .

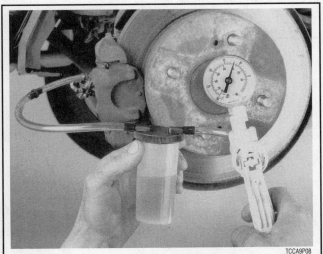

TCCA9P08

Fig. 32 There are tools, such as this Mighty-Vac, available to assist in proper brake system bleeding

90889P22

. . . then separate the caliper, pads and mounting bracket together from the rotor

Install two 8mm bolts in the holes in the rotor . . .

. . . then slowly, and evenly, tighten the 8mm bolts to draw the rotor off of the hub

Once the rotor is loosened from the hub, completely remove it from the vehicle

1. Loosen all of the front wheel lug nuts Ê turn.
2. Apply the parking brake, block the rear wheels, then raise and safely support the front of the vehicle on jackstands.
3. Remove the front wheels.
4. Remove the brake caliper/pads mounting bracket (with the caliper and the brake line attached) by loosening the two mounting bracket-to-backing plate bolts. Then, support it aside with strong cord or wire.

❊❊ WARNING

Do not allow the caliper to hang from the brake hose. Support it with strong cord or wire out of the way.

5. Install two 8 mm bolts into the threaded holes in the brake rotor and tighten them evenly; this will slowly draw the rotor off of the hub assembly.
To install:
6. Slide the brake rotor onto the hub, then position the caliper/pads/mounting bracket assembly over the brake rotor.
7. Install and tighten the two pad mounting bracket-to-backing plate bolts to 51–72 ft. lbs. (70–100 Nm).
8. Install the front wheels.
9. Lower the vehicle, then fully tighten the lug nuts.

INSPECTION

♦ See Figure 33

To inspect the brake rotor, remove the caliper (without disconnecting the flexible brake hose) and the pads. Inspect the rotor surface for numerous or excessive deep scratches. If such scratches are evident, have the brake rotor machine cut by a automotive machine shop.

Use a micrometer to measure the thickness of the brake rotor. The minimum allowable thickness should be as follows:
- All Samurai models—0.334 in. (8.5mm) minimum
- 1989–93 2-door Sidekick and Tracker models—0.315 in. (8mm)
- 1992–93 4-door Sidekick and Tracker models—0.591 in. (15mm)
- 1994–95 Sidekick and Tracker models—0.591 in. (15mm)
- 1996–98 2-door Sidekick, Tracker and X-90 models—0.315 in. (8mm)
- 1996–98 4-door Sidekick and Tracker models—0.590 in. (15mm)
- 1996–98 Sidekick Sport models—0.787 in. (20mm)

If the rotor is thinner than specified, it must be replaced with a new one.

Use a dial indicator to measure the amount of rotor run-out, while turning the brake rotor. The maximum amount of allowable run-out is 0.006 in. (0.15mm); if the run-out is greater than this, replace the rotor with a good one.

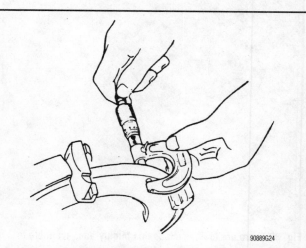

Fig. 33 Use a micrometer to measure the thickness of the brake rotor. If even only one spot on the rotor is too thin, it must be replaced with a good rotor

DRUM BRAKES

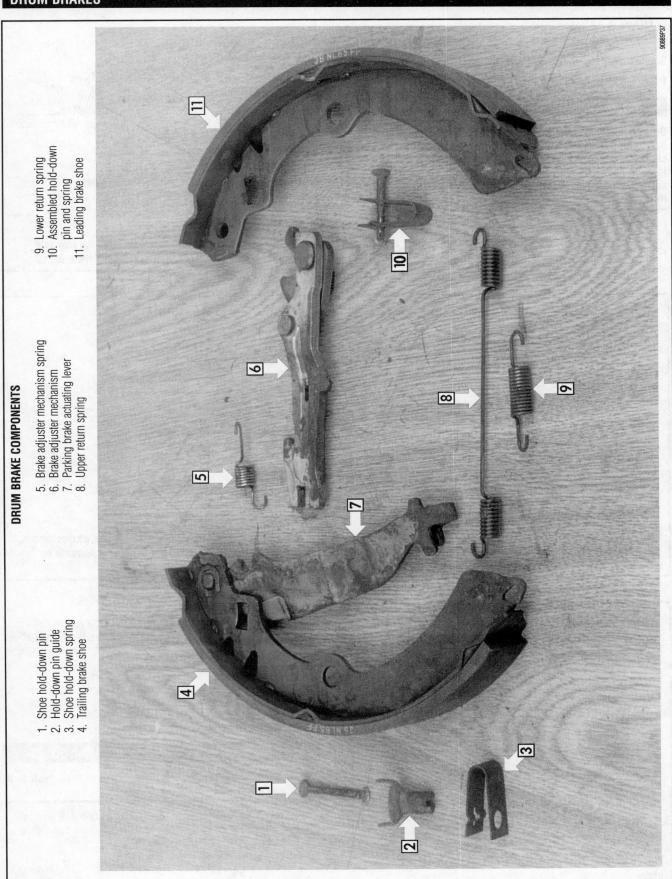

DRUM BRAKE COMPONENTS

1. Shoe hold-down pin
2. Hold-down pin guide
3. Shoe hold-down spring
4. Trailing brake shoe
5. Brake adjuster mechanism spring
6. Brake adjuster mechanism
7. Parking brake actuating lever
8. Upper return spring
9. Lower return spring
10. Assembled hold-down pin and spring
11. Leading brake shoe

Brake Drums

REMOVAL & INSTALLATION

Samurai Models

♦ See Figures 34, 35, 36 and 37

☀ CAUTION

Older brake pads or shoes may contain asbestos, which has been determined to be a cancer causing agent. Never clean the brake surfaces with compressed air! Avoid inhaling any dust from any brake surface! When cleaning brake surfaces, use a commercially available brake cleaning fluid.

1. Loosen all of the rear wheel lug nuts ½ turn.
2. Block the rear wheels, then raise and safely support the rear of the vehicle on jackstands.
3. If engaged, release the parking brake.

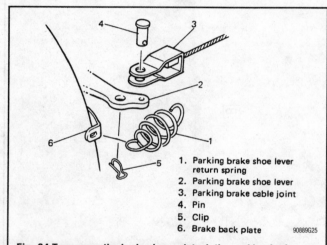

1. Parking brake shoe lever return spring
2. Parking brake shoe lever
3. Parking brake cable joint
4. Pin
5. Clip
6. Brake back plate

Fig. 34 To remove the brake drum, detach the parking brake cable from the parking brake shoe lever by removing the pin and clip . . .

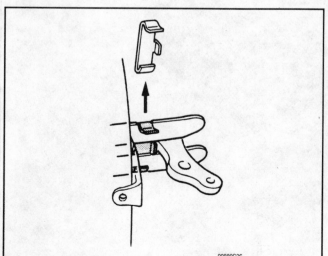

Fig. 35 . . . then remove the parking brake shoe lever stopper plate

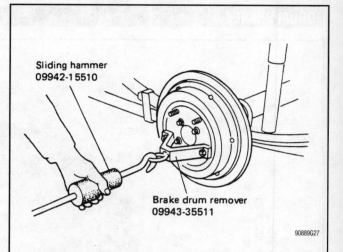

Fig. 36 If the drum is difficult to remove from the rear axle shaft, use a slide hammer and adapter to pull the drum off

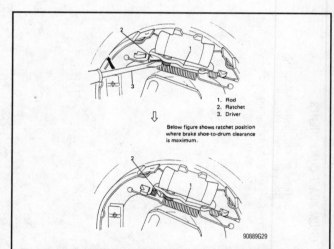

1. Rod
2. Ratchet
3. Driver

Below figure shows ratchet position where brake shoe-to-drum clearance is maximum.

Fig. 37 Use a small prytool to depress the ratchet mechanism, which will maximize the brake shoe-to-drum clearance for assembly

4. Remove the rear wheels.
5. If equipped, remove the rear drum nuts from the vehicle.
6. To increase the clearance between the brake shoe and drum, remove the parking brake shoe lever return spring, and detach the parking brake cable joint from the shoe lever.
7. Remove the parking brake shoe lever stopper plate.
8. Pull the brake drum off of the rear axle shaft flange. If the brake drum is difficult to separate from the axle flange, use a slide hammer.

To install:

9. Install the parking brake shoe lever stopper plate.

☀ WARNING

Inspect the joint pin clip for deformation or breakage; replace it with a new one if any damage is evident.

10. Connect the brake cable joint to the parking brake shoe lever by using the joint pin. Insert the pin down from the top, then install the clip into the joint pin hole.
11. Install the parking brake lever return spring.
12. Insert a small prytool between the rod and ratchet of the brake shoe adjuster mechanism, then push the ratchet down.

13. Install the brake drum, and tighten the brake drum nuts to 58 ft. lbs. (79 Nm).

14. Install the rear wheels, and lower the vehicle.

15. Before driving the vehicle, depress the brake pedal 4 or 5 times to seat the rear drum brake shoes.

16. Raise and safely support the rear of the vehicle on jackstands. Spin the rear wheels to ensure that the brakes are not adjusted too tightly. Lower the vehicle and remove the front wheel blocks.

Sidekick, Tracker, Sidekick Sport and X-90 Models

▶ See Figures 38 and 39

✳✳ CAUTION

Brake pads or shoes may contain asbestos, which has been determined to be a cancer causing agent. Never clean the brake surfaces with compressed air! Avoid inhaling any dust from any brake surface! When cleaning brake surfaces, use a commercially available brake cleaning fluid.

1. Loosen all of the rear wheel lug nuts ½ turn.

2. Block the front wheels, then raise and safely support the rear of the vehicle on jackstands.

3. Remove the wheel and tire assembly.

4. On 1989–95 models, remove the four brake drum nuts from the brake drum.

5. From inside the passenger's compartment, relieve the parking brake cable tension by removing the parking brake lever cover screws and pulling up on the brake lever cover. Loosen the parking brake cable lock-nut.

6. On 1989–95 models, from under the rear of the vehicle, remove the plug from the backing plate to gain access to the hold-down spring. Once the plug is removed, insert a brake spoon tool or flat prytool into the plug hole until its tip contacts the brake shoe hold-down spring. Push the spring in to release the parking brake shoe lever from the hold-down spring, which will backs the brake shoes off from the brake drum.

7. On 1989–95 models, pull the brake drum off of the rear axle flange. If the brake drum is difficult to remove, use a slide hammer and a special tool (such as Suzuki tool 09943–35511) to pull the brake drum off.

8. On 1996–98 models, install two 8mm bolts into the brake drum holes and uniformly tighten each bolt. Tighten each bolt until the brake drum is removed from the vehicle. If there is difficulty in removing the drum, insert a small tool through the hole in the rear of the backing plate,

Loosen the four brake drum retaining bolts. A large prytool can hold the drum steady during nut loosening

90889P28

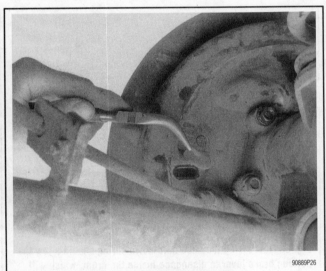

Remove the access plug from the backing plate . . .

90889P26

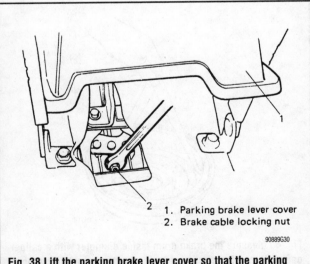

1. Parking brake lever cover
2. Brake cable locking nut

90889G30

Fig. 38 Lift the parking brake lever cover so that the parking brake cable adjusting nut can be loosened

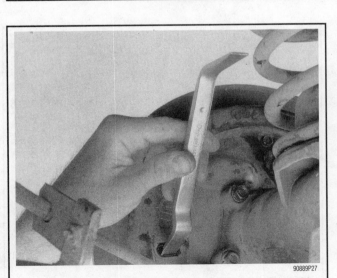

. . . then use a brake "spoon" to depress the brake shoe hold-down spring (located inside the drum)

90889P27

and hold the automatic adjusting lever away from the adjuster. Using another narrow, flat tool at the same time, reduce the brake shoe adjuster by turning the adjusting wheel.

9. Inspect the brake drum for wear and/or scoring. Machine or replace, as necessary.

To install:

10. On 1989–95 models, before installing the brake drum, maximize the brake shoe-to-drum clearance by inserting a small prytool between the rod and ratchet of the brake shoe adjuster mechanism, then pushing the ratchet down.

11. On 1996–98 models, perform the following to automatically adjust the brake shoes:

a. Install the brake drum and pull the parking brake lever all the way up until a clicking sound can no longer be heard.

b. Verify that the rear wheels will not turn. If the rear wheels turn, adjust the parking brake cable as necessary.

c. Release the parking brake and remove the brake drum. Using a caliper gauge, measure the outside diameter of the brake shoes. Outside diameter should be as follows:

- For 2-door models—8.637–8.639 in. (21.87–21.93cm)
- For 4-door models—9.972–9.988 in. (25.33–25.37cm)

d. If the brake shoe clearance is not correct, adjust the brake shoes (by turning the star wheel) until the clearance is correct.

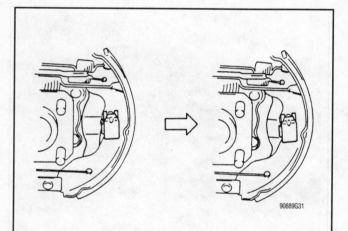

Fig. 39 Depressing the shoe hold-down spring should allow the parking brake lever to disengage inside the drum, which will provide more brake shoe-to-drum clearance for drum removal

Pull the brake drum off of the rear axle flange

12. On 1989–95 models, move the brake shoe hold-down spring back into its original position.

13. Slide the brake drum onto the axle flange.

14. On 1989–95 models, install the four drum retaining nuts. Tighten the drum retaining nuts to 37–57 ft. lbs. (50–80 Nm).

15. If necessary, install the plug in the brake backing plate.

16. Install the wheel and tire assembly, then lower the vehicle.

17. Fully tighten the lug nuts.

18. Before driving the vehicle, depress the brake pedal hard 4 or 5 times to seat the rear drum brake shoes.

19. Raise and safely support the rear of the vehicle on jackstands. Spin the rear wheels to ensure that the brakes are not adjusted too tightly. Lower the vehicle and remove the front wheel blocks.

INSPECTION

▶ **See Figure 40**

➡ **While the brake drum is removed from the vehicle, inspect the wheel cylinder for damage and leakage.**

1. Remove the brake drum from the vehicle.

❄❄ CAUTION

Older brake pads or shoes may contain asbestos, which has been determined to be a cancer causing agent. Never clean the brake surfaces with compressed air! Avoid inhaling any dust from any brake surface! When cleaning brake surfaces, use a commercially available brake cleaning fluid.

2. Thoroughly clean the brake drum.

3. Inspect the brake drum for cracks, scores deep grooves, etc. A damaged drum is unsafe for use, and should be replaced immediately. Do not attempt to weld a cracked drum. If the drum exhibits scoring, and there is enough metal left on the inside diameter of the drum, have the drum cut by a qualified automotive machine shop. Slight scoring can be smoothed using emery cloth.

4. Inspect the drum for excessive wear by measuring the inside diameter of the brake drum with a caliper gauge. The maximum inside drum diameter allowable is as follows:

- Samurai models—8.74 in. (22.2cm)
- 1989–91 Sidekick and Tracker models—8.74 in. (22.2cm)
- 1992–93 2-door Sidekick and Tracker models—8.74 in. (22.2cm)
- 1992–93 4-door Sidekick and Tracker models—10.07 in. (25.6cm)
- 1994–95 Sidekick and Tracker models—10.07 in. (25.6cm)

Fig. 40 Measure the brake drum inside diameter with a caliper gauge. If the diameter is too large, the drum must be replaced with a new one

• 1996–98 2-door Sidekick, Tracker, Sidekick Sport and X-90 models—8.74 in. (22.2cm)
• 1996–98 4-door Sidekick, Sidekick Sport and Tracker models—10.07 in. (25.6cm)

5. If the brake drum exhibits damage, or if the inside diameter is larger than specified, replace it with a new one.

Brake Shoes

✳✳ CAUTION

Brake pads or shoes may contain asbestos, which has been determined to be a cancer causing agent. Never clean the brake surfaces with compressed air! Avoid inhaling any dust from any brake surface! When cleaning brake surfaces, use a commercially available brake cleaning fluid.

INSPECTION

▶ See Figure 41

1. Remove the brake drum.
2. Use a vernier caliper to measure the thickness of the brake shoe lining and shoe backing. The minimum allowable lining/backing thickness (for all models) is 0.12 in. (3mm).
3. If one of the brake linings is worn to or beyond the allowable limit, all four of the rear brake shoes must be replaced.

✳✳ WARNING

Never polish the shoe lining with sandpaper, because hard particles from the sandpaper will become imbedded in the lining, which will damage the brake drum. If the shoe lining is damaged or worn excessively or unevenly, replace the shoes with new ones.

4. Install the brake drum.

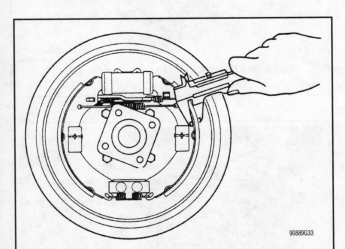

Fig. 41 The combined thickness of the shoe lining material and shoe backing should be greater than 0.12 in. (3mm). Otherwise, install new brake shoes

REMOVAL & INSTALLATION

➡Only service one side of the vehicle at a time, so that the other side can be used as a reference if you forget the proper arrangement of the brake items.

Samurai and 1989–95 Sidekick/Tracker Models

▶ See Figure 42

✳✳ CAUTION

Older brake pads or shoes may contain asbestos, which has been determined to be a cancer causing agent. Never clean the brake surfaces with compressed air! Avoid inhaling any dust from any brake surface! When cleaning brake surfaces, use a commercially available brake cleaning fluid.

1. Remove the brake drum.
2. Remove the brake shoe hold-down springs by rotating the retaining pins 90 degrees.
3. On 1989–95 Sidekick and Tracker models, disengage the parking brake cable from the parking brake actuating lever.
4. Remove the shoes, return springs and strut from the backing plate.
5. Detach the upper and lower return springs, and the strut from the brake shoes.

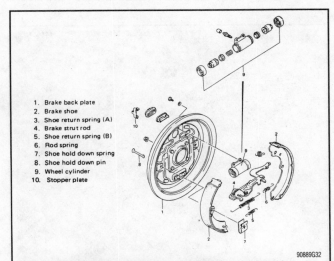

1. Brake back plate
2. Brake shoe
3. Shoe return spring (A)
4. Brake strut rod
5. Shoe return spring (B)
6. Rod spring
7. Shoe hold down spring
8. Shoe hold down pin
9. Wheel cylinder
10. Stopper plate

Fig. 42 Exploded view of the rear drum brake components—Samurai and 1989–95 Sidekick and Tracker models

To remove the brake shoes, first remove the brake drum from the rear axle

Clean the brake parts with commercially available solvent. NEVER use compressed air to clean the parts

90889P32

Remove the shoes and springs from the backing plate and wheel cylinder . . .

90889P35

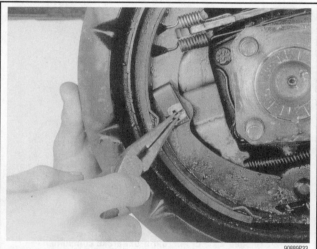

Grasp the shoe hold-down spring retaining pins, then turn them 90 degrees . . .

90889P33

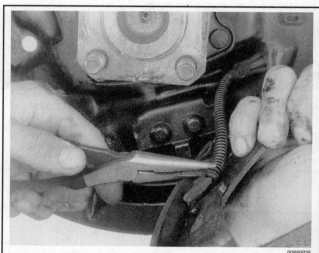

. . . then detach the parking brake cable from the actuating lever

90889P36

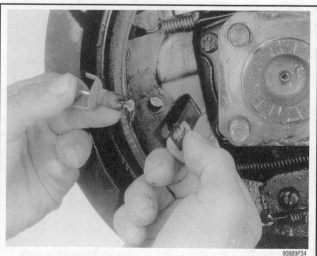

. . . and remove the hold-down springs and retaining pins from both brake shoes

90889P34

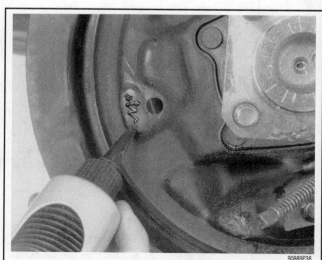

Before installing the brake shoes, apply grease to the backing plate-to-brake shoe contact points

90889P38

6. On 1989–95 Sidekick and Tracker models, separate the parking brake lever from the trailing brake shoe by prying the C-clip off of the parking brake lever stud.

7. Thoroughly clean the backing plate, the brake springs and the strut.

To install:

8. Apply a thin coat of high temperature, multi-purpose grease to the backing plate where the shoes rub against it.

9. On 10989–95 Sidekick and Tracker models, apply a small amount of high temperature, multi-purpose grease to the parking brake lever where it rubs against the parking brake cable end.

10. On 1989–95 Sidekick and Tracker models, install the parking brake lever on the trailing shoe by inserting the lever stud through the brake shoe hole, then by installing and crimping a NEW C-clip onto the stud.

11. Assemble the return springs, strut and brake shoes, then position the new brake shoes on the backing plate.

12. On 1989–95 Sidekick and Tracker models, reattach the parking brake cable to the lever.

13. Install the shoe hold-down springs by pushing them down in place, and turning the retaining pins.

14. Install the rear brake drum, as described earlier in this section.

1996–98 Sidekick, Tracker, Sidekick Sport and X-90 Models

➡The 1996–98 Sidekick, Tracker and X-90 models equipped with the Anti-Lock Brake System (ABS) require a scan tool to properly bleed the brake system. If you are servicing such a vehicle, please refer to the applicable ABS section located at the end of this section BEFORE you perform any brake procedures.

1. Remove the brake drum.
2. Remove the pawl lever and adjusting spring.
3. Remove the upper shoe return spring and adjuster.
4. Remove the shoe hold-down springs by depressing the spring and rotating it 90 degrees.
5. Remove the brake shoes and lower spring from the backing plate.
6. Detach the lower return spring from both brake shoes, then detach the parking brake cable from the actuating lever, mounted on the trailing shoe.
7. Separate the parking brake lever from the trailing brake shoe by prying the C-clip off of the parking brake lever stud.
8. Thoroughly clean the backing plate, the brake springs and the strut.

To install:

9. Apply a thin coat of high temperature, multi-purpose grease to the backing plate where the shoes rub against it.

10. Apply a small amount of high temperature, multi-purpose grease to the parking brake lever where it rubs against the parking brake cable end.

11. Install the parking brake actuating lever on the trailing shoe by inserting the lever stud through the brake shoe hole, then by installing and crimping a NEW C-clip onto the stud.

12. Assemble the two brake shoes and the lower return spring, then position them on the backing plate.

13. Install the shoe hold-down springs by positioning them over the retaining pins, depressing them and turning them 90 degrees.

✳✳ CAUTION

Be very careful when installing the upper return spring; if it is not installed properly, it may come dislodged from one of the shoes and cause injury.

14. Install the upper shoe return spring and adjuster.
15. Install the pawl lever and adjusting spring.
16. Install the rear brake drum, as described earlier in this section.

ADJUSTMENTS

All of the drum brakes used on these vehicles adjust automatically. No manual adjustment is necessary.

Wheel Cylinders

✳✳ CAUTION

Brake pads or shoes may contain asbestos, which has been determined to be a cancer causing agent. Never clean the brake surfaces with compressed air! Avoid inhaling any dust from any brake surface! When cleaning brake surfaces, use a commercially available brake cleaning fluid.

REMOVAL & INSTALLATION

➡The 1996–98 Sidekick, Tracker and X-90 models equipped with the Anti-Lock Brake System (ABS) require a scan tool to properly bleed the brake system. If you are servicing such a vehicle, please refer to the applicable ABS section located at the end of this section BEFORE you perform any brake procedures.

1. Loosen all of the rear wheel lug nuts ½ turn.
2. Block the front wheels, then raise and safely support the rear of the vehicle on jackstands.
3. Remove the rear wheels, brake drums and the rear brake shoes from the vehicle.
4. Detach and plug the brake line from the rear of the wheel cylinder.
5. Remove the 2 rear wheel cylinder mounting bolts, then separate the rear wheel cylinder from the backing plate.

To install:

6. Install the wheel cylinder onto the backing plate, then tighten the mounting bolts to 84 inch lbs. (9.5 Nm).
7. Reattach the brake line to the wheel cylinder, then tighten the flare nut to 124–150 inch lbs. (14–17 Nm).
8. Install the rear brake shoes, drums and wheels.
9. Lower the vehicle.
10. Bleed the brake system and check for any leaks when finished.

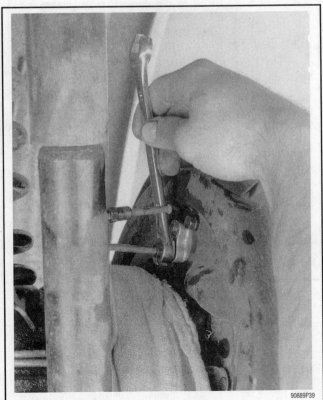

90889P39

To remove a wheel cylinder, remove the brake shoes, then detach the brake line(s) from the wheel cylinder

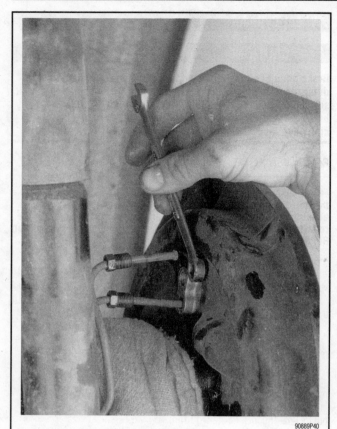

Loosen the wheel cylinder retaining bolts . . .

90889P40

. . . then separate the wheel cylinder from the backing plate

90889P41

OVERHAUL

Wheel cylinder overhaul kits may be available, but often at little or no savings over a reconditioned wheel cylinder. It often makes sense with these components to substitute a new or reconditioned part instead of attempting an overhaul.

If no replacement is available, or you would prefer to overhaul your wheel cylinders, the following procedure may be used. When rebuilding and installing wheel cylinders, avoid getting any contaminants into the sys-

tem. Always use clean, new, high quality brake fluid. If dirty or improper fluid has been used, it will be necessary to drain the entire system, flush the system with proper brake fluid, replace all rubber components, then refill and bleed the system.

1. Remove the wheel cylinder from the vehicle and place on a clean workbench.

2. First remove and discard the old rubber boots, then withdraw the pistons. Piston cylinders are equipped with seals and a spring assembly, all located behind the pistons in the cylinder bore.

3. Remove the remaining inner components, seals and spring assembly. Compressed air may be useful in removing these components. If no compressed air is available, be VERY careful not to score the wheel cylinder bore when removing parts from it. Discard all components for which replacements were supplied in the rebuild kit.

4. Wash the cylinder and metal parts in denatured alcohol or clean brake fluid.

✳✳ WARNING

Never use a mineral-based solvent such as gasoline, kerosene or paint thinner for cleaning purposes. These solvents will swell rubber components and quickly deteriorate them.

Remove the outer boots from the wheel cylinder

TCCA9P13

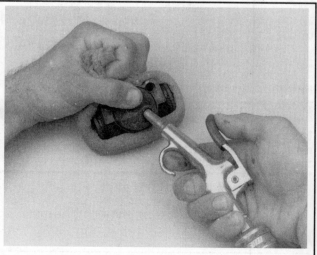

Compressed air can be used to remove the pistons and seals

TCCA9P14

Remove the pistons, cup seals and spring from the cylinder

Once cleaned and inspected, the wheel cylinder is ready for assembly

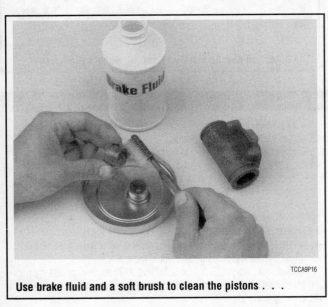

Use brake fluid and a soft brush to clean the pistons . . .

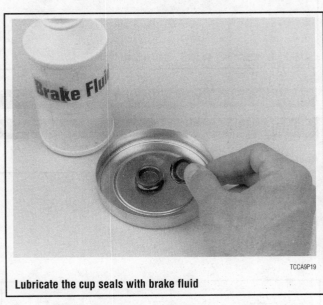

Lubricate the cup seals with brake fluid

. . . and the bore of the wheel cylinder

Install the spring, then the cup seals in the bore

5. Allow the parts to air dry or use compressed air. Do not use rags for cleaning, since lint will remain in the cylinder bore.

6. Inspect the piston and replace it if it shows scratches.

7. Lubricate the cylinder bore and seals using clean brake fluid.

8. Position the spring assembly.

9. Install the inner seals, then the pistons.

10. Insert the new boots into the counterbores by hand. Do not lubricate the boots.

11. Install the wheel cylinder.

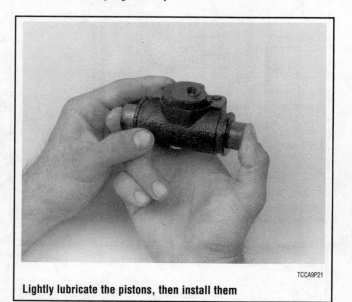

Lightly lubricate the pistons, then install them

TCCA9P21

The boots can now be installed over the wheel cylinder ends

TCCA9P22

PARKING BRAKE

Cable(s)

ADJUSTMENT

▶ **See Figure 43**

1. Ensure the following conditions are met before adjusting the parking brake cable:
- No air is trapped in the brake system.
- Brake pedal travel in within specifications.

- The brake pedal has been depressed a few times with about 44 lbs. (20 kg) of force applied and released.
- The parking brake lever has been applied up a few times with about 44 lbs. (20 kg) of force applied and released.
- Rear brakes are not worn beyond the limits and the self adjusting mechanism operates properly.

For Samurai models, loosen the stopper nut, then adjust the parking brake lever by loosening or tightening the self locking nut at the parking brake lever. While turning the adjusting nut, secure the holding nut with a wrench to prevent the inner cable from twisting. After the adjustment is complete, tighten the stopper nut against the pin.

For Sidekick, Tracker, Sidekick Sport and X-90 models, adjust the parking brake cable by loosening or tightening the self locking nut at the rear of the parking brake lever.

For all models, proper adjustment is when the parking brake lever engages 3–8 notches from the released position, when the lever is pulled up with a force of 44 lbs. (20 kg).

When the lever is applied to the aforementioned number of notches, the rear wheels should not move. The rear wheels should turn freely after the parking brake is released. Check the rear drum for dragging after adjustment.

REMOVAL & INSTALLATION

Samurai Models

1. Disconnect the parking brake cable from the parking lever.

2. Loosen all of the rear wheel lug nuts ½ turn.

3. Block the front wheels, then raise and safely support the rear of the vehicle.

4. Remove the rear wheels and brake drums from the vehicle.

5. Remove the rear brake shoes and disconnect the parking brake cable from the parking brake shoe lever.

6. Remove the cable from the brake backing plate by squeezing the parking brake cable stop ring. Often an appropriately-sized box end wrench compresses the stop ring easily for removal.

7. Remove the parking brake cable from its chassis holding clamps.

Fig. 43 Parking brake routing, retaining clip location and component identification—Samurai shown, others similar

90889G34

To install:

8. Install the cable to the backing plate and to the brake shoe lever. Make sure to route the cable through its chassis holding clamps.

9. Install the brake shoes and install the rear brake drums.

10. Install the rear wheels and connect the cable to the parking brake lever.

11. Lower the vehicle.

12. Ensure the parking brake is functioning properly, and adjust the cable if necessary.

Sidekick, Tracker, Sidekick Sport and X-90 Models

1. Block the vehicle wheels and release the parking brake lever.

2. Remove the two screws and one clip securing the parking brake lever cover in place and remove the cover.

3. Remove the parking brake cable locknut and washer.

4. Disconnect the connecting rod from the equalizer.

5. Loosen all of the rear wheel lug nuts ½ turn.

6. Block the rear wheels, then raise and safely support the rear of the vehicle on jackstands.

7. Remove the rear wheels and brake drums from the vehicle.

8. Remove the rear brake shoes.

9. Disconnect the parking brake cable from the parking brake shoe lever.

10. Remove the cable from the brake backing plate by squeezing the parking brake cable stop ring. Often an appropriately-sized box end wrench compresses the stop ring easily for removal.

11. Remove the four bolts securing the cable housing to the underbelly of the vehicle.

12. Remove the cable from the vehicle.

To install:

13. Position the cable in the vehicle and install the four underbelly mounting bolts. Feed the cable up through the hole in the floor and seat the grommet in place.

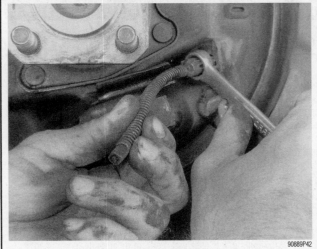

90889P42

When removing the cable from the backing plate, a box end wrench works well to depress the cable retaining clip fingers

14. Connect the cable housing to the backing plate and install the cable stopper ring. Connect the cable end to the brake shoe lever.

15. Install the brake shoes and install the rear brake drums.

16. Install the rear wheels.

17. Lower the vehicle.

18. Connect the parking brake cable to the equalizer.

19. Connect the equalizer to the connecting rod and install the washer and nut. DO NOT tighten the nut at this time.

20. Adjust the parking brake, and tighten the nut.

21. Install the brake lever cover and install the clip and two mounting bolts.

22. Apply the parking brake and remove the wheel blocks.

REAR WHEEL ANTI-LOCK (RWAL) BRAKE SYSTEM

General Description

♦ **See Figure 44**

The Kelsey Hayes RWAL system was available as an option on 1990–95 Sidekick and 1991 Tracker models. The system is particularly useful because of the wide variations of loading the vehicle may experience. Preventing rear wheel lock-up often makes the difference in controlling the vehicle during hard or sudden stops.

Found on both 2WD and 4WD vehicles, the RWAL system is designed to regulate rear hydraulic brake line pressure, preventing wheel lock-up at the rear. Pressure regulation is managed by the proportioning and differential (control) valve, located under the master cylinder. The control valve is capable of holding, increasing or decreasing brake line pressure based on electrical commands from the RWAL Electronic Control Unit (ECU) or Electronic Brake Control Module (EBCM).

The RWAL ECU is a separate and dedicated microcomputer mounted next to the master cylinder; it is not to be confused with the engine management ECU. The RWAL ECU receives signals from the speed sensor. The speed sensor sends its signals to the Vehicle Speed Sensor buffer (previously known as the Digital Ratio Adapter Controller or DRAC) within the instrument cluster. The buffer translates the sensor signal into a form usable by the ECU. The RWAL ECU reads this signal and commands the control valve to function. If commanded to release pressure, the dump valve releases pressurized fluid into the accumulator where it is held under pressure. If a pressure increase is called for, the isolator valve within the control valve pulses, releasing pressurized fluid into the system.

The RWAL system is connected to the BRAKE warning lamp on the instrument cluster. A RWAL self-check and a bulb test are performed every time the ignition switch is turned to **ON**. The BRAKE warning lamp should illuminate for about 2 seconds and then go off. Problems within the RWAL system will be indicated by the BRAKE warning lamp staying illuminated.

If a fault is detected within the system, the RWAL ECU will assign a fault code and store the code in memory. The code may be read to aid in diagnosis.

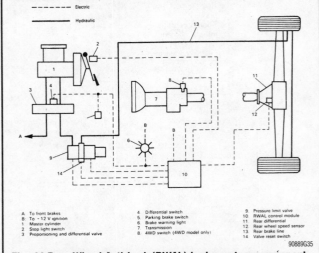

90889G35

Fig. 44 Rear Wheel Anti-Lock (RWAL) brake system component identification and locations

Diagnosis and Testing

SYSTEM PRECAUTIONS

• If the vehicle is equipped with air bag (SIR or SRS) system, always properly disable the system before commencing work on the ABS system.

• Certain components within the RWAL system are not intended to be serviced or repaired. Only those components with removal & Installation procedures should be serviced.

• Do not use rubber hoses or other parts not specifically specified for the RWAL system. When using repair kits, replace all parts included in the kit. Partial or incorrect repair may lead to functional problems.

• Lubricate rubber parts with clean, fresh brake fluid to ease assembly. Do not use lubricated shop air to clean parts; damage to rubber components may result.

• Use only brake fluid from an unopened container. Use of suspect or contaminated brake fluid can reduce system performance and/or durability.

• A clean repair area is essential. Perform repairs after components have been thoroughly cleaned; use only denatured alcohol to clean components. Do not allow components to come into contact with any substance containing mineral oil; this includes used shop rags.

• The RWAL ECU is a microprocessor similar to other computer units in the vehicle. Insure that the ignition switch is **OFF** before removing or installing controller harnesses. Avoid static electricity discharge at or near the controller.

• Never disconnect any electrical connection with the ignition switch **ON** unless instructed to do so in a test.

• Always wear a grounded wrist strap when servicing any control module or component labeled with a Electrostatic Discharge (ESD) symbol.

• Avoid touching module connector pins.

• Leave new components and modules in the shipping package until ready to install them.

• To avoid static discharge, always touch a vehicle ground after sliding across a vehicle seat or walking across carpeted or vinyl floors.

• Never allow welding cables to lie on, near or across any vehicle electrical wiring.

• Do not allow extension cords for power tools or droplights to lie on, near or across any vehicle electrical wiring.

PRELIMINARY DIAGNOSIS

♦ **See Figures 45, 46, 47 and 48**

Before reading trouble codes, perform the general system inspection according to the chart. This test will aid in separating RWAL system problems from common problems in the hydraulic brake system. The diagnostic circuit check will direct the reading of trouble codes as necessary.

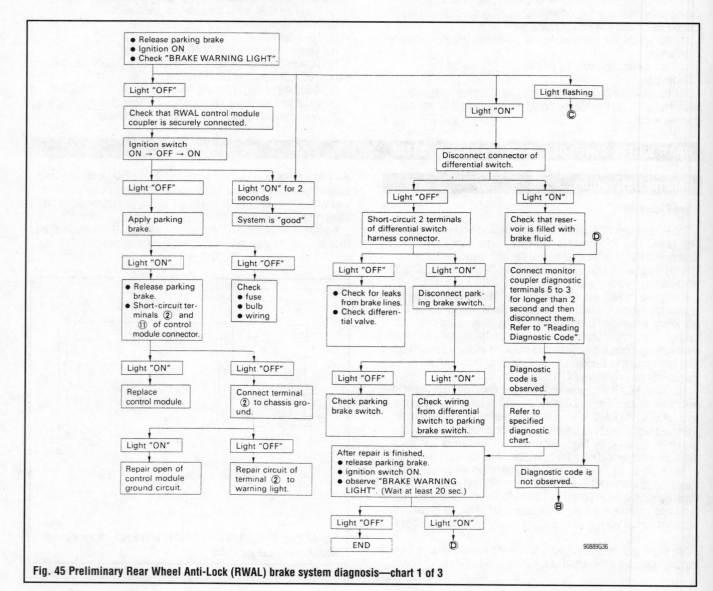

Fig. 45 Preliminary Rear Wheel Anti-Lock (RWAL) brake system diagnosis—chart 1 of 3

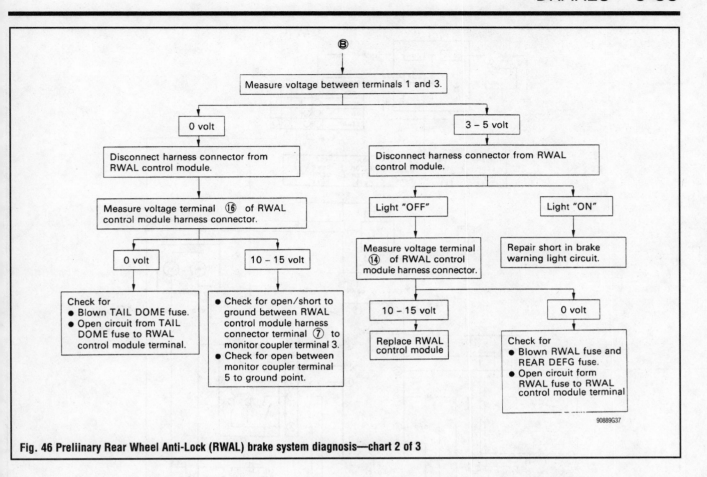

Fig. 46 Preliinary Rear Wheel Anti-Lock (RWAL) brake system diagnosis—chart 2 of 3

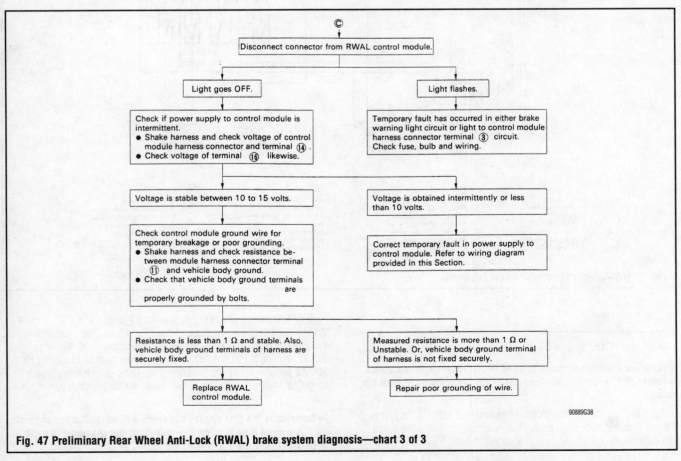

Fig. 47 Preliminary Rear Wheel Anti-Lock (RWAL) brake system diagnosis—chart 3 of 3

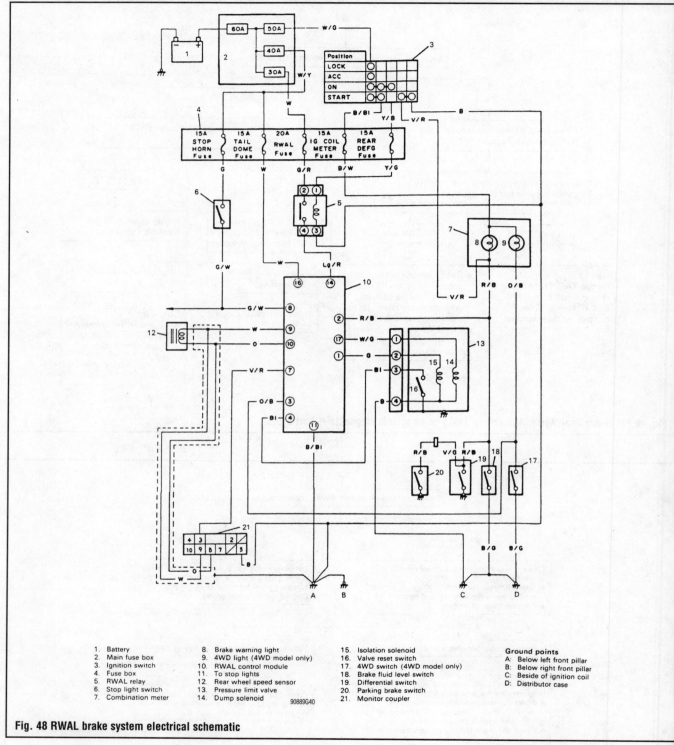

Fig. 48 RWAL brake system electrical schematic

1. Battery	8. Brake warning light	15. Isolation solenoid
2. Main fuse box	9. 4WD light (4WD model only)	16. Valve reset switch
3. Ignition switch	10. RWAL control module	17. 4WD switch (4WD model only)
4. Fuse box	11. To stop lights	18. Brake fluid level switch
5. RWAL relay	12. Rear wheel speed sensor	19. Differential switch
6. Stop light switch	13. Pressure limit valve	20. Parking brake switch
7. Combination meter	14. Dump solenoid	21. Monitor coupler

Ground points
A: Below left front pillar
B: Below right front pillar
C: Beside of ignition coil
D: Distributor case

90889G40

READING CODES

▶ **See Figures 49, 50 and 51**

➡**Since the trouble codes are cleared whenever the ignition switch is turned OFF, avoid turning the switch OFF if you intend to read the codes.**

The RWAL ECU will assign a code to the first fault found in the system. If there is more than 1 fault, only the first recognized code will the stored and transmitted.

Trouble codes may be read by connecting a jumper wire from terminal **3** to terminal **5** on the diagnostic monitor for at least 2 seconds, then releasing it. The fault code(s) will be displayed through the flashing of the BRAKE warning lamp on the dash. The terminals must be connected for about 2 seconds before the display begins. The display will begin with 1 long flash followed by shorter ones—count the long flash as part of the display.

➡**Sometimes the first display sequence will be inaccurate or short; so it is a good idea to allow the code flash-out sequence to cycle a couple of times while you read the codes.**

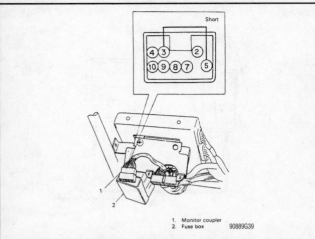

Fig. 49 To initiate the warning light flash-out of brake-related trouble codes, connect terminals 3 and 5 of the monitor coupler with a jumper wire for at least 2 seconds

CLEARING CODES

Stored trouble codes are cleared every time the ignition switch is turned **OFF**.

RWAL Electronic Control Unit (ECU)

REMOVAL & INSTALLATION

▶ **See Figures 52 and 53**

1. Disconnect the negative battery cable.
2. Remove the radio speaker cover from the underside of the lower, left-hand side of the instrument panel.
3. Remove the radio speaker from the instrument panel.
4. Remove the Engine Control Module (ECM) along with the cover, bracket and fuse box from the steering column holder.
5. Detach the wiring harness connector from the RWAL ECU, then remove the unit from the dash panel.

To install:

6. Position the RWAL ECU on the dash panel, then install and tighten the retaining nuts to 35 inch lbs. (4 Nm).

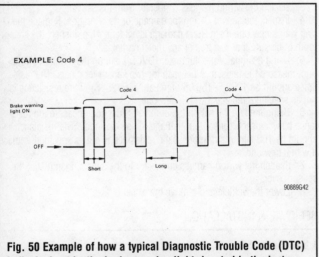

Fig. 50 Example of how a typical Diagnostic Trouble Code (DTC) is flashed out by the brake warning light, located in the instrument cluster

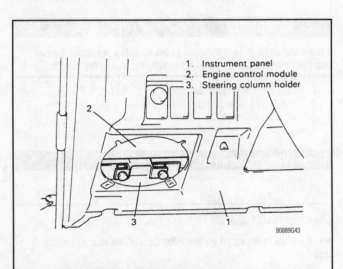

1. Instrument panel
2. Engine control module
3. Steering column holder

Fig. 52 Remove the left-hand radio speaker grille from the underside of the instrument panel to gain access to the RWAL ECU

NOTE:
When RWAL control module detects two or more of the following conditions, only the smallest one among their corresponding codes is indicated repeatedly.

DIAGNOSTIC CODE NO.	CONDITION	ACTION TO TAKE
2	Open isolation solenoid circuit	Diagnose according to diagnosis procedure for each code.
3	Open dump solenoid circuit	
4	Valve reset switch closed	
5	System dumps too many times (Condition occurs when brake is applied during driving.)	
6	Rear wheel speed sensor signal changed rapidly (Condition only occurs while driving.)	
7	Shorted isolation solenoid circuit	
8	Shorted dump solenoid circuit	
9	Open rear wheel speed sensor circuit	
10	Stop light switch remains ON	
11	Shorted rear wheel speed sensor circuit	
13	RWAL control module malfunction	

Fig. 51 Rear Wheel Anti-Lock (RWAL) brake system Diagnostic Trouble Codes (DTCs)

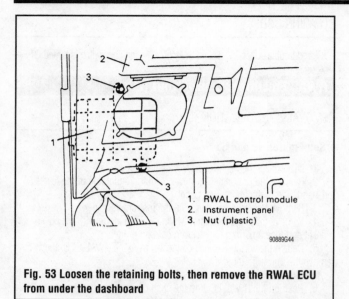

Fig. 53 Loosen the retaining bolts, then remove the RWAL ECU from under the dashboard

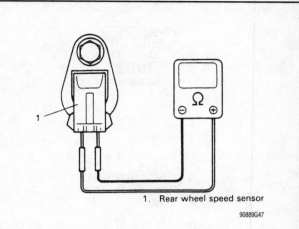

Fig. 55 Use a DVOM to measure the resistance between the two RWSS terminals. Replace it with a new one if the resistance is out of specifications

1. RWAL control module
2. Instrument panel
3. Nut (plastic)

90889G44

1. Rear wheel speed sensor

90889G47

✳✳ WARNING

If the nuts cannot be tightened to 35 inch lbs. (4 Nm), do not attempt to force them; this will break the mounting studs.

7. Reattach the wiring harness connector to the RWAL ECU.
8. Install the ECM, along with the fuse panel, bracket and cover.
9. Install the radio speaker and speaker grille.
10. Connect the negative battery cable.

Rear Wheel Speed Sensor (RWSS)

INSPECTION

◆ See Figures 54 and 55

➡ The RWSS is mounted on the front face of the rear differential case.

1. Block the front wheels, then raise and safely support the rear of the vehicle on jackstands.
2. Remove the sensor cover.

3. Detach the wiring harness connector from the sensor.
4. Inspect the sensor O-ring for damage or deterioration. Replace the O-ring with a new one if any such damage is evident. Also, inspect the sensor tooth to be sure that it is free of any metal particles.
5. Using a Digital Volt-Ohmmeter (DVOM), set on the ohmmeter function, measure the resistance between the two sensor terminals. The resistance should be 1282.5–1567.5 ohms at 77°F (25°C); if the resistance is not as specified, replace it with a new one.
6. Using the DVOM, set on the ohmmeter function, measure the resistance between each sensor terminal and the sensor body. The resistance should be 100 kilohms or more; if the resistance is not as specified, replace it with a new one.
7. Reattch the wiring harness connector to the sensor, then install the sensor cover.
8. Lower the vehicle and remove the wheel blocks.

REMOVAL & INSTALLATION

◆ See Figure 56

The speed sensor is not serviceable and must replaced if malfunctioning. The sensor is mounted on the front face of the rear differential case.

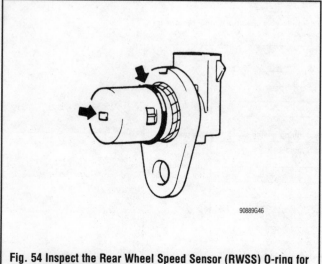

Fig. 54 Inspect the Rear Wheel Speed Sensor (RWSS) O-ring for damage, and the RWSS tooth for metal particles

90889G46

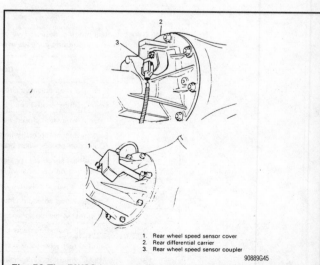

1. Rear wheel speed sensor cover
2. Rear differential carrier
3. Rear wheel speed sensor coupler

90889G45

Fig. 56 The RWSS is mounted on the front face of the rear differential assembly

1. Ensure that the ignition switch is **OFF**.
2. Block the front wheels, then raise and safely support the rear of the vehicle on jackstands.
3. Remove the sensor cover.
4. Detach the wiring harness connector from the sensor by gently prying outward on the connector plastic retaining tabs.
5. Remove the sensor retaining bolt, then pull the sensor out of the differential case.
6. Clean the sensor mounting surface on the differential case thoroughly.

To install:

7. Prior to installation, inspect the sensor.
8. Apply sealant to the sensor, then insert the sensor into the differential case.
9. Install and tighten the sensor, retaining bolt to 159–248 inch lbs. (18–28 Nm).
10. Reattch the wiring harness connector to the sensor, then install the sensor cover.
11. Lower the vehicle and remove the wheel blocks.

RWAL Relay

INSPECTION

▶ **See Figures 57 and 58**

1. Disconnect the negative battery cable.
2. Remove the monitor coupler bracket (located next to the ECM under the left-hand side of the instrument panel).
3. Detach the yellow wiring harness from the RWAL relay.
4. Using a Digital Volt-Ohmmeter (DVOM) set on the ohmmeter function, measure the resistance between relay terminals A and B, and between terminals C and D. The resistance between terminals A and B should register infinite resistance (no continuity). The resistance between terminals C and D should be 90–110 ohms at 77°F (25°C). If the resistances were not as indicated, replace the relay.
5. Connect a the negative lead of a 12 volt DC battery to terminal D of the relay, and the positive lead to terminal C of the relay. With the relay energized, measure terminals A and B for continuity. There should now be continuity between terminals A and B. If there is no continuity, replace the relay with a new one. Otherwise, the relay is functioning properly.
6. Reattach the yellow wiring harness connector to the relay.
7. Install the monitor coupler bracket.
8. Connect the negative battery cable.

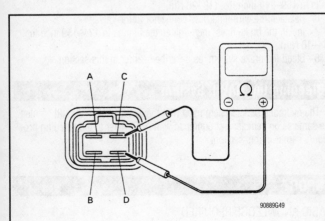

Fig. 57 Use a DVOM, set on the ohmmeter function, to measure the resistance between terminals A and B, and terminals C and D of the relay—if the resistances are not as specified, replace the relay

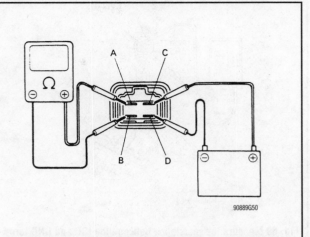

Fig. 58 Apply 12 volt DC power to terminals C and D, then measure the resistance between terminals A and B again—there should now be continuity evident

REMOVAL & INSTALLATION

▶ **See Figure 59**

1. Disconnect the negative battery cable.
2. Remove the ECM from the vehicle.
3. Remove the relay from the ECM.

To install:

4. Install the relay onto the ECM, then install the ECM in the vehicle.
5. Connect the negative battery cable.

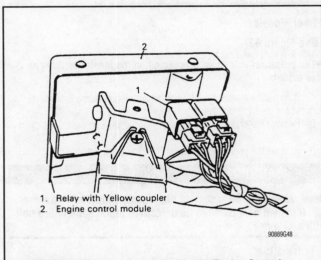

1. Relay with Yellow coupler
2. Engine control module

Fig. 59 The RWAL relay is mounted on the Engine Control Module (ECM), as shown

Pressure Limit (Isolation/Dump) Valve

INSPECTION

▶ **See Figure 60**

1. Ensure the ignition switch is turned **OFF**.
2. Detach the wiring harness connector from the pressure limit valve.

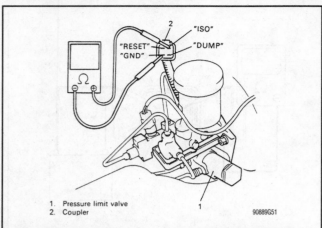

1. Pressure limit valve
2. Coupler

90889G51

Fig. 60 Measure the resistance between the ISO and GND terminals, the DUMP and GND terminals, and the RESET terminal and valve body—replace the valve if the resistance values are not within the specified ranges

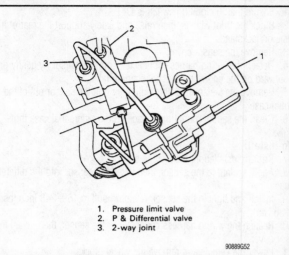

1. Pressure limit valve
2. P & Differential valve
3. 2-way joint

90889G52

Fig. 61 On 2-door models, the pressure limit valve is mounted on the underside of the master cylinder

3. Using a Digital Volt-Ohmmeter (DVOM) set on the ohmmeter function, measure the resistance between valve terminals ISO and GND, terminals DUMP and GND, and between the valve body and terminal RESET. The resistance between terminals ISO and GND should register 3–6 ohms at 68°F (20°C). The resistance between terminals DUMP and GND should be 1–3 ohms at 68°F (20°C). The resistance between the valve body and terminal RESET should register infinite resistance (no continuity). If the resistances were not as indicated, replace the valve.

4. Reattach the wiring harness connector to the valve.

REMOVAL & INSTALLATION

2-Door Models

▶ **See Figure 61**

➡The pressure limit valve is mounted on the master cylinder on 2-door models.

1. Remove the master cylinder (along with the pressure limit valve) from the brake power booster.
2. Remove the brake fluid lines attaching the valve to the master cylinder.
3. Remove the pressure limit valve from the master cylinder.

※※ WARNING

Never attempt to disassemble the pressure limit valve assembly. If the valve is found to be defective, replace the entire unit with a new one.

To install:

4. Install the valve on the master cylinder and reattach the brake fluid lines. Tighten the brake fluid line fittings to 124–159 inch lbs. (14–18 Nm).
5. Install the master cylinder, as described earlier in this section.

4-WHEEL ANTI-LOCK BRAKE SYSTEM—EXCEPT SIDEKICK SPORT

General Information

This ABS system, which is as an option on 1996–98 Sidekick, Tracker and X-90 models, is known as the DELCO ABS-VI system. It has been designed to improve the control and steering of a vehicle during braking that would cause one or more wheels to lock. ABS accomplishes this objective by controlling the hydraulic pressure applied to each wheel brake.

4-Door Models

➡The pressure limit valve is mounted next to the battery on 4-door models.

1. Disconnect the brake line fittings at the valve, then plug the brake lines. Protect the surrounding paintwork from brake fluid spillage.
2. Detach the wiring harness connector from the valve.
3. Remove the bolts holding the valve to the bracket.

➡**Do not touch the electrical connectors or pins; do not allow them to contact brake fluid. If contaminated with brake fluid, clean them with water followed by isopropyl alcohol.**

4. Carefully remove the valve from the vehicle.

※※ WARNING

Never attempt to disassemble the pressure limit valve assembly. If the valve is found to be defective, replace the entire unit with a new one.

To install:

5. Place the valve in position and install the retaining bolts. Tighten the bolts to 159–248 inch lbs. (18–28 Nm).
6. Reattach the wiring harness connector to the valve.
7. Install the brake lines, then tighten the fittings to 124–159 inch lbs. (14–18 Nm).
8. Bleed the brake system, as described earlier in this section.

Bleeding the RAWL System

The hydraulic brake system used with the RAWL system should be bled the same as on vehicles not equipped with ABS. Refer to the bleeding procedure earlier in this section.

BASIC KNOWLEDGE REQUIRED

Before using this section, it is important that you have a basic knowledge of the following items. Without this basic knowledge, it will be difficult to use the diagnostic procedures contained in this section.

Basic Electrical Circuits—You should understand the basic theory of electricity and know the meaning of voltage, current (amps) and resistance (ohms). You should understand what happens in a circuit with an open or shorted wire. You should be able to read and understand a wiring diagram.

Use Of Circuit Testing Tools—You should know how to use a test light and how to use jumper wires to bypass components to test circuits. You should be familiar with a Digital Volt-Ohmmeter (DVOM). You should be able to measure voltage, resistance and current and be familiar with the meter controls and how to use them correctly.

PRECAUTIONS

➡**Failure to observe the following precautions may result in system damage.**

• Before performing electric arc welding on the vehicle, disconnect the Electronic Brake Control Module (EBCM) and the hydraulic modulator connectors.

• When performing painting work on the vehicle, do not expose the Electronic Brake Control Module (EBCM) to temperatures in excess of 185°F (85°C) for longer than 2 hours. The system may be exposed to temperatures up to 200°F (95°C) for less than 15 min.

• Never disconnect or connect the Electronic Brake Control Module (EBCM) or hydraulic modulator connectors with the ignition switch **ON**.

• Never disassemble any component of the Anti-Lock Brake System (ABS) which is designated non-serviceable; the component must be replaced as an assembly.

• When filling the master cylinder, always use brake fluid, which meets DOT-3 specifications; petroleum base fluid will destroy the rubber parts.

Diagnosis and Testing

ON-BOARD DIAGNOSTICS

The ABS contains sophisticated on-board diagnostics that, when accessed with a TECH 1® or equivalent "Scan" tool, are designed to identify the source of any system fault as specifically as possible, including whether or not the fault is intermittent. There are over 50 diagnostic fault codes to assist the service technician with diagnosis. The last diagnostic fault code to occur is specifically identified, and specific ABS data is stored at the time of this fault, also, the first five codes set. Additionally, using the scan tool, each input and output can be monitored, thus enabling fault confirmation and repair verification. Manual control of components and automated functional tests are also available when using a scan tool. Details of many of these functions are contained in the following sections.

ENHANCED DIAGNOSTICS

Enhanced Diagnostic Information, found in the CODE HISTORY function of the scan tool is designed to provide the service technician with specific fault occurrence information. For each of the first five (5) and the very last diagnostic fault codes stored, data is stored to identify the specific fault code number, the number of failure occurrences, and the number of drive cycles since the failure first and last occurred (a drive cycle occurs when the ignition is turned **ON** and the vehicle is driven faster than 10 mph). However, if a fault is present, the drive cycle counter will increment by turning the ignition **ON** and **LOCK**. These first five (5) diagnostic fault codes are also stored in the order of occurrence. The order in which the first 5 faults occurred can be useful in determining if a previous fault is linked to the most recent faults, such as an intermittent wheel speed sensor which later becomes completely open.

During difficult diagnosis situations, this information can be used to identify fault occurrence trends. Does the fault occur more frequently now than it did during the last time when it only failed 1 out of 35 drive cycles? Did the fault only occur once over a large number of drive cycles, indicating unusual condition present when the fault occurred? Does the fault occur infrequently over a large number of drive cycles, indicating special diagnosis techniques may be required to identify the source of the fault?

If a fault occurred 1 out of 20 drive cycles, the fault is intermittent and has not reoccurred for 19 drive cycles. This fault may be difficult or impossible to duplicate and may have been caused by a severe vehicle impact (large pot hole, speed bump at high speed, etc.) that momentarily opened an electrical connector or caused unusual vehicle suspension movement. Problem resolution is unlikely, and the problem may never reoccur. If the fault occurred 3 out of 15 drive cycles, the odds of finding the cause are still not good, but you know how often it occurs and you can determine whether or not the fault is becoming more frequent based on an additional or past occurrences if the source of the problem can not or could not be found. If the fault occurred 10 out of 20 drive cycles, the odds of finding the cause are much better, as the fault may be easily reproduced.

By using the additional fault data, you can also determine if a failure is randomly intermittent or if it has not reoccurred for long periods of time due to weather changes or a prior repair. Say a diagnostic fault code occurred 10 of 20 drive cycles but has not reoccurred for 10 drive cycles. This means the failure occurred 10 of 10 drive cycles but has not reoccurred since. A significant environmental change or a repair may have occurred 10 drive cycles ago. A repair may not be necessary if a recent repair can be confirmed. If no repair was made, the service can focus on diagnosis techniques used to locate difficult to recreate problems.

INTERMITTENT FAILURES

As with most electronic systems, intermittent failures may be difficult to accurately diagnose. The following is a method to try to isolate an intermittent failure especially wheel speed circuitry failures.

If an ABS fault occurs, the ABS warning light indicator will be ON during the ignition cycle in which the fault was detected. If it is an intermittent problem which seems to have corrected itself (ABS warning light OFF), a history trouble code will be stored. Also stored will be the history data of the code at the time the fault occurred. The scan tool must be used to read ABS history data.

INTERMITTENTS & POOR CONNECTIONS

Most intermittent faults, or problems, are caused by faulty electrical connections or wiring, although occasionally a sticking relay or solenoid can be a problem. Some items to check are:

1. Poor mating of connector halves, or terminals not fully seated in the connector body (backed out).

2. Dirt or corrosion on the terminals. The terminals must be clean and free of any foreign material which could impede proper terminal contact.

3. Damaged connector body, exposing the terminals to moisture and dirt, as well as not maintaining proper terminal orientation with the component or mating connector.

4. Improperly formed or damaged terminals. All connector terminals in problem circuits should be checked carefully to ensure good contact tension. Use a corresponding mating terminal to check for proper tension. Refer to Checking Terminal Contact in this section for the specific procedure.

5. The J-35616-A Connector Test Adapter Kit must be used whenever a diagnostic procedure requests checking or probing a terminal. Using the adapter will ensure that no damage to the terminal will occur, as well as giving an idea of whether contact tension is sufficient. If contact tension seems incorrect, refer to Checking Terminal Contact in this section for specifics.

6. Poor terminal-to-wire connection. Checking this requires removing the terminal from the connector body. Some conditions which fall under this description are poor crimps, poor solder joints, crimping over wire insulation rather than the wire itself, corrosion in the wire-to-terminal contact area, etc.

7. Wire insulation which is rubbed through, causing an intermittent short as the bare area touches other wiring or parts of the vehicle.

8. Wiring broken inside the insulation. This condition could cause a continuity check to show a good circuit, but if only 1 or 2 strands of a multi-strand-type wire are intact, resistance could be far too high.

Checking Terminal Contact

When diagnosing an electrical system that uses Metri-Pack 150/280/480/630 series terminals (refer to Terminal Repair Kit J-38125-A instruction manual J-38125-4 for terminal identification), it is important to check terminal contact between a connector and component, or between in-line connectors, before replacing a suspect component.

Frequently, a diagnostic chart leads to a step that reads Check for poor connection. Mating terminals must be inspected to ensure good terminal contact. A poor connection between the male and female terminal at a connector may be the result of contamination or deformation.

Contamination is caused by the connector halves being improperly connected, a missing or damaged connector seal, or damage to the connector itself, exposing the terminals to moisture and dirt. Contamination, usually in underhood or underbelly connectors, leads to terminal corrosion, causing an open circuit or an intermittently open circuit.

Deformation is caused by probing the mating side of a connector terminal without the proper adapter, improperly joining the connector halves or repeatedly separating and joining the connector halves. Deformation, usually to the female terminal contact tang, can result in poor terminal contact causing an open or intermittently open circuit.

Follow the procedure below to check terminal contact:

1. Separate the connector halves. Refer to Terminal Repair Kit J-38125-A instruction manual J-38125-4, if available.

2. Inspect the connector halves for contamination. Contamination will result in a white or green buildup within the connector body or between terminals, causing high terminal resistance, intermittent contact or an open circuit. An underhood or underbelly connector that shows signs of contamination should be replaced in its entirety: terminals, seals, and connector body.

3. Using an equivalent male terminal from the Terminal Repair Kit J-38125-A, check the retention force of the female terminal in question by inserting and removing the male terminal to the female terminal in the connector body. Good terminal contact will require a certain amount of force to separate the terminals.

4. Using an equivalent female terminal from the Terminal Repair Kit J-38125-A, compare the retention force of this terminal to the female terminal in question by joining and separating the male terminal to the female terminal in question. If the retention force is significantly different between the two female terminals, replace the female terminal in question, using a terminal from Terminal Repair Kit J-38125-A.

DISPLAYING CODES

▶ See Figures 62 and 63

Diagnostic fault codes can only be read through the use of a TECH 1® or equivalent bi-directional scan tool. There are no provisions for flash code diagnostics.

CLEARING CODES

The trouble codes in EBCM memory are erased in one of two ways:
1. Scan tool Clear Codes selection.
2. Ignition cycle default.

These two methods are detailed below. Be sure to verify proper system operation and absence of codes when clearing procedure is completed.

The EBCM will not permit code clearing until all of the codes have been displayed. Also, codes cannot be cleared by unplugging the EBCM, disconnecting the battery cables, or turning the ignition to **LOCK** (except on an ignition cycle default).

''Clear Codes'' Method

After codes have been viewed completely, scan tool will ask, "CLEAR ABS CODES?" Press "YES." scan tool will then read, "HISTORY DATA WILL BE LOST. CLEAR DATA?" Answer "YES" and the codes will be cleared.

Ignition Cycle Default

If no diagnostic fault code occurs for 100 drive cycles (a drive cycle occurs when the ignition is turned **ON** and the vehicle is driven faster than 10 mph), any existing fault codes are cleared from the EBCM memory.

DIAGNOSTIC PROCESS

▶ See Figures 64 thru 74

When servicing the ABS, the following steps should be followed in order. Failure to follow these steps may result in the loss of important diagnostic data and may lead to difficult and time consuming diagnosis procedures.

1. Using the scan tool, read all current and history Diagnostic Trouble Codes (DTCs). Be certain to note which codes are current diagnostic code failures. DO NOT CLEAR CODES unless directed to do so.

2. Using a scan tool, read the CODE HISTORY data. Note the diagnostic fault codes stored and their frequency of failure. Specifically note the last failure that occurred and the conditions present when this failure occurred. This "last failure" should be the starting point for diagnosis and repair.

3. Perform a vehicle preliminary diagnosis inspection. This should include:

   a. Inspection of the compact master cylinder for proper brake fluid level.

   b. Inspection of the ABS hydraulic modulator for any leaks or wiring damage.

   c. Inspection of brake components at all four (4) wheels. Verify no drag exists. Also verify proper brake apply operation.

   d. Inspection for worn or damaged wheel bearings that allow a wheel to "wobble."

   e. Inspection of the wheel speed sensors and their wiring. Verify correct air gap range, solid sensor attachment, undamaged sensor toothed ring, and undamaged wiring, especially at vehicle attachment points.

   f. Verify tires meet legal tread depth requirements.

4. If no codes are present, or mechanical component failure codes are present, perform the automated modulator test using the scan tool to isolate the cause of the problem. If the failure is intermittent and not reproducible, test drive the vehicle while using the automatic snapshot feature of the scan tool.

Perform normal acceleration, stopping, and turning maneuvers. If this does not reproduce the failure, perform an ABS stop, on a low coefficient surface such as gravel, from approximately 30–50 mph while triggering on any ABS code. If the failure is still not reproducible, use the enhanced diagnostic information found in CODE HISTORY to determine whether or not this failure should be further diagnosed.

5. Once all system failures have been corrected, clear the ABS codes.

The scan tool, when plugged into the ALDL connector, becomes part of the vehicle's electronic system. The scan tool can also perform the following functions on components linked by the Serial Data Link (SDL):
- Display ABS data
- Display and clear ABS Diagnostic Trouble Codes (DTCs)
- Control ABS components
- Perform extensive ABS diagnosis
- Provide diagnostic testing for Intermittent ABS conditions.

Each test mode has specific diagnosis capabilities which depend upon various keystrokes. In general, five (5) keys control sequencing: YES, NO, EXIT, UP arrow and DOWN arrow. The F0 through F9 keys select operating modes, perform functions within an operating mode, or enter trouble code or model year designations.

In general, most scan tools have six (6) test modes for diagnosing the anti-lock brake system. The six (6) test modes are as follows:
- **MODE F0: DATA LIST**—In this test mode, the scan tool continuously monitors wheel speed data, brake switch status and other inputs and outputs.
- **MODE F1: CODE HISTORY**—In this mode, fault code history data is displayed. This data includes how many ignition cycles since the fault code occurred, along with other ABS information. The first five (5) and last fault codes set are included in the ABS history data.

DIAGNOSTIC TROUBLE CODE	DESCRIPTION	ABS Operate: ○ Not operate: X	ABS Warning light	BRAKE Warning light
14	ABS enable relay contact circuit open	X	ON NOTE 2	OFF NOTE 1
15	ABS enable relay circuit shorted to battery or always closed	○	OFF	OFF
16	ABS enable relay coil circuit open	X	ON NOTE 2	OFF NOTE 1
17	ABS enable relay coil circuit shorted to ground	○	OFF	OFF
18	ABS enable relay coil circuit shorted to battery	X	ON NOTE 2	OFF NOTE 1
21	Left front wheel speed – 0 or unreasonable	X	ON	OFF
22	Right front wheel speed – 0 or unreasonable	X	ON	OFF
24	Rear wheel speed – 0 or unreasonable	X	ON	OFF
25	Left front excessive wheel speed variation	X	ON	OFF
26	Right front excessive wheel speed variation	X	ON	OFF
28	Rear excessive wheel speed variation	X	ON	OFF
32	Left front wheel speed sensor circuit open or shorted to battery or ground	X	ON	OFF
33	Right front wheel speed sensor circuit open or shorted to battery or ground	X	ON	OFF
35	Rear wheel speed sensor circuit open or shorted to battery or ground	X	ON	OFF
36	Low system voltage	X	ON NOTE 2	OFF NOTE 1
37	High system voltage	X	ON	OFF
38	Left front ESB will not hold motor	X	ON	OFF
41	Right front ESB will not hold motor	X	ON	OFF
42	Rear ESB will not hold motor	X	ON NOTE 2	ON
44	Left front channel will not move	X	ON	OFF
45	Right front channel will not move	X	ON	OFF
46	Rear channel will not move	X	ON NOTE 2	ON
47	Left front motor free spin	X	ON	OFF
48	Right front motor free spin	X	ON	OFF
51	Rear motor free spin	X	ON	OFF
52	Left front channel in release too long	X	ON	OFF
53	Right front channel in release too long	X	ON	OFF
54	Rear channel in release too long	X	ON	OFF
55	EBCM malfunction	X	ON NOTE 2	OFF NOTE 1
56	Left front motor circuit open	X	ON	OFF
57	Left front motor circuit shorted to ground	X	ON	OFF
58	Left front motor circuit shorted to battery	X	ON	OFF

90889G64

Fig. 62 Diagnostic Trouble Codes (DTC's)—chart 1 of 2

DIAGNOSTIC TROUBLE CODE	DESCRIPTION	ABS Operate: ○ Not operate: X	ABS Warning light	BRAKE Warning light
61	Right front motor circuit open	X	ON	OFF
62	Right front motor circuit shorted to ground	X	ON	OFF
63	Right front motor circuit shorted to battery	X	ON	OFF
64	Rear motor circuit open	X	ON NOTE 2	ON NOTE 1
65	Rear motor circuit shorted to ground	X	ON NOTE 2	OFF NOTE 1
66	Rear motor circuit shorted to battery	X	ON NOTE 2	OFF NOTE 1
76	Left front solenoid circuit open or shorted to battery	X	ON	OFF
77	Left front solenoid circuit shorted to ground	X	ON	OFF
78	Right front solenoid circuit open or shorted to battery	X	ON	OFF
81	Right front solenoid circuit shorted to ground	X	ON	OFF
82	Calibration malfunction	X	ON	OFF
83	Idle up circuit malfunction	○	OFF	OFF
85	Base brake malfunction (Brake warning light turns ON)	X	ON	ON
86	EBCM turned on red brake warning light	X	OFF NOTE 2	ON
87	Brake warning light circuit open	X	ON	OFF
88	Brake warning light circuit shorted to battery	X	ON	OFF
91	Open brake switch during deceleration	X	ON	OFF
92	Open brake switch when ABS was required	X	ON	OFF
93	Code 91 or 92 set in current or previous ignition cycle	X	ON	OFF
94	Brake switch contacts always closed	○	OFF	OFF
95	Brake switch circuit open	X	ON	OFF
96	4WD switch circuit open	○	OFF	OFF
97	G sensor circuit shorted to ground	X	ON	OFF
98	G sensor circuit open or shorted to battery or ground	X	ON	OFF

90889G65

NOTE 1: If the rear piston is not in the home position, the BRAKE warning light will be illuminated.
NOTE 2: The ABS warning light will flash if the EBCM cannot illuminate the BRAKE warning light.

Fig. 63 Diagnostic Trouble Codes (DTC's)—chart 2 of 2

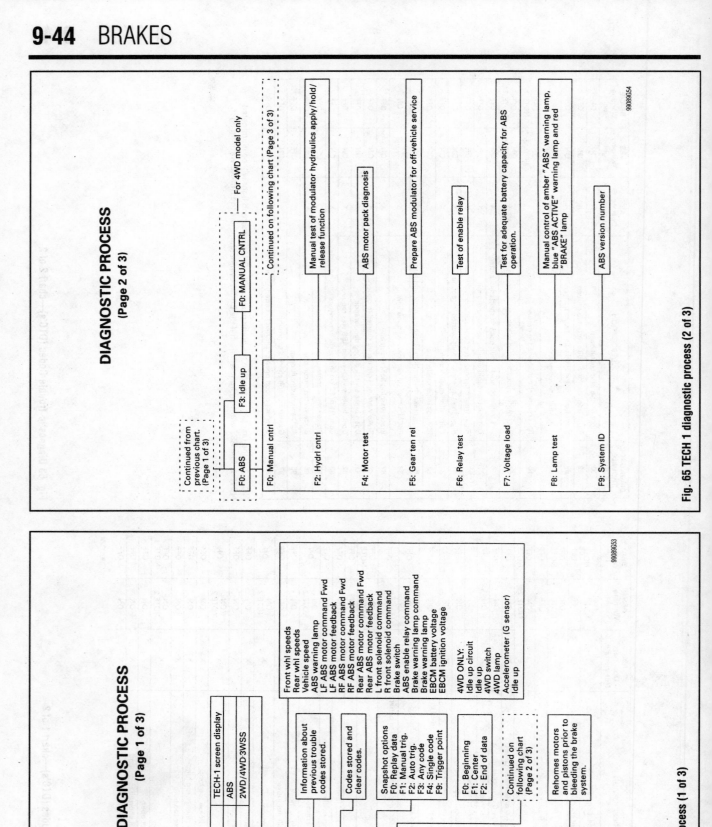

DIAGNOSTIC PROCESS
(Page 2 of 3)

Continued from previous chart. (Page 1 of 3)		

F3: Idle up — For 4WD model only

F0: ABS   F0: MANUAL CNTRL — Continued on following chart (Page 3 of 3)

F0: Manual cntrl

F2: Hydrl cntrl — Manual test of modulator hydraulics apply/hold/release function

F4: Motor test — ABS motor pack diagnosis

F5: Gear ten rel — Prepare ABS modulator for off-vehicle service

F6: Relay test — Test of enable relay

F7: Voltage load — Test for adequate battery capacity for ABS operation.

F8: Lamp test — Manual control of amber "ABS" warning lamp, blue "ABS ACTIVE" warning lamp and red "BRAKE" lamp

F9: System ID — ABS version number

99089G54

Fig. 65 TECH 1 diagnostic process (2 of 3)

DIAGNOSTIC PROCESS
(Page 1 of 3)

ABS cartridge section	TECH-1 screen display
STEP 1 Select system	ABS
STEP 2 Select ABS type	2WD/4WD/3WSS
STEP select mode (First Screen)	

F0: Data list —
Front whl speeds
Rear whl speeds
Vehicle speed
ABS warning lamp
LF ABS motor command Fwd
LF ABS motor feedback
RF ABS motor command Fwd
RF ABS motor feedback
Rear ABS motor command Fwd
Rear ABS motor feedback
L front solenoid command
R front solenoid command
Brake switch
ABS enable relay command
Brake warning lamp command
Brake warning lamp
EBCM battery voltage
EBCM ignition voltage

4WD ONLY:
Idle up circuit
Idle up
4WD switch
4WD lamp
Accelerometer (G sensor)
Idle up

F1: DTC history — Information about previous trouble codes stored.

F2: DTC(s) — Codes stored and clear codes.

F3: Snapshot — Snapshot options
F0: Replay data
F1: Manual trig.
F2: Auto trig.
F3: Any code
F4: Single code
F9: Trigger point

F4: Misc. test —
F0: Beginning
F1: Center
F2: End of data

Continued on following chart (Page 2 of 3)

F5: Motor rehome — Rehomes motors and pistons prior to bleeding the brake system.

99089G53

Fig. 64 TECH 1 diagnostic process (1 of 3)

DIAGNOSTIC CIRCUIT CHECK

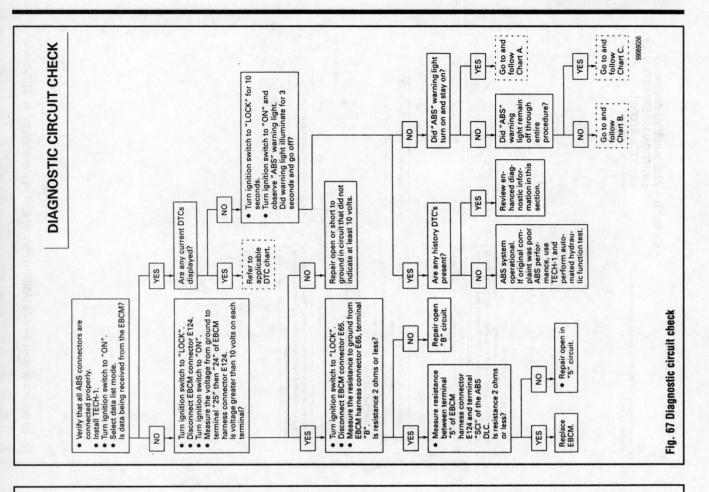

Fig. 67 Diagnostic circuit check

DIAGNOSTIC PROCESS
(Page 3 of 3)

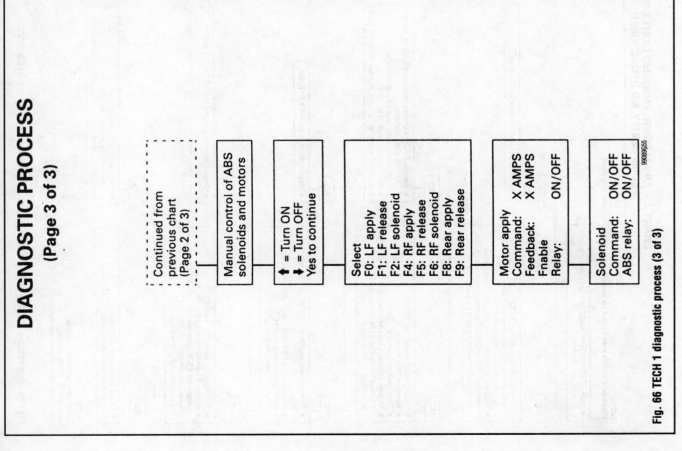

Fig. 66 TECH 1 diagnostic process (3 of 3)

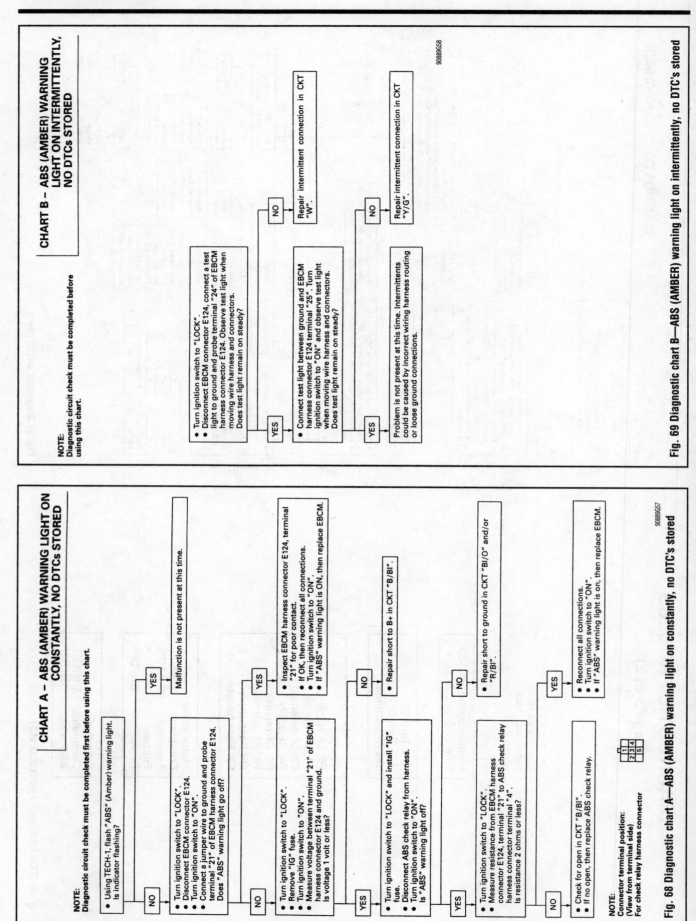

CHART B – ABS (AMBER) WARNING LIGHT ON INTERMITTENTLY, NO DTCs STORED

NOTE:
Diagnostic circuit check must be completed before using this chart.

- Turn ignition switch to "LOCK".
- Disconnect EBCM connector E124, connect a test light to ground and probe terminal "24" of EBCM harness connector E124. Observe test light when moving wire harness and connectors.
  Does test light remain on steady?

YES / NO

NO → Repair intermittent connection in CKT "W".

- Connect test light between ground and EBCM harness connector E124 terminal "25". Turn ignition switch to "ON" and observe test light when moving wire harness and connectors.
  Does test light remain on steady?

YES / NO

NO → Repair intermittent connection in CKT "Y/G".

Problem is not present at this time. Intermittents could be caused by incorrect wiring harness routing or loose ground connections.

90889G58

Fig. 69 Diagnostic chart B—ABS (AMBER) warning light on intermittently, no DTC's stored

CHART A – ABS (AMBER) WARNING LIGHT ON CONSTANTLY, NO DTCs STORED

NOTE:
Diagnostic circuit check must be completed first before using this chart.

- Using TECH-1, flash "ABS" (Amber) warning light.
  Is indicator flashing?

YES → Malfunction is not present at this time.

NO

- Turn ignition switch to "LOCK".
- Disconnect EBCM connector E124.
- Turn ignition switch to "ON".
- Connect a jumper wire to ground and probe terminal "21" of EBCM harness connector E124.
  Does "ABS" warning light go off?

YES

- Inspect EBCM harness connector E124, terminal "21" for poor contact.
- If OK, then reconnect all connections.
- Turn ignition switch to "ON".
- If "ABS" warning light is ON, then replace EBCM.

NO

- Turn ignition switch to "LOCK".
- Remove "IG" fuse.
- Turn ignition switch to "ON".
- Measure voltage between terminal "21" of EBCM harness connector E124 and ground.
  Is voltage 1 volt or less?

NO → • Repair short to B+ in CKT "B/Bl".

YES

- Turn ignition switch to "LOCK" and install "IG" fuse.
- Disconnect ABS check relay from harness.
- Turn ignition switch to "ON".
  Is "ABS" warning light off?

NO → • Repair short to ground in CKT "Bl/O" and/or "R/Bl".

YES

- Turn ignition switch to "LOCK".
- Measure resistance from EBCM harness connector E124, terminal "21" to ABS check relay harness connector terminal "4".
  Is resistance 2 ohms or less?

YES

- Reconnect all connections.
- Turn ignition switch to "ON".
- If "ABS" warning light is on, then replace EBCM.

NO

- Check for open in CKT "B/Bl".
- If no open, then replace ABS check relay.

NOTE:
Connector terminal position:
(View from terminal side)
For check relay harness connector

1 | | 4
2 3
| 5

90889G57

Fig. 68 Diagnostic chart A—ABS (AMBER) warning light on constantly, no DTC's stored

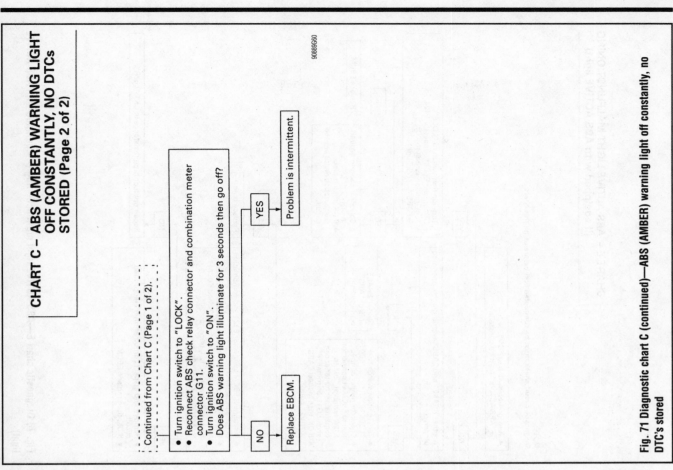

CHART C – ABS (AMBER) WARNING LIGHT OFF CONSTANTLY, NO DTCs STORED (Page 2 of 2)

Continued from Chart C (Page 1 of 2).

- Turn ignition switch to "LOCK".
- Reconnect ABS check relay connector and combination meter connector G11.
- Turn ignition switch to "ON".
- Does ABS warning light illuminate for 3 seconds then go off?

YES → Problem is intermittent.

NO → Replace EBCM.

90889G60

Fig. 71 Diagnostic chart C (continued)—ABS (AMBER) warning light off constantly, no DTC's stored

CHART C – ABS (AMBER) WARNING LIGHT OFF CONSTANTLY, NO DTCs STORED (Page 1 of 2)

NOTE:
Diagnostic circuit check must be completed first before using this chart.

- Turn ignition switch to "ON".
- Using TECH-1, select LAMP TEST and command the ABS warning light "ON".
- Is ABS warning light on?

YES → Malfunction is not present at this time.

NO →
- Turn ignition switch to "LOCK".
- Disconnect ABS check relay from harness connector.
- Turn ignition switch to "ON".
- With a fused jumper, with a 3 amp fuse, connect terminal "3" of ABS check relay harness connector to ground.
- Is "ABS" warning light on?

YES →
- Turn ignition switch to "LOCK".
- Disconnect combination meter harness connector G11.
- Measure resistance between terminal "3" of ABS check relay harness connector and terminal "7" of combination meter harness connector G11.
- Is resistance 2 ohms or less?

NO → Repair open or high resistance in CKT "Bl/O" and/or "R/Bl".

YES →
- Inspect ABS warning light bulb.
- Is bulb open?

YES → Replace bulb.

NO →
- Turn ignition switch to "ON".
- Connect test light between ground and terminal "3" of ABS check relay harness connector.
- Is test light on?

YES →
- Repair short to B+ on CKT "Bl/O" and/or "R/Bl".
- Replace ABS check relay.

NO → Go to following page of this chart (Page 2 of 2).

YES →
- Turn ignition switch to "LOCK".
- Measure resistance between terminal "5" of ABS check relay harness connector and chassis ground.
- Is resistance 2 ohms or less?

NO → Repair open from terminal "5" of ABS check relay connector to chassis ground.

YES →
- Turn ignition switch to "ON".
- Measure voltage between terminal "3" of ABS check relay harness connector and chassis ground.
- Is voltage 10 volts or less?

YES →
- Check for short to ground in CKT "Bl/Bl".
- If OK, then replace ABS check relay.

NO → Repair open or high resistance in CKT "Bl/O" and/or "R/Bl".

NOTE:
Connector terminal position: (View from terminal side) For ABS check relay harness connector.

For combination meter harness connector G11.

90889G59

Fig. 70 Diagnostic chart C—ABS (AMBER) warning light off constantly, no DTC's stored

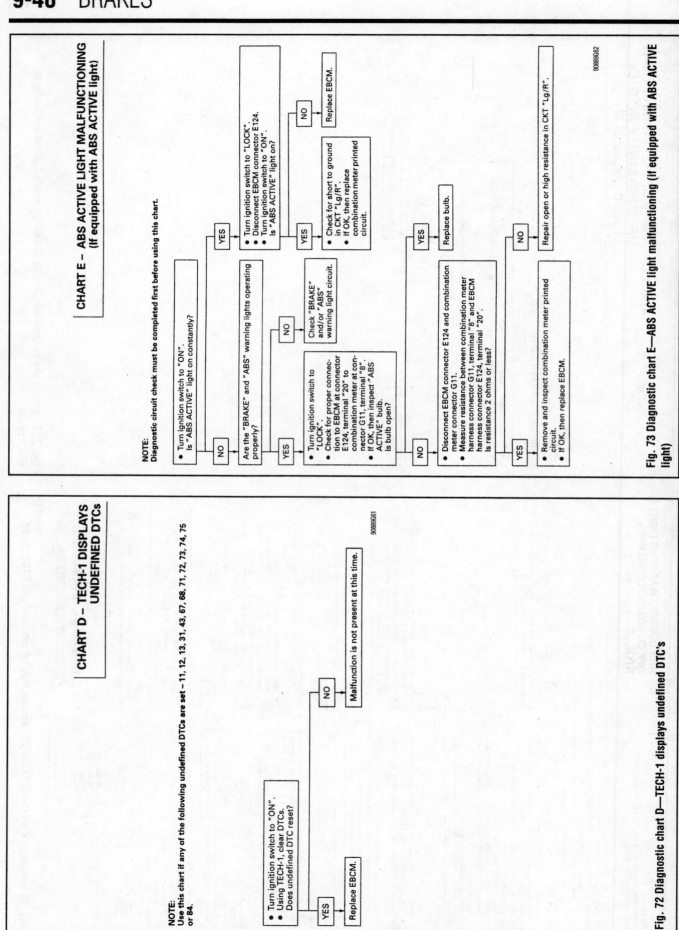

CHART E – ABS ACTIVE LIGHT MALFUNCTIONING
(If equipped with ABS ACTIVE light)

NOTE:
Diagnostic circuit check must be completed first before using this chart.

- Turn ignition switch to "ON".
  Is "ABS ACTIVE' light on constantly?

NO — Are the "BRAKE" and "ABS" warning lights operating properly?

NO — Check "BRAKE" and/or "ABS" warning light circuit.

YES —
- Turn ignition switch to "LOCK".
- Check for proper connection to EBCM at connector E124, terminal "20" to combination meter at connector G11, terminal "8".
- If OK, then inspect "ABS ACTIVE" bulb.
  Is bulb open?

YES — Replace bulb.

NO —
- Disconnect EBCM connector E124 and combination meter connector G11.
- Measure resistance between combination meter harness connector G11, terminal "8" and EBCM harness connector E124, terminal "20".
  Is resistance 2 ohms or less?

YES —
- Remove and inspect combination meter printed circuit.
- If OK, then replace EBCM.

NO — Repair open or high resistance in CKT "Lg/R".

YES —
- Turn ignition switch to "LOCK".
- Disconnect EBCM connector E124.
- Turn ignition switch to "ON".
  Is "ABS ACTIVE" light on?

NO — Replace EBCM.

YES —
- Check for short to ground in CKT "Lg/R".
- If OK, then replace combination meter printed circuit.

90889662

Fig. 73 Diagnostic chart E—ABS ACTIVE light malfunctioning (if equipped with ABS ACTIVE light)

CHART D – TECH-1 DISPLAYS UNDEFINED DTCs

NOTE:
Use this chart if any of the following undefined DTCs are set – 11, 12, 13, 31, 43, 67, 68, 71, 72, 73, 74, 75 or 84.

- Turn ignition switch to "ON".
- Using TECH-1, clear DTCs.
  Does undefined DTC reset?

YES — Replace EBCM.

NO — Malfunction is not present at this time.

90889661

Fig. 72 Diagnostic chart D—TECH-1 displays undefined DTC's

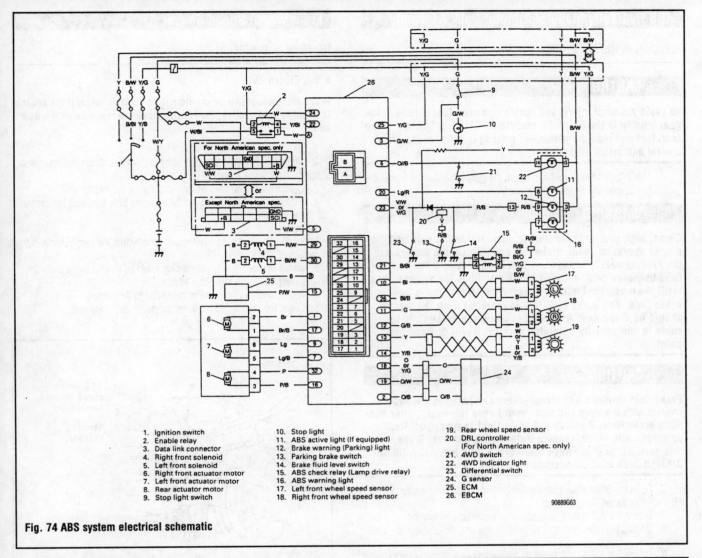

Fig. 74 ABS system electrical schematic

1. Ignition switch
2. Enable relay
3. Data link connector
4. Right front solenoid
5. Left front solenoid
6. Right front actuator motor
7. Left front actuator motor
8. Rear actuator motor
9. Stop light switch
10. Stop light
11. ABS active light (If equipped)
12. Brake warning (Parking) light
13. Parking brake switch
14. Brake fluid level switch
15. ABS check relay (Lamp drive relay)
16. ABS warning light
17. Left front wheel speed sensor
18. Right front wheel speed sensor
19. Rear wheel speed sensor
20. DRL controller
    (For North American spec. only)
21. 4WD switch
22. 4WD indicator light
23. Differential switch
24. G sensor
25. ECM
26. EBCM

90889G63

- **MODE F2: TROUBLE CODES**—In this test mode, trouble codes stored by the EBCM, both current ignition cycle and history, may be displayed or cleared.
- **MODE F3: ABS SNAPSHOT**—In this test mode, scan tool captures ABS data before and after a fault occurrence or a forced manual trigger.
- **MODE F4: ABS TESTS**—In this test mode, the scan tool performs hydraulic modulator functional tests to assist in problem isolation during troubleshooting. Included here is manual control of the motors which is used prior to bleeding the brake system.
- **MODE F5: MOTOR REHOME**—In this test mode, the scan tool commands the EBCM to rehome the motors on the hydraulic modulator assembly. This mode should always be used prior to bleeding the brake system.

ABS Enable/ABS Check Relays

REMOVAL & INSTALLATION

♦ **See Figure 75**

1. Disconnect the negative battery cable.
2. Remove the electronic brake control relay cover.
3. Detach the electronic brake control relay from the connector.

1. ABS enable relay
2. ABS check relay

90889G66

Fig. 75 The two ABS relays are mounted next to the hydraulic modulator assembly, in the engine compartment

To install:

4. Attach the electronic brake control relay to the connector.
5. Install the relay cover.
6. Connect the negative battery cable.

ABS Hydraulic Modulator/Motor Pack Assembly

REMOVAL & INSTALLATION

✳✳ CAUTION

To avoid personal injury, you must use a scan tool to relieve the gear tension in the hydraulic modulator. This is a function of the scan tool and must be performed prior to removal of the brake control and motor assembly.

1. Use a Tech 1® scan tool to perform the gear tension relief sequence.
2. Disconnect the negative battery cable.

✳✳ WARNING

Clean, high quality brake fluid is essential to the safe and proper operation of the brake system. You should always buy the highest quality brake fluid that is available. If the brake fluid becomes contaminated, drain and flush the system, then refill the master cylinder with new fluid. Never reuse any brake fluid. Any brake fluid that is removed from the system should be discarded. Also, do not allow any brake fluid to come in contact with a painted surface; it will damage the paint.

✳✳ CAUTION

Brake fluid contains polyglycol ethers and polyglycols. Avoid contact with the eyes and wash your hands thoroughly after handling brake fluid. If you do get brake fluid in your eyes, flush your eyes with clean, running water for 15 minutes. If eye irritation persists, or if you have taken brake fluid internally, IMMEDIATELY seek medical assistance

3. Drain the brake fluid from the fluid reservoir, master cylinder and ABS actuator assembly.
4. Detach the ABS brake solenoid valve electrical connectors.
5. Unplug the brake pressure differential warning switch electrical connector.
6. Detach the 6-way ABS brake motor pack electrical connector.
7. Wrap a shop towel around the hydraulic brake lines and disconnect the 5 brake lines (2 to master cylinder and 3 to wheel brakes) from the modulator. Do not let fluid to enter the bottom of the motor pack or electrical connectors.

➡**Cap the disconnected lines to prevent the loss of fluid and the entry of moisture and contaminants.**

8. Remove the clamps from the brake pipes.
9. Unfasten the ABS hydraulic modulator/motor pack assembly retaining bolts, then remove the ABS hydraulic modulator/motor pack assembly from the vehicle.

To install:

10. Position the ABS hydraulic modulator/motor pack assembly in the vehicle. Install the attaching bolt and tighten to 88 inch lbs. (10 Nm).
11. Uncap and connect the 5 brake pipes to the modulator assembly, then tighten the brake line fittings to 142 inch lbs. (16 Nm).
12. Attach the 6-way ABS brake motor pack electrical connector.
13. Plug in the brake pressure differential warning switch electrical connector.
14. Attach the 2 ABS brake solenoid valve electrical connectors.
15. Fill the master cylinder with new DOT 3 brake fluid.
16. Properly bleed the brake system.
17. Tighten the two brake combination valve tube nuts to 13 ft. lbs. (18 Nm) and the 3 hydraulic modulator tube nuts to 24 ft. lbs. (32 Nm).
18. Connect the negative battery cable.

Front Wheel Speed Sensor

REMOVAL & INSTALLATION

▶ **See Figure 76**

➡The front wheel sensor should not be disassembled; if the sensor is found to be defective, the sensor should be replaced with a new one.

1. Disconnect the negative battery cable.
2. Apply the parking brake, block the rear wheels, then raise and safely support the front of the vehicle on jackstands.
3. Detach the wiring harness connector from the sensor.
4. Remove the wheel speed sensor retaining bolt, then pull the sensor out of the steering knuckle.

To install:

5. Inspect the sensor for damage, especially that the sensor tooth is free of metal particles.
6. Install the sensor into the steering knuckle, then install and tighten the retaining bolt to 88 inch lbs. (10 Nm).
7. Reattach the wiring harness connector to the sensor.
8. Lower the vehicle, and connect the negative battery cable.

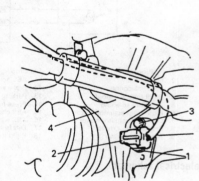

1. ABS wheel speed sensor
2. Connector
3. Bolt
4. Steering Knuckle

90889G67

Fig. 76 The front wheel speed sensors are mounted in the steering knuckles, as shown

Rear Wheel Speed Sensor (RWSS) Assembly

REMOVAL & INSTALLATION

▶ **See Figures 77 and 78**

The speed sensor is not serviceable and must replaced if malfunctioning. The sensor is mounted on the front face of the rear differential case.

1. Ensure that the ignition switch is **OFF**.
2. Block the front wheels, then raise and safely support the rear of the vehicle on jackstands.
3. Remove the sensor cover.
4. Detach the wiring harness connector from the sensor by gently prying outward on the connector plastic retaining tabs.
5. Remove the sensor retaining bolt, then pull the sensor out of the differential case.
6. Clean the sensor mounting surface on the differential case thoroughly.

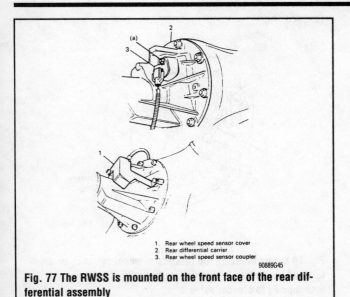

1. Rear wheel speed sensor cover
2. Rear differential carrier
3. Rear wheel speed sensor coupler

90889G45

Fig. 77 The RWSS is mounted on the front face of the rear differential assembly

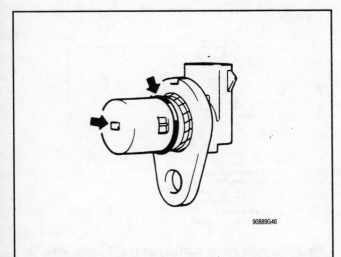

90889G46

Fig. 78 Inspect the Rear Wheel Speed Sensor (RWSS) O-ring for damage, and the RWSS tooth for metal particles

To install:

7. Prior to installation, inspect the O-ring for damage or deterioration. Replace the O-ring with a new one if any such damage is evident. Also, inspect the sensor tooth to be sure that it is free of any metal particles.

8. Apply sealant to the sensor, then insert the sensor into the differential case.

9. Install and tighten the sensor retaining bolt to 159–248 inch lbs. (18–28 Nm).

10. Reattch the wiring harness connector to the sensor, then install the sensor cover.

11. Lower the vehicle and remove the wheel blocks.

Electronic Brake Control Module (EBCM)

REMOVAL & INSTALLATION

▶ **See Figure 79**

1. Disconnect the negative battery cable.

2. Remove the fasteners on the lower steering column cover, then remove the cover.

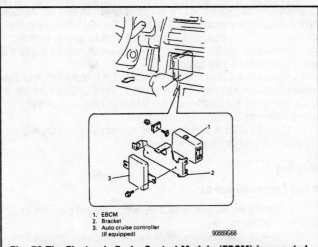

1. EBCM
2. Bracket
3. Auto cruise controller
   (If equipped)

90889G68

Fig. 79 The Electronic Brake Control Module (EBCM) is mounted under the center of the instrument panel, slightly toward the right

3. If equipped, remove the auto cruise controller.

4. Unfasten the wiring harness connector from the EBCM.

5. Remove the EBCM and bracket from under the instrument panel.

To install:

6. Reattach the wiring harness connector to the EBCM.

7. Position the EBCM and EBCM bracket into its mounting position.

8. Install the nut securing the bracket to the upper instrument panel and tighten to 18.5 ft. lbs. (25 Nm).

9. Install the lower steering column cover.

10. Connect the negative battery cable.

Bleeding the ABS System

❊❊ WARNING

Do NOT allow brake fluid to spill on or come in contact with the vehicle's finish as it will remove the paint. In case of a spill, immediately flush the area with water.

SYSTEM FILLING

The master cylinder reservoirs must be kept properly filled to prevent air from entering the system. No special filling procedures are required because of the anti-lock system.

When adding fluid, use only DOT 3 fluid; the use of DOT 5 or silicone fluids is specifically prohibited. Use of improper or contaminated fluid may cause the fluid to boil or cause the rubber components in the system to deteriorate. Never use any fluid with a petroleum base or any fluid which has been exposed to water or moisture.

SYSTEM BLEEDING

Before bleeding the ABS brake system, the front and rear displacement cylinder pistons must be returned to the topmost position. If brake related DTC's are present, the vehicle must be repaired and DTC's cleared before performing the motor rehome function.

Rehome Procedure

1. Raise and safely support the vehicle on jackstands so that the drive wheels are off the ground.

2. Start the engine, engage the transmission and run the vehicle above 3 mph (5 km/h) for at least 10 seconds.

3. Observe the ABS light on the instrument panel. Be sure that indicator light goes out after approximately 3 seconds. If the ABS light remains illuminated, the TECH-1 scan tool (or equivalent) must be used to diagnose the malfunction. If the ABS light goes out and stays off, stop the engine and repeat Steps 2 and 3 once again.

4. Using a Tech 1® or T-100® (CAMS), select "F5: Motor Rehome." The motor rehome function cannot be performed if current DTC's are present. If DTC's are present, the vehicle must be repaired and the codes cleared before performing the motor rehome function.

5. The entire brake system should now be bled using the manual bleeding procedures outlined later in this section.

Bleeding

♦ **See Figures 80 and 81**

1. Clean the master cylinder fluid reservoir cover and surrounding area, then remove the cover.

2. Add fluid, if necessary to obtain a proper fluid level, then put the reservoir cover back on.

3. Prime the ABS hydraulic modulator/master cylinder assembly as follows:

a. Attach a bleeder hose to bleeder valve (A) on the ABS hydraulic modulator, then submerge the opposite hose end in a clean container partially filled with clean brake fluid.

b. Slowly open bleeder valve (A) one half to one full turn.

c. Depress and hold the brake pedal until the fluid begins to flow.

d. Close the valve, then release the brake pedal.

e. Repeat Steps 3b–3d until no air bubbles are present.

f. Relocate the bleeder hose to bleeder valve (B), then repeat Steps 3a–3e.

4. Once the fluid is seen to flow from both modulator bleeder valves, the ABS modulator/master cylinder assembly is sufficiently full of fluid. However, it may not be completely purged of air. At this point, move to the wheel brakes and bleed them. This ensures that the lowest points in the system are completely free of air and then the assembly can purged of any remaining air.

5. Remove the fluid reservoir cover. Fill to the correct level, if necessary, then fasten the cover.

6. Raise and safely support the vehicle.

7. Proceed, as outlined in the following steps, to bleed the wheel brakes in the following sequence: left rear, right front, then left front.

a. Attach a clear plastic bleeder hose to the bleeder valve at the wheel, then submerge the opposite hose end in a clean container partially filled with clean brake fluid.

b. Open the bleeder valve.

c. Have an assistant slowly depress the brake pedal.

d. Close the valve and slowly release the release the brake pedal.

e. Wait 5 seconds.

f. Repeat Steps 7a–7e until the brake pedal feels firm at half travel and no air bubbles are observed in the bleeder hose. To assist in freeing the entrapped air, tap lightly on the caliper or braking plate to dislodge any trapped air bubbles.

8. Repeat Step 7 for the remaining brakes in the sequence given earlier.

9. Carefully lower the vehicle.

10. Remove the reservoir cover, then fill to the correct level with brake fluid and replace the cap.

11. Bleed the ABS hydraulic modulator as follows:

a. Attach a clear plastic bleeder hose to the rearward bleeder valve on the modulator, then submerge the opposite hose end in a clean container partially filled with clean brake fluid.

b. Have an assistant depress the brake pedal with moderate force.

c. Slowly open the rearward bleeder valve one half to one full turn, and allow the fluid to flow.

d. Close the valve, then slowly release the brake pedal.

e. Wait 5 seconds.

f. Repeat Steps 14b–14e until no air bubbles are present.

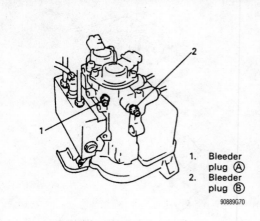

1. Bleeder plug Ⓐ
2. Bleeder plug Ⓑ

90889G70

Fig. 80 Before bleeding the calipers or wheel cylinder, be sure to bleed the hydraulic module, starting with bleeder valve A then moving to bleeder valve B

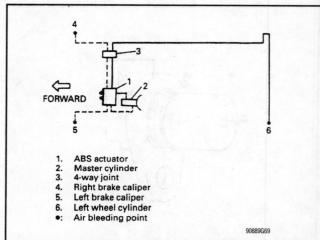

1. ABS actuator
2. Master cylinder
3. 4-way joint
4. Right brake caliper
5. Left brake caliper
6. Left wheel cylinder
●: Air bleeding point

90889G69

Fig. 81 The brake system must be bled at all 5 points, in the following order: Hydraulic Module (HM) valve A, HM valve B, left rear, right front, left front

g. Relocate the bleeder hose to the forward hydraulic modulator bleeder valve, then repeat Steps 11a–11f.

12. Check the brake fluid and add if necessary. Don't forget to put the reservoir cap back on.

13. With the ignition turned to the **RUN** position, apply the brake pedal with moderate force and hold it. Note the pedal travel and feel. If the pedal feels firm and constant and the pedal travel is not excessive, start the engine. With the engine running, recheck the pedal travel. If it's still firm and constant and pedal travel is not excessive, go to the next step.

14. If the pedal feels soft or has excessive travel either initially or after the engine is started, the following procedure may be used:

a. With the Tech 1® scan tool, "release" then "apply" each ABS motor 2–3 times and cycle each ABS solenoid 5–10 times. When finished, be sure to "apply" the front and rear motors on the ABS hydraulic modulator. This will ensure all trapped air has been removed from the hydraulic modulator bores.

b. Repeat the bleeding procedure, starting with Step 1.

15. Road test the vehicle. Make several normal (non-ABS) stops and from a moderate speed to be sure the brakes are operating properly.

4-WHEEL ANTI-LOCK BRAKE SYSTEM—SIDEKICK SPORT

General Information

▶ **See Figures 82 and 83**

The 4-wheel Anti-lock Brake System (ABS) used on Sidekick Sport models controls the fluid pressure applied to each wheel from the master cylinder so that the wheels will not lock even during hard braking. The 4-wheel ABS consists of the following components:

- Four wheel speed sensors (one at each wheel)
- ABS control module
- ABS hydraulic unit
- Fail-safe (solenoid valve) relay
- Pump motor relay
- ABS warning light
- G sensor

The wheel speed sensors detect wheel rotation, and sends this information to the ABS control module. The ABS control module receives this incoming signal, and a signal from the G sensor, and operates the ABS hydraulic unit to prevent wheel lock up.

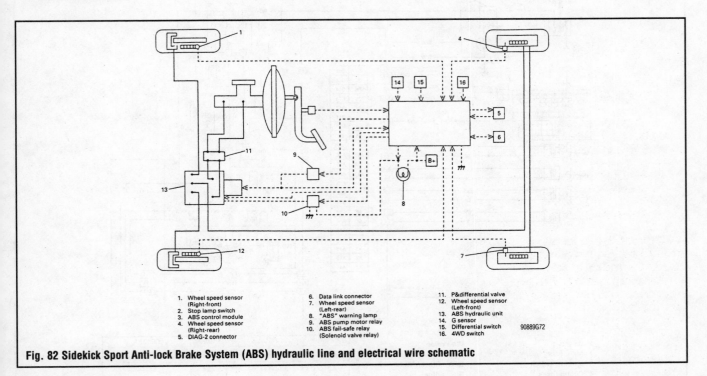

1. Wheel speed sensor (Right-front)
2. Stop lamp switch
3. ABS control module
4. Wheel speed sensor (Right-rear)
5. DIAG-2 connector
6. Data link connector
7. Wheel speed sensor (Left-rear)
8. "ABS" warning lamp
9. ABS pump motor relay
10. ABS fail-safe relay (Solenoid valve relay)
11. P&differential valve
12. Wheel speed sensor (Left-front)
13. ABS hydraulic unit
14. G sensor
15. Differential switch
16. 4WD switch

90889G72

Fig. 82 Sidekick Sport Anti-lock Brake System (ABS) hydraulic line and electrical wire schematic

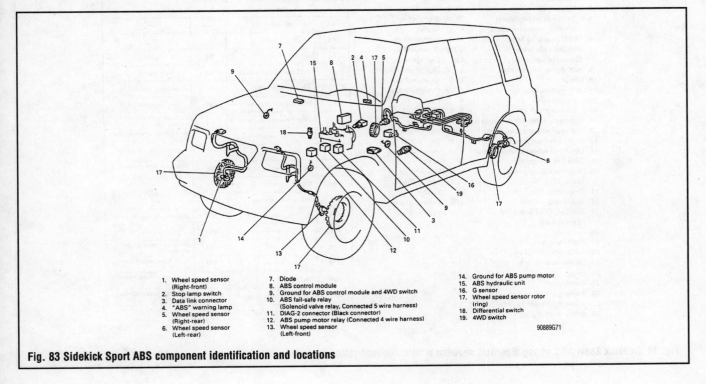

1. Wheel speed sensor (Right-front)
2. Stop lamp switch
3. Data link connector
4. "ABS" warning lamp
5. Wheel speed sensor (Right-rear)
6. Wheel speed sensor (Left-rear)
7. Diode
8. ABS control module
9. Ground for ABS control module and 4WD switch
10. ABS fail-safe relay (Solenoid valve relay, Connected 5 wire harness)
11. DIAG-2 connector (Black connector)
12. ABS pump motor relay (Connected 4 wire harness)
13. Wheel speed sensor (Left-front)
14. Ground for ABS pump motor
15. ABS hydraulic unit
16. G sensor
17. Wheel speed sensor rotor (ring)
18. Differential switch
19. 4WD switch

90889G71

Fig. 83 Sidekick Sport ABS component identification and locations

The ABS hydraulic unit controls the brake fluid pressure applied to each of the four wheels, to prevent wheel lock up.

The fail-safe relay supplies power to the solenoid valve in the ABS hydraulic unit and pump motor relay. The pump motor relay supplies power to the pump motor in the ABS hydraulic unit.

The ABS warning light is located in the instrument t cluster and informs the driver of any detected abnormality in the ABS system.

The G sensor detects vehicle deceleration, and provides this information to the ABS control module.

Testing and Diagnosis

♦ See Figure 84

The ABS Control Module (ABS CM) is programmed with a self-diagnostic routine, which constantly monitors the ABS components for problems or erratic behavior. If such a problem or behavior is noted, the control module saves a corresponding Diagnostic Trouble Code (DTC). The DTC, when retrieved, indicates in which component AND circuit the problem lies.

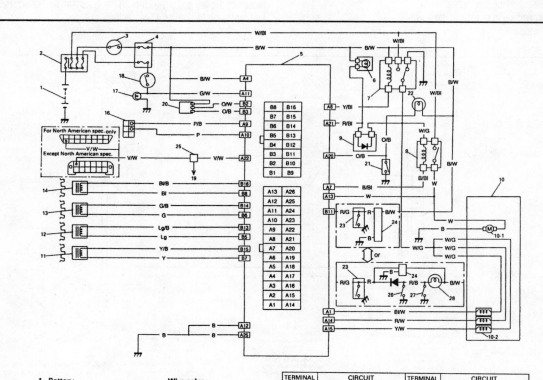

1. Battery
2. Main fuses
3. Ignition switch
4. Circuit fuses
5. ABS control module
5-1. Terminal arrangement for ABS control module
6. "ABS" warning lamp
7. ABS fail-safe relay (Solenoid valve relay)
8. ABS pump motor relay
9. Diode
10. ABS hydraulic unit
10-1. Pump motor
10-2. Solenoid valves
11. Right-rear wheel speed sensor
12. Left-rear wheel speed sensor
13. Right-front wheel speed sensor
14. Left-front wheel speed sensor
15. Data link connector
16. Diagnosis-2 connector (DIAG-2)
17. Stop lamp
18. Stop lamp switch
19. To ECM, TCM and SDM (if equipped)
20. G sensor
21. 4WD switch
22. 4WD indicator lamp
23. Differential switch
24. Filter
25. Connector
26. Parking brake switch
27. Brake fluid level switch
28. Brake warning (parking) light

Wire color

B : Black
B/W : Black/White
Bl : Blue
Bl/B : Blue/Black
Bl/W : Blue/White
G : Green
G/B : Green/Black
G/W : Green/White
Lg : Lightgreen
Lg/B : Lightgreen/Black
O/B : Orange/Black
O/W : Orange/White
P : Pink
P/B : Pink/Black
R/Bl : Red/Blue
R/G : Red/Green
R/W : Red/White
V/W : Violet/White
W : White
W/Bl : White/Blue
W/G : White/Green
Y : Yellow
Y/B : Yellow/Black
Y/Bl : Yellow/Blue

TERMINAL	CIRCUIT	TERMINAL	CIRCUIT
A1	Left-front solenoid valve	A23	———
A2		A24	
A3	———	A25	Ground
A4	Ignition switch	A26	———
A5			
A6		B1	
A7	ABS pump motor relay	B2	G sensor signal
A8	ABS fail-safe relay	B3	G sensor ground
A9	Diagnosis switch terminal	B4	———
A10	Diagnosis output terminal	B5	Left-rear wheel speed sensor (−)
A11	Stop lamp switch	B6	Right-front wheel speed sensor (−)
A12	Ground	B7	Right-rear wheel speed sensor (−)
A13	Motor voltage monitor	B8	Left-front wheel speed sensor (−)
A14	Right-front solenoid valve	B9	———
A15	Rear solenoid valve	B10	
A16		B11	Differential switch
A17	———	B12	
A18	———	B13	Left-rear wheel speed sensor (+)
A19	———	B14	Right-front wheel speed sensor (+)
A20	4WD switch	B15	Right-rear wheel speed sensor (+)
A21	"ABS" warning lamp	B16	Left-front wheel speed sensor (+)
A22	Data link connector		

90889G77

Fig. 84 Sidekick Sport ABS wiring diagram, showing terminal identification for testing

Remember that the problem may not be in the component, rather in its circuit. Therefore, it is just as important to inspect the component's circuit as it is to inspect the component itself.

The driver of the vehicle is alerted whenever the ABS CM stores such a DTC: the ABS warning light illuminates during vehicle operation. Normally the warning light should illuminate for approximately 2 seconds when the ignition switch is turned **ON**, after which the light should turn off. If the light stays on after the 2 seconds, or if during driving, the light illuminates, the ABS CM has detected a problem and stored a DTC.

ABS WARNING LAMP CHECK

▶ **See Figure 85**

Turn the ignition switch **ON** and observe the warning light. The light should turn off after 2 seconds. If the light does not turn on at all refer to the accompanying ABS light inspection chart.

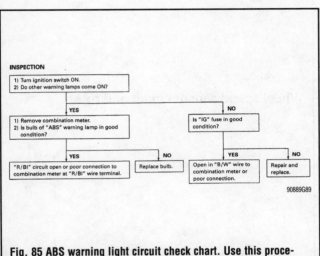

Fig. 85 ABS warning light circuit check chart. Use this procedure when the warning light does not turn on when the ignition switch is turned ON

READING DIAGNOSTIC TROUBLE CODES (DTC)

ABS Warning Light Method

▶ **See Figures 86, 87 and 88**

1. Locate the DIAG-2 connector, mounted next to the hydraulic unit in the engine compartment.
2. Use a jumper wire to connect the diag. switch terminal to ground.
3. Turn the ignition switch **ON**.
4. Read and note the flashes of the warning light. Each of the DTC's is composed of two digits, which are represented by the warning light as flashes. Therefore, a code 21 would be comprised of two flashes close together, then one flash after a one second pause. Each code is flashed three times in a row (separated by 3 second pauses), then the control module flashes the next code (if another one is stored).

➡ **If the DTC No. 12 is flashed, this indicates that the system is functioning normally. If your warning light indicates that a DTC was stored, there may be a problem with the warning light circuit.**

Scan Tool (TECH-1) Method

A scan tool can be used to read the DTC's for your ABS system. Follow the scan tool manufacturer's instructions to properly read the DTC's.

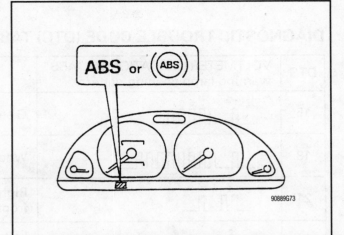

Fig. 86 The ABS warning light is located in the instrument cluster, and illuminates when the ABS computer stores a trouble code

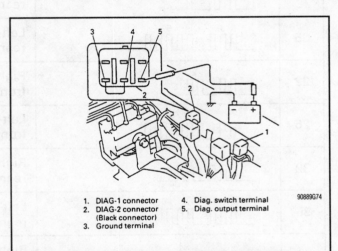

1. DIAG-1 connector
2. DIAG-2 connector (Black connector)
3. Ground terminal
4. Diag. switch terminal
5. Diag. output terminal

Fig. 87 Use a jumper wire to ground the Diag. Switch terminal of the DIAG-2 connector to a good ground. This enables the ABS warning light to flash out any stored codes

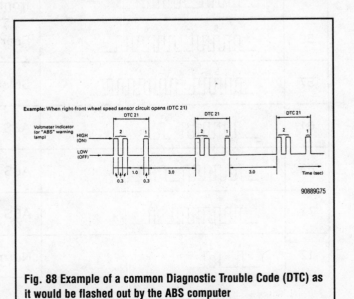

Fig. 88 Example of a common Diagnostic Trouble Code (DTC) as it would be flashed out by the ABS computer

DIAGNOSTIC TROUBLE CODE (DTC) TABLE

DTC	VOLTMETER INDICATION (or "ABS" warning lamp flashing pattern)	DIAGNOSTIC AREA	
15		G sensor (if equipped) or ABS control module	
18		Wheel speed sensor and/or rotor or hydraulic unit	
21		Right-front	Wheel speed sensor circuit and rotor
25		Left-front	
31		Right-rear	
35		Left-rear	
22		Right-front	
26		Left-front	
32		Right-rear	
36		Left-rear	
41		Right-front	Solenoid (in hydraulic unit) circuit
45		Left-front	
56		Rear	
57		Solenoid and pump motor power circuit	
61		ABS pump motor (in hydraulic unit) circuit	
63		ABS fail-safe relay circuit	
71		ABS control module	
12		Normal	

90889G76

CLEARING DIAGNOSTIC TROUBLE CODES (DTC)

To clear any stored DTC's after the repairs or service has been performed, do the following:

1. Check the part supply No. on your ABS control module. If the part No. is 33940–77E00, skip to Step 4. If the ABS CM No. is 33940–77E01, proceed to the next step.

2. If DTC's 21, 22, 25, 26, 31, 32, 35, or 36 existed prior to repairing the component or circuit, proceed to the next step. Otherwise, skip to Step 4.

3. Drive the vehicle between 6.5–12.5 mph (10–20 km/h), then stop the vehicle and turn the ignition switch **OFF**. The ABS warning light should turn off at this point; if it does not, there are DTC's still stored in the ABS CM, or there is a circuit problem with the warning light. Proceed to the next step, if the warning light turned off.

4. If not already done, turn the ignition switch **OFF**.

5. Using a jumper wire, connect the diag. switch terminal of the DIAG-2 connector to the diag. output terminal.

6. Turn the ignition switch **ON**, and leave it **ON** for at least 10 seconds.

7. Perform the DTC reading procedure to ensure that only DTC No. 12 (system normal) is indicated by the ABS warning light.

➡ **If you have any continued problems, have the system inspected by a qualified automotive technician with ABS training. The brake system is a very important system to maintain at optimum performance to avoid an accident.**

ABS Hydraulic Unit

REMOVAL & INSTALLATION

▶ **See Figure 89**

> ✳✳ **WARNING**
>
> **Clean, high quality brake fluid is essential to the safe and proper operation of the brake system. You should always buy the highest quality brake fluid that is available. If the brake fluid becomes contaminated, drain and flush the system, then refill the master cylinder with new fluid. Never reuse any brake fluid. Any brake fluid that is removed from the system should be discarded. Also, do not allow any brake fluid to come in contact with a painted surface; it will damage the paint.**

> ✳✳ **CAUTION**
>
> **Brake fluid contains polyglycol ethers and polyglycols. Avoid contact with the eyes and wash your hands thoroughly after handling brake fluid. If you do get brake fluid in your eyes, flush your eyes with clean, running water for 15 minutes. If eye irritation persists, or if you have taken brake fluid internally, IMMEDIATELY seek medical assistance**

1. Disconnect the negative battery cable.

2. Use a special wrench (such as Suzuki tool 09950–78210) to loosen the brake fluid lines from the hydraulic unit, then plug the brake lines to prevent fluid loss or fluid contamination.

3. Detach the wiring harness connectors from the unit.

4. Remove the three retaining nuts, then lift the unit from the mounting bracket.

> ✳✳ **WARNING**
>
> **Do not subject the unit to sudden impacts, do not allow dust to enter the unit, and do not set the hydraulic unit on its side or upside down. Handling it in these ways will result in unit damage.**

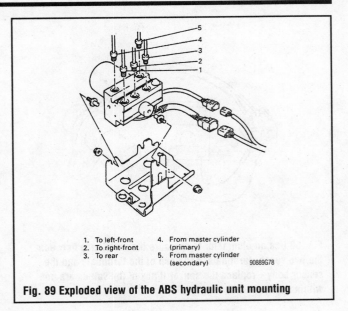

1. To left-front
2. To right-front
3. To rear
4. From master cylinder (primary)
5. From master cylinder (secondary)

90889G78

Fig. 89 Exploded view of the ABS hydraulic unit mounting

To install:

5. Position the unit in the mounting bracket, then install the retaining nuts. Tighten the nuts to 186 inch lbs. (21 Nm).

6. Reattch the brake fluid lines to the hydraulic unit, ensuring that the lines are attached to their original ports on the unit. Tighten the brake line fittings to 141 inch lbs. (16 Nm).

7. Reattach the wiring harness connectors to the unit.

8. Connect the negative battery cable.

9. Bleed the hydraulic brake system, as described earlier in this section. (This ABS system is bled in the same manner as the same vehicle not equipped with the ABS system.)

ABS Control Module (ABS CM)

REMOVAL & INSTALLATION

> ✳✳ **WARNING**
>
> **The ABS Control Module (ABS CM) is designed with precision parts, therefore do not expose the module to shocks.**

1. Disconnect the negative battery cable.

2. Remove the lower steering column cover.

3. Detach the wiring harness connectors from the ABS CM.

4. Remove the ABS CM retaining bolts, then remove the module from beneath the instrument panel.

To install:

5. Install the module under the instrument panel, then install the retaining bolts snugly.

6. Reattach the wiring harness connectors to the module.

7. Install the lower steering column cover.

8. Connect the negative battery cable.

Front Wheel Speed Sensor

INSPECTION

▶ **See Figures 90 and 91**

1. Remove the sensor from the steering knuckle. Inspect the sensor for physical damage, such as cracks or missing pieces. If any such damage is evident, replace the sensor with a new one.

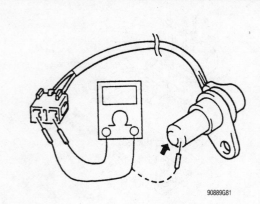

Fig. 90 Use an ohmmeter to measure the resistance between the two sensor terminals, and each of the terminals and the sensor body—replace the sensor if any of the values are not within specifications

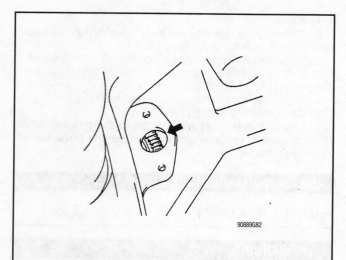

Fig. 91 Also be sure to inspect the sensor wheel teeth for damage, such as missing teeth or cracks

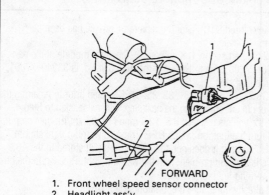

1. Front wheel speed sensor connector
2. Headlight ass'y.

Fig. 92 The front wheel sensor wiring harness connectors are located near the front headlight assemblies

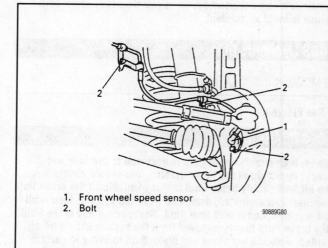

1. Front wheel speed sensor
2. Bolt

Fig. 93 The wheel sensors themselves are mounted in the front steering knuckles

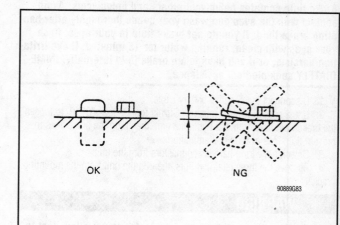

Fig. 94 When installing the sensors, ensure that the sensor mounting tab is not bent—if it is bent, replace the sensor with a new one

2. Using a Digital Volt-Ohmmeter (DVOM), set to the ohmmeter function, measure the resistance between the sensor terminals, which should be 1.2–1.6 kilohms at 68°F (20°C). If the resistance is not as specified, replace the sensor with a new one.

3. Measure the resistance between each sensor terminal and the sensor metal body, which should be 1 megohm or more. If the resistance is not as specified, replace the sensor with a new one.

4. Install the sensor in the steering knuckle.

REMOVAL & INSTALLATION

▶ **See Figures 92, 93 and 94**

➡The front wheel sensor should not be disassembled; if the sensor is found to be defective, the sensor should be replaced with a new one.

1. Disconnect the negative battery cable.
2. Loosen all of the front wheel lug nuts ½ turn.
3. Apply the parking brake, block the rear wheels, then raise and safely support the front of the vehicle on jackstands.
4. Remove the front wheel(s).
5. Detach the wiring harness connector from the sensor.

6. Remove the wheel speed sensor retaining bolt, then pull the sensor out of the steering knuckle.

To install:

7. Inspect the sensor and rotor for damage, especially that the sensor and rotor teeth are free of metal particles.

8. Install the sensor into the steering knuckle, then install and tighten the retaining bolt to 88 inch lbs. (10 Nm).

9. Reattach the wiring harness connector to the sensor.

10. Install the front wheel(s).

11. Lower the vehicle, and connect the negative battery cable.

12. Fully tighten the front wheel lug nuts.

Rear Wheel Speed Sensor

INSPECTION

▶ **See Figure 95**

1. Remove the sensor from the rear axle. Inspect the sensor for physical damage, such as cracks or missing pieces. If any such damage is evident, replace the sensor with a new one.

2. Using a Digital Volt-Ohmmeter (DVOM), set to the ohmmeter function, measure the resistance between the sensor terminals, which should be 1.2–1.6 kilohms at 68°F (20°C). If the resistance is not as specified, replace the sensor with a new one.

3. Measure the resistance between each sensor terminal and the sensor metal body, which should be 1 megohm or more. If the resistance is not as specified, replace the sensor with a new one.

4. Install the sensor in the rear axle.

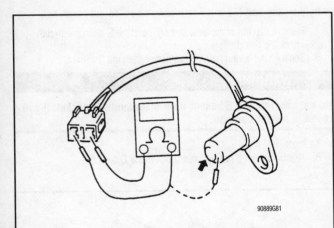

Fig. 95 Use an ohmmeter to measure the resistance between the two sensor terminals, and each of the terminals and the sensor body—replace the sensor if any of the values are not within specifications

REMOVAL & INSTALLATION

▶ **See Figure 96**

➡**The rear wheel sensor should not be disassembled; if the sensor is found to be defective, the sensor should be replaced with a new one.**

1. Disconnect the negative battery cable.

2. Block the front wheels, then raise and safely support the rear of the vehicle on jackstands.

3. Detach the wiring harness connector from the sensor.

4. Remove the wheel speed sensor retaining bolt, then pull the sensor out of the axle.

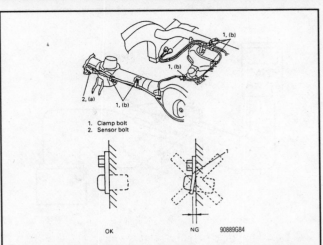

Fig. 96 The rear wheel speed sensors are mounted at either end of the rear axle assembly—during installation, ensure that the sensor mounting tab is not bent, otherwise replace the sensor

1. Clamp bolt
2. Sensor bolt

To install:

5. Inspect the sensor and rotor for damage, especially that the sensor and rotor teeth are free of metal particles.

6. Install the sensor into the rear axle, then install and tighten the retaining bolt to 186 inch lbs. (21 Nm).

7. Reattach the wiring harness connector to the sensor.

8. Lower the vehicle, and connect the negative battery cable.

ABS Fail-Safe/ABS Pump Motor Relays

INSPECTION

▶ **See Figures 97 and 98**

1. Remove the relay from the vehicle.

2. Using a Digital Volt-Ohmmeter (DVOM), set to the ohmmeter function, measure the resistance between relay terminals 1 and 3, terminals 2 and 5, and terminals 4 and 5. The resistance between terminals 1 and 3 should be 70–90 ohms at 68°F (20°C). The resistance between terminals 2 and 5 should register as zero ohms, or continuity. The resistance

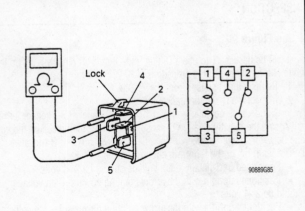

Fig. 97 Measure the resistance between the specified terminals of the relay—if the resistance values were not as specified, replace the relay with a new one

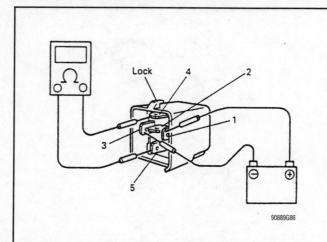

Fig. 98 Apply 12 volt DC current to terminals 1 and 3, then measure for continuity between terminals 4 and 5—if there is no continuity, replace the relay with a new one

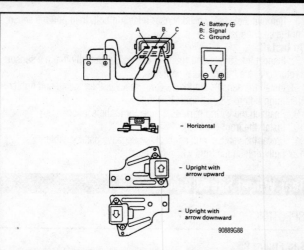

Fig. 99 To test the G sensor, measure the terminal resistance in all three positions (as shown)—if the values were not as specified, replace the sensor with a new one

between terminals 4 and 5 should indicate no continuity, or infinite ohms. If the resistance is not as specified, replace the relay with a new one.

3. Connect a 12 volt DC battery to relay terminal 1 (battery positive) and terminal 3 (battery negative), then measure the resistance between terminals 4 and 5 again. There should now be continuity (zero ohms) between these two terminals. If the resistance is not as specified, replace the relay with a new one.

4. Install the relay in the vehicle.

REMOVAL & INSTALLATION

1. Disconnect the negative battery cable.
2. If applicable, remove the relay cover.
3. Detach the relay from the connector.
To install:
4. Attach the relay to the connector.
5. If necessary, install the relay cover.
6. Connect the negative battery cable.

G Sensor

INSPECTION

▶ **See Figure 99**

It will be necessary to use a Digital Volt-Ohmmeter (DVOM), set on the voltmeter function, for this procedure.

1. Remove the G sensor from the vehicle.
2. Inspect the G sensor bracket for bends.
3. Connect the positive lead of a 12 volt DC battery to G sensor terminal A, and the negative lead to G sensor terminal C, then measure the voltage between sensor terminals B (positive DVOM lead) and C (negative DVOM lead) under the following circumstances:

• Positioned horizontally—teh voltage should be 2–3 volts
• Positioned upright with the arrow pointing upward—teh voltage should be 3–4 volts
• Positioned upright with the arrow pointing downward—teh voltage should be 1–2 volts

If the voltage was not as specified, replace the G sensor with a new one.

4. Install the G sensor.

REMOVAL & INSTALLATION

▶ **See Figure 100**

1. Turn the ignition switch **OFF**.
2. Disconnect the negative battery cable.
3. Remove the rear center console from the inside of the vehicle.

➡ **Only loosen bolt (B) in the following step—do not remove it.**

4. Remove parking brake lever bolts (A) and the G sensor with the bracket from the vehicle floor.
5. Separate the wiring harness connector from the G sensor.

✳✳ WARNING

Do not separate the G sensor from the mounting bracket; it will result in sensor damage.

To install:
6. Attach the wiring harness connector to the G sensor.

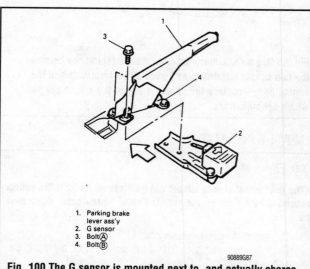

1. Parking brake lever ass'y
2. G sensor
3. Bolt(A)
4. Bolt(B)

Fig. 100 The G sensor is mounted next to, and actually shares two mounting bolts with, the parking brake handle

7. Install the parking brake lever bolts (A) and the G sensor with the bracket.
8. Install the rear center console.
9. Connect the negative battery cable.

Bleeding the ABS System

The ABS system used with Sidekick Sport models is bled the same as Sidekick Sport models without ABS. Please refer to the bleeding procedure earlier in this section.

BRAKE SPECIFICATIONS

All measurements in inches unless noted

Year	Model	Master Cylinder Bore	Brake Disc			Brake Drum Diameter			Min. Lining Thickness ①	
			Original Thickness	Min. Thickness	Max. Run-out	Original Inside Diameter	Max. Wear Limit	Max. Machine Diameter	Front	Rear
1986	Samurai	NA	0.394	0.334	0.006	8.66	8.74	8.74	0.236	0.120
1987	Samurai	NA	0.394	0.334	0.006	8.66	8.74	8.74	0.236	0.120
1988	Samurai	NA	0.394	0.334	0.006	8.66	8.74	8.74	0.236	0.120
1989	Samurai	NA	0.394	0.334	0.006	8.66	8.74	8.74	0.236	0.120
	Sidekick	NA	0.394	0.315	0.006	8.66	8.74	8.74	0.315	0.120
	Tracker	NA	0.394	0.315	0.006	8.66	8.74	8.74	0.315	0.120
1990	Samurai	NA	0.394	0.334	0.006	8.66	8.74	8.74	0.236	0.120
	Sidekick	NA	0.394	0.315	0.006	8.66	8.74	8.74	0.315	0.120
	Tracker	NA	0.394	0.315	0.006	8.66	8.74	8.74	0.315	0.120
1991	Samurai	NA	0.394	0.334	0.006	8.66	8.74	8.74	0.236	0.120
	Sidekick	NA	0.394	0.315	0.006	8.66	8.74	8.74	0.315	0.120
	Tracker	NA	0.394	0.315	0.006	8.66	8.74	8.74	0.315	0.120
1992	Samurai	NA	0.394	0.334	0.006	8.66	8.74	8.74	0.236	0.120
	Sidekick ②	NA	0.394	0.315	0.006	8.66	8.74	8.74	0.315	0.120
	Sidekick ③	NA	0.669	0.591	0.006	10.00	10.07	10.07	0.315	0.120
	Tracker	NA	0.394	0.315	0.006	8.66	8.74	8.74	0.315	0.120
1993	Samurai	NA	0.394	0.334	0.006	8.66	8.74	8.74	0.236	0.120
	Sidekick ②	NA	0.394	0.315	0.006	8.66	8.74	8.74	0.315	0.120
	Sidekick ③	NA	0.669	0.591	0.006	10.00	10.07	10.07	0.315	0.120
	Tracker	NA	0.394	0.315	0.006	8.66	8.74	8.74	0.315	0.120
1994	Samurai	NA	0.394	0.334	0.006	8.66	8.74	8.74	0.236	0.120
	Sidekick ②	NA	0.669	0.591	0.006	10.00	10.07	10.07	0.315	0.120
	Sidekick ③	NA	0.669	0.591	0.006	10.00	10.07	10.07	0.315	0.120
	Tracker	NA	0.394	0.315	0.006	8.66	8.74	8.74	0.315	0.120
1995	Samurai	NA	0.394	0.334	0.006	8.66	8.74	8.74	0.236	0.120
	Sidekick ②	NA	0.669	0.591	0.006	10.00	10.07	10.07	0.315	0.120
	Sidekick ③	NA	0.669	0.591	0.006	10.00	10.07	10.07	0.315	0.120
	Tracker	NA	0.394	0.315	0.006	8.66	8.74	8.74	0.315	0.120
1996	X-90	NA	0.394	0.315	0.006	8.66	8.74	8.74	0.240	0.120
	Sidekick ②	NA	0.394	0.315	0.006	8.66	8.74	8.74	0.240	0.120
	Sidekick ③	NA	0.670	0.590	0.006	10.00	10.07	10.07	0.295	0.120
	Sidekick Sport	NA	0.866	0.787	0.006	10.00	10.07	10.07	0.275	0.120
	Tracker ②	NA	0.394	0.315	0.006	8.66	8.74	8.74	0.240	0.120
	Tracker ③	NA	0.670	0.590	0.006	10.00	10.07	10.07	0.295	0.120

90889C00

BRAKE SPECIFICATIONS

All measurements in inches unless noted

Year	Model	Master Cylinder Bore	Brake Disc			Brake Drum Diameter			Min. Lining Thickness ①	
			Original Thickness	Min. Thickness	Max. Run-out	Original Inside Diameter	Max. Wear Limit	Max. Machine Diameter	Front	Rear
1997	X-90	NA	0.394	0.315	0.006	8.66	8.74	8.74	0.240	0.120
	Sidekick ②	NA	0.394	0.315	0.006	8.66	8.74	8.74	0.240	0.120
	Sidekick ③	NA	0.670	0.590	0.006	10.00	10.07	10.07	0.295	0.120
	Sidekick Sport	NA	0.866	0.787	0.006	10.00	10.07	10.07	0.275	0.120
	Tracker ②	NA	0.394	0.315	0.006	8.66	8.74	8.74	0.240	0.120
	Tracker ③	NA	0.670	0.590	0.006	10.00	10.07	10.07	0.295	0.120
1998	X-90	NA	0.394	0.315	0.006	8.66	8.74	8.74	0.240	0.120
	Sidekick ②	NA	0.394	0.315	0.006	8.66	8.74	8.74	0.240	0.120
	Sidekick ③	NA	0.670	0.590	0.006	10.00	10.07	10.07	0.295	0.120
	Sidekick Sport	NA	0.866	0.787	0.006	10.00	10.07	10.07	0.275	0.120
	Tracker ②	NA	0.394	0.315	0.006	8.66	8.74	8.74	0.240	0.120
	Tracker ③	NA	0.670	0.590	0.006	10.00	10.07	10.07	0.295	0.120

① This measurement includes the shoe/pad lining material as well as the backing plate.
② 2-door models only.
③ 4-door models only.

90889C01

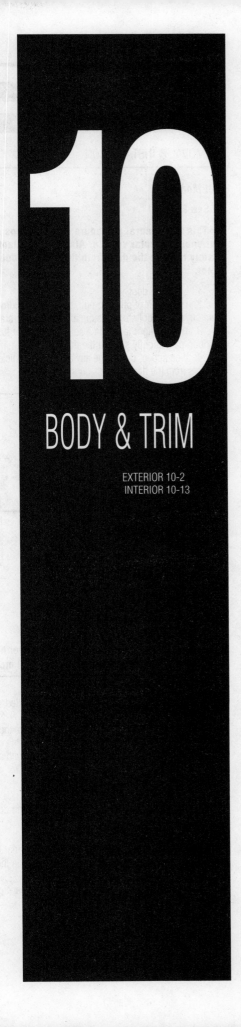

10
BODY & TRIM

EXTERIOR 10-2
INTERIOR 10-13

EXTERIOR

Front and Rear Doors

REMOVAL & INSTALLATION

All Models

▶ **See Figure 1**

➡This is a general procedure; certain steps may need alteration for your particular vehicle. Also, an assistant is required to safely remove the door from the vehicle, due to the weight of the door.

1. Open the door.
2. Use a pair of pliers to pull, or a mallet to drive, the retaining pin up and out of the door stopper strap and door pillar bracket.
3. Using a floor jack with a soft-faced pad or folded towel on the jack support pad, slightly support the door.
4. If equipped, disengage any applicable vehicle wiring harness connectors from the door harness connectors.

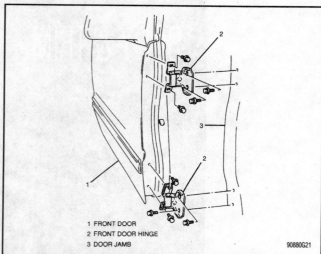

1 FRONT DOOR
2 FRONT DOOR HINGE
3 DOOR JAMB

90880G21

Fig. 1 Exploded view of the upper and lower hinge mounting— Sidekick, Tracker, Sidekick Sport and X-90 models

5. If the original door is going to be reinstalled, matchmark the hinges to the door.
6. Remove the hinge-to-door retaining bolts, then carefully lift the door away from the vehicle.
7. If the front door is going to be replaced with another door, transfer the following components to the new door:
  • Front door trim panel and watershield
  • Door lock and door latch
  • Window regulator, equalizer arm bracket and door glass
  • Door wiring harness
To install:
8. Using your assistant's help, support the door on the padded floor jack and maneuver it close to the vehicle. Position the door so that the hinges can be situated against the door.
9. Install the door hinge retaining bolts finger-tight.

10. Align the door in the door opening, as described later in this section.
11. Tighten the hinge-to-door bolts securely.
12. Reattach all applicable wiring harness connectors.
13. Reinstall the retaining pin so that the door stopper strap is properly engaged with the door pillar bracket.
14. Carefully close and open the door to ensure that it is properly aligned to the body.

ADJUSTMENT

▶ **See Figures 2, 3, 4 and 5**

The door hinges allow sufficient movement to correct most door misalignment conditions. The hinge mounting holes are elongated to provide movement for door alignment.

➡**Never attempt to remedy door misalignment solely by repositioning the latch striker.**

1. To adjust the up-down position of the entire door, or to adjust the in-out position of the front edge of the door, perform the following:
  a. Determine which hinge bolts are to be loosened and back them out just enough to allow movement.
  b. Move the door safely by using a padded pry bar to correct the misalignment condition. When the door is in the proper position, tighten the bolts securely, then check door operation. There should be no binding or other interference when the door is either closed or opened.
  c. Repeat sub-steps 1a and 1b until the door is properly aligned in the door opening. The gap between the edge of the door and the body should be uniform all around the door's perimeter.
2. To adjust the in-out position of the rear edge of the door, perform the following:
  a. Loosen the door latch striker mounting screws, then position the striker up and down until the center of the striker is aligned with the center of groove C on the door latch.
  b. Move the striker in or out so that the door will be flush with the body metal when closed.
  c. If it is necessary to move the striker fore or aft, add or remove

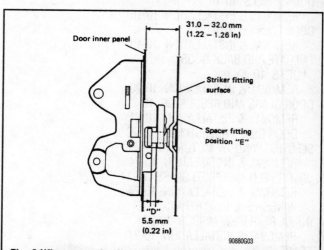

Door inner panel

31.0 – 32.0 mm
(1.22 – 1.26 in)

Striker fitting surface

Spacer fitting position "E"

"D"

5.5 mm
(0.22 in)

90880G03

Fig. 2 When properly aligned, the distance between the door edge and the door pillar surface should be 1.22–1.26 in. (31–32mm)—Samurai models

To fine-tune the striker position, loosen the mounting screws, then move the striker as necessary

90880P03

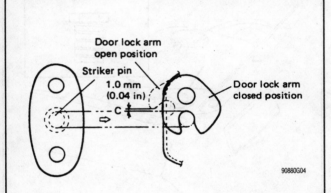

Fig. 3 The striker should be positioned so that the clearance (C) between the top of the striker bar and the bottom edge of the door lock arm (when the door is open) is 0.04 in. (1mm)— Samurai models

90880G04

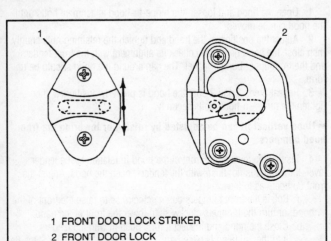

1 FRONT DOOR LOCK STRIKER
2 FRONT DOOR LOCK

90880G22

Fig. 4 On Sidekick, Tracker, Sidekick and X-90 models, the striker should be positioned so that it properly engages the door lock arm, as shown

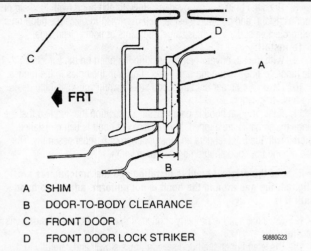

A   SHIM
B   DOOR-TO-BODY CLEARANCE
C   FRONT DOOR
D   FRONT DOOR LOCK STRIKER

90880G23

Fig. 5 Although not normally necessary, the striker can be adjusted fore-and-aft by adding or removing shims, respectively

shims from beneath the striker plate. The distance between the rear face of the door should be 0.499–0.579 in. (12.7–14.7mm) for Samurai models, 0.50–0.57 in. (12.6–14.6mm) for Sidekick, Tracker and Sidekick Sport models, or 0.44–0.51 in. (11.1–13.1mm) for X-90 models from the front face of the body in the door opening.

    d. Tighten the striker screws securely.

3. Lubricate the striker joints with oil or multi-purpose grease.

Hood

REMOVAL & INSTALLATION

All Models

➡This is a general procedure; certain steps may need alteration for your particular vehicle.

1. Open and support the hood. You can use an old broom handle or other long piece of wood with clean rags or padding wrapped around the ends to protect the vehicle from scratches or chips.

2. Position fenders covers or old blankets over both fenders to protect the paint in case the hood accidentally strikes the painted surface of the fenders.

3. If equipped with an underhood light, it may be necessary to remove the underhood insulation pad to access the underhood lamp wiring harness. To remove this pad, pry the plastic retainers out of the hood, then pull the pad off of the underside of the hood. The old plastic retainers can be reused if they are not damaged during removal, otherwise new ones may be purchased at many automotive parts retailers, or from your local factory dealership parts department.

4. If equipped, detach the hood ground strap by removing the retaining bolt.

5. If equipped, detach the underhood lamp wiring harness connector.

6. Matchmark the hood-to-hinge positions—this will make aligning the hood easier during installation.

7. Have an assistant support the hood while you remove the hinge-to-hood bolts.

✳✳ WARNING

An assistant is needed to keep the hood from sliding back and damaging the windshield once the nuts are removed. Positioning a folded-up old blanket on the bottom 10–12 in. (25–30cm) of the windshield may help protect it in the event that the hood slips and hits it.

8. Once the bolts are removed, carefully lift the hood (with the help or your assistant) and position it aside. You may wish to place the hood on a soft protective surface such as carpet remnants or some clean rags.

To install:

9. With the aid of your helper, position the hood on the vehicle so that the hinge-to-hood mounting bolt holes align with the holes in the hinges.

10. Have your helper hold the hood steady while you install the retaining bolts finger-tight.

11. If the original hood is being installed, position the hood so that the hinge matchmarks are aligned. If a replacement hood is being installed, align it with the front fenders and the upper, front bumper assembly. The gap around the hood should be uniform in width.

➡️**If, after the original hood is installed and the matchmarks are aligned, the gap around the hood is not uniform, adjust the hood until it is.**

12. Once the hood is properly aligned, tighten the hood-to-hinge bolts securely.

13. Close and open the hood several times slowly and carefully to ensure that there is not binding or interference between the hood, the fend-ers and the upper bumper panel. If there is interference or binding realign the hood until these symptoms no longer exist.

14. Open the hood.

15. If equipped, reattach the hood ground strap and the underhood lamp wiring harness.

16. If applicable, with the help of an assistant, position the insulator pad on the underside of the hood so that the mounting holes are aligned. Insert the plastic retainers through the pad and into the hood sheet metal until fully engaged. If any of the old retainers are damaged so that they will not hold the pad securely against the hood, purchase and install new retainers.

17. If necessary, adjust the hood latch by loosening the attaching bolts and moving it accordingly. Tighten the hood latch bolts to 49 inch lbs. (5.5 Nm).

ADJUSTMENT

◗ **See Figure 6**

➡️**Side-to-side and fore-aft adjustments can be made by loosening the hood-to-hinge attachment bolts, then by positioning the hood as necessary.**

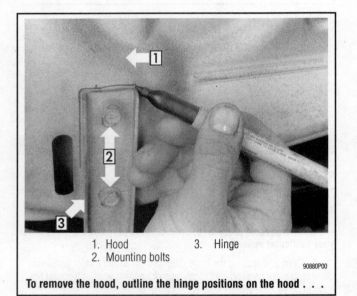

1. Hood   3. Hinge
2. Mounting bolts

90880P00

To remove the hood, outline the hinge positions on the hood . . .

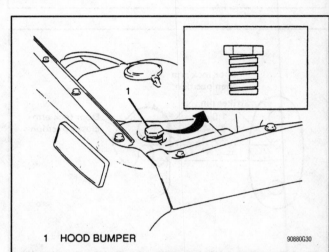

1   HOOD BUMPER   90880G30

Fig. 6 There are two bumpers located at the front corners of the hood—to adjust them, simply turn them until the desired height is reached

1. Open the hood and loosen the hinge-to-hood attachment bolts until the hood can be moved.

2. Adjust the position of the hood and tighten the retaining nuts snugly, then close the hood gently and check its alignment with the front fenders and the front upper bumper panel. The gap around the hood should be uniform.

3. Repeat Steps 1 and 2 until the hood is properly positioned, then tighten the hinge-to-hood bolts securely.

➡️**Hood vertical fit can be adjusted by raising or lowering the front hood bumpers.**

4. Inspect the level of the front of the hood in relation to the fender level. If the hood is not flush with the fenders, open the hood. Adjust the front bumpers as follows:

   a. Rotate the front bumpers counterclockwise to raise the front of the hood, or turn the bumpers clockwise to lower the front of the hood.

   b. Close the hood and inspect it for a flush fit with the fenders.

   c. If further aligning is necessary, open the hood and repeat Steps 6a and 6b until the hood is properly adjusted.

   d. If equipped, tighten the bumper lower jam nut until secure.

5. Close the hood once again to ensure that it is properly adjusted side-to-side, fore-and-aft, and up-and-down. Realign the hood, if necessary.

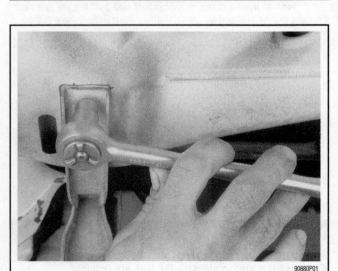

90880P01

. . . then, while your assistant supports the hood, loosen all of the hinge-to-hood bolts

Tailgate

➡Only soft-top Samurai, Sidekick and Tracker models are equipped with tailgates; the hard-top Samurai, Sidekick, Tracker and Sidekick Sport models are equipped with a back door, and the X-90 model is equipped with a trunk lid.

REMOVAL & INSTALLATION

▶ **See Figures 7 and 8**

➡An assistant is necessary to safely remove the tailgate, because of its weight, from the vehicle.

Before proceeding with this procedure, purchase new inner tailgate panel retainers from a dealership or an aftermarket automotive parts store. The retainers are plastic, and the old ones will most likely break during panel removal.

1. Remove the spare tire from the mounting bracket.
2. Open the tailgate.
3. Use a pair of pliers to pull, or a mallet to drive, the retaining pin up and out of the tailgate stopper strap and body bracket.

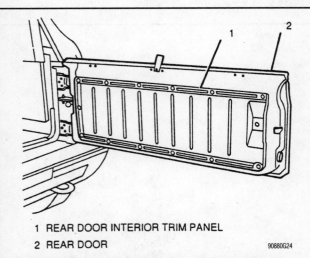

1 REAR DOOR INTERIOR TRIM PANEL
2 REAR DOOR   90880G24

Fig. 7 To remove the tailgate from the vehicle, first open the tailgate and remove the inner trim panel . . .

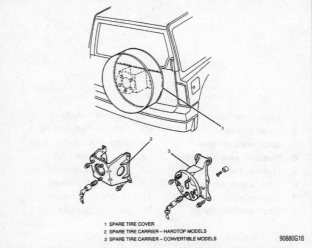

1 SPARE TIRE COVER
2 SPARE TIRE CARRIER—HARDTOP MODELS
3 SPARE TIRE CARRIER—CONVERTIBLE MODELS   90880G16

Fig. 8 . . . then remove the spare tire and carrier—note that only soft-top models use a tailgate

4. Using a floor jack with a soft-faced pad or folded towel on the jack support pad, slightly support the tailgate.
5. Remove the inner tailgate panel plastic retainers by pressing the center pin of the retainer in until the retainer is fully disengaged, then pull the entire retainer out of the inner tailgate panel. Separate the panel from the tailgate.
6. Disengage the license plate light wiring harness connectors from the vehicle wiring harness connectors. Then, pull the vehicle wiring harness out of the tailgate, making sure not to damage the rubber boot seal.
7. Remove the spare tire mounting bracket from the outside of the tailgate by loosening the mounting bolts.
8. If the original tailgate is going to be reinstalled, matchmark the hinges to the tailgate.
9. Remove the hinge-to-tailgate retaining bolts, then carefully lift the tailgate away from the vehicle.
10. If the tailgate is going to be replaced with another tailgate, transfer the following components to the new tailgate:
- Tailgate trim panel and watershield
- Tailgate lock and latch
- Spare tire mounting bracket
- License plate holder
- License plate light and tailgate handle housing
- Tailgate wiring harness

To install:
11. Using your assistant's help, support the tailgate on the padded floor jack and maneuver it close to the vehicle. Position the tailgate so that the hinges can be situated against the tailgate.
12. Install the tailgate hinge retaining bolts finger-tight.
13. Align the tailgate in the tailgate opening, as described later in this section.
14. Tighten the hinge-to-tailgate bolts securely.
15. Route the vehicle wiring harness into the tailgate, ensuring that you do not damage the rubber boot seal, then reattach all of the applicable wiring harness connectors.
16. Position the spare tire mounting bracket against the outside of the tailgate, then install the mounting bolts. Tighten the bolts securely.
17. Position the inner tailgate panel against the inside of the tailgate, then insert new plastic retainers in the panel mounting holes. Engage the retainers by depressing the retainer center pins until they are flush the rest of the retainer.
18. Reinstall the retaining pin so that the tailgate stopper strap is properly engaged with the tailgate pillar bracket.
19. Carefully close and open the tailgate to ensure that it is properly aligned to the body.
20. Install the spare tire onto the mounting bracket.

ADJUSTMENT

▶ **See Figure 9**

The tailgate hinges allow sufficient movement to correct most tailgate misalignment conditions. The hinge mounting holes are elongated to provide movement for tailgate alignment.

➡Never attempt to remedy tailgate misalignment solely by repositioning the latch striker.

1. To adjust the up-down position of the tailgate and the in-out position of the right-hand side of the tailgate, perform the following:
  a. Determine which hinge bolts are to be loosened and back them out just enough to allow movement.
  b. Move the tailgate safely by using a padded pry bar to correct the misalignment condition. When the tailgate is in the proper position, tighten the bolts securely, then check tailgate operation. There should be no binding or other interference when the tailgate is either closed or opened.
  c. Repeat Sub-Steps a and b until the tailgate is properly aligned in the tailgate opening. The gap between the edge of the tailgate and the body should be uniform all around the tailgate's perimeter.
2. To adjust the in-out position, and to fine-tune the up-down position, of the left-hand edge of the tailgate, perform the following:

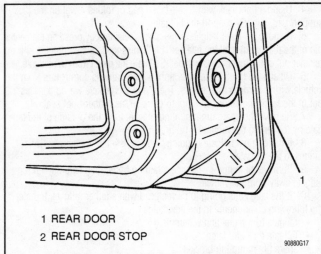

1 REAR DOOR
2 REAR DOOR STOP

90880G17

Fig. 9 To adjust the rear door stop, loosen the center retaining bolt and move the stop as desired

a. Loosen the tailgate latch striker and door stop mounting screws, then position the striker up and down until the center of the striker is aligned with the center of groove C on the tailgate latch. Move the door stop so that it engages properly with the C-shaped cup on the tailgate opening frame.

b. Move the striker in or out so that the tailgate will be flush with the body metal when closed.

c. If it is necessary to move the striker fore or aft, add or remove shims from beneath the striker plate.

d. Tighten all mounting screws securely.

3. Lubricate the striker joints with oil or multi-purpose grease.

Back Door

➡ Only hard-top Samurai, Sidekick, Tracker and Sidekick Sport models are equipped with a back door; soft-top Samurai, Sidekick and Tracker models are equipped with tailgates, and the X-90 model is equipped with a trunk lid.

REMOVAL & INSTALLATION

◆ See Figures 10, 11, 12 and 13

➡ An assistant is necessary to safely remove the back door, because of its weight, from the vehicle.

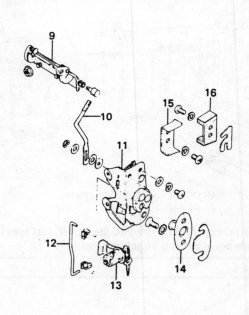

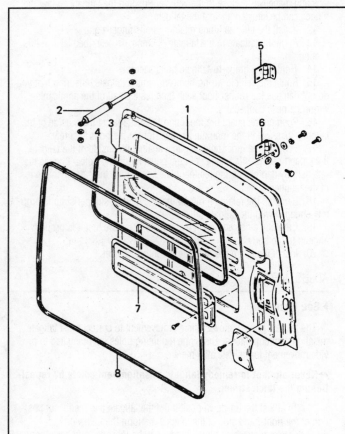

1. Back door panel	9. Outside handle
2. Door balancer	10. Outside handle rod
3. Back window glass	11. Back door lock
4. Window weatherstrip	12. Control rod
5. Door upper hinge	13. Door lock key set
6. Door lower hinge	14. Door lock striker
7. Service hole lid	15. Door stop female
8. Door weatherstrip	16. Door stop male

90880G05

Fig. 10 Exploded view of the common back door and lock mechanism

If you own a Sidekick, Tracker or Sidekick Sport, before proceeding with this procedure, purchase new inner back door panel retainers from a dealership or an aftermarket automotive parts store. The retainers are plastic, and the old ones will most likely break during panel removal.

1. If applicable, remove the spare tire from the mounting bracket.
2. Open the back door.
3. Remove the back door balancer from the door and vehicle body.
4. Using a floor jack with a soft-faced pad or folded towel on the jack support pad, slightly support the back door.
5. On Samurai models, remove the inner back door trim panel by loosening all of the retaining screws. Separate the panel from the back door.
6. On Sidekick, Tracker and Sidekick Sport models, remove the inner back door panel plastic retainers by pressing the center pin of the retainer in until the retainer is fully disengaged, then pull the entire retainer out of the inner back door panel. Separate the panel from the back door.
7. Carefully remove the watershield from the inside of the back door. If the watershield is not damaged during removal, it can be reused. Otherwise a new one must be purchased, or you can fabricate one out of a plastic lawn bag.
8. Disengage the license plate light wiring harness connectors from the vehicle wiring harness connectors. Then, pull the vehicle wiring harness out of the back door, making sure not to damage the rubber boot seal.
9. If equipped, remove the spare tire mounting bracket from the outside of the back door by loosening the mounting bolts.
10. If the original back door is going to be reinstalled, matchmark the hinge positions on the back door.
11. Remove the hinge-to-back door retaining bolts, then carefully lift the back door away from the vehicle.
12. If the back door is going to be replaced with another back door, transfer the following components to the new back door:
- Back door trim panel and watershield
- Back door lock and latch
- Spare tire mounting bracket
- License plate holder
- License plate light and back door handle housing
- Back door wiring harness

To install:

13. Using your assistant's help, support the back door on the padded floor jack and maneuver it close to the vehicle. Position the back door so that the hinges can be situated against the back door and vehicle body.
14. Install the back door hinge retaining bolts finger-tight.
15. Align the back door in the back door opening, as described later in this section.
16. Tighten the hinge-to-back door bolts securely.
17. Route the vehicle wiring harness into the back door, ensuring that you do not damage the rubber boot seal, then reattach all of the applicable wiring harness connectors.
18. If equipped, position the spare tire mounting bracket against the outside of the back door, then install the mounting bolts. Tighten the bolts securely.
19. Apply a continuos bead of sealant on the inside of the back door, then install the watershield.
20. Position the inner back door panel against the inside of the back door.
21. On Samurai models, install and tighten the inner door trim panel retaining screws.
22. On Sidekick, Tracker and Sidekick Sport models, insert new plastic retainers in the panel mounting holes. Engage the retainers by depressing the retainer center pins until they are flush the rest of the retainer.
23. Reinstall the back door balance to the vehicle body and back door.
24. Carefully close and open the back door to ensure that it is properly aligned to the body.
25. If equipped, install the spare tire onto the mounting bracket.

ADJUSTMENT

Adjust the back door in the same manner as the tailgate. Refer to the tailgate adjustment procedure.

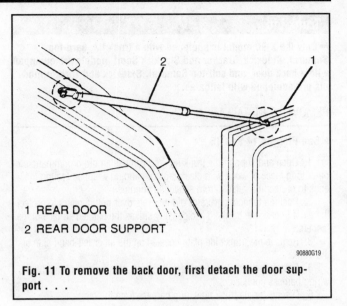

1 REAR DOOR
2 REAR DOOR SUPPORT

90880G19

Fig. 11 To remove the back door, first detach the door support . . .

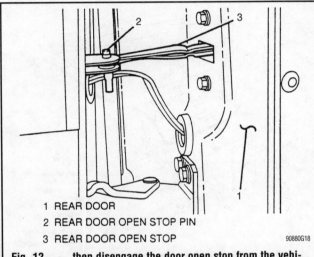

1 REAR DOOR
2 REAR DOOR OPEN STOP PIN
3 REAR DOOR OPEN STOP

90880G18

Fig. 12 . . . then disengage the door open stop from the vehicle body by removing the door open stop pin

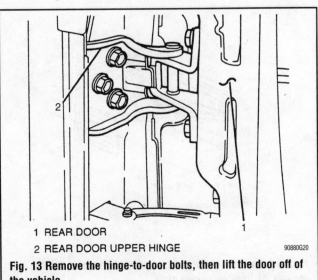

1 REAR DOOR
2 REAR DOOR UPPER HINGE

90880G20

Fig. 13 Remove the hinge-to-door bolts, then lift the door off of the vehicle

Trunk Lid

➡ Only the X-90 model is equipped with a trunk lid; hard-top Samurai, Sidekick, Tracker and Sidekick Sport models are equipped with a back door, and soft-top Samurai, Sidekick and Tracker models are equipped with tailgates.

REMOVAL & INSTALLATION

▸ See Figures 14 and 15

1. Open and support the trunk lid. You can use an old broom handle or other long piece of wood with clean rags or padding wrapped around the ends to protect the vehicle from scratches or chips.
2. Position fenders covers or old blankets over both fenders to protect the paint in case the trunk lid accidentally strikes the painted surface of the fenders.
3. Remove the trunk side plate, located on the inner left-hand side of the trunk.
4. Detach the vehicle wiring harness connectors from the trunk lid wiring harness connectors.
5. Disengage the trunk lid wiring harness from the hinge.

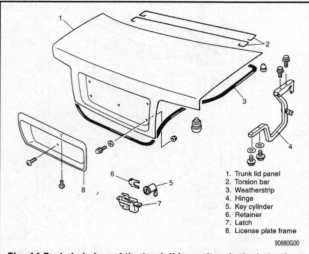

1. Trunk lid panel
2. Torsion bar
3. Weatherstrip
4. Hinge
5. Key cylinder
6. Retainer
7. Latch
8. License plate frame

90880G00

Fig. 14 Exploded view of the trunk lid, used exclusively by the X-90

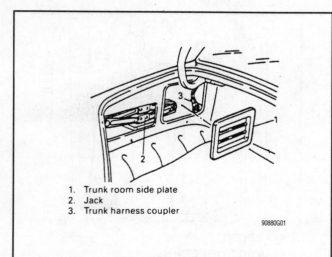

1. Trunk room side plate
2. Jack
3. Trunk harness coupler

90880G01

Fig. 15 For access to the trunk lid wiring harness connector, remove the trunk room side plate

6. Have an assistant support the trunk lid while you remove the trunk lid-to-hinge post bolts.

✳✳ WARNING

An assistant is needed to keep the trunk lid from sliding forward and damaging the rear window once the bolts are removed. Positioning a folded-up old blanket on the bottom 10–12 in. (25–30cm) of the rear window may help protect it in the event that the trunk lid slips and hits it.

7. Once the bolts are removed, carefully lift the trunk lid (with the help or your assistant) off of the vehicle and position it aside. You may wish to place the trunk lid on a soft protective surface such as carpet remnants or some clean rags.

To install:

8. With the aid of your helper, position the trunk lid on the vehicle so that the hinge-to-trunk lid mounting bolt holes align with the holes in the hinges.
9. Have your helper hold the trunk lid steady while you install and tighten the retaining bolts.
10. Close and open the trunk lid several times slowly and carefully to ensure that there is not binding or interference between the trunk lid latch and the latch striker. If there is interference or binding, align the trunk lid latch striker plate until these symptoms no longer exist. To adjust the striker plate, simply loosen the mounting screws and move the plate so that the striker shaft is approximately aligned with the center of the trunk lid latch groove, then retighten the bolts securely.
11. Open the trunk lid.
12. Reattach the trunk lid wiring harness to the hinge post.
13. Reattach the vehicle wiring harness and trunk lid wiring harness connectors.
14. Install the trunk side plate.
15. Close the trunk lid.

ADJUSTMENT

According to the manufacturer, the trunk lid does not require any adjustment other than the latch striker plate. To adjust the striker plate, simply loosen the mounting screws and move the plate so that the striker shaft is approximately aligned with the center of the trunk lid latch groove, then retighten the bolts securely.

Grille

REMOVAL & INSTALLATION

Samurai Model

To remove the grille from the vehicle, loosen the retaining screws (accessible from the front of the grille), then pull the grille out of the front body panel. During installation, tighten the retaining screws snugly.

Sidekick, Tracker and X-90 Models

▸ See Figure 16

1. Loosen the one grille retaining screw from the front of each wheel-housing.
2. Loosen the one top center grille retaining screw, which is accessible from the front of the grille.
3. Disconnect the two plastic grille retainer clips, then pull the grille away from the vehicle.

To install:

4. Position the grille in place and engage the two plastic retainer clips.
5. Install and tighten the top center, and two side mounting screws until snug.

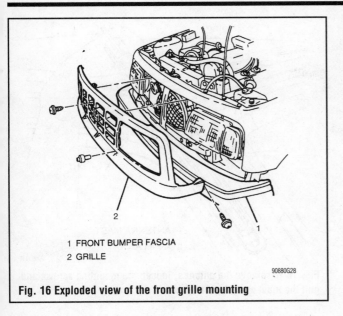

1 FRONT BUMPER FASCIA
2 GRILLE

90880G28

Fig. 16 Exploded view of the front grille mounting

90880P04

To remove the grille, first loosen the one screw in each wheel-housing opening . . .

90880P05

. . . then loosen the single top center retaining screw

90880P06

Remove the two plastic grille retainers . . .

90880P07

. . . then pull the grille out and away from the vehicle

Sidekick Sport Model

The front grille on the Sidekick Sport models is much smaller than that used on the Sidekick, Tracker and X-90 models. To remove it from the vehicle, loosen the retaining screws, which are accessible from the front of the grille, then pull the grille out of the front body panel. During installation, tighten the retaining screws snugly.

Outside Mirrors

REMOVAL & INSTALLATION

All Models

♦ See Figure 17

➡This is a general procedure; certain steps may need alteration for your particular vehicle.

1. Disconnect the negative battery cable.
2. Roll the door window down.
3. Using a plastic or wooden prytool, gently pry the inner mirror trim panel off of the door.

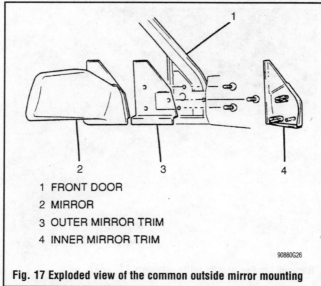

1 FRONT DOOR
2 MIRROR
3 OUTER MIRROR TRIM
4 INNER MIRROR TRIM

90880G26

Fig. 17 Exploded view of the common outside mirror mounting

4. While supporting the mirror with one hand, loosen the mirror-to-door mounting bolts or nuts with your other hand.

5. If equipped with power mirrors, disengage the wiring harness connector from the mirror.

6. Separate the mirror from the outside of the door, then, if equipped, remove the outer mirror trim panel from the mirror. Remove the mirror gasket and inspect it for brittleness and/or cracking; replace the gasket with a new one, if any such damage is found.

To install:

7. Thoroughly clean the portion of the door which is normally covered by the mirror base.

8. Install the gasket onto the mirror, then install the outer mirror trim panel.

9. If necessary, reattach the wiring harness connectors to the mirror assembly.

10. Position the mirror on the outside of the door.

11. Install the three mirror-to-door mounting bolts securely, then position the inner trim panel in place. Press the trim panel against the door until the retaining tabs are properly engaged.

12. Roll the door window up.

13. Connect the negative battery cable.

Antenna and Cable

REMOVAL & INSTALLATION

All Models

▶ **See Figures 18 and 19**

➡ **This is a general procedure; certain steps may need alteration for your particular vehicle.**

1. Disconnect the negative battery cable.

2. Remove the left heater duct from beneath the instrument panel. This will present better access for antenna installation.

3. Detach the antenna cable from the radio and the radio mounting bracket.

4. Attach the end of a long piece (at least 8–10 feet/2.4–3m) of firm wire to the radio end of the antenna cable BEFORE pulling the cable out through the A pillar. Be sure that the wire is securely fastened to the antenna cable; you do not want the two coming undone halfway through the A pillar. The wire will be used to run the antenna back through the A pillar during installation.

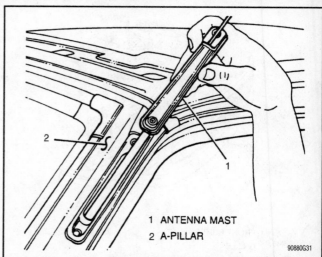

1 ANTENNA MAST
2 A-PILLAR

90880G31

Fig. 18 To remove the antenna, loosen the mounting screws and pull the mast away from the vehicle

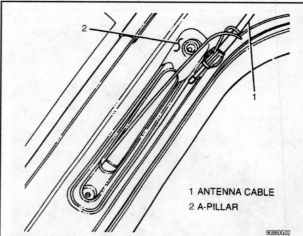

1 ANTENNA CABLE
2 A-PILLAR

90880G02

Fig. 19 Attach a piece of firm wire to the inner end of the antenna cable, then slowly withdraw the antenna cable from the vehicle

➡ **During the next step, do not pull the antenna cable so far out of the vehicle so that the inner end of the firm wire also comes out of the body; the inner end of the wire should stay inside the vehicle so that it can be used to pull the antenna cable back into the vehicle.**

5. Remove the antenna mast screws, then slowly pull the antenna mast up and away from the outside of the A pillar, which will slowly draw the antenna cable through the A pillar opening. Slowly pull the antenna cable all the way through until the radio end exits the A pillar hole. An assistant inside the vehicle guiding the antenna cable, makes it much easier to pull the cable out through the vehicle body.

6. Detach the antenna cable from the firm wire. Leave the wire in the A pillar.

To install:

7. Reattach the exposed end of the long piece of firm wire to the radio end of the antenna cable. Be sure that the wire is securely fastened to the antenna cable; you do not want the two coming undone halfway through the A pillar.

8. Have an assistant slowly pull the firm wire into the vehicle interior while you guide the antenna cable down into the A pillar opening. Once all of the antenna cable is routed into the passengers' compartment, position the antenna mast on the vehicle body and install the mounting screws securely.

9. Detach the antenna cable from the firm wire.

10. Reattach the antenna cable to the radio and radio mounting bracket.
11. Install the left heater duct,
12. Connect the negative battery cable, turn the radio on, kick back and listen to some great tunes to ensure that the antenna is functioning properly.

Fenders

REMOVAL & INSTALLATION

All Models

▶ See Figures 20, 21 and 22

➡ This is a general procedure; certain steps may need alteration for your particular vehicle.

1. Disconnect the negative battery cable.
2. Unclip the front side marker light from the fender, then disengage the lamp socket from the side marker light housing. Remove the housing from the vehicle.
3. Loosen the inner wheelhousing retaining screws, then remove the wheelhousing from the fender.
4. Remove the retaining fasteners from the front trim cover on the rocker panel, then separate the trim cover from the vehicle. This may be necessary to gain access to the front fender lower mounting bolts.
5. Remove the front fender lower mounting bolts. It may be necessary to open the door for proper access to these bolts.
6. Loosen the bolts from the fender upper extension panel, and any screws from the front of the fender.
7. Remove the upper fender mounting bolts from along the top of the front fender.
8. Lift the fender up and off of the vehicle.

To install:
9. Position the front fender on the vehicle.

➡ All fender mounting bolts should be tightened to 177 inch lbs. (20 Nm).

10. Install the upper fender mounting bolts along the top of the front fender.
11. install the fender front bolts and the fender upper extension panel bolts.
12. If necessary, close the front door.
13. Install the fender lower mounting bolts.
14. Align the front fender with the vehicle panels so that the gap between the two is uniform, then tighten the fender mounting bolts securely.
15. If equipped, install the rocker panel trim piece.
16. Position the wheelhousing up inside the front fender, then install the wheelhousing-to-fender fasteners.
17. Insert the side marker light socket into the lamp assembly, then affix the lamp assembly onto the front fender.
18. Connect the negative battery cable.

Chassis and Cab Mount Bushings

REPLACEMENT

All Models

➡ This is a general procedure; certain steps may need alteration for your particular vehicle.

If certain procedures covered by this manual require the cab/body mount bolts to be removed so that the body may be raised, it is critical that the body NOT be raised any more than necessary for access. If the cab/body is lifted too high, twisting and damage could occur. The body must be properly supported at all times.

If a cab/body mount must be removed completely for replacement, ALL mounts on that side of the vehicle MUST be unbolted in order to prevent damage. Again, the body must be suitably supported at multiple points (near each of the mounts) in order to prevent damage.

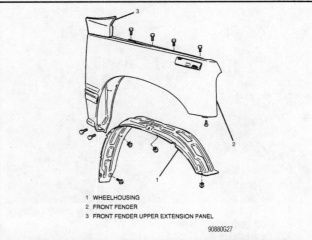

1 WHEELHOUSING
2 FRONT FENDER
3 FRONT FENDER UPPER EXTENSION PANEL

90880G27

Fig. 20 Exploded view of the front fender, showing the locations of the fender mounting fasteners—Sidekick, Tracker, Sidekick Sport and X-90 models

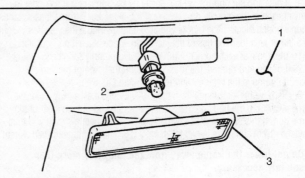

1 FRONT FENDER
2 FRONT SIDE MARKER LAMP BULB SOCKET
3 FRONT SIDE MARKER LAMP

90880G25

Fig. 21 Remove the side marker light assembly from the fender before attempting to pull it away from the body—otherwise you may damage the side marker light wiring

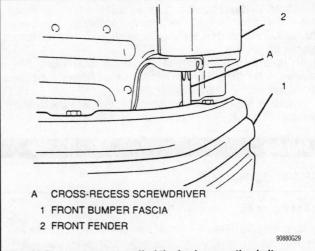

A   CROSS-RECESS SCREWDRIVER
1   FRONT BUMPER FASCIA
2   FRONT FENDER

90880G29

Fig. 22 Be sure to remove all of the fender mounting bolts, including the one front fender bolt

1. Vehicle body
2. Upper body mount bushing
3. Frame bracket
4. Lower body mount bushing
5. Washer

90880P02

With the vehicle body AND frame safely supported, remove the bushing bolts from one side of the vehicle only

1. Raise and support the vehicle safely by placing jackstands under the body at each of the mounts on that side. Protect the body from the jackstands using wooden blocks. The blocks will also help distribute the vehicle's weight on a larger area than the lips of the jackstand. Place at least one jackstand under the frame at each corner of the vehicle temporarily for safety.

2. Loosen and remove the mount bolts on that side of the vehicle. If possible, remove the retainer and lower cushion as well.

3. Remove the jackstands from the FRAME only, then slowly lower the frame away from the body on that side. Make sure you remain clear of the frame during this step. Also keep small children and pets away. (If you think ethylene glycol antifreeze is bad for them, a descending frame is even worse).

➡ **Do not lower the frame away from the body any more than absolutely necessary.**

4. Once the frame is lowered sufficiently, support it at this new height using two jackstands for safety.

5. Remove the upper cushion, spacer and shims, as applicable.

✳✳ WARNING

During installation remember that at NO point should you work under the vehicle unless both the body and frame are supported using jackstands. The floor jack is NOT sufficient to assure safety, even for short periods of time.

6. Install the upper body bushing, spacers and shims that were removed.

7. Raise the frame with the floor jack until it contacts the body. Support the frame with jackstands at this height. Install the lower bushings, spacers, washers and new nuts.

8. Tighten the nuts or bolts to the recommended torque values corresponding to their size and grade of manufacture, as presented in the torque specification chart at the end of this section.

9. Once all of the removed body mounts has been tightened, lower the vehicle to the ground. Repeat for the other side, if needed.

Soft Top

GENERAL INFORMATION

▶ **See Figure 23**

Many of the Suzuki and Geo models covered in this manual utilize a soft top. Although soft top fabric manufacturing processes have made great technological jumps since the early years of convertible top manufacturing, the soft tops used on these vehicles often wear out and require replacement.

If you need to purchase a new soft top for your Sidekick, Tracker or Samurai, you can buy one from a local dealership although neither Suzuki nor Geo manufactures the soft tops used on these models. The manufacturer for the Suzuki and Geo soft tops is a company called Bestop®. Soft tops can be purchased from Bestop® dealers directly, and have the added advantages of lower cost and different styles available. Purchasing a new soft top from a Bestop® dealer can often be 3 or 4 times less expensive than the same top purchased from a dealership parts department. Bestop® also offers many styles and colors of soft tops to choose from.

Therefore, if you need to purchase a replacement soft top for your vehicle, you may find it advantageous to investigate the possibility of buying one from Bestop® or another aftermarket manufacturer. For removal and installation of your soft top, refer to your owner's manual, which presents a very detailed procedure.

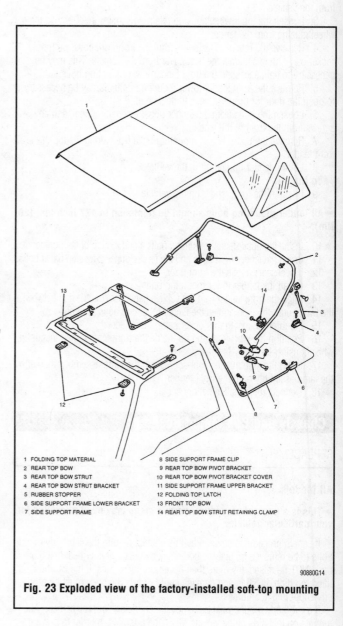

1 FOLDING TOP MATERIAL
2 REAR TOP BOW
3 REAR TOP BOW STRUT
4 REAR TOP BOW STRUT BRACKET
5 RUBBER STOPPER
6 SIDE SUPPORT FRAME LOWER BRACKET
7 SIDE SUPPORT FRAME
8 SIDE SUPPORT FRAME CLIP
9 REAR TOP BOW PIVOT BRACKET
10 REAR TOP BOW PIVOT BRACKET COVER
11 SIDE SUPPORT FRAME UPPER BRACKET
12 FOLDING TOP LATCH
13 FRONT TOP BOW
14 REAR TOP BOW STRUT RETAINING CLAMP

90880G14

Fig. 23 Exploded view of the factory-installed soft-top mounting

INTERIOR

Instrument Panel and Pad

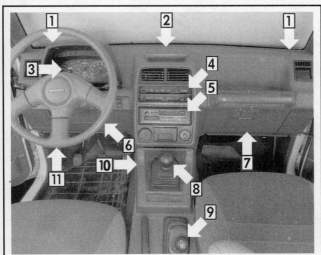

1. Upper side mounting bolt covers
2. Upper center mounting bolt cover
3. Instrument cluster
4. Heater-A/C control panel
5. Radio/tape/CD player
6. Lower steering column cover
7. Glove box
8. Transmission gearshift handle and boot (manual transmission shown)
9. Transfer case gearshift handle and boot (4WD models only)
10. Center console
11. Steering column and wheel

90880P24

Identification of some of the components related to instrument panel removal

REMOVAL & INSTALLATION

All Models

▶ See Figures 24, 25, 26 and 27

➡ This is a general procedure; certain steps may need alteration for your particular vehicle.

1. Disconnect the negative battery cable.

✳✳ WARNING

Before servicing a vehicle equipped with an air bag system, it is vital to read the precautions in Section 6 of this manual to avoid accidental injury or death.

2. Disable the air bag system, as described in Section 6.
3. Remove the center console.
4. Remove the lower steering column cover by loosening the mounting screws.
5. Remove the glove box.
6. Detach the wiring harness connectors from the heater unit and the blower motor assembly.
7. For Samurai models, remove the steering column as follows:
   a. Remove the combination switch, as described in Section 8 of this manual.
   b. Open the hood.
   c. Remove the upper-to-lower steering shaft attaching bolt.
   d. Loosen the steering column retaining bolts at the firewall and lower instrument panel brace.
   e. Remove the steering column from the vehicle.

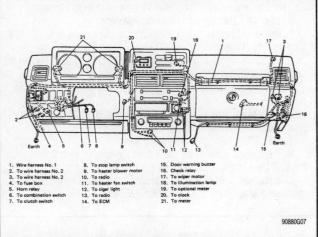

1. Wire harness No. 1
2. To wire harness No. 2
3. To wire harness No. 2
4. To fuse box
5. Horn relay
6. To combination switch
7. To clutch switch
8. To stop lamp switch
9. To heater blower motor
10. To radio
11. To heater fan switch
12. To cigar light
13. To radio
14. To ECM
15. Door warning buzzer
16. Check relay
17. To wiper motor
18. To illumination lamp
19. To optional meter
20. To clock
21. To meter

90880G07

Fig. 24 Before removing the mounting fasteners, be sure to detach and label all of the wiring harness connectors from the instrument panel—Samurai model shown

8. For Sidekick, Tracker, Sidekick Sport and X-90 models, remove the steering column as follows:
   a. Detach the wiring harness connectors from the ignition switch, contact coil and combination switch.
   b. Open the hood.
   c. Remove the steering column shaft joint bolt, then separate the steering column shaft from the lower steering shaft.
   d. Loosen all of the steering column-to-firewall and instrument panel brace bolts.
   e. If equipped, remove the shift (key) interlock cable screw. Disconnect the cable from the ignition switch.
   f. Remove the steering column from the vehicle.

✳✳ WARNING

Do not rest the steering column assembly on the steering wheel with the air bag module facing downward and the column vertical—personal injury may be the result.

9. Disconnect the speedometer cable from the speedometer, then remove the instrument cluster.
10. Remove the hood latch handle.
11. Remove the radio, the heater control panel and the heater control cables from the instrument panel.
12. Disconnect and label all wiring harness connectors from the instrument panel.
13. Remove the instrument panel mounting screws and bolts. Remove the side cover plates and the instrument panel mounting fasteners from the side of the assembly. Then, remove the upper cover plates and loosen the remaining mounting fasteners
14. Have an assistant help you carefully lift the instrument panel up and out of the vehicle. When separating the instrument panel from the firewall, ensure that all of the cables, wires and hoses are disconnected form the instrument panel.

   To install:
15. Have an assistant help you position the instrument panel in the vehicle. When installing the instrument panel on the firewall, ensure that all of the cables, wires and hoses are routed properly.
16. Install and tighten the instrument panel mounting screws and bolts.
17. Reattach all wiring harness connectors to the instrument panel.
18. Install the radio, the heater control panel and the heater control cables. Be sure to adjust the heater control cables as described in Section 6 of this manual.

19. Install the hood latch handle.

20. Install the instrument cluster, then connect the cable to the speedometer.

21. For Samurai models, install the steering column as follows:

a. Install the steering column in the vehicle.

b. Install and tighten the steering column retaining bolts to 97–150 inch lbs. (11–17 Nm).

c. Install the upper-to-lower steering shaft attaching bolt. Tighten the bolt to 177–265 inch lbs. (20–30 Nm).

d. Install the combination switch, as described in Section 8 of this manual.

22. For Sidekick, Tracker, Sidekick Sport and X-90 models, install the steering column as follows:

a. Install the steering column in the vehicle.

b. If equipped, connect the cable from the ignition switch, then install the shift (key) interlock cable screw.

c. Install and tighten all of the steering column-to-firewall and instrument panel brace bolts to 221 inch lbs. (25 Nm).

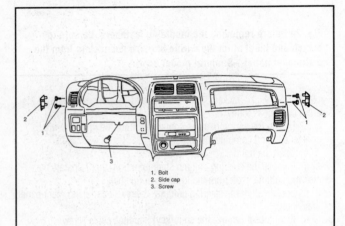

Fig. 25 Remove the side cover plates and the instrument panel mounting fasteners from the side of the assembly . . .

1. Bolt
2. Side cap
3. Screw

90880G40

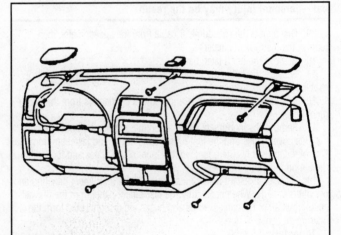

Fig. 26 . . . then remove the upper cover plates and loosen the remaining mounting fasteners

90880G39

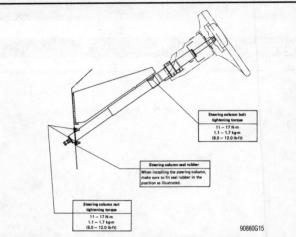

Fig. 27 During steering column installation, ensure that the mounting bolts are tightened to the proper values—Samurai model shown

90880G15

d. Install and tighten the steering column shaft joint bolt to 221 inch lbs. (25 Nm).

e. Reattach the wiring harness connectors to the ignition switch, contact coil and combination switch.

23. Reattach the wiring harness connectors to the heater unit and the blower motor assembly.

24. Install the glove box.

25. Install the lower steering column cover.

26. Install the center console.

27. Connect the negative battery cable.

28. Enable the air bag system, as described in Section 6.

Console

REMOVAL & INSTALLATION

Sidekick, Tracker, Sidekick Sport and X-90 Models

▶ See Figure 28

➡The Samurai model does not utilize a center console.

There are 3 separate boots on the shift lever assembly for these vehicles. An upper boot you can touch from the driver's seat and that is mostly for looks (called the upper boot by Geo or boot No. 3 by Suzuki), a middle boot that seals the passenger compartment from the hole in the vehicle's floor pan (called the lower boot by Geo or boot No. 2 by Suzuki) and a lower boot that seals the shift lever to the shift lever housing on the top of the transmission (called the lever case boot by Geo or boot No. 1 by Suzuki). For simplicity, the following procedure will refer to them as upper, middle and lower in reference to how they are physically mounted on the shift lever.

1. Disconnect the negative battery cable for safety.

2. For manual transmission models, remove the gearshift handle and boot.

3. For automatic transmission models, remove the shifter cover plate and handle.

4. From inside the passenger compartment remove the console cover or, on certain late-model vehicles, both the front and rear console covers. If equipped with 2 console covers, start at the rear one. To free a console cover, remove the 2 screws and the two plastic retainers, then carefully lift the cover from the floor of the vehicle.

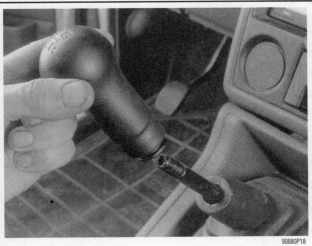

Fig. 28 Each center console is retained by 2 screws at the front and 2 snap retainers at the rear—Sidekick, Tracker, Sidekick Sport and X-90 models

1. Console box
2. Small allen wrench etc. for clip removal

90887G02

➡The plastic retainers are removed by first pushing the center inward using a small hex key or punch. The center will gently snap inward telling you that fastener is now free. At this point you should be able to pull it back and out by gently grabbing the edges. DO NOT force a retainer out using a prytool unless the center snap has pushed inwards releasing the fastener or it will break and require replacement.

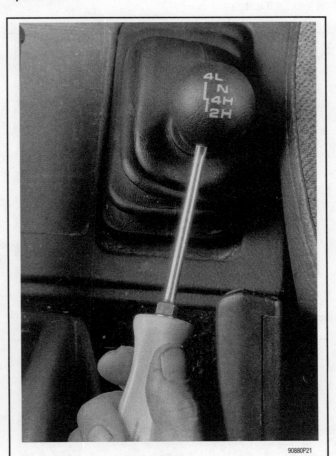

90880P21

. . . If equipped with 4WD, loosen the transfer case handle setscrew . . .

90880P18

To remove the console from a model equipped with a manual transmission, first unscrew the transmission gearshift handle . . .

90880P19

then remove the transmission gearshift handle boot from the console

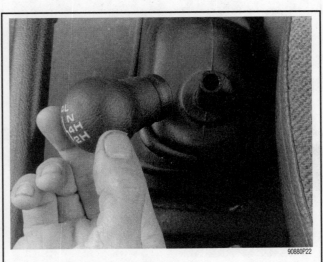

90880P22

. . . then remove the handle from the transfer case gearshift shaft

To install:

5. For manual transmission models, install the upper boot over the shift lever, then screw the gearshift knob back into place on top of the shift lever.

6. Install the console cover (or covers) using the retaining screws and snap fasteners. To secure the snap fasteners, remove the center portion and insert the large piece into the hole, then gently insert the center portion of the fastener until it is flush with the top of the outer portion. Pull back gently to assure it is secure.

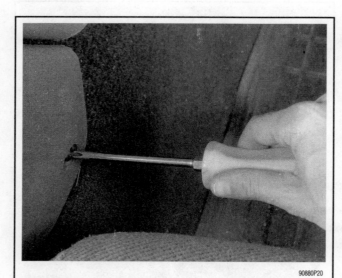

90880P20

Loosen the console side retaining screws . . .

90880P23

. . . then lift the console up and out of the vehicle

7. Check for the proper clearance between the front of the console cover and the bottom of the dash. There should be about 0.08 in. (2mm) of clearance. If not, the angled boot bracket may not be properly installed.

8. For manual models, make sure that the flare end of the upper boot is properly engaged with the console cover.

9. For automatic models, install the shifter handle and cover.

10. Connect the negative battery cable, but double-check shifter action before attempting to start the vehicle.

Door Panels

REMOVAL & INSTALLATION

Samurai Models

1. Remove the window regulator crank handle by using a tool designed specifically for this purpose.

2. Remove the inside door handle trim by loosening the retaining screw. Pull the door handle out and slide the trim off of the handle.

3. Loosen the two inside pull handle mounting screws, then separate the pull handle from the door panel.

4. Loosen the two screws retaining the stopper band to the door, then remove the stopper band.

5. Using a prytool, gently separate the trim panel from the door, disengaging the trim panel retaining clips.

To install:

6. Position the door panel on the door so that the retaining clips are aligned with the holes in the door, then press the door panel against the door until all of the retainers are completely engaged.

7. Install the snap-ring on the window crank handle, then press the handle onto the regulator shaft. The handle should be positioned so that when the window is fully closed, the handle points forward and upward at a 45 degree angle.

8. Position the pull handle against the door panel, then install and tighten the two mounting screws.

9. Install the stopper band and mounting screws.

10. Install the inside door handle trim and screw.

Sidekick, Tracker, Sidekick Sport and X-90 Models

▶ See Figures 29, 30 and 31

➡This is a general procedure; certain steps may need alteration for your particular vehicle.

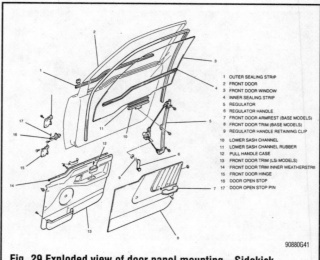

1 OUTER SEALING STRIP
2 FRONT DOOR
3 FRONT DOOR WINDOW
4 INNER SEALING STRIP
5 REGULATOR
6 REGULATOR HANDLE
7 FRONT DOOR ARMREST (BASE MODELS)
8 FRONT DOOR TRIM (BASE MODELS)
9 REGULATOR HANDLE RETAINING CLIP
10 LOWER SASH CHANNEL
11 LOWER SASH CHANNEL RUBBER
12 PULL HANDLE CASE
13 FRONT DOOR TRIM (LSi MODELS)
14 FRONT DOOR TRIM INNER WEATHERSTRII
15 FRONT DOOR HINGE
16 DOOR OPEN STOP
17 DOOR OPEN STOP PIN

90880G41

Fig. 29 Exploded view of door panel mounting—Sidekick, Tracker and Sidekick Sport models

1. Outer weatherstrip
2. Trim support
3. Inside pull handle bracket
4. Door sealing cover
5. Power window switch
6. Inner weatherstrip
7. Inside pull handle case
8. Door inside handle
9. Door hinge
10. Door open stop
11. Door panel
12. Door trim
13. Door center sash
14. Door window glass
15. Rear sash bracket sub ass'y
16. Door rear sash
17. Door glass stabilizer
18. Window regulator ass'y
19. Door glass stopper
20. Regulator bottom bolt
21. Window up stopper

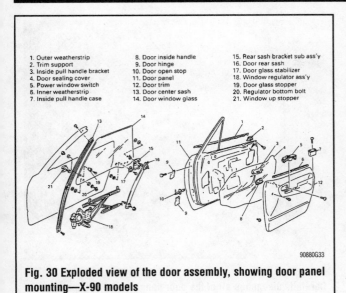

90880G33

Fig. 30 Exploded view of the door assembly, showing door panel mounting—X-90 models

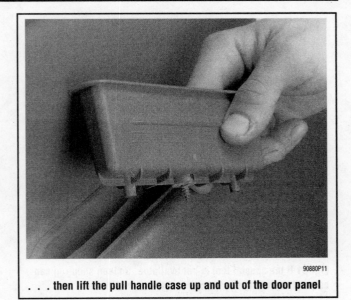

90880P11

. . . then lift the pull handle case up and out of the door panel

90880P09

To remove the door panel, loosen the inside door handle trim screw . . .

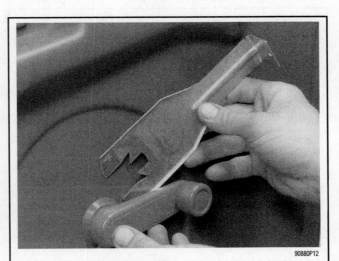

90880P12

This tool is specifically designed to remove window crank handle retaining snaprings

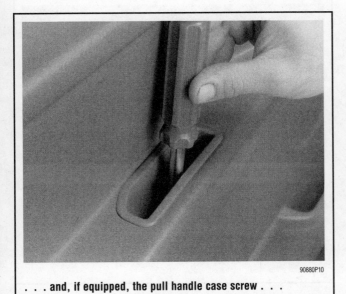

90880P10

. . . and, if equipped, the pull handle case screw . . .

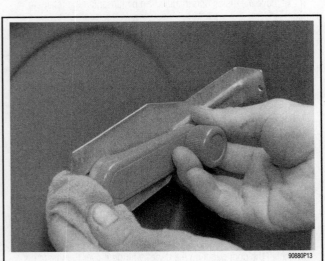

90880P13

Align the tool with the handle, then slide it underneath and disengage the snapring

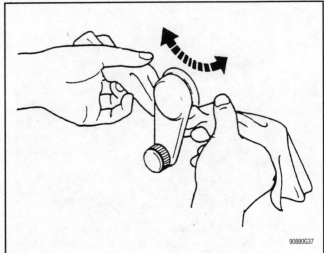

Fig. 31 If the special tool is not available, a clean shop rag can be used to work the snapring off of the crank handle

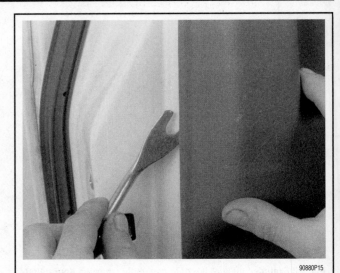

Carefully disengage all of the door panel retaining clips . . .

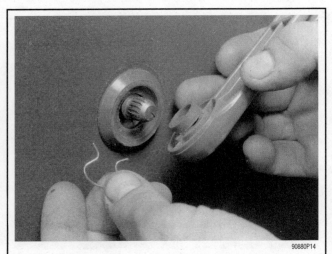

Do not lose the snapring—you will need it for handle installation

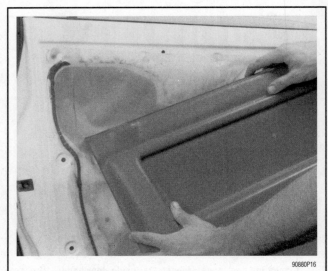

. . . then remove the trim panel from the door

1. Remove the inside door handle trim by loosening the retaining screw.

2. Remove the side mirror inner trim piece by gently prying it away from the door surface.

3. Loosen the two armrest mounting screws, then separate the armrest from the door panel.

4. If equipped, loosen the retaining screw from the pull handle case, then pull the case up and out of the door panel.

5. Remove the window regulator crank handle by using a tool designed specifically for this purpose. If the tool is not available, use a clean rag to disengage the retaining snapring, as shown in the accompanying illustration.

6. Using a prytool, gently separate the trim panel from the door, disengaging the trim panel retaining clips.

7. Pull the inside door handle inner bezel out from the door panel (almost at a 90 degree angle), then rotate the door trim panel in a counterclockwise direction so that the rear edge moves up and over the inside door handle inner bezel, and the front edge of the trim panel drops down beneath the bezel. In this position, remove the door trim panel from the door.

To install:

8. Install the door panel on the door by fitting it over the inside door handle inner bezel (as during removal), and then rotating it clockwise into position.

Install the snapring on the regulator crank handle before assembly

9. Position the door panel on the door so that the retaining clips are aligned with the holes in the door, then press the door panel against the door until all of the retainers are completely engaged.

10. Install the snapring on the window crank handle, then press the handle onto the regulator shaft. The handle should be positioned so that when the window is fully closed, the handle points forward and upward at a 45 degree angle.

11. If equipped, insert the pull handle case into the door panel, then install the retaining screw.

12. Position the armrest against the door panel, then install and tighten the two mounting screws.

13. Install the side mirror inside trim piece by aligning the retaining clips with the holes in the door, then press the trim piece against the door until all of the retainers are completely engaged.

14. Install the inside door handle trim.

Door Locks

REMOVAL & INSTALLATION

Samurai Models

▶ **See Figures 32, 33 and 34**

1. Remove the inner door panel.
2. Peel the watershield off of the inside face of the door. If the watershield is not excessively damaged during removal (rips or tears may be repaired with waterproof tape), it may be reused. Otherwise, a new one can be purchased or fabricated from a plastic lawn bag.
3. Disconnect all actuating rods from the door lock mechanism.
4. Remove the door lock mounting fasteners, then remove it from the door. The inside handle is removed along with the door lock assembly.

To install:

5. Position the door lock/inside handle mechanism in the door, then install the mounting fasteners. Tighten the fasteners securely.

➡ **When installing the door open rod to the lock mechanism, avoid depressing the push plate.**

6. Reattach all of the actuating rods to the door lock mechanism, keeping the following points in mind:
   • When installing the door open rod on the outside handle, adjust the rod play clearance to 0.000–0.079 in. (0–2mm) by turning the adjusting joint. (Refer to the accompanying illustration.)
   • Be sure to engage the lock rod with the rod pin as indicated in the accompanying illustration.

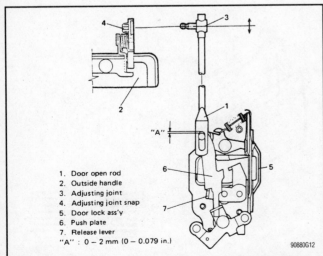

1. Door open rod
2. Outside handle
3. Adjusting joint
4. Adjusting joint snap
5. Door lock ass'y
6. Push plate
7. Release lever
"A" : 0 – 2 mm (0 – 0.079 in.)

90880G12

Fig. 32 Adjust the door open rod clearance (A) to 0.000–0.079 in. (0–2mm) by turning the adjusting joint (3)

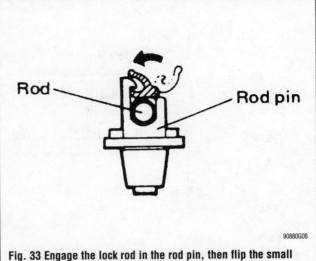

90880G08

Fig. 33 Engage the lock rod in the rod pin, then flip the small latch over to secure it in this position

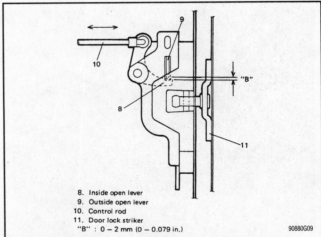

8. Inside open lever
9. Outside open lever
10. Control rod
11. Door lock striker
"B" : 0 – 2 mm (0 – 0.079 in.)

90880G09

Fig. 34 Adjust the clearance between the inside handle open lever and the outside lever by moving the control rod (10) in or out

   • If the inside door handle was detached from the door lock mechanism, adjust the clearance between the inside open lever and the outside open lever of the door lock to 0.000–0.079 in. (0–2mm) by moving the inside handle remote control rod in the direction of the arrow in the accompanying illustration.

After adjusting the various actuating rods, test the inside handle, the outside handle and the lock knob operation before installing the watershield on the door.

7. Apply a continuous bead of sealant to the inner face of the door, then install the watershield on the door.

8. Install the door panel.

Sidekick, Tracker, Sidekick Sport and X-90 Models

▶ **See Figures 35 and 36**

➡ **This is a general procedure; certain steps may need alteration for your particular vehicle.**

1. Roll the window up.
2. Remove the door panel.
3. Peel the watershield off of the inside face of the door. If the watershield is not excessively damaged during removal (rips or tears may be repaired with waterproof tape), it may be reused. Otherwise, a new one can be purchased or fabricated from a plastic lawn bag.

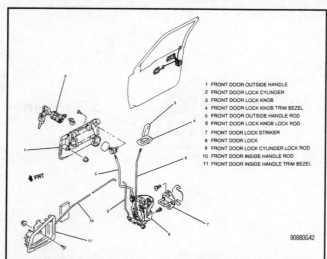

1 FRONT DOOR OUTSIDE HANDLE
2 FRONT DOOR LOCK CYLINDER
3 FRONT DOOR LOCK KNOB
4 FRONT DOOR LOCK KNOB TRIM BEZEL
5 FRONT DOOR OUTSIDE HANDLE ROD
6 FRONT DOOR LOCK KNOB LOCK ROD
7 FRONT DOOR LOCK STRIKER
8 FRONT DOOR LOCK
9 FRONT DOOR LOCK CYLINDER LOCK ROD
10 FRONT DOOR INSIDE HANDLE ROD
11 FRONT DOOR INSIDE HANDLE TRIM BEZEL

90880G42

Fig. 35 Exploded view of the common front door lock mechanism used on Sidekick, Tracker, Sidekick Sport and X-90 models

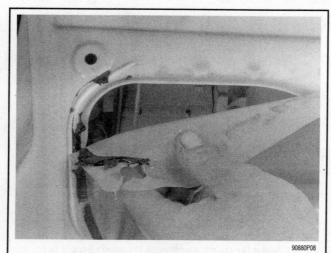

90880P08

If you want to reuse the old watershield, peel it off of the door carefully to avoid ripping or tearing it

4. Detach the inside and outside door handle rods from the door lock assembly.

5. Disengage the door lock cylinder lock rod from the door lock assembly.

6. Disconnect the door lock knob rod from the door lock assembly.

7. If equipped, detach the wiring harness connector from the door lock assembly.

8. Loosen the door lock assembly mounting screws, then remove the assembly from the door.

To install:

9. Position the door lock assembly in the door, then install and tighten the door lock assembly mounting screws securely.

10. Reattach the knob rod, cylinder lock rod, and the inside and outside door handle rods to the door lock assembly. Adjust the outside handle rod-to-door lock linkage distance to 0.00–0.08 in. (0–2mm).

11. If necessary, reattach the wiring harness connector to the door lock assembly.

12. Apply a continuous bead of sealant to the inner face of the door, then install the watershield on the door.

13. Install the door panel.

Tailgate and Back Door Locks

REMOVAL & INSTALLATION

Samurai Models

▶ See Figures 37 and 38

1. Remove the inner door panel.

2. Peel the watershield off of the inside face of the door. If the watershield is not excessively damaged during removal (rips or tears may be repaired with waterproof tape), it may be reused. Otherwise, a new one can be purchased or fabricated from a plastic lawn bag.

3. Disconnect all actuating rods from the door lock mechanism.

4. Remove the door lock mounting fasteners, then remove it from the door. The inside handle is removed along with the door lock assembly.

To install:

5. Position the door lock/inside handle mechanism in the door, then install the mounting fasteners. Tighten the fasteners securely.

➡**When installing the door open rod to the lock mechanism, avoid depressing the push plate.**

6. Reattach all of the actuating rods to the door lock mechanism, keeping the following points in mind:

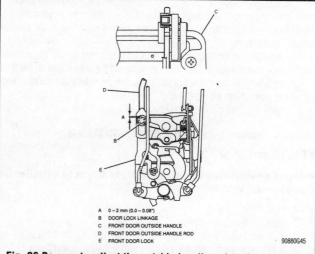

A 0 – 2 mm (0.0 – 0.08")
B DOOR LOCK LINKAGE
C FRONT DOOR OUTSIDE HANDLE
D FRONT DOOR OUTSIDE HANDLE ROD
E FRONT DOOR LOCK

90880G45

Fig. 36 Be sure to adjust the outside handle rod-to-door linkage clearance to 0.00–0.08 in. (0–2mm)

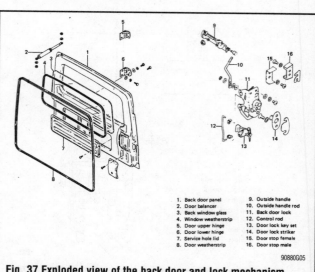

1. Back door panel
2. Door balancer
3. Back window glass
4. Window weatherstrip
5. Door upper hinge
6. Door lower hinge
7. Service hole lid
8. Door weatherstrip
9. Outside handle
10. Outside handle rod
11. Back door lock
12. Control rod
13. Door lock key set
14. Door lock striker
15. Door stop female
16. Door stop male

90880G05

Fig. 37 Exploded view of the back door and lock mechanism, showing all related linkage, used on hard-top Samurai models

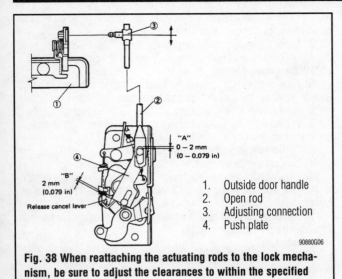

1. Outside door handle
2. Open rod
3. Adjusting connection
4. Push plate

90880G06

Fig. 38 When reattaching the actuating rods to the lock mechanism, be sure to adjust the clearances to within the specified ranges

• When installing the door open rod on the outside handle, adjust the rod play clearance to 0.000–0.079 in. (0–2mm) by turning the adjusting joint. (Refer to the accompanying illustration.)
• Be sure to engage the lock rod with the rod pin as indicated in the accompanying illustration.
• If the inside door handle was detached from the door lock mechanism, adjust the clearance between the inside open lever and the outside open lever of the door lock to 0.000–0.079 in. (0–2mm) by moving the inside handle remote control rod in the direction of the arrow in the accompanying illustration.

After adjusting the various actuating rods, test the inside handle, the outside handle and the lock knob operation before installing the watershield on the door.

7. Apply a continuous bead of sealant to the inner face of the door, then install the watershield on the door.
8. Install the door panel.

Sidekick, Tracker, Sidekick Sport and X-90 Models

▶ **See Figures 39 and 40**

Before proceeding with this procedure, purchase new inner tailgate panel retainers from a dealership or an aftermarket automotive parts store. The retainers are plastic, and the old ones will most likely break during panel removal.

1. On Samurai models, remove the inner back door trim panel by loosening all of the retaining screws. Separate the panel from the back door.
2. On Sidekick and Tracker models, remove the inner tailgate panel. Remove the inner tailgate panel plastic retainers by pressing the center pin of the retainer in until the retainer is fully disengaged, then pull the entire retainer out of the inner tailgate panel. Separate the panel from the tailgate.
3. Peel the watershield off of the inside face of the tailgate. If the watershield is not excessively damaged during removal (rips or tears may be repaired with waterproof tape), it may be reused. Otherwise, a new one can be purchased or fabricated from a plastic lawn bag.
4. Detach the outside tailgate handle rod from the tailgate lock assembly.
5. Disengage the lock cylinder lock rod from the tailgate lock assembly.
6. If equipped, detach the wiring harness connector from the tailgate lock assembly.
7. Loosen the lock assembly mounting screws, then remove the assembly from the tailgate.

To install:

8. Position the lock assembly in the tailgate, then install and tighten the tailgate lock assembly mounting screws securely.
9. Reattach the cylinder lock rod, and the outside tailgate handle rods to the tailgate lock assembly.

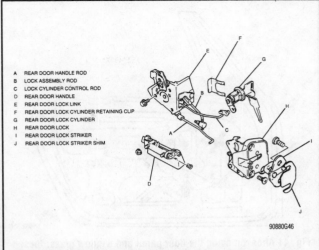

A REAR DOOR HANDLE ROD
B LOCK ASSEMBLY ROD
C LOCK CYLINDER CONTROL ROD
D REAR DOOR HANDLE
E REAR DOOR LOCK LINK
F REAR DOOR LOCK CYLINDER RETAINING CLIP
G REAR DOOR LOCK CYLINDER
H REAR DOOR LOCK
I REAR DOOR LOCK STRIKER
J REAR DOOR LOCK STRIKER SHIM

90880G46

Fig. 39 Exploded view of the back door lock mechanism used on hard-top Sidekick, Tracker and Sidekick Sport models

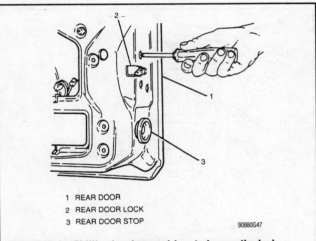

1 REAR DOOR
2 REAR DOOR LOCK
3 REAR DOOR STOP

90880G47

Fig. 40 Use a Phillips head screwdriver to loosen the lock mounting screws, then remove the lock mechanism from the door

10. If necessary, reattach the wiring harness connector to the tailgate lock assembly.
11. Apply a continuous bead of sealant to the inner face of the tailgate, then install the watershield on the tailgate.
12. On Samurai models, position the inner tailgate panel against the inside of the tailgate, then install the retaining screws.
13. On Sidekick and Tracker models, position the inner tailgate panel against the inside of the tailgate, then insert new plastic retainers in the panel mounting holes. Engage the retainers by depressing the retainer center pins until they are flush the rest of the retainer.

Door Glass and Regulator

REMOVAL & INSTALLATION

2-Door Models

▶ **See Figures 41, 42, 43, 44 and 45**

1. Remove the door trim panel.
2. Peel the watershield off of the inside face of the door. If the watershield is not excessively damaged during removal (rips or tears may be

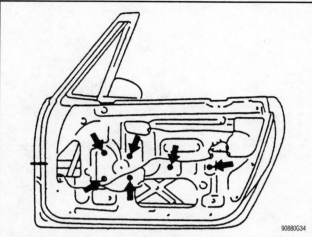

Fig. 41 After removing the door panel and window glass, loosen the regulator bolts (arrows) and remove the regulator through the large hole at the bottom of the door—X-90 model shown

repaired with waterproof tape), it may be reused. Otherwise, a new one can be purchased or fabricated from a plastic lawn bag.

3. Lower the window all the way down.

4. On X-90 models, remove the window glass stoppers from the top edge of the window opening.

5. Wrap electrical tape around the blade of a putty knife, then use the knife to gently pry the door outside weatherstripping off of the door.

6. Pry the inner weatherstripping off of the door.

7. Loosen the glass bottom channel mounting screws, then lift the glass and bottom channel up and out of the door.

8. Position the door glass on a clean, padded surface.

9. If necessary, the bottom channel can now be removed.

10. If equipped with power windows, detach the wiring harness connector from the regulator wiring harness connector, then loosen the regulator harness holding clamp.

11. Loosen the window regulator mounting bolts, then remove the regulator from the door through hole (A).

To install:

12. Prior to installation, apply multi-purpose grease to the lubrication points shown in the accompanying illustration.

13. Maneuver the window regulator through the hole in the door and into position. Install the regulator mounting bolts and tighten them securely.

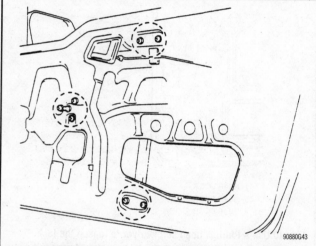

Fig. 42 Window regulator mounting screw locations—Sidekick and Tracker

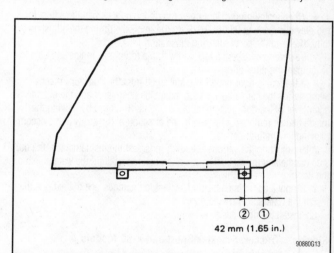

Fig. 44 If the bottom channel was removed from the glass, install it so that the rear hole is 1.65 in. (42mm) from the lower rear corner—Samurai models

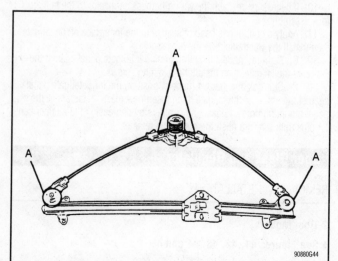

Fig. 43 Before installing the regulator, apply multi-purpose grease to the regulator at the points shown (A)

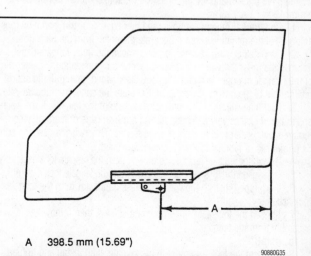

A   398.5 mm (15.69")

Fig. 45 On Sidekick and Tracker models, the rear hole of the bottom channel should be 15.69 in. (39.85cm) from the rear corner of the glass

14. If equipped with power windows, reattach the wiring harness connector to the regulator wiring harness.

15. If the bottom channel was removed from the glass, apply soapy water to the bottom channel and carefully tap the channel in place on the glass with a plastic hammer. The channel should be positioned so that the rear hole of the channel is 1.65 in. (42mm) from the bottom, rear corner of the window glass for Samurai models, or 15.69 in. (39.85cm) from the rear edge of the glass for Sidekick and Tracker models.

16. Lower the glass and channel down into the door.

17. Install the bottom channel mounting bolts securely.

18. Adjust the position of the window glass.

19. Install the inner and outer door weatherstripping.

20. On X-90 models, install the window glass stoppers onto the top edge of the window opening.

21. Apply a continuous bead of sealant to the inner face of the door, then install the watershield on the door.

22. Install the door panel.

4-Door Models

1. Remove the door trim panel.

2. Peel the watershield off of the inside face of the door. If the watershield is not excessively damaged during removal (rips or tears may be repaired with waterproof tape), it may be reused. Otherwise, a new one can be purchased or fabricated from a plastic lawn bag.

3. Lower the window all the way down.

4. Wrap electrical tape around the blade of a putty knife, then use the knife to gently pry the door outside weatherstripping off of the door.

5. Pry the inner weatherstripping off of the door.

6. Loosen the glass mounting screws, then lift the glass up and out of the door.

7. Position the door glass on a clean, padded surface.

8. If equipped with power windows, detach the wiring harness connector from the regulator wiring harness connector, then loosen the regulator harness holding clamp.

9. Loosen the window regulator mounting bolts, then remove the regulator from the door through hole (A).

To install:

10. Prior to installation, apply multi-purpose grease to the lubrication points shown in the accompanying illustration.

11. Manueveur the window regulator through the hole in the door and into position. Install the regulator mounting bolts and tighten them securely.

12. Adjust the position of the window glass.

13. If equipped with power windows, reattach the wiring harness connector to the regulator wiring harness.

14. Lower the glass down into the door.

15. Install the glass mounting bolts securely.

16. Install the outer door weatherstripping.

17. Apply a continuous bead of sealant to the inner face of the door, then install the watershield on the door.

18. Install the door panel.

DOOR GLASS ADJUSTMENT

X-90 Models

▶ **See Figure 46**

The window glass should be adjusted up and down so that the top edge of the window is level (as shown in the accompanying illustration). To adjust the front or rear of the window in the up-down orientation, fine-tune the positions of door stops A and B.

If the top edge of the window needs adjusting in or out from the vehicle, perform the following:

1. Loosen the trim support fixing screws.

2. Move the lower end of the rear sash by adjusting stud bolt B in or out as needed.

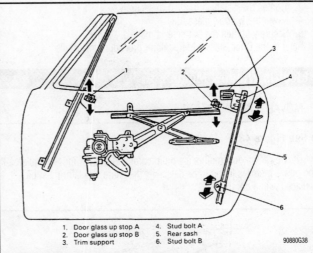

1. Door glass up stop A	4. Stud bolt A
2. Door glass up stop B	5. Rear sash
3. Trim support	6. Stud bolt B

90880G38

Fig. 46 Move the various door stops and sashes to adjust the position of the window glass—X-90 models

3. Move the upper end of the rear sash by moving stud bolt A in or out as necessary.

4. With the window glass fully raised, tighten the trim support fixing screw so that the window is no longer wobbly.

Except X-90 Models

FRONT DOORS

▶ **See Figure 47**

To adjust the position of the window glass, loosen the regulator mounting bolts and move the entire assembly until the glass is properly positioned. The top edge of the glass should be parallel with the top edge of the door, and the back edge of the glass should fit snugly in the rubber weatherstripping groove. Tighten the regulator bolts once the glass is properly adjusted.

REAR DOORS

During installation, adjust the window glass position as follows:

1. Loosen the five screws and two bolts.

2. Using the window regulator crank handle, raise the window completely.

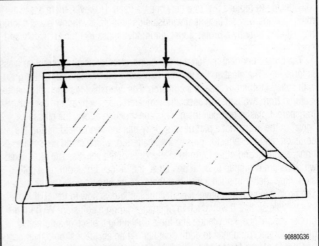

90880G36

Fig. 47 The window should be adjusted so that its top edge is parallel with the door frame edge, as shown

3. Tighten the fasteners marked ① securely.
4. Lower the window glass fully.
5. Securely tighten the two screws marked ②.
Refer to the Door Glass and Regulator procedure for details.

Electric Window Motor

REMOVAL & INSTALLATION

▶ **See Figure 48**

The power window motors are an integral part of the window regulator. If the power motor is found to be defective, the entire regulator must be replaced with a good one.

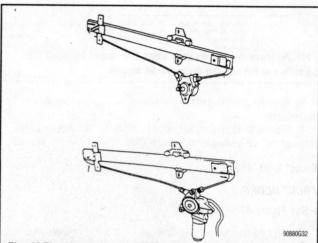

90880G32

Fig. 48 The electric motor, used with power windows, is an integral part of the regulator—in this illustration, the upper regulator is manual and the lower one is electric

Windshield and Fixed Glass

REMOVAL & INSTALLATION

If your windshield, or other fixed window, is cracked or chipped, you may decide to replace it with a new one yourself. However, there are two main reasons why replacement windshields and other window glass should be installed only by a professional automotive glass technician: safety and cost.

The most important reason a professional should install automotive glass is for safety. The glass in the vehicle, especially the windshield, is designed with safety in mind in case of a collision. The windshield is specially manufactured from two panes of specially-tempered glass with a thin layer of transparent plastic between them. This construction allows the glass to "give" in the event that a part of your body hits the windshield during the collision, and prevents the glass from shattering, which could cause lacerations, blinding and other harm to passengers of the vehicle. The other fixed windows are designed to be tempered so that if they break during a collision, they shatter in such a way that there are no large pointed glass pieces. The professional automotive glass technician knows how to install the glass in a vehicle so that it will function optimally during a collision. Without the proper experience, knowledge and tools, installing a piece of automotive glass yourself could lead to additional harm if an accident should ever occur.

Cost is also a factor when deciding to install automotive glass yourself. Performing this could cost you much more than a professional may charge for the same job. Since the windshield is designed to break under stress, an often life saving characteristic, windshields tend to break VERY easily when an inexperienced person attempts to install one. Do-it-yourselfers buying two, three or even four windshields from a salvage yard because they have broken them during installation are common stories. Also, since the automotive glass is designed to prevent the outside elements from entering your vehicle, improper installation can lead to water and air leaks. Annoying whining noises at highway speeds from air leaks or inside body panel rusting from water leaks can add to your stress level and subtract from your wallet. After buying two or three windshields, installing them and ending up with a leak that produces a noise while driving and water damage during rainstorms, the cost of having a professional do it correctly the first time may be much more alluring. We here at Chilton, therefore, advise that you have a professional automotive glass technician service any broken glass on your vehicle.

WINDSHIELD CHIP REPAIR

▶ **See Figures 49 thru 63**

➡**Check with your state and local authorities on the laws for state safety inspection. Some states or municipalities may not allow chip repair as a viable option for correcting stone damage to your windshield.**

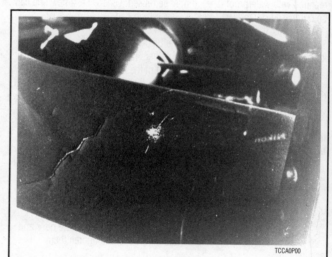

TCCA0P00

Fig. 49 Small chips on your windshield can be fixed with an aftermarket repair kit, such as the one from Loctite®

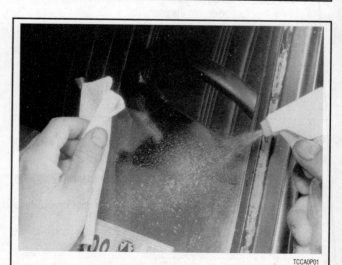

TCCA0P01

Fig. 50 To repair a chip, clean the windshield with glass cleaner and dry it completely

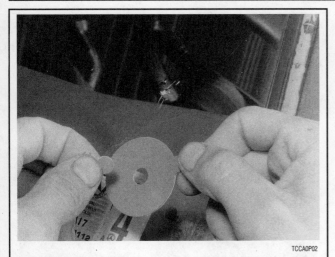

Fig. 51 Remove the center from the adhesive disc and peel off the backing from one side of the disc . . .

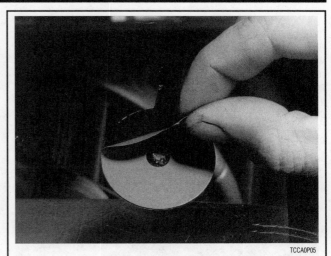

Fig. 54 Peel the backing off the exposed side of the adhesive disc . . .

Fig. 52 . . . then press it on the windshield so that the chip is centered in the hole

Fig. 55 . . . then position the plastic pedestal on the adhesive disc, ensuring that the tabs are aligned

Fig. 53 Be sure that the tab points upward on the windshield

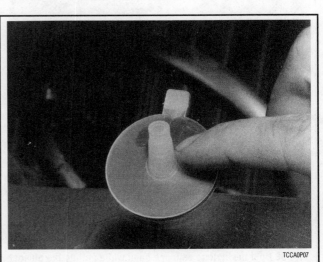

Fig. 56 Press the pedestal firmly on the adhesive disc to create an adequate seal . . .

Although severely cracked or damaged windshields must be replaced, there is something that you can do to prolong or even prevent the need for replacement of a chipped windshield. There are many companies which offer windshield chip repair products, such as Loctite's® Bullseye™ windshield repair kit. These kits usually consist of a syringe, pedestal and a sealing adhesive. The syringe is mounted on the pedestal and is used to create a vacuum which pulls the plastic layer against the glass. This helps make the chip transparent. The adhesive is then injected which seals the chip and helps to prevent further stress cracks from developing. Refer to the sequence of photos to get a general idea of what windshield chip repair involves.

➡**Always follow the specific manufacturer's instructions.**

TCCA0P08

Fig. 57 . . . then install the applicator syringe nipple in the pedestal's hole

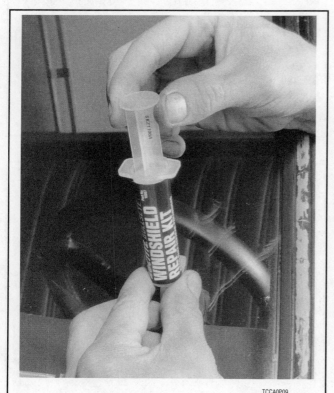

TCCA0P09

Fig. 58 Hold the syringe with one hand while pulling the plunger back with the other hand

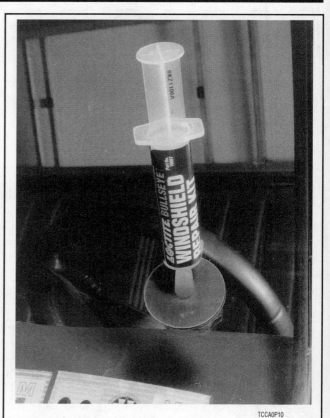

TCCA0P10

Fig. 59 After applying the solution, allow the entire assembly to sit until it has set completely

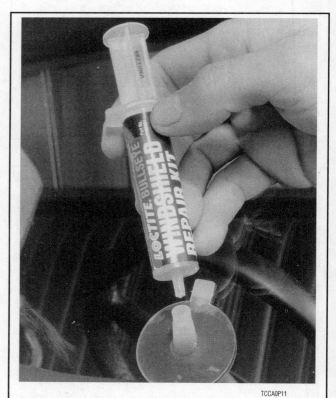

TCCA0P11

Fig. 60 After the solution has set, remove the syringe from the pedestal . . .

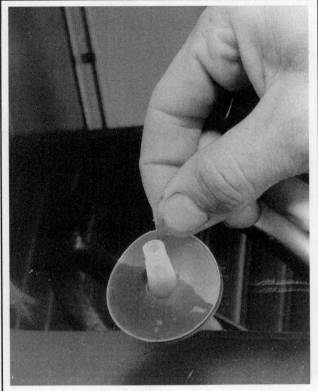

Fig. 61 . . . then peel the pedestal off of the adhesive disc . . .

Fig. 62 . . . and peel the adhesive disc off of the windshield

Inside Rear View Mirror

REMOVAL & INSTALLATION

▶ **See Figure 64**

1. Using a wooden or plastic prytool, carefully remove the trim piece from the inside rear view mirror base.

2. Loosen the mirror base mounting screws, then separate the mirror from the roof.

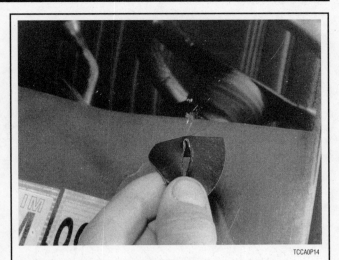

Fig. 63 The chip will still be slightly visible, but it should be filled with the hardened solution

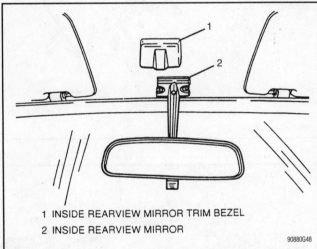

1 INSIDE REARVIEW MIRROR TRIM BEZEL
2 INSIDE REARVIEW MIRROR

Fig. 64 To remove the inside mirror, pry the base cover off, then loosen the mounting screws

To install:

3. Position the mirror base against the roof, then install and tighten the mounting screws until snug.

4. Install the mirror base trim piece.

Seats

REMOVAL & INSTALLATION

Front Seats

▶ **See Figures 65, 66 and 67**

➡**This is a general procedure; certain steps may need alteration for your particular vehicle.**

1. Remove the front seat adjuster trim cover by loosening the two retaining screws.

2. Remove the four front seat anchor bolt covers.

3. Loosen the four anchor bolts, then lift the seat up and out of the vehicle.

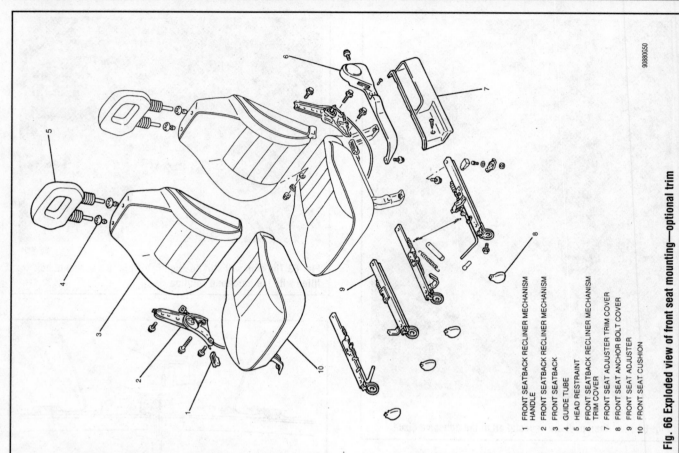

1 FRONT SEATBACK RECLINER MECHANISM
  HANDLE
2 FRONT SEATBACK RECLINER MECHANISM
3 FRONT SEATBACK
4 GUIDE TUBE
5 HEAD RESTRAINT
6 FRONT SEATBACK RECLINER MECHANISM
  TRIM COVER
7 FRONT SEAT ADJUSTER TRIM COVER
8 FRONT SEAT ANCHOR BOLT COVER
9 FRONT SEAT ADJUSTER
10 FRONT SEAT CUSHION

Fig. 66 Exploded view of front seat mounting—optional trim

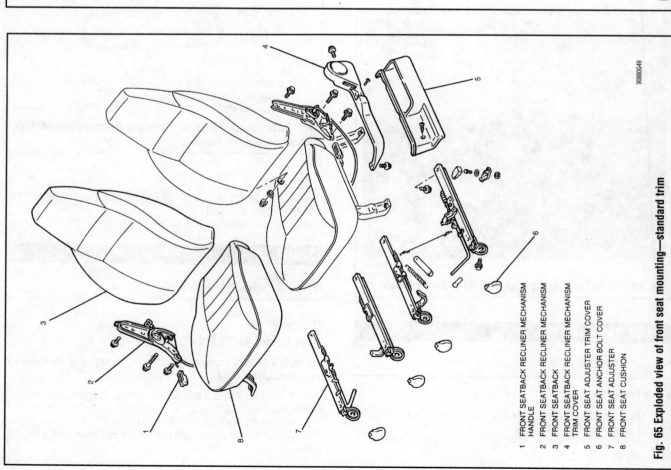

1 FRONT SEATBACK RECLINER MECHANISM
  HANDLE
2 FRONT SEATBACK RECLINER MECHANISM
3 FRONT SEATBACK
4 FRONT SEATBACK RECLINER MECHANISM
  TRIM COVER
5 FRONT SEAT ADJUSTER TRIM COVER
6 FRONT SEAT ANCHOR BOLT COVER
7 FRONT SEAT ADJUSTER
8 FRONT SEAT CUSHION

Fig. 65 Exploded view of front seat mounting—standard trim

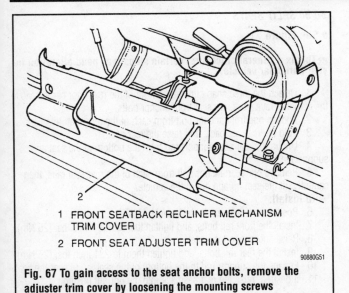

1 FRONT SEATBACK RECLINER MECHANISM
  TRIM COVER

2 FRONT SEAT ADJUSTER TRIM COVER

90880G51

Fig. 67 To gain access to the seat anchor bolts, remove the adjuster trim cover by loosening the mounting screws

To install:

4. Position the seat in the vehicle, then install and tighten the four anchor bolts to 221 inch lbs. (25 Nm).

5. Install the four anchor bolt covers.

6. Position the front seat adjuster trim cover in place, then install the two retaining screws.

Rear Seats

BENCH SEAT

▶ **See Figures 68, 69 and 70**

➡ **This is a general procedure; certain steps may need alteration for your particular vehicle.**

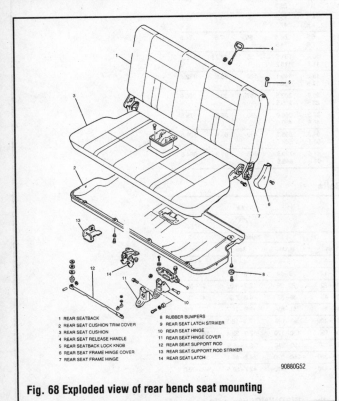

1 REAR SEATBACK
2 REAR SEAT CUSHION TRIM COVER
3 REAR SEAT CUSHION
4 REAR SEAT RELEASE HANDLE
5 REAR SEATBACK LOCK KNOB
6 REAR SEAT FRAME HINGE COVER
7 REAR SEAT FRAME HINGE
8 RUBBER BUMPERS
9 REAR SEAT LATCH STRIKER
10 REAR SEAT HINGE
11 REAR SEAT HINGE COVER
12 REAR SEAT SUPPORT ROD
13 REAR SEAT SUPPORT ROD STRIKER
14 REAR SEAT LATCH

90880G52

Fig. 68 Exploded view of rear bench seat mounting

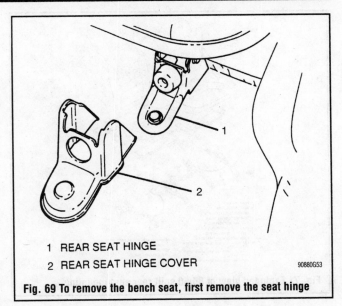

1 REAR SEAT HINGE
2 REAR SEAT HINGE COVER

90880G53

Fig. 69 To remove the bench seat, first remove the seat hinge

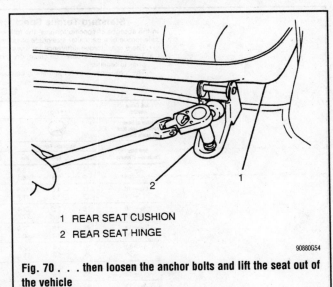

1 REAR SEAT CUSHION
2 REAR SEAT HINGE

90880G54

Fig. 70 . . . then loosen the anchor bolts and lift the seat out of the vehicle

1. Fold the rear seatback, pull the rear seat release handle and raise the rear seat.

2. Unclip the rear seat support rod from the bottom of the seat and support the seat

3. Remove one rear anchor bolt from each of the rear seat hinges.

4. Lower the seat, then gently pry the hinge cover off of each of the rear seat hinges.

5. Loosen one front anchor bolt from each of the rear seat hinges, then carefully lift the seat up and out of the vehicle.

To install:

6. Position the rear seat in the vehicle.

7. Install the two front hinge bolts, and tighten them to 221 inch lbs. (25 Nm).

8. Install the hinge cover on the front of each of the hinges, then raise and support the seat.

9. Install the two rear hinge bolts, and tighten them to 221 inch lbs. (25 Nm).

10. Engage the support rod to the bottom of the seat, and lower the seat.

11. If desired, raise the rear seatback into the upright position.

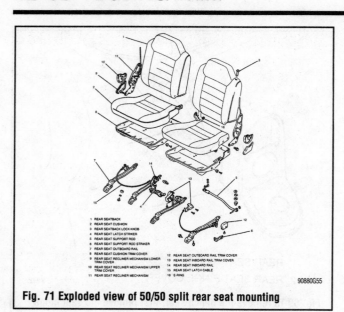

1 REAR SEATBACK
2 REAR SEAT CUSHION
3 REAR SEATBACK LOCK KNOB
4 REAR SEAT LATCH STRIKER
5 REAR SEAT SUPPORT ROD
6 REAR SEAT SUPPORT ROD STRIKER
7 REAR SEAT OUTBOARD RAIL
8 REAR SEAT CUSHION TRIM COVER
9 REAR SEAT RECLINER MECHANISM LOWER TRIM COVER
10 REAR SEAT RECLINER MECHANISM UPPER TRIM COVER
11 REAR SEAT RECLINER MECHANISM
12 REAR SEAT OUTBOARD RAIL TRIM COVER
13 REAR SEAT INBOARD RAIL TRIM COVER
14 REAR SEAT INBOARD RAIL
15 REAR SEAT LATCH CABLE
16 E-RING

90880G55

Fig. 71 Exploded view of 50/50 split rear seat mounting

50/50 SPLIT SEATS

♦ See Figure 71

➡ **This is a general procedure; certain steps may need alteration for your particular vehicle.**

1. Detach the three snap clips at the front of the rear floor carpet. Move the carpet to reveal the rear seat front anchor bolts.
2. Loosen one front anchor bolt from each of the rear seat rails.
3. Fold the rear seatback, and raise the rear seat.
4. Unclip the rear seat support rod from the bottom of the seat and support the seat
5. Remove one rear anchor bolt from each of the rear seat rails, then carefully lift the seat up and out of the vehicle.

To install:

6. Position the rear seat in the vehicle.
7. Install the front rail bolts, and tighten them to 221 inch lbs. (25 Nm).
8. Raise and support the seat.
9. Install the rear rail bolts, and tighten them to 221 inch lbs. (25 Nm).
10. Engage the support rod to the bottom of the seat, and lower the seat.
11. If desired, raise the rear seatback into the upright position.

Standard Torque Specifications and Fastener Markings

In the absence of specific torques, the following chart can be used as a guide to the maximum safe torque of a particular size/grade of fastener.
- There is no torque difference for fine or coarse threads.
- Torque values are based on clean, dry threads. Reduce the value by 10% if threads are oiled prior to assembly.
- The torque required for aluminum components or fasteners is considerably less.

U.S. Bolts

SAE Grade Number	1 or 2			5			6 or 7		
Number of lines always 2 less than the grade number.									
Bolt Size (Inches)—(Thread)	Ft./Lbs.	Kgm	Nm	Ft./Lbs.	Kgm	Nm	Ft./Lbs.	Kgm	Nm
¼ — 20	5	0.7	6.8	8	1.1	10.8	10	1.4	13.5
— 28	6	0.8	8.1	10	1.4	13.6			
5/16 — 18	11	1.5	14.9	17	2.3	23.0	19	2.6	25.8
— 24	13	1.8	17.6	19	2.6	25.7			
⅜ — 16	18	2.5	24.4	31	4.3	42.0	34	4.7	46.0
— 24	20	2.75	27.1	35	4.8	47.5			
7/16 — 14	28	3.8	37.0	49	6.8	66.4	55	7.6	74.5
— 20	30	4.2	40.7	55	7.6	74.5			
½ — 13	39	5.4	52.8	75	10.4	101.7	85	11.75	115.2
— 20	41	5.7	55.6	85	11.7	115.2			
9/16 — 12	51	7.0	69.2	110	15.2	149.1	120	16.6	162.7
— 18	55	7.6	74.5	120	16.6	162.7			
⅝ — 11	83	11.5	112.5	150	20.7	203.3	167	23.0	226.5
— 18	95	13.1	128.8	170	23.5	230.5			
¾ — 10	105	14.5	142.3	270	37.3	366.0	280	38.7	379.6
— 16	115	15.9	155.9	295	40.8	400.0			
⅞ — 9	160	22.1	216.9	395	54.6	535.5	440	60.9	596.5
— 14	175	24.2	237.2	435	60.1	589.7			
1 — 8	236	32.5	318.6	590	81.6	799.9	660	91.3	894.8
— 14	250	34.6	338.9	660	91.3	849.8			

Metric Bolts

Relative Strength Marking	4.6, 4.8			8.8		
Bolt Markings						
Bolt Size Thread Size x Pitch (mm)	Ft./Lbs.	Kgm	Nm	Ft./Lbs.	Kgm	Nm
6 x 1.0	2–3	.2–.4	3–4	3–6	4–.8	5–8
8 x 1.25	6–8	.8–1	8–12	9–14	1.2–1.9	13–19
10 x 1.25	12–17	1.5–2.3	16–23	20–29	2.7–4.0	27–39
12 x 1.25	21–32	2.9–4.4	29–43	35–53	4.8–7.3	47–72
14 x 1.5	35–52	4.8–7.1	48–70	57–85	7.8–11.7	77–110
16 x 1.5	51–77	7.0–10.6	67–100	90–120	12.4–16.5	130–160
18 x 1.5	74–110	10.2–15.1	100–150	130–170	17.9–23.4	180–230
20 x 1.5	110–140	15.1–19.3	150–190	190–240	26.2–46.9	160–320
22 x 1.5	150–190	22.0–26.2	200–260	250–320	34.5–44.1	340–430
24 x 1.5	190–240	26.2–46.9	260–320	310–410	42.7–56.5	420–550

TCCS1098

Fig. 72 Standard and metric bolt torque specifications based on bolt strengths—WARNING: use only as a guide

GLOSSARY

AIR/FUEL RATIO: The ratio of air-to-gasoline by weight in the fuel mixture drawn into the engine.

AIR INJECTION: One method of reducing harmful exhaust emissions by injecting air into each of the exhaust ports of an engine. The fresh air entering the hot exhaust manifold causes any remaining fuel to be burned before it can exit the tailpipe.

ALTERNATOR: A device used for converting mechanical energy into electrical energy.

AMMETER: An instrument, calibrated in amperes, used to measure the flow of an electrical current in a circuit. Ammeters are always connected in series with the circuit being tested.

AMPERE: The rate of flow of electrical current present when one volt of electrical pressure is applied against one ohm of electrical resistance.

ANALOG COMPUTER: Any microprocessor that uses similar (analogous) electrical signals to make its calculations.

ARMATURE: A laminated, soft iron core wrapped by a wire that converts electrical energy to mechanical energy as in a motor or relay. When rotated in a magnetic field, it changes mechanical energy into electrical energy as in a generator.

ATMOSPHERIC PRESSURE: The pressure on the Earth's surface caused by the weight of the air in the atmosphere. At sea level, this pressure is 14.7 psi at 32°F (101 kPa at 0°C).

ATOMIZATION: The breaking down of a liquid into a fine mist that can be suspended in air.

AXIAL PLAY: Movement parallel to a shaft or bearing bore.

BACKFIRE: The sudden combustion of gases in the intake or exhaust system that results in a loud explosion.

BACKLASH: The clearance or play between two parts, such as meshed gears.

BACKPRESSURE: Restrictions in the exhaust system that slow the exit of exhaust gases from the combustion chamber.

BAKELITE: A heat resistant, plastic insulator material commonly used in printed circuit boards and transistorized components.

BALL BEARING: A bearing made up of hardened inner and outer races between which hardened steel balls roll.

BALLAST RESISTOR: A resistor in the primary ignition circuit that lowers voltage after the engine is started to reduce wear on ignition components.

BEARING: A friction reducing, supportive device usually located between a stationary part and a moving part.

BIMETAL TEMPERATURE SENSOR: Any sensor or switch made of two dissimilar types of metal that bend when heated or cooled due to the different expansion rates of the alloys. These types of sensors usually function as an on/off switch.

BLOWBY: Combustion gases, composed of water vapor and unburned fuel, that leak past the piston rings into the crankcase during normal engine operation. These gases are removed by the PCV system to prevent the buildup of harmful acids in the crankcase.

BRAKE PAD: A brake shoe and lining assembly used with disc brakes.

BRAKE SHOE: The backing for the brake lining. The term is, however, usually applied to the assembly of the brake backing and lining.

BUSHING: A liner, usually removable, for a bearing; an anti-friction liner used in place of a bearing.

CALIPER: A hydraulically activated device in a disc brake system, which is mounted straddling the brake rotor (disc). The caliper contains at least one piston and two brake pads. Hydraulic pressure on the piston(s) forces the pads against the rotor.

CAMSHAFT: A shaft in the engine on which are the lobes (cams) which operate the valves. The camshaft is driven by the crankshaft, via a belt, chain or gears, at one half the crankshaft speed.

CAPACITOR: A device which stores an electrical charge.

CARBON MONOXIDE (CO): A colorless, odorless gas given off as a normal byproduct of combustion. It is poisonous and extremely dangerous in confined areas, building up slowly to toxic levels without warning if adequate ventilation is not available.

CARBURETOR: A device, usually mounted on the intake manifold of an engine, which mixes the air and fuel in the proper proportion to allow even combustion.

CATALYTIC CONVERTER: A device installed in the exhaust system, like a muffler, that converts harmful byproducts of combustion into carbon dioxide and water vapor by means of a heat-producing chemical reaction.

CENTRIFUGAL ADVANCE: A mechanical method of advancing the spark timing by using flyweights in the distributor that react to centrifugal force generated by the distributor shaft rotation.

CHECK VALVE: Any one-way valve installed to permit the flow of air, fuel or vacuum in one direction only.

CHOKE: A device, usually a moveable valve, placed in the intake path of a carburetor to restrict the flow of air.

CIRCUIT: Any unbroken path through which an electrical current can flow. Also used to describe fuel flow in some instances.

CIRCUIT BREAKER: A switch which protects an electrical circuit from overload by opening the circuit when the current flow exceeds a predetermined level. Some circuit breakers must be reset manually, while most reset automatically.

COIL (IGNITION): A transformer in the ignition circuit which steps up the voltage provided to the spark plugs.

COMBINATION MANIFOLD: An assembly which includes both the intake and exhaust manifolds in one casting.

COMBINATION VALVE: A device used in some fuel systems that routes fuel vapors to a charcoal storage canister instead of venting them into the atmosphere. The valve relieves fuel tank pressure and allows fresh air into the tank as the fuel level drops to prevent a vapor lock situation.

COMPRESSION RATIO: The comparison of the total volume of the cylinder and combustion chamber with the piston at BDC and the piston at TDC.

CONDENSER: 1. An electrical device which acts to store an electrical charge, preventing voltage surges. 2. A radiator-like device in the air conditioning system in which refrigerant gas condenses into a liquid, giving off heat.

CONDUCTOR: Any material through which an electrical current can be transmitted easily.

CONTINUITY: Continuous or complete circuit. Can be checked with an ohmmeter.

COUNTERSHAFT: An intermediate shaft which is rotated by a mainshaft and transmits, in turn, that rotation to a working part.

CRANKCASE: The lower part of an engine in which the crankshaft and related parts operate.

CRANKSHAFT: The main driving shaft of an engine which receives reciprocating motion from the pistons and converts it to rotary motion.

CYLINDER: In an engine, the round hole in the engine block in which the piston(s) ride.

CYLINDER BLOCK: The main structural member of an engine in which is found the cylinders, crankshaft and other principal parts.

CYLINDER HEAD: The detachable portion of the engine, usually fastened to the top of the cylinder block and containing all or most of the combustion chambers. On overhead valve engines, it contains the valves and their operating parts. On overhead cam engines, it contains the camshaft as well.

DEAD CENTER: The extreme top or bottom of the piston stroke.

DETONATION: An unwanted explosion of the air/fuel mixture in the combustion chamber caused by excess heat and compression, advanced timing, or an overly lean mixture. Also referred to as "ping".

DIAPHRAGM: A thin, flexible wall separating two cavities, such as in a vacuum advance unit.

DIESELING: A condition in which hot spots in the combustion chamber cause the engine to run on after the key is turned off.

DIFFERENTIAL: A geared assembly which allows the transmission of motion between drive axles, giving one axle the ability to turn faster than the other.

DIODE: An electrical device that will allow current to flow in one direction only.

DISC BRAKE: A hydraulic braking assembly consisting of a brake disc, or rotor, mounted on an axle, and a caliper assembly containing, usually two brake pads which are activated by hydraulic pressure. The pads are forced against the sides of the disc, creating friction which slows the vehicle.

DISTRIBUTOR: A mechanically driven device on an engine which is responsible for electrically firing the spark plug at a predetermined point of the piston stroke.

DOWEL PIN: A pin, inserted in mating holes in two different parts allowing those parts to maintain a fixed relationship.

DRUM BRAKE: A braking system which consists of two brake shoes and one or two wheel cylinders, mounted on a fixed backing plate, and a brake drum, mounted on an axle, which revolves around the assembly.

DWELL: The rate, measured in degrees of shaft rotation, at which an electrical circuit cycles on and off.

ELECTRONIC CONTROL UNIT (ECU): Ignition module, module, amplifier or igniter. See Module for definition.

ELECTRONIC IGNITION: A system in which the timing and firing of the spark plugs is controlled by an electronic control unit, usually called a module. These systems have no points or condenser.

END-PLAY: The measured amount of axial movement in a shaft.

ENGINE: A device that converts heat into mechanical energy.

EXHAUST MANIFOLD: A set of cast passages or pipes which conduct exhaust gases from the engine.

FEELER GAUGE: A blade, usually metal, or precisely predetermined thickness, used to measure the clearance between two parts.

FIRING ORDER: The order in which combustion occurs in the cylinders of an engine. Also the order in which spark is distributed to the plugs by the distributor.

FLOODING: The presence of too much fuel in the intake manifold and combustion chamber which prevents the air/fuel mixture from firing, thereby causing a no-start situation.

FLYWHEEL: A disc shaped part bolted to the rear end of the crankshaft. Around the outer perimeter is affixed the ring gear. The starter drive engages the ring gear, turning the flywheel, which rotates the crankshaft, imparting the initial starting motion to the engine.

FOOT POUND (ft. lbs. or sometimes, ft.lb.): The amount of energy or work needed to raise an item weighing one pound, a distance of one foot.

FUSE: A protective device in a circuit which prevents circuit overload by breaking the circuit when a specific amperage is present. The device is constructed around a strip or wire of a lower amperage rating than the circuit it is designed to protect. When an amperage higher than that stamped on the fuse is present in the circuit, the strip or wire melts, opening the circuit.

GEAR RATIO: The ratio between the number of teeth on meshing gears.

GENERATOR: A device which converts mechanical energy into electrical energy.

HEAT RANGE: The measure of a spark plug's ability to dissipate heat from its firing end. The higher the heat range, the hotter the plug fires.

HUB: The center part of a wheel or gear.

HYDROCARBON (HC): Any chemical compound made up of hydrogen and carbon. A major pollutant formed by the engine as a byproduct of combustion.

HYDROMETER: An instrument used to measure the specific gravity of a solution.

INCH POUND (inch lbs.; sometimes in.lb. or in. lbs.): One twelfth of a foot pound.

INDUCTION: A means of transferring electrical energy in the form of a magnetic field. Principle used in the ignition coil to increase voltage.

INJECTOR: A device which receives metered fuel under relatively low pressure and is activated to inject the fuel into the engine under relatively high pressure at a predetermined time.

INPUT SHAFT: The shaft to which torque is applied, usually carrying the driving gear or gears.

INTAKE MANIFOLD: A casting of passages or pipes used to conduct air or a fuel/air mixture to the cylinders.

JOURNAL: The bearing surface within which a shaft operates.

KEY: A small block usually fitted in a notch between a shaft and a hub to prevent slippage of the two parts.

MANIFOLD: A casting of passages or set of pipes which connect the cylinders to an inlet or outlet source.

MANIFOLD VACUUM: Low pressure in an engine intake manifold formed just below the throttle plates. Manifold vacuum is highest at idle and drops under acceleration.

MASTER CYLINDER: The primary fluid pressurizing device in a hydraulic system. In automotive use, it is found in brake and hydraulic clutch systems and is pedal activated, either directly or, in a power brake system, through the power booster.

MODULE: Electronic control unit, amplifier or igniter of solid state or integrated design which controls the current flow in the ignition primary circuit based on input from the pick-up coil. When the module opens the primary circuit, high secondary voltage is induced in the coil.

NEEDLE BEARING: A bearing which consists of a number (usually a large number) of long, thin rollers.

OHM: (Ω) The unit used to measure the resistance of conductor-to-electrical flow. One ohm is the amount of resistance that limits current flow to one ampere in a circuit with one volt of pressure.

OHMMETER: An instrument used for measuring the resistance, in ohms, in an electrical circuit.

OUTPUT SHAFT: The shaft which transmits torque from a device, such as a transmission.

OVERDRIVE: A gear assembly which produces more shaft revolutions than that transmitted to it.

OVERHEAD CAMSHAFT (OHC): An engine configuration in which the camshaft is mounted on top of the cylinder head and operates the valve either directly or by means of rocker arms.

OVERHEAD VALVE (OHV): An engine configuration in which all of the valves are located in the cylinder head and the camshaft is located in the cylinder block. The camshaft operates the valves via lifters and pushrods.

OXIDES OF NITROGEN (NOx): Chemical compounds of nitrogen produced as a byproduct of combustion. They combine with hydrocarbons to produce smog.

OXYGEN SENSOR: Use with the feedback system to sense the presence of oxygen in the exhaust gas and signal the computer which can reference the voltage signal to an air/fuel ratio.

PINION: The smaller of two meshing gears.

PISTON RING: An open-ended ring with fits into a groove on the outer diameter of the piston. Its chief function is to form a seal between the piston and cylinder wall. Most automotive pistons have three rings: two for compression sealing; one for oil sealing.

PRELOAD: A predetermined load placed on a bearing during assembly or by adjustment.

PRIMARY CIRCUIT: the low voltage side of the ignition system which consists of the ignition switch, ballast resistor or resistance wire, bypass, coil, electronic control unit and pick-up coil as well as the connecting wires and harnesses.

PRESS FIT: The mating of two parts under pressure, due to the inner diameter of one being smaller than the outer diameter of the other, or vice versa; an interference fit.

RACE: The surface on the inner or outer ring of a bearing on which the balls, needles or rollers move.

REGULATOR: A device which maintains the amperage and/or voltage levels of a circuit at predetermined values.

RELAY: A switch which automatically opens and/or closes a circuit.

RESISTANCE: The opposition to the flow of current through a circuit or electrical device, and is measured in ohms. Resistance is equal to the voltage divided by the amperage.

RESISTOR: A device, usually made of wire, which offers a preset amount of resistance in an electrical circuit.

RING GEAR: The name given to a ring-shaped gear attached to a differential case, or affixed to a flywheel or as part of a planetary gear set.

ROLLER BEARING: A bearing made up of hardened inner and outer races between which hardened steel rollers move.

ROTOR: 1. The disc-shaped part of a disc brake assembly, upon which the brake pads bear; also called, brake disc. 2. The device mounted atop the distributor shaft, which passes current to the distributor cap tower contacts.

SECONDARY CIRCUIT: The high voltage side of the ignition system, usually above 20,000 volts. The secondary includes the ignition coil, coil wire, distributor cap and rotor, spark plug wires and spark plugs.

SENDING UNIT: A mechanical, electrical, hydraulic or electro-magnetic device which transmits information to a gauge.

SENSOR: Any device designed to measure engine operating conditions or ambient pressures and temperatures. Usually electronic in nature and designed to send a voltage signal to an on-board computer, some sensors may operate as a simple on/off switch or they may provide a variable voltage signal (like a potentiometer) as conditions or measured parameters change.

SHIM: Spacers of precise, predetermined thickness used between parts to establish a proper working relationship.

SLAVE CYLINDER: In automotive use, a device in the hydraulic clutch system which is activated by hydraulic force, disengaging the clutch.

SOLENOID: A coil used to produce a magnetic field, the effect of which is to produce work.

SPARK PLUG: A device screwed into the combustion chamber of a spark ignition engine. The basic construction is a conductive core inside of a ceramic insulator, mounted in an outer conductive base. An electrical charge from the spark plug wire travels along the conductive core and jumps a preset air gap to a grounding point or points at the end of the conductive base. The resultant spark ignites the fuel/air mixture in the combustion chamber.

SPLINES: Ridges machined or cast onto the outer diameter of a shaft or inner diameter of a bore to enable parts to mate without rotation.

TACHOMETER: A device used to measure the rotary speed of an engine, shaft, gear, etc., usually in rotations per minute.

THERMOSTAT: A valve, located in the cooling system of an engine, which is closed when cold and opens gradually in response to engine heating, controlling the temperature of the coolant and rate of coolant flow.

TOP DEAD CENTER (TDC): The point at which the piston reaches the top of its travel on the compression stroke.

TORQUE: The twisting force applied to an object.

TORQUE CONVERTER: A turbine used to transmit power from a driving member to a driven member via hydraulic action, providing changes in drive ratio and torque. In automotive use, it links the driveplate at the rear of the engine to the automatic transmission.

TRANSDUCER: A device used to change a force into an electrical signal.

TRANSISTOR: A semi-conductor component which can be actuated by a small voltage to perform an electrical switching function.

TUNE-UP: A regular maintenance function, usually associated with the replacement and adjustment of parts and components in the electrical and fuel systems of a vehicle for the purpose of attaining optimum performance.

TURBOCHARGER: An exhaust driven pump which compresses intake air and forces it into the combustion chambers at higher than atmospheric pressures. The increased air pressure allows more fuel to be burned and results in increased horsepower being produced.

VACUUM ADVANCE: A device which advances the ignition timing in response to increased engine vacuum.

VACUUM GAUGE: An instrument used to measure the presence of vacuum in a chamber.

VALVE: A device which control the pressure, direction of flow or rate of flow of a liquid or gas.

VALVE CLEARANCE: The measured gap between the end of the valve stem and the rocker arm, cam lobe or follower that activates the valve.

VISCOSITY: The rating of a liquid's internal resistance to flow.

VOLTMETER: An instrument used for measuring electrical force in units called volts. Voltmeters are always connected parallel with the circuit being tested.

WHEEL CYLINDER: Found in the automotive drum brake assembly, it is a device, actuated by hydraulic pressure, which, through internal pistons, pushes the brake shoes outward against the drums.

MASTER
INDEX